Political Philosophy
Classic and Contemporary Readings

Nature, the art whereby God has made and governs the world, is by the *art* of man, as in many other things, so in this also imitated—that it can make an artificial animal. For seeing life is but a motion of limbs, the beginning whereof is in some principal part within, why may we not say that all *automata* (engines that move themselves by springs and wheels as does a watch) have an artificial life? For what is the *heart* but a *spring,* and the *nerves* but so many *strings,* and the *joints* but so many *wheels* giving motion to the whole body such as was intended by the artificer? *Art* goes yet further, imitating that rational and most excellent work of nature, *man.* For by art is created that great LEVIATHAN called a COMMONWEALTH or STATE—in Latin, CIVITAS—which is but an artificial man, though of greater stature and strength than the natural, for whose protection and defense it was intended; and in which the *sovereignty* is an artificial *soul,* as giving life and motion to the whole body; the *magistrates* and other *officers* of judicature and execution, artificial *joints;* *reward* and *punishment,* by which, fastened to the seat of the sovereignty, every joint and member is moved to perform his duty, are the *nerves,* that do the same in the body natural; the *wealth* and *riches* of all the particular members are the *strength; salus populi,* the people's safety, its *business; counselors,* by whom all things needful for it to know are suggested unto it, are the *memory; equity* and *laws,* an artificial reason and *will; concord, health; sedition, sickness;* and *civil war, death.* Lastly, the *pacts* and *covenants* by which the parts of this body politic were at first made, set together, and united resemble that *fiat,* or the *let us make man,* pronounced by God in the creation.

To describe the nature of this artificial man, I will consider

First, the *matter* thereof, and the *artificer,* both of which is *man.*

Secondly, *how* and by what *covenants* it is made, what are the *rights* and just *power* or *authority* of a *sovereign,* and what it is that preserves and *dissolves* it. Thirdly, what is a *Christian commonwealth.* Lastly, what is the *kingdom of darkness.*

—Thomas Hobbes, *Leviathan*

Political Philosophy

Classic and Contemporary Readings

Louis P. Pojman

Editor

Boston   Burr Ridge, IL   Dubuque, IA   Madison, WI   New York   San Francisco   St. Louis
Bangkok   Bogotá   Caracas   Kuala Lumpur   Lisbon   London   Madrid   Mexico City
Milan   Montreal   New Delhi   Santiago   Seoul   Singapore   Sydney   Taipei   Toronto

McGraw-Hill Higher Education

*A Division of The **McGraw-Hill** Companies*

POLITICAL PHILOSOPHY: CLASSIC AND CONTEMPORARY READINGS

Published by McGraw-Hill, a business unit of The McGraw-Hill Companies, Inc., 1221 Avenue of the Americas, New York, NY 10020. Copyright © 2002 by The McGraw-Hill Companies, Inc. All rights reserved. No part of this publication may be reproduced or distributed in any form or by any means, or stored in a database or retrieval system, without the prior written consent of The McGraw-Hill Companies, Inc., including, but not limited to, in any network or other electronic storage or transmission, or broadcast for distance learning.

Some ancillaries, including electronic and print components, may not be available to customers outside the United States.

This book is printed on acid-free paper.

1 2 3 4 5 6 7 8 9 0 QPF/QPF 0 9 8 7 6 5 4 3 2 1

ISBN 0–07–244811–3

Editorial director: *Jane E. Karpacz*
Sponsoring editor: *Monica Eckman*
Editorial coordinator*: Shannon Morrow*
Marketing manager: *Daniel M. Loch*
Senior project manager: *Mary E. Powers*
Production supervisor: *Enboge Chong*
Designer: *K. Wayne Harms*
Cover designer: *So Yon Kim*
Cover image: *Lafayette College Art Collection, Easton, Pennsylvania*
Media technology producer: *Lance Gerhart*
Compositor: ***TECHBOOKS***
Typeface: *10/12 Times Roman*
Printer: *Quebecor World Fairfield, PA*

Library of Congress Cataloging-in-Publication Data

Political philosophy : classic and contemporary readings / [edited by] Louis P. Pojman.—1st ed.
   p.   cm.
   ISBN 0–07–244811–3 (acid-free paper)
   1. Political science.   I. Pojman, Louis P.

JA66 .P635   2002
320′.01—dc21

                2001028749
                CIP

www.mhhe.com

Dedicated to

Ruth Freedom
and
Sergei

Contents

Preface

As we enter the twenty-first century, with the nations of the world experiencing more interconnection through an increasingly global economy, communications, and environmental problems—a world in which one nation's political problems are likely to affect many other nations—political philosophy takes on a renewed and vital importance. Whereas moral philosophy dominated philosophical interest from the 1960s through the early 1990s (including applied ethics, such as medical and environmental ethics), a shift is now taking place—spurred on by debates over the welfare state, affirmative action, and national health insurance—toward political philosophy. We want to know what justifies the State and how governments should be organized to maintain order, peace, liberty, and justice. Should the State exercise paternalism and aim at economic equality? Should the State be involved in making citizens moral, or should it be neutral with regard to visions of the good? What is the moral basis for our obligation to obey the State? What, if anything, justifies the existence of the State? And, even if the State is legitimate, is the Nation-State, as a sovereign institution, morally justified, or should we be moving toward some form of world government? How global should our moral vision be? Should it include sacrificing some State sovereignty, providing aid to underdeveloped countries, intervening in international crises? Is patriotism a provincial chauvinism, or does it have an ethical warrant in human affairs? These and similar questions have exercised the minds of political philosophers for decades, if not millennia, but now they are becoming so vital to our everyday social and political life that philosophy must address them with new urgency and concentration. This book is an anthology of the modern classics (beginning with Machiavelli, Hobbes, and Locke) and contemporary readings that sets forth a wide spectrum of theories about the justification and shape of government, including the ideals of liberty, justice, equality, and human rights, as well as the related issues of State paternalism and desert.

There are anthologies that cover ancient and modern classics, but, as far as I know, none that cover both modern classics and contemporary works. The issues covered in this work are what seem the burning philosophical issues of our time: the justification of the State; theories of justice and liberty; State neutrality versus moral perfectionism; equality and equal opportunity; the nature and scope of rights; national sovereignty, cosmopolitanism and world government; international politics, including foreign aid, military intervention, and immigration. I have endeavored to select the most cogent and accessible essays on various sides of these issues and to present them in a way that will engage the intelligent student.

I begin with a general introduction on political philosophy, after which follow some of the major modern classics—Machiavelli, Hobbes, Locke, Rousseau, Hume, Burke, Wollstonecraft, Marx and Engels, and Mill—which are important political documents in their own right but also connect with some of the subsequent eight topics. Each chapter begins with an introduction to the problems debated in that chapter. I introduce each selection with a biographical sketch of the author and an abstract of the reading, so that students can obtain an orientation to what they are about to read.

I have used many of the readings in my political philosophy classes at the University of Mississippi and at West Point over the past two decades, where I have had the joy of teaching some of the sharpest, most congenial, but critical, students one could ever hope to meet. I am indebted to them for stimulating discussion and sharp criticism. I am grateful to Steven Kershnar, State University of New York at Fredonia; Phil Fetzer, Cal Poly, San Luis Obispo; James Otteson, The University of Alabama; Stephen Nathanson, Northeastern University; Eloise Malone, U.S. Naval Academy; Charles Cochran, U.S. Naval Academy; Robert Westmoreland, University of Mississippi; John Kleinig, John Jay College of Criminal Justice; Bruce Landesman, University of Utah; Wallace Matson, University of California at Berkeley; James Sterba, University of Notre Dame; Christopher Morris, Bowling Green State University; especially John Kleinig, Douglas Olivant, and Stephen Kershnar, for their help in advising me on some of the latest material on many of these issues. I am grateful to my editor, Monica Eckman, who supported me in this project in an exemplary way. Mary Powers and Margo Quinto were very helpful in producing this book. Most of all, I thank my wife, Trudy, who has been the joy of my life, but also my sharpest constructive critic, and who helped me edit this work. This work is dedicated to my daughter, Ruth Freedom, and her husband, Sergei, who exemplify cosmopolitan citizenship, as they work together in Kyrgyzstan in the former Soviet Union for international peace and justice.

Louis P. Pojman
U.S. Military Academy
West Point, NY
November 2, 2000

General Introduction

If men were angels, no Government would be necessary.
If they were devils, no Government would be possible.
—Alexander Hamilton

Political philosophy inquires into the meaning of political concepts and the justification of theories about the nature and purpose of government. It seeks to provide understanding regarding such questions as, Why should I obey the laws of the State? How should the State be constituted? What is the justification of the State? What are the principal functions of the State? Should the State be a national or an international entity? Should the Nation-State be sovereign, or should we create a cosmopolitan government, transcending nationalism?

In seeking to answer, or at least understand, these questions and the conflicting answers to them, we encounter a series of secondary concepts and theories, including the nature and value of justice, liberty, equality, political obligation, moral perfectionism, nationalism, globalism, and sovereignty. In this book we will examine most of those concepts and the theories surrounding them.

Political philosophy, unlike political science, is not primarily descriptive, concerned with an explanation of why government exists the way it does (though it does consider this question), but is prescriptive or normative, dealing with how political institutions *ought* to function, concerned with setting forth arguments and justifications for the best or most morally justified ways of organizing society.

Before we can engage in considering the justification of political theories we need to clarify some concepts and inquire what we mean by *State, nation, justice, liberty, equality, sovereignty,* and the like. Those terms are examined in detail in this book, but here we may undertake an initial attempt.

Consider the fundamental concepts, *the State* and *the nation*. The State is an association that includes such formal ideas as a legislative body with an executive and judicial component. The State is the ultimate authority, a sovereign entity, having sole comprehensive authority over a geographical domain. A nation, on the other hand, is a group of people who are tied together through common sources of meaning and identity, through ethnic similarity, language, literature, history, myth, religion, and other cultural phenomena. A State may be made up of many nations, and one nation may be divided by many states. For example, Great Britain is a State made up of the nations of England, Wales, Scotland, and Northern Ireland. Canada is a State made up of two nations, the French-speaking people of Quebec and the English-speaking people of the rest of Canada. Until the early 1870s, when Bismarck united the German people, the German nation was divided into several separate States. After World War II, until the fall of the German Democratic Republic in 1991, the German nation was divided into two States, East Germany and West Germany. One could argue that Austria makes up yet another State of Germans. The ancient Greeks (a nation) were divided into several city-states, yet they joined in a military federation to defend their cities against the Persians. The distinction between *State* and *nation* is sometimes vague. Is Switzerland, with its three cultural and language groups, one State with three nations or one Nation-State or several mini-canton states? The goal of every nationalist is, in the words of the eighteenth-century Italian nationalist Giuseppe Mazzini, "Every nation a state, only one state for the entire nation."[1] When we read of the conflicts in Israel between Jew and Arab, in Northern Ireland between Protestant and Catholic, or the ethnic cleansing in Bosnia or Kosovo, we get a sense of just how penetrating and volatile nationalism can be. We shall examine these issues more closely in Chapter VIII.

In the nineteenth century, the German sociologist Ferdinand Tönnies (1855–1936) distinguished between *Gemeinschaft* (community) and *Gesellshaft* (society). The former refers to the natural, communal ties (such as friendship, family, and clan) that cause people to commit themselves to a common cause or way of life; the latter refers to those features of social organization constituted by contract and formal rules. Tönnies said that *Gemeinschaft* is formed by natural will, whereas *Gesellshaft* is formed by rational will. *Gemeinschaft* is constituted by a covenant rather than a contract, something informal and deeply rooted in human relationships, even sacred to its members, as is a religious heritage or a sacred myth. In the Old Testament, God does not contract but covenants with the people Israel. Indeed the very term *testament* means *covenant*. There is a relationship of personal loyalty, obedience, and trust on the part of the people of Israel that Yahweh will honor by his guidance and protection. When Israel becomes a formal State in I Samuel, choosing Saul as their king, the prophet Samuel deplores the act as a betrayal of the covenantal relationship between Yahweh and Israel but permits it as a concession to human weakness. It would be better to live in a relationship of direct trust in God, as a special community of faith, but since Israel's faith is weak, formal rules and an executive branch are permitted as a distant second best. The State, as a formal society, typically emerges from the nation or community when a formal structure of rules and a separation of powers are desired. Spontaneous acts of beneficence, as well as a notion of reciprocity, characterize the morality of the community, but it lacks the impartiality and consistent application of behavior. The State or society goes beyond such "natural morality" and formalizes rules of law, enforcing them impartially with sanctions. Whereas life in the community is characterized by virtue (or vice) and loyalty, society superimposes laws, rights, and contractual obligations.

When we organize a group of friends into a professional association or organization, giving it a constitution with goals and rules or laws, we superimpose society upon community. A group of hikers, trekking together in the mountains, form a community, but not a society, even though they may have a common purpose (say, climbing Giant Mountain); but when they agree upon a common set of rules and responsibilities, they are transformed into a primitive association, say the Adirondack Mountain Club or the Sierra Club, which gradually may lose many of its communal characteristics, becoming more powerful, but also more impersonal, bureaucratic, and legalistic. A group of tenants may constitute a caring community, but they become an association or society when they form a tenant's association with a constitution and a set of rules in order to fight more effectively for reduced rent and better maintenance. We can apply Tönnies's distinction to the concepts of the *Nation* and the *State*. When we refer to a State, we mean a large anonymous entity (the members need not know each other personally) that creates and enforces laws over a geographical area or over a group of people who, usually, reside in the geographical area. A nation, on the other hand, refers to the societal aspects, to the culture, and to the myths and history of the group. Nations, as communities, grow like trees, whereas States, as associations, are constructed like buildings. Typically, States, as artificial institutions, are invented, whereas nations are neither created by our will nor chosen, but are natural, primitive givens, based on shared history, beliefs, love and loyalty, constituting a vital part of our self-identity. One does not choose to be of German, French, or English ancestry with all that goes with that, but, rather, one is chosen by the lottery of nature. One then finds one's identity constituted by these factors. The fate of our nation is our fate, though we may not suffer physically or economically from its defeat or loss of power. In the community or nation, particular loyalties are the dominant motif. We have a special obligation to specific people, to a common identifiable tradition; whereas the society takes on a more universal aspect, characterized by a constitution, laws, and set of requirements for membership. It constructs rational principles, which have a universal aspect, and so applies impartially without respect for class or status. Whoever meets the abstract requirements is a citizen, a member of the society. Whoever breaches the law suffers the penalty.

Since the seventeenth century, we have been in a situation in which the two types of political groups are combined in the Nation-State. *Gesellshaft* and *Gemeinshaft* become one. The universal and the particular merge into a single political reality. However, it is useful to distinguish between these two aspects.

When we think of a nation, such as England or the United States, we think of its history, its wars, its language, its literature, folk songs, and stories, its architecture, including its churches and skyscrapers, its landscapes and cultural symbols—the flag, the Bald Eagle. When citizens travel abroad, they are soon reminded of their identity. The mores and manners are different in the foreign land and sometimes feel wrong. Travelers become nostalgic for the people, sights, sounds, and even smells and tastes of their native land. Americans abroad search for the *International Herald Tribune* to bring them news from home. And when they return, even if they have had a wonderful time abroad, they say, "It's good to be home." A sense of familiarity and wholeness spreads over them, even compensating for the jet lag they may experience. The nation, not the State provides our roots, our sense of belonging, our identity, our solidarity with others. So deep is this sense of communal covenant that many will risk their lives for the nation and even kill for it.

When we think of the State, on the other hand, we think of the laws, the institutions, including the constitution, that make up the State. These laws are impersonal and abstract though they can have powerful personal effects, especially if one is caught breaking one of them. The authority of the State consists in its *sovereignty*. It alone can make laws and enforce them within its jurisdiction. External associations are forbidden from interfering in its internal affairs, and no internal association may override its statutes. The State is supreme.

Politicians differ in their appeal to the electorate. Some appeal to societal and nationalistic sentiments—say family values, religion, and tradition; others appeal to institutional characteristics and propose changing specific laws, such as those governing Social Security or taxation. Of course, there is much overlap, for some of the laws touch deeply on our heritage, say a law against desecrating the flag. Still, the distinction is valid. Liberals, especially Libertarians, emphasize the formal State aspects, concentrating on the government's role as a protector (from both internal and external harm), whereas Conservatives and Communitarians emphasize the cultural communal aspects such as family values, patriotism, religious and cultural heritage. A Liberal may well tolerate, or even celebrate, wide differences in education, literature, and even language use ("multicultural diversity"), whereas a Conservative or Communitarian will seek to promote the tradition, a single language, "the core curriculum" in education. It is no accident that Conservatives call for immigration restrictions while Liberals promote open borders, or that Conservatives fight for making English the official language, while Liberals tolerate a diversity of language use. Liberals celebrate cultural diversity, whereas Conservatives identify so strongly with their own culture that they tend to be suspicious of diversity until a case for it is made. These distinctions will surface in many parts of this work.

In sum, the State is distinguished by its sovereignty, its authority to rule over its subjects, and its right to create laws and enforce them by coercive means. It is formal, abstract, legalistic, and dominated by the universal, but, because of its coercive authority, also potentially powerful for ill as well as for good. A nation, on the other hand, represents the communal, voluntary aspects of social life, stressing the particular over the universal. Whereas membership in the State is a matter of legal status, membership in a nation is a matter of passion or emotion, of personal commitment, which evokes the sentiment of patriotism.

You should review these concepts and distinctions and develop their implications as you go through this work, culminating in Chapter VIII, in which issues of global politics are examined.

OUTLINE OF THIS WORK

Chapter I consists of a set of modern classics in political philosophy, beginning with Niccolò Machiavelli's tract on political realism, *The Prince,* then turning to Thomas Hobbes's classic *Leviathan,* with its description of the state of nature and explanation of the need for a sovereign. Next, we examine John Locke's *Second Treatise of Government,* in which a natural rights theory of the justification of the State and political obligation is set forth, essentially arguing that we have an obligation to obey the State because we have tacitly consented to obey it. After this we present *The Social Contract,* Jean-Jacques Rousseau's version of democratic contractualism and, after that, David Hume's discussion of the origin of government and his critique of contractualism and the consent theory. Following this, we examine Edmund Burke's critique of French revolution egalitarianism, written prophetically before the Revolution got under way. Burke's essay may be the clearest defense of essential conservatism ever written. Thereupon follows Mary Wollstonecraft's nineteenth-century essay on why women should be given equal political rights. Then we examine Karl Marx and Friedrich Engels' *Communist Manifesto* and Marx's *Critique of the Gotha Program,* in which he rejects strong egalitarianism. Finally, we read the first chapters of John Stuart Mill's classic *On Liberty,* which sets forth the case for social liberty against all forms of state paternalism. These classics may be read separately or in conjunction with readings under the various topics in this book. For instance, Hobbes, Locke, Rousseau, and Hume are relevant to Chapter II on political obligation; Mill to Chapter III on liberty; and Wollstonecraft, Marx, and Engels to Chapter IV on justice.

Chapter II consists of essays on political obligation. It begins with Robert Paul Wolff's challenging essay on anarchism, which seeks to answer the question Why should I obey the law? Chapter III examines the value of liberty versus State paternalism. Chapter IV sets forth some of the most important readings on the nature of distributive justice, the principal political virtue. Chapter V examines the question of how deeply the State should involve itself in personal morality (moral perfectionism) or whether it should be neutral regarding the good. Chapter VI considers the concept of equality together with its related categories, equal opportunity, inheritance, and multicultural diversity. Chapter VII examines the nature of human rights and asks whether there really are any. Chapter VIII has to do with nationalism versus internationalism, or national sovereignty versus world government. We look at the arguments for world government and for national sovereignty, as well as the issue of patriotism.

I have tried to set before you the best argued, most accessible selections in the literature, representing many opposing points of view. I hope the book serves the purpose of advancing the discussion on these important and difficult issues.

As a kindness to modern readers, I have changed some punctuation and spelling, especially in the readings written in earlier centuries. Some notes have been edited or deleted. Unless otherwise noted, all endnotes were in the original.

---

[1]Quoted in Eric Hobsbawn, *Nations and Nationalism Since 1780* (Cambridge, England: Cambridge University Press, 1990), p. 101.

CHAPTER I

Modern Classics

There are a select few works of political philosophy with which every student should be thoroughly familiar. In the Ancient period these would include Plato's Republic and Aristotle's Politics. In the modern period, a period stretching from the late Renaissance until the late 19th century, nine works stand out. These are not only intrinsically significant but have been influential in shaping the nature of the succeeding debate, stretching into the present. They are very much living works, part of our patrimony. The first classic work is *The Prince* by Niccolò Machiavelli (1469–1527), wherein a new political vision is expounded, one which departs from the idealism of the Greek and Roman classics in favor of Realpolitik, a realistic assessment of human political intrigue, conspiracy and fallibility. The term "Machiavellian" has become synonymous with shrewd, cynical political realism, which deals with people as they are rather than as we might wish them to be. *The Prince* is a guide to one who governs, explaining how political power is acquired and how it's maintained. According to this vision, Reasons of state justify deception and fraudulent behavior which we would condemn in everyday human interactions. Machiavelli's claims and cynicism may not be the ultimate truth about human society, but they contain enough truth to warrant continued study.

The second classic work selected is the *Leviathan* of Thomas Hobbes (1588–1679), a work which sets forth a comprehensive political theory within the framework of a systematic account of human nature. Hobbes, a Royalist whose perceptions of the chaos and violence of the English Civil War (1641–44) led him to conclude that even an orderly *absolutism* is preferable to a *state of nature* in which life is "solitary, poor, nasty, brutish, and short. . . . a war of all against all," sets forth a contractualist theory of political obligation. Without the Sovereign State, in which subjects agree to sacrifice some liberties for peace, there is no hope of living a good life.

John Locke (1632–1704), the author of our third selection, the second of his *Two Treatises of Government* (1690), had a more optimistic view of human nature than Hobbes. In the work before us he sets forth a "natural rights" theory which became the intellectual foundation of our nation's Founding Fathers. For Locke all humans are endowed by God with the inalienable rights to life, liberty and property, the right to property adhering to anyone who mixes his labor with a segment of nature. Government rests on the consent of the governed, so that if it fails to meet its part of the bargain it may be dissolved by the citizenry. Locke also believed in an original contract which was the legitimate ancestor to all legitimate authority, a thesis rejected by David Hume in Reading 5.

Our fourth classic is the *Social Contract* (1762) by Jean-Jacques Rousseau (1712–78). If Locke's work is the manifesto of the American Revolution, Rousseau's is that of the French Revolution. He begins with the incendiary proclamation, "Man is born free but is everywhere in chains." Man is good by nature (a "Noble Savage") but social institutions corrupt him. Direct democracy is the only justified form of political decision making because it alone can express the General Will of the people in concrete form and for the common good. A form of majoritarianism dominates his thought which Mill (Reading 9) will later label "The Tyranny of the Majority", for it enables the majority to "force" the minority "to be free" by coercive action.

1

Our fifth classic author is the Scottish philosopher and historian David Hume (1711–76) whose two political essays, "On the Origin of Government" and "Of the Social Contract", break with the contractualism of the three previous writers. Hume argues that there never was an original social contract and that the idea of "tacit consent" is inapplicable to society. The poor uneducated peasant who knows no other language or set of customs is not free to leave his country for another, no matter how dissatisfied he becomes with it. "We may as well assert that a man, by remaining in a vessel, freely consents to the dominion of the master, though he was carried on board while asleep, and must leap into the ocean and perish, the moment he leaves her." Political obligation is not based on any abstract or *tacit* consent but on the fact that the government is the best institution for preserving our property and enforcing the law. That is, it has a broad utilitarian justification.

Edmund Burke (1729–97), the British statesman and philosopher, is the author of our next classic, *Reflection on the Recent Revolution in France*. In it he sets forth his brilliant but unsystematic defense of modern political conservatism. He not only predicts the course of the French Revolution, as an odyssey of violence ending in despotism, but shows how it loosens the citizen from his patrimony, the heritage which helps define an individual person. Radicalism is not only dangerous to life and limb but a form of social suicide. Burke rejects the radical egalitarianism embedded in the French Revolution, urging a benevolent, hierarchical aristocracy instead. Tradition is a treasure, which may be reformed, but ought never be abandoned.

Our seventh reading is a short selection from Mary Wollstonecraft's (1759–97) *Vindication of the Rights of Women* (1792), written only two years after Burke's work and a critique of it. Wollstonecraft defended the French Revolution as a move forward in defending civil and religious liberty and, hopefully, extending it to women. In this selection she argues for equal rights for women, contending that her lower level of ability is largely the consequence of inferior education and opportunity.

Our next selection, "The Communist Manifesto" (1848), the joint product of the German philosopher Karl Marx (1818–83) and Friedrich Engels (1820–95), is the *locus classicus* of the communist worker's movement. It is a wake-up call to the proletariat to rise from its slumber and overthrow the capitalist minions who enslave him. "Workers of the world unite, you have nothing to lose but your chains." It outlines the "specter" that haunted Europe until the end of the twentieth century. I have also included an excerpt from Marx's *Critique of the Gotha Program* (1875) in order to show the classical enlightenment (meritocratic) motif in his thought. Until the Communist Utopia is formed people should be rewarded according to their differential social contribution.

Finally, I have included a large selection from John Stuart Mill's (1806–73) *On Liberty* (1859), the classic defense of liberty which defends the principle that except to defend others from harm, one's personal liberty should be absolute. "The sole end for which mankind are warranted, individually or collectively, in interfering with liberty of action of any of their number is self-protection." All paternalistic reasons fail to override this absolute principle. Mill grounds his libertarianism in a broader utilitarianism in which liberty becomes the indispensable instrument to individual self-realization.

These nine selections constitute the most significant writings in political philosophy up to the beginning of the twentieth century in terms of philosophical acuity and influence on western society. They are valuable in their own right but can be related to the topics and readings that follow in this book: Hobbes, Locke, Rousseau and Hume can be read in connection with Part II, Justification of the State and Political Obligations. Mill connects with Part III, on Liberty; Hume, Burke, and Wollstonecraft with Part IV, on Justice; Mill with Part V on the debate over State neutrality and Perfectionism; Rousseau, Hume, and Marx with Part VI on Equality and Equal Opportunity; Locke with Part VII on Rights; Machiavelli, Hobbes, Locke and Marx and Engels with Part VIII, on Nationalism versus Internationalism in Politics.

These modern classics of political philosophy are our patrimony, to be neglected only at our peril.

READING 1

The Prince

Niccolò Machiavelli

Niccolò Machiavelli (1469 – 1527) was born in Florence and served as a diplomat in the court of Caesar Borgia until he was forced into retirement by a change of government.

His most famous work, *The Prince*, (written in 1513, published in 1532) was composed as advice for the young prince of Florence, Lorenzo de' Medici. In it, Machiavelli sets forth a realist and amoralist political philosophy. Idealism is fine in theory but not practical. He advises that if you want to succeed in office, you ought not to be preoccupied by normal moral rules. He distinguishes between man as he ought to be and man as he is and cautions us to take account of the latter, not the former, in our dealings.

The Prince must do whatever is necessary to stay in power: break promises, make friends of his enemies, betray his friends. To maintain power, he must have a strong military force that is loyal to him and always ready to defend him and his sovereignty when threatened. The successful prince is the political equivalent of the rapist.

Machiavelli is credited with being the founder of modern political realism.

This reading is taken from *The Prince* (London: J. M. Dent & Sons, 1908).

CHAPTER 15. CONCERNING THINGS FOR WHICH MEN, AND ESPECIALLY PRINCES, ARE PRAISED OR BLAMED

It remains now to see what ought to be the rules of conduct for a prince towards subject and friends. And as I know that many have written on this point, I expect I shall be considered presumptuous in mentioning it again, especially as in discussing it I shall depart from the methods of other people. But, it being my intention to write a thing which shall be useful to him who apprehends it, it appears to me more appropriate to follow up the real truth of a matter than the imagination of it; for many have pictured republics and principalities which in fact have never been known or seen, because how one lives is so far distant from how one ought to live, that he who neglects what is done for what ought to be done, sooner effects his ruin than his preservation; for a man who wishes to act entirely up to his professions of virtue soon meets with what destroys him among so much that is evil.

Hence it is necessary for a prince wishing to hold his own to know how to do wrong, and to make use of it or not according to necessity. Therefore, putting on one side imaginary things concerning a prince, and discussing those which are real, I say that all men when they are spoken of, and chiefly princes for being more highly placed, are remarkable for some of those qualities which bring them either blame or praise; and thus it is that one is reputed liberal, another miserly, using a Tuscan term (because an avaricious person in our language is still he who desires to possess by robbery, whilst we call one miserly who deprives himself too much of the use of his own); one is reputed generous, one rapacious; one cruel, one compassionate; one faithless, another faithful; one effeminate and cowardly, another bold and brave; one affable, another haughty; one lascivious, another chaste; one sincere, another cunning; one hard, another easy; one grave, another frivolous; one religious, another unbelieving, and the like. And I know that every one will confess that it would be most praiseworthy in a prince to exhibit all the above qualities that are considered good; but because they can neither be entirely possessed nor observed, for human conditions do not permit it, it is necessary for him to be sufficiently prudent that he may know how to avoid the reproach of those vices which would lose him his state; and also to keep himself, if it be possible, from those which would not lose him it; but this not being possible, he may with less hesitation abandon himself to them. And again, he need not make himself uneasy at incurring a reproach for those vices without which the state can only be saved with difficulty, for if everything is considered carefully, it will be found that something which looks like virtue, if followed, would be his ruin; whilst something else, which looks like vice, yet followed brings him security and prosperity.

CHAPTER 16. CONCERNING LIBERALITY AND MEANNESS

Commencing then with the first of the above-named characteristics, I say that it would be well to be reputed liberal. Nevertheless, liberality exercised in a way that does not bring you the reputation for it, injures you; for if one exercises it honestly and as it should be exercised, it may not become known, and you will not avoid the reproach of its opposite. Therefore, any one wishing to maintain among men the name of liberal is obliged to avoid no attribute of magnificence; so that a prince thus inclined will consume in such acts all his property, and will be compelled in the end, if he wish to maintain the name of liberal, to unduly weigh down his people, and tax them, and do everything he can to get money. This will soon make him odious to his subjects, and becoming poor he will be little valued by any one; thus, with his liberality, having offended many and rewarded few, he is affected by the very first trouble and imperilled by whatever may be the first danger; recognising this himself, and wishing to draw back from it, he runs at once into the reproach of being miserly.

Therefore, a prince, not being able to exercise this virtue of liberality in such a way that it is recognised, except to his cost, if he is wise he ought not to fear the reputation of being mean, for in time he will come to be more considered than if liberal, seeing that with his economy his revenues are enough, that he can defend himself against all attacks, and is able to engage in enterprises without burdening his people; thus it comes to pass that he exercises liberality towards all from whom he does not take, who are numberless, and meanness towards those to whom he does not give, who are few.

We have not seen great things done in our time except by those who have been considered mean; the rest have failed. Pope Julius the Second was assisted in reaching the papacy by a reputation for liberality, yet he did not strive afterwards to keep it up, when he made war on the King of France; and he made many wars without imposing any extraordinary tax on his subjects, for he supplied his additional expenses out of his long thriftiness. The present King of Spain would not have undertaken or conquered in so many enterprises if he had been reputed liberal. A prince, therefore, provided that he has not to rob his subjects, that he can defend himself, that he does not become poor and abject, that he is not forced to become rapacious, ought to hold of little account a reputation for being mean, for it is one of those vices which will enable him to govern.

And if any one should say: Caesar obtained empire by liberality, and many others have reached the highest positions by having been liberal, and by being considered so, I answer: Either you are a prince in fact, or in a way to become one. In the first case this liberality is dangerous, in the second it is very necessary to be considered liberal; and Caesar was one of those who wished to become pre-eminent in Rome; but if he had survived after becoming so, and had not moderated his expenses, he would have destroyed his government. And if any one should reply: Many have been princes, and have done great things with armies, who have been considered very liberal, I reply: Either a prince spends that which is his own or his subjects'

or else that of others. In the first case he ought to be sparing, in the second he ought not to neglect any opportunity for liberality. And to the prince who goes forth with his army, supporting it by pillage, sack, and extortion, handling that which belongs to others, this liberality is necessary, otherwise he would not be followed by soldiers. And of that which is neither yours nor your subjects' you can be a ready giver, as were Cyrus, Caesar, and Alexander; because it does not take away your reputation if you squander that of others, but adds to it; it is only squandering your own that injures you.

And there is nothing wastes so rapidly as liberality, for even whilst you exercise it you lose the power to do so, and so become either poor or despised, or else, in avoiding poverty, rapacious and hated. And a prince should guard himself, above all things, against being despised and hated; and liberality leads you to both. Therefore it is wiser to have a reputation for meanness which brings reproach without hatred, than to be compelled through seeking a reputation for liberality to incur a name for rapacity which begets reproach with hatred.

CHAPTER 17. CONCERNING CRUELTY AND CLEMENCY, AND WHETHER IT IS BETTER TO BE LOVED THAN FEARED

Coming now to the other qualities mentioned above, I say that every prince ought to desire to be considered clement and not cruel. Nevertheless he ought to take care not to misuse this clemency. Cesare Borgia was considered cruel; notwithstanding, his cruelty reconciled the Romagna, unified it, and restored it to peace and loyalty. And if this be rightly considered, he will be seen to have been much more merciful than the Florentine people, who, to avoid a reputation for cruelty, permitted Pistoia to be destroyed. Therefore a prince, so long as he keeps his subjects united and loyal, ought not to mind the reproach of cruelty; because with a few examples he will be more merciful than those who, through too much mercy, allow disorders to arise, from which follow murder or robbery; for these are wont to injure the whole people, whilst those executions which originate with a prince offend the individual only.

And of all princes, it is impossible for the new prince to avoid the imputation of cruelty, owing to new states being full of dangers. Hence Virgil, through the mouth of Dido, excuses the inhumanity of her reign owing to its being new. . . . Nevertheless he ought to be slow to believe and to act, nor should he himself show fear, but proceed in a temperate manner with prudence and humanity, so that too much confidence may not make him incautious and too much distrust render him intolerable.

Upon this a question arises: whether it be better to be loved than feared or feared than loved? It may be answered that one should wish to be both, but, because it is difficult to unite them in one person, it is much safer to be feared than loved, when, of the two, either must be dispensed with. Because this is to be asserted in general of men, that they are ungrateful, fickle, false, cowards, covetous, and as long as you succeed they are yours entirely; they will offer you their blood, property, life, and children, as is said above, when the need is far distant; but when it approaches they turn against you. And that prince who, relying entirely on their promises, has neglected other precautions, is ruined; because friendships that are obtained by payments, and not by greatness or nobility of mind, may indeed be earned, but they are not secured, and in time of need cannot be relied upon; and men have less scruple in offending one who is beloved than one who is feared, for love is preserved by the link of obligation which, owing to the baseness of men, is broken at every opportunity for their advantage; but fear preserves you by a dread of punishment which never fails.

Nevertheless a prince ought to inspire fear in such a way that, if he does not win love, he avoids hatred; because he can endure very well being feared whilst he is not hated, which will always be as long as he abstains from the property of his citizens and subjects and from their women. But when it is necessary for him to proceed against the life of some one, he must do it on proper justification and for manifest cause, but above all things he must keep his hands off the property of others, because men more quickly forget the death of their father than the loss of their patrimony. Besides, pretexts for taking away the property are never wanting; for he who has once begun to live by robbery will always find pretexts for seizing what belongs to others; but reasons for taking life, on the contrary, are more difficult to find and sooner lapse. But when a prince is with his army, and has under control a multitude of soldiers, then it is quite necessary for him to disregard the reputation of cruelty, for without it he would never hold his army united or disposed to its duties.

Among the wonderful deeds of Hannibal this one is enumerated: that having led an enormous army, composed of many various races of men, to fight in foreign lands, no dissensions arose either among them or against the prince, whether in his bad or in his good fortune. This arose from nothing else than his inhuman cruelty, which, with his boundless valour, made him revered and terrible in the sight of his soldiers, but without that cruelty, his other virtues were not sufficient to produce this effect. And short-sighted writers admire his deeds from one point of view and from another condemn the principal cause of them. That it is true his other virtues would not have been sufficient for him may be proved by the case of Scipio, that most excellent man, not only of his own times but within the memory of man, against whom, nevertheless, his army rebelled in Spain; this arose from nothing but his too great forbearance, which gave his soldiers more licence than is consistent with military discipline. For this he was upbraided in the Senate by Fabius Maximus, and called the corruptor of Roman soldiery. The Locrians were laid waste by a legate of Scipio, yet they were not avenged by him, nor was the insolence of the legate punished, owing entirely to his easy nature. Insomuch that some one in the Senate, wishing to excuse him, said there were many men who knew much better how not to err than to correct the errors of others. This disposition, if he had been continued in the command, would have destroyed in time the fame and glory of Scipio; but, he being under the control of the Senate, this injurious characteristic not only concealed itself, but contributed to his glory.

Returning to the question of being feared or loved, I come to the conclusion that, men loving according to their own will and fearing according to that of the prince, a wise prince should establish himself on that which is in his own control and not in that of others; he must endeavour only to avoid hatred, as is noted.

CHAPTER 18. CONCERNING THE WAY IN WHICH PRINCES SHOULD KEEP FAITH

Every one admits how praiseworthy it is in a prince to keep faith, and to live with integrity and not with craft. Nevertheless our experience has been that those princes who have done great things have held good faith of little account, and have known how to circumvent the intellect of men by craft, and in the end have overcome those who have relied on their word. You must know there are two ways of contesting, the one by the law, the other by force; the first method is proper to men, the second to beasts; but because the first is frequently not sufficient, it is necessary to have recourse to the second. Therefore it is necessary for a prince to understand how to avail himself of the beast and the man. This has been figuratively taught to princes by ancient writers, who describe how Achilles and many other princes of old were given to the Centaur Chiron to nurse, who brought them up in his discipline; which means solely that, as they had for a teacher one who was half beast and half man, so it is necessary for a prince to know how to make use of both natures, and that one without the other is not durable. A prince, therefore, being compelled knowingly to adopt the beast, ought to choose the fox and the lion; because the lion cannot defend himself against snares and the fox cannot defend himself against wolves. Therefore, it is necessary to be a fox to discover the snares and a lion to terrify the wolves. Those who rely simply on the lion do not understand what they are about. Therefore a wise lord cannot, nor ought he to, keep faith when such observance may be turned against him, and when the reasons that caused him to pledge it exist no longer. If men were entirely good this precept would not hold, but because they are bad, and will not keep faith with you, you too are not bound to observe it with them. Nor will there ever be wanting to a prince legitimate reasons to excuse this non-observance. Of this endless modern examples could be given, showing how many treaties and engagements have been made void and of no effect through the faithlessness of princes; and he who has known best how to employ the fox has succeeded best.

But it is necessary to know well how to disguise this characteristic, and to be a great pretender and dissembler; and men are so simple, and so subject to present necessities, that he who seeks to deceive will always find some one who will allow himself to be deceived. One recent example I cannot pass over in silence. Alexander the Sixth did nothing else but deceive men, nor ever thought of doing otherwise, and he always found victims; for there never was a man who had greater power in asserting, or who with greater oaths would affirm a thing, yet would observe it less; nevertheless his deceits always succeeded according to his wishes, because he well understood this side of mankind.

Therefore it is unnecessary for a prince to have all the good qualities I have enumerated, but it is very necessary to appear to have them. And I shall dare to say this also, that to have them and always to observe them is injurious, and that to appear to have them is useful; to appear merciful, faithful, humane, religious, upright, and to be so, but with a mind so framed that should you require not to be so, you may be able to know how to change to the opposite.

And you have to understand this, that a prince, especially a new one, cannot observe all those things for which men are esteemed, being often forced, in order to maintain the state, to act contrary to fidelity, friendship, humanity, and religion. Therefore it is necessary for him to have a mind ready to turn itself accordingly as the winds and variations of fortune force it, yet, as I have said above, not to diverge from the good if he can avoid doing so, but, if compelled, then to know how to set about it.

For this reason a prince ought to take care that he never lets anything slip from his lips that is not replete with the above-named five qualities, that he may appear to him who sees and hears him altogether merciful, faithful, humane, upright, and religious. There is nothing more necessary to appear to have than this last quality, inasmuch as men judge generally more by the eye than by the hand, because it belongs to everybody to see you, to few to come in touch with you. Every one sees what you appear to be, few really know what you are, and those few dare not oppose themselves to the opinion of the many, who have the majesty of the state to defend them; and in the actions of all men, and especially of princes, which it is not prudent to challenge, one judges by the result.

For that reason, let a prince have the credit of conquering and holding his state, the means will always be considered honest, and he will be praised by everybody; because the vulgar are always taken by what a thing seems to be and by what comes of it; and in the world there are only the vulgar, for the few find a place there only when the many have no ground to rest on.

One prince of the present time, whom it is not well to name, never preaches anything else but peace and good faith, and to both he is most hostile, and either, if he had kept it, would have deprived him of reputation and kingdom many a time. . . .

CHAPTER 25. WHAT FORTUNE CAN EFFECT IN HUMAN AFFAIRS, AND HOW TO WITHSTAND HER

It is not unknown to me how many men have had, and still have, the opinion that the affairs of the world are in such wise governed by fortune and by God that men with their wisdom cannot direct them and that no one can even help them; and because of this they would have us believe that it is not necessary to labour much in affairs, but to let chance govern them. This opinion has been more credited in our times because of the great changes in affairs which have been seen, and may still be seen, every day, beyond all human conjecture. Sometimes pondering over this, I am in some degree inclined to their opinion. Nevertheless, not to extinguish our free will, I hold it to be true that fortune is the arbiter of one half of our actions, but that she still leaves us to direct the other half, or perhaps a little less.

I compare her to one of those raging rivers, which when in flood overflows the plains, sweeping away trees and buildings, bearing away the soil from place to place; everything flies before it, all yield to its violence, without being able in any way to withstand it; and yet, though its nature be such, it does not follow therefore that men, when the weather becomes fair, shall not make provision, both with defences and barriers, in such a manner that, rising again, the waters may pass away by canal, and their force be neither so unrestrained nor so dangerous. So it happens with fortune, who shows her power where valour has not prepared to resist her, and thither she turns her forces where she knows that barriers and defences have not been raised to constrain her.

And if you will consider Italy, which is the seat of these changes, and which has given to them their impulse, you will see it to be an open country without barriers and without any defence. For if it had been defended by proper valour, as are Germany, Spain, and France, either this invasion would not have made the great changes it has made or it would not have come at all. And this I consider enough to say concerning resistance to fortune in general.

But confining myself more to the particular, I say that a prince may be seen happy to-day and ruined to-morrow without having shown any change of disposition or character. This, I believe, arises firstly from causes that have already been discussed at length, namely, that the prince who relies entirely upon fortune is lost when it changes. I believe also that he will be successful who directs his actions according to the spirit of the times, and that he whose actions do not accord with the times will not be successful. Because men are seen, in affairs that lead to the end which every man has before him, namely, glory and riches, to get there by various methods; one with caution, another with haste; one by force, another by skill; one by patience, another by its op-

posite; and each one succeeds in reaching the goal by a different method. One can also see of two cautious men the one attain his end, the other fail; and similarly, two men by different observances are equally successful, the one being cautious, the other impetuous; all this arises from nothing else than whether or not they conform in their methods to the spirit of the times. This follows from what I have said, that two men working differently bring about the same effect, and of two working similarly, one attains his object and the other does not.

Changes in estate also issue from this, for if, to one who governs himself with caution and patience, times and affairs converge in such a way that his administration is successful, his fortune is made; but if times and affairs change, he is ruined if he does not change his course of action. But a man is not often found sufficiently circumspect to know how to accommodate himself to the change, both because he cannot deviate from what nature inclines him to, and also because, having always prospered by acting in one way, he cannot be persuaded that it is well to leave it; and, therefore, the cautious man, when it is time to turn adventurous, does not know how to do it, hence he is ruined; but had he changed his conduct with the times fortune would not have changed.

Pope Julius the Second went to work impetuously in all his affairs, and found the times and circumstances conformed so well to that line of action that he always met with success. Consider his first enterprise against Bologna, Messer Giovanni Bentivogli being still alive. The Venetians were not agreeable to it, nor was the King of Spain, and he had the enterprise still under discussion with the King of France; nevertheless he personally entered upon the expedition with his accustomed boldness and energy, a move which made Spain and the Venetians stand irresolute and passive, the latter from fear, the former from desire to recover all the kingdom of Naples; on the other hand, he drew after him the King of France, because that king, having observed the movement, and desiring to make the Pope his friend so as to humble the Venetians, found it impossible to refuse him soldiers without manifestly offending him. Therefore Julius with his impetuous action accomplished what no other pontiff with simple human wisdom could have done; for if he had waited in Rome until he could get away, with his plans arranged and everything fixed, as any other pontiff would have done, he would never have succeeded. Because the King of France would have made a thousand excuses, and the others would have raised a thousand fears.

I will leave his other actions alone, as they were all alike, and they all succeeded, for the shortness of his life did not let him experience the contrary; but if circumstances had arisen which required him to go cautiously, his ruin would have followed, because he would never have deviated from those ways to which nature inclined him.

I conclude therefore that, fortune being changeful and mankind steadfast in their ways, so long as the two are in agreement men are successful, but unsuccessful when they fall out. For my part I consider that it is better to be adventurous than cautious, because fortune is a woman, and if you wish to keep her under it is necessary to beat and ill-use her; and it is seen that she allows herself to be mastered by the adventurous rather than by those who go to work more coldly. She is, therefore, always, woman-like, a lover of young men, because they are less cautious, more violent, and with more audacity command her.

READING 2

Leviathan

Thomas Hobbes

Thomas Hobbes of Malmesbury (1588–1679), considered by many to be the greatest English political philosopher, gave classic expression to the idea that morality and politics arise out of a social contract. The son of an eccentric vicar, he was born on Good Friday, April 5, 1588, in Westbury, England. On the day of his birth, the Spanish Armada, the greatest naval fleet the world had seen up to that time, was spotted off the coast of southern England. The chronicler John Aubrey reported that Hobbes's mother, only seven months pregnant, was so startled by the news that she fell into labor with Hobbes and delivered him. Hobbes wrote of his birth, "Unbeknownst to my mother at that time she gave birth to twins, myself and fear. And fear has been my constant companion throughout life." Hobbes's lifetime was filled with the dangers of war: the invading Spanish Armada, the religious wars of Europe, the civil wars in England. His po-

litical philosophy may be read as a cure against the fear and insecurity of people desperately in need of peace and tranquility.

Hobbes was educated at Oxford University and lived through an era of political revolutions as a scholar and tutor (he was tutor to Prince Charles II of England). He was widely traveled and was in communication with most of the intellectual luminaries of his day, both on the Continent (Galileo, Gassendi, Descartes) and in England (Bacon, Johnson, Harvey). He was regarded as a brilliant, if somewhat unorthodox and controversial, intellectual.

Hobbes is known today primarily for his masterpiece in political theory, *Leviathan* (1651), a book written during the English civil wars (1641–52), sometimes referred to as the Great Rebellion, which pitted the forces of monarchy (the Royalists) under Charles I against those of Parliament under Oliver Cromwell. Hobbes's work was intended to support the Royalists, as he believed that the monarchy was the best guarantee for orderly and stable government. Yet the Royalists misconstrued his interpretation as supporting the rebels, no doubt because Hobbes rejected the usual grounds for the monarchy, the divine right of kings. For this reason, and because the book conveyed a materialist view of human nature, thought to be dangerous to religion, it was suppressed or violently attacked throughout Hobbes's lifetime.

What were the doctrines his contemporaries found so controversial? First of all, Hobbes broke from the medieval notion that the State is a natural organism, based on natural devotion and interdependence. He developed a moral and political theory based not on natural affection but on psychological egoism. Hobbes argued that all people are egoists who always act in their own self-interest, to obtain gratification and avoid harm. However, we cannot obtain any of the basic goods because of the inherent fear of harm and death, the insecurity in an unregulated "state of nature," in which life is "solitary, poor, nasty, brutish, and short." We cannot relax our guard, for everyone is constantly in fear of everyone else. In this state of anarchy, the prudent person concludes that it really is in all our self-interests to make a contract to keep to a minimal morality of respecting human life, keeping covenants made, and obeying the laws of the society. This minimal morality, which Hobbes refered to as the "Laws of Nature," is nothing more than a set of maxims of prudence. In order to ensure that we all obey this covenant, Hobbes proposed a strong sovereign, or "Leviathan," to impose severe penalties on those who disobey the laws, for "covenants without the sword are but words." The term *Leviathan* refers to the sea monster (or whale) referred to in the Book of Job:

> Let those curse it who curse the day, who are skilled to rouse up Leviathan. (3:8)
>
> Can you draw out Leviathan with a fishhook, or press down his tongue with a cord?
>
> Can you put a rope in his nose, or pierce his jaw with a hook? . . .
>
> Will he make a covenant with you to take him for your servant for ever? . . .
>
> His sneezings flash forth light, and his eyes are like the eyelids of the dawn.
>
> Out of his mouth go flaming torches; sparks of fire leap forth.
>
> Out of his nostrils comes forth smoke, as from a boiling pot and burning rushes.
>
> His breath kindles coals, and a flame comes forth from his mouth. . . .
>
> When he raises himself up the mighty are afraid; at the crashing they are beside themselves. . . .
>
> Upon earth there is not his like, a creature without fear.
>
> He beholds everything that is high; he is king over all the sons of pride. (41)

The State is the great Leviathan, awesome and powerful, inspiring fear, but offering protection from violence and harm. We begin with Hobbes's discussion of human nature in Part 1 of *Leviathan* and move on through Part 2 on the Commonwealth.

This reading is taken from *Leviathan; or The Matter, Form, & Power of a Commonwealth Ecclesiastical and Civil.*

PART 1. OF MAN

Chapter 13. Of the Natural Condition of Mankind as Concerning Their Felicity, and Misery

Nature hath made men so equal in the faculties of body and mind as that though there be found one man sometimes manifestly stronger in body, or of quicker mind than another, yet when all is reckoned together, the difference between man and man is not so considerable as that one man can thereupon claim to himself any benefit, to which another may not pretend, as well as he. For as to the strength of body, the weakest has strength enough to kill the strongest, either by secret machination or by confederacy with others, that are in the same danger with himself.

And as to the faculties of the mind (setting aside the arts grounded upon words, and especially that skill of proceeding upon general, and infallible rules, called science; which very few have, and but in few things; as being not a native faculty, born with us; nor attained (as prudence) while we look after somewhat else) I find yet a greater equality amongst men, than that of strength. For prudence is but experience; which equal time, equally bestows on all men, in those things they equally apply themselves unto. That which may perhaps make such equality incredible is but a vain conceit of one's own wisdom, which almost all men think they have in a greater degree than the vulgar; that is, than all men but themselves, and a few others, whom by fame, or for concurring with themselves, they approve. For such is the nature of men, that howsoever they may acknowledge many others to be more witty, or more eloquent, or more learned; yet they will hardly believe there be many so wise as themselves: For they see their own wit at hand, and other men's at a distance. But this proves rather that men are in that point equal, than unequal. For there is not ordinarily a greater sign of the equal distribution of any thing, than that every man is contented with his share.

From this equality of ability arises equality of hope in the attaining of our ends. And therefore if any two men desire the same thing, which nevertheless they cannot both enjoy, they become enemies; and in the way to their end (which is principally their own conservation, and sometimes their delectation only) endeavor to destroy, or subdue one another. And from hence it comes to pass, that where an invader hath no more to fear than another man's single power; if one plant, sow, build, or possess a convenient seat, others may probably be expected to come prepared with forces united, to dispossess, and deprive him, not only of the fruit of his labour, but also of his life, or liberty. And the invader again is in the like danger of another.

And from this diffidence of one another, there is no way for any man to secure himself, so reasonable, as anticipation; that is, by force, or wiles, to master the persons of all men he can, so long, till he see no other power great enough to endanger him: and this is no more than his own conservation requires, and is generally allowed. Also because there be some, that taking pleasure in contemplating their own power in the acts of conquest, which they pursue farther than their security requires; if others, that otherwise would be glad to be at ease within modest bounds, should not by invasion increase their power, they would not be able, long time, by standing only on their defence, to subsist. And by consequence, such augmentation of dominion over men, being necessary to a man's conservation, it ought to be allowed him.

Again, men have no pleasure (but on the contrary a great deal of grief) in keeping company, where there is no power able to over-awe them all. For every man looks that his companion should value him at the same rate he sets upon himself: and upon all signs of contempt, or undervaluing, naturally endeavors, as far as he dares (which amongst them that have no common power to keep them in quiet, is far enough to make them destroy each other), to extort a greater value from his condemners, by damage; and from others, by the example.

So that in the nature of man, we find three principal causes of quarrel. First, competition; secondly, diffidence; thirdly, glory.

The first maketh men invade for gain; the second, for safety; and the third, for reputation. The first use violence, to make themselves masters of other men's persons, wives, children, and cattle; the second, to defend them; the third, for trifles, as a word, a smile, a different opinion, and any other sign of undervalue, either direct in their persons, or by reflection in their kindred, their friends, their nation, their profession, or their name.

Hereby it is manifest, that during the time men live without a common power to keep them all in awe, they are in that condition which is called war; and such a war, as is of every man, against every man. For WAR consists not in battle only, or the act of fighting; but in a tract of time, wherein the will to contend by battle is sufficiently known: and therefore the notion of time, is to be considered in the nature of war; as it is in the nature of weather. For as the nature of foul weather lies not in a shower or two of rain; but in an inclination thereto of many days together: so the nature of war consists not in actual fighting; but in the known disposition thereto, during all the time there is no assurance to the contrary. All other time is PEACE.

Whatsoever therefore is consequent to a time of war, where every man is enemy to every man; the same is consequent to the time, wherein men live without other security, than what their own strength, and their own invention shall furnish them withal. In such condition, there is no place for industry; because the fruit thereof is uncertain: and consequently no culture of the earth; no navigation, nor use of the commodities that may be imported by sea; no commodious building; no instruments of moving, and removing such things as require much force; no knowledge of the face of the earth; no account of time; no arts; no letters; no society; and which is worst of all, continual fear, and danger of violent death; and the life of man, solitary, poor, nasty, brutish, and short.

It may seem strange to some man, that has not well weighed these things; that nature should thus dissociate, and render men apt to invade, and destroy one another: and he may therefore, not trusting to this inference, made from the passions, desire perhaps to have the same confirmed by experience. Let him therefore consider with himself, when taking a journey, he arms himself, and seeks to go well accompanied; when going to sleep, he locks his doors; when even in his house he locks his chests; and this when he knows there be laws, and public officers, armed, to revenge all injuries that shall be done him; what opinion he has of his fellow subjects, when he rides armed; of his fellow citizens, when he locks his doors; and of his children, and servants, when he locks his chests. Does he not there as much accuse mankind by his actions, as I do by my words? But neither of us accuse man's nature in it. The desires, and other passions of man, are in themselves no sin. No more are the actions, that proceed from those passions, till they know a law that forbids them: which till laws be made they cannot know: nor can any law be made, till they have agreed upon the person that shall make it.

It may peradventure be thought, there was never such a time, nor condition of war as this; and I believe it was never generally so, over all the world: but there are many places, where they live so now. For the savage people in many places of America, except the government of small families, the concord whereof depends on natural lust, have no government at all; and live at this day in that brutish manner, as I said before. Howsoever, it may be perceived what manner of life there would be, where there were no common power to fear; by the manner of life, which men that have formerly lived under a peaceful government, use to degenerate into, in a civil war.

But though there had never been any time, wherein particular men were in a condition of war one against another; yet in all times, kings, and persons of sovereign authority, because of their independency, are in continual jealousies, and in the state and posture of gladiators; having their weapons pointing, and their eyes fixed on one another; that is, their forts, garrisons, and guns upon the frontiers of their kingdoms; and continual spies upon their neighbours; which is a posture of war. But because they uphold thereby, the industry of their subjects; there does not follow from it that misery which accompanies the liberty of particular men.

To this war of every man against every man, this also is consequent; that nothing can be unjust. The notions of right and wrong, justice and injustice have there no place. Where there is no common power, there is no law: where no law, no injustice. Force, and fraud, are in war the two cardinal virtues. Justice, and injustice are none of the faculties neither of the body, nor mind. If they were, they might be in a man that were alone in the world, as well as his senses, and passions. They are qualities that relate to men in society, not in solitude. It is consequent also to the same condition, that there be no propriety, no dominion, no mine and thine distinct; but only that to be every man's, that he can get; and for so long as he can keep it. And thus much for the ill condition, which man by mere nature is actually placed in; though with a possibility to come out of it, consisting partly in the passions, partly in his reason.

The passions that incline men to peace are fear of death; desire of such things as are necessary to commodious living; and a hope by their industry to obtain them. And reason suggests convenient articles of peace, upon which men may be drawn to agreement. These articles, are they, which otherwise are called the Laws of Nature: whereof I shall speak more particularly, in the two following chapters.

CHAPTER 14. OF THE FIRST AND SECOND NATURAL LAWS, AND OF CONTRACTS

The RIGHT OF NATURE, which writers commonly call jus naturale, is the liberty each man hath, to use his own power, as he will himself, for the preservation of his own nature; that is to say, of his own life; and consequently, of doing any thing, which in his own judgment, and reason, he shall conceive to be the aptest means thereunto.

By LIBERTY, is understood, according to the proper signification of the word, the absence of external impediments: which impediments, may oft take away part of a man's power to do what he would; but cannot hinder him from using the power left him, according as his judgment, and reason shall dictate to him.

A LAW OF NATURE (lex naturalis) is a precept, or general rule, found out by reason, by which a man is forbidden to do that, which is destructive of his life, or taketh away the means of preserving the same; and to omit that, by which he thinks it may be best preserved. For though they that speak of this subject, use to confound jus, and lex, right and law; yet they ought to be distinguished; because RIGHT, consists in liberty to do, or to forbear; whereas LAW, determines, and binds to one of them: so that law, and right, differ as much, as obligation, and liberty; which in one and the same matter are inconsistent.

And because the condition of man (as hath been declared in the precedent chapter) is a condition of war of every one against every one; in which case every one is governed by his own reason; and there is nothing he can make use of that may not be a help unto him, in preserving his life against his enemies; it followeth, that in such a condition, every man has a right to every thing; even to one another's body. And therefore, as long as this natural right of every man to every thing endures, there can be no security to any man (how strong or wise soever he be) of living out the time, which nature ordinarily allows men to live. And consequently it is a precept, or general rule of reason, that every man ought to endeavor peace, as far as he has hope of obtaining it; and when he cannot obtain it, that he may seek, and use, all helps, and advantages of war. The first branch of which rule, containeth the first, and fundamental law of nature; which is, to seek peace, and follow it. The second, the sum of the right of nature; which is, by all means we can, to defend ourselves.

From this fundamental law of nature, by which men are commanded to endeavor peace, is derived this second law; that a man be willing, when others are so too, as far-forth, as for peace, and defence of himself he shall think it necessary, to lay down this right to all things; and be contented with so much liberty against other men, as he would allow other men against himself. For as long as every man holds this right, of doing any thing he likes; so long are all men in the condition of war. But if other men will not lay down their right, as well as he; then there is no reason for any one to divest himself of his: for that were to expose himself to prey (which no man is bound to) rather than to dispose himself of peace. This is that law of the Gospel; whatsoever you require that others should do to you, that do ye to them. And that law of all men, [what you would not have done to you, do not do to others].

To lay down a man's right to any thing, is to divest himself of the liberty, of hindering another of the benefit of his own right to the same. For he that renounces or passeth away his right, giveth not to any other man a right which he had not before; because there is nothing to which every man had not right by nature: but only stands out of his way, that he may enjoy his own original right, without hindrance from him; not without hindrance from another. So that the effect which redounds to one man, by another man's defect of right, is but so much diminution of impediments to the use of his own right original.

Right is laid aside, either by simply renouncing it; or by transferring it to another. By simply RENOUNCING; when he cares not to whom the benefit thereof redounds. By TRANSFERRING; when he intends the benefit thereof to some certain person, or persons. And when a man hath in either manner abandoned, or granted away his right; then is he said to be OBLIGED, or BOUND, not to hinder those, to whom such right is granted, or abandoned, from the benefit of it: and that he ought, and it is his DUTY, not to make void that voluntary act of his own: and that such hindrance is INJUSTICE, and INJURY, as being sine jure; the right being before renounced, or transferred. So that injury, or in-

justice, in the controversies of the world, is somewhat like to that, which in the disputations of scholars is called absurdity. For as it is there called an absurdity, to contradict what one maintained in the beginning: so in the world, it is called injustice, and injury, voluntarily to undo that, which from the beginning he had voluntarily done. The way by which a man either simply renounces, or transfers his right, is a declaration, or signification, by some voluntary and sufficient sign, or signs, that he doth so renounce, or transfer; or hath so renounced, or transferred the same, to him that accepts it. And these signs are either words only, or actions only; or (as it happens most often) both words, and actions. And the same are the BONDS, by which men are bound, and obliged: bonds that have their strength, not from their own nature (for nothing is more easily broken than a man's word,) but from fear of some evil consequence upon the rupture.

Whensoever a man transfers his right, or renounces it; it is either in consideration of some right reciprocally transferred to himself; or for some other good he hopes for thereby. For it is a voluntary act: and of the voluntary acts of every man, the object is some good to himself. And therefore there be some rights, which no man can be understood by any words, or other signs, to have abandoned, or transferred. As first a man cannot lay down the right of resisting them, that assault him by force, to take away his life; because he cannot be understood to aim thereby, at any good to himself. The same may be said of wounds, and chains, and imprisonment; both because there is no benefit consequent to such patience; as there is to the patience of suffering another to be wounded, or imprisoned: as also because a man cannot tell, when he sees men proceed against him by violence, whether they intend his death or not. And lastly the motive, and end for which this renouncing, and transferring of right is introduced, is nothing else but the security of a man's person, in his life, and in the means of so preserving life, as not to be weary of it. And therefore if a man by words, or other signs, seem to despoil himself of the end, for which those signs were intended; he is not to be understood as if he meant it, or that it was his will; but that he was ignorant of how such words and actions were to be interpreted.

The mutual transferring of right, is that which men call CONTRACT.

There is difference between transferring of right to the thing; and transferring, or tradition, that is, delivery of the thing itself. For the thing may be delivered together with the translation of the right; as in buying and selling with ready money; or exchange of goods, or lands: and it may be delivered some time after.

Again, one of the contractors, may deliver the thing contracted for on his part, and leave the other to perform his part at some determinate time after, and in the mean time be trusted; and then the contract on his part, is called PACT, or COVENANT: or both parts may contract now, to perform hereafter: in which cases he that is to perform in time to come, being trusted, his performance is called keeping of promise, or faith; and the failing of performance (if it be voluntary) violation of faith.

When the transferring of right, is not mutual; but one of the parties transfers, in hope to gain thereby friendship, or service from another, or from his friends; or in hope to gain the reputation of charity, or magnanimity; or to deliver his mind from the pain of compassion; or in hope of reward in heaven; this is not contract, but GIFT, FREE-GIFT, GRACE: which words signify one and the same thing.

Signs of contract are either express, or by inference. Express, are words spoken with understanding of what they signify: and such words are either of the time present, or past; as, I give, I grant, I have given, I have granted, I will that this be yours: or of the future; as, I will give, I will grant: which words of the future are called PROMISE.

Signs by inference are sometimes the consequence of words; sometimes the consequence of silence; sometimes the consequence of actions; sometimes the consequence of forbearing an action: and generally a sign by inference, of any contract, is whatsoever sufficiently argues the will of the contractor.

Words alone, if they be of the time to come, and contain a bare promise, are an insufficient sign of a free-gift and therefore not obligatory. For if they be of the time to come, as, tomorrow I will give, they are a sign I have not given yet, and consequently that my right is not transferred, but remains till I transfer it by some other act. But if the words be of the time present, or past, as, I have given, or do give to be delivered tomorrow, then is my tomorrow's right given away today; and that by the virtue of the words, though there were no other argument of my will. And there is a great difference in the signification of these words, volo hoc tuum esse cras, and cras dabo; that is, between I will that this be thine tomorrow, and, I will give it thee tomorrow: for the word I will, in the former manner of speech, signifies an act of the will present; but in the latter, it signifies a promise of an act of the will to come: and therefore the former words, being of the

present, transfer a future right; the latter, that be of the future, transfer nothing. But if there be other signs of the will to transfer a right, besides words; then, though the gift be free, yet may the right be understood to pass by words of the future: as if a man propound a prize to him that comes first to the end of a race, the gift is free; and though the words be of the future, yet the right passeth: for if he would not have his words so be understood, he should not have let them run.

In contracts, the right passeth, not only where the words are of the time present, or past, but also where they are of the future: because all contract is mutual translation, or change of right; and therefore he that promises only, because he hath already received the benefit for which he promises, is to be understood as if he intended the right should pass: for unless he had been content to have his words so understood, the other would not have performed his part first. And for that cause, in buying, and selling, and other acts of contract, a promise is equivalent to a covenant; and therefore obligatory.

He that performs first in the case of a contract, is said to MERIT that which he is to receive by the performance of the other; and he hath it as due. Also when a prize is propounded to many, which is to be given to him only that wins; or money is thrown amongst many, to be enjoyed by them that catch it; though this be a free gift; yet so to win, or so to catch, is to merit, and to have it as DUE. For the right is transferred in the propounding of the prize, and in throwing down the money; though it be not determined to whom, but by the event of the contention. But there is between these two sorts of merit, this difference, that in contract, I merit by virtue of my own power, and the contractor's need; but in this case of free gift, I am enabled to merit only by the benignity of the giver: in contract, I merit at the contractor's hand that he should depart with his right; in this case of gift, I merit not that the giver should part with his right; but that when he has parted with it, it should be mine, rather than another's. . . .

If a covenant be made, wherein neither of the parties perform presently, but trust one another; in the condition of mere nature (which is a condition of war of every man against every man) upon any reasonable suspicion, it is void: but if there be a common power set over them both, with right and force sufficient to compel performance, it is not void. For he that performs first, has no assurance the other will perform after; because the bonds of words are too weak to bridle men's ambition, avarice, anger, and other passions, without the fear of some coercive power; which in the condition of mere nature, where all men are equal, and judges of the justness of their own fears, cannot possibly be supposed. And therefore he which performs first, does but betray himself to his enemy; contrary to the right (he can never abandon) of defending his life, and means of living.

But in a civil estate, where there is a power set up to constrain those that would otherwise violate their faith, that fear is no more reasonable; and for that cause, he which by the covenant is to perform first, is obliged so to do.

The cause of fear, which maketh such a covenant invalid, must be always something arising after the covenant made; as some new fact, or other sign of the will not to perform: else it cannot make the covenant void. For that which could not hinder a man from promising, ought not to be admitted as a hindrance of performing.

He that transfers any right, transfers the means of enjoying it, as far as lies in his power. As he that sells land is understood to transfer the herbage, and whatsoever grows upon it; nor can he that sells a mill turn away the stream that drives it. And they that give to a man the right of government in sovereignty are understood to give him the right of levying money to maintain soldiers; and of appointing magistrates for the administration of justice.

To make covenants with brute beasts is impossible; because not understanding our speech, they understand not, nor accept of any translation of right; nor can translate any right to another: and without mutual acceptation, there is no covenant.

To make covenant with God is impossible, but by mediation of such as God speaks to, either by revelation supernatural, or by his lieutenants that govern under him, and in his name: for otherwise we know not whether our covenants be accepted, or not. And therefore they that vow any thing contrary to any law of nature, vow in vain; as being a thing unjust to pay such vow. And if it be a thing commanded by the law of nature, it is not the vow, but the law that binds them.

The matter, or subject of a covenant, is always something that falls under deliberation; (for to covenant, is an act of the will; that is to say an act, and the last act, of deliberation;) and is therefore always understood to be something to come; and which is judged possible for him that covenants, to perform.

And therefore, to promise that which is known to be impossible is no covenant. But if that prove impossible afterwards, which before was thought possible, the covenant is valid, and binds (though not to the thing

itself) yet to the value; or, if that also be impossible, to the unfeigned endeavor of performing as much as is possible: for to more no man can be obliged.

Men are freed of their covenants two ways; by performing; or by being forgiven. For performance, is the natural end of obligation; and forgiveness, the restitution of liberty; as being a retransferring of that right, in which the obligation consisted.

Covenants entered into by fear, in the condition of mere nature, are obligatory. For example, if I covenant to pay a ransom, or service for my life, to an enemy; I am bound by it. For it is a contract, wherein one receives the benefit of life; the other is to receive money, or service for it; and consequently, where no other law (as in the condition of mere nature) forbids the performance, the covenant is valid. Therefore prisoners of war, if trusted with the payment of their ransom, are obliged to pay it: and if a weaker prince, make a disadvantageous peace with a stronger, for fear; he is bound to keep it; unless (as hath been said before) there arises some new, and just cause of fear, to renew the war. And even in commonwealths, if I be forced to redeem myself from a thief by promising him money, I am bound to pay it, till the civil law discharge me. For whatsoever I may lawfully do without obligation, the same I may lawfully covenant to do through fear: and what I lawfully covenant, I cannot lawfully break.

A former covenant makes void a later. For a man that hath passed away his right to one man today, hath it not to pass tomorrow to another: and therefore the later promise passeth no right, but is null.

A covenant not to defend myself from force, by force, is always void. For (as I have showed before) no man can transfer, or lay down his right to save himself from death, wounds, and imprisonment (the avoiding whereof is the only end of laying down any right, and therefore the promise of not resisting force, in no covenant transfers any right; nor is obliging). For though a man may covenant thus, unless I do so, or so, kill me; he cannot covenant thus, unless I do so, or so, I will not resist you, when you come to kill me. For man by nature chooses the lesser evil, which is danger of death in resisting; rather than the greater, which is certain and present death in not resisting. And this is granted to be true by all men, in that they lead criminals to execution, and prison, with armed men, notwithstanding that such criminals have consented to the law, by which they are condemned.

A covenant to accuse one self, without assurance of pardon, is likewise invalid. For in the condition of nature, where every man is judge, there is no place for accusation: and in the civil state, the accusation is followed with punishment; which being force, a man is not obliged not to resist. The same is also true, of the accusation of those, by whose condemnation a man falls into misery; as of a father, wife, or benefactor. For the testimony of such an accuser, if it be not willingly given, is presumed to be corrupted by nature; and therefore not to be received: and where a man's testimony is not to be credited, he is not bound to give it. Also accusations upon torture, are not to be reputed as testimonies. For torture is to be used but as means of conjecture, and light, in the further examination, and search of truth: and what is in that case confessed, tends to the ease of him that is tortured, not to the informing of the torturers: and therefore ought not to have the credit of a sufficient testimony: for whether he deliver himself by true, or false accusation, he does it by the right of preserving his own life.

The force of words, being (as I have formerly noted) too weak to hold men to the performance of their covenants; there are in man's nature, but two imaginable helps to strengthen it. And those are either a fear of the consequence of breaking their word; or a glory, or pride in appearing not to need to break it. This latter is a generosity too rarely found to be presumed on, especially in the pursuers of wealth, command, or sensual pleasure; which are the greatest part of mankind. The passion to be reckoned upon, is fear; whereof there be two very general objects: one, the power of spirits invisible; the other, the power of those men they shall therein offend. Of these two, though the former be the greater power, yet the fear of the latter is commonly the greater fear. The fear of the former is in every man, his own religion: which hath place in the nature of man before civil society. The latter hath not so; at least not place enough, to keep men to their promises; because in the condition of mere nature, the inequality of power is not discerned, but by the event of battle. So that before the time of civil society, or in the interruption thereof by war, there is nothing can strengthen a covenant of peace agreed on, against the temptations of avarice, ambition, lust, or other strong desire, but the fear of that invisible power, which they every one worship as God; and fear as a revenger of their perfidy. All therefore that can be done between two men not subject to civil power, is to put one another to swear by the God he fears: which swearing, or OATH, is a form of speech, added to a promise; by which he that promises, signifies, that unless he perform, he renounces the mercy of his God, or calleth to him for vengeance on himself. Such was the heathen form, Let

Jupiter kill me else, as I kill this beast. So is our form, I shall do thus, and thus, so help me God. And this, with the rites and ceremonies, which every one uses in his own religion, that the fear of breaking faith might be the greater.

By this it appears, that an oath taken according to any other form, or rite, than his, that swears, is in vain; and no oath: and that there is no swearing by any thing which the swearer thinks not God. For though men have sometimes used to swear by their kings, for fear, or flattery; yet they would have it thereby understood, they attributed to them divine honour. And that swearing unnecessarily by God, is but profaning of his name: and swearing by other things, as men do in common discourse, is not swearing, but an impious custom, gotten by too much vehemence of talking.

It appears also, that the oath adds nothing to the obligation. For a covenant, if lawful, binds in the sight of God, without the oath, as much as with it: if unlawful, binds not at all; though it be confirmed with an oath.

Chapter 15. Of Other Laws of Nature

From that law of nature, by which we are obliged to transfer to another, such rights, as being retained, hinder the peace of mankind, there followeth a third; which is this, that men perform their covenants made: without which, covenants are in vain, and but empty words; and the right of all men to all things remaining, we are still in the condition of war.

And in this law of nature, consists the fountain and original of JUSTICE. For where no covenant hath preceded, there hath no right been transferred, and every man has right to every thing; and consequently, no action can be unjust. But when a covenant is made, then to break it is unjust: and the definition of INJUSTICE is no other than the not performance of covenant. And whatsoever is not unjust, is just.

But because covenants of mutual trust, where there is a fear of non performance on either part (as hath been said in the former chapter) are invalid; though the original of justice be the making of covenants; yet injustice actually there can be none, till the cause of such fear be taken away; which while men are in the natural condition of war, cannot be done. Therefore before the names of just, and unjust can have place, there must be some coercive power, to compel men equally to the performance of their covenants, by the terror of some punishment, greater than the benefit they expect by the breach of their covenant; and to make good that propriety, which by mutual contract men acquire, in recompense of the universal right they abandon: and such power there is none before the erection of a commonwealth. And this is also to be gathered out of the ordinary definition of justice in the Schools: for they say, that justice is the constant will of giving to every man his own. And therefore where there is no own, that is, no propriety, there is no injustice; and where there is no coercive power erected, that is, where there is no commonwealth, there is no propriety; all men having right to all things: therefore where there is no commonwealth, there nothing is unjust. So that the nature of justice consists in keeping of valid covenants: but the validity of covenants begins not but with the constitution of a civil power, sufficient to compel men to keep them: and then it is also that propriety begins.

The fool hath said in his heart, there is no such thing as justice; and sometimes also with his tongue; seriously alleging, that every man's conservation, and contentment, being committed to his own care, there could be no reason why every man might not do what he thought conduced thereunto: and therefore also to make, or not make; keep, or not keep covenants, was not against reason, when it conduced to one's benefit. He does not therein deny, that there be covenants; and that they are sometimes broken, sometimes kept; and that such breach of them may be called injustice, and the observance of them justice: but he questions, whether injustice, taking away the fear of God (for the same fool hath said in his heart there is no God) may not sometimes stand with that reason, which dictates to every man his own good; and particularly then, when it conduces to such a benefit, as shall put a man in a condition, to neglect not only the dispraise, and revilings, but also the power of other men. The kingdom of God is gotten by violence: but what if it could be gotten by unjust violence? were it against reason so to get it, when it is impossible to receive hurt by it? and if it be not against reason, it is not against justice; or else justice is not to be approved for good. From such reasoning as this, successful wickedness hath obtained the name of virtue: and some that in all other things have disallowed the violation of faith; yet have allowed it, when it is for the getting of a kingdom. And the heathen that believed, that Saturn was deposed by his son Jupiter, believed nevertheless the same Jupiter to be the avenger of injustice: somewhat like to a piece of law in Coke's Commentaries on Littleton[1]; where he says, if the right heir of the crown be attainted of treason; yet the crown shall descend to him, and eo instante the attainder be void: from which instances a man will be very prone to infer; that when the heir apparent of a kingdom, shall kill him that is in possession, though his father; you may call it injustice, or by what other name you will; yet it can never be against reason, seeing all the voluntary actions of men tend to the benefit of themselves; and those actions are most reasonable, that conduce most to their ends. This specious reasoning is nevertheless false.

For the question is not of promises mutual, where there is no security of performance on either side; as when there is no civil power erected over the parties promising; for such promises are no covenants: but either where one of the parties has performed already; or where there is a power to make him perform; there is the question whether it be against reason, that is, against the benefit of the other to perform, or not. And I say it is not against reason. For the manifestation whereof, we are to consider; first, that when a man doth a thing, which notwithstanding any thing can be foreseen, and reckoned on, tends to his own destruction, howsoever some accident which he could not expect, arriving may turn it to his benefit; yet such events do not make it reasonably or wisely done. Secondly, that in a condition of war, wherein every man to every man, for want of a common power to keep them all in awe, is an enemy, there is no man can hope by his own strength, or wit, to defend himself from destruction, without the help of confederates; where every one expects the same defence by the confederation, that any one else does: and therefore he which declares he thinks it reason to deceive those that help him, can in reason expect no other means of safety, than what can be had from his own single power. He therefore that breaks his covenant, and consequently declares that he thinks he may with reason do so, cannot be received into any society, that unite themselves for peace and defence, but by the error of them that receive him; nor when he is received, be retained in it, without seeing the danger of their error; which errors a man cannot reasonably reckon upon as the means of his security: and therefore if he be left, or cast out of society, he perishes; and if he live in society, it is by the errors of other men, which he could not foresee, nor reckon upon; and consequently against the reason of his preservation; and so, as all men that contribute not to his destruction, forbear him only out of ignorance of what is good for themselves.

As for the instance of gaining the secure and perpetual felicity of heaven, by any way; it is frivolous:

there being but one way imaginable; and that is not breaking, but keeping of covenant.

And for the other instance of attaining sovereignty by rebellion; it is manifest, that though the event follow, yet because it cannot reasonably be expected, but rather the contrary; and because by gaining it so, others are taught to gain the same in like manner, the attempt thereof is against reason. Justice therefore, that is to say, keeping of covenant, is a rule of reason, by which we are forbidden to do any thing destructive to our life; and consequently a law of nature.

There be some that proceed further; and will not have the law of nature, to be those rules which conduce to the preservation of man's life on earth; but to the attaining of an eternal felicity after death; to which they think the breach of covenant may conduce; and consequently be just and reasonable; (such are they that think it a work of merit to kill, or depose, or rebel against, the sovereign power constituted over them by their own consent). But because there is no natural knowledge of man's estate after death; much less of the reward that is then to be given to breach of faith; but only a belief grounded upon other men's saying, that they know it supernaturally, or that they know those, that knew them, that knew others, that knew it supernaturally; breach of faith cannot be called a precept of reason, or nature.

Others, that allow for a law of nature, the keeping of faith, do nevertheless make exception of certain persons; as heretics, and such as use not to perform their covenant to others: and this also is against reason. For if any fault of a man, be sufficient to discharge our covenant made; the same ought in reason to have been sufficient to have hindered the making of it.

The names of just, and injust, when they are attributed to men, signify one thing; and when they are attributed to actions, another. When they are attributed to men, they signify conformity, or inconformity of manners, to reason. But when they are attributed to actions, they signify the conformity, or inconformity to reason, not of manners, or manner of life, but of particular actions. A just man therefore, is he that taketh all the care he can, that his actions may be all just: and an unjust man, is he that neglects it. And such men are more often in our language styled by the names of righteous, and unrighteous; than just, and unjust; though the meaning be the same. Therefore a righteous man, does not lose that title, by one, or a few unjust actions, that proceed from sudden passion, or mistake of things, or persons: nor does an unrighteous man, lose his character, for such actions, as he does, or forbears to do, for fear: because his will is not framed by the justice, but

by the apparent benefit of what he is to do. That which gives to human actions the relish of justice, is a certain nobleness or gallantness of courage, (rarely found,) by which a man scorns to be beholding for the contentment of his life, to fraud, or breach of promise. This justice of the manners, is that which is meant, where justice is called a virtue; and injustice a vice.

But the justice of actions denominates men, not just, but guiltless: and the injustice of the same, (which is also called injury,) gives them but the name of guilty.

Again, the injustice of manners, is the disposition, or aptitude to do injury; and is injustice before it proceed to act; and without supposing any individual person injured. But the injustice of an action, (that is to say injury,) supposes an individual person injured; namely him, to whom the covenant was made: and therefore many times the injury is received by one man, when the damage redounds to another. As when the master commands his servant to give money to a stranger; if it be not done, the injury is done to the master, whom he had before covenanted to obey; but the damage redounds to the stranger, to whom he had no obligation; and therefore could not injure him. And so also in commonwealths, private men may remit to one another their debts; but not robberies or other violences, whereby they are damaged; because the detaining of debt, is an injury to themselves; but robbery and violence, are injuries to the person of the commonwealth.

Whatsoever is done to a man, conformable to his own will signified to the doer, is no injury to him. For if he that doeth it, hath not passed away his original right to do what he please, by some antecedent covenant, there is no breach of covenant; and therefore no injury done him. And if he have; then his will to have it done being signified, is a release of that covenant: and so again there is no injury done him.

Justice of actions, is by writers divided into commutative, and distributive: and the former they say consists in proportion arithmetical; the latter in proportion geometrical. Commutative therefore, they place in the equality of value of the things contracted for; and distributive, in the distribution of equal benefit, to men of equal merit. As if it were injustice to sell dearer than we buy; or to give more to a man than he merits. The value of all things contracted for, is measured by the appetite of the contractors: and therefore the just value, is that which they be contented to give. And merit, (besides that which is by covenant, where the performance on one part, merits the performance of the other part, and falls under justice commutative, not distributive,) is not due by justice; but is rewarded of grace only. And therefore this distinction, in the sense wherein it uses to be expounded, is not right. To speak properly, commutative justice, is the justice of a contractor; that is, a performance of covenant, in buying, and selling; hiring, and letting to hire; lending, and borrowing; exchanging, bartering, and other acts of contract.

And distributive justice, the justice of an arbitrator; that is to say, the act of defining what is just. Wherein, (being trusted by them that make him arbitrator,) if he perform his trust, he is said to distribute to every man his own: and this is indeed just distribution, and may be called (though improperly) distributive justice; but more properly equity; which also is a law of nature, as shall be shown in due place.

As justice depends on antecedent covenant; so does GRATITUDE depend on antecedent grace; that is to say, antecedent free-gift: and is the fourth law of nature; which may be conceived in this form, that a man which receives benefit from another of mere grace, endeavor that he which giveth it, have no reasonable cause to repent him of his good will. For no man giveth, but with intention of good to himself; because gift is voluntary; and of all voluntary acts, the object is to every man his own good; of which if men see they shall be frustrated, there will be no beginning of benevolence, or trust; nor consequently of mutual help; nor of reconciliation of one man to another; and therefore they are to remain still in the condition of war; which is contrary to the first and fundamental law of nature, which commands men to seek peace. The breach of this law, is called ingratitude; and hath the same relation to grace, that injustice hath to obligation by covenant.

A fifth law of nature, is COMPLAISANCE; that is to say, that every man strive to accommodate himself to the rest. For the understanding whereof, we may consider, that there is in men's aptness to society, a diversity of nature, rising from their diversity of affections; not unlike to that we see in stones brought together for building of an edifice. For as that stone which by the asperity, and irregularity of figure, takes more room from others, than itself fills; and for the hardness, cannot be easily made plain, and thereby hinders the building, is by the builders cast away as unprofitable, and troublesome: so also, a man that by asperity of nature, will strive to retain those things which to himself are superfluous, and to others necessary; and for the stubbornness of his passions, cannot be corrected, is to be left, or cast out of society, as cumbersome thereunto. For seeing

every man, not only by right, but also by necessity of nature, is supposed to endeavor all he can, to obtain that which is necessary for his conservation; he that shall oppose himself against it, for things superfluous, is guilty of the war that thereupon is to follow; and therefore doth that, which is contrary to the fundamental law of nature, which commands to seek peace. The observers of this law, may be called SOCIABLE (the Latins call them *commodi*) the contrary, stubborn, unsociable, froward, intractable.

A sixth law of nature is this, that upon caution of the future time, a man ought to pardon the offences past of them that repenting, desire it. For PARDON, is nothing but granting of peace; which though granted to them that persevere in their hostility, be not peace, but fear; yet not granted to them that give caution of the future time, is sign of an aversion to peace; and therefore contrary to the law of nature.

A seventh is that in revenges (that is, retribution of evil for evil) men look not at the greatness of the evil past, but the greatness of the good to follow. Whereby we are forbidden to inflict punishment with any other design, than for correction of the offender, or direction of others. For this law is consequent to the next before it, that commands pardon, upon security of the future time. Besides, revenge without respect to the example, and profit to come, is a triumph, or glorying in the hurt of another, tending to no end (for the end is always somewhat to come); and glorying to no end, is vain-glory, and contrary to reason; and to hurt without reason, tends to the introduction of war; which is against the law of nature; and is commonly styled by the name of cruelty.

And because all signs of hatred, or contempt, provoke to fight; insomuch as most men choose rather to hazard their life, than not to be revenged; we may in the eighth place, for a law of nature, set down this precept, that no man by deed, word, countenance, or gesture, declare hatred, or contempt of another. The breach of which law, is commonly called contumely.

The question who is the better man has no place in the condition of mere nature; where (as has been shewn before) all men are equal. The inequality that now is, has been introduced by the laws civil. I know that Aristotle in the first book of his Politics, for a foundation of his doctrine, maketh men by nature, some more worthy to command, meaning the wiser sort (such as he thought himself to be for his philosophy), others to serve (meaning those that had strong bodies, but were not philosophers as he), as if master and servant were not introduced by consent of men, but by difference of wit: which is not only against reason; but also against experience. For there are very few so foolish that had not rather govern themselves than be governed by others: nor when the wise in their own conceit, contend by force, with them who distrust their own wisdom, do they always, or often, or almost at any time, get the victory. If nature therefore have made men equal, that equality is to be acknowledged: or if nature have made men unequal; yet because men that think themselves equal, will not enter into conditions of peace, but upon equal terms, such equality must be admitted. And therefore for the ninth law of nature, I put this, that every man acknowledge others for his equal by nature. The breach of this precept is pride.

On this law depends another, that at the entrance into conditions of peace, no man require to reserve to himself any right, which he is not content should be reserved to every one of the rest. As it is necessary for all men that seek peace, to lay down certain rights of nature; that is to say, not to have liberty to do all they list: so is it necessary for man's life, to retain some; as right to govern their own bodies; enjoy air, water, motion, ways to go from place to place; and all things else without which a man cannot live, or not live well. If in this case, at the making of peace, men require for themselves, that which they would not have to be granted to others, they do contrary to the precedent law, that commands the acknowledgment of natural equality, and therefore also against the law of nature. The observers of this law, are those we call modest, and the breakers arrogant men. The Greeks call the violation of this law *pleonexia;* that is, a desire of more than their share.

Also if a man be trusted to judge between man and man, it is a precept of the law of nature, that he deal equally between them. For without that, the controversies of men cannot be determined but by war. He therefore that is partial in judgment, doth what in him lies, to deter men from the use of judges, and arbitrators; and consequently (against the fundamental law of nature) is the cause of war.

The observance of this law, from the equal distribution to each man, of that which in reason belongs to him, is called EQUITY, and (as I have said before) distributive justice: the violation, acception of persons.

And from this followeth another law, that such things as cannot be divided, be enjoyed in common, if it can be; and if the quantity of the thing permit, without stint; otherwise proportionably to the number of them that have right. For otherwise the distribution is unequal, and contrary to equity.

But some things there be, that can neither be divided, nor enjoyed in common. Then, the law of nature, which prescribes equity, requires, that the entire right; or else (making the use alternate) the first possession be determined by lot. For equal distribution is of the law of nature; and other means of equal distribution cannot be imagined.

Of lots there be two sorts, arbitrary, and natural. Arbitrary is that which is agreed on by the competitors: natural is either primogeniture (which the Greek calls *kleronomia,* which signifies given by lot) or first seizure.

And therefore those things which cannot be enjoyed in common, nor divided, ought to be adjudged to the first possessor; and in some cases to the first-born, as acquired by lot.

It is also a law of nature, that all men that mediate peace, be allowed safe conduct. For the law that commands peace, as the end, commands intercession, as the means; and to intercession the means is safe conduct.

And because, though men be never so willing to observe these laws, there may nevertheless arise questions concerning a man's action; first, whether it were done, or not done; secondly (if done), whether against the law or not against the law; the former whereof, is called a question of fact; the latter a question of right; therefore unless the parties to the question, covenant mutually to stand to the sentence of another, they are as far from peace as ever. This other, to whose sentence they submit, is called an ARBITRATOR. And therefore it is of the law of nature, that they that are at controversy, submit their right to the judgment of an arbitrator.

And seeing every man is presumed to do all things in order to his own benefit, no man is a fit arbitrator in his own cause: and if he were never so fit; yet equity allowing to each party equal benefit, if one be admitted to be judge, the other is to be admitted also; and so the controversy, that is, the cause of war, remains, against the law of nature.

For the same reason no man in any cause ought to be received for arbitrator, to whom greater profit, or honour, or pleasure apparently arises out of the victory of one party, than of the other: for he hath taken (though an unavoidable bribe, yet) a bribe; and no man can be obliged to trust him. And thus also the controversy, and the condition of war remains, contrary to the law of nature.

And in a controversy of fact, the judge being to give no more credit to one, than to the other, (if there be no other arguments,) must give credit to a third; or to a third and fourth; or more: for else the question is undecided, and left to force, contrary to the law of nature.

These are the laws of nature, dictating peace, for a means of the conservation of men in multitudes; and which only concern the doctrine of civil society. There be other things tending to the destruction of particular men; as drunkenness, and all other parts of intemperance; which may therefore also be reckoned amongst those things which the law of nature hath forbidden; but are not necessary to be mentioned, nor are pertinent enough to this place.

And though this may seem too subtle a deduction of the laws of nature, to be taken notice of by all men; whereof the most part are too busy in getting food, and the rest too negligent to understand; yet to leave all men inexcusable, they have been contracted into one easy sum, intelligible, even to the meanest capacity; and that is, Do not that to another, which thou wouldest not have done to thyself; which shows him that he has no more to do in learning the laws of nature, but, when weighing the actions of other men with his own, they seem too heavy, to put them into the other part of the balance, and his own into their place, that his own passions, and self-love, may add nothing to the weight; and then there is none of these laws of nature that will not appear unto him very reasonable.

The laws of nature oblige in foro interno [in conscience]; that is to say, they bind to a desire they should take place: but in foro externo [in civil law]; that is, to the putting them in act, not always. For he that should be modest, and tractable, and perform all he promises, in such time, and place, where no man else should do so, should but make himself a prey to others, and procure his own certain ruin, contrary to the ground of all laws of nature, which tend to nature's preservation. And again, he that having sufficient security, that others shall observe the same laws towards him, observes them not himself, seeks not peace, but war; and consequently the destruction of his nature by violence.

And whatsoever laws bind in foro interno, may be broken, not only by a fact contrary to the law, but also by a fact according to it, in case a man think it contrary. For though his action in this case, be according to the law; yet his purpose was against the law; which, where the obligation is in foro interno, is a breach.

The laws of nature are immutable and eternal; for injustice, ingratitude, arrogance, pride, iniquity, acception of persons, and the rest, can never be made lawful. For it can never be that war shall preserve life, and peace destroy it.

The same laws, because they oblige only to a desire, and endeavor, I mean an unfeigned and constant endeavor, are easy to be observed. For in that they require nothing but endeavor; he that endeavors their performance, fulfills them; and he that fulfills the law, is just.

And the science of them is the true and only moral philosophy. For moral philosophy is nothing else but the science of what is good, and evil, in the conversation, and society of mankind. Good, and evil, are names that signify our appetites, and aversions; which in different tempers, customs, and doctrines of men, are different: and divers men, differ not only in their judgment, on the senses of what is pleasant, and unpleasant to the taste, smell, hearing, touch, and sight; but also of what is conformable, or disagreeable to reason, in the actions of common life. Nay, the same man, in divers times, differs from himself; and one time praises, that is, calleth good, what another time he dispraises, and calleth evil: from whence arise disputes, controversies, and at last war. And therefore so long a man is in the condition of mere nature, (which is a condition of war,) as private appetite is the measure of good, and evil: and consequently all men agree on this, that peace is good, and therefore also the way, or means of peace, which, (as I have shewed before) are justice, gratitude, modesty, equity, mercy, and the rest of the laws of nature, are good; that is to say, moral virtues; and their contrary vices, evil. Now the science of virtue and vice, is moral philosophy; and therefore the true doctrine of the laws of nature, is the true moral philosophy. But the writers of moral philosophy, though they acknowledge the same virtues and vices; yet not seeing wherein consisted their goodness; nor that they come to be praised, as the means of peaceable, sociable, and comfortable living; place them in a mediocrity of passions: as if not the cause, but the degree of daring, made fortitude; or not the cause, but the quantity of a gift, made liberality.

These dictates of reason, men used to call by the name of laws; but improperly: for they are but conclusions, or theorems concerning what conduces to the conservation and defence of themselves; whereas law, properly, is the word of him, that by right hath command over others. But yet if we consider the same theorems, as delivered in the word of God, that by right commands all things; then are they properly called laws. . . .

PART 2. OF COMMONWEALTH

Chapter 17. Of the Causes, Generation, and Definition of a Commonwealth

The final cause, end, or design of men (who naturally love liberty, and dominion over others) in the introduction of that restraint upon themselves (in which we see them live in commonwealths) is the foresight of their own preservation, and of a more contented life thereby; that is to say, of getting themselves out from that miserable condition of war, which is necessarily consequent (as hath been shown) to the natural passions of men, when there is no visible power to keep them in awe, and tie them by fear of punishment to the performance of their covenants, and observation of those laws of nature set down in the fourteenth and fifteenth chapters.

For the laws of nature (as justice, equity, modesty, mercy, and (in sum) doing to others, as we would be done to,) of themselves, without the terror of some power, to cause them to be observed, are contrary to our natural passions, that carry us to partiality, pride, revenge, and the like. And covenants, without the sword, are but words, and of no strength to secure a man at all. Therefore notwithstanding the laws of nature, (which every one hath then kept, when he has the will to keep them, when he can do it safely,) if there be no power erected, or not great enough for our security; every man will, and may lawfully rely on his own strength and art, for caution against all other men. And in all places, where men have lived by small families, to rob and spoil one another, has been a trade, and so far from being reputed against the law of nature, that the greater spoils they gained, the greater was their honour; and men observed no other laws therein, but the laws of honour; that is, to abstain from cruelty, leaving to men their lives, and instruments of husbandry. And as small families did then; so now do cities and kingdoms which are but greater families (for their own security) enlarge their dominions, upon all pretenses of danger, and fear of invasion, or assistance that may be given to invaders, endeavor as much as they can, to subdue, or weaken their neighbors, by open force, and secret arts, for want of other caution, justly; and are remembered for it in after ages with honour.

Nor is it the joining together of a small number of men, that gives them this security; because in small numbers, small additions on the one side or the other,

make the advantage of strength so great, as is sufficient to carry the victory; and therefore gives encouragement to an invasion. The multitude sufficient to confide in for our security, is not determined by any certain number, but by comparison with the enemy we fear; and is then sufficient, when the odds of the enemy is not of so visible and conspicuous moment, to determine the event of war, as to move him to attempt.

And be there never so great a multitude; yet if their actions be directed according to their particular judgments, and particular appetites, they can expect thereby no defence, nor protection, neither against a common enemy, nor against the injuries of one another. For being distracted in opinions concerning the best use and application of their strength, they do not help, but hinder one another; and reduce their strength by mutual opposition to nothing: whereby they are easily, not only subdued by a very few that agree together; but also when there is no common enemy, they make war upon each other, for their particular interests. For if we could suppose a great multitude of men to consent in the observation of justice, and other laws of nature, without a common power to keep them all in awe; we might as well suppose all mankind to do the same; and then there neither would be, nor need to be any civil government, or commonwealth at all; because there would be peace without subjection.

Nor is it enough for the security, which men desire should last all the time of their life, that they be governed, and directed by one judgment, for a limited time; as in one battle, or one war. For though they obtain a victory by their unanimous endeavor against a foreign enemy; yet afterwards, when either they have no common enemy, or he that by one part is held for an enemy, is by another part held for a friend, they must needs by the difference of their interests dissolve, and fall again into a war amongst themselves.

It is true, that certain living creatures, as bees, and ants, live sociably one with another, (which are therefore by Aristotle numbered amongst political creatures;) and yet have no other direction, than their particular judgments and appetites; nor speech, whereby one of them can signify to another, what he thinks expedient for the common benefit: and therefore some man may perhaps desire to know, why mankind cannot do the same. To which I answer,

First, that men are continually in competition for honour and dignity, which these creatures are not; and consequently amongst men there arises on that ground, envy and hatred, and finally war; but amongst these not so.

Secondly, that amongst these creatures, the common good differs not from the private; and being by nature inclined to their private, they procure thereby the common benefit. But man, whose joy consists in comparing himself with other men, can relish nothing but what is eminent.

Thirdly, that these creatures, having not, (as man) the use of reason, do not see, nor think they see any fault, in the administration of their common business; whereas amongst men, there are very many, that think themselves wiser, and abler to govern the public, better than the rest; and these strive to reform and innovate, one this way, another that way; and thereby bring it into distraction and civil war.

Fourthly, that these creatures, though they have some use of voice, in making known to one another their desires, and other affections; yet they want that art of words, by which some men can represent to others, that which is good, in the likeness of evil; and evil, in the likeness of good; and augment, or diminish the apparent greatness of good and evil; discontenting men, and troubling their peace at their pleasure.

Fifthly, irrational creatures cannot distinguish between injury, and damage; and therefore as long as they be at ease, they are not offended with their fellows: whereas man is then most troublesome, when he is most at ease: for then it is that he loves to shew his wisdom, and control the actions of them that govern the commonwealth.

Lastly, the agreement of these creatures is natural; that of men, is by covenant only, which is artificial: and therefore it is no wonder if there be somewhat else required (besides covenant) to make their agreement constant and lasting; which is a common power, to keep them in awe, and to direct their actions to the common benefit.

The only way to erect such a common power, as may be able to defend them from the invasion of foreigners, and the injuries of one another, and thereby to secure them in such sort, as that by their own industry, and by the fruits of the earth, they may nourish themselves and live contentedly; is, to confer all their power and strength upon one man, or upon one assembly of men, that may reduce all their wills, by plurality of voices, unto one will: which is as much as to say, to appoint one man, or assembly of men, to bear their person; and every one to own, and acknowledge himself to be author of whatsoever he that so beareth their person, shall act, or cause to be acted, in those things which concern the common peace and safety; and therein to submit their wills, every one to his will, and

their judgments, to his judgment. This is more than consent, or concord; it is a real unity of them all, in one and the same person, made by covenant of every man with every man, in such manner, as if every man should say to every man, I authorize and give up my right of governing myself, to this man, or to this assembly of men, on this condition, that thou give up thy right to him, and authorize all his actions in like manner. This done, the multitude so united in one person, is called a COMMONWEALTH, in Latin CIVITAS. This is the generation of that great LEVIATHAN, or rather (to speak more reverently) of that mortal god, to which we owe under the immortal God, our peace and defence. For by this authority, given him by every particular man in the commonwealth, he hath the use of so much power and strength conferred on him, that by terror thereof, he is enabled to form the wills of them all, to peace at home, and mutual aid against their enemies abroad. And in him consists the essence of the commonwealth; which (to define it,) is one person, of whose acts a great multitude, by mutual covenants one with another, have made themselves every one the author, to the end he may use the strength and means of them all, as he shall think expedient, for their peace and common defence.

And he that carries this person, is called SOVEREIGN, and said to have sovereign power; and every one besides, his SUBJECT.

The attaining to this sovereign power, is by two ways. One, by natural force; as when a man maketh his children, to submit themselves, and their children to his government, as being able to destroy them if they refuse; or by war subdues his enemies to his will, giving them their lives on that condition. The other, is when men agree amongst themselves, to submit to some man, or assembly of men, voluntarily, on confidence to be protected by him against all others. This latter, may be called a political commonwealth, or commonwealth by institution; and the former, a commonwealth by acquisition. And first, I shall speak of a commonwealth by institution.

Chapter 18. Of the Rights of Sovereigns by Institution

A commonwealth is said to be instituted, when a multitude of men do agree, and covenant, every one, with every one, that to whatsoever man, or assembly of men, shall be given by the major part, the right to present the person of them all, (that is to say, to be their representative;) every one, as well he that voted for it, as he that voted against it, shall authorize all the actions and judgments, of that man, or assembly of men, in the same manner, as if they were his own, to the end, to live peaceably amongst themselves, and be protected against other men.

From this institution of a commonwealth are derived all the rights, and faculties of him, or them, on whom the sovereign power is conferred by the consent of the people assembled.

First, because they covenant, it is to be understood, they are not obliged by former covenant to any thing repugnant hereunto. And consequently they that have already instituted a commonwealth, being thereby bound by covenant, to own the actions, and judgments of one, cannot lawfully make a new covenant, amongst themselves, to be obedient to any other, in any thing whatsoever, without his permission. And therefore, they that are subjects to a monarch, cannot without his leave cast off monarchy, and return to the confusion of a disunited multitude; nor transfer their person from him that beareth it, to another man, or other assembly of men: for they are bound, every man to every man, to own, and be reputed author of all, that he that already is their sovereign, shall do, and judge fit to be done: so that any one man dissenting, all the rest should break their covenant made to that man, which is injustice: and they have also every man given the sovereignty to him that beareth their person; and therefore if they depose him, they take from him that which is his own, and so again it is injustice. Besides, if he that attempts to depose his sovereign, be killed, or punished by him for such attempt, he is author of his own punishment, as being by the institution, author of all his sovereign shall do: and because it is injustice for a man to do any thing, for which he may be punished by his own authority, he is also upon that title, unjust. And whereas some men have pretended for their disobedience to their sovereign, a new covenant, made, not with men, but with God; this also is unjust: for there is no covenant with God, but by mediation of somebody that represents God's person; which none doth but God's lieutenant, who hath the sovereignty under God. But this pretence of covenant with God, is so evident a lie, even in the pretenders' own consciences, that it is not only an act of an unjust, but also of a vile, and unmanly disposition.

Secondly, because the right of bearing the person of them all, is given to him they make sovereign, by covenant only of one to another, and not of him to any of them; there can happen no breach of covenant on the part of the sovereign; and consequently none of his subjects, by any pretence of forfeiture, can be freed from his subjection. That he which is made sovereign maketh no covenant with his subjects beforehand, is manifest; because either he must make it with the whole multitude, as one party to the covenant; or he must make a several covenant with every man. With the whole, as one party, it is impossible; because as yet they are not one person: and if he make so many several covenants as there be men, those covenants after he hath the sovereignty are void, because what act soever can be pretended by any one of them for breach thereof, is the act both of himself, and of all the rest, because done in the person, and by the right of every one of them in particular. Besides, if any one, or more of them, pretend a breach of the covenant made by the sovereign at his institution; and others, or one other of his subjects, or himself alone, pretend there was no such breach, there is in this case, no judge to decide the controversy; it returns therefore to the sword again; and every man recovers the right of protecting himself by his own strength, contrary to the design they had in the institution. It is therefore in vain to grant sovereignty by way of precedent covenant. The opinion that any monarch receives his power by covenant, that is to say, on condition, proceeds from want of understanding this easy truth, that covenants being but words and breath, have no force to oblige, contain, constrain, or protect any man, but what it has from the public sword; that is, from the untied hands of that man, or assembly of men that hath the sovereignty, and whose actions are avouched by them all, and performed by the strength of them all, in him united. But when an assembly of men is made sovereign; then no man imagines any such covenant to have passed in the institution; for no man is so dull as to say, for example, the people of Rome made a covenant with the Romans, to hold the sovereignty on such or such conditions; which not performed, the Romans might lawfully depose the Roman people. That men see not the reason to be alike in a monarchy, and in a popular government, proceeds from the ambition of some, that are kinder to the government of an assembly, whereof they may hope to participate, than of monarchy, which they despair to enjoy.

Thirdly, because the major part hath by consenting voices declared a sovereign; he that dissented must now consent with the rest; that is, be contented to avow all the actions he shall do, or else justly be destroyed by the rest. For if he voluntarily entered into the congregation of them that were assembled, he sufficiently declared thereby his will, (and therefore tacitly covenanted) to stand to what the major part should ordain: and therefore if he refuse to stand thereto, or make protestation against any of their decrees, he does contrary to his covenant, and therefore unjustly. And whether he be of the congregation, or not; and whether his consent be asked, or not, he must either submit to their decrees, or be left in the condition of war he was in before; wherein he might without injustice be destroyed by any man whatsoever.

Fourthly, because every subject is by this institution author of all the actions, and judgments of the sovereign instituted; it follows, that whatsoever he doth, it can be no injury to any of his subjects; nor ought he to be by any of them accused of injustice. For he that doth any thing by authority from another, doth therein no injury to him by whose authority he acts: but by this institution of a commonwealth, every particular man is author of all the sovereign doth; and consequently he that complains of injury from his sovereign, complains of that whereof he himself is author; and therefore ought not to accuse any man but himself; no nor himself of injury; because to do injury to one's self, is impossible. It is true that they that have sovereign power, may commit iniquity; but not injustice, or injury in the proper signification.

Fifthly, and consequently to that which was said last, no man that hath sovereign power can justly be put to death, or otherwise in any manner by his subjects punished. For seeing every subject is author of the actions of his sovereign; he punishes another, for the actions committed by himself.

And because the end of this institution, is the peace and defence of them all; and whosoever has right to the end, has right to the means; it belongs of right, to whatsoever man, or assembly that hath the sovereignty, to be judge both of the means of peace and defence; and also of the hindrances, and disturbances of the same; and to do whatsoever he shall think necessary to be done, both beforehand, for the preserving of peace and security, by prevention of discord at home, and hostility from abroad; and, when peace and security are lost, for the recovery of the same. And therefore,

Sixthly, it is annexed to the sovereignty, to be judge of what opinions and doctrines are averse, and what conducing to peace; and consequently, on what occasions, how far, and what, men are to be trusted withal, in speaking to multitudes of people; and who shall examine the doctrines of all books before they be published. For the actions of men proceed from their opinions; and in the well-governing of opinions, consists the well-governing of men's actions, in order to their peace, and concord. And though in matter of doctrine, nothing ought to be regarded but the truth; yet this is not repugnant to regulating of the same by peace.

For doctrine repugnant to peace, can no more be true, than peace and concord can be against the law of nature. It is true, that in a commonwealth, where by the negligence, or unskillfulness of governors, and teachers, false doctrines are by time generally received; the contrary truths may be generally offensive: Yet the most sudden, and rough bustling in of a new truth, that can be, does never break the peace, but only sometimes awake the war. For those men that are so remissly governed, that they dare take up arms, to defend, or introduce an opinion, are still in war; and their condition not peace, but only a cessation of arms for fear of one another; and they live as it were, in the precincts of battle continually. It belongs therefore to him that hath the sovereign power, to be judge, or constitute all judges of opinions and doctrines, as a thing necessary to peace; thereby to prevent discord and civil war.

Seventhly, is annexed to the sovereignty, the whole power of prescribing the rules, whereby every man may know, what goods he may enjoy, and what actions he may do, without being molested by any of his fellow-subjects; and this is it men call propriety. For before constitution of sovereign power (as hath already been shown) all men had right to all things; which necessarily causes war: and therefore this propriety, being necessary to peace, and depending on sovereign power, is the act of that power, in order to the public peace. These rules of propriety (or meum and tuum [mine and thine]) and of good, evil, lawful, and unlawful in the actions of subjects, are the civil laws; that is to say, the laws of each commonwealth in particular; though the name of civil law be now restrained to the ancient civil laws of the city of Rome; which being the head of a great part of the world, her laws at that time were in these parts the civil law.

Eighthly, is annexed to the sovereignty, the right of judicature; that is to say, of hearing and deciding all controversies, which may arise concerning law, either civil, or natural; or concerning fact. For without the decision of controversies, there is no protection of one subject, against the injuries of another; the laws concerning meum and tuum are in vain; and to every man remains, from the natural and necessary appetite of his own conservation, the right of protecting himself by his private strength, which is the condition of war; and contrary to the end for which every commonwealth is instituted.

Ninthly, is annexed to the sovereignty, the right of making war and peace with other nations, and commonwealths; that is to say, of judging when it is for the public good, and how great forces are to be assembled, armed, and paid for that end; and to levy money upon the subjects, to defray the expenses thereof. For the power by which the people are to be defended, consists in their armies; and the strength of an army, in the union of their strength under one command; which command the sovereign instituted, therefore hath; because the command of the militia, without other institution, maketh him that hath it sovereign. And therefore whosoever is made general of an army, he that hath the sovereign power is always generalissimo.

Tenthly, is annexed to the sovereignty, the choosing of all counsellors, ministers, magistrates, and officers, both in peace, and war. For seeing the sovereign is charged with the end, which is the common peace and defence, he is understood to have power to use such means, as he shall think most fit for his discharge.

Eleventhly, to the sovereign is committed the power of rewarding with riches, or honour; and of punishing with corporal, or pecuniary punishment, or with ignominy every subject according to the law he hath formerly made; or if there be no law made, according as he shall judge most to conduce to the encouraging of men to serve the commonwealth, or deterring of them from doing disservice to the same.

Lastly, considering what values men are naturally apt to set upon themselves; what respect they look for from others; and how little they value other men; from whence continually arise amongst them, emulation, quarrels, factions, and at last war, to the destroying of one another, and diminution of their strength against a common enemy; it is necessary that there be laws of honour, and a public rate of the worth of such men as have deserved, or are able to deserve well of the commonwealth; and that there be force in the hands of some or other, to put those laws in execution. But it hath already been shown, that not only the whole militia, or forces of the commonwealth; but also the judicature of all controversies, is annexed to the sovereignty. To the sovereign therefore it belongs also to give titles of honour; and to appoint what order of place, and dignity, each man shall hold; and what signs of respect, in public or private meetings, they shall give to one another.

These are the rights, which make the essence of sovereignty; and which are the marks, whereby a man may discern in what man, or assembly of men, the sovereign power is placed, and resides. For these are incommunicable, and inseparable. The power to coin money; to dispose of the estate and persons of infant heirs; to have preemption in markets; and all other statute prerogatives, may be transferred by the sovereign; and yet the power to protect his subjects be retained. But if he transfer the militia, he retains the judicature in vain, for want of execution of the laws: or if he grant away the power of raising money; the militia is in vain: or if he give away the government of doctrines, men will be frightened into rebellion with the fear of spirits. And so if we consider any one of the said rights, we shall presently see, that the holding of all the rest will produce no effect, in the conservation of peace and justice, the end for which all commonwealths are instituted. And this division is it, whereof it is said, a kingdom divided in itself cannot stand: for unless this division precede, division into opposite armies can never happen. If there had not first been an opinion received of the greatest part of England, that these powers were divided between the King, and the Lords, and the House of Commons, the people had never been divided and fallen into this civil war; first between those that disagreed in politics; and after between the dissenters about the liberty of religion; which have so instructed men in this point of sovereign right, that there be few now (in England,) that do not see, that these rights are inseparable, and will be so generally acknowledged at the next return of peace[2]; and so continue, till their miseries are forgotten; and no longer, except the vulgar be better taught than they have hitherto been.

And because they are essential and inseparable rights, it follows necessarily, that in whatsoever words any of them seem to be granted away, yet if the sovereign power itself be not in direct terms renounced, and the name of sovereign no more given by the grantees to him that grants them, the grant is void: for when he has granted all he can, if we grant back the sovereignty, all is restored, as inseparably annexed thereunto.

This great authority being indivisible, and inseparably annexed to the sovereignty, there is little ground for the opinion of them, that say of sovereign kings, though they be singulis majores, of greater power than every one of their subjects, yet they be universis minores, of less power than them all together. For if by all together, they mean not the collective body as one person, then all together, and every one, signify the same; and the speech is absurd. But if by all together, they understand them as one person, (which person the sovereign bears,) then the power of all together, is the same with the sovereign's power; and so again the speech is absurd: which absurdity they see well enough, when the sovereignty is in an assembly of the people; but in a monarch they see it not; and yet the power of sovereignty is the same in whomsoever it be placed.

And as the power, so also the honour of the sovereign, ought to be greater, than that of any, or all the subjects. For in the sovereignty is the fountain of honour. The dignities of lord, earl, duke, and prince are his creatures. As in the presence of the master, the servants are equal, and without any honour at all; so are the subjects, in the presence of the sovereign. And though they shine some more, some less, when they are out of his sight; yet in his presence, they shine no more than the stars in presence of the sun.

But a man may here object that the condition of subjects is very miserable; as being obnoxious to the lusts, and other irregular passions of him, or them that have so unlimited a power in their hands. And commonly they that live under a monarch, think it the fault of monarchy; and they that live under the government of democracy, or other sovereign assembly, attribute all the inconvenience to that form of commonwealth; whereas the power in all forms, if they be perfect enough to protect them, is the same; not considering that the estate of man can never be without some incommodity or other; and that the greatest, that in any form of government can possibly happen to the people in general, is scarce sensible, in respect of the miseries, and horrible calamities, that accompany a civil war, or that dissolute condition of masterless men, without subjection to laws, and a coercive power to tie their hands from rapine and revenge: nor considering that the greatest pressure of sovereign governors, proceeds not from any delight, or profit they can expect in the damage or weakening of their subjects, in whose vigor, consists their own strength and glory; but in the restiveness of themselves, that unwillingly contributing to their own defence, make it necessary for their governors to draw from them what they can in time of peace, that they may have means on any emergent occasion, or sudden need, to resist, or take advantage on their enemies. For all men are by nature provided of notable multiplying glasses, (that is their passions and self-love,) through which, every little payment appears a great grievance; but are destitute of those prospective glasses, (namely moral and civil science,) to see afar off the miseries that hang over them, and cannot without such payments be avoided. . . .

Chapter 21. Of the Liberty of Subjects

LIBERTY, or FREEDOM, signifies (properly) the absence of opposition; (by opposition, I mean external impediments of motion;) and may be applied no less to irrational, and inanimate creatures, than to rational. For whatsoever is so tied, or environed, as it cannot move, but within a certain space, which space is determined by the opposition of some external body, we say it hath not liberty to go further. And so of all living creatures, whilst they are imprisoned, or restrained, with walls, or chains; and of the water whilst it is kept in by banks, or vessels, that otherwise would spread itself into a larger space, we used to say, they are not at liberty, to move in such manner, as without those external impediments they would. But when the impediment of motion, is in the constitution of the thing itself, we use not to say, it wants the liberty; but the power to move; as when a stone lies still, or a man is fastened to his bed by sickness.

And according to this proper, and generally received meaning of the word, a FREEMAN, is he, that in those things, which by his strength and wit he is able to do, is not hindered to do what he has a will to. But when the words free, and liberty, are applied to any thing but bodies, they are abused; for that which is not subject to motion, is not subject to impediment: and therefore, when it is said (for example) the way is free, no liberty of the way is signified, but of those that walk in it without stop. And when we say a gift is free, there is not meant any liberty of the gift, but of the giver, that was not bound by any law, or covenant to give it. So when we speak freely, it is not the liberty of voice, or pronunciation, but of the man, whom no law hath obliged to speak otherwise than he did. Lastly, from the use of the word free-will, no liberty can be inferred of the will, desire, or inclination, but the liberty of the man; which consists in this, that he finds no stop, in doing what he has the will, desire, or inclination to do.

Fear, and liberty are consistent; as when a man throws his goods into the sea for fear the ship should sink, he doth it nevertheless very willingly, and may refuse to do it if he will: it is therefore the action of one that was free: so a man sometimes pays his debt, only for fear of imprisonment, which because nobody hindered him from detaining, was the action of a man at liberty. And generally all actions which men do in commonwealths, for fear of the law, are actions, which the doers had liberty to omit.

Liberty, and necessity are consistent: as in the water, that hath not only liberty, but a necessity of descending by the channel; so likewise in the actions which men voluntarily do: which, because they proceed from their will, proceed from liberty; and yet, because every act of man's will, and every desire, and inclination proceeds from some cause, and that from another cause, in a continual chain, (whose first link is in the hand of God the first of all causes,) they proceed from necessity. So that to him that could see the connexion of those causes, the necessity of all men's voluntary actions, would appear manifest. And therefore God, that sees, and disposes all things, sees also that the liberty of man in doing what he will, is accompanied with the necessity of doing that which God will, and no more, nor less. For though men may do many things, which God does not command, nor is therefore author of them; yet they can have no passion, nor appetite to any thing, of which appetite God's will is not the cause. And did not his will assure the necessity of man's will, and consequently of all that on man's will depends, the liberty of men would be a contradiction, and impediment to the omnipotence and liberty of God. And this shall suffice, (as to the matter in hand) of that natural liberty, which only is properly called liberty.

But as men, for the attaining of peace, and conservation of themselves thereby, have made an artificial man, which we call a commonwealth; so also have they made artificial chains, called civil laws, which they themselves, by mutual covenants, have fastened at one end, to the lips of that man, or assembly, to whom they have given the sovereign power; and at the other end to their own ears. These bonds in their own nature but weak, may nevertheless be made to hold, by the danger, though not by the difficulty of breaking them.

In relation to these bonds only it is, that I am to speak now, of the liberty of subjects. For seeing there is no commonwealth in the world, wherein there be rules enough set down, for the regulating of all the actions, and words of men, (as being a thing impossible:) it followeth necessarily, that in all kinds of actions, by the laws pretermitted, men have the liberty, of doing what their own reasons shall suggest, for the most profitable to themselves. For if we take liberty in the proper sense, for corporal liberty; that is to say, freedom from chains, and prison, it were very absurd for men to clamor as they do, for the liberty they so manifestly enjoy. Again, if we take liberty, for an exemption from laws, it is no less absurd, for men to demand as they do, that liberty, by which all other men may be masters of their lives. And yet as absurd as it is, this is it they demand; not knowing that the laws are of no power to protect them, without a sword in the hands of a man, or men, to cause those laws to be put in execution. The liberty of a subject, lies therefore only in those things, which in regulating their actions, the sovereign hath pretermitted: such as is the liberty to buy, and sell, and otherwise contract with one another; to choose their own abode, their own diet, their own trade of life, and institute their children as they themselves think fit; and the like.

Nevertheless we are not to understand, that by such liberty, the sovereign power of life and death, is either abolished, or limited. For it has been already shown, that nothing the sovereign representative can do to a subject, on what pretence soever, can properly be called injustice, or injury; because every subject is author of every act the sovereign doth; so that he never wants right to any thing, otherwise, than as he himself is the subject of God, and bound thereby to observe the laws of nature. And therefore it may, and doth often happen in commonwealths, that a subject may be put to death, by the command of the sovereign power; and yet neither do the other wrong: as when Jephtha caused his daughter to be sacrificed: in which, and the like cases, he that so dies, had liberty to do the action, for which he is nevertheless, without injury put to death. And the same holds also in a sovereign prince, that puts to death an innocent subject. For though the action be against the law of nature, as being contrary to equity, (as was the killing of Uriah, by David;) yet it was not an injury to Uriah; but to God. Not to Uriah, because the right to do what he pleased, was given him by Uriah himself: and yet to God, because David was God's subject; and prohibited all iniquity by the law of nature. Which distinction, David himself, when he repented the fact, evidently confirmed, saying, To thee only have I sinned. In the same manner, the people of Athens, when they banished the most potent of their commonwealth for ten years, thought they committed no injustice; and yet they never questioned what crime he had done; but what hurt he would do: nay they commanded the banishment of they knew not whom; and every citizen bringing his oystershell into the market place, written with the name of him he desired should be banished, without actually accusing him, sometimes banished an Aristides, for his reputation of justice; and sometimes a scurrilous jester, as Hyperbolus, to make a jest of it. And yet a man cannot say, the sovereign people of Athens wanted the right to banish them; or an Athenian the liberty to jest, or to be just.[3]

The liberty, whereof there is so frequent and honorable mention, in the histories, and philosophy of the ancient Greeks, and Romans, and in the writings, and discourse of those that from them have received all their learning in the politics, is not the liberty of particular men; but the liberty of the commonwealth: which is the same with that, which every man then should have, if there were no civil laws, nor commonwealth at all. And the effects of it also be the same. For as amongst masterless men, there is perpetual war, of every man against his neighbor; no inheritance, to transmit to the son, nor to expect from the father; no propriety of goods, or lands; no security; but a full and absolute liberty in every particular man: so in states, and commonwealths not dependent on one another, every commonwealth, (not every man) has an absolute liberty, to do what it shall judge (that is to say, what that man, or assembly that represents it, shall judge) most conducing to their benefit. But withal, they live in the condition of a perpetual war, and upon the confines of battle, with their frontiers armed, and cannons planted against their neighbors round about. The Athenians, and Romans were free; that is, free commonwealths: not that any particular men had the liberty to resist their own representative; but that their representative had the liberty to resist, or invade other people. There is written on the turrets of the city of Lucca in great characters at this day, the word LIBERTAS; yet no man can thence infer, that a particular man has more liberty, or immunity from the service of the commonwealth there, than in Constantinople. Whether a commonwealth be monarchical, or popular, the freedom is still the same.

But it is an easy thing, for men to be deceived, by the specious name of liberty, and for want of judgment to distinguish, mistake that for their private inheritance, and birth right, which is the right of the public only. And when the same error is confirmed by the authority of men in reputation for their writings in this subject, it is no wonder if it produce sedition, and change of government. In these western parts of the world, we are made to receive our opinions concerning the institution, and rights of commonwealths, from Aristotle, Cicero, and other men, Greeks and Romans, that living under popular states, derived those rights, not from the principles of nature, but transcribed them into their books, out of the practice of their own commonwealths, which were popular; as the grammarians describe the rules of language, out of the practice of the time; or the rules of poetry, out of the poems of Homer and Virgil. And because the Athenians were taught, (to keep them from desire of changing their government,) that they were freemen, and all that lived under monarchy were slaves; therefore Aristotle puts it down in his Politics. In democracy, Liberty is to be supposed: for it is commonly held, that no man is Free in any other government. And as Aristotle; so Cicero, and other writers have grounded their civil doctrine, on the opinions of the Romans, who were taught to hate monarchy, at first, by them that having deposed their sovereign, shared amongst them the sovereignty of Rome; and afterwards by their successors. And by reading of these Greek, and Latin authors, men from their childhood have gotten a habit (under a false show of liberty,) of

favoring tumults, and of licentious controlling the actions of their sovereigns; and again of controlling those controllers, with the effusion of so much blood; as I think I may truly say, there was never any thing so dearly bought, as these western parts have bought the learning of the Greek and Latin tongues.

To come now to the particulars of the true liberty of a subject; that is to say, what are the things, which though commanded by the sovereign, he may nevertheless, without injustice, refuse to do; we are to consider, what rights we pass away, when we make a commonwealth; or (which is all one,) what liberty we deny ourselves, by owning all the actions (without exception) of the man, or assembly we make our sovereign. For in the act of our submission, consists both our obligation, and our liberty; which must therefore be inferred by arguments taken from thence; there being no obligation on any man, which arises not from some act of his own; for all men equally, are by nature free. And because such arguments, must either be drawn from the express words, I authorize all his actions, or from the intention of him that submits himself to his power, (which intention is to be understood by the end for which he so submits;) the obligation, and liberty of the subject, is to be derived, either from those words, (or others equivalent;) or else from the end of the institution of sovereignty, namely, the peace of the subjects within themselves, and their defence against a common enemy.

Men, women, a bird, a crocodile, a calf, a dog, a snake, an onion, a leek, deified. Besides that, they filled almost all places, with spirits called demons: the plains, with Pan, and Panises, or Satyrs; the woods, with Fawns, and Nymphs; the sea, with Tritons, and other Nymphs; every river, and fountain, with a ghost of his name, and with Nymphs; every house with its Lares, or familiars; every man with his Genius; hell with ghosts, and spiritual officers, as Charon, Cerberus, and the Furies; and in the night time, all places with larvae, lemures, ghosts of men deceased, and a whole kingdom of fairies and bugbears. They have also ascribed divinity, and built temples to meer accidents, and qualities; such as are time, night, day, peace, concord, love, contention, virtue, honour, health, lust, fever, and the like; which when they prayed for, or against, they prayed to, as if there were ghosts of those names hanging over their heads, and letting fall, or withholding that good, or evil, for, or against which they prayed. They invoked also their own wit, by the name of Muses; their own ignorance, by the name of Fortune; their own lust, by the name of Cupid; their own rage, by the name Furies; their own privy members, by the name of

Priapus, and attributed their pollutions, to Incubi, and Succubae: insomuch as there was nothing, which a poet could introduce as a person in his poem, which they did not make either a god, or a devil. . . .

First therefore, seeing sovereignty by institution, is by covenant of every one to every one; and sovereignty by acquisition, by covenants of the vanquished to the victor, or child to the parent; it is manifest, that every subject has liberty in all those things, the right whereof cannot by covenant be transferred. I have shewn before in the fourteenth chapter, that covenants, not to defend a man's own body, are void. Therefore, if the sovereign command a man (though justly condemned,) to kill, wound, or maim himself; or not to resist those that assault him; or to abstain from the use of food, air, medicine, or any other thing, without which he cannot live; yet hath that man the liberty to disobey.

If a man be interrogated by the sovereign, or his authority, concerning a crime done by himself, he is not bound (without assurance of pardon) to confess it; because no man (as I have shown in the same chapter) can be obliged by covenant to accuse himself.

Again, the consent of a subject to sovereign power, is contained in these words, I authorize, or take upon me, all his actions; in which there is no restriction at all, of his own former natural liberty: for by allowing him to kill me, I am not bound to kill myself when he commands me. It is one thing to say, kill me, or my fellow, if you please; another thing to say, I will kill myself, or my fellow. It followeth therefore, that No man is bound by the words themselves, either to kill himself, or any other man; and consequently, that the obligation a man may sometimes have, upon the command of the sovereign to execute any dangerous, or dishonorable office, depends not on the words of our submission; but on the intention, which is to be understood by the end thereof. When therefore our refusal to obey, frustrates the end for which the sovereignty was ordained; then there is no liberty to refuse: otherwise there is.

Upon this ground, a man that is commanded as a soldier to fight against the enemy, though his sovereign have right enough to punish his refusal with death, may nevertheless in many cases refuse, without injustice; as when he substitutes a sufficient soldier in his place: for in this case he deserts not the service of the commonwealth. And there is allowance to be made for natural timorousness; not only to women, (of whom no such dangerous duty is expected,) but also to men of feminine courage. When armies fight, there is on one side, or both, a running away; yet when they do it not out of treachery, but fear, they are not esteemed to do it un-

justly, but dishonorably. For the same reason, to avoid battle, is not injustice, but cowardice. But he that enrolls himself a soldier, or taketh imprest money, taketh away the excuse of a timorous nature; and is obliged, not only to go to the battle, but also not to run from it, without his captain's leave. And when the defence of the commonwealth, requires at once the help of all that are able to bear arms, every one is obliged; because otherwise the institution of the commonwealth, which they have not the purpose, or courage to preserve, was in vain.

To resist the sword of the commonwealth, in defence of another man, guilty, or innocent, no man hath liberty; because such liberty, takes away from the sovereign, the means of protecting us; and is therefore destructive of the very essence of government. But in case a great many men together, have already resisted the sovereign power unjustly, or committed some capital crime, for which every one of them expects death, whether have they not the liberty then to join together, and assist, and defend one another? Certainly they have: for they but defend their lives, which the guilty man may as well do, as the innocent. There was indeed injustice in the first breach of their duty; their bearing of arms subsequent to it, though it be to maintain what they have done, is no new unjust act. And if it be only to defend their persons, it is not unjust at all. But the offer of pardon taketh from them, to whom it is offered, the plea of self-defence, and maketh their perseverance in assisting, or defending the rest, unlawful.

As for other liberties, they depend on the silence of the law. In cases where the sovereign has prescribed no rule, there the subject hath the liberty to do, or forbear, according to his own discretion. And therefore such liberty is in some places more, and in some less; and in some times more, in other times less, according as they that have the sovereignty shall think most convenient. As for example, there was a time, when in England a man might enter into his own land, (and dispossess such as wrongfully possessed it,) by force. But in aftertimes, that liberty of forcible entry, was taken away by a statute made (by the king,) in parliament. And in some places of the world, men have the liberty of many wives: in other places, such liberty is not allowed.

If a subject have a controversy with his sovereign, of debt, or of right of possession of lands or goods, or concerning any service required at his hands, or concerning any penalty, corporal, or pecuniary, grounded on a precedent law; he hath the same liberty to sue for his right, as if it were against a subject; and before such judges, as are appointed by the sovereign. For seeing the sovereign demands by force of a former law, and not by virtue of his power; he declares thereby, that he requires no more, than shall appear to be due by that law. The suit therefore is not contrary to the will of the sovereign; and consequently the subject hath the liberty to demand the hearing of his cause; and sentence, according to that law. But if he demand, or take any thing by pretence of his power; there lies, in that case, no action of law: for all that is done by him in virtue of his power, is done by the authority of every subject, and consequently, he that brings an action against the sovereign, brings it against himself.

If a monarch, or sovereign assembly, grant a liberty to all, or any of his subjects, which grant standing, he is disabled to provide for their safety, the grant is void; unless he directly renounce, or transfer the sovereignty to another. For in that he might openly, (if it had been his will,) and in plain terms, have renounced, or transferred it, and did not; it is to be understood it was not his will; but that the grant proceeded from ignorance of the repugnancy between such a liberty and the sovereign power: and therefore the sovereignty is still retained; and consequently all those powers, which are necessary to the exercising thereof; such as are the power of war, and peace, of judicature, of appointing officers, and councilors, of levying money, and the rest named in the eighteenth chapter.

The obligation of subjects to the sovereign, is understood to last as long, and no longer, than the power lasts, by which he is able to protect them. For the right men have by nature to protect themselves, when none else can protect them, can by no covenant be relinquished. The sovereignty is the soul of the commonwealth; which once departed from the body, the members do no more receive their motion from it. The end of obedience is protection; which, wheresoever a man sees it, either in his own, or in another's sword, nature applies his obedience to it, and his endeavor to maintain it. And though sovereignty, in the intention of them that make it, be immortal; yet is it in its own nature, not only subject to violent death, by foreign war; but also through the ignorance, and passions of men, it hath in it, from the very institution, many seeds of a natural mortality, by intestine discord.

If a subject be taken prisoner in war; or his person, or his means of life be within the guards of the enemy, and hath his life and corporal liberty given him, on condition to be subject to the victor, he hath liberty to accept the condition; and having accepted it, is the subject of him that took him; because he had no other way to preserve himself. The case is the same, if he be detained on the same terms, in a foreign country. But if a man be held in prison, or bonds, or is not trusted with the liberty of his body; he cannot be understood to be bound by covenant to subjection; and therefore may, if he can, make his escape by any means whatsoever.

If a monarch shall relinquish the sovereignty, both for himself, and his heirs; his subjects return to the absolute liberty of nature; because, though nature may declare who are his sons, and who are the nearest of his kin; yet it depends on his own will, (as hath been said in the precedent chapter,) who shall be his heir. If therefore he will have no heir, there is no sovereignty, nor subjection. The case is the same, if he die without known kindred, and without declaration of his heir. For then there can no heir be known, and consequently no subjection be due.

If the sovereign banish his subject; during the banishment, he is not subject. But he that is sent on a message, or hath leave to travel, is still subject; but it is, by contract between sovereigns, not by virtue of the covenant of subjection. For whosoever enters into another's dominion, is subject to all the laws thereof; unless he have a privilege by the amity of the sovereigns, or by special license.

If a monarch subdued by war, render himself subject to the victor; his subjects are delivered from their former obligation, and become obliged to the victor. But if he be held prisoner, or have not the liberty of his own body; he is not understood to have given away the right of sovereignty; and therefore his subjects are obliged to yield obedience to the magistrates formerly placed, governing not in their own name, but in his. For, his right remaining, the question is only of the administration; that is to say, of the magistrates and officers; which, if he have not means to name, he is supposed to approve those, which he himself had formerly appointed.

READING 3

Second Treatise of Government

John Locke

John Locke (1632–1704) was a famous English philosopher and physician. His *Two Treatises of Government* (1689), from which this selection is taken, was an important factor in the development of parliamentary government in England and in the struggle for independence in the United States. Locke's ideas are reflected in the Declaration of Independence. Locke proposed that all humans, being created by God, possess equal natural rights. That is, in the *state of nature* they possess life, liberty, and property. Locke purports that our rights to property are based on mixing our labor with nature. It follows that society, if it is to be legitimate, must recognize these natural rights, which are bestowed on us by God. Because these rights are a gift of God, they are "inalienable" or "imprescribable"; that is, we do not give them to people, nor can we take them away or even give our own rights away (for example, we cannot give away our right to freedom by selling ourselves into slavery). They become the proper basis of all specific rights. Locke argues further that political legitimacy is based on the consent of the governed.

This reading is taken from *Two Treatises of Government*, 1689.

OF CIVIL GOVERNMENT

Book II. Chapter 1. Second Treatise of Government

3. Political power, then, I take to be a right of making laws and penalties of death, and consequently all less penalties for the regulating and preserving of property, and of employing the force of the community, in the execution of such laws, and in the defence of the commonwealth from foreign injury; and all this only for the public good.

Chapter 2. Of the State of Nature

4. To understand political power, right, and derive it from its original, we must consider what state all men are naturally in, and that is, a state of perfect freedom to order their actions, and dispose of their possessions and persons, as they think fit, within the bounds of the law of nature; without asking leave, or depending upon the will of any other man.

A state also of equality, wherein all the power and jurisdiction is reciprocal, no one having more than another; there being nothing more evident, than that creatures of the same species and rank, promiscuously born to all the same advantages of nature, and the use of the same faculties, should also be equal one amongst another without subordination or subjection; unless the lord and master of them all should, by any manifest declaration of his will, set one above another, and confer on him, by an evident and clear appointment, an undoubted right to dominion and sovereignty.

5. This equality of men by nature, the judicious Hooker[1] looks upon as so evident in itself, and beyond all question, that he makes it the foundation of that obligation to mutual love amongst men, on which he builds the duties we owe one another, and from whence he derives the great maxims of justice and charity. His words are, "The like natural inducement hath brought men to know, that it is no less their duty to love others than themselves; for seeing those things which are equal, must needs all have one measure; if I cannot but wish to receive good, even as much at every man's hands, as any man can wish unto his own soul, how should I look to have any part of my desire herein satisfied, unless myself be careful to satisfy the like desire, which is undoubtedly in other men, being of one and the same nature? To have any thing offered them repugnant to this desire, must needs in all respects grieve them as much as me; so that if I do harm, I must look to suffer, there being no reason that others should shew greater measure of love to me, than they have by me shewed unto them: my desire therefore to be loved of my equals in nature, as much as possibly may be, imposeth upon me a natural duty of bearing to them-ward fully the like affection: From which relation of equality between ourselves and them that are as ourselves, what several rules and canons natural reason hath drawn, for direction of life, no man is ignorant." Eccl. Pol. L. I.

6. But though this be a state of liberty, yet it is not a state of licence: though man in that state have an uncontrolable liberty to dispose of his person or possessions, yet he has not liberty to destroy himself, or so much as any creature in his possession, but where some nobler use than its bare preservation calls for it. The state of nature has a law of nature to govern it, which obliges every one: And reason, which is that law, teaches all mankind, who will but consult it, that being all equal and independent, no one ought to harm

another in his life, health, liberty, or possessions. For men being all the workmanship of one omnipotent and infinitely wise Maker; all the servants of one sovereign master, sent into the world by his order, and about his business; they are his property, whose workmanship they are, made to last during his, not another's pleasure. And being furnished with like faculties, sharing all in one community of nature, there cannot be supposed any such subordination among us, that may authorize us to destroy another, as if we were made for one another's uses, as the inferior ranks of creatures are for ours. Every one, as he is bound to preserve himself, and not to quit his station wilfully, so by the like reason, when his own preservation comes not in competition, ought he, as much as he can, to preserve the rest of mankind, and may not, unless it be to do justice to an offender, take away or impair the life, or what tends to the preservation of life, the liberty, health, limb, or goods of another.

7. And that all men may be restrained from invading others rights, and from doing hurt to one another, and the law of nature be observed, which willeth the peace and preservation of all mankind, the execution of the law of nature is, in that state, put into every man's hands, whereby every one has a right to punish the transgressors of that law to such a degree as may hinder its violation. For the law of nature would, as all other laws that concern men in this world, be in vain, if there were no body that in the state of nature had a power to execute that law, and thereby preserve the innocent and restrain offenders. And if any one in the state of nature may punish another for any evil he has done, every one may do so. For in that state of perfect equality, where naturally there is no superiority or jurisdiction of one over another, what any may do in prosecution of that law, every one must needs have a right to do.

8. And thus, in the state of nature, one man comes by a power over another; but yet no absolute or arbitrary power, to use a criminal, when he has got him in his hands, according to the passionate heats, or boundless extravagancy of his own will; but only to retribute to him, so far as calm reason and conscience dictate, what is proportionate to his transgression; which is so much as may serve for reparation and restraint. For these two are the only reasons, why one man may lawfully do harm to another, which is that we call punishment. In transgressing the law of nature, the offender declares himself to live by another rule than that of reason and common equity, which is that measure God has set to the actions of men, for their mutual security;

and so he becomes dangerous to mankind, the tye, which is to secure them from injury and violence, being slighted and broken by him. Which being a trespass against the whole species, and the peace and safety of it, provided for by the law of nature; every man upon this score, by the right he hath to preserve mankind in general, may restrain, or, where it is necessary, destroy things noxious to them, and so may bring such evil on any one, who hath transgressed that law, as may make him repent the doing of it, and thereby deter him, and by his example others, from doing the like mischief. And in this case, and upon this ground, every man hath a right to punish the offender, and be executioner of the law of nature.

9. I doubt not but this will seem a very strange doctrine to some men: but before they condemn it, I desire them to resolve me, by what right any prince or state can put to death, or punish an alien, for any crime he commits in their country. It is certain their laws, by virtue of any sanction they receive from the promulgated will of the legislative, reach not a stranger. They speak not to him, nor, if they did, is he bound to hearken to them. The legislative authority, by which they are in force over the subjects of that commonwealth, hath no power over him. Those who have the supreme power of making laws in England, France, or Holland, are to an Indian but like the rest of the world, men without authority: And therefore, if by the law of nature every man hath not a power to punish offences against it, as he soberly judges the case to require, I see not how the magistrates of any community can punish an alien of another country; since in reference to him, they can have no more power, than what every man naturally may have over another.

10. Besides the crime which consists in violating the law, and varying from the right rule of reason, whereby a man so far becomes degenerate, and declares himself to quit the principles of human nature, and to be a noxious creature, there is commonly injury done to some person or other, and some other man receives damage by his transgression, in which case he who hath received by any damage, has besides the right of punishment common to him with other men, a particular right to seek reparation from him that has done it. And any other person who finds it just, may also join with him that is injured, and assist him in recovering from the offender so much as may make satisfaction for the harm he has suffered.

11. From these two distinct rights, the one of punishing the crime for restraint, and preventing the like offence, which right of punishing is in every body; the

other of taking reparation, which belongs only to the injured party; comes it to pass that the magistrate, who by being magistrate, hath the common right of punishing put into his hands, can often, where the public good demands not the execution of the law, remit the punishment of criminal offences by his own authority, but yet cannot remit the satisfaction due to any private man, for the damage he has received. That, he who has suffered the damage has a right to demand in his own name, and he alone can remit: The damnified person has this power of appropriating to himself the goods or service of the offender, by right of self-preservation, as every man has a power to punish the crime, to prevent its being committed again, by the right he has of preserving all mankind; and doing all reasonable things he can in order to that end: And thus it is, that every man, in the state of nature, has a power to kill a murderer, both to deter others from doing the like injury, which no reparation can compensate, by the example of the punishment that attends it from every body, and also to secure men from the attempts of a criminal, who having renounced reason, the common rule and measure, God hath given to mankind, hath by the unjust violence and slaughter he hath committed upon one, declared war against all mankind; and therefore may be destroyed as a lion or a tiger, one of those wild savage beasts, with whom men can have no society nor security: And upon this is grounded the great law of nature, "Whoso sheddeth man's blood, by man shall his blood be shed." And Cain was so fully convinced, that every one had a right to destroy such a criminal, that after the murder of his brother, he cries out, "Every one that findeth me, shall slay me;" so plain was it writ in the hearts of all mankind.

12. By the same reason may a man in the state of nature punish the lesser breaches of that law. It will perhaps be demanded, with death? I answer, each transgression may be punished to that degree, and with so much severity, as will suffice to make it an ill bargain to the offender, give him cause to repent, and terrify others from doing the like. Every offence that can be committed in the state of nature, may in the state of nature be also punished equally, and as far forth as it may, in a commonwealth: for though it would be besides my present purpose, to enter here into the particulars of the law of nature, or its measures of punishment; yet it is certain there is such a law, and that too, as intelligible and plain to a rational creature, and a studier of that law, as the positive laws of commonwealths, nay possibly plainer; as much as reason is easier to be understood, than the fancies and intricate contrivances of men, following contrary and hidden interests put into

words; for so truly are a great part of the municipal laws of countries, which are only so far right, as they are founded on the law of nature, by which they are to be regulated and interpreted.

13. To this strange doctrine, viz. That in the state of nature every one has the executive power of the law of nature, I doubt not but it will be objected, that it is unreasonable for men to be judges in their own cases, that self-love will make men partial to themselves and their friends: And on the other side, that ill nature, passion and revenge will carry them too far in punishing others; and hence nothing but confusion and disorder will follow, and that therefore God hath certainly appointed government to restrain the partiality and violence of men. I easily grant, that civil government is the proper remedy for the inconveniencies of the state of nature, which must certainly be great, where men may be judges in their own case, since it is easy to be imagined, that he who was so unjust as to do his brother an injury, will scarce be so just as to condemn himself for it: But I shall desire those who make this objection, to remember, that absolute monarchs are but men, and if government is to be the remedy of those evils, which necessarily follow from men's being judges in their own cases, and the state of nature is therefore not to be endured, I desire to know what kind of government that is, and how much better it is than the state of nature, where one man commanding a multitude, has the liberty to be judge in his own case, and may do to all his subjects whatever he pleases, without the least liberty to any one to question or control those who execute his pleasure? and in whatsoever he doth, whether led by reason, mistake or passion, must be submitted to? Much better it is in the state of nature, wherein men are not bound to submit to the unjust will of another: And if he that judges, judges amiss in his own, or any other case, he is answerable for it to the rest of mankind.

14. It is often asked as a mighty objection, where are, or ever were, there any men in such a state of nature? To which it may suffice as an answer at present: That since all princes and rulers of independent governments, all through the world, are in a state of nature, it is plain the world never was, nor ever will be, without numbers of men in that state. I have named all governors of independent communities, whether they are, or are not, in league with others. For it is not every compact that puts an end to the state of nature between men, but only this one of agreeing together mutually to enter into one community, and make one body politic; other promises and compacts men may make one with another, and yet still be in the state of nature. The

promises and bargains for truck, &c. between the two men in the desert island, mentioned by Garcilasso de la Vega, in his history of Peru; or between a Swiss and an Indian, in the woods of America, are binding to them, though they are perfectly in a state of nature, in reference to one another. For truth and keeping of faith belongs to men as men, and not as members of society.

15. To those that say, there were never any men in the state of nature, I will not only oppose the authority of the judicious Hooker, Eccl. Pol. lib. I. sect. 10, where he says, "The laws which have been hitherto mentioned," i.e. the laws of nature, "do bind men absolutely, even as they are men, although they have never any settled fellowship, never any solemn agreeement amongst themselves what to do or not to do, but for as much as we are not by ourselves sufficient to furnish ourselves with competent store of things, needful for such a life, as our nature doth desire, a life fit for the dignity of man; therefore to supply those defects and imperfections which are in us, as living singly and solely by ourselves, we are naturally induced to seek communion and fellowship with others. This was the cause of men's uniting themselves at first in politic societies." But I moreover affirm, that all men are naturally in that state, and remain so, till by their own consents they make themselves members of some politic society; and I doubt not in the sequel of this discourse to make it very clear.

Chapter 3. Of The State of War

16. The state of war is a state of enmity and destruction: And therefore declaring by word or action, not a passionate and hasty, but a sedate settled design upon another man's life, puts him in a state of war with him against whom he has declared such an intention, and so has exposed his life to the other's power to be taken away by him, or any one that joins with him in his defence, and espouses his quarrel: it being reasonable and just I should have a right to destroy that which threatens me with destruction. For by the fundamental law of nature, man being to be preserved as much as possible, when all cannot be preserved, the safety of the innocent is to be preferred: And one may destroy a man who makes war upon him, or has discovered an enmity to his being, for the same reason that he may kill a wolf or a lion; because such men are not under the ties of the common law of reason, have no other rule, but that of force and violence, and so may be treated as beasts

of prey, those dangerous and noxious creatures, that will be sure to destroy him whenever he falls into their power.

17. And hence it is, that he who attempts to get another man into his absolute power, does thereby put himself into a state of war with him; it being to be understood as a declaration of a design upon his life. For I have reason to conclude, that he who would get me into his power without my consent, would use me as he pleased when he got me there, and destroy me too when he had a fancy to it; for no body can desire to have me in his absolute power unless it be to compel me by force to that which is against the right of my freedom, i.e. make me a slave. To be free from such force is the only security of my preservation; and reason bids me look on him, as an enemy to my preservation, who would take away that freedom which is the fence to it; so that he who makes an attempt to enslave me, thereby puts himself into a state of war with me. He that, in the state of nature, would take away the freedom that belongs to any one in that state, must necessarily be supposed to have a design to take away every thing else, that freedom being the foundation of all the rest: As he that, in the state of society, would take away the freedom belonging to those of that society or commonwealth, must be supposed to design to take away from them every thing else, and so be looked on as in a state of war.

18. This makes it lawful for a man to kill a thief, who has not in the least hurt him, nor declared any design upon his life, any farther, than by the use of force, so to get him in his power, as to take away his money, or what he pleases, from him; because using force, where he has no right, to get me into his power, let his pretence be what it will, I have no reason to suppose, that he, who would take away my liberty, would not, when he had me in his power, take away every thing else. And therefore it is lawful for me to treat him as one who has put himself into a state of war with me, i.e. kill him if I can; for to that hazard does he justly expose himself, whoever introduces a state of war, and is aggressor in it.

19. And here we have the plain difference between the state of nature and the state of war; which however some men have confounded, are as far distant, as a state of peace, good will, mutual assistance and preservation, and a state of enmity, malice, violence and mutual destruction, are one from another. Men living together according to reason, without a common superior on earth, with authority to judge between them, is properly the state of nature. But force, or a declared design

of force, upon the person of another, where there is no common superior on earth to appeal to for relief, is the state of war: And it is the want of such an appeal gives a man the right of war even against an aggressor, though he be in society and a fellow subject. Thus a thief, whom I cannot harm, but by appeal to the law, for having stolen all that I am worth, I may kill, when he sets on me to rob me but of my horse or coat; because the law, which was made for my preservation, where it cannot interpose to secure my life from present force, which, if lost, is capable of no reparation, permits me my own defence, and the right of war, a liberty to kill the aggressor, because the aggressor allows not time to appeal to our common judge, nor the decision of the law, for remedy in a case where the mischief may be irreparable. Want of a common judge with authority, puts all men in a state of nature: Force without right, upon a man's person, makes a state of war, both where there is, and is not, a common judge.

20. But when the actual force is over, the state of war ceases between those that are in society, and are equally on both sides subjected to the fair determination of the law; because then there lies open the remedy of appeal for the past injury, and to prevent future harm: but where no such appeal is, as in the state of nature, for want of positive laws, and judges with authority to appeal to, the state of war once begun, continues with a right to the innocent party to destroy the other whenever he can, until the aggressor offers peace, and desires reconciliation on such terms as may repair any wrongs he has already done, and secure the innocent for the future: nay, where an appeal to the law, and constituted judges, lies open, but the remedy is denied by a manifest perverting of justice, and a barefaced wresting of the laws to protect or indemnify the violence or injuries of some men, or party of men, there it is hard to imagine any thing but a state of war. For wherever violence is used, and injury done, though by hands appointed to administer justice, it is still violence and injury, however coloured with the name, pretences, or forms of law, the end whereof being to protect and redress the innocent, by an unbiassed application of it, to all who are under it; wherever that is not bona fide done, war is made upon the sufferers, who having no appeal on earth to right them, they are left to the only remedy in such cases, an appeal to heaven.

21. To avoid this state of war (where there is no appeal but to heaven, and wherein even the least difference is apt to end, where there is no authority to decide between the contenders) is one great reason of men's putting themselves into society, and quitting the state of nature. For where there is an authority, a power on earth, from which relief can be had by appeal, there the continuance of the state of war is excluded, and the controversy is decided by that power. Had there been any such court, any superior jurisdiction on earth, to determine the right between Jephthah and the Ammonites, they had never come to a state of war: But we see he was forced to appeal to heaven. "The Lord the Judge," says he, "be judge this day, between the children of Israel and the children of Ammon," Judg. xi. 27, and then prosecuting, and relying on his appeal, he leads out his army to battle: and therefore in such controversies, where the question is put, who shall be judge? it cannot be meant, who shall decide the controversy; every one knows what Jephthah here tells us, that "the Lord the Judge" shall judge. Where there is no judge on earth, the appeal lies to God in heaven. That question then cannot mean, who shall judge? whether another hath put himself in a state of war with me, and whether I may, as Jephthah did, appeal to heaven in it? of that I myself can only be judge in my own conscience, as I will answer it, at the great day, to the supreme judge of all men. . . .

Chapter 5. Of Property

25. Whether we consider natural reason, which tells us, that men, being once born, have a right to their preservation, and consequently to meat and drink, and such other things as nature affords for their subsistence: or revelation, which gives us an account of those grants God made of the world to Adam, and to Noah, and his sons, it is very clear, that God, as King David says, Psal. cxv. 16, "has given the earth to the children of men," given it to mankind in common. But this being supposed, it seems to some a very great difficulty how any one should ever come to have a property in any thing: I will not content myself to answer, that if it be difficult to make out property, upon a supposition, that God gave the world to Adam, and his posterity in common; it is impossible that any man, but one universal monarch, should have any property upon a supposition, that God gave the world to Adam, and his heirs in succession, exclusive of all the rest of his posterity. But I shall endeavour to shew, how men might come to have a property in several parts of that which God gave to mankind in common, and that without any express compact of all the commoners.

26. God, who hath given the world to men in common, hath also given them reason to make use of it to the

best advantage of life, and convenience. The earth, and all that is therein, is given to men for the support and comfort of their being. And though all the fruits it naturally produces, and beasts it feeds, belong to mankind in common, as they are produced by the spontaneous hand of nature; and no body has originally a private dominion, exclusive of the rest of mankind, in any of them, as they are thus in their natural state: yet being given for the use of men, there must of necessity be a means to appropriate them some way or other, before they can be of any use, or at all beneficial to any particular man. The fruit, or venison, which nourishes the wild Indian, who knows no enclosure, and is still a tenant in common, must be his, and so his, i.e. a part of him, that another can no longer have any right to it, before it can do him any good for the support of his life.

27. Though the earth, and all inferior creatures, be common to all men, yet every man has a property in his own person: this no body has any right to but himself. The labour of his body, and the work of his hands, we may say, are properly his. Whatsoever then he removes out of the state that nature hath provided, and left it in, he hath mixed his labour with, and joined to it something that is his own, and thereby makes it his property. It being by him removed from the common state nature hath placed it in, it hath by this labour something annexed to it, that excludes the common right of other men. For this labour being the unquestionable property of the labourer, no man but he can have a right to what that is once joined to, at least where there is enough, and as good, left in common for others.

28. He that is nourished by the acorns he picked up under an oak, or the apples he gathered from the trees in the wood, has certainly appropriated them to himself. No body can deny but the nourishment is his. I ask then, when did they begin to be his? When he digested? Or when he ate? Or when he boiled? Or when he brought them home? Or when he picked them up? And it is plain, if the first gathering made them not his, nothing else could. That labour put a distinction between them and common: that added something to them more than nature, the common mother of all, had done; and so they became his private right. And will any one say he had no right to those acorns or apples he thus appropriated, because he had not the consent of all mankind to make them his? Was it a robbery thus to assume to himself what belonged to all in common? If such a consent as that was necessary, man had starved, notwithstanding the plenty God had given him. We see in commons, which remain so by compact, that it is the taking any part of what is common, and re-

moving it out of the state nature leaves it in, which begins the property; without which the common is of no use. And the taking of this or that part does not depend on the express consent of all the commoners. Thus the grass my horse has bit; the turfs my servant has cut; and the ore I have digged in any place, where I have a right to them in common with others, become my property, without the assignation or consent of any body. The labour that was mine, removing them out of that common state they were in, hath fixed my property in them.

29. By making an explicit consent of every commoner necessary to any one's appropriating to himself any part of what is given in common, children or servants could not cut the meat, which their father or master had provided for them in common, without assigning to every one his peculiar part. Though the water running in the fountain be every one's, yet who can doubt, but that in the pitcher is his only who drew it out? His labour hath taken it out of the hands of nature, where it was common, and belonged equally to all her children, and hath thereby appropriated it to himself.

30. Thus this law of reason makes the deer that Indian's who hath killed it; it is allowed to be his goods, who hath bestowed his labour upon it, though before it was the common right of every one. And amongst those who are counted the civilized part of mankind, who have made and multiplied positive laws to determine property, this original law of nature, for the beginning of property, in what was before common, still takes place; and by virtue thereof, what fish any one catches in the ocean, that great and still remaining common of mankind; or what ambergreise any one takes up here, is by the labour that removes it out of that common state nature left it in, made his property, who takes that pains about it. And even amongst us, the hare that any one is hunting, is thought his who pursues her during the chase. For being a beast that is still looked upon as common, and no man's private possession; whoever has employed so much labour about any of that kind, as to find and pursue her, has thereby removed her from the state of nature, wherein she was common, and hath begun a property.

31. It will perhaps be objected to this, that if gathering the acorns, or other fruits of the earth, &c. makes a right to them, then any one may engross as much as he will. To which I answer, Not so. The same law of nature, that does by this means give us property, does also bound that property too. "God has given us all things richly," 1 Tim; vi. 17, is the voice of reason con-

firmed by inspiration. But how far has he given it us? To enjoy. As much as any one can make use of to any advantage of life before it spoils, so much he may by his labour fix a property in: whatever is beyond this, is more than his share, and belongs to others. Nothing was made by God for man to spoil or destroy. And thus, considering the plenty of natural provisions there was a long time in the world, and the few spenders; and to how small a part of that provision the industry of one man could extend itself, and engross it to the prejudice of others; especially keeping within the bounds, set by reason, of what might serve for his use; there could be then little room for quarrels or contentions about property so established.

32. But the chief matter of property being now not the fruits of the earth, and the beasts that subsist on it, but the earth itself; as that which takes in, and carries with it all the rest: I think it is plain, that property in that too is acquired as the former. As much land as a man tills, plants, improves, cultivates, and can use the product of, so much is his property. He by his labour does, as it were, enclose it from the common. Nor will it invalidate his right, to say every body else has an equal title to it; and therefore he cannot appropriate, he cannot enclose, without the consent of all his fellow commoners, all mankind. God, when he gave the world in common to all mankind, commanded man also to labour, and the penury of his condition required it of him. God and his reason commanded him to subdue the earth, i.e. improve it for the benefit of life, and therein lay out something upon it that was his own, his labour. He that, in obedience to this command of God, subdued, tilled, and sowed any part of it, thereby annexed to it something that was his property, which another had no title to, nor could without injury take from him.

33. Nor was this appropriation of any parcel of land, by improving it, any prejudice to any other man, since there was still enough, and as good left; and more than the yet unprovided could use. So that, in effect, there was never the less left for others because of his enclosure for himself. For he that leaves as much as another can make use of, does as good as take nothing at all. No body could think himself injured by the drinking of another man, though he took a good draught, who had a whole river of the same water left him to quench his thirst: And the case of land and water, where there is enough of both, is perfectly the same.

34. God gave the world to men in common; but since he gave it them for their benefit, and the greatest conveniences of life they were capable to draw from it,

it cannot be supposed he meant it should always remain common and uncultivated. He gave it to the use of the industrious and rational, (and labour was to be his title to it) not to the fancy or convetousness of the quarrelsome and contentious. He that had as good left for his improvement, as was already taken up, needed not complain, ought not to meddle with what was already improved by another's labour: If he did, it is plain he desired the benefit of another's pains, which he had no right to, and not the ground which God had given him in common with others to labour on, and whereof there was as good left, as that already possessed, and more than he knew what to do with, or his industry could reach to. . . .

Chapter 7. Of Political or Civil Society

77. God having made man such a creature, that in his own judgment, it was not good for him to be alone, put him under strong obligations of necessity, convenience, and inclination, to drive him into society, as well as fitted him with understanding and language to continue and enjoy it. The first society was between man and wife, which gave beginning to that between parents and children; to which, in time, that between master and servant came to be added; and though all these might, and commonly did meet together, and make up but one family, wherein the master or mistress of it had some sort of rule proper to a family; each of these, or all together, came short of political society, as we shall see, if we consider the different ends, ties, and bounds of each of these.

78. Conjugal society is made by a voluntary compact between man and woman; and though it consist chiefly in such a communion and right in one another's bodies as is necessary to its chief end, procreation; yet it draws with it mutual support and assistance, and a communion of interests too, as necessary not only to unite their care and affection, but also necessary to their common offspring, who have a right to be nourished and maintained by them, till they are able to provide for themselves.

79. For the end of conjunction between male and female being not barely procreation, but the continuation of the species; this conjunction betwixt male and female ought to last, even after procreation, so long as is necessary to the nourishment and support of the young ones, who are to be sustained by those that got them, till they are able to shift and provide for

themselves. This rule, which the infinite wise Maker hath set to the works of his hands, we find the inferior creatures steadily obey. In those viviparous animals which feed on grass, the conjunction between male and female lasts no longer than the very act of copulation; because the teat of the dam being sufficient to nourish the young, till it be able to feed on grass, the male only begets, but concerns not himself for the female or young, to whose sustenance he can contribute nothing. But in beasts of prey the conjunction lasts longer: because the dam not being able well to subsist herself, and nourish her numerous offspring by her own prey alone, a more laborious, as well as more dangerous way of living, than by feeding on grass; the assistance of the male is necessary to the maintenance of their common family, which cannot subsist till they are able to prey for themselves, but by the joint care of male and female. The same is to be observed in all birds (except some domestic ones, where plenty of food excuses the cock from feeding, and taking care of the young brood), whose young needing food in the nest, the cock and hen continue mates, till the young are able to use their wing, and provide for themselves.

80. And herein I think lies the chief, if not the only reason, why the male and female in mankind are tied to a longer conjunction than other creatures, viz. because the female is capable of conceiving, and de facto is commonly with child again, and brings forth too a new birth, long before the former is out of a dependency for support on his parents help, and able to shift for himself, and has all the assistance that is due to him from his parents: whereby the father, who is bound to take care for those he hath begot, is under an obligation to continue in conjugal society with the same woman longer than other creatures, whose young being able to subsist of themselves before the time of procreation returns again, the conjugal bond dissolves of itself, and they are at liberty, till Hymen at his usual anniversary season summons them again to choose new mates. Wherein one cannot but admire the wisdom of the great Creator, who having given to man foresight, and an ability to lay up for the future, as well as to supply the present necessity, hath made it necessary, that society of man and wife should be more lasting, than of male and female amongst other creatures; that so their industry might be encouraged, and their interest better united, to make provision and lay up goods for their common issue, which uncertain mixture, or easy and frequent solutions of conjugal society, would mightily disturb.

81. But though these are ties upon mankind, which make the conjugal bonds more firm and lasting in man,

than the other species of animals; yet it would give one reason to inquire, why this compact, where procreation and education are secured, and inheritance taken care for, may not be made determinable, either by consent, or at a certain time, or upon certain conditions, as well as any other voluntary compacts, there being no necessity in the nature of the thing, nor to the ends of it, that it should always be for life; I mean, to such as are under no restraint of any positive law, which ordains all such contracts to be perpetual.

82. But the husband and wife, though they have but one common concern, yet having different understandings, will unavoidably sometimes have different wills too; it therefore being necessary that the last determination, i.e. the rule, should be placed somewhere; it naturally falls to the man's share, as the abler and the stronger. But this reaching but to the things of their common interest and property, leaves the wife in the full and free possession of what by contract is her peculiar right, and gives the husband no more power over her life than she has over his. The power of the husband being so far from that of an absolute monarch, that the wife has in many cases a liberty to separate from him, where natural right or their contract allows it; whether that contract be made by themselves in the state of nature, or by the customs or laws of the country they live in; and the children upon such separation fall to the father's or mother's lot, as such contract does determine.

83. For all the ends of marriage being to be obtained under politic government, as well as in the state of nature, the civil magistrate doth not abridge the right or power of either naturally necessary to those ends, viz. procreation and mutual support and assistance whilst they are together; but only decides any controversy that may arise between man and wife about them. If it were otherwise, and that absolute sovereignty and power of life and death naturally belonged to the husband, and were necessary to the society between man and wife, there could be no matrimony in any of those countries where the husband is allowed no such absolute authority. But the ends of matrimony requiring no such power in the husband, the condition of conjugal society put it not in him, it being not at all necessary to that state. Conjugal society could subsist and attain its ends without it; nay, community of goods, and the power over them, mutual assistance and maintenance, and other things belonging to conjugal society, might be varied and regulated by that contract which unites man and wife in that society, as far as may consist with procreation and the bringing up of children till they could

shift for themselves; nothing being necessary to any society, that is not necessary to the ends for which it is made. . . .

86. Let us therefore consider a master of a family with all these subordinate relations of wife, children, servants, and slaves, united under the domestic rule of a family; which, what resemblance soever it may have in its order, offices, and number too, with a little commonwealth, yet is very far from it, both in its constitution, power, and end: or if it must be thought a monarchy, and the paterfamilias the absolute monarch in it, absolute monarchy will have but a very shattered and short power, when it is plain by what has been said before, that the master of the family has a very distinct and differently limited power, both as to time and extent, over those several persons that are in it. For excepting the slave (and the family is as much a family, and his power as paterfamilias as great, whether there be any slaves in his family or no) he has no legislative power of life and death over any of them, and none too but what a mistress of a family may have as well as he. And he certainly can have no absolute power over the whole family, who has but a very limited one over every individual in it. But how a family, or any other society of men, differ from that which is properly political society, we shall best see by considering wherein political society itself consists.

87. Man being born, as has been proved, with a title to perfect freedom, and an uncontrolled enjoyment of all the rights and privileges of the law of nature, equally with any other man, or number of men in the world, hath by nature a power, not only to preserve his property, that is, his life, liberty, and estate, against the injuries and attempts of other men; but to judge of and punish the breaches of that law in others, as he is persuaded the offence deserves, even with death itself, in crimes where the heinousness of the fact, in his opinion, requires it. But because no political society can be, nor subsist, without having in itself the power to preserve the property, and, in order thereunto, punish the offences of all those of that society; there and there only is political society, where every one of the members hath quitted his natural power, resigned it up into the hands of the community in all cases that excludes him not from appealing for protection to the law established by it. And thus all private judgment of every particular member being excluded, the community comes to be umpire by settled standing rules, indifferent, and the same to all parties; and by men having authority from the community, for the execution of those rules, decides all the differences that may happen between any members of that society concerning any matter of right; and punishes those offences which any member hath committed against the society, with such penalties as the law has established, whereby it is easy to discern, who are, and who are not, in political society together. Those who are united into one body, and have a common established law and judicature to appeal to, with authority to decide controversies between them, and punish offenders, are in civil society one with another: but those who have no such common appeal, I mean on earth, are still in the state of nature, each being, where there is no other, judge for himself, and executioner: which is, as I have before shewed, the perfect state of nature.

88. And thus the commonwealth comes by a power to set down what punishment shall belong to the several transgressions which they think worthy of it, committed amongst the members of that society (which is the power of making laws) as well as it has the power to punish any injury done unto any of its members, by any one that is not of it (which is the power of war and peace), and all this for the preservation of the property of all the members of that society, as far as is possible. But though every man who has entered into civil society, and is become a member of any commonwealth, has thereby quitted his power to punish offences against the law of nature, in prosecution of his own private judgment; yet with the judgment of offences, which he has given up to the legislative in all cases, where he can appeal to the magistrate, he has given a right to the commonwealth to employ his force, for the execution of the judgments of the commonwealth whenever he shall be called to it; which indeed are his own judgments, they being made by himself, or his representative. And herein we have the original of the legislative and executive power of civil society, which is to judge by standing laws, how far offences are to be punished, when committed within the commonwealth; and also to determine, by occasional judgments founded on the present circumstances of the fact, how far injuries from without are to be vindicated; and in both these to employ all the force of all the members, when there shall be need.

89. Whenever therefore any number of men are so united into one society, as to quit every one his executive power of the law of nature, and to resign it to the public, there and there only is a political, or civil society. And this is done, wherever any number of men, in the state of nature, enter into society to make one people, one body politic, under one supreme government; or else when any one joins himself to, and incorporates

with any government already made. For hereby he authorizes the society, or, which is all one, the legislative thereof, to make laws for him, as the public good of the society shall require; to the execution whereof, his own assistance (as to his own degrees) is due. And this puts men out of a state of nature into that of a commonwealth, by setting up a judge on earth, with authority to determine all the controversies, and redress the injuries that may happen to any member of the commonwealth: which judge is the legislative, or magistrate appointed by it. And wherever there are any number of men, however associated, that have no such decisive power to appeal to, there they are still in the state of nature.

90. Hence it is evident, that absolute monarchy, which by some men is counted the only government in the world, is indeed inconsistent with civil society, and so can be no form of civil government at all; for the end of civil society being to avoid and remedy these inconveniencies of the state of nature, which necessarily follow from every man's being judge in his own case, by setting up a known authority, to which every one of that society may appeal upon any injury received, or controversy that may arise, and which every one of the society ought to obey; wherever any persons are, who have not such an authority to appeal to for the decision of any difference between them, there those persons are still in the state of nature. And so is every absolute prince, in respect of those who are under his dominion.

91. For he being supposed to have all, both legislative and executive power in himself alone, there is no judge to be found, no appeal lies open to any one, who may fairly, and indifferently, and with authority decide, and from whose decision relief and redress may be expected of any injury or inconveniency that may be suffered from the prince, or by his order: so that such a man, however intitled, czar, or grand seignior, or how you please, is as much in the state of nature, with all under his dominion, as he is with the rest of mankind. For wherever any two men are, who have no standing rule, and common judge to appeal to on earth, for the determination of controversies of right betwixt them, there they are still in the state of nature, and under all the inconveniencies of it, with only this woful difference to the subject, or rather slave of an absolute prince; that whereas in the ordinary state of nature he has a liberty to judge of his right, and, according to the best of his power, to maintain it; now, whenever his property is invaded by the will and order of his monarch, he has not only no appeal, as those in society ought to have, but, as if he were degraded from the common state of

rational creatures, is denied a liberty to judge of, or to defend his right; and so is exposed to all the misery and inconveniencies that a man can fear from one, who being in the unrestrained state of nature, is yet corrupted with flattery, and armed with power.

92. For he that thinks absolute power purifies men's blood, and corrects the baseness of human nature, need read but the history of this or any other age, to be convinced of the contrary. He that would have been so insolent and injurious in the woods of America, would not probably be much better in a throne; where perhaps learning and religion shall be found out to justify all that he shall do to his subjects, and the sword presently silence all those that dare question it. For what the protection of absolute monarchy is, what kind of fathers of their countries it makes princes to be, and to what a degree of happiness and security it carries civil society, where this sort of government is grown to perfection; he that will look into the late relation of Ceylon, may easily see. . . .

Chapter 8. Of the Beginning of Political Societies

95. Men being, as has been said, by nature, all free, equal, and independent, no one can be put out of this estate, and subjected to the political power of another, without his own consent. The only way, whereby any one divests himself of his natural liberty, and puts on the bonds of civil society, is by agreeing with other men to join and unite into a community, for their comfortable, safe, and peaceable living one amongst another, in a secure enjoyment of their properties, and a greater security against any, that are not of it. This any number of men may do, because it injures not the freedom of the rest; they are left as they were in the liberty of the state of nature. When any number of men have so consented to make one community or government, they are thereby presently incorporated, and make one body politic, wherein the majority have a right to act and conclude the rest.

96. For when any number of men have, by the consent of every individual, made a community, they have thereby made that community one body, with a power to act as one body, which is only by the will and determination of the majority. For that which acts any community, being only the consent of the individuals of it, and it being necessary to that which is one body to move one way; it is necessary the body should move that way whither the greater force carries it, which is the consent of the majority: or else it is impossible it should act or continue one body, one community, which

the consent of every individual that united into it, agreed that it should; and so every one is bound by that consent to be concluded by the majority. And therefore we see, that in assemblies, impowered to act by positive laws, where no number is set by that positive law which impowers them, the act of the majority passes for the act of the whole, and of course determines, as having, by the law of nature and reason, the power of the whole.

97. And thus every man, by consenting with others to make one body politic under one government, puts himself under an obligation, to every one of that society, to submit to the determination of the majority, and to be concluded by it; or else this original compact, whereby he with others incorporate into one society, would signify nothing, and be no compact, if he be left free, and under no other ties than he was in before in the state of nature. For what appearance would there be of any compact? What new engagement if he were no farther tied by any decrees of the society, than he himself thought fit, and did actually consent to? This would be still as great a liberty, as he himself had before his compact, or any one else in the state of nature hath, who may submit himself, and consent to any acts of it if he thinks fit.

98. For if the consent of the majority shall not, in reason, be received as the act of the whole, and conclude every individual; nothing but the consent of every individual can make any thing to be the act of the whole: But such a consent is next to impossible ever to be had, if we consider the infirmities of health, and avocations of business, which in a number, though much less than that of a commonwealth, will necessarily keep many away from the public assembly. To which if we add the variety of opinions, and contrariety of interests, which unavoidably happen in all collections of men, the coming into society upon such terms would be only like Cato's coming into the theatre, only to go out again. Such a constitution as this would make the mighty leviathan of a shorter duration, than the feeblest creatures, and not let it outlast the day it was born in: which cannot be supposed, till we can think, that rational creatures should desire and constitute societies only to be dissolved. For where the majority cannot conclude the rest, there they cannot act as one body, and consequently will be immediately dissolved again.

99. Whosoever therefore out of a state of nature unite into a community, must be understood to give up all the power, necessary to the ends for which they unite into society, to the majority of the community, unless they expressly agreed in any number greater than the majority. And this is done by barely agreeing to unite into one political society, which is all the compact that is, or needs be, between the individuals, that enter into, or make up a commonwealth. And thus that, which begins and actually constitutes any political society, is nothing, but the consent of any number of freemen capable of a majority, to unite and incorporate into such a society. And this is that, and that only, which did, or could give beginning to any lawful government in the world.

100. To this I find two objections made.

First, That there are no instances to be found in story, of a company of men independent and equal one amongst another, that met together, and in this way began and set up a government.

Secondly, It is impossible of right, that men should do so, because all men being born under government, they are to submit to that, and are not at liberty to begin a new one.

101. To the first there is this to answer, That it is not at all to be wondered, that history gives us but a very little account of men, that lived together in the state of nature. The inconveniencies of that condition and the love and want of society, no sooner brought any number of them together, but they presently united and incorporated, if they designed to continue together. And if we may not suppose men ever to have been in the state of nature, because we hear not much of them in such a state, we may as well suppose the armies of Salmanasser or Xerxes were never children, because we hear little of them, till they were men, and embodied in armies. Government is every where antecedent to records, and letters seldom come in amongst a people till a long continuation of civil society has, by other more necessary arts, provided for their safety, ease, and plenty. And then they begin to look after the history of their founders, and search into their original, when they have outlived the memory of it. For it is with commonwealths, as with particular persons, they are commonly ignorant of their own births and infancies: and if they know any thing of their original, they are beholden for it to the accidental records that others have kept of it. And those that we have of the beginning of any politics in the world, excepting that of the Jews, where God himself immediately interposed, and which favours not at all paternal dominion, are all either plain instances of such a beginning as I have mentioned, or at least have manifest footsteps of it.

102. He must shew a strange inclination to deny evident matter of fact, when it agrees not with his hypothesis, who will not allow, that the beginning of

Rome and Venice were by the uniting together of several men free and independent one of another, amongst whom there was no natural superiority or subjection. And if Josephus Acosta's word may be taken, he tells us, that in many parts of America there was no government at all. "There are great and apparent conjectures," says he, "that these men, speaking of those of Peru, for a long time had neither kings nor commonwealths, but lived in troops, as they do this day in Florida, the Cheriquanas, those of Brasil, and many other nations, which have no certain kings, but as occasion is offered, in peace or war, they choose their captains as they please," 1. I. c. 25. If it be said, that every man there was born subject to his father, or the head of his family. That the subjection due from a child to a father took not away his freedom of uniting into what political society he thought fit, has been already proved. But be that as it will, these men, it is evident, were actually free; and whatever superiority some politicians now would place in any of them, they themselves claimed it not, but by consent were all equal, till by the same consent they set rulers over themselves. So that their politic societies all began from a voluntary union, and the mutual agreement of men freely acting in the choice of their governors, and forms of government.

103. And I hope those who went away from Sparta with Palantus, mentioned by Justin, 1. iii. c. 4, will be allowed to have been freemen, independent one of another, and to have set up a government over themselves, by their own consent. Thus I have given several examples out of history, of people free and in the state of nature, that being met together, incorporated and began a commonwealth. And if the want of such instances be an argument to prove that governments were not, nor could not be so begun, I suppose the contenders for paternal empire were better let it alone, than urge it against natural liberty. For if they can give so many instances out of history, of governments begun upon paternal right, I think (though at best an argument from what has been, to what should of right be, has no great force) one might, without any great danger, yield them the cause. But if I might advise them in the case, they would do well not to search too much into the original of governments, as they have begun de facto; lest they should find, at the foundation of most of them, something very little favourable to the design they promote, and such a power as they contend for.

104. But to conclude, reason being plain on our side, that men are naturally free, and the examples of history shewing, that the governments of the world,

that were begun in peace, had their beginning laid on that foundation, and were made by the consent of the people; there can be little room for doubt, either where the right is, or what has been the opinion, or practice of mankind, about the first erecting of governments.

105. I will not deny, that if we look back as far as history will direct us, towards the original of commonwealths, we shall generally find them under the government and administration of one man. And I am also apt to believe, that where a family was numerous enough to subsist by itself, and continued entire together, without mixing with others, as it often happens, where there is much land, and few people, the government commonly began in the father. For the father having, by the law of nature, the same power with every man else to punish, as he thought fit, any offences against that law, might thereby punish his transgressing children, even when they were men, and out of their pupilage; and they were very likely to submit to his punishment, and all join with him against the offender, in their turns, giving him thereby power to execute his sentence against any transgression, and so in effect make him the law maker, and governour over all that remained in conjunction with his family. He was fittest to be trusted; paternal affection secured their property and interest under his care; and the custom of obeying him, in their childhood, made it easier to submit to him, rather than to any other. If, therefore, they must have one to rule them, as government is hardly to be avoided amongst men that live together; who so likely to be the man as he that was their common father; unless negligence, cruelty, or any other defect of mind or body made him unfit for it? But when either the father died, and left his next heir, for want of age, wisdom, courage, or any other qualities, less fit for rule; or where several families met, and consented to continue together; there, it is not to be doubted, but they used their natural freedom to set up him whom they judged the ablest, and most likely to rule well over them. Conformable hereunto we find the people of America, who (living out of the reach of the conquering swords, and spreading domination of the two great empires of Peru and Mexico) enjoyed their own natural freedom, though, caeteris paribus, they commonly prefer the heir of their deceased king; yet, if they find him any way weak, or incapable, they pass him by, and set up the stoutest and bravest man for their ruler.

106. Thus, though looking back as far as records give us any account of peopling the world, and the history of nations, we commonly find the government to be in one hand; yet it destroys not that which I affirm,

viz. that the beginning of politic society depends upon the consent of the individuals, to join into, and make one society; who, when they are thus incorporated, might set up what form of government they thought fit. But this having given occasion to men to mistake, and think, that by nature government was monarchical, and belonged to the father; it may not be amiss here to consider, why people in the beginning generally pitched upon this form; which though perhaps the father's preeminency might, in the first institution of some commonwealth give rise to, and place in the beginning the power in one hand; yet it is plain that the reason, that continued the form of government in a single person, was not any regard or respect to paternal authority; since all petty monarchies, that is, almost all monarchies, near their original, have been commonly, at least upon occasion, elective.

107. First then, in the beginning of things, the father's government of the childhood of those sprung from him, having accustomed them to the rule of one man, and taught them that where it was exercised with care and skill, with affection and love to those under it, it was sufficient to procure and preserve to men all the political happiness they sought for in society. It was no wonder that they should pitch upon, and naturally run into that form of government, which from their infancy they had been all accustomed to; and which, by experience, they had found both easy and safe. To which, if we add, that monarchy being simple, and most obvious to men, whom neither experience had instructed in forms of government, nor the ambition or insolence of empire had taught to beware of the encroachments of prerogative, or the inconveniencies of absolute power, which monarchy in succession was apt to lay claim to, and bring upon them; it was not at all strange, that they should not much trouble themselves to think of methods of restraining any exorbitancies of those to whom they had given the authority over them, and of balancing the power of government, by placing several parts of it in different hands. They had neither felt the oppression of tyrannical dominion, nor did the fashion of the age, nor their possessions, or way of living, (which afforded little matter for covetousness or ambition) give them any reason to apprehend or provide against it; and therefore it is no wonder they put themselves into such a frame of government, as was not only, as I said, most obvious and simple, but also best suited to their present state and condition; which stood more in need of defence against foreign invasions and injuries, than of multiplicity of laws. The equality of a simple poor way of living, confining their desires within the narrow bounds of each man's small property, made few controversies, and so no need of many laws to decide them, or variety of officers to superintend the process, or look after the execution of justice, where there were but few trespasses, and few offenders. Since then those, who liked one another so well as to join into society, cannot but be supposed to have some acquaintance and friendship together, and some trust one in another; they could not but have greater apprehensions of others, than of one another: and therefore their first care and thought cannot but be supposed to be, how to secure themselves against foreign force. It was natural for them to put themselves under a frame of government which might best serve to that end, and choose the wisest and bravest man to conduct them in their wars, and lead them out against their enemies, and in this chiefly be their ruler.

108. Thus we see, that the kings of the Indians in America, which is still a pattern of the first ages in Asia and Europe, whilst the inhabitants were too few for the country, and want of people and money gave men no temptation to enlarge their possessions of land, or contest for wider extent of ground, are little more than generals of their armies; and though they command absolutely in war, yet at home and in time of peace they exercise very little dominion, and have but a very moderate sovereignty; the resolutions of peace and war being ordinarily either in the people, or in a council. Though the war itself, which admits not of plurality of governors, naturally devolves the command into the king's sole authority.

109. And thus, in Israel itself, the chief business of their judges, and first kings, seems to have been to be captains in war, and leaders of their armies; which (besides what is signified by going out and in before the people, which was to march forth to war, and home again at the heads of their forces) appears plainly in the story of Jephthah. The Ammonites making war upon Israel, the Gileadites in fear sent to Jephthah, a bastard of their family whom they had cast off, and article with him, if he will assist them against the Ammonites, to make him their ruler; which they do in these words, "And the people made him head and captain over them," Judg. xii. 11. which was, as it seems, all one as to be judge. "And he judged Israel," Judg. xii. 7. that is, was their captain-general, six years. So when Jotham upbraids the Shechemites with the obligation they had to Gideon, who had been their judge and ruler, he tells them, "He fought for you, and adventured his life far, and delivered you out of the hands of Midian," Judg. ix. 17. Nothing is mentioned of him, but what he did as a

general: and indeed that is all is found in his history, or in any of the rest of the judges. And Abimelech particularly is called king, though at most he was but their general. And when, being weary of the ill conduct of Samuel's sons, the children of Israel desired a king, "like all the nations, to judge them, and to go out before them, and to fight their battles," 1 Sam. viii. 20. God granting their desire, says to Samuel. "I will send thee a man, and thou shalt anoint him to be captain over my people Israel, that he may save my people out of the hands of the Philistines," c. ix. 16. As if the only business of a king had been to lead out their armies, and fight in their defence; and accordingly at his inauguration, pouring a vial of oil upon him, declares to Saul, that "the Lord had anointed him to be captain over his inheritance," c. x. 1. And therefore those who, after Saul's being solemnly chosen and saluted king by the tribes of Mispah, were unwilling to have him their king, made no other objection but this, "How shall this man save us?" v. 27. as if they should have said, this man is unfit to be our king, not having skill and conduct enough in war to be able to defend us. And when God resolved to transfer the government to David, it is in these words, "But now thy kingdom shall not continue: the Lord hath sought him a man after his own heart, and the Lord hath commanded him to be captain over his people," c. xiii. 14. As if the whole kingly authority were nothing else but to be their general: and therefore the tribes who had stuck to Saul's family, and opposed David's reign, when they came to Hebron with terms of submission to him, they tell him, amongst other arguments, they had to submit to him as their king, that he was in effect their king in Saul's time, and therefore they had no reason but to receive him as their king now. "Also" (say they,) "in time past, when Saul was king over us; thou wast he that leddest out, and broughtest in Israel, and the Lord said unto thee, Thou shalt feed my people Israel, and thou shalt be a captain over Israel."

110. Thus, whether a family by degrees grew up into a commonwealth, and the fatherly authority being continued on to the elder son, every one in his turn growing up under it, tacitly submitted to it; and the easiness and equality of it not offending any one, every one acquiesced, till time seemed to have confirmed it, and settled a right of succession by prescription: or whether several families, or the descendants of several families, whom chance, neighbourhood, or business brought together, uniting into society, the need of a general, whose conduct might defend them against their enemies in war, and the great confidence the innocence and sincerity of that poor but virtuous age (such as are almost all those which begin governments, that ever come to last in the world), gave men of one another, made the first beginners of commonwealths generally put the rule into one man's hand, without any other express limitation or restraint, but what the nature of the thing and the end of government required: Whichever of those it was that at first put the rule into the hands of a single person, certain it is that no body was entrusted with it but for the public good and safety, and to those ends, in the infancies of commonwealths, those who had it, commonly used it. And unless they had done so, young societies could not have subsisted; without such nursing fathers tender and careful of the public weal, all governments would have sunk under the weakness and infirmities of their infancy, and the prince and the people had soon perished together.

111. But though the golden age (before vain ambition, and amor sceleratus habendi, evil concupiscence, had corrupted men's minds into a mistake of true power and honour) had more virtue, and consequently better governors, as well as less vicious subjects; and there was then no stretching prerogative on the one side, to oppress the people; nor consequently on the other, any dispute about privilege, to lessen or restrain the power of the magistrate; and so no contest betwixt rulers and people about governors or government: yet when ambition and luxury in future ages would retain and increase the power, without doing the business for which it was given; and, aided by flattery, taught princes to have distinct and separate interests from their people; men found it necessary to examine more carefully the original and rights of government, and to find out ways to restrain the exorbitancies, and prevent the abuses of that power, which they having entrusted in another's hands only for their own good, they found was made use of to hurt them.

112. Thus we may see how probable it is, that people that were naturally free, and by their own consent either submitted to the government of their father, or united together out of different families to make a government, should generally put the rule into one man's hands, and choose to be under the conduct of a single person, without so much as by express conditions limiting or regulating his power, which they thought safe enough in his honesty and prudence. Though they never dreamed of monarchy being jure divino, which we never heard of among mankind, till it was revealed to us by the divinity of this last age; nor ever allowed paternal power to have a right to dominion, or to be the foundation of all government. And thus much may suffice to shew, that, as far as we have any light from

history, we have reason to conclude, that all peaceful beginnings of government have been laid in the consent of the people. I say peaceful, because I shall have occasion in another place to speak of conquest, which some esteem a way of beginning of governments.

The other objection I find urged against the beginning of polities, in the way I have mentioned, is this, viz.

113. That all men being born under government, some or other, it is impossible any of them should ever be free, and at liberty to unite together, and begin a new one, or ever be able to erect a lawful government.

If this argument be good, I ask, how came so many lawful monarchies into the world? for if any body, upon this supposition, can shew me any one man in any age of the world free to begin a lawful monarchy, I will be bound to shew him ten other free men at liberty at the same time to unite and begin a new government under a regal or any other form. It being demonstration, that if any one, born under the dominion of another, may be so free as to have a right to command others in a new and distinct empire, every one that is born under the dominion of another may be so free too, and may become a ruler, or subject of a distinct separate government. And so by this their own principle, either all men, however born, are free, or else there is but one lawful prince, one lawful government in the world. And then they have nothing to do, but barely to shew us which that is; which when they have done, I doubt not but all mankind will easily agree to pay obedience to him.

114. Though it be a sufficient answer to their objection, to shew that it involves them in the same difficulties that it doth those they use it against; yet I shall endeavour to discover the weakness of this argument a little farther.

"All men," say they, "are born under government, and therefore they cannot be at liberty to begin a new one. Every one is born a subject to his father, or his prince, and is therefore under the perpetual tie of subjection and allegiance." It is plain mankind never owned nor considered any such natural subjection that they were born in, to one or to the other, that tied them, without their own consents, to a subjection to them and their heirs.

115. For there are no examples so frequent in history, both sacred and profane, as those of men withdrawing themselves, and their obedience from the jurisdiction they were born under, and the family or community they were bred up in, and setting up new governments in other places, from whence sprang all

that number of petty commonwealths in the beginning of ages, and which always multiplied as long as there was room enough, till the stronger, or more fortunate, swallowed the weaker; and those great ones again breaking to pieces, dissolved into lesser dominions. All which are so many testimonies against paternal sovereignty, and plainly prove, that it was not the natural right of the father descending to his heirs, that made governments in the beginning, since it was impossible, upon that ground, there should have been so many little kingdoms; all must have been but only one universal monarchy, if men had not been at liberty to separate themselves from their families, and the government, be it what it will, that was set up in it, and go and make distinct commonwealths and other governments, as they thought fit.

116. This has been the practice of the world from its first beginning to this day; nor is it now any more hindrance to the freedom of mankind, that they are born under constituted and ancient polities, that have established laws, and set forms of government, than if they were born in the woods, amongst the unconfined inhabitants, that run loose in them. For those who would persuade us, that, by being born under any government, we are naturally subjects to it, and have no more any title or pretence to the freedom of the state of nature; have no other reason (bating that of paternal power, which we have already answered) to produce for it, but only, because our fathers of progenitors passed away their natural liberty, and thereby bound up themselves and their posterity to a perpetual subjection to the government which they themselves submitted to. It is true, that whatever engagements or promises any one has made for himself, he is under the obligation of them, but cannot, by any compact whatsoever, bind his children or posterity. For his son, when a man, being altogether as free as the father, any act of the father can no more give away the liberty of the son, than it can of any body else: he may indeed annex such conditions to the land he enjoyed as a subject of any commonwealth, as may oblige his son to be of that community, if he will enjoy those possessions which were his father's; because that estate being his father's property, he may dispose, or settle it, as he pleases.

117. And this has generally given the occasion to mistake in this matter; because commonwealths not permitting any part of their dominions to be dismembered, nor to be enjoyed by any but those of their community, the son cannot ordinarily enjoy the possessions of his father, but under the same terms his father did, by becoming a member of the society; whereby he puts

himself presently under the government he finds there established, as much as any other subject of that commonwealth. And thus the consent of freemen, born under government, which only makes them members of it, being given separately in their turns, as each comes to be of age, and not in a multitude together; people take no notice of it, and thinking it not done at all, or not necessary, conclude they are naturally subjects as they are men.

118. But, it is plain, governments themselves understand it otherwise; they claim no power over the son, because of that they had over the father; nor look on children as being their subjects, by their fathers being so. If a subject of England have a child, by an English woman in France, whose subject is he? Not the king of England's; for he must have leave to be admitted to the privileges of it. Nor the king of France's: for how then has his father a liberty to bring him away, and breed him as he pleases? And who ever was judged as a traitor or deserter, if he left, or warred against a country, for being barely born in it of parents that were aliens there? It is plain then, by the practice of governments themselves, as well as by the law of right reasons, that a child is born a subject of no country or government. He is under his father's tuition and authority, till he comes to age of discretion; and then he is a freeman, at liberty what government he will put himself under, what body politic he will unite himself to. For if an Englishman's son, born in France, be at liberty, and may do so, it is evident there is no tie upon him by his father's being a subject of this kingdom; nor is he bound up by any compact of his ancestors. And why then hath not his son, by the same reason, the same liberty, though he be born any where else? Since the power that a father hath naturally over his children is the same, wherever they be born, and the ties of natural obligations are not bounded by the positive limits of kingdoms and commonwealths.

119. Every man being, as has been shewed, naturally free, and nothing being able to put him into subjection to any earthly power, but only his own consent; it is to be considered, what shall be understood to be a sufficient declaration of a man's consent, to make him subject to the laws of any government. There is a common distinction of an express and a tacit consent, which will concern our present case. No body doubts but an express consent, of any man entering into any society, makes him a perfect member of that society, a subject of that government. The difficulty is, what ought to be looked upon as a tacit consent, and how far it binds, i.e. how far any one shall be looked on to have consented,

and thereby submitted to any government, where he has made no expressions of it at all. And to this I say, that every man, that hath any possessions, or enjoyment of any part of the dominions of any government, doth thereby give his tacit consent, and is as far forth obliged to obedience to the laws of that government, during such enjoyment, as any one under it; whether this his possession be of land, to him and his heirs for ever, or a lodging only for a week; or whether it be barely travelling freely on the highway: and, in effect, it reaches as far as the very being of any one within the territories of that government.

120. To understand this the better, it is fit to consider, that every man, when he at first incorporates himself into any commonwealth, he, by his uniting himself thereunto, annexed also, and submits to the community, those possessions which he has, or shall acquire, that do not already belong to any other government. For it would be a direct contradiction, for any one to enter into society with others for the securing and regulating of property, and yet to suppose, his land, whose property is to be regulated by the laws of the society, should be exempt from the jurisdiction of that government, to which he himself, the proprietor of the land, is a subject. By the same act therefore, whereby any one unites his person, which was before free, to any commonwealth; by the same he unites his possessions, which were before free, to it also: and they become, both of them, person and possession, subject to the government and dominion of that commonwealth, as long as it hath a being. Whoever therefore, from thenceforth, by inheritance, purchase, permission, or otherways, enjoys any part of the land so annexed to, and under the government of that commonwealth, must take it with the condition it is under; that is, of submitting to the government of the commonwealth, under whose jurisdiction it is, as far forth as any subject of it.

121. But since the government has a direct jurisdiction only over the land, and reaches the possessor of it, (before he has actually incorporated himself in the society) only as he dwells upon, and enjoys that; the obligation any one is under, by virtue of such enjoyment, to submit to the government, begins and ends with the enjoyment: so that whenever the owner, who has given nothing but such a tacit consent to the government, will, by donation, sale, or otherwise, quit the said possession, he is at liberty to go and incorporate himself into any other commonwealth; or to agree with others to begin a new one, in vacuis locis, in any part of the world they can find free and unpossessed: whereas he, that has once, by actual agreement, and

any express declaration, given his consent to be of any commonwealth, is perpetually and indispensably obliged to be, and remain unalterably a subject to it, and can never be again in the liberty of the state of nature; unless, by any calamity, the government he was under comes to be dissolved, or else by some public act cuts him off from being any longer a member of it.

122. But submitting to the laws of any country, living quietly, and enjoying privileges and protection under them, makes not a man a member of that society: this is only a local protection and homage due to and from all those, who, not being in a state of war, come within the territories belonging to any government, to all parts whereof the force of its laws extends. But this no more makes a man a member of that society, a perpetual subject of that commonwealth, than it would make a man a subject to another, in whose family he found it convenient to abide for some time, though, whilst he continued in it, he were obliged to comply with the laws, and submit to the government he found there. And thus we see, that foreigners, by living all their lives under another government, and enjoying the privileges and protection of it, though they are bound, even in conscience, to submit to its administration, as far forth as any denison; yet do not thereby come to be subjects or members of that commonwealth. Nothing can make any man so, but his actually entering into it by positive engagement, and express promise and compact. This is that, which I think, concerning the beginning of political societies, and that consent which makes any one a member of any commonwealth.

Chapter 9. Of the Ends of Political Society and Government

123. If man in the state of nature be so free, as has been said; if he be absolute lord of his own person and possessions, equal to the greatest, and subject to no body, why will he part with his freedom? Why will he give up this empire, and subject himself to the dominion and control of any other power? To which it is obvious to answer, that though in the state of nature he hath such a right, yet the enjoyment of it is very uncertain, and constantly exposed to the invasion of others. For all being kings as much as he, every man his equal, and the greater part no strict observers of equity and justice, the enjoyment of the property he has in this state is very unsafe, very unsecure. This makes him willing to quit this condition, which, however free, is full of fears and continual dangers: and it is not without rea-

son, that he seeks out, and is willing to join in society with others, who are already united, or have a mind to unite, for the mutual preservation of their lives, liberties, and estates, which I call by the general name, property.

124. The great and chief end, therefore, of men's uniting into commonwealths, and putting themselves under government, is the preservation of their property. To which in the state of nature there are many things wanting.

First, There wants an established, settled, known law, received and allowed by common consent to be the standard of right and wrong, and the common measure to decide all controversies between them. For though the law of nature be plain and intelligible to all rational creatures; yet men being biassed by their interest, as well as ignorant for want of studying it, are not apt to allow of it as a law binding to them in the application of it to their particular cases.

125. Secondly, In the state of nature there wants a known and indifferent judge, with authority to determine all differences according to the established law. For every one in that state being both judge and executioner of the law of nature, men being partial to themselves, passion and revenge is very apt to carry them too far, and with too much heat, in their own cases; as well as negligence, and unconcernedness, to make them too remiss in other men's.

126. Thirdly, In the state of nature, there often wants power to back and support the sentence when right, and to give it due execution. They who by any injustice offended, will seldom fail, where they are able, by force to make good their injustice; such resistance many times makes the punishment dangerous, and frequently destructive, to those who attempt it.

127. Thus mankind, notwithstanding all the privileges of the state of nature, being but in an ill condition, while they remain in it, are quickly driven into society. Hence it comes to pass that we seldom find any number of men live any time together in this state. The inconveniencies that they are therein exposed to, by the irregular and uncertain exercise of the power every man has of punishing the transgressions of others, make them take sanctuary under the established laws of government, and therein seek the preservation of their property. It is this makes them so willingly give up every one his single power of punishing, to be exercised by such alone, as shall be appointed to it amongst them; and by such rules as the community, or those authorized by them to that purpose, shall agree on. And in this we have the original right and rise of both the

legislative and executive power, as well as of the governments and societies themselves.

128. For in the state of nature, to omit the liberty he has of innocent delights, a man has two powers.

The first is to do whatsoever he thinks fit for the preservation of himself and others within the permission of the law of nature: by which law, common to them all, he and all the rest of mankind are one community, make up one society, distinct from all other creatures. And, were it not for the corruption and viciousness of degenerate men, there would be no need of any other; no necessity that men should separate from this great and natural community, and by positive agreements combine into smaller and divided associations.

The other power a man has in the state of nature, is the power to punish the crimes committed against that law. Both these he gives up, when he joins in a private, if I may so call it, or particular politic society, and incorporates into any commonwealth, separate from the rest of mankind.

129. The first power, viz. of doing whatsoever he thought fit for the preservation of himself, and the rest of mankind, he gives up to be regulated by laws made by the society, so far forth as the presevation of himself and the rest of that society shall require; which laws of the society in many things confine the liberty he had by the law of nature.

130. Secondly, The power of punishing he wholly gives up, and engages his natural force (which he might before employ in the execution of the law of nature, by his own single authority, as he thought fit) to assist the executive power of the society, as the law thereof shall require. For being now in a new state, wherein he is to enjoy many conveniencies, from the labour, assistance, and society of others in the same community, as well as protection from its whole strength; he is to part also, with as much of his natural liberty, in providing for himself, as the good, prosperity, and safety of the society shall require; which is not only necessary, but just, since the other members of the society do the like.

131. But though men, when they enter into society, give up the equality, liberty, and executive power they had in the state of nature, into the hands of the society, to be so far disposed of by the legislative, as the good of the society shall require; yet it being only with an intention in every one the better to preserve himself, his liberty and property; (for no rational creature can be supposed to change his condition with an intention to be worse) the power of the society, or legislative constituted by them, can never be supposed to extend farther, than the common good; but is obliged to secure every one's property, by providing against those three defects above mentioned, that made the state of nature so unsafe and uneasy. And so whoever has the legislative or supreme power of any commonwealth, is bound to govern by established standing laws, promulgated and known to the people, and not by extemporary decrees; by indifferent and upright judges, who are to decide controversies by those laws; and to employ the force of the community at home, only in the execution of such laws; or abroad to prevent or redress foreign injuries, and secure the community from inroads and invasion. And all this to be directed to no other end, but the peace, safety, and public good of the people. . . .

Chapter 19. Of The Dissolution of Government

211. He that will with any clearness speak of the dissolution of government, ought in the first place to distinguish between the dissolution of the society and the dissolution of the government. That which makes the community, and brings men out of the loose state of nature into one politic society, is the agreement which every one has with the rest to incorporate, and act as one body, and so be one distinct commonwealth. The usual, and almost only way whereby this union is dissolved, is the inroad of foreign force making a conquest upon them. For in that case, (not being able to maintain and support themselves, as one entire and independent body) the union belonging to that body which consisted therein, must necessarily cease, and so every one return to the state he was in before, with a liberty to shift for himself, and provide for his own safety, as he thinks fit, in some other society. Whenever the society is dissolved, it is certain the government of that society cannot remain. Thus conquerors swords often cut up governments by the roots, and mangle societies to pieces, separating the subdued or scattered multitude from the protection of, and dependence on, that society which ought to have preserved them from violence. The world is too well instructed in, and too forward to allow of, this way of dissolving of governments, to need any more to be said of it; and there wants not much argument to prove, that where the society is dissolved, the government cannot remain; that being as impossible, as for the frame of a house to subsist when the materials of it are scattered and dissipated by a whirlwind, or jumbled into a confused heap by an earthquake.

212. Besides this overturning from without, governments are dissolved from within.

First, when the legislative is altered. Civil society being a state of peace, amongst those who are of it, from whom the state of war is excluded by the umpirage, which they have provided in their legislative, for the ending all differences that may arise amongst any of them; it is in their legislative, that the members of a commonwealth are united, and combined together into one coherent living body. This is the soul that gives form, life, and unity to the commonwealth: from hence the several members have their mutual influence, sympathy, and connexion; and therefore, when the legislative is broken, or dissolved, dissolution and death follows. For, the essence and union of the society consisting in having one will, the legislative, when once established by the majority, has the declaring, and as it were keeping of that will. The constitution of the legislative is the first and fundamental act of society, whereby provision is made for the continuation of their union, under the direction of persons, and bonds of laws, made by persons authorized thereunto, by the consent and appointment of the people; without which no one man, or number of men, amongst them, can have authority of making laws that shall be binding to the rest. When any one, or more, shall take upon them to make laws, whom the people have not appointed so to do, they make laws without authority, which the people are not therefore bound to obey; by which means they come again to be out of subjection, and may constitute to themselves a new legislative, as they think best, being in full liberty to resist the force of those, who without authority would impose any thing upon them. Every one is at the disposure of his own will, when those who had, by the delegation of the society, the declaring of the public will, are excluded from it, and others usurp the place, who have no such authority or delegation. . . .

214. [W]hen such a single person, or prince, sets up his own arbitrary will in place of the laws, which are the will of the society, declared by the legislative, then the legislative is changed. For that being in effect the legislative, whose rules and laws are put in execution, and required to be obeyed; when other laws are set up, and other rules pretended, and enforced, than what the legislative, constituted by the society, have enacted, it is plain that the legislative is changed. Whoever introduces new laws, not being thereunto authorized, by the fundamental appointment of the society, or subverts the old, disowns and overturns the power by which they were made, and so sets up a new legislative.

215. Secondly, when the prince hinders the legislative from assembling in its due time, or from acting freely, pursuant to those ends for which it was constituted, the legislative is altered: for it is not a certain number of men, no, nor their meeting, unless they have also freedom of debating, and leisure of perfecting, what is for the good of the society, wherein the legislative consists: when these are taken away or altered, so as to deprive the society of the due exercise of their power, the legislative is truly altered. For it is not names that constitute governments, but the use and exercise of those powers that were intended to accompany them; so that he, who takes away the freedom, or hinders the acting of the legislative in its due seasons, in effect takes away the legislative, and puts an end to the government.

216. Thirdly, when, by the arbitrary power of the prince, the electors, or ways of election, are altered, without the consent, and contrary to the common interest of the people, there also the legislative is altered. For, if others than those whom the society hath authorized thereunto, do choose, or in another way than what the society hath prescribed, those chosen are not the legislative appointed by the people.

217. Fourthly, The delivery also of the people into the subjection of a foreign power, either by the prince, or by the legislative, is certainly a change of the legislative, and so a dissolution of the government. For the end why people entered into society being to be preserved one entire, free, independent society, to be governed by its own laws; this is lost, whenever they are given up into the power of another.

218. Why, in such a constitution as this, the dissolution of the government in these cases is to be imputed to the prince, is evident; because he, having the force, treasure, and offices of the state to employ, and often persuading himself, or being flattered by others, that as supreme magistrate, he is uncapable of control; he alone is in a condition to make great advances toward such changes, under pretence of lawful authority, and has it in his hands to terrify or suppress opposers, as factious, seditious, and enemies to the government: whereas no other part of the legislative, or people, is capable by themselves to attempt any alteration of the legislative, without open and visible rebellion, apt enough to be taken notice of; which, when, it prevails, produces effects very little different from foreign conquest. Besides, the prince in such a form of government having the power of dissolving the other parts of

the legislative, and thereby rendering them private persons, they can never in opposition to him, or without his concurrence, alter the legislative by a law, his consent being necessary to give any of their decrees that sanction. But yet, so far as the other parts of the legislative any way contribute to any attempt upon the government, and do either promote, or not, what lies in them, hinder such designs; they are guilty, and partake in this, which is certainly the greatest crime men can be guilty of one towards another.

219. There is one way more whereby such a government may be dissolved, and that is, when he who has the supreme executive power neglects and abandons that charge, so that the laws already made can no longer be put in execution. This is demonstratively to reduce all to anarchy, and so effectually to dissolve the government. For laws not being made for themselves, but to be, by their execution, the bonds of the society, to keep every part of the body politic in its due place and function; when that totally ceases, the government visibly ceases, and the people become a confused multitude, without order or connexion. Where there is no longer the administration of justice, for the securing of men's rights, nor any remaining power within the community to direct the force, or provide for the necessities of the public; there certainly is no government left. Where the laws cannot be executed, it is all one as if there were no laws; and a government without laws is, I suppose, a mystery in politics, inconceivable to human capacity, and inconsistent with human society.

220. In these and the like cases, when the government is dissolved, the people are at liberty to provide for themselves, by erecting a new legislative, differing from the other, by the change of persons, or form, or both, as they shall find it most for their safety and good. For the society can never, by the fault of another, lose the native and original right it has to preserve itself; which can only be done by a settled legislative, and a fair and impartial execution of the laws made by it. But the state of mankind is not so miserable that they are not capable of using this remedy, till it be too late to look for any. To tell people they may provide for themselves, by erecting a new legislative, when by oppression, artifice, or being delivered over to a foreign power, their old one is gone, is only to tell them, they may expect relief when it is too late, and the evil is past cure. This is in effect no more, than to bid them first be slaves, and then to take care of their liberty; and when their chains are on, tell them, they may act like freemen. This, if barely so, is rather mockery than relief; and men can never be secure from tyranny, if there

be no means to escape it, till they are perfectly under it: And therefore it is, that they have not only a right to get out of it, but to prevent it.

221. There is, therefore, secondly, another way whereby governments are dissolved, and that is, when the legislative, or the prince either of them, act contrary to their trust.

First, The legislative acts against the trust reposed in them, when they endeavour to invade the property of the subject, and to make themselves, or any part of the community, masters, or arbitrary disposers of the lives, liberties, or fortunes of the people.

222. The reason why men enter into society, is the preservation of their property; and the end why they choose and authorize a legislative, is, that there may be laws made, and rules set, as guards and fences to the properties of all the members of the society: to limit the power, and moderate the dominion, of every part and member of the society. For since it can never be supposed to be the will of the society, that the legislative should have a power to destroy that, which every one designs to secure, by entering into society, and for which the people submitted themselves to legislators of their own making, whenever the legislators endeavour to take away and destroy the property of the people, or to reduce them to slavery under arbitrary power, they put themselves into a state of war with the people, who are thereupon absolved from any farther obedience, and are left to the common refuge, which God hath provided for all men, against force and violence. Whensoever therefore the legislative shall transgress this fundamental rule of society; and either by ambition, fear, folly or corruption, endeavour to grasp themselves, or put into the hands of any other an absolute power over the lives, liberties, and estates of the people; by this breach of trust they forfeit the power, the people had put into their hands, for quite contrary ends, and it devolves to the people, who have a right to resume their original liberty, and, by the establishment of a new legislative, (such as they shall think fit) provide for their own safety and security, which is the end for which they are in society. What I have said here, concerning the legislative in general, holds true also concerning the supreme executor, who having a double trust put in him, both to have a part in the legislative, and the supreme execution of the law, acts against both, when he goes about to set up his own arbitrary will, as the law of the society. He acts also contrary to his trust, when he either employs the force, treasure, and offices of the society to corrupt the representatives, and gain them to his purposes; or openly pre-engages the elec-

51

tors, and prescribes to their choice, such, whom he has by solicitations, threats, promises, or otherwise, won to his designs: and employs them to bring in such, who have promised before-hand, what to vote, and what to enact. Thus to regulate candidates and electors, and new model the ways of election, what is it but to cut up the government by the roots, and poison the very fountatin of public security? for the people having reserved to themselves the choice of their representatives, as the fence to their properties, could do it for no other end, but that they might always be freely chosen, and so chosen, freely act, and advise, as the necessity of the commonwealth, and the public good should, upon examination and mature debate, be judged to require. This, those who give their votes before they hear the debate, and have weighed the reasons on all sides, are not capable of doing. To prepare such an assembly as this, and endeavour to set up the declared abettors of his own will, for the true representatives of the people, and the law-makers of the society, is certainly as great a breach of trust, and as perfect a declaration of a design to subvert the government, as is possible to be met with. To which if one shall add rewards and punishments visibly employed to the same end, and all the arts of perverted law made use of, to take off and destroy all that stand in the way of such a design, and will not comply and consent to betray the liberties of their country, it will be past doubt what he is doing. What power they ought to have in the society, who thus employ it contrary to the trust that went along with it in its first institution, is easy to determine; and one cannot but see, that he, who has once attempted any such thing as this, cannot any longer be trusted.

223. To this perhaps it will be said, that the people being ignorant, and always discontented, to lay the foundation of government in the unsteady opinion and uncertain humour of the people, is to expose it to certain ruin; and no government will be able long to subsist, if the people may set up a new legislative, whenever they take offence at the old one. To this I answer, quite the contrary. People are not so easily got out of their old forms as some are apt to suggest. They are hardly to be prevailed with to amend the acknowledged faults in the frame they have been accustomed to. And if there be any original defects, or adventitious ones introduced by time, or corruption: it is not an easy thing to get them changed, even when all the world sees there is an opportunity for it. This slowness and aversion in the people to quit their old constitutions, has in the many revolutions which have been seen in this kingdom, in this and former ages, still kept us to, or,

after some interval of fruitless attempts, still brought us back again to, our old legislative of king, lords, and commons: and whatever provocations have made the crown be taken from some of our princes' heads, they never carried the people so far as to place it in another line. . . .

243. To conclude, The power that every individual gave the society, when he entered into it, can never revert to the individuals gain, as long as the society lasts, but will always remain in the community; because without this there can be no community, no commonwealth, which is contrary to the original agreement: so also when the society hath placed the legislative in any assembly of men, to continue in them and their successors, with direction and authority for providing such successors, the legislative can never revert to the people whilst that government lasts: Because, having provided a legislative with power to continue for ever, they have given up their political power to the legislative, and cannot resume it. But if they have set limits to the duration of their legislative, and made this supreme power in any person, or assembly, only temporary; or else, when by the miscarriages of those in authority, it is forfeited; upon the forfeiture, or at the determination of the time set, it reverts to the society, and the people have a right to act as supreme, and continue the legislative in themselves; or erect a new form, or under the old form place it in new hands, as they think good.

READING 4

The Social Contract

Jean-Jacques Rousseau

Jean-Jacques Rousseau (1712–78) was born in Geneva, Switzerland. He was a self-educated genius whose most famous works are his *Confessions, Discourse on the Origin and Foundations of Inequality Among Men* (Reading 35), and *The Social Contract* (1962), from which this selection is taken.

He begins this work with his famous dictum, "Man is born free, and everywhere he is in chains." The origins, significance, and value of those "chains" are discussed in Book I, in which Rousseau delineates the differences between man's natural state—in which the strongest individuals benefit at the expense of others—and the civil state—in which all the members benefit. He does not think it possible for man to thrive in the state of nature; one must enter into a social contract to flourish. In Book II he discusses sovereignty and argues that by uniting our individual wills into a general will, we produce an optimal situation, in which both we and everyone else may flourish. In Books III (not included in this reading) and IV he distinguishes between legislative and executive power and discusses the general will regarding voting.

This reading is taken from *The Social Contract* (London: Swan Sonnenschein & Co., 1895).

BOOK I

Chapter I. Subject of the First Book

Man is born free, and everywhere he is in chains. Many a one believes himself the master of others, and yet he is a greater slave than they. How has this change come about? I do not know. What can render it legitimate? I believe that I can settle this question.

If I considered only force and the results that proceed from it, I should say that so long as a people is compelled to obey and does obey, it does well; but that, so soon as it can shake off the yoke and does shake it off, it does better; for, if men recover their freedom by virtue of the same right by which it was taken away, either they are justified in resuming it, or there was no justification for depriving them of it. But the social order is a sacred right which serves as a foundation for all others. This right, however, does not come from nature. It is therefore based on conventions. The question is to know what these conventions are. Before coming to that, I must establish what I have just laid down.

Chapter II. Primitive Societies

The earliest of all societies, and the only natural one, is the family; yet children remain attached to their father only so long as they have need of him for their own preservation. As soon as this need ceases, the natural bond is dissolved. The children being free from the obedience which they owed to their father, and the father from the cares which he owed to his children, become equally independent. If they remain united, it is no longer naturally but voluntarily; and the family itself is kept together only by convention.

This common liberty is a consequence of man's nature. His first law is to attend to his own preservation, his first cares are those which he owes to himself; and as soon as he comes to years of discretion, being sole judge of the means adapted for his own preservation, he becomes his own master. . . .

Chapter III. The Right of the Strongest

The strongest man is never strong enough to be always master, unless he transforms his power into right, and obedience into duty. Hence the right of the strongest—a right apparently assumed in irony, and really established in principle. But will this phrase never be explained to us? Force is a physical power; I do not see what morality can result from its effects. To yield to force is an act of necessity, not of will; it is at most an act of prudence. In what sense can it be a duty?

Let us assume for a moment this pretended right. I say that nothing results from it but inexplicable nonsense; for if force constitutes right, the effect changes with the cause, and any force which overcomes the first succeeds to its rights. As soon as men can disobey with impunity, they may do so legitimately; and since the strongest is always in the right, the only thing is to act in such a way that one may be the strongest. But what sort of a right is it that perishes when force ceases? If it is necessary to obey by compulsion, there is no need to obey from duty; and if men are no longer forced to obey, obligation is at an end. We see, then, that this word *right* adds nothing to force; it here means nothing at all.

Obey the powers that be. If that means, Yield to force, the precept is good but superfluous; I reply that it will never be violated. All power comes from God, I admit; but every disease comes from Him too; does it follow that we are prohibited from calling in a physician? If a brigand should surprise me in the recesses of a wood, am I bound not only to give up my purse when forced, but am I also morally bound to do so when I might conceal it? For, in effect, the pistol which he holds is a superior force.

Let us agree, then, that might does not make right, and that we are bound to obey none but lawful authorities. Thus my original question ever recurs.

Chapter IV. Slavery

Since no man has any natural authority over his fellow men, and since force is not the source of right, conventions remain as the basis of all lawful authority among men.

If an individual, says Grotius, can alienate his liberty and become the slave of a master, why should not a whole people be able to alienate theirs, and become subject to a king? In this there are many equivocal terms requiring explanation; but let us confine ourselves to the word *alienate*. To alienate is to give or sell. Now, a man who becomes another's slave does not give himself; he sells himself at the very least for his subsistence. But why does a nation sell itself? So far from a king supplying his subjects with their subsistence, he draws his from them; and, according to Rabelais, a king does not live on a little. Do subjects, then, give up their persons on condition that their property also shall be taken? I do not see what is left for them to keep.

It will be said that the despot secures to his subjects civil peace. Be it so; but what do they gain by that, if the wars which his ambition brings upon them, together with his insatiable greed and the vexations of his administration, harass them more than their own dissensions would? What do they gain by it if this tranquillity is itself one of their miseries? Men live tranquilly also in dungeons; is that enough to make them contented there? The Greeks confined in the cave of the Cyclops lived peacefully until their turn came to be devoured.

To say that a man gives himself for nothing is to say what is absurd and inconceivable; such an act is illegitimate and invalid, for the simple reason that he who performs it is not in his right mind. To say the same thing of a whole nation is to suppose a nation of fools; and madness does not confer rights.

Even if each person could alienate himself, he could not alienate his children; they are born free men; their liberty belongs to them, and no one has a right to dispose of it except themselves. Before they have come to years of discretion, the father can, in their name, stipulate conditions for their preservation and welfare, but not surrender them irrevocably and unconditionally; for such a gift is contrary to the ends of nature, and exceeds the rights of paternity. In order, then, that an arbitrary government might be legitimate, it would be necessary that the people in each generation should have the option of accepting or rejecting it; but in that case such a government would no longer be arbitrary.

To renounce one's liberty is to renounce one's quality as a man, the rights and also the duties of humanity. For him who renounces everything there is no possible compensation. Such a renunciation is incompatible with man's nature, for to take away all freedom from his will is to take away all morality from his actions. In short, a convention which stipulates absolute authority on the one side and unlimited obedience on the other is vain and contradictory. Is it not clear that we are under no obligations whatsoever towards a man from whom we have a right to demand everything? And does not this single condition, without equivalent, without exchange, involve the nullity of the act? For what right would my slave have against me, since all that he has belongs to me? His rights being mine, this right of me against myself is a meaningless phrase. . . .

Chapter V. That It Is Always Necessary to Go Back to a First Convention

If I should concede all that I have so far refuted, those who favor despotism would be no farther advanced. There will always be a great difference between subduing a multitude and ruling a society. When isolated men, however numerous they may be, are subjected one after another to a single person, this seems to me only a case of master and slaves, not of a nation and its chief; they form, if you will, an aggregation, but not an association, for they have neither public property nor a body politic. Such a man, had he enslaved half the world, is never anything but an individual; his interest, separated from that of the rest, is never anything but a private interest. If he dies, his empire after him is left disconnected and disunited, as an oak dissolves and becomes a heap of ashes after the fire has consumed it.

A nation, says Grotius, can give itself to a king. According to Grotius, then, a nation is a nation before it gives itself to a king. This gift itself is a civil act, and presupposes a public resolution. Consequently, before examining the act by which a nation elects a king, it would be proper to examine the act by which a nation becomes a nation; for this act, being necessarily anterior to the other, is the real foundation of the society.

In fact, if there were no anterior convention, where, unless the election were unanimous, would be the obligation upon the minority to submit to the decision of the majority? And whence do the hundred who desire a master derive the right to vote on behalf of ten who do not desire one? The law of the plurality of votes is itself established by convention, and presupposes unanimity once at least.

Chapter VI. The Social Pact

I assume that men have reached a point at which the obstacles that endanger their preservation in the state of nature overcome by their resistance the forces which each individual can exert with a view to maintaining himself in that state. Then this primitive condition can no longer subsist, and the human race would perish unless it changed its mode of existence.

Now, as men cannot create any new forces, but only combine and direct those that exist, they have no other means of self-preservation than to form by aggregation a sum of forces which may overcome the resistance, to put them in action by a single motive power, and to make them work in concert.

This sum of forces can be produced only by the combination of many; but the strength and freedom of each man being the chief instruments of his preservation, how can he pledge them without injuring himself, and without neglecting the cares which he owes to himself? This difficulty, applied to my subject, may be expressed in these terms:—

"To find a form of association which may defend and protect with the whole force of the community the person and property of every associate, and by means of which each, coalescing with all, may nevertheless obey only himself, and remain as free as before." Such is the fundamental problem of which the social contract furnishes the solution.

The clauses of this contract are so determined by the nature of the act that the slightest modification would render them vain and ineffectual; so that, although they have never perhaps been formally enunciated, they are everywhere the same, everywhere tacitly admitted and recognized, until, the social pact being violated, each man regains his original rights and recovers his natural liberty, while losing the conventional liberty for which he renounced it.

These clauses, rightly understood, are reducible to one only, viz., the total alienation to the whole community of each associate with all his rights; for, in the first place, since each gives himself up entirely, the conditions are equal for all; and, the conditions being equal for all, no one has any interest in making them burdensome to others.

Further, the alienation being made without reserve, the union is as perfect as it can be, and an individual associate can no longer claim anything; for, if any rights were left to individuals, since there would be no common superior who could judge between them and the public, each, being on some point his own judge, would soon claim to be so on all; the state of nature would still subsist, and the association would necessarily become tyrannical or useless.

In short, each giving himself to all, gives himself to nobody; and as there is not one associate over whom we do not acquire the same rights which we concede to him over ourselves, we gain the equivalent of all that we lose, and more power to preserve what we have.

If, then, we set aside what is not of the essence of the social contract, we shall find that it is reducible to the following terms: "Each of us puts in common his person and his whole power under the supreme direction of the general will; and in return we receive every member as an indivisible part of the whole."

Forthwith, instead of the individual personalities of all the contracting parties, this act of association produces a moral and collective body, which is composed of as many members as the assembly has voices, and which receives from this same act its unity, its common self *(moi),* its life, and its will. This public person, which is thus formed by the union of all the individual members, formerly took the name of *city,* and now takes that of *republic* or *body politic,* which is called by its members *State* when it is passive, *sovereign* when it is active, *power* when it is compared to similar bodies. With regard to the associates, they take collectively the name of *people,* and are called individually *citizens,* as participating in the sovereign power, and *subjects,* as subjected to the laws of the State. But these terms are often confused and are mistaken one for another; it is sufficient to know how to distinguish them when they are used with complete precision.

Chapter VII. The Sovereign

We see from this formula that the act of association contains a reciprocal engagement between the public and individuals, and that every individual, contracting so to speak with himself, is engaged in a double relation, viz., as a member of the sovereign towards individuals, and as a member of the State towards the sovereign. But we cannot apply here the maxim of civil law that no one is bound by engagements made with himself; for there is a great difference between being bound to oneself and to a whole of which one forms part.

We must further observe that the public resolution which can bind all subjects to the sovereign in consequence of the two different relations under which each of them is regarded cannot, for a contrary reason, bind the sovereign to itself; and that accordingly it is contrary to the nature of the body politic for the sovereign to impose on itself a law which it cannot transgress. As it can only be considered under one and the same relation, it is in the position of an individual contracting with himself; whence we see that there is not, nor can be, any kind of fundamental law binding upon the body of the people, not even the social contract. This does not imply that such a body cannot perfectly well enter into engagements with others in what does not derogate from this contract; for, with regard to foreigners, it becomes a simple being, an individual.

But the body politic or sovereign, deriving its existence only from the sanctity of the contract, can never bind itself, even to others, in anything that derogates from the original act, such as alienation of some portion of itself, or submission to another sovereign. To violate the act by which it exists would be to annihilate itself; and what is nothing produces nothing.

So soon as the multitude is thus united in one body, it is impossible to injure one of the members without attacking the body, still less to injure the body without the members feeling the effects. Thus duty and interest alike oblige the two contracting parties to give mutual assistance; and the men themselves should seek to combine in this twofold relationship all the advantages which are attendant on it.

Now, the sovereign, being formed only of the individuals that compose it, neither has nor can have any interest contrary to theirs; consequently the sovereign power needs no guarantee towards its subjects, because it is impossible that the body should wish to injure all its members; and we shall see hereafter that it can injure no one as an individual. The sovereign, for the simple reason that it is so, is always everything that it ought to be.

But this is not the case as regards the relation of subjects to the sovereign, which, notwithstanding the common interest, would have no security for the performance of their engagements, unless it found means to ensure their fidelity.

Indeed, every individual may, as a man, have a particular will contrary to, or divergent from, the general will which he has as a citizen; his private interest may prompt him quite differently from the common interest; his absolute and naturally independent existence may make him regard what he owes to the common cause as a gratuitous contribution, the loss of which will be less harmful to others than the payment of it will be burdensome to him; and, regarding the moral person that constitutes the State as an imaginary being

because it is not a man, he would be willing to enjoy the rights of a citizen without being willing to fulfil the duties of a subject. The progress of such injustice would bring about the ruin of the body politic.

In order, then, that the social pact may not be a vain formulary, it tacitly includes this engagement, which can alone give force to the others—that whoever refuses to obey the general will shall be constrained to do so by the whole body; which means nothing else than that he shall be forced to be free; for such is the condition which, uniting every citizen to his native land, guarantees him from all personal dependence, a condition that ensures the control and working of the political machine, and alone renders legitimate civil engagements, which, without it, would be absurd and tyrannical, and subject to the most enormous abuses.

Chapter VIII. The Civil State

The passage from the state of nature to the civil state produces in man a very remarkable change, by substituting in his conduct justice for instinct, and by giving his actions the moral quality that they previously lacked. It is only when the voice of duty succeeds physical impulse, and law succeeds appetite, that man, who till then had regarded only himself, sees that he is obliged to act on other principles, and to consult his reason before listening to his inclinations. Although, in this state, he is deprived of many advantages that he derives from nature, he acquires equally great ones in return; his faculties are exercised and developed; his ideas are expanded; his feelings are ennobled; his whole soul is exalted to such a degree that, if the abuses of this new condition did not often degrade him below that from which he has emerged, he ought to bless without ceasing the happy moment that released him from it for ever, and transformed him from a stupid and ignorant animal into an intelligent being and a man.

Let us reduce this whole balance to terms easy to compare. What man loses by the social contract is his natural liberty and an unlimited right to anything which tempts him and which he is able to attain; what he gains is civil liberty and property in all that he possesses. In order that we may not be mistaken about these compensations, we must clearly distinguish natural liberty, which is limited only by the powers of the individual, from civil liberty, which is limited by the general will; and possession, which is nothing but the result of force or the right of first occupancy, from property, which can be based only on a positive title.

Besides the preceding, we might add to the acquisitions of the civil state moral freedom, which alone renders man truly master of himself; for the impulse of mere appetite is slavery, while obedience to a self-prescribed law is liberty. But I have already said too much on this head, and the philosophical meaning of the term *liberty* does not belong to my present subject.

Chapter IX. Real Property

Every member of the community at the moment of its formation gives himself up to it, just as he actually is, himself and all his powers, of which the property that he possesses forms part. By this act, possession does not change its nature when it changes hands, and become property in those of the sovereign; but, as the powers of the State *(cité)* are incomparably greater than those of an individual, public possession is also, in fact, more secure and more irrevocable, without being more legitimate, at least in respect of foreigners; for the State, with regard to its members, is owner of all their property by the social contract, which, in the State, serves as the basis of all rights; but with regard to other powers, it is owner only by the right of first occupancy which it derives from individuals.

The right of first occupancy, although more real than that of the strongest, becomes a true right only after the establishment of that of property. Every man has by nature a right to all that is necessary to him; but the positive act which makes him proprietor of certain property excludes him from all the residue. His portion having been allotted, he ought to confine himself to it, and he has no further right to the undivided property. That is why the right of first occupancy, so weak in the state of nature, is respected by every member of a State. In this right men regard not so much what belongs to others as what does not belong to themselves.

In order to legalize the right of first occupancy over any domain whatsoever, the following conditions are, in general, necessary: first, the land must not yet be inhabited by any one; secondly, a man must occupy only the area required for his subsistence; thirdly, he must take possession of it, not by an empty ceremony, but by labor and cultivation, the only mark of ownership which, in default of legal title, ought to be respected by others.

Indeed, if we accord the right of first occupancy to necessity and labor, do we not extend it as far as it can go? Is it impossible to assign limits to this right? Will the mere setting foot on common ground be sufficient to give an immediate claim to the ownership of

it? Will the power of driving away other men from it for a moment suffice to deprive them forever of the right of returning to it? How can a man or a people take possession of an immense territory and rob the whole human race of it except by a punishable usurpation, since other men are deprived of the place of residence and the sustenance which nature gives to them in common? When Núñez de Balboa on the seashore took possession of the Pacific Ocean and of the whole of South America in the name of the crown of Castille, was this sufficient to dispossess all the inhabitants, and exclude from it all the princes in the world? On this supposition, such ceremonies might have been multiplied vainly enough; and the Catholic king in his cabinet might, by a single stroke, have taken possession of the whole world, only cutting off afterwards from his empire what was previously occupied by other princes.

We perceive how the lands of individuals, united and contiguous, become public territory, and how the right of sovereignty, extending itself from the subjects to the land which they occupy, becomes at once real and personal; which places the possessors in greater dependence, and makes their own powers a guarantee for their fidelity—an advantage which ancient monarchs do not appear to have clearly perceived, for, calling themselves only kings of the Persians or Scythians or Macedonians, they seem to have regarded themselves as chiefs of men rather than as owners of countries. Monarchs of today call themselves more cleverly kings of France, Spain, England, etc.; in thus holding the land they are quite sure of holding its inhabitants.

The peculiarity of this alienation is that the community, in receiving the property of individuals, so far from robbing them of it, only assures them lawful possession, and changes usurpation into true right, enjoyment into ownership. Also, the possessors being considered as depositaries of the public property, and their rights being respected by all the members of the State, as well as maintained by all its power against foreigners, they have, as it were, by a transfer advantageous to the public and still more to themselves, acquired all that they have given up—a paradox which is easily explained by distinguishing between the rights which the sovereign and the proprietor have over the same property, as we shall see hereafter.

It may also happen that men begin to unite before they possess anything, and that afterwards occupying territory sufficient for all, they enjoy it in common, or share it among themselves, either equally or in proportions fixed by the sovereign. In whatever way this acquisition is made, the right which every individual has over his own property is always subordinate to the right which the community has over all; otherwise there would be no stability in the social union, and no real force in the exercise of sovereignty.

I shall close this chapter and this book with a remark which ought to serve as a basis for the whole social system; it is that instead of destroying natural equality, the fundamental pact, on the contrary, substitutes a moral and lawful equality for the physical inequality which nature imposed upon men, so that, although unequal in strength or intellect, they all become equal by convention and legal right.[1]

BOOK II

Chapter I. That Sovereignty Is Inalienable

The first and most important consequence of the principles above established is that the general will alone can direct the forces of the State according to the object of its institution, which is the common good; for if the opposition of private interests has rendered necessary the establishment of societies, the agreement of these same interests has rendered it possible. That which is common to these different interests forms the social bond; and unless there were some point in which all interests agree, no society could exist. Now, it is solely with regard to this common interest that the society should be governed.

I say, then, that sovereignty, being nothing but the exercise of the general will, can never be alienated, and that the sovereign power, which is only a collective being, can be represented by itself alone; power indeed can be transmitted, but not will.

In fact, if it is not impossible that a particular will should agree on some point with the general will, it is at least impossible that this agreement should be lasting and constant; for the particular will naturally tends to preferences, and the general will to equality. It is still more impossible to have a security for this agreement; even though it should always exist, it would not be a result of art, but of chance. The sovereign may indeed say: "I will now what a certain man wills, or at least what he says that he wills"; but he cannot say: "What that man wills tomorrow, I shall also will," since it is absurd that the will should bind itself as regards the future, and since it is not incumbent on any will to consent to anything contrary to the welfare of the being that wills. If,

then, the nation simply promises to obey, it dissolves itself by that act and loses its character as a people; the moment there is a master, there is no longer a sovereign, and forthwith the body politic is destroyed.

This does not imply that the orders of the chiefs cannot pass for decisions of the general will, so long as the sovereign, free to oppose them, refrains from doing so. In such a case the consent of the people should be inferred from the universal silence. This will be explained at greater length.

Chapter II. That Sovereignty Is Indivisible

For the same reason that sovereignty is inalienable it is indivisible; for the will is either general, or it is not; it is either that of the body of the people, or that of only a portion. In the first case, this declared will is an act of sovereignty and constitutes law; in the second case, it is only a particular will, or an act of magistracy — it is at most a decree. . . .

Chapter III. Whether the General Will Can Err

It follows from what precedes that the general will is always right and always tends to the public advantage; but it does not follow that the resolutions of the people have always the same rectitude. Men always desire their own good, but do not always discern it; the people are never corrupted, though often deceived, and it is only then that they seem to will what is evil.

There is often a great deal of difference between the will of all and the general will; the latter regards only the common interest, while the former has regard to private interests, and is merely a sum of particular wills; but take away from these same wills the pluses and minuses which cancel one another[2] and the general will remains as the sum of the differences.

If the people came to a resolution when adequately informed and without any communication among the citizens, the general will would always result from the great number of slight differences, and the resolution would always be good. But when factions, partial associations, are formed to the detriment of the whole society, the will of each of these associations becomes general with reference to its members, and particular with reference to the State; it may then be said that there are no longer as many voters as there are men, but only as many voters as there are associations. The differences become less numerous and yield a less general result. Lastly, when one of these associations becomes so great that it predominates over all the rest, you no longer have as the result a sum of small differences, but a single difference; there is then no longer a general will, and the opinion which prevails is only a particular opinion.

It is important, then, in order to have a clear declaration of the general will, that there should be no partial association in the State, and that every citizen should express only his own opinion.[3] Such was the unique and sublime institution of the great Lycurgus. But if there are partial associations, it is necessary to multiply their number and prevent inequality, as Solon, Numa, and Servius did. These are the only proper precautions for ensuring that the general will may always be enlightened, and that the people may not be deceived.

Chapter IV. The Limits of the Sovereign Power

If the State or city is nothing but a moral person, the life of which consists in the union of its members, and if the most important of its cares is that of self-preservation, it needs a universal and compulsive force to move and dispose every part in the manner most expedient for the whole. As nature gives every man an absolute power over all his limbs, and the social pact gives the body politic an absolute power over all its members; and it is this same power which, when directed by the general will, bears, as I said, the name of sovereignty.

But besides the public person, we have to consider the private persons who compose it, and whose life and liberty are naturally independent of it. The question, then, is to distinguish clearly between the respective rights of the citizens and of the sovereign,[4] as well as between the duties which the former have to fulfill in their capacity as subjects and the natural rights which they ought to enjoy in their character as men.

It is admitted that whatever part of his power, property, and liberty each one alienates by social compact is only that part of the whole of which the use is important to the community; but we must also admit that the sovereign alone is judge of what is important.

All the services that a citizen can render to the State he owes to it as soon as the sovereign demands them; but the sovereign, on its part, cannot impose on its subjects any burden which is useless to the community; it cannot even wish to do so, for, by the law of reason, just as by the law of nature, nothing is done without a cause.

The engagements which bind us to the social body are obligatory only because they are mutual; and their nature is such that in fulfilling them we cannot work for others without also working for ourselves. Why is the general will always right, and why do all invariably desire the prosperity of each, unless it is because there is no one but appropriates to himself this word *each* and thinks of himself in voting on behalf of all? This proves that equality of rights and the notion of justice that it produces are derived from the preference which each gives to himself, and consequently from man's nature; that the general will, to be truly such, should be so in its object as well as in its essence; that it ought to proceed from all in order to be applicable to all; and that it loses its natural rectitude when it tends to some individual and determinate object, because in that case, judging of what is unknown to us, we have no true principle of equity to guide us.

Indeed, so soon as a particular fact or right is in question with regard to a point which has not been regulated by an anterior general convention, the matter becomes contentious; it is a process in which the private persons interested are one of the parties and the public the other, but in which I perceive neither the law which must be followed, nor judge who should decide. It would be ridiculous in such a case to wish to refer the matter for an express decision of the general will, which can be nothing but the decision of one of the parties, and which, consequently, is for the other party only a will that is foreign, partial, and inclined on such an occasion to injustice as well as liable to error. Therefore, just as a particular will cannot represent the general will, the general will in turn changes its nature when it has a particular end, and cannot, as general, decide about either a person or a fact. When the people of Athens, for instance, elected or deposed their chiefs, decreed honors to one, imposed penalties on another, and by multitudes of particular decrees exercised indiscriminately all the functions of government, the people no longer had any general will properly so called; they no longer acted as a sovereign power, but as magistrates. This will appear contrary to common ideas, but I must be allowed time to expound my own.

From this we must understand that what generalizes the will is not so much the number of voices as the common interest which unites them; for, under this system, each necessarily submits to the conditions which he imposes on others—an admirable union of interest and justice, which gives to the deliberations of the community a spirit of equity that seems to disappear in the discussion of any private affair, for want of a common interest to unite and identify the ruling principle of the judge with that of the party.

By whatever path we return to our principle we always arrive at the same conclusion, viz., that the social compact establishes among the citizens such an equality that they all pledge themselves under the same conditions and ought all to enjoy the same rights. Thus, by the nature of the compact, every act of sovereignty, that is, every authentic act of the general will, binds or favors equally all the citizens; so that the sovereign knows only the body of the nation, and distinguishes none of those that compose it.

What, then, is an act of sovereignty properly so called? It is not an agreement between a superior and an inferior, but an agreement of the body with each of its members; a lawful agreement, because it has the social contract as its foundation; equitable, because it is common to all; useful, because it can have no other object than the general welfare; and stable, because it has the public force and the supreme power as a guarantee. So long as the subjects submit only to such conventions, they obey no one, but simply their own will; and to ask how far the respective rights of the sovereign and citizens extend is to ask up to what point the latter can make engagements among themselves, each with all and all with each.

Thus we see that the sovereign power, wholly absolute, wholly sacred, and wholly inviolable as it is, does not, and cannot, pass the limits of general conventions, and that every man can fully dispose of what is left to him of his property and liberty by these conventions; so that the sovereign never has a right to burden one subject more than another, because then the matter becomes particular and his power is no longer competent.

These distinctions once admitted, so untrue is it that in the social contract there is on the part of individuals any real renunciation, that their situation, as a result of this contract, is in reality preferable to what it was before, and that, instead of an alienation, they have only made an advantageous exchange of an uncertain and precarious mode of existence for a better and more assured one, of natural independence for liberty, of the power to injure others for their own safety, and of their strength, which others might overcome, for a right which the social union renders inviolable. Their lives, also, which they have devoted to the State, are continually protected by it; and in exposing their lives for its

defense, what do they do but restore what they have received from it? What do they do but what they would do more frequently and with more risk in the state of nature, when, engaging in inevitable struggles, they would defend at the peril of their lives their means of preservation? All have to fight for their country in case of need, it is true; but then no one ever has to fight for himself. Do we not gain, moreover, by incurring, for what insures our safety, a part of the risks that we should have to incur for ourselves individually, as soon as we were deprived of it? . . .

Chapter VI. The Law

By the social compact we have given existence and life to the body politic; the question now is to endow it with movement and will by legislation. For the original act by which this body is formed and consolidated determines nothing in addition as to what it must do for its own preservation.

What is right and conformable to order is such by the nature of things, and independently of human conventions. All justice comes from God, He alone is the source of it; but could we receive it direct from so lofty a source, we should need neither government nor laws. Without doubt there is a universal justice emanating from reason alone; but this justice, in order to be admitted among us, should be reciprocal. Regarding things from a human standpoint, the laws of justice are inoperative among men for want of a natural sanction; they only bring good to the wicked and evil to the just when the latter observe them with every one, and no one observes them in return. Conventions and laws, then, are necessary to couple rights with duties and apply justice to its object. In the state of nature, where everything is in common, I owe nothing to those to whom I have promised nothing; I recognize as belonging to others only what is useless to me. This is not the case in the civil state, in which all rights are determined by law.

But then, finally, what is a law? So long as men are content to attach to this word only metaphysical ideas, they will continue to argue without being understood; and when they have stated what a law of nature is, they will know no better what a law of the State is.

I have already said that there is no general will with reference to a particular object. In fact, this particular object is either in the State or outside of it. If it is outside the State, a will which is foreign to it is not general in relation to it; and if it is within the State, it forms part of it; then there is formed between the whole and its part a relation which makes of it two separate beings, of which the part is one, and the whole, less this same part, is the other. But the whole less one part is not the whole, and so long as the relation subsists, there is no longer any whole, but two unequal parts; whence it follows that the will of the one is no longer general in relation to the other.

But when the whole people decree concerning the whole people, they consider themselves alone; and if a relation is then constituted, it is between the whole object under one point of view, without any division at all. Then the matter respecting which they decree is general like the will that decrees. It is this act that I call a law.

When I say that the object of the laws is always general, I mean that the law considers subjects collectively, and actions as abstract, never a man as an individual nor a particular action. Thus the law may indeed decree that there shall be privileges, but cannot confer them on any person by name; the law can create several classes of citizens, and even assign the qualifications which shall entitle them to rank in these classes, but it cannot nominate such and such persons to be admitted to them; it can establish a royal government and a hereditary succession, but cannot elect a king or appoint a royal family; in a word, no function which has reference to an individual object appertains to the legislative power.

From this standpoint we see immediately that it is no longer necessary to ask whose office it is to make laws, since they are acts of the general will; nor whether the prince is above the laws, since he is a member of the State; nor whether the law can be unjust, since no one is unjust to himself; nor how we are free and yet subject to the laws, since the laws are only registers of our wills.

We see, further, that since the law combines the universality of the will with the universality of the object, whatever any man prescribes on his own authority is not a law; and whatever the sovereign itself prescribes respecting a particular object is not a law, but a decree, not an act of sovereignty, but of magistracy.

I therefore call any State a republic which is governed by laws, under whatever form of administration it may be; for then only does the public interest predominate and the commonwealth count for something. Every legitimate government is republican;[5] I will explain hereafter what government is.

Laws are properly only the conditions of civil association. The people, being subjected to the laws, should be the authors of them; it concerns only the associates to determine the conditions of association. But how will they be determined? Will it be by a common agreement, by a sudden inspiration? Has the body politic an organ for expressing its will? Who will give it the foresight necessary to frame its acts and publish them at the outset? Or how shall it declare them in the hour of need? How would a blind multitude, which often knows not what it wishes because it rarely knows what is good for it, execute of itself an enterprise so great, so difficult, as a system of legislation? Of themselves, the people always desire what is good, but do not always discern it. The general will is always right, but the judgment which guides it is not always enlightened. It must be made to see objects as they are, sometimes as they ought to appear; it must be shown the good path that it is seeking, and guarded from the seduction of private interests; it must be made to observe closely times and places, and to balance the attraction of immediate and palpable advantages against the danger of remote and concealed evils. Individuals see the good which they reject; the public desire the good which they do not see. All alike have need of guides. The former must be compelled to conform their wills to their reason; the people must be taught to know what they require. Then from the public enlightenment results the union of the understanding and the will in the social body; and from that the close cooperation of the parts, and, lastly, the maximum power of the whole. Hence arises the need of a legislator.

Chapter VII. The Legislator

In order to discover the rules of association that are most suitable to nations, a superior intelligence would be necessary who could see all the passions of men without experiencing any of them; who would have no affinity with our nature and yet know it thoroughly; whose happiness would not depend on us, and who would nevertheless be quite willing to interest himself in ours; and, lastly, one who, storing up for himself with the progress of time a far-off glory in the future, could labor in one age and enjoy in another.[6] Gods would be necessary to give laws to men.

The same argument that Caligula adduced as to fact, Plato put forward with regard to right, in order to give an idea of the civil or royal man whom he is in quest of in his work the *Statesman*. But if it is true that a great prince is a rare man, what will a great legislator be? The first has only to follow the model which the other has to frame. The later is the mechanician who invents the machine, the former is only the workman who puts it in readiness and works it. "In the birth of societies," says Montesquieu, "it is the chiefs of the republics who frame the institutions, and afterwards it is the institutions which mold the chiefs of the republics."

He who dares undertake to give institutions to a nation ought to feel himself capable, as it were, of changing human nature; of transforming every individual, who in himself is a complete and independent whole, into part of a greater whole, from which he receives in some manner his life and his being; of altering man's constitution in order to strengthen it; of substituting a social and moral existence for the independent and physical existence which we have all received from nature. In a word, it is necessary to deprive man of his native powers in order to endow him with some which are alien to him, and of which he cannot make use without the aid of other people. The more thoroughly those natural powers are deadened and destroyed, the greater and more durable are the acquired powers, the more solid and perfect also are the institutions; so that if every citizen is nothing, and can be nothing, except in combination with all the rest . . .

The legislator is in all respects an extraordinary man in the State. If he ought to be so by his genius, he is not less so by his office. It is not magistracy nor sovereignty. This office which constitutes the republic, does not enter into its constitution; it is a special and superior office, having nothing in common with human government; for, if he who rules men ought not to control legislation, he who controls legislation ought not to rule men; otherwise his laws, being ministers of his passions, would often serve only to perpetuate his acts of injustice; he would never be able to prevent private interests from corrupting the sacredness of his work . . .

BOOK IV

Chapter I. That the General Will Is Indestructible

So long as a number of men in combination are considered as a single body, they have but one will, which relates to the common preservation and to the general well-being. In such a case all the forces of the State are vigorous and simple, and its principles are clear and luminous; it has no confused and conflicting interests; the common good is everywhere plainly manifest and only good sense is required to perceive it. Peace, union, and equality are foes to political subtleties. Upright and simpleminded men are hard to deceive because of their simplicity; allurements and refined pretexts do not impose upon them; they are not even cunning enough to be dupes. When, in the happiest nation in the world, we see troops of peasants regulating the affairs of the State under an oak and always acting wisely, can we refrain from despising the refinements of other nations, who make themselves illustrious and wretched with so much art and mystery?

A State thus governed needs very few laws; and in so far as it becomes necessary to promulgate new ones, this necessity is universally recognized. The first man to propose them only gives expression to what all have previously felt, and neither factions nor eloquence will be needed to pass into law what every one has already resolved to do, so soon as he is sure that the rest will act as he does.

What deceives reasoners is that, seeing only States that are ill-constituted from the beginning, they are impressed with the impossibility of maintaining such a policy in those States; they laugh to think of all the follies to which a cunning knave, an insinuating speaker, can persuade the people of Paris or London. They know not that Cromwell would have been put in irons by the people of Berne, and the Duke of Beaufort imprisoned by the Genevese.

But when the social bond begins to be relaxed and the State weakened, when private interests begin to make themselves felt and small associations to exercise influence on the State, the common interest is injuriously affected and finds adversaries; unanimity no longer reigns in the voting; the general will is no longer the will of all; opposition and disputes arise, and the best counsel does not pass uncontested.

Lastly, when the State, on the verge of ruin, no longer subsists except in a vain and illusory form, when the social bond is broken in all hearts, when the basest interest shelters itself impudently under the sacred name of the public welfare, the general will becomes dumb; all, under the guidance of secret motives, no more express their opinions as citizens than if the State had never existed; and, under the name of laws, they deceitfully pass unjust decrees which have only private interest as their end.

Does it follow from this that the general will is destroyed or corrupted? No; it is always constant, unalterable, and pure; but it is subordinated to others which get the better of it. Each, detaching his own interest from the common interest, sees clearly that he cannot completely separate it; but his share in the injury done to the State appears to him as nothing in comparison with the exclusive advantage which he aims at appropriating to himself. This particular advantage being excepted, he desires the general welfare for his own interests quite as strongly as any other. Even in selling his vote for money, he does not extinguish in himself the general will, but eludes it. The fault that he commits is to change the state of the question, and to answer something different from what he was asked; so that, instead of saying by a vote: "It is beneficial to the State," he says: "It is beneficial to a certain man or a certain party that such or such a motion should pass." Thus the law of public order in assemblies is not so much to maintain in them the general will as to ensure that it shall always be consulted and always respond.

I might in this place make many reflections on the simple right of voting in every act of sovereignty—a right which nothing can take away from the citizens—and on that of speaking, proposing, dividing, and discussing, which the government is always very careful to leave to its members only; but this important matter would require a separate treatise, and I cannot say everything in this one.

Chapter II. Voting

We see from the previous chapter that the manner in which public affairs are managed may give a sufficiently trustworthy indication of the character and health of the body politic. The more that harmony reigns in the assemblies, that is, the more the voting approaches unanimity, the more also is the general will predominant; but long discussions, dissensions, and uproar proclaim the ascendancy of private interests and the decline of the State.

This is not so clearly apparent when two or more orders enter into its constitution, as, in Rome, the patricians and plebeians, whose quarrels often disturbed the *comitia,* even in the palmiest days of the Republic; but this exception is more apparent than real, for, at that time, by a vice inherent in the body politic, there were, so to speak, two States in one; what is not true of the two together is true of each separately. And, indeed, even in the most stormy times, the *plebiscita* of the people, when the Senate did not interfere with them, always passed peaceably and by a large majority of votes; the citizens having but one interest, the people had but one will.

At the other extremity of the circle unanimity returns; that is, when the citizens, fallen into slavery, have no longer either liberty or will. Then fear and flattery change votes into acclamations; men no longer deliberate, but adore or curse. Such was the disgraceful mode of speaking in the Senate under the Emperors. Sometimes it was done with ridiculous precautions. Tacitus observes that under Otho the senators, in overwhelming Vitellius with execrations, affected to make at the same time a frightful noise, in order that, if he happened to become master, he might not know what each of them had said.

From these different considerations are deduced the principles by which we should regulate the method of counting votes and of comparing opinions, according as the general will is more or less easy to ascertain and the State more or less degenerate.

There is but one law which by its nature requires unanimous consent, that is, the social compact; for civil association is the most voluntary act in the world; every man being born free and master of himself, no one can, under any pretext whatever, enslave him without his assent. To decide that the son of a slave is born a slave is to decide that he is not born a man.

If, then, at the time of the social compact, there are opponents of it, their opposition does not invalidate the contract, but only prevents them from being included in it; they are foreigners among citizens. When the State is established, consent lies in residence; to dwell in the territory is to submit to the sovereignty.[7]

Excepting this original contract, the vote of the majority always binds all the rest, this being a result of the contract itself. But it will be asked how a man can be free and yet forced to conform to wills which are not his own. How are opponents free and yet subject to laws they have not consented to?

I reply that the question is wrongly put. The citizen consents to all the laws, even to those which are passed in spite of him, and even to those which punish him when he dares to violate any of them. The unvarying will of all the members of the State is the general will; it is through that that they are citizens and free. When a law is proposed in the assembly of the people, what is asked of them is not exactly whether they approve the proposition or reject it, but whether it is conformable or not to the general will, which is their own; each one in giving his vote expresses his opinion thereupon; and from the counting of the votes is obtained the declaration of the general will. When, therefore, the opinion opposed to my own prevails, that simply shows that I was mistaken, and that what I considered to be the general will was not so. Had my private opinion prevailed, I should have done something other than I wished; and in that case I should not have been free.

This supposes, it is true, that all the marks of the general will are still in the majority; when they cease to be so, whatever side we take, there is no longer any liberty.

In showing before how particular wills were substituted for general wills in public resolutions, I have sufficiently indicated the means practicable for preventing this abuse; I will speak of it again hereafter. With regard to the proportional number of votes for declaring this will, I have also laid down the principles according to which it may be determined. The difference of a single vote destroys unanimity; but between unanimity and equality there are many unequal divisions, at each of which this number can be fixed according to the condition and requirements of the body politic.

Two general principles may serve to regulate these proportions: the one, that the more important and weighty the resolutions, the nearer should the opinion which prevails approach unanimity; the other, that the greater the dispatch requisite in the matter under discussion, the more should we restrict the prescribed difference in the division of opinions; in resolutions which must be come to immediately, the majority of a single vote should suffice. The first of these principles appears more suitable to laws, the second to affairs. Be that as it may, it is by their combination that are established the best proportions which can be assigned for the decision of a majority.

READING 5

"Of the Origin of Government" and "Of the Original Contract"

David Hume

David Hume (1711–76) was born in Edinburgh, Scotland. A self-educated philosopher, he wrote his magnum opus, *Treatise of Human Nature*, while still in his early twenties. A friendly Renaissance man, he was denied a position as professor of philosophy at the University of Edinburgh because of his agnosticism.

The two essays presented here appeared in *Essays Moral, Political and Literary* (London, 1903). In the First essay, "Of the Origin of Government," Hume sets forth his theory of how governments originated from the basic unit of the family, meeting the needs of providing goods and maintaining peace and order. In the second essay, "Of the Original Contract," he criticizes the idea found in the works of Hobbes, Locke, and Rousseau (Readings 2, 3, and 4) that government is based on a social contract and the tacit consent of the governed. There was no such original contract and, even if there had been, it would not bind present members of society, who, for the most part, cannot be said to have freely consented to live under existing governments. For Hume's theory of justice see Reading 24.

This reading is taken from "Of the Origin of Government" (1777).

OF THE ORIGIN OF GOVERNMENT

Man, born in a family, is compelled to maintain society, from necessity, from natural inclination, and from habit. The same creature, in his farther progress, is engaged to establish political society, in order to administer justice; without which there can be no peace among them, nor safety, nor mutual intercourse. We are, therefore, to look upon all the vast apparatus of our government, as having ultimately no other object or purpose but the distribution of justice, or, in other words, the support of the twelve judges.[1] Kings and parliaments, fleets and armies, officers of the court and revenue, ambassadors, ministers, and privy-counsellors, are all subordinate in their end to this part of administration. Even the clergy, as their duty leads them to inculcate morality, may justly be thought, so far as regards this world, to have no other useful object of their institution.

All men are sensible of the necessity of justice to maintain peace and order; and all men are sensible of the necessity of peace and order for the maintenance of society. Yet, notwithstanding this strong and obvious necessity, such is the frailty or perverseness of our nature! It is impossible to keep men, faithfully and unerringly, in the paths of justice. Some extraordinary circumstances may happen, in which a man finds his interests to be more promoted by fraud or rapine, than hurt by the breach which his injustice makes in the social union. But much more frequently, he is seduced from his great and important, but distant interests, by the allurement of present, though often very frivolous temptations. This great weakness is incurable in human nature.

Men must, therefore, endeavor to palliate what they cannot cure. They must institute some persons, under the appellation of magistrates, whose peculiar office it is, to point out the decrees of equity, to punish transgressors, to correct fraud and violence, and to oblige men, however reluctant, to consult their own real and permanent interests. In a word, OBEDIENCE is a new duty which must be invented to support that of JUSTICE; and the ties of equity must be corroborated by those of allegiance.

But still, viewing matters in an abstract light, it may be thought, that nothing is gained by this alliance, and that the factitious duty of obedience, from its very nature, lays as feeble a hold of the human mind, as the primitive and natural duty of justice. Peculiar interests and present temptations may overcome the one as well as the other. They are equally exposed to the same inconvenience. And the man, who is inclined to be a bad neighbor, must be led by the same motives, well or ill understood, to be a bad citizen and subject. Not to mention, that the magistrate himself may often be negligent, or partial, or unjust in his administration.

Experience, however, proves, that there is a great difference between the cases. Order in society, we find, is much better maintained by means of government; and our duty to the magistrate is more strictly guarded by the principles of human nature, than our duty to our fellow-citizens. The love of dominion is so strong in the breast of man, that many, not only submit to, but court all the dangers, and fatigues, and cares of government; and men, once raised to that station, though often led astray by private passions, find, in ordinary cases, a visible interest in the impartial administration of justice. The persons, who first attain this distinction by the consent, tacit or express, of the people, must be endowed with superior personal qualities of valor, force, integrity, or prudence, which command respect and confidence: and after government is established, a regard to birth, rank, and station has a mighty influence over men, and enforces the decrees of the magistrate. The prince or leader exclaims against every disorder, which disturbs his society. He summons all his partisans and all men of probity to aid him in correcting and redressing it: and he is readily followed by all indifferent persons in the execution of his office. He soon acquires the power of rewarding these services; and in the progress of society, he establishes subordinate ministers and often a military force, who find an immediate and a visible interest, in supporting his authority. Habit soon consolidates what other principles of human nature had imperfectly founded; and men, once accustomed to obedience, never think of departing from that path, in which they and their ancestors have constantly trod, and to which they are confined by so many urgent and visible motives.

But though this progress of human affairs may appear certain and inevitable, and though the support which allegiance brings to justice, be founded on obvious principles of human nature, it cannot be expected that men should beforehand be able to discover them, or foresee their operation. Government commences more casually and more imperfectly. It is probable, that the first ascendant of one man over multitudes began during a state of war; where the superiority of courage and of genius discovers itself most visibly, where unanimity and concert are most requisite, and where the pernicious effects of disorder are most sensibly felt. The long continuance of that state, an incident common among savage tribes, inured the people to submission; and if the chieftain possessed as much equity as prudence and valor, he became, even during peace, the arbiter of all differences, and could gradually, by a mixture of force and consent, establish his authority. The benefit sensibly felt from his influence, made it be cherished by the people, at least by the peaceable and well disposed among them; and if his son enjoyed the same good qualities, government advanced the sooner to maturity and perfection; but was still in a feeble state, till the farther progress of improvement procured the magistrate a revenue, and enabled him to bestow rewards on the several instruments of his administration, and to inflict punishments on the refractory and disobedient. Before that period, each exertion of his influence must have been particular, and founded on the peculiar circumstances of the case. After it, submission was no longer a matter of choice in the bulk of the community, but was rigorously exacted by the authority of the supreme magistrate.

In all governments, there is a perpetual intestine struggle, open or secret, between AUTHORITY and LIBERTY; and neither of them can ever absolutely prevail in the contest. A great sacrifice of liberty must necessarily be made in every government; yet even the authority, which confines liberty, can never, and perhaps ought never, in any constitution, to become quite entire and uncontrollable. The sultan is master of the life and fortune of any individual; but will not be permitted to impose new taxes on his subjects: a French monarch can impose taxes at pleasure; but would find it dangerous to attempt to take the lives and fortunes of individuals. Religion also, in most countries, is commonly found to be a very intractable principle; and other principles or prejudices frequently resist all the authority of the civil magistrate; whose power, being founded on opinion, can never subvert other opinions, equally rooted with that of his title to dominion. The government, which, in common appellation, receives the appellation of free, is that which admits of a partition of power among several members, whose united authority is no less, or is commonly greater than that of any monarch; but who, in the usual course of administration, must act by general and equal laws, that are previously known to all the members and to all their subjects. In this sense, it must be owned, that liberty is the perfection of civil society; but still authority must be acknowledged essential to its very existence: and in those contests, which so often take place between the one and the other, the latter may, on that account, challenge the preference. Unless perhaps one may say (and it may be said with some reason) that a circumstance, which is essential to the existence of civil society, must always support itself, and needs be guarded with less jealousy, than one that contributes only to its perfection, which the indolence of men is so apt to neglect, or their ignorance to overlook.

OF THE ORIGINAL CONTRACT

As no party, in the present age, can well support itself, without a philosophical or speculative system of principles, annexed to its political or practical one; we accordingly find, that each of the factions, into which this nation is divided, has reared up a fabric of the former kind, in order to protect and cover that scheme of actions, which it pursues. The people being commonly very rude builders, especially in this speculative way, and more especially still, when actuated by party-zeal; it is natural to imagine, that their workmanship must be a little unshapely, and discover evident marks of that violence and hurry, in which it was raised. The one

party, by tracing up government to the DEITY, endeavor to render it so sacred and inviolate, that it must be little less than sacrilege, however tyrannical it may become, to touch or invade it, in the smallest article. The other party, by founding government altogether on the consent of the PEOPLE, suppose that there is a kind of *original contract,* by which the subjects have tacitly reserved the power of resisting their sovereign, whenever they find themselves aggrieved by that authority, with which they have, for certain purposes, voluntarily entrusted him. These are the speculative principles of the two parties; and these too are the practical consequences deduced from them.

I shall venture to affirm, *That both these* systems *of speculative principles are just; though not in the sense, intended by the parties:* And, *That both the* schemes *of practical consequences are prudent; though not in the extremes, to which each party, in opposition to the other, has commonly endeavoured to carry them.*

That the DIETY is the ultimate author of all government, will never be denied by any, who admit a general providence, and allow, that all events in the universe are conducted by an uniform plan, and directed to wise purposes. As it is impossible for the human race to subsist, at least in any comfortable or secure state, without the protection of government; this institution must certainly have been intended by that beneficent Being, who means the good of all his creatures. And as it has universally, in fact, taken place, in all countries, and all ages; we may conclude, with still greater certainty, that it was intended by that omniscient Being, who can never be deceived by any event or operation. But since he gave rise to it, not by any particular or miraculous interposition, but by his concealed and universal efficacy; a sovereign cannot, properly speaking, be called his vice-regent, in any other sense than every power or force, being derived from him, may be said to act by his commission. Whatever actually happens is comprehended in the general plan or intention of providence; nor has the greatest and most lawful prince any more reason, upon that account, to plead a peculiar sacredness or inviolable authority, than an inferior magistrate, or even an usurper, or even a robber and a pirate. The same divine superintendent, who, for wise purposes, invested a TITUS or a TRAJAN with authority, did also, for purposes, no doubt, equally wise, though unknown, bestow power on a BORGIA or an ANGRIA. The same causes, which gave rise to the sovereign power in every state, established likewise every petty jurisdiction in it, and every limited authority. A constable, therefore, no less than a king, acts by a divine commission, and possesses an indefeasible right.

When we consider how nearly equal all men are in their bodily force, and even in their mental powers and faculties, till cultivated by education; we must necessarily allow, that nothing but their own consent could, at first, associate them together, and subject them to any authority. The people, if we trace government to its first origin in the woods and deserts, are the source of all power and jurisdiction, and voluntarily, for the sake of peace and order, abandoned their native liberty, and received laws from their equal and companion. The conditions, upon which they were willing to submit, were either expressed, or were so clear and obvious, that it might well be esteemed superfluous to express them. If this, then, be meant by the *original contract,* it cannot be denied, that all government is, at first, founded on a contract, and that the most ancient rude combinations of mankind were formed chiefly by that principle. In vain, are we asked in what records this charter of our liberties is registered. It was not written on parchment, nor yet on leaves or barks of trees. It preceded the use of writing and all the other civilized arts of life. But we trace it plainly in the nature of man, and in the equality, or something approaching equality, which we find in all the individuals of that species. The force, which now prevails, and which is founded on fleets and armies, is plainly political, and derived from authority, the effect of established government. A man's natural force consists only in the vigor of his limbs, and the firmness of his courage; which could never subject multitudes to the command of one. Nothing but their own consent, and their sense of the advantages resulting from peace and order, could have had that influence.

Yet even this consent was long very imperfect, and could not be the basis of a regular administration. The chieftain, who had probably acquired his influence during the continuance of war, ruled more by persuasion than command; and till he could employ force to reduce the refractory and disobedient, the society could scarcely be said to have attained a state of civil government. No compact or agreement, it is evident, was expressly formed for general submission; an idea far beyond the comprehension of savages. Each exertion of authority in the chieftain must have been particular, and called forth by the present exigencies of the case. The sensible utility, resulting from his interposition, made these exertions become daily more frequent; and their frequency gradually produced an habitual, and, if you please to call it so, a voluntary, and therefore precarious, acquiescence in the people.

But philosophers, who have embraced a party (if that be not a contradiction in terms) are not contented with these concessions. They assert, not only that government in its earliest infancy arose from consent or rather the voluntary acquiescence of the people; but also, that, even at present, when it has attained full maturity, it rests on no other foundation. They affirm, that all men are still born equal, and owe allegiance to no prince or government, unless bound by the obligation and sanction of a *promise.* And as no man, without some equivalent, would forego the advantages of his native liberty, and subject himself to the will of another; this promise is always understood to be conditional, and imposes on him no obligation, unless he meet with justice and protection from his sovereign. These advantages the sovereign promises him in return; and if he fail in the execution, he has broken, on his part, the articles of engagement, and has thereby freed his subject from all obligations to allegiance. Such, according to these philosophers, is the foundation of authority in every government; and such the right of resistance, possessed by every subject.

But would these reasoners look abroad into the world, they would meet with nothing that, in the least, corresponds to their ideas, or can warrant so refined and philosophical a system. On the contrary, we find, everywhere, princes, who claim their subjects as their property, and assert their independent right of sovereignty, from conquest or succession. We find also, everywhere, subjects, who acknowledge this right in their prince, and suppose themselves born under obligations of obedience to a certain sovereign, as much as under the ties of reverence and duty to certain parents. These connections are always conceived to be equally independent of our consent, in PERSIA and CHINA; in FRANCE and SPAIN; and even in HOLLAND and ENGLAND, wherever the doctrines above-mentioned have not been carefully inculcated. Obedience or subjection becomes so familiar, that most men never make any inquiry about its origin or cause, more than about the principle of gravity, resistance, or the most universal laws of nature. Or if curiosity ever move them; as soon as they learn, that they themselves and their ancestors have, for several ages, or from time immemorial, been subject to such a form of government or such a family; they immediately acquiesce, and acknowledge their obligation to allegiance. Were you to preach, in most parts of the world, that political connections are founded altogether on voluntary consent or a mutual promise, the magistrate would soon imprison you, as seditious, for loosening the ties of obedience; if your friends did not before shut you up as delirious, for advancing such absurdities. It is strange, that an act of the mind, which every individual is supposed to have formed, and after he came to the use of reason too, otherwise it could have no authority; that this act, I say, should be so much unknown to all of them, that, over the face of the whole earth, there scarcely remain any traces or memory of it.

But the contract, on which government is founded, is said to be the *original contract;* and consequently may be supposed too old to fall under the knowledge of the present generation. If the agreement, by which savage men first associated and conjoined their force, be here meant, this is acknowledged to be real; but being so ancient, and being obliterated by a thousand changes of government and princes, it cannot now be supposed to retain any authority. If we would say anything to the purpose, we must assert, that every particular government, which is lawful, and which imposes any duty of allegiance on the subject, was, at first, founded on consent and a voluntary compact. But besides that this supposes the consent of the fathers to bind the children, even to the most remote generations (which republican writers will never allow), besides this, I say, it is not justified by history or experience, in any age or country of the world.

Almost all the governments, which exist at present, or of which there remains any record in story, have been founded originally, either on usurpation or conquest, or both, without any pretense of a fair consent, or voluntary subjection of the people. When an artful and bold man is placed at the head of an army or faction, it is often easy for him, by employing, sometimes violence, sometimes false pretenses, to establish his dominion over a people a hundred times more numerous than his partisans. He allows no such open communication, that his enemies can know, with certainty, their number or force. He gives them no leisure to assemble together in a body to oppose him. Even all those, who are the instruments of his usurpation, may wish his fall; but their ignorance of each other's intention keeps them in awe, and is the sole cause of his security. By such arts as these, many governments have been established; and this is all the *original contract,* which they have to boast of.

The face of the earth is continually changing, by the increase of small kingdoms into great empires, by the dissolution of great empires into smaller kingdoms, by the planting of colonies, by the migration of tribes. Is there anything discoverable in all these events, but *force* and *violence? Where is the mutual agreement* or voluntary association so much talked of?

Even the smoothest way, by which a nation may receive a foreign master, by marriage or a will, is not extremely honorable for the people; but supposes them to be disposed of, like a dowry or a legacy, according to the pleasure or interest of their rulers.

But where no force interposes, and election takes place; what is this election so highly vaunted? It is either the combination of a few great men, who decide for the whole, and will allow of no opposition, or it is the fury of a multitude, that follow a seditious ringleader, who is not known, perhaps, to a dozen among them, and who owes his advancement merely to his own impudence, or to the momentary caprice of his fellows.

Are these disorderly elections, which are rare too, of such mighty authority, as to be the only lawful foundation of all government and allegiance?

In reality, there is not a more terrible event, than a total dissolution of government, which gives liberty to the multitude, and makes the determination or choice of a new establishment depend upon a number, which nearly approaches to that of the body of the people. For it never comes entirely to the whole body of them. Every wise man, then, wishes to see, at the head of a powerful and obedient army, a general, who may speedily seize the prize, and give to the people a master, which they are so unfit to choose for themselves. So little correspondent is fact and reality to those philosophical notions.

Let not the establishment at the *Revolution* deceive us, or make us so much in love with a philosophical origin to government, as to imagine all others monstrous and irregular. Even that event was far from corresponding to these refined ideas. It was only the succession, and that only in the regal part of the government, which was then changed. And it was only the majority of seven hundred, who determined that change for near ten millions.[2] I doubt not, indeed, but the bulk of those ten millions acquiesced willingly in the determination: But was the matter left, in the least, to their choice? Was it not justly supposed to be, from that moment, decided, and every man punished, who refused to submit to the new sovereign? How otherwise could the matter have ever been brought to any issue or conclusion?

The republic of ATHENS was, I believe, the most extensive democracy, that we read of in history. Yet if we make the requisite allowances for the women, the slaves, and the strangers, we shall find, that that establishment was not, at first, made, nor any law ever voted, by a tenth part of those who were bound to pay obedience to it. Not to mention the islands and foreign dominions, which the ATHENIANS claimed as theirs by right of conquest. And as it is well known, that popular assemblies in that city were always full of license and disorder, notwithstanding the institutions and laws by which they were checked. How much more disorderly must they prove, where they form not the established constitution, but meet tumultuously on the dissolution of the ancient government, in order to give rise to a new one? How chimerical must it be to talk of a choice in such circumstances?

The ACHAEANS enjoyed the freest and most perfect democracy of all antiquity; yet they employed force to oblige some cities to enter into their league, as we learn from POLYBIUS.

HARRY the IVth and HARRY the VIIth of ENGLAND, had really no title to the throne but a parliamentary election; yet they never would acknowledge it, lest they should thereby weaken their authority. Strange, if the only real foundation of all authority be consent and promise!

It is in vain to say, that all governments are or should be, at first, founded on popular consent, as much as the necessity of human affairs will admit. This favors entirely my pretension. I maintain, that human affairs will never admit of this consent; seldom of the appearance of it. But that conquest or usurpation, that is, in plain terms, force, by dissolving the ancient governments, is the origin of almost all the new ones, which were ever established in the world. And that in the few cases, where consent may seem to have taken place, it was commonly so irregular, so confined, or so much intermixed either with fraud or violence, that it cannot have any great authority.

My intention here is not to exclude the consent of the people from being one just foundation of government where it has place. It is surely the best and most sacred of any. I only pretend, that it has very seldom had place in any degree, and never almost in its full extent. And that therefore some other foundation of government must also be admitted.

Were all men possessed of so inflexible a regard to justice, that, of themselves, they would totally abstain from the properties of others; they had forever remained in a state of absolute liberty, without subjection to any magistrate or political society. But this is a state of perfection, of which human nature is justly deemed incapable. Again, were all men possessed of so perfect an understanding, as always to know their own interests, no form of government had ever been submitted to, but what was established on

consent, and was fully canvassed by every member of the society. But this state of perfection is likewise much superior to human nature. Reason, history, and experience show us, that all political societies have had an origin much less accurate and regular; and were one to choose a period of time, when the people's consent was the least regarded in public transactions, it would be precisely on the establishment of a new government. In a settled constitution, their inclinations are often consulted; but during the fury of revolutions, conquests, and public convulsions, military force or political craft usually decides the controversy.

When a new government is established, by whatever means, the people are commonly dissatisfied with it, and pay obedience more from fear and necessity, than from any idea of allegiance or of moral obligation. The prince is watchful and jealous, and must carefully guard against every beginning or appearance of insurrection. Time, by degrees, removes all these difficulties, and accustoms the nation to regard, as their lawful or native princes, that family, which, at first, they considered as usurpers or foreign conquerors. In order to found this opinion, they have no recourse to any notion of voluntary consent or promise, which, they know, never was, in this case, either expected or demanded. The original establishment was formed by violence, and submitted to from necessity. The subsequent administration is also supported by power, and acquiesced in by the people not as a matter of choice, but of obligation. They imagine not that their consent gives their prince a title. But they willingly consent, because they think, that, from long possession, he has acquired a title, independent of their choice or inclination.

Should it be said, that, by living under the dominion of a prince, which one might leave, every individual has given a *tacit* consent to his authority, and promised him obedience; it may be answered, that such an implied consent can only have place, where a man imagines, that the matter depends on his choice. But where he thinks (as all mankind do who are born under established governments) that by his birth he owes allegiance to a certain prince or certain form of government; it would be absurd to infer a consent or choice, which he expressly, in this case, renounces and disclaims.

Can we seriously say, that a poor peasant or artisan has a free choice to leave his country, when he knows no foreign language or manners, and lives from day to day, by the small wages which he acquires? We may as well assert, that a man, by remaining in a vessel, freely consents to the dominion of the master; though he was carried on board while asleep, and must leap into the ocean, and perish, the moment he leaves her.

What if the prince forbid his subjects to quit his dominions; as in TIBERIUS's time, it was regarded as a crime in a ROMAN knight that he had attempted to fly to the PARTHIANS, in order to escape the tyranny of that emperor? Or as the ancient MUSCOVITES prohibited all travelling under pain of death? And did a prince observe, that many of his subjects were seized with the frenzy of migrating to foreign countries, he would doubtless, with great reason and justice, restrain them, in order to prevent the depopulation of his own kingdom. Would he forfeit the allegiance of all his subjects, by so wise and reasonable a law? Yet the freedom of their choice is surely, in that case, ravished from them.

A company of men, who should leave their native country, in order to people some uninhabited region, might dream of recovering their native freedom; but they would soon find, that their prince still laid claim to them, and called them his subjects, even in their new settlement. And in this he would but act conformably to the common ideas of mankind.

The truest *tacit* consent of this kind, that is ever observed, is when a foreigner settles in any country, and is beforehand acquainted with the prince, and government, and laws, to which he must submit. Yet is his allegiance, though more voluntary, much less expected or depended on, than that of a natural born subject? On the contrary, his native prince still asserts a claim to him. And if he punish not the renegade, when he seizes him in war with his new prince's commission; this clemency is not founded on the municipal law, which in all countries condemns the prisoner; but on the consent of princes, who have agreed to this indulgence, in order to prevent reprisals.

Did one generation of men go off the stage at once, and another succeed, as is the case with silkworms and butterflies, the new race, if they had sense enough to choose their government, which surely is never the case with men, might voluntarily; and by general consent, establish their own form of civil polity, without any regard to the laws or precedents, which prevailed among their ancestors. But as human society is in perpetual flux, one man every hour going out of the world, another coming into it, it is necessary, in order to preserve stability in government, that the new brood should conform themselves to the established constitution, and nearly follow the path

which their fathers, treading in the footsteps of theirs, had marked out to them. Some innovations must necessarily have place in every human institution, and it is happy where the enlightened genius of the age give these a direction to the side of reason, liberty, and justice: but violent innovations no individual is entitled to make: they are even dangerous to be attempted by the legislature: more ill than good is ever to be expected from them: and if history affords examples to the contrary, they are not to be drawn into precedent, and are only to be regarded as proofs, that the science of politics affords few rules, which will not admit of some exception, and which may not sometimes be controlled by fortune and accident. The violent innovations in the reign of HENRY VIII proceeded from an imperious monarch, seconded by the appearance of legislative authority. Those in the reign of CHARLES I were derived from faction and fanaticism; and both of them have proved happy in the issue. But even the former were long the source of many disorders, and still more dangers; and if the measures of allegiance were to be taken from the latter, a total anarchy must have place in human society, and a final period at once be put to every government.

Suppose, that a usurper, after having banished his lawful prince and royal family, should establish his dominion for ten or a dozen years in any country, and should preserve so exact a discipline in his troops, and so regular a disposition in his garrisons, that no insurrection had ever been raised, or even murmur heard, against his administration. Can it be asserted, that the people, who in their hearts abhor his treason, have tacitly consented to his authority, and promised him allegiance, merely because, from necessity, they live under his dominion? Suppose again their native prince restored, by means of an army, which he levies in foreign countries. They receive him with joy and exultation, and show plainly with what reluctance they had submitted to any other yoke. I may now ask, upon what foundation the prince's title stands? Not on popular consent surely. For though the people willingly acquiesce in his authority, they never imagine, that their consent made him sovereign. They consent; because they apprehend him to be already, by birth, their lawful sovereign. And as to that tacit consent, which may now be inferred from their living under his dominion, this is no more than what they formerly gave to the tyrant and usurper.

When we assert, that all lawful government arises from the consent of the people, we certainly do them a great deal more honor than they deserve, or even expect and desire from us. After the ROMAN dominions became too unwieldy for the republic to govern them, the people, over the whole known world, were extremely grateful to AUGUSTUS for that authority, which, by violence, he had established over them; and they showed an equal disposition to submit to the successor, whom he left them, by his last will and testament. It was afterwards their misfortune, that there never was, in one family, any long regular succession; but that their line of princes was continually broken, either by private assassinations or public rebellions. The *praetorian* bands, on the failure of every family, set up one emperor; the legions in the East a second; those in GERMANY, perhaps, a third: And the sword alone could decide the controversy. The condition of the people, in that mighty monarchy, was to be lamented, not because the choice of the emperor was never left to them; for that was impracticable: But because they never fell under any succession of masters, who might regularly follow each other. As to the violence and wars and bloodshed, occasioned by every new settlement; these were not blameable, because they were inevitable.

The house of LANCASTER ruled in this island about sixty years; yet the partisans of the white rose seemed daily to multiply in ENGLAND. The present establishment has taken place during a still longer period. Have all views of right in another family been utterly extinguished; even though scarce any man now alive had arrived at years of discretion, when it was expelled, or could have consented to its dominion, or have promised it allegiance? A sufficient indication surely of the general sentiment of mankind on this head. For we blame not the partisans of the abdicated family, merely on account of the long time, during which they have preserved their imaginary loyalty. We blame them for adhering to a family, which, we affirm, has been justly expelled, and which, from the moment the new settlement took place, had forfeited all title to authority.

But would we have a more regular, at least a more philosophical, refutation of this principle of an original contract or popular consent; perhaps, the following observations may suffice.

All *moral* duties may be divided into two kinds. The *first* are those, to which men are impelled by a natural instinct or immediate propensity, which operates on them, independent of all ideas of obligation, and of all views, either to public or private utility. Of this nature are, love of children, gratitude to benefactors, pity to the unfortunate. When we reflect on the advantage, which results to society from such humane instincts, we pay them the just tribute of moral ap-

probation and esteem: But the person, actuated by them, feels their power and influence, antecedent to any such reflection.

The *second* kind of moral duties are such as are not supported by any original instinct of nature, but are performed entirely from a sense of obligation, when we consider the necessities of human society, and the impossibility of supporting it, if these duties were neglected. It is thus *justice* or a regard to the property of others, *fidelity* or the observance of promises, become obligatory, and acquire an authority over mankind. For as it is evident, that every man loves himself better than any other person, he is naturally impelled to extend his acquisitions as much as possible; and nothing can restrain him in this propensity, but reflection and experience, by which he learns the pernicious effects of that license, and the total dissolution of society which must ensue from it. His original inclination, therefore, or instinct, is here checked and restrained by a subsequent judgment or observation.

The case is precisely the same with the political or civil duty of *allegiance,* as with the natural duties of justice and fidelity. Our primary instincts lead us either to indulge ourselves in unlimited freedom, or to seek dominion over others. And it is reflection only, which engages us to sacrifice such strong passions to the interests of peace and public order. A small degree of experience and observation suffices to teach us that society cannot possibly be maintained without the authority of magistrates, and that this authority must soon fall into contempt, where exact obedience is not payed to it. The observation of these general and obvious interests is the source of all allegiance, and of that moral obligation, which we attribute to it.

What necessity, therefore, is there to found the duty of *allegiance* or obedience to magistrates on that of *fidelity* or a regard to promises, and to suppose, that it is the consent of each individual, which subjects him to government; when it appears, that both allegiance and fidelity stand precisely on the same foundation, and are both submitted to by mankind, on account of the apparent interests and necessities of human society? We are bound to obey our sovereign, it is said; because we have given a tacit promise to that purpose. But why are we bound to observe our promise? It must here be asserted, that the commerce and intercourse of mankind, which are of such mighty advantage, can have no security where men pay no regard to their engagements. In like manner, may it be said, that men could not live at all in society, at least in a civilized society, without laws and magistrates and judges, to prevent the encroachments of the strong upon the weak, of the violent upon the just and equitable. The obligation to allegiance being of like force and authority with the obligation to fidelity, we gain nothing by resolving the one into the other. The general interests or necessities of society are sufficient to establish both.

If the reason be asked of that obedience, which we are bound to pay to government, I readily answer, *because society could not otherwise subsist:* And this answer is clear and intelligible to all mankind. Your answer is, *because we should keep our word.* But besides, that no body, till trained in a philosophical system, can either comprehend or relish this answer: Besides this, I say, you find yourself embarrassed, when it is asked, *why we are bound to keep our word?* Nor can you give any answer, but what would, immediately, without any circuit, have accounted for our obligation to allegiance.

But *to whom is allegiance due?* And *who is our lawful sovereign?* This question is often the most difficult of any, and liable to infinite discussions. When people are so happy, that they can answer, *Our present sovereign, who inherits, in a direct line, from ancestors, that have governed us for many ages;* this answer admits of no reply; even though historians, in tracing up to the remotest antiquity, the origin of that royal family, may find, as commonly happens, that its first authority was derived from usurpation and violence. It is confessed, that private justice, or the abstinence from the properties of others, is a most cardinal virtue. Yet reason tells us, that there is no property in durable objects, such as lands or houses, when carefully examined in passing from hand to hand, but must, in some period, have been founded on fraud and injustice. The necessities of human society, neither in private nor public life, will allow of such an accurate enquiry. And there is no virtue or moral duty, but what may, with facility, be refined away, if we indulge a false philosophy, in sifting and scrutinizing it, by every captious rule of logic, in every light or position, in which it may be placed.

The questions with regard to private property have filled infinite volumes of law and philosophy, if in both we add the commentators to the original text; and in the end, we may safely pronounce, that many of the rules, there established, are uncertain, ambiguous, and arbitrary. The like opinion may be formed with regard to the succession and rights of princes and forms of government. Several cases, no doubt, occur, especially in the infancy of any constitution, which admit of no determination from the laws of justice and equity. . . .

Nor can any thing be more unhappy than a despotic government of this kind; where the succession is disjointed and irregular, and must be determined, on every vacancy, by force or election. In a free government, the matter is often unavoidable, and is also much less dangerous. The interests of liberty may there frequently lead the people, in their own defense, to alter the succession of the crown. And the constitution, being compounded of parts, may still maintain a sufficient stability, by resting on the aristocratical or democratical members, though the monarchical be altered, from time to time, in order to accommodate it to the former.

In an absolute government, when there is no legal prince, who has a title to the throne, it may safely be determined to belong to the first occupant. Instances of this kind are but too frequent, especially in the eastern monarchies. When any race of princes expires, the will or destination of the last sovereign will be regarded as a title. Thus the edict of Lewis the XIVth, who called the bastard princes to the succession in case of the failure of all the legitimate princes, would, in such an event, have some authority. Thus the will of Charles the Second disposed of the whole Spanish monarchy. The cession of the ancient proprietor, especially when joined to conquest, is likewise deemed a good title. The general obligation, which binds us to government, is the interest and necessities of society; and this obligation is very strong. The determination of it to this or that particular prince or form of government is frequently more uncertain and dubious. Present possession has considerable authority in these cases, and greater than in private property; because of the disorders which attend all revolutions and changes of government.

We shall only observe, before we conclude, that, though an appeal to general opinion may justly, in the speculative sciences of metaphysics, natural philosophy, or astronomy, be deemed unfair and inconclusive, yet in all questions with regard to morals, as well as criticism, there is really no other standard, by which any controversy can ever be decided. And nothing is a clearer proof, that a theory of this kind is erroneous, than to find, that it leads to paradoxes, repugnant to the common sentiments of mankind, and to the practice and opinion of all nations and all ages. The doctrine, which founds all lawful government on an *original contract,* or consent of the people, is plainly of this kind; nor has the most noted of its partisans,[3] in prosecution of it, scrupled to affirm, *that absolute monarchy is inconsistent with civil society, and so can be no form of civil government at all; and that the supreme power in a state cannot take from any man, by taxes and impositions, any part of his property, without his own consent or that of his representatives.* What authority any moral reasoning can have; which leads into opinions so wide of the general practice of mankind, in every place but this single kingdom, it is easy to determine.

The only passage I meet with in antiquity, where the obligation of obedience to government is ascribed to a promise, is in PLATO's *Crito:* where SOCRATES refuses to escape from prison, because he had tacitly promised to obey the laws. Thus he builds a *Tory* consequence of passive obedience, on a *Whig* foundation of the original contract.

New discoveries are not to be expected in these matters. If scarce any man, till very lately, ever imagined that government was founded on compact, it is certain, that it cannot, in general, have any such foundation.

READING 6

Reflections on the Revolution in France

Edmund Burke

Edmund Burke (1729–97) was a political leader whose writings inspire everything from reverence to contempt more than two centuries after his death. For years a member of Parliament, Burke was best known before the French Revolution as a reformer who championed the rights of Ireland and the American colonies, hated the slave trade, and demanded decency in the administration of British India. He was an early admirer of the economic theory of Adam Smith. But it is his passionate opposition to the French Revolution that made him a central figure in modern political thought. Though a practicing politician rather than a systematic political thinker, Burke foresaw the course of that watershed event with astonishing accuracy. In his best-known work, *Reflections on the Revolution in France* (1790), Burke argued that the revolution was utopian in principle and would thus

become terrorist in fact. He expected terror to be supplanted by hope, inspired by someone on a white horse who would promise to rescue France from chaos. At the time the *Reflections* was published, the revolution had many admirers in England, and the work precipitated a split between long-time friends and political allies that presaged a deep modern ideological rift between champions and opponents of radical political change. The debate continues to this day as to whether the revolution transformed Burke from humane reformer to reactionary or whether he held fast to his principles while the political climate of Europe abruptly changed for the worse.

In any event, Burke's writings have been invoked by conservatives on both sides of the Atlantic in the struggle against comprehensive political reforms made in the name of equality. His view that simplistic "social engineering" squanders the wisdom embodied in gradually evolved institutions has inspired contemporary strands of political thought as different in temperament and detail as the romantic theistic conservativism of Russell Kirk and the austere secular classical liberalism of F. A. Hayek. A strenuous critic of Hobbes's approach to political and moral theory, Burke wrote in his *Speech on Conciliation with America* that "Aristotle, the great master of reasoning, cautions us, and with great weight and propriety, against this species of delusive geometrical accuracy in moral arguments, as the most fallacious of all sophistry."

This reading is taken from *Reflections on the Revolution in France* (1790).

A CRITIQUE OF REVOLUTIONARY EGALITARIANISM

Change and Conservation

A state without the means of some change is without the means of its conservation. Without such means it might even risk the loss of that part of the constitution which it wished the most religiously to preserve. The two principles of conservation and correction operated strongly at the two critical periods of the Restoration and Revolution, when England found itself without a king. At both those periods the nation had lost the bond of union in their ancient edifice; they did not, however, dissolve the whole fabric. On the contrary, in both cases they regenerated the deficient part of the old constitution through the parts which were not impaired. They kept these old parts exactly as they were, that the part recovered might be suited to them. They acted by the ancient organized states in the shape of their old organization, and not by the organic *molecules* of a disbanded people. At no time, perhaps, did the sovereign legislature manifest a more tender regard to that fundamental principle of British constitutional policy, than at the time of the Revolution, when it deviated from the direct line of hereditary succession. The crown was carried somewhat out of the line in which it had before moved; but the new line was derived from the same stock. It was still a line of hereditary descent; still an hereditary descent qualified with protestantism. When the legislature altered the direction, but kept the principle, they showed that they held it inviolable.

On this principle, the law of inheritance had admitted some amendment in the old time, and long before the era of the revolution. Some time after the conquest great questions arose upon the legal principles of hereditary descent. . . . This is the spirit of our constitution, not only in its settled course, but in all its revolutions. Whoever came in, or however he came in, whether he obtained the crown by law, or by force, the hereditary succession was either continued or adopted. . . . The same policy pervades all the laws which have since been made for the preservation of our liberties.

You will observe, that from Magna Carta to the Declaration of Right, it has been the uniform policy of our constitution to claim and assert our liberties, as an *entailed inheritance* derived to us from our forefathers, and to be transmitted to our posterity; as an estate specially belonging to the people of this kingdom, without any reference whatever to any other more general or prior right. By this means our constitution preserves a unity in so great a diversity of parts. We have an inheritable crown; an inheritable peerage; and a house of commons and a people inheriting privileges, franchises, and liberties, from a long line of ancestors.

The policy appears to me to be the result of profound reflection; or rather the happy effect of following nature, which is wisdom without reflection, and above it. A spirit of innovation is generally the result of a selfish temper, and confined views. People will not look forward to posterity, who never look backward to their ancestors. Besides, the people of England well know that the idea of inheritance furnishes a sure principle of conservation, and a sure principle of transmission; without at all excluding a principle of improvement. It leaves acquisition free; but it secures what it acquires. Whatever advantages are obtained by a state proceeding on these maxims, are locked fast as in a sort of family settlement; grasped as in a kind of mortmain for ever. By a constitutional policy working after the pattern of nature, we receive, we hold, we transmit our government and our privileges, in the same manner in which we enjoy and transmit our property and our lives. The institutions of policy, the goods of fortune, the gifts of Providence, are handed down to us, and from us, in the same course and order. Our political system is placed in a just correspondence and symmetry with the order of the world, and with the mode of existence decreed to a permanent body composed of transitory parts; wherein, by the disposition of a stupendous wisdom, moulding together the great mysterious incorporation of the human race, the whole, at one time, is never old, or middle-aged, or young, but, in a condition of unchangeable constancy, moves on through the varied tenour of perpetual decay, fall, renovation, and progression. Thus, by preserving the method of nature in the conduct of the state, in what we improve, we are never wholly new; in what we retain, we are never wholly obsolete. By adhering in this manner and on those principles to our forefathers, we are guided not by the superstition of antiquarians, but by the spirit of philosophic analogy. In this choice of inheritance we have given to our frame of polity the image of a relation in blood; binding up the constitution of our country with our dearest domestic ties; adopting our fundamental laws into the bosom of our family affections; keeping inseparable, and cherishing with the warmth of all their combined and mutually reflected charities, our state, our hearths, our sepulchres, and our altars.

Through the same plan of a conformity to nature in our artificial institutions, and by calling in the aid of her unerring and powerful instincts, to fortify the fallible and feeble contrivances of our reason, we have derived several other, and those no small benefits, from considering our liberties in the light of an inheritance. Always acting as if in the presence of canonized forefathers, the spirit of freedom, leading in itself to misrule and excess, is tempered with an awful gravity. This idea of a liberal descent inspires us with a sense of habitual native dignity, which prevents that upstart insolence almost inevitably adhering to and disgracing those who are the first acquirers of any distinction. By this means our liberty becomes a noble freedom. It carries an imposing and majestic aspect. It has a pedigree and illustrating ancestors. It has its bearings and its ensigns armorial. It has its gallery of portraits; its monumental inscriptions; its records, evidences, and titles. We procure reverence to our civil institutions on the principle upon which nature teaches us to revere individual men; on account of their age, and on account of those from whom they are descended. All your sophisters cannot produce any thing better adapted to preserve a rational and manly freedom than the course that we have pursued, who have chosen our nature rather than our speculations, our breasts rather than our inventions, for the great conservatories and magazines of our rights and privileges. . . .

Natural Rights and Real Rights

It is no wonder therefore, that with these ideas of every thing in their [the French Revolutionaries] constitution and government at home, either in church or state, as illegitimate and usurped, or, at best as a vain mockery, they look abroad with an eager and passionate enthusiasm. Whilst they are possessed by these notions, it is vain to talk to them of the practice of their ancestors, the fundamental laws of their country, the fixed form of a constitution, whose merits are confirmed by the solid test of long experience, and an encreasing public strength and national prosperity. They despise experience as the wisdom of unlettered men; and as for the rest, they have wrought under-ground a mine that will blow up, at one grand explosion, all examples of antiquity, all precedents, charters, and acts of parliament. They have "rights of men." Against these there can be no prescription [argument]; against these no argument is binding: these admit no temperament, and no compromise: any thing withheld from their full demand is so much of fraud and injustice. Against these their rights of men let no government look for security in the length of its continuance, or in the justice and lenity of its administration. The objections of these speculatists, if its forms do not quadrate with their theories, are as valid against such an old and beneficent government, as against the most violent tyranny, or the greenest usurpation. They are always at issue with governments, not on a question of abuse, but a question of competency, and a question of title. I have nothing to say to the clumsy subtilty of their political metaphysics. Let them be their amusement in the schools—"Illa *se jactat in aula—Eolus, et clauso ventorum carcere regnet.*"[1]—But let them not break prison to burst like a *Levanter,* to sweep the earth with their hurricane, and to break up the fountains of the great deep to overwhelm us.

Far am I from denying in theory, full as far is my heart from withholding in practice (if I were of power to give or to withhold) the *real* rights of men. In denying their false claims of right, I do not mean to injure those which are real, and are such as their pretended rights would totally destroy. If civil society be made for the advantage of man, all the advantages for which it is made become his right. It is an institution of beneficence; and law itself is only beneficence acting by a rule. Men have a right to live by that rule; they have a right to do justice; as between their fellows, whether their fellows are in politic function or in ordinary occupation. They have a right to the fruits of their industry; and to the means of making their industry fruitful. They have a right to the acquisitions of their parents; to the nourishment and improvement of their offspring; to instruction in life, and to consolation in death. Whatever each man can separately do, without trespassing upon others, he has a right to do for himself; and he has a right to a fair portion of all which society, with all its combinations of skill and force, can do in his favour. In this partnership all men have equal rights; but not to equal things. He that has but five shillings in the partnership, has as good a right to it, as he that has five hundred pounds has to his larger proportion. But he has not a right to an equal dividend in the product of the joint stock; and as to the share of power, authority, and direction which each individual ought to have in the management of the state, that I must deny to be amongst the direct original rights of man in civil society; for I have in my contemplation the civil social man, and no other. It is a thing to be settled by convention.

If civil society be the offspring of convention, that convention must be its law. That convention must limit and modify all the descriptions of constitution which are formed under it. Every sort of legislature, judicial, or executory power, are its creatures. They can have no being in any other state of things; and how can any man claim, under the conventions of civil society, rights which do not so much as suppose its existence? Rights which are absolutely repugnant to it? One of the first motives to civil society, and which becomes one of its fundamental rules, is, *that no man should be judge in his own cause.* By this each person has at once divested himself of the first fundamental right of uncovenanted man, that is, to judge for himself, and to assert his own cause. He abdicates all right to be his own governour. He inclusively, in a great measure abandons the right of self-defence, the first law of nature. Men cannot enjoy the rights of an uncivil and of a civil state together. That he may obtain justice, he gives up his right of determining, what it is in points the most essential to him. That he may secure some liberty, he makes a surrender in trust of the whole of it.

Government is not made in virtue of natural rights, which may and do exist in total independence of it; and exist in much greater clearness, and in a much greater degree of abstract perfection: but their abstract perfection is their practical defect. By having a right to every thing they want every thing. Government is a contrivance of human wisdom to provide for human *wants.* Men have a right that these wants should be provided for by this wisdom. Among these wants is to be reckoned the want, out of civil society, of a sufficient restraint upon their passions. Society requires not only that the passions of individuals should be subjected, but that even in the mass and body as well as in the individuals, the inclinations of men should frequently be thwarted, their will controlled, and their passions brought into subjection. This can only be done *by a power out of themselves;* and not, in the exercise of its function, subject to that will and to those passions which it is its office to bridle and subdue. In this sense the restraints on men, as well as their liberties, are to be reckoned among their rights. But as the liberties and the restrictions vary with times and circumstances, and admit of infinite modifications, they cannot be settled upon any abstract rule; and nothing is so foolish as to discuss them upon that principle.

The moment you abate any thing from the full rights of men, each to govern himself, and suffer any artificial, positive limitation upon those rights, from that moment the whole organization of government becomes a consideration of convenience. This it is which makes the constitution of a state, and the due distribution of its powers, a matter of the most delicate and complicated skill. It requires a deep knowledge of human nature and human necessities, and of the things which facilitate or obstruct the various ends, which are to be pursued by the mechanism of civil institutions. The state is to have recruits to its strength, and remedies to its distempers. What is the use of discussing a man's abstract right to food or medicine? The question is upon the method of procuring and administering them. In that deliberation I shall always advise to call in the aid of the farmer and the physician, rather than the professor of metaphysics.

The science of constructing a commonwealth, or renovating it, or reforming it, is, like every other experimental science, not to be taught *a priori.* Nor is it a short experience that can instruct us in that practical science; because the real effects of moral causes are not always immediate; but that which in the first instance is prejudicial may be excellent in its remoter operation; and its excellence may arise even from the ill effects it produces in the beginning. The reverse also happens; and very plausible schemes, with very pleasing commencements, have often shameful and lamentable conclusions. In states there are often some obscure and almost latent causes, things which appear at first view of little moment, on which a very great part of its prosperity or adversity may most essentially depend. The science of government being therefore so practical in itself, and intended for such practical purposes, a matter which requires experience, and even more experience than any person can gain in his whole life, however sagacious and observing he may be, it is with infinite caution that any man ought to venture upon pulling down an edifice, which has answered in any tolerable degree for ages the common purposes of society, or on building it up again, without having models and patterns of approved utility before his eyes.

These metaphysic rights entering into common life, like rays of light which pierce into a dense medium, are, by the laws of nature, refracted from their straight line. Indeed in the gross and complicated mass of human passions and concerns, the primitive rights of men undergo such a variety of refractions and reflections, that it becomes absurd to talk of them as if they continued in the simplicity of their original direction. The nature of man is intricate; the objects of society are of the greatest possible complexity: and therefore no simple disposition or direction of power can be suitable either to man's nature, or to the quality of his affairs. When I hear the simplicity of contrivance aimed at and boasted of in any new political constitutions, I am at no loss to decide that the artificers are grossly ignorant of their trade, or totally negligent of their duty. The simple governments are fundamentally defective, to say no worse of them. If you were to contemplate society in but one point of view, all these simple modes of polity are infinitely captivating. In effect each would answer its single end much more perfectly than the more complex is able to attain all its complex purposes. But it is better that the whole should be imperfectly and anomalously answered, than that, while some parts are provided for with great exactness, others might be totally neglected, or perhaps materially injured, by the over-care of a favorite member.

The pretended rights of these theorists are all extremes: and in proportion as they are metaphysically true, they are morally and politically false. The rights of men are in a sort of *middle,* incapable of definition, but not impossible to be discerned. The rights of men in governments are their advantages; and these are often in balances between differences of good; in compromises sometimes between good and evil, and sometimes between evil and evil. Political reason is a computing principle; adding, subtracting, multiplying, and dividing, morally and not metaphysically or mathematically, true moral denominations.

By these theorists the right of the people is almost always sophistically confounded with their power. The body of the community, whenever it can come to act, can meet with no effectual resistance; but till power and right are the same, the whole body of them has no right inconsistent with virtue, and the first of all virtues, prudence. Men have no right to what is not reasonable, and to what is not for their benefit. . . .

The kind of anniversary sermons to which a great part of what I write refers, if men are not shamed out of their present course, in commemorating the fact, will cheat many out of the principles, and deprive them of the benefits of the revolution they commemorate. I confess to you, Sir, I never liked this continual talk of resistance, and revolution, or the practice of making the extreme medicine of the constitution its daily bread. It renders the habit of society dangerously valetudinary: it is taking periodical doses of mercury sublimate, and swallowing down repeated provocatives of cantharides [toxic if used as an aphrodisiac] to our love of liberty.

The Moral Imagination

When ancient opinions and rules of life are taken away, the loss cannot possibly be estimated. From that moment we have no compass to govern us; nor can we know distinctly to what port we steer. Europe, undoubtedly, taken in a mass, was in a flourishing condition the day on which [the French Revolution] was completed. How much of that prosperous state was owing to the spirit of our old manners and opinions is not easy to say; but as such causes cannot be indifferent in their operation, we must presume, that, on the whole, their operation was beneficial.

We are but too apt to consider things in the state in which we find them, without sufficiently adverting to the causes by which they have been produced, and

possibly may be upheld. Nothing is more certain, than that our manners, our civilization, and all the good things which are connected with manners, and with civilization, have, in this European world of ours, depended for ages upon two principles; and were indeed the result of both combined; I mean the spirit of a gentleman, and the spirit of religion. The nobility and the clergy, the one by profession, the other by patronage, kept learning in existence, even in the midst of arms and confusions, and whilst governments were rather in their causes, than formed. Learning paid back what it received to nobility and to priesthood; and paid it with usury, by enlarging their ideas, and by furnishing their minds. Happy if they had all continued to know their indissoluble union, and their proper place! Happy if learning, not debauched by ambition, had been satisfied to continue the instructor, and not aspired to be the master! Along with its natural protectors and guardians, learning will be cast into the mire; and trodden down under the hoofs of a swinish multitude.

If, as I suspect, modern letters owe more than they are always willing to own to ancient manners, so do other interests which we value full as much as they are worth. Even commerce, and trade, and manufacture, the gods of our economical politicians, are themselves perhaps but creatures; are themselves but effects, which, as first causes, we choose to worship. They certainly grew under the same shade in which learning flourished. They too may decay with their natural protecting principles. With you, for the present at least, they all threaten to disappear together. Where trade and manufactures are wanting to a people, and the spirit of nobility and religion remains, sentiment supplies, and not always ill supplies, their place; but if commerce and the arts should be lost in an experiment to try how well a state may stand without these old fundamental principles, what sort of a thing must be a nation of gross, stupid, ferocious, and, at the same time, poor and sordid barbarians, destitute of religion, honour, or manly pride, possessing nothing at present, and hoping for nothing hereafter?

THE PEOPLE AND THE NATURAL ARISTOCRACY

When the supreme authority of the people is in question, before we attempt to extend or to confine it, we ought to fix in our minds, with some degree of distinctness, an idea of what it is we mean, when we say the PEOPLE.

In a state of *rude* nature there is no such thing as a people. A number of men in themselves have no collective capacity. The idea of a people is the idea of a corporation. It is wholly artificial; and made like all other legal fictions by common agreement. What the particular nature of that agreement was, is collected from the form into which the particular society has been cast. Any other is not *their* covenant. When men, therefore, break up the original compact or agreement which gives its corporate form and capacity to a state, they are no longer a people; they have no longer a corporate existence; they have no longer a legal, coactive force to bind within, nor a claim to be recognised abroad. They are a number of vague, loose individuals, and nothing more. With them all is to begin again. Alas! they little know how many a weary step is to be taken before they can form themselves into a mass, which has a true, politic personality.

We hear much from men, who have not acquired their hardiness of assertion from the profundity of their thinking, about the omnipotence of a *majority,* in such a dissolution of an ancient society as hath been taken place in France. But amongst men so disbanded, there can be no such thing as majority or minority; or power in any one person to bind another. The power of acting by a majority, which the gentlemen theorists seem to assume so readily, after they have violated the contract out of which it has arisen, (if at all it existed) must be grounded on two assumptions; first, that of an incorporation produced by unanimity; and secondly, an unanimous agreement, that the act of a mere majority (say of one) shall pass with them and with others as the act of the whole.

We are so little affected by things which are habitual, that we consider this idea of the decision of a *majority* as if it were a law of our original nature: but such constructive whole, residing in a part only, is one of the most violent fictions of positive law, that ever has been or can be made on the principles of artificial incorporation. Out of civil society nature knows nothing of it; nor are men, even when arranged according to civil order, otherwise than by very long training, brought at all to submit to it. The mind is brought far more easily to acquiesce in the proceedings of one man, or a few, who act under a general procuration for the state, than in the vote of a victorious majority in councils, in which every man has his share in the deliberation. For there the beaten party are exasperated and soured by the previous contention, and mortified by the conclusive defeat. This mode of decision, where wills may be so nearly equal, where, according to circumstances, the smaller number may be the stronger force, and where apparent reason may be all upon one side, and on the other little else than impetuous appetite; all this must be the result of a very particular and special convention, confirmed afterwards by long habits of obedience, by a sort of discipline in society, and by a strong hand, vested with stationary, permanent power, to enforce this sort of constructive general will. What organ it is that shall declare the corporate mind is so much a matter of positive arrangement, that several states, for the validity of several of their acts, have required a proportion of voices much greater than that of a mere majority. These proportions are so entirely governed by convention, that in some cases the minority decides. The laws in many countries to *condemn* require more than a mere majority; less than an equal number to *acquit.* In our judicial trials we require unanimity either to condemn or to absolve. In some incorporations one man speaks for the whole; in others, a few. Until the other day, in the constitution of Poland, unanimity was required to give validity to any act of their great national council or diet. This approaches much more nearly to rude nature than the institutions of any other country. Such, indeed, every commonwealth must be, without a positive law to recognise in a certain number the will of the entire body.

If men dissolve their ancient incorporation, in order to regenerate their community, in that state of things each man has a right, if he pleases, to remain an individual. Any number of individuals, who can agree upon it, have an undoubted right to form themselves into a state apart, and wholly independent. If any of these is forced into the fellowship of another, this is conquest and not compact. On every principle, which supposes society to be in virtue of a free covenant, this compulsive incorporation must be null and void.

As a people can have no right to a corporate capacity without universal consent, so neither have they a right to hold exclusively any lands in the name and title of a corporation. On the scheme of the present rulers in our neighbouring country, regenerated as they are, they have no more right to the territory called France than I have. I have a right to pitch my tent in any unoccupied place I can find for it; and I may apply to my own maintenance any part of their unoccupied soil. I may purchase the house or vineyard of any individual proprietor who refuses his consent (and most proprietors have, as far as they dared, refused it) to the new incorporation. I stand in his independent place. Who are these insolent men calling themselves the French nation, that would monopolize this fair domain of nature? Is it because they speak a certain jargon? Is it their mode of chattering, to me unintelligible, that forms their title to my land? Who are they who claim by prescription and descent from certain gangs of banditti called Franks, and Burgundians, and Visigoths, of whom I may have never heard, and ninety-nine out of an hundred of themselves certainly never have heard; whilst at the very time they tell me, that prescription and long possession form no title to property? Who are they that presume to assert that the land which I purchased of the individual, a natural person, and not a fiction of state, belongs to them who in the very capacity in which they make their claim can exist only as an imaginary being, and in virtue of the very prescription which they reject and disown? This mode of arguing might be pushed into all the detail, so as to leave no sort of doubt, that on their principles, and on the sort of footing on which they have thought proper to place themselves, the crowd of men, on the one side of the channel, who have the impudence to call themselves a people, can never be the lawful, exclusive possessors of the soil. By what they call reasoning without prejudice, they leave not one stone upon another in the fabric of human society. They subvert all the authority which they hold, as well as all that which they have destroyed.

As in the abstract, it is perfectly clear, that, out of a state of civil society, majority and minority are relations which can have no existence; and that, in civil society, its own specific conventions in each corporation determine what it is that constitutes the people, so as to make their act the signification of the general will: to come to particulars, it is equally clear, that neither in France nor in England has the original, or any subsequent compact of the state, expressed or implied, constituted *a majority of men, told by the head,* to be the acting people of their several communities. And I see as little of policy or utility, as there is of right, in laying down a principle that a majority of men told by the head are to be considered as the people, and that as such their will is to be law. What policy can there be found in arrangements made in defiance of every political principle? To enable men to act with the weight and character of a people, and to answer the ends for which they are incorporated into that capacity, we must suppose them (by means immediate or consequential) to be in that state of habitual social discipline, in which the wiser, the more expert, and the more opulent conduct, and by conducting enlighten and protect the weaker, the less knowing, and the less provided with the goods of fortune. When the multitude are not under this discipline, they can scarcely be said to be in civil society. Give once a certain constitution of things, which produces a variety of conditions and circumstances in a state, and there is in nature and reason a

principle which, for their own benefit, post-pones, not the interest but the judgment, of those who are *numero plures,* to those who are *virtute et honore majores.*[2] Numbers in a state (supposing, which is not the case in France, that a state does exist) are always of consideration—but they are not the whole consideration. It is in things more serious than a play, that it may be truly said *satis est equitatem mihi plaudere.*[3]

A true natural aristocracy is not a separate interest in the state, or separable from it. It is an essential integrant part of any large body rightly constituted. It is formed out of a class of legitimate presumptions, which, taken as generalities, must be admitted for actual truths. To be bred in a place of estimation; to see nothing low and sordid from one's infancy; to be taught to respect one's self; to be habituated to the censorial inspection of the public eye; to look early to public opinion; to stand upon such elevated ground as to be enabled to take a large view of the widespread and infinitely diversified combinations of men and affairs in a large society; to have leisure to read, to reflect, to converse; to be enabled to draw the court and attention of the wise and learned wherever they are to be found;—to be habituated in armies to command and to obey; to be taught to despise danger in the pursuit of honour and duty; to be formed to the greatest degree of vigilance, foresight, and circumspection, in a state of things in which no fault is committed with impunity, and the slightest mistakes draw on the most ruinous consequences—to be led to a guarded and regulated conduct, from a sense that you are considered as an instructor of your fellow-citizens in their highest concerns, and that you act as a reconciler between God and man—to be employed as an administrator of law and justice, and to be thereby amongst the first benefactors to mankind—to be a professor of high science, or of liberal and ingenuous art—to be amongst rich traders, who from their success are presumed to have sharp and vigorous understandings, and to possess the virtues of diligence, order, constancy, and regularity, and to have cultivated an habitual regard to commutative justice—these are the circumstances of men, that form what I should call a *natural* aristocracy, without which there is no nation.

The state of civil society, which necessarily generates this aristocracy, is a state of nature; and much more truly so than a savage and incoherent mode of life. For man is by nature reasonable; and he is never perfectly in his natural state, but when he is placed where reason may be best cultivated, and most predominates. Art is man's nature. We are as much, at least, in a state of nature in formed manhood, as in the immature and helpless infancy. Men, qualified in the manner I have just described, form in nature, as she operates in the common modification of society, the leading, guiding, and governing part. It is the soul to the body, without which the man does not exist. To give therefore no more importance, in the social order, to such descriptions of men, than that of so many units, is a horrible usurpation.

When great multitudes act together, under that discipline of nature, I recognise the PEOPLE. I acknowledge something that perhaps equals, and ought always to guide the sovereignty of convention. In all things the voice of this grand chorus of national harmony ought to have a mighty and decisive influence. But when you disturb this harmony; when you break up this beautiful order, this array of truth and nature, as well as of habit and prejudice; when you separate the common sort of men from their proper chieftains so as to form them into an adverse army, I no longer know that venerable object called the people in such a disbanded race of deserters and vagabonds. For a while they may be terrible indeed; but in such a manner as wild beasts are terrible. The mind owes to them no sort of submission. They are, as they have always been reputed, rebels. They may lawfully be fought with, and brought under, whenever an advantage offers. Those who attempt by outrage and violence to deprive men of any advantage which they hold under the laws, and to destroy the natural order of life, proclaim war against them.

READING 7

A Vindication of the Rights of Women

Mary Wollstonecraft

Mary Wollstonecraft (1759–97), political writer and novelist, was an outspoken advocate for the rights of women. Brought up in an abusive home, she found loving support in her relationship with the English philosopher William Godwin, whom she married. She had two children; the second was a daughter named Mary who married the poet Percy Bysshe Shelley and wrote *Frankenstein*. Wollstonecraft wrote *A Vindication of the Rights of Men* (1790) in support of the French Revolution and in opposition to Burke's critique of it (see Reading 6). Her most famous work is *A Vindication of the Rights of Women* (1792).

Wollstonecraft deplored the sycophantic deference women paid to men, and, while conceding the superior physical prowess of men, called on society to restructure the educational system to allow women to develop their rational capacities, which constitute the most salient feature of our common humanity. She opposed the ideas of Rousseau that boys and girls should have separate educations, purporting that, on the contrary, our common humanity calls for a common intellectual education. In her view, the so-called unique *feminine virtues*, docility and delicacy of sentiment, are really vices that allow women to be treated as inferior beings.

This reading is taken from *A Vindication of the Rights of Women* (1792).

INTRODUCTION

After considering the historic page, and viewing the living world with anxious solicitude, the most melancholy emotions of sorrowful indignation have depressed my spirits, and I have sighed when obliged to confess, that either nature has made a great difference between man and man, or that the civilization which has hitherto taken place in the world has been very partial. I have turned over various books written on the subject of education, and patiently observed the conduct of parents and the management of schools; but what has been the result?—a profound conviction that the neglected education of my fellow creatures is the grand source of the misery I deplore; and that women, in particular, are rendered weak and wretched by a variety of concurring causes, originating from one hasty conclusion. The conduct and manners of women, in fact, evidently prove that their minds are not in a healthy state; for, like the flowers which are planted in too rich a soil, strength and usefulness are sacrificed to beauty; and the flaunting leaves, after having pleased a fastidious eye, fade, disregarded on the stalk, long before the season when they ought to have arrived at maturity,—One cause of this barren blooming I attribute to a false system of education, gathered from the books written on this subject by men who, considering females rather as women than human creatures, have been more anxious to make them alluring mistresses than affectionate wives and rational mothers; and the understanding of the sex has been so bubbled by this specious homage, that the civilized women of the present century, with a few exceptions, are only anxious to inspire love, when they ought to cherish a nobler ambition, and by their abilities and virtues exact respect.

In a treatise, therefore, on female rights and manners, the works which have been particularly written for their improvement must not be overlooked; especially when it is asserted, in direct terms, that the minds of women are enfeebled by false refinement; that the books of instruction, written by men of genius, have had the same tendency as more frivolous productions; and that, in the true style of Mahometanism, they are treated as a kind of subordinate beings, and not as a part of the human species, when improveable reason is allowed to be the dignified distinction which raises men above the brute creation, and puts a natural sceptre in a feeble hand.

Yet, because I am a woman, I would not lead my readers to suppose that I mean violently to agitate the contested question respecting the equality or inferiority of the sex; but as the subject lies in my way, and I cannot pass it over without subjecting the main tendency of my reasoning to misconstruction, I shall stop a moment to deliver, in a few words, my opinion.—In the government of the physical world it is observable that the female in point of strength is, in general, inferior to the male. This is the law of nature; and it does not appear to be suspended or abrogated in favour of woman. A degree of physical superiority cannot, therefore, be denied—and it is a noble prerogative! But not content with this natural pre-eminence, men endeavour to sink us still lower, merely to render us alluring objects for a moment; and women, intoxicated by the adoration which men, under the influence of their senses, pay them, do not seek to obtain a durable interest in their hearts, or to become the friends of the fellow creatures who find amusement in their society.

I am aware of an obvious inference—from every quarter have I heard exclamations against masculine women; but where are they to be found? If by this appellation men mean to inveigh against their ardour in hunting, shooting, and gaming, I shall most cordially join in the cry; but if it be against the imitation of manly virtues, or, more properly speaking, the attainment of those talents and virtues, the exercise of which ennobles the human character, and which raise females

in the scale of animal being, when they are comprehensively termed mankind;—all those who view them with a philosophic eye must, I should think, wish with me, that they may every day grow more and more masculine.

This discussion naturally divides the subject. I shall first consider women in the grand light of human creatures, who, in common with men, are placed on this earth to unfold their faculties; and afterwards I shall more particularly point out their peculiar designation.

I wish also to steer clear of an error which many respectable writers have fallen into; for the instruction which has hitherto been addressed to women, has rather been applicable to *ladies,* if the little indirect advice, that is scattered through Sandford and Merton, be excepted; but, addressing my sex in a firmer tone, I pay particular attention to those in the middle class, because they appear to be in the most natural state. Perhaps the seeds of false-refinement, immorality, and vanity, have ever been shed by the great. Weak, artificial beings, raised above the common wants and affections of their race, in a premature unnatural manner, undermine the very foundation of virtue, and spread corruption through the whole mass of society! As a class of mankind they have the strongest claim to pity; the education of the rich tends to render them vain and helpless, and the unfolding mind is not strengthened by the practice of those duties which dignify the human character.—They only live to amuse themselves, and by the same law which in nature invariably produces certain effects, they soon only afford barren amusement.

But as I propose taking a separate view of the different ranks of society, and of the moral character of women, in each, this hint is, for the present, sufficient; and I have only alluded to the subject, because it appears to me to be the very essence of an introduction to give a cursory account of the contents of the work it introduces.

My own sex, I hope, will excuse me, if I treat him like rational creatures, instead of flattering their *fascinating* graces, and viewing them as if they were in a state of perpetual childhood, unable to stand alone. I earnestly wish to point out in what true dignity and human happiness consists—I wish to persuade women to endeavour to acquire strength, both of mind and body, and to convince them that the soft phrases, susceptibility of heart, delicacy of sentiment, and refinement of taste, are almost synonymous with epithets of weakness, and that those beings who are only the objects of pity and that kind of love, which has been termed its sister, will soon become objects of contempt.

Dismissing then those pretty feminine phrases, which the men condescendingly use to soften our slavish dependence, and despising that weak elegancy of mind, exquisite sensibility, and sweet docility of manners, supposed to be the sexual characteristics of the weaker vessel, I wish to shew that elegance is inferior to virtue, that the first object of laudable ambition is to obtain a character as a human being, regardless of the distinction of sex; and that secondary views should be brought to this simple touchstone.

This is a rough sketch of my plan; and should I express my conviction with the energetic emotions that I feel whenever I think of the subject, the dictates of experience and reflection will be felt by some of my readers. Animated by this important object, I shall disdain to cull my phrases or polish my style;—I aim at being useful, and sincerity will render me unaffected; for, wishing rather to persuade by the force of my arguments, than dazzle by the elegance of my language, I shall not waste my time in rounding periods, or in fabricating the turgid bombast of artificial feelings, which, coming from the head, never reach the heart.—I shall be employed about things, not words!—and, anxious to render my sex more respectable members of society, I shall try to avoid that flowery diction which has slided from essays into novels, and from novels into familiar letters and conservation.

These pretty superlatives, dropping glibly from the tongue, vitiate the taste, and create a kind of sickly delicacy that turns away from simple unadorned truth; and a deluge of false sentiments and overstretched feelings, stifling the natural emotions of the heart, render the domestic pleasures insipid, that ought to sweeten the exercise of those severe duties, which educate a rational and immortal being for a nobler field of action.

The education of women has, of late, been more attended to than formerly; yet they are still reckoned a frivolous sex, and ridiculed or pitied by the writers who endeavour by satire or instruction to improve them. It is acknowledged that they spend many of the first years of their lives in acquiring a smattering of accomplishments; meanwhile strength of body and mind are sacrificed to libertine notions of beauty, to the desire of establishing themselves—the only way women can rise in the world—by marriage. And this desire making mere animals of them, when they marry they act as such children may be expected to act:— they dress; they paint, and nickname God's creatures.—Surely these weak beings are only fit for a seraglio!—Can they be expected to govern a family with judgment, or take care of the poor babes whom they bring into the world?

If then it can be fairly deduced from the present conduct of the sex, from the prevalent fondness for pleasure which takes [the] place of ambition and those nobler passions that open and enlarge the soul; that the instruction which women have hitherto received has only tended, with the constitution of civil society, to render them insignificant objects of desire—mere propagators of fools!—if it can be proved that in aiming to accomplish them, without cultivating their understandings, they are taken out of their sphere of duties, and made ridiculous and useless when the short-lived bloom of beauty is over, I presume that *rational* men will excuse me for endeavouring to persuade them to become more masculine and respectable.

Indeed the word masculine is only a bugbear: there is little reason to fear that women will acquire too much courage or fortitude; for their apparent inferiority with respect to bodily strength, must render them, in some degree, dependent on men in the various relations of life; but why should it be increased by prejudices that give a sex to virtue, and confound simple truths with sensual reveries?

Women are, in fact, so much degraded by mistaken notions of female excellence, that I do not mean to add a paradox when I assert, that this artificial weakness produces a propensity to tyrannize, and give birth to cunning, the natural opponent of strength, which leads them to play off those contemptible infantine airs that undermine esteem even whilst they excite desire. Let men become more chaste and modest, and if women do not grow wiser in the same ratio, it will be clear that they have weaker understandings. It seems scarcely necessary to say, that I now speak of the sex in general. Many individuals have more sense than their male relatives; and, as nothing preponderates where there is a constant struggle for an equilibrium, without it has naturally more gravity, some women govern their husbands without degrading themselves, because intellect will always govern.

OBSERVATIONS ON THE STATE OF DEGRADATION TO WHICH WOMAN IS REDUCED BY VARIOUS CAUSES

That woman is naturally weak, or degraded by a concurrence of circumstances, is, I think, clear. But this position I shall simply contrast with a conclusion, which I have frequently heard fall from sensible men in favour of an aristocracy: that the mass of mankind cannot be anythings, or the obsequious slaves, who patiently allow themselves to be driven forward, would feel their own consequence, and spurn their chains. Men, they further observe, submit every where to oppression, when they have only to lift up their heads to throw off the yoke; yet, instead of asserting their birthright, they quietly lick the dust, and say, let us eat and drink, for to-morrow we die. Women, I argue from analogy, are degraded by the same propensity to enjoy the present moment; and, at last, despise the freedom which they have not sufficient virtue to struggle to attain. But I must be more explicit. . . .

The stamen of immortality, if I may be allowed the phrase, is the perfectibility of human reason; for, were man created perfect, or did a flood of knowledge break in upon him, when he arrived at maturity, the precluded error, I should doubt whether his existence would be continued after the dissolution of the body. But, in the present state of things, every difficulty in morals that escapes from human discussion, and equally baffles the investigation of profound thinking, and the lightning glance of genius, is an argument on which I build my belief of the immortality of the soul. Reason is, consequentially, the simple power of improvement; or, more properly speaking, of discerning truth. Every individual is in this respect a world in itself. More or less may be conspicuous in one being than another; but the nature of reason must be the same in all, if it be an emanation of divinity, the tie that connects the creature with the Creator; for, can that soul be stamped with heavenly image, that is not perfected by the exercise of its own reason? Yet outwardly ornamented with elaborate care, and so adorned to delight man, "that with honour he may love," the soul of woman is not allowed to have this distinction, and man, ever placed between her and reason, she is always represented as only created to see through a gross medium, and to take things on trust. But dismissing these fanciful theories, and considering woman as a whole, let it be what it will, instead of a part of man, the inquiry is whether she have reason or not. If she have, which, for a moment, I will take for granted, she was not created merely to be the solace of man, and the sexual should not destroy the human character.

Into this error men have, probably, been led by viewing education in a false light; not considering it as the first step to form a being advancing gradually towards perfection; but only as a preparation for life. . . .

The power of generalizing ideas, of drawing comprehensive conclusions from individual observations, is the only acquirement, for an immortal being, that really deserves the name of knowledge. Merely to observe, without endeavouring to account for any thing, may (in a very incomplete manner) serve as the common sense of life; but where is the store laid up that is to clothe the soul when it leaves the body?

This power has not only been denied to women; but writers have insisted that it is inconsistent, with a few exceptions, with their sexual character. Let men prove this, and I shall grant that woman only exists for man. I must, however, previously remark, that the power of generalizing ideas, to any great extent, is not very common amongst men or women. But this exercise is the true cultivation of the understanding; and every thing conspires to render the cultivation of the understanding more difficult in the female than the male world. . . .

Necessity has been proverbially termed the mother of invention—the aphorism may be extended to virtue. It is an acquirement, and an acquirement to which pleasure must be sacrificed—and who sacrifices pleasure when it is within the grasp, whose mind has not been opened and strengthened by adversity, or the pursuit of knowledge goaded on by necessity?—Happy is it when people have the cares of life to struggle with; for these struggles prevent their becoming a prey to enervating vices, merely from idleness! But, if from their birth men and women be placed in a torrid zone, with the meridian sun of pleasure darting directly upon them, how can they sufficiently brace their minds to discharge the duties of life, or even to relish the affections that carry them out of themselves?

Pleasure is the business of woman's life, according to the present modification of society, and while it continues to be so, little can be expected from such weak beings. Inheriting, in a lineal descent from the first fair defect in nature, the sovereignty of beauty, they have, to maintain their power, resigned the natural rights, which the exercise of reason might have procured them, and chosen rather to be short-lived queens than labour to obtain the sober pleasures that arise from equality. . . .

Lewis the XIVth, in particular, spread factitious manners, and caught, in a specious way, the whole nation in his toils; for, establishing an artful chain of despotism, he made it the interest of the people at large, individually to respect his station and support his power. And women, whom he flattered by a puerile attention to the whole sex, obtained in his reign that prince-like distinction so fatal to reason and virtue.

A king is always a king—and a woman always a woman: his authority and her sex, ever stand between them and rational converse. . . . [I]f, excepting warriors, no great men, of any denomination, have ever appeared amongst the nobility, may it not be fairly inferred that their local situation swallowed up the man, and produced a character similar to that of women, who are *localized,* if I may be allowed the word, by the rank they are placed in, by *courtesy?* Women, commonly called Ladies, are not to be contradicted in company, are not allowed to exert any manual strength; and from them the negative virtues only are expected, when any virtues are expected, patience, docility, good-humour, and flexibility; virtues incompatible with any vigorous exertion of intellect. Besides, by living more with each other, and being seldom absolutely alone, they are more under the influence of sentiments than passions. Solitude and reflection are necessary to give to wishes the force of passions, and to enable the imagination to enlarge the object, and make it the most desirable. The same may be said of the rich; they do not sufficiently deal in general ideas, collected by impassioned thinking, or calm investigation, to acquire that strength of character on which great resolves are built. . . .

In the middle rank of life, to continue the comparison, men, in their youth, are prepared for professions, and marriage is not considered as the grand feature in their lives; whilst women, on the contrary, have no other scheme to sharpen their faculties. It is not business, extensive plans, or any of the excursive flights of ambition, that engross their attention; no, their thoughts are not employed in rearing such noble structures. To rise in the world, and have the liberty of running from pleasure to pleasure, they must marry advantageously, and to this object their time is sacrificed, and their persons often legally prostituted. A man when he enters any profession has his eye steadily fixed on some future advantage (and the mind gains great strength by having all its efforts directed to one point), and, full of his business, pleasure is considered as mere relaxation; whilst women seek for pleasure as the main purpose of existence. In fact, from the education, which they receive from society, the love of pleasure may be said to govern them all; but does this prove that there is a sex in souls? It would be just as rational to declare that the courtiers in France, when a destructive system of despotism had formed their character, were not men, because liberty, virtue, and humanity, were sacrificed to pleasure and vanity.—Fatal passions, which have ever domineered over the *whole* race!

The same love of pleasure, fostered by the whole tendency of their education, gives a trifling turn to the conduct of women in most circumstances. . . .

In short, women, in general, as well as the rich of both sexes, have acquired all the follies and vices of civilization, and missed the useful fruit. It is not necessary for me always to premise, that I speak of the condition of the whole sex, leaving exceptions out of the question. Their senses are inflamed, and their understandings neglected, consequently they become the prey of their senses, delicately termed sensibility, and are blown about by every momentary gust of feeling. Civilized women are, therefore, so weakened by false refinement, that, respecting morals, their condition is much below what it would be were they left in a state nearer to nature. . . . Riches and honours prevent a man from enlarging his understanding, and enervate all his powers by reversing the order of nature, which has ever made true pleasure the reward of labour. Pleasure—enervating pleasure is, likewise, within women's reach without earning it. . . .

Let an enlightened nation[1] then try what effect reason would have to bring them back to nature, and their duty; and allowing them to share the advantages of education and government with man, see whether they will become better, as they grow wiser and become free. They cannot be injured by the experiment; for it is not in the power of man to render them more insignificant than they are at present.

To render this practicable, day schools, for particular ages, should be established by government, in which boys and girls might be educated together. The school for the younger children, from five to nine years of age, ought to be absolutely free and open to all classes.[2] A sufficient number of masters should also be chosen by a select committee, in each parish, to whom any complaint of negligence, &c. might be made, if signed by six of the children's parents.

Ushers would then be unnecessary; for I believe experience will ever prove that this kind of subordinate authority is particularly injurious to the morals of youth. What, indeed, can tend to deprave the character more than outward submission and inward contempt? Yet how can boys be expected to treat an usher with respect, when the master seems to consider him in the light of a servant, almost to countenance the ridicule which becomes the chief amusement of the boys during the play hours?

But nothing of this kind could occur in an elementary day-school, where boys and girls, the rich and poor, should meet together. And to prevent any of the distinctions of vanity, they should be dressed alike, and all obliged to submit to the same discipline, or leave the school. The school-room ought to be surrounded by a large piece of ground, in which the children might be usefully exercised, for at this age they should not be confined to any sedentary employment for more than an hour at a time. But these relaxations might all be rendered a part of elementary education, for many things improve and amuse the senses, when introduced as a kind of show, to the principles of which, dryly laid down, children would turn a deaf ear. For instance, botany, mechanics, and astronomy. Reading, writing, arithmetic, natural history, and some simple experiments in natural philosophy, might fill up the day; but these pursuits should never encroach on gymnastic plays in the open air. The elements of religion, history, the history of man, and politics, might also be taught by conversations, in the socratic form.

After the age of nine, girls and boys, intended for domestic employments, or mechanical trades, ought to be removed to other schools, and receive instruction, in some measure appropriated to the destination of each individual, the two sexes being still together in the morning; but in the afternoon, the girls should attend a school, where plain-work, mantua-making, millinery, &c. would be their employment.

The young people of superior abilities, or fortune, might now be taught, in another school, the dead and living languages, the elements of science, and continue the study of history and politics, on a more extensive scale, which would not exclude polite literature.

Girls and boys still together? I hear some readers ask: yes. And I should not fear any other consequence than that some early attachment might take place: which, whilst it had the best effect on the moral character of the young people, might not perfectly agree with the views of the parents, for it will be a long time, I fear, before the world will be so far enlightened that parents, only anxious to render their children virtuous, shall allow them to choose companions for life themselves.

Besides, this would be a sure way to promote early marriages, and from early marriages the most salutary physical and moral effects naturally flow. What a different character does a married citizen assume from the selfish coxcomb, who lives, but for himself, and who is often afraid to marry lest he should not be able to live in a certain style. Great emergencies excepted, which would rarely occur in a society of which equality was the basis, a man can only be prepared to discharge the duties of public life, by the habitual practice of those inferiour ones which form the man.

In this plan of education the constitution of boys would not be ruined by the early debaucheries, which now make men so selfish, or girls rendered weak and vain, by indolence, and frivolous pursuits. But, I presuppose, that such a degree of equality should be established between the sexes as would shut out gallantry and coquetry, yet allow friendship and love to temper the heart for the discharge of higher duties.

These would be schools of morality—and the happiness of man, allowed to flow from the pure springs of duty and affection, what advances might not the human mind make? Society can only be happy and free in proportion as it is virtuous; but the present distinctions, established in society, corrode all private, and blast all public virtue.

READING 8

The Communist Manifesto

Karl Marx and Friedrich Engels

Friedrich Engels (1820 – 95) was born the son of a German industrialist who moved to Manchester, England. He had considerable experience of the workings of British industry during the Industrial Revolution and was able to provide Marx with a firsthand insight of industrial realities. Harold Laski described the co-founder of the Marxist movement as

> always friendly, usually optimistic, with great gifts both for practical action and for getting on with others. . . . Widely read, with a very real talent for moving rapidly through a great mass of material, Engels was facile rather than profound. He was utterly devoid of jealousy or vanity. He had a happy nature which never agonized over the difficulty of thought. . . . It never occurred to him, during the friendship of forty years, marked only by one brief misunderstanding, to question his duty to serve Marx in every way he could.[1]

Karl Marx (1818–83) was born in Trier, Germany, and was educated in

Catholic schools and at the University of Berlin, where he received his doctorate. He began his career in 1842 as a journalist for the liberal *Rheinische Zeitung* and soon distinguished himself as a brilliant and radical thinker. In 1843 he married Jenny Westphalen, the close friend of his boyhood. Later that year, he and Jenny moved to Paris, where he studied French communism and met Engels, who became his lifelong friend and benefactor. Being exiled from Paris, he eventually found political asylum in London, where he spent the rest of his life in research and writing and in organizing the First International Workingmen's Association. He was described by a contemporary as follows: "He combines the deepest philosophical seriousness with the most biting wit. Imagine Rousseau, Voltaire, Holbach, Lessing, Heine, and Hegel fused into one person—I say fused, not juxtaposed— and you have Dr. Marx."[2] His principal works are *Economic and Philosophical Manuscripts of 1844, The Communist Manifesto* (with Friedrich Engels, 1848), and *Capital,* 3 volumes (1867, 1885, 1895).

As a young man, Marx wrote, "Hitherto, the various philosophies have only interpreted the world in various ways; the point is to change it." The message of our selection from *the Communist Manifesto* embodies that thesis. It combines socioeconomic analysis of the class struggle with a plan of action for overthrowing the existing oppressive government. It argues that the struggle between classes is the essential catalyst of historical change; in earlier times, the structure of society was a complicated arrangement of hierarchical classes, but in the present period of the bourgeoisie, the social structure is developing toward a simple division of two classes: the bourgeoisie, owners of the means of production and ruling class, and the proletariat, the worker-slaves. The proletariat are fast becoming self-conscious of their exploited state, and an international drama is unfolding in which they will create a violent revolution, throwing off their chains and, as new

dictators, instantiate a new era of justice, a classless society in which everyone freely and equally participates, "in which the free development of each is the condition for the free development of all."

The attraction of Marxism is that it appeals to a set of simple theses and gives low-paid workers, the proletariat, a feeling of hope and power, a sense that history is ineluctably on their side in the fight for justice. Perhaps the best way of understanding Marxism is to examine the basic ideas. Here is a summary of two elements of Marx's theses.

1. *Determinism.* Socialism is inevitable. Necessary economic laws will lead inevitably to communistic economic laws, which in turn determine history. Economic determination causes a dialectical process in which internal contradictions lead to self-destruction of each stage of social history and the creation of a new economic stage—until the end of history in creation of the communist state. This is a *one-directional* and *totally materialistic* order. The causal process is entirely from the economic foundations to the cultural superstructure (the walls and floors of the social edifice). Religion, law, morality, and cultural artifacts are completely determined by the economic, materialist base, but they have no effect on the materialist order. Law and morality are totally relativistic; their validity is limited to the culture itself; and they are the creation of the dominant class. In a capitalist society, morality and laws are the creation of the bourgeoisie and reflect their interests. Depending on the economic base and ruling class, the content of morality changes; so what is moral in one society may well be immoral in another where the material conditions are different. Some Marxists hold that in the final communist state, where class interest is abolished, an absolute morality will arise.

    The determinism thesis has the virtue of appearing to make the goal of communism as inevitable as the physical laws of nature. Its liability is that the same logic would seem to entail that we do not have free will and that we are pawns in history's dialectical struggle.

2. *Class struggle*. The driving determinist force in history is that of class struggle. People identify primarily with their socio-economic class (not race, gender, or religion), and each class is antagonistic to the others. Marx divided the history of humankind into five epochs: (1) the primitive communal society, (2) the slave society, (3) the feudal society, (4) the capitalist society, and, still to come, (5) the communist society. He argued that each of the first four phases has inner contradictions, or antagonisms, that lead to the next phase of history. As lords struggled against the bourgeoisie in feudalism, the bourgeoisie are presently pitted against the proletariat in capitalism.

We see this point in the first chapter of the *Communist Manifesto*.

This reading is taken from Karl Marx and Friedrich Engels, *Manifesto of the Communist Party*, translated by Samuel Moore in 1888 from the original German text of 1848 and edited by Friedrich Engels (Moscow: Progress Publishers).

A spectre is haunting Europe—the spectre of Communism. All the powers of old Europe have entered into a holy alliance to exorcise this spectre; Pope, Czar, Metternich and Guizot, French Radicals and German police-spies. Where is the party in opposition that has not been decried as communistic by its opponents in power? Where is the Opposition that has not hurled back the branding reproach of Communism against the more advanced opposition's parties, as well as against its reactionary adversaries?

Two things result from this fact:

1. Communism is already acknowledged by all European Powers to be itself a Power.
2. It is high time that Communists should openly, in the face of the whole world, publish their views, their aims, their tendencies, and meet the nursery tale of the Spectre of Communism with a Manifesto of the party itself.

To this end, Communists of various nationalities have assembled in London, and sketched the following manifesto, to be published in English, French, German, Italian, Flemish, and Danish languages.

I. BOURGEOIS AND PROLETARIANS

The history of all hitherto existing society is the history of class struggles.

Freeman and slave, patrician and plebeian, lord and serf, guildmaster and journeyman, in a word, oppressor and oppressed, stood in constant opposition to one another, carried on an uninterrupted, now hidden, now open fight, a fight that each time ended, either in a revolutionary re-constitution of society at large, or in the common ruin of the contending classes.

In the earlier epochs of history, we find almost everywhere a complicated arrangement of society into various orders, a manifold gradation of social rank. In ancient Rome we have patricians, knights, plebeians, slaves; in the Middle Ages, feudal lords, vassals, guildmasters, journeymen, apprentices, serfs; in almost all of these classes, again, subordinate gradations.

The modern bourgeois society that has sprouted from the ruins of feudal society has not done away with class antagonisms. It has but established new classes, new conditions of oppression, new forms of struggle in place of the old ones.

Our epoch, the epoch of the bourgeoisie, possesses, however, this distinctive feature: it has simplified the class antagonisms. Society as a whole is more and more splitting up into two great hostile camps, into two great classes directly facing each other: Bourgeoisie and Proletariat.

From the serfs of the Middle Ages sprang the chartered burghers of the earliest towns. From the burgesses the first elements of the bourgeoisie were developed.

The discovery of America, the rounding of the Cape, opened up fresh ground for the rising bourgeoisie. The East-Indian and Chinese markets, the colonisation of America, trade with the colonies, the increase in the means of exchange and in commodities generally, gave to commerce, to navigation, to industry, an impulse never before known, and thereby, to the revolutionary element in the tottering feudal society, a rapid development.

The feudal system of industry, under which industrial production was monopolised by closed guilds, now no longer sufficed for the growing wants of the new markets. The manufacturing system took its place. The guild-masters were pushed on one side by the manufacturing middle class; division of labour between the different corporate guilds vanished in the face of division of labour in each single workshop.

Meantime the markets kept ever growing, the demand ever rising. Even manufacture no longer sufficed. Thereupon, steam and machinery revolutionised industrial production. The place of manufacture was taken by the giant, Modern Industry, the place of the industrial middle class, by industrial millionaires, the leaders of whole industrial armies, the modern bourgeois.

Modern industry has established the world market, for which the discovery of America paved the way. This market has given an immense development to commerce, to navigation, to communication by land. This development has, in its turn, reacted on the extension of industry; and in proportion as industry, commerce, navigation, railways extended, in the same proportion the bourgeoisie developed, increased its capital, and pushed into the background every class handed down from the Middle Ages.

We see, therefore, how the modern bourgeoisie is itself the product of a long course of development, of a series of revolutions in the modes of production and of exchange. . . .

The bourgeoisie, wherever it has got the upper hand, has put an end to all feudal, patriarchal, idyllic relations. It has pitilessly torn asunder the motley feudal ties that bound man to his "natural superiors," and has left remaining no other nexus between man and man than naked self-interest, than callous "cash payment." It has drowned the most heavenly ecstasies of religious fervour, of chivalrous enthusiasm, of philistine sentimentalism, in the icy water of egotistical calculation. It has resolved personal worth into exchange value, and in place of the numberless indefeasible chartered freedoms, has set up that single, unconscionable freedom—Free Trade. In one word, for exploitation, veiled by religious and political illusions, it has substituted naked, shameless, direct, brutal exploitation.

The bourgeoisie has stripped of its halo every occupation hitherto honoured and looked up to with reverent awe. It has converted the physician, the lawyer, the priest, the poet, the man of science, into its paid wage-labourers.

The bourgeoisie has torn away from the family its sentimental zeal and has reduced the family relation to a mere money relation. . . .

The bourgeoisie cannot exist without constantly revolutionising the instruments of production, and thereby the relations of production, and with them the whole relations of society. Conservation of the old modes of production in unaltered form, was, on the contrary, the first condition of existence for all earlier industrial classes. Constant revolutionising of production, uninterrupted disturbance of all social conditions, everlasting uncertainty and agitation distinguished the bourgeois epoch from all earlier ones. All fixed, fast-frozen relations, with their train of ancient and venerable prejudices and opinions are swept away, all new-formed ones become antiquated before they can ossify. All that is solid melts into air, all that is holy is profaned, and man is at last compelled to face with sober senses, his real conditions of life, and his relations with his kind.

The need of a constantly expanding market for its products chases the bourgeoisie over the whole surface of the globe. It must nestle everywhere, settle everywhere, establish connexions everywhere.

The bourgeoisie has through its exploitation of the world market given a cosmopolitan character to production and consumption in every country. To the great chagrin of Reactionists, it has drawn from under the feet of industry the national ground on which it stood. All old-established national industries have been destroyed or are daily being destroyed. They are dislodged by new industries, whose introduction becomes a life and death question for all civilized nations, by industries that no longer work up indigenous raw material, but raw material drawn from the remotest zones; industries whose products are consumed, not only at home, but in every quarter of the globe. In place of the old wants, satisfied by the productions of the country, we find new wants, requiring for their satisfaction the products of distant lands and climes. In place of the old local and national seclusion and self-sufficiency, we have intercourse in every direction, universal interdependence of nations. And as in material, so also in intellectual production. The intellectual creations of individual nations become common property. National one-sidedness and narrow-mindedness become more and more impossible, and from the numerous national and local literatures there arises a world literature.

The bourgeoisie, by the rapid improvement of all instruments of production, by the immensely facilitated means of communication, draws all, even the most barbarian, nations into civilization. The cheap prices of its commodities are the heavy artillery with which it batters down all Chinese walls, with which it forces the barbarians' intensely obstinate hatred of foreigners to capitulate. It compels all nations, on pain of extinction, to adopt the bourgeois mode of production; it compels them to introduce what it calls civilization into their midst, *i.e.,* to become bourgeois themselves. In one word, it creates a world after its own image.

The bourgeoisie has subjected the country to the rule of the towns. It has created enormous cities, has greatly increased the urban population as compared with the rural, and has thus rescued a considerable part of the population from the idiocy of rural life. Just as it has made the country dependent on the towns, so it has made barbarian and semi-barbarian countries dependent on the civilized ones, nations of peasants on nations of bourgeois, the East on the West.

The bourgeoisie keeps more and more doing away with the scattered state of the population, of the means of production, and of property. It has agglomerated population, centralized means of production, and has concentrated property in a few hands. The necessary consequence of this was political centralization. Independent, or but loosely connected, provinces with separate interests, laws, governments and systems of taxation, became lumped together into one nation, with one government, one code of laws, one national class-interest, one frontier and one customs-tariff.

The bourgeoisie, during its rule of scarce one hundred years, has created more massive and more colossal productive forces than have all preceding generations together. Subjection of Nature's forces to man, machinery, application of chemistry to industry and agriculture, steam-navigation, railways, electric telegraphs, clearing of whole continents for cultivation, canalization of rivers, whole populations conjured out of the ground—what earlier century had even a presentiment that such productive forces slumbered in the lap of social labour?

We see then: the means of production and of exchange, on whose foundation the bourgeoisie built itself up, were generated in feudal society. At a certain stage in the development of these means of production and of exchange, the conditions under which feudal society produced and exchanged, the feudal organization of agriculture and manufacturing industry, in one word, the feudal relations of property became no longer compatible with the already developed productive forces; they became so many fetters. They had to be burst asunder; they were burst asunder.

Into their place stepped free competition, accompanied by a social and political constitution adapted to it, and by the economical and political sway of the bourgeois class.

A similar movement is going on before our own eyes. Modern bourgeois society with its relations of production, of exchange and of property, a society that has conjured up such gigantic means of production and of exchange, is like the sorcerer, who is no longer able to control the powers of the nether world whom he has called up by his spells. For many a decade past the history of industry and commerce is but the history of the revolt of modern productive forces against modern conditions of production, against the property relations that are the conditions for the existence of the bourgeoisie and of its rule. It is enough to mention the commercial crises that by their periodical return put on its trial, each time more threateningly, the existence of the entire bourgeois society. In these crises a great part not only of the existing products, but also of the previously created productive forces, are periodically destroyed. In these crises there breaks out an epidemic that, in all earlier epochs, would have seemed an absurdity—the epidemic of overproduction. Society suddenly finds itself put back into a state of momentary barbarism; it appears as if a famine, a universal war of devastation had cut off the supply of every means of subsistence; industry and commerce seem to be destroyed; and why? Because there is too much civilization, too much means of subsistence, too much industry, too much commerce. The productive forces at the disposal of society no longer tend to further the development of the conditions of bourgeois property; on the contrary, they have become too powerful for these conditions, by which they are fettered, and so soon as they overcome these fetters, they bring disorder into the whole of bourgeois society, endanger the existence of bourgeois property. The conditions of bourgeois society are too narrow to compromise the wealth created by them. And how does the bourgeoisie get over these crises? On the one hand by enforced destruction of a mass of productive forces; on the other, by the conquest of new markets, and by the more thorough exploitation of the old ones. That is to say, by paving the way for more extensive and more destructive crises, and by diminishing the means whereby crises are prevented.

The weapons with which the bourgeoisie felled feudalism to the ground are now turned against the bourgeoisie itself.

But not only has the bourgeoisie forged the weapons that bring death to itself; it has also called into existence the men who are to wield those weapons—the modern working class—the proletarians.

In proportion as the bourgeoisie, *i.e.,* capital, is developed, in the same proportion is the proletariat, the modern working class, developed—a class of labourers who live only so long as they find work, and who find work only so long as their labour increases capital. The labourers, who must sell themselves piecemeal, are a commodity, like every other article of commerce, and are consequently exposed to all the vicissitudes of competition, to all the fluctuations of the market.

Owing to the extensive use of machinery and to division of labour, the work of the proletarians has lost all individual character, and, consequently, all charm for the workman. He becomes an appendage of the machine, and it is only the most simple, most monotonous, and most easily acquired knack, that is required of him. Hence, the cost of production of a workman is restricted, almost entirely, to the means of subsistence that he requires for his maintenance, and for the propagation of his race. But the price of a commodity, and therefore also of labour, is equal to its cost of production. In proportion, therefore, as the repulsiveness of the work increases, the wage decreases. Nay more, in proportion as the use of machinery and division of labour increases, in the same proportion the burden of toil also increases, whether by prolongation of the working hours, by increase of the work exacted in a given time or by increased speed of the machinery, etc.

Modern industry has converted the little workshop of the patriarchal master into the great factory of the industrial capitalist. Masses of labourers, crowded into the factory, are organized like soldiers. As privates of the industrial army they are placed under the command of a perfect hierarchy of officers and sergeants. Not only are they slaves of the bourgeois class, and of the bourgeois State; they are daily and hourly enslaved by the machine, by the overlooker, and, above all, by the individual bourgeois manufacturer himself. The more openly this despotism proclaims gain to be its end and aim, the more petty, the more hateful and more embittering it is.

The less the skill and exertion of strength implied in manual labour, in other words, the more modern industry becomes developed, the more is the labour of men superseded by that of women. Differences of age and sex have no longer any distinctive social validity for the working class. All are instruments of labour, more or less expensive to use, according to their age and sex. No sooner is the exploitation of the labourer by the manufacturer, so far, at an end, that he receives his wages in cash, than he is set upon by the other portions of the bourgeoisie, the landlord, the storekeeper, the pawnbroker, etc.

The lower strata of the middle class—the small tradespeople, shopkeepers, and retired tradesmen generally, the handicraftsmen and peasants—all these sink gradually into the proletariat, partly because their diminutive capital does not suffice for the scale on which Modern Industry is carried on, and is swamped in the competition with the large capitalists, partly because their specialized skill is rendered worthless by new methods of production. Thus the proletariat is recruited from all classes of the population.

The proletariat goes through various stages of development. With its birth begins its struggle with the bourgeoisie. At first the contest is carried on by individual labourers, then by the workpeople of a factory, then by the operatives of one trade, in one locality, against the individual bourgeois who directly exploits them. They direct their attacks not against the bourgeois conditions of production, but against the instruments of production themselves; they destroy imported wares that compete with their labour, they smash to pieces machinery, they set factories ablaze, they seek to restore by force the vanished status of the workman of the Middle Ages.

At this stage the labourers still form an incoherent mass scattered over the whole country, and broken up by their mutual competition. If anywhere they unite to form more compact bodies, this is not yet the consequence of their own active union, but of the union of the bourgeoisie, which class, in order to attain its own political ends, is compelled to set the whole proletariat in motion, and is moreover yet, for a time, able to do so. At this stage, therefore, the proletarians do not fight their enemies, but the enemies of their enemies, the remnants of absolute monarchy, the landowners, the nonindustrial bourgeois, the petty bourgeoisie. Thus the whole historical movement is concentrated in the hands of the bourgeoisie; every victory so obtained is a victory for the bourgeoisie.

But with the development of industry the proletariat not only increases in number; it becomes concentrated in greater masses, its strength grows, and it feels that strength more. The various interests and conditions of life within the ranks of the proletariat are more and more equalized, in proportion as machinery obliterates all distinctions of labour, and nearly everywhere reduces wages to the same low level. The growing competition among the bourgeois, and the resulting commercial crises, make the wages of the workers ever more fluctuating. The unceasing improvement of machinery, ever more rapidly developing, makes their livelihood more and more precarious; the collisions between individual workmen and individual bourgeois take more and more the character of collisions between two classes. Thereupon the workers begin to form combinations (Trades' Unions) against the bourgeois; they club together in order to keep up the rate of wages; they found permanent associations in order to make provision beforehand for these occasional revolts. Here and there the contest breaks out into riots.

Now and then the workers are victorious, but only for a time. The real fruit of their battles lies, not in the immediate result, but in the ever-expanding union of the workers. This union is helped on by the improved means of communication that are created by modern industry and that place the workers of different localities in contact with one another. It was just this contact that was needed to centralize the numerous local struggles, all of the same character, into one national struggle between classes. But every class struggle is a political struggle. . . .

This organization of the proletarians into a class, and consequently into a political party, is continually being upset again by the competition between the workers themselves. But it ever rises up again, stronger, firmer, mightier. It compels legislative recognition of particular interests of the workers, by taking advantage of the divisions among the bourgeoisie itself. . . .

Altogether, collisions between the classes of the old society further, in many ways, the course of development of the proletariat. The bourgeoisie finds itself involved in a constant battle. At first with the aristocracy; later on, with those portions of the bourgeoisle itself, whose interests have become antagonistic to the progress of industry; at all times, with the bourgeoisie of foreign countries. In all these battles it sees itself compelled to appeal to the proletariat, to ask for its help, and thus, to drag it into the political arena. The bourgeoisie itself, therefore, supplies the proletariat with its own elements of political and general educaion, in other words, it furnishes the proletariat with weapons for fighting the bourgeoisie.

Further, as we have already seen, entire sections of the ruling classes are, by the advance of industry, precipitated into the proletariat, or are at least threatened in their conditions of existence. These also supply the proletariat with fresh elements of enlightenment and progress.

Finally, in times when the class struggle nears the decisive hour, the process of dissolution going on within the ruling class, in fact within the whole range of old society, assumes such a violent, glaring character, that a small section of the ruling class cuts itself adrift, and

joins the revolutionary class, the class that holds the future in its hands. Just as, therefore, at an earlier period, a section of the nobility went over to the bourgeoisie, so now a portion of the bourgeoisie goes over to the proletariat, and in particular, a portion of the bourgeoisie ideologists, who have raised themselves to the level of comprehending theoretically the historical movement as a whole.

Of all the classes that stand face to face with the bourgeoisie today, the proletariat alone is a really revolutionary class. The other classes decay and finally disappear in the face of modern industry; the proletariat is its special and essential product.

The lower middle class, the small manufacturer, the shopkeeper, the artisan, the peasant, all these fight against the bourgeoisie, to save from extinction their existence as fractions of the middle class. They are therefore not revolutionary, but conservative. Nay more, they are reactionary, for they try to roll back the wheel of history. If by chance they are revolutionary, they are so only in view of their impending transfer into the proletariat, they thus defend not their present, but their future interests, they desert their own standpoint to place themselves at that of the proletariat. . . .

In the conditions of the proletariat, those of old society at large are already virtually swamped. The proletarian is without property; his relation to his wife and children has no longer anything in common with the bourgeoisie family relations; modern industrial labour, modern subjection to capital, the same in England as in France, in America as in Germany, has stripped him of every trace of national character. Law, morality, religion, are to him so many bourgeois prejudices, behind which lurk in ambush just as many bourgeois interests.

All the preceding classes that got the upper hand, sought to fortify their already acquired status by subjecting society at large to their conditions of appropriation. The proletarians cannot become masters of the productive forces of society, except by abolishng their own previous mode of appropriation, and thereby also every other previous mode of appropriation. They have nothing of their own to secure and to fortify; their mission is to destroy all previous securities for, and insurances of, individual property. All previous historical movements were movements of minorities, or in the interest of minorities. The proletarian movement is the self-conscious, independent movement of the immense majority, in the interest of the immense majority. The proletariat, the lowest stratum of our present society, cannot stir, cannot raise itself up, without the whole superincumbent strata of official society being sprung into the air.

Though not in substance, yet in form, the struggle of the proletariat with the bourgeoisie is at first a national struggle. The proletariat of each country must, of course, first of all settle matters with its own bourgeoisie.

In depicting the most general phases of the development of the proletariat, we traced the more or less veiled civil war, raging within existing society, up to the point where that war breaks out into open revolution, and where the violent overthrow of the bourgeoisie lays the foundation for the sway of the proletariat.

Hitherto, every form of society has been based, as we have already seen, on the antagonism of oppressing and oppressed classes. But in order to oppress a class, certain conditions must be assured to it under which it can, at least, continue its slavish existence. The serf, in the period of serfdom, raised himself to membership in the commune, just as the petty bourgeois, under the yoke of feudal absolutism, managed to develop into a bourgeois. The modern labourer, on the contrary, instead of rising with the progress of industry, sinks deeper and deeper below the conditions of existence of his own class. He becomes a pauper, and pauperism develops more rapidly than population and wealth. And here it becomes evident that the bourgeoisie is unfit any longer to be the ruling class in society, and to impose its conditions of existence upon society as an over-riding law. It is unfit to rule because it is incompetent to assure an existence to its slave within his slavery, because it cannot help letting him sink into such a state, that it has to feed him, instead of being fed by him. Society can no longer live under this bourgeoisie, in other words, its existence is no longer compatible with society.

The essential condition for the existence, and for the sway of the bourgeois class, is the formation and augmentation of capital; the condition for capital is wage labour. Wage labour rests exclusively on competition between the labourers. The advance of industry, whose involuntary promoter is the bourgeoisie, replaces the isolation of the labourers, due to competition, by their revolutionary combination, due to association. The development of Modern Industry, therefore, cuts from under its feet the very foundation on which the bourgeoisie produces and appropriates products. What the bourgeoisie, therefore, produces, above all, is its own gravediggers. Its fall and the victory of the proletariat are equally inevitable.

II. PROLETARIANS AND COMMUNISTS

In what relation do the Communists stand to the proletarians as a whole?

The Communists do not form a separate party opposed to other working-class parties.

They have no interests separate and apart from those of the proletariat as a whole.

They do not set up any sectarian principles of their own, by which to shape and mould the proletarian movement.

The Communists are distinguished from the other working-class parties by this only: 1. In the national struggles of the proletarians of the different countries, they point out and bring to the front the common interests of the entire proletariat, independently of all nationality. 2. In the various stages of development which the struggle of the working class against the bourgeoisie has to pass through, they always and everywhere represent the interests of the movement as a whole.

The Communists, therefore, are on the one hand, practically, the most advanced and resolute section of the working-class parties of every country, that section which pushes forward all others; on the other hand, theoretically, they have over the great mass of the proletariat the advantage of clearly understanding the line of march, the conditions, and the ultimate general results of the proletarian government.

The immediate aim of the Communists is the same as that of all the other proletarian parties: formation of the proletariat into a class, overthrow of the bourgeois supremacy, conquest of political power by the proletariat. . . .

The proletariat will use its political supremacy to wrest, by degrees, all capital from the bourgeoisie, to centralize all instruments of production in the hands of the State, *i.e.,* of the proletariat organized as the ruling class; and to increase the total of productive forces as rapidly as possible.

Of course, in the beginning, this cannot be effected except by means of despotic inroads on the rights of property, and on the conditions of bourgeois production; by means of measures, therefore, which appear economically insufficient and untenable, but which, in the course of the movement, outstrip themselves, necessitate further inroads upon the old social order, and are unavoidable as a means of entirely revolutionizing the mode of production.

These measures will of course be different in different countries.

Nevertheless in the most advanced countries, the following will be pretty generally applicable.

1. Abolition of property in land and application of all rents of land to public purposes.
2. A heavy progressive or graduated income tax.
3. Abolition of all right of inheritance.
4. Confiscation of the property of all emigrants and rebels.
5. Centralization of credit in the hands of the State by means of a national bank with State capital and an exclusive monopoly.
6. Centralization of the means of communication and transport in the hands of the State.
7. Extension of factories and instruments of production owned by the State; the bringing into cultivation of waste-lands, and the improvement of the soil generally in accordance with a common plan.
8. Equal liability of all to labour. Establishment of industrial armies, especially for agriculture.
9. Combination of agriculture with manufacturing industries; gradual abolition of the distinction between town and country, by a more equable distribution of the population over the country.
10. Free education for all children in public schools. Abolition of children's factory labour in its present form. Combination of education with industrial production. . . .

When, in the course of development, class distinctions have disappeared, and all production has been concentrated in the hands of a vast association of the whole nation, the public power will lose its political character. Political power, properly so called, is merely the organized power of one class for oppressing another. If the proletariat during its contest with the bourgeoisie is compelled, by the force of circumstances, to organize itself as a class, if, by means of a revolution, it makes itself the ruling class, and, as such, sweeps away by force the old conditions of production, then it will, along with these conditions, have swept away the conditions for the existence of class antagonisms and of classes generally, and will thereby have abolished its own supremacy as a class.

In place of the old bourgeois society, with its classes and class antagonisms, we shall have an association, in which the free development of each is the condition for the free development of all. . . .

The Communists disdain to conceal their views and aims. They openly declare that their ends can be attained only by the forcible overthrow of all existing social conditions. Let the ruling classes tremble at a Communistic revolution. The proletarians have nothing to lose but their chains. They have a world to win.

WORKING MEN OF ALL COUNTRIES, UNITE!

READING 9

Critique of the Gotha Program

Karl Marx

For Marx's biography, see Reading 8. In this selection, Marx criticizes what he considers the utopian heresy of his fellow socialist Ferdinand la Salle, leader or the General Union of German Workers, who in 1875 formed a union with other Social Democrats in Gotha, Germany. In this famous essay (published in 1875) Marx rejects la Salle's strong egalitarianism, contending that in the intermediate socialist society, before the full emergence of communism, productivity must be the criterion of economic distribution. A person should receive, not according to a formula of need or equal distribution, but according to his or her contribution, according to one's true labor value.

This reading is taken from *Karl Marx/Friederich Engels Collected Works* (Moscow: International Publishing Company, 1975).

"The emancipation of labour demands the promotion of the instruments of labour to the common property of society and the cooperative regulation of the total labour with a fair distribution of the proceeds of labour."

"Promotion of the instruments of labour to the common property" ought obviously to read their "conversion into the common property;" but this only in passing.

What are "proceeds of labour"? The product of labour or its value? And in the latter case, is it the total value of the product or only that part of the value which labour has newly added to the value of the means of production consumed?

"Proceeds of labour" is a loose notion which Lassalle has put in the place of definite economic conceptions.

What is "a fair distribution"?

Do not the bourgeois assert that the present-day distribution is "fair"? And is it not, in fact, the only "fair" distribution on the basis of the present-day mode of production? Are economic relations regulated by legal conceptions or do not, on the contrary, legal relations arise from economic ones? Have not also the socialist sectarians the most varied notions about "fair" distribution?

To understand what is implied in this connection by the phrase "fair distribution", we must take the first paragraph and this one together. The latter presupposes a society wherein "the instruments of labour are common property and the total labour is co-operatively regulated", and from the first paragraph we learn that "the proceeds of labour belong undiminished with equal right to all members of society".

"To all members of society"? To those who do not work as well? What remains then of the "undiminished proceeds of labour"? Only to those members of society who work? What remains then of the "equal right" of all members of society?

But "all members of society" and "equal right" are obviously mere phrases. The kernel consists in this, that in this communist society every worker must receive the "undiminished" Lassallean "proceeds of labour".

Let us take first of all the words "proceeds of labour" in the sense of the product of labour; then the co-operative proceeds of labour are the *total social product.*

From this must now be deducted:

First, cover for replacement of the means of production used up.

Secondly, additional portion for expansion of production.

Thirdly, reserve or insurance funds to provide against accidents, dislocations caused by natural calamities, etc.

These deductions from the "undiminished proceeds of labour" are an economic necessity and their magnitude is to be determined according to available means and forces, and partly by computation of probabilities, but they are in no way calculable by equity.

There remains the other part of the total product, intended to serve as means of consumption.

Before this is divided among the individuals, there has to be deducted again, from it:

First, the general costs of administration not belonging to production.

This part will, from the outset, be very considerably restricted in comparison with present-day society and it diminishes in proportion as the new society develops.

Secondly, that which is intended for the common satisfaction of needs, such as schools, health services, etc.

From the outset this part grows considerably in comparison with present-day society and it grows in proportion as the new society develops.

Thirdly, funds for those unable to work, etc., in short, for what is included under so-called official poor relief today.

Only now do we come to the "distribution" which the programme, under Lassallean influence, alone has in view in its narrow fashion, namely, to that part of the means of consumption which is divided among the individual producers of the co-operative society.

The "undiminished proceeds of labour" have already unnoticeably become converted into the "diminished" proceeds, although what the producer is deprived of in his capacity as a private individual benefits him directly or indirectly in his capacity as a member of society.

Just as the phrase of the "undiminished proceeds of labour" has disappeared, so now does the phrase of the "proceeds of labour" disappear altogether.

Within the co-operative society based on common ownership of the means of production, the producers do not exchange their products; just as little does the labour employed on the products appear here *as the value* of these products, as a material quality possessed by them, since now, in contrast to capitalist society, individual labour no longer exists in an indirect fashion but directly as a component part of the total labour. The phrase "proceeds of labour", objectionable also today on account of its ambiguity, thus loses all meaning.

What we have to deal with here is a communist society, not as it has *developed* on its own foundations, but, on the contrary, just as it *emerges* from capitalist society; which is thus in every respect, economically, morally, and intellectually, still stamped with the birth marks of the old society from whose womb it emerges. Accordingly, the individual producer receives back from society—after the deductions have been made—exactly what he gives to it. What he has given to it is his individual quantum of labour. For example, the so-cial working day consists of the sum of the individual hours of work; the individual labour time of the indi-vidual producer is the part of the social working day contributed by him, his share in it. He receives a cer-tificate from society that he has furnished such and such an amount of labour (after deducting his labour for the common funds), and with this certificate he draws from the social stock of means of consumption as much as costs the same amount of labour. The same amount of labour which he has given to society in one form he receives back in another.

Here obviously the same principle prevails as that which regulates the exchange of commodities, as far as this is exchange of equal values. Content and form are changed, because under the altered circumstances no one can give anything except his labour, and because, on the other hand, nothing can pass to the ownership of individuals except individual means of consumption. But, as far as the distribution of the latter among the individual producers is concerned, the same principle prevails as in the exchange of commodity equivalents: a given amount of labour in one form is exchanged for an equal amount of labour in another form.

Hence, *equal right* here is still in principle—*bour-geois right,* although principle and practice are no longer at loggerheads, while the exchange of equiva-lents in commodity exchange only exists *on the aver-age* and not in the individual case.

In spite of this advance, this *equal right* is still constantly stigmatized by a bourgeois limitation. The right of the producers is *proportional* to the labour they supply; the equality consists in the fact that measure-ment is made with an *equal standard,* labour.

But one man is superior to another physically or mentally and so supplies more labour in the same time, or can labour for a longer time; and labour, to serve as a measure, must be defined by its duration or intensity, otherwise it ceases to be a standard of measurement. This *equal* right is an unequal right for unequal labour. It recognizes no class differences, because everyone is only a worker like everyone else; but it tacitly recog-nizes unequal individual endowment and thus produc-tive capacity as natural privileges. *It is, therefore, a right of inequality, in its content, like every right.* Right by its very nature can consist only in the application of an equal standard; but unequal individuals (and they would not be different individuals if they were not un-equal) are measurable only by an equal standard in so far as they are brought under an equal point of view, are taken from one *definite* side only, for instance, in

the present case, are regarded *only as workers* and nothing more is seen in them, everything else being ig-nored. Further, one worker is married, another not; one has more children than another, and so on and so forth. Thus, with an equal performance of labour, and hence an equal share in the social consumption fund, one will in fact receive more than another, one will be richer than another, and so on. To avoid all these defects, right instead of being equal would have to be unequal.

But these defects are inevitable in the first phase of communist society as it is when it has just emerged after prolonged birth pangs from capitalist society. Right can never be higher than the economic structure of society and its cultural development conditioned thereby.

In a higher phase of communist society, after the enslaving subordination of the individual to the divi-sion of labour, and therewith also the antithesis be-tween mental and physical labour, has vanished; after labour has become not only a means of life but life's prime want; after the productive forces have also in-creased with the all-round development of the individ-ual, and all the springs of co-operative wealth flow more abundantly—only then can the narrow horizon of bourgeois right be crossed in its entirety and society in-scribe on its banner: from each according to his ability, to each according to his needs!

I have dealt more at length with the "undiminished proceeds of labour", on the one hand, and with "equal right" and "fair distribution", on the other, in order to show what a crime it is to attempt, on the one hand, to force on our Party again, as dogmas, ideas which in a certain period had some meaning but have now become obsolete verbal rubbish, while again perverting, on the other, the realistic outlook, which it cost so much ef-fort to instil into the Party but which has now taken root in it, by means of ideological nonsense about right and other trash so common among the democrats and French Socialists.

Quite apart from the analysis so far given, it was in general a mistake to make a fuss about so-called *dis-tribution* and put the principal stress on it.

Any distribution whatever of the means of con-sumption is only a consequence of the distribution of the conditions of production themselves. The latter dis-tribution, however, is a feature of the mode of produc-tion itself. The capitalist mode of production, for ex-ample, rests on the fact that the material conditions of production are in the hands of non-workers in the form of property in capital and land, while the masses are only owners of the personal condition of production, of labour power. If the elements of production are so distributed, then the present-day distribution of the means of consumption results automatically. If the material conditions of production are the co-operative property of the workers themselves, then there likewise results a distribution of the means of consumption different from the present one. Vulgar socialism (and from it in turn a section of the democracy) has taken over from the bourgeois economists the consideration and treatment of distribution as independent of the mode of production and hence the presentation of socialism as turning principally on distribution. After the real relation has long been made clear, why retrogress again?

READING 10

On Liberty

John Stuart Mill

John Stuart Mill (1806–73), one of the most important British philosophers of the nineteenth century, was born in London and educated by his philosopher father, James Mill, who taught his son Greek at the age of three and Latin at the age of eight. By the time he was fourteen, he had received a thorough classical education, entirely at home. At the age of seventeen he began work as a clerk for the East India Company, eventually working his way up to the directorship. He was elected to Parliament in 1865. He married Harriet Taylor, with whom he collaborated in many ventures. A remarkably comprehensive philosopher, Mill made significant contributions to logic, epistemology, philosophy of science, philosophy of religion, and moral philosophy, as well as political philosophy. His treatise on Utilitarianism is the most fully developed work on the subject before the twentieth century. His principal works are *Utilitarianism* (1863), *The Subjection of Women* (1869), and *On Liberty* (1859), from which this selection is taken.

In the first four chapters of *On Liberty* (excerpted here), Mill argues that the State has a duty to protect the liberty of its subjects, so that in civilized countries,

an adult should be free to do whatever he or she wants to do, so long as the actions do not directly and unjustly harm others. He defends individual eccentricity and the right to be different, as he opposes the "tyranny of the majority" in defense of the individual's right to express unorthodox opinions and live according to his own lights. In Chapter II of *On Liberty* Mill defends an encompassing principle of freedom of thought and expression. In Chapter III he develops his thesis within the broader scope of his theory of human nature. Liberty is a necessary condition for developing one's deepest potential. In Chapter IV he sums up his theory by discussing the nature of the area that the right to liberty covers.

This reading is taken from *On Liberty* (1859)

CHAPTER I:
INTRODUCTORY

The subject of this Essay is not the so-called Liberty of the Will, so unfortunately opposed to the misnamed doctrine of Philosophical Necessity; but Civil, or Social Liberty: the nature and limits of the power which can be legitimately exercised by society over the individual. A question seldom stated, and hardly ever discussed, in general terms, but which profoundly influences the practical controversies of the age by its latent presence, and is likely soon to make itself recognized as the vital question of the future. It is so far from being new, that, in a certain sense, it has divided mankind, almost from the remotest ages, but in the stage of progress into which the more civilized portions of the species have now entered, it presents itself under new conditions, and requires a different and more fundamental treatment.

The struggle between Liberty and Authority is the most conspicuous feature in the portions of history with which we are earliest familiar, particularly in that of Greece, Rome, and England. But in old times this contest was between subjects, or some classes of subjects, and the government. By liberty, was meant protection against the tyranny of the political rulers. The rulers were conceived (except in some of the popular governments of Greece) as in a necessarily antagonistic position to the people whom they ruled. They consisted of a governing One, or a governing tribe or caste, who derived their authority from inheritance or conquest; who, at all events, did not hold it at the pleasure of the governed, and whose supremacy men did not venture, perhaps did not desire, to contest, whatever precautions might be taken against its oppressive exercise. Their power was regarded as necessary, but also as highly dangerous; as a weapon which they would attempt to use against their subjects, no less than against external enemies. To prevent the weaker members of the community from being preyed upon by innumerable vultures, it was needful that there should be an animal of prey stronger than the rest, commissioned to keep them down. But as the king of the vultures would be no less bent upon preying upon the flock than any of the minor harpies, it was indispensable to be in a perpetual attitude of defense against his beak and claws. The aim, therefore, of patriots, was to set limits to the power which the ruler should be suffered to exercise over the community; and this limitation was what they meant by liberty. It was attempted in two ways. First, by obtaining a recognition of certain immunities, called political liberties or rights, which it was to be regarded as a breach of duty in the ruler to infringe, and which, if he did infringe, specific resistance, or general rebellion, was held to be justifiable. A second, and generally a later expedient, was the establishment of constitutional checks; by which the consent of the community, or of a body of some sort supposed to represent its interests, was made a necessary condition to some of the more important acts of the governing power. To the first of these modes of limitation, the ruling power, in most European countries, was compelled, more or less, to submit. It was not so with the second; and to attain this, or when already in some degree possessed, to attain it more completely, became everywhere the principal object of the lovers of liberty. And so long as mankind were content to combat one enemy by another, and to be ruled by a master, on condition of being guaranteed more or less efficaciously against his tyranny, they did not carry their aspirations beyond this point.

A time, however, came in the progress of human affairs, when men ceased to think it a necessity of nature that their governors should be an independent power, opposed in interest to themselves. It appeared to them much better that the various magistrates of the State should be their tenants or delegates, revocable at their pleasure. In that way alone, it seemed, could they have complete security that the powers of government would never be abused to their disadvantage. By de-

grees, this new demand for elective and temporary rulers became the prominent object of the exertions of the popular party, wherever any such party existed; and superseded, to a considerable extent, the previous efforts to limit the power of rulers. As the struggle proceeded for making the ruling power emanate from the periodical choice of the ruled, some persons began to think that too much importance had been attached to the limitation of the power itself. That (it might seem) was a resource against rulers whose interests were habitually opposed to those of the people. What was now wanted was, that the rulers should be identified with the people; that their interest and will should be the interest and will of the nation. The nation did not need to be protected against its own will. There was no fear of its tyrannizing over itself. Let the rulers be effectually responsible to it, promptly removable by it, and it could afford to trust them with power of which it could itself dictate the use to be made. Their power was but the nation's own power, concentrated, and in a form convenient for exercise. This mode of thought, or rather perhaps of feeling, was common among the last generation of European liberalism, in the Continental section of which, it still apparently predominates. Those who admit any limit to what a government may do, except in the case of such governments as they think ought not to exist, stand out as brilliant exceptions among the political thinkers of the Continent. A similar tone of sentiment might by this time have been prevalent in our own country, if the circumstances which for a time encouraged it had continued unaltered.

But, in political and philosophical theories, as well as in persons, success discloses faults and infirmities which failure might have concealed from observation. The notion, that the people have no need to limit their power over themselves, might seem axiomatic, when popular government was a thing only dreamed about, or read of as having existed at some distant period of the past. Neither was that notion necessarily disturbed by such temporary aberrations as those of the French Revolution, the worst of which were the work of an usurping few, and which, in any case, belonged, not to the permanent working of popular institutions, but to a sudden and convulsive outbreak against monarchical and aristocratic despotism. In time, however, a democratic republic came to occupy a large portion of the earth's surface, and made itself felt as one of the most powerful members of the community of nations; and elective and responsible government became subject to the observations and criticisms which wait upon a great existing fact. It was now perceived that such phrases as "self-government" and "the power of the people over themselves," do not express the true state of the case. The "people" who exercise the power, are not always the same people with those over whom it is exercised, and the "self-government" spoken of, is not the government of each by himself, but of each by all the rest. The will of the people, moreover, practically means, the will of the most numerous or the most active part of the people; the majority, or those who succeed in making themselves accepted as the majority; the people, consequently, may desire to oppress a part of their number; and precautions are as much needed against this, as against any other abuse of power. The limitation, therefore, of the power of government over individuals, loses none of its importance when the holders of power are regularly accountable to the community, that is, to the strongest party therein. This view of things, recommending itself equally to the intelligence of thinkers and to the inclination of those important classes in European society to whose real or supposed interests democracy is adverse, has had no difficulty in establishing itself; and in political speculations "the tyranny of the majority" is now generally included among the evils against which society requires to be on its guard.

Like other tyrannies, the tyranny of the majority was at first, and is still vulgarly, held in dread, chiefly as operating through the acts of the public authorities. But reflecting persons perceived that when society is itself the tyrant—society collectively, over the separate individuals who compose it—its means of tyrannizing are not restricted to the acts which it may do by the hands of its political functionaries. Society can and does execute its own mandates: and if it issues wrong mandates instead of right, or any mandates at all in things with which it ought not to meddle, it practices a social tyranny more formidable than many kinds of political oppression, since, though not usually upheld by such extreme penalties, it leaves fewer means of escape, penetrating much more deeply into the details of life, and enslaving the soul itself. Protection, therefore, against the tyranny of the magistrate is not enough; there needs protection also against the tyranny of the prevailing opinion and feeling; against the tendency of society to impose, by other means than civil penalties, its own ideas and practices as rules of conduct on those who dissent from them; to fetter the development, and, if possible, prevent the formation, of any individuality not in harmony with its ways, and compel all characters to fashion themselves upon the model of its own. There is a limit to the legitimate interference of collective opinion with individual independence; and to find that limit, and maintain it against encroachment, is as indispensable to a good condition of human affairs, as protection against political despotism.

But though this proposition is not likely to be contested in general terms, the practical question, where to place the limit—how to make the fitting adjustment between individual independence and social control—is a subject on which nearly everything remains to be done. All that makes existence valuable to any one, depends on the enforcement of restraints upon the actions of other people. Some rules of conduct, therefore, must be imposed, by law in the first place, and by opinion on many things which are not fit subjects for the operation of law. What these rules should be, is the principal question in human affairs; but if we except a few of the most obvious cases, it is one of those which least progress has been made in resolving. No two ages, and scarcely any two countries, have decided it alike; and the decision of one age or country is a wonder to another. Yet the people of any given age and country no more suspect any difficulty in it, than if it were a subject on which mankind had always been agreed. The rules which obtain among themselves appear to them self-evident and self-justifying. This all but universal illusion is one of the examples of the magical influence of custom, which is not only, as the proverb says a second nature, but is continually mistaken for the first. The effect of custom, in preventing any misgiving respecting the rules of conduct which mankind impose on one another, is all the more complete because the subject is one on which it is not generally considered necessary that reasons should be given, either by one person to others, or by each to himself. People are accustomed to believe and have been encouraged in the belief by some who aspire to the character of philosophers, that their feelings, on subjects of this nature, are better than reasons, and render reasons unnecessary. The practical principle which guides them to their opinions on the regulation of human conduct, is the feeling in each person's mind that everybody should be required to act as he, and those with whom he sympathizes, would like them to act. No one, indeed, acknowledges to himself that his standard of judgment is his own liking; but an opinion on a point of conduct, not supported by reasons, can only count as one person's preference; and if the reasons, when given, are a mere appeal to a similar preference; felt by other people, it is still only many people's liking instead of one. To an ordinary man, however, his own preference, thus supported, is not only a perfectly satisfactory reason, but the only one he generally has for any of his notions of morality, taste, or propriety, which are not expressly written in his religious creed; and his chief guide in the interpretation even of that. Men's opinions, accordingly, on what is laudable or blamable, are affected by all the multifarious causes which influence their wishes in regard to the conduct of others, and which are as numerous as those which determine their wishes on any other subject. Sometimes their reason—at other times their prejudices or superstitions: often their social affections, not seldom their antisocial ones, their envy or jealousy, their arrogance or contemptuousness: but most commonly, their desires or fears for themselves—their legitimate or illegitimate self-interest. Wherever there is an ascendant class, a large portion of the morality of the country emanates from its class interests, and its feelings of class superiority. The morality between Spartans and Helots, between planters and negroes, between princes and subjects, between nobles and commoners, between men and women, has been for the most part the creation of these class interests and feelings: and the sentiments thus generated, react in turn upon the moral feelings of the members of the ascendant class, in their relations among themselves. Where, on the other hand, a class, formerly ascendant, has lost its ascendency, or where its ascendency is unpopular, the prevailing moral sentiments frequently bear the impress of an impatient dislike of superiority. Another grand determining principle of the rules of conduct, both in act and forbearance which have been enforced by law or opinion, has been the servility of mankind towards the supposed preferences or aversions of their temporal masters, or of their gods. This servility though essentially selfish, is not hypocrisy; it gives rise to perfectly genuine sentiments of abhorrence; it made men burn magicians and heretics. Among so many baser influences, the general and obvious interests of society have of course had a share, and a large one, in the direction of the moral sentiments: less, however, as a matter of reason, and on their own account, than as a consequence of the sympathies and antipathies which grew out of them: and sympathies and antipathies which had little or nothing to do with the interests of society, have made themselves felt in the establishment of moralities with quite as great force.

The likings and dislikings of society, or of some powerful portion of it, are thus the main thing which has practically determined the rules laid down for general observance, under the penalties of law or opinion. And in general, those who have been in advance of society in thought and feeling, have left this condition of things unassailed in principle, however they may have come into conflict with it in some of its details. They have occupied themselves rather in inquiring what things society ought to like or dislike, than in questioning whether its likings or dislikings should be a law to individuals. They preferred endeavouring to alter the feelings of mankind on the particular points on which they were themselves heretical, rather than make common cause in defense of freedom, with heretics generally. The only case in which the higher ground has been taken on principle and maintained with consistency, by any but an individual here and there, is that of religious belief: a case instructive in many ways, and not least so as forming a most striking instance of the fallibility of what is called the moral sense: for the odium theologicum, in a sincere bigot, is one of the most unequivocal cases of moral feeling. Those who first broke the yoke of what called itself the Universal Church, were in general as little willing to permit difference of religious opinion as that church itself. But when the heat of the conflict was over, without giving a complete victory to any party, and each church or sect was reduced to limit its hopes to retaining possession of the ground it already occupied; minorities, seeing that they had no chance of becoming majorities, were under the necessity of pleading to those whom they could not convert, for permission to differ. It is accordingly on this battle-field, almost solely, that the rights of the individual against society have been asserted on broad grounds of principle, and the claim of society to exercise authority over dissentients openly controverted. The great writers to whom the world owes what religious liberty it possesses, have mostly asserted freedom of conscience as an indefeasible right, and denied absolutely that a human being is accountable to others for his religious belief. Yet so natural to mankind is intolerance in whatever they really care about, that religious freedom has hardly anywhere been practically realized, except where religious indifference, which dislikes to have its ease disturbed by theological quarrels, has added its weight to the scale. In the minds of almost all religious persons, even in the most tolerant countries, the duty of toleration is admitted with the tacit reserves. One person will bear with dissent in matters of church government, but not of dogma; another can tolerate everybody, short of a Papist or an Unitarian; another, every one who believes in revealed religion; a few extend their charity a little further, but stop at the belief in a God and in a future state. Wherever the sentiment of the majority is still genuine and intense, it is found to have abated little of its claim to be obeyed.

In England, from the peculiar circumstances of our political history, though the yoke of opinion is perhaps heavier, that of law is lighter, than in most other countries of Europe; and there is considerable jealousy of direct interference, by the legislative or the executive power with private conduct; not so much from any just regard for the independence of the individual, as from the still subsisting habit of looking on the government as representing an opposite interest to the public. The majority have not yet learnt to feel the power of the government their power, or its opinions their opinions. When they do so, individual liberty will probably be as much exposed to invasion from the government, as it already is from public opinion. But, as yet, there is a considerable amount of feeling ready to be called forth against any attempt of the law to control individuals in things in which they have not hitherto been accustomed to be controlled by it; and this with very little discrimination as to whether the matter is, or is not, within the legitimate sphere of legal control; insomuch that the feeling, highly salutary on the whole, is perhaps quite as often misplaced as well grounded in the particular instances of its application.

There is, in fact, no recognized principle by which the propriety or impropriety of government interference is customarily tested. People decide according to their personal preferences. Some, whenever they see any good to be done, or evil to be remedied, would willingly instigate the government to undertake the business; while others prefer to bear almost any amount of social evil, rather than add one to the departments of human interests amenable to governmental control. And men range themselves on one or the other side in any particular case, according to this general direction of their sentiments; or according to the degree of interest which they feel in the particular thing which it is proposed that the government should do; or according to the belief they entertain that the government would, or would not, do it in the manner they prefer; but very rarely on account of any opinion to which they consistently adhere, as to what things are fit to be done by a government. And it seems to me that, in consequence of this absence of rule or principle, one side is at present as often wrong as the other; the interference of government is, with about equal frequency, improperly invoked and improperly condemned.

The object of this Essay is to assert one very simple principle, as entitled to govern absolutely the dealings of society with the individual in the way of compulsion and control, whether the means used be physical force in the form of legal penalties, or the moral coercion of public opinion. That principle is, that the sole end for which mankind are warranted, individually or collectively in interfering with the liberty of action of any of their number, is self-protection. That the only purpose for which power can be rightfully exercised over any member of a civilized community, against his will, is to prevent harm to others. His own good, either physical or moral, is not a sufficient warrant. He cannot rightfully be compelled to do or forbear because it will be better for him to do so, because it will make him happier, because, in the opinions of others, to do so would be wise, or even right. These are good reasons for remonstrating with him, or reasoning with him, or persuading him, or entreating him, but not for compelling him, or visiting him with any evil, in case he do otherwise. To justify that, the conduct from which it is desired to deter him must be calculated to produce evil to some one else. The only part of the conduct of any one, for which he is amenable to society, is that which concerns others. In the part which merely concerns himself, his independence is, of right, absolute. Over himself, over his own body and mind, the individual is sovereign.

It is, perhaps, hardly necessary to say that this doctrine is meant to apply only to human beings in the maturity of their faculties. We are not speaking of children, or of young persons below the age which the law may fix as that of manhood or womanhood. Those who are still in a state to require being taken care of by others, must be protected against their own actions as well as against external injury. For the same reason, we may leave out of consideration those backward states of society in which the race itself may be considered as in its nonage. The early difficulties in the way of spontaneous progress are so great, that there is seldom any choice of means for overcoming them; and a ruler full of the spirit of improvement is warranted in the use of any expedients that will attain an end, perhaps otherwise unattainable. Despotism is a legitimate mode of government in dealing with barbarians, provided the end be their improvement, and the means justified by actually effecting that end. Liberty, as a principle, has no application to any state of things anterior to the time when mankind have become capable of being improved by free and equal discussion. Until then, there is nothing for them but implicit obedience to an Akbar or a Charlemagne, if they are so fortunate as to find one. But as soon as mankind have attained the capacity of being guided to their own improvement by conviction or persuasion (a period long since reached in all nations with whom we need here concern ourselves), compulsion, either in the direct form or in that of pains and penalties for non-compliance, is no longer admissible as a means to their own good, and justifiable only for the security of others.

It is proper to state that I forego any advantage which could be derived to my argument from the idea of abstract right as a thing independent of utility. I regard utility as the ultimate appeal on all ethical questions; but it must be utility in the largest sense, grounded on the permanent interests of man as a progressive being. Those interests, I contend, authorize the subjection of individual spontaneity to external control, only in respect to those actions of each, which concern the interest of other people. If any one does an act hurtful to others, there is a prima facie case for punishing him, by law, or, where legal penalties are not safely applicable, by general disapprobation. There are also many positive acts for the benefit of others, which he may rightfully be compelled to perform; such as, to give evidence in a court of justice; to bear his fair share in the common defense, or in any other joint work necessary to the interest of the society of which he enjoys the protection; and to perform certain acts of individual beneficence, such as saving a fellow-creature's life, or interposing to protect the defenseless against ill-usage, things which whenever it is obviously a man's duty to do, he may rightfully be made responsible to society for not doing. A person may cause evil to others not only by his actions but by his inaction, and in either case he is justly accountable to them for the injury. The latter case, it is true, requires a much more cautious exercise of compulsion than the former. To make any one answerable for doing evil to others, is the rule; to make him answerable for not preventing evil, is, comparatively speaking, the exception. Yet there are many cases clear enough and grave enough to justify that exception. In all things which regard the external relations of the individual, he is de jure amenable to those whose interests are concerned, and if need be, to society as their protector. There are often good reasons for not holding him to the responsibility; but these reasons must arise from the special expediencies of the case: either because it is a kind of case in which he is on the whole likely to act better, when left to his own discretion, than when controlled in any way in which society have it in their power to control him; or because the attempt to exercise control would produce other evils, greater than those which it would prevent. When such reasons as these preclude the enforcement of responsibility, the conscience of the agent himself should step into the vacant judgment-seat, and protect those interests of others which have no external protection; judging himself all the more rigidly, because the case does not admit of his being made accountable to the judgment of his fellow creatures.

But there is a sphere of action in which society, as distinguished from the individual, has, if any, only an indirect interest; comprehending all that portion of a person's life and conduct which affects only himself, or, if it also affects others, only with their free, voluntary, and undeceived consent and participation. When I say only himself, I mean directly, and in the first instance: for whatever affects himself, may affect others through himself; and the objection which may be grounded on this contingency, will receive consideration in the sequel. This, then, is the appropriate region of human liberty. It comprises, first, the inward domain of consciousness; demanding liberty of conscience, in the most comprehensive sense; liberty of thought and feeling; absolute freedom of opinion and sentiment on all subjects, practical or speculative, scientific, moral, or theological. The liberty of expressing and publishing opinions may seem to fall under a different principle, since it belongs to that part of the conduct of an individual which concerns other people; but, being almost of as much importance as the liberty of thought itself, and resting in great part on the same reasons, is practically inseparable from it. Secondly, the principle requires liberty of tastes and pursuits; of framing the plan of our life to suit our own character; of doing as we like, subject to such consequences as may follow; without impediment from our fellow-creatures, so long as what we do does not harm them even though they should think our conduct foolish, perverse, or wrong. Thirdly, from this liberty of each individual, follows the liberty, within the same limits, of combination among individuals; freedom to unite, for any purpose not involving harm to others: the persons combining being supposed to be of full age, and not forced or deceived.

No society in which these liberties are not, on the whole, respected, is free, whatever may be its form of government; and none is completely free in which they do not exist absolute and unqualified. The only freedom which deserves the name, is that of pursuing our own good in our own way, so long as we do not attempt to deprive others of theirs, or impede their efforts to obtain it. Each is the proper guardian of his own health, whether bodily, or mental or spiritual. Mankind are greater gainers by suffering each other to live as seems good to themselves, than by compelling each to live as seems good to the rest.

Though this doctrine is anything but new, and, to some persons, may have the air of a truism, there is no doctrine which stands more directly opposed to the general tendency of existing opinion and practice. Society has expended fully as much effort in the attempt (according to its lights) to compel people to conform to its notions of personal, as of social excellence. The ancient commonwealths thought themselves entitled to practice, and the ancient philosophers countenanced, the regulation of every part of private conduct by public authority, on the ground that the State had a deep interest in the whole bodily and mental discipline of every one of its citizens, a mode of thinking which may have been admissible in small republics surrounded by powerful enemies, in constant peril of being subverted by foreign attack or internal commotion, and to which even a short interval of relaxed energy and self-command might so easily be fatal, that they could not afford to wait for the salutary permanent effects of freedom. In the modern world, the greater size of political communities, and above all, the separation between the spiritual and temporal authority (which placed the direction of men's consciences in other hands than those which controlled their worldly affairs), prevented so great an interference by law in the details of private life; but the engines of moral repression have been wielded more strenuously against divergence from the reigning opinion in self-regarding, than even in social matters; religion, the most powerful of the elements which have entered into the formation of moral feeling, having almost always been governed either by the ambition of a hierarchy, seeking control over every department of human conduct, or by the spirit of Puritanism. And some of those modern reforms who have placed themselves in strongest opposition to the religions of the past, have been no way behind either churches or sects in their assertion of the right of spiritual domination: M. Comte, in particular, whose social system, as unfolded in his Traite de Politique Positive, aims at establishing (though by moral more than by legal appliances) a despotism of society over the individual, surpassing anything contemplated in the political ideal of the most rigid disciplinarian among the ancient philosophers.

Apart from the peculiar tenets of individual thinkers, there is also in the world at large an increasing inclination to stretch unduly the powers of society over the individual, both by the force of opinion and even by that of legislation: and as the tendency of all the changes taking place in the world is to strengthen society, and diminish the power of the individual, this encroachment is not one of the evils which tend spontaneously to disappear, but, on the contrary, to grow more and more formidable. The disposition of mankind, whether as rulers or as fellow-citizens, to impose their own opinions and inclinations as a rule of conduct on others, is so energetically supported by some of the best and by some of the worst feelings incident to human nature, that it is hardly ever kept under restraint by anything but want of power; and as the power is not declining, but growing, unless a strong barrier of moral conviction can be raised against the mischief, we must expect, in the present circumstances of the world, to see it increase.

It will be convenient for the argument, if, instead of at once entering upon the general thesis, we confine ourselves in the first instance to a single branch of it, on which the principle here stated is, if not fully, yet to a certain point, recognized by the current opinions. This one branch is the Liberty of Thought: from which it is impossible to separate the cognate liberty of speaking and of writing. Although these liberties, to some considerable amount, form part of the political morality of all countries which profess religious toleration and free institutions, the grounds, both philosophical and practical, on which they rest, are perhaps not so familiar to the general mind, nor so thoroughly appreciated by many even of the leaders of opinion, as might have been expected. Those grounds, when rightly understood, are of much wider application than to only one division of the subject, and a thorough consideration of this part of the question will be found the best introduction to the remainder. Those to whom nothing which I am about to say will be new, may therefore, I hope, excuse me, if on a subject which for now three centuries has been so often discussed, I venture on one discussion more.

CHAPTER II: OF THE LIBERTY OF THOUGHT AND DISCUSSION

The time, it is to be hoped, is gone by when any defense would be necessary of the "liberty of the press" as one of the securities against corrupt or tyrannical government. No argument, we may suppose, can now be needed, against permitting a legislature or an executive, not identified in interest with the people, to prescribe opinions to them, and determine what doctrines or what arguments they shall be allowed to hear. This aspect of the question, besides, has been so often and so triumphantly enforced by preceding writers, that it needs not be specially insisted on in this place. Though the law of England, on the subject of the press, is as servile to this day as it was in the time of the Tudors, there is little danger of its being actually put in force against political discussion, except during some temporary panic, when fear of insurrection drives ministers and judges from their propriety; and, speaking generally, it is not, in constitutional countries, to be apprehended that the government, whether completely responsible to the people or not, will often attempt to control the expression of opinion, except when in doing so it makes itself the organ of the general intolerance of the public. Let us suppose, therefore, that the government is entirely at one with the people, and never thinks of exerting any power of coercion unless in agreement with what it conceives to be their voice. But I deny the right of the people to exercise such coercion, either by themselves or by their government. The power itself is illegitimate. The best government has no more title to it than the worst. It is as noxious, or more noxious, when exerted in accordance with public opinion, than when in opposition to it. If all mankind minus one, were of one opinion, and only one person were of the contrary opinion, mankind would be no more justified in silencing that one person, than he, if he had the power, would be justified in silencing mankind. Were an opinion a personal possession of no value except to the owner; if to be obstructed in the enjoyment of it were simply a private injury, it would make some difference whether the injury was inflicted only on a few persons or on many. But the peculiar evil of silencing the expression of an opinion is, that it is robbing the human race; posterity as well as the existing generation; those who dissent from the opinion, still more than those who hold it. If the opinion is right, they are deprived of the opportunity of exchanging error for truth: if wrong, they lose, what is almost as great a benefit, the clearer perception and livelier impression of truth, produced by its collision with error.

It is necessary to consider separately these two hypotheses, each of which has a distinct branch of the argument corresponding to it. We can never be sure that the opinion we are endeavouring to stifle is a false opinion; and if we were sure, stifling it would be an evil still.

First: the opinion which it is attempted to suppress by authority may possibly be true. Those who desire to suppress it, of course deny its truth; but they are not infallible. They have no authority to decide the question

for all mankind, and exclude every other person from the means of judging. To refuse a hearing to an opinion, because they are sure that it is false, is to assume that their certainty is the same thing as absolute certainty. All silencing of discussion is an assumption of infallibility. Its condemnation may be allowed to rest on this common argument, not the worse for being common.

Unfortunately for the good sense of mankind, the fact of their fallibility is far from carrying the weight in their practical judgment, which is always allowed to it in theory; for while every one well knows himself to be fallible, few think it necessary to take any precautions against their own fallibility, or admit the supposition that any opinion of which they feel very certain, may be one of the examples of the error to which they acknowledge themselves to be liable. Absolute princes, or others who are accustomed to unlimited deference, usually feel this complete confidence in their own opinions on nearly all subjects. People more happily situated, who sometimes hear their opinions disputed, and are not wholly unused to be set right when they are wrong, place the same unbounded reliance only on such of their opinions as are shared by all who surround them, or to whom they habitually defer: for in proportion to a man's want of confidence in his own solitary judgment, does he usually repose, with implicit trust, on the infallibility of "the world" in general. And the world, to each individual, means the part of it with which he comes in contact; his party, his sect, his church, his class of society: the man may be called, by comparison, almost liberal and large minded to whom it means anything so comprehensive as his own country or his own age. Nor is his faith in this collective authority at all shaken by his being aware that other ages, countries, sects, churches, classes, and parties have thought, and even now think, the exact reverse. He devolves upon his own world the responsibility of being in the right against the dissentient worlds of other people; and it never troubles him that mere accident has decided which of these numerous worlds is the object of his reliance, and that the same causes which make him a Churchman in London, would have made him a Buddhist or a Confucian in Pekin. Yet it is as evident in itself as any amount of argument can make it, that ages are no more infallible than individuals; every age having held many opinions which subsequent ages have deemed not only false but absurd; and it is as certain that many opinions, now general, will be rejected by future ages, as it is that many, once general, are rejected by the present.

The objection likely to be made to this argument, would probably take some such form as the following. There is no greater assumption of infallibility in forbidding the propagation of error, than in any other thing which is done by public authority on its own judgment and responsibility. Judgment is given to men that they may use it. Because it may be used erroneously, are men to be told that they ought not to use it at all? To prohibit what they think prenicious, is not claiming exemption from error, but fulfilling the duty incumbent on them, although fallible, of acting on their conscientious conviction. If we were never to act on our opinions, because those opinions may be wrong, we should leave all our interests uncared for, and all our duties unperformed. An objection which applies to all conduct can be no valid objection to any conduct in particular.

It is the duty of governments, and of individuals, to form the truest opinions they can; to form them carefully, and never impose them upon others unless they are quite sure of being right. But when they are sure (such reasoners may say), it is not conscientiousness but cowardice to shrink from acting on their opinions, and allow doctrines which they honestly think dangerous to the welfare of mankind, either in this life or in another, to be scattered abroad without restraint, because other people, in less enlightened times, have persecuted opinions now believed to be true. Let us take care, it may be said, not to make the same mistake: but governments and nations have made mistakes in other things, which are not denied to be fit subjects for the exercise of authority: they have laid on bad taxes, made unjust wars. Ought we therefore to lay on no taxes, and, under whatever provocation, make no wars? Men, and governments, must act to the best of their ability. There is no such thing as absolute certainty, but there is assurance sufficient for the purposes of human life. We may, and must, assume our opinion to be true for the guidance of our own conduct: and it is assuming no more when we forbid bad men to pervert society by the propagation of opinions which we regard as false and pernicious.

I answer, that it is assuming very much more. There is the greatest difference between presuming an opinion to be true, because, with every opportunity for contesting it, it has not been refuted, and assuming its truth for the purpose of not permitting its refutation. Complete liberty of contradicting and disproving our opinion, is the very condition which justifies us in assuming its truth for purposes of action; and on no other terms can a being with human faculties have any rotational assurance of being right.

When we consider either the history of opinion, or the ordinary conduct of human life, to what is it to be ascribed that the one and the other are no worse than they are? Not certainly to the inherent force of the human understanding; for, on any matter not self-evident, there are ninety-nine persons totally incapable of judging of it, for one who is capable; and the capacity of the hundredth person is only comparative; for the majority of the eminent men of every past generation held many opinions now known to be erroneous, and did or approved numerous things which no one will now justify. Why is it, then, that there is on the whole a preponderance among mankind of rational opinions and rational conduct? If there really is this preponderance— which there must be, unless human affairs are, and have always been, in an almost desperate state—it is owing to a quality of the human mind, the source of everything respectable in man, either as an intellectual or as a moral being, namely, that his errors are corrigible. He is capable of rectifying his mistakes by discussion and experience. Not by experience alone. There must be discussion, to show how experience is to be interpreted. Wrong opinions and practices gradually yield to fact and argument: but facts and arguments, to produce any effect on the mind, must be brought before it. Very few facts are able to tell their own story, without comments to bring out their meaning. The whole strength and value, then, of human judgment, depending on the one property, that it can be set right when it is wrong, reliance can be placed on it only when the means of setting it right are kept constantly at hand. In the case of any person whose judgment is really deserving of confidence, how has it become so? Because he has kept his mind open to criticism of his opinions and conduct. Because it has been his practice to listen to all that could be said against him; to profit by as much of it as was just, and expound to himself, and upon occasion to others, the fallacy of what was fallacious. Because he has felt, that the only way in which a human being can make some approach to knowing the whole of a subject, is by hearing what can be said about it by persons of every variety of opinion, and studying all modes in which it can be looked at by every character of mind. No wise man ever acquired his wisdom in any mode but this; nor is it in the nature of human intellect to become wise in any other manner. The steady habit of correcting and completing his own opinion by collating it with those of others, so far from causing doubt and hesitation in carrying it into practice, is the only stable foundation for a just reliance on it: for, being cognizant of all that can, at least obviously, be said against him, and having taken up his position against all gainsayers knowing that he has sought for objections and difficulties, instead of avoiding them, and has shut out no light which can be thrown upon the subject from any quarter—he has a right to think his judgment better than that of any person, or any multitude, who have not gone through a similar process.

It is not too much to require that what the wisest of mankind, those who are best entitled to trust their own judgment, find necessary to warrant their relying on it, should be submitted to by that miscellaneous collection of a few wise and many foolish individuals, called the public. The most intolerant of churches, the Roman Catholic Church, even at the canonization of a saint, admits, and listens patiently to, a "devil's advocate." The holiest of men, it appears, cannot be admitted to posthumous honors, until all that the devil could say against him is known and weighed. If even the Newtonian philosophy were not permitted to be questioned, mankind could not feel as complete assurance of its truth as they now do. The beliefs which we have most warrant for, have no safeguard to rest on, but a standing invitation to the whole world to prove them unfounded. If the challenge is not accepted, or is accepted and the attempt fails, we are far enough from certainty still; but we have done the best that the existing state of human reason admits of; we have neglected nothing that could give the truth a chance of reaching us: if the lists are kept open, we may hope that if there be a better truth, it will be found when the human mind is capable of receiving it; and in the meantime we may rely on having attained such approach to truth, as is possible in our own day. This is the amount of certainty attainable by a fallible being, and this the sole way of attaining it.

Strange it is, that men should admit the validity of the arguments for free discussion, but object to their being "pushed to an extreme;" not seeing that unless the reasons are good for an extreme case, they are not good for any case. Strange that they should imagine that they are not assuming infallibility when they acknowledge that there should be free discussion on all subjects which can possibly be doubtful, but think that some particular principle or doctrine should be forbidden to be questioned because it is so certain, that is, because they are certain that it is certain. To call any proposition certain, while there is any one who would deny its certainty if permitted, but who is not permitted, is to assume that we ourselves, and those who agree with us, are the judges of certainty, and judges without hearing the other side.

In the present age—which has been described as "destitute of faith, but terrified at scepticism,"—in which people feel sure, not so much that their opinions are true, as that they should not know what to do without them—the claims of an opinion to be protected from public attack are rested not so much on its truth, as on its importance to society. There are, it is alleged, certain beliefs, so useful, not to say indispensable to well-being, that it is as much the duty of governments to uphold those beliefs, as to protect any other of the interests of society. In a case of such necessity, and so directly in the line of their duty, something less than infallibility may, it is maintained, warrant, and even bind, governments, to act on their own opinion, confirmed by the general opinion of mankind. It is also often argued, and still oftener thought, that none but bad men would desire to weaken these salutary beliefs; and there can be nothing wrong, it is thought, in restraining bad men, and prohibiting what only such men would wish to practice. This mode of thinking makes the justification of restraints on discussion not a question of the truth of doctrines, but of their usefulness; and flatters itself by that means to escape the responsibility of claiming to be an infallible judge of opinions. But those who thus satisfy themselves, do not perceive that the assumption of infallibility is merely shifted from one point to another. The usefulness of an opinion is itself a matter of opinion: as disputable, as open to discussion and requiring discussion as much, as the opinion itself. There is the same need of an infallible judge of opinions to decide an opinion to be noxious, as to decide it to be false, unless the opinion condemned has full opportunity of defending itself. And it will not do to say that the heretic may be allowed to maintain the utility or harmlessness of his opinion, though forbidden to maintain its truth. The truth of an opinion is part of its utility. If we would know whether or not it is desirable that a proposition should be believed, is it possible to exclude the consideration of whether or not it is true? In the opinion, not of bad men, but of the best men, no belief which is contrary to truth can be really useful: and can you prevent such men from urging that plea, when they are charged with culpability for denying some doctrine which they are told is useful, but which they believe to be false? Those who are on the side of received opinion, never fail to take all possible advantage of this plea; you do not find them handling the question of utility as if it could be completely abstracted from that of truth: on the contrary, it is, above all, because their doctrine is "the truth," that the knowledge or the belief of it is held to be so indispensable.

There can be no fair discussion of the question of usefulness, when an argument so vital may be employed on one side, but not on the other. And in point of fact, when law or public feeling do not permit the truth of an opinion to be disputed, they are just as little tolerant of a denial of its usefulness. The utmost they allow is an extenuation of its absolute necessity or of the possitive guilt of rejecting it.

Mankind can hardly be too often reminded, that there was once a man named Socrates, between whom and the legal authorities and public opinion of his time, there took place a memorable collision. Born in an age and country abounding in individual greatness, this man has been handed down to us by those who best knew both him and the age, as the most virtuous man in it; while we know him as the head and prototype of all subsequent teachers of virtue, the source equally of the lofty inspiration of Plato and the judicious utilitarianism of Aristotle, "i maestri di color che sanno," [the master of them that know] the two headsprings of ethical as of all other philosophy. This acknowledged master of all the eminent thinkers who have since lived—whose fame, still growing after more than two thousand years, all but outweighs the whole remainder of the names which make his native city illustrious—was put to death by his countrymen, after a judicial conviction, for impiety and immorality. Impiety, in denying the gods recognized by the State; indeed his accuser asserted (see the "Apologia") that he believed in no gods at all. Immorality, in being, by his doctrines and instructions, a "corrupter of youth." Of these charges the tribunal, there is every ground for believing, honestly found him guilty, and condemned the man who probably of all then born had deserved best of mankind, to be put to death as a criminal.

To pass from this to the only other instance of judicial iniquity, the mention of which, after the condemnation of Socrates, would not be an anti-climax: the event which took place on Calvary rather more than eighteen hundred years ago. The man who left on the memory of those who witnessed his life and conversation, such an impression of his moral grandeur, that eighteen subsequent centuries have done homage to him as the Almighty in person, was ignominiously put to death, as what? As a blasphemer. Men did not merely mistake their benefactor; they mistook him for the exact contrary of what he was, and treated him as that prodigy of impiety, which they themselves are now held to be, for their treatment of him. The feelings with which mankind now regard these lamentable transactions, especially the latter of the two, render them extremely unjust in their judgment of the unhappy actors. These were, to all appearance, not bad men—not worse than men most commonly are, but rather the contrary; men who possessed in a full, or somewhat more than a full measure, the religious, moral, and patriotic feelings of their time and people: the very kind of men who, in all times our own included, have every chance of passing through life blameless and respected. The high-priest who rent his garments when the words were pronounced, which, according to all the ideas of his country, constituted the blackest guilt, was in all probability quite as sincere in his horror and indignation, as the generality of respectable and pious men now are in the religious and moral sentiments they profess; and most of those who now shudder at his conduct, if they had lived in his time and been born Jews, would have acted precisely as he did. Orthodox Christians who are tempted to think that those who stoned to death the first martyrs must have been worse men than they themselves are, ought to remember that one of those persecutors was Saint Paul. . . .

Aware of the impossibility of defending the use of punishment for restraining irreligious opinions . . . the enemies of religious freedom, when hard pressed, occasionally accept this consequence, and say, with Dr. Johnson, that the persecutors of Christianity were in the right; that persecution is an ordeal through which truth ought to pass, and always passes successfully, legal penalties being, in the end, powerless against truth, though sometimes beneficially effective against mischievous errors. This is a form of the argument for religious intolerance, sufficiently remarkable not to be passed without notice.

A theory which maintains that truth may justifiably be persecuted because persecution cannot possibly do it any harm, cannot be charged with being intentionally hostile to the reception of new truths; but we cannot commend the generosity of its dealing with the persons to whom mankind are indebted for them. To discover to the world something which deeply concerns it, and of which it was previously ignorant; to prove to it that it had been mistaken on some vital point of temporal or spiritual interest, is as important a service as a human being can render to his fellow-creatures, and in certain cases, as in those of the early Christians and of the Reformers, those who think with Dr. Johnson believe it to have been the most precious gift which could be bestowed on mankind. That the authors of such splendid benefits shoud be requited by martydom; that their reward should be to be dealt with as the vilest of criminals, is not, upon this theory, a deplorable error and misfortune for which humanity should mourn in sackcloth and ashes, but the normal and justifiable state of things. The propounder of a new truth, according to this doctrine, should stand, as stood, in the legislation of the Locrians, the proposer of a new law, with a halter round his neck, to be instantly tightened if the public assembly did not, on hearing his reasons, then and there adopt his proposition. People who defend this mode of treating benefactors, can not be supposed to set much value on the benefit; and I believe this view of the subject is mostly confined to the sort of persons who think that new truths may have been desirable once, but that we have had enough of them now.

But, indeed, the dictum that truth always triumphs over persecution, is one of those pleasant falsehoods which men repeat after one another till they pass into commonplaces, but which all experience refutes. History teems with instances of truth put down by persecution. If not suppressed forever, it may be thrown back for centuries. To speak only of religious opinions: the Reformation broke out at least twenty times before Luther, and was put down. Arnold of Brescia was put down. Fra Dolcino was put down. Savonarola was put down. The Albigenses were put down. The Vaudois were put down. The Lollards were put down. The Hussites were put down. Even after the era of Luther, wherever persecution was persisted in, it was successful. In Spain, Italy, Flanders, the Austrian empire, Protestantism was rooted out; and, most likely, would have been so in England, had Queen Mary lived, or Queen Elizabeth died. Persecution has always succeeded, save where the heretics were too strong a party to be effectually persecuted. No reasonable person can doubt that Christianity might have been extirpated in the Roman empire. It spread, and became predominant, because the persecutions were only occasional, lasting but a short time, and separated by long intervals of almost undisturbed propagandism. It is a piece of idle sentimentality that truth, merely as truth, has any inherent power denied to error, of prevailing against the dungeon and the stake. Men are not more zealous for truth than they often are for error, and a sufficient application of legal or even of social penalties will generally succeed in stopping the propagation of either. The real advantage which truth has, consists in this, that when an opinion is true, it may be extinguished once, twice, or many times, but in the course of ages there will generally be found persons to rediscover it, until some one of its reappearances falls on a time when from favourable circumstances it escapes persecution until it has made such head as to withstand all subsequent attempts to suppress it. . . .

Let us now pass to the second division of the argument, and dismissing the Supposition that any of the received opinions may be false, let us assume them to be true, and examine into the worth of the manner in which they are likely to be held, when their truth is not freely and openly canvassed. However unwillingly a person who has a strong opinion may admit the possibility that his opinion may be false, he ought to be moved by the consideration that however true it may be, if it is not fully, frequently, and fearlessly discussed, it will be held as a dead dogma, not a living truth.

There is a class of persons (happily not quite so numerous as formerly) who think it enough if a person assents undoubtingly to what they think true, though he has no knowledge whatever of the grounds of the opinion, and could not make a tenable defense of it against the most superficial objections. Such persons, if they can once get their creed taught from authority, naturally think that no good, and some harm, comes of its being allowed to be questioned. Where their influence prevails, they make it nearly impossible for the received opinion to be rejected wisely and considerately, though it may still be rejected rashly and ignorantly; for to shut out discussion entirely is seldom possible, and when it once gets in, beliefs not grounded on conviction are apt to give way before the slightest semblance of an argument. Waiving, however, this possibility—assuming that the true opinion abides in the mind, but abides as a prejudice, a belief indepedent of, and proof against, argument—this is not the way in which truth ought to be held by a rational being. This is not knowing the truth. Truth, thus held, is but one superstition the more, accidentally clinging to the words which enunciate a truth.

If the intellect and judgment of mankind ought to be cultivated, a thing which Protestants at least do not deny, on what can these faculties be more appropriately exercised by any one, than on the things which concern him so much that it is considered necessary for him to hold opinions on them? If the cultivation of the understanding consists in one thing more than in another, it is surely in learning the grounds of one's own opinions. Whatever people believe, on subjects on which it is of the first importance to believe rightly, they ought to be able to defend against at least the common objections. But, some one may say, "Let them be taught the grounds of their opinions. It does not follow that opinions must be merely parroted because they are never heard controverted. Persons who learn geometry do not simply commit the theorems to memory, but understand and learn likewise the demonstrations; and it would be absurd to say that they remain ignorant of the grounds of geometrical truths, because they never hear any one deny, and attempt to disprove them." Undoubtedly: and such teaching suffices on a subject like mathematics, where there is nothing at all to be said on the wrong side of the question. The peculiarity of the evidence of mathematical truths is, that all the argument is on one side. There are no objections, and no answers to objections. But on every subject on which difference of opinion is possible, the truth depends on a balance to be struck between two sets of conflicting reasons. Even in natural philosophy, there is always some other explanation possible of the same facts; some geocentric theory instead of heliocentric, some phlogiston instead of oxygen; and it has to be shown why that other theory cannot be the true one: and until this is shown and until we know how it is shown, we do not understand the grounds of our opinion. But when we turn to subjects infinitely more complicated, to morals, religion, politics, social relations, and the business of life, three-fourths of the arguments for every disputed opinion consist in dispelling the appearances which favor some opinion different from it. The greatest orator, save one, of antiquity, has left it on record that he always studied his adversary's case with as great, if not with still greater, intensity than even his own. What Cicero practiced as the means of forensic success, requires to be imitated by all who study any subject in order to arrive at the truth.

He who knows only his own side of the case, knows little of that. His reasons may be good; and no one may have been able to refute them. But if he is equally unable to refute the reasons on the opposite side; if he does not so much as know what they are, he has no ground for preferring either opinion. The rational position for him would be suspension of judgment, and unless he contents himself with that, he is either led by authority, or adopts, like the generality of the world, the side to which he feels most inclination. Nor is it enough that he should hear the arguments of adversaries from his own teachers, presented as they state them, and accompanied by what they offer as refutations. This is not the way to do justice to the arguments, or bring them into real contact with his own mind. He must be able to hear them from persons who actually believe them; who defend them in earnest, and do their very utmost for them. He must know them in their most plausible and persuasive form; he must feel the whole force of the difficulty which the true view of

the subject has to encounter and dispose of, else he will never really possess himself of the portion of truth which meets and removes that difficulty. Ninety-nine in a hundred of what are called educated men are in this condition, even of those who can argue fluently for their opinions. Their conclusion may be true, but it might be false for anything they know: they have never thrown themselves into the mental position of those who think differently from them, and considered what such persons may have to say; and consequently they do not, in any proper sense of the word, know the doctrine which they themselves profess. They do not know those parts of it which explain and justify the remainder; the considerations which show that a fact which seemingly conflicts with another is reconcilable with it, or that, of two apparently strong reasons, one and not the other ought to be preferred. All that part of the truth which turns the scale, and decides the judgment of a completely informed mind, they are strangers to; nor is it ever really known, but to those who have attended equally and impartially to both sides, and endeavored to see the reasons of both in the strongest light. So essential is this discipline to a real understanding of moral and human subjects, that if opponents of all important truths do not exist, it is indispensable to imagine them and supply them with the strongest arguments which the most skilful devil's advocate can conjure up.

To abate the force of these considerations, an enemy of free discussion may be supposed to say, that there is no necessity for mankind in general to know and understand all that can be said against or for their opinions by philosophers and theologians. That it is not needful for common men to be able to expose all the misstatements or fallacies of an ingenious opponent. That it is enough if there is always somebody capable of answering them, so that nothing likely to mislead uninstructed person remains unrefuted. That simple minds, having been taught the obvious grounds of the truths inculcated on them, may trust to authority for the rest, and being aware that they have neither knowledge nor talent to resolve every difficulty which can be raised, may repose in the assurance that all those which have been raised have been or can be answered, by those who are specially trained to the task.

Conceding to this view of the subject the utmost that can be claimed for it by those most easily satisfied with the amount of understanding of truth which ought to accompany the belief of it; even so, the argument for free discussion is no way weakened. For even this doctrine acknowledges that mankind ought to have a rational assurance that all objections have been satis-factorily answered; and how are they to be answered if that which requires to be answered is not spoken? or how can the answer be known to be satisfactory, if the objectors have no opportunity of showing that it is un-satisfactory? If not the public, at least the philosophers and theologians who are to resolve the difficulties, must make themselves familiar with those difficulties in their most puzzling form; and this cannot be ac-complished unless they are freely stated, and placed in the most advantageous light which they admit of. The Catholic Church has its own way of dealing with this embarrassing problem. It makes a broad separation be-tween those who can be permitted to receive its doc-trines on conviction, and those who must accept them on trust. Neither, indeed, are allowed any choice as to what they will accept; but the clergy, such at least as can be fully confided in, may admissibly and meritori-ously make themselves acquainted with the arguments of opponents, in order to answer them, and may, there-fore, read heretical books; the laity, not unless by spe-cial permission, hard to be obtained. This discipline recognizes a knowledge of the enemy's case as benefi-cial to the teachers, but finds means, consistent with this, of denying it to the rest of the world: thus giving to the elite more mental culture, though not more men-tal freedom, than it allows to the mass. By this device it succeeds in obtaining the kind of mental superiority which its purposes require; for though culture without freedom never made a large and liberal mind, it can make a clever nisi prius advocate of a cause. But in countries professing Protestantism, this resource is de-nied; since Protestants hold, at least in theory, that the responsibility for the choice of a religion must be borne by each for himself, and cannot be thrown off upon teachers. Besides, in the present state of the world, it is practically impossible that writings which are read by the instructed can be kept from the uninstructed. If the teachers of mankind are to be cognizant of all that they ought to know, everything must be free to be written and published without restraint.

If, however, the mischievous operation of the ab-sence of free discussion, when the received opinions are true, were confined to leaving men ignorant of the grounds of those opinions, it might be thought that this, if an intellectual, is no moral evil, and does not affect the worth of the opinions, regarded in their influence on the character. The fact, however, is, that not only the grounds of the opinion are forgotten in the absence of discussion, but too often the meaning of the opinion it-self. The words which convey it, cease to suggest ideas, or suggest only a small portion of those they were orig-inally employed to communicate. Instead of a vivid conception and a living belief, there remain only a few phrases retained by rote; or, if any part, the shell and husk only of the meaning is retained, the finer essence being lost. The great chapter in human history which this fact occupies and fills, cannot be too earnestly studied and meditated on.

It is illustrated in the experience of almost all eth-ical doctrines and religious creeds. They are all full of meaning and vitality to those who originate them, and to the direct disciples of the originators. Their mean-ing continues to be felt in undiminished strength, and is perhaps brought out into even fuller consciousness, so long as the struggle lasts to give the doctrine or creed an ascendency over other creeds. At last it either prevails, and becomes the general opinion, or its progress stops; it keeps possession of the ground it has gained, but ceases to spread further. When either of these results has become apparent, controversy on the subject flags, and gradually dies away. The doctrine has taken its place, if not as a received opinion, as one of the admitted sects or divisions of opinion: those who hold it have generally inherited, not adopted it; and conversion from one of these doctrines to another, being now an exceptional fact, occupies little place in the thoughts of their professors. Instead of being, as at first, constantly on the alert either to defend them-selves against the world, or to bring the world over to them, they have subsided into acquiescence, and nei-ther listen, when they can help it, to arguments against their creed, nor trouble dissentients (if there be such) with arguments in its favor. From this time may usu-ally be dated the decline in the living power of the doctrine. We often hear the teachers of all creeds lamenting the difficulty of keeping up in the minds of believers a lively apprehension of the truth which they nominally recognize, so that it may penetrate the feel-ings, and acquire a real mastery over the conduct. No such difficulty is complained of while the creed is still fighting for its existence: even the weaker combatants then know and feel what they are fighting for, and the difference between it and other doctrines; and in that period of every creed's existence, not a few persons may be found, who have realized its fundamental prin-ciples in all the forms of thought, have weighed and considered them in all their important bearings, and have experienced the full effect on the character, which belief in that creed ought to produce in a mind thor-oughly imbued with it. But when it has come to be an hereditary creed and to be received passively, not actively—when the mind is no longer compelled, in the same degree as at first, to exercise its vital powers on the questions which its belief presents to it, there is a progressive tendency to forget all of the belief except the formularies, or to give it a dull and torpid assent, as if accepting it on trust dispensed with the necessity of realizing it in consciousness, or testing it by personal experience; until it almost ceases to connect itself at all with the inner life of the human being. Then are seen the cases, so frequent in this age of the world as almost to form the majority, in which the creed remains as it were outside the mind, encrusting and petrifying it against all other influences addressed to the higher parts of our nature; manifesting its power by not suffering any fresh and living conviction to get in, but itself doing nothing for the mind or heart, except standing sentinel over them to keep them vacant.

To what an extent doctrines intrinsically fitted to make the deepest impression upon the mind may remain in it as dead beliefs, without being ever realized in the imagination, the feelings, or the understanding, is exemplified by the manner in which the majority of believers hold the doctrines of Christianity. By Christianity I here mean what is accounted such by all churches and sects—the maxims and precepts contained in the New Testament. These are considered sacred, and accepted as laws, by all professing Christians. Yet it is scarcely too much to say that not one Christian in a thousand guides or tests his individual conduct by reference to those laws. The standard to which he does refer it, is the custom of his nation, his class, or his religious profession. He has thus, on the one hand, a collection of ethical maxims, which he believes to have been vouchsafed to him by infallible wisdom as rules for his government; and on the other, a set of every-day judgments and practices, which go a certain length with some of those maxims, not so great a length with others, stand in direct opposition to some, and are, on the whole, a compromise between the Christian creed and the interests and suggestions of worldly life. To the first of these standards he gives his homage; to the other his real allegiance. All Christians believe that the blessed are the poor and humble, and those who are ill-used by the world; that it is easier for a camel to pass through the eye of a needle than for a rich man to enter the kingdom of heaven; that they should judge not, lest they be judged; that they should swear not at all; that they should love their neighbor as themselves; that if one take their cloak, they should give him their coat also; that they should take no thought for the morrow; that if they would be perfect, they should sell all that

they have and give it to the poor. They are not insincere when they say that they believe these things. They do believe them, as people believe what they have always heard lauded and never discussed. But in the sense of that living belief which regulates conduct, they believe these doctrines just up to the point to which it is usual to act upon them. The doctrines in their integrity are serviceable to pelt adversaries with; and it is understood that they are to be put forward (when possible) as the reasons for whatever people do that they think laudable. But any one who reminded them that the maxims require an infinity of things which they never even think of doing would gain nothing but to be classed among those very unpopular characters who affect to be better than other people. The doctrines have no hold on ordinary believers—are not a power in their minds. They have an habitual respect for the sound of them, but no feeling which spreads from the words to the things signified, and forces the mind to take them in, and make them conform to the formula. Whenever conduct is concerned, they look round for Mr. A and B to direct them how far to go in obeying Christ.

Now we may be well assured that the case was not thus, but far otherwise, with the early Christians. Had it been thus, Christianity never would have expanded from an obscure sect of the despised Hebrews into the religion of the Roman empire. When their enemies said, "See how these Christians love one another" (a remark not likely to be made by anybody now), they assuredly had a much livelier feeling of the meaning of their creed than they have ever had since. And to this cause, probably, it is chiefly owing that Christianity now makes so little progress in extending its domain, and after eighteen centuries, is still nearly confined to Europeans and the descendants of Europeans. Even with the strictly religious, who are much in earnest about their doctrines, and attach a greater amount of meaning to many of them than people in general, it commonly happens that the part which is thus comparatively active in their minds is that which was made by Calvin, or Knox, or some such person much nearer in character to themselves. The sayings of Christ coexist passively in their minds, producing hardly any effect beyond what is caused by mere listening to words so amiable and bland. There are many reasons, doubtless, why doctrines which are the badge of a sect retain more of their vitality than those common to all recognized sects, and why more pains are taken by teachers to keep their meaning alive; but one reason certainly is, that the peculiar doctrines are more questioned, and have to be oftener defended against open gainsayers. Both teachers and learners go to sleep at their post, as soon as there is no enemy in the field.

The same thing holds true, generally speaking, of all traditional doctrines—those of prudence and knowledge of life, as well as of morals or religion. All languages and literatures are full of general observations on life, both as to what it is, and how to conduct oneself in it; observations which everybody knows, which everybody repeats, or hears with acquiescence, which are received as truisms, yet of which most people first truly learn the meaning, when experience, generally of a painful kind, has made it a reality to them. How often, when smarting under some unforeseen misfortune or disappointment, does a person call to mind some proverb or common saying familiar to him all his life, the meaning of which, if he had ever before felt it as he does now, would have saved him from the calamity. There are indeed reasons for this, other than the absence of discussion: there are many truths of which the full meaning cannot be realized, until personal experience has brought it home. But much more of the meaning even of these would have been understood, and what was understood would have been far more deeply impressed on the mind, if the man had been accustomed to hear it argued pro and con by people who did understand it. The fatal tendency of mankind to leave off thinking about a thing when it is no longer doubtful, is the cause of half their errors. A contemporary author has well spoken of "the deep slumber of a decided opinion."

But what! (it may be asked) Is the absence of unanimity an indispensable condition of true knowledge? Is it necessary that some part of mankind should persist in error, to enable any to realize the truth? Does a belief cease to be real and vital as soon as it is generally received—and is a proposition never thoroughly understood and felt unless some doubt of it remains? As soon as mankind have unanimously accepted a truth, does the truth perish within them? The highest aim and best result of improved intelligence, it has hitherto been thought, is to unite mankind more and more in the acknowledgment of all important truths: and does the intelligence only last as long as it has not achieved its object? Do the fruits of conquest perish by the very completeness of the victory?

I affirm no such thing. As mankind improve, the number of doctrines which are no longer disputed or doubted will be constantly on the increase: and the well-being of mankind may almost be measured by the number and gravity of the truths which have reached the point of being uncontested. The cessation, on one question after another, of serious controversy, is one of the necessary incidents of the consolidation of opinion; a consolidation as salutary in the case of true opinions, as it is dangerous and noxious when the opinions are erroneous. But though this gradual narrowing of the bounds of diversity of opinion is necessary in both senses of the term, being at once inevitable and indispensable, we are not therefore obliged to conclude that all its consequences must be beneficial. The loss of so important an aid to the intelligent and living apprehension of a truth, as is afforded by the necessity of explaining it to, or defending it against, opponents, though not sufficient to outweigh, is no trifling drawback from, the benefit of its universal recognition. Where this advantage can no longer be had, I confess I should like to see the teachers of mankind endeavoring to provide a substitute for it; some contrivance for making the difficulties of the question as present to the learner's consciousness, as if they were pressed upon him by a dissentient champion, eager for his conversion.

But instead of seeking contrivances for this purpose, they have lost those they formerly had. The Socratic dialectics, so magnificently exemplified in the dialogues of Plato, were a contrivance of this description. They were essentially a negative discussion of the great questions of philosophy and life, directed with consummate skill to the purpose of convincing any one who had merely adopted the commonplaces of received opinion, that he did not understand the subject—that he as yet attached no definite meaning to the doctrines he professed; in order that, becoming aware of his ignorance, he might be put in the way to attain a stable belief, resting on a clear apprehension both of the meaning of doctrines and of their evidence. The school disputations of the Middle Ages had a somewhat similar object. They were intended to make sure that the pupil understood his own opinion, and (by necessary correlation) the opinion opposed to it, and could enforce the grounds of the one and confute those of the other. These last-mentioned contests had indeed the incurable defect, that the premises appealed to were taken from authority, not from reason; and, as a discipline to the mind, they were in every respect inferior to the powerful dialectics which formed the intellects of the "Socratici viri:" but the modern mind owes far more to both than it is generally willing to admit, and the present modes of education contain nothing which in the smallest degree supplies the place either of the one or of the other. A person who derives all his instruction from teachers or books, even if he escape the besetting temptation of contenting himself with cram, is under no compulsion to hear both sides; accordingly it is far from a frequent accomplishment, even among thinkers, to know both sides; and the weakest part of what everybody says in defense of his opinion, is what he intends as a reply to antagonists. It is the fashion of the present time to disparage negative logic—that which points out weaknesses in theory or errors in practice, without establishing positive truths. Such negative criticism would indeed be poor enough as an ultimate result; but as a means to attaining any positive knowledge or conviction worthy the name, it cannot be valued too highly; and until people are again systematically trained to it, there will be few great thinkers, and a low general average of intellect, in any but the mathematical and physical departments of speculation. On any other subject no one's opinions deserve the name of knowledge, except so far as he has either had forced upon him by others, or gone through of himself, the same mental process which would have been required of him in carrying on an active controversy with opponents. That, therefore, which when absent, it is so indispensable, but so difficult, to create, how worse than absurd is it to forego, when spontaneously offering itself! If there are any persons who contest a received opinion, or who will do so if law or opinion will let them, let us thank them for it, open our minds to listen to them, and rejoice that there is some one to do for us what we otherwise ought, if we have any regard for either the certainty or the vitality of our convictions, to do with much greater labor for ourselves.

It still remains to speak of one of the principal causes which make diversity of opinion advantageous, and will continue to do so until mankind shall have entered a stage of intellectual advancement which at present seems at an incalculable distance. We have hitherto considered only two possibilities: that the received opinion may be false, and some other opinion, consequently, true; or that, the received opinion being true, a conflict with the opposite error is essential to a clear apprehension and deep feeling of its truth. But there is a commoner case than either of these; when the conflicting doctrines, instead of being one true and the other false, share the truth between them; and the nonconforming opinion is needed to supply the remainder of the truth, of which the received doctrine embodies only a part. Popular opinions, on subjects not palpable to sense, are often true, but seldom or never the whole truth. They are a part of the truth; sometimes a greater, sometimes a smaller part, but exaggerated, distorted, and disjoined from the truths by which they ought to

be accompanied and limited. Heretical opinions, on the other hand, are generally some of these suppressed and neglected truths, bursting the bonds which kept them down, and either seeking reconciliation with the truth contained in the common opinion, or fronting it as enemies, and setting themselves up, with similar exclusiveness, as the whole truth. The latter case is hitherto the most frequent, as, in the human mind, one-sidedness has always been the rule, and many-sidedness the exception. Hence, even in revolutions of opinion, one part of the truth usually sets while another rises. Even progress, which ought to superadd, for the most part only substitutes one partial and incomplete truth for another; improvement consisting chiefly in this, that the new fragment of truth is more wanted, more adapted to the needs of the time, than that which it displaces. Such being the partial character of prevailing opinions, even when resting on a true foundation; every opinion which embodies somewhat of the portion of truth which the common opinion omits, ought to be considered precious, with whatever amount of error and confusion that truth may be blended. No sober judge of human affairs will feel bound to be indignant because those who force on our notice truths which we should otherwise have overlooked, overlook some of those which we see. Rather, he will think that so long as popular truth is one-sided, it is more desirable than otherwise that unpopular truth should have one-sided asserters too; such being usually the most energetic, and the most likely to compel reluctant attention to the fragment of wisdom which they proclaim as if it were the whole.

Thus, in the eighteenth century, when nearly all the instructed, and all those of the uninstructed who were led by them, were lost in admiration of what is called civilization, and of the marvels of modern science, literature, and philosophy, and while greatly overrating the amount of unlikeness between the men of modern and those of ancient times, indulged the belief that the whole of the difference was in their own favor; with what a salutary shock did the paradoxes of Rousseau explode like bombshells in the midst, dislocating the compact mass of one-sided opinion, and forcing its elements to recombine in a better form and with additional ingredients. Not that the current opinions were on the whole farther from the truth than Rousseau's were; on the contrary, they were nearer to it; they contained more of positive truth, and very much less of error. Nevertheless there lay in Rousseau's doctrine, and has floated down the stream of opinion along with it, a considerable amount of exactly those truths which the popular opinion wanted; and these are the deposit which was left behind when the flood subsided. The superior worth of simplicity of life, the enervating and demoralizing effect of the trammels and hypocrisies of artificial society, are ideas which have never been entirely absent from cultivated minds since Rousseau wrote; and they will in time produce their due effect, though at present needing to be asserted as much as ever, and to be asserted by deeds, for words, on this subject, have nearly exhausted their power.

In politics, again, it is almost a commonplace, that a party of order or stability, and a party of progress or reform, are both necessary elements of a healthy state of political life; until the one or the other shall have so enlarged its mental grasp as to be a party equally of order and of progress, knowing and distinguishing what is fit to be preserved from what ought to be swept away. Each of these modes of thinking derives its utility from the deficiencies of the other; but it is in a great measure the opposition of the other that keeps each within the limits of reason and sanity. Unless opinions favorable to democracy and to aristocracy, to property and to equality, to co-operation and to competition, to luxury and to abstinence, to sociality and individuality, to liberty and discipline, and all the other standing antagonisms of practical life, are expressed with equal freedom, and enforced and defended with equal talent and energy, there is no chance of both elements obtaining their due; one scale is sure to go up, and the other down. Truth, in the great practical concerns of life, is so much a question of the reconciling and combining of opposites, that very few have minds sufficiently capacious and impartial to make the adjustment with an approach to correctness, and it has to be made by the rough process of a struggle between combatants fighting under hostile banners. On any of the great open questions just enumerated, if either of the two opinions has a better claim than the other, not merely to be tolerated, but to be encouraged and countenanced, it is the one which happens at the particular time and place to be in a minority. That is the opinion which, for the time being, represents the neglected interests, the side of human well-being which is in danger of obtaining less than its share. I am aware that there is not, in this country, any intolerance of differences of opinion on most of these topics. They are adduced to show, by admitted and multiplied examples, the universality of the fact, that only through diversity of opinion is there, in the existing state of human intellect, a chance of fair play to all sides of the truth. When there are persons to be found, who form an exception to the apparent unanimity of the world on any subject, even if the world is in the right, it is always probable that dissentients have something worth hearing to say for themselves, and that truth would lose something by their silence.

It may be objected, "But some received principles, especially on the highest and most vital subjects, are more than half-truths. The Christian morality, for instance, is the whole truth on that subject and if any one teaches a morality which varies from it, he is wholly in error." As this is of all cases the most important in practice, none can be fitter to test the general maxim. But before pronouncing what Christian morality is or is not, it would be desirable to decide what is meant by Christian morality. If it means the morality of the New Testament, I wonder that any one who derives his knowledge of this from the book itself, can suppose that it was announced, or intended, as a complete doctrine of morals. The Gospel always refers to a preexisting morality, and confines its precepts to the particulars in which that morality was to be corrected, or superseded by a wider and higher; expressing itself, moreover, in terms most general, often impossible to be interpreted literally, and possessing rather the impressiveness of poetry or eloquence than the precision of legislation. To extract from it a body of ethical doctrine, has never been possible without eking it out from the Old Testament, that is, from a system elaborate indeed, but in many respects barbarous, and intended only for a barbarous people. St. Paul, a declared enemy to this Judaical mode of interpreting the doctrine and filling up the scheme of his Master, equally assumes a preexisting morality, namely, that of the Greeks and Romans; and his advice to Christians is in a great measure a system of accommodation to that; even to the extent of giving an apparent sanction to slavery. What is called Christian, but should rather be termed theological, morality, was not the work of Christ or the Apostles, but is of much later origin, having been gradually built up by the Catholic Church of the first five centuries, and though not implicitly adopted by moderns and Protestants, has been much less modified by them than might have been expected. For the most part, indeed, they have contented themselves with cutting off the additions which had been made to it in the Middle Ages, each sect supplying the place by fresh additions, adapted to its own character and tendencies. That mankind owe a great debt to this morality, and to its early teachers, I should be the last person to deny; but I do not scruple to say of it, that it is, in many important points, incomplete and one-sided, and that unless ideas and feelings, not sanctioned by it, had contributed to the formation of European life and character, human affairs would have been in a worse condition than they now are. Christian morality (so called) has all the characters of a reaction; it is, in great part, a protest against Paganism. Its ideal is negative rather than positive; passive rather than active; Innocence rather than Nobleness; Abstinence from Evil, rather than energetic Pursuit of Good: in its precepts (as has been well said) "thou shalt not" predominates unduly over "thou shalt." In its horror of sensuality, it made an idol of asceticism, which has been gradually compromised away into one of legality. It holds out the hope of heaven and the threat of hell, as the appointed and appropriate motives to a virtuous life: in this falling far below the best of the ancients, and doing what lies in it to give to human morality an essentially selfish character, by disconnecting each man's feelings of duty from the interests of his fellow-creatures, except so far as a self-interested inducement is offered to him for consulting them. It is essentially a doctrine of passive obedience; it inculcates submission to all authorities found established; who indeed are not to be actively obeyed when they command what religion forbids, but who are not to be resisted, far less rebelled against, for any amount of wrong to ourselves. And while, in the morality of the best Pagan nations, duty to the State holds even a disproportionate place, infringing on the just liberty of the individual; in purely Christian ethics that grand department of duty is scarcely noticed or acknowledged. It is in the Koran, not the New Testament, that we read the maxim—"A ruler who appoints any man to an office, when there is in his dominions another man better qualified for it, sins against God and against the State." What little recognition the idea of obligation to the public obtains in modern morality, is derived from Greek and Roman sources, not from Christian; as, even in the morality of private life, whatever exists of magnanimity, high-mindedness, personal dignity, even the sense of honor, is derived from the purely human, not the religious part of our education, and never could have grown out of a standard of ethics in which the only worth, professedly recognized, is that of obedience.

I am as far as any one from pretending that these defects are necessarily inherent in the Christian ethics, in every manner in which it can be conceived, or that the many requisites of a complete moral doctrine which it does not contain, do not admit of being reconciled with it. Far less would I insinuate this of the doctrines and precepts of Christ himself. I believe that the sayings of Christ are all, that I can see any evidence of their having been intended to be; that they are irreconcilable with nothing which a comprehensive morality requires; that everything which is excellent in ethics may be brought within them, with no greater violence to their language than has been done to it by all who have attempted to deduce from them any practical system of conduct whatever. But it is quite consistent with this, to believe that they contain and were meant to contain, only a part of the truth; that many essential elements of the highest morality are among the things which are not provided for, nor intended to be provided for, in the recorded deliverances of the Founder of Christianity, and which have been entirely thrown aside in the system of ethics erected on the basis of those deliverances by the Christian Church. And this being so, I think it a great error to persist in attempting to find in the Christian doctrine that complete rule for our guidance, which its author intended it to sanction and enforce, but only partially to provide. I believe, too, that this narrow theory is becoming a grave practical evil, detracting greatly from the value of the moral training and instruction, which so many well-meaning persons are now at length exerting themselves to promote. I much fear that by attempting to form the mind and feelings on an exclusively religious type, and discarding those secular standards (as for want of a better name they may be called) which heretofore coexisted with and supplemented the Christian ethics, receiving some of its spirit, and infusing into it some of theirs, there will result, and is even now resulting, a low, abject, servile type of character, which, submit itself as it may to what it deems the Supreme Will, is incapable of rising to or sympathizing in the conception of Supreme Goodness. I believe that other ethics than any one which can be evolved from exclusively Christian sources, must exist side by side with Christian ethics to produce the moral regeneration of mankind; and that the Christian system is no exception to the rule that in an imperfect state of the human mind, the interests of truth require a diversity of opinions. It is not necessary that in ceasing to ignore the moral truths not contained in Christianity, men should ignore any of those which it does contain. Such prejudice, or oversight, when it occurs, is altogether an evil; but it is one from which we cannot hope to be always exempt, and must be regarded as the price paid for an inestimable good. The exclusive pretension made by a part of the truth to be the whole, must and ought to be protested against, and if a re-actionary impulse should make the protestors unjust in their turn, this one-sidedness, like the other, may be lamented, but must be tolerated. If Christians would teach infidels to be just to Christianity, they should themselves be just to infidelity. It can do truth no service to blink the fact, known to all who have the most ordinary acquaintance with literary history, that a large portion of the noblest and most valuable moral teaching has been the work, not only of men who did not know, but of men who knew and re-jected, the Christian faith.

I do not pretend that the most unlimited use of the freedom of enunciating all possible opinions would put an end to the evils of religious or philosophical sectar-ianism.

Every truth which men of narrow capacity are in earnest about, is sure to be asserted, inculcated, and in many ways even acted on, as if no other truth existed in the world, or at all events none that could limit or qualify the first. I acknowledge that the tendency of all opinions to become sectarian is not cured by the freest discussion, but is often heightened and exacerbated thereby; the truth which ought to have been, but was not, seen, being rejected all the more violently because proclaimed by persons regarded as opponents. But it is not on the impassioned partisan, it is on the calmer and more disinterested bystander, that this collision of opin-ions works its salutary effect. Not the violent conflict between parts of the truth, but the quiet suppression of half of it, is the formidable evil: there is always hope when people are forced to listen to both sides; it is when they attend only to one that errors harden into prejudices, and truth itself ceases to have the effect of truth, by being exaggerated into falsehood. And since there are few mental attributes more rare than that ju-dicial faculty which can sit in intelligent judgment be-tween two sides of a question, of which only one is represented by an advocate before it, truth has no chance but in proportion as every side of it, every opin-ion which embodies any fraction of the truth, not only finds advocates, but is so advocated as to be listened to.

We have now recognized the necessity to the men-tal well-being of mankind (on which all their other well-being depends) of freedom of opinion, and free-dom of the expression of opinion, on four distinct grounds; which we will now briefly recapitulate.

First, if any opinion is compelled to silence, that opinion may, for aught we can certainly know, be true. To deny this is to assume our own infallibility.

Secondly, though the silenced opinion be an error, it may, and very commonly does, contain a portion of truth; and since the general or prevailing opinion on any object is rarely or never the whole truth, it is only by the collision of adverse opinions that the remainder of the truth has any chance of being supplied.

Thirdly, even if the received opinion be not only true, but the whole truth; unless it is suffered to be, and actually is, vigorously and earnestly contested, it will, by most of those who receive it, be held in the manner of a prejudice, with little comprehension or feeling of its rational grounds. And not only this, but, fourthly, the meaning of the doctrine itself will be in danger of being lost, or enfeebled, and deprived of its vital effect on the character and conduct: the dogma becoming a mere formal profession, inefficacious for good, but cumbering the ground, and preventing the growth of any real and heartfelt conviction, from reason or per-sonal experience.

CHAPTER III: ON INDIVIDUALITY, AS ONE OF THE ELEMENTS OF WELL-BEING

Such being the reasons which make it imperative that human beings should be free to form opinions, and to express their opinions without reserve; and such the baneful consequences to the intellectual, and through that to the moral nature of man, unless this liberty is either conceded, or asserted in spite of prohibition; let us next examine whether the same reasons do not re-quire that men should be free to act upon their opin-ions—to carry these out in their lives, without hin-drance, either physical or moral, from their fellow-men, so long as it is at their own risk and peril. This last pro-viso is of course indispensable. No one pretends that actions should be as free as opinions. On the contrary, even opinions lose their immunity, when the circum-stances in which they are expressed are such as to con-stitute their expression a positive instigation to some mischievous act. An opinion that corndealers are starvers of the poor, or that private property is robbery, ought to be unmolested when simply circulated through the press, but may justly incur punishment when deliv-ered orally to an excited mob assembled before the house of a corn-dealer, or when handed about among the same mob in the form of a placard. Acts of what-ever kind, which, without justifiable cause, do harm to others, may be, and in the more important cases absolutely require to be, controlled by the unfavorable sentiments, and, when needful, by the active interference of mankind. The liberty of the individual must be thus far limited; he must not make himself a nuisance to other people. But if he refrains from molesting others in what concerns them, and merely acts according to his own inclination and judgment in things which concern himself, the same reasons which show that opinion should be free, prove also that he should be allowed, without molestation, to carry his opinions into practice at his own cost. That mankind are not infallible; that their truths, for the most part, are only half-truths; that unity of opinion, unless resulting from the fullest and freest comparison of opposite opinions, is not desirable, and diversity not an evil, but a good, until mankind are much more capable than at present of recognizing all sides of the truth, are principles applicable to men's modes of action, not less than to their opinions. As it is useful that while mankind are imperfect there should be different opinions, so is it that there should be different experiments of living; that free scope should be given to varieties of character, short of injury to others; and that the worth of different modes of life should be proved practically, when any one thinks fit to try them. It is desirable, in short, that in things which do not primarily concern others, individuality should assert itself. Where, not the person's own character, but the traditions or customs of other people are the rule of conduct, there is wanting one of the principal ingredients of human happiness, and quite the chief ingredient of individual and social progress.

In maintaining this principle, the greatest difficulty to be encountered does not lie in the appreciation of means towards an acknowledged end, but in the indifference of persons in general to the end itself. If it were felt that the free development of individuality is one of the leading essentials of well-being; that it is not only a coordinate element with all that is designated by the terms civilization, instruction, education, culture, but is itself a necessary part and condition of all those things; there would be no danger that liberty should be undervalued, and the adjustment of the boundaries between it and social control would present no extraordinary difficulty. But the evil is, that individual spontaneity is hardly recognized by the common modes of thinking as having any intrinsic worth, or deserving any regard on its own account. The majority, being satisfied with the ways of mankind as they now are (for it is they who make them what they are), cannot com-

prehend why those ways should not be good enough for everybody; and what is more, spontaneity forms no part of the ideal of the majority of moral and social reformers, but is rather looked on with jealousy, as a troublesome and perhaps rebellious obstruction to the general acceptance of what these reformers, in their own judgment, think would be best for mankind. Few persons, out of Germany, even comprehend the meaning of the doctrine which Wilhelm von Humboldt, so eminent both as a savant and as a politician, made the text of a treatise—that "the end of man, or that which is prescribed by the eternal or immutable dictates of reason, and not suggested by vague and transient desires, is the highest and most harmonious development of his powers to a complete and consistent whole," that, therefore, the object "towards which every human being must ceaselessly direct his efforts, and on which especially those who design to influence their fellow-men must ever keep their eyes, is the individuality of power and development;" that for this there are two requisites, "freedom, and a variety of situations;" and that from the union of these arise "individual vigor and manifold diversity," which combine themselves in "originality."

Little, however, as people are accustomed to a doctrine like that of Von Humboldt, and surprising as it may be to them to find so high a value attached to individuality, the question, one must nevertheless think, can only be one of degree. No one's idea of excellence in conduct is that people should do absolutely nothing but copy one another. No one would assert that people ought not to put into their mode of life, and into the conduct of their concerns, any impress whatever of their own judgment, or of their own individual character. On the other hand, it would be absurd to pretend that people ought to live as if nothing whatever had been known in the world before they came into it; as if experience had as yet done nothing towards showing that one mode of existence, or of conduct, is preferable to another. Nobody denies that people should be so taught and trained in youth, as to know and benefit by the ascertained results of human experience. But it is the privilege and proper condition of a human being, arrived at the maturity of his faculties, to use and interpret experience in his own way. It is for him to find out what part of recorded experience is properly applicable to his own circumstances and character. The traditions and customs of other people are, to a certain extent, evidence of what their experience has taught them; presumptive evidence, and as such, have a claim to this deference: but, in the first place, their experience may be too narrow; or they may not have interpreted it rightly. Secondly, their interpretation of experience may be correct but unsuitable to him. Customs are made for customary circumstances, and customary characters: and his circumstances or his character may be uncustomary. Thirdly, though the customs be both good as customs, and suitable to him, yet to conform to custom, merely as custom, does not educate or develop in him any of the qualities which are the distinctive endowment of a human being. The human faculties of perception, judgment, discriminative feeling, mental activity, and even moral preference, are exercised only in making a choice. He who does anything because it is the custom, makes no choice. He gains no practice either in discerning or in desiring what is best. The mental and moral, like the muscular powers, are improved only by being used. The faculties are called into no exercise by doing a thing merely because others do it, no more than by believing a thing only because others believe it. If the grounds of an opinion are not conclusive to the person's own reason, his reason, cannot be strengthened, but is likely to be weakened by his adopting it: and if the inducements to an act are not such as are consentaneous to his own feelings and character (where affection, or the rights of others are not concerned), it is so much done towards rendering his feelings and character inert and torpid, instead of active and energetic.

He who lets the world, or his own portion of it, choose his plan of life for him, has no need of any other faculty than the ape-like one of imitation. He who chooses his plan for himself, employs all his faculties. He must use observation to see, reasoning and judgment to foresee, activity to gather materials for decision, discrimination to decide, and when he has decided, firmness and self-control to hold to his deliberate decision. And these qualities he requires and exercises exactly in proportion as the part of his conduct which he determines according to his own judgment and feelings is a large one. It is possible that he might be guided in some good path, and kept out of harm's way, without any of these things. But what will be his comparative worth as a human being? It really is of importance, not only what men do, but also what manner of men they are that do it. Among the works of man, which human life is rightly employed in perfecting and beautifying, the first in importance surely is man himself. Supposing it were possible to get houses built, corn grown, battles fought, causes tried, and even churches erected and prayers said, by machinery—by automations in human form—it would be a consider-

able loss to exchange for these automatons even the men and women who at present inhabit the more civilized parts of the world, and who assuredly are but starved specimens of what nature can and will produce. Human nature is not a machine to be built after a model, and set to do exactly the work prescribed for it, but a tree, which requires to grow and develop itself on all sides, according to the tendency of the inward forces which make it a living thing.

It will probably be conceded that it is desirable people should exercise their understandings, and that an intelligent following of custom, or even occasionally an intelligent deviation from custom, is better than a blind and simply mechanical adhesion to it. To a certain extent it is admitted, that our understanding should be our own: but there is not the same willingness to admit that our desires and impulses should be our own, likewise; or that to possess impulses of our own, and of any strength, is anything but a peril and a snare. Yet desires and impulses are as much a part of a perfect human being, as beliefs and restraints: and strong impulses are only perilous when not properly balanced; when one set of aims and inclinations is developed into strength, while others, which ought to coexist with them, remain weak and inactive. It is not because men's desires are strong that they act ill; it is because their consciences are weak. There is no natural connection between strong impulses and a weak conscience. The natural connection is the other way. To say that one person's desires and feelings are stronger and more various than those of another, is merely to say that he has more of the raw material of human nature, and is therefore capable, perhaps of more evil, but certainly of more good. Strong impulses are but another name for energy. Energy may be turned to bad uses; but more good may always be made of an energetic nature, than of an indolent and impassive one. Those who have most natural feeling, are always those whose cultivated feelings may be made the strongest. The same strong susceptibilities which make the personal impulses vivid and powerful, are also the source from whence are generated the most passionate love of virtue, and the sternest selfcontrol. It is through the cultivation of these, that society both does its duty and protects its interests: not by rejecting the stuff of which heroes are made, because it knows not how to make them. A person whose desires and impulses are his own—are the expression of his own nature, as it has been developed and modified by his own culture—is said to have a character. One whose desires and impulses are not his own, has no character, no more than a steam-engine has a character. If, in addition to being his own, his impulses are strong, and are under the government of a strong will, he has an energetic character. Whoever thinks that individuality of desires and impulses should not be encouraged to unfold itself, must maintain that society has no need of strong natures—is not the better for containing many persons who have much character—and that a high general average of energy is not desirable.

In some early states of society, these forces might be, and were, too much ahead of the power which society then possessed of disciplining and controlling them. There has been a time when the element of spontaneity and individuality was in excess, and the social principle had a hard struggle with it. The difficulty then was, to induce men of strong bodies or minds to pay obedience to any rules which required them to control their impulses. To overcome this difficulty, law and discipline, like the Popes struggling against the Emperors, asserted a power over the whole man, claiming to control all his life in order to control his character—which society had not found any other sufficient means of binding. But society has now fairly got the better of individuality; and the danger which threatens human nature is not the excess, but the deficiency, of personal impulses and preferences. Things are vastly changed, since the passions of those who were strong by station or by personal endowment were in a state of habitual rebellion against laws and ordinances, and required to be rigorously chained up to enable the persons within their reach to enjoy any particle of security. In our times, from the highest class of society down to the lowest every one lives as under the eye of a hostile and dreaded censorship. Not only in what concerns others, but in what concerns only themselves, the individual, or the family, do not ask themselves—what do I prefer? or, what would suit my character and disposition? or, what would allow the best and highest in me to have fair play, and enable it to grow and thrive? They ask themselves, what is suitable to my position? what is usually done by persons of my station and pecuniary circumstances? or (worse still) what is usually done by persons of a station and circumstances superior to mine? I do not mean that they choose what is customary, in preference to what suits their own inclination. It does not occur to them to have any inclination, except for what is customary. Thus the mind itself is bowed to the yoke: even in what people do for pleasure, conformity is the first thing thought of; they like [people] in crowds, exercise choice only among things commonly done: peculiarity of taste, eccentricity of conduct, are shunned equally with crimes: until by dint of not following their own nature, they have no nature to follow: their human capacities are withered and starved: they become incapable of any strong wishes or native pleasures, and are generally without either opinions or feelings of human growth, or properly their own. Now is this, or is it not, the desirable condition of human nature?

It is so, on the Calvinistic theory. According to that, the one great offence of man is Self-will. All the good of which humanity is capable, is comprised in Obedience. You have no choice; thus you must do, and no otherwise; "whatever is not a duty is a sin." Human nature being radically corrupt, there is no redemption for any one until human nature is killed within him. To one holding this theory of life, crushing out any of the human faculties, capacities, and susceptibilities, is no evil: man needs no capacity, but that of surrendering himself to the will of God: and if he uses any of his faculties for any other purpose but to do that supposed will more effectually, he is better without them. That is the theory of Calvinism; and it is held, in a mitigated form, by many who do not consider themselves Calvinists; the mitigation consisting in giving a less ascetic interpretation to the alleged will of God; asserting it to be his will that mankind should gratify some of their inclinations; of course not in the manner they themselves prefer, but in the way of obedience, that is, in a way prescribed to them by authority; and, therefore, by the necessary conditions of the case, the same for all.

In some such insidious form there is at present a strong tendency to this narrow theory of life, and to the pinched and hidebound type of human character which it patronizes. Many persons, no doubt, sincerely think that human beings thus cramped and dwarfed, are as their Maker designed them to be; just as many have thought that trees are a much finer thing when clipped into pollards, or cut out into figures of animals, than as nature made them. But if it be any part of religion to believe that man was made by a good Being it is more consistent with that faith to believe, that this Being gave all human faculties that they might be cultivated and unfolded, not rooted out and consumed, and that he takes delight in every nearer approach made by his creatures to the ideal conception embodied in them, every increase in any of their capabilities of comprehension, of action, or of enjoyment. There is a different type of human excellence from the Calvinistic; a conception of humanity as having its nature bestowed on it for other purposes than merely to be abnegated.

"Pagan self-assertion" is one of the elements of human worth, as well as "Christian self-denial." There is a Greek ideal of self-development, which the Platonic and Christian ideal of self-government blends with, but does not supersede. It may be better to be a John Knox than an Alcibiades, but it is better to be a Pericles than either; nor would a Pericles, if we had one in these days, be without anything good which belonged to John Knox.

It is not by wearing down into uniformity all that is individual in themselves, but by cultivating it and calling it forth, within the limits imposed by the rights and interests of others, that human beings become a noble and beautiful object of contemplation; and as the works partake the character of those who do them, by the same process human life also becomes rich, diversified, and animating, furnishing more abundant aliment to high thoughts and elevating feelings, and strengthening the tie which binds every individual to the race, by making the race infinitely better worth belonging to. In proportion to the development of his individuality, each person becomes more valuable to himself, and is therefore capable of being more valuable to others. There is a greater fulness of life about his own existence, and when there is more life in the units there is more in the mass which is composed of them. As much compression as is necessary to prevent the stronger specimens of human nature from encroaching on the rights of others, cannot be dispensed with; but for this there is ample compensation even in the point of view of human development. The means of development which the individual loses by being prevented from gratifying his inclinations to the injury of others, are chiefly obtained at the expense of the development of other people. And even to himself there is a full equivalent in the better development of the social part of his nature, rendered possible by the restraint put upon the selfish part. To be held to rigid rules of justice for the sake of others, develops the feelings and capacities which have the good of others for their object. But to be restrained in things not affecting their good, by their mere displeasure, develops nothing valuable, except such force of character as may unfold itself in resisting the restraint. If acquiesced in, it dulls and blunts the whole nature. To give any fair play to the nature of each, it is essential that different persons should be allowed to lead different lives. In proportion as this latitude has been exercised in any age, has that age been noteworthy to posterity. Even despotism does not produce its worst effects, so long as Individuality exists under it; and whatever crushes individuality is despotism, by whatever name it may be called, and whether it professes to be enforcing the will of God or the injunctions of men.

Having said that Individuality is the same thing with development, and that it is only the cultivation of individuality which produces, or can produce, well-developed human beings, I might here close the argument: for what more or better can be said of any condition of human affairs, than that it brings human beings themselves nearer to the best thing they can be? or what worse can be said of any obstruction to good, than that it prevents this? Doubtless, however, these considerations will not suffice to convince those who most need convincing; and it is necessary further to show, that these developed human beings are of some use to the undeveloped—to point out to those who do not desire liberty, and would not avail themselves of it, that they may be in some intelligible manner rewarded for allowing other people to make use of it without hindrance.

In the first place, then, I would suggest that they might possibly learn something from them. It will not be denied by anybody, that originality is a valuable element in human affairs. There is always need of persons not only to discover new truths, and point out when what were once truths are true no longer, but also to commence new practices, and set the example of more enlightened conduct, and better taste and sense in human life. This cannot well be gainsaid by anybody who does not believe that the world has already attained perfection in all its ways and practices. It is true that this benefit is not capable of being rendered by everybody alike: there are but few persons, in comparison with the whole of mankind, whose experiments, if adopted by others, would be likely to be any improvement on established practice. But these few are the salt of the earth; without them, human life would become a stagnant pool. Not only is it they who introduce good things which did not before exist; it is they who keep the life in those which already existed. If there were nothing new to be done, would human intellect cease to be necessary? Would it be a reason why those who do the old things should forget why they are done, and do them like cattle, not like human beings? There is only too great a tendency in the best beliefs and practices to degenerate into the mechanical; and unless there were a succession of persons whose ever-recurring originality prevents the grounds of those beliefs and practices from becoming merely traditional, such dead matter would not resist the smallest shock from anything really alive, and there would be no reason why civilization should not die out, as in the Byzantine Empire. Persons of genius, it is true, are, and are always likely to be, a small minority; but in order to have them, it is necessary to preserve the soil in which they grow. Genius can only breathe freely in an atmosphere of freedom. Persons of genius are, ex vi termini, more individual than any other people—less capable, consequently, of fitting themselves, without hurtful compression, into any of the small number of moulds which society provides in order to save its members the trouble of forming their own character. If from timidity they consent to be forced into one of these moulds, and to let all that part of themselves which cannot expand under the pressure remain unexpanded, society will be little the better for their genius. If they are of a strong character, and break their fetters they become a mark for the society which has not succeeded in reducing them to common-place, to point at with solemn warning as "wild," "erratic," and the like; much as if one should complain of the Niagara river for not flowing smoothly between its banks like a Dutch canal.

I insist thus emphatically on the importance of genius, and the necessity of allowing it to unfold itself freely both in thought and in practice, being well aware that no one will deny the position in theory, but knowing also that almost every one, in reality, is totally indifferent to it. People think genius a fine thing if it enables a man to write an exciting poem, or paint a picture. But in its true sense, that of originality in thought and action though no one says that it is not a thing to be admired, nearly all, at heart, think they can do very well without it. Unhappily this is too natural to be wondered at. Originality is the one thing which unoriginal minds cannot feel the use of. They cannot see what it is to do for them: how should they? If they could see what it would do for them, it would not be originality. The first service which originality has to render them, is that of opening their eyes: which being once fully done, they would have a chance of being themselves original. Meanwhile, recollecting that nothing was ever yet done which some one was not the first to do, and that all good things which exist are the fruits of originality, let them be modest enough to believe that there is something still left for it to accomplish, and assure themselves that they are more in need of originality, the less they are conscious of the want.

In sober truth, whatever homage may be professed, or even paid, to real or supposed mental superiority, the general tendency of things throughout the world is to render mediocrity the ascendant power among mankind. In ancient history, in the Middle Ages, and in a diminishing degree through the long transition from feudality to the present time, the individual was a power in himself; and If he had either great talents or a high social position, he was a considerable power. At present individuals are lost in the crowd. In politics it is almost a triviality to say that public opinion now rules the world. The only power deserving the name is that of masses, and of governments while they make themselves the organ of the tendencies and instincts of masses. This is as true in the moral and social relations of private life as in public transactions. Those whose opinions go by the name of public opinion, are not always the same sort of public: in America, they are the whole white population; in England, chiefly the middle class. But they are always a mass, that is to say, collective mediocrity. And what is still greater novelty, the mass do not now take their opinions from dignitaries in Church or State, from ostensible leaders, or from books. Their thinking is done for them by men much like themselves, addressing them or speaking in their name, on the spur of the moment, through the newspapers. I am not complaining of all this. I do not assert that anything better is compatible, as a general rule, with the present low state of the human mind. But that does not hinder the government of mediocrity from being mediocre government. No government by a democracy or a numerous aristocracy, either in its political acts or in the opinions, qualities, and tone of mind which it fosters ever did or could rise above mediocrity, except in so far as the sovereign Many have let themselves be guided (which in their best times they always have done) by the counsels and influence of a more highly gifted and instructed One or Few. The initiation of all wise or noble things, comes and must come from individuals; generally at first from some one individual. The honor and glory of the average man is that he is capable of following that initiative; that he can respond internally to wise and noble things, and be led to them with his eyes open. I am not countenancing the sort of "hero-worship" which applauds the strong man of genius for forcibly seizing on the government of the world and making it do his bidding in spite of itself. All he can claim is, freedom to point out the way. The power of compelling others into it, is not only inconsistent with the freedom and development of all the rest, but corrupting to the strong man himself. It does seem, however, that when the opinions of masses of merely average men are everywhere become or becoming the dominant power, the counterpoise and corrective to that tendency would be the more and more pronounced individuality of those who stand on the higher eminences of thought. It is in these circumstances most especially that exceptional individuals, instead of being deterred, should be encouraged in acting differently from the mass. In other times there was no advantage in their doing so, unless they acted not only differently, but better. In this age the mere example of non-conformity, the mere refusal to bend the knee to custom, is itself a service. Precisely because the tyranny of opinion is such as to make eccentricity a reproach, it is desirable, in order to break through that tyranny, that people should be eccentric. Eccentricity has always abounded when and where strength of character has abounded; and the amount of eccentricity in a society has generally been proportional to the amount of genius, mental vigor, and moral courage which it contained. That so few now dare to be eccentric, marks the chief danger of the time.

I have said that it is important to give the freest scope possible to uncustomary things, in order that it may in time appear which of these are fit to be converted into customs. But independence of action, and disregard of custom are not solely deserving of encouragement for the chance they afford that better modes of action, and customs more worthy of general adoption, may be struck out; nor is it only persons of decided mental superiority who have a just claim to carry on their lives in their own way. There is no reason that all human existences should be constructed on some one, or some small number of patterns. If a person possesses any tolerable amount of common sense and experience, his own mode of laying out his existence is the best, not because it is the best in itself, but because it is his own mode. Human beings are not like sheep; and even sheep are not undistinguishably alike. A man cannot get a coat or a pair of boots to fit him, unless they are either made to his measure, or he has a whole warehouseful to choose from: and is it easier to fit him with a life than with a coat, or are human beings more like one another in their whole physical and spiritual conformation than in the shape of their feet? If it were only that people have diversities of taste that is reason enough for not attempting to shape them all after one model. But different persons also require different conditions for their spiritual development; and can no more exist healthily in the same moral, than all the variety of plants can in the same physical atmosphere and climate. The same things which are helps to one person towards the cultivation of his higher nature, are hindrances to another. The same mode of life is a healthy excitement to one, keeping all his faculties of action and enjoyment in their best order, while to another it is a distracting burden, which suspends or

crushes all internal life. Such are the differences among human beings in their sources of pleasure, their susceptibilities of pain, and the operation on them of different physical and moral agencies, that unless there is a corresponding diversity in their modes of life, they neither obtain their fair share of happiness, nor grow up to the mental, moral, and aesthetic stature of which their nature is capable. Why then should tolerance, as far as the public sentiment is concerned, extend only to tastes and modes of life which extort acquiescence by the multitude of their adherents? Nowhere (except in some monastic institutions) is diversity of taste entirely unrecognized; a person may without blame, either like or dislike rowing, or smoking, or music, or athletic exercises, or chess, or cards, or study, because both those who like each of these things, and those who dislike them, are too numerous to be put down. But the man, and still more the woman, who can be accused either of doing "what nobody does," or of not doing "what everybody does," is the subject of as much depreciatory remark as if he or she had committed some grave moral delinquency. Persons require to possess a title, or some other badge of rank, or the consideration of people of rank, to be able to indulge somewhat in the luxury of doing as they like without detriment to their estimation. To indulge somewhat, I repeat: for whoever allow themselves much of that indulgence, incur the risk of something worse than disparaging speeches—they are in peril of a commission de lunatico, and of having their property taken from them and given to their relations.

There is one characteristic of the present direction of public opinion, peculiarly calculated to make it intolerant of any marked demonstration of individuality. The general average of mankind are not only moderate in intellect, but also moderate in inclinations: they have no tastes or wishes strong enough to incline them to do anything unusual, and they consequently do not understand those who have, and class all such with the wild and intemperate whom they are accustomed to look down upon. Now, in addition to this fact which is general, we have only to suppose that a strong movement has set in towards the improvement of morals, and it is evident what we have to expect. In these days such a movement has set in; much has actually been effected in the way of increased regularity of conduct, and discouragement of excesses; and there is a philanthropic spirit abroad, for the exercise of which there is no more inviting field than the moral and prudential improvement of our fellow-creatures. These tendencies of the times cause the public to be more disposed than at most former periods to prescribe general rules of conduct, and endeavor to make every one conform to the approved standard. And that standard, express or tacit, is to desire nothing strongly. Its ideal of character is to be without any marked character; to maim by compression, like a Chinese lady's foot, every part of human nature which stands out prominently, and tends to make the person markedly dissimilar in outline to commonplace humanity.

As is usually the case with ideals which exclude one half of what is desirable, the present standard of approbation produces only an inferior imitation of the other half. Instead of great energies guided by vigorous reason, and strong feelings strongly controlled by a conscientious will, its result is weak feelings and weak energies, which therefore can be kept in outward conformity to rule without any strength either of will or of reason. Already energetic characters on any large scale are becoming merely traditional. There is now scarcely any outlet for energy in this country except business. The energy expended in that may still be regarded as considerable. What little is left from that employment, is expended on some hobby; which may be a useful, even a philanthropic hobby, but is always some one thing, and generally a thing of small dimensions. The greatness of England is now all collective: individually small, we only appear capable of anything great by our habit of combining; and with this our moral and religious philanthropists are perfectly contented. But it was men of another stamp than this that made England what it has been; and men of another stamp will be needed to prevent its decline.

The despotism of custom is everywhere the standing hindrance to human advancement, being in unceasing antagonism to that disposition to aim at something better than customary, which is called, according to circumstances, the spirit of liberty, or that of progress or improvement. The spirit of improvement is not always a spirit of liberty, for it may aim at forcing improvements on an unwilling people; and the spirit of liberty, in so far as it resists such attempts, may ally itself locally and temporarily with the opponents of improvement; but the only unfailing and permanent source of improvement is liberty, since by it there are as many possible independent centres of improvement as there are individuals. The progressive principle, however, in either shape, whether as the love of liberty or of improvement, is antagonistic to the sway of Custom, involving at least emancipation from that yoke; and the contest between the two constitutes the chief interest of the history of mankind. The greater part of the world has, properly speaking, no history, because the despotism of Custom is complete. This is the case over the whole East. Custom is there, in all things, the final appeal; Justice and right mean conformity to custom; the argument of custom no one, unless some tyrant intoxicated with power, thinks of resisting. And we see the result. Those nations must once have had originality; they did not start out of the ground populous, lettered, and versed in many of the arts of life; they made themselves all this, and were then the greatest and most powerful nations in the world. What are they now? The subjects or dependents of tribes whose forefathers wandered in the forests when theirs had magnificent palaces and gorgeous temples, but over whom custom exercised only a divided rule with liberty and progress. A people, it appears, may be progressive for a certain length of time, and then stop: when does it stop? When it ceases to possess individuality. If a similar change should befall the nations of Europe, it will not be in exactly the same shape: the despotism of custom with which these nations are threatened is not precisely stationariness. It proscribes singularity, but it does not preclude change, provided all change together. We have discarded the fixed costumes of our forefathers; every one must still dress like other people, but the fashion may change once or twice a year. We thus take care that when there is change, it shall be for change's sake, and not from any idea of beauty or convenience; for the same idea of beauty or convenience would not strike all the world at the same moment, and be simultaneously thrown aside by all at another moment. But we are progressive as well as changeable: we continually make new inventions in mechanical things, and keep them until they are again superseded by better; we are eager for improvement in politics, in education, even in morals, though in this last our idea of improvement chiefly consists in persuading or forcing other people to be as good as ourselves. It is not progress that we object to; on the contrary, we flatter ourselves that we are the most progressive people who ever lived. It is individuality that we are against: we should think we had done wonders if we had made ourselves all alike; forgetting that the unlikeness of one person to another is generally the first thing which draws the attention of either to the imperfection of his own type, and the superiority of another, or the possibility, by combining the advantages of both, of producing something better than either. We have a warning example in China—a nation of much talent, and, in some respects, even wisdom, owing to the rare good fortune of having been provided at an early period with a particularly good set of customs, the work, in some measure, of men to whom even the most enlightened European must accord, under certain limitations, the title of sages and philosophers. They are remarkable, too, in the excellence of their apparatus for impressing, as far as possible, the best wisdom they possess upon every mind in the community, and securing that those who have appropriated most of it shall occupy the posts of honor and power. Surely the people who did this have discovered the secret of human progressiveness, and must have kept themselves steadily at the head of the movement of the world. On the contrary, they have become stationary—have remained so for thousands of years; and if they are ever to be farther improved, it must be by foreigners. They have succeeded beyond all hope in what English philanthropists are so industriously working at—in making a people all alike, all governing their thoughts and conduct by the same maxims and rules; and these are the fruits. The modern regime of public opinion is, in an unorganized form, what the Chinese educational and political systems are in an organized; and unless individuality shall be able successfully to assert itself against this yoke, Europe, notwithstanding its noble antecedents and its professed Christianity, will tend to become another China.

What is it that has hitherto preserved Europe from this lot? What has made the European family of nations an improving, instead of a stationary portion of mankind? Not any superior excellence in them, which when it exists, exists as the effect, not as the cause; but their remarkable diversity of character and culture. Individuals, classes, nations, have been extremely unlike one another: they have struck out a great variety of paths, each leading to something valuable; and although at every period those who travelled in different paths have been intolerant of one another, and each would have thought it an excellent thing if all the rest could have been compelled to travel his road, their attempts to thwart each other's development have rarely had any permanent success, and each has in time endured to receive the good which the others have offered. Europe is, in my judgment, wholly indebted to this plurality of paths for its progressive and many-sided development. But it already begins to possess this benefit in a considerably less degree. It is decidedly advancing towards the Chinese ideal of making all people alike. M. de Tocqueville, in his last important work, remarks how much more the Frenchmen of the present day resemble one another, than did those even of the last generation. The same remark might be made of Englishmen in a far greater degree. In a passage already quoted from Wilhelm von Humboldt, he points out two things as necessary conditions of human development, because necessary to render people unlike one another; namely, freedom, and variety of situations. The second of these

two conditions is in this country every day diminishing. The circumstances which surround different classes and individuals, and shape their characters, are daily becoming more assimilated. Formerly, different ranks, different neighborhoods, different trades and professions lived in what might be called different worlds; at present, to a great degree, in the same. Comparatively speaking, they now read the same things, listen to the same things, see the same things, go to the same places, have their hopes and fears directed to the same objects, have the same rights and liberties, and the same means of asserting them. Great as are the differences of position which remain, they are nothing to those which have ceased. And the assimilation is still proceeding. All the political changes of the age promote it, since they all tend to raise the low and to lower the high. Every extension of education promotes it, because education brings people under common influences, and gives them access to the general stock of facts and sentiments. Improvements in the means of communication promote it, by bringing the inhabitants of distant places into personal contact, and keeping up a rapid flow of changes of residence between one place and another. The increase of commerce and manufactures promotes it, by diffusing more widely the advantages of easy circumstances, and opening all objects of ambition, even the highest, to general competition, whereby the desire of rising becomes no longer the character of a particular class, but of all classes. A more powerful agency than even all these, in bringing about a general similarity among mankind, is the complete establishment, in this and other free countries, of the ascendancy of public opinion in the State. As the various social eminences which enabled persons entrenched on them to disregard the opinion of the multitude, gradually became levelled; as the very idea of resisting the will of the public, when it is positively known that they have a will, disappears more and more from the minds of practical politicians; there ceases to be any social support for non-conformity—any substantive power in society, which, itself opposed to the ascendancy of numbers, is interested in taking under its protection opinions and tendencies at variance with those of the public.

The combination of all these causes forms so great a mass of influences hostile to Individuality, that it is not easy to see how it can stand its ground. It will do so with increasing difficulty, unless the intelligent part of the public can be made to feel its value—to see that it is good there should be differences, even though not for the better, even though, as it may appear to them, some should be for the worse. If the claims of

Individuality are ever to be asserted, the time is now, while much is still wanting to complete the enforced assimilation. It is only in the earlier stages that any stand can be successfully made against the encroachment. The demand that all other people shall resemble ourselves, grows by what it feeds on. If resistance waits till life is reduced nearly to one uniform type, all deviations from that type will come to be considered impious, immoral, even monstrous and contrary to nature Mankind speedily become unable to conceive diversity, when they have been for some time unaccustomed to see it.

CHAPTER IV: OF THE LIMITS TO THE AUTHORITY OF SOCIETY OVER THE INDIVIDUAL

What, then, is the rightful limit to the sovereignty of the individual over himself? Where does the authority of society begin? How much of human life should be assigned to individuality, and how much to society?

Each will receive its proper share, if each has that which more particularly concerns it. To individuality should belong the part of life in which it is chiefly the individual that is interested; to society, the part which chiefly interests society.

Though society is not founded on a contract, and though no good purpose is answered by inventing a contract in order to deduce social obligations from it, every one who receives the protection of society owes a return for the benefit, and the fact of living in society renders it indispensable that each should be bound to observe a certain line of conduct towards the rest. This conduct consists, first, in not injuring the interests of one another; or rather certain interests, which, either by express legal provision or by tacit understanding, ought to be considered as rights; and secondly, in each person's bearing his share (to be fixed on some equitable principle) of the labors and sacrifices incurred for defending the society or its members from injury and molestation. These conditions society is justified in enforcing, at all costs to those who endeavor to withhold fulfillment. Nor is this all that society may do. The acts of an individual may be hurtful to others, or wanting in due consideration for their welfare, without going the length of violating any of their constituted rights. The offender may then be justly punished by opinion, though not by law. As soon as any part of a person's

conduct affects prejudicially the interests of others, society has jurisdiction over it, and the question whether the general welfare will or will not be promoted by interfering with it, becomes open to discussion. But there is no room for entertaining any such question when a person's conduct affect the interests of no persons besides himself, or needs not affect them unless they like (all the persons concerned being of full age, and the ordinary amount of understanding). In all such cases there should be perfect freedom, legal and social, to do the action and stand the consequences.

It would be a great misunderstanding of this doctrine, to suppose that it is one of selfish indifference, which pretends that human beings have no business with each other's conduct in life, and that they should not concern themselves about the well-doing or well-being of one another, unless their own interest is involved. Instead of any diminution, there is need of a great increase of disinterested exertion to promote the good of others. But disinterested benevolence can find other instruments to persuade people to their good, than whips and scourges, either of the literal or the metaphorical sort. I am the last person to undervalue the self-regarding virtues; they are only second in importance, if even second, to the social. It is equally the business of education to cultivate both. but even education works by conviction and persuasion as well as by compulsion, and it is by the former only that, when the period of education is past, the self-regarding virtues should be inculcated. Human beings owe to each other help to distinguish the better from the worse, and encouragement to choose the former and avoid the latter. They should be forever stimulating each other to increased exercise of their higher faculties, and increased direction of their feelings and aims towards wise instead of foolish, elevating instead of degrading, objects and contemplations. But neither one person, nor any number of persons, is warranted in saying to another human creature of ripe years, that he shall not do with his life for his own benefit what he chooses to do with it. He is the person most interested in his own well-being, the interest which any other person, except in cases of strong personal attachment, can have in it, is trifling; compared with that which he himself has; the interest which society has in him individually (except as to his conduct to others) is fractional, and altogether indirect: while, with respect to his own feelings and circumstances, the most ordinary man or woman has means of knowledge immeasurably surpassing those that can be possessed by any one else. The interference of society to overrule his judgment and purposes in what only regards himself, must be grounded on general presumptions; which may be altogether wrong, and even if right, are as likely as not to be misapplied to individual cases, by persons no better acquainted with the circumstances of such cases than those are who look at them merely from without. In this department, therefore, of human affairs, Individuality has its proper field of action. In the conduct of human beings towards one another, it is necessary that general rules should for the most part be observed, in order that people may know what they have to expect; but in each person's own concerns, his individual spontaneity is entitled to free exercise. Considerations to aid his judgment, exhortations to strengthen his will, may be offered to him, even obtruded on him, by others; but he, himself, is the final judge. All errors which he is likely to commit against advice and warning, are far outweighed by the evil of allowing others to constrain him to what they deem his good.

I do not mean that the feelings with which a person is regarded by others, ought not to be in any way affected by his self-regarding qualities or deficiencies. This is neither possible nor desirable. If he is eminent in any of the qualities which conduce to his own good, he is, so far, a proper object of admiration. He is so much the nearer to the ideal perfection of human nature. If he is grossly deficient in those qualities, a sentiment the opposite of admiration will follow. There is degree of folly, and a degree of what may be called (though the phrase is not unobjectionable) lowness or depravation of taste, which, though it cannot justify doing harm to the person who manifests it, renders him necessarily and properly a subject of distaste, or, in extreme cases, even of contempt: a person could not have the opposite qualities in due strength without entertaining these feelings. Though doing no wrong to any one, a person may so act as to compel us to judge him, and feel towards him, as a fool, or as a being of an inferior order: and since this judgment and feeling are a fact which he would prefer to avoid, it is doing him a service to warn him of it beforehand, as of any other disagreeable consequence to which he exposes himself. It would be well, indeed, if this good office were much more freely rendered than the common notions of politeness at present permit, and if one person could honestly point out to another that he thinks him at fault, without being considered unmannerly or presuming. We have a right, also, in various ways, to act upon our unfavorable opinion of any one, not to the oppression of his individuality, but in the exercise of ours. We are not bound, for example, to seek his society; we have a right to avoid it (though not to parade the avoidance), for we have a right to choose the society most acceptable to us. We have a right, and it may be our duty, to caution others against him, if we think his example or conversation likely to have a pernicious effect on those with whom he associates. We may give others a preference over him in optional good offices, except those which tend to his improvement. In these various modes a person may suffer very severe penalties at the hands of others, for faults which directly concern only himself; but he suffers these penalties only in so far as they are the natural, and, as it were, the spontaneous consequences of the faults themselves, not because they are purposely inflicted on him for the sake of punishment. A person who shows rashness, obstinacy, self-conceit—who cannot live within moderate means—who cannot restrain himself from hurtful indulgences—who pursues animal pleasures at the expense of those of feeling and intellect—must expect to be lowered in the opinion of others, and to have a less share of their favorable sentiments, but of this he has no right to complain, unless he has merited their favor by special excellence in his social relations, and has thus established a title to their good offices, which is not affected by his demerits towards himself.

What I contend for is, that the inconveniences which are strictly inseparable from the unfavorable judgment of others, are the only ones to which a person should ever be subjected for that portion of his conduct and character which concerns his own good, but which does not affect the interests of others in their relations with him. Acts injurious to others require a totally different treatment. Encroachment on their rights; infliction on them of any loss or damage not justified by his own rights; falsehood or duplicity in dealing with them; unfair or ungenerous use of advantages over them; even selfish abstinence from defending them against injury— these are fit objects of moral reprobation, and, in grave cases, of moral retribution and punishment. And not only these acts, but the dispositions which lead to them, are properly immoral, and fit subjects of disapprobation which may rise to abhorrence. Cruelty of disposition; malice and ill-nature; that most anti-social and odious of all passions, envy; dissimulation and insincerity, irascibility on insufficient cause, and resentment disproportioned to the provocation; the love of domineering over others; the desire to engross more than one's share of advantages (the pleonexia of the Greeks); the pride which derives gratification from the abasement of others; the egotism which thinks self and its concerns more important than everything else, and decides all doubtful questions in his own favor;—these are moral vices, and constitute a bad and odious moral character: unlike the self-regarding faults previously mentioned, which are not properly immoralities, and to whatever pitch they may be carried, do not constitute wickedness. They may be proofs of any amount of folly, or want of personal dignity and self-respect; but they are only a subject of moral reprobation when they involve a breach of duty to others, for whose sake the individual is bound to have care for himself. What are called duties to ourselves are not socially obligatory, unless circumstances render them at the same time duties to others. The term duty to oneself, when it means anything more than prudence, means self-respect or self-development; and for none of these is any one accountable to his fellow-creatures, because for none of them is it for the good of mankind that he be held accountable to them.

The distinction between the loss of consideration which a person may rightly incur by defect of prudence or of personal dignity, and the reprobation which is due to him for an offence against the rights of others, is not a merely nominal distinction. It makes a vast difference both in our feelings and in our conduct towards him, whether he displeases us in things in which we think we have a right to control him, or in things in which we know that we have not. If he displeases us, we may express our distaste, and we may stand aloof from a person as well as from a thing that displeases us; but we shall not therefore feel called on to make his life uncomfortable. We shall reflect that he already bears, or will bear, the whole penalty of his error; if he spoils his life by mismanagement, we shall not, for that reason, desire to spoil it still further: instead of wishing to punish him, we shall rather endeavor to alleviate his punishment, by showing him how he may avoid or cure the evils his conduct tends to bring upon him. He may be to us an object of pity, perhaps of dislike, but not of anger or resentment; we shall not treat him like an enemy of society: the worst we shall think ourselves justified in doing is leaving him to himself, if we do not interfere benevolently by showing interest or concern for him. It is far otherwise if he has infringed the rules necessary for the protection of his fellow-creatures, individually or collectively. The evil consequences of his acts do not then fall on himself, but on others; and society, as the protector of all its members, must retaliate on him; must inflict pain on him for the express purpose of punishment, and must take care that it be sufficiently severe. In the one case, he is an offender at our bar, and we are called on not only to sit in judgment on him, but, in one shape or another, to execute our own sentence: in the other case, it is not our part to inflict any suffering on him, except what may incidentally follow from our using the same liberty in the regulation of our own affairs, which we allow to him in his.

The distinction here pointed out between the part of a person's life which concerns only himself, and that which concerns others, many persons will refuse to admit. How (it may be asked) can any part of the conduct of a member of society be a matter of indifference to the other members? No person is an entirely isolated being; it is impossible for a person to do anything seriously or permanently hurtful to himself, without mischief reaching at least to his near connections, and often far beyond them. If he injures his property, he does harm to those who directly or indirectly derived support from it, and usually diminishes, by a greater or less amount, the general resources of the community. If he deteriorates his bodily or mental faculties, he not only brings evil upon all who depended on him for any portion of their happiness, but disqualifies himself for rendering the services which he owes to his fellow-creatures generally; perhaps becomes a burden on their affection or benevolence; and if such conduct were very frequent, hardly any offence that is committed would detract more from the general sum of good. Finally, if by his vices or follies a person does no direct harm to others, he is nevertheless (it may be said) injurious by his example; and ought to be compelled to control himself, for the sake of those whom the sight or knowledge of his conduct might corrupt or mislead.

And even (it will be added) if the consequences of misconduct could be confined to the vicious or thoughtless individual, ought society to abandon to their own guidance those who are manifestly unfit for it? If protection against themselves is confessedly due to children and persons under age, is not society equally bound to afford it to persons of mature years who are equally incapable of self-government? If gambling, or drunkenness, or incontinence, or idleness, or uncleanliness, are as injurious to happiness, and as great a hindrance to improvement, as many or most of the acts prohibited by law, why (it may be asked) should not law, so far as is consistent with practicability and social convenience, endeavor to repress these also? And as a supplement to the unavoidable imperfections of law, ought not opinion at least to organize a powerful police against these vices, and visit rigidly with social penalties those who are known to practice them? There is no question here (it may be said) about restricting individuality, or impeding the trial of new and original experiments in living. The only things it is sought to prevent are things which have been tried and condemned from the beginning of the world until now; things which experience has shown not to be useful or suitable to any person's individuality. There must be some length of time and amount of experience, after which a moral or prudential truth may be regarded as established, and it is merely desired to prevent generation after generation from falling over the same precipice which has been fatal to their predecessors.

I fully admit that the mischief which a person does to himself, may seriously affect, both through their sympathies and their interests, those nearly connected with him, and in a minor degree, society at large. When, by conduct of this sort, a person is led to violate a distinct and assignable obligation to any other person or persons, the case is taken out of the self-regarding class, and becomes amenable to moral disapprobation in the proper sense of the term. If, for example, a man, through intemperance or extravagance, becomes unable to pay his debts, or, having undertaken the moral responsibility of a family, becomes from the same cause incapable of supporting or educating them, he is deservedly reprobated, and might be justly punished; but it is for the breach of duty to his family or creditors, not for the extravagence. If the resources which ought to have been devoted to them, had been diverted from them for the most prudent investment, the moral culpability would have been the same. George Barnwell murdered his uncle to get money for his mistress, but if he had done it to set himself up in business, he would equally have been hanged. Again, in the frequent case of a man who causes grief to his family by addiction to bad habits, he deserves reproach for his unkindness or ingratitude; but so he may for cultivating habits not in themselves vicious, if they are painful to those with whom he passes his life, or who from personal ties are dependent on him for their comfort. Whoever fails in the consideration generally due to the interests and feelings of others, not being compelled by some more imperative duty, or justified by allowable self-preference, is a subject of moral disapprobation for that failure, but not for the cause of it, nor for the errors, merely personal to himself, which may have remotely led to it. In like manner, when a person disables himself, by conduct purely self-regarding, from the performance of some definite duty incumbent on him to the public, he is guilty of a social offence. No person ought to be punished simply for being drunk; but a soldier or a policeman should be punished for being drunk on duty. Whenever, in short, there is a definite damage, or a definite risk of damage, either to an individual or to the public, the case is taken out of the province of liberty, and placed in that of morality or law.

But with regard to the merely contingent or, as it may be called, constructive injury which a person causes to society, by conduct which neither violates any specific duty to the public, nor occasions percepti-

ble hurt to any assignable individual except himself; the inconvenience is one which society can afford to bear, for the sake of the greater good of human freedom. If grown persons are to be punished for not taking proper care of themselves, I would rather it were for their own sake, than under pretence of preventing them from impairing their capacity of rendering to society benefits which society does not pretend it has a right to exact. But I cannot consent to argue the point as if society had no means of bringing its weaker members up to its ordinary standard of rational conduct, except waiting till they do something irrational, and then punishing them, legally or morally, for it. Society has had absolute power over them during all the early portion of their existence: it has had the whole period of childhood and nonage in which to try whether it could make them capable of rational conduct in life. The existing generation is master both of the training and the entire circumstances of the generation to come; it cannot indeed make them perfectly wise and good, because it is itself so lamentably deficient in goodness and wisdom; and its best efforts are not always, in individual cases, its most successful ones; but it is perfectly well able to make the rising generation, as a whole, as good as, and a little better than, itself. If society lets any considerable number of its members grow up mere children, incapable of being acted on by rational consideration of distant motives, society has itself to blame for the consequences. Armed not only with all the powers of education, but with the ascendency which the authority of a received opinion always exercises over the minds who are least fitted to judge for themselves; and aided by the natural penalties which cannot be prevented from falling on those who incur the distaste or the contempt of those who know them; let not society pretend that it needs, besides all this, the power to issue commands and enforce obedience in the personal concerns of individuals, in which, on all principles of justice and policy, the decision ought to rest with those who are to abide the consequences. Nor is there anything which tends more to discredit and frustrate the better means of influencing conduct, than a resort to the worse. If there be among those whom it is attempted to coerce into prudence or temperance, any of the material of which vigorous and independent characters are made, they will infallibly rebel against the yoke. No such person will ever feel that others have a right to control him in his concerns, such as they have to prevent him from injuring them in theirs; and it easily comes to be considered a mark of spirit and courage to fly in the face of such usurped authority, and do with ostentation the exact opposite of what it enjoins; as in the fashion of grossness which succeeded, in the time of Charles II, to the fanatical moral intolerance of the Puritans. With respect to what is said of the necessity of protecting society from the bad example set to others by the vicious or the self-indulgent; it is true that bad example may have a pernicious effect, especially the example of doing wrong to others with impunity to the wrong-doer. But we are now speaking of conduct which, while it does no wrong to others, is supposed to do great harm to the agent himself; and I do not see how those who believe this, can think otherwise than that the example, on the whole, must be more salutary than hurtful, since, if it displays the misconduct, it displays also the painful or degrading consequences which, if the conduct is justly censured, must be supposed to be in all or most cases attendant on it.

But the strongest of all the arguments against the interference of the public with purely personal conduct, is that when it does interfere, the odds are that it interferes wrongly, and in the wrong place. On questions of social morality, of duty to others, the opinion of the public, that is, of an overruling majority, though often wrong, is likely to be still oftener right; because on such questions they are only required to judge of their own interests; of the manner in which some mode of conduct, if allowed to be practiced, would affect themselves. But the opinion of a similar majority, imposed as a law on the minority, on questions of self-regarding conduct, is quite as likely to be wrong as right; for in these cases public opinion means, at the best, some people's opinion of what is good or bad for other people; while very often it does not even mean that; the public, with the most perfect indifference, passing over the pleasure or convenience of those whose conduct they censure, and considering only their own preference. There are many who consider as an injury to themselves any conduct which they have a distaste for, and resent it as an outrage to their feelings; as a religious bigot, when charged with disregarding the religious feelings of others, has been known to retort that they disregard his feelings, by persisting in their abominable worship or creed. But there is no parity between the feeling of a person for his own opinion, and the feeling of another who is offended at his holding it; no more than between the desire of a thief to take a purse, and the desire of the right owner to keep it. And a person's taste is as much his own peculiar concern as his opinion or his purse. It is easy for any one to imagine an ideal public, which leaves the freedom and choice of individuals in all uncertain matters undisturbed, and only requires them to abstain from modes of conduct which universal experience has condemned. But where

has there been seen a public which set any such limit to its censorship? or when does the public trouble itself about universal experience? In its interferences with personal conduct it is seldom thinking of anything but the enormity of acting or feeling differently from itself; and this standard of judgment, thinly disguised, is held up to mankind as the dictate of religion and philosophy, by nine tenths of all moralists and speculative writers. These teach that things are right because they are right; because we feel them to be so. They tell us to search in our own minds and hearts for laws of conduct binding on ourselves and on all others. What can the poor public do but apply these instructions, and make their own personal feelings of good and evil, if they are tolerably unanimous in them, obligatory on all the world?

The evil here pointed out is not one which exists only in theory; and it may perhaps be expected that I should specify the instances in which the public of this age and country improperly invests its own preferences with the character of moral laws. I am not writing an essay on the aberrations of existing moral feeling. That is too weighty a subject to be discussed parenthetically, and by way of illustration. Yet examples are necessary, to show that the principle I maintain is of serious and practical moment, and that I am not endeavoring to erect a barrier against imaginary evils. And it is not difficult to show, by abundant instances, that to extend the bounds of what may be called moral police, until it encroaches on the most unquestionably legitimate liberty of the individual, is one of the most universal of all human propensities.

As a first instance, consider the antipathies which men cherish on no better grounds than that persons whose religious opinions are different from theirs, do not practice their religious observances, especially their religious abstinences. To cite a rather trivial example, nothing in the creed or practice of Christians does more to envenom the hatred of Mahomedans against them, than the fact of their eating pork. There are few acts which Christians and Europeans regard with more unaffected disgust, than Mussulmans regard this particular mode of satisfying hunger. It is, in the first place, an offence against their religion; but this circumstance by no means explains either the degree or the kind of their repugnance; for wine also is forbidden by their religion, and to partake of it is by all Mussulmans accounted wrong, but not disgusting. Their aversion to the flesh of the "unclean beast" is, on the contrary, of that peculiar character, resembling an instinctive antipathy, which the idea of uncleanness, when once it thoroughly sinks into the feelings, seems always to excite even in those whose personal habits are anything but scrupulously clean and of which the sentiment of religious impurity, so intense in the Hindoos, is a remarkable example. Suppose now that in a people, of whom the majority were Mussulmans, that majority should insist upon not permitting pork to be eaten within the limits of the country. This would be nothing new in Mahomedan countries. Would it be a legitimate exercise of the moral authority of public opinion? and if not, why not? The practice is really revolting to such a public. They also sincerely think that it is forbidden and abhorred by the Deity. Neither could the prohibition be censured as religious persecution. It might be religious in its origin, but it would not be persecution for religion, since nobody's religion makes it a duty to eat pork. The only tenable ground of condemnation would be, that with the personal tastes and self-regarding concerns of individuals the public has no business to interfere.

To come somewhat nearer home: the majority of Spaniards consider it a gross impiety, offensive in the highest degree to the Supreme Being, to worship him in any other manner than the Roman Catholic; and no other public worship is lawful on Spanish soil. The people of all Southern Europe look upon a married clergy as not only irreligious, but unchaste, indecent, gross, disgusting. What do Protestants think of these perfectly sincere feelings, and of the attempt to enforce them against non-Catholics? Yet, if mankind are justified in interfering with each other's liberty in things which do not concern the interests of others, on what principle is it possible consistently to exclude these cases? or who can blame people for desiring to suppress what they regard as a scandal in the sight of God and man?

No stronger case can be shown for prohibiting anything which is regarded as a personal immorality, than is made out for suppressing these practices in the eyes of those who regard them as impieties; and unless we are willing to adopt the logic of persecutors, and to say that we may persecute others because we are right, and that they must not persecute us because they are wrong, we must beware of admitting a principle of which we should resent as a gross injustice the application to ourselves.

The preceding instances may be objected to, although unreasonably, as drawn from contingencies impossible among us: opinion, in this country, not being likely to enforce abstinence from meats, or to interfere with people for worshipping, and for either marrying or not marrying, according to their creed or inclination. The next example, however, shall be taken from an interference with liberty which we have by no means

passed all danger of. Wherever the Puritans have been sufficiently powerful, as in New England, and in Great Britain at the time of the Commonwealth, they have endeavored, with considerable success, to put down all public, and nearly all private, amusements: especially music, dancing, public games, or other assemblages for purposes of diversion, and the theatre. There are still in this country large bodies of persons by whose notions of morality and religion these recreations are condemned; and those persons belonging chiefly to the middle class, who are the ascendant power in the present social and political condition of the kingdom, it is by no means impossible that persons of these sentiments may at some time or other command a majority in Parliament. How will the remaining portion of the community like to have the amusements that shall be permitted to them regulated by the religious and moral sentiments of the stricter Calvinists and Methodists? Would they not, with considerable peremptoriness, desire these intrusively pious members of society to mind their own business? This is precisely what should be said to every government and every public, who have the pretension that no person shall enjoy any pleasure which they think wrong. But if the principle of the pretension be admitted, no one can reasonably object to its being acted on in the sense of the majority, or other preponderating power in the country; and all persons must be ready to conform to the idea of a Christian commonwealth, as understood by the early settlers in New England, if a religious profession similar to theirs should ever succeed in regaining its lost ground, as religions supposed to be declining have so often been known to do.

To imagine another contingency, perhaps more likely to be realized than the one last mentioned. There is confessedly a strong tendency in the modern world towards a democratic constitution of society, accompanied or not by popular political institutions. It is affirmed that in the country where this tendency is most completely realized—where both society and the government are most democratic—the United States—the feeling of the majority, to whom any appearance of a more showy or costly style of living than they can hope to rival is disagreeable, operates as a tolerably effectual sumptuary law, and that in many parts of the Union it is really difficult for a person possessing a very large income, to find any mode of spending it, which will not incur popular disapprobation. Though such statements as these are doubtless much exaggerated as a representation of existing facts, the state of things they describe is not only a conceivable and possible, but a probable result of democratic feeling, combined with the notion that the public has a right to a veto on the manner in which individuals shall spend their incomes. We have only further to suppose a considerable diffusion of Socialist opinions, and it may become infamous in the eyes of the majority to possess more property than some very small amount, or any income not earned by manual labor. Opinions similar in principle to these, already prevail widely among the artisan class, and weigh oppressively on those who are amenable to the opinion chiefly of that class, namely, its own members. It is known that the bad workmen who form the majority of the operatives in many branches of industry, are decidedly of opinion that bad workmen ought to receive the same wages as good, and that no one ought to be allowed, through piecework or otherwise, to earn by superior skill or industry more than others can without it. And they employ a moral police, which occasionally becomes a physical one, to deter skilful workmen from receiving, and employers from giving, a larger remuneration for a more useful service. If the public have any jurisdiction over private concerns, I cannot see that these people are in fault, or that any individual's particular public can be blamed for asserting the same authority over his individual conduct, which the general public asserts over people in general.

END NOTES

Hobbes

[1]Sir Edward Coke (1552 – 1634) was the first Lord Chief Justice of England. His Commentaries on Littleton refer to Sir Thomas de Littleton's (1422 – 1481) *Treatise on Tenures.* [Ed.]

[2]Hobbes wrote this work in the midst of the English civil wars (1641–46; 1648–52), in which Parliament fought King Charles I (the Royalists), which Parliament won. [Ed.]

[3]The Athenians in the fifth century B.C. expelled innocent men thought to be dangerous to the state. The names of the men deemed dangerous were written on pieces of broken pottery. The famous general Aristides was expelled in 483 B.C. but was recalled a few years later. The demagogue Hyperbolus was expelled in 417 B.C. [Ed.]

Locke

[1]Richard Hooker (1553 – 1600) was a prominent English theologian and political philosopher, who greatly influenced Locke.

Rousseau

[1]Under bad governments this equality is only apparent and illusory; it serves only to keep the poor in their misery and the rich in their usurpations. In fact, laws are always useful to those who possess and

injurious to those that have nothing; whence it follows that the social state is advantageous to men only so far as they all have something, and none of them has too much.

[2]"Every interest," says the Marquis d'Argenson, "has different principles. An identity of interests between any two given persons is established by reason of their opposition to the interests of a third." He might have added that the identity of the interests of all is established by reason of their opposition to the interests of each. Did individual interests not exist, the idea of a common interest could scarcely be entertained, for there would be nothing to oppose it. Society would become automatic, and politics would cease to be an art.

[3]"It is true," says Machiavelli, "that some divisions injure the State, while some are beneficial to it; those are injurious to it which are accompanied by cabals and factions; those assist it which are maintained without cabals, without factions. Since, therefore, no founder of a State can provide against enmities in it, he ought at least to provide that there shall be no cabals" (*History of Florence,* Book VII).

[4]Attentive readers, do not, I beg you, hastily charge me with contradiction here. I could not avoid it in terms owing to the poverty of the language, but wait.

[5]I do not mean by this word an aristocracy or democracy only, but in general any government directed by the general will, which is the law. To be legitimate, the government must not be combined with the sovereign power, but must be its minister; then monarchy itself is a republic. This will be made clear in the next book.

[6]A nation becomes famous only when its legislation is beginning to decline. We are ignorant during how many centuries the institutions of Lycurgus conferred happiness on the Spartans before they were known in the rest of Greece.

[7]This must always be understood to relate to a free State; for otherwise family, property, want of an asylum, necessity, or violence, may detain an inhabitant in a country against his will; and then his residence alone no longer supposes his consent to the contract or to the violation of it.

Hume

[1]i.e., of Israel, who dispensed justice. [Ed.]

[2]In England, following the Glorious Revolution. [Ed.]

[3] Locke. [Ed.]

Burke

[1]"Let Aeolus boast in that hall and reign in the locked prison of the winds." (Virgil, *Aeneid* I. 140–1.) [Ed.]

[2]*Numero plures:* greater in number. *Virtute et honore majores:* greater in virtue and honor. [Ed.]

[3]"It is enough for me to applaud justice." [Ed.]

Wollstonecraft

[1]France.

[2]Treating this part of the subject, I have borrowed some hints from a very sensible pamphlet, written by the late bishop of Autun on Public Education. [The reference is to Talleyrand's *Rapport sur L'Instruction Publique* (Paris, 1791)—Ed.]

Marx and Engels

[1]Harold Laski, *Introduction to "The Communist Manifesto"* (New York: Random House, 1967).

[2]Quoted in David McClellan, *Karl Marx* (New York: Viking Press, 1975). p. 3.

CHAPTER II

Justification of the State and Political Obligation:

Why Should I Obey the Law?

You are filling out your yearly federal income tax forms and become irritated at the large sum of money that you are going to have to pay, $5000. If that weren't bad enough, you don't believe in the programs for which most of the money will be spent. You ask yourself, "What right does the government have to demand payment of me?" But you don't like the probable consequences of not paying—a heavy fine or even a prison sentence—so you reluctantly write out a check for $5000, realizing that you will not be able to afford needed house repairs or a vacation this year.

You put your tax forms, with a check, into an envelope and go out to mail it at the nearest mailbox. On your way home, a man accosts you with a gun. "Your money or your life," he roughly demands. You open your wallet and hand him the $100 therein. You continue home, beaten in spirit, feeling twice robbed, and wondering which is the greater robber, the gunman or the government?

You ask yourself if that feeling is justified. Is the government with its laws only a gunman, but one who observes reliable rituals and procedures and, unlike the robber, warns you in advance that a percentage of your money will be taken at a certain time every year? You've always been a law-abiding citizen, but now you wonder, By what right does the government demand my obedience? Why should I obey the State? What is the justification of government? What are the limits of governmental authority in light of my right or need to be free? Is taxation legitimate?

First, let us survey seven classic answers to these related questions:

1. The Anarchist answer. Your autonomy is a moral absolute, and no amount of efficiency, utility, or stability justifies the State overriding it. All States are without moral authority. We begin this chapter with Robert Paul Wolff's *In Defense of Anarchism*.

2. The Absolutist answer. Anarchy—*the state of nature* without political security—is so dangerous, barbarous, and impoverished—wherein "life is solitary, poor, nasty, brutish, and short—a war of all against all"—that it is rational to give up significant freedom to the state in order to obtain peace and security. Since anarchy is unspeakably terrible, any government (even a despotism) is better than none. This is Hobbes' answer (see Reading 2).

3. The Classical Liberal answer. Our obligation to obey the State is based on free consent. Government is based on the consent of the governed. Locke agrees with Hobbes in that we contract with the State to give up some freedom for security, but he disagrees on the degree of the surrender. In consenting to obey the State, we do not give up our natural rights to life, property, representation, and other goods—better a state of nature, which is not as bad as Hobbes makes out, than slavery to the state! (See Locke's essay, Reading 3. Hume criticizes the consent theory in Reading 5, and M. B. E. Smith argues against it in Reading 15. Harry Beran, however, defends it in Reading 12).

4. The Libertarian answer. This answer, represented by Robert Nozick in Reading 25, goes further than

the Lockean answer in honoring freedom, especially our right to own property, and therefore in insisting that the only function of the state is to protect us from external and internal enemies—otherwise, the government that governs least, governs best.

5. The Marxist answer. Diametrically opposite the libertarian position, the Marxist answer argues that property should belong to the State so that it may use the property for human good, taking from each as he or she is able and giving to each as he or she has need. In other words, the function that justifies political authority is that of justice, of justly distributing the goods of the society in a radical egalitarian manner. Because capitalist societies fail to promote this state of justice, the proletariat is justified in overthrowing the State by revolutionary means. (See Readings 8 and 9.)

6. The Fair Play answer. The function of the state is to promote justice as fairness, an arrangement of institutions whereby maximal liberty consistent with equal opportunity and a principle to benefit the worst-off prevails. Our obligation to the State is based on the principle of fairness. If within a social scheme, which depends on social cooperation, you are accepting the benefits of that scheme, it's fair that you do your part to cooperate with others in doing your part to produce benefits. (This answer is put forth by H. L. A. Hart in Reading 49 and John Rawls in Reading 13. Smith criticizes it in Reading 15).

7. The Utilitarian or Consequentialist answer. Government is a tool for enabling us to coordinate our activities and live a harmonious social life. Any government that is carrying out this function is legitimate and should be obeyed. At least it has a prima facie right to be obeyed. This is Hume's position in Reading 5 and David Copp's position in Reading 14.

The two pivotal questions here are, What exactly grounds the State's authority, making it legitimate? Do we have a general moral obligation to obey the law? This last question may be seen as the mirror image of the question that precedes it, and it is discussed by most of the authors in this chapter. M. B. E. Smith (Reading 15) attempts to show that none of the standard theories succeed in establishing a general prima facie obligation to obey the law. He seeks to separate the question of State legitimacy from the question, Is there a prima facie obligation to obey the law?

READING 11

In Defense of Anarchism

Robert Paul Wolff

Robert Paul Wolff was for many years Professor of Philosophy at Columbia University and presently is Professor of Philosophy at the University of Massachusetts at Amherst. He is the author of many articles and books but is best known for his In Defense of Anarchism. Wolff's argument (and essay) can be divided into two parts. In the first, he describes the meaning of political authority, distinguishing it from mere power. In the second part, he defines autonomy and argues that it is incompatible with accepting authority.

Wolff distinguishes an authoritative command from a persuasive argument. I may choose to do exactly as a sovereign commands because I see it as my moral duty, but the commanding or arguing party has no authority in himself.

This reading is taken from In Defense of Anarchism (New York: Harper & Row, 1970).

THE CONCEPT OF AUTHORITY

Politics is the exercise of the power of the state, or the attempt to influence that exercise. Political philosophy is therefore, strictly speaking, the philosophy of the state. If we are to determine the content of political philosophy, and whether indeed it exists, we must begin with the concept of the state.

The state is a group of persons who have and exercise supreme authority within a given territory. Strictly, we should say that a state is a group of persons who have supreme authority within a given territory *or over a certain population.* A nomadic tribe may exhibit the authority structure of a state, so long as its subjects do not fall under the superior authority of a territorial state. The state may include all the persons who fall under its authority, as does the democratic state according to its theorists; it may also consist of a single individual to whom all the rest are subject. We may doubt whether the one-person state has ever actually existed, although Louis XIV evidently thought so when he announced, "L'etat c'est moi" [I am the State]. The distinctive characteristic of the state is supreme authority.

Authority is the right to command, and correlatively, the right to be obeyed. *It must be distinguished from power,* which is the ability to compel compliance, either through the use or threat of force. When I turn over my wallet to a thief who is holding me at gunpoint, I do so because the fate with which he threatens me is worse than the loss of money which I am made to suffer. I grant that he has power over me, but I would hardly suppose that he has *authority,* that is, that he has a right to demand my money and that I have an obligation to give it to him. When the government presents me with a bill for taxes, on the other hand, I pay it (normally) even though I do not wish to and even if I think I can get away with not paying. It is after all, the duly constituted government, and hence it has a *right* to tax me. It has *authority* over me. Sometimes, of course, I cheat the government, but even so, I acknowledge its authority, for who would speak of "cheating" a thief?

To claim authority is to claim the right to be obeyed. To *have* authority is then—what? It may mean to have that right, or it may mean to have one's claim acknowledged and accepted by those at whom it is directed. The term "authority" is ambiguous, having both a descriptive and a normative sense. Even the descriptive sense refers to norms or obligations, of course, but it does so by *describing* what men believe they ought to do rather than by *asserting* that they ought to do it. . . .

What is meant by *supreme* authority? Some political philosophers have held that the true state has ultimate authority over all matters whatsoever that occur within its venue. Jean-Jacques Rousseau, for example, asserted that the social contract by which a just political community is formed "gives to the body absolute command over the members of which it is formed; and it is this power, when directed by the general will, that bears . . . the name of 'sovereign.'" John Locke, on the other hand, held that the supreme authority of the just state extends only to those matters which it is proper for a state to control. The state is, to be sure, the highest authority, but its right to command is less than absolute. One of the questions which political philosophy must answer is whether there is any limit to the range of affairs over which a just state has authority.

An authoritative command must also be distinguished from a persuasive argument. When I am commanded to do something, I may choose to comply even though I am not being threatened, because I am brought to believe that it is something which I ought to do. If that is the case, then I am not, strictly speaking, obeying a command, but rather acknowledging the force of an argument or the rightness of a prescription. The person who issues the "command" functions merely as the *occasion* for my becoming aware of my duty, and his role might in other instances be filled by an admonishing friend, or even by my own conscience. I might, by an extension of the term, say that the prescription has authority over me, meaning simply that I ought to act in accordance with it. But the person himself has no authority—or, to be more precise, my complying with his command does not constitute an acknowledgment on my part of any such authority. Thus authority resides in persons; they possess it—if indeed they do at all—by virtue of who they are and not by virtue of what they command. My duty to obey is a duty owed to them, not to the moral law or to the beneficiaries of the actions I may be commanded to perform.

There are, of course, many reasons why men actually acknowledge claims of authority. The most common, taking the whole of human history, is simply the prescriptive force of tradition. The fact that something has always been done in a certain way strikes most men as a perfectly adequate reason for doing it that way again. Why should we submit to a king? Because we have always submitted to kings. But why should the oldest son of the king become king in turn? Because oldest sons have always been heirs to the throne. The force of the traditional is engraved so deeply on men's minds that even a study of the violent and haphazard origins of a ruling family will not weaken its authority in the eyes of its subjects.

Some men acquire the aura of authority by virtue of their own extraordinary characteristics, either as great military leaders, as men of saintly character, or as forceful personalities. Such men gather followers and disciples around them who willingly obey without consideration of personal interest or even against its dictates. The followers believe that the leader has a *right to command,* which is to say, *authority.*

Most commonly today, in a world of bureaucratic armies and institutionalized religions, when kings are few in number and the line of prophets has run out, authority is granted to those who occupy official positions. As Weber has pointed out, these positions appear authoritative in the minds of most men because they are defined by certain sorts of bureaucratic regulations having the virtues of publicity, generality, predictability, and so forth. We become conditioned to respond to the visible signs of officiality, such as printed forms and badges. Sometimes we may have clearly in mind the justification for a legalistic claim to authority, as when we comply with a command because its author is an *elected* official. More often the mere sight of a uniform is enough to make us feel that the man inside it has a right to be obeyed.

That men accede to claims of supreme authority is plain. That men *ought* to accede to claims of supreme authority is not so obvious. Our first question must therefore be, Under what conditions and for what reasons does one man have supreme authority over another? The same question can be restated, Under what conditions can a state (understood normatively) exist?

Kant has given us a convenient title for this sort of investigation. He called it a "deduction," meaning by the term not a proof of one proposition from another, but a demonstration of the legitimacy of a concept. When a concept is empirical, its deduction is accomplished merely by pointing to instances of its objects. For example, the deduction of the concept of a horse consists in exhibiting a horse. Since there are horses, it must be legitimate to employ the concept. Similarly, a deduction of the descriptive concept of a state consists simply in pointing to the innumerable examples of human communities in which some men claim supreme authority over the rest and are obeyed. But when the concept in question is nonempirical, its deduction must proceed in a different manner. All normative concepts are nonempirical, for they refer to what ought to be rather than to what is. Hence, we cannot justify the use of the concept of (normative) supreme authority by presenting instances. We must demonstrate by an *a priori* argument that there can be forms of human community in which some men have a moral right to rule. In short, the fundamental task of political philosophy is to provide a *deduction of the concept of the state.*

To complete this deduction, it is not enough to show that there are circumstances in which men have an obligation to do what the *de facto* authorities command. Even under the most unjust of governments there are frequently good reasons for obedience rather than defiance. It may be that the government has commanded its subjects to do what in fact they already have an independent obligation to do; or it may be that the evil consequences of defiance far outweigh the indignity of submission. A government's commands may promise beneficent effects, either intentionally or not. For these

reasons, and for reasons of prudence as well, a man may be right to comply with the commands of the government under whose *de facto* authority he finds himself. But none of this settles the question of legitimate authority. That is a matter of the *right* to command, and of the correlative obligation *to obey the person who issues the command.*

The point of the last paragraph cannot be too strongly stressed. Obedience is not a matter of doing what someone tells you to do. It is a matter of doing what he tells you to do *because he tells you to do it.* Legitimate, or *de jure,* authority thus concerns the grounds and sources of moral obligation.

Since it is indisputable that there are men who believe that others have authority over them, it might be thought that we could use that fact to prove that somewhere, at some time or other, there must have been men who really did possess legitimate authority. We might think, that is to say, that although some claims to authority might be wrong, it could not be that *all* such claims were wrong, since then we never would have had the concept of legitimate authority at all. By a similar argument, some philosophers have tried to show that not all our experiences are dreams, or more generally that in experience not everything is mere appearance rather than reality. The point is that terms like "dream" and "appearance" are defined by contrast with "waking experience" or "reality." Hence we could only have developed a use for them by being presented with situations in which some experiences were dreams and others not, or some things mere appearance and others reality.

Whatever the force of that argument in general, it cannot be applied to the case of *de facto* versus *de jure* authority, for the key component of both concepts, namely "right," is imported into the discussion from the realm of moral philosophy generally. Insofar as we concern ourselves with the possibility of a just state, we *assume* that moral discourse is meaningful and that adequate deductions have been given of concepts like "right," "duty," and "obligation."

What can be inferred from the existence of *de facto* states is that men *believe* in the existence of legitimate authority, for of course a *de facto* state is simply a state whose subjects believe it to be legitimate (i.e., really to have the authority which it claims for itself). They may be wrong. Indeed, *all* beliefs in authority may be wrong—there may be not a single state in the history of mankind which has now or ever has had a right to be obeyed. It might even be impossible for such a state to exist; that is the question we must try to settle. But so long as men believe in the authority of states, we can conclude that they possess the concept of *de jure* authority.[1]

The normative concept of the state as the human community which possesses rightful authority within a territory thus defines the subject matter of political philosophy proper. However, even if it should prove impossible to present a deduction of the concept—if, that is, there can be no *de jure* state—still a large number of moral questions can be raised concerning the individual's relationship with *de facto* states. We may ask, for example, whether there are any moral principles which ought to guide the state in its lawmaking, such as the principle of utilitarianism, and under what conditions it is right for the individual to obey the laws. We may explore the social ideals of equality and achievement, or the principles of punishment, or the justifications for war. All such investigations are essentially applications of general moral principles to the particular phenomena of (*de facto*) politics. Hence, it would be appropriate to reclaim a word which has fallen on bad days, and call that branch of the study of politics *casuistical politics*. Since there are men who acknowledge claims to authority, there are *de facto* states. Assuming that moral discourse in general is legitimate, there must be moral questions which arise in regard to such states. Hence, casuistical politics as a branch of ethics does exist. It remains to be decided whether political philosophy proper exists.

THE CONCEPT OF AUTONOMY

The fundamental assumption of moral philosophy is that men are responsible for their actions. From this assumption it follows necessarily, as Kant pointed out, that men are metaphysically free, which is to say that in some sense they are capable of choosing how they shall act. Being able to choose how he acts makes a man responsible, but merely choosing is not in itself enough to constitute *taking* responsibility for one's actions. Taking responsibility involves attempting to determine what one ought to do, and that, as philosophers since Aristotle have recognized, lays upon one the additional burdens of gaining knowledge, reflecting on motives, predicting outcomes, criticizing principles, and so forth.

The obligation to take responsibility for one's actions does not derive from man's freedom of will alone, for more is required in taking responsibility than freedom of choice. Only because man has the capacity to reason about his choices can he be said to stand under a continuing obligation to take responsibility for them. It is quite appropriate that moral philosophers should group together children and madmen as beings not fully responsible for their actions, for as madmen are thought to lack freedom of choice, so children do not yet possess the power of reason in a developed form. It is even just that we should assign a greater degree of responsibility to children, for madmen, by virtue of their lack of free will, are completely without responsibility, while children, insofar as they possess reason in a partially developed form, can be held responsible (i.e., can be required to take responsibility) to a corresponding degree.

Every man who possesses both free will and reason has an obligation to take responsibility for his actions, even though he may not be actively engaged in a continuing process of reflection, investigation, and deliberation about how he ought to act. A man will sometimes announce his willingness to take responsibility for the consequences of his actions, even though he has not deliberated about them, or does not intend to do so in the future. Such a declaration is, of course, an advance over the refusal to take responsibility; it at least acknowledges the existence of the obligation. But it does not relieve the man of the duty to engage in the reflective process which he has thus far shunned. It goes without saying that a man may take responsibility for his actions and yet act wrongly. When we describe someone as a responsible individual, we do not imply that he always does what is right, but only that he does not neglect the duty of attempting to ascertain what is right.

The responsible man is not capricious or anarchic, for he does acknowledge himself bound by moral constraints. But he insists that he alone is the judge of those constraints. He may listen to the advice of others, but he makes it his own by determining for himself whether it is good advice. He may learn from others about his moral obligations, but only in the sense that a mathematician learns from other mathematicians—namely by hearing from them arguments whose validity he recognizes even though he did not think of them himself. He does not learn in the sense that one learns from an explorer, by accepting as true his accounts of things one cannot see for oneself.

Since the responsible man arrives at moral decisions which he expresses to himself in the form of imperatives, we may say that he gives laws to himself, or is self-legislating. In short, he is *autonomous*. As Kant argued, moral autonomy is a combination of freedom and responsibility; it is a submission to laws which one has made for oneself. The autonomous man, insofar as he is autonomous, is not subject to the will of another. He may do what another tells him, but not *because* he has been told to do it. He is therefore, in the political sense of the word, *free*.

Since man's responsibility for his actions is a consequence of his capacity for choice, he cannot give it up or put it aside. He can refuse to acknowledge it, however, either deliberately or by simply failing to recognize his moral condition. All men refuse to take responsibility for their actions at some time or other during their lives, and some men so consistently shirk their duty that they present more the appearance of overgrown children than of adults. Inasmuch as moral autonomy is simply the condition of taking full responsibility for one's actions, it follows that men can forfeit their autonomy at will. That is to say, a man can decide to obey the commands of another without making any attempt to determine for himself whether what is commanded is good or wise.

This is an important point, and it should not be confused with the false assertion that a man can give up responsibility for his actions. Even after he has subjected himself to the will of another, an individual remains responsible for what he does. But by refusing to engage in moral deliberation, by accepting as final the commands of the others, he forfeits his autonomy. Rousseau is therefore right when he says that a man cannot become a slave even through his own choice, if he means that even slaves are morally responsible for their acts. But he is wrong if he means that men cannot place themselves voluntarily in a position of servitude and mindless obedience.

There are many forms and degrees of forfeiture of autonomy. A man can give up his independence of judgment with regard to a single question, or in respect of a single type of question. For example, when I place myself in the hands of my doctor, I commit myself to whatever course of treatment he prescribes, but only in regard to my health. I do not make him my legal counselor as well. A man may forfeit autonomy on some or all questions for a specific period of time, or during his entire life. He may submit himself to all commands, whatever they may be, save for some specified acts (such as killing) which he refuses to perform. From the example of the doctor, it is obvious that there are at least some situations in which it is reasonable to give up one's autonomy. Indeed, we may wonder whether, in a complex world of technical expertise, it is ever reasonable *not* to do so!

Since the concept of taking and forfeiting responsibility is central to the discussion which follows, it is worth devoting a bit more space to clarifying it. Taking responsibility for one's actions means making the final decisions about what one should do. For the autonomous man, there is no such thing, strictly speaking, as a *command*. If someone in my environment is issuing what are intended as commands, and if he or others expect those commands to be obeyed, that fact will be taken account of in my deliberations. I may decide that I ought to do what that person is commanding me to do, and it may even be that his issuing the command is the factor in the situation which makes it desirable for me to do so. For example, if I am on a sinking ship and the captain is giving orders for manning the life-boats, and if everyone else is obeying the captain *because he is the captain,* I may decide that under the circumstances I had better do what he says, since the confusion caused by disobeying him would be generally harmful. But insofar as I make such a decision, I am not *obeying his command;* that is, I am not acknowledging him as having authority over me. I would make the same decision, for exactly the same reasons, if one of the passengers had started to issue "orders" and had, in the confusion, come to be obeyed.

In politics, as in life generally, men frequently forfeit their autonomy. There are a number of causes for this fact, and also a number of arguments which have been offered to justify it. Most men, as we have already noted, feel so strongly the force of tradition or bureaucracy that they accept unthinkingly the claims to authority which are made by their nominal rulers. It is the rare individual in the history of the race who rises even to the level of questioning the right of his masters to command and the duty of himself and his fellows to obey. Once the dangerous question has been started, however, a variety of arguments can be brought forward to demonstrate the authority of the rulers. Among the most ancient is Plato's assertion that men should submit to the authority of those with superior knowledge, wisdom, or insight. A sophisticated modern version has it that the educated portion of a democratic population is more likely to be politically active, and that it is just as well for the ill-informed segment of the electorate to remain passive, since its entrance into the political arena only supports the efforts of demagogues and extremists.

A number of American political scientists have gone so far as to claim that the apathy of the American masses is a cause of stability and hence a good thing.

The moral condition demands that we acknowledge responsibility and achieve autonomy wherever and whenever possible. Sometimes this involves moral deliberation and reflection; at other times, the gathering of special, even technical, information. The contemporary American citizen, for example, has an obligation to master enough modern science to enable him to follow debates about nuclear policy and come to an independent conclusion.[2] There are great, perhaps insurmountable, obstacles to the achievement of a complete and rational autonomy in the modern world. Nevertheless, so long as we recognize our responsibility for our actions, and acknowledge the power of reason within us, we must acknowledge as well the continuing obligation to make ourselves the authors of such commands as we may obey. The paradox of man's condition in the modern world is that the more fully he recognizes his right and duty to be his own master, the more completely he becomes the passive object of a technology and bureaucracy whose complexities he cannot hope to understand. It is only several hundred years since a reasonably well-educated man could claim to understand the major issues of government as well as his king or parliament. Ironically, the high school graduate of today, who cannot master the issues of foreign and domestic policy on which he is asked to vote, could quite easily have grasped the problems of eighteenth-century statecraft.

THE CONFLICT BETWEEN AUTHORITY AND AUTONOMY

The defining mark of the state is authority, the right to rule. The primary obligation of man is autonomy, the refusal to be ruled. It would seem, then, that there can be no resolution of the conflict between the autonomy of the individual and the putative authority of the state. Insofar as a man fulfills his obligation to make himself the author of his decisions, he will resist the state's claim to have authority over him. That is to say, he will deny that he has a duty to obey the laws of the state *simply because they are the laws*. In that sense, it would seem that anarchism is the only political doctrine consistent with the virtue of autonomy.

Now, of course, an anarchist may grant the necessity of *complying* with the law under certain circum-

stances or for the time being. He may even doubt that there is any real prospect of eliminating the state as a human institution. But he will never view the commands of the state as *legitimate,* as having a binding moral force. In a sense, we might characterize the anarchist as a man without a country, for despite the ties which bind him to the land of his childhood, he stands in precisely the same moral relationship to "his" government as he does to the government of any other country in which he might happen to be staying for a time. When I take a vacation in Great Britain, I obey its laws, both because of prudential self-interest and because of the obvious moral considerations concerning the value of order, the general good consequences of preserving a system of property, and so forth. On my return to the United States, I have a sense of reentering *my* country, and if I think about the matter at all, I imagine myself to stand in a different and more intimate relation to American laws. They have been promulgated by *my* government, and I therefore have a special obligation to obey them. But the anarchist tells me that my feeling is purely sentimental and has no objective moral basis. All authority is equally illegitimate, although of course not therefore equally worthy or unworthy of support, and my obedience to American laws, if I am to be morally autonomous, must proceed from the same considerations which determine me abroad.

The dilemma which we have posed can be succinctly expressed in terms of the concept of a *de jure* state. If all men have a continuing obligation to achieve the highest degree of autonomy possible, then there would appear to be no state whose subjects have a moral obligation to obey its commands. Hence, the concept of a *de jure* legitimate state would appear to be vacuous, and philosophical anarchism would seem to be the only reasonable political belief for an enlightened man.

READING 12

Political Obligation and Consent

Harry Beran

Harry Beran is Professor of Philosophy at the University of Wollongong in Australia. In this article he defends the consent theory of political obligation and authority, providing the Classical Liberal answer. Beran seeks to throw light on the reasons for our obligation to obey the State. He limits his thesis to consent as a necessary condition for political obligation. He does not defend the stronger thesis that it is also a sufficient condition. He begins by attempting to answer skeptics such as H. A. Prichard and Thomas Weldon, who think the question of whether one is obligated to obey the State is wrongheaded or unanswerable. Then he moves on to answer the great critic of consent theories, David Hume. He concedes that most members of a society may not actually have consented, explicitly or implicitly, to their government.

This reading is taken from "A Contemporary Defense of the Consent Theory of Obligation," *Ethics* (1994), by permission of the publisher.

I

The consent theory of political obligation and authority (the Consent Theory below) is much more plausible than its many critics have realized. However, its plausibility can only be appreciated if the precise and limited scope of the theory within a complete theory of reasons for political obedience is recognized. These are the two claims I will try to substantiate in this paper.

To understand the scope of the Consent Theory let us note the following characteristics of political obligation and political authority.

1. To have political authority is for someone, A, to be in authority over some others, B and C; and for A to have authority over B and C is necessarily for A to have the right to make demands (in certain areas of conduct) on B and C and for the latter to have an obligation to meet these demands. The right of A to make these demands and B's and C's obligation to meet them are the correlatives. Hence, if a state has political authority, the right to govern, then there must be someone who has a correlative obligation. It is this particular obligation of the citizens to obey the state, the correlative of political authority, to which I refer by the term "political obligation." Since political obligation and political authority are correlatives, whatever is the logical basis of one must also be the logical

basis of the other. When I speak, below, of a political authority relationship, I will be referring to the two correlatives which make it up.

2. One can distinguish between conclusive reasons for doing something and a (not necessarily conclusive) reason for doing it. To be under political obligation is for there to be a (not necessarily conclusive) reason for obeying the state. This must be so since it is possible to be under political obligation and yet to be morally justified in disobeying the state. Two sorts of cases are worth mentioning. One is morally justified civil disobedience, that is, disobedience of a law because it is morally objectionable. For unlike rebellion, which typically involves a denial that one is under political obligation, civil disobedience typically does not involve such a denial but rather the assertion that there are moral reasons for disobeying the state which override one's political obligation. The other sort of case is disobedience of a law which is not morally objectionable. Even if one is under political obligation one may be morally justified in breaking such a law, say the law against theft, if this is necessary for the sake of a greater good, say, saving a child from starvation. Since political obligation and political authority are correlatives, a state's having political authority is also only a (not necessarily conclusive) reason for obeying it.[1]

3. "Political obligation" refers not just to any reason for obeying the state but to one specific reason: that reason which is logically related both to political obligation and its correlative, political authority. If I promise my mother to obey state *S* then there is a reason for my obeying it and, moreover, I am under an obligation to obey it. But clearly this obligation has nothing to do with political obligation, since my promising my mother to obey state *S* does not give it authority to govern me.

From the above three points the scope of the Consent Theory can be understood. Within a theory of reasons for political obedience the Consent Theory distinguishes between obeying a state because it stands in an authority to its members and obeying it for other reasons. The Consent Theory merely claims that consent is a necessary condition for there being an authority relationship between a state and its members (and possibly also a sufficient condition, but this stronger claim cannot be considered in this paper). It does not claim that consent is either a necessary or a sufficient condition for there being conclusive reasons for obeying the state. The Consent Theory can deny this since the existence of a political authority relationship is neither a sufficient condition for the existence of conclusive reasons for political obedience (as has been shown already) nor a necessary condition for the existence of such reasons (as will be shown in Section II).

II

Recognition of the precise scope of the Consent Theory resolves some of the traditional disputes about the theory. However, before I can demonstrate this, I have to make some further preliminary points.

I must grant that, in using the term "political obligation" to refer to that obligation which is the correlative of political authority, I am using it in a narrower sense than that in which some others have used it. Still, this is surely one proper sense of "political obligation" and, moreover, an important one, since the authority relationship between a state and its members is an important political phenomenon. Also, it is a sense of "political obligation" which suits my aim in this paper, which is to find a sense of "political obligation" and of "consent" such that it can plausibly be claimed that consent is (at least) a necessary condition of political obligation.

What do I mean by "consent" in the Consent Theory? Consent consists in acceptance of membership in a state by each person who is under political obligation. For in accepting membership in an association, be it a state or some other association, one agrees to obey the rules of that association; and in agreeing to obey the rules of the state, one puts oneself under an obligation to obey its rules and gives it authority to govern. Naturalized citizens explicitly agree to obey the state in the naturalization ceremony. Native-born citizens implicitly agree to obey when they cease to be political minors and accept adult status, that is, full membership, in the state. I wish this model of consent as acceptance of membership in an association to be taken quite literally. There is at least one other kind of association where a particularly important obligation to obey the association's rules rests on implicit acceptance of membership: namely, churches. Very plausibly the obligation of Anglicans to obey the rules of their church is based on their acceptance of membership in the Church of England. Most members of the Anglican church are baptized into it, and hence become members of it, as infants; but such members' obligation to obey the church as adults can hardly be grounded in in-

fant baptism or confirmation at the age of twelve and, therefore, most plausibly, is grounded in implicit (continuing) acceptance of membership at the age when such acceptance can be morally binding.

Agreeing to do something is either a form of promising or something analogous to promising; and promissory obligations are moral obligations. Hence agreeing to do *X,* like promising to do *X,* gives rise to a moral obligation to do *X.* So the Consent Theory subsumes political obligation and the right involved in political authority under moral obligation and moral right, that is, the kind of moral obligation and moral right which arise out of a promise. Since consenting and agreeing to do something are either forms of promising or analogous to promising, I do not, in this article, distinguish between consenting, agreeing, and promising to do something.

Recognition of the precise and limited scope of the Consent Theory makes possible convincing replies to some of the traditional objections to the Consent Theory.

H. A. Prichard, Margaret MacDonald, T. D. Weldon, J. C. Rees, and Thomas MacPherson have all claimed that classical political philosophy rests on a mistake. Their argument for this claim runs roughly thus: The problem of political obligation—Why should I or anyone obey the state?—is the fundamental problem of political philosophy. Classical philosophy assumed that there is a single answer to this question, for example, that the state has the consent of its members or that it promotes the general good. But there is no single answer to this question, for reasons why one should obey (or disobey) the law depend on the circumstances of particular cases. Deeply committed democrats may (rightly) think they ought to obey a dictator if this is the least evil possible under certain circumstances; and they may (also rightly) think they are not morally required to obey a genuinely democratic government which refuses, for no sufficient reasons, to let them leave the country. As MacDonald puts it "there is no general criterion" of political obligation (no "sole justification for accepting any or every law") "but an indefinite set of vaguely shifting criteria, different for different times and circumstances. . . ." She adds, "No general criterion of all right actions can be supplied. Similarly, the answer to 'Why should I obey *any* law, acknowledge the authority of *any* State or support *any* Government?' is that this is a senseless question."

As a criticism of the Consent Theory this objection is misconceived. For the Consent Theory distinguishes between authoritative and nonauthoritative states and merely claims that consent is (at least) a necessary condition for a state being authoritative and, therefore, that consent is a necessary condition for the members of a state being under political obligation. Thus while the Consent Theory does propose a criterion for any state being authoritative, it does not propose to answer the question, Why should I obey *any* law . . . or support *any* government? The Consent Theory is quite consistent with MacDonald's claim that the answer to the last question cannot be given in terms of necessary and sufficient conditions, without, however, being committed to this claim.

It may be thought that a state which does not have *authority* to govern cannot be morally justified in exercising political power. But this is not so. A group of people cannot have *authority* to govern without the consent of the governed, but they may be morally justified in exercising *power* without consent. According to the Consent Theory this must be at least logically possible. For one of the starting points of this theory is the claim that not just any moral reason for obeying the state constitutes a political authority relationship (cf. Section I). Hence there may be reasons for obeying the state other than the reason which is involved in the existence of a political authority relationship; and these reasons may sometimes be conclusive.

Let me illustrate this through an example. According to classical Marxism there will be a dictatorship of the proletariat between the overthrow of capitalism and the withering away of the state; this is thought to be necessary, *interalia,* to prevent a counterrevolution by the expropriated capitalists. According to Leninism this dictatorship may be exercised by the vanguard of the proletariat, that is, by the leaders of the Communist party; in other words a dictatorship by a small minority of the population. If such a dictatorship did not have the support of the people it would not be an authoritative government; however, if such a dictatorship really were a necessary condition for the creation of a just society of free and unalienated human beings, it would perhaps be morally justified despite its lack of authority.

The plausibility of Hume's objection to the "unnecessary shuffle" [Rawls's term] (see "Of the Original Contract" [Reading 5]) also depends on a failure to recognize the precise scope of the Consent Theory. Consent Theorists, Hume claims, ask:

1. Why are we bound to obey our government? and answer: Because
2. We have promised to obey our government, and

3. We are bound to keep our promises.
   Hume challenges this argument by asking:
4. Why should we keep our word? and answering: Because
5. It is necessary for civilized life.

But, Hume continues, 5 is in itself a sufficient answer to 1; so there is no need to derive 1 from 3 by means of a highly speculative act of promising. In fact, Hume claims, 1 and 3 are principles which "stand precisely on the same foundations"; both obligations, that to obey one's government and that to keep one's promises, are established by their necessity for civilized life.

Hume does not establish his conclusion. Married people have an obligation to love and support each other because they promise to do so in the marriage ceremony. I hope no one would want to challenge this "consent theory or marital obligation" on the ground that marital obligation can be derived directly from the necessity of the family for civilized life. No one should be swayed by such a challenge, since it tried to make do with one answer to two distinct questions:

Why do we have the institution of marriage?

Why do individuals A and B have certain marital obligations to each other?

The answer to the first question may well be that the institution of the family is necessary for civilized life. But this answer cannot explain why two particular individuals have certain marital obligations to each other. The answer to this question is that they have promised to love and support each other.

Similarly, it may well be the case that we have the institution of the state because of its utility—because the state is necessary for civilized life. But, on the face of it, the utility of the state cannot in itself explain why a particular state stands in an authority relation to some particular individuals. Hence, both the question of utility (Is the state worth having?) and the question of fidelity (Do the members of a particular state owe it obedience?) have to be asked and answered. And just as A's marital obligations to a certain woman cannot be explained directly in terms of the utility of the institution of marriage, so A's political obligation to a certain state cannot be explained directly in terms of the utility of the state.

Hume simply assumes that political obligation, unlike marital obligation, can be explained directly in terms of the utility of the state. Thus he assumes, but does not show, that there is no need to distinguish between a state's authority relationship to its members as a reason for obedience and other possible reasons for obedience. Hence Hume has not shown that the admittedly speculative appeal to an act of promising is an unnecessary shuffle.

III

Even if it is granted that recognition of the limited scope of the Consent Theory shows that the above objections to it are misconceived, there are further well-known objections which may be regarded as fatal to the Consent Theory even as now understood. To these objections I now turn.

S. I. Benn and R. S. Peters argue thus:

> . . . if consent is a *necessary* condition for political obligation, it would deny a government any rightful authority over anyone who dissented from the basic principles of the constitution. Force used against Communists in a liberal democracy, or against liberals in a "people's democracy," would alike be naked aggression, for the law authorizing it would not be *their* law. In this form, no one who chose to contract out could be legitimately coerced.
>
> And is it reasonable to assume that all members of a state subscribe to its constitution? In the 1946 referendum, eight million Frenchmen voted against the constitution of the Fourth Republic, and a further eight million did not vote at all. In what sense, then, did they consent to it? Some may have rejected even the majority principle.[2]

This objection does not get a grip on the version of the Consent Theory I defend. I identify consent with acceptance of membership in the state; and one can (continue to) accept membership in a state although one votes against a constitution or abstains from a referendum on a constitution.

One must distinguish between the statements "A *agrees with* the constitution" and "A *agrees to obey* the constitution." The second statement can be true, though the first is false. But why would those who vote against a constitution yet agree to obey it? Well perhaps because they would rather (continue to) be members of a particular state, though it has a constitution with which they disagree, than not to be members of that state at all. After all, what true Frenchman, though he be a communist and given that he cannot have a Communist France now, would not rather live in Capitalist France than Communist Russia!

But perhaps some of those who dissent from the constitution do not wish to agree to obey it. There are

three ways in which they can avoid agreeing to obey the constitution: secession, migration, or a public declaration that they are not accepting membership in the state in whose territory they are living. I will discuss each option in turn.

It is true, these days, that a repressed or disenchanted minority cannot found a new state of their own liking or an anarchist community by migrating to hitherto unoccupied territory. But they can, and I am inclined to think they have a moral right to, found a new state or an anarchist community by secession. The number of new independent communities which can be founded by discovering unoccupied territory is necessarily limited; but that which can be founded by secession is, for all practical purposes, not. Politically speaking, new Americas can always be found *within* America.

The claim that there is a moral right to secession is congenial to the Consent Theory. The claim needs, nevertheless, to be supported by argument. However, instead of supplying such an argument now, I will merely note that secession is a topic completely neglected by contemporary philosophers. Hence I am not making a claim against which there exist arguments in the literature (or otherwise known to me). Despite Katanga, Biafra, Rhodesia, Northern Ireland, and Bangla Desh—not to mention Scottish and Welsh Nationalists, French Canadians, Spanish Basques, and Croatian Yugoslavs—there does not seem to be a single recent philosophical contribution to the problem of the justification of secession. Nor have the major classical political philosophers had much to say on the topic.

Migration, as a way of avoiding political obligation to a particular state, raises some well-known objections. Hume [see Reading 5] put one of them thus: "Should it be said, that, by living under the dominion of a prince, which one might leave, every individual has given a tacit consent to his authority, and promised him obedience; it may be answered, that such an implied consent can only have place, where one imagines, that the matter depends on his choice. . . . [But] can we seriously say, that a poor peasant . . . has a free choice to leave his country, when he knows no foreign language or manners, and lives from day to day, by the small wages he acquires?"

I take the point of the objection to be that if the peasant cannot leave his state then his putative implicit agreement to obey is not made freely and, therefore, cannot create a promissory obligation. Hence the Consent Theory is committed to the implausible claim that the peasant is not under political obligation simply because he is too poor and ignorant to leave his state.

Well, is the peasant in a position, despite his predicament, to make a morally binding promise to obey the state? H. L. A. Hart has made extremely plausible the view that the serious utterance of "I promise to do X" counts as a morally binding promise, provided none of certain defeating conditions are present. Some of the more important conditions which defeat a claim that a morally binding promise has been made are deception, mental incapacity, coercion or undue influence, and unfair bargaining position. The claim that "free choice" is a necessary condition for the creation of a promissory obligation can be regarded as a compendious way of claiming that a promissory obligation is created only if none of the defeating conditions hold.

The Consent Theory is committed to the view that one's agreement to obey the state does not create an obligation if there obtains one or more of the conditions which defeat the claim that a promissory obligation has been created. But there is nothing in the peasant's predicament that defeats the claim that his acceptance of membership in the state counts as putting himself under a promissory obligation to obey. Not even the coercion defense applies: P is coerced by A to do X only if P's doing X is (partly) brought about by A threatening P, or a third party, with harm unless P does X. But Hume's peasant is prevented from leaving his state not by any threat of harm by the state should he attempt to leave, but by his ignorance and poverty. He accepts membership in the state not because of the state's threat of harm should he do otherwise, but because of his poverty and ignorance.

In general, it simply does not follow from one's being unable to leave a state that there is present one or more of the conditions which prevent one's promise to obey that state from creating an obligation.

What if a government did coerce citizens into staying within its territory? Would this be a case where the citizens are no longer under political obligation? Hume did not think so; he wrote: "And did a prince observe, that many of his subjects were seized with a frenzy of migrating to foreign countries, he would doubtless, with great reason and justice, restrain them, in order to prevent the depopulation of his kingdom. Would he forfeit the allegiance of all his subjects, by so wise and reasonable a law? Yet the freedom of their choice is surely, in that case, ravished for them." Unlike the case of the poor, ignorant peasant, now it is the government which has "ravished free choice," not circumstances for which the government is not responsible.

The trouble with this objection lies in our knowing a "prince" whose subjects were seized with a frenzy

of migrating to foreign countries. To make this frenzy ineffective he built a wall across the main escape route from his "kingdom" and put sharpshooters on it with orders to shoot anyone who tried to get over it. I do think this "prince" has forfeited the right to the allegiance of those of the people in his "kingdom" who stay in it out of fear of being killed if they try to leave without permission. These people are obliged to stay under his rule, but they are not under political obligation.

According to the United Nations Universal Declaration of Human Rights, people have the moral right to leave their country permanently and to change their nationality and should have the corresponding legal rights. Now, if people are forcibly denied the exercise of the moral right to leave the state of which they are citizens, then surely it is not implausible to claim that they cease to be under political obligation. Or at least it is not implausible to claim this, provided that they have not put themselves under some special obligation which they cannot fulfill if they leave, that they have not broken the law and not yet met the penalty, and that their leaving is compatible with the government fulfilling its constitutional functions.

Political minors present a further problem for the claim that one can escape political obligation through migration. Assume there is an authoritative state. It would seem plausible that the adolescent as well as the adult members of this state are under political obligation. Assume further that there is some age, say fourteen, at which adolescents, while sufficiently mature to be under an obligation to obey the law, are not sufficiently mature to choose their place of residence; hence they would not have the moral or legal right to emigrate without their parents' consent; hence they could be coerced to remain in a state without ceasing to be under political obligation. It seems that these political minors are under political obligation without anything having created that obligation that can plausibly be regarded as morally binding consent.

This objection forces a qualification on the Consent Theory. Some philosophers distinguish between logically primary and logically secondary cases falling under a concept. D. M. Armstrong offers this definition of "logically secondary": "Let it be given that there is a class of things of the sort X, and a subclass of X: the class of things Y. Y's are then logically secondary instances of X if, and only if, (i) it is logically possible that there should be no Y's and yet there still be X's; but (ii) it is logically impossible that Y's should be the only X's which exist."[3]

If this definition of "logically secondary" is tenable then the political obligation of political minors is a logically secondary instance of political obligation. For it is logically impossible for all the members of the class "persons who are under political obligation to state S" to be political minors; if this were so there could not be a state S (though there could be a society S not politically organized) since, by definition, political minors cannot fill the positions which must be filled for a state to exist. On the other hand, it is logically possible that this class should consist of full members only.

So, the claim that consent is a necessary condition of political obligation and authority has to be qualified thus: consent is a necessary condition of political obligation and authority in logically primary cases. This qualification is to be understood as required whenever I claim that consent is a necessary condition of political obligation and authority.

Let me now deal with a difficulty which brings us back to the importance of recognizing the precise and limited scope of the Consent Theory. The version of the Consent Theory which I defend relies on the notion of implicit consent. But nothing A does in situation S can count as A's implicit consent to do X, unless it is in fact possible for A in S to do something that would count as refusing to agree to do X. For implicit consent to do X simply consists in the absence of explicit refusal to agree to do it in a context which gives such absence of (explicit) refusal the significance of (implicit) consent. Hence, I must grant that at least persons who are unable to leave their state, for example, Hume's poor ignorant peasant, can avoid political obligation by, say, declaring publicly and to the appropriate officials that they are not accepting membership in the state. I do grant this, but subject to the following remarks. If some people neither agree to obey the state, nor emigrate, nor secede, then though they would not be under political obligation, the state may well be justified in banishing them to a "Dissenters' Territory" (i.e., a no-man's land created by an adjustment of existing borders) where those who do not agree to obey the state may live.

If the state does not banish them then they would indeed live within its territory, yet not be under political obligation. Needless to say, they would still be morally required to act in accordance with the law in many cases because of moral reasons for doing what is legally required which are independent of the existence of the law. One is not morally justified in killing people just because one is not under political obligation not to do so.

While the admission just made again reveals the limited scope of the Consent Theory, this limited scope does not trivialize it. Let P be someone who lives in a given state but is not under political obligation to it. What difference does this absence of political obligation make to the justification of political action? If one is under political obligation then there is a (not necessarily conclusive) reason for obeying the law. Hence there is one reason for obeying the law, for those who are under political obligation, which does not hold for P. Hence P may be morally justified in disobeying the law in some cases where those who are under political obligation would not be. For example, assume that there is a law against doing X and there are no moral reasons for or against doing X independent of the possible political obligation to do X. (Regrettably states do sometimes ban actions which are not morally wrong.) Then those who are under political obligation have a moral reason against doing X, no moral reasons for doing X, and, therefore, ought, morally speaking, not to do X. On the other hand, P is not under political obligation, and, therefore, it is morally indifferent whether P does X or not.

One further objection has to be considered. The Consent Theory claims that what creates the political obligation of native-born citizens is their acceptance of full membership in the state when they cease to be political minors. This acceptance of full membership in the state is what counts as their implicit agreement to obey it. In other words, staying in the state when one gets the legal right to leave counts as implicit agreement to obey it. Now surely ordinary people are not aware that their remaining within a state when they cease to be political minors counts as their implicit agreement to obey. But if they are not aware of this, then this act cannot give rise to an obligation. For if one does not know that doing W counts as agreeing to do X, then although one does W does not thereby make a morally binding agreement to do X—the claim that one has created an obligation to do X can be defeated by an epistemological defense. So according to the Consent Theory only those few who hold this theory are under political obligation!

This is a very persuasive objection, but it is not conclusive. Adults in contemporary states with universal education do know the following propositions.

1. In remaining within the territory of a state when one comes of age one accepts full membership in it.

2. In accepting membership in a rule-governed association (in the absence of coercion, deception, etc.,) one puts oneself under an obligation to obey its rules.

3. The state is a rule-governed association.

From 1–3 it follows that

4. In remaining within the territory of a state when one comes of age (in the absence of coercion, deception, etc.) one puts oneself under an obligation to obey its rules.

Now either citizens make the inference to 4 or they do not. If they do, then the key premise of the present objection is false. If they do not, it may yet be true that they are under political obligation and that this obligation rests on their acceptance of membership in the state when they come of age. For ignorance that doing W counts as agreeing to do X is only a conclusive defense against the claim that one has agreed to do X if such ignorance is not negligent. If one's ignorance that doing W counts as agreeing to do X is negligent then one's doing W may count as a morally binding agreement despite one's ignorance. Now may one not be negligent in not making the inference from propositions 1, 2, and 3 to proposition 4 when one assumes full adult status, including the legal right to leave the state? It may well be negligent, since people should consider what moral significance there is in their new status and their new rights. So, even if there are some citizens who do not make the inference to proposition 4, this ignorance may not defeat the claim that in accepting full membership of a state when they come of age they put themselves under political obligation.

IV

I have tried to defend the claim that consent is a necessary condition of political obligation and authority; but I have done so without asserting that this condition has in fact held for the majority of the members of any state that has ever existed.

Such caution was not due to timidity but to a desire to separate the theory of political obligation and authority from an application of the theory to particular cases. The agreement to obey the state only gives rise to political obligation if it is free from the conditions which defeat an agreement's giving rise to an obligation, for example, if the agreement is due neither to coercion nor deception. At least two things are necessary for an application of this theory to particular cases. First, what absence of coercion and deception (as well as the other defeating conditions) amounts to would have to be specified much more clearly than I have done in this paper. Second, much empirical information on how much coercion and deception exist in a particular state would have to be available to make it possible to say whether that state has the uncoerced and undeceived consent of the governed.

I cannot attempt to apply the Consent Theory to particular states now beyond noting obvious differences between, for example, Australia and the USSR. Australian citizens are virtually never prevented by their governments from exercising their legal right to leave Australia permanently, and there seems to be very little political censorship by the government. Citizens of the USSR who wish to leave Russia permanently are usually prevented from doing so (except for Jews, many of whom have recently been permitted to leave), and there is a very high level of political censorship in Russia. Hence, even from an armchair, there must be much greater doubt about the extent of uncoerced and undeceived consent by the governed in Russia than in Australia.

READING 13

Legal Obligation and the Duty of Fair Play

John Rawls

John Rawls (1921–) is Professor Emeritus of Philosophy at Harvard University and the author of several works in moral and political philosophy, including one of the most influential works of our time, *A Theory of Justice* (1971), a selection of which is included as Reading 26.

In this earlier essay, Rawls seeks to show how receiving benefits from a social group obligates one to bear one's fair burden within the group for the common good. It conveys the fundamental concepts of the Fair Play answer.

This reading is taken from "Legal Obligation and the Duty of Fair Play," *in Law and Philosophy*, ed. Sidney Hook (New York University Press, 1964), by permission.

1. The subject of law and morality suggests many different questions. In particular, it may consider the historical and sociological question as to the way and manner in which moral ideas influence and are influenced by the legal system; or it may involve the question whether moral concepts and principles enter into an adequate definition of law. Again, the topic of law and morality suggests the problem of the legal enforcement of morality and whether the fact that certain conduct is immoral by accepted precepts is sufficient to justify making that conduct a legal offense. Finally, there is the large subject of the study of the rational principles of moral criticism of legal institutions and the moral grounds of our acquiescence in them. I shall be concerned solely with a fragment of this last question: with the grounds for our moral obligation to obey the law, that is, to carry out our legal duties and to fulfill our legal obligations. My thesis is that the moral obligation to obey the law is a special case of the prima facie duty of fair play.

I shall assume, as requiring no argument, that there is, at least in a society such as ours, a moral obligation to obey the law, although it may, of course, be overridden in certain cases by other more stringent obligations. I shall assume also that this obligation must rest on some general moral principle; that is, it must depend on some principle of justice or upon some principle of social utility or the common good, and the like. Now, it may appear to be a truism, and let us suppose it is, that a moral obligation rests on some moral principle. But I mean to exclude the possibility that the obligation to obey the law is based on a special principle of its own. After all, it is not, without further argument, absurd that there is a moral principle such that when we find ourselves subject to an existing system of rules satisfying the definition of a legal system, we have an obligation to obey the law; and such a principle might be final, and not in need of explanation, in the way in which the principles of justice or of promising and the like are final. I do not know of anyone who has said that there is a special principle of legal obligation in this sense. Given a rough agreement, say, on the possible principles as being those of justice, of social utility, and the like, the question has been on which of one or several is the obligation to obey the law founded, and which,

if any, has a special importance. I want to give a special place to the principle defining the duty of fair play.

2. In speaking of one's obligation to obey the law, I am using the term "obligation" in its more limited sense, in which, together with the notion of a duty and of a responsibility, it has a connection with institutional rules. Duties and responsibilities are assigned to certain positions and offices, and obligations are normally the consequence of voluntary acts of persons, and while perhaps most of our obligations are assumed by ourselves, through the making of promises and the accepting of benefits, and so forth, others may put us under obligation to them (as when on some occasion they help us, for example, as children). I should not claim that the moral grounds for our obeying the law is derived from the duty of fair-play except insofar as one is referring to an obligation in this sense. It would be incorrect to say that our duty not to commit any of the legal offenses, specifying crimes of violence, is based on the duty of fair play, at least entirely. These crimes involve wrongs as such, and with such offenses, as with the vices of cruelty and greed, our doing them is wrong independently of there being a legal system the benefits of which we have voluntarily accepted.

I shall assume several special features about the nature of the legal order in regard to which a moral obligation arises. In addition to the generally strategic place of its system of rules, as defining and relating the fundamental institutions of society that regulate the pursuit of substantive interests, and to the monopoly of coercive powers, I shall suppose that the legal system in question satisfies the concept of the *rule of law* (or what one may think of as justice as regularity). By this I mean that its rules are public, that similar cases are treated similarly, that there are no bills of attainder, and the like. These are all features of a legal system insofar as it embodies without deviation the notion of a public system of rules addressed to rational beings for the organization of their conduct in the pursuit of their substantive interests. This concept imposes, by itself, no limits on the *content* of legal rules, but only on their regular administration. Finally, I shall assume that the legal order is that of a constitutional democracy: that is, I shall suppose that there is a constitution establishing a position of equal citizenship and securing freedom of the person, freedom of thought and liberty of conscience, and such political equality as in suffrage and the right to participate in the political process. Thus I am confining discussion to a legal system of a special kind, but there is no harm in this.

3. The moral grounds of legal obligation may be brought out by considering what at first seem to be two anomalous facts: first, that sometimes we have an obligation to obey what we think, and think correctly, is an unjust law; and second, that sometimes we have an obligation to obey a law even in a situation where more good (thought of as a sum of social advantages) would seem to result from not doing so. If the moral obligation to obey the law is founded on the principle of fair play, how can one become bound to obey an unjust law, and what is there about the principle that explains the grounds for forgoing the greater good?

It is, of course, a familiar situation in a constitutional democracy that a person finds himself morally obligated to obey an unjust law. This will be the case whenever a member of the minority, on some legislative proposal, opposes the majority view for reasons of justice. Perhaps the standard case is where the majority, or a coalition sufficient to constitute a majority, takes advantage of its strength and votes in its own interests. But this feature is not essential. A person belonging to the minority may be advantaged by the majority proposal and still oppose it as unjust, yet when it is enacted he will normally be bound by it.

Some have thought that there is ostensibly a paradox of a special kind when a citizen, who votes in accordance with his moral principles (conception of justice), accepts the majority decision when he is in the minority. Let us suppose the vote is between two bills, A and B, each establishing an income tax procedure, rates of progression, or the like, which are contrary to one another. Suppose further that one thinks of the constitutional procedure for enacting legislation as a sort of machine that yields a result when the votes are fed into it—the result being that a certain bill is enacted. The question arises as to how a citizen can accept the machine's choice, which (assuming that B gets a majority of the votes) involves thinking that B ought to be enacted when, let us suppose, he is of the declared opinion that A ought to be enacted. For some the paradox seems to be that in a constitutional democracy a citizen is often put in a situation of believing that both A and B should be enacted when A and B are contraries: that A should be enacted because A is the best policy, and that B should be enacted because B has a majority—and moreover, and this is essential, that this conflict is different from the usual sort of conflict between prima facie duties.

There are a number of things that may be said about this supposed paradox, and there are several ways in which it may be resolved, each of which brings out an aspect of the situation. But I think the simplest thing to say is to deny straightaway that there is anything different in this situation than in any other situation where there is a conflict of prima facie principles. The essential of the matter seems to be as follows: (1) Should A or B be enacted and implemented, that is, administered? Since it is supposed that everyone accepts the outcome of the vote, within limits, it is appropriate to put the enactment and implementation together. (2) Is A or B the best policy? It is assumed that everyone votes according to his political opinion as to which is the best policy and that the decision as to how to vote is not based on personal interest. There is no special conflict in this situation: the citizen who knows that he will find himself in the minority believes that, taking into account only the relative merits of A and B as prospective statutes, and leaving aside how the vote will go, A should be enacted and implemented. Moreover, on his own principles he should vote for what he thinks is the best policy, and leave aside how the vote will go. On the other hand, given that a majority will vote for B, B should be enacted and implemented, and he may know that a majority will vote for B. These judgments are relative to different principles (different arguments). The first is based on the person's conception of the best social policy; the second is based on the principles on which he accepts the constitution. The real decision, then, is as follows: A person has to decide, in each case where he is in the minority, whether the nature of the statute is such that, given that it will get, or has got, a majority vote, he should oppose its being implemented, engage in civil disobedience, or take equivalent action. In this situation he simply has to balance his obligation to oppose an unjust statute against his obligation to abide by a just constitution. This is, of course, a difficult situation, but not one introducing any deep logical paradox. Normally, it is hoped that the obligation to the constitution is clearly the decisive one.

Although it is obvious, it may be worthwhile mentioning, since a relevant feature of voting will be brought out, that the result of a vote is that a rule of law is enacted, and although given the fact of its enactment, everyone agrees that it should be implemented, no one is required to believe that the statute enacted represents the best policy. It is consistent to say that another statute would have been better. The vote does not result in a statement to be believed: namely, that B is superior, on its merits, to A. To get this interpretation one would have to suppose that the principles of the constitution specify a device which gathers information as to what citizens think should be done and that the device is so constructed that it always produces from this information the morally correct opinion as to which is the best policy. If in accepting a constitution it was so interpreted, there would, indeed, be a serious paradox: for a citizen would be torn between believing, on his own principles, that *A* is the best policy, and believing at the same time that *B* is the best policy as established by the constitutional device, the principles of the design of which he accepts. This conflict could be made a normal one only if one supposed that a person who made his own judgment on the merits was always prepared to revise it given the opinion constructed by the machine. But it is not possible to determine the best policy in this way, nor is it possible for a person to give such an undertaking. What this misinterpretation of the constitutional procedure shows, I think, is that there is an important difference between voting and spending. The constitutional procedure is not, in an essential respect, the same as the market: Given the usual assumptions of perfect competition of price theory, the actions of private persons spending according to their interests will result in the best situation, as judged by the criterion of Pareto. But in a perfectly just constitutional procedure, people voting their political opinions on the merits of policies may or may not reflect the best policy. What this misinterpretation brings out, then, is that when citizens vote for policies on their merits, the constitutional procedure cannot be viewed as acting as the market does, even under ideal conditions. A constitutional procedure does not reconcile differences of opinion into an opinion to be taken as true—this can only be done by argument and reasoning—but rather it decides whose opinion is to determine legislative policy.

4. Now to turn to the main problem, that of understanding how a person can properly find himself in a position where, by his own principles, he must grant that, given a majority vote, *B* should be enacted and implemented even though *B* is unjust. There is, then, the question as to how it can be morally justifiable to acknowledge a constitutional procedure for making legislative enactments when it is certain (for all practical purposes) that laws will be passed that by one's own principles are unjust. It would be impossible for a person to undertake to change his mind whenever he found himself in the minority; it is not impossible, but entirely reasonable, for him to undertake to abide by the enactments made, whatever they are, provided that they are within certain limits. But what more exactly are the conditions of this undertaking?

First of all, it means, as previously suggested, that the constitutional procedure is misinterpreted as a procedure for making legal rules. It is a process of social decision that does not produce a statement to be believed (that *B* is the best policy) but a rule to be followed. Such a procedure, say involving some form of majority rule, is necessary because it is certain that there will be disagreement on what is the best policy. This will be true even if we assume, as I shall, that everyone has a similar sense of justice and everyone is able to agree on a certain constitutional procedure as just. There will be disagreement because they will not approach issues with the same stock of information, they will regard different moral features of situations as carrying different weights, and so on. The acceptance of a constitutional procedure is, then, a necessary political device to decide between conflicting legislative proposals. If one thinks of the constitution as a fundamental part of the scheme of social cooperation, then one can say that if the constitution is just, and if one has accepted the benefits of its working and intends to continue doing so, and if the rule enacted is within certain limits, then one has an obligation, based on the principle of fair play, to obey it when it comes one's turn. In accepting the benefits of a just constitution one becomes bound to it, and in particular one becomes bound to one of its fundamental rules: given a majority vote in behalf of a statute, it is to be enacted and properly implemented.

The principle of fair play may be defined as follows. Suppose there is a mutually beneficial and just scheme of social cooperation, and that the advantages it yields can only be obtained if everyone, or nearly everyone, cooperates. Suppose further that cooperation requires a certain sacrifice from each person, or at least involves a certain restriction of his liberty. Suppose finally that the benefits produced by cooperation are, up to a certain point, free: that is, the scheme of cooperation is unstable in the sense that if any one person knows that all (or nearly all) of the others will continue to do their part, he will still be able to share a gain from the scheme even if he does not do his part. Under these conditions a person who has accepted the benefits of the scheme is bound by a duty of fair play to do his part and not to take advantage of the free benefit by not cooperating. The reason one must abstain from this attempt is that the existence of the benefit is the result of everyone's effort, and prior to some understanding as to how it is to be shared, if it can be shared at all, it belongs in fairness to no one. (I return to this question on next page.)

Now I want to hold that the obligation to obey the law, as enacted by a constitutional procedure, even when the law seems unjust to us, is a case of the duty of fair play as defined. It is, moreover, an obligation in the more limited sense in that it depends upon our having accepted and our intention to continue accepting the benefits of a just scheme of cooperation that the constitution defines. In this sense it depends on our own voluntary acts. Again, it is an obligation owed to our fellow citizens generally: that is, to those who cooperate with us in the working of the constitution. It is not an obligation owed to public officials, although there may be such obligations. That it is an obligation owed by citizens to one another is shown by the fact that they are entitled to be indignant with one another for failure to comply. Further, an essential condition of the obligation is the justice of the constitution and the general system of law being roughly in accordance with it. Thus the obligation to obey (or not to resist) an unjust law depends strongly on there being a just constitution. Unless one obeys the law enacted under it, the proper equilibrium, or balance, between competing claims defined by the constitution will not be maintained. Finally, while it is true enough to say that the enactment by a majority binds the minority, so that one may be bound by the acts of others, there is no question of their binding them in conscience to certain beliefs as to what is the best policy, and it is a necessary condition of the acts of others binding us that the constitution is just, that we have accepted its benefits, and so forth.

5. Now a few remarks about the principles of a just constitution. Here I shall have to presuppose a number of things about the principles of justice. In particular, I shall assume that there are two principles of justice that properly apply to the fundamental structure of institutions of the social system and, thus, to the constitution. The first of these principles requires that everyone have an equal right to the most extensive liberty compatible with a like liberty for all; the second is that inequalities are arbitrary unless it is reasonable to expect that they will work out for everyone's advantage and provided that the positions and offices to which they attach or from which they may be gained are open to all. I shall assume that these are the principles that can be derived by imposing the constraints of morality upon rational and mutually self-interested persons when they make conflicting claims on the basic form of their common institutions: that is, when questions of justice arise.

The principle relevant at this point is the first principle, that of equal liberty. I think it may be argued with some plausibility that it requires, where it is possible, the various equal liberties in constitutional democracy. And once these liberties are established and constitutional procedures exist, one can view legislation as rules enacted that must be ostensibly compatible with both principles. Each citizen must decide as best he can whether a piece of legislation, say the income tax, violates either principle; and this judgment depends on a wide body of social facts. Even in a society of impartial and rational persons, one cannot expect agreement on these matters.

Now recall that the question is this: How is it possible that a person, in accordance with his own conception of justice, should find himself bound by the acts of another to obey an unjust law (not simply a law contrary to his interests)? Put another way: Why, when I am free and still without my chains, should I accept certain a priori conditions to which any social contract must conform, a priori conditions that rule out all constitutional procedures that would decide in accordance with my judgment of justice against everyone else? To explain this (Little has remarked), we require two hypotheses: that among the very limited number of procedures that would stand any chance of being established, none would make my decision decisive in this way; and that all such procedures would determine social conditions that I judge to be better than anarchy. Granting the second hypothesis, I want to elaborate on this in the following way: the first step in the explanation is to derive the principles of justice that are to apply to the basic form of the social system and, in particular, to the constitution. Once we have these principles, we see that no just constitutional procedure would make my judgment as to the best policy decisive (would make me a dictator in Arrow's sense).[1] It is not simply that, among the limited number of procedures actually possible as things are, no procedure would give me this authority. The point is that even if such were possible, given some extraordinary social circumstances, it would not be just. (Of course it is not possible for everyone to have this authority.) Once we see this, we see how it is possible that within the framework of a just constitutional procedure to which we are obligated, it may nevertheless happen that we are bound to obey what seems to us to be and is an unjust law. Moreover, the possibility is present even though everyone has the same sense of justice (that is, accepts the same principles of justice) and everyone regards the constitutional procedure itself as just. Even the most efficient constitution cannot prevent the enactment of unjust laws if, from the complexity of the social situation and like conditions, the majority decides to enact them. A just constitutional procedure cannot foreclose all injustice; this depends on those who carry out the procedure. A constitutional procedure is not like a market reconciling interests to an optimum result.

6. So far I have been discussing the first mentioned anomaly of legal obligation, namely, that though it is founded on justice, we may be required to obey an unjust law. I should now like to include the second anomaly: that we may have an obligation to obey the law even though more good (thought of as a sum of advantages) may be gained by not doing so. The thesis I wish to argue is that not only is our obligation to obey the law a special case of the principle of fair play, and so dependent upon the justice of the institutions to which we are obligated, but also the principles of justice are absolute with respect to the principle of utility (as the principle to maximize the net sum of advantages). By this I mean two things. First, unjust institutions cannot be justified by an appeal to the principle of utility. A greater balance of net advantages shared by some cannot justify the injustice suffered by others; and where unjust institutions are tolerable it is because a certain degree of injustice sometimes cannot be avoided, that social necessity requires it, there would be greater injustice otherwise, and so on. Second, our obligation to obey the law, which is a special case of the principle of fair play, cannot be overridden by an appeal to utility, though it may be overridden by another duty of justice. These are sweeping propositions and most likely false, but I should like to examine them briefly.

I do not know how to establish these propositions. They are not established by the sort of argument used above to show that the two principles, previously mentioned, are the two principles of justice, that is, when the subject is the basic structure of the social system. What such an argument might show is that, if certain natural conditions are taken as specifying the concept of justice, then the two principles of justice are the principles logically associated with the concept when the subject is the basic structure of the social system. The argument might prove, if it is correct, that the principles of justice are incompatible with the principle of utility. The argument might establish that our intuitive notions of justice must sometimes conflict with the principle of utility. But it leaves unsettled what the more general notion of right requires when this conflict occurs. To prove that the concept of justice should have

an absolute weight with respect to that of utility would require a deeper argument based on an analysis of the concept of right, at least insofar as it relates to the concepts of justice and utility. I have no idea whether such an analysis is possible. What I propose to do instead is to try out the thought that the concept of justice does have an absolute weight, and to see whether this suggestion, in view of our considered moral opinions, leads to conclusions that we cannot accept. It would seem as if to attribute to justice an absolute weight is to interpret the concept of right as requiring that a special place be given to persons capable of a sense of justice and to the principle of their working out together, from an initial position of equality, the form of their common institutions. To the extent that this idea is attractive, the concept of justice will tend to have an absolute weight with respect to utility.

7. Now to consider the two anomalous cases. First: In the situation where the obligation requires obedience to an unjust law, it seems true to say that the obligation depends on the principle of fair play and, thus, on justice. Suppose it is a matter of a person being required to pay an income tax of a kind that he thinks is unjust, not simply by reference to his interests. He would not want to try to justify the tax on the ground that the net gain to certain groups in society is such as to outweigh the injustice. The natural argument to make is to his obligation to a just constitution.

But in considering a particular issue, a citizen has to make two decisions: how he will vote (and I assume that he votes for what he thinks is the best policy, morally speaking), and, in case he should be in the minority, whether his obligation to support, or not obstruct, the implementation of the law enacted is not overridden by a stronger obligation that may lead to a number of courses including civil disobedience. Now in the sort of case imagined, suppose there is a real question as to whether the tax law should be obeyed. Suppose, for example, that it is framed in such a way that it seems deliberately calculated to undermine unjustly the position of certain social or religious groups. Whether the law should be obeyed or not depends, if one wants to emphasize the notion of justice, on such matters as (1) the justice of the constitution and the real opportunity it allows for reversal; (2) the depth of the injustice of the law enacted; (3) whether the enactment is actually a matter of calculated intent by the majority and warns of further such acts; and (4) whether the political sociology of the situation is such as to allow of hope that the law may be repealed.

Certainly, if a social or religious group reasonably (not irrationally) and correctly supposes that a permanent majority, or majority coalition, has deliberately set out to undercut its basis and that there is no chance of successful constitutional resistance, then the obligation to obey that particular law (and perhaps other laws more generally) ceases. In such a case a minority may no longer be obligated by the duty of fair play. There may be other reasons, of course, at least for a time, for obeying the law. One might say that disobedience will not improve the justice of their situation or of their descendants' situation; or that it will result in injury and harm to innocent persons (that is, members not belonging to the unjust majority). In this way, one might appeal to the balance of justice, if the principle of not causing injury to the innocent is a question of justice; but, in any case, the appeal is not made to the greater net balance of advantages (irrespective of the moral position of those receiving them). The thesis I want to suggest then, is that in considering whether we are obligated to obey an unjust law, one is led into no absurdity if one simply throws out the principle of utility altogether, except insofar as it is included in the general principle requiring one to establish the most efficient just institutions.

Second: Now the other sort of anomaly arises when the law is just and we have a duty of fair play to follow it, but a greater net balance of advantages could be gained from not doing so. Again, the income tax will serve to illustrate this familiar point: The social consequences of any one person (perhaps even many people) not paying his tax are unnoticeable, and let us suppose zero in value, but there is a noticeable private gain for the person himself, or for another to whom he chooses to give it (the institution of the income tax is subject to the first kind of instability). The duty of fair play binds us to pay our tax, nevertheless, since we have accepted, and intend to continue doing so, the benefits of the fiscal system to which the income tax belongs. Why is this reasonable and not a blind following of a rule, when a greater net sum of advantages is possible?—because the system of cooperation consistently followed by everyone else itself produces the advantages generally enjoyed, and in the case of a practice such as the income tax there is no reason to give exemptions to anyone so that they might enjoy the possible benefit. (An analogous case is the moral obligation to vote and so to work the constitutional procedure from which one has benefited. This obligation cannot be overridden by the fact that our vote never makes a difference in the outcome of an election; it may be overridden, however, by a number of

other considerations, such as a person being disenchanted with all parties, being excusably uninformed, and the like.)

There are cases, on the other hand, where a certain number of exemptions can be arranged for in a just or fair way; and if so, the practice, including the exemptions, is more efficient, and when possible it should be adopted (waiving problems of transition) in accordance with the principle of establishing the most efficient just practice. For example, in the familiar instance of the regulation to conserve water in a drought, it might be ascertained that there would be no harm in a certain extra use of water over and above the use for drinking. In this case some rotation scheme can be adopted that allots exemptions in a fair way, such as houses on opposite sides of the street being given exemptions on alternate days. The details are not significant here. The main idea is simply that if the greater sum of advantages can effectively and fairly be distributed among those whose cooperation makes these advantages possible, then this should be done. It would indeed be irrational to prefer a lesser to a more efficient just scheme of cooperation; but this fact is not to be confused with justifying an unjust scheme by its greater efficiency or excusing ourselves from a duty of fair play by an appeal to utility. If there is no reason to distribute the possible benefit, as in the case of the income tax, or in the case of voting, or if there is no way to do so that does not involve such problems as excessive costs, then the benefit should be forgone. One may disagree with this view, but it is not irrational, not a matter of rule worship: it is, rather, an appeal to the duty of fair play, which requires one to abstain from an advantage that cannot be distributed fairly to those whose efforts have made it possible. That those who make the efforts and undergo the restrictions of their liberty should share in the benefits produced is a consequence of the assumption of an initial position of equality, and it falls under the second principle. But the question of distributive justice is too involved to go into here. Moreover, it is unlikely that there is any substantial social benefit for the distribution of which some fair arrangement cannot be made.

8. To summarize, I have suggested that the following propositions may be true:

First, that our moral obligation to obey the law is a special case of the duty of fair play. This means that the legal order is construed as a system of social cooperation to which we become bound because: first, the scheme is just (that is, it satisfies the two principles of justice), and no just scheme can ensure against our ever being in the minority in a vote; and second, we have accepted, and intend to continue to accept, its benefits. If we failed to obey the law, to act on our duty of fair play, the equilibrium between conflicting claims, as defined by the concept of justice, would be upset. The duty of fair play is not, of course, intended to account for its being wrong for us to commit crimes of violence, but it is intended to account, in part, for the obligation to pay our income tax, to vote, and so on.

Second, I then suggested that the concept of justice has an absolute weight with respect to the principle of utility (not necessarily with respect to other moral concepts). By that I meant that the union of the two concepts of justice and utility must take the form of the principle of establishing the most efficient just institution. This means that an unjust institution or law cannot be justified by an appeal to a greater net sum of advantages, and that the duty of fair play cannot be analogously overridden. An unjust institution or law or the overriding of the duty of fair play can be justified only by a greater balance of justice. I know of no way to prove this proposition. It is not proved by the analytic argument to show that the principles of justice are indeed the principles of justice. But I think it may be shown that the principle to establish the most efficient just institutions does not lead to conclusions counter to our intuitive judgments and that it is not in any way irrational. It is, moreover, something of a theoretical simplification, in that one does not have to balance justice against utility. But this simplification is no doubt not a real one, since it is as difficult to ascertain the balance of justice as anything else.

READING 14

The Idea of a Legitimate State

David Copp

David Copp is Professor of Philosophy and a Senior Research Fellow at the Social Philosophy and Policy Center at Bowling Green State University. He taught previously at the University of California–Davis, the University of Illinois at Chicago, and Simon Fraser University. He is author of *Morality, Normativity, and Society* and of many articles in moral and political philosophy. He is an associate editor of the journal *Ethics*. In this essay, he presents the basic elements of the Utilitarian, or Consequentialist, answer.

This reading is Copp's abridged version of a paper that was published in *Philosophy and Public Affairs* 28 (1999).

Imagine that a drug smuggling cartel organizes a coup and overthrows the democratically elected government of Exemplar. It establishes a dictatorship under a new constitution with the leading members of the cartel in the key political positions. Call this the Coup Example. The cartel has created a rogue state, and we want to say that this state is not "legitimate." What would we mean by this, and why would we want to say it? At root, the idea is surely as follows. Prior to the coup, as a mere band of criminals, the members of the cartel had no right to impose their will on the people, and nothing has been added to their credentials that would give them a right to do this. Simply to overthrow the state and replace it with a state of their own design does not give them this right. Of course, they can now dress their demands in the trappings of law, but this does not add any moral authority to their actions. Hence, the members of the cartel have no right to rule the people of Exemplar, and neither does their newly constituted state. To be sure, other states will eventually come to treat the cartel as the "legitimate" government of Exemplar—they will "recognize" the cartel as the government. Our point, however, is a normative one about the relation between the rogue state that has been newly founded by the cartel and the people and territory of Exemplar. It is about the moral authority of the rogue state, not about the likelihood that other states will treat it a certain way.

Unfortunately, reasoning similar to our reasoning in the example might force us to conclude that virtually no state is legitimate, for virtually every state owes its existence to some combination of events that includes a share of skullduggery, or worse. Therefore, unless we agree that virtually no state is legitimate, we need to explain how a state can become morally rehabilitated, even if it began by being illegitimate. The first question that I need to address, however, is what the legitimacy of a state would consist in.

When we evaluate a state for its legitimacy, our concern is to assess its moral authority to govern. The laws of a state require or prohibit us to act in certain ways, and the state typically enforces its law by attaching punishments or penalties to failures to comply. Criminal law is only one example, and it is not a typical example, since unlike other parts of law, much of the criminal law requires actions or forbearances that would be morally required in any event. In other parts of the law, such as the traffic code, some actions that are legally required would not be morally required in the absence of the law. In all of these cases, there is the problem of explaining by what right the state imposes requirements and by what right it enforces them. Moreover, states are territorial.[1] A state may apply its law to anyone within its territory, including many who have no special attachment to it, such as illegal immigrants and their children, and temporary visitors. A state may attempt to control the use of land and resources within its territory, and states define the rules of property. Moreover, states enforce their boundaries by controlling entry into and exit from their territories. The territoriality of the state raises the problem of explaining by what right the state takes jurisdiction in these ways throughout a given territory.

The problem of legitimacy is, then, to explain how a state can have the moral authority to do the kinds of things involved in governing. In part, it is the problem of explaining how a state could be morally entitled to impose and to enforce its law throughout its territory and to enforce its borders. In John Simmons's words, a legitimate state would have "the right to rule." The problem is to understand, first, precisely what this right amounts to, and second, under what conditions a state would have it. According to the traditional account, the legitimacy of a state is to be explained in terms of its subjects' obligation to obey the law. In section 2 of this paper, I argue that this account is inadequate. In section 3, I take an inventory of various kinds of rights, and, in section 4, I propose that the legitimacy of a state would consist in its having a bundle of rights of various kinds, which I attempt to specify. In sections 5 and 6, I discuss familiar accounts of the circumstances under which a state would be legitimate, and I argue that none is satisfactory, given my proposal as to what the legitimacy of a state would consist in. Finally, in section 7, I propose an argument from societal needs which, I claim, supports a presumption that states are legitimate. Before we can begin exploring the idea of legitimacy, however, we need to understand the notion of the state. What is a state?

1. THE IDEA OF A STATE

Part of the problem is terminological. Speakers of contemporary English, especially North Americans, tend to use the term "state" to refer to things that are not states in my sense of the word. For example, the "states" of the United States and of Australia are subordinate

political units or jurisdictions of the United States and of Australia, respectively, but they are not states in my sense of the term. The United States is a state in my sense of the term, however, as are Australia, Mexico and France.

According to the characterization I would give of the state, one state would be replaced by another state if the legal system or institutions of government were destroyed and replaced by another legal system or set of institutions. In the Coup Example, I stipulated that Exemplar was overthrown and replaced by the rogue state. This seems the correct way to describe a situation in which the original constitution and government were replaced abruptly and unconstitutionally by a different kind of constitution and government. In more ordinary situations, changes in the law or in the institutions of government occur gradually and in accord with the constitution, and it is accordingly plausible to think that the original state continues to exist. Of course there can be borderline cases, but nothing turns on whether we can find a sharp line between situations in which one state is replaced by another state and those in which a state merely undergoes change.

On my account, a state is to be distinguished both from the territory that it governs and from the people that it governs. It is worth noticing, however, a feature of the way that we use names such as "France" and "the United States." We may ask, for instance, about the constitution of "France," the size of the population of "France," and the total land area of "France." On my analysis, these questions are about the state, the group governed by the state, and the territory governed by the state, respectively. Yet the ease with which we view all three questions as about "France" suggests how natural it is to suppose that there is a single entity called "France" that in some way essentially involves not only the state, but the land and the people as well. I will reserve the term "country" for such entities. We may view a country as a state together with the group of people it governs and its territory. Legitimacy, however, is a property of states.

2. THE TRADITIONAL ACCOUNT: THE OBLIGATION TO OBEY

The traditional view is that the legitimacy of a state would consist in its subjects' having a moral obligation to obey its law. Corresponding to this obligation would be the state's right to the obedience of its subjects. On this view, then, the right to rule is a right against relevant persons that they obey the law.[2] There are two chief problems with this idea.

First, the idea of an obligation is more specialized than is necessary to capture the idea that the subjects of a legitimate state would have a moral duty to obey the law. In the sense at issue, an "obligation" is a special kind of moral requirement. An obligation is owed to some agent, and it corresponds in a precise way to a right possessed by that agent. Obligations correspond to "claim-rights," as they are often called. But obligations are not the only kind of requirement. Other moral requirements, including duties, are not owed to any agent and do not correspond in this way to rights. If an obligation to obey the law would be sufficient for the legitimacy of a state, then surely it would be sufficient as well if people had a duty to obey the law, even if they did not owe their obedience to the state. This is the first problem with the traditional view. It would not be an interesting problem except that, as I will explain, the traditional view seems to lead to a form of philosophical anarchism according to which it is doubtful that any actual state is legitimate. And the arguments that support this anarchistic conclusion turn on the traditional identification of the legitimacy of a state with an obligation of its subjects to obey the law. Unless, therefore, we are inclined to accept this anarchistic conclusion, which I am not, we must question the traditional identification of legitimacy with a moral requirement of this special kind.

Since obligations correspond to claim-rights, we can carry on the discussion in terms of the idea of a claim-right. In effect, the traditional view identifies legitimacy with a claim-right to obedience, for a state has a claim-right against its citizens that they obey just in case its subjects have an obligation to obey. There are two kinds of claim-rights. There are "special rights," which some agents acquire as a result of others' voluntarily assuming or otherwise acquiring the corresponding obligations, and there are "fundamental rights," which are possessed by things of a relevant kind without having been acquired. The traditional view is that a legitimate state's right to obedience would be a special right, grounded in the consent of its subjects.

The arguments to show that the traditional view leads to an anarchistic result are presented most clearly by John Simmons. Simmons [in *Moral Principles and Political Obligations*] argues that a special right against an agent must be derived either from the agent's voluntary commitment or from her voluntary acceptance of benefits. As for the first possibility, Simmons argues

that it is implausible that the subjects of states have voluntarily committed themselves to obey the law. Actual undertakings would be required, not merely hypothetical ones, for hypothetical commitments do not bind us. To commit oneself voluntarily to obey the law would be to do something with the intention to obligate oneself to obey, and very few subjects of any state have done any such thing. The other possibility is that the state's right to obedience is grounded in an obligation of its subjects to reciprocate for benefits they have received. Simmons points out, however, that the goods provided by a state that are available to all of its residents, such as national defense, public safety, clean air, and so on, are "public goods."[3] If a state provides such goods, it provides them to everyone in a relevant territory. It is implausible that a person who receives such benefits is thereby obligated to reciprocate. She may have had no real opportunity to avoid receiving the benefit or to stop the state from producing it. It is even less plausible that she is obligated to reciprocate by obeying the law. For the benefits may be worth less to her than the cost of obeying. In this case, [says Simmons] adequate reciprocation, if such were required, would involve less than obeying the law. For these reasons, Simmons argues, it is implausible that any actual state has a special right to the obedience of its residents.

The alternative is that a legitimate state's right to obedience would be a fundamental right. Since it is not plausible that every state is legitimate, a viable defense of this alternative would have to identify a property that distinguishes states that are plausibly held to be legitimate from states that are not. It might seem that the property of being a just state is a candidate for this role, given the plausible idea that we have a duty to support just institutions.[4] But, first, as I will argue later in this paper, it is implausible that only just states are legitimate. Moreover, if there is a duty to support just institutions, it would seem to be a duty incumbent on everyone, not specifically on those who are subject to just institutions. Finally, it is doubtful that this duty would be owed to those institutions. What has to be grounded is not merely a duty to obey the law, but an obligation owed to the state specifically by its subjects, and it is quite unclear what property of a state might ground such a thing, given the objections to the traditional view. It therefore seems doubtful that any actual state has a fundamental right to obedience.

For these reasons, it is doubtful that any actual state has a claim-right to the obedience of its subjects. On the traditional view, it follows that it is doubtful that any actual state is legitimate. But, as we have seen, the arguments for this anarchistic result turn on the traditional identification of the legitimacy of a state with its having a claim-right to obedience, or with its subjects' having an obligation to obey. And there is no reason to accept this identification, for there is no reason to think that a state's legitimacy depends on its citizens' having an obligation as opposed to some other kind of moral requirement to obey the law. The traditional view is on the right track in insisting that the citizens of a legitimate state would be morally required to obey the law. But they could be required to obey even if they do not owe their obedience to the state, even if the state has no claim-right to their obedience.

The second problem with the traditional view is that its account of legitimacy is too slim to ground an adequate account of the territoriality of the state.[5] First, a state purports to have the right to govern its territory, which includes enforcing its laws against any members of other states who live in its territory as well as controlling access across its borders. But even if the members of state A have an obligation to obey the laws of A, members of state B who live in state A might have no such obligation on the traditional view. Consider, for instance, Betty, a member of B who has entered state A illegally. She might not have explicitly consented to obey the laws of A, and she might not have lived there long enough to have benefitted from living in A. Yet state A would claim the right to apply its law to her. A defender of the traditional view might argue that, in entering A, Betty must have "tacitly" consented to obey the laws of A. But in order for Betty's mere crossing of the border to have put her under an obligation to obey the law of A, Betty would have to have crossed the border with some relevant intention or understanding, such as the intention thereby to obligate herself to obey, and it is unlikely that Betty had any such intention. It is especially unlikely that she intended to obligate herself to obey the very law that prohibited her act of crossing the border, since, for one thing, she presumably could be deported under that law. Indeed, state A would claim to have had the right to refuse to allow her to enter even before she actually attempted to enter. It is difficult to see how the traditional view could account for A's having any such right since it would be quite implausible to maintain, even before she entered A, that she must already have consented to obey the laws of A, even if only "tacitly." Moreover, second, state A purports to have a right not to be interfered with by any other state in governing its territory. It is difficult to see how the traditional view

could explain this, especially since, for example, Betty might have consented to B's intervention on her behalf and, again, we are assuming that she has not explicitly consented to obey the laws of A and that merely crossing A's border is not sufficient to obligate her. It is difficult, therefore, to see how a state's claims regarding its borders could be given a plausible explanation on the traditional view. The situation is not improved if we turn to the idea that our obligation to obey the law is grounded in a duty to reciprocate for benefits received, for the benefits of a state's investments in public goods can spill over into territories that it has no right to rule on any plausible account. For example, state A's attempts to prevent air pollution can benefit the downwind members of state B. State A does not acquire a right to the obedience of members of state B on this basis. The traditional view therefore is inadequate to account for the territoriality of states.

This problem is deeper than it might appear to be, for the traditional view cannot adequately explain the sense in which a legitimate state would be associated with a territory. It explains legitimacy in terms of an obligation to obey the law on the part of those people who have consented to obey the law. The subjects of a legitimate state therefore would have an obligation to obey its laws regarding their property. Given this, it would be natural to add to the traditional view the idea that a state's territory consists in the aggregated property of its members. But it is not necessary that the territory associated with a state in this sense should coincide with the territory that is intuitively associated with a state—i.e., the territory throughout which the state's legal system is enforced. Anyone could in principle commit herself to obeying the law of any state. It is not necessary that all the people living in the territory intuitively associated with a state, nor even that only the people living in this territory, should commit themselves to obeying its law. Suppose that Alice has spent her life on her large property, which lies within the territory intuitively associated with A. But suppose she has freely committed herself to obey the law of B rather than to obey the law of A. The traditional view must see her as a citizen of state B, and, on the proposed account of territory, her property is part of the territory of B rather than the territory of A. Unless we are given some other account of legitimate territory, it cannot be argued that Alice must have tacitly consented to obey the law of A since she resides in the territory of A, for the proposed account of territory implies to the contrary that she resides in B. Yet, of course, B will view her as a subject of state A, and A will treat her the way it treats all of its subjects. It will enforce its laws against her, and purport to have the right to do so. It seems, then, that the traditional view does not give us an intuitively plausible account of the territoriality of the state.

Of course, the traditional view could reply that the most I have shown is that states have neither the rights nor the territories that we intuitively take them to have. I think, however, that my discussion of the difficulties facing the traditional view suggests that we need to rethink the traditional analysis of legitimacy. For the arguments we discussed which show it is doubtful that any actual state is legitimate turn on the idea that legitimacy requires the citizens of the state to have an obligation to obey the law, rather than any other kind of duty to obey. And the argument that even a legitimate state might lack the rights over territory that we intuitively would expect turns on the fact that the traditional analysis seeks to explain legitimacy entirely in terms of moral relations derivable from the obligation to obey and the consent on which this obligation is thought to be based. A different account of legitimacy might yield a more plausible overall picture.

3. HOHFELDIAN RIGHTS

We are looking for an account of what the legitimacy of a state would consist in, and I am assuming that the legitimacy of a state would consist in its having a right to rule. What are rights?

Wesley Newcomb Hohfeld observed that lawyers use the term "right" to refer to four different kinds of legal "advantage," which he called "claims," "privileges," "powers," and "immunities."[6] I will use Hohfeld's distinctions in sorting out various possible interpretations of the purported right to rule.

A claim is a right of the familiar kind that corresponds to an obligation owed to the right-bearer by the person against whom the right is held. Promises and contracts can give rise to claim-rights. For example, if I promise you to dance under the moon, then I have an obligation to do this; I owe this to you, and you have a claim against me that I do it. In general, a person A has a claim against B that such and such if and only if B has an obligation to A that such and such. A Hohfeldian privilege is simply an absence of relevant obligations and claims. Person A has a privilege (against B) to do something if and only if there is no claim against A (on the part of B) that A not do the thing. For example, if I hadn't made the promise to dance under the moon,

then presumably no one would have had a right that I dance under the moon, and so I presumably would have had a privilege not to dance under the moon. Even if my promise to you means that I am obligated to you to dance, there may be no one else to whom I am obligated to dance. If so, I have a privilege with respect to everyone else that I not dance.

The third kind of Hohfeldian right is a power. Person A has a power if and only if A has the ability to alter the rights or duties of some person by performing some (permitted) action. For example, the right of the United States Congress to legislate in the area of interstate commerce consists of a legal power to create valid law in this area, thereby altering people's legal duties, claims, privileges, or powers. The fourth kind of Hohfeldian right, an immunity, is simply the absence of a relevant power in others. The constitutional right to free speech in the United States, for example, can be understood as an immunity against congressional legislation of certain kinds. These are legal powers and immunities, but there are also moral powers and immunities. For instance, I have the power to put myself under an obligation to dance under the moon by promising, but I have an immunity against being put under such an obligation by anything you do. You have a power to obligate yourself, but no power to obligate me.

I must emphasize here that I do not view rights, obligations, or duties as "absolute." I have a claim to my privacy, and you have no privilege to break down my door. Yet if you were being chased by a grizzly bear, and if your only hope of surviving were to break down my door and enter my home, you would be morally permitted to do so, all things considered, despite my claim and your obligation. And if you were being chased by a grizzly, I would be wrong not to open my door to you even though you have no claim against me that I open it. Rights, obligations, and duties support propositions about what agents ought to do *pro tanto,* but although *pro tanto* duties are genuine duties, they can be outweighed by other moral factors in a determination of what an agent ought to do all things considered.[7]

4. THE RIGHT TO RULE

Armed with this inventory of kinds of rights, we can now turn to the central question, What is the right to rule? What rights and powers do states purport to have simply in virtue of being states? What rights and powers would a state need to have in order to have the moral authority to do the kinds of things that states must do in ruling their people and their territories? There appear to be three basic aspects to this. First, a state claims to be morally entitled to impose and to enforce legal requirements on its subjects. Second, a state claims to have a jurisdictional right over its territory, including a right to enforce its borders. Third, a state claims a right not to be interfered with by other states. The idea of legitimacy involves all three of these aspects, and the right to rule is, then, a bundle of Hohfeldian rights. Let us begin with the first aspect, the right to impose and enforce legal requirements.

(1) The Right to Command Persons

In order to distinguish a legitimate state from a rogue state, we must suppose that the laws of a legitimate state have some significant normative status. They must be more than simply enactments since that is all that the laws of a rogue state are. The traditional view, expressed in Hohfeldian terms, is that a legitimate state would have a moral claim that its subjects obey the law, but this is implausible, as I argued before. The subjects of a legitimate state would have a duty to obey the laws, but this does not entail that the state would have a claim to their obedience.

Consider the idea that we would have a *pro tanto* duty to obey the morally unobjectionable laws of a legitimate state. If so, then a legitimate state would have a qualified Hohfeldian power to put its citizens under a duty to do something by enacting a morally unobjectionable law requiring them to do it.[8] To explain this, I need to explain the state's right to legislate, which involves a Hohfeldian privilege.

A state is not morally free to enact any law whatsoever, for people have claims that would be violated by certain laws, including laws interfering with the choice of religion. Nevertheless, the idea that a state is entitled to enforce and enact law can be understood in Hohfeldian terms as the idea that there is a sphere within which it has a privilege to legislate. And it surely must be true, if a state is legitimate, that there is a sphere within which it has a privilege to legislate—a privilege with respect to all of its subjects to enact and enforce laws affecting them. If a state is legitimate, there surely must be some matters such that the state would not violate any of its subjects' claims by enacting and enforcing laws pertaining to these matters.

Suppose that we restrict attention to laws that are "morally innocent" in that enacting and enforcing them is within the sphere of privilege of the state and they are in no way unjust. I propose that a legitimate state would have the power to put its residents under a *pro tanto* duty to do something simply by enacting a law, provided that the law is morally innocent.[9] The fact that a legitimate state would possess such a power distinguishes it from a rogue state. The duty to comply with the morally innocent law of a legitimate state gives its laws a special normative status by comparison with the laws of a rogue state. In addition, a legitimate state would have the power to make it permissible for its officials to enforce the law simply by enacting laws that provide for the enforcement of law, provided again that these laws are morally innocent.

My view implies that a legitimate state can in principle change the moral status of actions. A legitimate state can put us under duties to perform actions that, in the absence of law, would merely have been morally permissible, provided that the relevant laws are morally innocent. For example, we are under a duty to pay the taxes required by a legitimate state assuming the moral innocence of the tax law. The view also implies that a legitimate state can place its officials under duties to do things that would otherwise have been prohibited, provided that the relevant laws are morally innocent. For example, in the absence of law, it would be wrong to harm people in the guise of "punishing" them, or to exact money from them in the guise of "taxation." But the law of a legitimate state can give officials a permission and even a duty to do such things, assuming that coercive tax laws and criminal laws can be morally innocent.

One might object that it is implausible to suppose that I violate a moral duty when I exceed the speed limit by a trivial amount on a deserted highway. But we do feel that we need to excuse or justify ourselves for lawbreaking. At least we feel this way if we believe that our state is legitimate. The objection does, however, point to various ways in which my account could be made more subtle and complex. I want to say that a legitimate state has the power to put us under duties, but perhaps it does not *exercise* this power each and every time that it enacts a law. Many laws are not strictly enforced, and some of the less important laws are enforced merely by threatened penalties, rather than by threatened punishment. Perhaps we should say that in order to exercise its power to put us under a duty, a state must not only enact a law, it must enforce the law and do so by threatening to punish violations of it. It must in effect announce in some conventionally understood way that the law is meant to put us under a duty and not merely to change our incentives by attaching a penalty to an action.

(2) The Right to Control Territory

The territory of a state is the entire territory in which its legal system is "in force." This territory is "its" simply in the sense that it is the territory in which it has "positivistic" jurisdiction—a jurisdiction that consists in a complex non-moral historical and sociological fact about the territory and the relationships among its residents. A legitimate state, however, would have more than simply a positivistic jurisdiction. It would have a moral jurisdiction or authority both over its territory and over residents of the territory. There are at least three aspects to this.

To begin with, states are territorial in the sense that they apply their law to all those who reside in their territory. A legitimate state would have to have the moral authority to do so. That is, the class of persons relative to which a legitimate state would have the moral powers and privileges that I discussed in the preceding section would include all residents of its territory. These people would be the "moral citizens" of the state, provided it were legitimate.

Second, states presume that their authority over their territory includes a right to control uses of the territory. This right presumably includes the privilege to enact a regime of property law, including laws governing the transfer of property, as well as a regime of ordinary criminal law, which presumably would prohibit the use of force or fraud to seize property. States also presume that they have a privilege to restrict or control the uses to which owners put their property. The question, then, is whether this presumption is correct. What kinds of restrictions or controls on the uses of property, if any, fall within the sphere of privilege of a legitimate state?

There are a variety of views on this question. At one end of the spectrum is the position that any moral property rights that we have are derivative from the laws of legitimate states. On this view, there are no antecedent moral property rights that limit the state's sphere of privilege. At the other end of the spectrum is the idea that there are what we might call "full natural property rights"—property rights that prohibit the state from placing any limits or controls on how people use land in which they have such rights. On this view, if all the land were owned by individuals who had "full natural prop-

erty rights" in their land, then the state would have no privilege to legislate land-use policy. For my part, I think that there are not in fact full natural property rights and that legitimate states would have the privilege to control how people use their land within certain limits. For present purposes, however, we do not need to decide whether there are full natural property rights.

It is nevertheless important to see that the idea that private property can be justified is not the same as the idea that there are full natural property rights. It seems plausible that a legitimate state would have a privilege to construct a law of property that gives owners only a restricted set of rights regarding the use of their land.

The third respect in which states are territorial is that they purport to have the right to control movement across their borders. Would legitimate states have any such right? Would the borders of a legitimate state have a moral significance of this kind? It is widely assumed that people who have no legal claim to be in the territory of a state have no moral claim either. This is almost certainly false, but it is quite unclear what rights people do have in this area. Does any interesting category of non-resident non-citizens have a claim to move into the territory of a legitimate state and establish a home there? Does a legitimate state have the privilege to control immigration and movement across its borders?

These questions raise deep issues about global economic justice. These issues are relevant to our question about the moral significance of borders because, at least arguably, the enforcement of borders contributes to global inequality. Some might argue on this basis that all borders ought to be opened to all people. Even if this is correct, however, it does not follow that legitimate states would have no privilege to control access to their territory or to restrict immigration. A privilege to do something is the absence of a claim on the part of others that one not do that thing. Perhaps, then, even though a better-off country ought to admit the poor, the poor have no claim against the better-off countries that they be admitted. In the grizzly bear example, I have the privilege to lock my door against you even though, all things considered, I ought not to do so. In a similar way, states might have the privilege to control access to their territories even if they ought to have open borders in the interest of contributing to global equality. An alternative view would be that a wealthy state has the privilege to exclude the poor from less well-off states, and does no wrong in excluding them, but only if it contributes in an appropriate way to a just scheme for the global redistribution of wealth. The general point is that even if the existence of global economic injustice limits the rights of legitimate states to enforce their borders, this is compatible with the idea that states have a privilege to control movement across their borders. The thesis that legitimate states have a privilege to exclude a broad category of non-resident non-citizens from their territory is compatible with the idea that justice requires redistribution in the interest of global equality.

In any event, the issue here is what the legitimacy of a state would consist in, and I think that a legitimate state would have a privilege to control access to its territory across its borders. For I think that our notion of a state is of a thing that governs a bounded territory and that does at least purport to have the privilege to control access to its territory.[10] The idea of a privilege to control access to territory is puzzling. In enforcing its borders, a state restricts the movement of people who are not residents of its territory, and it is puzzling how a state could have a right to enforce laws against non-residents who, presumably, stand in no special relation to it. But this puzzle is about the grounding of a state's legitimacy, not about what the legitimacy of a state would consist in. At this point, I am only concerned with what legitimacy would consist in.

(3) Sovereignty: The Right to Non-Interference

The final aspect of the right to rule is the state's moral relation to other states. A legitimate state's sphere of privilege, as so far defined, is presumably a sphere within which it could govern without violating any claim of another state since other states have no claim to legislate with respect to its territory or people. Plausibly, too, a legitimate state would have a claim against other states that they not interfere with its governing within this sphere of privilege. This means that it would have a claim that it not be interfered with in governing its residents and territory. A legitimate state therefore does not merely have a privilege to govern its territory; it has a "protected privilege," a privilege that is protected from interference by the *pro tanto* obligation of other states not to interfere.

For similar reasons, it is plausible that a legitimate state would have an immunity to having any of its rights extinguished by any other state, or, for that matter, by any person. Moral agents have no power to extinguish their obligations nor therefore do they have a power to extinguish claims held against them by others. So I think that an immunity to extinction of the cluster of Hohfeldian rights that compose the right to rule is as plausible as the other rights in the cluster.[11]

The moral sovereignty of a legitimate state is its immunity to having its right to rule extinguished by any other state plus its claim against other states that they not interfere with its governing its residents and territory. It is perhaps worth adding that a legitimate state presumably also has the moral power to modify and perhaps to extinguish certain of its own rights. For example, the members of the European Union have altered by treaty their privileges to control movements across their borders.

(4) The Right to Rule—Summary

Let me bring these ideas together. I have used the varieties of Hohfeldian rights to explain the idea of a legitimate state. I call the territory in which a state has positivistic jurisdiction, "its territory," and the residents of the state's territory, "its residents." I propose that the legitimacy of a state would consist in its having roughly the following cluster of Hohfeldian "advantages": (1) a sphere within which it has a privilege to enact and enforce laws applying to the residents of its territory; (2) a power to put people residing in its territory under a *pro tanto* duty to do something simply by enacting a law that requires them to do that thing, provided that the law falls within its sphere of privilege and is otherwise morally innocent; (3) a privilege to control access to its territory by people who are not residents and have no moral claim to live or travel there; (4) a claim against other states that they not interfere with its governing its territory; (5) an immunity to having any of these rights extinguished by any action of any other state or person.

All of the claims and privileges of a legitimate state are defeasible; they are not absolute. And the power of a legitimate state is merely to put its subjects under *pro tanto* duties. No other state can extinguish these rights, but in cases of extreme injustice or violations of human rights, it is plausible to think that a state would forfeit its legitimacy. In less extreme cases of injustice, however, a state might retain its legitimacy even though, because of the injustice, its subjects have no duty to obey any but the most benign laws, such as laws against force and fraud or traffic laws. And other states might even have a duty, all things considered, to interfere with its internal affairs in order to protect human rights. The state might still be legitimate, but its legitimacy would not protect it from efforts by the international community to ensure that its people are treated justly.

This, then, is my account of what the legitimacy of a state would consist in. I agree with the traditional view that a legitimate state would have a "right to rule," and I agree that the traditional view is on the right track in thinking that the subjects of a legitimate state would be morally required to obey the law. But both more and less than this is involved in legitimacy. A legitimate state has a power to put its subjects under duties, but only if it legislates within its sphere of privilege. A legitimate state has such a sphere of privilege. There are laws it can enact and enforce without violating any claims. Legitimacy includes as well privileges regarding territory and a right to non-interference. There are two parts to the traditional view, however. The first part is the traditional account of what the legitimacy of a state would consist in; the second part is the thesis that the legitimacy of a state must be grounded in its subjects' consent. My own account of legitimacy will remain incomplete until I provide a story about the circumstances under which a state would have the cluster of Hohfeldian advantages that, as I have claimed, would constitute it as legitimate. Under what circumstances would a state be legitimate?

5. "LIBERAL LEGITIMACY" AND CONSENT

On the traditional view, as we saw, consent is required for legitimacy because consent is needed in order to ground an obligation to obey the law. Recently, however, John Rawls and others have proposed views that would give due recognition to the idea of the person's prerogative but without requiring actual consent as a condition of legitimacy. Rawls has proposed that "our exercise of political power is justifiable only when it is exercised in accordance with a constitution the essentials of which all citizens may reasonably be expected to endorse in the light of principles and ideals acceptable to them as reasonable and rational."[12] He calls this principle the "liberal principle of legitimacy."

This principle is best viewed as a proposal regarding the circumstances under which a state would be legitimate rather than as an account of what the legitimacy of a state would consist in. The view is that a state is legitimate only if its constitution meets a certain test. One could combine the test with my Hohfeldian account of what legitimacy would consist in.

Unfortunately, the test is unsuccessful. It is not sufficient to establish the legitimacy of a state. For even if all reasonable citizens may be expected to endorse a state's constitution, it does not follow that the state is legitimate. It does not follow, for example, that

the citizens have a *pro tanto* duty to obey morally innocent laws. Moreover, a state might be legitimate even if its constitution does not pass the test. The constitution of Britain presumably would not pass, for example, for we cannot reasonably expect all reasonable citizens to endorse the monarchy and the House of Lords. Nevertheless, I believe that Britain is a legitimate state if any is.

6. HISTORY AND PERFORMANCE

We have now seen that unless we can accept the anarchical conclusion that virtually no state is legitimate, we must reject the idea that consent of the governed is necessary for the legitimacy of a state. We must also reject the idea that the legitimacy of a state is settled by the moral credentials it establishes at its origin. Virtually every state owes its existence to some combination of events that includes a share of force or fraud. Because of this, reasoning similar to the reasoning that led us to conclude that the rogue state in the Coup Example is illegitimate might force us to conclude that virtually no state is legitimate. Since I do not believe that this conclusion would be correct, I need to deny that the legitimacy of a state is settled by the process by which it came to exist, or by its "pedigree."

As an alternate to the pedigree view, one might suggest a consequentialist view according to which the legitimacy of a state is determined by how well it serves the goals of its citizens by comparison with how well their goals would otherwise be served. There are two variants of this view. One postulates a threshold of efficiency such that a state that surpasses the threshold is legitimate. The other, a maximizing view, holds that a state is legitimate just in case it is more efficient than any available alternative. Neither variant is plausible. Suppose that the rogue state serves the goals of its residents just as well as did the former state of Exemplar. Then on either the threshold view or the maximizing view, the rogue state would be just as legitimate as Exemplar. But our intuition is that although Exemplar was legitimate, the rogue state at least initially was not. To have the right to rule is to have a moral property importantly different from that of being efficient in ruling, which is (roughly) the property at issue in these consequentialist views. How could efficiency give the rogue state the right to rule? Many things that we are good at doing we have no right to do.

There is a fundamental problem with attempts to ground the legitimacy of states in facts about their performance. What we need to ground is a state's possession of the complex cluster of Hohfeldian rights that would constitute its legitimacy. States that efficiently serve the goals of their citizens might deserve our support, or they might meet some minimal condition for deserving support, but this is a different matter from having the Hohfeldian cluster of rights that constitutes the right to rule. This point seems to undermine not only arguments from efficiency as such, but also arguments that turn on the special ability of states to provide public goods.

The basic idea of "public goods" justifications of the state is found in the following famous passage from David Hume's *Treatise of Human Nature*. Hume says:

> . . . bridges are built; harbours open'd; ramparts raid'd; canals form'd; fleets equip'd; and armies disciplin'd; every where, by the care of government, which, tho' compos'd of men subject to all human infirmities, becomes, by one of the finest and most subtle inventions imaginable, a composition, that is, in some measure, exempted from all these infirmities.[13]

Public goods arguments are intended to justify the state, in the sense of showing that the state is permitted to tax people coercively in order to produce public goods whether or not people have explicitly consented, on the basis that it is in people's interest to have these goods provided. It is intended to support the legitimacy of states by supporting the permissibility of coercive taxation.

The most important public good provided by a state is surely the rule of law, which, ideally at least, supports our security and protects us in our basic moral rights. Protection of our basic rights is a *moral* good. In addition, if there are certain duties that our society has, such as a duty to ensure that its members are able at least to meet their basic needs, then a state that fulfills such duties on behalf of the society promotes a moral good. The good in question here is justice, broadly construed. Insofar as we have a duty to support just institutions, and to support the establishment of justice, we presumably then have a duty to support a just state. The question is whether states that were just in all respects other than being legitimate would necessarily also be legitimate.[14] The argument from moral public goods does go some way toward supporting an affirmative answer to this question, but I want to press two objections.

First, the argument does not suffice to show that (otherwise) just states have the full panoply of Hohfeldian rights that constitute legitimacy. It does support the proposition that we have a duty to obey laws that are essential to the recognition of human rights, or that are constitutive of a state's program to establish justice, such as its scheme of redistributive taxation. But a legitimate state would have a broad power to put its citizens under a duty to obey morally innocent law, and the argument does not show that a just state would have this broad power. The argument also does not support the right, even of (otherwise) just states, to govern their people and territory without interference. Perhaps a neighboring state would do just as well as our state at serving justice. In that case, the argument appears to provide no reason why the neighboring state would be wrong to take over the job. The moral public goods argument provides no account of sovereignty.

Second, the moral public goods argument does not provide any support for the legitimacy of (otherwise) unjust states. But I think that even an unjust state might be legitimate. I agree of course that no-one had any duty to obey the morally bankrupt laws of Nazi Germany, and no-one had any duty to obey the fugitive slave laws that figured as law in the United States before the Civil War. These were unjust laws in unjust states. Yet I believe that people did have a duty even in these states to obey morally innocent law, such as laws against murder and rape, theft from the mails, smuggling, and so on. And these states had the right to enforce such laws. In saying this, I do not mean to restrict attention to laws which prohibit actions that would be morally prohibited in the absence of law, such as murder and rape. For I think that citizens have a duty to obey other kinds of laws as well, even in a state that is deeply unjust. They have a duty, for example, to obey laws requiring them to have a driver's license before driving a car, and laws requiring them to buy a ticket before riding the subway. Of course, the duty to obey morally innocent law is merely *pro tanto*. If disobedience to law can help to support the establishment of justice, by drawing attention to injustice, for instance, or by demonstrating the serious commitment of those who believe there is injustice and want to see it corrected, then such disobedience might well be justified, all things considered. I do not mean to say that people in unjust states ought all things considered to obey the law and go about their business as if their states were perfectly just. But I do think that civil disobedience needs a serious justification because it typically involves the violation of morally innocent law, such as prohibitions on parading in the streets without a permit, and we have a duty to obey morally innocent law. The view that unjust states can be legitimate can help to explain why civil disobedience needs a serious justification even in an unjust state.

I think, therefore, that arguments from efficiency or from public goods, even from moral public goods, are not fully adequate accounts of the circumstances under which a state would be legitimate. Performance based arguments of these kinds are unsuccessful. I argued before that arguments from consent, or from historical pedigree, also are unsuccessful. I would now like to suggest a new way to think of the state and its rights.

7. THE SOCIETAL NEEDS ARGUMENT

I have argued elsewhere for a moral theory that I call the "society-centered theory of moral justification." According to this theory, morality is at bottom a system of norms or "standards" that are justified to the extent that their currency in society enables society to get along, and to meet its basic needs. The underlying intuition can be expressed as follows: We live in societies, and we need to live in societies. We order our lives partly on the basis of standards that we share, where the fact that we share them facilitates beneficial cooperation and coordination among us. To the extent that these standards actually function as well as can be to make things go well in society, they are justified, and corresponding moral judgments are true. This is the central idea.[15] It can helpfully be viewed as a kind of ideal moral code consequentialism. Such a view obviously raises many questions, and, equally obviously, I cannot hope to answer them here. My goal here is merely to explain how the issue of the legitimacy of the state can be handled within this framework.

To explain my approach, I need to introduce the idea of a society. In the relevant sense, the populations of states are typically societies. A society is a population comparable in size and in social and economic complexity to the population of a state. A society has a multi-generational history. It is characterized by a relatively self-contained network of social relationships, such as relationships of family, friendship, and commerce, and by norms of cooperation and coordination that are salient to its members. It is comprehensive of the entire population of permanent residents of a relevant territory, with the exception of recent arrivals who may not yet fit into the group's network of social relationships. A society is, roughly speaking, a multi-generational temporally extended population of persons embracing a relatively closed network of social relationships, and limited by the widest boundary of a distinctive system of instrumental interaction.

The idea of society-centered theory is that societies need to have shared moral norms, and that a society's basic needs can better be served by the currency of some such norms than the currency of others. A society's needs can be classified as needs for "physical integrity," including the continued existence of the multi-generational population that it is, needs for "cooperative integrity," including internal social harmony, and needs for peaceful and cooperative relationships with neighboring societies. The question of how best to promote societal needs clearly depends on empirical matters, and this means that the moral implications of the society-centered theory are both contingent and somewhat speculative. I think we can see nevertheless, at least in broad outlines, the kinds of considerations that would support the legitimacy of a state.

To begin, I think it is clear enough that a society that is organized into a state, or that is at least included in a state, will tend to do better at satisfying its basic needs than it otherwise could expect to do. This seems to be true at least of societies at the present time in our world. This is the basic justification of the state.[16] After all, a state is essentially the administrative apparatus of a legal system. To think that societies could do better at meeting their needs in the absence of states, one would have to think that societies could do better in the absence of law. This is certainly dubious.

In order for a state to further the satisfaction of societal needs by means of law, the law must obviously be obeyed with sufficient likelihood. Moreover, in most circumstances, laws must be enforced in order to ensure a sufficient likelihood that they will be obeyed. This is the basic justification of a standard permitting the state to enforce morally innocent law. But it is a familiar point that the expense of sanctions and of enforcement could be avoided if people obeyed voluntarily, as a matter of their subscribing to a moral standard that required them to obey. The advantage of voluntary compliance with the state's arrangements to realize society's needs is the basic justification of a moral standard requiring citizens to obey the law, at least in cases where the law is morally innocent. It underwrites a Hohfeldian power, on the part of legitimate states, to put their residents under a *pro tanto* duty to do something by enacting morally innocent law.[17]

My argument responds to many of the intuitions that drive the argument from efficiency and the public goods argument. The key to it is the society-centered theory of moral justification, which provides a bridge between facts about the performance of the state and the moral credentials of the state, thereby overcoming what I called before the "fundamental problem" facing attempts to ground the legitimacy of states in facts about their performance. The state is justified, in my view, if the society as a whole benefits from what it does. And what is thereby justified more specifically is a standard that requires our obedience to morally innocent law, as well as standards that permit the enforcement of morally innocent law and that underwrite the other moral aspects of legitimacy.

Consider the thesis that a legitimate state would have a (qualified) privilege to control access to its territory. The simplest argument for this thesis turns on the fact that at least some of the projects that a state undertakes in order to serve the needs of society might not be successful without some restriction on the entry of people into its territory. For example, a state-operated health care insurance scheme perhaps could not be financed successfully if anyone at all could enter the state and gain access to medical care under the scheme. Suppose that a state were faced with massive immigration on the order of fifty percent of the population per year. The state would not even be able to house the new immigrants adequately. For reasons such as this, if a state's success at serving the needs of society requires it to have programs of these kinds that are available to all its members, it might need to restrict access to its territory.

A more interesting and controversial argument turns on the idea of a "home." Michael Hardimon has suggested that there is a basic human need to "be at home" in one's "social world."[18] What is relevant here is the idea of a "home" as a familiar and comfortable social and physical environment. If our homeland became less familiar and comfortable to us as a result of massive immigration, we might feel threatened. If enough people came to feel this way, the result might be to undermine the society's internal harmony. Given that societies need to ensure their internal social harmony, it follows that a state's success in serving the needs of society might require it to restrict immigra-

tion. If so, then, leaving aside issues of redistribution, non-resident non-citizens of a state would not in general have a claim to be permitted to immigrate.

This argument needs to be assessed with care. For one thing, societies actually tend to benefit from immigration. For another thing, it is all too easy to exaggerate the impact of immigration policies on a society's internal harmony. When people are able to work together successfully, and generally to achieve their goals, then it cannot seriously be maintained that a somewhat increasing degree of cultural diversity in a country is undermining its harmony. Perhaps it is true, however, that a society's internal harmony would be undermined by a continuing massive immigration of people who spoke many different languages and came from many cultures, and who increased a society's population by, say, fifty percent per year. This thought suggests that there is a threshold rate of immigration such that the harmony of a society would be damaged by immigration in excess of that rate. If so, a state has the privilege to restrict immigration to a level below the threshold.

In any event, given how controversial immigration policy can be, I want to stress that the issue I am addressing here is whether states have the privilege to place any controls on the movement of people across their borders. The argument shows that a state can have morally legitimate reasons to regulate immigration, but it does not show that borders may be hermetically sealed.

Why should we think that other states have an obligation not to interfere with a state's governing its people and its territory? As I said, each society needs to have peaceful and cooperative relationships with neighboring societies. A norm prohibiting the state from interfering with other states would tend to preserve a peaceful relationship between the corresponding society and its neighbors. Moreover, I believe that at least the bulk of the Earth's population constitutes a society. This global society's need to secure internal harmony would be well served by a norm against interference. It is each state's job, as it were, to serve the needs of the society it governs, subject to its obligation to respect the rights of its residents and others. Other states have no right to get involved except to assist a society whose government is failing in some significant way to meet its needs. For these reasons, it is plausible to attribute to a state a defeasible claim to non-interference by other states.

This completes the societal needs argument. It rests on a debatable moral theory as well as on contestable empirical claims, including especially, the claim that societies need to be organized into states. What, then, should we make of it? I make two claims on its behalf. First, it illustrates how one could support the thesis that there are legitimate states, given my Hohfeldian account of legitimacy. Second, and more controversially, I claim that the argument supports the plausibility of a presumption that states are legitimate.

The conclusion of the argument is that there is a presumption that states are legitimate. The argument did not depend on details that distinguish one state from another, so if it supports the legitimacy of any state, it supports the legitimacy of all states. Nevertheless, the case it makes for the legitimacy of any given state could be undermined by detailed considerations having to do with how well that state is doing at furthering the needs of the society that it governs. There must presumably be a threshold of efficiency at serving societal needs such that states falling below the threshold are not legitimate. I confess that I do not know how to specify this threshold, but it seems to me that matters would have to be very bad for a state not to be legitimate. Note that even if an existing state is legitimate, if things are bad enough, we might be justified overall in violating morally innocent laws, and other states might be justified overall in intervening in the affairs of our state. It is as if we were at sea in a leaky boat. Unless there is another boat available to which we could easily move, there are strong considerations in favor of following the orders of the captain. Even so, if the captain is incompetent and unjust, we might be justified overall to mutiny, although mutiny would need a serious justification.

Similarly, an extremely unjust state might be illegitimate, for it may be that the society's needs are likely to be best served if, say, citizens viewed themselves as under no duty at all to obey the law. But more typically, we are under a *pro tanto* duty to obey morally innocent law. Even if the existing state is legitimate, we might be justified overall in attempting to replace one government with another, even if by unconstitutional means.

Let me return briefly to the Coup Example. The rogue state clearly began by being illegitimate. Given the rights of Exemplar, the rogue state initially had no sphere of privilege within which it could rule. With time, however, and perhaps in a very short time, it established *de facto* control over the territory of Exemplar. The society that once was ruled by Exemplar

came to be ruled by the rogue state, and once Exemplar ceased to exist, the society's needs had to be served by the rogue state, if by any state. Moreover, once Exemplar ceased to exist, its rights ceased to put barriers in the way of the rogue state's having a sphere of privilege. The rogue state therefore came to be legitimate.

8. CONCLUSION

In summary, I have argued that the legitimacy of a state would consist in its having a cluster of Hohfeldian rights. First, a legitimate state would have a sphere of privilege within which to enact and enforce laws applying to the residents of its territory. Second, a legitimate state would have the power to put its residents under a *pro tanto* duty to do something simply by enacting a law that requires its residents to do that thing, provided that the law falls within its sphere of privilege and is otherwise morally innocent. Third, a legitimate state would have the privilege to control access to its territory by non-resident non-citizens who have no claim to live or travel there. Fourth, a legitimate state would have a claim against other states that they not interfere with its governing its territory. Fifth, a legitimate state would have an immunity to having any of these rights extinguished by any other state or by any person. A legitimate state's right to rule has at least these components.

I offered the societal needs argument to show that there is a presumption that states are legitimate. If the argument is successful, it establishes a justification for moral standards that require people to obey morally innocent laws of their state, that permit the state to control access to its territory, and the like. As I said, however, the argument turns on contestable empirical claims as well as a debatable moral theory. So although I claim to have made a case for the presumption that existing states are legitimate, I cannot claim to have established it.

It is a sad fact that most states were founded in a way that involved wrongful exercises of force and fraud. And it is sad as well that many people, and perhaps most people in the world, live in states that they would not voluntarily consent to obey. But this does not mean that most states are illegitimate. It means that most states are unjust, or at least that they began by being unjust. Yet unjust or not, they are the ships in which we find ourselves, and we must try to make them just and to make them serve our needs.

READING 15

Is There a Prima Facie Obligation to Obey the Law?

M. B. E. Smith

M. B. E. Smith is Professor of Law at Yale University. In this comprehensive article, Smith considers the widely accepted thesis that there exists a general prima facie obligation to obey the law. He defines a prima facie obligation as one for which there is a moral reason for someone to do a thing, unless he has a moral reason, at least as strong, not to do it. Smith then examines all of the arguments discussed in the other readings in this chapter, as well as a few more, and finds them all problematic, if not unsound. Smith seeks to separate the question of whether a State can be legitimate from the question of whether we have a prima facie duty to obey the law. His stance is that none of the standard justifications for the State obligate us to obey the law.

This reading is taken From "Is There a Prima Facie Obligation to Obey the Law?" Yale Law Journal 82 (19): 950 – 76, by permission.

It isn't a question of whether it was legal or illegal. That isn't enough. The question is, what is morally wrong.
—Richard Nixon, "Checkers Speech" 1952

Many political philosophers have thought it obvious that there is a prima facie obligation to obey the law; and so, in discussing this obligation, they have thought their task to be more that of explaining its basis than of arguing for its existence. John Rawls has, for example, written:

> I shall assume, as requiring no argument, that there is, at least in a society such as ours, a moral obligation to obey the law, although it may, of course, be overridden in certain cases by other more stringent obligations. [See Reading 13:, p. 144.]

As against this, I suggest that it is not at all obvious that there is such an obligation, that this is something that must be shown, rather than so blithely assumed. Indeed, were he uninfluenced by conventional wisdom,

a reflective man might on first considering the question be inclined to deny any such obligation: As H. A. Prichard once remarked, "the mere receipt of an order backed by force seems, if anything, to give rise to the duty of resisting, rather than obeying."[1]

I shall argue that, although those subject to a government often have a prima facie obligation to obey particular laws (e.g., when disobedience has seriously untoward consequences or involves an act that is *mala in se*), they have no prima facie obligation to obey all its laws. I do not hope to prove this contention beyond a reasonable doubt. My goal is rather the more modest one of showing that it is a reasonable position to maintain by first criticizing arguments that purport to establish the obligation and then presenting some positive argument against it.

First, however, I must explain how I use the phrase "prima facie obligation." I shall say that a person S has a prima facie obligation to do an act X if, and only if, there is a moral reason for S to do X which is such that, unless he has a moral reason not to do X at least as strong as his reason to do X, S's failure to do X is wrong.[2] In this discussion it will also be convenient to distinguish two kinds of prima facie obligation via the difference between the two kinds of statement which ascribe them. A specific statement asserts that some particular person has a prima facie obligation to perform some particular act. In contrast, a generic statement (e.g., "Parents have a prima facie obligation to care for their infant children") asserts that everyone who meets a certain description has a prima facie obligation to perform a certain kind of act whenever he has an opportunity to do so. I shall therefore say that a person S has a *specific* prima facie obligation to do X if, and only if, the specific statement "S has a prima facie obligation to do X" is true; and that he has a *generic* prima facie obligation to do X if, and only if, S meets some description D and the generic statement. "Those who are D have a prima facie obligation to do X." is true.

Now, the question of whether there is a prima facie obligation to obey the law is clearly about a generic obligation. Everyone, even the anarchist, would agree that in many circumstances individuals have specific prima facie obligations to obey specific laws. Since it is clear that there is in most circumstances a specific prima facie obligation to refrain from murder, rape, or breach of contract, it is plain that in these circumstances each of us has a specific prima facie obligation not to violate laws which prohibit these acts. Again, disobeying the law often has seriously untoward consequences; and, when this is so, virtually everyone would agree that there is a specific prima facie obligation to obey. Therefore, the interesting question about our obligation vis-à-vis the law is not "Do individual citizens ever have specific prima facie obligations to obey particular laws?," but rather "Is the moral relation of any government to its citizens such that they have a prima facie obligation to do certain things merely because they are legally required to do so?" This is, of course, equivalent to asking "Is there a generic prima facie obligation to obey the law?" Hereafter, when I use the phrase "the prima facie obligation to obey the law" I shall be referring to a generic obligation.

One final point in clarification: As used here, the phrase "prima facie" bears a different meaning than it does when used in legal writing. In legal materials, the phrase frequently refers to evidence sufficiently persuasive so as to require rebuttal. Hence, were a lawyer to ask "Is there a prima facie obligation to obey the law?," a reasonable interpretation of his question might be "May a reasonable man take mere illegality to be sufficient evidence that an act is morally wrong, so long as there is no specific evidence tending to show it is right?" Let us call this the "lawyer's question." Now, the question of primary concern in this inquiry is "Is there any society in which mere illegality is a moral reason for an act's being wrong?" The difference between these questions is that, were there a prima facie obligation to obey the law in the lawyer's sense, mere illegality would, in the absence of specific evidence to the contrary, be evidence of wrongdoing, but it would not necessarily be relevant to a determination of whether lawbreaking is wrong where there is reason to think such conduct justified or even absolutely obligatory. In contrast, if there is a prima facie obligation to obey the law in the sense in which I am using the phrase, the mere illegality of an act is always relevant to the determination of its moral character, despite whatever other reasons are present. Hence, there may be a prima facie obligation to obey the law in the lawyer's sense and yet be no such obligation in the sense of the phrase used here. Near the end of this article I shall return briefly to the lawyer's question; for the present, I raise it only that it may not be confused with the question I wish to examine.

I

The arguments I shall examine fall into three groups: First, those which rest on the benefits each individual receives from government; second, those relying on implicit consent or promise; third, those which appeal to utility or the general good. I shall consider each group in turn.

Of those in the first group, I shall begin with the argument from gratitude. Although they differ greatly in the amount of benefits they provide, virtually all governments do confer substantial benefits on their subjects. Now, it is often claimed that, when a person accepts benefits from another, he thereby incurs a debt of gratitude towards his benefactor. Thus, if it be maintained that obedience to the law is the best way of showing gratitude towards one's government, it may with some plausibility be concluded that each person who has received benefits from his government has a prima facie obligation to obey the law.

On reflection, however, this argument is unconvincing. First, it may reasonably be doubted whether most citizens have an obligation to act gratefully towards their government. Ordinarily, if someone confers benefits on me without any consideration of whether I want them, and if he does this in order to advance some purpose other than promotion of my particular welfare, I have no obligation to be grateful towards him. Yet the most important benefits of government are not accepted by its citizens, but are rather enjoyed regardless of whether they are wanted. Moreover, a government typically confers these benefits, not to advance the interests of particular citizens, but rather as a consequence of advancing some purpose of its own. At times, its motives are wholly admirable, as when it seeks to promote the general welfare; at others, they are less so, as when it seeks to stay in power by catering to the demands of some powerful faction. But, such motives are irrelevant: Whenever government forces benefits on me for reasons other than my particular welfare, I clearly am under no obligation to be grateful to it.

Second, even assuming *arguendo* that each citizen has an obligation to be grateful to his government, the argument still falters. It is perhaps true that cheerful and willing obedience is the best way to show one's gratitude towards government, in that it makes his gratitude unmistakable. But, when a person owes a debt of gratitude towards another, he does not necessarily acquire a prima facie obligation to display his gratitude in the most convincing manner: A person with demanding, domineering parents might best display his gratitude towards them by catering to their every whim, but he surely has no prima facie obligation to do so. Without undertaking a lengthy case-by-case examination, one cannot delimit the prima facie obligation of acting gratefully, for its existence and extent depend on such factors as the nature of the benefits received, the manner in which they are conferred, the motives of the benefactor, and so forth. But, even without such an examination, it is clear that the mere fact that a person has conferred on me even the most momentous benefits does not establish his right to dictate all of my behavior; nor does it establish that I always have an obligation to consider his wishes when I am deciding what I shall do. If, then, we have a prima facie obligation to act gratefully towards government, we undoubtedly have an obligation to promote its interests when this does not involve great sacrifice on our part and to respect some of its wishes concerning that part of our behavior which does not directly affect its interests. But, our having this obligation to be grateful surely does not establish that we have a prima facie obligation to obey the law.

A more interesting argument from the benefits individuals receive from government is the argument from fair play. It differs from the argument from gratitude in contending that the prima facie obligation to obey the law is owed, not to one's government but rather to one's fellow citizens. Versions of this argument have been offered by H. L. A. Hart and John Rawls.

According to Hart, the mere existence of cooperative enterprise gives rise to a certain prima facie obligation. He argues that:

> when a number of persons conduct any joint enterprise according to rules and thus restrict their liberty, those who have submitted to these restrictions when required have a right to a similar submission from those who have benefited by their submission. The rules may provide that officials should have authority to enforce obedience and make further rules, and this will create a structure of legal rights and duties, but the moral obligation to obey the rules in such circumstances is *due* to the cooperating members of the society, and they have the correlative moral right to obedience.[3] [See Reading, 49]

Rawls's account of this obligation in his essay Legal Obligation and the Duty of Fair Play," is rather more complex. Unlike Hart, he sets certain requirements on the kinds of cooperative enterprises that give rise to the obligation: First, that success of the enterprise depends on near-universal obedience to its rules, but not on universal cooperation; second, that obedience to its rules involves some sacrifice, in that obeying the rules restricts one's liberty; and finally, that the

enterprise conform to the principles of justice. Rawls also offers an explanation of the obligation: He argues, that, if a person benefits from participating in such an enterprise and if he intends to continue receiving its benefits, he acts unfairly when he refuses to obey its rules. With Hart, however, Rawls claims that this obligation is owed not to the enterprise itself, nor to its officials, but rather to those members whose obedience has made the benefits possible. Hart and Rawls also agree that this obligation of fair play—"fair play" is Rawls's term—is a fundamental obligation, not derived from utility or from mutual promise or consent. Finally, both Hart and Rawls conceive of legal systems, at least those in democratic societies, as complex practices of the kind which give rise to the obligation of fair play; and they conclude that those who benefit from such legal systems have a prima facie obligation to obey their laws.

These arguments deserve great respect. Hart and Rawls appear to have isolated a kind of prima facie obligation overlooked by other philosophers and have thereby made a significant contribution to moral theory. However, the significance of their discovery to jurisprudence is less clear. Although Hart and Rawls have discovered the obligation of fair play, they do not properly appreciate its limits. Once these limits are understood, it is clear that the prima facie obligation to obey the law cannot be derived from the duty of fair play.

The obligation of fair play seems to arise most clearly within small, voluntary cooperative enterprises. Let us suppose that a number of persons have gone off into the wilderness to carve out a new society, and that they have adopted certain rules to govern their communal life. Their enterprise meets Rawls's requirements on success, sacrifice, and justice. We can now examine the moral situation of the members of that community in a number of circumstances, taking seriously Hart's insistence that cooperating members have a right to the obedience of others and Rawls's explanation of this right and its correlative obligation on grounds of fairness.

Let us take two members of the community, *A* and *B. B,* we may suppose, has never disobeyed the rules, and *A* has benefitted from *B*'s previous submission. Has *B* a right to *A*'s obedience? It would seem necessary to know the consequences of *A*'s obedience. If, in obeying the rules, *A* will confer on *B* a benefit roughly equal to those he has received from *B*, it would be plainly unfair for *A* to withhold it from *B*; and so, in this instance, *B*'s right to *A*'s obedience is clear. Similarly, if, in disobeying the rule, *A* will harm the community, B's right to A's obedience is again clear. This is because in harming the community A will harm B indirectly, by threatening the existence or efficient functioning of an institution on which B's vital interests depend. Since A has benefitted from B's previous submission to the rules, it is unfair for A to do something which will lessen B's chances of receiving like benefits in the future. However, if A's compliance with some particular rule does not benefit B and if his disobedience will not harm the community, it is difficult to see how fairness to B could dictate that A must comply. Surely, the fact that A has benefitted from B's submission does not give B the right to insist that A obey when B's interests are unaffected. A may in this situation have an obligation to obey, perhaps because he has promised or because his disobedience would be unfair to some other member; but, if he does disobey, he has surely not been unfair to B.

We may generalize from these examples. Considerations of fairness apparently do show that, when cooperation is perfect and when each member has benefitted from the submission of every other, each member of an enterprise has a prima facie obligation to obey its rules when obedience benefits some other member or when disobedience harms the enterprise. For, if in either circumstance a member disobeys, he is unfair to at least one other member and is perhaps unfair to them all. However, if a member disobeys when his obedience would have benefitted no other member and when his disobedience does no harm, his moral situation is surely different. If his disobedience is then unfair, it must be unfair to the group but not to any particular member. But this, I take it, is impossible: Although the moral properties of a group are not always a simple function of the moral properties of its members, it is evident that one cannot be unfair to a group without being unfair to any of its members. It would seem, then, that even when cooperation is perfect, considerations of fairness do not establish that members of a cooperative enterprise have a simple obligation to obey all of its rules, but have rather the more complex obligation to obey when obedience benefits some other member or when disobedience harms the enterprise. This does not, it is worth noting, reduce the obligation of fair play to a kind of utilitarian obligation, for it may well be that fair play will dictate in certain circumstances that a man obey when disobedience would have better consequences. My point is merely that the obligation of fair play governs a man's actions only when some benefit or harm turns on whether he obeys. Surely, this is as it should be, for

questions of fairness typically arise from situations in which burdens or benefits are distributed or in which some harm is done.

The obligation of fair play is therefore much more complex than Hart or Rawls seem to have imagined. Indeed, the obligation is even more complex than the above discussion suggests, for the assumption of perfect cooperation is obviously unrealistic. When that assumption is abandoned, the effect of previous disobedience considered, and the inevitable disparity among the various members' sacrifice in obeying the rules taken into account, the scope of the obligation is still further limited; we shall then find that it requires different things of different members, depending on their previous pattern of compliance and the amount of sacrifice they have made. These complications need not detain us, however, for they do not affect the fact that fairness requires obedience only in situations where noncompliance would withhold benefits from someone or harm the enterprise. Now it must be conceded that all of this makes little difference when we confine our attention to small, voluntary, cooperative enterprises. Virtually any disobedience may be expected to harm such enterprises to some extent, by diminishing the confidence of other members in its probable success and therefore reducing their incentive to work diligently towards it. Moreover, since they are typically governed by a relatively small number of rules, none of which ordinarily require behavior that is useless to other members, we may expect that when a member disobeys he will probably withhold a benefit from some other member and that he has in the past benefitted significantly from that member's obedience. We may therefore expect that virtually every time the rules of a small, voluntary enterprise call on a member to obey he will have a specific prima facie obligation to do so because of his obligation of fair play.

In the case of legal systems, however, the complexity of the obligation makes a great deal of difference. Although their success may depend on the "habit of obedience" of a majority of their subjects, all legal systems are designed to cope with a substantial amount of disobedience. Hence, individual acts of disobedience to the law only rarely have an untoward effect on legal systems. What is more, because laws must necessarily be designed to cover large numbers of cases, obedience to the law often benefits no one. Perhaps the best illustration is obedience of the traffic code: Very often I benefit no one when I stop at a red light or observe the speed limit. Finally, virtually every legal system contains a number of pointless or even pos-

itively harmful laws, obedience to which either benefits no one or, worse still, causes harm. Laws prohibiting homosexual activity or the dissemination of
birth control information are surely in this category.
Hence, even if legal systems are the kind of cooperative enterprise that gives rise to the obligation of fair
play, in a great many instances that obligation will not
require that we obey specific laws. If, then, there is a
generic prima facie obligation to obey the laws of any
legal system, it cannot rest on the obligation of fair
play. The plausibility of supposing that it does depends on an unwarranted extrapolation from what is
largely true of our obligations within small, cooperative enterprises to what must always be true of our
obligations within legal systems.

In his recent book, Rawls has abandoned the argument from fair play as proof that the entire citizenry
of even just governments has a prima facie obligation
to obey the law. He now distinguishes between obligations (e.g., to be fair or to keep promises) and natural
duties (e.g., to avoid injury to others). Obligations, according to Rawls, are incurred only by one's voluntary
acts, whereas this is not true of natural duties. In his
book, A Theory of Justice [see Reading 26], he retains
the obligation of fair play (now "fairness"); but he now
thinks that this obligation applies only to those citizens
of just governments who hold office or who have advanced their interests through the government. He excludes the bulk of the citizenry from having a prima facie obligation to obey the law on the ground that, for
most persons, receiving benefits from government is
nothing they do voluntarily, but is rather something
that merely happens to them. He does not, however,
take this to imply that most citizens of a reasonably
just government are morally free to disobey the law:
He maintains that everyone who is treated by such a
government with reasonable justice has a natural duty
to obey all laws that are not grossly unjust, on the
ground that everyone has a natural duty to uphold and
to comply with just institutions.

It is tempting to criticize Rawls's present position
in much the same way that I criticized his earlier one.
One might argue that, while it is true that officehold-
ers and those who have profited by invoking the rules
of a just government must in fairness comply with its
laws when disobedience will result in harm to that
government or when it withholds a benefit from some
person who has a right to it, it is simply false that fairness dictates obedience when disobedience does no
harm or withholds no benefit. One might further argue
that the utility of a just government is such that one

has a prima facie duty to obey when disobedience is
harmful to it, but that, so long as disobedience does no
harm, the government's character is irrelevant to the
question of whether one has a prima facie obligation
to obey. These criticisms would, I think, show that if
we are to base our normative ethics on an appeal to intuitively reasonable principles of duty and obligation,
Rawls's present position is no more satisfying than is
his earlier one. However, although certainly relevant to
an assessment of Rawls's present position, these arguments cannot be regarded as decisive, for in his book
Rawls does not rely on a bare appeal to moral intuition. He does not disregard the evidence of intuition,
and he is glad to enlist its aid when he can; but, in
putting forward particular principles of duty and obligation, he is more concerned with showing that they
follow from his general theory of justice. Hence, to refute Rawls's present position, one would have to set
out his elaborate theory and then show either that it is
mistaken or that the particular claims he makes on its
basis do not follow from it. Such a task is beyond the
scope of this article; and I shall therefore be content to
observe that Rawls's present position lacks intuitive
support and, hence, that it rests solely on a controversial ethical theory and a complicated argument based
upon it, neither of which has as yet emerged unscathed
from the fire of critical scrutiny. His view deserves
great respect and demands extended discussion, but it
is not one which we must now accept, on pain of being unreasonable.

II

The second group of arguments are those from implicit
consent or promise. Recognizing that among the clearest cases of prima facie obligation are those in which a
person voluntarily assumes the obligation, some
philosophers have attempted to found the citizen's
obligation to obey the law upon his consent or promise
to do so. There is, of course, a substantial difficulty in
any such attempt, viz., the brute fact that many persons
have never so agreed. To accommodate this fact, some
philosophers have invoked the concept of implicit
promise or consent. In the *Second Treatise* [see Reading
3], Locke argued that mere residence in a country,
whether for an hour or a lifetime, constitutes implicit
consent to its law. Plato in the *Dialogues* and W. D.
Ross[4] made the similar argument that residence in a
country and appeal to the protection of its laws constitute an implicit promise to obey.

Nevertheless, it is clear that residence and use of the protection of the law do not constitute any usual kind of promise to obey its laws. The phrases "implicit consent" and "implicit promise" are somewhat difficult to understand, for they are not commonly used; nor do Locke, Plato, or Ross define them. Still, a natural way of understanding them is to assume that they refer to acts which differ from explicit consent or promise only in that, in the latter cases, the person has said "I consent . . ." or "I promise . . . ," whereas in the former, he has not uttered such words but has rather performed some act which counts as giving consent or making a promise. Now, as recent investigation in the philosophy of language has shown, certain speech acts are performed only when someone utters certain words (or performs some other conventional act) with the intention that others will take what he did as being an instance of the particular act in question. And it is certain that, in their ordinary usage, "consenting" and "promising" refer to speech acts of this kind. If I say to someone, "I promise to give you fifty dollars," but it is clear from the context that I do not intend that others will take my utterance as a promise, no one would consider me as having promised. Bringing this observation to bear on the present argument, it is perhaps possible that some people reside in a country and appeal to the protection of its laws with the intention that others will take their residence and appeal as consent to the laws or as a promise to obey; but this is surely true only of a very small number, consisting entirely of those enamoured with social contract theory.

It may be argued, however, that my criticism rests on an unduly narrow reading of the words "consent" and "promise." Hence, it may be supposed that, if I am to refute the implicit consent or promise arguments, I must show that there is no other sense of the words "consent" or "promise" in which it is true that citizens, merely by living in a state and going about their usual business, thereby consent or promise to obey the law. This objection is difficult to meet, for I know of no way to show that there is no sense of either word that is suitable for contractarian purposes. However, I can show that two recent attempts, by John Plamenatz and Alan Gewirth, to refurbish the implicit consent argument along this line have been unsuccessful. I shall not quarrel with their analyses of "consent," though I am suspicious of them; rather, I shall argue that given their definitions of "consent" the fact that a man consents to government does not establish that he has a prima facie obligation to obey the law.

Plamenatz claims that there are two kinds of consent. The first, which is common-garden variety consent, he terms "direct." He concedes that few citizens directly consent to their government. He suggests, however, that there is another kind of consent, which he calls "indirect," and that, in democratic societies, consent in this sense is widespread and establishes a prima facie obligation to obey the law. Indirect consent occurs whenever a person freely votes or abstains from voting. Voting establishes a prima facie obligation of obedience because:

> Even if you dislike the system and wish to change it, you put yourself by your vote under a *prima facie* obligation to obey whatever government comes legally to power. . . . For the purpose of an election is to give authority to the people who win it and, if you vote knowing what you are doing and without being compelled to do it, you voluntarily take part in a process which gives authority to these people.[5]

Plamenatz does not explain why abstention results in a prima facie obligation, but perhaps his idea is that, if a person abstains, he in effect acknowledges the authority of whoever happens to win.

The key premise then in the argument is that "the purpose of an election is to give authority to the people who win it," and it is clear that Plamenatz believes that this implies that elections do give authority to their winners. In assessing the truth of these contentions, it is, of course, vital to know what Plamenatz means by "authority." Unfortunately, he does not enlighten us, and we must therefore speculate as to his meaning. To begin, the word "authority," when used without qualification, is often held to mean the same as "legitimate authority." Since prima facie obligation is the weakest kind of obligation, part of what we mean when we ascribe authority to some government is that those subject to it have at least a prima facie obligation to obey. However, if this is what Plamenatz means by "authority," his argument simply begs the question: For, in order to be justified in asserting that the purpose of an election is to confer authority and that elections succeed in doing this, he must first show that everyone subject to an elected government has a prima facie obligation to obey its law, both those eligible to vote and those ineligible.

It is possible, however, that Plamenatz is using "authority" in some weaker sense, one that does not entail that everyone subject to it has a prima facie obligation to obey. If this is so, his premises will perhaps pass, but he must then show that those who are eligible to take part in conferring authority have a prima facie obligation to obey it. However, it is difficult to see how this can be done. First, as Plamenatz recognizes, voting is not necessarily consenting in the "direct" or usual sense, and merely being eligible to vote is even more clearly not consenting. Hence, the alleged prima facie obligation of obedience incurred by those eligible to vote is not in consequence of their direct consent. Second, Plamenatz cannot appeal to "common moral sentiment" to bolster his argument: This is because if we really believed that those eligible to vote have a prima facie obligation to obey, an obligation not incurred by the ineligible, we should then believe that the eligible have a stronger obligation than those who are ineligible. But, as far as I can tell, we do not ordinarily think that this is true. Finally, Plamenatz cannot rely on a purely conceptual argument to make his point. It is by no means an analytic truth that those subject to elected governments have a prima facie obligation to obey the law. The radical who says, "The present government of the United States was freely elected, but because it exploits people its citizens have no obligation to obey it," has perhaps said something false, but he has not contradicted himself. Plamenatz's argument is therefore either question-begging or inconclusive, depending on what he means by "authority."

Gewirth's argument is similar to Plamenatz's in that he also holds that a person's vote establishes his prima facie obligation of obedience. He argues that men consent to government when "certain institutional arrangements exist in the community as a whole," including "the maintenance of a method which leaves open to every sane, noncriminal adult the opportunity to discuss, criticize, and vote for or against the government." He holds that the existence of such consent "justifies" government and establishes the subject's prima facie obligation to obey because:

> The method of consent combines and safeguards the joint values of freedom and order as no other method does. It provides a choice in the power of government which protects the rights of the electorate more effectively than does any other method. It does more justice to man's potential rationality than does any other method, for it gives all men the opportunity to participate in a reasoned discussion of the problem of society and to make their discussion effective in terms of political control.[6]

As it stands, Gewirth's argument is incomplete. He makes certain claims about the benefits of government by consent which are open to reasonable doubt.

Some communists, for example, would hold that Gewirth's method of consent has led to exploitation, and that human rights and freedom are better protected by the rule of the party. This aside, Gewirth's argument still needs strengthening. The fact that certain benefits are given only by government with a method of consent establishes only that such a government is better than one which lacks such a method. But, to show that one government is better than another, or even to show that it is the best possible government, does not prove that its subjects have a prima facie obligation to obey its laws: There is a prior question, which remains to be settled, as to whether there can be a prima facie obligation to obey any government. Gewirth does not carry the argument farther in his discussion of "consent," but earlier in his paper he hints as to how he would meet this objection. He argues that "government as such" is justified, or made legitimate, by its being necessary to avoid certain evils. Indeed, although he does not explicitly so state, he seems to think that utilitarian considerations demonstrate that there is a prima facie obligation to obey any government that protects its subjects from these evils, but that there is an additional prima facie obligation to obey a government with a method of consent because of the more extensive benefits it offers. In the next section, I shall discuss whether a direct appeal to utility can establish a prima facie obligation to obey the law.

III

I shall consider three utilitarian arguments: the first appealing to a weak form of act-utilitarianism, the second and third to rule-utilitarian theories. To my knowledge, the first argument has never been explicitly advanced. It is nevertheless worth considering, both because it possesses a certain plausibility and because it has often been hinted at when philosophers, lawyers, and political theorists have attempted to derive an obligation to obey the law from the premise that government is necessary to protect society from great evil. The argument runs as follows:

> There is obviously a prima facie obligation to perform acts which have good consequences. Now, government is absolutely necessary for securing the general good: The alternative is the state of nature in which everyone is miserable, in which life is "solitary, poor, nasty, brutish and short." But, no government can long stand in the face of

widespread disobedience, and government can therefore promote the general good only so long as its laws are obeyed. Therefore, obedience to the law supports the continued existence of government and, hence, always has good consequences. From that it follows that there is a prima facie obligation to obey the law.

On even brief scrutiny, however, this argument quickly disintegrates. The first thing to be noticed is that its principle of prima facie obligation is ambiguous. It may be interpreted as postulating either (a) an obligation to perform those acts which have any good consequences, or (b) an obligation to perform optimific acts (i.e., those whose consequences are better than their alternatives). Now, (a) and (b) are in fact very different principles. The former is obviously absurd. It implies, for example, that I have a prima facie obligation to kill whomever I meet, since this would have the good consequence of helping to reduce overpopulation. Thus, the only weak act-utilitarian principle with any plausibility is (b). But, regardless of whether (b) is acceptable—and some philosophers would not accept it—the conclusion that there is a prima facie obligation to obey the law cannot be derived from it, inasmuch as there are obvious and familiar cases in which breach of a particular law has better consequences than obedience. The only conclusion to be derived from (b) is that there is a specific prima facie obligation to obey the law whenever obedience is optimific. But no generic prima facie obligation to obey can be derived from weak act-utilitarianism.

The second utilitarian argument appeals not to the untoward consequences of individual disobedience, but rather to those of general disobedience. Perhaps the most common challenge to those who defend certain instances of civil disobedience is "What would happen if everyone disobeyed the law?" One of the arguments implicit in this question is the generalization argument, which may be expanded as follows:

No one can have a right to do something unless everyone has a right to do it. Similarly, an act cannot be morally indifferent unless it would be morally indifferent if everyone did it. But, everyone's breaking the law is not a matter of moral indifference; for no government can survive in such a circumstance and, as we have already agreed, government is necessary for securing and maintaining the general good. Hence, since the consequences of general disobedience would be disastrous, each person subject to law has a prima facie obligation to obey it.

In assessing this argument, we must first recognize that the generalization argument is a moral criterion to be applied with care, as virtually everyone who has discussed it has recognized. If we simply note that if everyone committed a certain act there would be disastrous consequences and thereupon conclude that there is a prima facie obligation not to commit acts of that kind, we will be saddled with absurdities. We will have to maintain, for example, that there is a prima facie obligation not to eat dinner at five o'clock, for if everyone did so, certain essential services could not be maintained. And, for similar reasons, we will have to maintain that there is a prima facie obligation not to produce food. Now, those who believe that the generalization argument is valid argue that such absurdities arise when the criterion is applied to acts which are either too generally described or described in terms of morally irrelevant features. They would argue that the generalization argument appears to go awry when applied to these examples because the description "producing food" is too general to give the argument purchase and because the temporal specification in "eating dinner at five o'clock" is morally irrelevant.

However, such a restriction on the generalization argument is fatal to its use in proving a prima facie obligation to obey the law. This is because a person who denies any such obligation is surely entitled to protest that the description "breaking the law" is overly general, on the ground that it refers to acts of radically different moral import. Breaking the law perhaps always has some bad consequences; but sometimes the good done by it balances the bad or even outweighs it. And, once we take these differences in consequences into account, we find that utilitarian generalization, like weak act-utilitarianism, can only establish a specific prima facie obligation to obey the law when obedience is optimific. Were everyone to break the law when obedience is optimific, the consequences would undoubtedly be disastrous; but it is by no means clear that it would be disastrous if everyone broke the law when obedience is not optimific. Since no one knows, with respect to any society, how often obedience is not optimific, no one can be certain as to the consequences of everyone acting in this way. Indeed, for all we know, if everyone broke the law when obedience was not optimific the good done by separate acts of law-breaking might more than compensate for any public disorder which might result. In sum, even if the generalization argument is regarded as an acceptable principle of prima facie obligation, the most it demonstrates is that there is a specific prima facie obligation to obey the law whenever the consequences of obedience are optimific.

Some readers—especially those unfamiliar with the recent literature on utilitarianism—may suspect that this last argument involves sleight of hand. They may object:

> In your discussion of the generalization argument, you argued that we have no way of knowing the consequences if everyone disobeyed when obedience was not optimific. But, your argument rests on the premise that the act-utilitarian formula can be perfectly applied, whereas this is in fact impossible: The consequences of many acts are difficult or impossible to foretell; and so, were we all to attempt to be act-utilitarians, we would either make horrendous mistakes or be paralyzed into inaction. In constructing a rule-utilitarian theory of prima facie obligations, we should therefore concentrate not on the consequences of everyone following certain rules, but rather on the consequences of everyone trying to follow them. And it seems reasonable to believe that, in such a theory, the rule "Obey the law" would receive utilitarian blessing.

As it stands, this objection is overdrawn. My argument does not presuppose that persons can generally succeed in applying the act-utilitarian formula: I merely speculated on the consequences of everyone behaving in a certain way; and I made no assumption as to what made them act that way. Moreover, the objection severely overestimates the difficulty in being a confirmed act-utilitarian. Still, the objection makes one substantial point that deserves further attention. Rule-utilitarian theories which focus on the consequences of everyone accepting (although not always following) a certain set of rules do differ markedly from the generalization argument; and so the question remains as to whether such a theory could establish a prima facie obligation to obey the law. I shall therefore discuss whether the most carefully developed such theory, that given by R. B. Brandt, does just this.

In Brandt's theory, one's obligations are (within certain limits) relative to his society and are determined by the set of rules whose acceptance in that society would have better consequences than would acceptance of any other set.[7] According to this theory, then, there can be a generic prima facie obligation to obey the law within a given society if, and only if, general acceptance of the rule "Obey the law," as a rule of prima facie obligation, would have better consequences than were no rule accepted with respect to obeying the law, as well as better consequences than were some alternative rule accepted (e.g., "Obey the law when obedience to the law is optimific," or "Obey the law so long as it is just").

Now, to many it may seem obvious that the ideal set of rules for any society will contain the rule "Obey the law," on the ground that, were its members not generally convinced of at least a prima facie obligation to obey, disobedience would be widespread, resulting in a great many crimes against person and property. But, there are two reasons to doubt such a gloomy forecast. First, we must surely suppose that in this hypothetical society the laws are still backed by sanctions, thereby giving its members a strong incentive to obey its laws. Second, we must also assume that the members of that society accept other moral rules (e.g., "Do not harm others," "Keep promises," "Tell the truth") which will give them a moral incentive to obey the law in most circumstances. It is, in short, a mistake to believe that unless people are convinced that they have a generic prima facie obligation to obey the law, they cannot be convinced that in most circumstances they have a specific prima facie obligation to obey particular laws. We may therefore expect that, even though members of our hypothetical society do not accept a moral rule about obedience to the law per se, they will still feel a prima facie obligation to act in accordance with the law, save when disobedience does no harm. There is, then, no reason to think that an orgy of lawbreaking would ensue were no rule about obedience to the law generally recognized; nor, I think, is there any good reason to believe that acceptance of the rule "Obey the law" would in any society have better consequences than recognition of some alternative rule. In sum, Brandt's theory requires that we be able to determine the truth-value of a large number of counter-factual propositions about what would happen were entire societies persuaded of the truth of certain moral rules. But, even if we assume—and it is hardly clear that we should—that we can reliably determine the truth-value of such counter-factuals through "common sense" and our knowledge of human nature, Brandt's form of rule-utilitarianism gives no support for the proof of a prima facie obligation to obey the law.

IV

In the foregoing discussion, I have played the skeptic, contending that no argument has as yet succeeded in establishing a prima facie obligation to obey the law. I want now to examine this supposed obligation directly. I shall assume *arguendo* that such an obligation exists in order to inquire as to how it compares in moral weight with other prima facie obligations. As we shall see, this question is relevant to whether we should hold that such an obligation exists.

To discuss this question, I must, of course, first specify some test for determining the weight of a prima facie obligation. It will be recalled that I defined "prima facie obligation" in terms of wrongdoing: To say that a person S has a prima facie obligation to do an act X is to say that S has a moral reason to do X which is such that, unless he has a reason not to do X that is at least as strong, S's failure to do X is wrong. Now, we are accustomed, in our reflective moral practice, to distinguish degrees of wrongdoing. And so, by appealing to this notion, we can formulate two principles that may reasonably be held to govern the weight of prima facie obligations: First, that a prima facie obligation is a serious one if, and only if, an act which violates that obligation and fulfils no other is seriously wrong; and, second, that a prima facie obligation is a serious one if, and only if, violation of it will make considerably worse an act which on other grounds is already wrong. These principles, which constitute tests for determining an obligation's weight, are closely related, and application of either to a given prima facie obligation is a sufficient measure; but I shall apply both to the presumed prima facie obligation to obey the law in order to make my argument more persuasive.

First, however, we should convince ourselves of the reliability of these tests by applying them to some clear cases. I suppose it will be granted that we all have a prima facie obligation not to kill (except perhaps in self-defense), and that this obligation is most weighty. Our first test corroborates this, for, if a person kills another when he is not defending himself and if he has no specific prima facie obligation to kill that person, his act is seriously wrong. By contrast, our prima facie obligation to observe rules of etiquette—if indeed there is any such obligation—is clearly trifling. This is borne out by our test, for if I belch audibly in the company of those who think such behavior rude, my wrongdoing is at most trivial. The same results are obtained under our second test. If I attempt to extort money from someone my act is much worse if I kill one of his children and threaten the rest than if I merely threatened them all; and so the obligation not to kill again counts as substantial. Similarly, the prima facie obligation to observe the rules of etiquette is again trivial, for if I am rude during the extortion my act is hardly worse than it would have been had I been polite.

By neither of these tests, however, does the prima facie obligation to obey the law count as substantial. As for the first test, let us assume that while driving home at two o'clock in the morning I run a stop sign. There is no danger, for I can see clearly that there was no one approaching the intersection, nor is there any impres-

sionable youth nearby to be inspired to a life of crime by my flouting of the traffic code. Finally, we may assume that I nevertheless had no specific prima facie obligation to run the stop sign. If, then, my prima facie obligation to obey the law is of substantial moral weight, my action must have been a fairly serious instance of wrongdoing. But clearly it was not. If it was wrong at all—and to me this seems dubious—it was at most a mere peccadillo. As for the second test, we may observe that acts which are otherwise wrong are not made more so—if they are made worse at all—by being illegal. If I defraud someone my act is hardly worse morally by being illegal than it would have been were it protected by some legal loophole. Thus, if there is a prima facie obligation to obey the law, it is at most of trifling weight.

This being so, I suggest that considerations of simplicity indicate that we should ignore the supposed prima facie obligation to obey the law and refuse to count an act wrong merely because it violates some law. There is certainly nothing to be lost by doing this, for we shall not thereby recommend or tolerate any conduct that is seriously wrong, nor shall we fail to recommend any course of action that is seriously obligatory. Yet, there is much to be gained, for in refusing to let trivialities occupy our attention, we shall not be diverted from the important questions to be asked about illegal conduct, viz., "What kind of act was it?," "What were its consequences?," "Did the agent intend its consequences?," and so forth. Morality is, after all, a serious business; and we are surely right not to squander our moral attention and concern on matters of little moral significance.

To illustrate what can be gained, let us consider briefly the issue of civil disobedience. Most philosophers who have written on the subject have argued that, at least in democratic societies, there is always a strong moral reason to obey the law. They have therefore held that civil disobedience is a tactic to be employed only when all legal means of changing an unjust law have failed, and that the person who engages in it must willingly accept punishment as a mark of respect for the law and recognition of the seriousness of lawbreaking. However, once we abandon the notion that civil disobedience is morally significant per se, we shall judge it in the same way we judge most other kinds of acts, that is, on the basis of their character and consequences. Indeed, we can then treat civil disobedience just as we regard many other species of illegal conduct. If breaking the law involves an act which is *mala in se* or if it has untoward consequences, we are ordinarily prepared to condemn it and to think that the malefactor ought to accept punishment. But if lawbreaking does not involve an act that is *mala in se* and if it has no harmful consequences, we do not ordinarily condemn it, nor do we think that its perpetrator must accept punishment, unless evading punishment itself has untoward consequences. If we adopt this view of civil disobedience, we shall have done much to escape the air of mystery that hovers about most discussions of it.

Of course, this is not to say it will be easy to determine when civil disobedience is justified. Some have maintained that the civil disobedience of the last decade has led to increasing violation of laws which safeguard people and property. If this is true, each instance of disobedience which has contributed to this condition has a share in the evil of the result. Others maintain that such disobedience has had wholly good consequences, that it has helped to remedy existing injustice. Still others think its consequences are mixed. Which position is correct is difficult to determine. I myself am inclined to believe that, although the consequences have been mixed, the good far outweigh the bad; but I would be hard pressed to prove it. What is clear, however, is that either abandoning or retaining the supposed prima facie obligation to obey the law will not help settle these questions about consequences. But, if we do abandon it, we shall then at least be able to focus on these questions without having to worry about a prima facie obligation of trivial weight that must nevertheless somehow be taken into account. Finally, if we abandon the prima facie obligation to obey the law, we shall perhaps look more closely at the character of acts performed in the course of civil disobedience, and this may, in turn, lead to fruitful moral speculation. For example, we shall be able to distinguish between acts which cannot conceivably violate the obligation of fair play (e.g., burning one's draft card) and acts which may do so (e.g., tax refusal or evasion of military service). This in turn may provide an incentive to reflect further on the obligation of fair play, to ask, for example, whether Rawls is right in his present contention that a person can incur the obligation of fair play only so long as his acceptance of the benefits of a cooperative enterprise is wholly voluntary.

V

It is now time to take stock. I initially suggested that it is by no means obvious that there is any prima facie obligation to obey the law. In the foregoing, I have rejected a number of arguments that purport to establish its existence. The only plausible argument I have not rejected is the one of Rawls that purports to prove that there is a natural duty to obey the laws of reasonably just governments. However, I did note that his position lacks intuitive support and rests on a controversial ethical theory which has not yet withstood the test of critical scrutiny. Finally, I have shown that even if such an obligation is assumed, it is of trivial weight and that there are substantial advantages in ignoring it. I suggest that all of this makes it reasonable to maintain that there is in no society a prima facie obligation to obey the law.

Before I conclude my discussion, however, I want to tie up one loose thread. Near the beginning of my argument I distinguished the question to be discussed from that which I called the lawyer's question, "May a reasonable man take mere illegality to be sufficient evidence that an act is morally wrong, so long as he lacks specific evidence that tends to show that it is right?" Since I have raised the question, I believe that, for the sake of completeness, I should consider it, if only briefly. To begin, it seems very doubtful that there is, in the lawyer's sense, a prima facie obligation to obey the law. It is undoubtedly true that most instances of lawbreaking are wrong, but it is also true that many are not: This is because there are, as Lord Devlin once remarked, "many fussy regulations whose breach it would be pedantic to call immoral," and because some breaches of even non-fussy regulations are justified. Now, unless—as in a court of law—there is some pressing need to reach a finding, the mere fact that most *A*s are also *B* does not, in the absence of evidence that a particular *A* is not *B,* warrant an inference that the *A* in question is also a *B*: In order for this inference to be reasonable, one must know that virtually all *A*s are *B*s. Since, then, it rarely happens that there is a pressing need to reach a moral finding, and since to know merely that an act is illegal is not to know very much of moral significance about it, it seems clear that, if his only information about an act was that it was illegal, a reasonable man would withhold judgment until he learned more about it. Indeed, this is not only what the fictitious reasonable man would do, it is what we should expect the ordinary person to do. Suppose we were to ask a large number of people: "Jones has broken a law; but I won't tell you whether what he did is a serious crime or merely violation of a parking regulation, nor whether he had good reason for his actions. Would you, merely on the strength of what I have just told you, be willing to say that what he did was morally wrong?" I have conducted only an informal poll; but, on its basis, I would wager that the great majority would answer "I can't yet say—you must tell me more about what Jones did."

More importantly, it appears to make little difference what answer we give to the lawyer's question. While an affirmative answer establishes a rule of inference that an illegal act is wrong in the absence of specific information tending to show it to be right, it is a rule that would in fact virtually never be applied in any reasonable determination of whether an illegal act is wrong. If, on the one hand, we have specific information about an illegal act which tends to show it to be right, then the rule is irrelevant to our determination of the act's moral character. Should we be inclined, in this instance, to hold the act wrong we must have specific information which tends to show this; and it is clear that our conclusions about its moral character must be based on this specific information, and not on the supposed reasonableness of holding illegal conduct wrong in the absence of specific information tending to show it is right. On the other hand, if we have specific information tending to show that an illegal act is wrong and no information tending to show it is right, the rule is applicable but otiose: Since we have ample specific reason to condemn the act, the rule is superfluous to our judgment. It would seem, then, that the rule is relevant only when we have no specific information about the illegal conduct's rightness or wrongness; and this, I suggest, is something that virtually never occurs. When we are prompted to make a moral judgment about an illegal act, we virtually always know something of its character or at least its consequences; and it is these that we consider important in determining the rightness or wrongness of lawbreaking. In short, it seems to make little difference what answer we give to the lawyer's question; I raise it here only that it may hereafter be ignored.

In conclusion, it is, I think, important to recognize that there is nothing startling in what I am recommending, nothing that in any way outrages common sense. Even the most conscientious men at times violate trivial and pointless laws for some slight gain in convenience and, when they do so, they do not feel shame or remorse. Similarly, when they observe other men behaving in a like fashion, they do not think of passing moral censure. For most people, violation of the law becomes a matter for moral concern only when it involves an act which is believed to be wrong on grounds apart from its illegality. Hence, anyone who believes that the purpose of normative ethics is to organize and clarify our reflective moral practice should be skeptical of any argument purporting to show that there is a prima facie obligation to obey the law. It is necessary to state this point with care: I am not contending that reflective and conscientious citizens would, if asked, deny that there is a prima facie obligation to obey the law. Indeed, I am willing to concede that many more would affirm its existence than deny it. But, this is in no way inconsistent with my present point. We often find that reflective people will accept general statements which are belied by their actual linguistic practice. That they also accept moral generalizations that are belied by their actual reflective moral practice should occasion no surprise.

This last point may, however, be challenged on the ground that it implies that there is in our reflective moral practice no distinction between raw power and legitimate authority. As I noted above, the concept of legitimate authority is often analyzed in terms of the right to command, where "right" is used in the strict sense as implying some correlative obligation of obedience. Given this definition, if it is true that the principle "There is a prima facie obligation to obey the law" is not observed in our reflective moral practice, it follows that we do not really distinguish between governments which possess legitimate authority (e.g., that of the United States) and those which do not (e.g., the Nazi occupation government of France). And this, it may justly be held, is absurd. What I take this argument to show, however, is not that the principle is enshrined in our reflective morality, but rather that what we ordinarily mean when we ascribe legitimate authority to some government is not captured by the usual analysis of "legitimate authority." It is a mistake to believe that, unless we employ the concept of authority as it is usually analyzed, we cannot satisfactorily distinguish between the moral relation of the government of the United States vis-à-vis Americans and the moral relation of the Nazi occupation government vis-à-vis Frenchmen. One way of doing this, for example, is to define "legitimate authority" in terms of "the right to command and to enforce obedience," where "right" is used in the sense of "what is morally permissible." Thus, according to this analysis of the notion, the government of the United States counts as having legitimate authority over its subjects because within certain limits there is nothing wrong in its issuing commands to them and enforcing their obedience, whereas the Nazi occupation government lacked such authority because its issuing commands to Frenchmen was morally impermissible. It is not my intention to proffer this as an adequate analysis of the notion of legitimate authority or to suggest that it captures what we ordinarily mean when we ascribe such authority to some government. These are difficult matters, and I do not wish to address myself to them here. My point is rather that the questions "What governments enjoy legitimate authority?" and "Have the citizens of any government a prima facie obligation to obey the law?" both can be, and should be, kept separate.

END NOTES

Wolff

[1]This point is so simple that it may seem unworthy of such emphasis. Nevertheless, a number of political philosophers, including Hobbes and John Austin, have supposed that *the concept* as well as the principles of authority could be derived from the concepts of power or utility. For example, Austin defines a command as a signification of desire, uttered by someone who will visit evil on those who do not comply with it (*The Providence of Jurisprudence Determined*, Lecture I).

[2]This is not quite so difficult as it sounds, since policy very rarely turns on disputes over technical or theoretical details. Still, the citizen who, for example, does not understand the nature of atomic radiation cannot even pretend to have an opinion on the feasibility of bomb shelters; and since the momentous choice between first-strike and second-strike nuclear strategies depends on the possibility of a successful shelter system, the uninformed citizen will be as completely at the mercy of his "representatives" as the lowliest slave.

Beran

[1]Within the field of moral reasons for action the distinction between a reason for action and conclusive reason for action has been marked since W. D. Ross by speaking of a prima facie obligation or ought (a reason for action) and an actual obligation or ought (conclusive reason for action). In "Ought, Obligation, and Duty" (*Australasian Journal of Philosophy* 50 [1972]: 207–21), I argued for the view that this way of making the distinction is unnecessary and confused. I claimed there that the "prima facie/actual" terminology is unnecessary, since the distinction between a reason for action and conclusive reason for action is already embodied in ordinary language through obligation statements always having the former force and (unqualified) ought statements always having the latter force. Throughout this article I will use "obligation" with the force of a reason for action and "ought" with the force of a conclusive reason for action. However, the arguments which follow merely depend on the distinction between a reason for action and a conclusive reason for action itself, not on the terminology used to mark the distinction.

[2]S.I. Benn and R.S. Peters, *Principles and the Democratic State* (London, 1969), p. 332.

[3]D. M. Armstrong, *Belief, Truth, and Knowledge* (Cambridge, 1973), p. 28.

Rawls

[1]The metaphor of being free and without one's chains is taken from I. M. D. Little's review of Kenneth Arrow's book *Social Choice and Individual Values* (New York: John Wiley, 1951), which appeared in *Journal of Political Economy*, 60 (1952). My argument follows his in all essential respects, the only addition being that I have introduced the concept of justice in accounting for what is, in effect, Arrow's non-dictatorship condition.

Copp

[1]It may seem that states are not necessarily territorial. I will address this worry in what follows.

[2]See A. John Simmons, *Moral Principles and Political Obligations* (Princeton: Princeton University Press, 1979), pp. 195–196, 29. Simmons describes the "traditional" view as the idea that the subjects of a legitimate state have a moral obligation to obey its law and he holds that every "obligation" is "correlated" with "a right" (p. 14). This traditional idea is implicit in John Locke's *Two Treatises of Government*.

[3]Technically, the notion of a public good is the notion of a good "characterized by *nonrivalry in consumption* (i.e., its use by one person does not interfere with its use by others)," and "the consumption of which is *nonexclusive* (i.e., if the good is available to one person, it will be available to all, including those who do not help to produce it)." See David Schmidtz, *The Limits of Government: An Essay on the Public Goods Argument* (Boulder: Westview Press, 1991), p. 55. Consider lighthouses, for example.

[4]A legitimate state would presumably be just at least in that one respect, for it would have the right to rule. What I have in mind is the idea that the property of being just in other respects might ground the legitimacy of a state.

[5]The idea that a legitimate state would have a claim to obedience is also too weak by itself to explain the state's entitlement to enforce legal requirements.

[6]Wesley Newcomb Hohfeld, *Fundamental Legal Conceptions*, Walter Wheeler Cook, ed., (New Haven: Yale University Press, 1919). The term "liberty" could be used in place of the term "privilege." In the following paragraphs, I follow the account given by Judith Jarvis Thomson, *The Realm of Rights* (Cambridge: Harvard University Press, 1990), chapter 1.

[7]In place of the term, "pro tanto," one could use "prima facie."

[8]If a legitimate state would have the power to impose a duty on us to do something, it might seem that we would in some sense "owe" the duty to do that thing "to" the state after all. The duty would at least owe its existence to the state. I have no objection to this way of using the phrase "owed to." The traditional view was that the citizens of a legitimate state would "owe" an obligation "to" the state in a sense which entailed that the state would have a claim-right to obedience. It is not part of my view that a legitimate state would have a claim-right to obedience. Christopher Morris suggested understanding legitimacy in terms of a power possessed by the state. See Christopher W. Morris, *An Essay on the Modern State* (Cambridge: Cambridge University Press, 1998), chapter 4.

[9]Even in a legitimate state, controversy about whether a law has been properly enacted, or about whether a law is morally innocent, would ground controversy about whether there is a *pro tanto* duty to comply with its requirements.

[10]It does not follow that there could not be a single global state. What follows is that such a state, if it were legitimate, would have a privilege to control access to Earth on the part of any extraterrestrials.

[11]To say that a legitimate state would have an immunity—relative to other states and relative to individuals—against losing its right to rule is to say that no individual and no other state has the *moral* power to strip it of its right to rule. The drug smugglers destroyed Exemplar, but to destroy a state is not to exercise a *moral* power.

[12]John Rawls, *Political Liberalism* (New York: Columbia University Press, 1993), p. 137. For present purposes, I assume an intuitive notion of the reasonable person. I take the Rawlsian test of an arrangement to be whether any reasonable person *would* endorse it.

[13]David Hume, *A Treatise of Human Nature,* L. Selby-Bigge, ed. (Oxford: Clarendon Press, 1978 [1739–40]), p. 539.

[14]In what follows, I speak of states that are "just" when I mean to refer to states that are just (at least) in all respects other than being legitimate. Two paragraphs ahead, when I discuss "unjust" states, I mean to refer to states that exemplify injustices other than being illegitimate.

[15]See David Copp, *Morality, Normativity, and Society* (New York: Oxford University Press, 1995). In this summary, I ignore various complications and qualifications.

[16]I need to make two qualifications. (1) Some large societies are the sum of smaller societies, which are themselves organized into states. Such societies may not need to be organized into states. (2) It may be true that in certain periods of history there were forms of social organization that better served the needs of societies than states would have done. If so, my justification of the state in terms of societal needs is restricted to a certain range of historical circumstances.

[17]It might be more plausible to postulate a power to put citizens under a *pro tanto* duty by creating morally innocent law and threatening to *punish* violations of it, rather than merely to penalize violations of it. This amendment would respond to the objection I discussed before that it would be implausible to suppose I violate a moral duty when I exceed the speed limit by a trivial amount on a deserted highway.

[18]Michael O. Hardimon, "The Project of Reconciliation: Hegel's Social Philosophy," *Philosophy and Public Affairs,* 21 (1992), pp. 165–95.

Smith

[1]H. A. Prichard, "Green's Principles of Political Obligation," *Moral Obligation* 54 (1949).

[2]The distinction between prima facie and absolute obligation was first made by W. D. Ross in *The Right and the Good,* ch. 2 (1930). My account of prima facie obligation differs somewhat from Ross'; but I believe it adequately captures current philosophical usage. As for absolute obligation, I shall not often speak of it; but when I do, what I shall mean by "S has an absolute obligation to do X" is that "S's failure to do X is wrong."

[3]I must note that Hart does not use the phrase "prima facie obligation," maintaining that his argument establishes an obligation *sans phrase* to comply with the rules of cooperative enterprises. However, since his use of "obligation" seems much the same as my use of "prima facie obligation," I shall ignore his terminological scruples.

[4]Ross, *supra* note 2.

[5]J. Plamenatz, *Man and Society* 228, 238–39, 349–40 (1963).

[6]A. Gewirth, "Political Justice," in *Social Justice* 138 (R. Brandt, ed., 1962), 139, 135.

[7]Brandt, "Toward a Credible Utilitarianism," in *Morality and the Language of Conduct 107* (H. N. Castenada & G. Nakhnikian, eds., 1963). In the following I shall not be attacking a position Brandt holds, but only an argument that might be offered on the basis of his theory. According to Brandt's theory, there is an absolute obligation to perform an act if it "conforms with that learnable set of rules the recognition of which is morally binding—roughly at the time of the act—by everyone in the society of the agent, except for the retention by individuals of already formed and decided moral convictions, would maximize intrinsic value."

CHAPTER III

Liberty

The Limits of the State and State Paternalism

I know not what course others may take; but as for me, Give me liberty or give me death.
—Patrick Henry at the Second Virginia Convention, 1775.

[T]he only purpose for which power can be rightfully exercised over any member of a civilized community, against his will, is to prevent harm to others.

—John Stuart Mill, On Liberty

According to Mill (see Reading 10), Utilitarian moral theory requires that each rational adult in a civilized society be given maximum liberty to do whatever he or she wishes, so long as the person is not harming other people in a manner that violates their rights. The only justification for the State's interference in one's life is to protect others from unjustified harm. Some of your free acts may harm me in a way that does not infringe my rights. For instance, you and I both want to be president of Company C, which offers lucrative benefits. You win the position in fair competition (i.e., you were better qualified), thus ruining my self-esteem and sending me into a deep depression, which, in turn destroys my marriage; my divorce, in turn, creates such a dysfunctional family that my children become criminals, wreaking havoc over society. From a Utilitarian perspective it would have been better if I had gotten the job, for the negative consequences would not have been half as bad. Yet Mill has faith in meritocracy as a principle derivative from a Utilitarian theory. In the long run, hiring the best candidate for the position will have the best social consequences. We ought to adhere to a system of Utilitarian rights, including the right to hire the person best qualified for a position, even if, in the short run, hiring a mediocre candidate might have had better consequences.

But the principle of noninterference is dominant. If a man chooses to be drunk, the State should not punish him, but if he gets drunk while on police duty or mili-

tary watch, he should be severely punished, not because he got drunk, but because he is unable to fulfill his duty (Reading 10). Mill does not go as far as the anarchists, who would abolish government. Human beings need an overarching political authority to assist them in making the conditions of life better, but there are severe limits on the State's authority. A strong burden of proof always rests on the State or society at large to justify intervention into the lives of individuals.

But, although Mill holds that we ought not paternalistically to interfere in people's private lives, he does not hold to State neutrality regarding the morally good.

> [T]here is need of a great increase of disinterested exertion to promote the good of others. . . . Human beings owe to each other help to distinguish the better from the worse, and encouragement to choose the former and avoid the latter. They should be forever stimulating each other to increased exercise of their higher faculties, and increased direction of their feelings and aims towards wise instead of foolish, elevating instead of degrading, objects and contemplations. (Reading 10)

Mill roots his idea of human freedom in his theory of human nature as stating that human beings are progressive beings who need to be free to develop their highest potential. This potential requires a moral

177

community and personal moral development with deep virtuosity, but the period in which to inculcate character is childhood. We can remonstrate and argue with each other about moral improvement, but after childhood, the State should not intervene in protecting people from themselves, rather it should tolerate offensive behavior as well as personally destructive behavior. Mill believed that liberty required us to tolerate offensive behavior. Virtually everyone is offended by some behavior — some by homosexual conduct, others by men wearing earrings, others by public nudity, and some by different religious practices—but those eccentricities may be meaningful to the bearers, so if we want others to tolerate our eccentricities, we ought likewise to tolerate theirs.

You should read Mill's *On Liberty* (Reading 10) before you read the selections in this chapter, for Mill's essay forms the background for discussion on the nature and limits of liberty and legitimate State intervention. In Reading 16 Isaiah Berlin distinguishes between two kinds of liberty, *negative* and *positive*. *Negative liberty* is simply the absence of external coercion on a person. It is the freedom to do whatever we want, without being interfered with by others. This is the liberty that Mill was talking about. It is political liberty. *Positive liberty*, on the other hand, is the genuine freedom to become your real or rational self. It is what Rousseau meant by one's true self and Hegel by one's real self. Rousseau went so far as to endorse the society to "force people to become free" (see Reading 4). Berlin argues that it is a contradiction in terms to say that one can be "coerced to be free." We ought not call "positive liberty" liberty at all, but something else. "Liberty is liberty, not equality or fairness or justice or culture, or human happiness of a quiet conscience." We ought not to conflate or confuse these two types of liberty; political liberty must be confined to negative liberty. This idea is relevant to Reading 20, by James Sterba, who argues for a type of positive liberty. In Reading 21, Jan Narveson tries to rebut Sterba.

Mill's defense of liberty seems quite plausible when we read it. Certainly we want to be free and not enslaved (we identify with Patrick Henry's dictum quoted above), autonomous and not coerced. But consider Clement Atlee's criticism of the notion:

> The prime minister [Winston Churchill] made much play last night with the rights of the individual and the dangers of people being ordered about by officials. I entirely agree that people should have the greatest freedom compatible with the freedom of others. There was a time when employers were free

to work little children for sixteen hours a day. I remember when employers were free to employ sweated women workers on finishing trousers at a penny halfpenny a pair. There was a time when people were free to neglect sanitation so that thousands died of preventable diseases. For years every attempt to remedy these crying evils was blocked by the same plea of freedom for the individual. It was in fact freedom for the rich and slavery for the poor. Make no mistake, it has only been through the power of the State, given to it by Parliament, that the general public has been protected against the greed of ruthless profit-makers and property owners.[1]

Atlee, leader of the Labor party during the British General Election campaign of 1945 arguing that State intervention, *paternalism*, is sometimes justified in order to prevent exploitation of the poor and powerless. Such considerations motivate Reading 18, by Gerald Dworkin, and Reading 20 by James Sterba.

Reading 17, by Joel Feinberg, on the grounds for state coercion, may be read as an insightful commentary of Mill's theory, arguing for a presumption of liberty and relating it to the harm principle, as well as analyzing other criticisms of Mill's position.

In Reading 18 Gerald Dworkin argues that even by Mill's own premises paternalism, intervention by others for one's own good, may be justified. He cites Odysseus, who in the Odyssey asks his sailors to bind him to the mast lest he be tempted to be influenced by the melodious singing of the Sirens and drive his ship into the rocks. Sometimes adults need to be protected from their own behavior, and we rationally would consent to some paternalistic interventions. Furthermore, sometimes the State is justified in limiting the liberty of the powerful to prevent exploitation of the vulnerable.

In Reading 19, the Czech economist-philosopher F. A. Hayek contrasts liberty, equality, and merit and argues that liberty (of a free market) ought to be the sole mechanism for the distribution of wealth. People are not equal in any significant way, and to force a situation of equal results is tyrannical. Distribution according to merit may seem more reasonable, but first of all most of the talents one has are not merited, but given, and second, no human is wise enough to decide just what each of us morally deserves. Liberty to compete and thus have the chance to succeed in a market economy is the only mechanism worthy of a humane society, one that would be free from the despotism of social engineers. Hayek's position is developed by Robert Nozick (Reading 25).

Traditionally, Mill's near absolute position on liberty (called *libertarianism*) has been viewed as the opposite of welfarism, the thesis that the State is required to assist the worst off who are below the poverty line, but in Reading 20 James Sterba argues that even on a libertarian's own premises we can argue for a welfare state. In Reading 21, Jan Narveson disagrees with Sterba's argument.

In Reading 22, Stanley Fish argues that our notion of free speech, including that specified in the First Amendment to the U.S. Constitution, does not exist but is "just a name we give to verbal behavior that serves the substantive agendas we wish to advance." When speech departs from our social agenda, as hate speech and racist speech do, we ought to prohibit it and punish it. In other words, we give the title *free speech* to speech that fits the reigning political ideology. He cites contemporary Canadian law, especially the case of *R. v. Keegstra*, in which a teacher, James Keegstra, denigrated Jews and was convicted of a criminal offense, as a decision more accurate than much American liberal and conservative thinking about speech.

Reading 23, by Russell Roberts, is a criticism of government-sponsored programs that, he argues, give us the illusion of giving us something for nothing, when they are really making most of us worse off by depriving us of freedom in terms of taxation.

READING 16

Two Concepts of Liberty

Isaiah Berlin

Isaiah Berlin (1909–97) was a fellow at All Souls College Oxford University and later became the president of Wolfson College. He was the president of the British Academy from 1974 to 1978 and the author of many works in political philosophy, including *Four Essays on Liberty*, from which this essay is taken. In this essay Berlin distinguishes between *negative*, or political *liberty* (the absence of external coercion on a person) and *positive liberty* (the ability to be one's own master). However valuable *positive liberty* is, it should not be confused with political liberty, as within the concern of the State.

This reading is excerpted from *Four Essays on Liberty* (Oxford University Press, 1969), by permission.

I.

To coerce a man is to deprive him of freedom—freedom from what? Almost every moralist in human history has praised freedom. Like happiness and goodness, like nature and reality, the meaning of this term is so porous that there is little interpretation that it seems able to resist. I do not propose to discuss either the history or the more than two hundred senses of this protean word recorded by historians of ideas. I propose to examine no more than two of these senses—but those central ones, with a great deal of human history behind them, and, I dare say, still to come. The first of these political senses of freedom or liberty (I shall use both words to mean the same), which (following much precedent) I shall call the "negative" sense, is involved in the answer to the question "What is the area within which the subject—a person or group of persons—is or should be left to do or be what he is able to do or be, without interference by other persons?" The second, which I shall call the positive sense, is involved in the answer to the question "What, or who, is the source of control or interference that can determine someone to do, or be, this rather than that?" The two questions are clearly different, even though the answers to them may overlap.

THE NOTION OF "NEGATIVE" FREEDOM

I am normally said to be free to the degree to which no man or body of men interferes with my activity. Political liberty in this sense is simply the area within which a man can act unobstructed by others. If I am prevented by others from doing what I could otherwise do, I am to that degree unfree; and if this area is contracted by other men beyond a certain minimum, I can be described as being coerced, or, it may be, enslaved. Coercion is not, however, a term that covers every form of inability. If I say that I am unable to jump more than ten feet in the air, or cannot read because I am blind, or cannot understand the darker pages of Hegel, it would be eccentric to say that I am to that degree enslaved or coerced. Coercion implies the deliberate interference of other human beings within the area in which I could otherwise act. You lack political liberty or freedom only if you are prevented from attaining a goal by human beings. Mere incapacity to attain a goal is not lack of political freedom. This is brought out by the use of such modern expressions as "economic freedom" and its counterpart, "economic slavery." It is argued, very plausibly, that if a man is too poor to afford something on which there is no legal ban—a loaf of bread, a journey round the world, recourse to the law courts—he is as little free to have it as he would be if it were forbidden him by law. If my poverty were a kind of disease, which prevented me from buying bread, or paying for the journey round the world or getting my case heard, as lameness prevents me from running, this inability would not naturally be described as a lack of freedom, least of all political freedom. It is only because I believe that my inability to get a given thing is due to the fact that other human beings have made arrangements whereby I am, whereas others are not, prevented from having enough money with which to pay for it, that I think myself a victim of coercion or slavery. In other words, this use of the term depends on a particular social and economic theory about the causes of my poverty or weakness. If my lack of material means is due to my lack of mental or physical capacity, then I begin to speak of being deprived of freedom (and not simply about poverty) only if I accept the theory. If, in addition, I believe that I am being kept in want by a specific arrangement which I consider unjust or unfair, I speak of economic slavery or oppression. "The nature of things does not madden us, only ill will does," said Rousseau. The criterion of oppression is the part that I believe to be played by other human beings, directly or indirectly, with or without the intention of doing so, in frustrating my wishes. By being free in this sense I mean not being interfered with by others. The wider the area of non-interference the wider my freedom.

This is what the classical English political philosophers meant when they used this word. They disagreed about how wide the area could or should be. They supposed that it could not, as things were, be unlimited, because if it were, it would entail a state in which all men could boundlessly interfere with all other men; and this kind of "natural" freedom would lead to social chaos in which men's minimum needs would not be satisfied; or else the liberties of the weak would be suppressed by the strong. Because they perceived that human purposes and activities do not automatically harmonize with one another, and because (whatever their official doctrines) they put high value on other goals, such as justice, or happiness, or culture, or security, or varying degrees of equality, they were prepared to curtail freedom in the interests of other values and, indeed, of freedom itself. For, without this, it was impossible to create the kind of association that they thought desirable. Consequently, it is assumed by these thinkers that the area of men's free action must be limited by law. But equally it is assumed, especially by such libertarians as Locke and Mill in England, and Constant and Tocqueville in France, that there ought to exist a certain minimum area of personal freedom which must on no account be violated; for if it is overstepped, the individual will find himself in an area too narrow for even that minimum development of his natural faculties which alone makes it possible to pursue, and even to conceive, the various ends which men hold good or right or sacred. It follows that a frontier must be drawn between the area of private life and that of public authority. Where it is to be drawn is a matter of argument, indeed of haggling. Men are largely interdependent, and no man's activity is so completely private as never to obstruct the lives of others in any way. "Freedom for the pike is death for the minnows;" the liberty of some must depend on the restraint of others. "Freedom for an Oxford don," others have been known to add, "is a very different thing from freedom for an Egyptian peasant."

This proposition derives its force from something that is both true and important, but the phrase itself remains a piece of political claptrap. It is true that to offer political rights, or safeguards against intervention by the state, to men who are half-naked, illiterate, underfed, and diseased is to mock their condition; they need medical help or education before they can understand, or make use of, an increase in their freedom. What is freedom to those who cannot make use of it? Without adequate conditions for the use of freedom, what is the value of freedom? First things come first: there are situations, as a nineteenth-century Russian radical writer declared, in which boots are superior to the works of Shakespeare; individual freedom is not everyone's primary need. For freedom is not the mere absence of frustration of whatever kind; this would inflate the meaning of the word until it meant too much or too little. The Egyptian peasant needs clothes or medicine before, and more than, personal liberty, but the minimum freedom that he needs today, and the greater degree of freedom that he may need tomorrow, is not some species of freedom peculiar to him, but identical with that of professors, artists, and millionaires.

What troubles the consciences of Western liberals

is not, I think, the belief that the freedom that men seek differs according to their social or economic conditions, but that the minority who possess it have gained it by exploiting, or, at least, averting their gaze from, the vast majority who do not. They believe, with good reason, that if individual liberty is an ultimate end for human beings, none should be deprived of it by others; least of all that some should enjoy it at the expense of others. Equality of liberty; not to treat others as I should not wish them to treat me; repayment of my debt to those who alone have made possible my liberty or prosperity or enlightenment; justice, in its simplest and most universal sense—these are the foundations of liberal morality. Liberty is not the only goal of men. I can, like the Russian critic Belinsky, say that if others are to be deprived of it—if my brothers are to remain in poverty, squalor, and chains—then I do not want it for myself, I reject it with both hands and infinitely prefer to share their fate. But nothing is gained by a confusion of terms. To avoid glaring inequality or widespread misery I am ready to sacrifice some, or all, of my freedom: I may do so willingly and freely: but it is freedom that I am giving up for the sake of justice or equality or the love of my fellow men. I should be guilt-stricken, and rightly so, if I were not, in some circumstances, ready to make this sacrifice. But a sacrifice is not an increase in what is being sacrificed, namely freedom, however great the moral need or the compensation for it. Everything is what it is: liberty is liberty, not equality or fairness or justice or culture, or human happiness or a quiet conscience. If the liberty of myself or my class or nation depends on the misery of a number of other human beings, the system which promotes this is unjust and immoral. But if I curtail or lose my freedom, in order to lessen the shame of such inequality, and do not thereby materially increase the individual liberty of others, an absolute loss of liberty occurs. This may be compensated for by a gain in justice or in happiness or in peace, but the loss remains, and it is a confusion of values to say that although my "liberal," individual freedom may go by the board, some other kind of freedom—"social" or "economic"—is increased. Yet it remains true that the freedom of some must at times be curtailed to secure the freedom of others. Upon what principle should this be done? If freedom is a sacred, untouchable value, there can be no such principle. One or other of these conflicting rules or principles must, at any rate in practice, yield: not always for reasons which can be clearly stated, let alone generalized into rules or universal maxims. Still, a practical compromise has to be found.

Philosophers with an optimistic view of human nature and a belief in the possibility of harmonizing human interests, such as Locke or Adam Smith and, in some moods, Mill, believe that social harmony and progress were compatible with reserving a large area for private life over which neither the state nor any other authority must be allowed to trespass. Hobbes, and those who agreed with him, especially conservative or reactionary thinkers, argued that if men were to be prevented from destroying one another and making social life a jungle or a wilderness, greater safeguards must be instituted to keep them in their places; he wished correspondingly to increase the area of centralized control and decrease that of the individual. But both sides agreed that some portion of human existence must remain independent of the sphere of social control. To invade that preserve, however small, would be despotism. The most eloquent of all defenders of freedom and privacy, Benjamin Constant, who had not forgotten the Jacobin dictatorship, declared that at the very least the liberty of religion, opinion, expression, property, must be guaranteed against arbitrary invasion. Jefferson, Burke, Paine, Mill, compiled different catalogues of individual liberties, but the argument for keeping authority at bay is always substantially the same. We must preserve a minimum area of personal freedom if we are not to "degrade or deny our nature." We cannot remain absolutely free, and must give up some of our liberty to preserve the rest. But total self-surrender is self-defeating. What then must the minimum be? That which a man cannot give up without offending against the essence of his human nature. What is this essence? What are the standards which it entails? This has been, and perhaps always will be, a matter of infinite debate. But whatever the principle in terms of which the area of non-interference is to be drawn, whether it is that of natural law or natural rights, or of utility or the pronouncements of a categorical imperative, or the sanctity of the social contract, or any other concept with which men have sought to clarify and justify their convictions, liberty in this sense means liberty *from;* absence of interference beyond the shifting, but always recognizable, frontier. "The only freedom which deserves the name is that of pursuing our own good in our own way," said the most celebrated of its champions. If this is so, is compulsion ever justified? Mill had no doubt that it was. Since justice demands that all individuals be entitled to a minimum of freedom, all other individuals were of necessity to be restrained, if need be by force, from depriving anyone of it. Indeed, the whole function of law was the prevention of just such collisions: the state was reduced to what Lassalle contemptuously described as the functions of a night-watchman or traffic policeman.

What made the protection of individual liberty so sacred to Mill? In his famous essay he declares that, unless men are left to live as they wish "in the path which merely concerns themselves," civilization cannot advance; the truth will not, for lack of a free market in ideas, come to light; there will be no scope for spontaneity, originality, genius, for mental energy, for moral courage. Society will be crushed by the weight of "collective mediocrity." Whatever is rich and diversified will be crushed by the weight of custom, by men's constant tendency to conformity, which breeds only "withered capacities," "pinched and hidebound," "cramped and warped" human beings. "Pagan self-assertion is as worthy as Christian self-denial." "All the errors which a man is likely to commit against advice and warning are far outweighed by the evil of allowing others to constrain him to what they deem is good." The defence of liberty consists in the "negative" goal of warding off interference. To threaten a man with persecution unless he submits to a life in which he exercises no choices of his goals; to block before him every door but one, no matter how noble the prospect upon which it opens, or how benevolent the motives of those who arrange this, is to sin against the truth that he is a man, a being with a life of his own to live. This is liberty as it has been conceived by liberals in the modern world from the days of Erasmus (some would say of Occam) to our own. Every plea for civil liberties and individual rights, every protest against exploitation and humiliation, against the encroachment of public authority, or the mass hypnosis of custom or organized propaganda, springs from this individualistic, and much disputed, conception of man.

Three facts about this position may be noted. In the first place Mill confuses two distinct notions. One is that all coercion is, insofar as it frustrates human desires, bad as such, although it may have to be applied to prevent other, greater evils; while non-interference, which is the opposite of coercion, is good as such, although it is not the only good. This is the "negative" conception of liberty in its classical form. The other is that men should seek to discover the truth, or to develop a certain type of character of which Mill approved—critical, original, imaginative, independent, non-conforming to the point of eccentricity, and so on—and that truth can be found, and such character can be bred, only in conditions of freedom. Both these

are liberal views, but they are not identical, and the connexion between them is, at best, empirical. No one would argue that truth or freedom of self-expression could flourish where dogma crushes all thought. But the evidence of history tends to show (as, indeed, was argued by James Stephen in his formidable attack on Mill in his *Liberty, Equality, Fraternity*) that integrity, love of truth, and fiery individualism grow at least as often in severely disciplined communities among, for example, the puritan Calvinists of Scotland or New England, or under military discipline, as in more tolerant or indifferent societies; and if this is so, Mill's argument for liberty as a necessary condition for the growth of human genius falls to the ground. If his two goals proved incompatible, Mill would be faced with a cruel dilemma, quite apart from the further difficulties created by the inconsistency of his doctrines with strict utilitarianism, even in his own humane version of it.

In the second place, the doctrine is comparatively modern. There seems to be scarcely any discussion of individual liberty as a conscious political ideal (as opposed to its actual existence) in the ancient world. Condorcet had already remarked that the notion of individual rights was absent from the legal conceptions of the Romans and Greeks; this seems to hold equally of the Jewish, Chinese, and all other ancient civilizations that have since come to light. The domination of this ideal has been the exception rather than the rule, even in the recent history of the West. Nor has liberty in this sense often formed a rallying cry for the great masses of mankind. The desire not to be impinged upon, to be left to oneself, has been a mark of high civilization both on the part of individuals and communities. The sense of privacy itself, of the area of personal relationships as something sacred in its own right, derives from a conception of freedom which, for all its religious roots, is scarcely older, in its developed state, than the Renaissance or the Reformation. Yet its decline would mark the death of a civilization, of an entire moral outlook.

The third characteristic of this notion of liberty is of greater importance. It is that liberty in this sense is not incompatible with some kinds of autocracy, or at any rate with the absence of self-government. Liberty in this sense is principally concerned with the area of control, not with its source. Just as a democracy may, in fact, deprive the individual citizen of a great many liberties which he might have in some other form of society, so it is perfectly conceivable that a liberal-minded despot would allow his subjects a large measure of personal freedom. The despot who leaves his subjects a wide area of liberty may be unjust, or encourage the wildest inequalities, care little for order, or virtue, or knowledge; but provided he does not curb their liberty, or at least curbs it less than many other régimes, he meets with Mill's specification. Freedom in this sense is not, at any rate logically, connected with democracy or self-government. Self-government may, on the whole, provide a better guarantee of the preservation of civil liberties than other régimes, and has been defended as such by libertarians. But there is no necessary connexion between individual liberty and democratic rule. The answer to the question "Who governs me?" is logically distinct from the question "How far does government interfere with me?" It is in this difference that the great contrast between the two concepts of negative and positive liberty, in the end, consists. For the "positive" sense of liberty comes to light if we try to answer the question, not "What am I free to do or be?" but "By whom am I ruled?" or "Who is to say what I am, and what I am not, to be or do?" The connexion between democracy and individual liberty is a good deal more tenuous than it seemed to many advocates of both. The desire to be governed by myself, or at any rate to participate in the process by which my life is to be controlled, may be as deep a wish as that of a free area for action, and perhaps historically older. But it is not a desire for the same thing. So different is it, indeed, as to have led in the end to the great clash of ideologies that dominates our world. For it is this—the "positive" conception of liberty: not freedom from, but freedom to—to lead one prescribed form of life—which the adherents of the "negative" notion represent as being, at times, no better than a specious disguise for brutal tyranny.

II. THE NOTION OF "POSITIVE" FREEDOM

The "positive" sense of the word "liberty" derives from the wish on the part of the individual to be his own master. I wish my life and decisions to depend on myself, not on external forces of whatever kind. I wish to be the instrument of my own, not of other men's, acts of will. I wish to be a subject, not an object; to be moved by reasons, by conscious purposes, which are my own, not by causes which affect me, as it were, from outside. I wish to be somebody, not nobody; a doer—deciding, not being decided for, self-directed and not acted upon by external nature or by other men as if I were a thing, or an animal, or a slave incapable

of playing a human role, that is, of conceiving goals and policies of my own and realizing them. This is at least part of what I mean when I say that I am rational, and that it is my reason that distinguishes me as a human being from the rest of the world. I wish, above all, to be conscious of myself as a thinking, willing, active being, bearing responsibility for my choices and able to explain them by references to my own ideas and purposes. I feel free to the degree that I believe this to be true, and enslaved to the degree that I am made to realize that it is not.

The freedom which consists in being one's own master, and the freedom which consists in not being prevented from choosing as I do by other men, may, on the face of it, seem concepts at no great logical distance from each other—no more than negative and positive ways of saying much the same thing. Yet the "positive" and "negative" notions of freedom historically developed in divergent directions not always by logically reputable steps, until, in the end, they came into direct conflict with each other.

One way of making this clear is in terms of the independent momentum which the, initially perhaps quite harmless, metaphor of self-mastery acquired. "I am my own master;" "I am slave to no man;" but may I not (as Platonists or Hegelians tend to say) be a slave to nature? Or to my own "unbridled" passions? Are these not so many species of the identical genus "slave"—some political or legal, others moral or spiritual? Have not men had the experience of liberating themselves from spiritual slavery, or slavery to nature, and do they not in the course of it become aware, on the one hand, of a self which dominates, and, on the other, of something in them which is brought to heel? This dominant self is then variously identified with reason, with my "higher nature," with the self which calculates and aims at what will satisfy it in the long run, with my "real"; or "ideal," or "autonomous" self, or with my self "at its best;" which is then contrasted with irrational impulse, uncontrolled desires, my "lower" nature, the pursuit of immediate pleasures, my "empirical" or "heteronomous" self, swept by every gust of desire and passion, needing to be rigidly disciplined if it is ever to rise to the full height of its "real" nature. Presently the two selves may be represented as divided by an even larger gap: the real self may be conceived as something wider than the individual (as the term is normally understood), as a social "whole" of which the individual is an element or aspect: a tribe, a race, a church, a state, the great society of the living and the dead and the yet unborn. This entity is then identified as being the "true" self which, by imposing its collective, or "organic," single will upon its recalcitrant "members," achieves its own, and therefore their, "higher" freedom. The perils of using organic metaphors to justify the coercion of some men by others in order to raise them to a "higher" level of freedom have often been pointed out. But what gives such plausibility as it has to this kind of language is that we recognize that it is possible, and at times justifiable, to coerce men in the name of some goal (let us say, justice or public health) which they would, if they were more enlightened, themselves pursue, but do not, because they are blind or ignorant or corrupt. This renders it easy for me to conceive of myself as coercing others for their own sake, in their, not my, interest. I am then claiming that I know what they truly need better than they know it themselves. What, at most, this entails is that they would not resist me if they were rational and as wise as I and understood their interests as I do. But I may go on to claim a good deal more than this. I may declare that they are actually aiming at what in their benighted state they consciously resist, because there exists within them an occult entity—their latent rational will, or their "true" purpose—and that this entity, although it is belied by all that they overtly feel and do and say, is their "real" self, of which the poor empirical self in space and time may know nothing or little; and that this inner spirit is the only self that deserves to have its wishes taken into account. Once I take this view, I am in a position to ignore the actual wishes of men or societies, to bully, oppress, torture them in the name, and on behalf, of their "real" selves, in the secure knowledge that whatever is the true goal of man (happiness, performance of duty, wisdom, a just society, self-fulfilment) must be identical with his freedom—the free choice of his "true," albeit often submerged and inarticulate, self.

This paradox has been often exposed. It is one thing to say that I know what is good for X, while he himself does not; and even to ignore his wishes for its—and his—sake; and a very different one to say that he has *eo ipso* chosen it, not indeed consciously, not as he seems in everyday life, but in his role as a rational self which his empirical self may not know— the "real" self which discerns the good, and cannot help choosing it once it is revealed. This monstrous impersonation, which consists in equating what X would choose if he were something he is not, or at least not yet, with what X actually seeks and chooses, is at the heart of all political theories of self-realization. It is one thing to say that I may be coerced for my own good which I am too blind to see: this may, on occasion, be for my benefit; indeed it may enlarge the scope of my liberty. It is another to say that if it is my good, then I am not being coerced, for I have willed it, whether I know this or not, and am free (or "truly" free) even while my poor earthly body and foolish mind bitterly reject it, and struggle against those who seek however benevolently to impose it, with the greatest desperation.

This magical transformation, or sleight of hand (for which William James so justly mocked the Hegelians), can no doubt be perpetrated just as easily with the "negative" concept of freedom, where the self that should not be interfered with is no longer the individual with his actual wishes and needs as they are normally conceived, but the "real" man within, identified with the pursuit of some ideal purpose not dreamed of by his empirical self. And, as in the case of the "positively" free self, this entity may be inflated into some super-personal entity—a state, a class, a nation, or the march of history itself, regarded as a more "real" subject of attributes than the empirical self. But the "positive" conception of freedom as self-mastery, with its suggestion of a man divided against himself, has, in fact, and as a matter of history, of doctrine and of practice, lent itself more easily to this splitting of personality into two: the transcendent, dominant controller, and the empirical bundle of desires and passions to be disciplined and brought to heel. It is this historical fact that has been influential. This demonstrates (if demonstration of so obvious a truth is needed) that conceptions of freedom directly derive from views of what constitutes a self, a person, a man. Enough manipulation with the definition of man, and freedom can be made to mean whatever the manipulator wishes. Recent history has made it only too clear that the issue is not merely academic.

The consequences of distinguishing between two selves will become even clearer if one considers the two major forms which the desire to be self-directed— directed by one's "true" self—has historically taken: the first, that of self-abnegation in order to attain independence; the second, that of self-realization, or total self-identification with a specific principle or ideal in order to attain the selfsame end.

III. THE RETREAT TO THE INNER CITADEL

I am the possessor of reason and will; I conceive ends and I desire to pursue them; but if I am prevented from attaining them I no longer feel master of the situation.

I may be prevented by the laws of nature, or by accidents, or the activities of men, or the effect, often undesigned, of human institutions. These forces may be too much for me. What am I to do to avoid being crushed by them? I must liberate myself from desires that I know I cannot realize. I wish to be master of my kingdom, but my frontiers are long and insecure, therefore I contract them in order to reduce or eliminate the vulnerable area. I begin by desiring happiness, or power, or knowledge, or the attainment of some specific object. But I cannot command them. I choose to avoid defeat and waste, and therefore decide to strive for nothing that I cannot be sure to obtain. I determine myself not to desire what is unattainable. The tyrant threatens me with the destruction of my property, with imprisonment, with the exile or death of those I love. But if I no longer feel attached to property, no longer care whether or not I am in prison, if I have killed within myself my natural affections, then he cannot bend me to his will, for all that is left of myself is no longer subject to empirical fears or desires. It is as if I had performed a strategic retreat into an inner citadel—my reason, my soul, my "noumenal" self—which, do what they may, neither external blind force, nor human malice, can touch. I have withdrawn into myself; there, and there alone, I am secure. It is as if I were to say: "I have a wound in my leg. There are two methods of freeing myself from pain. One is to heal the wound. But if the cure is too difficult or uncertain, there is another method. I can get rid of the wound by cutting off my leg. If I train myself to want nothing to which the possession of my leg is indispensable, I shall not feel the lack of it." This is the traditional self-emancipation of ascetics and quietists, of stoics or Buddhist sages, men of various religions or of none, who have fled the world, and escaped the yoke of society or public opinion, by some process of deliberate self-transformation that enables them to care no longer for any of its values, to remain, isolated and independent, on its edges, no longer vulnerable to its weapons. All political isolationism, all economic autarky, every form of autonomy, has in it some element of this attitude. I eliminate the obstacles in my path by abandoning the path; I retreat into my own sect, my own planned economy, my own deliberately insulated territory, where no voices from outside need be listened to, and no external forces can have effect. This is a form of the search for security; but it has also been called the search for personal or national freedom or independence. . . .

It is perhaps worth remarking that in its individualistic form the concept of the rational sage who has escaped into the inner fortress of his true self seems to arise when the external world has proved exceptionally arid, cruel, or unjust. "He is truly free," said Rousseau, "who desires what he can perform, and does what he desires." In a world where a man seeking happiness or justice or freedom (in whatever sense) can do little, because he finds too many avenues of action blocked to him, the temptation to withdraw into himself may become irresistible. It may have been so in Greece, where the Stoic ideal cannot be wholly unconnected with the fall of the independent democracies before centralized Macedonian autocracy. It was so in Rome, for analogous reasons, after the end of the Republic. It arose in Germany in the seventeenth century, during the period of the deepest national degradation of the German states that followed the Thirty Years' War, when the character of public life, particularly in the small principalities, forced those who prized the dignity of human life, not for the first or last time, into a kind of inner emigration. The doctrine that maintains that what I cannot have I must teach myself not to desire; that a desire eliminated, or successfully resisted, is as good as a desire satisfied, is a sublime, but, it seems to me, unmistakable, form of the doctrine of sour grapes: what I cannot be sure of, I cannot truly want.

This makes it clear why the definition of negative liberty as the ability to do what one wishes—which is, in effect, the definition adopted by Mill—will not do. If I find that I am able to do little or nothing of what I wish, I need only contract or extinguish my wishes, and I am made free. If the tyrant (or "hidden persuader") manages to condition his subjects (or customers) into losing their original wishes and embrace ("internalize") the form of life he has invented for them, he will, on this definition, have succeeded in liberating them. He will, no doubt, have made them *feel* free—as Epictetus feels freer than his master (and the proverbial good man is said to feel happy on the rack). But what he has created is the very antithesis of political freedom.

Ascetic self-denial may be a source of integrity or serenity and spiritual strength, but it is difficult to see how it can be called an enlargement of liberty. If I save myself from an adversary by retreating indoors and locking every entrance and exit, I may remain freer than if I had been captured by him, but am I freer than if I had defeated or captured him? If I go too far, contract myself into too small a space, I shall suffocate and die. The logical culmination of the process of destroying everything through which I can possibly be wounded is suicide. While I exist in the natural world,

I can never be wholly secure. Total liberation in this sense (as Schopenhauer correctly perceived) is conferred only by death. . . .

IV. SELF-REALIZATION

. . . Marx and his disciples maintained that the path of human beings was obstructed not only by natural forces, or the imperfections of their own character, but, even more, by the workings of their own social institutions, which they had originally created (not always consciously) for certain purposes, but whose functioning they systematically came to misconceive, and which thereupon became obstacles in their creators' progress. He offered social and economic hypotheses to account for the inevitability of such misunderstanding, in particular of the illusion that such man-made arrangements were independent forces, as inescapable as the laws of nature. As instances of such pseudo-objective forces, he pointed to the laws of supply and demand, or of the institution of property, or of the eternal division of society into rich and poor, or owners and workers, as so many unaltering human categories. Not until we had reached a stage at which the spells of these illusions could be broken, that is, until enough men reached a social stage that alone enabled them to understand that these laws and institutions were themselves the work of human minds and hands, historically needed in their day, and later mistaken for inexorable, objective powers, could the old world be destroyed, and more adequate and liberating social machinery substituted.

We are enslaved by despots—institutions or beliefs or neuroses—which can be removed only by being analysed and understood. We are imprisoned by evil spirits which we have ourselves—albeit not consciously—created, and can exorcize them only by becoming conscious and acting appropriately: indeed, for Marx understanding *is* appropriate action. I am free if, and only if, I plan my life in accordance with my own will; plans entail rules; a rule does not oppress me or enslave me if I impose it on myself consciously, or accept it freely, having understood it, whether it was invented by me or by others, provided that it is rational, that is to say, conforms to the necessities of things. To understand why things must be as they must be is to will them to be so. Knowledge liberates not by offering us more open possibilities amongst which we can make our choice, but by preserving us from the frustration of attempting the impossible. To want necessary laws to be other than they are is to be prey to an irrational desire—a desire that what must be X should also be not X. To go further, and believe these laws to be other than what they necessarily are, is to be insane. That is the metaphysical heart of rationalism. The notion of liberty contained in it is not the "negative" conception of a field (ideally) without obstacles, a vacuum in which nothing obstructs me, but the notion of self-direction or self-control. I can do what I will with my own. I am a rational being; whatever I can demonstrate to myself as being necessary, as incapable of being otherwise in a rational society—that is, in a society directed by rational minds, towards goals such as a rational being would have—I cannot, being rational, wish to sweep out of my way. I assimilate it into my substance as I do the laws of logic, of mathematics, of physics, the rules of art, the principles that govern everything of which I understand, and therefore will, the rational purpose, by which I can never be thwarted, since I cannot want it to be other than it is.

This is the positive doctrine of liberation by reason. Socialized forms of it, widely disparate and opposed to each other as they are, are at the heart of many of the nationalist, communist, authoritarian, and totalitarian creeds of our day. It may, in the course of its evolution, have wandered far from its rationalist moorings. Nevertheless, it is this freedom that, in democracies and in dictatorships, is argued about, and fought for, in many parts of the earth today. Without attempting to trace the historical evolution of this idea, I should like to comment on some of its vicissitudes.

V. THE TEMPLE OF SARASTRO

Those who believed in freedom as rational self-direction were bound, sooner or later, to consider how this was to be applied not merely to a man's inner life, but to his relations with other members of his society. Even the most individualistic among them—and Rousseau, Kant, and Fichte certainly began as individualists—came at some point to ask themselves whether a rational life not only for the individual, but also for society, was possible, and if so, how it was to be achieved. I wish to be free to live as my rational will (my "real self") commands, but so must others be. How am I to avoid collisions with their wills? Where is the frontier that lies between my (rationally determined) rights and the identical rights of others? For if I am rational, I cannot deny that what is right for me must, for the same reasons, be right for others who are rational like me. A rational (or free) state would be a state governed by such laws as all rational men would freely accept; that is to say, such laws as they would themselves have enacted had they been asked what, as rational beings, they demanded; hence the frontiers would be such as all rational men would consider to be the right frontiers for rational beings. But who, in fact, was to determine what these frontiers were? Thinkers of this type argued that if moral and political problems were genuine—as surely they were—they must in principle be soluble; that is to say, there must exist one and only one true solution to any problem. All truths could in principle be discovered by any rational thinker, and demonstrated so clearly that all other rational men could not but accept them; indeed, this was already to a large extent the case in the new natural sciences. On this assumption, the problem of political liberty was soluble by establishing a just order that would give to each man all the freedom to which a rational being was entitled. My claim to unfettered freedom can prima facie at times not be reconciled with your equally unqualified claim; but the rational solution of one problem cannot collide with the equally true solution of another, for two truths cannot logically be incompatible; therefore a just order must in principle be discoverable—an order of which the rules make possible correct solutions to all possible problems that could arise in it. This ideal, harmonious state of affairs was sometimes imagined as a Garden of Eden before the Fall of Man, from which we were expelled, but for which we were still filled with longing; or as a golden age still before us, in which men, having become rational, will no longer be "other-directed," nor "alienate" or frustrate one another. In existing societies justice and equality are ideals which still call for some measure of coercion, because the premature lifting of social controls might lead to the oppression of the weaker and the stupider by the stronger or abler or more energetic and unscrupulous. But it is only irrationality on the part of men (according to this doctrine) that leads them to wish to oppress or exploit or humiliate one another. Rational men will respect the principle of reason in each other, and lack all desire to fight or dominate one another. The desire to dominate is itself a symptom of irrationality, and can be explained and cured by rational methods. Spinoza offers one kind of explanation and remedy, Hegel another, Marx a third. Some of these theories may perhaps, to some degree, supplement each other, others are not combinable. But

they all assume that in a society of perfectly rational beings the lust for domination over men will be absent or ineffective. The existence of, or craving for, oppression will be the first symptom that the true solution to the problems of social life has not been reached.

This can be put in another way. Freedom is self-mastery, the elimination of obstacles to my will, whatever these obstacles may be—the resistance of nature, of my ungoverned passions, of irrational institutions, of the opposing wills or behaviour of others. Nature I can, at least in principle, always mould by technical means, and shape to my will. But how am I to treat recalcitrant human beings? I must, if I can, impose my will on them too, "mould" them to my pattern, cast parts for them in my play. But will this not mean that I alone am free, while they are slaves? They will be so if my plan has nothing to do with their wishes or values, only with my own. But if my plan is fully rational, it will allow for the full development of their "true" natures, the realization of their capacities for rational decisions "for making the best of themselves"— as a part of the realization of my own "true" self. All true solutions to all genuine problems must be compatible: more than this, they must fit into a single whole: for this is what is meant by calling them all rational and the universe harmonious. Each man has his specific character, abilities, aspirations, ends. If I grasp both what these ends and natures are, and how they all relate to one another, I can, at least in principle, if I have the knowledge and the strength, satisfy them all, so long as the nature and the purposes in question are rational. Rationality is knowing things and people for what they are: I must not use stones to make violins, nor try to make born violin players play flutes. If the universe is governed by reason, then there will be no need for coercion; a correctly planned life for all will coincide with full freedom—the freedom of rational self-direction—for all. This will be so if, and only if, the plan is the true plan—the one unique pattern which alone fulfils the claims of reason. Its laws will be the rules which reason prescribes: they will only seem irksome to those whose reason is dormant, who do not understand the true "needs" of their own "real" selves. So long as each player recognizes and plays the part set him by reason—the faculty that understands his true nature and discerns his true ends—there can be no conflict. Each man will be a liberated, self-directed actor in the cosmic drama. Thus Spinoza tells us that "children, although they are coerced, are not slaves," because "they obey orders given in their own interests," and that "The subject of a true commonwealth is no slave, because the common interests must include his own." Similarly, Locke says "Where there is no law there is no freedom," because rational laws are directions to a man's "proper interests" or "general good"; and adds that since such laws are what "hedges us from bogs and precipices" they "ill deserve the name of confinement," and speaks of desires to escape from such laws as being irrational, forms of "licence," as "brutish," and so on. Montesquieu, forgetting his liberal moments, speaks of political liberty as being not permission to do what we want, or even what the law allows, but only "the power of doing what we ought to will," which Kant virtually repeats. Burke proclaims the individual's "right" to be restrained in his own interest, because "the presumed consent of every rational creature is in unison with the predisposed order of things." The common assumption of these thinkers (and of many a schoolman before them and Jacobin and Communist after them) is that the rational ends of our "true" natures must coincide, or be made to coincide, however violently our poor, ignorant, desire-ridden, passionate, empirical selves may cry out against this process. Freedom is not freedom to do what is irrational, or stupid, or wrong. To force empirical selves into the right pattern is no tyranny, but liberation. Rousseau tells me that if I freely surrender all the parts of my life to society, I create an entity which, because it has been built by an equality of sacrifice of all its members, cannot wish to hurt any one of them; in such a society, we are informed, it can be nobody's interest to damage anyone else. "In giving myself to all, I give myself to none," and get back as much as I lose, with enough new force to preserve my new gains. Kant tells us that when "the individual has entirely abandoned his wild, lawless freedom, to find it again, unimpaired, in a state of dependence according to law," that alone is true freedom, "for this dependence is the work of my own will acting as a lawgiver." Liberty, so far from being incompatible with authority, becomes virtually identical with it. This is the thought and language of all the declarations of the rights of man in the eighteenth century, and of all those who look upon society as a design constructed according to the rational laws of the wise lawgiver, or of nature, or of history, or of the Supreme Being. Bentham, almost alone, doggedly went on repeating that the business of laws was not to liberate but to restrain: "Every law is an infraction of liberty"—even if such "infraction" leads to an increase of the sum of liberty.

If the underlying assumptions had been correct—if the method of solving social problems resembled the way in which solutions to the problems of the natural sciences are found, and if reason were what rationalists said that it was, all this would perhaps follow. In the ideal case, liberty coincides with law: autonomy with authority. A law which forbids me to do what I could not, as a sane being, conceivably wish to do is not a restraint of my freedom. In the ideal society, composed of wholly responsible beings, rules, because I should scarcely be conscious of them, would gradually wither away. Only one social movement was bold enough to render this assumption quite explicit and accept its consequences—that of the Anarchists. But all forms of liberalism founded on a rationalist metaphysics are less or more watered-down versions of this creed.

In due course, the thinkers who bent their energies to the solution of the problem on these lines came to be faced with the question of how in practice men were to be made rational in this way. Clearly they must be educated. For the uneducated are irrational, heteronomous, and need to be coerced, if only to make life tolerable for the rational if they are to live in the same society and not be compelled to withdraw to a desert or some Olympian height. But the uneducated cannot be expected to understand or co-operate with the purposes of their educators. Education, says Fichte, must inevitably work in such a way that "you will later recognize the reasons for what I am doing now." Children cannot be expected to understand why they are compelled to go to school, nor the ignorant—that is, for the moment, the majority of mankind—why they are made to obey the laws that will presently make them rational. "Compulsion is also a kind of education." You learn the great virtue of obedience to superior persons. If you cannot understand your own interests as a rational being, I cannot be expected to consult you, or abide by your wishes, in the course of making you rational. I must, in the end, force you to be protected against smallpox, even though you may not wish it. Even Mill is prepared to say that I may forcibly prevent a man from crossing a bridge if there is not time to warn him that it is about to collapse, for I know, or am justified in assuming, that he cannot wish to fall into the water. Fichte knows what the uneducated German of his time wishes to be or do better than he can possibly know them for himself. The sage knows you better than you know yourself, for you are the victim of your passions, a slave living a heteronomous life, purblind, unable to understand your true goals.

You want to be a human being. It is the aim of the state to satisfy your wish. "Compulsion is justified by education for future insight." The reason within me, if it is to triumph, must eliminate and suppress my "lower" instincts, my passions and desires, which render me a slave; similarly (the fatal transition from individual to social concepts is almost imperceptible) the higher elements in society—the better educated, the more rational, those who "possess the highest insight of their time and people"—may exercise compulsion to rationalize the irrational section of society. For—so Hegel, Bradley, Bosanquet have often assured us—by obeying the rational man we obey ourselves: not indeed as we are, sunk in our ignorance and our passions, weak creatures afflicted by diseases that need a healer, wards who require a guardian, but as we could be if we were rational; as we could be even now, if only we would listen to the rational element which is, *exhypothesi,* within every human being who deserves the name. . . .

The same attitude was pointedly expressed by Auguste Comte, who asked "If we do not allow free thinking in chemistry or biology, why should we allow it in morals or politics?" Why indeed? If it makes sense to speak of political truths—assertions of social ends which all men, because they are men, must, once they are discovered, agree to be such; and if, as Comte believed, scientific method will in due course reveal them; then what case is there for freedom of opinion or action—at least as an end in itself, and not merely as a stimulating intellectual climate, either for individuals or for groups? Why should any conduct be tolerated that is not authorized by appropriate experts? Comte put bluntly what had been implicit in the rationalist theory of politics from its ancient Greek beginnings. There can, in principle, be only one correct way of life; the wise lead it spontaneously, that is why they are called wise. The unwise must be dragged towards it by all the social means in the power of the wise; for why should demonstrable error be suffered to survive and breed? The immature and untutored must be made to say to themselves: "Only the truth liberates, and the only way in which I can learn the truth is by doing blindly today, what you, who know it, order me, or coerce me, to do, in the certain knowledge that only thus will I arrive at your clear vision, and be free like you."

We have wandered indeed from our liberal beginnings. This argument, employed by Fichte in his latest phase, and after him by other defenders of authority, from Victorian schoolmasters and colonial administra-tors to the latest nationalist or communist dictator, is precisely what the Stoic and Kantian morality protests against most bitterly in the name of the reason of the free individual following his own inner light. In this way the rationalist argument, with its assumption of the single true solution, has led by steps which, if not logically valid, are historically and psychologically intelligible, from an ethical doctrine of individual responsibility and individual self-perfection to an authoritarian state obedient to the directives of an *élite* of Platonic guardians. . . .

If this leads to despotism, albeit by the best or the wisest—to Sarastro's temple in the *Magic Flute*—but still despotism, which turns out to be identical with freedom, can it be that there is something amiss in the premises of the argument? that the basic assumptions are themselves somewhere at fault? Let me state them once more: first, that all men have one true purpose, and one only, that of rational self-direction; second, that the ends of all rational beings must of necessity fit into a single universal, harmonious pattern, which some men may be able to discern more clearly than others; third, that all conflict, and consequently all tragedy, is due solely to the clash of reason with the irrational or the insufficiently rational—the immature and undeveloped elements in life—whether individual or communal, and that such clashes are, in principle, avoidable, and for wholly rational beings impossible; finally, that when all men have been made rational, they will obey the rational laws of their own natures, which are one and the same in them all, and so be at once wholly law-abiding and wholly free. Can it be that Socrates and the creators of the central Western tradition in ethics and politics who followed him have been mistaken, for more than two millennia, that virtue is not knowledge, nor freedom identical with either? That despite the fact that it rules the lives of more men than ever before in its long history, not one of the basic assumptions of this famous view is demonstrable, or, perhaps, even true?

VI. THE SEARCH FOR STATUS

. . . No doubt every interpretation of the word liberty, however unusual, must include a minimum of what I have called "negative" liberty. There must be an area within which I am not frustrated. No society literally suppresses all the liberties of its members; a being who is prevented by others from doing anything at all on his own is not a moral agent at all, and could not either legally or morally be regarded as a human being, even if a physiologist or a biologist, or even a psychologist, felt inclined to classify him as a man. But the fathers of liberalism—Mill and Constant—want more than this minimum: they demand a maximum degree of non-interference compatible with the minimum demands of social life. It seems unlikely that this extreme demand for liberty has ever been made by any but a small minority of highly civilized and self-conscious human beings. The bulk of humanity has certainly at most times been prepared to sacrifice this to other goals: security, status, prosperity, power, virtue, rewards in the next world; or justice, equality, fraternity, and many other values which appear wholly, or in part, incompatible with the attainment of the greatest degree of individual liberty, and certainly do not need it as a pre-condition for their own realization. It is not a demand for *Lebensraum* for each individual that has stimulated the rebellions and wars of liberation for which men were ready to die in the past, or, indeed, in the present. Men who have fought for freedom have commonly fought for the right to be governed by themselves or their representatives—sternly governed, if need be, like the Spartans, with little individual liberty, but in a manner which allowed them to participate, or at any rate to believe that they were participating, in the legislation and administration of their collective lives. And men who have made revolutions have, as often as not, meant by liberty no more than the conquest of power and authority by a given sect of believers in a doctrine, or by a class, or by some other social group, old or new. Their victories certainly frustrated those whom they ousted, and sometimes repressed, enslaved, or exterminated vast numbers of human beings. Yet such revolutionaries have usually felt it necessary to argue that, despite this, they represented the party of liberty, or "true" liberty, by claiming universality for their ideal, which the "real selves" of even those who resisted them were also alleged to be seeking, although they were held to have lost the way to the goal, or to have mistaken the goal itself owing to some moral or spiritual blindness. All this has little to do with Mill's notion of liberty as limited only by the danger of doing harm to others. It is the non-recognition of this psychological and political fact (which lurks behind the apparent ambiguity of the term "liberty") that has, perhaps, blinded some contemporary liberals to the world in which they live. Their plea is clear, their cause is just. But they do not allow for the variety of basic human needs. Nor yet for the ingenuity with which men can prove to their own satisfaction that the road to one ideal also leads to its contrary. . . .

VIII. THE ONE AND THE MANY

One belief, more than any other, is responsible for the slaughter of individuals on the altars of the great historical ideals—justice or progress or the happiness of future generations, or the sacred mission or emancipation of a nation or race or class, or even liberty itself, which demands the sacrifice of individuals for the freedom of society. This is the belief that somewhere, in the past or in the future, in divine revelation or in the mind of an individual thinker, in the pronouncements of history or science, or in the simple heart of an uncorrupted good man, there is a final solution. This ancient faith rests on the conviction that all the positive values in which men have believed must, in the end, be compatible, and perhaps even entail one another. "Nature binds truth, happiness, and virtue together as by an indissoluble chain," said one of the best men who ever lived, and spoke in similar terms of liberty, equality, and justice. But is this true? It is a commonplace that neither political equality nor efficient organization nor social justice is compatible with more than a modicum of individual liberty, and certainly not with unrestricted *laissez-faire*; that justice and generosity, public and private loyalties, the demands of genius and the claims of society, can conflict violently with each other. And it is no great way from that to the generalization that not all good things are compatible, still less all the ideals of mankind. But somewhere, we shall be told, and in some way, it must be possible for all these values to live together, for unless this is so, the universe is not a cosmos, not a harmony; unless this is so, conflicts of values may be an intrinsic, irremovable element in human life. To admit that the fulfilment of some of our ideals may in principle make the fulfilment of others impossible is to say that the notion of total human fulfilment is a formal contradiction, a metaphysical chimera. For every rationalist metaphysician, from Plato to the last disciples of Hegel or Marx, this abandonment of the notion of a final harmony in which all riddles are solved, all contradictions reconciled, is a piece of crude empiricism, abdication before brute facts, intolerable bankruptcy of reason before things as they are, failure to explain and to justify, to reduce everything to a system, which "reason" indignantly rejects. But if we are not armed with an *a priori* guarantee of the proposition that a total harmony of true values is somewhere to be found—perhaps in some ideal realm the characteristics of which we can, in our finite state, not so much as conceive—we must fall back on the ordinary resources of empirical observation and ordinary human knowledge. And these certainly give us no warrant for supposing (or even understanding what would be meant by saying) that all good things, or all bad things for that matter, are reconcilable with each other. The world that we encounter in ordinary experience is one in which we are faced with choices between ends equally ultimate, and claims equally absolute, the realization of some of which must inevitably involve the sacrifice of others. Indeed, it is because this is their situation that men place such immense value upon the freedom to choose; for if they had assurance that in some perfect state, realizable by men on earth, no ends pursued by them would ever be in conflict, the necessity and agony of choice would disappear, and with it the central importance of the freedom to choose. Any method of bringing this final state nearer would then seem fully justified, no matter how much freedom were sacrificed to forward its advance. It is, I have no doubt, some such dogmatic certainty that has been responsible for the deep, serene, unshakeable conviction in the minds of some of the most merciless tyrants and persecutors in history that what they did was fully justified by its purpose. I do not say that the ideal of self-perfection—whether for individuals or nations or churches or classes—is to be condemned in itself, or that the language which was used in its defence was in all cases the result of a confused or fraudulent use of words, or of moral or intellectual perversity. Indeed, I have tried to show that it is the notion of freedom in its "positive" sense that is at the heart of the demands for national or social self-direction which animate the most powerful and morally just public movements of our time, and that not to recognize this is to misunderstand the most vital facts and ideas of our age. But equally it seems to me that the belief that some single formula or principle can be found whereby all the diverse ends of men can be harmoniously realized is demonstrably false. If, as I believe, the ends of men are many, and not all of them are in principle compatible with each other, then the possibility of conflict—and of tragedy—can never wholly be eliminated from human life, either personal or social. The necessity of choosing between absolute claims is then an inescapable characteristic of the human condition. This gives its value to freedom as

Acton had conceived of it—as an end in itself, and not as a temporary need, arising out of our confused notions and irrational and disordered lives, a predicament which a panacea could one day put right. . . .

Pluralism, with the measure of "negative" liberty that it entails, seems to me a truer and more humane ideal than the goals of those who seek in the great, disciplined, authoritarian structures the ideal of "positive" self-mastery by classes, or peoples, or the whole of mankind. It is truer, because it does, at least, recognize the fact that human goals are many, not all of them commensurable, and in perpetual rivalry with one another. To assume that all values can be graded on one scale, so that it is a mere matter of inspection to determine the highest, seems to me to falsify our knowledge that men are free agents, to represent moral decision as an operation which a slide-rule could, in principle, perform. To say that in some ultimate, all-reconciling, yet realizable synthesis, duty *is* interest, or individual freedom *is* pure democracy or an authoritarian state, is to throw a metaphysical blanket over either self-deceit or deliberate hypocrisy. It [pluralism] is more humane because it does not (as the system builders do) deprive men, in the name of some remote, or incoherent, ideal, of much that they have found to be indispensable to their life as unpredictably self-transforming human beings. In the end, men choose between ultimate values; they choose as they do, because their life and thought are determined by fundamental moral categories and concepts that are, at any rate over large stretches of time and space, a part of their being and thought and sense of their own identity; part of what makes them human.

It may be that the ideal of freedom to choose ends without claiming eternal validity for them, and the pluralism of values connected with this, is only the late fruit of our declining capitalist civilization: an ideal which remote ages and primitive societies have not recognized, and one which posterity will regard with curiosity, even sympathy, but little comprehension. This may be so; but no sceptical conclusions seem to me to follow. Principles are not less sacred because their duration cannot be guaranteed. Indeed, the very desire for guarantees that our values are eternal and secure in some objective heaven is perhaps only a craving for the certainties of childhood or the absolute values of our primitive past. "To realise the relative validity of one's convictions," said an admirable writer of our time, "and yet stand for them unflinchingly, is what distinguishes a civilised man from a barbarian." To demand more than this is perhaps a deep and incurable metaphysical need; but to allow it to determine one's practice is a symptom of an equally deep, and more dangerous, moral and political immaturity.

READING 17

Liberty and the Grounds For Coercion

Joel Feinberg

Joel Feinberg is Professor of Philosophy emeritus at the University of Arizona and the author of several works in ethical, legal, and political theory. In this essay, Feinberg, commenting on James Fitzjames Stephen's criticism of Mill's theory of liberty, concedes that sometimes political coercion is warranted but argues for a fundamental presumption of liberty. He discusses the harm principle and considers other objections to Mill's theory.

This reading is taken from Feinberg's *Social Philosophy* (Prentice Hall, 1973), by permission.

1. THE PRESUMPTIVE CASE FOR LIBERTY

Whatever else we believe about freedom, most of us believe it is something to be praised, or so luminously a Thing of Value that it is beyond praise. What is it that makes freedom a good thing? Some say that freedom is good in itself quite apart from its consequences. On the other hand, James Fitzjames Stephen wrote that ". . . the question whether liberty is a good or a bad thing appears as irrational as the question whether fire is a good or a bad thing." Freedom, according to Stephen, is good (when it is good) only because of what it does, not because of what it is.

It would be impossible to demonstrate that freedom is good for its own sake, and indeed, this proposition is far from self-evident. Still, Stephen's analogy to fire seems an injustice to freedom. Fire has no constant and virtually invariant effects that tend to make it, on balance, a good thing whenever and wherever it occurs, and bad only when its subsequent remoter effects are so evil as to counterbalance its direct and immediate ones. Thus, a fire in one's bed while one is sleeping is dreadful because its effects are evil, but a fire under the pot on the stove is splendid because it makes possible a hot cup of coffee when one wants it. The direct effect of fire in these and all other cases is to oxidize material objects and raise the temperature in its immediate environment; but *these* effects, from the point of view of human interests, and considered just in themselves, are neither good nor bad.

Freedom has seemed to most writers quite different in this respect. When a free man violates his neighbor's interests, then his freedom, having been put to bad use, was, on balance, a bad thing, but unlike the fire in the bed, it was not an unalloyed evil. Whatever the harmful consequences of freedom in a given case, there is always a direct effect on the person of its possessor which must be counted a positive good. Coercion may prevent great evils, and be wholly justified on that account, but it always has its price. Coercion may be on balance a great gain, but its direct effects always, or nearly always, constitute a definite loss. If this is true, there is always a *presumption* in favor of freedom, even though it can in some cases be overridden by more powerful reasons on the other side.

The presumption in favor of freedom is usually said to rest on freedom's essential role in the development of traits of intellect and character which constitute the good of individuals and are centrally important means to the progress of societies. One consensus argument, attributable with minor variations to Von Humboldt, Mill, Hobhouse, and many others, goes roughly as follows. The highest good for man is neither enjoyment nor passive contentment, but rather a dynamic process of growth and self-realization. This can be called "happiness" if we mean by that term what the Greeks did, namely, "The exercise of vital powers along lines of excellence in a life affording them scope.[1] The highest social good is then the greatest possible amount of individual self-realization and (assuming that different persons are inclined by their natures in different ways) the resultant diversity and fullness of life. Self-realization consists in the actualization of certain uniquely human potentialities, the bringing to full development of certain powers and abilities. This in turn requires constant practice in making difficult choices among alternative hypotheses, policies, and actions—and the more difficult the better. John Stuart Mill explained why:

The human faculties of perception, judgment, discriminative feeling, mental activity, and even moral preference are exercised only in making a choice. He who does anything because it is the custom makes no choice. He gains no practice either in discerning or in desiring what is best. The mental and moral, like the muscular, powers are improved only by being used. [See Reading 10]

In short, one does not realize what is best in oneself when social pressures to conform to custom lead one mindlessly along. Even more clearly, one's growth will be stunted when one is given no choice in the first place, either because of being kept in ignorance or because one is terrorized by the wielders of bayonets.

Freedom to decide on one's own while fully informed of the facts thus tends to promote the good of the person who exercises it, even if it permits him to make foolish or dangerous mistakes. Mill added to this argument the citation of numerous social benefits that redound indirectly but uniformly to those who grant freedom as well as those who exercise it. We all profit from the fruits of genius, he maintained, and genius, since it often involves doggedness and eccentricity, is likely to flourish only where coercive pressures toward conformity are absent. Moreover, social progress is more likely to occur where there is free criticism of prevailing ways and adventurous experiments in living. Finally, true understanding of human nature requires freedom, since without liberty there will be little diversity, and without diversity *all* aspects of the human condition will be ascribed to fixed nature rather than to the workings of a particular culture.

Such are the grounds for holding that there is always a presumption in favor of freedom, that whenever we are faced with an option between forcing a person to do something and letting him decide on his own whether or not to do it, other things being equal, we should always opt for the latter. If a strong general presumption for freedom has been established, the burden of proof rests on the shoulders of the advocate of coercion, and the philosopher's task will be to state the conditions under which the presumption can be overridden.

2. THE ANARCHISTIC PRINCIPLE

It will be instructive to see why certain very simple statements of the conditions for justified social and political coercion are unsatisfactory. The first of these, which might with propriety be called "anarchistic," insists that society and the state should grant to every cit-

izen "complete liberty to do whatever he wishes." In this view, no coercive power exercised by state or society is ever justified. What then of the coercion imposed by one individual or group on another? If every man is free to do whatever he wishes, it follows that all men are free to inflict blows on John Doe, to hold noisy parties under his window every night, and to help themselves to his possessions. How can it then be true that John Doe is free at the same time to come and go as he pleases, to sleep at night, and to enjoy exclusive use of his possessions?

There is no *logical* inconsistency in holding both that Doe is dispositionally free to do something and that someone else, Roe, is dispositionally free to prevent him from doing that thing. (I am considering these judgments only when made from the sociological, not the juridical, perspective.) Consider the statements that Doe is free to go to Chicago and Roe is free to keep Doe from going anywhere. It would be something of an oversimplification, but useful for our present purposes, to regard these statements as equivalent to the following hypotheticals: (1) If Doe chooses to go to Chicago, he will in fact go to Chicago, and (2) If Roe chooses to have Doe stay at home, Doe will in fact stay at home. There are conceivable circumstances in which both of these statements would be true. One set of facts that would make them both true would be those obtaining when Roe has the power to prevent Doe from leaving home, but does *not* choose to exercise that power, and no other obstacle stands in Doe's way. Thus, (1) is true because if, in these circumstances, Doe chooses to go to Chicago, there is nothing to stop him; (2) is true because if (contrary to fact) Roe were to choose to keep Doe at home, Doe would be kept at home. For any Doe and any Roe, whether or not (1) and (2) are true together depends upon what the facts happen to be. The conjunction of (1) and (2), therefore, cannot be logically contradictory.

There is no logical barrier to its being true that *everyone* is free (from coercion) to do whatever he may choose. One can conceive of logically possible worlds in which this would be the case. But in order for it to be true of our actual world, there would have to be a disappearance of conflict between choices: as soon as two men attempt to acquire what only one can have, or one man desires something that can be acquired only by frustrating the desires of someone else, then one man's freedom is possible only at the cost of another man's constraint. The anarchistic principle, in short, would be workable only in a world in which human desires and choices, through a miracle of preestablished harmony, could never conflict. In our own world, where conflict and rivalry are ineradicable facts, "complete liberty for all" on the anarchist formula would mean greater freedom for the strong then the weak, and no very stable freedoms for anyone.

Given that the important desires of men can and usually do conflict, one person will be free to act on a desire only to the extent that others are unfree to act on conflicting desires; if the state is to guarantee to all men the freedom to do one certain kind of thing, then, in all likelihood, it must make all men unfree to prevent others from doing that sort of thing. "As against the coercion applicable by individual to individual," wrote Bentham, "no liberty can be given to one man but in proportion as it is taken away from another. All coercive laws, therefore, and in particular all laws creative of liberty, are as far as they go abrogative of liberty."[2] But if prohibitive laws destroy a liberty for every liberty they confer or protect, while the anarchistic principle would neither add nor subtract liberties from the natural situation of men, don't they yield precisely the same net totals of liberty and constraint, differing merely in the manner of distribution? This conclusion is yet another trap we can fall into by interpreting usefully loose talk about "amounts" of freedom in a precise quantitative way.

Most civilized societies have prohibitive laws or other social devices to prevent individuals from inflicting blows on the faces of other individuals. There is sometimes a great deal of pleasure to be derived from bopping someone in the nose, but most of us think that this pleasure is worth sacrificing for the greater good of security from physical attack by others. Suppose, however, that some rugged individualist complains that our law infringes on his freedom, making it virtually impossible for him to enjoy the thrill of smashing noses, and just because of the scruples of a lot of weak-kneed, lily-livered sissies. "Since the days of the frontier," he might say, "there hasn't been any real freedom in this country." We should no doubt try to explain to him that the interest people have in the physical integrity of their noses is *more important* than their aggressive interests, and therefore more worthy of protection.

Now suppose that we had quite different rules, and that more people were free to hit others in the nose, and correspondingly fewer were free to enjoy the full beauty and utility of their own unbloodied proboscises. Would this new arrangement have a greater or smaller "amount" of freedom in it, on balance? Perhaps it is least misleading to say that there would be not "less" freedom but freedom of a morally inferior kind. Most

societies have recognized that there are some relatively permanent desires present in all men that must be singled out, given precedence, and made legally sacrosanct. When these interests are so recognized and protected by law, they come to be called *rights* (see Chapter 4). Selection of those interests important enough to be protected in this way is made in accordance with the settled value judgments of the community by application of some standard other than that of "simple freedom" itself, which is quite insufficient. To receive "complete liberty" from society and its government would be to incur other constraints from private individuals, and almost all who have thought about this exchange consider it a bad trade.

3. THE FORMALISTIC PRINCIPLE

The second unsatisfactory principle of freedom distribution does not have such obvious failings. In fact, many have spoken as if it were a self-evident truth. Society, it says, should grant to every person "full liberty to do what he pleases providing only that he does not interfere with the like liberty of another."[3] This principle is the right answer to the wrong question. It insists that liberty should be distributed impartially, and that no individual take exception to the general prohibitive laws. But if it is taken as an answer to our question—when is political or social coercion justified?—it is entirely formal and empty, and consistent with any system of legal constraints that is not arbitrary. A general rule permitting nose-bopping would satisfy it just as well as one prohibiting it; the anarchistic principle conforms to it, as well as a principle prohibiting all aggressive behavior. The principle employs a sound maxim of justice, insisting as it does on non-discriminatory legislation and impartial enforcement, but it provides no guide to the proper *content* of the law. Its inadequacy as a substantive principle of freedom distribution was well appreciated by L. T. Hobhouse, who wrote, "My right to keep my neighbor awake by playing the piano all night is not satisfactorily counterbalanced by his right to keep a dog which howls all the time the piano is being played."[4] Each party in this example would use his freedom to the detriment of the other under a law which recognizes a "like liberty" for the other party to do the same if he can. That the law is nondiscriminatory would be small consolation to either party if it permitted his interests to be seriously harmed.

4. THE CONCEPT OF HARM

If social and political coercion is a harm-causing evil, then one way to justify it is to show that it is necessary for the prevention of even greater evils. That is the generating insight of the "harm to others principle" (henceforth called simply "the harm principle") which permits society to restrict the liberty of some persons in order to prevent harm to others. Two versions of this principle can be distinguished. The first would justify restriction of one person's liberty to prevent injury to other specific individuals, and can therefore be called "the private harm principle." The second can be invoked to justify coercion on the distinct ground that it is necessary to prevent impairment of institutional practices and regulatory systems that are in the public interest; thus it can be called "the public harm principle." That the private harm principle (whose chief advocate was J. S. Mill) states at least one of the acceptable grounds for coercion is virtually beyond controversy. Hardly anyone would deny the state the right to make criminal such directly injurious conduct as willful homicide, assault and battery, and robbery. Mill often wrote as if prevention of private harm is the *sole* valid ground for state coercion, but this must not have been his considered intention. He would not have wiped from the books such crimes as tax evasion, smuggling, and contempt of court, which need not injure any specific individuals, except insofar as they weaken public institutions in whose health we all have a stake. I shall assume that Mill held both the public and private versions of the harm principle.

In its simplest formulations, the harm principle is still a long way from being a precise guide to the ideal legislator, especially in those difficult cases where harms of different orders, magnitudes, and probabilities must be balanced against one another. Even when made fully explicit and qualified in appropriate ways, however, the unsupplemented harm principle cannot be fairly assessed until it is known precisely what is meant by "harm."

(i) Harm as the Invasion of an Interest

It has become common, especially in legal writings, to take the object of harm always to be an *interest*. The *Restatement of the Law of Torts* gives one sense of the term "interest" when it defines it as "anything which is the object of human desire,"[5] but this seems much too broad to be useful for our present purposes. A person is often said to "have an interest" in something he does not presently desire. A dose of medicine may be "in a man's interest" even when he is struggling and kicking to avoid it. In this sense, an object of an interest is "what is truly good for a person whether he desires it or not." Even interest defined in this second way may be indirectly but necessarily related to desires. The only way to argue that X is in Doe's interest even though Doe does not want X may be to show that X would effectively integrate Doe's total set of desires leading to a greater net balance of desire-fulfillment in the long run. If most of Doe's acknowledged important desires cannot be satisfied so long as he is ill, and he cannot become well unless he takes the medicine, then taking the medicine is in Doe's interest in this desire-related sense.

Legal writers classify interests in various ways. One of the more common lists "Interests of Personality," "Interests of Property," "Interest in Reputation," "Interest in Domestic Relations," and "Interest in Privacy," among others. A humanly inflicted harm is conceived as the violation of one of a person's interests, an injury to something in which he has a genuine stake. In the lawyer's usage, an interest is something a person always possesses in some condition, something that can grow and flourish or diminish and decay, but which can rarely be totally lost. Other persons can be said to promote or hinder an individual's interest in bodily health, or in the avoidance of damaging or offensive physical contacts, or in the safety and security of his person, his family, his friends, and his property. One advantage of this mode of speaking is that it permits us to appraise harms by distinguishing between more and less important interests, and between those interests which are, and those which are not, worthy of legal recognition and/or protection.

(ii) Harm vs. Hurt: The Role of Knowledge

Is it true that "what a person doesn't know can't *harm* him?" For most cases, this maxim certainly does *not* apply, and it is one of the merits of the "interest" analysis of harm that it explains why. Typically, having one's interests violated is one thing, and knowing that one's interests have been violated is another. The rich man is harmed at the time his home is burgled, even though he may not discover the harm for months; similarly, a soldier is harmed the moment he is wounded, though in the heat of the battle he may not discover even his serious wounds for some time. The law does not permit a burglar to plead "He will never miss it" even when that plea is true, for the crime of burglary consists in inflicting a forbidden harm, whether or not it will be discovered or will hurt. It is true that not all harms *hurt,* partly because not all harms ever come to be noticed. There may well be a relatively narrow and precise sense of "harm" in ordinary usage such that "being harmed" can be contrasted with being hurt (as well as with "being shocked" and "being offended"). However, if harm is understood as the violation of an interest, and all men have an interest in not being hurt, it follows that hurt is one species of harm. Hence, even though not all harms hurt, all hurts do harm (or more accurately, are themselves harm), and the harm principle could conceivably be used to justify coercion when it is necessary to prevent hurts, even when the hurts do not lead to any *further* harm.

There are some special cases where the maxim "What a person does't know can't hurt him" seems quite sound. In these cases, knowledge of some fact, such as the adulterous infidelities of one's spouse, is itself hurtful; indeed, the whole hurt consists in the knowledge and is inseparable from it. Here knowledge is both a necessary and sufficient condition of a hurt: What the cuckolded husband doesn't know "can't *hurt* him." That is not to say that he cannot be *harmed* unless he is hurt. An undetected adultery damages one of the victim's "interests in domestic relations," just as an unknown libelous publication can damage his interest in a good reputation, or an undetected trespass on his land can damage his interest in "the exclusive enjoyment and control" of that land. In all these cases, violation of the interest in question is itself a harm even though no *further* harm may result to any other interests.

The distinction between hurt and (generic) harm raises one additional question. We must include in the category of "hurts" not only physical pains but also forms of mental distress. Our question is whether, in applying the harm principle, we should permit coercion designed to prevent mental distress when the distress is not likely to be followed by hurt or harm of any other kind. Some forms of mental distress (e.g., "hurt feelings") can be ruled out simply on the ground that they are too minor or trivial to warrant interference. Others are so severe that they can lead to mental breakdowns. In such cases, however, it is the consequential harm to mental health and not the mere fact of distress that clearly warrants interference on the ground of harmfulness. Thus, a convenient criterion for deter-

mining whether a hurt is sufficiently harmful to justify preventive coercion on that ground suggests itself: the hurt is serious enough if and only if it is either a symptom of a prior or concurrent harm of another order (as a pain in an arm may be the result and sign of a broken bone), or is in itself the cause of a consequential harm (e.g., mental breakdown) of another order. . . .

5. LINES OF ATTACK ON MILL

Arguments against Mill's unsupplemented harm principle (his claim that the private and public harm principles state the *only* grounds for justified interference with liberty) have been mainly of two different kinds.[6] Many have argued that the harm principle justifies too much social and political interference in the affairs of individuals. Others allow that the prevention of individual and social harm is always a ground for interference, but insist that it is by no means the only ground.

(i) "No Man is an Island"

Mill maintained in *On Liberty* that social interference is never justified in those of a man's affairs that concern himself only. But no man's affairs have effects on himself alone. There are a thousand subtle and indirect ways in which every individual act, no matter how private and solitary, affects others. It would therefore seem that society has a right, on Mill's own principles, to interfere in every department of human life. Mill anticipated this objection and took certain steps to disarm it. Let it be allowed that no human conduct is entirely, exclusively, and to the last degree self-regarding. Still, Mill insisted, we can distinguish between actions that are plainly other-regarding and those that are "directly," or "chiefly," or "primarily" self-regarding. There will be a twilight area of cases difficult to classify, but that is true of many other workable distinctions, including that between night and day.

It is essential to Mill's theory that we make a distinction between two different kinds of consequences of human actions: the consequences *directly* affecting the interests of others, and those of primarily self-regarding behavior which only *indirectly* or *remotely* affect the interests of others. "No person ought to be punished simply for being drunk," Mill wrote, "but a soldier or policeman should be punished for being drunk on duty." [Reading 10] A drunk policeman directly harms the interests of others. His conduct gives opportunities to criminals and thus creates grave risk of harm to other citizens. It brings the police into disrepute, and makes the work of his colleagues more dangerous. Finally, it may lead to loss of the policeman's job, with serious consequences for his wife and children.

Consider, on the other hand, a hard working bachelor who habitually spends his evening hours drinking himself into a stupor, which he then sleeps off, rising fresh in the morning to put in another hard day's work. His drinking does not *directly* affect others in any of the ways of the drunk policeman's conduct. He has no family; he drinks alone and sets no direct example; he is not prevented from discharging any of his public duties; he creates no substanital risk of harm to the interests of other individuals. Although even his private conduct will have some effects on the interests of others, these are precisely the sorts of effects Mill would call "indirect" and "remote." First, in spending his evenings the way he does, our solitary tippler is *not* doing any number of other things that might be of greater utility to others. In not earning and spending more money, he is failing to stimulate the economy (except for the liquor industry) as much as he might. Second, he fails to spend his evening time improving his talents and making himself a better person. Perhaps he has a considerable native talent for painting or poetry, and his wastefulness is depriving the world of some valuable art. Third, he may make those of his colleagues who like him sad on his behalf. Finally, to those who know of his habits, he is a "bad example."[7] All of these "indirect harms" together, Mill maintained, do not outweigh the direct and serious harm that would result from social or legal coercion.

Mill's critics have never been entirely satisfied by this. Many have pointed out that Mill is concerned not only with political coercion and legal punishment but also with purely social coercion—moral pressure, social avoidance, ostracism. No responsible critic would wish the state to punish the solitary tippler, but social coercion is another matter. We can't prevent people from disapproving of an individual for his self-regarding faults or from expressing that disapproval to others, without undue restriction on *their* freedom. Such expressions, in Mill's view, are inevitably coercive, constituting a "milder form of punishment." Hence "social punishment" of individuals for conduct that directly concerns only themselves—the argument concludes—is both inevitable and, according to Mill's own principles, proper.

Mill anticipated this objection, too, and tried to cope with it by making a distinction between types of social responses. We cannot help but lower in our estimation a person with serious self-regarding faults. We will think ill of him, judge him to be at fault, and make him the inevitable and proper object of our disapproval, distaste, even contempt. We may warn others about him, avoid his company, and withhold gratuitous benefits from him—"not to the oppression of his individuality but in the exercise of ours." Mill concedes that all of these social responses can function as "penalties"—but they are suffered "only insofar as they are the natural and, as it were, the spontaneous consequences of the faults themselves, not because they are purposely inflicted on him for the sake of punishment." Other responses, on the other hand, add something to the "natural penalties"—pointed snubbing, economic reprisals, gossip campaigns, and so on. The added penalties, according to Mill, are precisely the ones that are never justified as responses to merely self-regarding flaws—"if he displeases us, we may express our distaste; and we may stand aloof from a person as well as from a thing that displeases us, but we shall not therefore feel called on to make his life uncomfortable."

(ii) Other Proposed Grounds for Coercion

The distinction between self-regarding and other-regarding behavior, as Mill intended it to be understood, does seem at least roughly serviceable, and unlikely to invite massive social interference in private affairs. I think most critics of Mill would grant that, but reject the harm principle on the opposite ground that it doesn't permit enough interference. These writers would allow at least one, and as many as five or more, additional valid grounds for coercion. Each of these proposed grounds is stated in a principle listed below. One might hold that restriction of one person's liberty can be justified:

1. To prevent harm to others, either
   a. injury to individual persons (*The Private Harm Principle*), or
   b. impairment of institutional practices that are in the public interest (*The Public Harm Principle*);
2. To prevent offense to others (*The Offense Principle*);
3. To prevent harm to self (*Legal Paternalism*);

4. To prevent or punish sin, i.e., to "enforce morality as such" (*Legal Moralism*);
5. To benefit the self (*Extreme Paternalism*);
6. To benefit others (*The Welfare Principle*).

The liberty-limiting principles on this list are best understood as stating neither necessary nor sufficient conditions for justified coercion, but rather specifications of the *kinds* of reasons that are always relevant or acceptable in support of proposed coercion, even though in a given case they may not be conclusive. Each principle states that interference might be permissible *if* (but not *only if*) a certain condition is satisfied. Hence the principles are not mutually exclusive; it is possible to hold two or more of them at once, even all of them together, and it is possible to deny all of them. Moreover, the principles cannot be construed as stating sufficient conditions for legitimate interference with liberty, for even though the principle is satisfied in a given case, the general presumption against coercion might not be outweighed. The harm principle, for example, does not justify state interference to prevent a tiny bit of inconsequential harm. Prevention of minor harm always counts in favor of proposals (as in a legislature) to restrict liberty, but in a given instance it might not count *enough* to outweigh the general presumption against interference, or it might be outweighed by the prospect of practical difficulties in enforcing the law, excessive costs, and forfeitures of privacy. A liberty-limiting principle states considerations that are always good reasons for coercion, though neither exclusively nor, in every case, decisively good reasons.

It will not be possible to examine each principle in detail here, and offer "proofs" and "refutations." The best way to defend one's selection of principles is to show to which positions they commit one on such issues as censorship of literature, "morals offenses," and compulsory social security programs. General principles arise in the course of deliberations over particular problems, especially in the efforts to defend one's judgments by showing that they are consistent with what has gone before. If a principle commits one to an antecedently unacceptable judgment, then one has to modify or supplement the principle in a way that does the least damage to the harmony of one's particular and general opinions taken as a group. On the other hand, when a solid, well-entrenched principle entails a change in a particular judgment, the overriding claims of consistency may require that the judgment be adjusted. This sort of dialectic is similar to the reasonings that are prevalent in law courts. When similar cases are decided in opposite ways, it is incumbent on the court to distinguish them in some respect that will reconcile the separate decisions with each other and with the common rule applied to each. Every effort is made to render current decisions consistent with past ones unless the precedents seem so disruptive of the overall internal harmony of the law that they must, reluctantly, be revised or abandoned. In social and political philosophy every person is on his own, and the counterparts to "past decisions" are the most confident judgments one makes in ordinary normative discourse. The philosophical task is to extract from these "given" judgments the principles that render them consistent, adjusting and modifying where necessary in order to convert the whole body of opinions into an intelligible, coherent system. There is no *a priori* way of refuting another's political opinions, but if our opponents are rational men committed to the ideal of consistency, we can always hope to show them that a given judgment is inconsistent with one of their own acknowledged principles. Then something will have to give.

READING 18

Paternalism

Gerald Dworkin

Gerald Dworkin (1931–20) is Professor of Philosophy at the University of California–Davis and a former editor of the Journal *Ethics*. He is the author of *Theory and Practice of Autonomy* and *Morality, Harm and the Law*. In this essay Dworkin analyzes Mill's harm principle and argues that Mill's blanket prohibition against paternalism needs to be corrected. Dworkin seeks to provide criteria for deciding when the State or another person may justly intervene to override a person's free choice.

This reading is taken from the *Monist* 56, no. 1 (1972), by permission.

I take as my starting point the "one very simple principle" proclaimed by Mill in *On Liberty* . . . "That principle is, that the sole end for which mankind are warranted, individually or collectively, in interfering with the liberty of action of any of their number, is self-protection. That the only purpose for which power can be rightfully exercised over any member of a civilized community, against his will, is to prevent harm to others. He cannot rightfully be compelled to do or forbear because it will be better for him to do so, because it will make him happier, because, in the opinion of others, to do so would be wise, or even right." [See Reading 10]

This principle is neither "one" nor "very simple." It is at least two principles; one asserting that self-protection or the prevention of harm to others is sometimes a sufficient warrant and the other claiming that the individual's own good is *never* a sufficient warrant for the exercise of compulsion either by the society as a whole or by its individual members. I assume that no one with the possible exception of extreme pacifists or anarchists questions the correctness of the first half of the principle. This essay is an examination of the negative claim embodied in Mill's principle—the objection to paternalistic interferences with a man's liberty.

I

By paternalism I shall understand roughly the interference with a person's liberty of action justified by reasons referring exclusively to the welfare, good, happiness, needs, interests or values of the person being coerced. One is always well-advised to illustrate one's definitions by examples but it is not easy to find "pure" examples of paternalistic interferences. For almost any piece of legislation is justified by several different kinds of reasons and even if historically a piece of legislation can be shown to have been introduced for purely paternalistic motives, it may be that advocates of the legislation with an anti-paternalistic outlook can find sufficient reasons justifying the legislation without appealing to the reasons which were originally adduced to support it. Thus, for example, it may be that the original legislation requiring motorcyclists to wear safety helmets was introduced for purely paternalistic reasons. But the Rhode Island Supreme Court recently upheld such legislation on the grounds that it was "not persuaded that the legislature is powerless to prohibit individuals from pursuing a course of conduct which could conceivably result in their becoming public charges," thus clearly introducing reasons of a quite different kind. Now I regard this decision as being based on reasoning of a very dubious nature but it illustrates the kind of problem one has in finding examples. The following is a list of the kinds of interferences I have in mind as being paternalistic.

II

1. Laws requiring motorcyclists to wear safety helmets when operating their machines.
2. Laws forbidding persons from swimming at a public beach when lifeguards are not on duty.
3. Laws making suicide a criminal offense.
4. Laws making it illegal for women and children to work at certain types of jobs.
5. Laws regulating certain kinds of sexual conduct, e.g. homosexuality among consenting adults in private.
6. Laws regulating the use of certain drugs which may have harmful consequences to the user but do not lead to anti-social conduct.
7. Laws requiring a license to engage in certain professions, with those not receiving a license subject to fine or jail sentence if they do engage in the practice.
8. Laws compelling people to spend a specified fraction of their income on the purchase of retirement annuities. (Social Security)
9. Laws forbidding various forms of gambling (often justified on the grounds that the poor are more likely to throw away their money on such activities than the rich, who can afford to).
10. Laws regulating the maximum rates of interest for loans.
11. Laws against duelling.

In addition to laws which attach criminal or civil penalties to certain kinds of action there are laws, rules, regulations, decrees, which make it either difficult or impossible for people to carry out their plans and which are also justified on paternalistic grounds. Examples of this are:

1. Laws regulating the types of contracts which will be upheld as valid by the courts, e.g. (an example of Mill's to which I shall return) no man may make a valid contract for perpetual involuntary servitude.
2. Not allowing as a defense to a charge of murder or assault the consent of the victim.
3. Requiring members of certain religious sects to have compulsory blood transfusions. This is made possible by not allowing the patient to have recourse to civil suits for assault and battery and by means of injunctions.
4. Civil commitment procedures when these are specifically justified on the basis of preventing the person being committed from harming himself.

(The D.C. Hospitalization of the Mentally Ill Act provides for involuntary hospitalization of a person who "is mentally ill, and because of that illness, is likely to injure *himself* or others if allowed to remain at liberty." The term injure in this context applies to unintentional as well as intentional injuries.)

5. Putting fluorides in the community water supply.

All of my examples are of existing restrictions on the liberty of individuals. Obviously one can think of interferences which have not yet been imposed. Thus one might ban the sale of cigarettes, or require that people wear safety-belts in automobiles (as opposed to merely having them installed) enforcing this by not allowing motorists to sue for injuries even when caused by other drivers if the motorist was not wearing a seat-belt at the time of the accident.

I shall not be concerned with activities which though defended on paternalistic grounds are not interferences with the liberty of persons, e.g. the giving of subsidies in kind rather than in cash on the grounds that the recipients would not spend the money on the goods which they really need, or not including a $1000 deductible provision in a basic protection automobile insurance plan on the ground that the people who would elect it could least afford it. Nor shall I be concerned with measures such as "truth-in-advertising" acts and the Pure Food and Drug legislation which are often attacked as paternalistic but which should not be considered so. In these cases all that is provided—it is true by the use of compulsion—is information which it is presumed that rational persons are interested in having in order to make wise decisions. There is no interference with the liberty of the consumer unless one wants to stretch a point beyond good sense and say that his liberty to apply for a loan without knowing the true rate of interest is diminished. It is true that sometimes there is sentiment for going further than providing information, for example when laws against usurious interest are passed preventing those who might wish to contract loans at high rates of interest from doing so, and these measures may correctly be considered paternalistic.

III

Bearing these examples in mind let me return to a characterization of paternalism. I said earlier that I meant by the term, roughly, interference with a person's liberty for his own good. But as some of the examples show the class of persons whose good is involved is not always identical with the class of persons whose freedom is restricted. Thus in the case of professional licensing it is the practitioner who is directly interfered with and it is the would-be patient whose interests are presumably being served. Not allowing the consent of the victim to be a defense to certain types of crime primarily affects the would-be aggressor but it is the interests of the willing victim that we are trying to protect. Sometimes a person may fall into both classes as would be the case if we banned the manufacture and sale of cigarettes and a given manufacturer happened to be a smoker as well.

Thus we may first divide paternalistic interferences into "pure" and "impure" cases. In "pure" paternalism the class of persons whose freedom is restricted is identical with the class of persons whose benefit is intended to be promoted by such restrictions. Examples: the making of suicide a crime, requiring passengers in automobiles to wear seat-belts, requiring a Christian Scientist to receive a blood transfusion. In the case of "impure" paternalism in trying to protect the welfare of a class of persons we find that the only way to do so will involve restricting the freedom of other persons besides those who are benefitted. Now it might be thought that there are no cases of "impure" paternalism since any such case could always be justified on non-paternalistic grounds, i.e., in terms of preventing harms to others. Thus we might ban cigarette manufacturers from continuing to manufacture their product on the grounds that we are preventing them from causing illness to others in the same way that we prevent other manufacturers from releasing pollutants into the atmosphere, thereby causing danger to the members of the community. The difference is, however, that in the former but not the latter case the harm is of such a nature that it could be avoided by those individuals affected if they so chose. The incurring of the harm requires, so to speak, the active co-operation of the victim. It would be mistaken theoretically and hypocritical in practice to assert that our interference in such cases is just like our interference in standard cases of protecting others from harm. At the very least someone interfered with in this way can reply that no one is complaining about his activities. It may be that impure paternalism requires arguments or reasons of a stronger kind in order to be justified since there are persons who are losing a portion of their liberty and they do not even have the solace of having it be done "in their own interest." Of course in some sense, if paternalistic justifications are ever correct then we are protecting others, we are preventing some from injuring others, but it is important to see the differences between this and the standard case.

Paternalism then will always involve limitations on the liberty of some individuals in their own interest but it may also extend to interferences with the liberty of parties whose interests are not in question.

IV

Finally, by way of some more preliminary analysis, I want to distinguish paternalistic interferences with liberty from a related type with which it is often confused. Consider, for example, legislation which forbids employees to work more than, say, 40 hours per week. It is sometimes argued that such legislation is paternalistic for if employees desired such a restriction on their hours of work they could agree among themselves to impose it voluntarily. But because they do not the society imposes its own conception of their best interests upon them by the use of coercion. Hence this is paternalism.

Now it may be that some legislation of this nature is, in fact, paternalistically motivated. I am not denying that. All I want to point out is that there is another possible way of justifying such measures which is not paternalistic in nature. It is not paternalistic because as Mill puts it in a similar context such measures are "required not to overrule the judgment of individuals respecting their own interest, but to give effect to that judgment: they being unable to give effect to it except by concert, which concert again cannot be effectual unless it receives validity and sanction from the law." [See Reading 10]

The line of reasoning here is a familiar one first found in Hobbes and developed with great sophistication by contemporary economists in the last decade or so. There are restrictions which are in the interests of a class of persons taken collectively but are such that the immediate interest of each individual is furthered by his violating the rule when others adhere to it. In such cases the individuals involved may need the use of compulsion to give effect to their collective judgment of their own interest by guaranteeing each individual compliance by the others. In these cases compulsion is not used to achieve some benefit which is not recognized to be a benefit by those concerned, but rather because it is the only feasible means of achieving some benefit which *is* recognized as such by all concerned. This way of viewing mat-

ters provides us with another characterization of paternalism in general. Paternalism might be thought of as the use of coercion to achieve a good which is not recognized as such by those persons for whom the good is intended. Again while this formulation captures the heart of the matter—it is surely what Mill is objecting to in *On Liberty*—the matter is not always quite like that. For example when we force motorcyclists to wear helmets we are trying to promote a good—the protection of the person from injury—which is surely recognized by most of the individuals concerned. It is not that a cyclist doesn't value his bodily integrity; rather, as a supporter of such legislation would put it, he either places, perhaps irrationally, another value or good (freedom from wearing a helmet) above that of physical well-being or, perhaps, while recognizing the danger in the abstract, he either does not fully appreciate it or he underestimates the likelihood of it occurring. But now we are approaching the question of possible justifications of paternalistic measures and the rest of this essay will be devoted to that question.

V

I shall begin for dialectical purposes by discussing Mill's objections to paternalism and then go on to discuss more positive proposals.

An initial feature that strikes one is the absolute nature of Mill's prohibitions against paternalism. It is so unlike the carefully qualified admonitions of Mill and his fellow Utilitarians on other moral issues. He speaks of self-protection as the *sole* end warranting coercion, of the individual's own goals as *never* being a sufficient warrant. Contrast this with his discussion of the prohibition against lying in *Util[itarianism]*.

> Yet that even this, rule, sacred as it is, admits of possible exception, is acknowledged by all moralists, the chief of which is where the with-holding of some fact . . . would save an individual . . . from great and unmerited evil.

The same tentativeness is present when he deals with justice.

> It is confessedly unjust to break faith with any one: to violate an engagement, either express or implied, or disappoint expectations raised by our own conduct, at least if we have raised these expectations knowingly and voluntarily. Like all the other obligations of justice already spoken of, this one is

not regarded as absolute, but as capable of being overruled by a stronger obligation of justice on the other side.

This anomaly calls for some explanation. The structure of Mill's argument is as follows:

1. Since restraint is an evil the burden of proof is on those who propose such restraint.
2. Since the conduct which is being considered is purely self-regarding, the normal appeal to the protection of the interests of others is not available.
3. Therefore we have to consider whether reasons involving reference to the individual's own good, happiness, welfare, or interests are sufficient to overcome the burden of justification.
4. We either cannot advance the interests of the individual by compulsion, or the attempt to do so involves evil which outweighs the good done.
5. Hence the promotion of the individual's own interests does not provide a sufficient warrant for the use of compulsion.

Clearly the operative premise here is 4 and it is bolstered by claims about the status of the individual as judge and appraiser of his welfare, interests, needs, etc.

> With respect to his own feelings and circumstances, the most ordinary man or woman has means of knowledge immeasurably surpassing those that can be possessed by any one else.
>
> He is the man most interested in his own well-being: the interest which any other person, except in cases of strong personal attachment, can have in it, is trifling, compared to that which he himself has.

These claims are used to support the following generalizations concerning the utility of compulsion for paternalistic purposes.

> The interferences of society to overrule his judgment and purposes in what only regards himself must be grounded on general presumptions; which may be altogether wrong, and even if right, are as likely as not to be misapplied to individual cases.
>
> But the strongest of all the arguments against the interference of the public with purely personal conduct is that when it does interfere, the odds are that it interferes wrongly and in the wrong place.
>
> All errors which the individual is likely to commit against advice and warning are far outweighed by the evil of allowing others to constrain him to what they deem his good.

Performing the utilitarian calculation by balancing the advantages and disadvantages we find that:

> Mankind are greater gainers by suffering each other to live as seems good to themselves, than by compelling each other to live as seems good to the rest.

From which follows the operative premise 4.

This classical case of a utilitarian argument with all the premises spelled out is not the only line of reasoning present in Mill's discussion. There are asides, and more than asides, which look quite different and I shall deal with them later. But this is clearly the main channel of Mill's thought and it is one which has been subjected to vigorous attack from the moment it appeared—most often by fellow Utilitarians. The link that they have usually seized on is, as Fitzjames Stephen put it, the absence of proof that the "mass of adults are so well acquainted with their own interests and so much disposed to pursue them that no compulsion or restraint put upon them by any others for the purpose of promoting their interest can really promote them." Even so sympathetic a critic as Hart is forced to the conclusion that:

> In Chapter 5 of his essay Mill carried his protests against paternalism to lengths that may now appear to us as fantastic. . . . No doubt if we no longer sympathise with this criticism this is due, in part, to a general decline in the belief that individuals know their own interest best.
>
> Mill endows the average individual with "too much of the psychology of a middle-aged man whose desires are relatively fixed, not liable to be artificially stimulated by external influences; who knows what he wants and what gives him satisfaction of happiness; and who pursues these things when he can."

Now it is interesting to note that Mill himself was aware of some of the limitations on the doctrine that the individual is the best judge of his own interests. In his discussion of government intervention in general (even where the intervention does not interfere with liberty but provides alternative institutions to those of the market) after making claims which are parallel to those just discussed, e.g.,

> People understand their own business and their own interests better, and care for them more, than the government does, or can be expected to do.

He goes on to an intelligent discussion of the "very large and conspicuous exceptions" to the maxim that:

Most persons take a juster and more intelligent view of their own interest, and of the means of promoting it than can either be prescribed to them by a general enactment of the legislature, or pointed out in the particular case by a public functionary.

Thus there are things

of which the utility does not consist in ministering to inclinations, nor in serving the daily uses of life, and the want of which is least felt where the need is greatest. This is peculiarly true of those things which are chiefly useful as tending to raise the character of human beings. The uncultivated cannot be competent judges of cultivation. Those who most need to be made wiser and better, usually desire it least, and, if they desired it, would be incapable of finding the way to it by their own lights.

... A second exception to the doctrine that individuals are the best judges of their own interest, is when an individual attempts to decide irrevocably now what will be best for his interest at some future and distant time. The presumption in favor of individual judgment is only legitimate, where the judgment is grounded on actual, and especially on present, personal experience; not where it is formed antecedently to experience, and not suffered to be reversed even after experience has condemned it.

The upshot of these exceptions is that Mill does not declare that there should never be government interference with the economy but rather that

... in every instance, the burden of making out a strong case should be thrown not on those who resist but on those who recommend government interference. Letting alone, in short, should be the general practice: every departure from it, unless required by some great good, is a certain evil.

In short, we get a presumption not an absolute prohibition. The question is why doesn't the argument against paternalism go the same way?

I suggest that the answer lies in seeing that in addition to a purely utilitarian argument Mill uses another as well. As a Utilitarian Mill has to show, in Fitzjames Stephen's words, that:

Self-protection apart, no good object can be attained by any compulsion which is not in itself a greater evil than the absence of the object which the compulsion obtains.

To show this is impossible; one reason being that it isn't true. Preventing a man from selling himself into slavery (a paternalistic measure which Mill himself accepts as legitimate), or from taking heroin, or from driving a car without wearing seat-belts may constitute a lesser evil than allowing him to do any of these things. A consistent Utilitarian can only argue against paternalism on the grounds that it (as a matter of fact) does not maximize the good. It is always a contingent question that may be refuted by the evidence. But there is also a non-contingent argument which runs through *On Liberty*. When Mill states that "there is a part of the life of every person who has come to years of discretion, within which the individuality of that person ought to reign uncontrolled either by any other person or by the public collectively" he is saying something about what it means to be a person, an autonomous agent. It is because coercing a person for his own good denies this status as an independent entity that Mill objects to it so strongly and in such absolute terms. To be able to choose is a good that is independent of the wisdom of what is chosen. A man's "mode of laying out his existence is the best, not because it is the best in itself, but because it is his own mode."

It is the privilege and proper condition of a human being, arrived at the maturity of his faculties, to use and interpret experience in his own way. [See Reading 10]

As further evidence of this line of reasoning in Mill consider the one exception to his prohibition against paternalism.

In this and most civilised countries, for example, an engagement by which a person should sell himself, or allow himself to be sold, as a slave, would be null and void; neither enforced by law nor by opinion. The ground for thus limiting his power of voluntarily disposing of his own lot in life, is apparent, and is very clearly seen in this extreme case. The reason for not interfering, unless for the sake of others, with a person's voluntary acts, is consideration for his liberty. His voluntary choice is evidence that what he so chooses is desirable, or at least endurable, to him, and his good is on the whole best provided for by allowing him to take his own means of pursuing it. But by selling himself for a slave, he abdicates his liberty; he foregoes any future use of it beyond that single act.

He therefore defeats, in his own case, the very purpose which is the justification of allowing him to dispose of himself. He is no longer free; but is thenceforth in a position which has no longer the presumption in its favour, that would be afforded by his voluntarily remaining in it. The principle of freedom cannot require that he should be free not to be free. It is not freedom to be allowed to alienate his freedom.

Now leaving aside the fudging on the meaning of freedom in the last line it is clear that part of this argument is incorrect. While it is true that *future* choices of the slave are not reasons for thinking that what he chooses then is desirable for him, what is at issue is limiting his immediate choice; and since this choice is made freely, the individual may be correct in thinking that his interests are best provided for by entering such a contract. But the main consideration for not allowing such a contract is the need to preserve the liberty of the person to make future choices. This gives us a principle—a very narrow one—by which to justify some paternalistic interferences. Paternalism is justified only to preserve a wider range of freedom for the individual in question. How far this principle could be extended, whether it can justify all the cases in which we are inclined upon reflection to think paternalistic measures justified remains to be discussed. What I have tried to show so far is that there are two strains of argument in Mill—one a straight-forward Utilitarian mode of reasoning and one which relies not on the goods which free choice leads to but on the absolute value of the choice itself. The first cannot establish any absolute prohibition but at most a presumption and indeed a fairly weak one given some fairly plausible assumptions about human psychology; the second while a stronger line of argument seems to me to allow on its own grounds a wider range of paternalism than might be suspected. I turn now to a consideration of these matters.

VI

We might begin looking for principles governing the acceptable use of paternalistic power in cases where it is generally agreed that it is legitimate. Even Mill intends his principles to be applicable only to mature individuals, not those in what he calls "non-age." What is it that justifies us in interfering with children? The fact that they lack some of the emotional and cognitive capacities required in order to make fully rational decisions. It is an empirical question to just what extent children have an adequate conception of their own present and future interests but there is not much doubt that there are many deficiencies. For example it is very difficult for a child to defer gratification for any considerable period of time. Given these deficiencies and given the very real and permanent dangers that may befall the child it becomes not only permissible but even a duty of the parent to restrict the child's freedom in various ways. There is however an important moral limitation on the exercise of such parental power which is provided by the notion of the child eventually coming to see the correctness of his parent's interventions. Parental paternalism may be thought of as a wager by the parent on the child's subsequent recognition of the wisdom of the restrictions. There is an emphasis on what could be called future-oriented consent—on what the child will come to welcome, rather than on what he does welcome.

The essence of this idea has been incorporated by idealist philosophers into various types of "real-will" theory as applied to fully adult persons. Extensions of paternalism are argued for by claiming that in various respects, chronologically mature individuals share the same deficiencies in knowledge, capacity to think rationally, and the ability to carry out decisions that children possess. Hence in interfering with such people we are in effect doing what they would do if they were fully rational. Hence we are not really opposing their will, hence we are not really interfering with their freedom. The dangers of this move have been sufficiently exposed by Berlin in his Two Concepts of Liberty. I see no gain in theoretical clarity nor in practical advantage in trying to pass over the real nature of the interferences with liberty that we impose on others. Still the basic notion of consent is important and seems to me the only acceptable way of trying to delimit an area of justified paternalism.

Let me start by considering a case where the consent is not hypothetical in nature. Under certain conditions it is rational for an individual to agree that others should force him to act in ways in which, at the time of action, the individual may not see as desirable. If, for example, a man knows that he is subject to breaking his resolves when temptation is present, he may ask a friend to refuse to entertain his requests at some later stage.

A classical example is given in the Odyssey when Odysseus commands his men to tie him to the mast and refuse all future orders to be set free, because he knows the power of the Sirens to enchant men with their songs. Here we are on relatively sound ground in later refusing Odysseus' request to be set free. He may even claim to have changed his mind but since it is just such changes that he wished to guard against we are entitled to ignore them.

A process analogous to this may take place on a social rather than individual basis. An electorate may mandate its representatives to pass legislation which when it comes time to "pay the price" may be unpalatable. I may believe that a tax increase is necessary to halt inflation though I may resent the lower pay check each month. However, in both this case and that of Odysseus the measure to be enforced is specifically requested by the party involved and at some point in time there is genuine consent and agreement on the part of those persons whose liberty is infringed. Such is not the case for the paternalistic measures we have been speaking about. What must be involved here is not consent to specific measures but rather consent to a system of government, run by elected representatives, with an understanding that they may act to safeguard our interests in certain limited ways.

I suggest that since we are all aware of our irrational propensities, deficiencies in cognitive and emotional capacities and avoidable and unavoidable ignorance it is rational and prudent for us to in effect take out "social insurance policies." We may argue for and against proposed paternalistic measures in terms of what fully rational individuals would accept as forms of protection. Now, clearly since the initial agreement is not about specific measures we are dealing with a more-or-less blank check and therefore there have to be carefully defined limits. What I am looking for are certain kinds of conditions which make it plausible to suppose that rational men could reach agreement to limit their liberty even when other men's interests are not affected.

Of course as in any kind of agreement schema there are great difficulties in deciding what rational individuals would or would not accept. Particularly in sensitive areas of personal liberty, there is always a danger of the dispute over agreement and rationality being a disguised version of evaluative and normative disagreement.

Let me suggest types of situations in which it seems plausible to suppose that fully rational individuals would agree to having paternalistic restrictions imposed upon them. It is reasonable to suppose that there are "goods" such as health which any person would want to have in order to pursue his own good—no matter how that good is conceived. This is an argument that is used in connection with compulsory education for children but it seems to me that it can be extended to other goods which have this character. Then one could agree that the attainment of such goods should be promoted even when not recognized to be such, at the moment, by the individuals concerned.

An immediate difficulty that arises stems from the fact that men are always faced with competing goods and that there may be reasons why even a value such as health—or indeed life—may be overridden by competing values. Thus the problem with the Christian Scientist and blood transfusions. It may be more important for him to reject "impure substances" than to go on living. The difficult problem that must be faced is whether one can give sense to the notion of a person irrationally attaching weights to competing values.

Consider a person who knows the statistical data on the probability of being injured when not wearing seat-belts in an automobile and knows the types and gravity of the various injuries. He also insists that the inconvenience attached to fastening the belt every time he gets in and out of the car outweighs for him the possible risks to himself. I am inclined in this case to think that such a weighing is irrational. Given his life-plans, which we are assuming are those of the average person, his interests and commitments already undertaken, I think it is safe to predict that we can find inconsistencies in his calculations at some point. I am assuming that this is not a man who for some conscious or unconscious reasons is trying to injure himself nor is he a man who just likes to "live dangerously." I am assuming that he is like us in all the relevant respects but just puts an enormously high negative value on inconvenience—one which does not seem comprehensible or reasonable.

It is always possible, of course to assimilate this person to creatures like myself. I, also, neglect to fasten my seat-belt and I concede such behavior is not rational but not because I weigh the inconvenience differently from those who fasten the belts. It is just that having made (roughly) the same calculation as everybody else I ignore it in my actions. (Note: a much better case of weakness of the will than those usually given in ethics texts.) A plausible explanation for this deplorable habit is that although I know in some intellectual sense what the probabilities and risks are I do not fully appreciate them in an emotionally genuine manner.

We have two distinct types of situations in which a man acts in a non-rational fashion. In one case he attaches incorrect weights to some of his values; in the other he neglects to act in accordance with his actual preferences and desires. Clearly there is a stronger and more persuasive argument for paternalism in the latter situation. Here we are really not—by assumption—imposing a good on another person. But why may we not extend our interference to what we might call evaluative delusions? After all in the case of cognitive delusions we are prepared, often, to act against the expressed will of the person involved. If a man believes that when he jumps out the window he will float upwards—Robert Nozick's example—would not we detain him, forcibly if necessary? The reply will be that this man doesn't wish to be injured and if we could convince him that he is mistaken as to the consequences of his action he would not wish to perform the action. But part of what is involved in claiming that a man who doesn't fasten his seat-belts is attaching an irrational weight to the inconvenience of fastening them is that if he were to be involved in an accident and severely injured he would look back and admit that the inconvenience wasn't as bad as all that. So there is a sense in which if I could convince him of the consequences of his action he also would not wish to continue his present course of action. Now the notion of consequences being used here is covering a lot of ground. In one case it's being used to indicate what will or can happen as a result of a course of action and in the other it's making a prediction about the future evaluation of the consequences—in the first sense—of a course of action. And whatever the difference between facts and values—whether it be hard and fast or soft and slow—we are genuinely more reluctant to consent to interferences where evaluative differences are the issue. Let me now consider another factor which comes into play in some of these situations which may make an important difference in our willingness to consent to paternalistic restrictions.

Some of the decisions we make are of such a character that they produce changes which are in one or another way irreversible. Situations are created in which it is difficult or impossible to return to anything like the initial stage at which the decision was made. In particular some of these changes will make it impossible to continue to make reasoned choices in the future. I am thinking specifically of decisions which involve taking drugs that are physically or psychologically addictive and those which are destructive of one's mental and physical capacities.

I suggest we think of the imposition of paternalistic interferences in situations of this kind as being a kind of insurance policy which we take out against making decisions which are far-reaching, potentially dangerous and irreversible. Each of these factors is important. Clearly there are many decisions we make that are relatively irreversible. In deciding to learn to play chess I could predict in view of my general interest in games that some portion of my free-time was going to be preempted and that it would not be easy to give up

the game once I acquired a certain competence. But my whole life-style was not going to be jeopardized in an extreme manner. Further it might be argued that even with addictive drugs such as heroin one's normal life plans would not be seriously interfered with if an inexpensive and adequate supply were readily available. So this type of argument might have a much narrower scope than appears to be the case at first.

A second class of cases concerns decisions which are made under extreme psychological and sociological pressures. I am not thinking here of the making of the decision as being something one is pressured into—e.g., a good reason for making duelling illegal is that unless this is done many people might have to manifest their courage and integrity in ways in which they would rather not do so—but rather of decisions such as that to commit suicide which are usually made at a point where the individual is not thinking clearly and calmly about the nature of his decision. In addition, of course, this comes under the previous heading of all-too-irrevocable decisions. Now there are practical steps which a society could take if it wanted to decrease the possibility of suicide—for example not paying social security benefits to the survivors or, as religious institutions do, not allowing such persons to be buried with the same status as natural deaths. I think we may count these as interferences with the liberty of persons to attempt suicide and the question is whether they are justifiable.

Using my argument schema the question is whether rational individuals would consent to such limitations. I see no reason for them to consent to an absolute prohibition but I do think it is reasonable for them to agree to some kind of enforced waiting period. Since we are all aware of the possibility of temporary states, such as great fear or depression, that are inimical to the making of well-informed and rational decisions, it would be prudent for all of us if there were some kind of institutional arrangement whereby we were restrained from making a decision which is (all too) irreversible. What this would be like in practice is difficult to envisage and it may be that if no practical arrangements were feasible then we would have to conclude that there should be no restriction at all on this kind of action. But we might have a "cooling off" period, in much the same way that we now require couples who file for divorce to go through a waiting period. Or, more far-fetched, we might imagine a Suicide Board composed of a psychologist and another member picked by the applicant. The Board would be required to meet and talk with the person proposing to take his life, though its approval would not be required.

A third class of decisions—these classes are not supposed to be disjoint—involves dangers which are either not sufficiently understood or appreciated correctly by the persons involved. Let me illustrate, using the example of cigarette smoking, a number of possible cases.

1. A man may not know the facts—e.g., smoking between 1 and 2 packs a day shortens life expectancy 6.2 years, the costs and pain of the illness caused by smoking, etc.
2. A man may know the facts, wish to stop smoking, but not have the requisite will-power.
3. A man may know the facts but not have them play the correct role in his calculation because, say, he discounts the danger psychologically because it is remote in time and/or inflates the attractiveness of other consequences of his decision which he regards as beneficial.

In case 1 what is called for is education, the posting of warnings, etc. In case 2 there is no theoretical problem. We are not imposing a good on someone who rejects it. We are simply using coercion to enable people to carry out their own goals. (Note: There obviously is a difficulty in that only a subclass of the individuals affected wish to be prevented from doing what they are doing.) In case 3 there is a sense in which we are imposing a good on someone since given his current appraisal of the facts he doesn't wish to be restricted. But in another sense we are not imposing a good since what is being claimed—and what must be shown or at least argued for—is that an accurate accounting on his part would lead him to reject his current course of action. Now we all know that such cases exist, that we are prone to disregard dangers that are only possibilities, that immediate pleasures are often magnified and distorted.

If in addition the dangers are severe and far-reaching we could agree to allowing the state a certain degree of power to intervene in such situations. The difficulty is in specifying in advance, even vaguely, the class of cases in which intervention will be legitimate.

A related difficulty is that of drawing a line so that it is not the case that all ultra-hazardous activities are ruled out, e.g. mountain-climbing, bull-fighting, sports-car racing, etc. There are some risks—even very great ones—which a person is entitled to take with his life.

A good deal depends on the nature of the deprivation—e.g., does it prevent the person from engaging in the activity completely or merely limit his participation—and how important to the nature of the activity is the absence of restriction when this is weighed against the role that the activity plays in the life of the person. In the case of automobile seat-belts, for example, the restriction is trivial in nature, interferes not at all with the use or enjoyment of the activity, and does, I am assuming, considerably reduce a high risk of serious injury. Whereas, for example, making mountain-climbing illegal prevents completely a person engaging in an activity which may play an important role in his life and his conception of the person he is.

In general the easiest cases to handle are those which can be argued about in the terms which Mill thought to be so important—a concern not just for the happiness or welfare, in some broad sense, of the individual but rather a concern for the autonomy and freedom of the person. I suggest that we would be most likely to consent to paternalism in those instances in which it preserves and enhances for the individual his ability to rationally consider and carry out his own decisions.

I have suggested in this essay a number of types of situations in which it seems plausible that rational men would agree to granting the legislative powers of a society the right to impose restrictions on what Mill calls "self-regarding" conduct. However, rational men knowing something about the resources of ignorance, ill-will and stupidity available to the lawmakers of a society—a good case in point is the history of drug legislation in the United States—will be concerned to limit such intervention to a minimum. I suggest in closing two principles designed to achieve this end.

In all cases of paternalistic legislation there must be a heavy and clear burden of proof placed on the authorities to demonstrate the exact nature of the harmful effects (or beneficial consequences) to be avoided (or achieved) and the probability of their occurrence. The burden of proof here is twofold—what lawyers distinguish as the burden of going forward and the burden of persuasion. That the authorities have the burden of going forward means that it is up to them to raise the question and bring forward evidence of the evils to be avoided. Unlike the case of new drugs where the manufacturer must produce some evidence that the drug has been tested and found not harmful, no citizen has to show with respect to self-regarding conduct that it is not harmful or promotes his best interests. In addition the nature and cogency of the evidence for the harmfulness of the course of action must be set at a high level. To paraphrase a formulation of the burden of proof for criminal proceedings—better 10 men ruin themselves than one man be unjustly deprived of liberty.

Finally I suggest a principle of the least restrictive alternative. If there is an alternative way of accomplishing the desired end without restricting liberty then although it may involve great expense, inconvenience, etc., the society must adopt it.

READING 19

Liberty, Equality, and Merit

F. A. Hayek

I have no respect for the passion for equality, which seems to me merely idealizing envy.
Oliver Wendell Holmes, Jr.

F. A. Hayek (1899–1992) was a Czech economist and philosopher who emigrated to England and then to the United States. He was a professor at the University of London and the University of Chicago. He is the foremost libertarian philosopher of the twentieth century. Among his works are *The Road to Serfdom* (1944) and *The Constitution of Liberty,* from which this selection is taken.

In this selection Hayek contrasts equality before the law with equality of economic outcomes and contends that only the former is defensible. He argues that people are not equal and that, given equality before the law and freedom to develop one's talents, different people will do better than others. Although this position may seem to resemble meritocracy, merit presupposes an agency wise enough to decide our individual worth, but no human is. So maximal liberty of a free market is the sole way to avoid coercion and tyranny. Inequalities in wealth, including inheritance, while they may exacerbate differences in wealth, are worth those inequalities.

This reading is taken from *The Constitution of Liberty* (University of Chicago Press, 1960), by permission.

1. The great aim of the struggle for liberty has been equality before the law. This equality under the rules which the state enforces may be supplemented by a similar equality of the rules that men voluntarily obey in their relations with one another. This extension of the principle of equality to the rules of moral and social conduct is the chief expression of what is commonly called the democratic spirit—and probably that aspect of it that does most to make inoffensive the inequalities that liberty necessarily produces.

Equality of the general rules of law and conduct, however, is the only kind of equality conducive to liberty and the only equality which we can secure without destroying liberty. Not only has liberty nothing to do with any other sort of equality, but it is even bound to produce inequality in many respects. This is the necessary result and part of the justification of individual liberty: if the result of individual liberty did not demonstrate that some manners of living are more successful than others, much of the case for it would vanish.

It is neither because it assumes that people are in fact equal nor because it attempts to make them equal that the argument for liberty demands that government treat them equally. This argument not only recognizes that individuals are very different but in a great measure rests on that assumption. It insists that these individual differences provide no justification for government to treat them differently. And it objects to the differences in treatment by the state that would be necessary if persons who are in fact very different were to be assured equal positions in life.

Modern advocates of a more far-reaching material equality usually deny that their demands are based on any assumption of the factual equality of all men. It is nevertheless still widely believed that this is the main justification for such demands. Nothing, however, is more damaging to the demand for equal treatment than to base it on so obviously untrue an assumption as that of the factual equality of all men. To rest the case for equal treatment of national or racial minorities on the assertion that they do not differ from other men is implicitly to admit that factual inequality would justify unequal treatment; and the proof that some differences do, in fact, exist would not be long in forthcoming. It is of the essence of the demand for equality before the law that people should be treated alike in spite of the fact that they are different.

2. The boundless variety of human nature—the wide range of differences in individual capacities and potentialities—is one of the most distinctive facts about the human species. Its evolution has made it probably the most variable among all kinds of creatures. It has been well said that "biology, with variability as its cornerstone, confers on every human individual a unique set of attributes which give him a dignity he could not otherwise possess. Every newborn baby is an unknown quantity so far as potentialities are concerned because there are many thousands of unknown interrelated genes and gene-patterns which contribute to his makeup. As a result of nature and nurture the newborn infant may become one of the greatest of men or women ever to have lived. In every case he or she has the making of a distinctive individual. . . . If the differences are not very important, then freedom is not very important and the idea of individual worth is not very important." The writer justly adds that the widely held uniformity theory of human nature, "which on the surface appears to accord with democracy . . . would in time undermine the very basic ideals of freedom and individual worth and render life as we know it meaningless."

It has been the fashion in modern times to minimize the importance of congenital differences between men and to ascribe all the important differences to the influence of environment. However important the latter may be, we must not overlook the fact that individuals are very different from the outset. The importance of individual differences would hardly be less if all people were brought up in very similar environments. As a statement of fact, it just is not true that "all men are born equal." We may continue to use this hallowed phrase to express the ideal that legally and morally all men ought to be treated alike. But if we want to understand what this ideal of equality can or should mean, the first requirement is that we free ourselves from the belief in factual equality.

From the fact that people are very different it follows that, if we treat them equally, the result must be inequality in their actual position, and that the only way to place them in an equal position would be to treat them differently. Equality before the law and material equality are therefore not only different but are in conflict with each other; and we can achieve either the one or the other, but not both at the same time. The equality before the law which freedom requires leads to material inequality. Our argument will be that, though where the state must use coercion for other reasons, it should treat all poeple alike, the desire of making people more alike in their condition cannot be accepted in a free society as a justification for further and discriminatory coercion.

We do not object to equality as such. It merely happens to be the case that a demand for equality is the professed motive of most of those who desire to impose upon society a preconceived pattern of distribution. Our objection is against all attempts to impress upon society a deliberately chosen pattern of distribution, whether it be an order of equality or of inequality. We shall indeed see that many of those who demand an extension of equality do not really demand equality but a distribution that conforms more closely to human conceptions of individual merit and that their desires are as irreconcilable with freedom as the more strictly egalitarian demands.

If one objects to the use of coercion in order to bring about a more even or a more just distribution, this does not mean that one does not regard these as desirable. But if we wish to preserve a free society, it is essential that we recognize that the desirability of a particular object is not sufficient justification for the use of coercion. One may well feel attracted to a community in which there are no extreme contrasts between rich and poor and may welcome the fact that the general increase in wealth seems gradually to reduce those differences. I fully share these feelings and certainly regard the degree of social equality that the United States has achieved as wholly admirable.

There also seems no reason why these widely felt preferences should not guide policy in some respects. Wherever there is a legitimate need for government action and we have to choose between different methods of satisfying such a need, those that incidentally also reduce inequality may well be preferable. If, for example, in the law of intestate succession one kind of provision will be more conducive to equality than another, this may be a strong argument in its favor. It is a different matter, however, if it is demanded that, in order to produce substantive equality, we should abandon the basic postulate of a free society, namely, the limitation of all coercion by equal law. Against this we shall hold that economic inequality is not one of the evils which justify our resorting to discriminatory coercion or privilege as a remedy.

3. Our contention rests on two basic propositions which probably need only be stated to win fairly general assent. The first of them is an expression of the belief in a certain similarity of all human beings: it is the proposition that no man or group of men possesses the capacity to determine conclusively the potentialities of

other human beings and that we should certainly never trust anyone invariably to exercise such a capacity. However great the differences between men may be, we have no ground for believing that they will ever be so great as to enable one man's mind in a particular instance to comprehend fully all that another responsible man's mind is capable of.

The second basic proposition is that the acquisition by any member of the community of additional capacities to do things which may be valuable must always be regarded as a gain for that community. It is true that particular people may be worse off because of the superior ability of some new competitor in their field; but any such additional ability in the community is likely to benefit the majority. This implies that the desirability of increasing the abilities and opportunities of any individual does not depend on whether the same can also be done for the others—provided, of course, that others are not thereby deprived of the opportunity of acquiring the same or other abilities which might have been accessible to them had they not been secured by that individual.

Egalitarians generally regard differently those differences in individual capacities which are inborn and those which are due to the influences of environment, or those which are the result of "nature" and those which are the result of "nurture." Neither, be it said at once, has anything to do with moral merit. Though either may greatly affect the value which an individual has for his fellows, no more credit belongs to him for having been born with desirable qualities than for having grown up under favorable circumstances. The distinction between the two is important only because the former advantages are due to circumstances clearly beyond human control, while the latter are due to factors which we might be able to alter. The important question is whether there is a case for so changing our institutions as to eliminate as much as possible those advantages due to environment. Are we to agree that "all inequalities that rest on birth and inherited property ought to be abolished and none remain unless it is an effect of superior talent and industry?"

The fact that certain advantages rest on human arrangements does not necessarily mean that we could provide the same advantages for all or that, if they are given to some, somebody else is thereby deprived of them. The most important factors to be considered in this connection are the family, inheritance, and education, and it is against the inequality which they produce that criticism is mainly directed. They are, however, not the only important factors of environment.

Geographic conditions such as climate and landscape, not to speak of local and sectional differences in cultural and moral traditions, are scarcely less important. We can, however, consider here only the three factors whose effects are most commonly impugned.

So far as the family is concerned, there exists a curious contrast between the esteem most people profess for the institution and their dislike of the fact that being born into a particular family should confer on a person special advantages. It seems to be widely believed that, while useful qualities which a person acquires because of his native gifts under conditions which are the same for all are socially beneficial, the same qualities become somehow undesirable if they are the result of environmental advantages not available to others. Yet it is difficult to see why the same useful quality which is welcomed when it is the result of a person's natural endowment should be less valuable when it is the product of such circumstances as intelligent parents or a good home.

The value which most people attach to the institution of the family rests on the belief that, as a rule, parents can do more to prepare their children for a satisfactory life than anyone else. This means not only that the benefits which particular people derive from their family environment will be different but also that these benefits may operate cumulatively through several generations. What reason can there be for believing that a desirable quality in a person is less valuable to society if it has been the result of family background than if it has not? There is, indeed, good reason to think that there are some socially valuable qualities which will be rarely acquired in a single generation but which will generally be formed only by the continuous efforts of two or three. This means simply that there are parts of the cultural heritage of a society that are more effectively transmitted through the family. Granted this, it would be unreasonable to deny that a society is likely to get a better elite if ascent is not limited to one generation, if individuals are not deliberately made to start from the same level, and if children are not deprived of the chance to benefit from the better education and material environment which their parents may be able to provide. To admit this is merely to recognize that belonging to a particular family is part of the individual personality, that society is made up as much of families as of individuals, and that the transmission of the heritage of civilization within the family is as important a tool in man's striving toward better things as is the heredity of beneficial physical attributes.

4. Many people who agree that the family is desirable as an instrument for the transmission of morals, tastes, and knowledge still question the desirability of the transmission of material property. Yet there can be little doubt that, in order that the former may be possible, some continuity of standards, of the external forms of life, is essential, and that this will be achieved only if it is possible to transmit not only immaterial but also material advantages. There is, of course, neither greater merit nor any greater injustice involved in some people being born to wealthy parents than there is in others being born to kind or intelligent parents. The fact is that it is no less of an advantage to the community if at least some children can start with the advantages which at any given time only wealthy homes can offer than if some children inherit great intelligence or are taught better morals at home.

We are not concerned here with the chief argument for private inheritance, namely, that it seems essential as a means to preserve the dispersal in the control of capital and as an inducement for its accumulation. Rather, our concern here is whether the fact that it confers unmerited benefits on some is a valid argument against the institution. It is unquestionably one of the institutional causes of inequality. In the present context we need not inquire whether liberty demands unlimited freedom of bequest. Our problem here is merely whether people ought to be free to pass on to children or others such material possessions as will cause substantial inequality.

Once we agree that it is desirable to harness the natural instincts of parents to equip the new generation as well as they can, there seems no sensible ground for limiting this to non-material benefits. The family's function of passing on standards and traditions is closely tied up with the possibility of transmitting material goods. And it is difficult to see how it would serve the true interest of society to limit the gain in material conditions to one generation.

There is also another consideration which, though it may appear somewhat cynical, strongly suggests that if we wish to make the best use of the natural partiality of parents for their children, we ought not to preclude the transmission of property. It seems certain that among the many ways in which those who have gained power and influence might provide for their children, the bequest of a fortune is socially by far the cheapest. Without this outlet, these men would look for other ways of providing for their children, such as placing them in positions which might bring them the income and the prestige that a fortune would have done; and

this would cause a waste of resources and an injustice much greater than is caused by the inheritance of property. Such is the case with all societies in which inheritance of property does not exist, including the Communist. Those who dislike the inequalities caused by inheritance should therefore recognize that, men being what they are, it is the least of evils, even from their point of view.

5. Though inheritance used to be the most widely criticized source of inequality, it is today probably no longer so. Egalitarian agitation now tends to concentrate on the unequal advantages due to differences in education. There is a growing tendency to express the desire to secure equality of conditions in the claim that the best education we have learned to provide for some should be made gratuitously available for all and that, if this is not possible, one should not be allowed to get a better education than the rest merely because one's parents are able to pay for it, but only those and all those who can pass a uniform test of ability should be admitted to the benefits of the limited resources of higher education.

The problem of educational policy raises too many issues to allow of their being discussed incidentally under the general heading of equality. For the present we shall only point out that enforced equality in this field can hardly avoid preventing some from getting the education they otherwise might. Whatever we might do, there is no way of preventing those advantages which only some can have, and which it is desirable that some should have, from going to people who neither individually merit them nor will make as good a use of them as some other person might have done. Such a problem cannot be satisfactorily solved by the exclusive and coercive powers of the state.

It is instructive at this point to glance briefly at the change that the ideal of equality has undergone in this field in modern times. A hundred years ago, at the height of the classical liberal movement, the demand was generally expressed by the phrase *la carrière ouverte aux talents* "careers open to talent". It was a demand that all man-made obstacles to the rise of some should be removed, that all privileges of individuals should be abolished, and that what the state contributed to the chance of improving one's conditions should be the same for all. That so long as people were different and grew up in different families this could not assure an equal start was fairly generally accepted. It was understood that the duty of government was not to ensure that everybody had the same prospect of reaching a given position but merely to make available to all on equal terms those facilities which in their nature depended on government action. That the results were bound to be different, not only because the individuals were different, but also because only a small part of the relevant circumstances depended on government action, was taken for granted.

This conception that all should be allowed to try has been largely replaced by the altogether different conception that all must be assured an equal start and the same prospects. This means little less than that the government, instead of providing the same circumstances for all, should aim at controlling all conditions relevant to a particular individual's prospects and so adjust them to his capacities as to assure him of the same prospects as everybody else. Such deliberate adaptation of opportunities to individual aims and capacities would, of course, be the opposite of freedom. Nor could it be justified as a means of making the best use of all available knowledge except on the assumption that government knows best how individual capacities can be used.

When we inquire into the justification of these demands, we find that they rest on the discontent that the success of some people often produces in those that are less successful, or, to put it bluntly, on envy. The modern tendency to gratify this passion and to disguise it in the respectable garment of social justice is developing into a serious threat to freedom. Recently an attempt was made to base these demands on the argument that it ought to be the aim of politics to remove all sources of discontent. This would, of course, necessarily mean that it is the responsibility of government to see that nobody is healthier or possesses a happier temperament, a better-suited spouse or more prospering children, than anybody else. If really all unfulfilled desires have a claim on the community, individual responsibility is at an end. However human, envy is certainly not one of the sources of discontent that a free society can eliminate. It is probably one of the essential conditions for the preservation of such a society that we do not countenance envy, not sanction its demands by camouflaging it as social justice, but treat it, in the words of John Stuart Mill, as "the most anti-social and evil of all passions."

6. While most of the strictly egalitarian demands are based on nothing better than envy, we must recognize that much that on the surface appears as a demand for greater equality is in fact a demand for a juster distribution of the good things of this world and springs therefore from much more creditable motives. Most people will object not to the bare fact of inequality but to the fact that the differences in reward do not correspond to any recognizable differences in the merits of those who receive them. The answer commonly given to this is that a free society on the whole achieves this kind of justice. This, however, is an indefensible contention if by justice is meant proportionality of reward to moral merit. Any attempt to found the case for freedom on this argument is very damaging to it, since it concedes that material rewards ought to be made to correspond to recognizable merit and then opposes the conclusion that most people will draw from this by an assertion which is untrue. The proper answer is that in a free system it is neither desirable nor practicable that material rewards should be made generally to correspond to what men recognize as merit and that it is an essential characteristic of a free society that an individual's position should not necessarily depend on the views that his fellows hold about the merit he has acquired.

This contention may appear at first so strange and even shocking that I will ask the reader to suspend judgment until I have further explained the distinction between value and merit. The difficulty in making the point clear is due to the fact that the term "merit," which is the only one available to describe what I mean, is also used in a wider and vaguer sense. It will be used here exclusively to describe the attributes of conduct that make it deserving of praise, that is, the moral character of the action and not the value of the achievement.

As we have seen throughout our discussion, the value that the performance or capacity of a person has to his fellows has no necessary connection with its ascertainable merit in this sense. The inborn as well as the acquired gifts of a person clearly have a value to his fellows which does not depend on any credit due to him for possessing them. There is little a man can do to alter the fact that his special talents are very common or exceedingly rare. A good mind or a fine voice, a beautiful face or a skilful hand, and a ready wit or an attractive personality are in a large measure as independent of a person's efforts as the opportunities or the experiences he has had. In all these instances the value which a person's capacities or services have for us and for which he is recompensed has little relation to anything that we can call moral merit or deserts. Our problem is whether it is desirable that people should enjoy advantages in proportion to the benefits which their fellows derive from their activities or whether the distribution of these advantages should be based on other men's views of their merits.

Reward according to merit must in practice mean reward according to assessable merit, merit that other people can recognize and agree upon and not merit merely in the sight of some higher power. Assessable merit in this sense presupposes that we can ascertain that a man has done what some accepted rule of conduct demanded of him and that this has cost him some pain and effort. Whether this has been the case cannot be judged by the result: merit is not a matter of the objective outcome but of subjective effort. The attempt to achieve a valuable result may be highly meritorious but a complete failure, and full success may be entirely the result of accident and thus without merit. If we know that a man has done his best, we will often wish to see him rewarded irrespective of the result; and if we know that a most valuable achievement is almost entirely due to luck or favorable circumstances, we will give little credit to the author.

We may wish that we were able to draw this distinction in every instance. In fact, we can do so only rarely with any degree of assurance. It is possible only where we possess all the knowledge which was at the disposal of the acting person, including a knowledge of his skill and confidence, his state of mind and his feelings, his capacity for attention, his energy and persistence, etc. The possibility of a true judgment of merit thus depends on the presence of precisely those conditions whose general absence is the main argument for liberty. It is because we want people to use knowledge which we do not possess that we let them decide for themselves. But insofar as we want them to be free to use capacities and knowledge of facts which we do not have, we are not in a position to judge the merit of their achievements. To decide on merit presupposes that we can judge whether people have made such use of their opportunities as they ought to have made and how much effort of will or self-denial this has cost them; it presupposes also that we can distinguish between that part of their achievement which is due to circumstances within their control and that part which is not.

7. The incompatibility of reward according to merit with freedom to choose one's pursuit is most evident in those areas where the uncertainty of the outcome is particularly great and our individual estimates of the chances of various kinds of effort very different. In those speculative efforts which we call "research" or "exploration," or in economic activities which we commonly describe as "speculation," we cannot expect to attract those best qualified for them unless we give the successful ones all the credit or gain, though many others may have striven as meritoriously. For the same reason that nobody can know beforehand who will be the successful ones, nobody can say who has earned greater merit. It would clearly not serve our purpose if we let all who have honestly striven share in the prize. Moreover, to do so would make it necessary that somebody have the right to decide who is to be allowed to strive for it. If in their pursuit of uncertain goals people are to use their own knowledge and capacities, they must be guided, not by what other people think they ought to do, but by the value others attach to the result at which they aim.

What is so obviously true about those undertakings which we commonly regard as risky is scarcely less true of any chosen object we decide to pursue. Any such decision is beset with uncertainty, and if the choice is to be as wise as it is humanly possible to make it, the alternative results anticipated must be labeled according to their value. If the remuneration did not correspond to the value that the product of a man's efforts has for his fellows, he would have no basis for deciding whether the pursuit of a given object is worth the effort and risk. He would necessarily have to be told what to do, and some other person's estimate of what was the best use of his capacities would have to determine both his duties and his remuneration.

The fact is, of course, that we do not wish people to earn a maximum of merit but to achieve a maximum of usefulness at a minimum of pain and sacrifice and therefore a minimum of merit. Not only would it be impossible for us to reward all merit justly, but it would not even be desirable that people should aim chiefly at earning a maximum of merit. Any attempt to induce them to do this would necessarily result in people being rewarded differently for the same service. And it is only the value of the result that we can judge with any degree of confidence, not the different degrees of effort and care that it has cost different people to achieve it.

The prizes that a free society offers for the result serve to tell those who strive for them how much effort they are worth. However, the same prizes will go to all those who produce the same result, regardless of effort. What is true here of the remuneration for the same services rendered by different people is even more true of the relative remuneration for different services requiring different gifts and capacities: they will have little relation to merit. The market will generally offer for services of any kind the value they will have for those who benefit from them; but it will rarely be known whether it was necessary to offer so much in order to obtain these services, and often, no doubt, the community could have had them for much less. The pianist who was reported not long ago to have said that he would perform even if he had to pay for the privilege probably described the position of many who earn large incomes from activities which are also their chief pleasure.

8. Though most people regard as very natural the claim that nobody should be rewarded more than he deserves for his pain and effort, it is nevertheless based on a colossal presumption. It presumes that we are able to judge in every individual instance how well people use the different opportunities and talents given to them and how meritorious their achievements are in the light of all the circumstances which have made them possible. It presumes that some human beings are in a position to determine conclusively what a person is worth and are entitled to determine what he may achieve. It presumes, then, what the argument for liberty specifically rejects: that we can and do know all that guides a person's action.

A society in which the position of the individuals was made to correspond to human ideas of moral merit would therefore be the exact opposite of a free society. It would be a society in which people were rewarded for duty performed instead of for success, in which every move of every individual was guided by what other people thought he ought to do, and in which the individual was thus relieved of the responsibility and the risk of decision. But if nobody's knowledge is sufficient to guide all human action, there is also no human being who is competent to reward all efforts according to merit.

In our individual conduct we generally act on the assumption that it is the value of a person's performance and not his merit that determines our obligation to him. Whatever may be true in more intimate relations, in the ordinary business of life we do not feel that, because a man has rendered us a service at a great sacrifice, our debt to him is determined by this, so long as we could have had the same service provided with ease by somebody else. In our dealings with other men we feel that we are doing justice if we recompense value rendered with equal value, without inquiring what it might have cost the particular individual to supply us with these services. What determines our responsibility is the advantage we derive from what others offer us, not their merit in providing it. We also expect in our dealings with others to be remunerated not according

to our subjective merit but according to what our services are worth to them. Indeed, so long as we think in terms of our relations to particular people, we are generally quite aware that the mark of the free man is to be dependent for his livelihood not on other people's views of his merit but solely on what he has to offer them. It is only when we think of our position or our income as determined by "society" as a whole that we demand reward according to merit.

Though moral value or merit is a species of value, not all value is moral value, and most of our judgments of value are not moral judgments. That this must be so in a free society is a point of cardinal importance; and the failure to distinguish between value and merit has been the source of serious confusion. We do not necessarily admire all activities whose product we value; and in most instances where we value what we get, we are in no position to assess the merit of those who have provided it for us. If a man's ability in a given field is more valuable after thirty years' work than it was earlier, this is independent of whether these thirty years were most profitable and enjoyable or whether they were a time of unceasing sacrifice and worry. If the pursuit of a hobby produces a special skill or an accidental invention turns out to be extremely useful to others, the fact that there is little merit in it does not make it any less valuable than if the result had been produced by painful effort.

This difference between value and merit is not peculiar to any one type of society—it would exist anywhere. We might, of course, attempt to make rewards correspond to merit instead of value, but we are not likely to succeed in this. In attempting it, we would destroy the incentives which enable people to decide for themselves what they should do. Moreover, it is more than doubtful whether even a fairly successful attempt to make rewards correspond to merit would produce a more attractive or even a tolerable social order. A society in which it was generally presumed that a high income was proof of merit and a low income of the lack of it, in which it was universally believed that position and remuneration corresponded to merit, in which there was no other road to success than the approval of one's conduct by the majority of one's fellows, would probably be much more unbearable to the unsuccessful ones than one in which it was frankly recognized that there was no necessary connection between merit and success.

It would probably contribute more to human happiness if, instead of trying to make remuneration correspond to merit, we made clearer how uncertain is the connection between value and merit. We are probably all much too ready to ascribe personal merit where there is, in fact, only superior value. The possession by an individual or a group of a superior civilization or education certainly represents an important value and constitutes an asset for the community to which they belong; but it usually constitutes little merit. Popularity and esteem do not depend more on merit than does financial success. It is, in fact, largely because we are so used to assuming an often non-existent merit wherever we find value that we balk when, in particular instances, the discrepancy is too large to be ignored.

There is every reason why we ought to endeavor to honor special merit where it has gone without adequate reward. But the problem of rewarding action of outstanding merit which we wish to be widely known as an example is different from that of the incentives on which the ordinary functioning of society rests. A free society produces institutions in which, for those who prefer it, a man's advancement depends on the judgment of some superior or of the majority of his fellows. Indeed, as organizations grow larger and more complex, the task of ascertaining the individual's contribution will become more difficult; and it will become increasingly necessary that, for many, merit in the eyes of the managers rather than the ascertainable value of the contribution should determine the rewards. So long as this does not produce a situation in which a single comprehensive scale of merit is imposed upon the whole society, so long as a multiplicity of organizations compete with one another in offering different prospects, this is not merely compatible with freedom but extends the range of choice open to the individual.

9. Justice, like liberty and coercion, is a concept which, for the sake of clarity, ought to be confined to the deliberate treatment of men by other men. It is an aspect of the intentional determination of those conditions of people's lives that are subject to such control. Insofar as **we want the effort**s of individuals to be guided by their own views about prospects and chances, the results of the individual's efforts are necessarily unpredictable, and the question as to whether the resulting distribution of incomes is just has no meaning. Justice does require that those conditions of people's lives that are determined by government be provided equally for all. But equality of those conditions must lead to inequality of results. Neither the equal provision of particular public facilities nor the equal treatment of different partners in our voluntary dealings with one another will secure reward that is proportional to merit. Reward for merit is reward for obeying the wishes of others in what we do, not compensation for the benefits we have conferred upon them by doing what we thought best.

It is, in fact, one of the objections against attempts by government to fix income scales that the state must attempt to be just in all it does. Once the principle of reward according to merit is accepted as the just foundation for the distribution of incomes, justice would require that all who desire it should be rewarded according to that principle. Soon it would also be demanded that the same principle be applied to all and that incomes not in proportion to recognizable merit not be tolerated. Even an attempt merely to distinguish between those incomes or gains which are "earned" and those which are not will set up a principle which the state will have to try to apply but cannot in fact apply generally. And every such attempt at deliberate control of some remunerations is bound to create further demands for new controls. The principle of distributive justice, once introduced, would not be fulfilled until the whole of society was organized in accordance with it. This would produce a kind of society which in all essential respects would be the opposite of a free society—a society in which authority decided what the individual was to do and how he was to do it.

10. In conclusion we must briefly look at another argument on which the demands for a more equal distribution are frequently based, though it is rarely explicitly stated. This is the contention that membership in a particular community or nation entitles the individual to a particular material standard that is determined by the general wealth of the group to which he belongs. This demand is in curious conflict with the desire to base distribution on personal merit. There is clearly no merit in being born into a particular community, and no argument of justice can be based on the accident of a particular individual's being born in one place rather than another. A relatively wealthy community in fact regularly confers advantages on its poorest members unknown to those born in poor communities. In a wealthy community the only justification its members can have for insisting on further advantages is that there is much private wealth that the government can confiscate and redistribute and that men who

constantly see such wealth being enjoyed by others will have a stronger desire for it than those who know of it only abstractly, if at all.

There is no obvious reason why the joint efforts of the members of any group to ensure the maintenance of law and order and to organize the provision of certain services should give the members a claim to a particular share in the wealth of this group. Such claims would be especially difficult to defend where those who advanced them were unwilling to concede the same rights to those who did not belong to the same nation or community. The recognition of such claims on a national scale would in fact only create a new kind of collective (but not less exclusive) property right in the resources of the nation that could not be justified on the same grounds as individual property. Few people would be prepared to recognize the justice of these demands on a world scale. And the bare fact that within a given nation the majority had the actual power to enforce such demands, while in the world as a whole it did not yet have it, would hardly make them more just.

There are good reasons why we should endeavor to use whatever political organization we have at our disposal to make provision for the weak or infirm or for the victims of unforeseeable disaster. It may well be true that the most effective method of providing against certain risks common to all citizens of a state is to give every citizen protection against those risks. The level on which such provisions against common risks can be made will necessarily depend on the general wealth of the community.

It is an entirely different matter, however, to suggest that those who are poor, merely in the sense that there are those in the same community who are richer, are entitled to a share in the wealth of the latter or that being born into a group that has reached a particular level of civilization and comfort confers a title to a share in all its benefits. The fact that all citizens have an interest in the common provision of some services is no justification for anyone's claiming as a right a share in all the benefits. It may set a standard for what some ought to be willing to give, but not for what anyone can demand.

National groups will become more and more exclusive as the acceptance of this view that we have been contending against spreads. Rather than admit people to the advantages that living in their country offers, a nation will prefer to keep them out altogether; for, once admitted, they will soon claim as a right a particular share in its wealth. The conception

that citizenship or even residence in a country confers a claim to a particular standard of living is becoming a serious source of international friction. And since the only justification for applying the principle within a given country is that its government has the power to enforce it, we must not be surprised if we find the same principle being applied by force on an international scale. Once the right of the majority to the benefits that minorities enjoy is recognized on a national scale, there is no reason why this should stop at the boundaries of the existing states.

READING 20

Welfare Libertarianism

James P. Sterba

James P. Sterba is Professor of Philosophy at the University of Notre Dame. He has written more than 150 articles and published twenty-one books, including *How to Make People Just, Earth Ethics, Feminist Philosophies,* and *Morality in Practice.* His book *Justice for Here and Now* was awarded the 1998 Book of the Year Award of the North American Society for Social Philosophy. His most recent book is *Three Challenges to Ethics: Environmentalism, Feminism and Multiculturalism.*

In this selection, Sterba shows how the libertarian view can be used to support arguments for a welfare state, despite most interpretations, which claim libertanism argues against welfare

This selection has been written for this work and appears here in print for the first time.

Libertarians have interpreted their ideal of liberty in two basically different ways. Some, following Herbert Spencer, have (1) taken a right to liberty as basic and (2) derived all other rights from this right to liberty. Others, following John Locke, have (1) taken a set of rights, including typically a right to life and a right to property, as basic and (2) defined liberty as the absence of constraints in the exercise of these rights. Both groups of libertarians regard liberty as the ultimate political ideal, but they do so for different reasons. For Spencerian libertarians, liberty is the ultimate political ideal because all other rights are derived from a right to liberty. For Lockean libertarians, liberty is the ultimate political ideal because liberty is just the absence of constraints in the exercise of people's fundamental rights.

One could, of course, develop the libertarian view in directions that libertarians are happy to go. For example, one could derive a range of nonpaternalistic policies, including the legalization of drugs, from a libertarian foundation. Unfortunately, developing libertarianism in such directions would do little to reconcile the differences between libertarians and welfare liberals over the provision of welfare in society, given that libertarians think their own ideal requires the rejection of a right to welfare, while welfare liberals endorse this right as a basic requirement of their ideals. Accordingly, I propose to develop the libertarian view in a direction that libertarians have yet to recognize by showing that their ideal requires the right to welfare endorsed by welfare liberals, or, put another way, that libertarianism leads to welfare libertarianism.

I. SPENCERIAN AND LOCKEAN LIBERTARIANS

Let us begin by considering the view of Spencerian libertarians, who take a right to liberty to be basic and define all other rights in terms of this right to liberty. According to this view, liberty is usually interpreted as being unconstrained by other persons from doing what one wants or is able to do. Interpreting liberty this way, libertarians like to limit constraints to positive acts (that is, acts of commission) that prevent people from doing what they otherwise want or are able to do. In contrast, welfare liberals and socialists interpret constraints to include, in addition, negative acts (acts of omission) that prevent people from doing what they otherwise want or are able to do. In fact, this is one way to understand the debate between defenders of "negative liberty" and defenders of "positive liberty." This is because defenders of negative

liberty interpret constraints to include only positive acts of others that prevent people from doing what they otherwise want or are able to do, while defenders of positive liberty interpret constraints to include both positive and negative acts of others that prevent people from doing what they otherwise want or are able to do.

In order not to beg the question against libertarians, suppose we interpret constraints in the manner favored by libertarians to include only positive acts by others that prevent people from doing what they otherwise want or are able to do. Libertarians go on to characterize their political ideal as requiring that each person should have the greatest amount of liberty commensurate with the same liberty for all.[1] From this ideal, they claim that a number of more specific requirements, in particular a right to life, a right to freedom of speech, press, and assembly, and a right to property, can be derived.

Here it is important to observe that the libertarian's right to life is not a right to receive from others the goods and resources necessary for preserving one's life. It is not a right to welfare: It is simply a right not to be killed unjustly. Correspondingly, the libertarian's right to property is not a right to receive from others the goods and resources necessary to meet one's basic needs, but rather a right to acquire goods and resources either by initial acquisitions or by voluntary agreements.

Of course, libertarians would allow that it would be nice of the rich to share their surplus goods and resources with the poor. Nevertheless, they deny that government has a duty to provide for such needs. Some good things, such as providing welfare to the needy, are requirements of charity rather than justice, libertarians claim. Accordingly, failure to make such provisions is neither blameworthy nor punishable. As a consequence, libertarians contend that such acts of charity should not be coercively required. For this reason, they are opposed to any coercively supported welfare program.

The same opposition to coercively supported welfare programs characterizes Lockean libertarians, who take a set of rights, typically including a right to life and a right to property, as basic and then interpret liberty as being unconstrained by other persons from doing what one has a right to do. According to this view, a right to life is simply a right not to be killed unjustly; it is not a right to receive welfare. Correspondingly, a right to property is a right to acquire property either by initial acquisitions or by voluntary transactions; it is not a right to receive from others whatever goods and resources one needs to maintain oneself. Understanding a right to life and a right to property in this way, libertarians reject coercively supported welfare programs as violations of liberty.

II. SPENCERIAN LIBERTARIANS AND THE PROBLEM OF CONFLICT

To evaluate the libertarian view, let us begin with the ideal of liberty as defended by Spencerian libertarians and consider a typical conflict situation between the rich and the poor. In this situation, the rich have more than enough goods and resources to satisfy their basic needs. By contrast, the poor lack the goods and resources to meet their most basic needs, even though they have tried all the means available to them that Spencerian libertarians regard as legitimate for acquiring such goods and resources. Under circumstances like these, libertarians usually maintain that the rich should have the liberty to use their goods and resources to satisfy their luxury needs if they so wish. Spencerian libertarians recognize that this liberty might well be enjoyed at the expense of the satisfaction of the most basic needs of the poor; they just think that liberty always has priority over other political ideals, and since they assume that the liberty of the poor is not at stake in such conflict situations, it is easy for them to conclude that the rich should not be required to sacrifice their liberty so that the basic needs of the poor may be met.

Spencerian libertarians also allow that it would be nice of the rich to share their surplus goods and resources with the poor. Nevertheless, according to Spencerian libertarians, such acts of charity cannot be required, because the liberty of the poor is not thought to be at stake in such conflict situations.

In fact, however, the liberty of the poor is at stake in such conflict situations. What is at stake is the liberty of the poor not to be interfered with in taking from the surplus possessions of the rich what is necessary to satisfy their basic needs.[2] Needless to say, Spencerian libertarians would want to deny that the poor have this liberty. But how could they justify such a denial? As this liberty of the poor has been specified, it is not a positive right to receive something but a negative right of noninterference. Nor will it do for Spencerian libertarians to appeal to a right to life or a right to property to rule out such a liberty, because on the Spencerian view liberty is basic and all other rights are derived from a right to liberty. Clearly, what Spencerian libertarians must do is recognize the existence of such a liberty and then claim that it conflicts with other liberties of the rich. But when Spencerian libertarians see that this is the case, they are often genuinely surprised— one might even say rudely awakened—for they had not previously seen the conflict between the rich and the poor as a conflict of liberties.

When the conflict between the rich and the poor is viewed as a conflict of liberties, either we can say that the rich should have the liberty not to be interfered with in using their surplus goods and resources for luxury purposes or we can say that the poor should have the liberty not to be interfered with in taking from the rich what they require to meet their basic needs. If we choose one liberty, we must reject the other. What needs to be determined, therefore, is which liberty is morally preferable: the liberty of the rich or the liberty of the poor.

Two Principles

In order to see that the liberty of the poor not to be interfered with in taking from the surplus resources of the rich what is required to meet their basic needs is morally preferable to the liberty of the rich not to be interfered with in using their surplus goods and resources for luxury purposes, we need to appeal to one of the most fundamental principles of morality, one that is common to all political perspectives. This is the "ought" implies "can" principle:

> People are not morally required to do what they lack the power to do or what would involve so great a sacrifice that it would be unreasonable to ask them to perform such an action and/or, in the case of severe conflicts of interest, unreasonable to require them to perform such an action.

For example, suppose I promised to attend a departmental meeting on Friday, but on Thursday I am involved in a serious car accident that leaves me in a coma. Surely, it is no longer the case that I ought to attend the meeting now that I lack the power to do so. Or suppose that on Thursday I develop a severe case of pneumonia for which I am hospitalized. Surely, I could legitimately claim that I cannot attend the meeting, on the grounds that the risk to my health involved in attending is a sacrifice that it would be unreasonable to ask me to bear. Or suppose the risk to my health from having pneumonia is not so great that it would be unreasonable to ask me to attend the meeting (a supererogatory request), it still might be serious enough to be unreasonable to require my attendance at the meeting (a demand that is backed up by blame or coercion).

What is distinctive about this formulation of the "ought" implies "can" principle is that it claims that the requirements of morality cannot, all things considered, be unreasonable to ask, and/or, in cases of severe conflict of interest, unreasonable to require people to abide by. The principle claims that reason and morality must be linked in an appropriate way, especially if we are going to be able justifiably to use blame or coercion to get people to abide by the requirements of morality. It should be noted, however, that although major figures in the history of philosophy, and most philosophers today, including virtually all libertarian philosophers, accept this linkage between reason and morality, this linkage is not usually conceived to be part of the "ought" implies "can" principle. Nevertheless, I claim that there are good reasons for associating this linkage with the principle, namely, our use of the word "can" as in the example just given, and the natural progression from logical, physical, and psychological possibility found in the traditional "ought" implies "can" principle to the notion of moral possibility found in this formulation of the principle. In any case, the acceptability of this formulation of the "ought" implies "can" principle is determined by the virtually universal acceptance of its components and not by the manner in which I have proposed to join those components together.

Now applying the "ought" implies "can" principle to the case at hand, it seems clear that the poor have it within their power willingly to relinquish such an important liberty as the liberty not to be interfered with in taking from the rich what they require to meet their basic needs. Nevertheless, it would be unreasonable to ask or require them to make so great a sacrifice. In the extreme case, it would involve asking or requiring the poor to sit back and starve to death. Of course, the poor may have no real alternative to relinquishing this liberty. To do anything else may involve worse consequences for themselves and their loved ones and may invite a painful death. Accordingly, we may expect that the poor would acquiesce, albeit unwillingly, to a political system that denies them the right to welfare supported by such a liberty at the same time that we recognize that such a system imposes an unreasonable sacrifice upon the poor—a sacrifice that we cannot morally blame the poor for trying to evade. Analogously, we might expect that a woman whose life was threatened would submit to a rapist's demands at the same time that we recognize the utter unreasonableness of those demands.

By contrast, it would not be unreasonable to ask and require the rich to sacrifice the liberty to meet some of their luxury needs so that the poor could have the liberty to meet their basic needs. Naturally, we might expect that the rich, for reasons of self-interest and past contribution, might be disinclined to make such a sacrifice. We might even suppose that the past contribution of the rich provides a good reason for not sacrificing their liberty to use their surplus for luxury purposes. Yet, unlike the poor, the rich can not claim that relinquishing such a liberty would involve so great a sacrifice that it would be unreasonable to ask and require them to make it; unlike the poor, the rich can be morally blameworthy for failing to make such a sacrifice.

Notice that by virtue of the "ought" implies "can" principle, this argument establishes that:

> (1a) Because it would be unreasonable to ask or require the poor to sacrifice the liberty not to be interfered with when taking from the surplus goods and resources of the rich what is necessary to meet their basic needs, (1b) it is not the case that the poor are morally required to make such a sacrifice.

> (2a) Because it would not be unreasonable to ask and require the rich to sacrifice the liberty not to be interfered with when using their surplus goods and resources for luxury purposes, (2b) it may be the case that the rich are morally required to make such a sacrifice.

What the argument does not establish is that the rich are *morally required* to sacrifice (some of) their surplus so that the basic needs of the poor can be met. To establish that conclusion clearly, we need to appeal to a principle that is, in fact, simply the contrapositive of the "ought" implies "can" principle. It is the conflict resolution principle:

> What people are morally required to do is what is either reasonable to ask them to do or, in the case of severe conflicts of interest, reasonable to require them to do.

While the "ought" implies "can" principle claims that if any action is *not reasonable to ask or require* a person to do, all things considered, that action is *not morally required* for that person, all things considered. The conflict resolution principle claims that if any action is *morally required* for a person to do, all things considered, that action is *reasonable to ask or require* that person to do, all things considered.

This conflict resolution principle accords with the generally accepted view of morality as a system of reasons for resolving interpersonal conflicts of interest. Of course, morality is not limited to such a system of reasons. Most surely it also includes reasons of self-development. All that is being claimed by the principle is that moral resolutions of interpersonal conflicts of interest cannot be contrary to reason to ask everyone affected to accept or, in the case of severe interpersonal conflicts of interest, unreasonable to require everyone affected to accept. The reason for the distinction between the two kinds of cases is that when interpersonal conflicts of interest are not severe, moral resolutions must still be reasonable to ask everyone affected to accept, but they need not be reasonable to *require* everyone affected to accept. This is because not all moral resolutions can be justifiably enforced; only moral resolutions of severe interpersonal conflicts of interest can and *should* be justifiably enforced. Furthermore, the reason why moral resolutions of severe interpersonal conflicts of interest should be enforced is that if the parties are simply asked but not required to abide by a moral resolution in such cases of conflict, then it is likely that the stronger party will violate the resolution and that would be unreasonable to ask or require the weaker party to accept.

When we apply the conflict resolution principle to our example of severe conflict between the rich and the poor, there are three possible moral resolutions:

I. a moral resolution that would require the rich to sacrifice the liberty not to be interfered with when using their surplus goods and resources for luxury purposes so that the poor can have the liberty not to be interfered with when taking from the surplus resources of the rich what is necessary to meet their basic needs;

II. a moral resolution that would require the poor to sacrifice the liberty not to be interfered with when taking from the surplus goods and resources of the rich what is necessary to meet their basic needs so

that the rich can have the liberty not to be interfered with when using their surplus resources for luxury purposes;

III. a moral resolution that would require the rich and the poor to accept the results of a power struggle in which both the rich and the poor are at liberty to appropriate and use the surplus goods and resources of the rich.

Applying our previous discussion of the "ought" implies "can" principle to these three possible moral resolutions, it is clear that (1a) (it would be unreasonable to ask or require the poor . . .) rules out II, but (2a) (it would not be unreasonable to ask and require the rich . . .) does not rule out I. But what about III? Some libertarians have contended that III is the proper resolution of severe conflicts of interest between the rich and the poor. But a resolution, like III, that sanctions the results of a power struggle between the rich and the poor is a resolution which, by and large, favors the rich over the poor. So all things considered, it would be no more reasonable to require the poor to accept III than it would be to require them to accept II. This means that only I satisfies the conflict resolution principle by being a resolution that is reasonable to require everyone affected to accept. Consequently, if we assume that however else we specify the requirements of morality, they cannot violate the "ought" implies "can" principle or the conflict resolution principle, it follows that despite what Spencerian libertarians claim, the basic right to liberty endorsed by them, as determined by a weighing of the relevant competing liberties according to these two principles, actually favors the liberty of the poor over the liberty of the rich. Yet couldn't Spencerian libertarians object to this conclusion, claiming that it would be unreasonable to require the rich to sacrifice the liberty to meet some of their luxury needs so that the poor could have the liberty to meet their basic needs? As has been pointed out, libertarians don't usually see the situation as a conflict of liberties, but suppose they did. How plausible would such an objection be? Not very plausible at all.

Consider: What are Spencerian libertarians going to say about the poor? Isn't it clearly unreasonable to require the poor to sacrifice the liberty to meet their basic needs so that the rich can have the liberty to meet their luxury needs? Isn't it clearly unreasonable to require the poor to sit back and starve to death? If it is, then there is no resolution of this conflict that it would be reasonable to require both the rich and the poor to accept. But that would mean that libertarians could not be putting forth a moral resolution because, according to the conflict resolution principle in cases of severe conflict of interest, a moral resolution resolves conflicts of interest in ways that it would be reasonable to require everyone affected to accept. Therefore, as long as libertarians think of themselves as putting forth a moral resolution for cases of severe conflict of interest, they cannot allow that it would be unreasonable *both* to require the rich to sacrifice the liberty to meet some of their luxury needs in order to benefit the poor and to require the poor to sacrifice the liberty to meet their basic needs in order to benefit the rich. But I submit that if one of these requirements is to be judged reasonable, then, by any neutral assessment, it must be the requirement that the rich sacrifice the liberty to meet some of their luxury needs so that the poor can have the liberty to meet their basic needs. There is no other plausible resolution if libertarians intend to be putting forth a moral resolution.

It should also be noted that this case for restricting the liberty of the rich depends upon the willingness of the poor to take advantage of whatever opportunities are available to them to engage in mutually beneficial work, so that failure of the poor to take advantage of such opportunities would normally cancel, or at least significantly reduce, the obligation of the rich to restrict their own liberty for the benefit of the poor. In addition, the poor would be required to return the equivalent of any surplus possessions they have taken from the rich once they are able to do so and still satisfy their basic needs. Nor would the poor be required to keep the liberty to which they are entitled. They could give up part of it, or all of it, or risk losing it on the chance of gaining a greater share of liberties or other social goods.[3] Consequently, the case for restricting the liberty of the rich for the benefit of the poor is neither unconditional nor inalienable.

Of course, there will be cases in which the poor fail to satisfy their basic needs, not because of any direct restriction of liberty on the part of the rich, but because the poor are in such dire need that they are unable even to attempt to take from the rich what they require to meet their basic needs. In such cases, the rich would not be performing any act of commission that would prevent the poor from taking what they require. Yet, even in such cases, the rich would normally be performing acts of commission that would prevent other persons from taking part of the rich's own surplus possessions and using it to aid the poor. And when assessed from a moral point of view, restricting the liberty of these allies or agents of the poor would not be morally justified for the very same reason that restricting the liberty of the poor to meet their own basic needs would not be morally justified: It would not be reasonable to require all of those affected to accept such a restriction of liberty.

III. LOCKEAN LIBERTARIANS AND THE PROBLEM OF CONFLICT

Let us now consider whether these same conclusions can be established against Lockean libertarians, who take a set of rights, typically including a right to life and a right to property, as basic and then interpret liberty as being unconstrained by other persons from doing what one has a right to do. According to this view, a right to life is understood as a right not to be killed unjustly, and a right to property is understood as a right to acquire goods and resources either by initial acquisition or by voluntary agreement. In order to evaluate this view, we must determine what is entailed by these rights.

Presumably, a right to life understood as a right not to be killed unjustly would not be violated by defensive measures designed to protect one's person from life-threatening attacks. Yet would this right be violated when the rich prevent the poor from taking what they require to satisfy their basic needs? Obviously, as a consequence of such preventive actions poor people sometimes do starve to death. Have the rich, then, in contributing to this result, killed the poor, or have they simply let them die; and, if they have killed the poor, have they done so unjustly?

Sometimes the rich, in preventing the poor from taking what they require to meet their basic needs, would not in fact be killing the poor but would only be causing them to be physically or mentally debilitated. Yet because such preventive acts involve resisting the life-preserving activities of the poor, when the poor do die as a consequence of such acts, it seems clear that the rich would be killing the poor, whether intentionally or unintentionally.

Of course, libertarians would want to argue that such killing is simply a consequence of the legitimate exercise of property rights and, hence, is not unjust.

But to understand why libertarians are mistaken in this regard, let us appeal again to those fundamental principles of morality, the "ought" implies "can" principle and the conflict resolution principle. In this context, these principles can be used to assess two opposing accounts of property rights. According to the first account, a right to property is not conditional upon whether other persons have sufficient opportunities and resources to satisfy their basic needs. This view holds that the initial acquisition and voluntary agreement of some can leave others, through no fault of their own, dependent upon charity for the satisfaction of their most basic needs. By contrast, according to the second account, initial acquisition and voluntary agreement can confer title of property on all goods and resources except those surplus goods and resources of the rich that are required to satisfy the basic needs of those poor who, through no fault of their own, lack opportunities and resources to satisfy their own basic needs.

Recall that there were two interpretations of the basic right to liberty on which the Spencerian view is grounded. One interpretation ignores the liberty of the poor not be interfered with when taking from the surplus possessions of the rich what they require to meet their basic needs; the other gives that liberty priority over the liberty of the rich not to be interfered with when using their surplus for luxury purposes. Here, too, there are two interpretations of the right to property on which the Lockean view is grounded. One interpretation regards the right to property as *not* conditional upon the resources and opportunities available to others, and the other regards the right to property as conditional upon the resources and opportunities available to others. And, just as in the case of the Spencerian view, here we need to appeal to those fundamental principles of morality, the "ought" implies "can" principle and the conflict resolution principle, to decide which interpretation is morally acceptable.

It is clear that only the unconditional interpretation of property rights would generally justify the killing of the poor as a legitimate exercise of the property rights of the rich. Yet it would be unreasonable to require the poor to accept anything other than some version of the conditional interpretation of property rights. Moreover, according to the conditional interpretation, it does not matter whether the poor would actually die or are only physically or mentally debilitated as a result of such acts of prevention. Either result would preclude property rights from arising. Of course, the poor may have no real alternative to acquiescing to a political system modeled after the unconditional interpretation of property rights, even though such a system imposes an unreasonable sacrifice upon them—a sacrifice that we could not blame them for trying to evade. At the same time, although the rich may be disinclined to do so, it would not be unreasonable to require them to accept a political system modeled after the conditional interpretation of property rights—the interpretation favored by the poor. Consequently, if we assume that, however else we specify the requirements of morality, they cannot violate the "ought" implies "can" principle and the conflict resolution principle, it follows that, despite what Lockean libertarians claim, the right to life and the right to property endorsed by them actually support a right to welfare.

Now it might be objected that the right to welfare which this argument establishes from libertarian premises is not the same as the right to welfare endorsed by welfare liberals. This is correct. We could mark this difference by referring to the right that this argument establishes as "a negative welfare right" and by referring to the right endorsed by welfare liberals as "a positive welfare right." The significance of this difference is that a person's negative welfare right can be violated only when other people through acts of commission interfere with its exercise, whereas a person's positive welfare right can be violated not only by such acts of commission but by acts of omission as well. Nonetheless, this difference will have little practical import, for in recognizing the legitimacy of negative welfare rights, libertarians will come to see that virtually any use of their surplus possessions is likely to violate the negative welfare rights of the poor by preventing the poor from rightfully appropriating (some part of) their surplus goods and resources. So, in order to ensure that they will not be engaging in such wrongful actions, it will be incumbent on them to set up institutions guaranteeing adequate positive welfare rights for the poor. Only then will they be able to use legitimately any remaining surplus possessions to meet their own nonbasic needs. Furthermore, in the absence of adequate positive welfare rights, the poor, either acting by themselves or through their allies or agents, would have some discretion in determining when and how to exercise their negative welfare rights. In order not to be subject to that discretion, libertarians will tend to favor the only morally legitimate way of preventing the exercise of such rights: They will set up institutions guaranteeing adequate positive welfare rights that will then take precedence over the exercise of negative welfare rights. For these reasons, recognizing the negative welfare rights of the poor will ultimately lead libertarians to endorse the same sort of welfare institutions favored by welfare liberals.

IV. CHALLENGES TO LIBERTARIAN EGALITARIANISM

In a recent article, Ruth Sample has challenged my argument for welfare libertarianism.[4] She argues that the ideal of liberty endorsed by libertarians does not lead to a general right to welfare and that the proper response to libertarianism is to simply reject it as an implausible view. Two defenders of libertarianism, Tibor Machan and Jan Narveson, have also challenged my attempt to derive a right to welfare from libertarian premises.[5] Their challenges focus on whether a libertarianism without a right to welfare would be acceptable to the poor. I will show how these new challenges to my argument can be met, and also how they proceed from different understandings of what a proper defense of libertarianism would be like.

Ruth Sample begins her discussion of my attempt to derive a right to welfare from libertarian premises by noting that I distinguish two different kinds of libertarianism: Spencerian libertarianism and Lockean libertarianism. As I characterize them, Spencerian libertarians take a right to liberty as basic and derive all other rights from this right to liberty, while Lockean libertarians take a set of rights, including typically a right to life and a right to property, as basic and define liberty as the absence of constraints in the exercise of these rights. Sample then goes on to interpret Spencerian libertarianism as seeking the maximization of liberty and then rejects it on the grounds that a "truly libertarian" view is rights-based, nonconsequentualist, and does not recognize the possibility of conflicting rights. Unfortunately, Sample does not seem to realize that the Spencerian libertarianism I discuss does meet two of the three conditions she proposes for being a "truly libertarian" view, the only two she actually defends as being essential to libertarianism, that is, it is nonconsequentialist and it does not recognize the possibility of conflicting rights.[6] The fact that Spencerian libertarianism is liberty-based rather than rights-based I don't think is a sufficient reason to reject the view as a "truly libertarian" view.[7] Nor do I think that Sample believes that it is either.

Actually, the distinction between Spencerian libertarianism and Lockean libertarianism was suggested to me by libertarians as a way of improving on my earlier discussions. These libertarians thought that these two forms of libertarianism deserve separate treatment although they regarded them both as viable forms of libertarianism. Fortunately, nothing much is lost from Sample's neglect of my argument that Spencerian libertarianism would lead to welfare rights. This is because my argument that Lockean libertarianism would lead to welfare rights and my argument that Spencerian libertarianism would lead to welfare rights take the same form.

So why then does Sample object to my argument that Lockean libertarianism would lead to welfare rights? Surprisingly, one of her first objections is that we really don't need it because if we understand the Lockean libertarianism to incorporate the Lockean proviso, a right of self-subsistence would already be guaranteed, at least for those who are capable of working. What is so surprising about this objection is that it undercuts Sample's grounds for thinking that (Lockean) libertarianism rests on "implausible premises" given that its premises, so interpreted, would be supporting a right to welfare for the able-bodied.

Of course, Sample could reply that there is still something implausible about the premises of Lockean libertarianism because, on her interpretation, while these premises secure a right to welfare for those who are capable of working, they do not secure a right to welfare for those who are incapable of working. Yet Sample gets this result only by misinterpreting the Lockean proviso. The proviso simply requires that "enough and as good be left in common for others." It does not specify whether what is left is to be used for production or for consumption, and so does not distinguish between those who are capable of working and those who are only capable of consuming.[8] So properly understood, the Lockean proviso would guarantee a fairly general right to welfare.

But the relative ease with which Lockean libertarianism can be seen to support a right to welfare once it is interpreted as endorsing the Lockean proviso was the main reason I had for not wanting to interpret Lockean libertarianism in that way. I wanted to see if a right to welfare still could be derived from Lockean libertarianism without the benefit of the welfare-friendly Lockean proviso. Most libertarians today also seem to favor this approach.

Sample goes on to consider two other objections to my interpretation of Lockean libertarianism, which

I don't think she realizes are actually inconsistent with thinking of libertarianism as endorsing the Lockean proviso. First, she claims that when there are serious conflicts between the rich and the poor—just when the Lockean proviso would be thought to apply—libertarians could maintain that we are not in the circumstances of justice where people's rights can be determined, and so neither the rich nor the poor would have a right to anything.

One problem with this objection is that it denies the existence of property rights to a surplus whenever there are severe conflicts of interest between the rich and the poor, without recognizing any alternative (welfare) rights as applicable in those circumstances. This means that property rights to a surplus would be justified only in those rare cases in which they equally serve the interest of both the rich and the poor. In all other cases, no property rights to a surplus would be justified. But surely this is not the real-world justification of property rights that libertarians had promised us.

Another problem with this way of dealing with severe conflict-of-interest situations is that it requires the poor to accept the results of a power struggle in which both the rich and the poor are at liberty to appropriate and use the surplus resources of the rich insofar as they are able to do so. Obviously, such a resolution favors the rich over the poor. Consequently, it would be no more reasonable to require the poor to accept this resolution than it would be to require them to accept the resolution that secures for the rich property rights to their surplus. This implies that for severe conflict-of-interest situations only a resolution that guarantees the poor a right to welfare would satisfy the "ought" implies "can" principle.

Moreover, this is just the sort of resolution that the contrapositive of the "ought" implies "can" principle, the conflict resolution principle, requires. This principle requires that moral resolutions of severe conflicts of interest must be reasonable to require everyone affected to accept. So in the severe conflict-of-interest situations we are considering, only a moral resolution that guaranteed the poor a right to welfare would be reasonable for both the rich and the poor to accept. Thus, for such conflict situations, only a moral resolution that guarantees the poor a right to welfare would satisfy both the "ought" implies "can" principle and its contrapositive, the conflict resolution principle.

The second objection that Sample raises to my interpretation of Lockean libertarianism, which is also inconsistent with thinking of libertarianism as endorsing the Lockean proviso, is derived from Judith Jarvis Thomson's work on abortion.[9] As is well known, Thomson defends a women's right to have an abortion even on the assumption that the fetus is a person. Thomson asks us to imagine that we have been kidnapped and attached to an unconscious violinist who needs the use of our kidneys for nine months in order to survive. Thomson argues that it would be within our rights to detach ourselves from the violinist despite the fact that the violinist would die as a result. Analogously, Sample argues that libertarians could maintain that it would be within the rights of the rich to detach themselves from the poor who need their help to sustain their lives.

But the situation of the poor is not analogous to that of the unconscious violinist because most of the poor, if not interfered with, are clearly capable of taking from the rich what they need for survival. So the question arises, should the poor have the liberty not to be interfered with in taking from the rich what they need for survival or should the rich have the liberty not to be interfered with in using their surplus of luxury purposes? Here I argue that the "ought" implies "can" principle actually favors the liberty of the poor over the liberty of the rich, which provides the grounds for a right to welfare.

Sample does not challenge any of this, but rather focuses on just those unusual cases of conflict between the rich and the poor that are more analogous to Thomson's unconscious violinist example—cases where the poor are incapable of taking from the rich what they need for survival. For these cases, I argue that there are likely to be allies and agents of the poor whose liberty not to be interfered with in taking from the rich what the poor need for survival would have priority over the liberty of the rich not to be interfered with in using their surplus for luxury purposes. But would this resolution imply an analogous resolution for the case of the unconscious violinist? Would it imply that the liberty of the allies or agents of the unconscious violinist not to be interfered with in keeping us bodily attached to the violinist has priority over our liberty not to be interfered with respect to the use of our kidneys? Thinking that it would not turns on ignoring what would be a reasonable response of the violinist if he or she were conscious, or a reasonable response of allies and agents of the violinist on the assumption that the violinist in not conscious.

In Thomson's example, one is being asked to remain in bed with one's kidney's attached to the unconscious violinist for nine months. In the case of the conflict between the rich and the poor, the rich are being asked to relinquish claim to some of the surplus goods they have produced so that the basic needs of the poor may be met. Obviously, the sacrifice involved in sharing the use of one's kidneys and remaining bed-ridden for nine months is far greater than the sacrifice involved in redistributing goods from the rich to the poor. Nevertheless, in either case, if the sacrifice is not made far greater harm would result.

I claim that in order to properly resolve these cases, we need to consider what would be the reasonable response of the violinist if he or she were conscious, or the reasonable response of allies or agents of the violinist on the assumption that the violinist is not conscious. Similarly, we need to consider what would be a reasonable response of the poor or their allies or agents who, if not interfered with, are capable of taking from the rich what is required to meet the basic needs of the poor. If we apply the "ought" implies "can" principle taking these reasonable responses into account, I think we will come down in favor of the liberty of the violinist and his or her allies and agents just as we would, I think, come down in favor of the liberty of the poor and their allies and agents. Of course, the sacrifice involved in sharing the use of one's kidneys and remaining bed-ridden for nine months is far greater than the sacrifice involved in redistributing goods from the rich to the poor. Nevertheless, it does seem to be a sacrifice we can reasonably impose given that the alternatives involve putting an end to other people's lives. At some point, if the sacrifices on both sides were equally grave, we would be in a lifeboat-like situation where maybe only a chance mechanism could provide reasonable resolution. But Thomson's unconscious violinist example is not a lifeboat case. By assumption, only the violinist is in a life-threatening situation.

Nor is being kidnapped and attached to an unconscious violinist analogous to being raped. Rape is a crime of sexual domination. In Thomson's example, those who kidnap you and attach you to the unconscious violinist have selected you because you alone have the right blood type to help save the life of the violinist. You are surely being coerced but the reason why you are being coerced is to save the life of the violinist. It is not an act of sexual domination. So as long as we keep in mind that the unconscious violinist is a full-fledged person with all the rights of any other person, it is hard to see how your sacrifice for the sake of the violinist would not be required, as would the sacrifice of the rich to provide a right to welfare for the poor.[10]

Previously, Tibor Machan has also criticized my argument that a libertarian ideal of liberty leads to a right to welfare, accepting its theoretical thrust but

denying its practical significance. He does appreciate the force of the argument enough to grant that if the type of conflict cases that we have described between the rich and the poor actually obtained, the poor would have a right to welfare. But he denies that such cases—in which the poor have done all they legitimately can to satisfy their basic needs in a libertarian society—actually obtain. "Normally," he writes, "persons do not lack the opportunities and resources to satisfy their basic needs."[11]

This response, however, virtually concedes everything that my argument intended to establish, for the poor's right to welfare is not claimed to be unconditional. Rather, it is said to be conditional principally upon the poor doing all that they legitimately can to meet their own basic needs. So it follows that only when the poor lack sufficient opportunity to satisfy their own basic needs would their right to welfare have any practical moral force. Accordingly, on libertarian grounds, Machan has conceded the legitimacy of just the kind of right to welfare that the preceding argument hoped to establish.

The only difference that remains is a practical one. Machan thinks that virtually all of the poor have sufficient opportunities and resources to satisfy their basic needs and that, therefore, a right to welfare has no practical moral force. In contrast, I think that many of the poor do not have sufficient opportunities and resources to satisfy their basic needs and that, therefore, a right to welfare has considerable practical moral force.

But isn't this practical disagreement resolvable? Who could deny that most of the 1.2 billion people [worldwide] who are currently living in conditions of absolute poverty "lack the opportunities and resources to satisfy their basic needs?" And even within our own country, it is estimated that some 32 million Americans live below the official poverty index, and that one-fifth of American children are growing up in poverty.[12] Surely, it is impossible to deny that many of these Americans also "lack the opportunities and resources to satisfy their basic needs." Given the impossibility of reasonably denying these factual claims, Machan would have to concede that the right to welfare, which he grants can be theoretically established on libertarian premises, also has practical moral force.

Recently, however, Machan, seeking to undercut the practical force of my argument, has contended that when we compare economic systems to determine which produce more poverty, "No one can seriously dispute that the near-libertarian systems have fared much better than those going in the opposite direction, including the welfare state." Here one would think that Machan has the U.S. in mind as a "near-libertarian system" because earlier in the same paragraph he claims: "America is still the freest of societies, with many of its legal principles giving expression to classical liberal, near-libertarian ideas." Yet apparently this is not what Machan thinks because in a footnote to the same text he writes, "It is notable that the statistics that Sterba cites" (in my above response to Machan's critique) "are drawn from societies, including the United States of America, which are far from libertarian in their legal construction and are far closer to the welfare state, if not to outright socialism."[13]

Obviously, then, Machan is surprisingly unclear as to whether he wants to call the U.S. a near-libetarian state, a welfare state, or a socialist state. Yet, whichever of these designations is most appropriate, what is clear is that the poor do less well in the U.S. than they do in the welfare liberal or socialist states of Western Europe such as Germany, Sweden, and Switzerland.[14] For example, 22.4% of children live below the poverty line in the U.S. as compared to 4.9% in Germany, 5% in Sweden, and 7.8% in Switzerland, and the U.S shares with Italy the highest infant mortality rate of the major industrialized nations. The U.S. also ranks 67 among all nations in the percentage of national income received by the poorest 20% of its population, ranking the absolute lowest among industrialized nations.[15] Accordingly, the success that welfare liberal and socialist states have had, especially in Western Europe, in coming close to truly meeting the basic needs of their deserving poor should give us good reason to doubt what Machan proclaims is the superior practical effectiveness of "near-libertarian states" in dealing with poverty.

In his latest responses, Machan challenges the statistical evidence on which I based my above claim that "the poor do less well in the U.S. than they do in the welfare liberal or socialist states of Western Europe such as Germany, Sweden, and Switzerland".[16] Part of Machan's challenge consists of a series of speculations as to how the statistical evidence I provide could be correct and still the conclusion I want to draw would not follow. Thus, Machan considers how the U.S. could rank low (67th) with respect to the percentage of national income received by the poorest 20% of its population, and still the poor could be doing better off in the U.S. than in some country which ranks higher on the same scale. We are asked to imagine a relatively egalitarian Haiti (nothing like the real Haiti which is actually very inegalitarian) in which the poorest 20% of its population receive a higher

percentage of national income, but are still worse off than the poor in the U.S. But while this is certainly the case with respect to some of the 66 countries that rank higher than the U.S. in this comparison, it is not true of the welfare liberal or socialist countries of Western Europe, such as Germany, Sweden and Switzerland, which rank significantly higher than the U.S. on this scale.

Machan also considers the possibility that the fact that the U.S. shares with Italy the highest infant mortality rate of the major industrialized nations may be explained in terms of our superior medical care which allows children to be born in the U.S. who would die at or before birth in other countries. But Machan makes no effort to see whether this factor does actually account for the difference rather than the lack of prenatal care for the poor or the fact that roughly 40 million Americans have no health care insurance, and so typically have poor health care.[17]

Machan also cites the fact that the poor in America have a higher incidence of car ownership than any other country in the world other than Germany, and with 0.56 persons per room are less crowded "today" (the figures are from 1987) than the average West European household in 1980. But the lack of adequate public transportation in most places in the U.S. makes owning a car a necessity in a way that is not true in much of Western Europe, and Americans who live in places like New York City where adequate public transportation is available probably have similar person-per-room statistics to those in Western Europe.[18] Moreover, from an environmental perspective, the Western European lesser reliance on the automobile for transportation is clearly preferable. Although Machan offers other speculations and bits of evidence, nowhere does he provide the kind of evidence that is needed to back up his original claim that "no one can seriously dispute that the near-libertarian systems have fared much better than those going in the opposite direction, including the welfare state." In fact, the more closely one looks at the relevant evidence it seems clear that it better supports my claim that "the poor do less well in the U.S. than they do in the welfare liberal or socialist states of Western Europe." Or as sociologist Nathan Glazer puts the claim:

> The American welfare state came under attack long before it reached the levels of the European welfare states, whether measured in percentage of gross national product (GNP) taken for social purposes; in percentage of population in poverty, or by extensiveness of protection by public programs

against unemployment, ill health or loss of wages in sickness, or of child care services; or by degree of subsidization for housing, Indeed, possibly in only one respect, pensions for the aged, is the American welfare state comparable to the advanced European states, Without ever having reached European levels, the American welfare state has been in retreat since 1981.[19]

In his latest challenge to my liberty to welfare argument, Jan Narveson offers us a distinctive way to conceive of and justify libertarianism.[20] Narveson thinks of libertarianism as a fixed doctrine with absolute property rights and then sees justification for it proceeding externally by showing that everyone, the rich and particularly the poor, would have the best of reasons to endorse libertarianism, so construed, in comparison to all other political ideals. By contrast, I think of libertarianism not as a fixed doctrine but as open to a number of interpretations, some with absolute property rights and others with conditional property rights, some favoring the liberty of the rich and others favoring the liberty of the poor. I then see justification for libertarianism proceeding internally by showing that everyone, the rich and particularly the poor, would have the best reasons to endorse libertarianism under a certain interpretation. But since Narveson's and my standard of justification is the same—what everyone, particularly the poor, would have the best reasons to endorse—it turns out that the differences in the way we conceive of and justify libertarianism don't amount to much. Where we really do differ, however, is with respect to what political ideal we think our commonly shared standard of justification picks out. Narveson thinks it picks out what I would call absolute property rights libertarianism (a version of Lockean libertarianism), what he would call just plain libertarianism. By contrast, I think our shared standard of justification picks out what I would call conditional property rights libertarianism (another version of Lockean libertarianism), what Narveson would call welfare liberalism or socialism. Clearly, one of us is misapplying our shared standard of justification, and, of course, I have my suspicions as to who it is.

Just consider how Narveson tries to show how the poor have the best reasons to endorse (absolute propety rights) libertarianism. What he argues is that the poor will be better off under (absolute property rights) libertarianism than they would be under any other political ideal. Now my response to this argument is the same response I gave to a similar argument raised by John Hospers a few years ago.

Hospers had cited the example of Ernst Mahler, an entrepreneurial genius who employed more than 100,000 and produced newsprint and tissue products that are now used by more than 2 billion people. Hospers had suggested that requiring Mahler to contribute to a welfare system for the deserving poor would not only "decrease his own wealth but that of countless other people."

Responding to this objection, I contended that if the more talented members of a society provided sufficient employment opportunities and voluntary welfare assistance to enable the poor to meet their basic needs, then the conditions for invoking a right to welfare would not arise, since the poor are first required to take advantage of whatever employment opportunities and voluntary welfare assistance are available to them before they can legitimately invoke such a right. Consequently, if sufficient employment opportunities and voluntary welfare assistance obtained, there would be no practical difference in this regard between a libertarian society and a welfare or socialist state, as neither would justify invoking a right to welfare. Only when insufficient employment opportunities and voluntary welfare assistance obtained would there be a practical difference between a libertarian society and a welfare or socialist state, and then it would clearly benefit the poor to be able to invoke the right to welfare. Consequently, given the practical possibility, and in most cases, the actuality of insufficient employment opportunities and voluntary welfare assistance obtaining, there is no reason to think that the poor would be better off without the enforcement of such a right. In fact, historically, tax-supported welfare systems have come into existence because voluntary giving turned out to be insufficient.[21]

It is also difficult to see how Narveson could think that the poor would be better off under (absolute property rights) libertarianism given the way that he rails against my view and existing welfare programs for providing the poor with too high a welfare minimum. Narveson points out that persons living below the poverty line in the United States (a standard which is based on a food plan that was developed for "temporary or emergency use" and is inadequate for a permanent diet) have a monetary income several times the median income of people in India. Of course, what Narveson ignores here is that the costs of meeting basic needs can vary between different societies and within the same society at different times. This is due to the way that the means most readily available for satisfying basic needs are produced. For example, in more affluent societies, the most readily available means for satisfying a person's basic needs are usually processed so as to satisfy nonbasic needs at the same time as they satisfy basic needs. This processing is carried out to make the means more attractive to persons in higher income brackets who can easily afford the extra cost. As a result, the most readily available means for satisfying basic needs are much more costly in more affluent societies than in less affluent societies, thus requiring a higher welfare minimum in more affluent societies than in less affluent societies.

Yet even if Narveson were to recognize the need to fix welfare minimums differently in different societies and differently within the same society at different times, he would still want to drastically cut welfare minimums virtually everywhere. Given that Narveson contends that my arguments for welfare only have whatever force they have when the poor are actually starving to death, it would appear that he would only support a welfare minimum limited to preventing starvation. Narveson must have had such a minimum in mind when at a recent meeting at the Cato Institute, he argued against my view by claiming that 75 cents a day would suffice to take care of the poor's nutritional needs in the U.S. Unfortunately, by putting the welfare minimum this low, Narveson fails to meet what he rightly takes to be a requirement of our shared standard of justification, namely, that the poor must be better off under his version of libertarianism than they would be under any other political ideal. For surely the poor who are just avoiding starving to death are not better off than they would be under many existing welfare programs or under the basic-needs welfare minimum they would be guaranteed in the form of libertarianism that I defend. This is why my conditional rights libertarianism, what I call here welfare libertarianism, is preferable to Narveson's absolute rights libertarianism when judged by our shared standard of justification.

Ruth Sample presents us with a bifurcated view of libertarianism. On the one hand, she interprets the view as endorsing the Lockean proviso and so easily leading to a right to welfare. On the other hand, she interprets the view as holding a position analogous to Thomson's position on abortion, and so easily capable of turning a blind eye to the welfare needs of the poor. In contrast, Machan and Narveson are far more concerned to interpret libertarianism in a way that would be acceptable to the poor. Obviously, my own interpretation of libertarianism is closer to that of Machan and Narveson than it is to Sample's. By alternating between a welfare-friendly and a morality-unfriendly interpretation of libertarianism, Sample makes the task of deriving a

right to welfare either too easy or impossible because a right to welfare needs to be grounded in morality. Admirably, Machan and Narveson both seek to provide a morally defensible interpretation of libertarianism that would be acceptable to the poor. The thrust of my work in this area has been to show that libertarians can only succeed in this endeavor by endorsing a right to welfare. Hopefully, these responses to the recent challenges raised by Sample, Machan and Narveson will help to provide further support for this understanding of libertarianism.

READING 21

A Critique of Sterba's Defense of the Welfare State

Jan Narveson

Jan Narveson is Professor of Philosophy at the University of Waterloo in Canada and the author of several works in moral and political philosophy. In this response to Sterba's position in Reading 20, he concludes that the welfare state is not supported by Sterba's proposed arguments.

Although this work is based on other articles Jan Narveson has written, this essay has been commissioned for this work and appears in print here for the first time.

1. AN ALLEGED DIVISION OF LIBERTARIANISMS

Professor Sterba begins with us libertarians, proposing a distinction between two sorts of us.

> Some, following Herbert Spencer, have (1) taken a right to liberty as basic and (2) derived all other rights from this right to liberty. Others, following John Locke, have (1) taken a set of rights, including typically a right to life and a right to property, as basic and (2) defined liberty as the absence of constraints in the exercise of these rights. Both groups of libertarians regard liberty as the ultimate political ideal, but they do so for different reasons.

For Spencerian libertarians, liberty is the ultimate political ideal because all other rights are derived from a right to liberty. For Lockean libertarians, liberty is the ultimate political ideal because liberty is just the absence of constraints in the exercise of people's fundamental rights.

I don't accept this claimed distinction. Locke's Law of Nature requires us to refrain from harming others in respect of life, health, liberty, or property. But in his view, all these come to the same thing in the end: what we have a right to is ourselves, which is to say, to our life, health, goings-on, and acquirings. (In the *Treatise,* Locke refers to "his Property, that is, his Life, Liberty and Estate" [#87]; again: "their Lives, Liberties and Estates, which I call by the general name, Property."[123]. Locke's Law of Nature asserts that we own ourselves: that is to say, that others must ask permission before they can use our bodies or enlist our actions. But our having the right to them is, by definition, its being the case that, to quote Locke, "no one ought to harm another in his Life, Health, Liberty or Possessions." [#6] Life, health, and property, then, are not things distinct from liberty such that the latter is "based on" one or more of the former. The assertion of a fundamental right to liberty is the assertion of exactly the same thing as the ownership of oneself, namely the right to do as one will with one's self; and that is exactly what a fundamental right of liberty is. Which is exactly what Spencer held. There is only one position to consider, not two.

Sterba appreciates that the libertarian's proposed rights are negative, as Locke's wording makes clear: they are not rights to be supplied by others and at their expense, with the means of life, health, liberty, and property. They are, only, protections (if respected) against damages to any of those—rights "not to be harmed." And he sees what follows from the libertarian claim: that helping others—with food, clothing, medical supplies, or whatever—while meritorious, may not be forcibly required of anyone, unless and until they have taken on, by their own voluntary commitments, obligations to do so.

2. A FAULTY "CONFLICT OF LIBERTIES"

Nevertheless, Sterba proposes to argue that the libertarian is inconsistent in opposing the welfare state. He asks us to suppose a "conflict situation" between the liberties of the rich and of the poor. The conflict is supposed to lie in the fact that "the rich have more than enough goods and resources to satisfy their basic needs. By contrast, the poor lack the goods and resources to meet their most basic needs." In such a case, he asks, how can it be consistent to maintain that the rich have the liberty to spend their money on superfluities, while the poor do not have the liberty to take what they need from the well-stocked cupboards of the rich? The implication of conflict is emphasized in this passage: "Spencerian libertarians recognize that this liberty might well be enjoyed at the expense of the satisfaction of the most basic needs of the poor; they just think that liberty always has priority over other political ideals." Libertarians, such as myself, deny that there are conflicting rights here. In our basic view, neither of these good people has the right to take anything from the other. But according to Sterba, "In fact, however, the liberty of the poor is at stake in such conflict situations. What is at stake is the liberty of the poor not to be interfered with in taking from the surplus possessions of the rich what is necessary to satisfy their basic needs."

In a footnote, Sterba says, "It is not being assumed here that the surplus possessions of the rich are either justifiably or unjustifiably possessed by the rich. Moreover, according to Spencerian libertarians, it is an assessment of the liberties involved that determines whether the possession is justifiable." Now, in the latter sentence he is absolutely correct: it is precisely the general, basic principle of a uniform right of all to liberty that determines which holdings are legitimate and which not. But how are we to understand the claim that the liberties of the rich are enjoyed "at the expense of" the poor? It is true, of course, that for any given poor person, I could give him my car. Yet we do not say, on this ground, that I have my car "at the expense" of this stranger to whom I didn't give it. That phrase suggests that I actually stole it from this man, or exacted it from him, perhaps by slave labor. But, of course, I did not. So none of that will do. If Sterba's example is to be of any use in the present discussion, it must be assumed that the rich in question have acquired their riches without doing any violence to the poor or to anyone else. In some real situations, of course, this would be false— there are, certainly, some successful larcenists out there. But in many, I and all of us presume, it is true. What matters for the present discussion is that, as I say, his case is pointless unless he assumes that in it, the rich did not violate any liberties of anyone in the course of becoming rich; for if they did, of course, the libertarian will cheerfully agree that he owes somebody compensation for his previous impositions on them. There are some critics, to be sure, who think that the way the rich get rich is by imposing costs on the poor— by robbing them, then—and so, by violating their liberties in fact. Needless to say, the libertarian agrees that theft is not an acceptable way of getting rich. But then, they also deny, for the excellent reason that it is obviously false, that in a capitalist economy the rich had to do it that way.

What the libertarian proposes is that it is the principle of liberty itself that shows us when and why the rich are entitled to their wealth (when they are). In saying this, we recognize something that Sterba pays too little attention to: the rich get rich by virtue of what they do and have done. The wealth they have would not exist if those people had not done those things: people create wealth. Wealth isn't just there, more being taken by some people (who are thus "the rich") and less by others ("the poor"). Wealth is made, created, by effort, careful investment, ingenious invention, and so on— doubtless with a bit of luck thrown in, but that is minor by comparison with the other factors. These are all activities of persons, and the libertarian holds that so long as none of those activities aggresses against any other person, the persons who engage in those activities are to be inviolate against force exerted by others. This means that those who steal from persons whose wealth has been come by in this nonviolent way are in fact commandeering the work of those people, without their consent. If we make Sterba's case relevant in this way, so that the "rich" we are considering became so via activities that harmed no innocent person, then it is also clearly not true that we have here a conflict of the sort of rights proclaimed by libertarians. The rich never had a right to invade and despoil the poor or anyone else, and by hypothesis did not have it in this case. The poor, who we will suppose are equally innocent, consequently have no right to help themselves to the wealth of the rich. They may ask, of course, but the rich have the right to refuse, just as the poor have the right to refuse any services asked of them, by the rich or anyone else.

So there simply is no conflict of the sort he wants to describe, and therefore no inconsistency in the libertarian's case. In order to generate such a conflict, you need positive rights, or you need a history of previous violations of libertarian rights to appeal to. Given neither, there is no conflict of rights of the libertarian type. There is, of course, a conflict of desires: the poor would like to have more, and the rich, we'll suppose in this case, would prefer not to have the poor get that "more" by taking it from them, though they are happy to have

the poor become less poor by methods that don't involve force and fraud against others. But then, what else is new? No one can think that everyone has the right to do just anything, to satisfy their desires of whatever kind, by just any means. The point of rights is to provide a structure superior to the unimpeded operation of sheer desires—including the desires we might want to classify as "needs."

3. THE QUESTION: WOULD WE CONTRACT FOR LIBERTY?

However, I think it is clear that the previous discussion is really just preliminary sparring, for the appeal to consistency, as such, isn't really Sterba's main argument. The real question, as we both agree, is whether we should, as rational people, go for the general right to liberty, along with the libertarians; or should we instead adopt one of the split principles so popular with present-day philosophers, who mostly sit, as they suppose, at the feet of Rawls. On their view, people will be allowed to work and save and trade, for such purposes as they see fit, up to a point—but this liberty is substantially restricted, for they will also be required to devote some of their activities to the maintenance of the otherwise-poor, and the more successful they have been, the more of those activities they will have to devote to that. What we are asking here is: Why? This certainly gets us into the foundations of moral and political principles. Which principles ought we to embrace, and why? Many theorists apparently think that we do not really need to answer the second question: we hold these truths to be self-evident, they say. Or they say that the test of a moral principle is whether it hangs together with one's other moral principles and the whole thing somehow feels right. I am not impressed with either of these ideas, and happily, neither is Sterba. We both agree that the test of a moral principle is this: Would all reasonable people embrace it, given their choice? More precisely: Would everyone embrace it, on condition that everyone else does so too?

An essential point about this test is that it is to be uniform for all. That is the Hobbesian-Kantian idea. Nobody gets to have a principle that somebody else won't go along with, given the facts. Now, all of us, we presume, have sets of preferences, or values, on the basis of which we choose what we do. The beauty of the contractarian approach to morals is that it is those very same sets of preferences that are used to appraise proposals in morals—thus providing motivation for the results. But at the same time, we are required to look at things from the points of view of all others. A moral rule is an imposition on all. It says to everybody, "You are to do this, like it or not!" None of us will accept any such thing unless, somehow, there's a payoff for the impositions it makes on us. That is because we are independent rational beings who do what we judge best—nobody can push us around until we say they may.

Where is this payoff to come from? There can be but one answer: from the commitments of others. Trees and gophers don't care what we propose; it is only other people whose actions can be influenced by what we propose, and vice versa. If I am asked to forgo some advantage, it must be that someone else, in forgoing it as well, thereby leaves me better off, and does so in respect of things that matter to me. Person A accepts a duty only if he believes that he benefits from B's acceptance of a similar duty, or some other one. The rewards of A's onerous duties are A's advantageous rights—they are what make it worthwhile to bear the costs that duties impose. The question before us, then, is this: Would we all do best sticking to a single fundamental right of general liberty as our basic principle insofar as it concerns the use of force among people, or should we accept additional restrictions on our liberty, over and above those that the principle of liberty itself imposes on us?

Those restrictions are, of course, extensive. Respecting everyone's liberty, granting them a general right to it, means forgoing whatever advantages could be gained by using violence against others: no killing or wounding, and no threat of same, except in defense against aggressors; and no lying, cheating, or other forms of what we may call verbal violence. It is easy to see the gains from an agreement with all others to refrain from those things: nobody inflicts any damage on me. That leaves me free to use my resources as I will, including using them in cooperation with others. The result, as Hobbes says, is that we have all the advantages not available in a condition where none can trust anyone else in those respects: now we can till the soil, build universities, engage in commerce with peoples far away, and on and on. It is almost impossible to overestimate the benefits of peace, which is what the fundamental principle of liberty requires us all to pursue.

But Sterba claims this is not enough. He claims that the cost of this is too high for certain people, namely, the poor. This vaguely defined set of people allegedly lacks the "basic needs" of humans. He can't quite mean that literally, of course, since if they did, they would all be dead. And if he were to try to be precise about this, his results would run a severe danger of being arbitrary. If the people he has in mind have made it to here and now, what is his criterion of being in basic need? That they will only last five minutes longer without the involuntarily garnered help in question? Or five days? Or weeks? Years? Decades? We aren't told. And, of course, many of the non-poor will also last only a few days, weeks, years, or decades. If we aim to minister, collectively, to needs, disregarding the matter of who actually produced the means of meeting them, how do we rationally set the levels of provision supposedly required by the basic rights being proposed?

4. TOO MUCH TO ASK?

But for the present, we will not press him on this extreme, and probably (as we shall see) crucial vagueness. We will instead consider Sterba's claim that it is just too much to ask these people to refrain from theft, when hunger impels them. This, he claims, runs afoul of what he calls the "ought" implies "can" principle.

Now in fact, to begin with, his claim that respecting the liberty of others is "too much to ask" cannot be literally true. Many a brave soldier has sacrificed life or limb to the call of duty. If anything is too much to ask, surely it should be too much to ask of any man that he literally sacrifice his life for others. And yet, down through the centuries, millions of them have done just that—done what they saw to be their duty, at cost of life itself. Does Sterba think that the poor are being asked something more difficult than that? No doubt death by slow starvation would be dreadful, but is it really more dreadful than the prospect of being blown to bits in the immediate future or having a couple of limbs torn from one's body? That it is, is hardly obvious.

Another fundamental question, and, in a way, for present purposes, by far the most important question is: What does it do to the prospects of improvement from any such condition that nobody is either prevented from extending or required to extend a helping hand to such people? The alternative to the libertarian principle recommended by Sterba, and almost everybody in contemporary Anglo-American academia, is that we will compel everyone to help such people.

This answer raises two questions. The first is whether it is plausible to think that every rational person would prefer a system in which his own efforts are commandeered for the benefit of the designated "poor"—which, remember, on both of our views is the question whether it is just to exact these services from those capable of providing them.

But there is another question. This second question is, Is it plausible to think that the system in which these nice services are exacted from others, with threat of jail or worse upon noncompliance, would in fact work out better, or even as well, for the intended recipients of this extracted assistance? That question brings up a third question: Might the intended recipients actually do better if normal human interest and sympathy were permitted to exert themselves, without compulsion? There is an important question about the relation between those two considerations, which are not identical. If the liberty system can plausibly claim to supply an affirmative answer to the third one, then that would seem to settle the whole issue. For no one, surely, can prefer a system in which force is employed to one in which it is not if the results of the latter are otherwise at least as good as the results of the former. But I shall argue that that is the position that contemporary "welfare liberals" occupy today.

What if it were not so? What if forced labor actually works—as so many social systems in the past have assumed? We would then have a divergence between justice and the interests of some people, the poor, as against some others, the rich. But this is hardly unusual. There is, after all, always a divergence between justice and the interests of some. Justice is the interest of all, not of some at the expense of others. To be just, a policy must be such as to accord with principles that every reasonable person subscribes to, given the options of the others.

5. LIBERTY AND PROPERTY

Contemporary theorists such as Sterba load the dice in these matters in favor of the supposedly poor. To appraise their arguments, we must make a short detour. For perhaps, it will be said, the general right to liberty won't uphold private property after all. Perhaps the holdings of the well-off don't really belong to them.

Whether they do belong to them on the libertarian view means this: Is the right to use, at will, certain particular durable objects, derivable from a general right of liberty? The right to use things at will is what property consists of. For me to own X is for it to be the case that anything done with X, by anyone, needs my approval. My use of it, of course, is in turn limited by the

rights of others to their persons and properties. (Indeed, their persons, as noted above, are their property. Nobody is to be used by others without his own consent.) But how do we come to be in a condition such that we enjoy this right over certain things outside our own bodies? The short answer is that it is our own actions that were responsible for the objects in question. Almost always, nowadays, these actions have consisted in purchasing the things from others, but of course, that only pushes the question back farther. At the end of the line, we have people using things, found in nature, which in turn consists in using their own minds and bodies to relate to those things.

All free actions of persons that do not in turn consist in inflicting damage to others are actions that they have the right to perform: others are not to invade and despoil people in peaceful pursuits. When someone's actions, in particular, consist in bringing it about that useful things exist which otherwise would not have, then for outsiders to appropriate those things is, in effect, for those outsiders to commandeer the efforts of the creators. And that is what is forbidden by the liberty principle. This is, I believe, the correct account of the situation in regard to the "original acquisition" of property. It is no doubt also true that the system of recognizing people's property rights is of immense social value. That has been demonstrated time and again down through the years, though it is still underappreciated (or even just blindly ignored) by too many of today's thinkers about social matters. But we should appreciate the very close connection there is between the abstract-sounding general libertarian principle of justice and the social benefits of the free enterprise system. It has become popular of late to make a large issue of a supposed limitation on original acquisition, as in the "Lockean Proviso" on acquisition. It would take this essay much too far afield to discuss this issue at length. It is, I have argued elsewhere, a non-issue, in the end, and is ignored here partly for that reason, and mainly because it really has no bearing on the question of poverty. No poverty-stricken person today is so because of some kind of maldivision of natural resources.

6. LIBERTY AND PROSPERITY

When enterprise and exchange are genuinely free, with property rights being respected by all, we can expect an enormous amount of exchange to occur. And that is what we actually see. All of these exchanges are distinguished by being of mutual benefit, in the view of the parties to them—benefit to both or all parties to the exchanges in question, and characteristically to others not immediately involved as well.

In consequence, of course, those who we say are "rich" can only, apart from the larcenists who are deplored by the liberty principle, have become so by having engaged in a great deal of activity that is beneficial to a great many people, or in some few cases highly beneficial to some few. But the former option is overwhelmingly the more frequent and the most basic. "The wealthy" manufacture, or provide other services for, large numbers of people, each of whom has judged that the service or item purchased was worth buying, in comparison with all other available options at the time. The free enterprise picture, then, is not a picture of the rich getting rich at the expense of the poor. On the contrary: it is a picture of the rich getting richer by enabling a great many people to become richer, or anyway slightly less poor, than previously. More generally, everyone gains income by doing useful services, such as providing wanted goods, for other people. An enterprise system is looked on as a "land of opportunity" precisely because, and insofar as, there are no obstacles to the doing of business, on terms agreeable to all concerned. Freedom of enterprise makes the providing of opportunities a profitable undertaking: small wonder that so many of them are in fact provided.

All this works only insofar as the use of force is effectively prohibited in human affairs, except as necessary to prevent and control the use of force against the innocent. The use of force, by contrast, is socially inefficient. Instead of engaging in mutually beneficial activities, those who use force at most benefit themselves at the expense of others. For force to benefit anyone, it must harm someone; to make anyone better off, it entails that some others are made worse off. This is, of course, an invitation to the potential victims to be less productive, in one way or another. The main way is that it induces them to find ways of circumventing or avoiding or counteracting the threat of force by others. In contemporary society, we can point to the enormous amount of time spent by most money-earners in minimizing the extraction of taxes; also in seeking ways to incorporate into the law ways of shoring up their own economic positions at the expense of others; as well, of course, as the time and effort invested in guards, security systems, and the like.

The prosperity stemming from reasonably well-functioning free-enterprise systems has a rather important implication for our purposes. People with a lot of money to spend can spend it on things like charity—

can, and as we shall see shortly, do. That is a main reason why the connection between general liberty and the welfare of the less fortunate is so strong—contrary, it would seem, to widely held preconceptions.

7. A DILEMMA FOR DEMOCRATIC WELFARE STATES

The right to liberty does not include, nor does it entail, a positive right to welfare, even at the level of "subsistence." In a social system based on mutual voluntary benefit, those not capable of producing much will not be entitled, as a result of their activities, to anything of the "need-satisfying" type from others. They won't be entitled to it—but it doesn't follow that they won't get it. What reasons are there for supposing that even quite unproductive people will be taken care of?

The first point to make and emphasize here is one that welfare-rights advocates seem to have almost uniformly ignored: namely, that such people are, no matter what the social system, de facto dependent on the good will of others. Social philosophers tend to talk as though they themselves are absolute despots, whose commands are sufficient to get things done even though no one willingly responds to them and in fact follows those orders only because of the evils that the commander is able to threaten them with if they don't comply.

Well, surely social philosophers don't—I hope!—really think that. Yet they talk as if they do. For otherwise they would realize that in order for their ends to be accomplished, a great many people would have to share them. Consider the Welfare State, for example. All advocates of this propose it as an outcome of democracy. The dictator doesn't command the welfare state, by himself: rather, he is elected to do so, by millions of people who must, evidently, sympathize or feel morally impelled to do something for the supposedly poor and helpless.

This presents the welfare-state advocate with a very interesting dilemma. Each of those allegedly well-meaning people votes to impose a tax on all, including himself, in order to bring this result about. Does that, or does it not, imply that those people are willing to spend that much for that purpose? It's their own money—or at least, it was, prior to being forcibly extracted from them by the taxman. They are free to vote either way. They do in fact tend to vote for the welfare state. If they didn't have either the sympathy or the moral impulsion in question, why on earth would they do so? After all, it's going to cost them a lot of money over the years.

Perhaps they think that it's only other people who will pay the bills. This is an economic absurdity, of course, but it is not beyond the realm of possibility that ordinary people don't realize that there is a connection between what they do in the voting booth and what happens to their paycheck every month. We will suppose, however, that they aren't quite that far out of it. If we charitably assume that the voters aren't that ignorant, then my question remains pertinent.

But if they are, and they vote only under the illusion that the programs they vote for aren't costing them anything, then the welfare-state advocates have another problem: they are advocating a program based on fraud and mendacity. True, politicians routinely engage in such things, and talk as though these grand giveaway programs don't cost anything. But does Sterba think that most people actually believe them? Worse yet, does he think we should encourage this fraudulent basis? Does he regard this as a Platonic Lie? Is the welfare-state liberal so enamored of his idea that he's ready to see it undertaken on the basis of fraud and deception? Has it come to that?

Let us suppose not. Then we are back to my point, that in a democratic society, welfare systems can exist only if most people willingly pay large sums of money to support their fellows who are in need. But obviously they could do that without a welfare state. Indeed, we do! For even now we are daily deluged with appeals from charitable organizations, to fight cancer, heart disease, starvation in distant countries—and all sorts of other useful things which, by the way, the current welfare-state apparatus is not taking care of. And not only are we besieged by those people, but, despite heavy taxation, this system works! People respond to these appeals. The cover of a prominent news journal a few years ago featured a major article on American charitable expenditure—easily the highest in the world, per capita as well as in absolute terms, at something like $160 billions in that year (it's surely higher now). Assuming that the officially poor give nothing to charity—though they probably give quite a lot—that means that the average American gave something like $700 to charitable causes in that year—which means that the average family gave about $2800. Details here don't matter. What matters is that even in a country where virtually all wage earners pay hefty income taxes and many taxes of other kinds, they still devote thousands of dollars to charitable causes not catered to by governments.

It's quite true that many of those contributions were tax-deductible and reduced the tax bills of the contributors. But it's also true (a) that many of them were not, too, and (b) that if you pay $1000 and get $250 back, you have still contributed $750 of your own hard-earned money. It would bespeak even greater delusion if people thought they were actually saving money, net, by giving to charity on a tax-deductible basis.

It is remarkably common for leftists to belittle voluntary charity. For example, Alan Gewirth tells us that "Charity while very valuable, cannot do the normative work accomplished by rights." Or hear Robert Goodin: "What is wrong with the charity-based approach to welfare is that charitable contributions are discretionary, and being discretionary they are . . . utterly unreliable." Such belittlement fits in, I think, with a fundamentally negative picture of human nature. But the facts are clear and not disputable: people do help other people, voluntarily. We didn't really need those spectacular figures to reveal the fact either. A bit of ordinary interaction with your fellows will show you people who are generally helpful to others, in large ways and small, as a matter of routine. For those inclined to dispute this familiar fact of social life, I remind the reader that there is absolutely no way that a social system can incorporate help to anyone, poor or otherwise, in the absence of substantial basically voluntary support from individual people—the more so in a democracy. And as we have just seen, the highest level of individual voluntary charitable expenditure is found in the world's oldest and wealthiest democracy. (Perhaps not coincidentally, the United States is also among the latest-comers into the welfare-state syndrome.)

A great deal of empirical work, done by many writers, demonstrates that this recent charitable trend is no fluke and that, by and large, people help each other. Not only do they help their families and loved ones, but they also help miscellaneous people, including people in distant lands whom they have never met and never will. Under the circumstances, Sterba's hypothetical examples need to be put in perspective. The thesis that in an area in which economic activity is at least predominantly voluntary, there would be "starving people" whose only option was to steal from "the rich" belongs in the realm of fantasy, not reality. Those who do steal from the rich are by no means poverty-stricken, and those who are poverty-stricken get handouts from amiable passersby and a large variety of private associations, such as churches of many denominations.

In an unbiased view of the matter, this would settle the issue so far as real-world questions go. In the real world, if the welfare state were turned off entirely (though not, of course, overnight), what we should expect is that the poor and hopeless would continue to be taken care of, as always. Whether they would be taken better care of than the State manages to is, of course, an interesting question, but affirmative answers to that are certainly not wanting. Whatever, it is perfectly clear that the issue, in real-world terms, has nothing to do with starvation. The welfare payments of contemporary wealthy countries such as the United States are far above the subsistence level.

What, now, is Sterba's case? He envisages the possibility that in a free-market social world, nobody would be willing to help the poor. But he fails to draw the obvious conclusion: that in that case, if there were any poor—as there might not be, of course—those poor would starve, period. They would not be taken care of by the welfare state, because there would be no welfare state—no way to get state welfare initiatives off the ground, for lack of voters with the necessary sympathies. And, by hypothesis, they would not be taken care of by individuals acting on their own either. What this shows is a familiar thing: that if you make your premises absurd enough, there is no problem deducing absurd conclusions from them. But it is a more serious point when the absurd premises, imported in order to refute an opposing position, also refute one's own.

The issue, then, has to come to this: given a choice between a world in which there is no institutionalized enforceable requirement that people help the poor, although in fact a great many of them would, and a world in which there was such an institutionalized requirement, would the prospectively poor choose the latter or the former? Now, in political terms, they tend to choose the state-imposed method, as the experiences of recent democracies make clear. But this, we may point out, is due to the fact that, *pace* Lincoln, you can fool a lot of the people a lot of the time. However, it is also irrelevant, when stacked up against the terms of our discussion that Sterba subscribes to: namely, the demonstration that there would be a unanimous preference for the compulsory system. And how could he possibly think that?

There are two overwhelmingly good reasons to think that as between the welfare state and the voluntary state, the latter would get unanimous preference rather than the former. We won't count the fact that, for instance, I wouldn't go for the welfare state, so we know that we would be at least one short of unanimity

(in fact, several thousand nonphilosophical libertarians wouldn't go for it, and probably many millions of others if the alternatives were clear and if they thought they could actually do anything about it). But the two things I have in mind are more general than that.

First, the rational poor would be aware of the dismal record of actual socialist societies claiming to guarantee sustenance to the poor. Given the thirty-some millions known to have starved in Mao's China and the ten or so millions intentionally starved in Stalin's Russia, the many thousands facing starvation in North Korea but for foreign beneficence, and so on, an intelligent poor person armed with the facts would be ready to distrust "guarantees" by states. Going on a bit further, this person would note the unreliable character, and the extremely alienated character, of welfare assistance in contemporary welfare states. He would note the many thousands of people who voluntarily refuse its assistance, preferring to throw themselves upon private charity. And he would ask himself, "Do I really think I am better off having force used against the breadwinners in this society to see to it that I am fed, than I would be if people were even richer than they are now, and quite capable of advertising my plight to them, in hopes of voluntary relief?" To me, it seems obvious that the answer is in the negative. I should note that on my side of this are thousands of the "homeless" in the United States and Canada, people who prefer taking to the streets and bridges rather than facing the army of state welfare bureaucrats who stand ready to assist them.

I have, of course, deliberately biased the above account in the same way that Sterba has, by looking at it only from the point of view of the prospectively poor. That is a bias, and an outrageous one. The correct account of this is to look at it from every person's point of view, and seek a principle on which all would rationally agree, the alternative being no-agreement with its general welfare. It is quite obvious that the people who provide all this welfare have no reason to prefer compulsory welfare extraction from themselves. Only a biased social contract could possibly be thought to support the welfarist result. That is the account which, under the influence of Rawls, almost all current theorists do use, in fact. But to be fair, we should realize that it's a fraud. In the nonfraudulent account, the welfare state comes a cropper. Nevertheless, the point of this exercise has been to demonstrate that looking at it from this biased point of view still gives us excellent reason to prefer the voluntary system. The welfare state is worse for the poor, not just for everyone else.

8. A PREMISE-CONCLUSION GAP

Relieving poverty at the level of genuine subsistence isn't what Sterba means to support in his conclusions. He thinks, I am sure, that his arguments support government policies and programs such as the U.S. "War on Poverty," Medicare, and the rest of it. He isn't really talking about starvation at all. What contemporary intellectuals mean by people's "starving" is generally that the individuals in question don't have as much money left over after buying the VCR, beer, and cigarettes to live in the manner that intellectuals think is a decent minimum for every human—somewhere around the Assistant Professor level, roughly.

Yet even the homeless on the streets of New York and Toronto are by no means starving. They aren't living as comfortably as you or I—though one hears of exceptions—but to say that they are starving is in general false. An adept beggar in either of those cities can actually make a decent income these days; in any case, there are ample numbers of people around who are willing to keep such people fed, if that was what is in question. And that's all that was supposed to be in question, if we take Sterba strictly at his word.

Sterba's premise includes a clause to the effect that the poor "have tried all the means available to them that Spencerian libertarians regard as legitimate for acquiring such resources." If he really meant that, then he should be opposed to the American welfare state. For in hardly any cases, if any, is it true that the "poor" aren't working because they "can't find" work—most unemployed today are people who prefer drawing unemployment compensation or welfare checks to the sort of jobs, at the sort of rates of pay, that they might have to take if they did have to take any. And as for the rest, the resource left to them by the libertarian is voluntary, private charity—a source that is superabundant in relation to demand. It is fairly likely, actually, that the characteristic generosity of the American generates much of the problem as well as solving it. If people know they can make a living by begging, a good many of them will not be motivated to try to do better by working; indeed, they may well regard begging as "their job," take a good deal of pride in it, and regard handouts as a right. Sterba's principles simply have no bearing on these cases. On his own statement of the case, then, he should be against the contemporary welfare state, not for it.

Sterba's premise is really meant to be the thin edge of a wedge prizing open the door to policies immensely more "generous" (in the welfare-state liberal's peculiar sense of "generous," in which generosity consists of forcing everybody else to "contribute" to the worthy causes you have selected for their involuntary support). Consider, for example, people who "need" a $100,000 kidney dialysis job. If they don't get it, they will die. So of course they, or rather their Liberal Establishment friends, get to gang up on the rest of us and extract from us the necessary $100,000 (at the inflated prices caused by the deep-pockets welfare state—medical costs in the United States have skyrocketed since the onset of government handouts in the medical field).

This application to medicine serves well as an example of both the premise-conclusion chasm and the incoherence of American welfare liberalism. Sterba apparently thinks that life or death is a simple, yes or no matter, life being a "necessity" to assert against the "luxuries" of people like ourselves, who have books and computers and battered '89 Chevs instead of boomboxes, cigarettes, and battered '83 Cadillacs. Now, it is possible, like John Locke and Sterba, to think it obvious that justice requires us to give bread to a starving man at our door. But Locke would have found it laughably unobvious that you ought to give two-thirds of your estate to a man at your door who needs a kidney transplant.

It has to be pointed out that if you're going to include any and all possible medical services for prolonging life among the "necessities" Sterba seems to want to talk about, then he should appreciate that there is literally no limit to what can possibly be spent on the prolonging of life. If we want to get into this compulsion to prolong life—anybody's life, no matter whose, and regardless of that person's resources, or even his interest in prolonging it—then you can justify a tax approaching 100 percent on all productive people to toss into this bottomless pit.

No matter whether you look at it individually or collectively, this means that you are going to have to make some decision about quality of life. It's not a matter of the "luxurious" against the "starving," but, for example, of one person's living an interesting, useful, and enjoyable life for another thirty years against another person's living a boring, painful, drug-besotted life for another six weeks. Of course people have the right to prefer the latter to the former—but why should the rest of us have to pay in order to support that choice?

The American Welfare Liberal's proclivity these days is to think that such decisions must be made collectively. I suggest that that is absurd and, perhaps more to the point here, inhumane, indeed inhuman.

Once you have a life of your own, and (thus) a set of resources to devote as best you can to making that life as good as possible, then you are in a position to decide between a more interesting but possibly shorter life and a poverty-stricken but longer one (poverty-stricken because you are devoting three-fourths of your income to medical insurance against that awful day when you need a $100,000 operation to give you another few weeks of miserable life). Most of us, I am sure, would make that decision in favor of the former rather than the latter. Indeed, all smokers do so, choosing to lower their own life expectancy by several years on the average, so we are led to believe nowadays, in preference to the longer but alas, smoke-free life they could otherwise have. In my view, this should indeed be their choice—as long as they can keep the smoke out of my eyes, lungs, and clothing. Does Sterba think so too? If he does, that's very odd, for he nevertheless thinks that the rest of us can be compelled to spend vast amounts of money treating the lung cancer that awaits a hefty proportion of those smokers. Finally, if we turn back to the "War on Poverty" syndrome, we should appreciate that poverty comes in many forms. I grew up in a small community in Minnesota, in which, I daresay, fairly close to 100 percent of the people were "poor" by official contemporary standards—probably including my own family, even though my father was in a moderately prominent position in that community. But in no reasonable judgment of well-being were these people worse off than the typical American inner-city welfare occupant, dependent on the State for her check, plus the sale of crack by her twelve-year-old. Living in a violent, depressed, angry social environment of utterly dependent, listless, slatternly, and contemptuous people with nothing to do and nowhere to go, almost all of it courtesy of American "Liberals" in Congress who can think of nothing better to do with your and my money than support precisely such an environment for such people—how could anybody think that this is a good life for anyone? How could anyone think that it is better than being "poor" merely in the sense of not having very much money? It is easy enough to see why many people prefer the life of the beggar to that.

At the bottom of these policies, it seems to me, lies a kind of Olympian contempt for ordinary people, felt by way too many philosophers nowadays. They "know" what is good for them, and that it can be "provided" with a sufficient infusion of well-meaning bureaucracy fueled by other people's money. The possibility that the people we are trying to benefit might be people, like ourselves, instead of incompetent children,

is not one that readily occurs to us. The contemporary so-called liberal philosopher goes on about an alleged duty of "equal opportunity"—and out of this emerges the American ghetto and the impoverishment of ordinary people. To detail the unhappy course from Sterba's premises to that conclusion would take too long, but that, I think, is what we are ultimately talking about here. It wouldn't be so bad if political welfarism were just a conceptual fraud; the trouble is, it has consequences for real people, and those consequences are largely evil, though so thick is the haze of ideology that we have become almost unable to see them.

9. BOTTOMLESS PITS

Let us start with the case of Robinson Crusoe, who has done very well for himself and is enjoying his comfortable life on the island. Note that he could not conceivably be accused of having used force against anyone else to acquire his hard-earned luxuries—there wasn't anybody around. Now, however, the island next door suddenly becomes densely populated with ravenous people. Question for Sterba: How many of them does Robinson have to feed? Sterba's idea is that we have the rich with their "abundance," their "luxuries," their "superfluities," and the poor with their needs for "minimum" calories, or whatever. So the rich don't owe the poor very much, you see. Still, when you multiply one beggar, with his modest request, by a hundred thousand, you have a problem. Robinson may be wealthy, but he isn't that wealthy: a couple of dozen and he's reduced to pauperdom himself. And then what?

Sterba now has to face the old familiar question posed by resolute marketeers: How much must he part with? If the answer is that he has to part with everything, up to the point where his marginal contribution to the others is matched by his marginal deprivation to himself, then, for one thing, the appearance that Sterba is running a liberal, nonegalitarian theory goes down the drain in this special case.

Interpreting the right-to-enough principle leads the welfare enthusiast into a dilemma. He insists on a general, positive right to a "minimum." It therefore makes a draw on resources—unlike a negative right, which does not. When the resources are grossly inadequate, then the outcome is, say, that of two million poor people, a million people starve, and two dozen are saved by the action of our rich man, turning himself into a near-pauper in the interests of "justice." But what is the situation, in Sterba's terms, of the other million? Does he want to say that their rights have been violated? Not if he is serious about the "ought" implies "can" principle: Crusoe has done all he can, we will suppose. But it isn't nearly enough. The supposed right of the remaining million has done them no good. Is that important? Ask anybody in any previously socialist country, whose "right" to all sorts of stuff hasn't kept things from getting into a state where he had to wait three hours in line for his loaf of bread—which he probably wouldn't have had at all if it weren't for burgeoning capitalist granaries in Canada and the United States.

In addition, there would be the question of capital. If the ne'er-do-wells' clamoring is enough to generate a demand in justice for all of one's "surplus," then what about all of Robinson's carefully planned gardens, his seed grains, his workshops? If all of this is converted to consumption immediately, then all of the starvelings, plus Robinson himself, will starve a little later. If none of it is, then a good many will starve now, but a good many will be able to go to work for Robinson, increasing his stock for himself as well as for them. If Sterba has a calculated answer to this, what is the basis of his calculation? Perhaps a utilitarian one? But whatever it is, it isn't Robinson's. Indeed, Robinson's agreement to the proceedings went by the boards some time ago, didn't it? In fact, it seems that on the welfarist view, the only people who count are the poor; Robinson has no say until he himself becomes one of them—an odd result for what started out as a view that morals are supposed to be agreements among reasonable people. It seems that you are "reasonable," you are only consulted, only if you are poor!

Even then, we might note, it seems that only the poor in one's own country are actually consulted. Those next door, or on the other side of the world, do not come in for a cut. And if they did, the problem broached above becomes pretty overwhelming. Keeping the entire world's population at the American Assistant Professor level would take a good deal more than the entire GNPs of the United States, Canada, and probably all of Europe while we're at it.

10. THE ARGUMENT AT A MORE ABSTRACT LEVEL

These considerations bring up the question of what kind of exercise the recourse to a hypothetical rational decision really is, and whether it is possibly relevant to the real world. Thus far I have couched it in substantially real-world terms. But we may gain some insight by being a bit more general. It is much too easy to construe alternatives presented in such discussions in the terms, and with the assumptions, of prevailing institutions and orthodoxies of thought. The original Social Contract idea, however, was a great deal sparer than that, especially for the very good reason that the welfare state was very much a thing of the future in, say, seventeenth-century England.

Contractarian theory has been greatly infected in the past few decades by the work of Rawls, who tells us that he is trying to "generalize and carry to a higher order of abstraction the traditional theory of the social contract as represented by Locke, Rousseau, and Kant." Conspicuously missing from that list, it should be noted, is Hobbes, the modern originator of the social contract approach and arguably the only theorist who stuck to his guns. Hobbes uses, and imports, no moral assumptions into his theorizing—especially, no "veils of ignorance" of the kind Rawls imports with a view to shoring up his own academic "liberal" prejudices, as I think it only fair to describe them.

This purer theory of the social contract has it that we should contemplate how things might be if we had no morality at all, though we were otherwise recognizably human. Hobbes expounded the theory, confusingly, in political terms, identifying a hypothetical condition of man without government instead of the more fundamental case of the condition of man without morality. Yet it is perfectly clear that his Laws of Nature do address precisely that possibility. He expounds those laws on the assumptions that people are self-interested and rational, that they do not live in the Garden of Eden, but do live in a world that can be indefinitely improved, for all, by the application of human intelligence, skill, and energy. The trouble with the utterly amoral situation is that nobody could rely on anyone else, not only in minor cases, as when A scratches B's back in return for B's scratching A's, but also in the very much more far-reaching case in which A refrains from killing B whenever it may serve A's individual interest to do so, provided that B will likewise refrain from killing A whenever it serves B's similarly individual interest to do so. In the absence of the general disposition to refrain from violence, the consequences Hobbes attributes to the absence of a sovereign really do seem likely. There can indeed, in that case, be "no place for Industry; because the fruit thereof is uncertain; and consequently no Culture of the Earth, no Navigation, . . . no commodious Building . . . no

Knowledge of the face of the Earth . . . no Arts; no Letters; no Society; and which is worst of all, continual fear, and danger of violent death; And the life of man, solitary, poor, nasty, brutish, and short." These sentences, I think, affirm obvious truths, and are too often dismissed as paranoid or silly. Understood as the thought experiment it obviously is, the point stands out with impressive clarity. We do, absolutely, depend on others around us not resorting readily to violence whenever they should happen to think it would be useful to do so.

The power of the social contract idea, then, is straightforward: no agreement, and we are all dead (to put it overdramatically)—that is, dead a lot sooner than we'd like to be and could be, and in the meantime enormously poorer than we'd like to be and could be. I take it as obvious that any rational person must prefer the situation in which we can depend on each other in that particular way to the situation in which we can't depend on each other at all. And if the dependency in question can be secured only by general acknowledgment of the justifiability of resort to force in defense against those who would use violence nevertheless, well, so be it. That is a price easily worth paying.

But the welfare state is another matter altogether. The incompetent and weak have the same stake as the rich in being immune from the depredations of others. It is always possible to make someone worse off, no matter how badly off he is at present, up to the very point of death. And it is always in our interests that others refrain from doing so—possibly more so if we are weak and poor than if we are strong and wealthy. But it is very far from obvious that we would all be better off if we were all to agree, not just to provide for others voluntarily, as our sentiments and estimates of our resources prescribe, but to do so at the point of a gun or in the shadow of a prison's gate.

"Far from obvious," however, is too weak an expression here, for this is an abstract exercise. That being so, the conclusion has to be that the welfare-state contract is a non-starter. It simply is not in the interests of the competent and the strong to sign this sort of a contract. The welfare state is of little likely benefit to them, and they have, we are assuming, no great interest in the well-being of the weak as a class (we have to assume that, for otherwise a welfare state would, by definition, be unnecessary). This being so, they must expect that the costs of the welfare state must fall upon them, the relatively more competent. So a rough cost-benefit analysis suggests, straight off, that they would not rationally go for it.

If that is true, however, then the welfare state is, at this abstract level, dead in the water. There is another option that is better for everyone than the no-agreement condition, and anything "stronger" is probably not going to get unanimity.

CONCLUSION

Our general conclusion remains, then, that the welfare state simply is not supported by the arguments Sterba proposes, as compared with the libertarian society in which, just because there are no forcibly imposed duties to do good to others at cost to the doer, more and better good is in fact done to those others, because it is done by persons who act voluntarily and enthusiastically because self-interestedly. And it is an advantage to my libertarian view that it runs into no special difficulties when we cross borders.

All this is, as I have noted, predicated on a highly biased idea about the social contract, whose ideological profile has been thoroughly biased of late by confining the theorist's view, myopically, to the unfortunate and incompetent. Were we instead to take all people as they are, the superior claims of general peace for all against partial peace with war against the rich would, I think, be too obvious to require so lengthy a treatment as the foregoing.

READING 22

There's No Such Thing As Free Speech and It's a Good Thing Too

Stanley Fish

Stanley Fish is Arts and Science Professor of English and Professor of Law at Duke University and the author of several works, including *Surprised by Sin and Doing What Comes Naturally, There's No Such Thing As Free Speech and It's a Good Thing Too*. Fish argues that the so-called

First Amendment right of free speech is no right at all and never was. What we call free speech is merely a "political" prize.

This reading is taken from Fish's *There's No Such Thing As Free Speech and It's a Good Thing Too* (Oxford University Press, 1994), by permission.

Lately, many on the liberal and progressive left have been disconcerted to find that words, phrases, and concepts thought to be their property and generative of their politics have been appropriated by the forces of neoconservatism. This is particularly true of the concept of free speech, for in recent years First Amendment rhetoric has been used to justify policies and actions the left finds problematical if not abhorrent: pornography, sexist language, campus hate speech. How has this happened? The answer I shall give in this essay is that abstract concepts like free speech do not have any "natural" content but are filled with whatever content and direction one can manage to put into them. "Free speech" is just the name we give to verbal behavior that serves the substantive agendas we wish to advance; and we give our preferred verbal behaviors *that* name when we can, when we have the power to do so, because in the rhetoric of American life, the label "free speech" is the one you want your favorites to wear. Free speech, in short, is not an independent value but a political prize, and if that prize has been captured by a politics opposed to yours, it can no longer be invoked in ways that further your purposes, for it is now an obstacle to those purposes. This is something that the liberal left has yet to understand, and what follows is an attempt to pry its members loose from a vocabulary that may now be a disservice to them.

Not far from the end of his *Areopagitica,* and after having celebrated the virtues of toleration and unregulated publication in passages that find their way into every discussion of free speech and the First Amendment, John Milton catches himself up short and says, of course I didn't mean Catholics, them we exterminate:

> I mean not tolerated popery, and open superstition, which as it extirpates all religious and civil supremacies, so itself should be extirpate . . . that also which is impious or evil absolutely against faith or manners no law can possibly permit that intends not to unlaw itself.

Notice that Milton is not simply stipulating a single exception to a rule generally in place; the kinds of utterance that might be regulated and even prohibited on pain of trial and punishment constitute an open set; popery is named only as a particularly perspicuous instance of the advocacy that cannot be tolerated. No doubt there are other forms of speech and action that might be categorized as "open superstitions" or as subversive of piety, faith, and manners, and presumably these too would be candidates for "extirpation." Nor would Milton think himself culpable for having failed to provide a list of unprotected utterances. The list will fill itself out as utterances are put to the test implied by his formulation: would this form of speech or advocacy, if permitted to flourish, tend to undermine the very purposes for which our society is constituted? One cannot answer this question with respect to a particular utterance in advance of its emergence on the world's stage; rather, one must wait and ask the question in the full context of its production and (possible) dissemination. It might appear that the result would be ad hoc and unprincipled, but for Milton the principle inheres in the core values in whose name individuals of like mind came together in the first place. Those values, which include the search for truth and the promotion of virtue, are capacious enough to accommodate a diversity of views. But at some point—again impossible of advance specification—capaciousness will threaten to become shapelessness, and at that point fidelity to the original values will demand acts of extirpation.

I want to say that all affirmations of freedom of expression are like Milton's, dependent for their force on an exception that literally carves out the space in which expression can then emerge. I do not mean that expression (saying something) is a realm whose integrity is sometimes compromised by certain restrictions but that restriction, in the form of an underlying articulation of the world that necessarily (if silently) negates alternatively possible articulations, is constitutive of expression. Without restriction, without an inbuilt sense of what it would be meaningless to say or wrong to say, there could be no assertion and no reason for asserting it. The exception to unregulated expression is not a negative restriction but a positive hollowing out of value—we are for *this,* which means we are against *that*—in relation to which meaningful assertion can then occur. It is in reference to that value—constituted as all values are by an act of exclusion—that some forms of speech will be heard as (quite literally) intolerable. Speech, in short, is never a value in and of itself but is always produced within the precincts of some assumed conception of the good to which it must yield in the event of conflict. When the pinch comes (and sooner or later it will always come) and the institution (be it church, state, or university) is confronted by behavior subversive of its core rationale, it will respond by declaring "of course we mean not tolerated — — , that we extirpate," not because an exception to a general freedom has suddenly and contradictorily been announced, but because the freedom has never been general and has always been understood against the background of an originary exclusion that gives it meaning.

This is a large thesis, but before tackling it directly I want to buttress my case with another example, taken not from the seventeenth century but from the charter and case law of Canada. Canadian thinking about freedom of expression departs from the line usually taken in the United States in ways that bring that country very close to the *Areopagitica* as I have expounded it. The differences are fully on display in a recent landmark case, *R. v. Keegstra*. James Keegstra was a high school teacher in Alberta who, it was established by evidence, "systematically denigrated Jews and Judaism in his classes." He described Jews as treacherous, subversive, sadistic, money loving, power hungry, and child killers. He declared them "responsible for depressions, anarchy, chaos, wars and revolution" and required his students "to regurgitate these notions in essays and examinations." Keegstra was indicted under Section 319(2) of the Criminal Code and convicted. The Court of Appeal reversed, and the Crown appealed to the Supreme Court, which reinstated the lower court's verdict.

Section 319(2) reads in part, "Every one who, by communicating statements other than in private conversation, willfully promotes hatred against any identifiable group is guilty of . . . an indictable offense and is liable to imprisonment for a term not exceeding two years." In the United States, this provision of the code would almost certainly be struck down because, under the First Amendment, restrictions on speech are apparently prohibited without qualification. To be sure, the Canadian charter has its own version of the First Amendment, in Section 2(b): "Everyone has the following fundamental freedoms . . . (b) freedom of thought, belief, opinion, and expression, including freedom of the press and other media of communication." But Section 2(b), like every other section of the charter, is qualified by Section 1: "The Canadian Charter of Rights and Freedoms guarantees the rights and freedoms set out in it subject only to such reasonable limits prescribed by law as can be demonstrably justified in a free and democratic society." Or in other words, every right and freedom herein granted can be trumped if its exercise is found to be in conflict with the principles that underwrite the society.

This is what happens in *Keegstra* as the majority finds that Section 319(2) of the Criminal Code does in fact violate the right of freedom of expression guaranteed by the charter but is nevertheless a *permissible* restriction because it accords with the principles proclaimed in Section 1. There is, of course, a dissent that reaches the conclusion that would have been reached by most, if not all, U.S. courts; but even in dissent the minority is faithful to Canadian ways of reasoning. "The question," it declares, "is always one of balance," and thus even when a particular infringement of the charter's Section 2(b) has been declared unconstitutional, as it would have been by the minority, the question remains open with respect to the next case. In the United States the question is presumed closed and can only be pried open by special tools. In our legal culture as it is now constituted, if one yells "free speech" in a crowded courtroom and makes it stick, the case is over.

Of course, it is not that simple. Despite the apparent absoluteness of the First Amendment, there are any number of ways of getting around it, ways that are known to every student of the law. In general, the preferred strategy is to manipulate the distinction, essential to First Amendment jurisprudence, between speech and action. The distinction is essential because no one would think to frame a First Amendment that began "Congress shall make no law abridging freedom of action," for that would amount to saying "Congress shall make no law," which would amount to saying "There shall be no law," only actions uninhibited and unregulated. If the First Amendment is to make any sense, have any bite, speech must be declared not to be a species of action, or to be a special form of action lacking the aspects of action that cause it to be the object of regulation. The latter strategy is the favored one and usually involves the separation of speech from consequences. This is what Archibald Cox does when he assigns to the First Amendment the job of protecting "expressions separable from conduct harmful to other individuals and the community." The difficulty of managing this segregation is well known: speech always seems to be crossing the line into action, where it becomes, at least potentially, consequential. In the face of this categorical instability, First Amendment theorists and jurists fashion a distinction within the speech/action distinction: some forms of speech are not really speech because their purpose is to incite violence or because they are, as the court declares in *Chaplinsky v. New Hampshire* (1942), "fighting words," words "likely to provoke the average person to retaliation, and thereby cause a breach of the peace."

The trouble with this definition is that it distinguishes not between fighting words and words that remain safely and merely expressive but between words that are provocative to one group (the group that falls under the rubric "average person") and words that might be provocative to other groups, groups of persons not now considered average. And if you ask what words are likely to be provocative to those nonaverage groups, what are likely to be *their* fighting words, the answer is anything and everything, for as Justice Holmes said long ago (in *Gitlow v. New York*), every idea is an incitement to somebody, and since ideas come packaged in sentences, in words, every sentence is potentially, in some situation that might occur tomorrow, a fighting word and therefore a candidate for regulation.

This insight cuts two ways. One could conclude from it that the fighting words exception is a bad idea because there is no way to prevent clever and unscrupulous advocates from shoveling so many forms of speech into the excepted category that the zone of constitutionally protected speech shrinks to nothing and is finally without inhabitants. Or, alternatively, one could conclude that there was never anything in the zone in the first place and that the difficulty of limiting the fighting words exception is merely a particular instance of the general difficulty of separating speech from action. And if one opts for this second conclusion, as I do, then a further conclusion is inescapable: insofar as the point of the First Amendment is to identify speech separable from conduct and from the consequences that come in conduct's wake, there is no such speech and therefore nothing for the First Amendment to protect. Or, to make the point from the other direction, when a court invalidates legislation because it infringes on protected speech, it is not because the speech in question is without consequences but because the consequences have been discounted in relation to a good that is judged to outweigh them. Despite what they say, courts are never in the business of protecting speech per se, "mere" speech (a nonexistent animal); rather, they are in the business of classifying speech (as protected or regulatable) in relation to a value—the health of the republic, the vigor of the economy, the maintenance of the status quo, the undoing of the status quo— that is the true, if unacknowledged, object of their protection.

But if this is the case, a First Amendment purist might reply, why not drop the charade along with the malleable distinctions that make it possible, and declare up front that total freedom of speech is our primary value and trumps anything else, no matter what?

The answer is that freedom of expression would only be a primary value if it didn't matter what was said, didn't matter in the sense that no one gave a damn but just liked to hear talk. There are contexts like that, a Hyde Park corner or a call-in talk show where people get to sound off for the sheer fun of it. These, however, are special contexts, artificially bounded spaces designed to assure that talking is not taken seriously. In ordinary contexts, talk is produced with the goal of trying to move the world in one direction rather than another. In these contexts—the contexts of everyday life—you go to the trouble of asserting that X is Y only because you suspect that some people are wrongly asserting that X is Z or that X doesn't exist. You assert, in short, because you give a damn, not about assertion—as if it were a value in and of itself—but about what your assertion is about. It may seem paradoxical, but free expression could only be a primary value if what you are valuing is the right to make noise; but if you are engaged in some purposive activity in the course of which speech happens to be produced, sooner or later you will come to a point when you decide that some forms of speech do not further but endanger that purpose.

Take the case of universities and colleges. Could it be the purpose of such places to encourage free expression? If the answer were "yes," it would be hard to say why there would be any need for classes, or examinations, or departments, or disciplines, or libraries, since freedom of expression requires nothing but a soapbox or an open telephone line. The very fact of the university's machinery—of the events, rituals, and procedures that fill its calendar—argues for some other, more substantive purpose. In relation to that purpose (which will be realized differently in different kinds of institutions), the flourishing of free expression will in almost all circumstances be an obvious good; but in some circumstances, freedom of expression may pose a threat to that purpose, and at that point it may be necessary to discipline or regulate speech, lest, to paraphrase Milton, the institution sacrifice itself to one of its *accidental* features.

Interestingly enough, the same conclusion is reached (inadvertently) by Congressman Henry Hyde, who is addressing these very issues in a recently offered amendment to Title VI of the Civil Rights Act. The first section of the amendment states its purpose, to protect "the free speech rights of college students" by prohibiting private as well as public educational institutions from "subjecting any student to disciplinary sanctions solely on the basis of conduct that is speech."

The second section enumerates the remedies available to students whose speech rights may have been abridged; and the third, which is to my mind the nub of the matter, declares as an exception to the amendment's jurisdiction any "educational institution that is controlled by a religious organization," on the reasoning that the application of the amendment to such institutions "would not be consistent with the religious tenets of such organizations." In effect, what Congressman Hyde is saying is that at the heart of these colleges and universities is a set of beliefs, and it would be wrong to require them to tolerate behavior, including speech behavior, inimical to those beliefs. But insofar as this logic is persuasive, it applies across the board, for all educational institutions rest on some set of beliefs—no institution is "just there" independent of any purpose—and it is hard to see why the rights of an institution to protect and preserve its basic "tenets" should be restricted only to those that are religiously controlled. Read strongly, the third section of the amendment undoes sections one and two—the exception becomes, as it always was, the rule—and points us to a balancing test very much like that employed in Canadian law: given that any college or university is informed by a core rationale, an administrator faced with complaints about offensive speech should ask whether damage to the core would be greater if the speech were tolerated or regulated.

The objection to this line of reasoning is well known and has recently been reformulated by Benno Schmidt, former president of Yale University. According to Schmidt, speech codes on campuses constitute "well intentioned but misguided efforts to give values of community and harmony a higher place than freedom" (*Wall Street Journal,* May 6, 1991). "When the goals of harmony collide with freedom of expression," he continues, "freedom must be the paramount obligation of an academic community." The flaw in this logic is on display in the phrase "academic community," for the phrase recognizes what Schmidt would deny, that expression only occurs in communities—if not in an academic community, then in a shopping mall community or a dinner party community or an airplane ride community or an office community. In these communities and in any others that could be imagined (with the possible exception of a community of major league baseball fans), limitations on speech in relation to a defining and deeply assumed purpose are inseparable from community membership.

Indeed, "limitations" is the wrong word because it suggests that expression, as an activity and a value, has a pure form that is always in danger of being compromised by the urgings of special interest communities; but independently of a community context informed by interest (that is, purpose), expression would be at once inconceivable and unintelligible. Rather than being a value that is threatened by limitations and constraints, expression, in any form worth worrying about, is a *product* of limitations and constraints, of the already-in-place presuppositions that give assertions their very particular point. Indeed, the very act of thinking of something to say (whether or not it is subsequently regulated) is already constrained—rendered impure, and because impure, communicable—by the background context within which the thought takes its shape. (The analysis holds too for "freedom," which in Schmidt's vision is an entirely empty concept referring to an urge without direction. But like expression, freedom is a coherent notion only in relation to a goal or good that limits and, by limiting, shapes its exercise.)

Arguments like Schmidt's only get their purchase by first imagining speech as occurring in no context whatsoever, and then stripping particular speech acts of the properties conferred on them by contexts. The trick is nicely illustrated when Schmidt urges protection for speech "no matter how obnoxious in content." "Obnoxious" at once acknowledges the reality of speech-related harms and trivializes them by suggesting that they are *surface* injuries that any large-minded ("liberated and humane") person should be able to bear. The possibility that speech-related injuries may be grievous and *deeply* wounding is carefully kept out of sight, and because it is kept out of sight, the fiction of a world of weightless verbal exchange can be maintained, at least withing the confines of Schmidt's carefully denatured discourse.

To this Schmidt would no doubt reply, as he does in his essay, that harmful speech should be answered not by regulation but by more speech; but that would make sense only if the effects of speech could be canceled out by additional speech, only if the pain and humiliation caused by racial or religious epithets could be ameliorated by saying something like "So's your old man." What Schmidt fails to realize at every level of his argument is that expression is more than a matter of proffering and receiving propositions, that words do work in the world of a kind that cannot be confined to a purely cognitive realm of "mere" ideas.

It could be said, however, that I myself mistake the nature of the work done by freely tolerated speech because I am too focused on short-run outcomes and fail to understand that the good effects of speech will be realized, not in the present, but in a future whose emergence regulation could only inhibit. This line of reasoning would also weaken one of my key points, that speech in and of itself cannot be a value and is only worth worrying about if it is in the service of something with which it cannot be identical. My mistake, one could argue, is to equate the something in whose service speech is with some locally espoused value (e.g., the end of racism, the empowerment of disadvantaged minorities), whereas in fact we should think of that something as a now-inchoate shape that will be given firm lines only by time's pencil. That is why the shape now receives such indeterminate characterizations (e.g., true self-fulfillment, a more perfect polity, a more capable citizenry, a less partial truth); we cannot now know it, and therefore we must not prematurely fix it in ways that will bind successive generations to error.

This forward-looking view of what the First Amendment protects has a great appeal, in part because it continues in a secular form the Puritan celebration of millenarian hopes, but it imposes a requirement so severe that one would except more justification for it than is usually provided. The requirement is that we endure whatever pain racist and hate speech inflicts for the sake of a future whose emergence we can only take on faith. In a specifically religious vision like Milton's, this makes perfect sense (it is indeed the whole of Christianity), but in the context of a politics that puts its trust in the world and not in the Holy Spirit, it raises more questions than it answers and could be seen as the second of two strategies designed to delegitimize the complaints of victimized groups. The first strategy, as I have noted, is to define speech in such a way as to render it inconsequential (on the model of "sticks and stones will break my bones, but . . ."); the second strategy is to acknowledge the (often grievous) consequences of speech but declare that we must suffer them in the name of something that cannot be named. The two strategies are denials from slightly different directions of the *present* effects of racist speech; one confines those effects to a closed and safe realm of pure mental activity; the other imagines the effects of speech spilling over into the world but only in an ever-receding future for whose sake we must forever defer taking action.

I find both strategies unpersuasive, but my own skepticism concerning them is less important than the fact that in general they seem to have worked; in the parlance of the marketplace (a parlance First Amendment commentators love), many in the society

seemed to have bought them. Why? The answer, I think, is that people cling to First Amendment pieties because they do not wish to face what they correctly take to be the alternative. That alternative is *politics,* the realization (at which I have already hinted) that decisions about what is and is not protected in the realm of expression will rest not on principle or firm doctrine but on the ability of some persons to interpret—recharacterize or rewrite—principle and doctrine in ways that lead to the protection of speech they want heard and the regulation of speech they want heard and the regulation of speech they want silenced. (That is how George Bush can argue *for* flag-burning statutes and *against* campus hate-speech codes.) When the First Amendment is successfully invoked, the result is not a victory for free speech in the face of a challenge from politics but a *political victory* won by the party that has managed to wrap its agenda in the mantle of free speech.

It is from just such a conclusion—a conclusion that would put politics *inside* the First Amendment— that commentators recoil, saying things like "This could render the First Amendment a dead letter," or "This would leave us with no normative guidance in determining when and what speech to protect," or "This effaces the distinction between speech and action," or "This is incompatible with any viable notion of freedom of expression." To these statements (culled more or less at random from recent law review pieces) I would reply that the First Amendment has always been a dead letter if one understood its "liveness" to depend on the identification and protection of a realm of "mere" expression distinct from the realm of regulatable conduct; the distinction between speech and action has always been effaced in principle, although in practice it can take whatever form the prevailing political conditions mandate; we have never had any normative guidance for marking off protected from unprotected speech; rather, the guidance we have has been fashioned (and refashioned) in the very political struggles over which it then (for a time) presides. In short, the name of the game has always been politics, even when (indeed, especially when) it is played by stigmatizing politics as the area to be avoided.

In saying this, I would not be heard as arguing either for or against regulation and speech codes as a matter of general principle. Instead my argument turns away from general principle to the pragmatic (anti)principle of considering each situation as it emerges. The question of whether or not to regulate will always be a local one, and we can not rely on abstractions that are either empty of content or filled with the content of some partisan agenda to generate a "principled" answer. Instead we must consider in every case what is at stake and what are the risks and gains of alternative courses of action. In the course of this consideration many things will be of help, but among them will not be phrases like "freedom of speech" or "the right of individual expression," because, as they are used now, these phrases tend to obscure rather than clarify our dilemmas. Once they are deprived of their talismanic force, once it is no longer strategically effective simply to invoke them in the act of walking away from a problem, the conversation could continue in directions that are now blocked by a First Amendment absolutism that has only been honored in the breach anyway. To the student reporter who complains that in the wake of the promulgation of a speech code at the University of Wisconsin there is now something in the back of his mind as he writes, one could reply, "There was always something in the back of your mind, and perhaps it might be better to have this code in the back of your mind than whatever was in there before." And when someone warns about the slippery slope and predicts mournfully that if you restrict one form of speech, you never know what will be restricted next, one could reply, "Some form of speech is always being restricted, else there could be no meaningful assertion; we have always and already slid down the slippery slope; someone is always going to be restricted next, and it is your job to make sure that the someone is not you." And when someone observes, as someone surely will, that antiharassment codes chill speech, one could reply that since speech only becomes intelligible against the background of what isn't being said, the background of what has already been silenced, the only question is the political one of which speech is going to be chilled, and, all things considered, it seems a good thing to chill speech like "nigger," "cunt," "kike," and "faggot." And if someone then says, "But what happened to free-speech principles?" one could say what I have now said a dozen times, free-speech principles don't exist except as a component in a bad argument in which such principles are invoked to mask motives that would not withstand close scrutiny.

An example of a wolf wrapped in First Amendment clothing is an advertisement that ran recently in the Duke University student newspaper, the *Chronicle*. Signed by Bradley R. Smith, well known as a purveyor of anti-Semitic neo-Nazi propaganda, the ad is packaged as a scholarly treatise: four densely packed columns complete with "learned" references, undocu-

mented statistics, and an array of so-called authorities. The message of the ad is that the Holocaust never occurred and that the German state never "had a policy to exterminate the Jewish people (or anyone else) by putting them to death in gas chambers." In a spectacular instance of the increasingly popular "blame the victim" strategy, the Holocaust "story" or "myth" is said to have been fabricated in order "to drum up world sympathy for Jewish causes." The "evidence" supporting these assertions is a slick blend of supposedly probative facts—"not a single autopsied body has been shown to be gassed"—and sly insinuations of a kind familiar to readers of *Mein Kampf* and *The Protocols of the Elders of Zion*. The slickest thing of all, however, is the presentation of the argument as an exercise in free speech—the ad is subtitled "The Case for Open Debate"—that could be objected to only by "thought police" and censors. This strategy bore immediate fruit in the decision of the newspaper staff to accept the ad despite a long-standing (and historically honored) policy of refusing materials that contain ethnic and racial slurs or are otherwise offensive. The reasoning of the staff (explained by the editor in a special column) was that under the First Amendment advertisers have the "right" to be published. "American newspapers are built on the principles of free speech and free press, so how can a newspaper deny these rights to anyone?" The answer to this question is that an advertiser is not denied his rights simply because a single media organ declines his copy so long as other avenues of publication are available and there has been no state suppression of his views. This is not to say that there could not be a case for printing the ad, only that the case cannot rest on a supposed First Amendment obligation. One might argue, for example, that printing the ad would foster healthy debate, or that lies are more likely to be shown up for what they are if they are brought to the light of day, but these are precisely the arguments the editor *disclaims* in her eagerness to take a "principled" free-speech stand.

What I find most distressing about this incident is not that the ad was printed but that it was printed by persons who believed it to be a lie and a distortion. If the editor and her staff were in agreement with Smith's views or harbored serious doubts about the reality of the Holocaust, I would still have a quarrel with them, but it would be a different quarrel; it would be a quarrel about evidence, credibility, documentation. But since on these matters the editors and I are in agreement, my quarrel is with the reasoning that led them to act in opposition to what they believed to be true. That reasoning, as I understand it, goes as follows: although we ourselves are certain that the Holocaust was a fact, facts are notoriously interpretable and disputable; therefore nothing is ever really settled, and we have no right to reject something just because we regard it as pernicious and false. But the fact—if I can use that word—that settled truths can always be upset, at least theoretically, does not mean that we cannot affirm and rely on truths that according to our present lights seem indisputable; rather, it means exactly the opposite: in the absence of absolute certainty of the kind that can only be provided by revelation (something I do not rule out but have not yet experienced), we must act on the basis of the certainty we have so far achieved. Truth may, as Milton said, always be in the course of emerging, and we must always be on guard against being so beguiled by its present shape that we ignore contrary evidence; but, by the same token, when it happens that the present shape of truth is compelling beyond a reasonable doubt, it is our moral obligation to act on it and not defer action in the name of an interpretative future that may never arrive. By running the First Amendment up the nearest flagpole and rushing to salute it, the student editors defaulted on that obligation and gave over their responsibility to a so-called principle that was not even to the point.

Let me be clear. I am not saying that First Amendment principles are inherently bad (they are *inherently* nothing), only that they are not always the appropriate reference point for situations involving the production of speech, and that even when they are the appropriate reference point, they do not constitute a politics-free perspective because the shape in which they are invoked will always be political, will always, that is, be the result of having drawn the relevant line (between speech and action, or between high-value speech and low-value speech, or between words essential to the expression of ideas and fighting words) in a way that is favorable to some interests and indifferent or hostile to others. This having been said, the moral is not that First Amendment talk should be abandoned, for even if the standard First Amendment formulas do not and could not perform the function expected of them (the elimination of political considerations in decisions about speech), they still serve a function that is not at all negligible: they slow down outcomes in an area in which the fear of overhasty outcomes is justified by a long record of abuses of power. It is often said that history shows (itself a formula) that even a minimal restriction on the right of expression too easily

leads to ever-larger restrictions; and to the extent that this is an empirical fact (and it is a question one could debate), there is some comfort and protection to be found in a procedure that requires you to jump through hoops—do a lot of argumentative work—before a speech regulation will be allowed to stand.

I would not be misunderstood as offering the notion of "jumping through hoops" as a new version of the First Amendment claim to neutrality. A hoop must have a shape—in this case the shape of whatever binary distinction is representing First Amendment "interests"—and the shape of the hoop one is asked to jump through will in part determine what kinds of jumps can be regularly made. Even if they are only mechanisms for slowing down outcomes, First Amendment formulas by virtue of their substantive content (and it is impossible that they be without content) will slow down some outcomes more easily than others, and that means that the form they happen to have at the present moment will favor some interests more than others. Therefore, even with a reduced sense of the effectivity of First Amendment rhetoric (it can not assure any particular result), the counsel with which I began remains relevant: so long as so-called free-speech principles have been fashioned by your enemy (so long as it is *his* hoops you have to jump through), contest their relevance to the issue at hand; but if you manage to refashion them in line with your purposes, urge them with a vengeance.

It is a counsel that follows from the thesis that there is no such thing as free speech, which is not, after all, a thesis as startling or corrosive as may first have seemed. It merely says that there is no class of utterances separable from the world of conduct and that therefore the identification of some utterances as members of that nonexistent class will always be evidence that a political line has been drawn rather than a line that denies politics entry into the forum of public discourse. It is the job of the First Amendment to mark out an area in which competing views can be considered without state interference; but if the very marking out of that area is itself an interference (as it always will be), First Amendment jurisprudence is inevitably self-defeating and subversive of its own aspirations. That's the bad news. The good news is that precisely *because* speech is never "free" in the two senses required—free of consequences and free from state pressure—speech always matters, is always doing work; because everything we say impinges on the world in ways indistinguishable from the effects of physical action, we must take responsibility for our verbal performances—*all* of them—and not assume that they are being taken care of by a clause in the Constitution. Of course, with responsibility comes risks, but they have always been our risks, and no doctrine of free speech has ever insulated us from them. They are the risks, respectively, of permitting speech that does obvious harm and of shutting off speech in ways that might deny us the benefit of Joyce's *Ulysses* or Lawrence's *Lady Chatterly's Lover* or Titian's paintings. Nothing, I repeat, can insulate us from those risks. (If there is no normative guidance in determining when and what speech to protect, there is no normative guidance in determining what is art—like free speech a category that includes everything and nothing—and what is obscenity.) Moreover, nothing can provide us with a principle for deciding which risk in the long run is the best to take. I am persuaded that at the present moment, right now, the risk of not attending to hate speech is greater than the risk that by regulating it we will deprive ourselves of valuable voices and insights or slide down the slippery slope toward tyranny. This is a judgment for which I can offer reasons but no guarantees. All I am saying is that the judgments of those who would come down on the other side carry no guarantees either. They urge us to put our faith in apolitical abstractions, but the abstractions they invoke—the marketplace of ideas, speech alone, speech itself—only come in political guises, and therefore in trusting to them we fall (unwittingly) under the sway of the very forces we wish to keep at bay. It is not that there are no choices to make or means of making them; it is just that the choices as well as the means are inextricable from the din and confusion of partisan struggle. There is no safe place.

READING 23

If You're Paying, I'll Have Top Sirloin

Russell Roberts

Russell Roberts is director of the Management Center at Washington University in St. Louis. In this short essay from the *Wall Street Journal*, Roberts applies the lesson of the tragedy of the commons to government spending. The

tragedy of the commons, an idea developed by Garret Hardin in an article by that name, shows that what may be rational self-interested behavior for one person becomes in time a ruinous catastrophe, if too many people engage in it. Hardin's example is farmers who own cattle which are overgrazing a common field. If only one farmer overgrazes, he reaps a net gain, but if a lot of farmers overgraze, disaster for all eventually obtains. Hardin argues that self-restraint is unlikely to occur because everyone thinks he is profiting, although eventually, such self-interested reasoning defeats itself. What we need is mutually agreed upon mutually coercive rules to enforce restraint.

Roberts, without mentioning the tragedy of the commons, illustrates the theory in the way people support government projects such as public transportation systems or local arts centers. Given that maintaining expensive government organizations siphons off a large amount of tax dollars, the average person is really worse off, despite some worthy government-subsidized projects.

As Congress tries to cut spending, I am reminded of an evening last fall at the St. Louis Repertory Theater, our local company. Before the curtain rose, the company's director appeared and encouraged us to vote against a ballot proposition to limit state taxes. He feared it would lead to reduced funding for the company.

I turned to the woman sitting next to me and asked her if she felt guilty knowing that her ticket was subsidized by some farmer in the "boot heel" of Missouri. No, she answered, he's probably getting something, too. She seemed to be implying that somehow it all evened out.

I left her alone. But I wanted to say: No, it doesn't even out. That's the whole idea behind much of what the government does. The subsidized theatergoer thinks she's getting a good deal, and so does the farmer. If it "evened out" for everybody, then matters would really be depressing: all that money shuffled around, all those people working for the IRS, all those marginal tax rates discouraging work effort just to get everybody to get the same deal.

Here in St. Louis we recently completed the Metrolink, a light rail system. It cost $380 million to build. We locals contributed zero out of pocket, except for the usual federal taxes. Shouldn't we feel guilty making people in California pay for our trips to the hockey arena downtown? No, say the beneficiaries. After all, we paid for BART in San Francisco, MARTA in Atlanta and all the other extraordinarily expensive, underutilized public transportation systems whose benefits fall far short of their costs. It's only fair that we get our turn at the trough.

This destructive justification reminds me of a very strange restaurant.

When you eat there, you usually spend about $6. You have a sandwich, fries and a drink. Of course you'd also enjoy dessert and a second drink, but they would cost an additional $4. The extra food isn't worth $4 to you, so you stick with the $6 meal.

Sometimes, you go to the restaurant with three friends. The four of you split the check evenly. You realize after a while that the $4 drink and dessert will end up costing you only $1 because the total tab is split four ways. Should you order the drink and dessert? If you're a nice person, you might want to spare your friends from having to subsidize your extravagance. Then it dawns on you that they may be ordering extras financed out of your pocket. But they're your friends. You wouldn't do that to each other.

But now suppose the tab is split not at each table but across the 100 diners at all the tables. Now adding the $4 drink and dessert costs only four cents. Splurging is easy to justify now. In fact, you won't just add a drink and dessert, you'll upgrade to the steak and add a bottle of wine.

Suppose you and everybody else orders $40 worth of food. The tab for the entire restaurant will be $4,000. Divided by the 100 diners, your bill comes to $40. Like my neighbor at the theater, you'll get your "fair share." But this outcome is a disaster. When you dined alone, you spent $6. The extra $34 of steak and other treats was not worth it. But in competition with the others, you chose a meal far out of your price range whose enjoyment fell far short of its cost.

Self-restraint goes unrewarded. If you go back to ordering your $6 meal in hopes of saving money, your tab will be close to $40 anyway, unless the other 99 diners cut back also. The good citizen starts to feel like a chump.

And so we read of the freshmen congressman eager to cut pork out of the budget but in trouble back home because local projects will also come under the

knife. Instead of being proud to lead the way, he is forced to fight for the projects, to make sure his district gets its "fair share."

Matters get much worse when there are gluttons and drunkards at the restaurant mixing with dieters and teetotalers. The average tab might be $40, but some are eating $80 worth of food while others are stuck with salad and an iced tea. Those with modest appetites would like to flee the premises, but suppose it's the only restaurant in town and you're forced to eat there every night. Resentment and anger come naturally. And since it's the only restaurant in town, you can imagine the quality of the service.

Such a restaurant can be a happy place if the light eaters enjoy watching the gluttony of those who eat and drink with gusto. Many government programs generate a comparable range of support. But many do not.

How many Americans other than farmers benefit from agriculture subsidies? How many Americans other than train riders benefit from the Amtrak subsidy? How many Americans outside of the theater and its patrons benefit from the susbsidy to the arts?

People who are overeating at the expense of others should be ashamed. The only way to avoid national indigestion is to close the government restaurant where few benefit at the expense of many.

END NOTES

Introduction

[1]Clement Atlee's speech is quoted in *the Open University* course book *Political Philosophy* (Milton Keynes, 1973), p. 54. The Labor party defeated the Tory party under the leadership of Winston Churchill, and Clement Atlee became prime minister.

Feinberg

[1]See Edith Hamilton, *The Greek Way* (New York: W. W. Norton & Company, Inc., 1942), pp. 35 ff.

[2]Jeremy Bentham, "Anarchical Fallacies" in *The Works of Jeremy Bentham*, vol. 2, ed. John Bowring (Edinburgh, 1843).

[3]L. T. Hobhouse, *The Elements of Social Justice* (London: George Allen & Unwin Ltd., 1922), p. 60. Hobhouse rejects this formula, and I have adapted his argument against it in the text.

[4]L. T. Hobhouse, *Liberalism* (New York: Holt, Rinehart and Winston, Inc., 1911), pp. 63–64.

[5]*Restatement of the Law of Torts* (St. Paul: American Law Institute, 1939), p. 1.

[6] Cf. H. L. A. Hart, *Law, Liberty, and Morality* (Stanford: Stanford University Press, 1963), p. 5.

[7] Mill has a ready rejoinder to this last point: If the conduct in question is supposed to be greatly harmful to the actor himself,

"the example, on the whole must be more salutory" than harmful socially, since it is a warning lesson, rather than an alluring model, to others.

Sterba

[1]See John Hospers, "The Libertarian Manifesto" in *Morality in Practice,* edited by James P. Sterba, Fifth Edition, (Belmont: Wadsworth Publishing Co. 1997) p. 21.

[2]It is not being assumed here that the surplus possessions of the rich are either justifiably or unjustifiably possessed by the rich. Moreover, according to Spencerian libertarians, it is an assessment of the liberties involved that determines whether the possession is justifiable.

[3]The poor cannot, however, give up the liberty to which their children are entitled.

[4]Ruth Sample, "Libertarian Rights and Welfare Rights," *Social Theory and Practice* 24 (1998): 393–418.

[5]Tibor Machan, "Does Libertarianism Imply the Welfare State?" *Res Publica* (1997): 131–148; Jan Narveson, "Sterba's Program of Philosophical Reconciliation," *Journal of Social Philosophy* (1999).

[6]Lockean libertarianism, as I interpret it, requires a ranking of liberties in conflict cases, but it is nonconsequentialist because it does not require that we maximize liberty. Nor does the view recognize the possibility of conflicting rights once the relevant rights are determined by a weighing of the relevant liberties.

[7]To say that a view is liberty-based is to say that it is grounded on a right to liberty. To say that a view is rights-based is to say that the view is grounded on a set of rights other than a right to liberty.

[8]As further evidence that Locke did not intend to exclude those who are incapable of working from his proviso, consider this passage from the *First Treatise:* "But we know God hath not left man so to the mercy of another that he may starve him if he please: God the Lord and Father of all, has given no one of his children such a property in his peculiar portion of the things of this world, but that he has given his needy brother a right to the surplusage of his goods; so that it cannot justly be denied him, when his pressing wants call for it." *Two Treatises of Government,* ed. Peter Laslett (New York: New American Library, 1960), Book I, chapter 3, section 42. [See Reading 3]

[9]Judith Thomson, "A Defense of Abortion," *Philosophy and Public Affairs* (1971).

[10]By supposedly parallelling this case to that of abortion, Thomson makes it difficult for us to think of the unconscious violinist as a full-fledged person.

[11]Tibor Machan, *Individuals and Their Rights* (La Salle, Illinois: Open Court, 1989), pp. 100–111, 107.

[12]Alan Durning, "Life on the Brink," *World Watch,* 3 (1990): 24, 29.

[13]Tibor Machan, "The Nonexistence of Welfare Rights," in *Liberty for the 21st Century,* ed. Tibor Machan and Douglas Rasmussen for the Social, Political and Legal Philosophy Series edited by James P. Sterba (Lanham, Maryland: Rowman and Littlefield, 1995), pp. 218–220.

[14]Richard Rose and Rei Shiratori, eds., *The Welfare State East and West* (Oxford University Press, 1986). In fact, the living standards of poor children in Switzerland, Sweden, Finland, Denmark, Belgium, Norway, Luxembourg, Germany, the Netherlands, Austria, Canada, France, Italy, the United Kingdom, and Australia are all better than they are in the United States. See James Carville, *We're Right They're Wrong* (New York: Random House, 1996), pp. 31–32.

[15]Michael Wolff, *Where We Stand* (New York: Bantam Books, 1992) pp. 23 and 115; George Kurian, *The New Book of World Rankings,* 3rd ed. (New York: Facts on File, 1990), p. 73; *New York Times,* April 17, 1995.

[16]Machan, "Does Libertarianism imply the Welfare State?"

[17]Wolff, *Where We Stand,* p. 110. For an interesting discussion of infant mortality as a useful international criterion of welfare, see Richard Rose, "Making Progress and Catching Up: Comparative Analysis for Social Policy Making," in *UNESCO 1995* (Oxford: Blackwell Publishers, 1995), pp. 118–119.

[18]It is also not clear how relevant such statistics are to judging overall welfare. Afganistan, for example, currently ranks higher than the U.S. and, in fact, third in the world with respect to the number of rooms per dwelling. See George Kurian, *The Illustrated Book of World Rankings* (Amonk, N.Y.: M.E. Sharpe, 1997), pp. 254–255.

[19]Nathan Glazer, "Welfare" and "Welfare in America," in Rose and Shiratori, *The Welfare State East and West,* p. 44.

[20]Narveson, "Sterba's Program of Philosophical Reconciliation."

[21]Joel Handler, *Poverty of Welfare Reform* (New Haven, Conn.: Yale University Press, 1995); Herbert Gans, *The War Against the Poor* (New York: Basic Books, 1995).

CHAPTER IV

Theories of Justice

. . . Impartiality implies a kind of equality—not that all cases should be treated alike but that the onus rests on who-ever would treat them differently to distinguish them in relevant ways. . . . That is what is really meant by the right to equal consideration—to be treated alike unless relevant differences have been proved.

—Stanley Benn
"Justice," in *The Encyclopedia of Philosophy*, ed. Paul Edwards, Macmillan, 1967, vol. 3, p. 299

It is only from the selfishness and confined generosity of men, along with the scanty provision nature has made for his wants, that justice derives its origin.

—David Hume
A Treatise of Human Nature

Problems of justice typically arise, as David Hume (see Reading 24) pointed out over two centuries ago, when in situations of scarcity we seek to adjudicate between competing claims for limited goods. This refers to distributive justice. (Retributive or compensatory justice have different structures.) Consider this example: Suppose one hundred candidates apply for a highly desirable position (e.g., university professorship, position of chief surgeon in a medical center, airline pilot, or CEO). What are the correct moral and legal criteria by which to decide who should get the job? Should the selection be based on merit, need, utility, previous effort, likely contribution to be made, or individual need? Or should the decision be left to market forces, giving the hiring group unlimited discretion in making their choice? Should race, ethnicity, and gender be taken into consideration? If in the past blacks and women or the disabled have been systematically discriminated against, should affirmative action programs be utilized, which would engage in reverse discrimination, showing favor to less qualified women and blacks over more qualified white males (who themselves, though innocent of wrong-doing, may have profited from past favoritism)? (See Chapter VI for readings on this issue).

Or consider the use of kidney dialysis machines in a county hospital that can afford only five machines but has a waiting list of twenty or thirty people. How should we decide which five should be treated? By lottery? By a process of first come–first served? By greatest need? By merit? By desert? By utility (for example, one of the candidates is the mayor of one of the towns and has served the community well for many years)? Or should a complex set of factors (including age, contribution, responsibilities, merit, and need) be used?

The most significant and contested issue in the debate over distributive justice is that of economic justice. How should wealth be divided up in society? Should we simply allow the free enterprise system to determine how much money and wealth people end up with, or should we redistribute wealth through some sort of income tax policy? Should there be a vigorous welfare program, ensuring that no one falls below a certain economic threshold?

Theories of justice may be divided into *formal* and *material* types. A formal theory of justice provides the formula or definition of justice without directly filling in the content or criteria of application. Material theories of justice specify the relevant content to be inserted into the formulas. They tell us what the relevant criterion is. The classical principle of formal justice, based on Book V of Aristotle's *Nicomachean Ethics,* is that "equals should be treated equally and unequals unequally," in proportion to their relevant differences. The formula is one of proportionality:

$$\frac{\text{A has X of P}}{\text{B has Y of P}} = \frac{\text{A should have X of Q}}{\text{B should have Y of Q}}$$

That is, if person A has X units of a relevant property (P), and B has Y units (where Y is more or less than X), then A should have proportionally more or less of the relevant reward or good (Q) than B. If A has worked eight hours at a job and B only four hours, and working time is the relevant criterion of reward, then A should be paid twice as much as B.

The formal principle is used in law in the guise of *stare decisis,* the rule of precedent—like cases should be decided in like manner. The principle applies not only to the case of distributive justice but also to the case of retributive justice (punishment—"an eye for an eye, a tooth for a tooth, a life for a life") and commutative justice (obligation is based on a promise or contract that requires fulfillment). In this chapter we will concentrate on the central type of justice, distributive justice.

The formal principle of justice seems reducible to the principle of universalizability—treat like cases similarly unless there is a relevant difference—which itself is simply the principle of consistency. Be consistent in your decisions. If you can't find a relevant difference between agents, treat them similarly (e.g., what's good for the goose is good for the gander). If it's alright for boys to engage in premarital sex, then it's alright for girls to do so too, since there is no relevant moral difference between the genders when it comes to the morality of sexual relations. If it is all right for Jack to engage in premarital sex, then it is also alright for Jill to engage in premarital sex; but if it is immoral for Jill to engage in premarital sex, it is also immoral for Jack. The formal principle of justice doesn't tell us whether some act is right or wrong; it simply calls for consistency. If we were content to live only with the formal principle, we might treat people very badly and still be considered just. As one of his players once said of Vince Lombardi, the former coach of football's Green Bay Packers, "He treated us all equally—like dogs."

Some philosophers, such as Stanley Benn (quoted at the beginning of this chapter) believe that the formal principle of equal treatment for equals implies a kind

of *presumption* of equal treatment of people. But there are problems with this viewpoint. As Joel Feinberg points out, sometimes the presumption is instead for unequal treatment of people. Suppose that a father suddenly decides to share his fortune, and he divides it in two and gives half each to his oldest son and his neighbor's oldest son.[1] We should say that this kind of impartiality is misguided and, in reality, unjust. We need to specify the respect in which people are equal and so deserve the same kind of treatment, and this seems to be a material problem, not a purely formal one. In other words, Benn confuses an *exceptive principle* ("Treat all people alike except when there are relevant differences among them") that is formal with a *presumptive principle* ("Treat all people alike *until it can be shown* that there are relevant differences among them").

The formal principle does not tell us which qualities determine which kinds of distribution of goods or treatment. Thus, material principles are needed to supplement the formal definition. Aristotle's own material principle involved merit: each person is to be given what he or she deserves. So, a coach could justly treat his players like dogs only if they were doglike. Otherwise, he should treat them more humanely.

Material theories of justice may be further divided into patterned and nonpatterned types of justice. A patterned principle chooses some trait that indicates how the proper distribution is to be accomplished. It has the form:

To each according to . . .

To quote from Robert Nozick's *Anarchy, State, and Utopia* (Reading 25) "Let us call a principle of distribution *patterned* if it specifies that a distribution is to vary along with some natural dimension, weighted sum of natural dimensions, or lexicographic ordering of natural dimensions." Nozick rejects patterned types of principles, such as those of John Rawls (Reading 26) and Nicholas Rescher (Reading 29), because patterned attempts to regulate distribution constitute a violation of liberty. He illustrates this point by considering how a great basketball player, Wilt Chamberlain, can justly upset the patterned balance and in so doing violate the liberty of others. Nozick's point is that, in order to maintain a pattern, one must either "continually interfere to stop people from transferring resources as they wish to, or continually interfere to take from some persons resources that others for some reason chose to transfer to them."

Nozick argues for a libertarian view of nonpatterned justice, which he calls the "theory of entitlement." A distribution is just if everyone has that to which he is entitled. To determine what people are entitled to, we must have a historical understanding of what the original position of holdings or possessions was and what constitutes a just transfer of holdings. Borrowing from John Locke's theory of property rights, Nozick argues that we have a right to any possession so long as ownership does not worsen the position of anyone else.

In Reading 26, John Rawls agrees that patterned versions of justice are faulty, but he disagrees with libertarian views like Nozick's. Instead, he presents a version of the social contract that is broadly Kantian, in which a theory of just procedures takes the place of substantive principles. Rawls asks us to imagine being behind a "veil of ignorance" in which we have very little, if any, knowledge of who we are, and he then asks us to choose the general principles that will govern our social policies. Rawls argues that the principles that rational people will choose are those that maximize individual freedom, that arrange social and economic inequalities in ways that are to everyone's advantage, and that guarantee equal opportunity in attaining privileged positions.

In Reading 27, Wallace Matson, by a series of imaginative tales, contrasts natural justice (the authentic type) against paternalistic justice. The former is "bottom-up" and is based on voluntary agreements; the latter is "top-down," based on the will of government. In the former, freedom is the starting point and property the necessary good; in the latter equality is the goal and the government effectively owns all property. The mistake of paternalistic, or top-down, justice is to suppose that the love and egalitarianism of the family can be extended to society at large. Matson illustrates the tension between these two motifs that exists in the philosophy of Rawls, who, with his first principle of liberty, expresses bottom-up justice, but with his second "difference" principle—which distributes all inequalities in favor of the parties that are worst off—expresses top-down, paternalistic justice.

In Reading 28, Alasdair MacIntyre discusses our changing notions of justice. In Reading 29, Nicholas Rescher argues for a pluralist theory of justice wherein various criteria (canons) play a role, all fitting under the classical formula: render to each his due. The difficulty consists in how to decide which canon applies to which situation.

In Chapter VI we will continue studying justice under the concept of Equality.

Justice As Convention

David Hume

See Reading 5 for a biosketch of David Hume. In this selection Hume characterizes justice as an artificial virtue invented by society for utilitarian purposes, namely to mitigate the limited benevolence of human beings and the scanty provisions of nature. If either of these conditions were changed, justice would not be required. If people were completely altruistic, as is often the case in families, or if nature's resources were more abundant, there would be no need of this virtue. Given the human condition as it really is, however, justice is a necessary institution, providing stability and reliable expectations to people. Hume notes that an equal distribution of property has certain attractiveness, but history and common sense show us that it is, at bottom, impracticable, impossible to maintain, except under the most rigorous tyranny.

This reading is taken from *An Enquiry Concerning the Principles of Morals* (1751) and *A Treatise of Human Nature* (1739).

That justice is useful to society, and consequently that *part* of its merit, at least, must arise from that consideration, it would be a superfluous undertaking to prove. That public utility is the *sole* origin of Justice, and that reflections on the beneficial consequences of this virtue are the *sole* foundation of its merit; this proposition, being more curious and important, will better deserve our examination and inquiry.

Let us suppose, that nature has bestowed on the human race such profuse *abundance* of all *external* conveniences, that, without any uncertainty in the event, without any care or industry on our part, every individual finds himself fully provided with whatever his most voracious appetites can want, or luxurious imagination wish or desire. His natural beauty, we shall suppose, surpasses all acquired ornaments. The perpetual clemency of the seasons renders useless all clothes or covering. The raw herbage affords him the most delicious fare; the clear fountain, the richest beverage. No laborious occupation required. No tillage. No navigation. Music, poetry, and contemplation, form his sole business. Conversation, mirth, and friendship, his sole amusement.

It seems evident, that, in such a happy state, every other social virtue would flourish, and receive tenfold increase; but the cautious, jealous virtue of justice, would never once have been dreamed of. For what purpose make a partition of goods, where every one has already more than enough? Why give rise to property, where there cannot possibly be any injury? Why call this object *mine,* when, upon the seizing of it by another, I need but stretch out my hand to possess myself of what is equally valuable? Justice, in that case, being totally USELESS, would be an idle ceremonial, and could never possibly have place in the catalogue of virtues.

We see, even in the present necessitous condition of mankind, that, wherever any benefit is bestowed by nature in an unlimited abundance, we leave it always in common among the whole human race, and make no subdivisions of right and property. Water and air, though the most necessary of all objects, are not challenged as the property of individuals; nor can any man commit injustice by the most lavish use and enjoyment of these blessings. In fertile extensive countries, with few inhabitants, land is regarded on the same footing. And no topic is so much insisted on by those who defend the liberty of the seas, as the unexhausted use of them in navigation. Were the advantages procured by navigation as inexhaustible, these reasoners had never had any adversaries to refute; nor had any claims ever been advanced of a separate, exclusive dominion over the ocean.

It may happen, in some countries, at some periods, that there be established a property in water, none in land; if the latter be in greater abundance than can be used by the inhabitants, and the former be found with difficulty, in very small quantities.

Again: Suppose, that though the necessities of the human race continue the same as at present, yet the mind is so enlarged, and so replete with friendship and generosity, that every man has the utmost tenderness for every man, and feels no more concern for his own interest than for that of his fellows. It seems evident, that the USE of Justice would, in this case, be suspended by such an extensive benevolence, nor would the divisions and barriers of property and obligation have ever been thought of. Why should I bind another, by a deed or promise, to do me any good office, when I know that he is already prompted, by the strongest in-

clination, to seek my happiness, and would, of himself, perform the desired service; except the hurt he thereby receives be greater than the benefit accruing to me. In which case he knows that, from my innate humanity and friendship, I should be the first to oppose myself to his imprudent generosity. Why raise landmarks between my neighbor's field and mine, when my heart has made no division between our interests; but shares all his joys and sorrows with the same force and vivacity as if originally my own? Every man, upon this supposition, being a second self to another, would trust all his interests to the discretion of every man; without jealousy, without partition, without distinction. And the whole human race would form only one family; where all would lie in common, and be used freely, without regard to property; but cautiously too, with an entire regard to the necessities of each individual, as if our own interests were most intimately concerned.

In the present disposition of the human heart, it would perhaps be difficult to find complete instances of such enlarged affections; but still we may observe, that the case of families approaches towards it; and the stronger the mutual benevolence is among the individuals, the nearer it approaches; till all distinction of property be, in a great measure, lost and confounded among them. Between married persons, the cement of friendship is by the laws supposed so strong as to abolish all division of possessions, and has often, in reality, the force ascribed to it. And it is observable, that, during the ardor of new enthusiasms, when every principle is inflamed into extravagance, the community of goods has frequently been attempted; and nothing but experience of its inconveniences, from the returning or disguised selfishness of men, could make the imprudent fanatics adopt anew the ideas of justice and of separate property. So true is it that this virtue derives its existence entirely from its necessary *use* to the intercourse and social state of mankind.

To make this truth more evident, let us reverse the foregoing suppositions; and, carrying every thing to the opposite extreme, consider what would be the effect of these new situations. Suppose a society to fall into such want of all common necessaries, that the utmost frugality and industry cannot preserve the greater number from perishing, and the whole from extreme misery. It will readily, I believe, be admitted, that the strict laws of justice are suspended, in such a pressing emergence, and give place to the stronger motives of necessity and self-preservation. Is it any crime, after a shipwreck, to seize whatever means or instrument of safety one can lay hold of, without regard to former limitations of property? Or if a city besieged were perishing with hunger; can we imagine that men will see any means of preservation before them, and lose their lives, from a scrupulous regard to what, in other situations, would be the rules of equity and justice? The USE and TENDENCY of that virtue is to procure happiness and security, by preserving order in society. But where the society is ready to perish from extreme necessity, no greater evil can be dreaded from violence and injustice, and every man may now provide for himself by all the means which prudence can dictate, or humanity permit. The public, even in less urgent necessities, open granaries without the consent of proprietors; as justly supposing, that the authority of magistracy may, consistent with equity, extend so far. But were any number of men to assemble, without the tie of laws or civil jurisdiction; would an equal partition of bread in a famine, though effected by power and even violence, be regarded as criminal or injurious?

Suppose, likewise, that it should be a virtuous man's fate to fall into the society of ruffians; remote from the protection of laws and government; what conduct must he embrace in that melancholy situation? He sees such a desperate rapaciousness prevail; such a disregard to equity, such contempt of order, such stupid blindness to future consequences, as must immediately have the most tragical conclusion, and must terminate in destruction to the greater number, and in a total dissolution of society to the rest, He meanwhile, can have no other expedient than to arm himself, to whomever the sword he seizes, or the buckler, may belong, to make provision of all means of defence and security. And his particular regard to justice being no longer of USE to his own safety or that of others, he must consult the dictates of self-preservation alone, without concern for those who no longer merit his care and attention.

When any man, even in political society, renders himself by his crimes obnoxious to the public, he is punished by the laws in his goods and person; that is, the ordinary rules of justice are, with regard to him, suspended for a moment; and it becomes equitable to inflict on him, for the *benefit* of society, what otherwise he could not suffer without wrong or injury.

The rage and violence of public war; what is it but a suspension of justice among the warring parties, who perceive that this virtue is now no longer of any *use* or advantage to them? The laws of war, which then succeed to those of equity and justice, are rules calculated for the *advantage* and *utility* of that particular state in which men are now placed. And were a civilized nation engaged with barbarians, who observed no rules even of war; the former must also suspend their observance of them, where they no longer serve to any purpose; and must render every action or encounter as bloody and pernicious as possible to the first aggressors.

Thus, the rules of equity or justice depend entirely on the particular state and condition in which men are placed, and owe their origin and existence to that UTILITY, which results to the public from their strict and regular observance. Reverse, in any considerable circumstance, the condition of men. Produce extreme abundance or extreme necessity. Implant in the human breast perfect moderation and humanity, or perfect rapaciousness and malice. By rendering justice totally *useless,* you thereby totally destroy its essence, and suspend its obligation upon mankind.

The common situation of society is a medium amidst all these extremes. We are naturally partial to ourselves and to our friends; but are capable of learning the advantage resulting from a more equitable conduct. Few enjoyments are given us from the open and liberal hand of nature; but by art, labor, and industry, we can extract them in great abundance. Hence the ideas of property become necessary in all civil society. Hence justice derives its usefulness to the public. And hence alone arises its merit and moral obligation.

These conclusions are so natural and obvious, that they have not escaped even the poets in their descriptions of the felicity attending the golden age or the reign of Saturn. The seasons, in that first period of nature, were so temperate, if we credit these agreeable fictions, that there was no necessity for men to provide themselves with clothes and houses, as a security against the violence of heat and cold. The rivers flowed with wine and milk. The oaks yielded honey. And Nature spontaneously produced her greatest delicacies. Nor were these the chief advantages of that happy age. Tempests were not alone removed from nature; but those more furious tempests were unknown to human breasts, which now cause such uproar, and engender such confusion. Avarice, ambition, cruelty, selfishness, were never heard of. Cordial affection, compassion, sympathy, were the only movements with which the mind was yet acquainted. Even the punctilious distinction of *mine* and *thine* was banished from among that happy race of mortals, and carried with it the very notion of property and obligation, justice and injustice.

This *poetical* fiction of the *golden age* is, in some respects, of a piece with the *philosophical* fiction of the *state of nature;* only that the former is represented as the most charming and most peaceable condition which can possibly be imagined; whereas the latter is painted out as a state of mutual war and violence, attended with the most extreme necessity. On the first origin of mankind, we are told, their ignorance and savage nature were so prevalent, that they could give no mutual trust, but must each depend upon himself, and his own force or cunning for protection and security. No law was heard of. No rule of justice known. No distinction of property regarded. Power was the only measure of right; and a perpetual war of all against all was the result of men's untamed selfishness and barbarity.

Whether such a condition of human nature could ever exist, or, if it did, could continue so long as to merit the appellation of a state, may justly be doubted. Men are necessarily born in a family-society at least; and are trained up by their parents to some rule of conduct and behaviour. But this must be admitted, that, if such a state of mutual war and violence was ever real, the suspension of all laws of justice, from their absolute inutility, is a necessary and infallible consequence.

The more we vary our views of human life, and the newer and more unusual the lights are in which we survey it, the more shall we be convinced, that the origin here assigned for the virtue of justice is real and satisfactory.

Were there a species of creatures intermingled with men, which, though rational, were possessed of such inferior strength, both of body and mind, that they were incapable of all resistance, and could never, upon the highest provocation, make us feel the effects of their resentment; the necessary consequence, I think, is, that we should be bound, by the laws of humanity, to give gentle usage to these creatures, but should not, properly speaking, lie under any restraint of justice, with regard to them, nor could they possess any right or property exclusive of such arbitrary lords. Our intercourse with them could not be called society, which supposes a degree of equality; but absolute command on the one side, and servile obedience on the other. Whatever we covet, they must instantly resign. Our permission is the only tenure by which they hold their possessions. Our compassion and kindness the only check by which they curb our lawless will. And as no inconvenience ever results from the exercise of a power so firmly established in nature, the restraints of justice and property, being totally *useless,* would never have place in so unequal a confederacy.

This is plainly the situation of men with regard to animals; and how far these may be said to possess reason, I leave it to others to determine. The great superiority of civilized Europeans above barbarous Indians, tempted us to imagine ourselves on the same footing with regard to them, and made us throw off all restraints of justice, and even of humanity, in our treatment of them. In many nations, the female sex are reduced to like slavery, and are rendered incapable of all property, in opposition to their lordly masters. But though the males, when united, have in all countries bodily force sufficient to maintain this severe tyranny; yet such are the insinuations, address, and charms of their fair companions, that women are commonly able to break the confederacy, and share with the other sex in all the rights and privileges of society.

Were the human species so framed by nature as that each individual possessed within himself every faculty, requisite both for his own preservation, and for the propagation of his kind: Were all society and intercourse cut off between man and man, by the primary intention of the Supreme Creator: It seems evident, that so solitary a being would be as much incapable of justice as of social discourse and conversation. Where mutual regards and forbearance serve to no manner of purpose, they would never direct the conduct of any reasonable man. The headlong course of the passions would be checked by no reflection on future consequences. And as each man is here supposed to love himself alone, and to depend only on himself and his own activity for safety and happiness, he would, on every occasion, to the utmost of his power, challenge the preference above every other being, to none of which he is bound by any ties, either of nature or of interest.

But suppose the conjunction of the sexes to be established in nature, a family immediately arises; and particular rules being found requisite for its subsistence, these are immediately embraced, though without comprehending the rest of mankind within their prescriptions. Suppose that several families unite together into one society, which is totally disjoined from all others, the rules which preserve peace and order enlarge themselves to the utmost extent of that society; but becoming then entirely useless, lose their force when carried one step farther. But again, suppose that several distinct societies maintain a kind of intercourse for mutual convenience and advantage, the boundaries of justice still grow larger, in proportion to the largeness of men's views, and the force of their mutual connection. History, experience, reason, sufficiently instruct us in this natural progress of human sentiments, and in the gradual enlargement of our regards to justice, in proportion as we become acquainted with the extensive utility of that virtue.

If we examine the *particular* laws by which justice is directed and property determined we shall still be presented with the same conclusion. The good of mankind is the only object of all these laws and regulations. Not only is it requisite for the peace and interest of society that men's possessions should be separated but the rules, which we follow in making the separation are such as can best be contrived to serve further the interests of society.

We shall suppose that a creature possessed of reason but unacquainted with human nature, deliberates with himself that rules of justice or property would best promote public interest, and establish peace and security among mankind. His most obvious thought would be, to assign the largest possessions to the most extensive virtue, and give everyone the power of doing good, proportioned to his inclination. In a perfect theocracy where a being infinitely intelligent governs by particular volitions, this rule would certainly have place and might serve to the wisest purposes. But were mankind to execute such a law, so great is the uncertainty of merit, both from its natural obscurity, and from the self-conceit of each individual, that no determinate rule of conduct would ever result from it; and the total dissolution of society must be the immediate consequence. Fanatics may suppose *that dominion is founded on grace,* and *that saints alone inherit the earth,* but the civil magistrate very justly puts these sublime theorists on the same footing with common robbers, and teaches them by the severest discipline that a rule which, in speculation, may seem the most advantageous to society, may yet be found in practice totally pernicious and destructive.

That there were *religious* fanatics of this kind in England, during the civil wars, we learn from history; though it is probable, that the obvious *tendency* of these principles excited such horror in mankind, as soon obliged the dangerous enthusiasts to renounce, or at least conceal their tenets. Perhaps the *levellers,* who claimed an equal distribution of property, were a kind of *political* fanatics which arose from the religious species and more openly avowed their pretensions; as carrying a more plausible appearance, of being practicable in themselves as well as useful to human society.

It must, indeed, be confessed that nature is so liberal to mankind that, were all her presents equally divided among the species, and improved by art and industry, every individual would enjoy all the necessaries, and even most of the comforts of life, nor would ever be liable to any ills, but such as might accidentally arise from the sickly frame and constitution of his body. It must also be confessed that wherever we depart from this equality, we rob the poor of more satisfaction than we add to the rich, and that the slight gratification of a frivolous vanity in one individual frequently costs more than bread to many families, and even provinces. It

may appear withal, that the rule of equality, as it would be highly *useful,* is not altogether *impracticable,* but has taken place, at least in an imperfect degree, in some republics, particularly that of Sparta, where it was attended, it is said, with the most beneficial consequences. Not to mention that the Agrarian laws, so frequently claimed in Rome, and carried into execution in many Greek cities, proceeded all of them from a general idea of the utility of this principle.

But historians and even common sense may inform us, that, however specious these ideas of *perfect* equality may seem, they are really, at bottom, *impracticable;* and were they not so, would be extremely *pernicious* to human society. Render possessions ever so equal, men's different degrees of art, care, and industry will immediately break that equality. Or if you check these virtues, you reduce society to the most extreme indigence; and instead of preventing want and beggary in a few, render it unavoidable to the whole community. The most rigorous inquisition too is requisite to watch every inequality on its first appearance; and the most severe jurisdiction to punish and redress it. But besides that so much authority must soon degenerate into tyranny and be exerted with great partialities; who can possibly be possessed of it in such a situation as is here supposed? Perfect equality of possessions destroying all subordination weakens extremely the authority of magistracy and must reduce all power nearly to a level, as well as property.

We may conclude, therefore, that in order to establish laws for the regulation of property we must be acquainted with the nature and situation of man; must reject appearances, which may be false, though specious; and must search for those rules, which are, on the whole, most *useful* and *beneficial*. Vulgar sense and slight experience are sufficient for this purpose; where men give not way to too selfish avidity or too extensive enthusiasm. . . .

READING 25

A Libertarian Theory of Justice

Robert Nozick

Robert Nozick is Professor of Philosophy at Harvard University and the author of several works in political philosophy and epistemology. In this selection from

Anarchy, State and Utopia, Nozick distinguishes between two types of material principles of justice: patterned and nonpatterned. A patterned principle selects a trait (or traits: e.g., desert, need, or interest) that directs the proper distribution of benefits and burdens. It takes the form: "To each according to . . . " where the trait is filled in, as in Marx's formula: "From each according to his ability, to each according to his need." Nozick rejects all patterned principles of justice, including Rawls's contractualist version, and argues for a nonpatterned, libertarian theory, which he calls the "theory of entitlement." A distribution is just if everyone has that to which he is entitled. To determine what people are entitled to, we must understand what the original position of holdings or possessions was and whether the subsequent transfers were done in a morally acceptable manner, violating no one's rights. Borrowing from Locke's theory of property (see Reading 3), he argues that we have a right to any possession so long as ownership does not in itself worsen the position of anyone else.

This reading is taken from *Anarchy, State and Utopia* (Basic Books, 1974). Copyright © 1974 by Basic Books, Inc. Reprinted by permission of Basic Books, a division of HarperCollins Publishers, Inc.

The minimal state is the most extensive state that can be justified. Any state more extensive violates people's rights. Yet many persons have put forth reasons purporting to justify a more extensive state. It is impossible within the compass of this book to examine all the reasons that have been put forth. Therefore, I shall focus upon those generally acknowledged to be most weighty and influential, to see precisely wherein they fail. In this chapter we consider the claim that a more extensive state is justified, because [it is] necessary (or the best instrument) to achieve distributive justice; in the next chapter we shall take up diverse other claims.

The term "distributive justice" is not a neutral one. Hearing the term "distribution," most people presume that some thing or mechanism uses some principle or criterion to give out a supply of things. Into this process of distributing shares some error may have crept. So it is an open question, at least, whether *re*distribution should take place; whether we should do again what

has already been done once, though poorly. However, we are not in the position of children who have been given portions of pie by someone who now makes last minute adjustments to rectify careless cutting. There is no *central* distribution, no person or group entitled to control all the resources, jointly deciding how they are to be doled out. What each person gets, he gets from others who give to him in exchange for something, or as a gift. In a free society, diverse persons control different resources, and new holdings arise out of the voluntary exchanges and actions of persons. There is no more a distributing or distribution of shares than there is a distributing of mates in a society in which persons choose whom they shall marry. The total result is the product of many individual decisions which the different individuals involved are entitled to make. Some uses of the term "distribution," it is true, do not imply a previous distributing appropriately judged by some criterion (for example, "probability distribution"); nevertheless, despite the title of this chapter, it would be best to use a terminology that clearly is neutral. We shall speak of people's holdings; a principle of justice in holdings describes (part of) what justice tells us (requires) about holdings. I shall state first what I take to be the correct view about justice in holdings, and then turn to the discussion of alternative views.

THE ENTITLEMENT THEORY

The subject of justice in holdings consists of three major topics. The first is the *original acquisition of holdings,* the appropriation of unheld things. This includes the issues of how unheld things may come to be held, the process, or processes, by which unheld things may come to be held, the things that may come to be held by these processes, the extent of what comes to be held by a particular process, and so on. We shall refer to the complicated truth about this topic, which we shall not formulate here, as the principle of justice in acquisition. The second topic concerns the *transfer of holdings* from one person to another. By what processes may a person transfer holdings to another? How may a person acquire a holding from another who holds it? Under this topic come general descriptions of voluntary exchange, and gift and (on the other hand) fraud, as well as reference to particular conventional details fixed upon in a given society. The complicated truth about this subject (with placeholders for conventional details) we shall call the principle of justice in transfer. (And we shall suppose it also includes principles governing how a person may divest himself of a holding, passing it into an unheld state.)

If the world were wholly just, the following inductive definition would exhaustively cover the subject of justice in holdings.

1. A person who acquires a holding in accordance with the principle of justice in acquisition is entitled to that holding.
2. A person who acquires a holding in accordance with the principle of justice in transfer, from someone else entitled to the holding, is entitled to the holding.
3. No one is entitled to a holding except by (repeated) applications of 1 and 2.

The complete principle of distributive justice would say simply that a distribution is just if everyone is entitled to the holdings they possess under the distribution.

A distribution is just if it arises from another just distribution by legitimate means. The legitimate means of moving from one distribution to another are specified by the principle of justice in transfer. The legitimate first "moves" are specified by the principle of justice in acquisition.[1] Whatever arises from a just situation by just steps is itself just. The means of change specified by the principle of justice in transfer preserve justice. As correct rules of inference are truth-preserving and any conclusion deduced via repeated application of such rules from only true premises is itself true, so the means of transition from one situation to another specified by the principle of justice in transfer are justice-preserving, and any situation actually arising from repeated transitions in accordance with the principle from a just situation is itself just. The parallel between justice-preserving transformations and truth-preserving transformations illuminates where it fails as well as where it holds. That a conclusion could have been deduced by truth-preserving means from premises that are true suffices to show its truth. That from a just situation a situation *could* have arisen via justice-preserving means does *not* suffice to show its justice. The fact that a thief's victims voluntarily *could* have presented him with gifts does not entitle the thief to his ill-gotten gains. Justice in holdings is historical; it depends upon what actually has happened. We shall return to this point later.

Not all actual situations are generated in accordance with the two principles of justice in holdings: the principle of justice in acquisition and the principle of justice in transfer. Some people steal from others, or defraud them, or enslave them, seizing their product and preventing them from living as they choose, or forcibly exclude others from competing in exchanges. None of these are permissible modes of transition from one situation to another. And some persons acquire holdings by means not sanctioned by the principle of justice in acquisition. The existence of past injustice (previous violations of the first two principles of justice in holdings) raises the third major topic under justice in holdings: the rectification of injustice in holdings. If past injustice has shaped present holdings in various ways, some identifiable and some not, what now, if anything, ought to be done to rectify these injustices? What obligations do the performers of injustice have toward those whose position is worse than it would have been had the injustice not been done? Or, than it would have been had compensation been paid promptly? How, if at all, do things change if the beneficiaries and those made worse off are not the direct parties in the act of injustice, but, for example, their descendants? Is an injustice done to someone whose holding was itself based upon an unrectified injustice? How far back must one go in wiping clean the historical slate of injustices? What may victims of injustice permissibly do in order to rectify the injustices being done to them, including the many injustices done by persons acting through their government? I do not know of a thorough or theoretically sophisticated treatment of such issues. Idealizing greatly, let us suppose theoretical investigation will produce a principle of rectification. This principle uses historical information about previous situations and injustices done in them (as defined by the first two principles of justice and rights against interference), and information about the actual course of events that flowed from these injustices, until the present, and it yields a description (or descriptions) of holdings in the society. The principle of rectification presumably will make use of its best estimate of subjunctive information about what would have occurred (or a probability distribution over what might have occurred, using the expected value) if the injustice had not taken place. If the actual description of holdings turns out not to be one of the descriptions yielded by the principle, then one of the descriptions yielded must be realized.[2]

The general outlines of the theory of justice in holdings are that the holdings of a person are just if he is entitled to them by the principles of justice in acquisition and transfer, or by the principle of rectification of injustice (as specified by the first two principles). If each person's holdings are just, then the total set (distribution) of holdings is just. To turn these general outlines into a specific theory we would have to specify the details of each of the three principles of justice in holdings: the principle of acquisition of holdings, the principle of transfer of holdings, and the principle of rectification of violations of the first two principles. I shall not attempt that task here. (Locke's principle of justice in acquisition is discussed below.)

HISTORICAL PRINCIPLES AND END-RESULT PRINCIPLES

The general outlines of the entitlement theory illuminate the nature and defects of other conceptions of distributive justice. The entitlement theory of justice in distribution is *historical;* whether a distribution is just depends upon how it came about. In contrast, *current time-slice principles* of justice hold that the justice of a distribution is determined by how things are distributed (who has what) as judged by some *structural* principle(s) of just distribution. A utilitarian who judges between any two distributions by seeing which has the greater sum of utility and, if the sums tie, applies some fixed equality criterion to choose the more equal distribution would hold a current time-sliced principle of justice. As would someone who had a fixed schedule of trade-offs between the sum of happiness and equality. According to a current time-slice principle, all that needs to be looked at, in judging the justice of a distribution, is who ends up with what; in comparing any two distributions one need look only at the matrix presenting the distributions. No further information need be fed into a principle of justice. It is a consequence of such principles of justice that any two structurally identical distributions are equally just. (Two distributions are structurally identical if they present the same profile, but perhaps have different persons occupying the particular slots. My having ten and your having five, and my having five and your having ten are structurally identical distributions.) Welfare economics is the theory of current time-slice principles of justice. The subject is conceived as operating on matrices representing only current information about distribution. This, as well as some of the usual conditions (for example, the choice of distribution is invariant under relabeling of columns), guarantees that welfare economics will be a current time-slice theory, with all of its inadequacies.

Most persons do not accept current time-slice principles as constituting the whole story about distributive shares. They think it relevant in assessing the justice of a situation to consider not only the distribution it embodies, but also how that distribution came about. If some persons are in prison for murder or war crimes, we do not say that to assess the justice of the distribution in the society we must look only at what this person has, and that person has, and that person has, . . . at the current time. We think it relevant to ask whether someone did something so that he *deserved* to be punished, deserved to have a lower share. Most will agree to the relevance of further information with regard to punishments and penalties. Consider also desired things. One traditional socialist view is that workers are entitled to the product and full fruits of their labor; they have earned it; a distribution is unjust if it does not give the workers what they are entitled to. Such entitlements are based upon some past history. No socialist holding this view would find it comforting to be told that because the actual distribution A happens to coincide structurally with the one he desires D, A therefore is no less just than D; it differs only in that the "parasitic" owners of capital received under A what the workers are entitled to under D, and the workers receive under A what the owners are entitled to under D, namely very little. This socialist rightly, in my view, holds onto the notions of earning, producing, entitlement, desert, and so forth, and he rejects current time-slice principles that look only to the structure of the resulting set of holdings. (The set of holdings resulting from what? Isn't it implausible that how holdings are produced and come to exist has no effect at all on who should hold what?) His mistake lies in his view of what entitlements arise out of what sorts of productive processes.

We construe the position we discuss too narrowly by speaking of *current* time-slice principles. Nothing is changed if structural principles operate upon a time sequence of current time-slice profiles and, for example, give someone more now to counterbalance the less he has had earlier. A utilitarian or an egalitarian or any mixture of the two over time will inherit the difficulties of his more myopic comrades. He is not helped by the fact that *some* of the information others consider relevant in assessing a distribution is reflected, unrecoverably, in past matrices. Henceforth, we shall refer to such unhistorical principles of distributive justice, including the current time-slice principles, as *end-result principles* or *end-state principles*.

In contrast to end-result principles of justice, *historical principles* of justice hold that past circumstances or actions of people can create differential entitlements or differential deserts to things. An injustice can be worked by moving from one distribution to another structurally identical one, for the second, in profile the same, may violate people's entitlements or deserts; it may not fit the actual history.

PATTERNING

The entitlement principles of justice in holdings that we have sketched are historical principles of justice. To better understand their precise character, we shall distinguish them from another subclass of the historical principles. Consider, as an example, the principle of distribution according to moral merit. This principle requires that total distributive shares vary directly with moral merit; no person should have a greater share than anyone whose moral merit is greater. (If moral merit could be not merely ordered but measured on an interval or ratio scale, stronger principles could be formulated.) Or consider the principle that results by substituting "usefulness to society" for "moral merit" in the previous principle. Or instead of "distribute according to moral merit," or "distribute according to usefulness to society," we might consider "distribute according to the weighted sum of moral merit, usefulness to society, and need," with the weights of the different dimensions equal. Let us call a principle of distribution patterned if it specifies that a distribution is to vary along with some natural dimension, weighted sum of natural dimensions, or lexicographic ordering of natural dimensions. And let us say a distribution is patterned if it accords with some patterned principle. (I speak of natural dimensions, admittedly without a general criterion for them, because for any set of holdings some artificial dimensions can be gimmicked up to vary along with the distribution of the set.) The principle of distribution in accordance with moral merit is a patterned historical principle, which specifies a patterned distribution. "Distribute according to I.Q." is a patterned principle that looks to information not contained in distributional matrices. It is not historical, however, in that it does not look to any past actions creating differential entitlements to evaluate a distribution; it requires only distributional matrices whose columns are labeled by I.Q. scores. The distribution in a society, however, may be composed of such simple patterned distributions, without itself being simply patterned. Different sectors may operate different patterns, or some combination of patterns may operate in different proportions across a society. A distribution composed in this manner, from a small number of patterned distributions, we also shall term "patterned." And we extend the use of "pattern" to include the overall designs put forth by combinations of end-state principles.

Almost every suggested principle of distributive justice is patterned: to each according to his moral merit, or needs, or marginal product, or how hard he tries, or the weighted sum of the foregoing, and so on. The principle of entitlement we have sketched is *not* patterned.[3] There is no one natural dimension or weighted sum or combination of a small number of natural dimensions that yields the distributions generated in accordance with the principle of entitlement. The set of holdings that results when some persons receive their marginal products, others win at gambling, others receive a share of their mate's income, others receive gifts from foundations, others receive interest on loans, others receive gifts from admirers, others receive returns on investment, others make for themselves much of what they have, others find things, and so on, will not be patterned. Heavy strands of patterns will run through it; significant portions of the variance in holdings will be accounted for by pattern-variables. If most people most of the time choose to transfer some of their entitlement to others only in exchange for something from them, then a large part of what many people hold will vary with what they held that others wanted. More details are provided by the theory of marginal productivity. But gifts to relatives, charitable donations, bequests to children, and the like, are not best conceived, in the first instance, in this manner. Ignoring the strands of pattern, let us suppose for the moment that a distribution actually arrived at by the operation of the principle of entitlement is random with respect to any pattern. Though the resulting set of holdings will be unpatterned, it will not be incomprehensible, for it can be seen as arising from the operation of a small number of principles. These principles specify how an initial distribution may arise (the principle of acquisition of holdings) and how distributions may be transformed into others (the principle of transfer of holdings). The process whereby the set of holdings is generated will be intelligible, though the set of holdings itself that results from this process will be unpatterned.

The writings of F. A. Hayek focus less than is usually done upon what patterning distributive justice requires. Hayek argues that we cannot know enough about each person's situation to distribute to each according to his moral merit (but would justice demand we do so if we did have this knowledge?); and he goes on to say, "Our objection is against all attempts to impress upon society a deliberately chosen pattern of distribution, whether it be an order of equality or of inequality."[4] However, Hayek concludes that in a free society there will be distribution in accordance with value rather than moral merit; that is, in accordance with the perceived value of a person's actions and services to others. Despite his rejection of a patterned conception of distributive justice, Hayek himself suggests a pattern he thinks justifiable: distribution in accordance with the perceived benefits given to others, leaving room for the complaint that a free society does not realize exactly this pattern. Stating this patterned strand of a free capitalist society more precisely, we get "To each according to how much he benefits others who have the resources for benefiting those who benefit them." This will seem arbitrary unless some acceptable initial set of holdings is specified, or unless it is held that the operation of the system over time washes out any significant effects from the initial set of holdings. As an example of the latter, if almost anyone would have bought a car from Henry Ford, the supposition that it was an arbitrary matter who held the money then (and so bought) would not place Henry Ford's earnings under a cloud. In any event, *his* coming to hold it is not arbitrary. Distribution according to benefits to others *is* a major patterned strand in a free capitalist society, as Hayek correctly points out, but it is only a strand and does not constitute the whole pattern of a system of entitlements (namely, inheritance, gifts for arbitrary reasons, charity, and so on) or a standard that one should insist society fit. Will people tolerate for long a system yielding distributions that they believe are unpatterned?[5] No doubt people will not long accept a distribution they believe is *unjust*. People want their society to be and to look just. But must the look of justice reside in a resulting pattern rather than in the underlying generating principles? We are in no position to conclude that the inhabitants of a society embodying an entitlement conception of justice in holdings will find it unacceptable. Still, it must be granted that were people's reasons for transferring some of their holdings to others always irrational or arbitrary, we would find this disturbing. (Suppose people always determined what holdings they would transfer, and to whom, by using a random device.) We feel more comfortable upholding the justice of an entitlement system if most of the transfers under it are done for reasons. This does not mean necessarily that all deserve what holdings they receive. It means only that there is a pur-

pose or point to someone's transferring a holding to one person rather than to another; that usually we can see what the transferrer thinks he's gaining, what cause he thinks he's serving, what goals he thinks he's helping to achieve, and so forth. Since in a capitalist society people often transfer holdings to others in accordance with how much they perceive these others benefiting them, the fabric constituted by the individual transactions and transfers is largely reasonable and intelligible.[6] (Gifts to loved ones, bequests to children, charity to the needy also are nonarbitrary components of the fabric.) In stressing the large strand of distribution in accordance with benefit to others, Hayek shows the point of many transfers, and so shows that the system of transfer of entitlements is not just spinning its gears aimlessly. The system of entitlements is defensible when constituted by the individual aims of individual transactions. No overarching aim is needed, no distributional pattern is required.

To think that the task of a theory of distributive justice is to fill in the blank in "to each according to his _____" is to be predisposed to search for a pattern; and the separate treatment of "from each according to his _____" treats production and distribution as two separate and independent issues. On an entitlement view these are *not* two separate questions. Whoever makes something, having bought or contracted for all other held resources used in the process (transferring some of his holdings for these cooperating factors), is entitled to it. The situation is *not* one of something's getting made, and there being an open question of who is to get it. Things come into the world already attached to people having entitlements over them. From the point of view of the historical entitlement conception of justice in holdings, those who start afresh to complete "to each according to his _____" treat objects as if they appeared from nowhere, out of nothing. A complete theory of justice might cover this limit case as well; perhaps here is a use for the usual conceptions of distributive justice.[7]

So entrenched are maxims of the usual form that perhaps we should present the entitlement conception as a competitor. Ignoring acquisition and rectification, we might say:

> From each according to what he chooses to do, to each according to what he makes for himself (perhaps with the contracted aid of others) and what others choose to do for him and choose to give him of what they've been given previously (under this maxim) and haven't yet expended or transferred.

This, the discerning reader will have noticed, has its defects as a slogan. So as a summary and great simplification (and not as a maxim with any independent meaning) we have:

From each as they choose, to each as they are chosen.

HOW LIBERTY UPSETS PATTERNS

It is not clear how those holding alternative conceptions of distributive justice can reject the entitlement conception of justice in holdings. For suppose a distribution favored by one of these nonentitlement conceptions is realized. Let us suppose it is your favorite one and let us call this distribution $D1$; perhaps everyone has an equal share, perhaps shares vary in accordance with some dimension you treasure. Now suppose that Wilt Chamberlain is greatly in demand by basketball teams, being a great gate attraction. (Also suppose contracts run only for a year, with players being free agents.) He signs the following sort of contract with a team: In each home game, twenty-five cents from the price of each ticket of admission goes to him. (We ignore the question of whether he is "gouging" the owners, letting them look out for themselves.) The season starts, and people cheerfully attend his team's games; they buy their tickets, each time dropping a separate twenty-five cents of their admission price into a special box with Chamberlain's name on it. They are excited about seeing him play; it is worth the total admission price to them. Let us suppose that in one season one million persons attend his home games, and Wilt Chamberlain winds up with $250,000, a much larger sum than the average income and larger even than anyone else has. Is he entitled to this income? Is this new distribution $D2$, unjust? If so, why? There is *no* question about whether each of the people was entitled to the control over the resources they held in $D1$, because that was the distribution (your favorite) that (for the purposes of argument) we assumed was acceptable. Each of these persons *chose* to give twenty-five cents of their money to Chamberlain. They could have spent it on going to the movies, or on candy bars, or on copies of *Dissent* magazine, or of *Monthly Review*. But they all, at least one million of them, converged on giving it to Wilt Chamberlain in exchange for watching him play basketball. If $D1$ was a just distribution, and people voluntarily moved from it to $D2$ transferring

parts of their shares they were given under $D1$ (what was it for if not to do something with?), isn't $D2$ also just? If people were entitled to dispose of the resources to which they were entitled (under $D1$), didn't this include their being entitled to give it to, or exchange it with, Wilt Chamberlain? Can anyone else complain on grounds of justice? Each other person already has his legitimate share under $D1$. Under $D1$, there is nothing that anyone has that anyone else has a claim of justice against. After someone transfers something to Wilt Chamberlain, third parties *still* have their legitimate shares; *their* shares are not changed. By what process could such a transfer among two persons give rise to a legitimate claim of distributive justice on a portion of what was transferred, by a third party who had no claim of justice on any holding of the others *before* the transfer? To cut off objections irrelevant here, we might imagine the exchanges occurring in a socialist society, after hours: After playing whatever basketball he does in his daily work, or doing whatever other daily work he does, Wilt Chamberlain decides to put in *overtime* to earn additional money. (First his work quota is set; he works time over that.) Or imagine it is a skilled juggler people like to see, who puts on shows after hours.

Why might someone work overtime in a society in which it is assumed their needs are satisfied? Perhaps because they care about things other than needs. I like to write in books that I read, and to have easy access to books for browsing at odd hours. It would be very pleasant and convenient to have the resources of Widener Library in my backyard. No society, I assume, will provide such resources close to each person who would like them as part of his regular allotment (under $D1$). Thus, persons either must do without some extra things that they want, or be allowed to do something extra to get some of these things. On what basis could the inequalities that would eventuate be forbidden? Notice also that small factories would spring up in a socialist society, unless forbidden. I melt down some of my personal possessions (under $D1$) and build a machine out of the material. I offer you, and others, a philosophy lecture once a week in exchange for your cranking the handle on my machine, whose products I exchange for yet other things, and so on. (The raw materials used by the machine are given to me by others who possess them under $D1$, in exchange for hearing lectures.) Each person might participate to gain things over and above their allotment under $D1$. Some persons even might want to leave their job in socialist industry and work full time in this private sector. [In any case] I wish merely to note how private property even in means of production would occur in a socialist society that did not forbid people to use as they wished some of the resources they are given under the socialist distribution *D1*. The socialist society would have to forbid capitalist acts between consenting adults.

The general point illustrated by the Wilt Chamberlain example and the example of the entrepreneur in a socialist society is that no end-state principle or distributional patterned principle of justice can be continuously realized without continuous interference with people's lives. Any favored pattern would be transformed into one unfavored by the principle, by people choosing to act various ways; for example, by people exchanging goods and services with other people, or giving things to other people, things the transferrers are entitled to under the favored distributional pattern. To maintain a pattern one must either continually interfere to stop people from transferring resources as they wish to, or continually (or periodically) interfere to take from some persons resources that others for some reason chose to transfer to them. (But if some time limit is to be set on how long people may keep resources others voluntarily transfer to them, why let them keep these resources for *any* period of time? Why not have immediate confiscation?) It might be objected that all persons voluntarily will choose to refrain from actions which would upset the pattern. This presupposes unrealistically (1) that all will most want to maintain the pattern (are those who don't, to be "reeducated" or forced to undergo "self-criticism"?), (2) that each can gather enough information about his own actions and the ongoing activities of others to discover which of his actions will upset the pattern, and (3) that diverse and far-flung persons can coordinate their actions to dovetail into the pattern. Compare the manner in which the market is neutral among persons' desires, as it reflects and transmits widely scattered information via prices, and coordinates persons' activities.

It puts things perhaps a bit too strongly to say that every patterned (or end-state) principle is liable to be thwarted by the voluntary actions of the individual parties transferring some of their shares they receive under the principle. For perhaps some *very* weak patterns are not so thwarted. Any distributional pattern with any egalitarian component is overturnable by the voluntary actions of individual persons over time; as is every patterned condition with sufficient content so as actually to have been proposed as presenting the central core of distributive justice. Still, given the possibility that some weak conditions or patterns may not be unstable in this way, it would be better to formulate an explicit description of the kind of interesting and contentful patterns under discussion, and to prove a theorem about their instability. Since the weaker the patterning, the more likely it is that the entitlement system itself satisfies it, a plausible conjecture is that any patterning either is unstable or is satisfied by the entitlement system. . . .

REDISTRIBUTION AND PROPERTY RIGHTS

Apparently, patterned principles allow people to choose to expend upon themselves, but not upon others, those resources they are entitled to (or rather, receive) under some favored distributional pattern *D1*. For if each of several persons chooses to expend some of his *D1* resources upon one other person, then that other person will receive more than his *D1* share, disturbing the favored distributional pattern. Maintaining a distributional pattern is individualism with a vengeance! Patterned distributional principles do not give people what entitlement principles do, only better distributed. For they do not give the right to choose what to do with what one has; they do not give the right to choose to pursue an end involving (intrinsically, or as a means) the enhancement of another's position. To such views, families are disturbing; for within a family occur transfers that upset the favored distributional pattern. Either families themselves become units to which distribution takes place, the column occupiers (on what rationale?), or loving behavior is forbidden. We should note in passing the ambivalent position of radicals toward the family. Its loving relationships are seen as a model to be emulated and extended across the whole society, at the same time that it is denounced as a suffocating institution to be broken and condemned as a focus of parochial concerns that interfere with achieving radical goals. Need we say that it is not appropriate to enforce across the wider society the relationships which are voluntarily undertaken? Incidentally, love is an interesting instance of another relationship that is historical, in that (like justice) it depends upon what actually occurred. An adult may come to love another because of the other's characteristics; but it is the other person, and not the characteristics, that is loved. The love is not transferable to someone else with the same characteristics, even to one who "scores" higher for these characteristics. And the love endures through changes of the characteristics that gave rise to it. One loves the particular person one actually encountered. Why love is historical, attaching to persons in this way and not to characteristics, is an interesting and puzzling question.

Proponents of patterned principles of distributive justice focus upon criteria for determining who is to receive holdings; they consider the reasons for which someone should have something, and also the total picture of holdings. Whether or not it is better to give than to receive, proponents of patterned principles ignore giving altogether. In considering the distribution of goods, income, and so forth, their theories are theories of recipient justice; they completely ignore any right a person might have to give something to someone. Even in exchanges where each party is simultaneously giver and recipient, patterned principles of justice focus only upon the recipient role and its supposed rights. Thus discussions tend to focus on whether people (should) have a right to inherit, rather than on whether people (should) have a right to bequeath or on whether persons who have a right to hold also have a right to choose that others hold in their place. I lack a good explanation of why the usual theories of distributive justice are so recipient oriented; ignoring givers and transferrers and their rights is of a piece with ignoring producers and their entitlements. But why is it *all* ignored?

Patterned principles of distributive justice necessitate *re*distributive activities. The likelihood is small that any actual freely-arrived-at set of holdings fits a given pattern; and the likelihood is nil that it will continue to fit the pattern as people exchange and give. From the point of view of an entitlement theory, redistribution is a serious matter indeed, involving, as it does, the violation of people's rights. (An exception is those takings that fall under the principle of the rectification of injustices.) From other points of view, also, it is serious.

Taxation of earnings from labor is on a par with forced labor. Some persons find this claim obviously true: taking the earnings of *n* hours labor is like taking *n* hours from the person; it is like forcing the person to work *n* hours for another's purpose. Others find the claim absurd. But even these, *if* they object to forced labor, would oppose forcing unemployed hippies to work for the benefit of the needy. And they would also object to forcing each person to work five extra hours each week for the benefit of the needy. But a system that takes five hours' wages in taxes does not seem to them like one that forces someone to work five hours, since it offers the person forced a wider range of choice in activities than does taxation in kind with the particular labor specified. (But we can imagine a gradation of systems of forced labor, from one that specifies a particular activity, to one that gives a choice among two activities, to . . . ; and so on up.) Furthermore, people envisage a system with something like a proportional tax on everything above the amount necessary for basic needs. Some think this does not force someone to work extra hours, since there is no fixed number of extra hours he is forced to work, and since he can avoid the tax entirely by earning only enough to cover his basic needs. This is a very uncharacteristic view of forcing for those who *also* think people are forced to do something *whenever* the alternatives they face are considerably worse. However, *neither* view is correct. The fact that others intentionally intervene, in violation of a side constraint against aggression, to threaten force to limit the alternatives, in this case to paying taxes or (presumably the worse alternative) bare subsistence, makes the taxation system one of forced labor and distinguishes it from other cases of limited choices which are not forcings.

The man who chooses to work longer to gain an income more than sufficient for his basic needs prefers some extra goods or services to the leisure and activities he could perform during the possible nonworking hours; whereas the man who chooses not to work the extra time prefers the leisure activities to the extra goods or services he could acquire by working more. Given this, if it would be illegitimate for a tax system to seize some of a man's leisure (forced labor) for the purpose of serving the needy, how can it be legitimate for a tax system to seize some of a man's goods for that purpose? Why should we treat the man whose happiness requires certain material goods or services differently from the man whose preferences and desires make such goods unnecessary for his happiness? Why should the man who prefers seeing a movie (and who has to earn money for a ticket) be open to the required call to aid the needy, while the person who prefers looking at a sunset (and hence need earn no extra money) is not? Indeed, isn't it surprising that redistributionists choose to ignore the man whose pleasures are so easily attainable without extra labor, while adding yet another burden to the poor unfortunate who must work for his pleasures? If anything, one would have expected the reverse. Why is the person with the nonmaterial or nonconsumption desire allowed to proceed unimpeded to his most favored feasible alternative, whereas the man whose pleasures or desires involve material things and who must work for extra money (thereby serving whomever considers his activities valuable enough to pay him) is constrained in what he can realize? Perhaps there is no difference in principle. And perhaps some think the answer concerns merely administrative convenience. (These questions and issues will not disturb those who think that forced labor to serve the needy or to realize some favored end-state pattern is acceptable.) In a fuller discussion we would have (and want) to extend our argument to include interest, entrepreneurial profits, and so on. Those who doubt that this extension can be carried through, and who draw the line here at taxation of income from labor, will have to state rather complicated patterned *historical* principles of distributive justice, since end-state principles would not distinguish *sources* of income in any way. It is enough for now to get away from end-state principles and to make clear how various patterned principles are dependent upon particular views about the sources or the illegitimacy or the lesser legitimacy of profits, interest, and so on; which particular views may well be mistaken.

What sort of right over others does a legally institutionalized end-state pattern give one? The central core of the notion of a property right in *X*, relative to which other parts of the notion are to be explained, is the right to choose which of the constrained set of options concerning *X* shall be realized or attempted. The constraints are set by other principles or laws operating in the society; in our theory, by the Lockean rights people possess (under the minimal state). My property rights in my knife allow me to leave it where I will, but not in your chest. I may choose which of the acceptable options involving the knife is to be realized. This notion of property helps us to understand why earlier theorists spoke of people as having property in themselves and their labor. They viewed each person as having a right to decide what would become of himself and what he would do, and as having a right to reap the benefits of what he did.

This right of selecting the alternative to be realized from the constrained set of alternatives may be held by an *individual* or by a *group* with some procedure for reaching a joint decision; or the right may be passed back and forth, so that one year I decide what's to become of *X*, and the next year you do (with the alternative of destruction, perhaps, being excluded). Or, during the same time period, some types of decisions about *X* may be made by me, and others by you. And so on. We lack an adequate, fruitful, analytical apparatus for classifying the *types* of constraints on the set of the options among which choices are to be made, and the *types* of ways decision powers can be held, divided, and amalgamated. A *theory* of property would, among

other things, contain such a classification of constraints and decision modes, and from a small number of principles would follow a host of interesting statements about the *consequences* and effects of certain combinations of constraints and modes of decision.

When end-result principles of distributive justice are built into the legal structure of a society, they (as do most patterned principles) give each citizen an enforceable claim to some portion of the total social product; that is, to some portion of the sum total of the individually and jointly made products. This total product is produced by individuals laboring, using means of production others have saved to bring into existence, by people organizing production or creating means to produce new things or things in a new way. It is on this batch of individual activities that patterned distributional principles give each individual an enforceable claim. Each person has a claim to the activities and the products of other persons, independently of whether the other persons enter into particular relationships that give rise to these claims, and independently of whether they voluntarily take these claims upon themselves, in charity or in exchange for something.

Whether it is done through taxation on wages or on wages over a certain amount, or through seizure of profits, or through there being a big *social pot* so that it's not clear what's coming from where and what's going where, patterned principles of distributive justice involve appropriating the actions of other persons. Seizing the results of someone's labor is equivalent to seizing hours from him and directing him to carry on various activities. If people force you to do certain work, or, unrewarded work, for a certain period of time, they decide what you are to do and what purposes your work is to serve apart from your decisions. This process whereby they take this decision from you makes them a *part owner* of you; it gives them a property right in you. Just as having such partial control and power of decision, by right, over an animal or inanimate object would be to have a property right in it.

End-state and most patterned principles of distributive justice institute (partial) ownership by others of people and their actions and labor. These principles involve a shift from the classical liberals' notion of self-ownership to a notion of (partial) property rights in *other* people.

Considerations such as these confront end-state and other patterned conceptions of justice with the question of whether the actions necessary to achieve the selected pattern don't themselves violate moral side constraints. Any view holding that there are moral side constraints on actions, that not all moral considerations can be built into end-states that are to be achieved . . . must face the possibility that some of its goals are not achievable by any morally permissible available means. An entitlement theorist will face such conflicts in a society that deviates from the principles of justice for the generation of holdings, if and only if the only actions available to realize the principles themselves violate some moral constraints. Since deviation from the first two principles of justice (in acquisition and transfer) will involve other persons' direct and aggressive intervention to violate rights, and since moral constraints will not exclude defensive or retributive action in such cases, the entitlement theorist's problem rarely will be pressing. And whatever difficulties he has in applying the principle of rectification to persons who did not themselves violate the first two principles are difficulties in balancing the conflicting considerations so as correctly to formulate the complex principle of rectification itself; he will not violate moral side constraints by applying the principle. Proponents of patterned conceptions of justice, however, often will face head-on clashes (and poignant ones if they cherish each party to the clash) between moral side constraints on how individuals may be treated and their patterned conception of justice that presents an end-state or other pattern that *must* be realized.

May a person emigrate from a nation that has institutionalized some end-state or patterned distributional principle? For some principles (for example, Hayek's) emigration presents no theoretical problem. But for others it is a tricky matter. Consider a nation having a compulsory scheme of minimal social provision to aid the neediest (or one organized so as to maximize the position of the worst-off group); no one may opt out of participating in it. (None may say, "Don't compel me to contribute to others and don't provide for me via this compulsory mechanism if I am in need.") Everyone above a certain level is forced to contribute to aid the needy. But if emigration from the country were allowed, anyone could choose to move to another country that did not have compulsory social provision but otherwise was (as much as possible) identical. In such a case, the person's *only* motive for leaving would be to avoid participating in the compulsory scheme of social provision. And if he does leave, the needy in his initial country will receive no (compelled) help from him. What rationale yields the result that the person be permitted to emigrate, yet forbidden to stay and opt out of the compulsory scheme of social provision? If providing for the needy is of overriding importance, this does militate against allowing internal opting out; but it also speaks against allowing external emigration. (Would it also support, to some extent, the kidnapping of persons living in a place without compulsory social provision, who could be forced to make a contribution to the needy in your community?) Perhaps the crucial component of the position that allows emigration solely to avoid certain arrangements, while not allowing anyone internally to opt out of them, is a concern for fraternal feelings within the country. "We don't want anyone here who doesn't contribute, who doesn't care enough about the others to contribute." That concern, in this case, would have to be tied to the view that forced aiding tends to produce fraternal feelings between the aided and the aider (or perhaps merely to the view that the knowledge that someone or other voluntarily is not aiding produces unfraternal feelings).

LOCKE'S THEORY OF ACQUISITION

Before we turn to consider other theories of justice in detail, we must introduce an additional bit of complexity into the structure of the entitlement theory. This is best approached by considering Locke's attempt to specify a principle of justice in acquisition. Locke views property rights in an unowned object as originating through someone's mixing his labor with it. This gives rise to many questions. What are the boundaries of what labor is mixed with? If a private astronaut clears a place on Mars, has he mixed his labor with (so that he comes to own) the whole planet, the whole uninhabited universe, or just a particular plot? Which plot does an act bring under ownership? The minimal (possibly disconnected) area such that an act decreases entropy in that area, and not elsewhere? Can virgin land (for the purposes of ecological investigation by high-flying airplanes) come under ownership by a Lockean process? Building a fence around a territory presumably would make one the owner of only the fence (and the land immediately underneath it).

Why does mixing one's labor with something make one the owner of it? Perhaps because one owns one's labor, and so one comes to own a previously unowned thing that becomes permeated with what one owns. Ownership seeps over into the rest. But why isn't mixing what I own with what I don't own a way of losing what I own rather than a way of gaining what I don't? If I own a can of tomato juice and spill it in the sea so that its molecules (made radioactive, so I can check this) mingle evenly throughout the sea, do I thereby come to own the sea, or have I foolishly dissipated my tomato juice? Perhaps the idea, instead, is that laboring on something improves it and makes it more valuable; and anyone is entitled to own a thing whose value he has created. (Reinforcing this, perhaps, is the view that laboring is unpleasant. If some people made things effortlessly, as the cartoon characters in *The Yellow Submarine* trail flowers in their wake, would they have lesser claim to their own products whose making didn't *cost* them anything?) Ignore the fact that laboring on something may make it less valuable (spraying pink enamel paint on a piece of driftwood that you have found). Why should one's entitlement extend to the whole object rather than just to the *added value* one's labor has produced? (Such reference to value might also serve to delimit the extent of ownership; for example, substitute "increases the value of" for "decreases entropy in" in the above entropy criterion.) No workable or coherent value added property scheme has yet been devised, and any such scheme presumably would fall to objections (similar to those) that fell to the theory of Henry George.

It will be implausible to view improving an object as giving full ownership to it, if the stock of unowned objects that might be improved is limited. For an object's coming under one person's ownership changes the situation of all others. Whereas previously they were at liberty (in Hohfeld's sense) to use the object, they now no longer are. This change in the situation of others (by removing their liberty to act on a previously unowned object) need not worsen their situation. If I appropriate a grain of sand from Coney Island, no one else may now do as they will with *that* grain of sand. But there are plenty of other grains of sands left for them to do the same with. Or if not grains of sand, then other things. Alternatively, the things I do with the grain of sand I appropriate might improve the position of others, counterbalancing their loss of liberty to use that grain. The crucial point is whether appropriation of an unowned object worsens the situation of others.

Locke's proviso that there be "enough and as good left in common for others" . . . is meant to ensure that the situation of others is not worsened. (If this proviso is met is there any motivation for his further condition of nonwaste?) It is often said that this proviso once held but now no longer does. But there appears to be an argument for the conclusion that if the proviso no longer holds, then it cannot ever have held so as to yield permanent and inheritable property rights.

Consider the first person Z for whom there is not enough and as good left to appropriate. The last person Y to appropriate left Z without his previous liberty to act on an object, and so worsened Z's situation. So Y's appropriation is not allowed under Locke's proviso. Therefore the next to last person X to appropriate left Y in a worse position, for X's act ended permissible appropriation. Therefore X's appropriation wasn't permissible. But then the appropriator two from last, W, ended permissible appropriation and so, since it worsened X's position, W's appropriation wasn't permissible. And so on back to the first person A to appropriate a permanent property right.

This argument, however, proceeds too quickly. Someone may be made worse off by another's appropriation in two ways: first, by losing the opportunity to improve his situation by a particular appropriation of any one; and second, by no longer being able to use freely (without appropriation) what he previously could. A *stringent* requirement that another not be made worse off by an appropriation would exclude the first way if nothing else counterbalances the diminution in opportunity, as well as the second. A *weaker* requirement would exclude the second way, though not the first. With the weaker requirement, we cannot zip back so quickly from Z to A, as in the above argument; for though person Z can no longer *appropriate,* there may remain some for him to *use* as before. In this case Y's appropriation would not violate the weaker Lockean condition. (With less remaining that people are at liberty to use, users might face more inconvenience, crowding, and so on; in that way the situation of others might be worsened, unless appropriation stopped far short of such a point.) It is arguable that no one legitimately can complain if the weaker provision is satisfied. However, since this is less clear than in the case of the more stringent proviso, Locke may have intended this stringent proviso, by "enough and as good" remaining, and perhaps he meant the nonwaste condition to delay the end point from which the argument zips back.

Is the situation of persons who are unable to appropriate (there being no more accessible and useful unowned objects) worsened by a system allowing appropriation and permanent property? Here enter the various familiar social considerations favoring private property: it increases the social product by putting means of production in the hands of those who can use them most efficiently (profitably); experimentation is encouraged, because with separate persons controlling resources, there is no one person or small group whom someone with a new idea must convince to try it out; private property enables people to decide on the pattern and types of risks they wish to bear, leading to specialized types of risk bearing; private property protects future persons by leading some to hold back resources from current consumption for future markets; it provides alternate sources of employment for unpopular persons who don't have to convince any one person or small group to hire them, and so on. These considerations enter a Lockean theory to support the claim that appropriation of private property satisfies the intent behind the "enough and as good left over" proviso, *not* as a utilitarian justification of property. They enter to rebut the claim that because the proviso is violated no natural right to private property can arise by a Lockean process. The difficulty in working such an argument to show that the proviso is satisfied is in fixing the appropriate baseline for comparison. Lockean appropriation makes people no worse off than they would be *how*? This question of fixing the baseline needs more detailed investigation than we are able to give it here. It would be desirable to have an estimate of the general economic importance of original appropriation in order to see how much leeway there is for differing theories of appropriation and of the location of the baseline. Perhaps this importance can be measured by the percentage of all income that is based upon untransformed raw materials and given resources (rather than upon human actions), mainly rental income representing the unimproved value of land, and the price of raw material *in situ,* and by the percentage of current wealth which represents such income in the past.

We should note that it is not only persons favoring *private* property who need a theory of how property rights legitimately originate. Those believing in collective property, for example those believing that a group of persons living in an area jointly own the territory, or its mineral resources, also must provide a theory of how such property rights arise; they must show why the persons living there have rights to determine what is done with the land and resources there that persons living elsewhere don't have (with regard to the same land and resources).

THE PROVISO

Whether or not Locke's particular theory of appropriation can be spelled out so as to handle various difficulties, I assume that any adequate theory of justice in ac-

quisition will contain a proviso similar to the weaker of the ones we have attributed to Locke. A process normally giving rise to a permanent bequeathable property right in a previously unowned thing will not do so if the position of others no longer at liberty to use the thing is thereby worsened. It is important to specify *this* particular mode of worsening the situation of others, for the proviso does not encompass other modes. It does not include the worsening due to more limited opportunities to appropriate (the first way above, corresponding to the more stringent condition), and it does not include how I "worsen" a seller's position if I appropriate materials to make some of what he is selling, and then enter into competition with him. Someone whose appropriation otherwise would violate the proviso still may appropriate provided he compensates the others so that their situation is not thereby worsened; unless he does compensate these others, his appropriation will violate the proviso of the principle of justice in acquisition and will be an illegitimate one. A theory of appropriation incorporating this Lockean proviso will handle correctly the cases (objections to the theory lacking the proviso) where someone appropriates the total supply of something necessary for life.

A theory which includes this proviso in its principle of justice in acquisition must also contain a more complex principle of justice in transfer. Some reflection of the proviso about appropriation constrains later actions. If my appropriating all of a certain substance violates the Lockean proviso, then so does my appropriating some and purchasing all the rest from others who obtained it without otherwise violating the Lockean proviso. If the proviso excludes someone's appropriating all the drinkable water in the world, it also excludes his purchasing it all. (More weakly, and messily, it may exclude his charging certain prices for some of his supply.) This proviso (almost?) never will come into effect; the more someone acquires of a scare substance which others want the higher the price of the rest will go, and the more difficult it will become for him to acquire it all. But still, we can imagine, at least, that something like this occurs: someone makes simultaneous secret bids to the separate owners of a substance, each of whom sells assuming he can easily purchase more from the other owners; or some natural catastrophe destroys all of the supply of something except that in one person's possession. The total supply could not be permissibly appropriated by one person at the beginning. His later acquisition of it all does not show that the original appropriation violated the proviso (even by a reverse argument similar to the one above that tried to zip back from Z to A). Rather, it is the combination of the original appropriation *plus* all the later transfers and actions that violates the Lockean proviso.

Each owner's title to his holding includes the historical shadow of the Lockean proviso on appropriation. This excludes his transferring it into an agglomeration that does violate the Lockean proviso and excludes his using it in a way, in coordination with others or independently of them, so as to violate the proviso by making the situation of others worse than their baseline situation. Once it is known that someone's ownership runs afoul of the Lockean proviso, there are stringent limits on what he may do with (what it is difficult any longer unreservedly to call) "his property." Thus a person may not appropriate the only water hole in a desert and charge what he will. Nor may he charge what he will if he possesses one, and unfortunately it happens that all the water holes in the desert dry up, except for his. This unfortunate circumstance, admittedly no fault of his, brings into operation the Lockean proviso and limits his property rights. Similarly, an owner's property right in the only island in an area does not allow him to order a castaway from a shipwreck off his island as a trespasser, for this would violate the Lockean proviso.

Notice that the theory does not say that owners do have these rights, but that the rights are overridden to avoid some catastrophe. (Overridden rights do not disappear; they leave a trace of a sort absent in the cases under discussion.) There is no such external (and *ad hoc*?) overriding. Considerations internal to the theory of property itself, to its theory of acquisition and appropriation, provide the means for handling such cases. The results, however, may be coextensive with some condition about catastrophe, since the baseline for comparison is so low as compared to the productiveness of a society with private appropriation that the question of the Lockean proviso being violated arises only in the case of catastrophe (or a desert-island situation).

The fact that someone owns the total supply of something necessary for others to stay alive does *not* entail that his (or anyone's) appropriation of anything left some people (immediately or later) in a situation worse than the baseline one. A medical researcher who synthesizes a new substance that effectively treats a certain disease and who refuses to sell except on his terms does not worsen the situation of others by depriving them of whatever he has appropriated. The others easily can possess the same materials he appropri-

ated; the researcher's appropriation or purchase of chemicals didn't make those chemicals scarce in a way so as to violate the Lockean proviso. Nor would someone else's purchasing the total supply of the synthesized substance from the medical researcher. The fact that the medical researcher uses easily available chemicals to synthesize the drug no more violates the Lockean proviso than does the fact that the only surgeon able to perform a particular operation eats easily obtainable food in order to stay alive and to have the energy to work. This shows that the Lockean proviso is not an "end-state principle;" it focuses on a particular way that appropriative actions affect others, and not on the structure of the situation that results.

Intermediate between someone who takes all of the public supply and someone who makes the total supply out of easily obtainable substances is someone who appropriates the total supply of something in a way that does not deprive the others of it. For example, someone finds a new substance in an out-of-the-way place. He discovers that it effectively treats a certain disease and appropriates the total supply. He does not worsen the situation of others; if he did not stumble upon the substance no one else would have, and the others would remain without it. However, as time passes, the likelihood increases that others would have come across the substance; upon this fact might be based a limit to his property right in the substance so that others are not below their baseline position; for example, its bequest might be limited. The theme of someone worsening another's situation by depriving him of something he otherwise would possess may also illuminate the example of patents. An inventor's patent does not deprive others of an object which would not exist if not for the inventor. Yet patents would have this effect on others who independently invent the object. Therefore, these independent inventors, upon whom the burden of proving independent discovery may rest, should not be excluded from utilizing their own invention as they wish (including selling it to others). Furthermore, a known invention drastically lessens the chances of actual independent invention. For persons who know of an invention usually will not try to reinvent it, and the notion of independent discovery here would be murky at best. Yet we may assume that in the absence of the original invention, sometime later someone else would have come up with it. This suggests placing a time limit on patents, as a rough rule of thumb to approximate how long it would have taken, in the absence of knowledge of the invention, for independent discovery.

I believe that the free operation of a market system will not actually run afoul of the Lockean proviso. (Recall that crucial to our story in Part I of how a protective agency becomes dominant and a *de facto* monopoly is the fact that it wields force in situations of conflict, and is not merely in competition, with other agencies. A similar tale cannot be told about other businesses.) If this is correct, the proviso will not play a very important role in the activities of protective agencies and will not provide a significant opportunity for future state action. Indeed, were it not for the effects of previous *illegitimate* state action, people would not think of the possibility of the proviso's being violated as of more interest than any other logical possibility. (Here I make an empirical historical claim; as does someone who disagrees with this.) This completes our indication of the complication in the entitlement theory introduced by the Lockean proviso.

READING 26

Justice As Fairness

John Rawls

For a biosketch of Rawls see Reading 13. No twentieth-century work in moral and political philosophy has had greater influence in our time than Rawls's *A Theory of Justice* (1971). Robert Nisbett calls it the "long awaited successor to Rousseau's *Social Contract*, the Rock on which the Church of Equality can properly be founded in our time." In scope and power it rivals the classics of Hobbes, Locke, and Rousseau. Fundamentally egalitarian, it seeks to justify the welfare state.

In *A Theory of Justice*, from which this reading is taken, Rawls sets forth a hypothetical contract theory in which the bargainers go behind a *veil of ignorance* in order to devise a set of fundamental agreements that will govern society. Behind the metaphorical veil "no one knows his or her place in society, class, gender, race, religion, social status, fortune in the distribution of natural assets and abilities, [or even] intelligence." Parties to the contract are to act as rationally self-interested agents and choose the basic principles that will govern their

society. Rawls thinks that these conditions ensure objectivity and impartiality of judgment. He calls his system "Justice as Fairness" because he seeks a contract on whose fairness all parties will agree. In effect, the parties to the contract should choose the kind of principles they could live with if their enemies were assigning them positions in society. Rawls begins *A Theory of Justice* with a declaration of equal human worth:

> Each person possesses an inviolability founded on justice that even the welfare of society as a whole cannot override. For this reason justice denies that the loss of freedom for some is made right by a greater good shared by others. It does not allow that the sacrifices imposed on a few are outweighed by the larger sum of advantages enjoyed by the many. Therefore, in a just society the liberties of equal citizenship are taken as settled; the rights secured by justice are not subject to political bargaining or the calculus of social interests. . . .

Rawls is an egalitarian, one who believes that each minimally rational human being who has a conception of the good and is able to act justly (sometimes called "moral person") is valuable and all such persons are equally valuable.

This reading is taken from *A Theory of Justice* (Harvard University Press, 1971), by permission.

My aim is to present a conception of justice which generalizes and carries to a higher level of abstraction the familiar theory of the social contract as found, say, in Locke, Rousseau, and Kant. In order to do this we are not to think of the original contract as one to enter a particular society or to set up a particular form of government. Rather, the guiding idea is that the principles of justice for the basic structure of society are the object of the original agreement. They are the principles that free and rational persons concerned to further their own interests would accept in an initial position of equality as defining the fundamental terms of their association. These principles are to regulate all further agreements; they specify the kinds of social cooperation that can be entered into and the forms of government that can be established. This way of regarding the principles of justice I shall call justice as fairness.

Thus we are to imagine that those who engage in social cooperation choose together, in one joint act, the principles which are to assign basic rights and duties and to determine the division of social benefits. Men are to decide in advance how they are to regulate their claims against one another and what is to be the foundation charter of their society. Just as each person must decide by rational reflection what constitutes his good—that is, the system of ends which it is rational for him to pursue—so a group of persons must decide once and for all what is to count among them as just and unjust. The choice which rational men would make in this hypothetical situation of equal liberty, assuming for the present that this choice problem has a solution, determines the principles of justice.

In justice as fairness the original position of equality corresponds to the state of nature in the traditional theory of the social contract. This original position is not, of course, thought of as an actual historical state of affairs, much less as a primitive condition of culture. It is understood as a purely hypothetical situation characterized so as to lead to a certain conception of justice. Among the essential features of this situation is that no one knows his place in society, his class position or social status, nor does any one know his fortune in the distribution of natural assets and abilities, his intelligence, strength, and the like. I shall even assume that the parties do not know their conceptions of the good or their special psychological propensities. The principles of justice are chosen behind a veil of ignorance. This ensures that no one is advantaged or disadvantaged in the choice of principles by the outcome of natural chance or the contingency of social circumstances. Since all are similarly situated and no one is able to design principles to favor his particular condition, the principles of justice are the result of a fair agreement or bargain. For given the circumstances of the original position, the symmetry of everyone's relations to each other, this initial situation is fair between individuals as moral persons; that is, as rational beings with their own ends and capable, I shall assume, of a sense of justice. The original position is, one might say, the appropriate initial status quo, and thus the fundamental agreements reached in it are fair. This explains the propriety of the name "justice as fairness;" it conveys the idea that the principles of justice are agreed to in an initial situation that is fair. The name does not mean that the concepts of justice and fairness are the

same, any more than the phrase "poetry as metaphor" means that the concepts of poetry and metaphor are the same.

Justice as fairness begins, as I have said, with one of the most general of all choices which persons might make together, namely, with the choice of the first principles of a conception of justice which is to regulate all subsequent criticism and reform of institutions. Then, having chosen a conception of justice, we can suppose that they are to choose a constitution and a legislature to enact laws, and so on, all in accordance with the principles of justice initially agreed upon. Our social situation is just if it is such that by this sequence of hypothetical agreements we would have contracted into the general system of rules which defines it. Moreover, assuming that the original position does determine a set of principles (that is, that a particular conception of justice would be chosen), it will then be true that whenever social institutions satisfy these principles those engaged in them can say to one another that they are cooperating on terms to which they would agree if they were free and equal persons whose relations with respect to one another were fair. They could all view their arrangements as meeting the stipulations which they would acknowledge in an initial situation that embodies widely accepted and reasonable constraints on the choice of principles. The general recognition of this fact would provide the basis for a public acceptance of the corresponding principles of justice. No society can, of course, be a scheme of cooperation which men enter voluntarily in a literal sense; each person finds himself placed at birth in some particular position in some particular society, and the nature of this position materially affects his life prospects. Yet a society satisfying the principles of justice as fairness comes as close as a society can to being a voluntary scheme, for it meets the principles which free and equal persons would assent to under circumstances that are fair. In this sense its members are autonomous and the obligations they recognize self-imposed.

One feature of justice as fairness is to think of the parties in the initial situation as rational and mutually disinterested. This does not mean that the parties are egoists; that is, individuals with only certain kinds of interests, say in wealth, prestige, and domination. But they are conceived as not taking an interest in one another's interests. They are to presume that even their spiritual aims may be opposed, in the way that the aims of those of different religions may be opposed. Moreover, the concept of rationality must be interpreted as far as possible in the narrow sense, standard in economic theory, of taking the most effective means to given ends. I shall modify this concept to some extent . . . , but one must try to avoid introducing into it any controversial ethical elements. The initial situation must be characterized by stipulations that are widely accepted.

In working out the conception of justice as fairness one main task clearly is to determine which principles of justice would be chosen in the original position. To do this we must describe this situation in some detail and formulate with care the problem of choice which it presents. It may be observed, however, that once the principles of justice are thought of as arising from an original agreement in a situation of equality, it is an open question whether the principle of utility would be acknowledged. Offhand it hardly seems likely that persons who view themselves as equals, entitled to press their claims upon one another, would agree to a principle which may require lesser life prospects for some simply for the sake of a greater sum of advantages enjoyed by others. Since each desires to protect his interests, his capacity to advance his conception of the good, no one has a reason to acquiesce in an enduring loss for himself in order to bring about a greater net balance of satisfaction. In the absence of strong and lasting benevolent impulses, a rational man would not accept a basic structure merely because it maximized the algebraic sum of advantages irrespective of its permanent effects on his own basic rights and interests. Thus it seems that the principle of utility is incompatible with the conception of social cooperation among equals for mutual advantage. It appears to be inconsistent with the idea of reciprocity implicit in the notion of a well-ordered society. Or, at any rate, so I shall argue.

I shall maintain instead that the persons in the initial situation would choose two rather different principles: the first requires equality in the assignment of basic rights and duties, while the second holds that social and economic inequalities; for example, inequalities of wealth and authority; are just only if they result in compensating benefits for everyone, and in particular for the least advantaged members of society. These principles rule out justifying institutions on the grounds that the hardships of some are offset by a greater good in the aggregate. It may be expedient but it is not just that some should have less in order that others may prosper. But there is no injustice in the greater benefits earned by a few provided that the situation of persons not so fortunate is thereby improved. The intuitive idea

is that since everyone's well-being depends upon a scheme of cooperation without which no one could have a satisfactory life, the division of advantages should be such as to draw forth the willing cooperation of everyone taking part in it, including those less well situated. Yet this can be expected only if reasonable terms are proposed. The two principles mentioned seem to be a fair agreement on the basis of which those better endowed, or more fortunate in their social position, neither of which we can be said to deserve, could expect the willing cooperation of others when some workable scheme is a necessary condition of the welfare of all. Once we decide to look for a conception of justice that nullifies the accidents of natural endowment and the contingencies of social circumstance as counters in quest for political and economic advantage, we are led to these principles. They express the result of leaving aside those aspects of the social world that seem arbitrary from a moral point of view.

The problem of the choice of principles, however, is extremely difficult. I do not expect the answer I shall suggest to be convincing to everyone. It is, therefore, worth noting from the outset that justice as fairness, like other contract views, consists of two parts: (1) an interpretation of the initial situation and of the problem of choice posed there, and (2) a set of principles which, it is argued, would be agreed to. One may accept the first part of the theory (or some variant thereof), but not the other, and conversely. The concept of the initial contractual situation may seem reasonable although the particular principles proposed are rejected. To be sure, I want to maintain that the most appropriate conception of this situation does lead to principles of justice contrary to utilitarianism and perfectionism, and therefore that the contract doctrine provides an alternative to these views. Still, one may dispute this contention even though one grants that the contractarian method is a useful way of studying ethical theories and of setting forth their underlying assumptions.

Justice as fairness is an example of what I have called a contract theory. Now there may be an objection to the term "contract" and related expressions, but I think it will serve reasonably well. Many words have misleading connotations which at first are likely to confuse. The terms "utility" and "utilitarianism" are surely no exception. They too have unfortunate suggestions which hostile critics have been willing to exploit; yet they are clear enough for those prepared to study utilitarian doctrine. The same should be true of the term "contract" applied to moral theories. As I have mentioned, to understand it one has to keep in mind that it implies a certain level of abstraction. In particular, the content of the relevant agreement is not to enter a given society or to adopt a given form of government, but to accept certain moral principles. Moreover, the undertakings referred to are purely hypothetical: a contract view holds that certain principles would be accepted in a well-defined initial situation.

The merit of the contract terminology is that it conveys the idea that principles of justice may be conceived as principles that would be chosen by rational persons, and that in this way conceptions of justice may be explained and justified. The theory of justice is a part, perhaps the most significant part, of the theory of rational choice. Furthermore, principles of justice deal with conflicting claims upon the advantages won by social cooperation; they apply to the relations among several persons or groups. The word "contract" suggests this plurality as well as the condition that the appropriate division of advantages must be in accordance with principles acceptable to all parties. The condition of publicity for principles of justice is also connoted by the contract phraseology. Thus, if these principles are the outcome of an agreement, citizens have a knowledge of the principles that others follow. It is characteristic of contract theories to stress the public nature of political principles. Finally there is the long tradition of the contract doctrine. Expressing the tie with this line of thought helps to define ideas and accords with natural piety. There are then several advantages in the use of the term "contract." With due precautions taken, it should not be misleading.

A final remark. Justice as fairness is not a complete contract theory. For it is clear that the contractarian idea can be extended to the choice of more or less an entire ethical system; that is, to a system including principles for all the virtues and not only for justice. Now for the most part I shall consider only principles of justice and others closely related to them; I make no attempt to discuss the virtues in a systematic way. Obviously if justice as fairness succeeds reasonably well, a next step would be to study the more general view suggested by the name "rightness as fairness." But even this wider theory fails to embrace all moral relationships, since it would seem to include only our relations with other persons and to leave out of account how we are to conduct ourselves toward animals and the rest of nature. I do not contend that the contract notion offers a way to approach these questions, which are certainly of the first importance; and I shall have to

put them aside. We must recognize the limited scope of justice as fairness and of the general type of view that it exemplifies. How far its conclusions must be revised once these other matters are understood cannot be decided in advance.

THE ORIGINAL POSITION AND JUSTIFICATION

I have said that the original position is the appropriate initial status quo which ensures that the fundamental agreements reached in it are fair. This fact yields the name "justice as fairness." It is clear, then, that I want to say that one conception of justice is more reasonable than another, or justifiable with respect to it, if rational persons in the initial situation would choose its principles over those of the other for the role of justice. Conceptions of justice are to be ranked by their acceptability to persons so circumstanced. Understood in this way the question of justification is settled by working out a problem of deliberation: we have to ascertain which principles it would be rational to adopt given the contractual situation. This connects the theory of justice with the theory of rational choice.

If this view of the problem of justification is to succeed, we must, of course, describe in some detail the nature of this choice problem. A problem of rational decision has a definite answer only if we know the beliefs and interests of the parties, their relations with respect to one another, the alternatives between which they are to choose, the procedure whereby they make up their minds, and so on. As the circumstances are presented in different ways, correspondingly different principles are accepted. The concept of the original position, as I shall refer to it, is that of the most philosophically favored interpretation of this initial choice situation for the purposes of a theory of justice.

But how are we to decide what is the most favored interpretation? I assume, for one thing, that there is a broad measure of agreement that principles of justice should be chosen under certain conditions. To justify a particular description of the initial situation one shows that it incorporates these commonly shared presumptions. One argues from widely accepted but weak premises to more specific conclusions. Each of the presumptions should by itself be natural and plausible; some of them may seem innocuous or even trivial. The aim of the contract approach is to establish that taken together they impose significant bounds on acceptable principles of justice. The ideal outcome would be that these conditions determine a unique set of principles; but I shall be satisfied if they suffice to rank the main traditional conceptions of social justice.

One should not be misled, then, by the somewhat unusual conditions which characterize the original position. The idea here is simply to make vivid to ourselves the restrictions that it seems reasonable to impose on arguments for principles of justice, and therefore on these principles themselves. Thus it seems reasonable and generally acceptable that no one should be advantaged or disadvantaged by natural fortune or social circumstances in the choice of principles. It also seems widely agreed that it should be impossible to tailor principles to the circumstances of one's own case. We should ensure further that particular inclinations and aspirations, and persons' conceptions of their good, do not affect the principles adopted. The aim is to rule out those principles that it would be rational to propose for acceptance, however little the chance of success, only if one knew certain things that are irrelevant from the standpoint of justice. For example, if a man knew that he was wealthy, he might find it rational to advance the principle that various taxes for welfare measures be counted unjust; if he knew that he was poor, he would most likely propose the contrary principle. To represent the desired restrictions one imagines a situation in which everyone is deprived of this sort of information. One excludes the knowledge of those contingencies which sets men at odds and allows them to be guided by their prejudices. In this manner the veil of ignorance is arrived at in a natural way. This concept should cause no difficulty if we keep in mind the constraints on arguments that it is meant to express. At any time we can enter the original position, so to speak, simply by following a certain procedure; namely, by arguing for principles of justice in accordance with these restrictions.

It seems reasonable to suppose that the parties in the original position are equal. That is, all have the same rights in the procedure for choosing principles; each can make proposals, submit reasons for their acceptance, and so on. Obviously the purpose of these conditions is to represent equality between human beings as moral persons, as creatures having a conception of their good and capable of a sense of justice. The basis of equality is taken to be similarity in these two respects. Systems of ends are not ranked in value; and each man is presumed to have the requisite ability to understand and to act upon whatever principles are adopted. Together with the veil of ignorance, these conditions define the principles of justice as those which rational persons concerned to advance their interests would consent to as equals when none are known to be advantaged or disadvantaged by social and natural contingencies.

There is, however, another side to justifying a particular description of the original position. This is to see if the principles which would be chosen match our considered convictions of justice or extend them in an acceptable way. We can note whether applying these principles would lead us to make the same judgments about the basic structure of society which we now make intuitively and in which we have the greatest confidence; or whether, in cases where our present judgments are in doubt and given with hesitation, these principles offer a resolution which we can affirm on reflection. There are questions which we feel sure must be answered in a certain way. For example, we are confident that religious intolerance and racial discrimination are unjust. We think that we have examined these things with care and have reached what we believe is an impartial judgment not likely to be distorted by an excessive attention to our own interests. These convictions are provisional fixed points which we presume any conception of justice must fit. But we have much less assurance as to what is the correct distribution of wealth and authority. Here we may be looking for a way to remove our doubts. We can check an interpretation of the initial situation, then, by the capacity of its principles to accommodate our firmest convictions and to provide guidance where guidance is needed.

In searching for the most favored description of this situation we work from both ends. We begin by describing it so that it represents generally shared and preferably weak conditions. We then see if these conditions are strong enough to yield a significant set of principles. If not, we look for further premises equally reasonable. But if so, and these principles match our considered convictions of justice, then so far well and good. But presumably there will be discrepancies. In this case we have a choice. We can either modify the account of the initial situation or we can revise our existing judgments, for even the judgments we take provisionally as fixed points are liable to revision. By going back and forth, sometimes altering the conditions of the contractual circumstances, at others withdrawing our judgments and conforming them to principle, I assume that eventually we shall find a description of the initial situation that both expresses reasonable conditions and yields principles which match our considered judgments duly pruned and adjusted. This state of affairs I refer to as reflective equilibrium. It is an equilibrium because at last our principles and judgments coincide; and it is reflective since we know to what principles our judgments conform and the premises of their derivation. At the moment everything is in order. But this equilibrium is not necessarily stable. It is liable to be upset by further examination of the conditions which should be imposed on the contractual situation and by particular cases which may lead us to revise our judgments. Yet for the time being we have done what we can to render coherent and to justify our convictions of social justice. We have reached a conception of the original position.

I shall not, of course, actually work through this process. Still, we may think of the interpretation of the original position that I shall present as the result of such a hypothetical course of reflection. It represents the attempt to accommodate within one scheme both reasonable philosophical conditions on principles as well as our considered judgments of justice. In arriving at the favored interpretation of the initial situation there is no point at which an appeal is made to self-evidence in the traditional sense either of general conceptions or particular convictions. I do not claim for the principles of justice proposed that they are necessary truths or derivable from such truths. A conception of justice cannot be deduced from self-evident premises or conditions on principles; instead, its justification is a matter of the mutual support of many considerations, of everything fitting together into one coherent view.

A final comment. We shall want to say that certain principles of justice are justified because they would be agreed to in an initial situation of equality. I have emphasized that this original position is purely hypothetical. It is natural to ask why, if this agreement is never actually entered into, we should take any interest in these principles, moral or otherwise. The answer is that the conditions embodied in the description of the original position are ones that we do in fact accept. Or if we do not, then perhaps we can be persuaded to do so by philosophical reflection. Each aspect of the contractual situation can be given supporting grounds. Thus what we shall do is to collect together into one conception a number of conditions on principles that we are ready upon due consideration to recognize as reasonable. These constraints express what we are prepared to regard as limits on fair terms of social cooperation. One way to look at the idea of the original position, therefore, is to see it as an expository device which sums up the meaning of these conditions and helps us to extract their consequences. On the other hand, this conception is also an intuitive notion that suggests its own elaboration, so that led on by it we are drawn to define more clearly the standpoint from which we can best interpret moral relationships. We need a conception that enables us to envision our objective from afar: the intuitive notion of the original position is to do this for us. . . .

TWO PRINCIPLES OF JUSTICE

I shall now state in a provisional form the two principles of justice that I believe would be chosen in the original position. In this section I wish to make only the most general comments, and therefore the first formulation of these principles is tentative. As we go on I shall run through several formulations and approximate step by step the final statement to be given much later. I believe that doing this allows the exposition to proceed in a natural way.

The first statement of the two principles reads as follows:

> First: each person is to have an equal right to the most extensive basic liberty compatible with a similar liberty for others.

> Second: Social and economic inequalities are to be arranged so that they are both (a) reasonably expected to be to everyone's advantage, and (b) attached to positions and offices open to all.

There are two ambiguous phrases in the second principle, namely "everyone's advantage" and "open to all." Determining their sense more exactly will lead to a second formulation of the principle. . . .

By way of general comment, these principles primarily apply, as I have said, to the basic structure of society. They are to govern the assignment of rights and duties and to regulate the distribution of social and economic advantages. As their formulation suggests, these principles presuppose that the social structure can be divided into two more or less distinct parts, the first principle applying to the one, the second to the other. They distinguish between those aspects of the social system that define and secure the equal liberties of citizenship and those that specify and establish social and economic inequalities. The basic liberties of citizens are, roughly speaking, political liberty (the right to vote and to be eligible for public office) together with freedom of speech and assembly; liberty of conscience and freedom of thought; freedom of the person along with the right to hold (personal) property; and freedom from arbitrary arrest and seizure as defined by the concept of the rule of law. These liberties are all required to be equal by the first principle, since citizens of a just society are to have the same basic rights.

The second principle applies, in the first approximation, to the distribution of income and wealth and to the design of organizations that make use of differences in authority and responsibility; or chains of command. While the distribution of wealth and income need not be equal, it must be to everyone's advantage, and at the same time, positions of authority and offices of command must be accessible to all. One applies the second principle by holding positions open, and then, subject to this constraint, arranges social and economic inequalities so that everyone benefits.

These principles are to be arranged in a serial order with the first principle prior to the second. This ordering means that a departure from the institutions of equal liberty required by the first principle cannot be justified by, or compensated for, by greater social and economic advantages. The distribution of wealth and income, and the hierarchies of authority, must be consistent with both the liberties of equal citizenship and equality of opportunity.

It is clear that these principles are rather specific in their content, and their acceptance rests on certain assumptions that I must eventually try to explain and justify. A theory of justice depends upon a theory of society in ways that will become evident as we proceed. For the present, it should be observed that the two principles (and this holds for all formulations) are a special case of a moral general conception of justice that can be expressed as follows:

> All social values—liberty and opportunity, income and wealth, and the bases of self-respect—are to be distributed equally unless an unequal distribution of any, or all, of these values is to everyone's advantage.

Injustice, then, is simply inequalities that are not to the benefit of all. Of course, this conception is extremely vague and requires interpretation.

As a first step, suppose that the basic structure of society distributes certain primary goods, that is, things that every rational man is presumed to want. These goods normally have a use whatever a person's rational plan of life. For simplicity, assume that the chief primary goods at the disposition of society are rights and liberties, powers and opportunities, income and wealth. (Later on . . . the primary good of self-respect has a central place.) These are the social primary goods. Other primary goods such as health and vigor, intelligence and imagination, are natural goods; although their possession is influenced by the basic structure, they are not so directly under its control. Imagine, then, a hypothetical initial arrangement in which all the social primary goods are equally distributed: everyone has similar rights and duties, and income and wealth are evenly shared. This state of affairs provides a benchmark for judging improvements. If certain inequalities of wealth and organizational powers would make everyone better off than in this hypothetical starting situation, then they accord with the general conception.

Now it is possible, at least theoretically, that by giving up some of their fundamental liberties men are sufficiently compensated by the resulting social and economic gains. The general conception of justice imposes no restrictions on what sort of inequalities are permissible; it only requires that everyone's position be improved. We need not suppose anything so drastic as consenting to a condition of slavery. Imagine instead that men forgo certain political rights when the economic returns are significant and their capacity to influence the course of policy by the exercise of these rights would be marginal in any case. It is this kind of exchange which the two principles as stated rule out; being arranged in serial order they do not permit exchanges between basic liberties and economic and social gains. The serial ordering of principles expresses an underlying preference among primary social goods. When this preference is rational so likewise is the choice of these principles in this order.

In developing justice as fairness I shall, for the most part, leave aside the general conception of justice and examine instead the special case of the two principles in serial order. The advantage of this procedure is that from the first the matter of priorities is recognized and an effort made to find principles to deal with it. One is led to attend throughout to the conditions under which the acknowledgement of the absolute weight of liberty with respect to social and economic advantages, as defined by the lexical order of the two principles, would be reasonable. Offhand, this ranking appears extreme and too special a case to be of much interest; but there is more justification for it than would appear at first sight. Or at any rate, so I shall maintain. Furthermore, the distinction between fundamental rights and liberties and economic and social benefits marks a difference among primary social goods that one should try to exploit. It suggests an important division in the social system. Of course, the distinctions drawn and the ordering proposed are bound to be at best only approximations. There are surely circumstances in which they fail. But it is essential to depict clearly the main lines of a reasonable conception of justice; and under many conditions, anyway, the two principles in serial order may serve well enough. When necessary we can fall back on the more general conception.

The fact that the two principles apply to institutions has certain consequences. Several points illustrate this. First of all, the rights and liberties referred to by these principles are those that are defined by the public rules of the basic structure. Whether men are free is determined by the rights and duties established by the major institutions of society. Liberty is a certain pattern of social forms. The first principle simply requires that certain sorts of rules, those defining basic liberties, apply to everyone equally and that they allow the most extensive liberty compatible with a like liberty for all. The only reason for circumscribing the rights defining liberty and making men's freedom less extensive than it might otherwise be is that these equal rights as institutionally defined would interfere with one another.

Another thing to bear in mind is that when principles mention persons, or require that everyone gain from an inequality, the reference is to representative persons holding the various social positions, or offices, or whatever, established by the basic structure. Thus in applying the second principle I assume that it is possible to assign an expectation of well-being to representative individuals holding these positions. This expectation indicates their life prospects as viewed from their social station. In general, the expectations of representative persons depend upon the distribution of rights and duties throughout the basic structure. When this changes, expectations change. I assume, then, that expectations are connected: by raising the prospects of the representative man in one position we presumably increase or decrease the prospects of representative men in other positions. Since it applies to institutional forms, the second principle (or rather the first part of it) refers to the expectations of representative individuals. As I shall discuss below, neither principle applies to distributions of particular goods to particular individuals who may be identified by their proper names. The situation where someone is considering how to allocate certain commodities to needy persons who are known to him is not within the scope of the principles. They are meant to regulate basic institutional arrangements. We must not assume that there is much similarity from the standpoint of justice between an administrative allotment of goods to specific persons and the appropriate design of society. Our commonsense intuitions for the former may be a poor guide to the latter.

Now the second principle insists that each person benefit from permissible inequalities in the basic structure. This means that it must be reasonable for each relevant representative man defined by this structure, when he views it as a going concern, to prefer his prospects with the inequality to his prospects without it. One is not allowed to justify differences in income or organizational powers on the ground that the disadvantages of those in one position are outweighed by the greater advantages of those in another. Much less can infringements of liberty be counterbalanced in this way. Applied to the basic structure, the principle of utility would have us maximize the sum of expectations of representative men (weighted by the number of persons they represent, on the classical view); and this would permit us to compensate for the losses of some by the gains of others. Instead, the two principles require that everyone benefit from economic and social inequalities.

THE REASONING LEADING TO THE TWO PRINCIPLES OF JUSTICE

It will be recalled that the general conception of justice as fairness requires that all primary social goods will be distributed equally unless an unequal distribution would be to everyone's advantage. No restrictions are placed on exchanges of these goods and therefore a lesser liberty can be compensated for by greater social and economic benefits. Now looking at the situation from the standpoint of one person selected arbitrarily, there is no way for him to win special advantages for himself. Nor, on the other hand, are there grounds for his acquiescing in special disadvantages. Since it is not reasonable for him to expect more than an equal share in the division of social goods, and since it is not rational for him to agree to less, the sensible thing for him to do is to acknowledge as the first principle of justice one requiring an equal distribution. Indeed, this principle is so obvious that we would expect it to occur to anyone immediately.

Thus, the parties start with a principle of establishing equal liberty for all, including equality of opportunity, as well as an equal distribution of income and wealth. But there is no reason why this acknowledgment should be final. If there are inequalities in the basic structure that work to make everyone better off in comparison with the benchmark of initial equality, why not permit them? The immediate gain which a greater equality might allow can be regarded as intelligently invested in view of its future return.

If, for example, these inequalities set up various incentives which succeed in eliciting more productive efforts, a person in the original position may look upon them as necessary to cover the costs of training and to encourage effective performance. One might think that ideally individuals should want to serve one another. But since the parties are assumed not to take an interest in one another's interests, their acceptance of these inequalities is only the acceptance of the relations in which men stand in the circumstances of justice. They have no grounds for complaining of one another's motives. A person in the original position would, therefore, concede the justice of these inequalities. Indeed, it would be shortsighted of him not to do so. He would hesitate to agree to these regularities only if he would be dejected by the bare knowledge or perception that others were better situated; and I have assumed that the parties decide as if they are not moved by envy. In order to make the principle regulating inequalities determinate, one looks at the system from the standpoint of the least advantaged representative man. Inequalities are permissible when they maximize, or at least all contribute to, the long-term expectations of the least fortunate group in society.

Now this general conception imposes no constraints on what sorts of inequalities are allowed, whereas the special conception, by putting the two principles in serial order (with the necessary adjustments in meaning), forbids exchanges between basic liberties and economic and social benefits. I shall not try to justify this ordering here. . . . But roughly, the idea underlying this ordering is that if the parties assume that their basic liberties can be effectively exercised, they will not exchange a lesser liberty for an improvement in economic well-being. It is only when social conditions do not allow the effective establishment of these rights that one can concede their limitation; and these restrictions can be granted only to the extent that they are necessary to prepare the way for a free society. The denial of equal liberty can be defended only if it is necessary to raise the level of civilization so that in due course these freedoms can be enjoyed. Thus in adopting a serial order we are in effect making a special assumption in the original position, namely, that the parties know that the conditions of their society, whatever they are, admit the effective realization of the equal liberties. The serial ordering of the two principles of justice eventually comes to be reasonable if the general conception is consistently followed. This lexical ranking is the long-run tendency of the general view. For the most part I shall assume that the requisite circumstances for the serial order obtain.

It seems clear from these remarks that the two principles are at least a plausible conception of justice. The question, though, is how one is to argue for them more systematically. Now there are several things to do. One can work out their consequences for institutions and note their implications for fundamental social policy. In this way they are tested by a comparison with our considered judgments of justice. . . . But one can also try to find arguments in their favor that are decisive from the standpoint of the original position. In order to see how this might be done, it is useful as a heuristic device to think of the two principles as the maximin solution to the problem of social justice. There is an analogy between the two principles and the maximin rule for choice under uncertainty. This is evident from the fact that the two principles are those a person would choose for the design of a society in which his enemy is to assign him his place. The maximin rule tells us to rank alternatives by their worst possible outcomes; we are to adopt the alternative the worst outcome of which is superior to the worst outcomes of the others. The persons in the original position do not, of course, assume that their initial place in society is decided by a malevolent opponent. As I note below, they should not reason from false premises. The veil of ignorance does not violate this idea, since an absence of information is not misinformation. But that the two principles of justice would be chosen if the parties were forced to protect themselves against such a contingency explains the sense in which this conception is the maximin solution. And this analogy suggests that if the original position has been described so that it is rational for the parties to adopt the conservative attitude expressed by this rule, a conclusive argument can indeed be constructed for these principles. Clearly the maximin rule is not, in general, a suitable guide for choices under uncertainty. But it is attractive in situations marked by certain special features. My aim, then, is to show that a good case can be made for the two principles based on the fact that the original position manifests these features to the fullest possible degree, carrying them to the limit, so to speak.

Consider the gain-and-loss table below. It represents the gains and losses for a situation which is not a game of strategy. There is no one playing against the person making the decision; instead he is faced with several possible circumstances which may or may not obtain. Which circumstances happen to exist does not depend upon what the person choosing decides or whether he announces his moves in advance. The numbers in the table are monetary values (in hundreds of dollars) in comparison with some initial situation. The gain (g) depends upon the individual's decision (d) and the circumstances (c). Thus $g = f(d,c)$. Assuming that there are three possible decisions and three possible circumstances, we might have this gain-and-loss table.

Decisions	Circumstances		
	c_1	c_2	c_3
d_1	−7	8	12
d_2	−8	7	14
d_3	5	6	8

The maximin rule requires that we make the third decision. For in this case the worst that can happen is that one gains five hundred dollars, which is better than the worst for the other actions. If we adopt one of these we may lose either eight or seven hundred dollars. Thus, the choice of d_3 maximizes $f(d,c)$ for that value of c which for a given d, minimizes f. The term "maximin" means the *maximum minimorum;* and the rule directs our attention to the worst that can happen under any proposed course of action, and to decide in the light of that.

Now there appear to be three chief features of situations that give plausibility to this unusual rule. First, since the rule takes no account of the likelihoods of the possible circumstances, there must be some reason for sharply discounting estimates of these probabilities. Offhand, the most natural rule of choice would seem to be to compute the expectation of monetary gain for each decision and then to adopt the course of action with the highest prospect. (This expectation is defined as follows: let us suppose that g_{ij} represents the numbers in the gain-and-loss table, where i is the row index and j is the column index; and let p_jj = 1, 2, 3, be the likelihoods of the circumstances, with $\Sigma p_j = 1$. Then the expectation for the decision is equal to $\Sigma p_j g_{ij}$.) Thus it must be, for example, that the situation is one in which a knowledge of likelihoods is impossible, or at best extremely insecure. In this case it is unreasonable not to be skeptical of probabilistic calculations unless there is no other way out, particularly if the decision is a fundamental one that needs to be justified to others.

The second feature that suggests the maximin rule is the following: the person choosing has a conception

of the good such that he cares very little, if anything, for what he might gain above the minimum stipend that he can, in fact, be sure of by following the maximin rule. It is not worthwhile for him to take a chance for the sake of a further advantage, especially when it may turn out that he loses much that is important to him. This last provision brings in the third feature; namely, that the rejected alternatives have outcomes that one can hardly accept. The situation involves grave risks. Of course, these features work most effectively in combination. The paradigm situation for following the maximin rule is when all three features are realized to the highest degree. This rule does not, then, generally apply, nor of course is it self-evident. Rather, it is a maxim, a rule of thumb, that comes into its own in special circumstances. Its application depends upon the qualitative structure of the possible gains and losses in relation to one's conception of the good, all this against a background in which it is reasonable to discount conjectural estimates of likelihoods.

It should be noted, as the comments on the gain-and-loss table say, that the entries in the table represent monetary values and not utilities. This difference is significant since for one thing computing expectations on the basis of such objective values is not the same thing as computing expected utility and may lead to different results. The essential point, though, is that in justice as fairness the parties do not know their conception of the good and cannot estimate their utility in the ordinary sense. In any case, we want to go behind de facto preferences generated by given conditions. Therefore expectations are based upon an index of primary goods and the parties make their choice accordingly. The entries in the example are in terms of money and not utility to indicate this aspect of the contract doctrine.

Now, as I have suggested, the original position has been defined so that it is a situation in which the maximin rule applies. In order to see this, let us review briefly the nature of this situation with these three special features in mind. To begin with, the veil of ignorance excludes all but the vaguest knowledge of likelihoods. The parties have no basis for determining the probable nature of their society, or their place in it. Thus they have strong reasons for being wary of probability calculations if any other course is open to them. They must also take into account the fact that their choice of principles should seem reasonable to others, in particular their descendants, whose rights will be deeply affected by it. There are further grounds for discounting that I shall mention as we go along. For the present it suffices to note that these considerations are strengthened by the fact that the parties know very little about the gain-and-loss table. Not only are they unable to conjecture the likelihoods of the various possible circumstances, they cannot say much about what the possible circumstances are, much less enumerate them and foresee the outcome of each alternative available. Those deciding are much more in the dark than the illustration by a numerical table suggests. It is for this reason that I have spoken of an analogy with the maximin rule.

Several kinds of arguments for the two principles of justice illustrate the second feature. Thus, if we can maintain that these principles provide a workable theory of social justice, and that they are compatible with reasonable demands of efficiency, then this conception guarantees a satisfactory minimum. There may be, on reflection, little reason for trying to do better. Thus much of the argument . . . is to show, by their application to the main questions of social justice, that the two principles are a satisfactory conception. These details have a philosophical purpose. Moreover, this line of thought is practically decisive if we can establish the priority of liberty, the lexical ordering of the two principles. For this priority implies that the persons in the original position have no desire to try for greater gains at the expense of the equal liberties. The minimum assured by the two principles in lexical order is not one that the parties wish to jeopardize for the sake of greater economic and social advantages. . . .

Finally, the third feature holds if we can assume that other conceptions of justice may lead to institutions that the parties would find intolerable. For example, it has sometimes been held that under some conditions the utility principle (in either form) justifies, if not slavery or serfdom, at any rate serious infractions of liberty for the sake of greater social benefits. We need not consider here the truth of this claim, or the likelihood that the requisite conditions obtain. For the moment, this contention is only to illustrate the way in which conceptions of justice may allow for outcomes which the parties may not be able to accept. And having the ready alternative of the two principles of justice which secure a satisfactory minimum, it seems unwise, if not irrational, for them to take a chance that these outcomes are not realized.

So much, then, for a brief sketch of the features of situations in which the maximin rule comes into its own and of the way in which the arguments for the two principles of justice can be subsumed under them. . . .

THE TENDENCY TO EQUALITY

I wish to conclude this discussion of the two principles by explaining the sense in which they express an egalitarian conception of justice. Also I should like to forestall the objection to the principle of fair opportunity that it leads to a callous meritocratic society. In order to prepare the way for doing this, I note several aspects of the conception of justice that I have set out.

First we may observe that the difference principle gives some weight to the considerations singled out by the principle of redress. This is the principle that undeserved inequalities call for redress; and since inequalities of birth and natural endowment are undeserved, these inequalities are to be somehow compensated for. Thus the principle holds that in order to treat all persons equally, to provide genuine equality of opportunity, society must give more attention to those with fewer native assets and to those born into the less favorable social positions. The idea is to redress the bias of contingencies in the direction of equality. In pursuit of this principle greater resources might be spent on the education of the less rather than the more intelligent, at least over a certain time of life, say the earlier years of school.

Now the principle of redress has not to my knowledge been proposed as the sole criterion of justice, as the single aim of the social order. It is plausible as most such principles are only as a prima facie principle, one that is to be weighed in the balance with others. For example, we are to weigh it against the principle to improve the average standard of life, or to advance the common good. But whatever other principles we hold, the claims of redress are to be taken into account. It is thought to represent one of the elements in our conception of justice. Now the difference principle is not of course the principle of redress. It does not require society to try to even out handicaps as if all were expected to compete on a fair basis in the same race. But the difference principle would allocate resources in education, say, so as to improve the long-term expectation of the least favored. If this end is attained by giving more attention to the better endowed, it is permissible; otherwise not. And in making this decision, the value of education should not be assessed solely in terms of economic efficiency and social welfare. Equally if not more important is the role of education in enabling a person to enjoy the culture of his society and to take part in its affairs, and in this way to provide for each individual a secure sense of his own worth.

Thus although the difference principle is not the same as that of redress, it does achieve some of the intent of the latter principle. It transforms the aims of the basic structure so that the total scheme of institutions no longer emphasizes social efficiency and technocratic values. We see then that the difference principle represents, in effect, an agreement to regard the distribution of natural talents as a common asset and to share in the benefits of this distribution whatever it turns out to be. Those who have been favored by nature, whoever they are, may gain from their good fortune only on terms that improve the situation of those who have lost out. The naturally advantaged are not to gain merely because they are more gifted, but only to cover the costs of training and education and for using their endowments in ways that help the less fortunate as well. No one deserves his greater natural capacity nor merits a more favorable starting place in society. But it does not follow that one should eliminate these distinctions. There is another way to deal with them. The basic structure can be arranged so that these contingencies work for the good of the least fortunate. Thus we are led to the difference principle if we wish to set up the social system so that no one gains or loses from his arbitrary place in the distribution of natural assets or his initial position in society without giving or receiving compensating advantages in return.

In view of these remarks we may reject the contention that the ordering of institutions is always defective because the distribution of natural talents and the contingencies of social circumstance are unjust, and this injustice must inevitably carry over to human arrangements. Occasionally this reflection is offered as an excuse for ignoring injustice, as if the refusal to acquiesce in injustice is on a par with being unable to accept death. The natural distribution is neither just nor unjust; nor is it unjust that persons are born into society at some particular position. These are simply natural facts. What is just and unjust is the way that institutions deal with these facts. Aristocratic and caste societies are unjust because they make these contingencies the ascriptive basis for belonging to more or less enclosed and privileged social classes. The basic structure of these societies incorporates the arbitrariness found in nature. But there is no necessity for men to resign themselves to these contingencies. The social system is not an unchangeable order beyond human control but a pattern of human action. In justice as fairness men agree to share one another's fate. In designing institutions they undertake to avail themselves of the accidents of nature and social circumstance only when doing so is for the common benefit. The two principles are a fair way of meeting the arbitrariness of fortune; and while no doubt imperfect in other ways, the institutions which satisfy these principles are just.

A further point is that the difference principle expresses a conception of reciprocity. It is a principle of mutual benefit. We have seen that, at least when chain connection holds, each representative man can accept the basic structure as designed to advance his interests. The social order can be justified to everyone, and in particular to those who are least favored; and in this sense it is egalitarian. But it seems necessary to consider in an intuitive way how the condition of mutual benefit is satisfied. Consider any two representative men A and B, and let B be the one who is less favored. Actually, since we are most interested in the comparison with the least favored man, let us assume that B is this individual. Now B can accept A's being better off since A's advantages have been gained in ways that improve B's prospects. If A were not allowed his better position, B would be even worse off than he is. The difficulty is to show that A has no grounds for complaint. Perhaps he is required to have less than he might since his having more would result in some loss to B. Now what can be said to the more favored man? To begin with, it is clear that the well-being of each depends on a scheme of social cooperation without which no one could have a satisfactory life. Secondly, we can ask for the willing cooperation of everyone only if the terms of the scheme are reasonable. The difference principle, then, seems to be a fair basis on which those better endowed, or more fortunate in their social circumstances, could expect others to collaborate with them when some workable arrangement is a necessary condition of the good of all.

There is a natural inclination to object that those better situated deserve their greater advantages whether or not they are to the benefit of others. At this point it is necessary to be clear about the notion of desert. It is perfectly true that given a just system of cooperation as a scheme of public rules and the expectations set up by it, those who, with the prospect of improving their condition, have done what the system announces that it will reward are entitled to their advantages. In this sense the more fortunate have a claim to their better situation; their claims are legitimate expectations established by social institutions, and the community is

obligated to meet them. But this sense of desert presupposes the existence of the cooperative scheme; it is
irrelevant to the question whether in the first place the
scheme is to be designed in accordance with the difference principle or some other criterion.

Perhaps some will think that the person with
greater natural endowments deserves those assets and
the superior character that made their development possible. Because he is more worthy in this sense, he deserves the greater advantages that he could achieve
with them. This view, however, is surely incorrect. It
seems to be one of the fixed points of our considered
judgments that no one deserves his place in the distribution of native endowments, any more than one deserves one's initial starting place in society. The assertion that a man deserves the superior character that
enables him to make the effort to cultivate his abilities
is equally problematic; for his character depends in
large part upon fortunate family and social circumstances for which he can claim no credit. The notion of
desert seems not to apply to these cases. Thus the more
advantaged representative man cannot say that he deserves and therefore has a right to a scheme of cooperation in which he is permitted to acquire benefits in
ways that do not contribute to the welfare of others.
There is no basis for his making this claim. From the
standpoint of common sense, then, the difference principle appears to be acceptable both to the more advantaged and to the less advantaged individual. Of course,
none of this is strictly speaking an argument for the
principle, since in a contract theory arguments are made
from the point of view of the original position. But
these intuitive considerations help to clarify the nature
of the principle and the sense in which it is egalitarian.

I noted earlier that a society should try to avoid the
region where the marginal contributions of those better
off to the well-being of the less favored are negative. It
should operate only on the upward rising part of the
contribution curve (including of course the maximum).
One reason for this, we can now see, is that on this segment of the curve the criterion of mutual benefit is always fulfilled. Moreover, there is a natural sense in
which the harmony of social interests is achieved; representative men do not gain at one another's expense
since only reciprocal advantages are allowed. To be
sure, the shape and slope of the contribution curve [are]
determined in part at least by the natural lottery in native assets, and as such it is neither just nor unjust. But
suppose we think of the forty-five degree line as representing the ideal of a perfect harmony of interests; it
is the contribution curve (a straight line in this case)

along which everyone gains equally. Then it seems that
the consistent realization of the two principles of justice tends to raise the curve closer to the ideal of a perfect harmony of interests. Once a society goes beyond
the maximum it operates along the downward sloping
part of the curve and a harmony of interests no longer
exists. As the more favored gain the less advantaged
lose, and vice versa. The situation is analogous to being on an efficiency frontier. This is far from desirable
when the justice of the basic structure is involved. Thus
it is to realize the ideal of the harmony of interests on
terms that nature has given us, and to meet the criterion of mutual benefit, that we should stay in the region
of positive contributions.

A further merit of the difference principle is that
it provides an interpretation of the principle of fraternity. In comparison with liberty and equality, the idea
of fraternity has had a lesser place in democratic theory. It is thought to be less specifically a political concept, not in itself defining any of the democratic rights
but conveying instead certain attitudes of mind and
forms of conduct without which we would lose sight of
the values expressed by these rights. Or closely related
to this, fraternity is held to represent a certain equality
of social esteem manifest in various public conventions
and in the absence of manners of deference and servility. No doubt fraternity does imply these things, as well
as a sense of civic friendship and social solidarity, but
so understood it expresses no definite requirement. We
have yet to find a principle of justice that matches the
underlying idea. The difference principle, however,
does seem to correspond to a natural meaning of fraternity: namely, to the idea of not wanting to have
greater advantages unless this is to the benefit of others who are less well off. The family, in its ideal conception and often in practice, is one place where the
principle of maximizing the sum of advantages is rejected. Members of a family commonly do not wish to
gain unless they can do so in ways that further the interests of the rest. Now wanting to act on the difference
principle has precisely this consequence. Those better
circumstanced are willing to have their greater advantages only under a scheme in which this works out for
the benefit of the less fortunate.

The ideal of fraternity is sometimes thought to involve ties of sentiment and feeling which it is unrealistic to expect between members of the wider society.
And this is surely a further reason for its relative neglect in democratic theory. Many have felt that it has
no proper place in political affairs. But if it is interpreted
as incorporating the requirements of the difference

principle, it is not an impracticable conception. It does seem that the institutions and policies which we most confidently think to be just satisfy its demands, at least in the sense that the inequalities permitted by them contribute to the well-being of the less favored. On this interpretation, then, the principle of fraternity is a perfectly feasible standard. Once we accept it we can associate the traditional ideas of liberty, equality, and fraternity with the democratic interpretation of the two principles of justice as follows: liberty corresponds to the first principle, equality to the idea of equality in the first principle together with equality of fair opportunity, and fraternity to the difference principle. In this way we have found a place for the conception of fraternity in the democratic interpretation of the two principles, and we see that it imposes a definite requirement on the basic structure of society. The other aspects of fraternity should not be forgotten, but the difference principle expresses its fundamental meaning from the standpoint of social justice.

Now it seems evident in the light of these observations that the democratic interpretation of the two principles will not lead to a meritocratic society. This form of social order follows the principle of careers open to talents and uses equality of opportunity as a way of releasing men's energies in the pursuit of economic prosperity and political dominion. There exists a marked disparity between the upper and lower classes in both means of life and the rights and privileges of organizational authority. The culture of the poorer strata is impoverished while that of the governing and technocratic elite is securely based on the service of the national ends of power and wealth. Equality of opportunity means an equal chance to leave the less fortunate behind in the personal quest for influence and social position. Thus a meritocratic society is a danger for the other interpretations of the principles of justice but not for the democratic conception. For, as we have just seen, the difference principle transforms the aims of society in fundamental respects. This consequence is even more obvious once we note that we must when necessary take into account the essential primary good of self-respect and the fact that a well-ordered society is a social union of social unions. It follows that the confident sense of their own worth should be sought for the least favored and this limits the forms of hierarchy and the degrees of inequality that justice permits. Thus, for example, resources for education are not to be allotted solely or necessarily mainly according to their return as estimated in productive trained abilities, but also according to their worth in enriching the personal and social life of citizens, including here the less favored. As a society progresses the latter consideration becomes increasingly more important.

THE BASIS OF EQUALITY

We have yet to consider what sorts of beings are owed the guarantees of justice. . . . The natural answer seems to be that it is precisely the moral persons who are entitled to equal justice. Moral persons are distinguished by two features: first they are capable of having (and are assumed to have) a conception of their good (as expressed by a rational plan of life); and second they are capable of having (and assumed to acquire) a sense of justice, a normally effective desire to apply and to act upon the principles of justice, at least to a certain minimum degree. We use the characterization of the persons in the original position to single out the kind of beings to whom the principles chosen apply. After all, the parties are thought of as adopting these criteria to regulate their common institutions and their conduct toward one another; and the description of their nature enters into the reasoning by which these principles are selected. Thus equal justice is owed to those who have the capacity to take part in and to act in accordance with the public understanding of the initial situation. One should observe that moral personality is here defined as a potentiality that is ordinarily realized in due course. It is this potentiality which brings the claims of justice into play. . . .

We see, then, that the capacity for moral personality is a sufficient condition for being entitled to equal justice. Nothing beyond the essential minimum is required. . . .

It should be stressed that the sufficient condition for equal justice, the capacity for moral personality, is not at all stringent. When someone lacks the requisite potentiality either from birth or accident, this is regarded as a defect or deprivation. There is no race or recognized group of human beings that lacks this attribute. Only scattered individuals are without this capacity, or its realization to the minimum degree, and the failure to realize it is the consequence of unjust and impoverished social circumstances, or fortuitous contingencies. Furthermore, while individuals presumably have varying capacities for a sense of justice, this fact is not a reason for depriving those with a lesser capacity of the full protection of justice. Once a certain minimum is met, a person is entitled to equal liberty on a par with everyone else. . . . It is sometimes thought that basic rights and liberties should vary with capacity, but justice as fairness denies this: provided the minimum for moral personality is satisfied, a person is owed all the guarantees of justice.

This account of the basis of equality calls for a few comments. First of all, it may be objected that equality cannot rest on natural attributes. There is no natural feature with respect to which all human beings are equal, that is, which everyone has (or which sufficiently many have) to the same degree. It might appear that if we wish to hold a doctrine of equality, we must interpret it in another way, namely as a purely procedural principle. Thus to say that human beings are equal is to say that none has a claim to preferential treatment in the absence of compelling reasons. The burden of proof favors equality: it defines a procedural presumption that persons are to be treated alike. Departures from equal treatment are in each case to be defended and judged impartially by the same system of principles that hold for all: the essential equality is thought to be equality of consideration.

There are several difficulties with this procedural interpretation. For one thing, it is nothing more than the precept of treating similar cases similarly applied at the highest level, together with an assignment of the burden of proof. Equality of consideration puts no restrictions upon what grounds may be offered to justify inequalities. There is no guarantee of substantive equal treatment, since slave and caste systems (to mention extreme cases) may satisfy this conception. The real assurance of equality lies in the content of the principles of justice and not in these procedural presumptions. The placing of the burden of proof is not sufficient. But further, even if the procedural interpretation imposed some genuine restriction on institutions, there is still the question why we are to follow the procedure in some instances and not others. Surely it applies to creatures who belong to some class, but which one? We still need a natural basis for equality so that this class can be identified.

Moreover, it is not the case that founding equality on natural capacities is incompatible with an egalitarian view. All we have to do is select a range property (as I shall say) and to give equal justice to those meeting its conditions. For example, the property of being in the interior of the unit circle is a range property of points in the plane. All points inside this circle have this property although their coordinates vary within a certain range. And they equally have this property,

since no point interior to a circle is more or less interior to it than any other interior point. Now whether there is a suitable range property for singling out the respect in which human beings are to be counted equal is settled by the conception of justice. But the description of the parties in the original position identifies such a property, and the principles of justice assure us that any variations in ability within the range are to be regarded as any other natural asset. There is no obstacle to thinking that a natural capacity constitutes the basis of equality.

Mutual respect is a natural duty due to a moral agent as a being with a sense of justice and a conception of the good. . . . Mutual respect is shown in several ways: in our willingness to see the situation of others from their point of view, from the perspective of their conception of their good; and in our being prepared to give reasons for our actions whenever the interests of others are materially affected. . . .

[T]he public recognition of the two principles gives greater support to men's self-respect and this in turn increases the effectiveness of social cooperation. Both effects are reasons for choosing these principles. It is clearly rational for men to secure their self-respect. A sense of their own worth is necessary if they are to pursue their conception of the good with zest and to delight in its fulfillment. Self-respect is not so much a part of any rational plan of life as the sense that one's plan is worth carrying out. Now our self-respect normally depends upon the respect of others. Unless we feel that our endeavors are honored by them, it is difficult if not impossible for us to maintain the conviction that our ends are worth advancing. Hence for this reason the parties would accept the natural duty of mutual respect which asks them to treat one another civilly and to be willing to explain the grounds of their actions, especially when the claims of others are overruled. Moreover, one may assume that those who respect themselves are more likely to respect each other and conversely. Self-contempt leads to contempt of others and threatens their good as much as envy does. Self-respect is reciprocally self-supporting. . . .

[People need] to be assured by the esteem of their associates. Their self-respect and their confidence in the value of their own system of ends cannot withstand the indifference much less the contempt of others. Everyone benefits then from living in a society where the duty of mutual respect is honored. The cost to self-interest is minor in comparison with the support for the sense of one's own worth.

THE FINAL FORMULATION OF THE PRINCIPLES OF JUSTICE

I now wish to give the final statement of the two principles of justice for institutions. For the sake of completeness, I shall give a full statement including earlier formulations.

First Principle Each person is to have an equal right to the most extensive total system of equal basic liberties compatible with a similar system of liberty for all.

Second Principle Social and economic inequalities are to be arranged so that they are both

a. to the greatest benefit of the least advantaged, consistent with the just savings principle, and

b. attached to offices and positions open to all under conditions of fair equality of opportunity.

First Priority Rule (The Priority of Liberty) The principles of justice are to be ranked in lexical order and therefore liberty can be restricted only for the sake of liberty. There are two cases:

a. a less extensive liberty must strengthen the total system of liberty shared for all;

b. a less than equal liberty must be acceptable to those with the lesser liberty.

Second Priority Rule (The Priority of Justice over Efficiency and Welfare) The second principle of justice is lexically prior to the principle of efficiency and to that of maximizing the sum of advantages; and fair opportunity is prior to the difference principle. There are two cases:

a. an inequality of opportunity must enhance the opportunities of those with the lesser opportunity;

b. an excessive rate of saving must on balance mitigate the burden of those bearing this hardship.

General Conception All social primary goods—liberty and opportunity, income and wealth, and the bases of self-respect—are to be distributed equally unless an unequal distribution of any or all of these goods is to the advantage of the least favored.

By way of comment, these principles and priority rules are no doubt incomplete. Other modifications will surely have to be made, but I shall not further complicate the statement of the principles. It suffices to observe that when we come to nonideal theory, we do not fall back straightway upon the general conception of justice. The lexical ordering of the two principles, and the valuations that this ordering implies, suggest priority rules which seem to be reasonable enough in many cases. By various examples I have tried to illustrate how these rules can be used and to indicate their plausibility. Thus the ranking of the principles of justice in ideal theory reflects back and guides the application of these principles to nonideal situations. It identifies which limitations need to be dealt with first. The drawback of the general conception of justice is that it lacks the definite structure of the two principles in serial order. In more extreme and tangled instances of nonideal theory there may be no alternative to it. At some point the priority of rules for nonideal cases will fail; and indeed, we may be able to find no satisfactory answer at all. But we must try to postpone the day of reckoning as long as possible, and try to arrange society so that it never comes. . . .

READING 27

Justice: A Funeral Oration

Wallace Matson

Wallace Matson is Professor Emeritus of Philosophy at the University of California–Berkeley and is the author of several books including *A New History of Philosophy* (1987) and *The Existence of God* (1965).

Matson claims that "philosophers such as John Rawls [Reading 26] have filched the name Justice from rendering-each-his-due and bestowed it on doling-out - pleasure - experiences - equally - all-around, the doling to be done by philosopher kings. These thinkers either do not perceive or do not care about the incompatibility of pseudojustice with liberty." In this reading, Matson contrasts justice based on voluntary agreements with justice based on the will of government.

This reading is taken from *Social Philosophy and Policy* 1 (1983), by permission.

> The auncient Ciuilians do say justice is a wille perpetuall and constaunt, which gyueth to euery man his right.
>
> —Sir Thomas Elyot, 1531

TAX JUSTICE: IT'S IN YOUR INTEREST! . . . The military budget seems to have replaced human needs as a priority. . . . UC employees have a right to a job and a living wage. . . . To insure this right, AFSCME is asking UC employees to support the *Split Roll Tax Initiative*, which will redistribute the benefits of Proposition 13 among residents and renters, while taking a fair share from commerce. Along with other tax equality measures . . . this will put the state budget back on its feet. . . . PUBLIC EMPLOYEES NEED TAX JUSTICE IN CALIFORNIA!

> —From a manifesto handed out in Berkeley, 1982

1. THRENODY

Is it any longer possible to talk seriously about justice and rights? Are these words corrupted and debased beyond redemption? There is no need to multiply examples of how anything that any pressure group has the chutzpah to lay claim to forthwith becomes a right, *nemine contradicente.* Nor is this Newspeak restricted to the vulgar. The President of the Pacific Division of the American Philosophical Association has granted permission to misuse words like *rights* and *justice* if you do so in the service of desirable political ends.[1] Our most universally acclaimed theoretician of justice [John Rawls, see Reading 26] has shown at length that justice is a will perpetual and constant to forcibly take goods from those who have earned them and give them to those who have not;[2] and the leading light of Anglo-American jurisprudence [Ronald Dworkin, see Reading 33] has constructed a "straightforward" argument proving that a citizen's right to equal protection of the laws is fully satisfied if only the bureaucrat denying him or her a public benefit on racial grounds shows "respect and concern" while processing the forms.[3]

Linguistic entropy makes it as futile to try to rehabilitate mutilated words as to put toothpaste back in the tube. The semantic battle has been lost; and with it a lot more than perspicuous speech. From Plato onward ideologues have sought to capture the vocabulary of justice, the paradigm of OK words, and tie it to schemes aiming at doing away with rights and justice. Now they have brought it off. A single generation has witnessed the movement of enlightened thought away from the position that any discrimination in treatment based merely on race is a grievous wrong, all the way to a consensus that forgetting about race and treating people as individuals is proof positive of racism, and people who advocate it should be ostracized and deprived of the protection of the First Amendment. It took the Supreme Court hardly a decade to discover that the Civil Rights Act of 1964, which in the plainest and clearest language ever seen in a statute [that] condemned racial quotas, really encouraged or even mandated them. Scarcely less abrupt has been the transformation of admiration and fostering of excellence into the vice of elitism. The deepest philosophico-legal thinker of the western United States has preached against the immorality of requiring any applicant for any job to possess qualifications for it.[4] At the other end of the country lives another heavyweight moralist who can imagine no worse injustice than paying smart people more than dumb people.[5]

Why then am I writing about justice? What can arguments accomplish anyway? The windmills of the *Zeitgeist* ["spirit of the times"] keep right on turning. I write also about the interpretation of Parmenides (5th century B.C.). The one activity is likely to produce about as much change in the world as the other.

2. A TALE OF THE SOUTH SEAS

The island of Alpha is not on any chart and is claimed by no nation. It is a delightful place with abundant vegetation which when properly cultivated yields delicious groceries. The lagoon abounds in succulent fish. There are plenty of materials for shelter, clothing, whatever you need or desire and know how to make.

A, the sole inhabitant, who arrived on Alpha quite by accident, works a not excessively fatiguing forty-hour week producing all he wants save companionship, and being satisfied, makes no attempt to attract rescuers.

In this situation, Aristotle has told us, no questions of just and unjust can arise. One cannot be unjust to oneself "except metaphorically," and there is no one else for A to be unjust to, or vice versa.

Beta is an island near Alpha but quite unlike it: barren, plagued by vermin. It too has but one inhabitant, B, who also arrived by accident. B lives at the brink of starvation, laboriously scratching the soil to grow the single, foul-tasting, barely edible plant found on the island.

A and B do not communicate nor even know of each other's existence.

The condition of B is pitiable, but there is no more cause for talk of injustice on Beta than on Alpha. Can it be said, however, that the state of affairs consisting of A on Alpha and B on Beta is an unjust state of affairs? A and B are certainly unequal, which condition benefits neither of them, and it has been said that injustice is simply inequalities that are not to the advantage of all. Nevertheless, it would be bizarre to contend that the situation contains injustice. B's condition is unfortunate but not unjust (nor just either). The mere coexistence of A without interaction cannot add a new moral dimension.

So let us add some interaction and see what happens.

There are no materials on Beta for making a boat or raft, and the strait between the islands is shark-infested. So B cannot go to Alpha. And A has no incentive to go to Beta. But now a volcano emerges from the sea, and when it has cooled there is a land bridge making Alpha and Beta one island.

Let us consider the time interval when B can enter the Alpha district but has not actually done so. We have then a single territory containing two inhabitants, one of whom is in possession of fewer goods than the other. Is this a condition of injustice?

The difference is only that now it is feasible to equalize the conditions of A and B whereas previously it was not. If there is injustice it consists in the unequal possessions of A and B and can be remedied by taking from A and giving to B. But then it cannot be the case that the injustice arose when the islands became connected; it must rather have existed previously but only at that moment become remediable. (Murder is murder whether or not it can be punished.) But this would be contrary to our conclusion that no injustice arose from the mere comparison of the two conditions.

None of this will surprise us. We knew that justice is a social concept; so as long as A and B were in-communicado the notion had no application. If we now arrange for them to meet and converse, no injustice can be deemed to have arisen here either. How could it? B is now conscious of being worse off than A, and will no doubt feel envy, will want to share in A's bounty. B may even complain of "unjust fate," but that can only be poetry. The change has been only in knowledge; and the previous absence of injustice did not depend on ignorance.

Various things may happen when B sets foot on Alpha territory. Let us consider some of the possibilities.

Case I. Suppose the Alpha territory is a land of such abundance that it cannot be exploited by A alone; there are resources that A does not need and cannot make use of. It is no injustice if B now appropriates some or all of these goods. Nothing has been taken to which A has established any claim, nor has A been harmed.

But what if A regards B as a threat or nuisance? Would injustice be committed if A chased B out of the area or took even more drastic measures? It is hard to see what the charge could be based on, if A and B have held no converse. On a right to be let alone if one is behaving peaceably? But what if A is a lady and B is a tiger?—a possibility not ruled out by any of our suppositions. Is it not permissible to drive tigers away from one's vicinity, even if in fact the tiger has only peaceable intentions? If so, how is the situation changed if instead of a tiger one is confronted with another human being of unknown intent?

Case II. Zucchini does not grow wild in Alpha; all that there is has been cultivated by A, but there is more of it than A can possibly make use of. Would injustice arise if B should appropriate some of the surplus without A's consent? Hardly, for the surplus does not constitute a good for A, even though he produced it. Whatever happens to it is a matter of indifference as far as A is concerned; and if A is not made any worse off there can be no injustice.

Case III. Is the moral situation altered if the produce with which B absconds is something necessary for A's dinner? Well, again, if B is a tiger, we should not want to say that it is guilty of injustice, however inconvenient its conduct may be for A. And how should it differ if B is human? Both the tiger and the man are hungry, perceive an opportunity to eat, and take it. If they do fight it out, "like animals," no question of justice arises. But if A and B are human (as we shall henceforth assume) they may have an alternative not generally available to the brute creature: they can communicate, talk things over, and reach some settlement of the question "Who gets what?" that is more advantageous for one or the other or both than direct and, perhaps, uncertain combat.

3. INTERMISSION

There are in Alpha two classes of things: those which exist, or exist in altered form, or in the place where they are, because of the labor of A; and those that do not, but would be just as they are even if A had never been there. The first class of things consists of cultivated plants, constructed shelter, utensils, fish hooks, woodpiles, and the like. Call them the Artifacts. It is characteristic of human beings to labor to produce artifacts. The essence of life—any kind of life—consists in doing, acting; production of things is one important kind of doing. This means, in the human case, experiencing a need or at least a desire for something; picturing to oneself the advantage of possessing that thing; making a plan to bring it into existence or into one's possession; and expending effort to that end according to a developed pattern of skill. We speak of this in terms of the Will and its satisfaction. When all goes well we end up having what we want, and sometimes we are better off thereby. Not to be able to carry out one's own projects in this way but to serve only the interests of others is so far not to live a human life. Extreme deprivation of this kind is slavery.

Most projects are recognized to be more or less chancy. The compassing of material ends may be frustrated by droughts, earthquakes, diseases, wild beasts, etc. Any animal can be viewed as a device for sorting out its dinner and other necessities from an environment in which the constituents occur more or less at random. And the whole process may be got through successfully and then at the last moment the desired product is snatched away, as with the Old Man in Hemingway's story. None of these frustrations is literally immoral. Tigers are not murderers and coyotes are not thieves.

To a certain extent the same attitude may be taken to other human beings, if they are strangers, not in one's group: forces of nature to be coped with as best one can. It is different, however, within the tribe. That is a group within which it is taken for granted that at least some cooperation will be extended.

People may help one another because they are forced to by threats or punishment, but that negates essential humanity. Voluntary assistance must be based on some community of goals.

4. THE TALE CONTINUED

Case IV. Let us now suppose that A and B confer. Let us suppose further that A has not produced any more artifacts than he can himself use and consume, but he has been so skillful and industrious that his production comprises considerably more than he requires for mere survival. Let us refer to the difference between A's total store and what he needs for bare survival as A's quasi-surplus.

This is what A has to bargain with. It seems that he cannot concede more than it to B, for if he does he cannot survive, so he might as well fight. A's aim in negotiating will be to give up as little of the quasi-surplus as possible to B, and to get in exchange for it as much as he can from B.

What can B bargain with? He has no surplus at all; indeed, to make the situation even starker we may assume that the earthquake destroyed Beta so that B is entirely destitute. This would, however, merely increase A's problem, for if no bargain can be struck, B will fight, which we assume A wants to avoid. Let us suppose that B can survive only if ceded 150% of A's quasi-surplus. Does it follow that there must be war to the death? No, fortunately, because if B pitches in and helps, the production of artifacts in Alpha may increase to the point where both A and B can survive. In other words, B can contribute his labor even if he lacks material resources. It turns out, then, that A can cede more than his quasi-surplus as long as the excess is made up by the added effort.

The upshot is that both A and B may be individually better off for making an agreement to share goods and labor than either one would have been if they fought winner-take-all.

Perhaps truce would be a better word than agreement for the arrangement that A and B set up. For the question of course arises, What is to prevent either party from violating the provisions of the pact when he sees fit? And the answer can only be: Nothing. We can expect no more than that each party will abide by the pact as long as it is in his interest to do so. But it was in the interest of both parties to conclude the treaty in the first place; it remains in the interest of each party to see to it that the other one remains in the same situation; and it will not be impossible in general for him to do so. Covenants without the sword are but words, true; but each of our covenantors has and retains his sword.

Even in this simplified situation the particulars of the compact might take indefinitely many different forms, depending on the amount of A's armaments and other resources in relation to B's, their bargaining skills, and their preferences. They might agree to pool their resources (notwithstanding A's initial advantage) and share alike; or erect a fence across the island not henceforth to be crossed by either without the other's permission; or agree that B should go to work for A five days in seven at a fixed wage. Or B might consent to become A's slave. What any such compact is, though, is an acquiescence of wills in the restriction of their own future objects. For A to cede a shovel to B is for A to renounce the satisfaction of any future desire he might have to dig with that particular shovel. B in his turn denies himself liberty to kill, disable, or maim A.

The transaction is fraught with momentous consequences. *First,* there are now obligations—bonds—between A and B; to this extent at least they form a community. They have set up rules, and they ought to abide by them. This ought, to be sure, is a prudential ought: the sanction, the consequence of nonconformity, is that the truce will be called off, and the parties will again be in danger of physical attack by each other, which they both want to avoid. To avoid resumption of war over minor infractions of the truce conditions, they may agree on methods of restitution. There will be problems about determining when a rule has been violated, as there are in tennis without an umpire, but they need not be insurmountable.

Second, A and B have invented property, at least if there are any clauses in the treaty specifying that any artifacts or other objects, or parcels of land, are to be off limits to one party without the consent of the other. Ownership is acknowledged, exclusive control of use or access.

But was there not already property before the truce? What about the artifacts A had labored to produce? Were not they, at least, already his?

John Locke's argument is that a man owns his own body; therefore he owns the labor of his body; therefore whatever he "mixes" that labor with becomes *pro tanto* an extension of his body; therefore he owns it too. The argument gets off to a bad start: "I own my own body" may look like a truism but it hardly is. It is a question of fact whether one has acknowledged, ex-

clusive control of the use of one's body, and there are people for whom the answer is No. No doubt that is not as it should be; but we are talking of how things are. And while it is true that before B appeared on the scene A had exclusive control of the use of his own body, the exclusive control was not acknowledged. It takes two to make property.

When A and B draw up their treaty there is no limitation in principle to what they may agree to be the property of one and of the other, or to be held in common or left subject to subsequent claim. There is nothing about the axe that A has laboriously constructed from scratch that makes it his property, or property at all: no more than a tree that he plans to cut down, perhaps, some time next year and saw into boards. Nevertheless, there is something more than sentiment making the relation between a man and that with which he has "mixed his labor" particularly intimate and fit to be legitimized, as it were, by acknowledgment of ownership. Labor need not be unpleasant always, but it is generally engaged in not for its own sake but because some comprehensive plan requires it; the agent envisages some end, the production of something, the enjoyment of which is viewed a good in itself; he plans how to get it; and realizing that work is indispensable, he works. To deprive a man of some good thing that he got by luck, without effort, is indeed to frustrate him; but to take away the product of his labor is to do double damage. He has undergone the hardship of toil, and in vain. He would not have put up with the drudgery if he had known of the outcome in advance. So it is impossible to suppose that anyone would voluntarily forgo the enjoyment—which means the ownership—of what he has mixed his labor with, unless in exchange for some other good perceived as of at least equivalent value. This means that in the terms of the truce between A and B, possession of their respective artifacts will be guaranteed to them unless they receive compensation. And since A and B begin their negotiations with each in physical possession of his artifacts, it is, to be sure, as if they had property to begin with. Moreover, this concern that each has for what he produces shapes the form that their agreement will take. It is to the continuing interest of each that each should keep on producing things. Therefore the truce will contain provisions for maintaining production, which must recognize and respect the producer's ownership of his product or allow compensation if it is to be taken from him; otherwise there could remain no motive to keep it going, unless sheer fear, which is incompatible with the primary aim of the agreement.

And so, *third* and finally, we see in this agreement the genesis of rights and justice. The truce once agreed to will remain in force only as long as both parties find its continuance to their advantage. Now, some truces are made for stipulated, definite periods of time, but not this one, since the motive for making it is to avoid combat altogether. Hence it has no expiration date and cannot be abrogated by mutual consent. Breaking it is a unilateral act of war and will provoke the indignation of the other party, who was willing to continue it and was living up to it. This is enough to generate the use of moral language, supposing it has not up to now been current. One has a *right* to have the terms adhered to; failure to observe the terms on which one has agreed is *injustice*. Even if derelictions in this regard are initially only violations of a prudential ought, they are very serious, as tending to bring about the dissolution of community. Moreover the prudence they offend against is primarily not that of the agent himself but of his fellow citizen; in consequence of which objections are bound to take on a moral tone.

Thomas Hobbes held that to enter into society is to give up at least some rights, whereas I am claiming that there are no rights outside community. This is perhaps a verbal point, but hardly of no consequence. Hobbes's Right of Nature, an absolute "right to all things," is anomalous in that it has no correlative duty. In the state of nature I have the right to appropriate your shovel or hit you over the head, but that does not mean that you have any duty to submit or to refrain from doing the same to me. The sense of "right" in this context, then, seems to be only "not subject to moral censure," or as a hockey player not in the penalty box has a right to pass the puck. But this is at least a misleading way of speaking; the thought is more straightforwardly conveyed simply by saying that before any agreements have been made, questions of right and wrong in the moral sense cannot arise.

The objection might be raised that this truce cannot be the origin of justice and rights, for it might be asked of the truce itself, Is it a just agreement? Does it not, or could it not, infringe on the rights of a party?

But it is a logical point about justice that injustice cannot be suffered voluntarily, as Aristotle saw. And the truce is not only concluded but maintained voluntarily.

This reply may be thought unsatisfactory on the ground that the parties are not equal in their bargaining positions. Hence one (A) may get the better of the bargain, i.e., be in a better position after concluding it than the other party (B). Indeed, as I admitted, one form the agreement might take would be for B to make himself A's slave. But this or any other inequitable arrangement would be manifestly unjust. And it is not only absurd but morally repugnant to suggest that a slave would be behaving unjustly, violating his master's rights, if he subsequently rebelled (broke the truce). Furthermore, no such desperate engagement could be voluntarily undertaken.

I answer: First, the view that any inequality is *ipso facto* unjust is mere dogma. It is certainly not self-evidently true, for *prima facie* it is not unjust to pay travel money and honoraria to learned persons who participate in enlightening conferences on justice. The objection based on slavery is more serious. I do not assert with complete confidence that a person might voluntarily agree to become a slave. In practice there are, of course, degrees of slavery; but I suppose the concept is of one whose will is entirely subordinate to another's, one who never makes plans of his own and carries them out. Galley slavery must approximate this condition. If that is so, then the question whether one can voluntarily become a slave seems to be the same as whether the will can voluntarily negate itself permanently. If as I maintain the essence of life is the exertion of will, then the slave is as good as dead.

But not quite. Where there is life there is hope. Probably the only circumstances in which one would choose slavery would be where the only alternative was death. And a choice being between unpleasant alternatives does not make it no choice. If the terms of our truce involve my becoming your slave, then we form a community within which you have a right to all my services and I have no right to pursue any interest of mine independent of yours; and *within that community* I act unjustly if I do anything for myself. But let us not forget that according to the view being presented I may choose at any time to abrogate the truce and bring the community to an end. In practice, then, a community consisting of one master and one slave is likely to be unstable, the slave always on the lookout for the opportune moment to get out of that status. In other words, it is a sort of degenerate case of community, hardly distinguishable from a lull in a state of war.

5. MORALS OF THE STORY

A novelist would tell the tale differently, but to much the same effect. Actual people in this sort of situation, if not murderously inclined or forced by extreme scarcity to climinate competition, will come to some agreement, perhaps tacit, of the form "I'll let you alone if you let me alone; and I'll help you out from time to time if you reciprocate." Appropriation by one of things the other had made, or even just found, would be regarded as stealing and if serious would lead to conflict.

That is to say, they would establish a community and a system of justice based on agreement. This can be called justice "from the bottom up:" it is not imposed on them by any superior force, for there isn't any. It comes from their mutual apprehension of necessary conditions for human beings, each with his own interests and plans, to dwell in close proximity without fighting. It can fittingly be called natural, being a direct consequence of what human life is about, the expression of human capabilities in achieving planned goals in those universal and unavoidable circumstances of existence of a semigregarious species.

However, there is, as we have seen, no constraint on the particular form of the truce. It must represent what the parties to it, not in some hypothetical and abstract condition but in concrete circumstances of their existence, can agree on as preferable to direct physical confrontation. In particular it does not presuppose equality of power in the bargaining situation, or of talents or industry, or of luck, or of the distribution of goods that result, or of anything except that all parties have equal rights to insist on the equal observance of those clauses of the treaty in which their particular interests are safeguarded. Nevertheless, natural justice if it does not (necessarily) start from an initial position of equality and does not guarantee eventual achievement of it, yet facilitates betterment of the individual's position through effort. That is what its main purpose is: to make it possible for plans to be carried out without arbitrary interference and frustration by fellow members of the community. Even in our story, destitute B will probably be able to come to terms with prosperous A that will make it possible for him through hard work to approach A's level of luxurious consumption. Remember: the harsher the terms A attempts to impose on B, the greater danger he runs of B's abrogating the truce.

The story is not a myth of the origin of government; it is Lockean, not Hobbist. There is no Sovereign set up to whom all owe deference and who has a monopoly of power wherewith to coerce the intractable; there are only the individuals with whatever resources they happen to command. As Locke noted, such an arrangement will be attended with certain inconveniences showing, for example, a need for impartial umpires and arbitrators. How it might come about (after a

few more castaways had landed) that a central authority would be set up, and what its functions would or should be, is another topic. But the institutions and conceptions of right and justice would antedate the formation of such an authority, the operations of which would be liable to criticism from the standpoint of justice. So much seems incontrovertible; the Hobbesian contention to the contrary is paradoxical and carries no conviction.

Lest this analysis be regarded as excessively hardboiled, note that the conception of justice as observance of rules agreed on from the motive of self-interest by no means precludes the existence and importance in the community of interactions in which the requirements of justice are voluntarily held in abeyance: love and charity. Indeed it is what makes them possible: one cannot simultaneously make love and war.

Finally we observe that nothing precludes the extension of the truce to later arrivals. The conditions may have to be modified for their benefit; the arrival of a third castaway would so perturb the relations of A and B that there might have to be a new constitutional convention, as it were. But not for every new immigrant; as population grows we may expect the weight of existing agreement to impose itself on latecomers in a take-it-or-leave-it fashion.

And what is the bearing of this story and its morals on actual human affairs? This: We have been examining the kinds of relations other than out-and-out no-holds-barred conflict that can subsist between human beings; we have concluded that peace might be based on agreement; that the agreement cannot be expected to outlast its advantageousness to all parties; that the terms of agreement define what justice is, and what the rights of the parties are, within the community of those in agreement—in particular and most importantly it creates the rights of property. The normative character of the rights so specified is derived from the fact—so we have contended—that persons wishing each to attain his own goals in the context of association with other persons, would agree to them.

However, we have been assuming that human plans to achieve particular separate goals sometimes lead to conflict; and that conflict if serious will be settled by force unless the rivals can arrive at some compromise. But is it the case that human animals are necessarily motivated by individual "selfish" interests? Is it not possible—maybe sometimes actual—that they could as it were submerge their own interests into one big interest, the general welfare, the pursuit of which would involve only peaceful cooperation?

6. SOUTH SEAS TALE II

B, oppressed by the harsh terms of the truce with A but impotent to revolt, has thought of a way out. Every week he spends the one afternoon he has to himself in collecting branches and vines from the little forest plot that A has not claimed. At last one day, having secretly made a raft, he scratches in the sand an insulting note to A and paddles off into the open sea.

After many hardships he struggles onto the shore of another island. From between the palms a majestic bearded figure appears.

Alas, B thinks to himself, here we go again. More truce terms!

But no. "Welcome to Gamma, O stranger" the figure intones in a kindly voice "I am G. You must be hungry and thirsty. Won't you join us for dinner?"

At the groaning board B is introduced to the other islanders; F, an old man confined to a wheelchair; H, a mature and handsome woman; J, a lad of seventeen or so; and two children, K and L.

Over the coffee and liqueurs B deems the time opportune for discussing their future arrangements. "I'm grateful for your tacit temporary truce," he begins, "and hope you can make it permanent."

"Truce? What ever do you mean?"

"Why, the usual—I won't try to kill you as long as you don't—"

Consternation and alarm among the Gammanians. H grasps K and L protectively in her arms. Desperately trying to scurry out of the way, F overturns his wheelchair. J grabs a silver candlestick and advances menacingly on B but is restrained by G, who at last restores a modicum of calm.

B then explains how things are done on Alpha. The Gammanians weep at the sad tale. H comforts him that he has arrived finally in a civilized community.

"But how can you get along without a truce?" B is still puzzled. "Don't you have your individual interests and goals, and don't you have to have some means of reconciling the conflicts to which they inevitably give rise?"

"Well," the youthful J begins to reply, "Sometimes I—"

But G cuts him off. "Not at all. We have only one goal, which is the good life for us all. Each of us helps to achieve it in any way that he or she can, and each gets all the help he or she needs from all the rest. From each according to his ability; to each according to his need."

"Just like one big happy family," B muses, dimly recalling childhood scenes.

"Of course," says G. "That's what we are—a family!"

"But what happens if you have different ideas about what your needs are?"

A suggestion of a frown appears on J's face, and he seems to exchange a significant glance with H; but G replies: "Oh, sometimes there is some perplexity about that, but when there is, we handle it democratically."

"You mean, you have a discussion and then vote on the different proposals?"

"Not exactly," says G. "I listen to what everybody has to say, and then I explain what the wise thing to do is. As everybody here is rational, they all concur, and that's that.—From now on, we all want you to feel that you are one of the family.—You must be tired. H will make your bed in the dormitory. Tomorrow after breakfast J will show you the woodpile and get you started—I take it you know something about wood-chopping?—"

And so they lived happily ever after.

7. ANOTHER BATCH OF MORALS

Within the family—I mean the "traditional" family as found (say) in the novels of Jane Austen and Samuel Butler—there is little concern for justice in the sense of giving each member his or her rights. Ordinarily there is one "breadwinner," the father, who is the sole or at least principal source of income, most of which is disbursed for the common benefit of all. Where it is used to buy things for individuals, the principle of distribution is need not merit; the snaggle-toothed daughter must have her orthodontia before the musical prodigy acquires a Steinway. And if the old folks and infants are helpless and only a drain on resources, their needs must nevertheless be provided. Competitiveness plays no part, or at least it is deplored when it does. This is called Love.

Most philosophers now writing experienced family life more or less along these lines when they were young, or at least were able to view it close up. And it may seem a more satisfactory way to order relations between people than "justice" with its stern judgments and devil-take-the-hindmost attitude. The transition from the warm nurturing environment of the family to the cold and impersonal rat-race in which the independent individual is caught up may be as traumatic as birth itself. That is doubtless one reason why the family is preferred by so many to the treaty as the proper model for human relationships.

Another is that it is inherently equalitarian. Within the ideal family all members are equal in a number of respects. There is no distinction of rich and poor; if one member has more expended on him, it is not so that he can enjoy a higher "standard of living." One does not have higher status than another or receive more deference. (Again, this is the ideal; but it is why we feel that something is wrong in the household where Cinderella lives.) Parents are careful to treat all their children fairly, which means dividing up benefits equally unless one has greater need than another; the notion of "earning" hardly enters except in comparatively trivial ways mostly concerned with putative training for the rat-race to come; and even here the experts tend to deprecate it. Granted that intrafamilial conflicts, notably sibling rivalry, have always occurred, they are—or used to be—considered superficial and due to immaturity. Universal brotherhood has been taken as synonymous with the elimination of human conflicts.

"Why can't the whole human race, or at least the whole nation, be like that?" the philosopher asks, and so do the plain man and woman. The plain man is likely to answer, "Because family relations are based on affection, which won't stretch that far." So do some philosophers, e.g., Hobbes in commenting on the perpetual state of war "in many places of *America,* except the government of small Families, the concord whereof dependeth on natural lust."[6] But many others, of whom the first and greatest was Plato, have maintained that the project is not impossible; all that is needed is a salutary revision of education and institutional arrangements, whereupon paternal, maternal, filial, fraternal, and sororal affection will become the cement binding together a completely unified and, therefore, happy social order in which everyone cares for everyone else.

These philosophers base their optimism on the belief that so-called human nature is all nurture, there is no limit to how outlooks and motivations can be altered by training. This is held as a dogma by many social thinkers, like creationism among fundamentalists. But also like creationism, it is an empirical question whether it is true. A lot of evidence is in, all of it adverse: the utter failure of every attempt whether on a large scale or small, to produce the requisite changes (with the doubtful and minor exception of Israeli kibbutzim).

The explanation of this dismal history is provided by the science of sociobiology. But is it altogether regrettable that human beings cannot be improved to fill the bill? If we scrutinize the family model more closely we may find that it has less pleasant aspects.

If there is no conflict within the ideal family, it is because there is only one will, or only one that counts: father's. Husband and wife being "one flesh," the woman's will is held to coincide with her man's. ("Man's happiness is: I will. Woman's happiness is: He wills."—Nietzsche.) The children are under tutelage, their wills are being formed, and are not to be regarded as competent in their own right. When in adolescence they begin to develop wills of their own and assert them, that is the well-known revolt against parental authority and the first step in exit from the familial hearth.

The totalitarian implications, when the family is held up as a model for emulation by the larger community, are obvious. If they are not seen immediately it is because within the family the will of the father is (sometimes) not regarded as merely the expression of the de facto dominant family member, but as the voice of Reason. "Father knows best." His macrocosmic analogue, then, is not looked upon as a vulgar tyrant but as the Philosopher King. And all his subjects, that is, all the children of the Philosopher Father's extended family, agree entirely with him insofar as they are rational—and that is all that matters, of course. Who wants to be irrational? Nevertheless, there is no getting around the fact that the expanded family, unlike the microcosm, must maintain its "children" in tutelage not for fifteen or twenty years but for all their lives. They cannot be allowed to grow up; all their important decisions must be made for them from above.

This has not bothered philosophers from Plato to Pol Pot who saw themselves as the loving fathers. It is, however, a stumbling block to Professor John Rawls (to his credit), and accounts for some incoherencies in his philosophy, as I shall explain presently.

Now, what will the conception of justice be according to the family model?

The short answer to this question is that there will be no such conception, although the word will be retained for propaganda effect. As we saw, there is little use for a notion of justice within the real family; and this will carry over. However, let us go the long way around to this conclusion.

The first thing to notice is that the adjective in the phrase "distributive justice" now receives emphasis. On the agreement model of justice the question of *distributing* anything hardly arises. The main idea of justice from the bottom up is that people are to keep what they produce unless they voluntarily exchange it for what others have made. It is no part of the agreement model that there will be a Master Distributor at all, distinct from the producers. That is one reason for calling it justice from the bottom up.

It is otherwise with the family model. In the (real) family there is a divorce between production and acquisition on the one hand and distribution on the other. With unimportant exceptions property is held in common; where all can make use of it as they do; where they cannot it is distributed (by Father, or at least according to his will) without special consideration for who in particular made, earned, or acquired it. The *fundamentum distributionis* being need, things will be thought of as rightly distributed when they go to the neediest; or if they are such that one member's need for them is no greater than another's, when the distribution is fair, that is, equal.

Second, fathers are *ex officio* utilitarians. The loving father's aim is that all his dependents should be happy, and equally so. He is a "good provider" and what he provides is satisfactions. That does not mean of course that he caters to every whim; he does not "spoil" his dependents. He may on occasion be judgmental and punishing, but it is for their own good; when he birches the unruly offspring it really does hurt him more than the wailing lad. If family members are in trouble, he is automatically on their side and will do all he can to get them out of it regardless of whether it is "their own fault."

Magnified to the scale of society this concern becomes what in contemporary jargon is called "compassion." Anyone who is hard up for whatever reason is to have his or her needs met at the expense of all who are not hard up. And so in this regard the paternalistic society will equate justice with compassion (a term which itself has undergone a curious transformation—one hardly tends to picture sleek politicians and bureaucrats as "suffering with" the objects of their solicitude). It is held that need entails the right to its fulfillment.

Natural justice on the other hand has no conceptual connection to utility, only a factual one. The idea of justice is that people should get what they deserve, what they have earned, and to find out what fits this specification it is not relevant to calculate the consequences of the award. But since the prospect of enjoying the fruits of one's labors is by and large the most potent incentive to labor, and labor by and large is what produces goods that satisfy desires, the observance of natural justice promotes utility demonstrably better for all concerned than "compassionate" redistribution.

Third, the characteristic concern of the father for his dependents is positive in the sense that it is not enough for him to keep them from harm, he must actively promote their welfare. Writ large, this means that the Philosopher King has not discharged his duty to his subjects when he has prevented or redressed wrongdoing among them; he must improve them, make them positively better off than they were, even if he knows that in so doing some inconveniences are regrettably bound to occur. Thus Dr. Goebbels mused:

> There can be no peace in Europe until the last Jews are eliminated from the continent.
>
> That, of course, raises a large number of exceedingly delicate questions. What is to be done with the half-Jews? What with those related to Jews? In-laws of Jews? Persons married to Jews? Evidently we still have quite a lot to do and undoubtedly a multitude of personal tragedies will ensue within the framework of the solution of this problem. But that is unavoidable. . . . We are doing a good work in proceeding radically and consistently. The task we are assuming today will be an advantage and a boon to our descendants.[7]

In contrast, the partisan of natural justice does not suppose that the reign of justice and the millennium are necessarily one and the same thing. Justice is no doubt desirable for its own sake, but its main value is instrumental: it is one important condition for the productive release of human energy. And in a way the negative is primary: all that the champion of justice is called upon to do is to eliminate *in*justice; once that has been done he can rest and allow those whom he has liberated from its shadow to go about the task of making a better world.

In sum: Every society must have some recognized rules for deciding questions of ownership. In a social structure based on agreement the rules will be those of natural justice, justice from the bottom up, providing for initial ownership and subsequent voluntary exchange of the products of one's own labor. In a paternalistic society, on the other hand, such considerations will not be decisive or paid much attention. The term "justice" will nevertheless be retained on account of its favorable associations to refer to the principles observed by the persons who have the power, authority, and wisdom to redistribute the goods taken from the producers and put into a common pot. These principles will emphasize the satisfaction of needs, the most urgent getting the highest priority. Where needs are equal, distribution will be equal as far as possible. Moreover the distribution is to be handled in such a way that a harmonious social pattern is produced, a "better world." This last principle applies especially to the distribution of intangibles such as status. A person will be said to have a "right" to X if and only if the distribution pattern assigns X to that person.

This is artificial justice or justice from the top down.

8. ILLUSTRATION: AFFIRMATIVE ACTION

Philosophy is sometimes said to have no practical consequences. If so, the theory of justice is not philosophy, for whether one holds one view or another of justice makes an enormous difference in practice. As an example, let us consider the ways in which justice from the bottom up and from the top down deal with the problem of racial discrimination in employment.

First, justice from the bottom up:

In a society recognizing this norm, citizens may make whatever agreements they choose, for any reason or none, as long as they do not infringe on the rights of other citizens. So if I am a Ruritanian widgetmaker, a manufacturer of widgets who detests Ruritanians may legitimately refuse to hire me. And if there are many more of his sort, we Ruritanian widgetmakers will be at a disadvantage, we will be discriminated against just because we are Ruritanians, and that is bad. But happily the problem will solve itself. We will offer our services to non-Ruritanophobe entrepreneurs for wages lower than the bigots must pay; and if we really are just as good workers, our unbiased employers will be put at a competitive advantage over the prejudiced ones. In the not very long run, then, the gap between Ruritanians and non-Ruritanian wage levels will disappear. And in the somewhat longer run the very idea of this sort of discrimination will begin to look silly, and we will be welcomed as fellow club members and sons-in-law by the former meanies. At any rate this is the pattern that has hitherto manifested itself time and again in the United States. It is well to note in this connection that slavery in the Southern states was, and South African apartheid is, imposed by government edict, i.e., they are interferences with freedom of contract.

Justice from the top down takes a different approach. Everybody is equal to everybody else (dogma), therefore, Ruritanians are just as good at making widgets as anyone else (non sequitur); therefore, if Ruritanian representation in the widget industry is not equal to the statistical expectation, it must be the work of prejudice (non sequitur), which if sincerely denied must be an unconscious aversion (absurdity). This is sin, which must be put down by force, viz., the imposition of a pro-Ruritanian quota (called something else) on widgetmakers. This will, of course, have two effects: it will disrupt the widget industry, already reeling from Japanese competition; and it will exacerbate resentment against Ruritanians.

9. SOME PARADOXES

The derivation of some main tenets of contemporary liberal (another word-corpse) opinion from the family model will no doubt strike some people as absurd, on the ground that liberals hold the old-fashioned family to be a pernicious institution which must be abolished or at least drastically overhauled. But hostility of derivative to original is hardly unheard of. Christianity with its anti-Semitism is after all in origin a Jewish sect. Nazism was a kind of socialism. And no one can deny that Plato's Republic is paternalistic; yet Plato was the first to propose the abolition of the family in order to eliminate emotional competition with his extended political family. Totalitarian liberalism finds no embarrassment in this.

It is otherwise, however, with John Rawls. The celebrated Difference Principle, that "social and economic inequalities are to be arranged so that they are . . . to the greatest benefit of the least advantaged," and its elaboration are all easily deducible from the family model. But we must not forget that there is another Rawlsian Principle of Justice, that of equal liberties—"each person is to have an equal right to the most extensive basic liberty compatible with a similar liberty for others"—which comes first and is required to be satisfied before one even starts thinking about fulfilling the Difference Principle. The sincerity of Rawls's advocacy of liberty, at least political liberty, and his rejection of a constitution where the Philosopher King runs everything, cannot be called in question. And that is why Rawls bases his philosophy on consent of self-interested parties; as we have seen, that is what generates a free society. But Rawls hedges his commitment. The personages behind the veil of ignorance are deprived of all flesh and blood, what is left being only the

abstract Voice of Reason, which might as well be a single Rational Person wishing equal happiness for all—
which as we have also seen is central to the paternalistic model.

Rawls's theory thus turns out, unsurprisingly, to
be a confection of incompatible elements. The principle of equal liberties is bottom-up, but the difference
principle is top-down. It would be humanly impossible
to instantiate both principles simultaneously: the redistribution required by the second can only be brought
about by force, thereby contravening the equal liberties. Rawls like many thinkers of today has failed to see
what was so clear to Locke and his contemporaries,
that without property rights there can be no rights at
all. For government, not being producer of anything,
has to be supported out of citizens' property. So if government has complete control of property there can be
no limit on its power. In particular, as the economist
Milton Friedman has emphasized, the dissenter from
official policy has no base of operations or even of
livelihood.

Perhaps the blindness of Rawls and so many others to this point, so obvious both in theory and in practice, results from their having convinced themselves
that if ever *they* were in power, of course *they* would
never abuse their position by clobbering the opposition,
but would behave as exemplary liberals.

10. IN AETERNAM?

We have compared two conceptions that claim the name
justice.

One is that of rendering every man his due. A
man's due is what he has acquired by his own efforts
and not taken from some other man without consent. A
community in which this conception is realized will be
one in which the members agree not to interfere in the
legitimate endeavors of each other to achieve their individual goals, and to help each other to the extent that
the conditions for doing so are mutually satisfactory.
These agreements obtain at the level of the individual
citizens, for which reason I call this conception justice
from the bottom up. ("Up": there may develop a hierarchical arrangement with those at the top having special duties of enforcing the agreements; but if so, the
decision concerning which agreements to enforce will
not originate with them.) Such a community will be
one giving the freest possible rein to all its members to
develop their particular capacities and use them to carry
out their plans for their own betterment. If this activity

is The Good for Man (and I hold with the Philosopher
that it is), then it is appropriate to call the associated
conception of justice natural.

The other conception holds justice to be the satisfaction of needs so as to bring everyone as far as possible onto the same plateau of pleasurable experience.
The view of human life underlying it is that life consists of two separable phases, production and consumption; the consumption phase is where The Good
lies; there is ultimately no reason why any individual
should have any more or less of this Good than any
other individual; and the problem of how to secure the
requisite production is merely technical. Society based
on this conception must be structured as a hierarchy of
authority, in order to solve the problem of production
and to administer justice, i.e., to adjust the satisfaction
quanta. Thus I have called this justice from the top
down (though of course I don't think it is really justice
at all).

Justice from the top down as I have described it
does not sound attractive. I have tried to account for the
fact that, nevertheless, it commands the enthusiastic
support of so many clever men and women and is everywhere on the march by showing its emotional basis in
the structure of the family, an institution that has been
felt to be, at its best, a warm, conflict-free, loving
refuge from fear and anxiety. Many people do not really *want* to grow up, and when they do they yearn for
a return to blissful dependence in the family or even in
the stage of development previous to that. I do not
think it can be controverted that this is part of the explanation for the popularity of top-down justice; but
nor can it be the whole, for such a complex phenomenon must be due to many factors. Among them are genuine compassion for the unfortunate and altruistic desire
to help them; fantasies of omnipotence, to which powerless academic intellectuals are exceptionally liable;
and envy. What the proportions are, is anybody's guess.

As there is no hope of lessening the influence of
these emotions in human affairs, the triumph of the
top-down cannot be stemmed unless there are yet more
powerful emotions to pit against them. What might
they be? I can think of three possibilities: the desire
that everyone has that he himself should be given his
due, and the concomitant outrage, with which more
and more people are becoming acquainted, when the
top-down authority denies it; revulsion witnessing the
actual, practical effects of top-down justice, e.g., in
Cambodia; and finally the life force itself, Spinoza's
conatus, the endeavor of each thing to persevere in its
being, and not (except in parasites) by sucking forever
but by getting proper solid nourishment. I *hope* these

are strong enough to prevail and show this funeral oration to have been premature: Justice is not dead, only mugged by intellectual hoods.

Justice As a Virtue: Changing Conceptions

Alasdair MacIntyre

Alasdair MacIntyre is Professor of Philosophy at the University of Notre Dame and the author of several works in ethics, political philosophy, and philosophy of religion. His work *After Virtue* is one of the most widely discussed books on ethics in recent years. In this selection from *After Virtue,* MacIntyre compares libertarian conceptions of justice and welfare liberal theories of justice, arguing that they are incommensurable with each other, as well as with the classical Aristotelian and Christian view which is based on a concept of desert. To illustrate his thesis, he examines Nozick's libertarian theory (see Reading 25) and contrasts it with Rawls's welfare liberal theory (see Reading 26). He concludes by arguing that our society is made of fragments of different traditions, but we have no single coherent theory of justice to steer us through difficult times and issues. He illustrates this fragmented reasoning by examining the 1979 Supreme Court Decision of *Regents of the University of California v. Bakke.*

This reading is taken from *After Virtue* (University of Notre Dame Press, 1981), by permission.

When Aristotle praised justice as the first virtue of political life, he did so in such a way as to suggest that a community which lacks practical agreement on a conception of justice must also lack the necessary basis for political community. But the lack of such a basis must therefore threaten our own society. For the outcome of that history . . . has not only been an inability to agree upon a catalogue of the virtues and an even more fundamental inability to agree upon the relative importance of the virtue concepts within a moral scheme in which notions of rights and of utility also have a key place. It has also been an inability to agree upon the content and character of particular virtues. For, since a virtue is now generally understood as a disposition or sentiment which will produce in us obedience to certain rules, agreement on what the relevant rules are to be is always a prerequisite for agreement upon the nature and content of a particular virtue. But this prior agreement in rules is . . . something which our individualist culture is unable to secure. Nowhere is this more marked and nowhere are the consequences more threatening than in the case of justice. Everyday life is pervaded by them and basic controversies cannot therefore be rationally resolved. Consider one such controversy, endemic in the politics of the United States today—I present it in the form of a debate between two ideal-typical characters unimaginatively named *A* and *B.*

A, who may own a store or be a police officer or a construction worker, has struggled to save enough from his earnings to buy a small house, to send his children to the local college, to pay for some special type of medical care for his parents. He now finds all of his projects threatened by rising taxes. He regards this threat to his projects as *unjust;* he claims to have a right to what he has earned and that nobody else has a right to take away what he acquired legitimately and to which he has a just title. He intends to vote for candidates for political office who will defend his property, his projects, *and* his conception of justice.

B, who may be a member of one of the liberal professions, or a social worker, or someone with inherited wealth, is impressed with the arbitrariness of the inequalities in the distribution of wealth, income, and opportunity. He is, if anything, even more impressed with the inability of the poor and the deprived to do very much about their own condition as a result of inequalities in the distribution of power. He regards both these types of inequality as *unjust* and as constantly engendering further injustice. He believes more generally that all inequality stands in need of justification and that the only possible justification for inequality is to improve the condition of the poor and the deprived— by, for example, fostering economic growth. He draws the conclusion that in present circumstances redistributive taxation which will finance welfare and the social services is what justice demands. He intends to vote for candidates for political office who will defend redistributive taxation *and* his conception of justice.

It is clear that in the actual circumstances of our social and political order A and B are going to disagree about policies and politicians. But *must* they so disagree? The answer seems to be that under certain types of economic conditions their disagreement need not manifest itself at the level of political conflict. If A and B belong to a society where economic resources are such, or are at least believed to be such, that B's public redistributive projects can be carried through at least to a certain point without threatening A's private life-plan projects, A and B might for some time vote for the same politicians and policies. Indeed they might on occasion be one and the same person. But if it is, or comes to be, the case that economic circumstances are such that either A's projects must be sacrificed to B's or vice versa, it at once becomes clear that A and B have views of justice which are not only logically incompatible with each other but which . . . invoke considerations which are incommensurable with those advanced by the adversary party.

The logical incompatibility is not difficult to identify. A holds that principles of just acquisition and entitlement set limits to redistributive possibilities. If the outcome of the application of the principles of just acquisition and entitlement is gross inequality, the toleration of such inequality is a price that has to be paid for justice. B holds that principles of just distribution set limits to legitimate acquisition and entitlement. If the outcome of the application of the principles of just distribution is interference—by means of taxation or such devices as eminent domain—with what has up till now been regarded in this social order as legitimate acquisition and entitlement, the toleration of such interference is a price that has to be paid for justice. We may note in passing—it will not be unimportant later—that in the case of both A's principle and B's principle the price for one person or group of persons receiving justice is always paid by someone else. Thus different identifiable social groups have an interest in the acceptance of one of the principles and the rejection of the other. Neither principle is socially or politically neutral.

Moreover it is not simply that A and B advance principles which produce incompatible practical conclusions. The type of concept in terms of which each frames his claim is so different from that of the other that the question of how and whether the dispute between them may be rationally settled begins to pose difficulties. For A aspires to ground the notion of justice in some account of what and how a given person is entitled to in virtue of what he has acquired and earned; B aspires to ground the notion of justice in

some account of the equality of the claims of each person in respect of basic needs and of the means to meet such needs. Confronted by a given piece of property or resource, A will be apt to claim that it is justly his because he owns it—he acquired it legitimately, he earned it; B will be apt to claim that it justly ought to be someone else's, because they need it much more, and if they do not have it, their basic needs will not be met. But our pluralist culture possesses no method of weighing, no rational criterion for deciding between claims based on legitimate entitlement against claims based on need. Thus these two types of claim are indeed, as I suggested, incommensurable, and the metaphor of "weighing" moral claims is not just inappropriate but misleading.

It is at this point that recent analytical moral philosophy makes important claims. For it aspires to provide rational principles to which appeal may be made by contending parties with conflicting interests. And the two most distinguished recent attempts to carry through this project have a special relevance for the argument between A and B. For Robert Nozick's account of justice [see Reading 25] is at least to some large degree a rational articulation of key elements in A's position, while John Rawls's account [see Reading 26] is in the same way a rational articulation of key elements in B's position. Thus, if the philosophical considerations which either Rawls or Nozick urge upon us turn out to be rationally compelling, the argument between A and B will have been rationally settled one way or another and my own characterization of the dispute will in consequence turn out to be quite false.

I begin with Rawls's account. [See Reading 26.] Rawls argues that the principles of justice are those which would be chosen by a rational agent "situated behind a veil of ignorance" such that he does not know what place in society he will occupy—that is, what his class or status will be, what talents and ability he will possess, what his conception of the good or his aims in life will be, what his temperament will be or what kind of economic, political, cultural, or social order he will inhabit. Rawls argues that any rational agent so situated will define a just distribution of goods in *any* social order in terms of two principles and a rule for allocating priorities when the two principles conflict.

The first principle is: "Each person is to have an equal right to the most extensive total system of equal basic liberties compatible with a similar system of liberty for all." The second principle is: "Social and economic inequalities are to be arranged so that they are both (a) to the greatest benefit of the least advantaged, consistent with the joint savings principle [the joint savings principle provides for fair investment in the interests of future generations], and (b) attached to offices and parties open to all under conditions of fair equality of opportunity." The first principle has priority over the second; liberty is to be restricted only for the sake of liberty. And justice generally has priority over efficiency. So Rawls arrives at his general conception: "All social primary goods—liberty and opportunity, income and wealth, and the bases of self-respect—are to be distributed equally unless an unequal distribution of any or all of these goods is to the advantage of the least favored."

Many critics of Rawls have focused their attention on the ways in which Rawls derives his principles of justice from his statement of the initial position of the rational agent "situated behind a veil of ignorance." Such critics have made a number of telling points, but I do not intend to dwell on them, if only because I take it not only that a rational agent in *some such* situation as that of the veil of ignorance would indeed choose *some such* principles of justice as Rawls claims, but also that it is *only* a rational agent in such a situation who would choose such principles. Later in my argument this point will become important. For the moment however I shall put it on one side in order to turn to a characterization of Nozick's view.

Nozick [see Reading 25] claims that "if the world were wholly just" the only people entitled to hold anything, that is to appropriate it for use as they and they alone wished, would be those who had justly acquired what they held by some just act of original acquisition and those who had justly acquired what they held by some just act of transfer from someone else who had either acquired it by some just act of original acquisition or by some just transfer . . . and so on. In other words, the justifiable answer to the question "Why are you entitled to use that seashell as you wish?" will either be "I picked it up on the seashore, where it belonged to no one and where there were plenty left for everyone else" (a just act of original acquisition), *or* "Someone else picked it up at the seashore and freely sold or gave it to someone . . . to someone . . . who freely sold or gave it to me" (a series of just acts of transfer). It follows from Nozick's view as he himself immediately notes that: "The complete principle of distributive justice would say simply that a distribution is just if everyone is entitled to the holdings that they possess under the distribution."

Nozick derives these conclusions from premises about the inalienable rights of each individual, premises for which he does not himself offer arguments.

As in the case of Rawls, I do not want to quarrel with Nozick's derivation of his principles from his premisses; once again I shall want to stress instead that it is *only* from some such premisses that such principles could be rationally derived. That is to say, in the case of both Nozick's account of justice and Rawls's account of justice the problems that I want to raise do not concern the coherence of the internal structure of their arguments. Indeed my own argument requires that their accounts do not lack such coherence.

What I want to argue is threefold: first, that the incompatibility of Rawls's and Nozick's accounts does up to a point genuinely mirror the incompatibility of A's position with B's, and that to this extent at least Rawls and Nozick successfully articulate at the level of moral philosophy the disagreement between such ordinary non-philosophical citizens as A and B; but that Rawls and Nozick also reproduce the very same type of incompatibility and incommensurability at the level of philosophical argument that made A's and B's debate unsettlable at the level of social conflict; and, secondly, that there is none the less an element in the position of both A and B which neither Rawls's account nor Nozick's captures, an element which survives from that older classical tradition in which the virtues were central. When we reflect on both these points, a third emerges: namely, that in their conjunction we have an important clue to the social presuppositions which Rawls and Nozick to some degree share.

Rawls makes primary what is in effect a principle of equality with respect to needs. His conception of "the worst off" sector of the community is a conception of those whose needs are gravest in respect of income, wealth, and other goods. Nozick makes primary what is a principle of equality with respect to entitlement. For Rawls how those who are now in grave need come to be in grave need is irrelevant; justice is made into a matter of present patterns of distribution to which the past is irrelevant. For Nozick only evidence about what has been legitimately acquired in the past is relevant; present patterns of distribution in themselves must be irrelevant to *justice* (although not perhaps to kindness or generosity). To say even this much makes it clear how close Rawls is to B and how close Nozick is to A. For A appealed against distributive canons to a justice of entitlement, and B appealed against canons of entitlement to a justice which regards needs. Yet it is also at once clear not only that Rawls's priorities are incompatible with Nozick's in a way parallel to that in which B's position is incompatible with A's, but also that Rawls's position is incommensurable with Nozick's in a way similarly parallel to that in which *B*'s is incommensurable with *A*'s. For how can a claim that gives priority to equality of needs be rationally weighed against one which gives priority to entitlements? If Rawls were to argue that anyone *behind the veil of ignorance,* who knew neither whether and how his needs would be met nor what his entitlements would be, ought rationally to prefer a principle which respects needs to one which respects entitlements, invoking perhaps principles of rational decision theory to do so, the immediate answer must be not only that *we* are *never* behind such a veil of ignorance, but also that this leaves unimpugned Nozick's premiss about inalienable rights. And if Nozick were to argue that any distributive principle, if enforced, could violate a freedom to which every one of us is entitled—as he does indeed argue—the immediate answer must be that in so interpreting the inviolability of basic rights he begs the question in favour of his own argument and leaves unimpugned Rawls's premisses.

None the less there is something important, if negative, which Rawls's account shares with Nozick's. Neither of them make any reference to *desert* in their account of justice, nor could they consistently do so. And yet both *A* and *B* did make such a reference—and it is imperative here to notice that "*A*" and "*B*" are not the names of mere arbitrary constructions of my own; their arguments faithfully reproduce, for example, a good deal of what was actually said in recent fiscal debates in California, New Jersey, and elsewhere. What *A* complains of on his own behalf is not merely that he is entitled to what he has earned, but that he *deserves* it in virtue of his life of hard work; what *B* complains of on behalf of the poor and deprived is that their poverty and deprivation [are] *undeserved* and therefore unwarranted. And it seems clear that in the case of the real-life counterparts of *A* and *B* it is the reference to desert which makes them feel strongly that what they are complaining about is injustice, rather than some other kind of wrong or harm.

Neither Rawls's account nor Nozick's allows this central place, or indeed any kind of place, for desert in claims about justice and injustice. Rawls allows that common-sense views of justice connect it with desert, but argues, first, that we do not know what anyone deserves until we have already formulated the rules of justice (and hence we cannot base our understanding of justice upon desert), and, secondly, that when we have formulated the rules of justice it turns out that it is not desert that is in question anyway, but only legitimate expectations. He also argues that to attempt to apply notions of desert would be impracticable—the ghost of Hume walks in his pages at this point.

Nozick is less explicit, but his scheme of justice being based exclusively on entitlements can allow no place for desert. He does at one point discuss the possibility of a principle for the rectification of injustice, but what he writes on that point is so tentative and cryptic that it affords no guidance for amending his general viewpoint. It is in any case clear that for both Nozick and Rawls a society is composed of individuals, each with his or her own interest, who then have to come together and formulate common rules of life. In Nozick's case there is the additional negative constraint of a set of basic rights. In Rawls's case the only constraints are those that a prudent rationality would impose. Individuals are thus in both accounts primary and society secondary, and the identification of individual interests is prior to, and independent of, the construction of any moral or social bonds between them. But we have already seen that the notion of desert is at home only in the context of a community whose primary bond is a shared understanding both of the good for man and of the good of that community and where individuals identify their primary interests with reference to those goods. Rawls explicitly makes it a presupposition of his view that we must expect to disagree with others about what the good life for man is and must therefore exclude any understanding of it that we may have from our formulation of the principles of justice. Only those goods in which everyone, whatever their view of the good life, takes an interest are to be admitted to consideration. In Nozick's argument, too, the concept of community required for the notion of desert to have application is simply absent. To understand this is to clarify two further points.

The first concerns the shared social presuppositions of Rawls and Nozick. It is, from both standpoints, as though we had been shipwrecked on an uninhabited island with a group of other individuals, each of whom is a stranger to me and to all the others. What have to be worked out are rules which will safeguard each one of us maximally in such a situation. Nozick's premiss concerning rights introduces a strong set of constraints; we do know that certain types of interference with each other are absolutely prohibited. But there is a limit to the bonds between us, a limit set by our private and competing interests. This individualistic view has of course, as I noticed earlier, a distinguished ancestry: Hobbes, Locke (whose views Nozick treats with great respect), Machiavelli, and others. And it contains within itself a certain note of realism about modern society;

modern society is indeed often, at least in surface appearance, nothing but a collection of strangers, each pursuing his or her own interests under minimal constraints. We still of course, even in modern society, find it difficult to think of families, colleges, and other genuine communities in this way; but even our thinking about those is now invaded to an increasing degree by individualist conceptions, especially in the law courts. Thus Rawls and Nozick articulate with great power a shared view which envisages entry into social life as—at least ideally—the voluntary act of at least potentially rational individuals with prior interests who have to ask the question "What kind of social contract with others is it reasonable for me to enter into?" Not surprisingly it is a consequence of this that their views exclude any account of human community in which the notion of desert in relation to contributions to the common tasks of that community in pursing shared goods could provide the basis for judgements about virtue and injustice.

Desert is ruled out too in another way. I have remarked upon how Rawls's distributive principles exclude reference to the past and so to claims to desert based on past actions and sufferings. Nozick too excludes that of the past on which such claims might be based, by making a concern for the legitimacy of entitlements the sole ground for taking an interest in the past in connection with justice. What makes this important is that Nozick's account serves the interest of a particular mythology about the past precisely by what it excludes from view. For central to Nozick's account is the thesis that all legitimate entitlements can be traced to legitimate acts of original acquisition. But, if that is so, there are in fact very few, and in some large areas of the world *no,* legitimate entitlements. The property-owners of the modern world are not the legitimate heirs of Lockean individuals who performed quasi-Lockean ("quasi" to allow for Nozick's emendations of Locke) acts of original acquisition; they are the inheritors of those who, for example, stole, and used violence to steal, the common lands of England from the common people, vast tracts of North America from the American Indian, much of Ireland from the Irish, and Prussia from the original non-German Prussians. This is the historical reality ideologically concealed behind any Lockean thesis. The lack of any principle of rectification is thus not a small side issue for a thesis such as Nozick's; it tends to vitiate the theory as a whole—even if we were to suppress the overwhelming objections to any belief in inalienable human rights.

A and *B* differ from Rawls and Nozick at the price of inconsistency. Each of them in conjoining either Rawls's principles or Nozick's with an appeal to desert exhibits an adherence to an older, more traditional, more Aristotelian and Christian view of justice. This inconsistency is thus a tribute to the residual power and influence of the tradition, a power and influence with two distinct sources. In the conceptual *melange* of moral thought and practice today fragments from the tradition—virtue concepts for the most part—are still found alongside characteristically modern and individualist concepts such as those of rights or utility. But the tradition also survives in a much less fragmented, much less distorted form in the lives of certain communities whose historical ties with their past remain strong. So the older moral tradition is discernible in the United States and elsewhere among, for example, some Catholic Irish, some Orthodox Greeks, and some Jews of an Orthodox persuasion, all of them communities that inherit their moral tradition not only through their religion, but also from the structure of the peasant villages and households which their immediate ancestors inhabited on the margins of modern Europe. Moreover it would be wrong to conclude from the stress that I have laid on the medieval background that Protestantism did not in some areas become the bearer of this very same moral tradition; in Scotland, for example, Aristotle's *Nicomachean Ethics* and *Politics* were the secular moral texts in the universities, coexisting happily with a Calvinist theology which was often elsewhere hostile to them until 1690 and after. And there are today both black and white Protestant communities in the United States, especially perhaps those in or from the South, who will recognize in the tradition of the virtues a key part of their own cultural inheritance.

Even, however, in such communities the need to enter into public debate enforces participation in the cultural *melange* in the search for a common stock of concepts and norms which all may employ and to which all may appeal. Consequently the allegiance of such marginal communities to the tradition is constantly in danger of being eroded, and this in search of what, if my argument is correct, is a chimera. For what analysis of *A*'s and *B*'s position reveals once again is that we have all too many disparate and rival moral concepts, in this case rival and disparate concepts of justice, and that the moral resources of the culture allow us no way of settling the issue between them rationally. Moral philosophy, as it is dominantly understood, reflects the debates and disagreements of the culture so faithfully that its controversies turn out to be unsettlable in just the way that the political and moral debates themselves are.

It follows that our society cannot hope to achieve moral consensus. For quite non-Marxist reasons Marx was in the right when he argued against the English trade unionists of the 1860s that appeals to justice were pointless, since there are rival conceptions of justice formed by and informing the life of rival groups. Marx was of course mistaken in supposing that such disagreements over justice are merely secondary phenomena, that they merely reflect the interests of rival economic classes. Conceptions of justice and allegiance to such conceptions are partly constitutive of the lives of social groups, and economic interests are often partially defined in terms of such conceptions and not vice versa. None the less Marx was fundamentally right in seeing conflict and not consensus at the heart of modern social structure. It is not just that we live too much by a variety and multiplicity of fragmented concepts; it is that these are used at one and the same time to express rival and incompatible social ideals and policies *and* to furnish us with a pluralist political rhetoric whose function is to conceal the depth of our conflicts.

Important conclusions follow for constitutional theory. Liberal writers such as Ronald Dworkin invite us to see the Supreme Court's function as that of invoking a set of consistent principles, most and perhaps all of them of moral import, in the light of which particular laws and particular decisions are to be evaluated. Those who hold such a view are bound to consider certain decisions of the Supreme Court inadequate in the light of these supposed principles. The type of decision which I have in mind is exemplified by the Bakke case, where two, at first sight strongly incompatible, views were held by members of the court, and Mr Justice Powell, who wrote the decision, was the one justice to hold both views. But, if my argument is correct, one function of the Supreme Court must be to keep the peace between rival social groups adhering to rival and incompatible principles of justice by displaying a fairness which consists in even-handedness in its adjudications. So the Supreme Court in Bakke both forbade precise ethnic quotas for admission to colleges and universities, but allowed discrimination in favour of previously deprived minority groups. Try to conjure up a set of consistent principles behind such a decision and ingenuity may or may not allow you to find the court not guilty of formal inconsistency. But even to make such an attempt is to miss the point. The Supreme

Court in *Bakke,* as on occasion in other cases, played the role of a peacemaking or truce-keeping body by negotiating its way through an impasse of conflict, not by invoking our shared moral first principles. For our society as a whole has none.

What this brings out is that modern politics cannot be a matter of genuine moral consensus. And it is not. Modern politics is civil war carried on by other means, and *Bakke* was an engagement whose antecedents were at Gettysburg and Shiloh. The truth on this matter was set out by Adam Ferguson: "We are not to expect that the laws of any country are to be framed as so many lessons of morality. . . . Laws, whether civil or political, are expedients of policy to adjust the pretensions of parties, and to secure the peace of society. The expedient is accommodated to special circumstances . . ." (*Principles of Moral and Political Science,* ii. 144). The nature of any society, therefore, is not to be deciphered from its laws alone, but from those understood as an index of its conflicts. What our laws show is the extent and degree to which conflict has to be suppressed.

Yet, if this is so, another virtue too has been displaced. Patriotism cannot be what it was because we lack in the fullest sense a *patria.* The point that I am making must not be confused with the commonplace liberal rejection of patriotism. Liberals have often— not always—taken a negative or even hostile attitude towards patriotism, partly because their allegiance is to values which they take to be universal and not local and particular, and partly because of a well-justified suspicion that in the modern world patriotism is often a façade behind which chauvinism and imperialism are fostered. But my present point is not that patriotism is good or bad as a sentiment, but that the practice of patriotism as a virtue is in advanced societies no longer possible in the way that it once was. In any society where government does not express or represent the moral community of the citizens, but is instead a set of institutional arrangements for imposing a bureaucratized unity on a society which lacks genuine moral consensus, the nature of political obligation becomes systematically unclear. Patriotism is or was a virtue founded on attachment primarily to a political and moral community and only secondarily to the government of that community; but it is characteristically exercised in discharging responsibility to and in such government. When, however, the relationship of government to the moral community is put in question both by the changed nature of government and the lack of moral consensus in the society, it becomes difficult any longer to have any clear, simple, and teachable conception of patriotism. Loyalty to my country, to my community—which remains unalterably a central virtue—becomes detached from obedience to the government which happens to rule me.

Just as this understanding of the displacement of patriotism must not be confused with the liberal critique of moral particularity, so this necessary distancing of the moral self from the governments of modern states must not be confused with any anarchist critique of the state. Nothing in my argument suggests, let alone implies, any good grounds for rejecting certain forms of government as necessary and legitimate; what the argument does entail is that the modern state is not such a form of government. It must have been clear from earlier parts of my argument that the tradition of the virtues is at variance with central features of the modern economic order and more especially its individualism, its acquisitiveness, and its elevation of the values of the market to a central social place. It now becomes clear that it also involves a rejection of the modern political order. This does not mean that there are not many tasks only to be performed in and through government which still require performing: the rule of law, so far as it is possible in a modern state, has to be vindicated, injustice and unwarranted suffering have to be dealt with, generosity has to be exercised, and liberty has to be defended, in ways that are sometimes only possible through the use of governmental institutions. But each particular task, each particular responsibility, has to be evaluated on its own merits. Modern systematic politics, whether liberal, conservative, radical, or socialist, simply has to be rejected from a standpoint that owes genuine allegiance to the tradition of the virtues; for modern politics itself expresses in its institutional forms a systematic rejection of that tradition.

READING 29

Distributive Justice

Nicholas Rescher

Nicholas Rescher is Professor of Philosophy at the University of Pittsburgh and has written prolifically in the field. In this essay he discusses seven candidates for material principles of distributive justice: people are to be treated (1) as equals; or according to their (2) needs, (3) merit or ability, (4) effort or sacrifices, (5) contribution, or (6) economic usefulness; or according to (7) the public good.

Rescher analyzes each of these candidates, including their strengths and weaknesses, and concludes that none of them is sufficient in itself as a criterion of distributive justice. Rescher argues for a complex, multifaceted approach to this issue. Different types of situations require giving predominance to different material principles. The question is, How do we decide which particular "canon" of justice applies in any given situation?

This reading is taken from *Distributive Justice* (Bobbs-Merrill, 1966), by permission.

In the course of the long history of discussions on the subject, distributive justice has been held to consist, wholly or primarily, in the treatment of all people:

1. as equals (except possibly in the case of certain "negative" distributions such as punishments)
2. according to their needs
3. according to their ability or merit or achievements
4. according to their efforts and sacrifices
5. according to their actual productive contribution
6. according to the requirements of the common good, or the public interest, or the welfare of mankind, or the greatest good of a greater number
7. according to a valuation of their socially useful services in terms of scarcity in the essentially economic terms of supply and demand

Correspondingly, seven "canons" of distributive justice result, depending upon which of these factors is taken as the ultimate or primary determination of individual claims; namely, the canons of equality, need, ability, effort, productivity, public utility, and supply and demand. Brief consideration must be given to each of these proposed conceptions of justice.[1]

THE CANON OF EQUALITY

This canon holds that justice consists in the treatment of people as equals. Here we have the *egalitarian* criterion of (idealistic) democratic theorists. The shortcomings of this canon have already been canvassed in considerable detail . . . to the effect that the principle is oblivious to the reality of differential claims and desert. It is vulnerable to all the same lines of objection which hold against the type of just-wage principle advocated by G. B. Shaw—to let all who contribute to the production of the social-economic product share in it equally. Moreover, the specification of the exact way in which equality is to be understood is by no means so simple and straightforward as it seems on first view. Is one, for example, to think of the type of fixed constant equality that is at issue in a sales tax, or the "equal burden" type of differential equality at issue in a graduated income tax; and more generally, is the "equality" at issue strict equality, equality of sacrifice, equality of opportunity-and-risk, equality of rights, or equality of "consideration," etc.?

A rule of strict equality violates the most elemental requisites of the concept of justice itself: justice not only requires the equal treatment of equals, as the canon at issue would certainly assure, but also under various circumstances requires the converse, the (appropriately measured) unequal treatment of unequals, a requisite which the canon violates blatantly. In any distribution among individuals whose legitimate claims with respect to this distribution are diverse, the treatment of people as equals without reference to their differential claims outrages rather than implements our sense of justice.

THE CANON OF NEED

This canon holds that justice consists in the treatment of people according to their needs. Here we have the *socialistic* principle of the idealistic socialistic and communist theoreticians: "to each according to his needs."[2] Basically this principle is closely allied with the preceding one, and is, like it, one of *rectification*: recognizing that as things stand, men come into the world with different possessions and opportunities as well as differences in natural endowments, the principle professes to treat them, not equally, but so as to *make* them as equal as possible.

Regarding this principle, it has been said:

> If the task of distribution were entirely independent of the process of production, this rule would be ideal [from the standpoint of justice]; for it would treat men as equal in those respects in which they are equal; namely, as beings endowed with the dignity and the potencies of personality; and it would

treat them as unequal in those respects in which they are unequal; that is, in their desires and capacities.[3]

This limitation of the rule is of itself too narrow. The principle does recognize inequalities, but it recognizes only one sort; it rides roughshod not only over the matter of productive contributions but over all other ways of grounding legitimate claims (e.g., those based on kinship, on [nonproductive] services rendered, on contracts and compacts, etc.) that make for relevant differences, i.e., inequalities, among the potential recipients of a distribution. Nor, for that matter, is the principle as clear-cut as it seems on first view: by the time anything like an adequate analysis of "need" has been provided, the principle covers a wide-ranging area. For example, are we to interpret the "needs" at issue as *real* needs or as *felt* needs?

THE CANON OF ABILITY AND/OR ACHIEVEMENT

This canon holds that justice consists in the treatment of people according to their abilities. Here we have the *meritarian* criterion going back to Aristotle and echoed by the (Jeffersonian) theorists of a "natural aristocracy of ability." Natural ability, however, is a latent quality which subsists in the mode of potentiality. It represents natural endowments that can be cultivated to varying degrees and may or may not become operative and actually put to work. To allocate rewards with reference solely to innate ability, unqualified by considerations of how the abilities in question are used or abused, would be to act in a way that is patently unjust. Moreover, a question can validly be raised as to the propriety of having natural ability—which is, after all, wholly a "gift of the gods" and in no way a matter of desert—count as the sole or even the primary basis of claims.

This objection might be countered by granting that it may hold for *natural* (or innate) ability, but that it fails to be applicable when the "ability" at issue is an *acquired* ability, or perhaps even more aptly, a *demonstrated* ability of the persons at issue, as determined by their achievements. This is the criterion naturally used in giving grades to students and prizes to tennis plays (where need, for instance, and effort are deliberately discounted). But in this case the canon becomes transformed, in its essentials, into the Canon of Productivity, which will be dealt with below.

THE CANON OF EFFORT

This canon holds that justice consists in the treatment of people according to their efforts and sacrifices on their own behalves, or perhaps on behalf of their group (family, society, fellowmen). Here we have the *puritanical* principal espoused by theorists of a "Puritan ethic," who hold that God helps (and men should help) those who help themselves. Burke lauded the "natural society" in which "it is an invariable law that a man's acquisitions are in proportion to his labors." Think also of the historic discussions of a just wage and the traditional justification of differential wage scales. On the question of wages, classical socialists such as Fourier and St. Simon argued that the wage should be inversely proportioned to the intrinsic pleasantness (interest, appeal, prestige) of the task. (Presumably, thus, the policeman walking the beat shall receive more than the captain sitting at headquarters.) But the difficulties of this standpoint lie on the surface, e.g., the difficulty of maintaining morale and discipline in a setting in which the claims of ability and responsibility go unrecognized.

Moreover, the principle ignores the fact that effort is of its very nature a many-sided thing: it can be either fruitful or vain, well-directed or misguided, properly applied or misapplied, availing or unavailing, etc. To allocate rewards by effort as such without reference to its nature and direction is to ignore a key facet of just procedure—to fail to make a distinction that makes a difference. Also, to reward by effort rather than achievement is socially undesirable: it weakens incentive and encourages the inefficient, the untalented, the incompetent.

single-factor criterion. The principle is prepared to put aside all considerations not only of unmerited claims in general, but also of merited claims when merited through extra-productive factors such as need and effort.

Yet one cannot fail to be impressed by the appeal to justice of such an argument as the following:

> When men of equal productive power are performing the same kind of labour, superior amounts of product do represent superior amounts of effort. . . . If men are unequal in productive power their products are obviously not in proportion to their efforts. Consider two men whose natural physical abilities are so unequal that they can handle with equal effort shovels differing in capacity by fifty per cent. Instances of this kind are innumerable in industry. If these two men are rewarded according to productivity, one will get fifty per cent more compensation than the other. Yet the surplus received by the more fortunate man does not represent any action or quality for which he is personally responsible. It corresponds to no larger output of personal effort, no superior exercise of will, no greater personal desert.[4]

Note here the criticism of a (restricted) purely economic application of the principle by an appeal to one's sense of justice. If such an appeal is to be given but the slightest (even if not ultimately decisive) weight, as I think it must, then the canon in question must *a fortiori* be at once abandoned as an exclusive and exhaustive general principle of distributive justice.

THE CANON OF PRODUCTIVITY

This canon holds that justice consists in the treatment of people according to their actual productive contribution to their group. Here we have the essentially economic principle of the social-welfare-minded *capitalistic* theoreticians. The claim-bases at issue here are primarily those traditionally considered in economics: services rendered, capital advanced, risks run, and the like. Much is to be said on behalf of this principle as a *restricted* rule, governing the division of proceeds and profits resulting from a common productive enterprise; but it is clearly defective as a general principle of distributive justice, simply because it is an overly limited

THE CANON OF SOCIAL UTILITY

This canon holds that justice consists in the treatment of people according to the best prospects for advancing the common good, or the public interest, or the welfare of mankind, or the greater good of a greater number. The theory has two basic variants, according as one resorts to a distinction between the common good of men considered *collectively*, as constituting a social group with some sort of life of its own, or merely *distributively*, as an aggregation of separate individuals. In the former case we have the "public interest," expedientialist variant of the canon with roots going back to Hebraic theology, Stoic philosophy, and Roman jurisprudence (*pro bono publico*). In the second case we have the *utilitarian* and more modern, individualistic version of the canon.

The same fundamental criticism (already dwelt upon at considerable length in our preceding discussion) can be deployed against both versions of the theory: an individual's *proper share viewed from the angle of the general good* cannot be equated with his *just share* pure and simple, because there is no "pre-established harmony" to guarantee that all of the individual's legitimate claims (the authoritative determinants of his just share) be recognized and acceded to when "the *general* good" becomes the decisive criterion. And insofar as these legitimate claims are disallowed—or *could* be disallowed—in a patently unjust (though socially advantageous) way, the principle of the primacy of the general good exhibits a feature which precludes its acceptance as a principle of justice.

THE CANON OF SUPPLY AND DEMAND

This canon holds that justice consists in the treatment of people according to a valuation of their socially useful—or perhaps merely desired—contributions, these being evaluated not on the basis of the value of the product (as with the Canon of Productivity, above), but on the basis of relative scarcity of the service. Here we have the essentially economic principle of the more hard-boiled "play of the market" school of laissez-faire theoreticians. The train dispatcher would thus deserve a larger part of the proceeds of the joint operation than the conductor, the general manager more than the section foreman, the buyer more than the sales-girl, because—while in each case both kinds of contribution are alike essential to the enterprise—the former type of labour calls for skills that are relatively scarcer, being less plentifully diffused throughout the working population. Such valuation then rests not upon the relative extent or intrinsic merit of the contribution made, but upon the fact that that contribution is viewed by the community as necessary or desirable, and can either be made successfully by fewer people, or else involves such expenditures, risks, hardships, or hazards that fewer people are willing to undertake the task. (Throughout recent years successful entertainers have been remunerated more highly than successful physicians—and on this principle, justly so.)

As a criterion of justice, this canon suffers from the general defects as does the Canon of Productivity

which it seeks to qualify. Not only does it put aside any accommodation of unmerited claims, but also any claims based upon factors (such as individual need and expenditure of effort) which have no basis in the making of a productive contribution to felt social needs.

OUR OWN POSITION: THE CANON OF CLAIMS

One and the same shortcoming runs through all of the above canons of distributive justice: they are all *monistic*. They all recognize but one solitary, homogeneous mode of claim production (be it need, effort, productivity, or whatever), to the exclusion of all others. A single specific ground of claim establishment is canonized as uniquely authoritative, and all the others dismissed. As a result, these canons all suffer the aristocratic fault of hyperexclusiveness. As we see it, they err not so much in commission as in omission.

To correct this failing requires that we go from a concept of claim establishment that is monistic and homogeneous to one that is pluralistic and heterogeneous. To do so we put forward, as representing (in essentials) our own position on the issue of distributive justice, the Canon of Claims: Distributive justice consists in the treatment of people *according to their legitimate claims,* positive and negative. This canon shifts the burden to—and thus its implementation hinges crucially upon—the question of the nature of legitimate claims, and of the machinery for their mutual accommodation in cases of plurality, and their reconciliation in cases of conflict. To say this is not a criticism of the principle, but simply the recognition of an inevitable difficulty which must be encountered by any theory of distributive justice at the penalty of showing itself grossly inadequate.

The Canon of Claims plainly avoids the fault of overrestrictiveness: indeed, it reaches out to embrace all the other canons. From its perspective each canon represents one particular sort of ground (need, effort, productivity, etc.) on whose basis certain legitimate claims—upon whose accommodation it insists—can be advanced. The evaluation of these claims in context, and their due recognition under the circumstances, is in our view the key element of distributive justice.

We must be prepared to take such a multifaceted approach to claims because of the propriety of recognizing different kinds of claims-grounds as appropriate types of distribution. Our society inclines to the view that in the case of wages, desert is to be measured according to productivity of contribution qualified by supply-and-demand considerations; in the case of property income, by productivity considerations; in public-welfare distributions, by need qualified to avoid the demoralization inherent in certain types of means-tests; and in the negative distributions of taxation, by ability-to-pay qualified by social-utility considerations. The list could be extended and refined at great length but is already extensive enough to lend support to our pluralistic view of claims.

One important consequence of our canon must be noted. With it, the concept of justice is no solitarily self-sufficient ultimate, but becomes dependent upon the articulation of certain coordinate ideas, namely, those relating to claims and their establishment. The unraveling of the short thesis that distributive justice requires (in general) the accommodation of legitimate claims is but the preface of a long story about claims, a story for which there is neither need nor space here. Moreover, since claims themselves are not (at any rate, not in general) established by considerations of abstract justice, but are in large part grounded in positive law, the heavy dependence of justice upon a body of positive law may be seen. Where abstract justice might countenance various alternative divisions, the law specifies one particular procedure that underwrites a certain specific set of claims. That law shall embody considerations of justice is a trite thesis, but that there is a converse requirement resulting in mutual dependence is less frequently observed.

In espousing the Canon of Claims we may note that the search for a canon of distributive justice is carried back to the Roman jurists' view that the definitive principle of justice is inherent in the dictum *suum cuique tribuens*—"giving each his own." To the question *What is his own?* we have given the answer *What he deserves!*; that is, a share ideally equal—or at any rate generally proportional—to his legitimate claims.

END NOTES

Introduction

[1] See Joel Feinberg, *Social Philosophy* (Englewood Cliffs, N.J.: Prentice Hall, 1973), pp. 100 f.

Nozick

[1] Applications of the principles of justice in acquisition may also occur as part of the move from one distribution to another. You may find an unheld thing now and appropriate it. Acquisitions also are to be understood as included when, to simplify, I speak only of transitions by transfers.

[2] If the principle of rectification of violations of the first two principles yields more than one description of holdings, then some choice must be made as to which of these is to be realized. Perhaps the sort of considerations about distributive justice and equality that I argue against play a legitimate role in *this* subsidiary choice. Similarly, there may be room for such considerations in deciding which otherwise arbitrary features a statute will embody, when such features are unavoidable because other considerations do not specify a precise line; yet a line must be drawn.

[3] One might try to squeeze a patterned conception of distributive justice into the framework of the entitlement conception, by formulating a gimmicky obligatory "principle of transfer" that would lead to the pattern. For example, the principle that if one has more than the mean income one must transfer everything one holds above the mean to persons below the mean so as to bring them up (but not over) the mean. We can formulate a criterion for a "principle of transfer" to rule out such obligatory transfers, or we can say that no correct principle of transfers, no principle of transfers in a free society will be like this. The former is probably the better course, though the latter also is true.

Alternatively, one might think to make the entitlement conception instantiate a pattern, by using matrix entries that express the relative strength of a person's entitlements as measured by some real-valued function. But even if the limitation to natural dimensions failed to exclude this function, the resulting edifice would *not* capture our system of entitlements to *particular* things.

[4] F. A. Hayek, *The Constitution of Liberty* (Chicago: University of Chicago Press, 1960), p. 87.

[5] This question does not imply that they will tolerate any and every patterned distribution. In discussing Hayek's views, Irving Kristol has recently speculated that people will not long tolerate a system that yields distributions patterned in accordance with value rather than merit. ("'When Virtue Loses All Her Loveliness'—Some Reflections on Capitalism and 'The Free Society.'" *The Public Interest* [Fall 1970]: 3–15.) Kristol, following some remarks of Hayek, equates the merit system with justice. Since some case can be made for the external standard of distribution in accordance with benefit to others, we ask about a weaker (and therefore more plausible) hypothesis.

[6] We certainly benefit because economic incentives operate to get others to spend much time and energy to figure out how to serve us by providing things we will want to pay for. It is not mere paradox mongering to wonder whether capitalism should be criticized for most rewarding and hence encouraging, not individuals like Thoreau who go about their own lives, but people who are occupied with serving others and winning them as customers. But to defend capitalism one need not think businessmen are the finest human types. (I do not mean to join here the general maligning of businessmen, either.) Those who think the finest should acquire the most can try to convince their fellows to transfer resources in accordance with *that* principle.

[7] Varying situations continuously from that limit situation to our own would force us to make explicit the underlying rationale of entitlements and to consider whether entitlement considerations

lexicographically precede the considerations of the usual theories of distributive justice, so that the slightest strand of entitlement outweighs the considerations of the usual theories of distributive justice.

Matson

[1]Joel Feinberg, *Rights, Justice, and the Bounds of Liberty* (Princeton: Princeton University Press, 1980), 141, 153.

[2]John Rawls, *A Theory of Justice* (Cambridge, MA: Harvard University Press, 1971), 277–280 *et passim.*

[3]Ronald Dworkin, *Taking Rights Seriously* (Cambridge: Harvard University Press, 1977), 227–229.

[4]Richard Wasserstrom, "A Defense of Programs of Preferential Treatment," in Vincent Barry, ed., *Applying Ethics* (Belmont, CA: Wadsworth, 1982), 332 f.

[5]Thomas Nagel, *Mortal Questions* (New Rochelle, N.Y.: Cambridge University Press, 1979), 99 f.

[6]*Leviathan,* Chapter 13.

[7]*The Goebbels Diaries,* ed. and trans. Louis P. Lochner (Westport, CT: Greenwood, 1971), 135 (March 7, 1942).

Rescher

[1]All of these canons except number 3 (the Canon of Ability) are competently and instructively discussed from an essentially economic point of view—from the special angle of the idea of a just wage or income—in Chapter 14 of John A. Ryan, *Distributive Justice,* 3rd ed. (New York: Macmillan, 1942).

[2]The formula "From each according to his abilities; to each according to his needs" was first advanced by the early French socialists of the Utopian school, and was officially adopted by German socialists in the Gotha Program of 1875 [see Reading 9 for an explanation of the Gotha Program].

[3]Ryan, *Distributive Justice,* p. 181.

[4]Ryan, *Distributive Justice,* pp. 183–84.

CHAPTER V

State Neutrality versus Perfectionism

Should the State Make People Moral?

[T]hose who care for good government take into consideration virtue and vice in states. Whence it may be further inferred that virtue must be the care of the state which is truly so called, and not merely enjoys the name, for without this end the community becomes a mere alliance. Aristotle, Politics *III.9*

Justice as fairness . . . [does not] try to evaluate the relative merits of different conceptions of the good. . . . There is no necessity to compare the worth of the conceptions of different persons once it is supposed they are compatible with the principles of justice. Everyone is assured an equal liberty to pursue whatever plan of life he pleases as long as it does not violate what justice demands. Rawls, A Theory of Justice *(Harvard University Press, 1971), p. 94*

In 1957 the Wolfenden Committee, mandated by the British government to draw up a recommendation regarding the practice of homosexuality, issued the famous Wolfenden Report, in which it argued that there existed a realm of private morality which is sacrosanct, so that the government may not intervene. Essentially, it was a Millian position (see Reading 10), proceeding on the premise that the only legitimate grounds for criminalizing behavior was protection of the society. Where the individual alone is involved, he is sovereign. A distinguished British judge, Lord Patrick Devlin, took exception to the report and in 1959 gave an equally famous lecture, "Morals and the Criminal Law" (Reading 30) in which he argued that the public/private morality distinction was bogus. Where society has widespread deeply shared values, it should legislate those values into criminal law. Just as laws against treason are necessary to protect the State from traitors, so laws against immoral private behavior are necessary to protect the community from corruption and, eventually, dissolution. Hence, since the reasonable person condemns homosexual behavior as immoral, the State has a right to criminalize such behavior. Soon after, Oxford University Professor of Jurisprudence H. L. A. Hart published a sharp critique of Devlin's lecture in the British weekly *The Listener* (Reading 31). Hart de-

fended the Wolfenden Report, taking a Millian position and arguing that the State ought not interfere in people's private lives. This debate inaugurated the present controversy of whether the State may or should criminalize what society perceives as immoral behavior. Reading 32, by Robert George, and Reading 33, by Ronald Dworkin, take up the debate as to whether the State should enforce morality. The debate has been extended by such philosophers as Rawls, Dworkin, George, and George Sher (Reading 43) to cover the issue of pluralism regarding a vision of the good and moral virtues in general.

There is a classical political tradition—going back to Plato, Aristotle, and Aquinas—that holds that a salient function of the State is to help citizens realize the good life, including making people virtuous. An objective theory of the Good is discoverable by reason, and the role of government is to inculcate this notion of the Good in its citizens. This tradition is sometimes referred to as *perfectionism,* since it aims at using the powers of the State to make citizens as morally excellent (or perfect) as possible. (See the opening quote from Aristotle *above.*)

This ideal has been under attack for some time. A rival to the perfectionist tradition—one emphasizing liberty and autonomy rather than a theory of the

Good—has replaced it in the minds of many political theorists. Although the roots of this more modern theory are found in Kant's ideal of autonomy, it was John Stuart Mill, who in his classic work *On Liberty* (Reading 10) argued that the role of government was to protect citizens from harm from others; they should be left alone to do whatever they want, so long as they do not unjustifiably harm others. This modern theory is referred to as the *protectionist* model of government as opposed to the Ancient Greek *perfectionist* model. Although the debate really gets a jump-start with the Devlin-Hart exchange, an earlier and perhaps more cogent defense of protectionism is Karl Popper's *The Open Society and Its Enemies,* volume 1 (1944), in which he attacks Plato's perfectionism as a kind of fascism (comparing it to Nazism), one that in the name of perfect justice would create a perfect hell of injustice (*summum justicia, summa injuria*). Rather than imposing a rigid straightjacket of a single vision of morality onto the world, it is more fitting that the State see its function as protecting people from harm and allowing them to work out their own visions of the Good. The assumption here is that there are many types of the good life, a plurality of visions of the Good, so that the perfectionist model not only deprives people of their legitimate autonomy but also falsely supposes that it has the only correct theory of how life should be lived. For Popper, the very notion of democracy entailed pluralism. Perfectionism is simply a euphemism for tyranny and oppression.

This protectionist model has been developed by contemporary liberal political philosophers, such as Rawls (see quotation at the head of this section), Ronald Dworkin (Reading 33), Bruce Ackerman, Charles Laremore, and Jeremy Waldron under the name of *neutralism.* (See the Bibliography for some of their works.) That is, the State should be neutral concerning particular theories of the Good. Governments ought to provide stability and minimal order in society, so that individual self-determination can flourish. Government and laws ought to be neutral between rival conceptions of the good life for humans, so that government is forbidden from imposing any one particular moral outlook.

The most celebrated neutralist theory is that of Rawls, who in his magnum opus, *A Theory of Justice* (1971; Reading 26), argued in the spirit of Kant and Mill that justice as fairness required that each citizen have maximal liberty to pursue his own notion of the good life. Rawls seems to reject perfectionism for two reasons: (1) because it violates the autonomy of citi-

zens and (2) because it lacks a comprehensive rational defense. Ronald Dworkin presents this liberal neutralist position: "Political decisions must be, so far as possible, independent of any particular conception of the good life, or of what gives value to life" [Reading 33].

Perfectionists, such as Robert George (Reading 32) and George Sher, have responded to the neutralist critique, arguing that neutralists are mistaken on both counts, as well as to the Popperian criticism that perfectionism is undemocratic and oppressive. Against (1) the charge of perfectionism's being inimical to autonomy, they argue that perfectionist policies correctly aim to enhance autonomy by providing the kind of moral education necessary for liberating citizens from slavish self-indulgence, so that they may have a greater possibility of reaching their potential as human beings. Against (2) the charge that perfectionism is indefensible, they argue that a commitment to an objective core morality, which liberal neutralists themselves are (or should be) committed to entails a coherent justification of the perfectionist platform. And against (3) Popper's accusation that perfectionism is oppressive, even fascist, they argue that, although this is a danger, it is not a necessary corollary of perfectionism. The rational ideal aimed for is one wherein progress and criticism are part of the rational program, so that diversity and difference are permitted and celebrated within the context of a comprehensive theory of the good. Whereas some antiperfectionists have accused perfectionists of being dogmatic regarding morality, rhetorically asking, "Who's to judge?" perfectionists respond that impartial reason necessitates moral judgment, pointing out that the kind of relativism implied in the rhetorical question is the nemesis of the neutralist's own program of liberty and tolerance. For, if there is no universal objective core morality, liberty and tolerance are not objectively justified either, so that there is no reason to prefer the liberal state to the fascist.

Sher puts his criticism of liberal neutrality this way:

> I am ambivalent toward contemporary liberalism. On the one hand, I believe that many of today's liberal thinkers are waging a necessary and courageous battle on behalf of certain vital but embattled Enlightenment attitudes—attitudes that include a willingness to abstract away from differences of background and culture to defend universally applicable standards of fairness and right; a commitment to such liberal values as civility, toleration, and respect for others; and, most impor-

tant, a confidence in the power of reason to resolve our disagreements.

But at the same time, contemporary liberal thought has taken a turn I find deeply problematic. For some important reason . . . many liberals have concluded that reason's scope is drastically limited. Though still confident about our ability to reach universally applicable conclusions about justice and rightness, these thinkers are much less sanguine about the prospects for reaching conclusions about goodness or value.[1]

Sher's ambivalence is characteristic of many political philosophers who see a core morality inseparable from a theory of the Good. The same objective reasoning that would lead us to support tolerance and justice as universal moral norms would seem to support a principle of honesty, including rational assessment of the evidence, a principle of promise keeping, a principle of beneficence, and a principle of sobriety and self-discipline. Perhaps some issues are simply matters of taste or free choice, such as what kind of music or art one prefers, one's sexual orientation, whether to marry or to remain single, one's religious preference, and whether one prefers to be a risk taker or a cautious player of life's game. But underlying these options, it seems, there ought to be a common denominator of integrity and self-control (*sophrosune*) necessary for the good life and the good society.

Indeed, most contemporary liberals, like Ronald Dworkin and Jeremy Waldron, accept the notion of an objective core morality but still fear the undermining of autonomy and the danger of an oppressive tyranny inherent in the perfectionist's vision. Rawls, as the quotation at the head of this introduction indicates, thinks that society needs a minimal level of tolerance and respect for others, but, within the scheme of justice, individuals must be let alone to develop their own particular theory of the good life [see Reading 26]. "A community is simply an arena in which individuals each pursue their own self-chosen conception of the good life, and political institutions exist to provide that degree of order which makes such self-determined activity possible."

We must also make a distinction between moral perfectionism, in which the State has an obligation to make people morally better, and legal perfectionism, in which the State has an obligation to make people better by instituting laws imposing sanctions on immoral behavior and, perhaps, rewarding virtuous behavior. It is not always easy to tell which kind of perfectionism a philosopher is advocating. Aristotle, Aquinas, Devlin,

and, to some degree, George seem to be advocating legal *and* moral perfectionism. George puts the matter this way:

> I defend the proposition that, though there are indeed global principles of justice and political morality (principles whose existence enables us to speak meaningfully of fundamental human rights), no such principles exclude the legal enforcement of true moral obligations. I shall argue that someone who has good reasons to believe that a certain act is immoral may support the legal prohibition of the act of protecting public morals without necessarily violating a norm of justice or political morality.

George does not say that the perfectionist must support a legal prohibition against an immoral act. In his book he uses our present antidrug legislation as an example, where a perfectionist may hold that drug use is a bad thing but should not be made illegal.

On the other side, philosophers like Rawls, Hart (Reading 31), Ackerman, and Ronald Dworkin hold that the State should not get into the value question but should let individuals determine their own conception of the Good. In the moral and legal zone, the State must remain neutral.

Reading 34, by William Galston, defends a form of perfectionism from a liberal political philosophy, arguing that liberalism, contrary to the most prominent contemporary liberals and even Kant, is really committed to a vision of the Good.

Who is right? The readings in this chapter, it is hoped, will throw light on that question.

READING 30

The Enforcement of Morals

Patrick Devlin

Patrick Devlin was a distinguished British judge from 1948 to 1960. In this famous lecture, originally entitled, "Morals and the Criminal Law" (1959) Devlin argues that Mill and the Wolfenden Report, which separated public from private morality, were misguided. Our morality is deeply and thoroughly woven into our social fabric, so that to tolerate private immorality (or to leave it unchallenged) is to encourage the dissolution of society from within, in the same way omitting an injunction against treason may encourage traitors to betray their country and so help destroy if from without.

This reading is taken from *The Enforcement of Morals* (Oxford University Press, 1965).

The report of the Committee on Homosexual Offences and Prostitution, generally known as the Wolfenden Report, is recognized to be an excellent study of two very difficult legal and social problems. But it has also a particular claim to the respect of those interested in jurisprudence; it does what law reformers so rarely do; it sets out clearly and carefully what in relation to its subjects it considers the function of the law to be. Statutory additions to the criminal law are too often made on the simple principle that "there ought to be a law against it." The greater part of the law relating to sexual offences is the creation of statute and it is difficult to ascertain any logical relationship between it and the moral ideas which most of us uphold. Adultery, fornication, and prostitution are not, as the Report points out, criminal offences: homosexuality between males is a criminal offence, but between females it is not. Incest was not an offence until it was declared so by statute only fifty years ago. Does the legislature select these offences haphazardly or are there some principles which can be used to determine what part of the moral law should be embodied in the criminal? . . . What is the connection between crime and sin and to what extent, if at all, should the criminal law of England concern itself with the enforcement of morals and punish sin or immorality as such?

The statements of principle in the Wolfenden Report provide an admirable and modern starting-point for such an inquiry. . . .

Early in the Report the Committee put forward

our own formulation of the function of the criminal law so far as it concerns the subjects of this inquiry. In this field, its function, as we see it, is to preserve public order and decency, to protect the citizen from what is offensive or injurious, and to provide sufficient safeguards against exploitation and corruption of others, particularly those who are specially vulnerable because they are young, weak in body or mind, inexperienced, or in a state of special physical, official or economic dependence.

It is not, in our view, the function of the law to intervene in the private lives of citizens, or to

seek to enforce any particular pattern of behavior, further than is necessary to carry out the purposes we have outlined.

The Committee preface their most important recommendation

that homosexual behavior between consenting adults in private should no longer be a criminal offence, [by stating the argument] which we believe to be decisive, namely, the importance which society and the law ought to give to individual freedom of choice and action in matters of private morality. Unless a deliberate attempt is to be made by society, acting through the agency of the law, to equate the sphere of crime with that of sin, there must remain a realm of private morality and immorality which is, in brief and crude terms, not the law's business. To say this is not to condone or encourage private immorality.

Similar statements of principle are set out in the chapters of the Report which deal with prostitution. No case can be sustained, the Report says, for attempting to make prostitution itself illegal. The Committee refer to the general reasons already given and add: "We are agreed that private immorality should not be the concern of the criminal law except in the special circumstances therein mentioned." They quote with approval the report of the Street Offences Committee, which says: "As a general proposition it will be universally accepted that the law is not concerned with private morals or with ethical sanctions." It will be observed that the emphasis is on *private* immorality. By this is meant immorality which is not offensive or injurious to the public in the ways defined or described in the first passage which I quoted. In other words, no act of immorality should be made a criminal offence unless it is accompanied by some other feature such as indecency, corruption, or exploitation. This is clearly brought out in relation to prostitution: "It is not the duty of the law to concern itself with immorality as such . . . it should confine itself to those activities which offend against public order and decency or expose the ordinary citizen to what is offensive or injurious."

These statements of principle are naturally restricted to the subject-matter of the Report. But they are made in general terms and there seems to be no reason why, if they are valid, they should not be applied to the criminal law in general. They separate very decisively crime from sin, the divine law from the secular, and the moral from the criminal. They do not signify any lack of support for the law, moral or criminal, and they do not represent an attitude that can be called either religious or irreligious. There are many schools of thought among those who may think that morals are not the law's business. There is first of all the agnostic or free-thinker. He does not of course disbelieve in morals, nor in sin if it be given the wider of the two meanings assigned to it in the *Oxford English Dictionary* where it is defined as "transgression against divine law or the principles of morality." He cannot accept the divine law; that does not mean that he might not view with suspicion any departure from moral principles that have for generations been accepted by the society in which he lives; but in the end he judges for himself. Then there is the deeply religious person who feels that the criminal law is sometimes more of a hindrance than a help in the sphere of morality, and that the reform of the sinner—at any rate when he injures only himself—should be a spiritual rather than a temporal work. Then there is the man who without any strong feeling cannot see why, where there is freedom in religious belief, there should not logically be freedom in morality as well. All these are powerfully allied against the equating of crime with sin.

I must disclose at the outset that I have as a judge an interest in the result of the inquiry which I am seeking to make as a jurisprudent. . . .

I think it is clear that the criminal law as we know it is based upon moral principle. In a number of crimes its function is simply to enforce a moral principle and nothing else. The law, both criminal and civil, claims to be able to speak about morality and immorality generally. Where does it get its authority to do this and how does it settle the moral principles which it enforces? Undoubtedly, as a matter of history, it derived both from Christian teaching. But I think that the strict logician is right when he says that the law can no longer rely on doctrines in which citizens are entitled to disbelieve. It is necessary therefore to look for some other source.

In jurisprudence . . . everything is thrown open to discussion and, in the belief that they cover the whole field, I have framed three interrogatories addressed to myself to answer:

1. Has society the right to pass judgment at all on matters of morals? Ought there, in other words, to be a public morality, or are morals always a matter for private judgment?
2. If society has the right to pass judgment, has it also the right to use the weapon of the law to enforce it?
3. If so, ought it to use that weapon in all cases or only in some; and if only in some, on what principles should it distinguish?

I shall begin with the first interrogatory and consider what is meant by the right of society to pass a moral judgment, that is, a judgment about what is good and what is evil. The fact that a majority of people may disapprove of a practice does not of itself make it a matter for society as a whole. Nine men out of ten may disapprove of what the tenth man is doing and still say that it is not their business. There is a case for a collective judgment (as distinct from a large number of individual opinions which sensible people may even refrain from pronouncing at all if it is upon somebody else's private affairs) only if society is affected. Without a collective judgment there can be no case at all for intervention. Let me take as an illustration the Englishman's attitude to religion as it is now and as it has been in the past. His attitude now is that a man's religion is his private affair; he may think of another man's religion that it is right or wrong, true or untrue, but not that it is good or bad. In earlier times that was not so; a man was denied the right to practice what was thought of as heresy, and heresy was thought of as destructive of society.

The . . . Wolfenden Report suggests the view that there ought not to be a collective judgment about immorality *per se.* Is this what is meant by "private morality" and "individual freedom of choice and action?" Some people sincerely believe that homosexuality is neither immoral nor unnatural. Is the "freedom of choice and action" that is offered to the individual, freedom to decide for himself what is moral or immoral, society remaining neutral; or is it freedom to be immoral if he wants to be? The language of the Report may be open to question, but the conclusions at which the Committee arrive answer this question unambiguously. If society is not prepared to say that homosexuality is morally wrong, there would be no basis for a law protecting youth from "corruption" or punishing a man for living on the "immoral" earnings of a homosexual prostitute, as the Report recommends. This attitude the Committee make even clearer when they come to deal with prostitution. In truth, the Report takes it for granted that there is in existence a public morality which condemns homosexuality and prostitution. What the Report seems to mean by private morality might perhaps be better described as private behavior in matters of morals.

This view—that there is such a thing as public morality—can also be justified by *a priori* argument. What makes a society of any sort is community of ideas, not only political ideas but also ideas about the way its members should behave and govern their lives; these latter ideas are its morals. Every society has a moral structure as well as a political one: or rather, since that might suggest two independent systems, I should say that the structure of every society is made up both of politics and morals. Take, for example, the institution of marriage. Whether a man should be allowed to take more than one wife is something about which every society has to make up its mind one way or the other. In England we believe in the Christian idea of marriage and therefore adopt monogamy as a moral principle. Consequently the Christian institution of marriage has become the basis of family life and so part of the structure of our society. It is there not because it is Christian. It has got there because it is Christian, but it remains there because it is built into the house in which we live and could not be removed without bringing it down. The great majority of those who live in this country accept it because it is the Christian idea of marriage and for them the only true one. But a non-Christian is bound by it, not because it is part of Christianity but because, rightly or wrongly, it has been adopted by the society in which he lives. It would be useless for him to stage a debate designed to prove that polygamy was theologically more correct and socially preferable; if he wants to live in the house, he must accept it as built in the way in which it is.

We see this more clearly if we think of ideas or institutions that are purely political. Society cannot tolerate rebellion; it will not allow argument about the rightness of the cause. Historians a century later may say that the rebels were right and the Government was wrong and a percipient and conscientious subject of the State may think so at the time. But it is not a matter which can be left to individual judgment.

The institution of marriage is a good example for my purpose because it bridges the division, if there is one, between politics and morals. Marriage is part of the structure of our society and it is also the basis of a moral code which condemns fornication and adultery. The institution of marriage would be gravely threatened if individual judgments were permitted about the morality of adultery; on these points there must be a public morality. But public morality is not to be confined to those moral principles which support institutions such as marriage. People do not think of monogamy as something which has to be supported because our society has chosen to organize itself upon it; they think of it as something that is good in itself and offering a good way of life and that it is for that reason that our society has adopted it. I return to the statement that I have already made, that society means a community of ideas; without shared ideas on politics, morals, and ethics no society can exist. Each one of us

has ideas about what is good and what is evil; they cannot be kept private from the society in which we live. If men and women try to create a society in which there is no fundamental agreement about good and evil they will fail; if, having based it on common agreement, the agreement goes, the society will disintegrate. For society is not something that is kept together physically; it is held by the invisible bonds of common thought. If the bonds were too far relaxed the members would drift apart. A common morality is part of the bondage. The bondage is part of the price of society; and mankind, which needs society, must pay its price. . . .

You may think that I have taken far too long in contending that there is such a thing as public morality, a proposition which most people would readily accept, and may have left myself too little time to discuss the next question which to many minds may cause greater difficulty: to what extent should society use the law to enforce its moral judgments? But I believe that the answer to the first question determines the way in which the second should be approached and may indeed very nearly dictate the answer to the second question. If society has no right to make judgments on morals, the law must find some special justification for entering the field of morality: if homosexuality and prostitution are not in themselves wrong, then the onus is very clearly on the lawgiver who wants to frame a law against certain aspects of them to justify the exceptional treatment. But if society has the right to make a judgment and has it on the basis that a recognized morality is as necessary to society as, say, a recognized government, then society may use the law to preserve morality in the same way as it uses it to safeguard anything else that is essential to its existence. If therefore the first proposition is securely established with all its implications, society has a *prima facie* right to legislate against immorality as such. . . .

I think, therefore, that it is not possible to set theoretical limits to the power of the State to legislate against immorality. It is not possible to settle in advance exceptions to the general rule or to define inflexibly areas of morality into which the law is in no circumstances to be allowed to enter. Society is entitled by means of its laws to protect itself from dangers, whether from within or without. Here again I think that the political parallel is legitimate. The law of treason is directed against aiding the king's enemies and against sedition from within. The justification for this is that established government is necessary for the existence of society and therefore its safety against violent overthrow must be secured. But an established morality is as necessary as good government to the welfare of society. Societies disintegrate from within more frequently than they are broken up by external pressures. There is disintegration when no common morality is observed and history shows that the loosening of moral bonds is often the first stage of disintegration, so that society is justified in taking the same steps to preserve its moral code as it does to preserve its government and other essential institutions. The suppression of vice is as much the law's business as the suppression of subversive activities; it is no more possible to define a sphere of private morality than it is to define one of private subversive activity. It is wrong to talk of private morality or of the law not being concerned with immorality as such or to try to set rigid bounds to the part which the law may play in the suppression of vice. There are no theoretical limits to the power of the State to legislate against treason and sedition, and likewise I think there can be no theoretical limits to legislation against immorality. You may argue that if a man's sins affect only himself it cannot be the concern of society. If he chooses to get drunk every night in the privacy of his own home, is any one except himself the worse for it? But suppose a quarter or a half of the population got drunk every night, what sort of society would it be? You cannot set a theoretical limit to the number of people who can get drunk before society is entitled to legislate against drunkenness. The same may be said of gambling. The Royal Commission on Betting, Lotteries, and Gaming took as their test the character of the citizen as a member of society. They said: "Our concern with the ethical significance of gambling is confined to the effect which it may have on the character of the gambler as a member of society. If we were convinced that whatever the degree of gambling this effect must be harmful we should be inclined to think that it was the duty of the state to restrict gambling to the greatest extent practicable."

In what circumstances the State should exercise its power is the third of the interrogatories I have framed. But before I get to it I must raise a point which might have been brought up in any one of the three. How are the moral judgments of society to be ascertained? By leaving it until now, I can ask it in the more limited form that is now sufficient for my purpose. How is the law-maker to ascertain the moral judgments of society? It is surely not enough that they should be reached by the opinion of the majority; it would be too much to require the individual assent of every citizen. English law has evolved and regularly uses a standard which does not depend on the counting of heads. It is that of the reasonable man. He is not to be confused with the

rational man. He is not expected to reason about anything and his judgment may be largely a matter of feeling. It is the viewpoint of the man in the street—or to use an archaism familiar to all lawyers—the man in the Clapham omnibus. He might also be called the right-minded man. For my purpose I should like to call him the man in the jury box, for the moral judgment of society must be something about which any twelve men or women drawn at random might after discussion be expected to be unanimous. . . .

Immorality then, for the purpose of the law, is what every right-minded person is presumed to consider to be immoral. Any immorality is capable of affecting society injuriously and in effect to a greater or lesser extent it usually does; this is what gives the law its *locus standi*. It cannot be shut out. But—and this brings me to the third question—the individual has a *locus standi* too; he cannot be expected to surrender to the judgment of society the whole conduct of his life. It is the old and familiar question of striking a balance between the rights and interests of society and those of the individual. This is something which the law is constantly doing in matters large and small. To take a very down-to-earth example, let me consider the right of the individual whose house adjoins the highway to have access to it; that means in these days the right to have vehicles stationary in the highway, sometimes for a considerable time if there is a lot of loading or unloading. There are many cases in which the courts have had to balance the private right of access against the public right to use the highway without obstruction. It cannot be done by carving up the highway into public and private areas. It is done by recognizing that each have rights over the whole; that if each were to exercise their rights to the full, they would come into conflict; and therefore that the rights of each must be curtailed so as to ensure as far as possible that the essential needs of each are safeguarded.

I do not think that one can talk sensibly of a public and private morality any more than one can of a public or private highway. Morality is a sphere in which there is a public interest and a private interest, often in conflict, and the problem is to reconcile the two. This does not mean that it is impossible to put forward any general statements about how in our society the balance ought to be struck. Such statements cannot of their nature be rigid or precise. . . . Nothing should be punished by the law that does not lie beyond the limits of tolerance; it is not nearly enough to say that a majority dislike a practice; there must be a real feeling of reprobation. Those who are dissatisfied with the present law on homosexuality often say that the opponents of reform are swayed simply by disgust. If that were so it would be wrong, but I do not think one can ignore disgust if it is deeply felt and not manufactured. Its presence is a good indication that the bounds of toleration are being reached. Not everything is to be tolerated. No society can do without intolerance, indignation, and disgust; they are the forces behind the moral law, and indeed it can be argued that if they or something like them are not present, the feelings of society cannot be weighty enough to deprive the individual of freedom of choice. I suppose that there is hardly anyone nowadays who would not be disgusted by the thought of deliberate cruelty to animals. No one proposes to relegate that or any other form of sadism to the realm of private morality or to allow it to be practiced in public or in private. It would be possible no doubt to point out that until a comparatively short while ago nobody thought very much of cruelty to animals and also that pity and kindliness and the unwillingness to inflict pain are virtues more generally esteemed now than they have ever been in the past. But matters of this sort are not determined by rational argument. Every moral judgment, unless it claims a divine source, is simply a feeling that no right-minded man could behave in any other way without admitting that he was doing wrong. It is the power of a common sense and not the power of reason that is behind the judgments of society. But before a society can put a practice beyond the limits of tolerance there must be a deliberate judgment that the practice is injurious to society. There is, for example, a general abhorrence of homosexuality. We should ask ourselves in the first instance whether, looking at it calmly and dispassionately, we regard it as a vice so abominable that its mere presence is an offence. If that is the genuine feeling of the society in which we live, I do not see how society can be denied the right to eradicate it. Our feeling may not be so intense as that. We may feel about it that, if confined, it is tolerable, but that if it spread it might be gravely injurious; it is in this way that most societies look upon fornication, seeing it as a natural weakness which must be kept within bounds but which cannot be rooted out. It becomes then a question of balance, the danger to society in one scale and the extent of the restriction in the other. . . .

The limits of tolerance shift. This is supplementary to what I have been saying but of sufficient importance in itself to deserve statement as a separate principle which law-makers have to bear in mind. I suppose that moral standards do not shift; so far as they come from divine revelation they do not, and I am willing to assume that the moral judgments made by a so-

ciety always remain good for that society. But the extent to which society will tolerate—I mean tolerate, not approve—departures from moral standards varies from generation to generation. It may be that over-all tolerance is always increasing. The pressure of the human mind, always seeking greater freedom of thought, is outwards against the bonds of society forcing their gradual relaxation. It may be that history is a tale of contraction and expansion and that all developed societies are on their way to dissolution. I must not speak of things I do not know; and anyway as a practical matter no society is willing to make provision for its own decay. I return therefore to the simple and observable fact that in matters of morals the limits of tolerance shift. Laws, especially those which are based on morals, are less easily moved. It follows as another good working principle that in any new matter of morals the law should be slow to act. By the next generation the swell of indignation may have abated and the law be left without the strong backing which it needs. But it is then difficult to alter the law without giving the impression that moral judgment is being weakened. This is now one of the factors that is strongly militating against any alteration to the law on homosexuality. . . .

It is that as far as possible privacy should be respected. This is not an idea that has ever been made explicit in the criminal law. Acts or words done or said in public or in private are all brought within its scope without distinction in principle. But there goes with this a strong reluctance on the part of judges and legislators to sanction invasions of privacy in the detection of crime. The police have no more right to trespass than the ordinary citizen has; there is no general right of search; to this extent an Englishman's home is still his castle. The Government is extremely careful in the exercise even of those powers which it claims to be undisputed. Telephone tapping and interference with the mails afford a good illustration of this. . . .

The part that the jury plays in the enforcement of the criminal law, the fact that no grave offence against morals is punishable without their verdict, these are of great importance in relation to the statements of principle that I have been making. They turn what might otherwise be pure exhortation to the legislature into something like rules that the law-makers cannot safely ignore. The man in the jury box is not just an expression; he is an active reality. It will not in the long run work to make laws about morality that are not acceptable to him.

This then is how I believe my third interrogatory should be answered—not by the formulation of hard and fast rules, but by a judgement in each case taking into account the sort of factors I have been mentioning. . . .

The true principle is that the law exists for the protection of society. It does not discharge its function by protecting the individual from injury, annoyance, corruption, and exploitation; the law must protect also the institutions and the community of ideas, political and moral, without which people cannot live together. Society cannot ignore the morality of the individual any more than it can his loyalty; it flourishes on both and without either it dies.

I have said that the morals which underlay the law must be derived from the sense of right and wrong which resides in the community as a whole; it does not matter whence the community of thought comes, whether from one body of doctrine or another or from the knowledge of good and evil which no man is without. If the reasonable man believes that a practice is immoral and believes also—no matter whether the belief is right or wrong, so be it that it is honest and dispassionate—that no right-minded member of his society could think otherwise, then for the purpose of the law it is immoral. This, you may say, makes immorality a question of fact—what the law would consider as self-evident fact no doubt, but still with no higher authority than any other doctrine of public policy. I think that that is so, and indeed the law does not distinguish between an act that is immoral and one that is contrary to public policy. But the law has never yet had occasion to inquire into the differences between Christian morals and those which every right-minded member of society is expected to hold. The inquiry would, I believe, be academic. Moralists would find differences; indeed they would find them between different branches of the Christian faith on subjects such as divorce and birth-control. But for the purpose of the limited entry which the law makes into the field of morals, there is no practical difference. It seems to me therefore that the free-thinker and the non-Christian can accept, without offence to his convictions, the fact that Christian morals are the basis of the criminal law and that he can recognize, also without taking offence, that without the support of the churches the moral order, which has its origin in and takes its strength from Christian beliefs, would collapse. . . .

I return now to the main thread of my argument and summarize it. Society cannot live without morals. Its morals are those standards of conduct which the reasonable man approves. A rational man, who is also a good man, may have other standards. If he has no standards at all he is not a good man and need not be further considered. If he has standards, they may be very different; he may, for example, not disapprove of homosexuality or abortion. In that case he will not share in the common morality; but that should not make him deny that it is a social necessity. A rebel may be rational in thinking that he is right but he is irrational if he thinks that society can leave him free to rebel.

A man who concedes that morality is necessary to society must support the use of those instruments without which morality cannot be maintained. The two instruments are those of teaching, which is doctrine, and of enforcement, which is the law. . . .

Freedom is not a good in itself. We believe it to be good because out of freedom there comes more good than bad. If a free society is better than a disciplined one, it is because—and this certainly was Mill's view—it is better for a man himself that he should be free to seek his own good in his own way and better too for the society to which he belongs, since thereby a way may be found to a greater good for all. But no good can come from a man doing what he acknowledges to be evil. The freedom that is worth having is freedom to do what you think to be good notwithstanding that others think it to be bad. Freedom to do what you know to be bad is worthless. . . .

Granted then that the law can play some part in the war against vice, ought it to be excluded for the reason that private vice cannot do any harm to society? I think that it is capable of doing both physical harm and spiritual harm. Tangible and intangible may be better words; body and soul a better simile.

Let me consider first the tangible harm. It is obvious that an individual may by unrestricted indulgence in vice so weaken himself that he ceases to be a useful member of society. It is obvious also that if a sufficient number of individuals so weaken themselves, society will thereby be weakened. That is what I mean by tangible harm to society. If the proportion grows sufficiently large, society will succumb either to its own disease or to external pressure. A nation of debauchees would not in 1940 have responded satisfactorily to Winston Churchill's call to blood and toil and sweat and tears. I doubt if any of this would be denied. The answer that is made to it is that the danger, if private immorality were tolerated, of vice spreading to such an extent as to affect society as a whole is negligible and in a free society ought to be ignored. . . .

In the same way, while a few people getting drunk in private cause no problem at all, widespread drunkenness, whether in private or public, would create a social problem. The line between drunkenness that creates a social problem of sufficient magnitude to justify the intervention of the law and that which does not, cannot be drawn on the distinction between private indulgence and public sobriety. It is a practical one, based on an estimate of what can safely be tolerated whether in public or in private, and shifting from time to time as circumstances change. The licensing laws coupled with high taxation may be all that is needed. But if more be needed there is no doctrinal answer even to complete prohibition. It cannot be said that so much is the law's business but more is not.

I move now to the consideration of intangible harm to society and begin by noting a significant distinction. When considering tangible damage to society we are concerned chiefly with immoral activity. Moral belief is relevant only in so far as the lack of it contributes to immoral activity. A vicious minority diminishes the physical strength of society even if all its members believe themselves to be sinning. But if they all believed that, they would not diminish the common belief in right and wrong which is the intangible property of society. When considering intangible injury to society it is moral belief that matters; immoral activity is relevant only in so far as it promotes disbelief.

It is generally accepted that some shared morality, that is, some common agreement about what is right and what is wrong, is an essential element in the constitution of any society. Without it there would be no cohesion. But polygamy can be as cohesive as monogamy and I am prepared to believe that a society based on free love and a community of children could be just as strong (though according to our ideas it could not be as good) as one based on the family. What is important is not the quality of the creed but the strength of the belief in it. The enemy of society is not error but indifference.

On this reasoning there is nothing inherently objectionable about the change of an old morality for a new one. Why then is the law used to guard existing moral beliefs? It is because an old morality cannot be changed for a new morality as an old coat for a new one. The old belief must be driven out by disbelief. . . .

It can be said in general terms, and often is, that law-makers are bound to legislate for the common good. The common good is perhaps a useful and compendious, if vague, description of all the things law-makers should have in mind when they legislate. But it does not constitute a clear limitation on the right to legislate. There may be a difference of opinion about what is for the common good which can be solved only by a judgment upon the conflicting values. Society alone

can make that judgment and if it makes it honestly, it is a judgment that cannot be impugned.

Can then the judgment of society sanction every invasion of a man's privacy, however extreme? Theoretically that must be so; there is no theoretical limitation. Society must be the judge of what is necessary to its own integrity if only because there is no other tribunal to which the question can be submitted. In a free society the understanding that men have with each other is that each shall retain for himself the greatest measure of personal freedom that is compatible with the integrity and good government of his society. In a free society men must trust each other and each man must put his trust in his fellows that they will not interfere with him unless in their honest judgment it is necessary to do so. Furthermore, in a free society checks are usually put upon the government, both the executive and the legislature, so that it is difficult for them to enact and enforce a law that takes away another's freedom unless in the honest judgment of society it is necessary to do so. One sort of check consists in the safeguarding of certain specific freedoms by the articles of a constitution; another consists in trial by jury. But the only certain security is the understanding in the heart of every man that he must not condemn what another does unless he honestly considers that it is a threat to the integrity or good government of their society.

If one man practices what he calls virtue and the others call vice and if he fails to convince the others that they are wrong, he has the right to make a further appeal. He has, in a free society, a right to claim that however much the others dislike and deplore what he does, they should allow him to do it unless they are genuinely convinced that it threatens the integrity of society. If the others reject that appeal, constitutionally that is the end. He must either submit or reject society. . . .

READING 31

Immorality and Treason

H. L. A. Hart

H. L. A. Hart (1907–92) was Professor of Jurisprudence at Oxford University from 1952 to 1968 and was arguably the most influential philosopher of law of his generation. His most significant works are *The Concept of Law* (1961) and *Punishment and Responsibility* (1968).

In this essay Hart critiques Patrick Devlin's argument (see Reading 30) against the Millian protectionist doctrine of protecting one's privacy. He argues that Devlin fails to offer sufficient reason for criminalizing *victimless crimes* (widespread personal disgust is inadequate to label behavior a crime) and that his comparison of private immorality with private treason is absurd.

This reading is taken from *The Listener,* July 30, 1959.

The most remarkable feature of Sir Patrick's lecture is his view of the nature of morality—the morality which the criminal law may enforce. Most previous thinkers who have repudiated the liberal point of view have done so because they thought that morality consisted either of divine commands or of rational principles of human conduct discoverable by human reason. Since morality for them had this elevated divine or rational status as the law of God or reason, it seemed obvious that the state should enforce it, and that the function of human law should not be merely to provide men with the opportunity for leading a good life, but actually to see that they lead it. Sir Patrick does not rest his repudiation of the liberal point of view on these religious or rationalist conceptions. Indeed much that he writes reads like an abjuration of the notion that reasoning or thinking has much to do with morality. English popular morality has no doubt its historical connection with the Christian religion: "That," says Sir Patrick, "is how it got there." But it does not owe its present status or social significance to religion any more than to reason.

What then, is it? According to Sir Patrick it is primarily a matter of feeling. "Every moral judgment," he says, "is a feeling that no right-minded man could act in any other way without admitting that he was doing wrong." Who then must feel this way if we are to have what Sir Patrick calls a public morality? He tells us that it is "the man in the street," "the man in the jury box," or (to use the phrase so familiar to English lawyers) "the man on the Clapham omnibus." For the moral judgments of society so far as the law is concerned are to be ascertained by the standards of the reasonable man, and he is not to be confused with the rational man. Indeed, Sir Patrick says "he is not expected to reason about anything and his judgment may be largely a matter of feeling."

INTOLERANCE, INDIGNATION, AND DISGUST

But what precisely are the relevant feelings, the feelings which may justify use of the criminal law? Here the argument becomes a little complex. Widespread dislike of a practice is not enough. There must, says Sir Patrick, be "a real feeling of reprobation." Disgust is not enough either. What is crucial is a combination of intolerance, indignation, and disgust. These three are the forces behind the moral law, without which it is not "weighty enough to deprive the individual of freedom of choice." Hence there is, in Sir Patrick's outlook, a crucial difference between the mere adverse moral judgment of society and one which is inspired by feeling raised to the concert pitch of intolerance, indignation, and disgust.

This distinction is novel and also very important. For on it depends the weight to be given to the fact that when morality is enforced individual liberty is necessarily cut down. Though Sir Patrick's abstract formulation of his views on this point is hard to follow, his examples make his position fairly clear. We can see it best in the contrasting things he says about fornication and homosexuality. In regard to fornication, public feeling in most societies is not now of the concert-pitch intensity. We may feel that it is tolerable if confined: only its spread might be gravely injurious. In such cases the question whether individual liberty should be restricted is for Sir Patrick a question of balance between the danger to society in the one scale, and the restriction of the individual in the other. But if, as may be the case with homosexuality, public feeling is up to concert pitch, if it expresses a "deliberate judgment" that a practice as such is injurious to society, if there is "a genuine feeling that it is a vice so abominable that its mere presence is an offence," then it is beyond the limits of tolerance, and society may eradicate it. In this case, it seems, no further balancing of the claims of individual liberty is to be done, though as a matter of prudence the legislator should remember that the popular limits of tolerance may shift: the concert-pitch feeling may subside. This may produce a dilemma for the law; for the law may then be left without the full moral backing that it needs, yet it cannot be altered without giving the impression that the moral judgment is being weakened. . . .

If this is what morality is—a compound of indignation, intolerance, and disgust—we may well ask what justification there is for taking it, and turning it as such, into criminal law with all the misery which criminal punishment entails. Here Sir Patrick's answer is very clear and simple. A collection of individuals is not a society; what makes them into a society is among other things a shared or public morality. This is as necessary to its existence as an organized government. So society may use the law to preserve its morality like anything else essential to it. "The suppression of vice is as much the law's business as the suppression of subversive activities." The liberal point of view which denies this is guilty of "an error in jurisprudence:" for it is no more possible to define an area of private morality than an area of private subversive activity. There can be no "theoretical limits" to legislation against immorality just as there are no such limits to the power of the state to legislate against treason and sedition.

Surely all this, ingenious as it is, is misleading. Mill's formulation of the liberal point of view may well be too simple. The grounds for interfering with human liberty are more various than the single criterion of "harm to others" suggests: cruelty to animals or organizing prostitution for gain do not, as Mill himself saw, fall easily under the description of harm to others. Conversely, even where there is harm to others in the most literal sense, there may well be other principles limiting the extent to which harmful activities should be repressed by law. So there are multiple criteria, not a single criterion, determining when human liberty may be restricted. Perhaps this is what Sir Patrick means by a curious distinction which he often stresses between theoretical and practical limits. But with all its simplicities the liberal point of view is a better guide than Sir Patrick to clear thought on the proper relation of morality to the criminal law: for it stresses what he obscures—namely, the points at which thought is needed before we turn popular morality into criminal law. . . .

No doubt we would all agree that a consensus of moral opinion on certain matters is essential if society is to be worth living in. Laws against murder, theft, and much else would be of little use if they were not supported by a widely diffused conviction that what these laws forbid is also immoral. So much is obvious. But it does not follow that everything to which the moral vetoes of accepted morality attach is of equal importance to society; nor is there the slightest reason for thinking of morality as a seamless web: one which will fall to pieces carrying society with it, unless all its emphatic vetoes are enforced by law. Surely even in the face of the moral feeling that is up to concert pitch—the trio of intolerance, indignation, and disgust—we must pause to think. We must ask a question at two different levels which Sir Patrick never clearly enough

identifies or separates. First, we must ask whether a practice which offends moral feeling is harmful, independently of its repercussion on the general moral code. Secondly, what about repercussion on the moral code? Is it really true that failure to translate this item of general morality into criminal law will jeopardize the whole fabric of morality and so of society?

We cannot escape thinking about these two different questions merely by repeating to ourselves the vague nostrum: "This is part of public morality and public morality must be preserved if society is to exist." Sometimes Sir Patrick seems to admit this, for he says in words which both Mill and the Wolfenden Report might have used, that there must be the maximum respect for individual liberty consistent with the integrity of society. Yet this, as his contrasting examples of fornication and homosexuality show, turns out to mean only that the immorality which the law may punish must be generally felt to be intolerable. This plainly is no adequate substitute for a reasoned estimate of the damage to the fabric of society likely to ensue if it is not suppressed.

Nothing perhaps shows more clearly the inadequacy of Sir Patrick's approach to this problem than his comparison between the suppression of sexual immorality and the suppression of treason or subversive activity. Private subversive activity is, of course, a contradiction in terms because "subversion" means overthrowing government, which is a public thing. But it is grotesque, even where moral feeling against homosexuality is up to concert pitch, to think of the homosexual behavior of two adults in private as in any way like treason or sedition either in intention or effect. We can make it *seem* like treason only if we assume that deviation from a general moral code is bound to affect that code, and to lead not merely to its modification but to its destruction. The analogy could begin to be plausible only if it was clear that offending against this item of morality was likely to jeopardize the whole structure. But we have ample evidence for believing that people will not abandon morality, will not think any better of murder, cruelty, and dishonesty, merely because some private sexual practice which they abominate is not punished by the law.

Because this is so the analogy with treason is absurd. Of course "No man is an island:" what one man does in private, if it is known, may affect others in many different ways. Indeed it may be that deviation from general sexual morality by those whose lives, like the lives of many homosexuals, are noble ones and in all other ways exemplary will lead to what Sir Patrick calls the shifting of the limits of tolerance. But if this has any analogy in the sphere of government it is not the overthrow of ordered government, but a peaceful change in its form. So we may listen to the promptings of common sense and of logic, and say that though there could not logically be a sphere of private treason there is a sphere of private morality and immorality.

Sir Patrick's doctrine is also open to a wider, perhaps a deeper, criticism. In his reaction against a rationalist morality and his stress on feeling, he has I think thrown out the baby and kept the bath water; and the bath water may turn out to be very dirty indeed. When Sir Patrick's lecture was first delivered *The Times* greeted it with these words: "There is a moving and welcome humility in the conception that society should not be asked to give its reason for refusing to tolerate what in its heart it feels intolerable." This drew from a correspondent in Cambridge the retort: "I am afraid that we are less humble than we used to be. We once burnt old women because, without giving our reasons, we felt in our hearts that witchcraft was intolerable."

This retort is a bitter one, yet its bitterness is salutary. We are not, I suppose, likely, in England, to take again to the burning of old women for witchcraft or to punishing people for associating with those of a different race or colour, or to punishing people again for adultery. Yet if these things were viewed with intolerance, indignation, and disgust, as the second of them still is in some countries, it seems that on Sir Patrick's principles no rational criticism could be opposed to the claim that they should be punished by law. We could only pray, in his words, that the limits of tolerance might shift. . . .

It is impossible to see what curious logic has led Sir Patrick to this result. For him a practice is immoral if the thought of it makes the man on the Clapham omnibus sick. So be it. Still, why should we not summon all the resources of our reason, sympathetic understanding, as well as critical intelligence, and insist that before general moral feeling is turned into criminal law it is submitted to scrutiny of a different kind from Sir Patrick's? Surely, the legislator should ask whether the general morality is based on ignorance, superstition, or misunderstanding; whether there is a false conception that those who practice what it condemns are in other ways dangerous or hostile to society; and whether the misery to many parties, the blackmail and the other evil consequences of criminal punishment, especially for sexual offences, are well understood. It is surely extraordinary that among the things which Sir Patrick says are to be considered before we legislate against immorality these appear nowhere; not even as "practical considerations," let alone "theoretical limits." To any

theory which, like this one, asserts that the criminal law may be used on the vague ground that the preservation of morality is essential to society and yet omits to stress the need for critical scrutiny, our reply should be: "Morality, what crimes may be committed in thy name!"

As Mill saw, and de Tocqueville showed in detail long ago in his critical but sympathetic study of democracy, it is fatally easy to confuse the democratic principle that power should be in the hands of the majority with the utterly different claim that the majority with power in their hands need respect no limits. Certainly there is a special risk in a democracy that the majority may dictate how all should live. This is the risk we run, and should gladly run; for it is the price of all that is so good in democratic rule. But loyalty to democratic principles does not require us to maximize this risk; yet this is what we shall do if we mount the man in the street on the top of the Clapham omnibus and tell him that if only he feels sick enough about what other people do in private to demand its suppression by law no theoretical criticism can be made of his demand.

READING 32

The Central Tradition: Classical Perfectionism

Robert George

Robert George is Professor of Philosophy at Princeton University and the author of several works in legal and political philosophy, including *How to Make Men Moral*, from which this selection is taken.

George describes and subscribes to what he calls the "central tradition" of political perfectionism, especially in the philosophy of Aristotle and Aquinas, in which governments through good laws and institutions (e.g., schools, religious establishments, and family) should be concerned to help citizens reach virtuous and worthwhile lives.

This reading is taken from *How to Make Men Moral: Civil Liberties and Public Morality* (Oxford University Press, 1993), by permission. [Notes edited. Ed.]

. . . Mainstream contemporary liberalism (which, after the demise of Marxism, is surely *the* principal rival) challenges the "perfectionism" of the central tradition as inconsistent with a due regard for human liberty. It rejects the central tradition's aspirations to "make men moral" on the ground that perfectionist laws and policies violate fundamental principles of justice and human rights. Orthodox liberals maintain that the moral perfection of human beings, while in itself desirable, is not a valid reason for *political* action. Hence, they advance "anti-perfectionist" theories of justice and political morality that rule out "morals laws" and other perfectionist policies as a matter of moral principle.

In the chapters that follow, I shall defend the perfectionism of the central tradition. I shall argue that sound politics and good law *are* concerned with helping people to lead morally upright and valuable lives, and, indeed, that a good political society may justly bring to bear the coercive power of public authority to provide people with some protection from the corrupting influences of vice.[1] I am not prepared, however, to endorse everything that the principal architects of the central tradition have said regarding the legitimacy of political action undertaken for the sake of leading people to virtue. So in this chapter I shall lay out what I accept (and mean to defend in the chapters that follow), and what I reject (finding it indefensible), and why.

I shall focus on the perfectionism of Aristotle and Aquinas, the two thinkers who have most profoundly influenced the tradition. Although the tradition, as embodied in actual laws and policies as well as in the thinking of later philosophers, has not followed their teachings in every respect, it is imbued with their perfectionist understandings of justice and political morality. In rejecting perfectionism, orthodox liberals deny the validity of essential tenets of Aristotelian and Thomistic political theory. I concede that liberalism is rightly critical of important elements of the political teachings of Aristotle and Aquinas, but shall argue that, stripped of these mistaken ideas, their perfectionism is sound and defensible.

II. ARISTOTLE ON THE ROLE OF THE *POLIS* IN MAKING MEN MORAL

No one deserves more credit (or blame) than Aristotle for shaping the central tradition's ideas about justice and political morality. Centuries before the liberal assault on the tradition got into full swing, Aristotle himself anticipated, criticized, and firmly rejected what has become the defining doctrine of mainstream contemporary liberalism, namely, the belief that the law of a political community (*polis*) should be merely "(in the phrase of the Sophist Lycophron) 'a guarantor of men's rights against one another'—instead of being as it should be, a rule of life such as will make the members of a polis good and just."[2] Aristotle's argument in his *Politics* was that:

> any polis which is truly so called, and is not merely one in name, must devote itself to the end of encouraging goodness. Otherwise a political association sinks into a mere alliance, which only differs in space [i.e. in the contiguity of its members] from other forms of alliance where the members live at a distance from one another . . . a polis is not an association for residence on a common site, or for the sake of preventing mutual injustice and easing exchange. There are indeed conditions which must be present before a polis can exist; but the presence of all these conditions is not enough, in itself, to constitute a polis. What constitutes a polis is an association of households and clans in a good life, for the sake of attaining a perfect and self-suffising existence. . . . It is therefore for the sake of good actions, and not for the sake of social life, that political associations must be considered to exist.[3]

Making men moral, Aristotle supposed, is a—if not *the*—central purpose of any genuine political community. Why?

To answer that question, we must turn to Aristotle's writing on moral goodness and virtue. Near the end of the *Nicomachean Ethics,* he pointedly asks why sound moral arguments are not in and of themselves sufficient to lead men away from vice and toward virtue. Having provided, at least in outline, a philosophical account of "the virtues, and also friendship and pleasure," Aristotle suggests the need for the project he undertakes in his *Politics,* observing that:

> while [moral arguments] seem to have power to encourage and stimulate the generous-minded among our youth, and to make a character which is gently born, and a true lover of what is noble, ready to be possessed by virtue, they are not able to encourage the *many* to nobility and goodness.[4]

Why not? Are "the many" too stupid to understand moral arguments? People obviously differ in native intelligence; and it is plausible to think that only a minority of people have the intellectual capacity to follow the most subtle and complex philosophical arguments. Is it the case that, when it comes to the power of moral arguments to encourage and stimulate people to nobility and goodness, the difference between "the many" for whom the arguments are insufficient, and the few for whom they are virtually all that is needed, is one in native intelligence?

No. While Aristotle suggests that "the many" and "the few" differ by nature, the relevant difference, as he sees it, is not, or at least not fundamentally, a difference in raw intellectual capacity to follow philosophical argumentation. Rather, it is from the start a difference in *character*. The problem with "the many" is that:

> these do not by nature obey the sense of shame, but only fear, and do not abstain from bad acts because of their baseness but through fear of punishment; living by passion they pursue their own pleasures and the means to them, and avoid the opposite pains, and have not even a conception of what is noble and truly pleasant, since they have never tasted it. [*Nic. Eth.*]

Is virtue, then, unattainable by "the many?" Is the average person, "living by passion," and lacking "a character which is gently born, and a true lover of what is noble," simply incapable of living virtuously? Aristotle indeed concludes that moral argument is futile with such people. It is pointless to argue with them. Argument can merely inform people of the right thing to do; it cannot motivate them to do it. Thus argument is sufficient only for the already "generous-minded" few who have been blessed by nature with a character "ready to be possessed by virtue." Nevertheless, Aristotle holds that other means may dispose those whose character is not "gently born" to attain some measure of moral goodness:

> It is hard if not impossible, to remove by argument the traits that have long since been incorporated in the character; and perhaps we must be content if, when all the influences by which we are thought to become good are present, we get some tincture of virtue. [*Nic. Eth.*]

What are these "influences by which we are thought to become good?" How can "the many" be brought under them? Plainly Aristotle supposes that character is, by and large, given by nature. Of nature's part in making men good, he says that it "evidently does not depend on us, but as a result of some divine causes is present in those who are truly fortunate." Nevertheless, he maintains that the character of the av-

erage person is not completely fixed by nature; it can be improved, if only slightly, by good influences. These influences can supply a bit (though apparently not much) of what nature has left out of the character of the average person, thus making it possible for him to "get some tincture of virtue."

Inasmuch, however, as the average person is moved by passion and not by reason, what is needed to prepare him for virtue is not argument, but coercion. "In general," Aristotle says, "passion seems to yield not to argument but to force." Therefore, if "the many" are to have even the small measure of moral goodness of which they are capable, they must be forbidden from doing what is morally wrong and required to do what morality requires; and these commands must be backed by threats of punishment. If people have passionate motives (e.g., love of pleasure) for doing what is morally bad, they must be presented with more powerful countervailing passionate motives (e.g., fear of pain) not to do it. While people motivated by love of what is morally good can be expected to do the right thing *because* it is the right thing (once they understand it to be the right thing), people motivated by passion cannot be expected to do the right thing when they have a passionate motive not to do it and no more powerful countervailing passionate motive to do it. They can be expected to do what is right only when their passionate motives for doing so are more powerful than any competing passionate motives for not doing so. A lively fear of a sufficient punishment typically provides the countervailing motive needed to get the average person to do what is right and avoid doing what is wrong.

Building thus on an analysis of character and its formation, Aristotle develops his view of the role of law in providing the influences necessary to make men moral. Here again I shall let Aristotle speak for himself:

> But it is difficult to get from youth up a right training for virtue if one has not been brought up under right laws; for to live temperately and hardily is not pleasant to most people, especially when they are young. For this reason their nurture and occupations should be fixed by law; for they will not be painful when they have become customary. But it is surely not enough that when they are young they should get the right nurture and attention; since they must, even when they are grown up, practise and be habituated to them, we shall need laws for this as well, and generally speaking to cover the whole of life; for most people obey necessity rather than argument, and punishments rather than the sense of what is noble. [*Nic. Eth.*]

Apparently referring to the teaching of Plato, he goes on to observe that:

> This is why some think that legislators ought to stimulate men to virtue and urge them forward by the motive of the noble, on the assumption that those who have been well advanced by the formation of habits will attend to such influences; and that punishments and penalties should be imposed on those who disobey and are of inferior nature, while the incurably bad should be completely banished. A good man . . . will submit to argument, while a bad man, whose desire is for pleasure, is corrected by pain like a beast of burden. This is, too, why they say the pains inflicted should be those that are most opposed to the pleasures men love. [*Nic. Eth.*]

It may seem from these passages that Aristotle has missed an elementary point about moral goodness, namely, that coercing people to do the right thing, even when it is successful, does not make them morally better; it does nothing more than produce external conformity to moral norms. Morality, however, is above all an internal matter, a matter of rectitude in choosing: one becomes morally good precisely, and only, by doing the right thing *for the right reason*. In other words, morality, unlike knowledge, or beauty, or even skillful performance, is a reflexive good, namely, a good that is (and can only be) realized in *choosing* uprightly, reasonably, well; a good into whose very definition *choice* enters. A coerced choice, however, does not adopt the good and the reason which might have shaped the chosen option; instead one adopts that option for the sake of avoiding pain, harm, or loss to oneself. So, someone is not "just and noble" for doing merely out of fear of punishment something that would truly be just and noble if done for the sake of what is good and right. If the legal enforcement of moral obligations does nothing more for the masses than present them with subrational motives for outward conformity with what morality requires, it does nothing toward making men moral.

Aristotle's point, however, is not that moral good is realized whenever the law produces in people outward behavior that conforms with what morality requires, even if that behavior is purely the product of fear of punishment. Rather, his point is that, given the natural tendency of the majority of people to act on passionate motives in preference to reason (i.e., love of the good), the law must first settle people down if it is to help them to gain some appreciation of the good, some grasp of the intrinsic value of morally upright choosing, some control by their reason of their pas-

sions. Mere arguments will not do the job, "for he who lives as passion directs will not hear argument that dissuades him, nor understand it if he does." It is precisely inasmuch as the average man is given to passions that, "like a beast of burden," he must be governed by fear of punishment. The law must combat his emotional motives for wrongdoing with countervailing emotional motives. Once the law is successful in calming his passions and habituating him to doing what is right and avoiding what is wrong, he—unlike a brute animal—may gain some intelligent, reasonable, and reflective control of his passion. Even the average person may then learn to appreciate the good a little, and in choosing for the sake of the good, become morally better.[5]

Someone might object to Aristotle's claim that legal coercion can help put people into shape to appreciate the value of moral uprightness by settling them down and habituating them to virtue, on the ground that the more likely effect of such coercion is to instill resentment in people, and even incline them to rebellion. Here, too, Aristotle has an answer: "While people hate *men* who oppose their impulses, even if they oppose them rightly, the law in its ordaining of what is good is not burdensome." What he appears to have in mind here is that, while resentment and rebellion can be expected where one person brings coercion to bear against another in an effort to prevent him from doing something morally wrong, people will accept coercion more readily when an immoral act is prohibited *generally,* that is, throughout a society, and by the *impersonal* force of the law.

Why, though, does Aristotle suppose that immoral acts must be prohibited by *public* authority as opposed to the authority of the head of the household or family? His argument is that:

> the paternal command . . . has not the required force or compulsive power (nor in general has the command of one man, unless he be king or something similar), but the law has compulsive power, while it is at the same time a rule proceeding from a sort of practical wisdom and reason. [*Nic. Eth.*]

It is, once again, the generality of legal prohibition that makes the difference. People, notably including children, are formed not only in households, but in neighborhoods, and wider communities. Parents can prohibit a certain act, but their likelihood of success in enforcing the prohibition, and transmitting to their children a genuine grasp of the wrongness of the prohibited act, will be lessened to the extent that others more or less freely perform the act.

For example, parents can forbid their teenage sons to look at pornographic magazines; if, however, other boys with whom they have contact are freely circulating such material, it will be difficult for the parents to enforce their prohibition. Moreover, the boys whose parents have forbidden them to have pornography are likely to experience that prohibition as more onerous to the extent of their knowledge that other boys are free to indulge their taste for pornography. They are more likely to feel resentment, and to rebel, when they are being deprived of a freedom that others enjoy. Whatever authority parents have over their own children, they lack the authority to deprive other people in the community, or other people's children, of the legal liberty to perform immoral acts; only public officials possess authority of that kind. If, however, public authorities fail to combat certain vices, the impact of widespread immorality on the community's moral environment is likely to make the task of parents who rightly forbid their own children from, say, indulging in pornography, extremely difficult.

Nevertheless, Aristotle argues that where the *polis* is failing to do its job, other institutions, including households, should do what they can to prevent immorality.

> Now it is best that there should be a public and proper care for such matters; but if they are neglected by the community it would seem right for each man to help his children and friends towards virtue, and that they should have the power, or at least the will, to do this. [*Nic. Eth.*]

Indeed, he seems to recognize that the kind of moral formation that goes on in families, whatever its limitations, has certain advantages in the formation of moral character.

> For as in cities laws and prevailing types of character have force, so in households do the injunctions and habits of the father, and these have even more because of the tie of blood and the benefits he confers; for the children start with a natural affection and disposition to obey. Further, private education has an advantage over public; for while in general rest and abstinence from food are good for a man in a fever, for a particular man they may not be. . . . It would seem, then, that the detail is worked out with more precision if the control is private; for each person is more likely to get what suits his case. [*Nic. Eth.*]

In short, families, unlike political authorities, can deal with individuals as individuals, taking into account their distinctive needs and circumstances. So, Aristotle finally implies, making men moral is not a task for the *polis* alone: political communities should do what they can to encourage virtue and prevent vice, while other institutions should do what they can to complement the work of the *polis*.[6]

III. AQUINAS ON THE MORAL AIMS OF LAW AND GOVERNMENT

More than fifteen hundred years after Aristotle's death, his greatest Christian disciple, St. Thomas Aquinas, made his own enquiry into the point and purposes of human law in his *Summa Theologiae,* and reached similar conclusions about the need for law to concern itself with making men moral.[7] While Aquinas certainly seems more optimistic, as, perhaps, a Christian should be, about the universality of what he calls man's "natural aptitude for virtue" he agrees with Aristotle that "the perfection of virtue must be acquired by man by means of some kind of training." Moreover, he shares Aristotle's doubts that "man could suffice for himself in the matter of this training, since the perfection of virtue consists chiefly in withdrawing man from undue pleasures, to which above all man is inclined, and especially the young who are more capable of being trained." With Aristotle, Aquinas acknowledges that there are some people "who are inclined to acts of virtue by their good natural disposition, or by custom, or rather by the gift of God;" as for these, "paternal training suffices, which is by admonitions." At the same time, however:

> since some are found to be dissolute and prone to vice, and not easily amenable to words, it was necessary for such to be restrained from evil by force and fear, in order that, at least, they might desist from evil-doing, and leave others in peace, and that they themselves, by being habituated in this way, might be brought to do willingly what hitherto they did from fear, and thus become virtuous. Now this kind of training, which compels through fear of punishment, is the discipline of laws. Therefore, in order that man might have peace and virtue, it was necessary for laws to be framed. [*Summa Theologiae*]

When Aquinas comments on the *Nicomachean Ethics,* he expounds what Aristotle says there without demurrer, suggesting that he is generally in agreement with it. In his advice to a Christian king, entitled *De*

Regno, however, he gives a different (though not necessarily incompatible) rationale for the legal enforcement of morality, a peculiarly Christian rationale which, of course, never would have occurred to Aristotle.

Aquinas's basic premiss in *De Regno* is that what is good for everybody, in the end, is getting to heaven. The attainment of heavenly beatitude is the central common good of the people. The realization of this good (or goal) is not only what the Church is there for, it is the ultimate reason for the existence of public authority as well. The king serves the common good by getting the community into shape so that people are meeting their obligations to love their neighbors, thus fulfilling the second table of the Decalogue, and, through the redemption effected by Christ, getting themselves into heaven.

> Therefore since the beatitude of heaven is the end of that virtuous life which we live at present, it pertains to the king's office to promote the good life of the multitude in such a way as to make it suitable for the attainment of heavenly happiness, that is to say, he should command those things which lead to the happiness of Heaven and, as far as possible, forbid the contrary.[8]

How is the king to determine what leads to heavenly happiness? Aquinas says that "What conduces to true beatitude and what hinders it are learned from the law of God, the teaching of which belongs to the office of the priest." Having been instructed by the priest as to the law of God, the king "should have for his principal concern the means by which the multitude subject to him shall live well." The task of the king is to lead people to virtue by a gradual process: "first of all, to establish a virtuous life in the multitude subject to him; second, to preserve it once established; and third, having preserved it, to promote its greater perfection."

Aquinas recognizes that a king who wishes to fulfill his duty to lead the people to virtue must establish and maintain the conditions for people to lead virtuous lives. These conditions are material as well as moral. First, he says, it is necessary for "the multitude [to] be established in the unity of peace." Second, the multitude, thus united, must be "directed to acting well." And third, "it is necessary that there be at hand a sufficient supply of the things required for proper living, procured by the ruler's efforts." The material conditions, that is, "a sufficiency of those bodily goods whose use is necessary for a virtuous life," while "secondary and instrumental" to a man's living in a virtuous manner, must be secured if the ruler is to fulfill his

duty. Without the unity of peace, and other material goods, the political order will lack the stability it needs to function for the common good of its members. Indeed, security as well as stability, is needed; hence, the king must "keep the multitude entrusted to him safe from the enemy, for it would be useless to prevent internal dangers, if the multitude could not be defended from external dangers."

In *De Regno* Aquinas declares that the king should "by his laws and orders, punishments and rewards . . . restrain the men subject to him from wickedness and induce them to virtuous deeds." Recognizing, however, that there are limits to what can be effectively and prudently commanded by public authority, he holds that evil-doing should be forbidden "as far as possible." In the *Summa Theologiae,* he explains these limits in reply to the famous question of whether it belongs to human law to repress all vices. His answer is that "human law rightly allows some vices, by not repressing them." His reasoning begins from the premiss that law should fit the condition of the people, many of whom will be quite imperfect in virtue and therefore incapable of living up to the highest standards of morality. "Many things," he says, "are permissible to men not perfect in virtue, which would be intolerable in a virtuous man."

> Now human law is framed for the multitude of human beings, the majority of whom are not perfect in virtue. Therefore human laws do not forbid all vices, from which the virtuous abstain, but only the more grievous vices, from which it is possible for the majority to abstain; and chiefly those that are injurious to others, without the prohibition of which human society could not be maintained. Thus the law prohibits murder, theft and the like. [*De Regno*]

Aquinas is not here opposing in principle, as Joel Feinberg supposes he is,[9] the criminalization of victimless immoralities. Rather, he is acknowledging the need for any legislator to tailor the criminal law to fit the character and state of his particular society. Of course, Aquinas recognizes that some things must be forbidden in every society, for the simple reason that social life is impossible unless they are prohibited. Thus, no society can afford to leave its members generally free to kill or steal from each other. According to Aquinas, the law can and should go beyond the prohibition of these evils, however, to prohibit other serious wrongs that average people in the society can generally abstain from committing. Aquinas does not in the least deviate from Aristotle's view that the lawgiver should try to lead men to virtue. He qualifies Aristotle's position merely to note the fact that the legal prohibition of their immoral acts cannot suddenly make men moral.

> The purpose of human law is to lead men to virtue, not suddenly, but gradually. Therefore it does not lay upon the multitude of imperfect men the burdens of those who are already virtuous, viz., that they should abstain from all evil. Otherwise these imperfect ones, being unable to bear such precepts, would break out into yet greater evils. . . . the precepts are despised, and those men, from contempt, break out into evils worse still. [*Summa Theologiae*]

The limits of legal prohibition of vice, for Aquinas, are not based on any supposed moral right of those whose actions might otherwise be prohibited. He does not suppose that people have a moral right to the legal liberty to perform immoral acts. He cites no principle of political morality which is transgressed by legislators who bring the coercive force of the law to bear against, say, putatively victimless immoralities. Rather, he judges it morally right to refrain from legally prohibiting vice where, given the condition of the people, the prohibition is likely to be futile or, worse yet, productive of more serious vices or wrongs. Citing Isidore, he holds that laws, if they are to serve the common good of leading the people to virtue, must be "according to the customs of the country," and "adapted to place and time."

What Aquinas appears to have in mind is that laws which the multitude of a people generally find too difficult to comply with will produce a negative attitude toward the law in general, and lead to resentment and hardening of hearts, and possibly even rebellion. If, as Aristotle thought, the project of leading people to virtue requires that the law "calm them down," and habituate them to doing the right thing, then the laws imposed on them toward these ends must be laws that they can bear. If a law provokes resentment and rebelliousness, then, far from calming passion-driven people so that they can become virtuous, the law will enflame their passions and make them less virtuous.[10] Hence, the prudent legislator will be careful to make the law fit the condition of the people, and not to make legal prohibitions too onerous.

Such reasoning might reasonably be described as prudential, and I will so describe it hereinafter. But its fundamentally moral character is made clear enough when later in the *Summa Theologiae* Aquinas discusses whether Christian rulers should tolerate the rites of Jews and infidels. Such rites, he thinks, are harmful to people, but should be tolerated when not doing so will either lead to worse things or interfere with the achievement of better things. He cites an example from St Augustine's writings of the need sometimes to tolerate prostitution "so that men do not break out in worse lusts."[11]

On the precise question whether Christian political authorities ought to prohibit non-Christian worship, Aquinas holds that the rites of Jews should be legally tolerated, despite his belief that all Jews should now be Christians. He argues that there is still value in Jewish worship, which foreshadows and prefigures the full truth, despite its imperfection in failing to acknowledge Christ. To forbid such worship would be to lose that genuine, if incomplete, good.

He has no such irenical view toward the rites of infidels, however; he sees nothing of value in their worship. Nevertheless, he argues that they can rightly be tolerated, not to preserve any good, but to avoid greater evils. Which evils? Aquinas seems to be concerned first of all with the disruption and division that would be caused when infidels violate laws that suppress their rites. Moreover, he suggests, forbidding their rites would tend to harden them toward Christianity, thus closing their ears to the Gospel and making the task of evangelization more difficult. In other words, coercing them to avoid what is wrong might have the effect of impeding them from eventually doing what is right, that is, becoming Christians and accepting the divine offer of eternal life. This consequence is worse, he says, than tolerating their valueless worship.

When he turns to the crucial question of compelling *belief,* Aquinas holds that, since belief is by nature voluntary, it is useless to attempt to compel people who are not believers to believe or make the commitment of faith. Nevertheless, he maintains that public authorities may rightly, and indeed should, compel Christians to hold to the religious commitments that they have made and to renounce heresy and apostasy. Apparently he supposes that, while belief cannot be compelled, fidelity to a commitment based on belief can be. He argues that to hold to the faith is "of necessity," that is, a matter of moral obligation. His view of the matter is undoubtedly influenced by the norms according to which medieval society functioned: having made a commitment of fealty, one is bound by it; and people to whom one has made the commitment can hold one strictly to it.

Plainly, Aquinas is not thinking of religion as people do today (or as his own Church has come to understand it),[12] that is, as a matter of belief which, as such, must be and remain fully voluntary, and, therefore, uncoerced, if it is to be authentic and have any value. Rather, he is thinking of it as a commitment one has made to God, to which one is bound, and can be held bound by ecclesiastical and civil authority. Indeed, Aquinas goes so far as to defend the executing of heretics on the ground that tolerating heresy permits a cancer to spread in the body politic of political communities ordered and integrated around a religious faith;[13] inasmuch as what heretics do is more damaging to society (whose ultimate goal, after all, is to get people to heaven) than what counterfeiters do, he approves of the harsh way that medieval society dealt with them.

At the same time, he makes a justice-based (or as we would nowadays say, rights-based) argument as to why Christians, and the Christian state, should refrain from requiring baptism of non-Christian children. Recall that the whole point of political society is to help people to fulfill the moral law so that they can get to heaven. The saving of souls is the whole reason for the law. Now, Aquinas believed that, without baptism, people could not attain heavenly beatitude. Nevertheless, he held strictly to the principle that it is wrong to baptize Jewish children, for example, against their parents' wishes, even if doing so is indispensable to their salvation.

His objection to this practice, which many in his day apparently supported, is not merely that "it would be detrimental to the [Christian] faith," because the forcibly baptized children, once they attain the age of reason, "might easily be persuaded by their parents to renounce what they had unknowingly embraced." More importantly, he maintains, the practice "is against natural justice." In *Summa Theologiae,* II-II, q. 10, a. 12, he sets out five arguments—more than the two or three he usually offers—for the proposition he means to reject. The number of these arguments, their seriousness, and the quality of the authorities he cites for them (including Augustine and Jerome) make it plain that he intends to take a strong stand on a live issue. His answer begins by putting forward the authority of the Church herself, whose traditions had rejected the idea of baptizing children against their parents' wishes, against her most esteemed theologians. He then argues that "the parents' duty to look after the salvation of their children," who are, in a sense, "a part of [them]" entails that "it would be contrary to natural justice, if a child, before coming to the use of reason, were to be taken away from its parents' custody, or anything done to it against its parents' wishes."

IV. A CRITIQUE OF ARISTOTLE AND AQUINAS

While Aquinas does not say so explicitly, his view of the need for political authorities to uphold public morality by forbidding serious vice is undoubtedly reinforced by the Christian picture of pre-Christian Rome. The idea of what it was like, and what a horrible alternative it is, was spelled out vividly by Augustine:

> The worshippers . . . of those gods, whom they delighted to imitate in their criminal wickedness, are unconcerned about the utter corruption of their country. "So long as . . . it enjoys material prosperity [they say], and the glory of victorious war, or, better, the security of peace, why should we worry? What concerns us is that we should get richer all the time, to have enough for extravagant spending every day, enough to keep our inferiors in their place. It is all right if the poor serve the rich, so as to get enough to eat and to enjoy a lazy life under their patronage; while the rich make use of the poor to ensure a crowd of hangers-on to minister to their pride; if the people applaud those who supply them with pleasures rather than those who offer salutary advice; if no one imposes disagreeable duties, or forbids perverted delights; if kings are interested not in the mortality but the docility of their subjects; if provinces are under rulers who are regarded not as directors of conduct but as controllers of material things and providers of material satisfactions, and are treated with servile fear instead of sincere respect. The laws should punish offences against another's property, not offences against a man's own personal character. No one should be brought to trial except for an offence, or threat of offence, against another's property, house, or person; but anyone should be free to do as he likes about his own, or with his own, or with others, if they consent. There should be a plentiful supply of public prostitutes, for the benefit of all those who prefer them, and especially for those who cannot keep private mistresses. It is a good thing to have imposing houses luxuriously furnished, where lavish banquets can be held, where people can, if they like, spend night and day in debauchery, and eat and drink till they are sick: to have the din of dancing everywhere, and theatres full of fevered shouts of degenerate pleasure and of every kind of cruel and degraded indulgence. Anyone who disapproves of this kind of happiness should rank as a public enemy: anyone who attempts to change it or get rid of it should be hustled out of hearing by the freedom-loving majority."[14]

In these passages, Augustine depicts the kind of public life that can be expected when the law prescinds from questions of "private" virtue and seeks only to protect one man from another as each struggles to achieve his own satisfactions. His view is that the law cannot be morally neutral in the way that orthodox contemporary liberalism supposes: either it will promote virtue, or it will facilitate vice.

Perhaps every generation must learn for itself that "private" immoralities have public consequences. In our own time, we have ample reason to doubt that orthodox liberalism's distinction between private and public immorality can be maintained, at least with respect to the types of immoral acts that the central tradition has proposed to forbid or restrict by law. It is plain that moral decay has profoundly damaged the morally valuable institutions of marriage and the family,[15] and has, indeed, largely undercut the understandings of the human person, marriage, and the family that are presupposed by the very idea of sexual immorality and by the ideals of chastity and fidelity which give family life its full sense and viability. It is one thing for radicals or relativists who believe that traditional marriage and family life are oppressive, or merely "one option among equally valid alternatives," to condemn laws premised on the idea of sexual vice; it is quite another thing, though, for liberals to maintain that even adherents of traditional moral views should accept their critique of morals laws on the ground that the legal prohibition of "private" immorality serves no public good.[16]

The idea that public morality is a public good, and that immoral acts—even between consenting adults—can therefore do public harm, has not been refuted by liberal critics of the central tradition. On the contrary, the idea is vindicated by the experiences of modern cultures which have premised their law on its denial. The institutions of marriage and the family have plainly been weakened in cultures in which large numbers of people have come to understand themselves as "satisfaction seekers" who, if they happen to desire it, may resort more or less freely to promiscuity, pornographic fantasies, prostitution, and drugs. Of course, recognition of the public consequences of putatively private vice does not mean that liberalism is wrong to be critical of morals legislation. For, as we shall see in later chapters, contemporary liberals make a variety of moral arguments against such legislation that do not depend on the propositions that public morality is not a public good or that private immorality cannot do public harm. It does mean, however, that a crucial premiss of the tra-

dition's case against moral *laissez-faire* remains unshaken: societies have reason to care about what might be called their "moral ecology."

The tradition, as embodied in the sorts of laws and public policies to which orthodox liberalism objects, has not followed Aristotle and Aquinas in every detail. It has come to give greater room to freedom, and to be more circumspect in the use of the law's coercive power, than Aristotle and Aquinas would have thought necessary or appropriate. I shall argue that, where the tradition has developed in these ways, it has been right to do so. Although Aristotle and Aquinas were correct in supposing that the law may justly and appropriately seek to combat vice and encourage virtue, and while the whole tradition, including Aristotle and Aquinas, is superior to liberalism in allowing, in principle at least, for the quasi-paternalistic (and, in some cases, even the paternalistic) and educative use of the law to forbid certain immoralities, their analyses of these questions were flawed in various ways. And, indeed, there are certain respects, especially those touching upon religious liberty, in which the influence of liberalism on the tradition has been salutary.

While ancient and medieval life was not without diversity, Isaiah Berlin is probably correct to criticize the tradition for failing to understand the diversity of basic forms of good and the range of valid pluralism. Aristotle, for example, plainly failed to allow room in his ethical and political theory for the diversity of irreducible human goods which, considered as providing basic reasons for action and options for choice, are the bases for a vast range of valuable, but mutually incompatible, choices, commitments, and plans and ways of life. And he lacked anything like a good argument for his view that there must be a single superior way of life, or a uniquely highest life for those capable of it; nor did he provide anything approaching a plausible theory of where those not capable of what he believed to be the highest life fit into a society that treats that way of life as the best.

Without adopting the relativistic view which sees the good as so radically diverse that whatever people happen to want is good, we can and should recognize a multiplicity of basic human goods and a multiplicity of ways that different people (and communities) can pursue and organize instantiations of those goods in living valuable and morally upright lives. Our recognition of (non-relativistic) value pluralism opens up something that Aristotle never clearly saw: people are not simply disposed by nature (and/or culture) well or badly; they dispose themselves, and can dispose themselves, well or badly, in a vast variety of ways. Human beings put their lives together in different ways by making different choices and commitments based on different values that provide different reasons for choice and action. There is no single pattern anyone can identify as the proper model of a human life, not because there is no such thing as good and bad, but because there are many goods. Moreover, people are fulfilled in part by deliberating and choosing for themselves a pattern of their own. Practical reasoning is not merely a human capacity; it is itself a fundamental aspect of human well-being and fulfillment: a basic dimension of the human good consists precisely in bringing reason to bear in deliberating and choosing among competing valuable possibilities, commitments, and ways of life.

Lacking an appreciation of the diversity of basic human goods, and thus the diversity of valuable ways of life ordinarily available to people, Aristotle wrongly supposed that people have preordained stations in life, and that the wise legislator who is concerned to promote virtue will therefore have the job of slotting people into their proper stations and seeing to it that each person fulfills the duties of his particular station. Working from an implausibly limited and hierarchical view of human good, Aristotle failed to perceive that persons, as loci of human goods and of rational capacity for self-determination by free choices, are *equal in dignity,* however unequal they are in ability, intelligence, and other gifts: hence his élitism, not to mention his notorious doctrine of "natural slaves."

Aristotelian élitism is a fundamental and gross error, which is itself rooted in a failure to appreciate the diversity of basic human goods that fulfill the persons in and by whom they are instantiated and realized. It is this diversity that confounds every attempt to identify a "highest" or "best" life to which those who are by nature suited to that life (and are thus the "highest" or "best" examples of human beings) should aspire. In any event, whatever may have been the case in Aristotle's Athens, legislators in modern representative democracies are unlikely to be morally superior to the people who elect them. One might even argue that, given what it takes to achieve public office, the average legislator today is likely to be generally less strict in the observance of certain moral norms than the average voter.

At the same time, there is in normal circumstances no reason to suppose, as Aristotle did, that the great mass of people are incapable of being reasonable and need to be governed by fear. Nor is there any reason to believe in the existence of a moral élite whose members need only understand moral truth in order to live up to its demands. The fact is that all rational human beings are capable of understanding moral reasons; yet all require guidance, support, and assistance from others. All are susceptible to moral failure, even serious moral failure; and all are capable of benefiting from a milieu which is more or less free from powerful inducements to vice. All require freedom if they are to flourish; but unlimited freedom is the enemy, not the friend, of everyone's well-being.

Once we have brought into focus the diversity of human goods, it becomes clear that legislators concerned to uphold morality cannot prohibit all that much. At most, they can legitimately proscribe only the fairly small number of acts and practices that are incompatible with any morally good life. Paternalism is strictly limited by the diversity of goods whose recognition makes nonsense of the idea of assigning people to "natural" or "appropriate" stations in life. Of course, there are morally valuable institutions, such as marriage, which, while not morally obligatory for everyone, are nevertheless worthy of protection. To defend such institutions from forces and developments in a society that may threaten them, legislators will need to understand their nature, value, and vulnerability. It will be complicated, then, for legislators to design laws that protect institutions such as marriage. To ban an act such as adultery on the ground of its intrinsic immorality is fairly straightforward (if difficult to enforce); to design just and good laws pertaining to marital break-up, divorce, and the care of children, however, is not so simple.

Of course, even where intrinsic immorality is not a question, political authorities can rightly regulate the pursuit of certain plans of life, and even forbid them to certain persons because of their lack of ability or appropriate training, in order to protect the public from, say, incompetent physicians, lawyers, accountants, or teachers. In any event, the recognition of a variegated human good, and the consequence of a multiplicity of possible good plans of life, will both limit the scope of the legislation validly aimed at encouraging virtue and discouraging vice, and render the job of legislators concerned to uphold public morality a task more complicated than Aristotle imagined.

Turning to Aquinas, the fundamental and (to the modern reader) obvious problem with his view is that it assumes the propriety of legislating not only morals, but also faith, and indeed of legislating morals precisely in so far as they are accepted on religious authority and are the means to an end (i.e., heavenly beatitude) that religious faith puts forward but reason by itself cannot identify. Aquinas makes the first principle of politics a matter of religious belief, thus proposing a radical establishment of religion that is utterly inconsistent with a due regard for religious liberty. I shall later argue that religion, considered as a basic human good within the grasp of practical reason, can indeed provide a reason for political action. It cannot, however, provide a reason for compelling or forbidding religious belief or practice. Aquinas's approach, in so far as it imperils religious freedom, jeopardizes (for reasons I shall later identify) the value of religion itself.

Aquinas himself, as we saw, perceives that justice, as well as prudence, requires respect for some measure of religious freedom: hence his willingness to tolerate the rites of non-Christians and his principled opposition to requiring the baptism of children against their parents' wishes. He fails, however, to see that the reasons for civil authorities to respect religious liberty extend to everybody, including heretics and apostates. Recognition of the moral grounds of the right to freedom of religion renders unacceptable Aquinas's semi-theocratic (or sacral/consecrational) view of political community and authority.

As we have seen, Aquinas does recognize important prudential limits to the political pursuit of beatitude. He astutely suggests that prudent legislators will tailor the criminal law to the character of the people and the moral state of their society in order to avoid the likely bad consequences of imposing on people burdens that they cannot bear. This point remains valid even when we consider laws to uphold public morality for the sake of virtue as such, rather than as means to getting people to heaven. Taking a cue from Aquinas, we can identify other prudential (and, as such, morally significant) considerations which might militate in favor of a policy of tolerating certain moral evils: for example, (1) the need to avoid placing dangerous powers in the hands of governments that are likely to abuse them; (2) the danger that criminalization of certain vices may have the effect of placing monopolies in the hands of organized criminals who will market and spread the vices more efficiently; (3) the risk of producing secondary crimes against innocent parties; (4) the risk of diverting police and judicial resources away from the prevention and prosecution of more serious crimes; (5) the concern that the power to enforce moral obligations will be exploited by puritanical, prudish, or disciplinarian elements in society to repress morally legitimate activities and ways of life whose genuine values these elements fail to appreciate; (6) the danger of establish-ing too much authority and creating a situation in which people relate primarily to a central authority whom they must constantly work to avoid offending, thus discouraging them from building genuine relationships with each other to the point of true friendships and valuable communities.

V. THE VALUE AND LIMITS OF PERFECTIONIST LAW AND POLICY

Aquinas is right to say that immorality must sometimes be tolerated in order to avoid morally worse evils, or because, in certain circumstances, the failure to tolerate a certain vice will impede the realization of important goods. These considerations have more extensive implications, however, than Aquinas works out or that people who agree with him in principle commonly suppose. Virtue is instantiated, and virtuous characters are established, by (and only by) choosing right against choosing wrong. Thus any tightly disciplinary regime of law, even if it succeeds in producing outward conformity to moral rules, will tend, as a result of overly aggressive efforts to combat some vices, to create a milieu in which other vices flourish. Wise legislators whose goal is to encourage true moral goodness, and not merely the outward behavior that mimics true virtue, will therefore seek to secure and maintain a moral ecology that is inhospitable not only to such vices as pornography, prostitution, and drug abuse, but also to the vices of moral infantilism, conformism, servility, mindless obedience to authority, and hypocrisy.

Commenting on the situation in Catholic colleges and universities in the United States in the late 1950s, Germain Grisez has remarked on the dangers posed to the moral and spiritual life by approaches to personal formation that fail to take full cognizance of the difference between mere outward conformity to moral rules and genuine moral action.

> This formation involved outward conformity to a detailed set of rules and practices, but it did not guarantee any inward acceptance or conversion. The freedom of the student was not elicited to make a commitment to values which might have grounded the practices he was expected to enact.[17]

Any legislator who understands the human good well enough to be trusted to legislate for any community—political, religious, or even familial—will recognize that there are many important goods that people ought to realize in their lives whose realization is possible only if people freely choose to do "the right thing"—more exactly, to adopt a morally upright option in situations where at least one option that they are rejecting would be to do the morally wrong thing. Moral goods are "reflexive" in that they are reasons to choose which include choice in their very meaning; one *cannot* participate in these goods otherwise than by acts of choice, that is, internal acts of will, and the internal disposition established by such choices. As internal acts, they are beyond legal compulsion. Such goods get instantiated precisely in people's choices to do things that they should do when they could willfully fail to do them, or to refrain from doing things that they should not do when they could choose to do them. In light of the reflexivity of moral goods, there would be a compelling reason not to even try to eliminate every opportunity for immorality. Even if, *per impossibile,* a government could do so without damaging people's participation in important non-moral human goods, such an attempt necessarily involves an effort to eliminate choice and directly impede people's participation in the reflexive good. It would therefore be unjust or, as we now say, a violation of a human right.

Moreover, governments have conclusive reasons not to attempt to enforce certain obligations which are essential to valuable social practices whose meaningfulness depends on the parties fulfilling their obligations freely. For example, compelling the expressing of gratitude, or the giving of gifts, or the acknowledging of achievements, where people ought to express gratitude, give gifts, or acknowledge achievements, would have the effect of robbing these important practices of their meaning and value in social life. The reasons for not bringing coercion to bear with respect to such practices do not depend on the circumstances; they are not merely prudential. And they place significant ranges of morality beyond the reach of legislation as a matter of principle.

Nevertheless, the existence of justice- or rights-based grounds, as well as prudential reasons, for "not repressing every vice," does not entail that there are never valid reasons to legally prohibit *any* vice on the ground of its immorality. The legal prohibition of a vice may be warranted precisely to protect people from the *moral* harm it does to them and their communities. I have already observed that people do not become morally good by merely conforming their outward behavior to moral rules. Someone who refrains from a vice merely to avoid being caught and punished under a law prohibiting the vice realizes no moral good

(though he may avoid further moral harm). Laws can compel outward behavior, not internal acts of the will; therefore, they cannot compel people to realize moral goods. They cannot, in any direct sense, "make men moral." Their contribution to making men moral must be indirect.

People become morally bad by yielding to vice; and they can be protected from the corrupting influence of powerfully seductive vices by laws that prohibit them (in so far as they are manifest in outward behavior) and prevent them from flourishing in the community. By suppressing industries and institutions that cater to moral weakness, and whose presence in the moral environment makes it difficult for people to choose uprightly, such laws can protect people from strong temptations and inducements to vice. To the extent that morals laws help to preserve the quality of the moral environment, they protect people from moral harm.

Any social environment will be constituted, in part, by a framework of understandings and expectations which will tend, sometimes profoundly, to influence the choices people actually make. People's choices, in turn, shape that framework. The significance of common understandings and expectations with respect to sex, marriage, and family life is obvious. The point extends well beyond these matters, however: the moral environment as constituted, in part, by the framework of understandings and expectations which exists in a particular society will affect everything from people's tendency to abuse drugs, to their driving habits on the highways, to their honesty or dishonesty in filling out their tax returns. If people's moral understandings are more or less sound, and if these understandings inform their expectations of one another, the moral environment thus constituted will be conducive to virtue. In contrast, if human relations are constituted according to morally defective understandings and expectations, the moral environment will seduce people into vice. In neither case will the moral environment eliminate the possibility of moral goodness and badness, for people can be good in bad moral environments and bad in good moral environments. The point remains, however, that a good moral ecology benefits people by encouraging and supporting their efforts to be good; a bad moral ecology harms people by offering them opportunities and inducements to do things that are wicked.

A physical environment marred by pollution jeopardizes people's physical health; a social environment abounding in vice threatens their moral well-being and integrity. A social environment in which vice abounds (and vice might, of course, abound in subtle ways) tends to damage people's moral understandings and weaken their characters as it bombards them with temptations to immorality. People who sincerely desire to avoid acts and dispositions which they know to be wrong may nevertheless find themselves giving in to prevalent vices and more or less gradually being corrupted by them. Even people who themselves stand fast in the face of powerful temptations may find their best efforts to instill in their children a sense of decency and moral integrity thwarted by a moral environment filled with activities and images or representations which, in the unfashionable but accurate phrase of the common law, "tend to corrupt and deprave."

Moreover, even people who wish to perform immoral acts but fear doing so lest they be caught and punished, or who would wish to perform them if their opportunities to do so had not been eliminated by the effective enforcement of a morals law, can be protected by effective laws from the (further) moral harm that they would do to themselves. A morals law may prevent moral harm, thus benefiting a potential wrongdoer, simply by protecting him from the (further) corrupting impact of acting out the vice. It is not that the person deterred solely by the law from wrongdoing realizes a moral good by not engaging in the vice. Moral goods cannot be realized by direct paternalism. Rather, it is that he avoids, albeit unwillingly, the bad impact of (further) involvement in the vice on his character.

Of course, it is a mistake to suppose that laws by themselves are sufficient to establish and maintain a healthy moral ecology. It is equally a mistake to suppose, however, that laws have nothing to contribute to that goal. Even apart from their more direct effects in discouraging particular vices or eliminating occasions for people to commit them, morals laws can help to shape the framework of understandings and expectations that helps to constitute the moral environment of any community. As Aristotle and Augustine rightly held, a community's laws will inevitably play an important educative role in the life of the community. They can powerfully reinforce, or fail to reinforce, the teachings of parents and families, teachers and schools, religious leaders and communities, and other persons and institutions who have the leading roles in the moral formation of each new generation.

Although Aristotle was correct in observing that parents sometimes require the assistance of the general and impersonal force of the law to provide their children with a sound moral upbringing, he was wrong to ascribe to the law the role of primary moral educator.

As he himself seemed dimly to perceive, sound moral education requires close attention to the moral development of persons who, as individual moral agents, instantiate moral goodness and badness in their choices and actions. Parents, teachers, and pastors can attend to, understand, and work with individual persons in ways that the law simply cannot. Law, as a more or less impersonal guide, must aspire to nothing more than a supporting or secondary role.

At the same time, inasmuch as vice itself often damages and weakens families, schools, and religious institutions, the contribution of law to upholding public morality may be crucial to enabling these institutions to flourish and fulfill their roles as primary moral educators. As modern exponents of the central tradition have carefully explained, however, law goes wrong— it weakens these valuable "subsidiary" institutions and damages people's moral well-being—when it usurps their role and sets itself up as the primary moral teacher.

Critics of morals legislation often point out that law is a "blunt instrument." There is truth in this claim: law really is poorly suited to dealing with the complexities and details of individuals' moral lives. Laws can forbid the grosser forms of vice, but certainly cannot prescribe the finer points of virtue. Nevertheless, laws that effectively uphold public morality may contribute significantly to the common good of any community by helping to preserve the moral ecology which will help to shape, for better or worse, the morally self-constituting choices by which people form their character, and in turn affect the milieu in which they *and others* will in future have to make such choices.

READING 33

Liberalism and Neutrality

Ronald Dworkin

Ronald Dworkin was for many years a Professor of Jurisprudence at Oxford University and is presently a professor of law at New York University. He is the author of several important works in the philosophy of law, including *Taking Rights Seriously* and *The Law's Empire*. In this essay, he characterizes Liberalism as a commitment to a certain kind of equality, which includes neutrality regarding a conception of the Good. "The liberal disapproves of enforcing morality through the criminal law." He argues that this neutrality regarding the good life distinguishes the liberal from the conservative and the socialist as well as from the Marxist.

This reading is taken from "Liberalism," in Stuart Hampshire, ed. *Public and Private Morality.* Cambridge University Press, 1978. [Notes deleted. Ed.]

I want to argue that a certain conception of equality, which I shall call the liberal conception of equality, is the nerve of liberalism. But that supposes that liberalism is an authentic and coherent political morality, so that it can make sense to speak of "its" central principle, and these developments may be taken to suggest that that is not. They may seem to support the following sceptical thesis instead. "The word 'liberalism' has been used, since the eighteenth century, to describe various distinct clusters of political positions, but with no important similarity of principle among the different clusters called 'liberal' at different times. The explanation of why different clusters formed in various circumstances, or why they were called 'liberal,' cannot be found by searching for any such principle. It must be found instead in complicated accidents of history, in which the self-interest of certain groups, the prevalence of certain political rhetoric, and many other discrete factors played different parts. One such cluster was formed, for such reasons, in the period of the New Deal: it combined an emphasis on less inequality and greater economic stability with more abundant political and civil liberty for the groups then compaigning for these goals. Our contemporary notion of 'liberal' is formed from that particular package of political aims."

These two issues—the connection of liberalism with economic growth and capitalism—are especially controversial, but we can locate similar problems of distinguishing what is fundamental from what is strategic in almost every corner of the New Deal liberal settlement. The liberal favors free speech. But is free speech a fundamental value, or is it only a means to some other goal like the discovery of truth (as Mill argued) or the efficient functioning of democracy (as Michaeljohn suggested)? The liberal disapproves of enforcing morality through the criminal law. Does this suggest that liberalism opposes the formation of a shared community sense of decency? Or is liberalism hostile only to using the criminal law to secure that shared community sense? I must say, perhaps out of unnecessary caution, that these questions cannot be answered, at the end of the day, apart from history and developed social theory; but it does not contradict that truism to insist that philosophical analysis of the idea of liberalism is an essential part of that very process.

So my original question—what is liberalism—turns out to be a question that must be answered, at least tentatively, before the more clearly historical questions posed by the sceptical thesis can be confronted. For my question is just the question of what morality is constitutive in particular liberal settlements like the New Deal package.

My project does take a certain view of the role of political theory in politics. It supposes that liberalism consists in some constitutive political morality that has remained roughly the same over some time, and that continues to be influential in politics. It supposes that distinct liberal settlements are formed when, for one reason or another, those moved by that constitutive morality settle on a particular scheme of derivative positions as appropriate to complete a practical liberal political theory, and others, for their own reasons, become allies in promoting that scheme. Such settlements break up, and liberalism is accordingly fragmented, when these derivative positions are discovered to be ineffective, or when economic or social circumstances change so as to make them ineffective, or when the allies necessary to make an effective political force are no longer drawn to the scheme. I do not mean that the constitutive morality of liberalism is the only force at work in forming liberal settlements, or even that it is the most powerful, but only that it is sufficiently distinct and influential to give sense to the idea, shared by liberals and their critics, that liberalism exists, and to give sense to the popular practice of arguing about what it is.

But the argument so far has shown that the claim that a particular position is constitutive rather than derivative in a political theory will be both controversial and complex. How shall I proceed? Any satisfactory description of the constitutive morality of liberalism must meet the following catalogue of conditions. (a) It must state positions that it makes sense to suppose might be constitutive of political programs for people in our culture. I do not claim simply that some set of constitutive principles could explain liberal settlements if people held those principles, but that a particular set does help to explain liberal settlements because people actually have held those principles. (b) It must be sufficiently well tied to the last clear liberal settlement—

the political positions I described at the outset as acknowledged liberal "causes" [see next paragraph] so that it can be seen to be constitutive for that entire scheme; so that the remaining positions in the scheme can be seen, that is, to be derivative given that constitutive morality. (c) It must state constitutive principles in sufficient detail so as to discriminate a liberal political morality from other, competing political moralities. If, for example, I say simply that it is constitutive of liberalism that the government must treat its citizens with respect, I have not stated a constitutive principle in sufficient detail, because, although liberals might argue that all their political schemes follow from that principle, conservatives, Marxists and perhaps even fascists would make the same claim for their theories. (d) Once these requirements of authenticity, completeness and distinction are satisfied, then a more comprehensive and frugal statement of constitutive principles meeting these requirements is to be preferred to a less comprehensive and frugal scheme, because the former will have greater explanatory power, and provide a fairer test of the thesis that these constitutive principles both precede and survive particular settlements.

The second of these four conditions provides a starting point. I must therefore repeat the list of what I take to be the political positions of the last liberal settlement, and I shall, for convenience, speak of "liberals" as these who support those positions. In economic policy, liberals demand that inequalities of wealth be reduced through welfare and other forms of redistribution financed by progressive taxes. They believe that government should intervene in the economy to promote economic stability, to control inflation, to reduce unemployment, and to provide services that would not otherwise be provided, but they favor a pragmatic and selective intervention over a dramatic change from free enterprise to wholly collective decisions about investment, production, prices and wages. They support racial equality, and approve government intervention to secure it, through constraints on both public and private discrimination in education, housing and employment. But they oppose other forms of collective regulation of individual decision: they oppose regulation of the content of political speech, even when such regulation might secure greater social order, and they oppose regulation of sexual literature and conduct even when such regulation has considerable majoritarian support. They are suspicious of the criminal law and anxious to reduce the extension of its provisions to behavior whose morality is controversial, and they support procedural constraints and devices, like rules against the admissi-

bility of confessions, that makes it more difficult to secure criminal convictions.

I do not mean that everyone who holds any of these positions will or did hold them all. Some people who call themselves liberal do not support several elements of this package; some who call themselves conservative support most of them. But these are the positions that we use as a touchstone when we ask how liberal or conservative someone is; and indeed on which we now rely when we say that the line between liberals and conservatives is more blurred than once it was. I have omitted those positions that are only debatably elements of the liberal package, like support for military intervention in Vietnam, or the present campaign in support of human rights in Communist countries, or concern for more local participation in government or for consumer protection against manufacturers, or for the environment. I have also omitted debatable extension of liberal doctrines, like busing and quotas that discriminate in favor of minorities in education and employment. I shall assume that the positions that are uncontroversially liberal positions are the core of the liberal settlement. If my claim is right, that a particular conception of equality can be shown to be constitutive for that core of positions, we shall have, in that conception, a device for stating and testing the claim that some debatable position is also "really" liberal.

II

Is there a thread of principle that runs through the core liberal positions, and that distinguishes these from the corresponding conservative positions? There is a familiar answer to this question that is mistaken, but mistaken in an illuminating way. The politics of democracies, according to this answer, recognizes several independent constitutive political ideals, the most important of which are the ideals of liberty and equality. Unfortunately, liberty and equality often conflict: sometimes the only effective means to promote equality require some limitation of liberty, and sometimes the consequences of promoting liberty are detrimental to equality. In these cases, good government consists in the best compromise between the competing ideals, but different politicians and citizens will make that compromise differently. Liberals tend relatively to favor equality more and liberty less than conservatives do, and the core set of liberal positions I described is the result of striking the balance that way.

This account offers a theory about what liberalism is. Liberalism shares the same constitutive principles with many other political theories, including conservatism, but is distinguished from these by attaching different relative importance to different principles. The theory therefore leaves room, on the spectrum it describes, for the radical who cares even more for equality and less for liberty than the liberal, and therefore stands even further away from the extreme conservative. The liberal becomes the man in the middle, which explains why liberalism is so often now considered wishy-washy, an untenable compromise between two more forthright positions.

No doubt this description of American politics could be made more sophisticated. It might make room for other independent constitutive ideals shared by liberalism and its opponents, like stability or security, so that the compromises involved in particular decisions are made out to be more complex. But if the nerve of the theory remains the competition between liberty and equality as constitutive ideals, then the theory cannot succeed. In the first place, it does not satisfy condition (b) in the catalogue of conditions I set out. It seems to apply, at best, to only a limited number of the political controversies it tries to explain. It is designed for economic controversies, but is either irrelevant or misleading in the case of censorship and pornography, and indeed, in the criminal law generally.

But there is a much more important defect in this explanation. It assumes that liberty is measurable so that, if two political decisions each invades the liberty of a citizen, we can sensibly say that one decision takes more liberty away from him than the other. That assumption is necessary, because otherwise the postulate, that liberty is a constitutive ideal of both the liberal and conservative political structures, cannot be maintained. Even firm conservatives are content that their liberty to drive as they wish (for example to drive uptown on Lexington Avenue) may be invaded for the sake, not of some important competing political ideal, but only for marginal gains in convenience or orderly traffic patterns. But since traffic regulation plainly involves some loss of liberty, the conservative cannot be said to value liberty as such unless he is able to show that, for some reason, less liberty is lost by traffic regulation than by restrictions on, for example, free speech, or the liberty to sell for prices others are willing to pay, or whatever other liberty he takes to be fundamental.

But that is precisely what he cannot show, because we do not have a concept of liberty that is quantifiable in the way that demonstration would require. He can-

not say, for example, that traffic regulations interfere less with what most men and women want to do than would a law forbidding them to speak out in favor of Communism, or a law requiring them not to fix their prices as they think best. Most people care more about driving than speaking for Communism, and have no occasion to fix prices even if they want to. I do not mean that we can make no sense of the idea of fundamental liberties, like freedom of speech. But we cannot argue in their favor by showing that they protect more liberty, taken to be an even roughly measurable commodity, than does the right to drive as we wish; the fundamental liberties are important because we value something else that they protect. But if that is so, then we cannot explain the difference between liberal and conservative political positions by supposing that the latter protect the commodity of liberty, valued for its own sake, more effectively than the former.

It might now be said, however, that the other half of the liberty–equality explanation may be salvaged. Even if we cannot say that conservatives value liberty, as such, more than liberals, we can still say that they value equality less, and that the different political positions may be explained in that way. Conservatives tend to discount the importance of equality when set beside other goals, like general prosperity or even security; while liberals, in contrast, value equality relatively more, and radicals more still. Once again, it is apparent that this explanation is tailored to the economic controversies, and fits poorly with the non-economic controversies. Once again, however, its defects are more general and more important. We must identify more clearly the sense in which equality could be a constitutive ideal for either liberals or conservatives. Once we do so we shall see that it is misleading to say that the conservative values equality, in that sense, less than the liberal. We shall want to say, instead, that he has a different conception of what equality requires.

We must distinguish between two different principles that take equality to be a political ideal. The first requires that the government treat all those in its charge *as equals,* that is, as entitled to its equal concern and respect. That is not an empty requirement: most of us do not suppose that we must, as individuals, treat our neighbor's children with the same concern as our own, or treat everyone we meet with the same respect. It is nevertheless plausible to think that any government should treat all its citizens as equals in that way. The second principle requires that the government treat all those in its charge *equally* in the distribution of some resource of opportunity, or at least work to secure the state of affairs in which they all are equal or more nearly equal in that respect. It is, of course, conceded by everyone that the government cannot make everyone equal in every respect, but people do disagree about how far government should try to secure equality in some particular resource; for example, in monetary wealth.

If we look only at the economic-political controversies, then we might well be justified in saying that liberals want more equality in the sense of the second principle than conservatives do. But it would be a mistake to conclude that they value equality in the sense of the first and more fundamental principle any more highly. I say that the first principle is more fundamental because I assume that, for both liberals and conservatives, the first is constitutive and the second derivative. Sometimes treating people equally is the only way to treat them as equals; but sometimes not. Suppose a limited amount of emergency relief is available for two equally populous areas injured by floods; treating the citizens of both areas as equals requires giving more aid to the more seriously devastated area rather than splitting the available funds equally. The conservative believes that in many other, less apparent, cases treating citizens equally amounts to not treating them as equals. He might concede, for example, that positive discrimination in university admissions will work to make the two races more nearly equal in wealth, but nevertheless maintain that such programs do not treat black and white university applicants as equals. If he is a utilitarian he will have a similar, though much more general, argument against any redistribution of wealth that reduces economic efficiency. He will say that the only way to treat people as equals is to maximize the average welfare of all members of community, counting gains and losses to all in the same scales, and that a free market is the only, or best, instrument for achieving that goal. This is not (I think) a good argument, but if the conservative who makes it is sincere he cannot be said to have discounted the importance of treating all citizens as equals.

So we must reject the simple idea that liberalism consists in a distinctive weighting between constitutive principles of equality and liberty. But our discussion of the idea of equality suggests a more fruitful line. I assume (as I said) that there is broad agreement within modern politics that the government must treat all its citizens with equal concern and respect. I do not mean to deny the great power of prejudice in, for example, American politics. But few citizens, and even fewer

politicians, would now admit to political convictions that contradict the abstract principle of equal concern and respect. Different people hold, however, as our discussion made plain, very different conceptions of what that abstract principle requires in particular cases.

III

What does it mean for the government to treat its citizens as equals? That is, I think, the same question as the question of what it means for the government to treat all its citizens as free, or as independent, or with equal dignity. In any case, it is a question that has been central to political theory at least since Kant.

It may be answered in two fundamentally different ways. The first supposes that government must be neutral on what might be called the question of the good life. The second supposes that government cannot be neutral on that question, because it cannot treat its citizens as equal human beings without a theory of what human beings ought to be. I must explain that distinction further. Each person follows a more-or-less articulate conception of what gives value to life. The scholar who values a life of contemplation has such a conception; so does the television-watching, beer-drinking citizen who is fond of saying "This is the life," though of course he has thought less about the issue and is less able to describe or defend his conception.

The first theory of equality supposes that political decisions must be, so far as is possible, independent of any particular conception of the good life, or of what gives value to life. Since the citizens of a society differ in their conceptions, the government does not treat them as equals if it prefers one conception to another, either because the officials believe that one is intrinsically superior, or because one is held by the more numerous or more powerful group. The second theory argues, on the contrary, that the content of equal treatment cannot be independent of some theory about the good for man or the good of life, because treating a person as an equal means treating him the way the good or truly wise person would wish to be treated. Good government consists in fostering or at least recognizing good lives; treatment as an equal consists in treating each person as if he were desirous of leading the life that is in fact good, at least so far as this is possible.

This distinction is very abstract, but it is also very important. I shall now argue that liberalism takes, as its constitutive political morality, the first conception of equality. I shall try to support that claim in this way. In the next section of this essay I shall show how it is plausible, and even likely, that a thoughtful person who accepted the first conception of equality would, given the economic and political circumstances of America in the last several decades, reach the positions I identified as the familiar core of liberal positions. If so, then the hypothesis satisfies the second of the conditions I described for a successful theory. In the following section I shall try to satisfy the third condition by showing how it is plausible and even likely that someone who held a particular version of the second theory of equality would reach what are normally regarded as the core of American conservative positions. I say "a particular version of" because American conservatism does not follow automatically from rejecting the liberal theory of equality. The second (or non-liberal) theory of equality holds merely that the treatment government owes citizens is at least partly determined by some conception of the good life. Many political theories share that thesis, including theories as far apart as, for example, American conservatism and various forms of socialism or Marxism, though these will of course differ in the conception of the good life they adopt, and hence in the political institutions and decisions they endorse. In this respect, liberalism is decidedly not some compromise or half-way house between more forceful positions, but stands on one side of an important line that distinguishes it from all competitors taken as a group.

I shall not provide arguments in this essay that my theory of liberalism meets the first condition I described—that the theory must provide a political morality that it makes sense to suppose people in our culture hold—though I think it plain that the theory does meet this condition. The fourth condition requires that a theory be as abstract and general as the first three conditions allow. I doubt there will be objections to my theory on that account.

IV

I now define a liberal as someone who holds the first, or liberal, theory of what equality requires. Suppose that a liberal is asked to found a new state. He is required to dictate its constitution and fundamental institutions. He must propose a general theory of political distribution, that is, a theory of how whatever the community has to assign, by way of goods or resources or

opportunities, should be assigned. He will arrive initially at something like this principle of rough equality: resources and opportunities should be distributed, so far as possible, equally, so that roughly the same share of whatever is available is devoted to satisfying the ambitions of each. Any other general aim of distribution will assume either that the fate of some people should be of greater concern than that of others, or that the ambitions or talents of some are more worthy, and should be supported more generously on that account.

Someone may object that this principle of rough equality is unfair because it ignores the fact that people have different tastes, and that some of these are more expensive to satisfy than others, so that, for example, the man who prefers champagne will need more funds if he is not to be frustrated than the man satisfied with beer. But the liberal may reply that tastes as to which people differ are, by and large, not afflictions, like diseases, but are rather cultivated, in accordance with each person's theory of what his life should be like. The most effective neutrality, therefore, requires that the same share be devoted to each, so that the choice between expensive and less expensive tastes can be made by each person for himself, with no sense that his overall share will be enlarged by choosing a more expensive life, or that, whatever he chooses, his choice will subsidize those who have chosen more expensively.

But what does the principle of rough equality of distribution require in practice? If all resources were distributed directly by the government through grants of food, housing, and so forth; if every opportunity citizens have were provided directly by the government through the provisions of civil and criminal law; if every citizen had exactly the same talents; if every citizen started his life with no more than what any other citizen had at the start; and if every citizen had exactly the same theory of the good life and hence exactly the same scheme of preferences as every other citizen, including preferences between productive activity of different forms and leisure, then the principle of rough equality of treatment could be satisfied simply by equal distributions of everything to be distributed and by civil and criminal laws of universal application. Government would arrange for production that maximized the mix of goods, including jobs and leisure, that everyone favored, distributing the product equally.

Of course, none of these conditions of similarity holds. But the moral relevance of different sorts of diversity are very different, as may be shown by the following exercise. Suppose all the conditions of similarity I mentioned did hold except the last: citizens have different theories of the good and hence different preferences. They therefore disagree about what product the raw materials and labor and savings of the community should be used to produce, and about which activities should be prohibited or regulated so as to make others possible or easier. The liberal, as lawgiver, now needs mechanisms to satisfy the principles of equal treatment in spite of these disagreements. He will decide that there are no better mechanisms available, as general political institutions, than the two main institutions of our own political economy: the economic market, for decisions about what goods shall be produced and how they shall be distributed, and representative democracy, for collective decisions about what conduct shall be prohibited or regulated so that other conduct might be made possible or convenient. Each of these familiar institutions may be expected to provide a more egalitarian division than any other general arrangement. The market, if it can be made to function efficiently, will determine for each product a price that reflects the cost in resources of material, labor and capital that might have been applied to produce something different that someone else wants. That cost determines, for anyone who consumes that product, how much his account should be charged in computing the egalitarian division of social resources. It provides a measure of how much more his account should be charged for a house than a book, and for one book rather than another. The market will also provide, for the laborer, a measure of how much should be credited to his account for his choice of productive activity over leisure, and for one activity rather than another. It will tell us, through the price it puts on his labor, how much he should gain or lose by his decision to pursue one career rather than another. These measurements make a citizen's own distribution a function of the personal preferences of others as well as of his own, and it is the sum of these personal preferences that fixes the true cost to the community of meeting his own preferences for goods and activities. The egalitarian distribution, which requires that the cost of satisfying one person's preferences should as far as is possible be equal to the cost of satisfying another's, cannot be enforced unless those measurements are made.

We are familiar with the anti-egalitarian consequences of free enterprise in practice; it may therefore seem paradoxical that the liberal as lawgiver should choose a market economy for reasons of equality rather than efficiency. But, under the special condition that people differ only in preferences for goods and activities, the market is more egalitarian than any alternative

of comparable generality. The most plausible alternative would be to allow decisions of production, investment, price and wage to be made by elected officials in a socialist economy. But what principles should officials use in making those decisions? The liberal might tell them to mimic the decisions that a market would make if it was working efficiently under proper competition and full knowledge. This mimicry would be, in practice, much less efficient than an actual market would be. In any case, unless the liberal had reason to think it would be much more efficient, he would have good reason to reject it. Any minimally efficient mimicking of an hypothetical market would require invasions of privacy to determine what decisions individuals would make if forced actually to pay for their investment, consumption and employment decisions at market rates, and this information gathering would be, in many other ways, much more expensive than an actual market. Inevitably, moreover, the assumptions officials make about how people would behave in a hypothetical market reflect the officials' own beliefs about how people should behave. So there would be, for the liberal, little to gain and much to lose in a socialist economy in which officials were asked to mimic a hypothetical market.

But any other instructions would be a direct violation of the liberal theory of what equality requires, because if a decision is made to produce and sell goods at a price below the price a market would fix, then those who prefer those goods are, *pro tanto,* receiving more than an equal share of the resources of the community at the expense of those who would prefer some other use of the resources. Suppose the limited demand for books, matched against the demand for competing uses for wood-pulp, would fix the price of books at a point higher than the socialist managers of the economy will charge; those who want books are having less charged to their account than the egalitarian principle would require. It might be said that in a socialist economy books are simply valued more, because they are inherently more worthy uses of social resources, quite apart from the popular demand for books. But the liberal theory of equality rules out that appeal to the inherent value of one theory of what is good in life.

In a society in which people differed only in preferences, then, a market would be favored for its egalitarian consequences. Inequality of monetary wealth would be the consequence only of the fact that some preferences are more expensive than others, including the preference for leisure time rather than the most lucrative productive activity. But we must now return to the real world. In the actual society for which the liberal must construct political institutions, there are all the other differences. Talents are not distributed equally, so the decision of one person to work in a factory rather than a law firm, or not to work at all, will be governed in large part by his abilities rather than his preferences for work or between work and leisure. The institutions of wealth, which allow people to dispose of what they receive by gift, means that children of the successful will start with more wealth than the children of the unsuccessful. Some people have special needs, because they are handicapped; their handicap will not only disable them from the most productive and lucrative employment, but will incapacitate them from using the proceeds of whatever employment they find as efficiently, so that they will need more than those who are not handicapped to satisfy identical ambitions.

These inequalities will have great, often catastrophic, effects on the distribution that a market economy will provide. But, unlike differences in preferences, the differences these inequalities make are indefensible according to the liberal conception of equality. It is obviously obnoxious to the liberal conception, for example, that someone should have more of what the community as a whole has to distribute because he or his father had superior skill or luck. The liberal lawgiver therefore faces a difficult task. His conception of equality requires an economic system that produces certain inequalities (those that reflect the true differential costs of goods and opportunities) but not others (those that follow from differences in ability, inheritance, etc.). The market produces both the required and the forbidden inequalities, and there is no alternative system that can be relied upon to produce the former without the latter.

The liberal must be tempted, therefore, to a reform of the market through a scheme of redistribution that leaves its pricing system relatively intact but sharply limits, at least, the inequalities in welfare that his initial principle prohibits. No solution will seem perfect. The liberal may find the best answer in a scheme of welfare rights financed through redistributive income and inheritance taxes of the conventional sort, which redistributes just to the Rawlsian point, that is, to the point at which the worst-off group would be harmed rather than benefited by further transfers. In that case, he will remain a reluctant capitalist, believing that a market economy so reformed is superior, from the standpoint of his conception of equality, to any practical socialist alternative. Or he may believe that the redistribution that is possible in a capitalist economy will be so inadequate, or will be purchased at the cost of such inefficiency, that it is better to proceed in a more radical way, by substituting socialist for market decisions over a large part of the economy, and then relying on the political process to ensure that prices are set in a manner at least roughly consistent with his conception of equality. In that case he will be a reluctant socialist, who acknowledges the egalitarian defects of socialism but counts them as less severe than the practical alternatives. In either case, he chooses a mixed economic system—either redistributive capitalism or limited socialism—not in order to compromise antagonistic ideals of efficiency and equality, but to achieve the best practical realization of the demands of equality itself.

Let us assume that in this manner the liberal either refines or partially retracts his original selection of a market economy. He must now consider the second of the two familiar institutions he first selected, which is representative democracy. Democracy is justified because it enforces the right of each person to respect and concern as an individual; but in practice the decisions of a democratic majority may often violate that right, according to the liberal theory of what the right requires. Suppose a legislature elected by a majority decides to make criminal some act (like speaking in favor of an unpopular political position, or participating in eccentric sexual practices) not because the act deprives others of opportunities they want, but because the majority disapproves of those views or that sexual morality. The political decision, in other words, reflects not simply some accommodation of the *personal* preferences of everyone, in such a way as to make the opportunities of all as nearly equal as may be, but the domination of one set of *external* preferences, that is, preferences people have about what others shall do or have. The decision invades rather than enforces the right of citizens to be treated as equals.

How can the liberal protect citizens against that sort of violation of their fundamental right? It will not do for the liberal simply to instruct legislators, in some constitutional exhortation, to disregard the external preferences of their constituents. Citizens will vote these preferences in electing their representatives, and a legislator who chooses to ignore them will not survive. In any case, it is sometimes impossible to distinguish, even by introspection, the external and personal components of a political position: this is the case, for example, with associational preferences, which are the preferences some people have for opportunities, like the opportunity to attend public schools, but only with others of the same "background."

The liberal, therefore, needs a scheme of civil rights, whose effect will be to determine those political decisions that are antecedently likely to reflect strong external preferences, and to remove those decisions from majoritarian political institutions altogether. Of course, the scheme of rights necessary to do this will depend on general facts about the prejudices and other external preferences of the majority at any given time, and different liberals will disagree about what is needed at any particular time. But the rights encoded in the Bill of Rights of the United States Constitution, as interpreted (on the whole) by the Supreme Court, are those that a substantial number of liberals would think reasonably well suited to what the United States now requires (though most would think that the protection of the individual in certain important areas, including sexual publication and practice, are much too weak).

The main parts of the criminal law, however, present a special problem not easily met by a scheme of civil rights that disable the legislature from taking certain political decisions. The liberal knows that many of the most important decisions required by an effective criminal law are not made by legislators at all, but by prosecutors deciding whom to prosecute for what crime, and by juries and judges deciding whom to convict and what sentences to impose. He also knows that these decisions are antecedently very likely to be corrupted by the external preferences of those who make these decisions because those they judge, typically, have attitudes and ways of life very different from their own. The liberal does not have available, as protection against these decisions, any strategy comparable to the strategy of civil rights that simply remove a decision from an institution. Decisions to prosecute, convict and sentence must be made by someone. But he has available, in the notion of procedural rights, a different device to protect equality in a different way. He will insist that criminal procedure be structured to achieve a margin of safety in decisions, so that the process is biased strongly against the conviction of the innocent. It would be a mistake to suppose that the liberal thinks that these procedural rights will improve the *accuracy* of the criminal process, that is, the probability that any particular decision about guilt or innocence will be the right one. Procedural rights intervene in the process, even at the cost of inaccuracy, to compensate in a rough way for the antecedent risk that a criminal process, especially if it is largely administered by one class against another, will be corrupted by the impact of external preferences that cannot be eliminated directly. This is, of course, only the briefest sketch of how various sub-

stantive and procedural civil rights follow from the liberal's initial conception of equality; it is meant to suggest, rather than demonstrate, the more precise argument that would be available for more particular rights.

So the liberal, drawn to the economic market and to political democracy for distinctly egalitarian reasons, finds that these institutions will produce inegalitarian results unless he adds to his scheme different sorts of individual rights. These rights will function as trump cards held by individuals; they will enable individuals to resist particular decisions in spite of the fact that these decisions are or would be reached through the normal workings of general institutions that are not themselves challenged. The ultimate justification for these rights is that they are necessary to protect equal concern and respect; but they are not to be understood as representing equality in contrast to some other goal or principle served by democracy or the economic market. The familiar idea, for example, that rights of redistribution are justified by an ideal of equality that overrides the efficiency ideals of the market in certain cases, has no place in liberal theory. For the liberal, rights are justified, not by some principle in competition with an independent justification of the political and economic institutions they qualify, but in order to make more perfect the only justification on which these other institutions may themselves rely. If the liberal arguments for a particular right are sound, then the right is an unqualified improvement in political morality, not a necessary but regrettable compromise of some other independent goal, like economic efficiency.

V

I said that the conservative holds one among a number of possible alternatives to the liberal conception of equality. Each of these alternatives shares the opinion that treating a person with respect requires treating him as the good man would wish to be treated. The conservative supposes that the good man would wish to be treated in accordance with the principles of a special sort of society, which I shall call the virtuous society. A virtuous society has these general features. Its members share a sound conception of virtue, that is, of the qualities and dispositions people should strive to have and exhibit. They share this conception of virtue not only privately, as individuals, but publicly: they believe their community, in its social and political activity, exhibits virtues, and that they have a responsibility, as citizens, to promote these virtues. In that sense they treat the lives of other members of their community as part of their own lives. The conservative position is not the only position that relies on this ideal of the virtuous society (some forms of socialism rely on it as well). But the conservative is distinct in believing that his own society, with its present institutions, is a virtuous society for the special reason that its history and common experience are better guides to sound virtue than any non-historical and therefore abstract deduction of virtue from first principles could provide.

Suppose a conservative is asked to draft a constitution for a society generally like ours, which he believes to be virtuous. Like the liberal, he will see great merit in the familiar institutions of political democracy and an economic market. The appeal of these institutions will be very different for the conservative, however. The economic market, in practice, assigns greater rewards to those who, because they have the virtues of talent and industry, supply more of what is wanted by the other members of the virtuous society; and that is, for the conservative, the paradigm of fairness in distribution. Political democracy distributes opportunities, through the provisions of the civil and criminal law, as the citizens of a virtuous society wish it to be distributed, and that process will provide more scope for virtuous activity and less for vice than any less democratic technique. Democracy has a further advantage, moreover, that no other technique could have. It allows the community to use the processes of legislation to reaffirm, as a community, its public conception of virtue.

The appeal of the familiar institutions to the conservative is, therefore, very different from their appeal to the liberal. Since the conservative and the liberal both find the familiar institutions useful, though for different reasons, the existence of these institutions, as institutions, will not necessarily be a point of controversy between them. But they will disagree sharply over which corrective devices, in the form of individual rights, are necessary in order to maintain justice, and the disagreement will not be a matter of degree. The liberal, as I said, finds the market defective principally because it allows morally irrelevant differences, like differences in talent, to affect distribution, and he therefore considers that those who have less talent, as the market judges talent, have a right to some form of redistribution in the name of justice. But the conservative prizes just the feature of the market that puts a premium on talents prized in the community, because these

are, in a virtuous community, virtues. So he will find no genuine merit, but only expediency, in the idea of redistribution. He will allow room, of course, for the virtue of charity, for it is a virtue that is part of the public catalogue; but he will prefer private charity to public, because it is a purer expression of that virtue. He may accept public charity as well, particularly when it seems necessary to retain the political allegiance of those who would otherwise suffer too much to tolerate a capitalist society at all. But public charity, justified either on grounds of virtue or expediency, will seem to the conservative a compromise with the primary justification of the market, rather than, as redistribution seems to the liberal, an improvement in that primary justification.

Nor will the conservative find the same defects in representative democracy that the liberal finds there. The conservative will not aim to exclude moralistic or other external preferences from the democratic process by any scheme of civil rights; on the contrary, it is the pride of democracy, for him, that external preferences are legislated into a public morality. But the conservative will find different defects in democracy, and he will contemplate a different scheme of rights to diminish the injustice they work.

The economic market distributes rewards for talents valued in the virtuous society, but since these talents are unequally distributed, wealth will be concentrated, and the wealthy will be at the mercy of an envious political majority anxious to take by law what it cannot take by talent. Justice requires some protection for the successful. The conservative will be (as historically he has been) anxious to hold some line against extensions of the vote to those groups most likely to be envious, but there is an apparent conflict between the ideals of abstract equality, even in the conservative conception, and disenfranchisement of large parts of the population. In any case, if conservatism is to be politically powerful, it must not threaten to exclude from political power those who would be asked to consent, formally or tacitly, to their own exclusion. The conservative will find more appeal in the different, and politically much more feasible, idea of rights to property.

These rights have the same force, though of course radically different content, as the liberal's civil rights. The liberal will, for his own purposes, accept some right to property, because he will count some sovereignty over a range of personal possessions essential to dignity. But the conservative will strive for rights to property of a very different order; he will want rights that protect, not some minimum dominion over a range of possessions independently shown to be desirable, but an unlimited dominion over whatever has been acquired through an institution that defines and rewards talent.

The conservative will not, of course, follow the liberal in the latter's concern for procedural rights in the criminal process. He will accept the basic institutions of criminal legislation and trial as proper; but he will see, in the possible acquittal of the guilty, not simply an inefficiency in the strategy of deterrence, but an affront to the basic principle that the censure of vice is indispensable to the honor of virtue. He will believe, therefore, that just criminal procedures are those that improve the antecedent probability that particular decisions of guilt or innocence will be accurate. He will support rights against interrogation or self-incrimination, for example, when such rights seem necessary to protect against torture or other means likely to elicit a confession from the innocent; but he will lose his concern for such rights when non-coercion can be guaranteed in other ways.

The fair-minded conservative will be concerned about racial discrimination, but his concern will differ from the concern of the liberal, and the remedies he will countenance will also be different. The distinction between equality of opportunity and equality of result is crucial to the conservative: the institutions of the economic market and representative democracy cannot achieve what he supposes they do unless each citizen has an equal opportunity to capitalize on his genuine talents and other virtues in the contest these institutions provide. But since the conservative knows that these virtues are unequally distributed, he also knows that equality of opportunity must have been denied if the outcome of the contest is equality of result.

The fair conservative must, therefore, attend to the charge that prejudice denies equality of opportunity between members of different races, and he must accept the justice of remedies designed to reinstate that equality, so far as this may be possible. But he will steadily oppose any form of "affirmative action" that offers special opportunities, like places in medical school or jobs, on criteria other than some proper conception of the virtue appropriate to the reward.

The issue of gun control, which I have thus far not mentioned, is an excellent illustration of the power of the conservative's constitutive political morality. He favors strict control of sexual publication and practice, but he opposes parallel control of the ownership or use of guns, though of course guns are more dangerous

than sex. President Ford, in the second Carter–Ford debate, put the conservative position of gun control especially clearly. Sensible conservatives do not dispute that private and uncontrolled ownership of guns leads to violence, because it puts guns in circulation that bad men may use badly. But (President Ford said) if we meet that problem by not allowing good men to have guns, we are punishing the wrong people. It is, of course, distinctive to the conservative's position to regard regulation as condemnation and hence as punishment. But he must regard regulation that way, because he believes that opportunities should be distributed, in a virtuous society, so as to promote virtuous acts at the expense of vicious ones.

VI

In place of a conclusion, I shall say something, though not much, about two of the many important questions raised by what I have said. The first is the question posed in the first section of the essay. Does the theory of liberalism I described answer the sceptical thesis? Does it explain our present uncertainty about what liberalism now requires, and whether it is a genuine and tenable political theory? A great part of that uncertainty can be traced, as I said, to doubts about the connections between liberalism and the suddenly unfashionable idea of economic growth. The opinion is popular that some form of utilitarianism, which does take growth to be a value in itself, is constitutive of liberalism; but my arguments, if successful, show that this opinion is a mistake. Economic growth, as conventionally measured, was a derivative element in New Deal liberalism. It seemed to play a useful role in achieving the complex egalitarian distribution of resources that liberalism requires. If it now appears that economic growth injures more than it aids the liberal conception of equality, then the liberal is free to reject or curtail growth as a strategy. If the effect of growth is debatable, as I believe it is, then liberals will be uncertain, and appear to straddle the issue.

But the matter is more complicated than that analysis makes it seem, because economic growth may be deplored for many different reasons, some of which are plainly not available to the liberal. There is a powerful sentiment that a simpler way of life is better, in itself, than the life of consumption most Americans have recently preferred; this simpler life requires living in harmony with nature, and is therefore disturbed when, for example, a beautiful mountainside is spoiled by strip mining for the coal that lies within it. Should the mountainside be saved, in order to protect a way of life that depends upon it, either by regulation that prohibits mining, or by acquisition with taxpayers' money for a national park? May a liberal support such policies, consistently with his constitutive political morality? If he believes that government intervention is necessary to achieve a fair distribution of resources, on the ground that the market does not fairly reflect the preferences of those who want a park against those who want what the coal will produce, then he has a standard, egalitarian reason for supporting intervention. But suppose he does not believe that, but rather believes that those who want the park have a superior conception of what a truly worthwhile life is. A nonliberal may support conservation on that theory; but a liberal may not.

Suppose, however, that the liberal holds a different, more complex, belief about the importance of preserving natural resources. He believes that the conquest of unspoilt terrain by the consumer economy is self-fueling and irreversible, and that this process will make a way of life that has been desired and found satisfying in the past unavailable to future generations, and indeed to the future of those who now seem unaware of its appeal. He fears that this way of life will become unknown, so that the process is not neutral amongst competing ideas of the good life, but in fact destructive of the very possibility of some of these. In that case the liberal has reasons for a program of conservation that are not only consistent with his constitutive morality, but in fact sponsored by it.

I raise these possible lines of argument, not to provide the liberal with an easier path to a popular political position, but to illustrate the complexity of the issues that the new politics has provided. Liberalism seems precise and powerful when it is relatively clear what practical political positions are derivative from its fundamental constitutive morality; on these occasions politics allows what I called a liberal settlement of political positions. But such a settlement is fragile, and when it dissolves liberals must regroup, first through study and analysis, which will encourage a fresh and deeper understanding of what liberalism is, and then through the formation of a new and contemporary program for liberals. The study and theory are not yet in progress, and the new program is not yet in sight.

The second question I wish to mention, finally, is a question I have not touched at all. What is to be said in favor of liberalism? I do not suppose that I have made liberalism more attractive by arguing that its con-

stitutive morality is a theory of equality that requires official neutrality amongst theories of what is valuable in life. That argument will provoke a variety of objections. It might be said that liberalism so conceived rests on scepticism about theories of the good, or that it is based on a mean view of human nature that assumes that human beings are atoms who can exist and find self-fulfillment apart from political community, or that it is self-contradictory because liberalism must itself be a theory of the good, or that it denies to political society its highest function and ultimate justification, which is that society must help its members to achieve what is in fact good. The first three of these objections need not concern us for long, because they are based on philosophical mistakes which I can quickly name if not refute. Liberalism cannot be based on scepticism. Its constitutive morality provides that human beings must be treated as equals by their government, not because there is no right and wrong in political morality, but because that is what is right. Liberalism does not rest on any special theory of personality, nor does it deny that most human beings will think that what is good for them is that they be active in society. Liberalism is not self-contradictory: the liberal conception of equality is a principle of political organization that is required by justice, not a way of life for individuals, and liberals, as such, are indifferent as to whether people choose to speak out on political matters, or to lead eccentric lives, or otherwise to behave as liberals are supposed to prefer.

But the fourth objection cannot so easily be set aside. These is no easy way to demonstrate the proper role of institutions that have a monopoly of power over the lives of others; reasonable and moral men will disagree. The issue is at bottom the issue I identified: what is the content of the respect that is necessary to dignity and independence?

That raises problems in moral philosophy and in the philosophy of mind that are fundamental for political theory though not discussed here; but this essay does bear on one issue sometimes thought to be relevant. It is sometimes said that liberalism must be wrong because it assumes that the opinions people have about the sort of lives they want are self-generated, whereas these opinions are in fact the products of the economic system or other aspects of the society in which they live. That would be an objection to liberalism if liberalism were based on some form of preference-utilitarianism which argued that justice in distribution consists in maximizing the extent to which people have what they happen to want. It is useful to point out, against that preference-utilitarianism, that since the preferences of people are formed by the system of distribution already in place, these preferences will tend to support that system, which is both circular and unfair. But liberalism, as I have described it, does not make the content of preferences the test of fairness in distribution. On the contrary, it is anxious to protect individuals whose needs are special or whose ambitions are eccentric from the fact that more popular preferences are institutionally and socially reinforced, for that is the effect and justification of the liberal's scheme of economic and political rights. Liberalism responds to the claim, that preferences are caused by systems of distribution, with the sensible answer that in that case it is all the more important that distribution be fair in itself, not as tested by the preferences it produces.

READING 34

Liberalism and the Neutral State

William Galston

William Galston is Senior Research Scholar at the Institute for Philosophy and Public Policy at the University of Maryland and the author of several works in political philosophy and public policy. His essay defending equal opportunity appears as Reading 40.

Galston defends the notion of the State being committed to a vision of the good against the neutralism of John Rawls, Ronald Dworkin, and Bruce Ackerman. What is distinctive about Galston's defense of perfectionism is that he argues for it, not from a conservative or natural law position, as does Robert George (see Reading 32), but from within liberalism itself. He argues that rationality itself leads us to support some views of the good as morally superior to others and that, whether recognized or not, every political system really "embodies at least a partial rank-order among individual ways of life."

This reading is taken from *Liberal Purposes* (Cambridge University Press, 1991), by permission.

I

There are, broadly speaking, two strategies for justifying the liberal state. The first begins by arguing for the worth of the way of life characterized by distinctively liberal or (as some say) bourgeois virtues and goals. The liberal state is justified, according to this view, because it is designed to foster liberal virtues, and to permit, insofar as possible, the unhindered pursuit of liberal goals.

This form of justification has its roots in classical antiquity. Aristotle, for example, virtually defined the *polis* as a tutelary community, based on a shared moral understanding, and directed toward a specific way of life. In our day, substantive justification has been defended by Brian Barry, who insists that every political partisan "must take his stand on the proposition that some ways of life, some types of character are more admirable than others. . . . He must hold that societies ought to be organized in such a way as to produce the largest possible proportion of people with an admirable type of character and the best possible chance to act in accordance with it." Liberalism, Barry asserts, rests on the worth of the Faustian vision: a life of self-mastery, self-expression, active pursuit of knowledge, unhesitating acceptance of moral responsibility.

The second strategy for justifying liberalism is very different. According to this view, the liberal state is desirable not because it promotes a specific way of life but precisely because it alone does not do so. The liberal state is "neutral" among different ways of life. It presides benignly over them, intervening only to adjudicate conflict, to prevent any particular way of life from tyrannizing over others, and to ensure that all adhere to the principles that constitute society's basic structure. Thus, in John Rawls's view, "the liberal state rests on a conception of equality between human beings as moral persons, as creatures having a conception of the good and capable of a sense of justice. . . . Systems of ends are not ranked in value." For Ronald Dworkin, the liberal state "must be neutral on . . . the question of the good life [and] political decisions must be, so far as is possible, independent of any particular conception of the good life, or of what gives value to life." Bruce Ackerman has advanced the "Neutrality Principle" as the centerpiece of liberal theory. It constrains the kinds of reasons that may validly be offered in defense of social arrangements, much as the Rawlsian veil of ignorance limits the considerations available to the denizens of the original position. According to the Neutrality Principle:

No reason [that purports to justify a social arrangement] is a good reason if it requires the power holder to assert (a) that his conception of the good is better than that asserted by any of his fellows, or (b) that, regardless of his conception of the good, he is intrinsically superior to one or more of his fellow citizens.

These defenders of the liberal state, then, assert that liberalism rejects—and can get along without—any substantive theory of the good as a determinate end for human endeavor. This position is, of course, compatible with a theory of the good as neutral universal means; in this vein, Dworkin speaks of "resources and opportunities," and Ackerman of infinitely malleable "manna." It is also compatible with—indeed, is thought by many (though not all) liberal theorists to require—moral principles governing our attitudes toward, and relations with, other human beings: fairness, equal respect, noncoercion, or rational dialogue, for example. In cases of conflict with individual ways of life, moreover, these principles are thought to take precedence. So the neutrality in question need not be a comprehensive moral neutrality but, rather, a wide neutrality concerning the worth of ways of life that individuals may define and pursue. . . .

Assuming for the moment that such neutrality is possible, why is it desirable? How does neutrality provide a justification for the liberal state?

There are three answers. First, it may be argued that there is in fact no rational basis for choosing among ways of life. Assertions about the good are personal and incorrigible. State neutrality is desirable because it is the only nonarbitrary response to this state of affairs. Second, it may be argued that even if knowledge about the good life is available, it is a breach of individual freedom—the highest value—for the state to impose this knowledge on its citizens. Of course, the best outcome occurs when individuals freely choose to pursue the good. But freely chosen error is preferable to the coerced pursuit of the good. Neutrality is justified because it is the practical expression of this priority of freedom over the good. Third, it may be argued that diversity is a basic fact of modern social life and that the practical costs of public efforts to constrain it would be unacceptably high. Just as the post-Reformation religious wars could be ended only by adopting policies of public toleration, present-day disagreements can be decently and peaceably accommodated only by a state that refrains from throwing its support to any of the contending parties.

Contemporary theorists of liberal neutrality typically rest their case on one or more of these arguments. In Chapter 5, I consider the third in detail. Here I argue that the first and second—the arguments from skepticism and from the lexical priority of freedom—both fail.

II

Kant offers the model argument for the liberal state based on the priority of freedom over the good. In *The Metaphysical Principles of Virtue,* he develops an account of the good life—the intellectual and moral perfection that each of us has a duty to pursue—and he argues that every individual is obligated to promote the well-being or happiness of others. Yet in his political writings, especially *The Metaphysical Elements of Justice* and "Theory and Practice," he propounds a full-blown and intransigent doctrine of the neutral state. The state is not in the business of teaching or enforcing morality, nor can it promote a specific conception of happiness. A paternalistic government, Kant insists, is the "greatest conceivable despotism." The substance of politics is not virtue, not happiness, but rather "freedom in the mutual external relationships of human beings." And the leading principle of politics is right: "the restriction of each individual's freedom so that it harmonizes with the freedom of everyone else."

The difficulty is that Kant does not and cannot simply posit external freedom as a value. Rather, he seeks to derive it from what is for him the unconditional value: moral autonomy. Kantian moral autonomy is (to adopt Isaiah Berlin's terms) a kind of *positive* freedom. [See Reading 16.] We are morally free when our will is open to, and determined by, moral rationality. But Kantian external freedom is a kind of negative freedom. We are externally free to the extent that we are not constrained by other human beings in the pursuit of our individual purposes. Kantian practical philosophy is the attempt to combine an ethics of positive freedom with a politics of negative freedom.

The attempt fails. External freedom cannot be derived from moral freedom because the two freedoms have different logics and lie in different spheres. They have different logics because while one individual's exercise of moral freedom can never conflict with another individual's moral freedom, the exercise of political freedom can—indeed, must—engender conflict. Thus, unlike moral freedom, the political freedom of each individual must be limited if the multiplicity of wills is to be harmonized. They lie in different spheres because the dignity, the infinite worth, of Kantian moral freedom consists in its elevation above the world of natural necessity, whereas external freedom is an aspect of that world. Thus, the dignity of moral freedom cannot be transferred to external freedom. To assign moral worth and inviolable priority to external freedom is to shift the ground of moral worth in a manner not merely unwarranted by, but actually impermissible within, the overall structure of Kantian theory.

This tension between positive and negative freedom is inevitably reflected in Kant's theory of the state. The strain shows in two ways: First, state policies compatible with negative freedom are nevertheless ruled out if they contradict positive freedom. Kant asks, for example, whether a people can impose on itself an ecclesiastical constitution "whereby certain accepted doctrines and outward forms of religion are declared permanent, [thus preventing] its own descendants from making further progress in religious understanding or from correcting any past mistakes." No, it cannot, he asserts: "It is clear that any original contract of the people which established such a law would itself be null and void, *for it would conflict with the appointed aim and purpose of mankind.*"

With this ringing declaration, Kant breaks through the limits of external freedom and of the neutral state. He appeals not just to historical tendencies but also to the teleological understanding of individual rational perfection that he develops in *The Metaphysical Principles of Virtue.* If human beings cannot, as individuals, deliberately undercut their potential for development, then they cannot, as citizens, do so collectively.

Second, Kant's arguments against the paternalistic state turn out, on close inspection, to constitute no real barrier to the tutelary state, directly engaged in the moral education of its citizens. Kant defines paternalism as state enforcement of an arbitrary conception of happiness, but given his sharp distinction between happiness and virtue, this definition can have no bearing on the issue of moral education. Equally, his insistence that morality cannot be coerced is irrelevant, for he distinguishes between coercion and education. And in spite of his emphasis on moral conscience, Kant affirms the possibility and necessity of moral education: "The fact that virtue must be acquired (and is not innate) is contained already in the concept of virtue. . . . That virtue can and must be taught follows from the fact that it is not innate."

We come, finally, to what I take to be Kant's official argument. The state cannot act for the people when the people cannot impose that action upon themselves, and, if no individual can so act, then the people as a collectivity cannot do so either. Kant argues:

> It is a contradiction to make the perfection of another my end and to deem myself obligated to promote his perfection. For the perfection of another man as a person consists precisely in his being able to set his end for himself according to his own concepts of duty. And it is a contradiction to require (to make it a duty for me) that I ought to do something which no one except another himself can do.

But this argument seems to rest on a confusion. To say that perfection consists in the capacity for autonomy is not to say that this capacity can be achieved autonomously. Kant appears to conflate perfection as an end state with the process whereby it is realized, a distinction clearly presupposed by his contention that virtue can and must be taught.

In the end, then, Kant gives no good arguments against a tutelary liberal state. This is not terribly surprising, for, as George Kelly has pointed out, there is a tutelary ideal at work in Kantian politics. Entrance into civil society is not a deduction from self-interest but, rather, a direct duty. Membership in civil society and participation in an advancing culture discipline our natural inclinations even as they help us to attain our ends. Political life, especially in a polity that heeds the precepts of republican legitimacy and liberates the life of the mind, is a preparation for morality. Kant's belief in a substantive doctrine of human perfection exerts an irresistible pressure on the limits of the neutral state.

This result is not just an idiosyncrasy of Kantian theory. To say that rational knowledge of the good life is available is to imply both that one ought to strive to lead that life and that one is harmed by deviating from it. It is to open up the possibility that B may understand what is good for A better than A does. It is to concede that negative freedom is not the only value and that its exercise may impede the pursuit of the good.

Still, the defender of negative freedom may seek to blunt the force of this concession by assigning negative freedom an absolute, lexical priority over the good. Freedom is inviolable in the sense that it may be restricted only by the requirements of others' freedom, never by teleological considerations.

These are two kinds of arguments that might be used to support this contention. First, one could reject Kant's strategy of deriving negative freedom from some more fundamental value and argue instead that negative freedom is an end in itself that does not require—indeed, cannot receive—external justification. Nothing is more important than pursuing my purposes, doing what I want, with a minimum of interference.

The difficulty with this line of argument is that it disregards the nature of freedom. Charles Taylor has reminded us: "Freedom is important to us because we are purposive beings." We are purposive in that we have goals whose attainment seems desirable and attainable—in some measure, anyway—through our striving. And freedom is valuable because it permits us to pursue our good.

But, *ex hypothesi,* the real good and the apparent good are not identical. Negative freedom allows us to pursue the apparent good even at the cost of losing the real good. But the real good is what we really want. It is the goal we would pursue if we had full intellectual clarity and emotional receptivity. To invade negative freedom in the name of the real good is to promote the individual's benefit over his or her harm, rationality over irrationality, truth over error. In practice, such invasions can be wrong *in principle* only if the mere fact that the impetus toward the good is external somehow negates the worth of the good end so achieved, that is, only if the consciously willed pursuit of a goal is a necessary condition of the value of attaining it.

As recent discussions of paternalism have shown, this proposition cannot be defended. Freeing an individual from heroin addiction is good even though the afflicted individual may not consciously will his or her liberation. Indeed, it may well be that the individual cannot affirm the worth of nonaddiction before having been coerced to attain it. Similarly, the outcome of education may be worthwhile, and students may retrospectively affirm its worth, even if the process of education frequently thwarts the exercise of their own inclinations.

This is not to deny, but rather to affirm, the superiority of the noncoerced over the coerced pursuit of the good. It is to deny that the noncoerced pursuit of the bad enjoys priority in principle—that is, in every case—over the coerced pursuit of the good. With this denial, the lexical priority of negative freedom vanishes. . . .

Perhaps further investigation will disclose some other grounding principle for negative freedom, but in the absence of plausible candidates, it seems sensible to conclude that the Kantian strategy for justifying the priority of negative freedom over the good is no more successful than was the direct strategy of justifying

negative freedom as an end in itself. We are, therefore, warranted in generalizing the conclusion to which the discussion of Kant's argument led us: Every substantive doctrine of the human good, or of human perfection, exerts irresistible pressure on the limits of the neutral state.

To avoid misunderstanding, let me state here what I argue at some length in Chapter 8: Negative freedom has a substantial, and legitimate, role within liberal theory. This is so because the liberal theory of the good is at most a partial account, one that leaves a considerable portion of life up to each individual's discretion. Freedom allows us to pursue this discretionary aspect of our lives, and it gains its worth from its contribution to the ends of life we have properly defined for ourselves. From this standpoint, a suitably constrained interpretation of negative freedom becomes an element of our good.

I should also repeat what I asserted in Chapter 1 (and defend in Chapter 8): What is distinctive about liberalism is not the absence of a substantive conception of the good, but rather a reluctance to move from this conception to full-blown public coercion of individuals. There are, I think, some excellent considerations of both prudence and principle that support this reluctance, and these considerations go some way toward staking out a sphere of individual freedom. My point is only that they do not add up to the kind of come-what-may defense of negative freedom that many liberals believe (wrongly, if I am right) is indispensable to their creed.

III

Contemporary liberal theorists, many of whom have been inspired by Kant, have endeavored to avoid the tension between individual perfection and state neutrality that we found at the heart of Kant's political theory and in every theory that contains these two elements. Many contemporary theorists are deeply skeptical about the rational status of any account of perfection or of the good life. For them, the defense of the neutral state rests in part on the unavailability of knowledge of the good, and they argue that liberal theory requires no substantive theory of the good whatever, but at most a "thin" or instrumental theory.

This argument takes two forms. The first is familiar: Ignorance about the good implies relativism, which mandates tolerance, which in turn requires the neutral state.

The fallacy of this chain of inference is equally familiar. Relativism, taken by itself, does not entail tolerance. B seeks to impose his way of life on A; A protests that B has no rational justification for his action; B replies, "What do I care about rational justification?" or (more moderately) "My way of life requires as a necessary condition a society in which others think and behave as I do." A can continue the argument only by appealing to some principle beyond ignorance of the good. Full skepticism about the good leads not to tolerance, not to liberal neutrality, but to an unconstrained struggle among different ways of life, a struggle in which force, not reason, is the final arbiter.

The second line of defense is more subtle but not more successful. Human beings, it is argued, must be judged and treated as equals unless there is some good reason to do otherwise. The only good reason would be a philosophic demonstration that some human beings are better than others, either in their moral character or in their conception of the good life, but we know that no such demonstration is possible. We must therefore treat all individuals as equals, and in a manner that neither presupposes nor imposes what we lack—a rational theory of the good. It is because individuals are morally equal that the state must be morally neutral.

This is a coherent argument as far as it goes, but it does not bring us to the liberal state. Liberals, after all, cannot be satisfied to say that all human lives are *equally* worthy. They must also say that each life has *positive* worth, greater than zero. So, for example, before Ronald Dworkin can arrive at his fundamental principle of liberalism—equality of concern and respect—he must assert that government is obligated to treat those whom it governs "with concern, that is, as human beings who are capable of suffering and frustration, and with respect, that is, as human beings who are capable of forming and acting on intelligent conceptions of how their lives should be lived."

It is not my purpose here to object to these contentions, but only to point out the grounds on which they rest. Our "respect" is for human existence itself, the ability to form and act on purposes, whatever they may be, taken as a positive good. Our "concern" is for the fulfillment of human purposes—the avoidance of pain, the achievement of our goals, whatever they may be—taken as positive goods. And we move from these positive valuations to equality of concern and respect through the commitment to rationality: Differences of moral weight among individuals can be justified only if they rest on relevant reasons, which are (by hypothesis) absent.

These features of Dworkin's argument are hardly idiosyncratic. The participants in Ackerman's neutral dialogue, from which all special conceptions of the good have allegedly been expelled, in fact share a conception of the good. They argue that life itself is preferable to death: "[None] of us is willing to starve to death while the other takes all the manna." They agree on the worth of human purposiveness, and on the worth of fulfilling purposes: "each of us is prepared to say that our own image of self-fulfillment has *some* value." And they agree that reason is preferable to force, as a guide for the constraint on action. They choose the rational life, and in so doing they endorse a specific conception of what is truly good for beings who wish to be human.

Matters are much the same in Rawls's theory. The distribution of primary goods takes on moral significance only if the fulfillment of the disparate individual purposes they serve is assumed to have intrinsic worth, that is, only if we as social theorists begin by accepting the evaluative standpoint of purposive agents. And clearly, the movement from individual purposiveness to principles of social justice rests on individuals' shared commitment to abide by the dictates of rationality in a suitably defined choice situation. The formal constraints on possible principles reflect this commitment to rationality as well.

This conclusion is confirmed and reinforced by Rawls's argument in the Dewey Lectures. Human beings are, he contends, characterized by "two moral powers and by two corresponding highest-order interests in realizing and exercising these powers. The first power is the capacity to understand, to apply, and to act from (and not merely in accordance with) the principles of justice. The second moral power is the capacity to form, to revise, and rationally to pursue a conception of the good. The gap separating this conception of moral agency from the perfectionism Rawls elsewhere castigates is exceedingly narrow. . . .

We can discern a recurrent pattern. Each of these contemporary liberal theories begins by promising to do without a substantive theory of the good; each ends by betraying that promise. All of them covertly rely on the same triadic theory of the good, which assumes the worth of human existence, the worth of human purposiveness and of the fulfillment of human purposes, and the worth of rationality as the chief constraint on social principles and social actions. If we may call the beliefs in the worth of human existence and in the worth of purposes and their fulfillment the root assumptions of humanism, then the theory of the good presupposed by these neutralist liberals is the theory of rationalist humanism.

In many ways this result is not terribly surprising, for it merely reemphasizes the line of descent from Enlightenment assumptions to present-day liberalism. Nor is it clear at first glance what the critical force of this finding may be. "Very well," we may imagine these theorists to retort, "we do have a more than instrumental theory of the good. Still, it is gratifyingly capacious and undemanding. To begin with, it expresses something like the minimum presuppositions of social philosophy, the convictions that all serious participants in discussions of social principles must hold. Liberalism is the theory not of the neutral state but of the minimally committed state. Moreover, much the same is true on the level of political practice. The liberal state rests solely on those beliefs about the good shared by all its citizens, whereas every other state must coercively espouse some controversial assumptions about the good life."

This is a powerful and important argument. On the theoretical plane, it calls our attention to a crucial ambiguity in the notion of neutrality. Strong neutrality implies the expulsion of any and all conceptions of the good from liberal theory. Weak neutrality, on the other hand, implies the rejection only of those theories that entail moral distinctions among individuals—that is, that preach the superiority of specific types of character and ways of life. But not all conceptions of the good imply hierarchical distinctions among individuals. In particular, neutralist liberals may argue, their theory of the good—the theory of rationalist humanism—does not do so. It is therefore neutral in the only sense that their thesis requires, and in the only sense that they ever intended, even though occasional linguistic infelicities may have led readers to expect that their thesis would be neutral in the strong sense.

But this clarification raises a new difficulty. It is one thing to propound a full-blown skepticism about the possibility of knowing the good in any philosophically or intersubjectively valid manner, and to endeavor to build social theory on this parsimonious foundation. It is a very different matter to assert that we can have usable knowledge of the good, but only up to a point. If we can proceed on the assumption that existence is preferable to nonexistence, that fulfillment of purposes is preferable to nonfulfillment, then why are we not free to enter into a fuller range of traditional arguments about the good life? On the basis of what considerations do we draw the line between objectivity and subjectivity just where most contemporary liberal theorists wish to draw it? In the absence of more explicit supporting arguments, the partial skepticism characteristic of neutralist liberalism has the appearance of an arbitrary arrangement of convenience rather than a principled position.

Versions of this problem have bedeviled liberal theory all the way back to Hobbes, whose robust skepticism gives way at the crucial point to the doctrine of the *summum malum*. Good and evil are relative to the individual, and variable within each individual,

> whence arise disputes, controversies, and at last war. And therefore so long as man is in the condition of mere nature, which is a condition of war, as private appetite is the measure of good, and evil: *and consequently all men agree on this, that peace is good,* and therefore also the [moral virtues,] as the means of *peaceable, sociable, and comfortable living.*

The difficulty is dual. Hobbes's skepticism comes to an abrupt end when he accepts the humanist theory of the good—the worth of existence and of the orderly pursuit of individual purposes—that he ascribes to all human beings. On the other hand, he does not and cannot simply appeal to an existing consensus. As he admits, many men—proud aristocrats, reckless desperados, religious fanatics, benighted fools—do not act on the belief that death is the worst of all evils. Liberal humanism is not only a substantive theory of the good but also an eminently contestable theory. The liberal commitment to individual existence and purposes can be challenged not solely by genocidal regimes but also by the traditions of secular heroism and, as we have rediscovered in the case of Iran, by the tradition of religious martyrdom as well.

Moreover, the liberal commitment to moral rationality is far from minimal in its implications for the scope and content of state activity. In Rawls's construction, for example, those who are to decide on general social arrangements are assumed to be able to reflect and to act in compliance with the dictates of rationality. Nevertheless, in formulating these arrangements, they must take into account the certainty that extensive moral education is essential if citizens of actual societies are to obtain the capacity for acting "on principle." A member of a well-ordered liberal society cannot object to state-governed tutelary practices designed to inculcate a sense of justice, for "in agreeing to principles of right the parties in the original position consent to the arrangements necessary to make these principles effective in their conduct." The more seriously liberalism takes its commitment to practical rationality, the more blurred becomes the line separating the liberal state from the tutelary, "perfectionist" state committed to a fuller theory of the good.

The path to defensible clarity in these matters leads *through,* not *around,* a direct consideration of the understanding of well-being on which liberalism rests. . . .

Moving from the theoretical to the practical plane, we must ask whether the minimally committed state is truly hospitable to all ways of life and conceptions of the good. . . . Rawls concedes that under liberal conditions certain forms of life—those that require control of the machinery of state—are likely systematically to lose out. Does this mean that liberal society is, contrary to its professed principles, systematically biased? No, he replies,

> a well-ordered society defines a fair background within which ways of life have a reasonable opportunity to establish themselves. If a conception of the good is unable to endure and gain adherents under institutions of equal freedom and mutual toleration, one must question whether it is a viable conception of the good, and whether its passing is to be regretted.

But (we may in turn reply) our fears cannot be allayed merely by invoking the sacred ghost of John Stuart Mill. Social competition is no more reliably benign than economic competition. Indeed, a kind of social Gresham's Law may operate, in which the pressure of seductively undemanding ways of life may make it very difficult, for example, for parents to raise children in accordance with norms of effort, conscientiousness, and self-restraint. The easy assumption that only "undeserving" ways of life lose out in a liberal society is unworthy of serious social philosophy. The line between ways of life that can flourish in the midst of social heterogeneity and those whose viability depends on a more hospitable homogeneity does not neatly divide valuable from worthless, or generous from repressive, conceptions of the good. The destruction of homogeneous and relatively self-contained subcommunities through the subtle corrosion of liberal society or through the direct assault of liberal social policy is not always to be welcomed. But this is not to say that, taken as a whole, we may not rightly choose the characteristic biases of the liberal polity over the biases inherent in the alternative forms of political organization actually available to us. It is not to say that these biases cannot be further ameliorated by more carefully distinguishing between what is and is not required for liberal public order. . . . And it is certainly not to say that the

bias of liberalism is as systematically constraining, as hostile to full human diversity, as are other forms of political life. Indeed, the relative capaciousness of liberal orders is an important element in the case for their relative superiority.

We need not look to the indirect effects of social heterogeneity to deny the full neutrality of the liberal state. There is a wide range of controverted issues over which, as a matter of both logic and practice, the contending parties cannot simply agree to differ and must instead arrive at binding determinations. Whatever its decision, the polity unavoidably commits itself to specific views of human personality and right conduct as well as to a range of external effects on other institutions and practices. In such cases, neutrality is never violated, because it is never possible. Every polity, then, embodies a more than minimal conception of the good that establishes at least a partial rank-order among individual ways of life and competing principles of right conduct.

END NOTES

Introduction

[1] George Sher, *Beyond Neutrality,* Cambridge University Press, 1999.

George

[1] As we shall see, certain influential contemporary thinkers have mounted a challenge from within the tradition of liberalism to the mainstream or orthodox view that excludes perfectionism from political theory. Joseph Raz, for example, has severely criticized anti-perfectionist liberalism, and proposed, as an alternative, a perfectionist theory of political morality, according to which "it is the goal of all political action to enable individuals to pursue valid conceptions of the good and to discourage evil or empty ones" (*The Morality of Freedom* (Oxford: Clarendon Press, 1986), 133). Raz stands with contemporary liberalism, and against the central tradition, however, in his view that "victimless immoralities" may not legitimately be forbidden by law.
[2] *Pol.* iii. 5. 1280[b]; quotations are from the translation by Ernest Barker, in *The Politics of Aristotle* (Oxford: Clarendon Press, 1946). Barker's use of the term "rights" here is somewhat anachronistic; the modern use of the term is foreign to Greek and Roman thought, and Aristotle's quotation from Lycophron would be more exactly rendered "guarantor of reciprocal justice."
[3] Ibid.
[4] *Nic. Eth.* x 9. 1179[b]; quotations are from the translation by W. D. Ross in *The Basic Works of Aristotle* (New York: Random House, 1941).
[5] Much later in the tradition, Aristotle's view is echoed by Kant: "Man must be trained, so as to become domesticated and

virtuous later on. The coercion of government and education make him supple, flexible and obedient to the laws; then reason will rule." *Gesammelte Schriften,* xv. 522–3 (Prussian Academy edn., 1923); quoted from the translation by G. Kelly, in *Idealism, Politics and History* (London: Cambridge University Press, 1969).

[6]Aristotle's view of the matter appears to be unstable, however, for in *Pol.* i. 1. 1252^b 13–30, he assumes that the household or family is merely an association for the sake of life, while the *polis* is an association for the sake of the good life; and, in *Pol.* viii. 1. 1337^a 23–32, he concludes that education is the responsibility of the *polis* and not (or at least not primarily) the responsibility of parents.

[7]*Summa Theologiae,* I-II, q. 95, a. 1; quotations are from the translation by the Fathers of the English Dominican Province, in *The "Summa Theologica" of St. Thomas Aquinas* (London: Burns, Oates & Washburn, 1915).

[8]*De Regno,* iv (i. 15) [115]; quotations are from the translation by Gerald B. Phelan, in *St. Thomas Aquinas On Kingship* (Toronto: The Pontifical Institute of Mediaeval Studies, 1949).

[9]See Joel Feinberg, *Harmless Wrongdoing* (New York: Oxford University Press, 1988); 341–2. For a critique of Feinberg's reading of Aquinas on this point, see Robert P. George, "Moralistic Liberalism and Legal Moralism," *Michigan Law Review,* 88 (1990), 1415–29, at 1421–2.

[10]Here Aquinas, as a Christian thinker, had the advantage of St. Paul's reflections in ch. 7 of the *Letter to the Romans* on the tendency of the law to make people rebellious.

[11]Citing Augustine, *De Ordine,* ii. 4. Whatever Augustine's view of the matter, one should not conclude that Aquinas is here endorsing the legalization of prostitution. Whether prostitution ought to be legally prohibited or tolerated is not the issue. He is simply exemplifying the prudential consideration that he has just laid down, and citing Augustine as an authority for it.

[12] See the Declaration on Religious Liberty of the Second Vatican Council, *Dignitatis Humanae.*

[13]On the "sacral" or "consecrational" nature of medieval political communities, see Jacques Maritain, *True Humanism* (London: Geoffrey Bles, 1941), 135–51.

[14]*De Civitate Dei,* ii. 20; quoted from the translation by Henry Bettenson, in *The City of God* (Harmondsworth: Penguin Books, 1972), 71.

[15]See William A. Galston, *Liberal Purposes* (Cambridge: Cambridge University Press, 1991), 283–7.

[16]In light of the data he considers regarding family break-up, out-of-wedlock births, and the tragic consequences of these phenomena for family life in contemporary America, Galston urges his fellow liberals to reject both "the proposition that different family structures represent nothing more than 'alternative life-styles,'" and "the thesis that questions of family structure are purely private matters not appropriate for public discussion and response" (ibid. 285).

[17]"American Catholic Higher Education: The Experience Evaluated," in George A. Kelly (ed.), *Why Should the Catholic University Survive?* (New York: St. John's University Press, 1973), 44.

CHAPTER VI

Equality: Its Nature and Value

"We hold these truths to be self-evident that all men are created equal" and are endowed by their Creator with certain inalienable rights, and among these the rights of life, liberty and the pursuit of happiness. Thomas Jefferson's words in the Declaration of Independence—it is an empirical fact that human beings are unequal in almost every way. They are of different shapes, sizes, and sexes, different genetic endowments, and different abilities. Take any characteristic you like—whether it be health, longevity, strength, athletic prowess, sense of humor, ear for music, intelligence, social sensitivity, ability to deliberate or do abstract thinking, sense of responsibility, self-discipline—and you will find vast differences between humans. Yet it is one of the basic tenets of almost all contemporary moral and political theories that humans are essentially equal, of equal worth, and that this fundamental "truth" should be reflected in the economic, social, and political structures of society. In the minds of many people, equality has come to be identified with *justice;* inequality with *injustice.* Why? And how can these opposing theses, empirical inequality and egalitarianism, be reconciled? And exactly what is "equality" in the first place? The essays in this chapter address these questions.

Another important question is, *What* exactly is to be "equalized?" Among the competing items to be equalized are welfare, preference satisfaction, primary goods, economic resources, social status, political power, capacity for personal fulfillment, opportunity for welfare, and opportunity for scarce resources and social positions. One is sometimes tempted to apply Hume's conclusion on competing theologies to competing egalitarian arguments: when they attack their rivals, they seem completely successful, the result being a mutual self-destruction.

The internal debate between egalitarians as to which version of egalitarianism is the correct one is in full bloom and the issue has not been decided. But there is an even more fundamental debate: the external debate between egalitarians and nonegalitarians, those who argue that equality has little or no moral significance. Despite an almost universal belief in equal human worth, a minority voice needs to be heard if we are to make progress in moral and political theory. In this volume, we have included readings that engage both the internal and the external debate.

What is the idea of equality? Essentially it involves a triadic relationship. Except with abstract ideas, such as numbers, there is no such thing as pure equality, equality per se. Two objects are always different in some way or other—even two Ping Pong balls are made up of different pieces of plastic and exist in different places. Two things A and B, if they are equal, are equal with respect to some property P. Two trees are of equal height, two baseball players have equal batting averages, two workers have produced the same amount of widgets in the same amount of time, and so forth. So statements of equality always must answer the question, Equal what? When the concept has a normative dimension, the relationship is quadratic: If A and B are equal with respect to the normative (merit-ascribing) property P, then A and B deserve equal amounts of desert D.

Given that people are unequal in many ways, we must also ask, Which ways are morally indefensible? And, Given that a type of inequality is morally indefensible, what, if anything, should the State do about it? Regarding the second question, socialists and liberals tend to be interventionists, calling for the State to act redistribute resources where a moral case can be made for mitigating the effects of inequality. Conservatives and libertarians tend to limit the State's role here, leaving the matter to voluntary action. With regard to the first question, a few idealists, such as Gracchus Babeuf and Sylvan Marechal, have called for the abolition of virtually all distinctions between persons.

> We declare that we can no longer suffer that the great majority of men shall labor and sweat to serve and pamper the extreme minority. . . . Let there be at length an end to this enormous scandal, which posterity will scarcely credit. Away for ever with the revolting distinctions of rich and poor, of great and little, of masters and servants, of *governors* and *governed.* Let there be no other differences between people than that of age or sex. Since all have the same needs and the same faculties, let them henceforth have the same education and the same diet. They are content with the same sun and the same air for all; why should not the same portion and the same quality of nourishment suffice for each of them.[1]

Babeuf's "Manifesto of the Equals" suggested even the elimination of the arts, since they hinder "that real equality" which Babeuf and Marechal would promote. The arts, of course, would reveal the difference between a Rembrandt or a Michelangelo and the rest of us. Sports and academic grades would have to be abolished for the same reason. We note below Christopher Jenck's suggestion that entitlements based on differences in native intelligence should likewise be abolished. John Rawls (see Reading 26) seems to think that our intelligence, temperament, and even our industriousness should be disregarded in matters of distribution, for they are outcomes of the natural lottery. Since we don't deserve our native endowments or our better family backgrounds, we don't deserve the results of what we do with those endowments.

Egalitarians generally agree that not all inequalities are morally repugnant. Differences in ethnicity, interests, aptitudes, and conceptions of the good may be innocent. Unlike Rawls, most egalitarians—e.g., Karl Marx (Reading 9) and Brian Barry (Reading 55)—would save a place for desert. People are entitled to the fruits of their labor and should be punished for their bad acts. The question becomes on what basis one distinguishes the morally innocent from the immoral differences between people. Criteria for such distinctions have not been worked out as well as one would like.

Let us then consider the question, What sort of inequalities are morally wrong and should be corrected by a more equal distribution? Candidates for such qualities identified in our readings include primary goods, resources, economic benefits (wealth), power, prestige, class, welfare, satisfaction of desire, satisfaction of interest, need, and opportunity. Some egalitarians emphasize great differences in wealth as the morally repugnant item. In most countries a small percentage of the population (the rich) own a disproportionate amount of the wealth, whereas a large percentage (the poor) own a small percentage of the wealth. Why should the poor suffer while the rich live in luxury? Other egalitarians emphasize political power as the item that should be equalized. Traditionally such egalitarians in the United States have fought for universal enfranchisement: for blacks (1870), for women (1920), for Native Americans (1924). Marxist and Socialist egalitarians, among others, argue that the franchise is insufficient for political equality. One needs such auxiliary traits as wealth, education, and leisure to participate effectively in the political process. Marx and Engels saw that so long as a State existed, political equality was impossible, since the rulers would always control the direction and speed of power more than the individual worker-citizen.

The question is: How is complete political equality possible, so long as there is the division between ruler and ruled—even if the rule be benevolent, enlightened, and voluntarily accepted by the governed? Government by its very nature seems to entail hierarchical chains of command, coercion, and authority of the governors over the governed. Rousseau recognized this point and so argued that political groups should be confined to small numbers wherein everyone had an equal input. Few egalitarians espouse the kind of anarchy required for political equality, so they would seem to opt for severely constrained political equality.

One important question that has often been sloughed over by participants in the debate over equality is whether equality of whatever substance is an intrinsic or simply an instrumental good. Thomas Nagel expresses the notion that equality is an intrinsic value when he writes, "The defense of economic equality on the ground that it is needed to protect political, legal, and social equality [is not] a defense of equality *per se*—equality in the possession of benefits in general. Yet the latter is a further moral idea of great importance. Its validity would provide an independent reason to favor economic equality as a good in its own right."[2] Even more strongly, Christopher Jencks in his famous report on American education, *Inequality,* writes, "Most educators lament and evidently feel that an individual's genes are his, and that they entitle him to whatever advantage he can get from them. . . . For a thoroughgoing egalitarian, however, inequality that derives from biology ought to be as *repulsive* as inequality that derives from early socialization."[3] And Richard Watson argues that equality of resources is such a transcendent value, at least for many purposes, that if equal distribution of food were to result in no one's getting enough to eat, we should nevertheless choose this annihilation of the human race rather than an unequal distribution.[4]

Watson's prescription illustrates the problem of treating equality as an intrinsic value, especially as an overriding one, for there are three ways in which we can achieve equality between people. We can bring the worst off and everyone in between up to the level of the best off. We can bring the best off and everyone in between down to the level of the worst off. And we can bring the worse off up and the better off down so that they meet somewhere in between. No doubt egalitarians would like to raise everyone up to the highest level, but with regard to many qualities this solution seems impossible. Given our present technology, there is no way we can raise imbeciles to the level of Einsteins or valetudinarians to the level of optimal health or the blind to the ability level of the sighted, so that the "thoroughgoing egalitarian," if equality is a transcendent value, as Jencks would have it, would have to dumb-down the brilliant, infuse the healthy with disease, and blind the sighted. An instructive satire of this position is Kurt Vonnegut's short story "Henry Bergeron," in which talented people are given burdensome handicaps in order to bring them down to the lowest common denominator. Few egalitarians want to go that far. Equality may be an intrinsic good, but it is not the only good. Others, both egalitarians and non-egalitarians, see equality as an instrumental good, relevant to achieve high welfare or justice.

There is no doubt but that the ideal of equality has inspired millions to protest undemocratic forms of government, monarchies, oligarchies, despotisms, and even republicanism. The sense that all individuals are of equal worth has been the basis for rights claims from the English Civil Wars (1641–52) to the civil rights movements in the United States and South Africa. Who can resist the appeal of Major William Rainborough of Cromwell's Parliamentary Army petitioning for political equality. "I think that the poorest he that is in England hath a life to live, as the greatest he; and therefore truly, sir, I think it's clear, that every man that is to live under a government ought first by his own consent to put himself under that government; and I do think that the poorest man in England is not at all bound in a strict sense to that government that he hath not had a voice to put himself under."[5] But the ideal of equality has dangers too. The French aristocrat Alexis de Tocqueville, in his visit to the United States in the 1830s, was amazed at the passion and preoccupation of Americans for equality. He saw in it both the promise of the future and a great danger.

> There is indeed a manly and legitimate passion for equality which rouses in all men a desire to be strong and respected. This passion tends to elevate the little man to the rank of the great. But the human heart also nourishes a debased taste for equality, which leads the weak to want to drag the strong down to their level and which induces men to prefer equality in servitude to inequality in freedom.[6]

We begin this chapter with Rousseau's essay (Reading 35) attributing the origins of inequality to the fact that humans have renounced their primitive natural ways of life and claimed property rights. Next, in Reading 36, the late great Plato scholar Gregory Vlastos, takes Aristotle's statement that "justice is equality, as all men believe it to be, quite apart from any argument," and argues that the two ideas are related in a way Aristotle never intended. Examining various candidates for distributive justice—need, worth, merit, work, and agreement—Vlastos argues that merit and agreement are inadequate principles and that equal human worth is the basis for just distributions and that it leads to an emphasis on allocation according to need. The worth of all persons is equal, however unequal may be their merit. This is so because that worth is of "infinite value," and human merit is of finite value; the intrinsic worth always overrides merit.

Harry Frankfurt, in Reading 37, opposes egalitarian theories, arguing that what morality requires is not equal distribution of resources but sufficiency. In an affluent society we have a duty to provide for people's minimal needs, but nothing further. Frankfurt's essay contains an interesting critique of the principle of diminishing marginal utility.

In Reading 38, I examine ten theories of equal human worth, upon which contemporary egalitarians base their theories of human rights, and argue that they are all unsound. I further argue that the notion of equal human worth is rooted in a deeper metaphysic, namely our religious heritage, and that by divorcing the thesis of human worth from that kind of metaphysic, the thesis, along with its entailments of rights, is left naked.

The next four readings deal with the principle of equal opportunity. There are at least two different notions of equal opportunity: (1) Weak Equal Opportunity (sometimes called "formal equal opportunity") holds that offices should be open to talent. This was classically set forth in postrevolutionary France by Napoleon Bonaparte, who chose officers not by class but by ability—"la carriere ouverte aux talents." It is meritocratic equal opportunity but does not address the advantages people have owing to natural or family resources. It leaves the matter of initial starting points untouched. (2) Strong Equal Opportunity (sometimes called "substantive equal opportunity") holds that individuals ought to have equal life chances to fulfill themselves or reach the same heights. It calls for compensation for those who had less fortune early in life to bring them to the level of those who had advantages. This kind of equal opportunity would support affirmative action programs and other compensatory policies. At the extreme end, as advocated by Onora O'Neill, this sort of equal opportunity would have to result in groups succeeding in obtaining coveted positions in proportion to their makeup in the population.[7] Equal opportunity would be equivalent to equal outcomes. Perhaps we should call this "Super Strong Equal Opportunity."

In a seminal article, "Equality of Opportunity and Beyond," John Schaar noted that the ideal of equal opportunity is the most popular of all the various conceptions of equality.[8] "The formula has few enemies—politicians, businessmen, social theorists, and freedom marchers all approve it—and it is rarely subjected to intellectual challenge." So much popularity might lead us to suspect that something is wrong, and Schaar argues that there is. Equality of opportunity is not egalitarian at all, but a deeply cruel conservative "debasement of a genuinely democratic understanding of equality." It actually militates against the ideals of equal worth, because it promotes meritocratic hierarchies wherein one is valued not for his or her humanity but according to how well he or she competes on the social playing field. Thoroughgoing equal opportunity would actually end up increasing inequalities between people.

James Fishkin, in Reading 39 points out a trilemma between strong equal opportunity (equal life chances), family values, and meritocracy. We can combine any two of these, but not all three, into viable social policy. We can have equal life chances and the family if we give up a commitment to excellence. We can preserve equal life chances and meritocracy if we give up our notion of the family and raise children in a Platonic commune or something that will assure an equal starting point for all. And we can preserve the family and merit if we give up the principle of equal life chances. The problem is not that we are not committed to significant moral values, but that these values compete with one another. We have one value too many.

William Galston (Reading 40) argues that despite its problems, the liberal idea of equal opportunity is morally significant, a necessary component of liberal democracy. Traditionally, four arguments have been given in support of the justification of equal opportunity. All are discussed in Galston's article. First, equal opportunity can be justified as producing *efficiency.* We want the best skilled people in positions necessary for the effective execution of social processes. All things being equal, a business that employs merely minimally capable workers will lose out to one which employs workers with high talent. Sometimes aggregate efficiency militates against the ideal of individual equal opportunity, but on the whole the principle of efficiency will support a presumption in favor of assigning positions to those most talented. The second justification for equal opportunity involves the notion of *desert.* There exists a deeply felt principle that people deserve to be treated in ways that follow from relevant antecedent activities. Equals should be treated equally according to their merits. Whereas the efficiency argument is teleological, forward looking, the desert argument is deontological, backward looking. In virtually every known culture people think that criminals should be punished in proportion to the seriousness of their crimes. They think that equal work deserves equal pay. They think that the good should prosper and the evil should suffer. The third justification for equal opportunity is that it enables people to *develop their talents* to the utmost. But, as Galston points out, this is a very general justification and is not an absolute. The fourth justification for equal opportunity is that it promotes *personal satisfaction.* By allowing people to compete for prizes and places, society promotes individual fulfillment. In this way, equal opportunity promotes excellence—strive for the highest achievement and you will experience deep satisfaction in attaining it. Of course, there are dangers here, for people may aim at things they have no chance at attaining and be doomed to disappointment. There is no social good without risk of evil. Excellence, self-discipline, and commitment, which equal opportunity supports, are all good things, but they do not guarantee against foolish calculations, failure, and envy in others who detest comparing themselves with their betters.

In the next two readings, Albert Mosley (Reading 41) and I (Reading 42) debate the case for affirmative action. Mosley bases his defense on a notion of compensation for past wrongs; I argue that two wrongs don't make a right. He argues that the compensation argument for preferential treatment is unsound, and that none of the other contemporary arguments for Strong Affirmative Action work either.

George Sher (Reading 43) critically examines one of the most popular egalitarian ideals of our time, the concept of "multicultural" diversity, the quest to have racial, gender, and ethnic diversity represented in every walk of life. He argues that the arguments for this position are fraught with difficulties. Finally, Sterling Harwood (Reading 44) analyzes the notion of inheritance of wealth and argues for a principle of limited inheritance.

READING 35

Discourse on the Origin and Foundations of Inequality Among Men

Jean-Jacques Rousseau

For Rousseau's biography, see Reading 4. Jean-Jacques Rousseau submitted *The Discourse on the Origin and Foundations of Inequality Among Men* to the Academy in Dijon, France, in 1754. Although his essay failed to win the Academy's prize, it established Rousseau as a leading social philosopher. In this essay, Rousseau opposes Hobbes's gloomy assessment of humans in the state of nature, where life is "solitary, poor, nasty, brutish, and short."

Rousseau describes the life of primitive humans as filled with spontaneous and simple pleasures, in a world in which healthy and hearty individuals, free and equal, far stronger and self-sufficient than civilized, domesticated beings, wander through forests, picking up food from nature's abundance. Enter property and with it the origins of inequality.

"The first person who, having enclosed a plot of land, took it into his head to say this is mine and found people simple enough to believe him, was the true founder of civil society." Thus ended the halcyon existence of the noble savage. A new stage of existence commenced, one that was based on vanity and the need for recognition and respect and that led to acquisitiveness. Yet Rousseau doesn't think it possible to go back to the state of nature. One must enter into a social contract to flourish in this artificial state of existence.

This reading is taken from The Social Contract and Discourses (London: Evergreen's Library, 1913)

QUESTION Proposed by the Academy of Dijon: What is the Origin of Inequality Among Men, and is it Authorized by the Natural Law?

I conceive of two kinds of inequality in the human species: one which I call natural or physical, because it is established by nature and consists in the difference of age, health, bodily strength, and qualities of mind or soul. The other may be called moral or political inequality, because it depends on a kind of convention and is established, or at least authorized, by the consent of men. This latter type of inequality consists in the different privileges enjoyed by some at the expense of others, such as being richer, more honored, more powerful than they, or even causing themselves to be obeyed by them.

There is no point in asking what the source of natural inequality is, because the answer would be found enunciated in the simple definition of the word. There is still less point in asking whether there would not be some essential connection between the two inequalities, for that would amount to asking whether those who command are necessarily better than those who obey, and whether strength of body or mind, wisdom or virtue are always found in the same individuals in proportion to power and wealth. Perhaps this is a good question for slaves to discuss within earshot of their masters, but it is not suitable for reasonable and free men who seek the truth.

Precisely what, then, is the subject of this discourse? To mark, in the progress of things, the moment when, right taking place of violence, nature was subjected to the law. To explain the sequence of wonders by which the strong could resolve to serve the weak, and the people to buy imaginary repose at the price of real felicity.

PART ONE

When I strip that being, thus constituted, of all the supernatural gifts he could have received and of all the artificial faculties he could have acquired only through long progress; when I consider him, in a word, as he must have left the hands of nature, I see an animal less strong than some, less agile than others, but all in all, the most advantageously organized of all. I see him satisfying his hunger under an oak tree, quenching his thirst at the first stream, finding his bed at the foot of the same tree that supplied his meal; and thus all his needs are satisfied.

When the earth is left to its natural fertility and covered with immense forests that were never mutilated by the axe, it offers storehouses and shelters at every step to animals of every species. Men, dispersed among the animals, observe and imitate their industry, and thereby raise themselves to the level of animal instinct, with the advantage that, whereas each species has only its own instincts, man, who may perhaps have none that belongs to him, appropriates all of them to himself, feeds himself equally well on most of the various foods which the other animals divide among themselves, and consequently finds his sustenance more easily than any of the rest can.

Accustomed from childhood to inclement weather and the rigors of the seasons, acclimated to fatigue, and forced, naked and without arms, to defend their lives and their prey against other ferocious beasts, or to escape them by taking flight, men develop a robust and nearly unalterable temperament. Children enter the world with the excellent constitution of their parents and strengthen it with the same exercises that produced it, thus acquiring all the vigor that the human race is capable of having. Nature treats them precisely the way the law of Sparta treated the children of its citizens: it renders strong and robust those who are well consti-

tuted and makes all the rest perish, thereby differing from our present-day societies, where the state, by making children burdensome to their parents, kills them indiscriminately before their birth.

Since the savage man's body is the only instrument he knows, he employs it for a variety of purposes that, for lack of practice, ours are incapable of serving. And our industry deprives us of the force and agility that necessity obliges him to acquire. If he had had an axe, would his wrists break such strong branches? If he had had a sling, would he throw a stone with so much force? If he had had a ladder, would he climb a tree so nimbly? If he had had a horse, would he run so fast? Give a civilized man time to gather all his machines around him, and undoubtedly he will easily overcome a savage man. But if you want to see an even more unequal fight, pit them against each other naked and disarmed, and you will soon realize the advantage of constantly having all of one's forces at one's disposal, of always being ready for any event, and of always carrying one's entire self, as it were, with one.

Hobbes maintains that man is naturally intrepid and seeks only to attack and to fight. On the other hand, an illustrious philosopher thinks, and Cumberland and Pufendorf also affirm, that nothing is as timid as man in the state of nature, and that he is always trembling and ready to take flight at the slightest sound he hears or at the slightest movement he perceives. That may be the case with regard to objects with which he is not acquainted. And I do not doubt that he is frightened by all the new sights that present themselves to him every time he can neither discern the physical good and evil he may expect from them nor compare his forces with the dangers he must run: rare circumstances in the state of nature, where everything takes place in such a uniform manner and where the face of the earth is not subject to those sudden and continual changes caused by the passions and inconstancy of peoples living together. But since a savage man lives dispersed among the animals and, finding himself early on in a position to measure himself against them, he soon makes the comparison; and, aware that he surpasses them in skillfulness more than they surpass him in strength, he learns not to fear them any more. Pit a bear or a wolf against a savage who is robust, agile, and courageous, as they all are, armed with stones and a hefty cudgel, and you will see that the danger will be at least equal on both sides, and that after several such experiences, ferocious beasts, which do not like to attack one another, will be quite reluctant to attack a man, having found him to be as ferocious as themselves. With regard to animals that actually have more strength than man has skillfulness, he is in the same position as other weaker species, which nevertheless subsist. Man has the advantage that, since he is no less adept than they at running and at finding almost certain refuge in trees, he always has the alternative of accepting or leaving the encounter and the choice of taking flight or entering into combat. Moreover, it appears that no animal naturally attacks man, except in the case of self-defense or extreme hunger, or shows evidence of those violent antipathies toward him that seem to indicate that one species is destined by nature to serve as food for another. . . .

With regard to illnesses, I will not repeat the vain and false pronouncements made against medicine by the majority of people in good health. Rather, I will ask whether there is any solid observation on the basis of which one can conclude that the average lifespan is shorter in those countries where the art of medicine is most neglected than in those where it is cultivated most assiduously. And how could that be the case, if we give ourselves more ills than medicine can furnish us remedies? The extreme inequality in our lifestyle: excessive idleness among some, excessive labor among others; the ease with which we arouse and satisfy our appetites and our sensuality; the overly refined foods of the wealthy, which nourish them with irritating juices and overwhelm them with indigestion; the bad food of the poor, who most of the time do not have even that, and who, for want of food, are inclined to stuff their stomachs greedily whenever possible; staying up until all hours, excesses of all kinds, immoderate outbursts of every passion, bouts of fatigue and mental exhaustion; countless sorrows and afflictions which are felt in all levels of society and which perpetually gnaw away at souls: these are the fatal proofs that most of our ills are of our own making, and that we could have avoided nearly all of them by preserving the simple, regular and solitary lifestyle prescribed to us by nature. If nature has destined us to be healthy, I almost dare to affirm that the state of reflection is a state contrary to nature and that the man who meditates is a depraved animal. When one thinks about the stout constitutions of the savages, at least of those whom we have not ruined with our strong liquors; when one becomes aware of the fact that they know almost no illnesses but wounds and old age, one is strongly inclined to believe that someone could easily write the history of human maladies by following the history of civil societies. . . .

With so few sources of ills, man in the state of nature hardly has any need therefore of remedies, much less of physicians. The human race is in no worse condition than all the others in this respect; and it is easy to learn from hunters whether in their chases they find many sick animals. They find quite a few that have received serious wounds that healed quite nicely, that have had bones or even limbs broken and reset with no other surgeon than time, no other regimen than their everyday life, and that are no less perfectly cured for not having been tormented with incisions, poisoned with drugs, or exhausted with fasting. Finally, however correctly administered medicine may be among us, it is still certain that although a sick savage, abandoned to himself, has nothing to hope for except from nature, on the other hand, he has nothing to fear except his illness. This frequently makes his situation preferable to ours.

Therefore we must take care not to confuse savage man with the men we have before our eyes. Nature treats all animals left to their own devices with a predilection that seems to show how jealous she is of that right. The horse, the cat, the bull, even the ass, are usually taller, and all of them have a more robust constitution, more vigor, more strength, and more courage in the forests than in our homes. They lose half of these advantages in becoming domesticated; it might be said that all our efforts at feeding them and treating them well only end in their degeneration. It is the same for man himself. In becoming habituated to the ways of society and a slave, he becomes weak, fearful, and servile; his soft and effeminate lifestyle completes the enervation of both his strength and his courage. Let us add that the difference between the savage man and the domesticated man should be still greater than that between the savage animal and the domesticated animal; for while animal and man have been treated equally by nature, man gives more comforts to himself than to the animals he tames, and all of these comforts are so many specific causes that make him degenerate more noticeably.

So far I have considered only physical man. Let us now try to look at him from a metaphysical and moral point of view. . . . Every animal has ideas, since it has senses; up to a certain point it even combines its ideas, and in this regard man differs from an animal only in degree. Some philosophers have even suggested that there is a greater difference between two given men than between a given man and an animal. Therefore it is not so much understanding which causes the specific distinction of man from all other animals as it is his being a free agent. Nature commands every animal, and beasts obey. Man feels the same impetus, but he knows he is free to go along or to resist; and it is above all in the awareness of this freedom that the spirituality of his soul is made manifest. For physics explains in some way the mechanism of the senses and the formation of ideas; but in the power of willing, or rather of choosing, and in the feeling of this power, we find only purely spiritual acts, about which the laws of mechanics explain nothing.

But if the difficulties surrounding all these questions should leave some room for dispute on this difference between man and animal, there is another very specific quality which distinguishes them and about which there can be no argument: the faculty of self-perfection, a faculty which, with the aid of circumstances, successively develops all the others, and resides among us as much in the species as in the individual. On the other hand, an animal, at the end of a few months, is what it will be all its life; and its species, at the end of a thousand years, is what it was in the first of those thousand years. Why is man alone subject to becoming an imbecile? Is it not that he thereby returns to his primitive state, and that, while the animal which has acquired nothing and which also has nothing to lose, always retains its instinct, man, in losing through old age or other accidents all that his perfectibility has enabled him to acquire, thus falls even lower than the animal itself? It would be sad for us to be forced to agree that this distinctive and almost unlimited faculty is the source of all man's misfortunes; that this is what, by dint of time, draws him out of that original condition in which he would pass tranquil and innocent days; that this is what, through centuries of giving rise to his enlightenment and his errors, his vices and his virtues, eventually makes him a tyrant over himself and nature.

Savage man, left by nature to instinct alone, or rather compensated for the instinct he is perhaps lacking by faculties capable of first replacing them and then of raising him to the level of instinct, will therefore begin with purely animal functions. Perceiving and feeling will be his first state, which he will have in common with all animals. Willing and not willing, desiring, and fearing will be the first and nearly the only operations of his soul until new circumstances bring about new developments in it.

Whatever the moralists may say about it, human understanding owes much to the passions, which, by common consensus, also owe a great deal to it. It is by their activity that our reason is perfected. We seek to know only because we desire to find enjoyment; and it is impossible to conceive why someone who had neither desires nor fears would go to the bother of reasoning. The passions in turn take their origin from our needs, and their progress from our knowledge. For one can desire or fear things only by virtue of the ideas one can have of them, or from the simple impulse of nature; and savage man, deprived of every sort of enlightenment, feels only the passion of this latter sort. His desires do not go beyond his physical needs. The only goods he knows in the universe are nourishment, a woman and rest; the only evils he fears are pain and hunger. I say pain and not death because an animal will never know what it is to die; and knowledge of death and its terrors is one of the first acquisitions that man has made in withdrawing from the animal condition. . . .

Whatever these origins may be, it is clear, from the little care taken by nature to bring men together through mutual needs and to facilitate their use of speech, how little she prepared them for becoming habituated to the ways of society, and how little she contributed to all that men have done to establish the bonds of society. In fact, it is impossible to imagine why, in that primitive state, one man would have a greater need for another man than a monkey or a wolf has for another of its respective species; or, assuming this need, what motive could induce the other man to satisfy it; or even, in this latter instance, how could they be in mutual agreement regarding the conditions. I know that we are repeatedly told that nothing would have been so miserable as man in that state; and if it is true, as I believe I have proved, that it is only after many centuries that men could have had the desire and the opportunity to leave that state, that would be a charge to bring against nature, not against him whom nature has thus constituted. But if we understand the word miserable properly, it is a word which is without meaning or which signifies merely a painful privation and suffering of the body or the soul. Now I would very much like someone to explain to me what kind of misery can there be for a free being whose heart is at peace and whose body is in good health? I ask which of the two, civil or natural life, is more likely to become insufferable to those who live it? We see about us practically no people who do not complain about their existence; many even deprive themselves of it to the extent they are able, and the combination of divine and human laws is hardly enough to stop this disorder. I ask if anyone has ever heard tell of a savage who was living in liberty ever dreaming of complaining about his life and of killing himself. Let the judgment therefore be made with less pride on which side real misery lies. On the other hand, nothing would have been so miserable as savage man, dazzled by enlightenment, tormented by passions, and reasoning about a state different from his own. It was by a very wise providence that the latent faculties he possessed should develop only as the occasion to exercise them presents itself, so that they would be neither superfluous nor troublesome to him beforehand, nor underdeveloped and useless in time of need. In instinct alone, man had everything he needed in order to live in the state of nature; in a cultivated reason, he has only what he needs to live in society. . . .

Above all, let us not conclude with Hobbes that because man has no idea of goodness he is naturally evil; that he is vicious because he does not know virtue; that he always refuses to perform services for his fellow men he does not believe he owes them; or that, by virtue of the right, which he reasonably attributes to himself, to those things he needs, he foolishly imagines himself to be the sole proprietor of the entire universe. Hobbes has very clearly seen the defect of all modern definitions of natural right, but the consequences he draws from his own definition show that he takes it in a sense that is no less false. Were he to have reasoned on the basis of the principles he establishes, this author should have said that since the state of nature is the state in which the concern for our self-preservation is the least prejudicial to that of others, that state was consequently the most appropriate for peace and the best suited for the human race. He says precisely the opposite, because he had wrongly injected into the savage man's concern for self-preservation the need to satisfy a multitude of passions which are the product of society and which have made laws necessary.

Man is weak when he is dependent, and he is emancipated from that dependence before he is robust. Hobbes did not see that the same cause preventing savages from using their reason, as our jurists claim, is what prevents them at the same time from abusing their faculties, as he himself maintains. Hence we could say that savages are not evil precisely because they do not know what it is to be good; for it is neither the development of enlightenment nor the restraint imposed by the law, but the calm of the passions and the ignorance of vice which prevents them from doing evil. *So much more profitable to these is the ignorance of vice than the knowledge of virtue is to those.* Moreover, there is another principle that Hobbes failed to notice, and which, having been given to man in order to mitigate, in certain circumstances, the ferocity of his egocentrism or the desire for self-preservation before this egocentrism of his came into being, tempers the ardor he

has for his own well-being by an innate repugnance to seeing his fellow men suffer. I do not believe I have any contradiction to fear in granting the only natural virtue that the most excessive detractor of human virtues was forced to recognize. I am referring to pity, a disposition that is fitting for beings that are as weak and as subject to ills as we are; a virtue all the more universal and all the more useful to man in that it precedes in him any kind of reflection, and so natural that even animals sometimes show noticeable signs of it. . . .

Reason is what turns man in upon himself. Reason is what separates him from all that troubles him and afflicts him. Philosophy is what isolates him and what moves him to say in secret, at the sight of a suffering man, "Perish if you will; I am safe and sound." No longer can anything but danger to the entire society trouble the tranquil slumber of the philosopher and yank him from his bed. His fellow man can be killed with impunity underneath his window. He has merely to place his hands over his ears and argue with himself a little in order to prevent nature, which rebels within him, from identifying him with the man being assassinated. Savage man does not have this admirable talent, and for lack of wisdom and reason he is always seen thoughtlessly giving in to the first sentiment of humanity. When there is a riot or a street brawl, the populace gathers together; the prudent man withdraws from the scene. It is the rabble, the women of the marketplace, who separate the combatants and prevent decent people from killing one another.

It is therefore quite certain that pity is a natural sentiment, which, by moderating in each individual the activity of the love of oneself, contributes to the mutual preservation of the entire species. Pity is what carries us without reflection to the aid of those we see suffering. Pity is what, in the state of nature, takes the place of laws, mores, and virtue, with the advantage that no one is tempted to disobey its sweet voice. Pity is what will prevent every robust savage from robbing a weak child or an infirm old man of his hard-earned subsistence, if he himself expects to be able to find his own someplace else. Instead of the sublime maxim of reasoned justice, *Do unto others as you would have them do unto you,* pity inspires all men with another maxim of natural goodness, much less perfect but perhaps more useful than the preceding one: *Do what is good for you with as little harm as possible to others.* In a word, it is in this natural sentiment, rather than in subtle arguments that one must search for the cause of the repugnance at doing evil that every man would experience, even independently of the maxims of education. Although it might be appropriate for Socrates and minds of his stature to acquire virtue through reason, the human race would long ago have ceased to exist, if its preservation had depended solely on the reasonings of its members. . . .

PART TWO

The first person who, having enclosed a plot of land, took it into his head to say this is mine and found people simple enough to believe him, was the true founder of civil society. What crimes, wars, murders, what miseries and horrors would the human race have been spared, had someone pulled up the stakes or filled in the ditch and cried out to his fellow men: "Do not listen to this impostor. You are lost if you forget that the fruits of the earth belong to all and the earth to no one!" But it is quite likely that by then things had already reached the point where they could no longer continue as they were. For this idea of property, depending on many prior ideas which could only have arisen successively, was not formed all at once in the human mind. It was necessary to make great progress, to acquire much industry and enlightenment, and to transmit and augment them from one age to another, before arriving at this final stage in the state of nature. Let us therefore take things farther back and try to piece together under a single viewpoint that slow succession of events and advances in knowledge in their most natural order.

Man's first sentiment was that of his own existence; his first concern was that of his preservation. The products of the earth provided him with all the help he needed; instinct led him to make use of them. With hunger and other appetites making him experience by turns various ways of existing, there was one appetite that invited him to perpetuate his species; and this blind inclination, devoid of any sentiment of the heart, produced a purely animal act. Once this need had been satisfied, the two sexes no longer took cognizance of one another, and even the child no longer meant anything to the mother once it could do without her.

Such was the condition of man in his nascent stage; such was the life of an animal limited at first to pure sensations, and scarcely profiting from the gifts nature offered him, far from dreaming of extracting anything from her. But difficulties soon presented themselves to him; it was necessary to learn to overcome them. The height of trees, which kept him from reaching their fruits, the competition of animals that sought to feed themselves on these same fruits, the ferocity of those animals that wanted to take his own life: everything obliged him to apply himself to bodily exercises. It was necessary to become agile, fleet-footed and vigorous in combat. Natural arms, which are tree branches and stones, were soon found ready at hand. He learned to surmount nature's obstacles, combat other animals when necessary, fight for his subsistence even with men, or compensate for what he had to yield to those stronger than himself.

In proportion as the human race spread, difficulties multiplied with the men. Differences in soils, climates and seasons could force them to inculcate these differences in their lifestyles. Barren years, long and hard winters, hot summers that consume everything required new resourcefulness from them. Along the seashore and the riverbanks they invented the fishing line and hook, and became fishermen and fish-eaters. In the forests they made bows and arrows, and became hunters and warriors. In cold countries they covered themselves with the skins of animals they had killed. Lightning, a volcano, or some fortuitous chance happening acquainted them with fire: a new resource against the rigors of winter. They learned to preserve this element, then to reproduce it, and finally to use it to prepare meats that previously they devoured raw.

This repeated appropriation of various beings to himself, and of some beings to others, must naturally have engendered in man's mind the perceptions of certain relations. These relationships which we express by the words "large," "small," "strong," "weak," "fast," "slow," "timorous," "bold," and other similar ideas, compared when needed and almost without thinking about it, finally produced in him a kind of reflection, or rather a mechanical prudence which pointed out to him the precautions that were most necessary for his safety.

The new enlightenment which resulted from this development increased his superiority over the other animals by making him aware of it. He trained himself to set traps for them; he tricked them in a thousand different ways. And although several surpassed him in fighting strength or in swiftness in running, of those that could serve him or hurt him, he became in time the master of the former and the scourge of the latter. Thus the first glance he directed upon himself produced within him the first stirring of pride; thus, as yet hardly knowing how to distinguish the ranks, and contemplating himself in the first rank by virtue of his species, he prepared himself from afar to lay claim to it in virtue of his individuality.

Although his fellowmen were not for him what they are for us, and although he had hardly anything more to do with them than with other animals, they were not forgotten in his observations. The conformities that time could make him perceive among them, his female, and himself, made him judge those he did not perceive. And seeing that they all acted as he would have done under similar circumstances, he concluded that their way of thinking and feeling was in complete conformity with his own. And this important truth, well established in his mind, made him follow, by a presentiment as sure as dialectic and more prompt, the best rules of conduct that it was appropriate to observe toward them for his advantage and safety.

Taught by experience that love of well-being is the sole motive of human actions, he found himself in a position to distinguish the rare occasions when common interest should make him count on the assistance of his fellowmen, and those even rarer occasions when competition ought to make him distrust them. In the first case, he united with them in a herd, or at most in some sort of free association, that obligated no one and that lasted only as long as the passing need that had formed it. In the second case, everyone sought to obtain his own advantage, either by overt force, if he believed he could, or by cleverness and cunning, if he felt himself to be the weaker.

This is how men could imperceptibly acquire some crude idea of mutual commitments and of the advantages to be had in fulfilling them, but only insofar as present and perceptible interests could require it, since foresight meant nothing to them, and far from concerning themselves about a distant future, they did not even give a thought to the next day. Were it a matter of catching a deer, everyone was quite aware that he must faithfully keep to his post in order to achieve this purpose; but if a hare happened to pass within reach of one of them, no doubt he would have pursued it without giving it a second thought, and that, having obtained his prey, he cared very little about causing his companions to miss theirs. . . .

Having previously wandered about the forests and having assumed a more fixed situation, men slowly came together and united into different bands, eventually forming in each country a particular nation, united by mores and characteristic features, not by regulations and laws, but by the same kind of life and foods and by the common influence of the climate. Eventually a permanent proximity cannot fail to engender some intercourse among different families. Young people of different sexes live in neighboring huts; the passing intercourse demanded by nature soon leads to another, through frequent contact with one another, no less sweet and more permanent. People become accustomed to consider different objects and to make comparisons. Imperceptibly they acquire the ideas of merit and beauty which produce feelings of preference. By dint of seeing one another, they can no longer get along without seeing one another again. A sweet and tender feeling insinuates itself into the soul and at the least opposition becomes an impetuous fury. Jealousy awakens with love; discord triumphs, and the sweetest passion receives sacrifices of human blood.

In proportion as ideas and sentiments succeed one another and as the mind and heart are trained, the human race continues to be tamed, relationships spread and bonds are tightened. People grew accustomed to gather in front of their huts or around a large tree; song and dance, true children of love and leisure, became the amusement or rather the occupation of idle men and women who had flocked together. Each one began to look at the others and to want to be looked at himself, and public esteem had a value. The one who sang or danced the best, the handsomest, the strongest, the most adroit or the most eloquent became the most highly regarded. And this was the first step toward inequality and, at the same time, toward vice. From these first preferences were born vanity and contempt on the one hand, and shame and envy on the other. And the fermentation caused by these new leavens eventually produced compounds fatal to happiness and innocence.

As soon as men had begun mutually to value one another, and the idea of esteem was formed in their minds, each one claimed to have a right to it, and it was no longer possible for anyone to be lacking it with impunity. From this came the first duties of civility, even among savages; and from this every voluntary wrong became an outrage, because along with the harm that resulted from the injury, the offended party saw in it contempt for his person, which often was more insufferable than the harm itself. Hence each man punished the contempt shown him in a manner proportionate to the esteem in which he held himself; acts of revenge became terrible, and men became bloodthirsty and cruel. This is precisely the stage reached by most of the savage people known to us; and it is for want of having made adequate distinctions among their ideas or of having noticed how far these peoples already were from the original state of nature that many have hastened to conclude that man is naturally cruel, and that he needs civilization in order to soften him. On the contrary, nothing is so gentle as man in his primitive state, when, placed by nature at an equal distance from the stupidity of brutes and the fatal enlightenment of civil man, and limited equally by instinct and reason to protecting himself from the harm that threatens him, he is restrained by natural pity from needlessly harming anyone himself, even if he has been harmed. For according to the axiom of the wise Locke, *where there is no property, there is no injury.* . . .

From the cultivation of land, there necessarily followed the division of land; and from property once recognized, the first rules of justice. For in order to render everyone what is his, it is necessary that everyone can have something. Moreover, as men began to look toward the future and as they saw that they all had goods to lose, there was not one of them who did not have to fear reprisals against himself for wrongs he might do to another. This origin is all the more natural as it is impossible to conceive of the idea of property arising from anything but manual labor, for it is not clear what man can add, beyond his own labor, in order to appropriate things he has not made. It is labor alone that, in giving the cultivator a right to the product of the soil he has tilled, consequently gives him a right, at least until the harvest, and thus from year to year. With this possession continuing uninterrupted, it is easily transformed into property. . . .

Things in this state could have remained equal, if talents had been equal, and if the use of iron and the consumption of foodstuffs had always been in precise balance. But this proportion, which was not maintained by anything, was soon broken. The strongest did the most work; the most adroit turned theirs to better advantage; the most ingenious found ways to shorten their labor. The farmer had a greater need for iron, or the blacksmith had a greater need for wheat; and in laboring equally, the one earned a great deal while the other barely had enough to live. Thus it is that natural inequality imperceptibly manifests itself together with inequality occasioned by the socialization process. Thus it is that the differences among men, developed by those of circumstances, make themselves more noticeable, more permanent in their effects, and begin to influence the fate of private individuals in the same proportion. . . .

Thus we find here all our faculties developed, memory and imagination in play, egocentrism looking out for its interests, reason rendered active, and the mind having nearly reached the limit of the perfection of which it is capable. We find here all the natural qualities put into action, the rank and fate of each man established not only on the basis of the quantity of goods and the power to serve or harm, but also on the basis of mind, beauty, strength or skill, on the basis of merit or talents. And since these qualities were the only ones that could attract consideration, he was soon forced to have them or affect them. It was necessary, for his advantage, to show himself to be something other than what he in fact was. Being something and appearing to be something became two completely different things; and from this distinction there arose grand ostentation, deceptive cunning, and all the vices that follow in their wake. On the other hand, although man had previously been free and independent, we find him, so to speak, subject, by virtue of a multitude of fresh needs, to all of nature and particularly to his fellowmen, whose slave in a sense he becomes even in becoming their master; rich, he needs their services; poor, he needs their help; and being midway between wealth and poverty does not put him in a position to get along without them. It is therefore necessary for him to seek incessantly to interest them in his fate and to make them find their own profit, in fact or in appearance, in working for his. This makes him two-faced and crooked with some, imperious and harsh with others, and puts him in the position of having to abuse everyone he needs when he cannot make them fear him and does not find it in his interests to be of useful service to them. Finally, consuming ambition, the zeal for raising the relative level of his fortune, less out of real need than in order to put himself above others, inspires in all men a wicked tendency to harm one another, a secret jealousy all the more dangerous because, in order to strike its blow in greater safety, it often wears the mask of benevolence; in short, competition and rivalry on the one hand, opposition of interest[s] on the other, and always the hidden desire to profit at the expense of someone else. All these ills are the first effect of property and the inseparable offshoot of incipient inequality. . . .

I have tried to set forth the origin and progress of inequality, the establishment and abuse of political societies, to the extent that these things can be deduced from the nature of man by the light of reason alone, and independently of the sacred dogmas that give to sovereign authority the sanction of divine right. It follows from this presentation that, since inequality is practically non-existent in the state of nature, it derives its force and growth from the development of our faculties and the progress of the human mind, and eventually becomes stable and legitimate through the establishment of property and laws. Moreover, it follows that moral inequality, authorized by positive right alone, is contrary to natural right whenever it is not combined in the same proportion with physical inequality: a distinction that is sufficient to determine what one should think in this regard about the sort of inequality that reigns among all civilized people, for it is obviously contrary to the law of nature, however it may be defined, for a child to command an old man, for an imbecile to lead a wise man, and for a handful of people to gorge themselves on superfluities while the starving multitude lacks necessities.

READING 36

Justice and Equality

Gregory Vlastos

Gregory Vlastos (1907–91) was Professor of Philosophy at Princeton University and the University of California–Berkeley. He began his career as a Congregational minister and became one of the outstanding scholars of Ancient Greek philosophy.

In this classic defense of egalitarianism, Vlastos imagines a Martian visitor inquiring why we would spend an inordinate amount of money helping a person in great need in order to give him equal chances in life. When the visitor is told that it is because of our commitment to equality, he responds, "But why do you want this sort of equality?" Vlastos answers, "Because the human worth of all persons is equal, however unequal may be their merit." All humans have equal positive worth; as Rawls might say, their worth is "inviolable" so that it may not be sacrificed to utilitarian consequences.

Vlastos examines five traditional canons of distributive justice, similar to those discussed by Rescher in Reading 29: need, worth, merit, work, and agreement made. Although each of these has a legitimate place, need is the most important criterion for distribution.

This reading is taken from *Social Justice*, ed. Richard Brandt (Englewood Cliffs, N.J.: Prentice Hall, 1962).

I

The close connection between justice and equality is manifest in both history and language. The great historic struggles for social justice have centered about some demand for equal rights: the struggle against slavery, political absolutism, economic exploitation, the disfranchisement of the lower and middle classes and the disfranchisement of women, colonialism, racial oppression. On the linguistic side let me mention a curiosity that will lead us into the thick of our problem. When Aristotle in Book V of the *Nicomachean Ethics* comes to grips with distributive justice, almost the first remark he has to make is that "justice is equality, as all men believe it to be, quite apart from any argument." And well they might if they are Greeks, for their ordinary word for equality, to *ison* or *isotes,* comes closer to being the right word for "justice" than does the word *dikaiosyne,* which we usually translate as "justice." Thus, when a man speaks Greek he will be likely to say "equality" and *mean* "justice." But it so happens that Aristotle, like Plato and others before him, believed firmly that a just distribution is in general an unequal one. And to say this, if "equal" is your word for "just," you would have to say that an "equal" distribution is an *unequal* one. A way had been found to hold this acrobatic linguistic posture by saying that in this connection *isotes* meant "geometrical equality," i.e., proportionality; hence the "equal" (just, fair) distribution to persons of unequal merit would have to be unequal. This tour de force must have provoked many an honest man at the time as much as it has enraged Professor Popper in ours. We may view it more dispassionately as classical testimony to the strength of the tie between equality and justice: even those who meant to break the conceptual link could not, or would not, break the verbal one. The meritarian view of justice paid reluctant homage to the equalitarian one by using the vocabulary of equality to assert the justice of inequality.

But when the equalitarian has drawn from this what comfort he may, he still has to face the fact that the expropriation of his word "equality" could be carried through so reputably and so successfully that its remote inheritance has made it possible for us to speak now in a perfectly matter of fact way of "equitable inequalities" or "inequitable equalities." This kind of success cannot be wholly due to the tactical skill of those who carried out the original maneuver; though one may envy the virtuosity with which Plato disposes of the whole notion of democratic equality in a single sentence (or rather less, a participial clause) when he speaks of democracy as "distributing an odd sort of equality to equals and unequals." The democrats themselves would have been intellectually defenseless against that quip. Their faith in democracy had no deep roots in any concept of human equality; the *isonomia* (equality of law) on which they prided themselves was the club-privilege of those who had had the good judgment to pick their ancestors from free Athenian stock of the required purity of blood. But even if we could imagine a precocious humanitarian in or before Plato's time, founding the rights of the citizen on the rights of man, it is not clear that even he would be proof against Plato's criticism. For what Plato would like to know is whether his equalitarian opponent really means to universalize equality: would he, would anyone, wish to say that there are no just inequalities? That there are no rights in respect of which men are unequal?

One would think that this would be among the first questions that would occur to equalitarians, and would have had long since a clear and firm answer. Strange as it may seem, this has not happened. The question has been largely evaded. Let me give an example: Article I of the Declaration of Rights of Man and Citizen (enacted by the Constituent Assembly of the First French Republic in 1791) reads: "Men are born and remain free and equal in rights. Social distinctions can be based only upon public utility." Bentham takes the first sentence to mean that men are equal in *all* rights. One would like to think that this was a wilful misunderstanding. For it would be only too obvious to the drafters of the Declaration that those "social distinctions" of which they go on to speak would entail many inequalities of right. Thus the holder of a unique political office (say, the president of a republic) would not be equal in all rights to all other men or even to one other man: no other man would have equal right to this office, or to as high an office; and many would not have equal right to any political office, even if they had, as they would according to the republican constitution, equal right of eligibility to all offices. But if this is in the writers' minds, why don't they come out and say that men are born and remain equal in some rights, but are either not born or do not remain equal in a great many others? They act as though they were afraid to say the latter on this excessively public occasion, lest their public construe the admission of some unequal rights as out of harmony with the ringing commitment to human rights which is the keynote of the Declaration. What is this? Squeamishness? Confusion? Something of both? Or has it perhaps a sound foundation and, if so, in what? Plato's question is not answered. It is allowed to go by default.

There is here, as so often in the tradition of natural rights, a lack of definiteness which is exasperating to those who look for plain and consecutive thinking in moral philosophy. Coming back to this tradition fresh from the systems of Plato or Hobbes or Hume, with their clean, functional lines, one feels that whether or not the case for inequality has ever been proved, it has at least been made clear from both the aristocratic and the utilitarian side; while the case for equality, housed in the rambling and somewhat rundown mansion of natural rights, has fared so poorly that when one puts a question like the one I just raised, one can't be sure of what the answer is, or even that there is supposed to be one. And much the same is true of several other questions that remain after one has completely cut out one earlier source of confusion: the mythological prehistory of a supposed state of nature. Taking "natural rights" to mean simply *human* rights—that is to say, rights which are human not in the trivial sense that those who have them are men, but in the challenging sense that in order to have them they need only be men—one would still like to know:

(1) What is the range of these rights? The French Declaration states: "these rights are liberty, property, security, and resistance to oppression." The imprudent beginning—"these rights are" instead of Jefferson's more cautious, "among these rights are"—makes it look as though the four natural rights named here are meant to be all the rights there are. If so, what happened to the pursuit of happiness? Is that the same as liberty? As for property, this was not a natural right before Locke, and not always after him, e.g., not for Jefferson. And what of welfare rights? They are not mentioned in the French document, nor are they implied by "security."

(2) Can the doctrine of natural rights find a place for each of the following well-known maxims of distributive justice:

1. To each according to his *need*.
2. To each according to his *worth*.
3. To each according to his *merit*.
4. To each according to his *work*.

And we might add a fifth which does not seem to have worked its way to the same level of adage-like respectability, but has as good a claim as some of the others:

5. To each according to the *agreements* he has made.

By making judicious selections from this list one can "justicize" extreme inequalities of distribution. It is thus that Plato concludes that the man who can no longer work has lost his right to live, and Bentham that no just limits can be set to the terms on which labor can be bought, used, and used up. Hobbes, most frugal of moral philosophers, operates with just the last of these maxims; making the keeping of covenants the defining element of justice, he decimates civil liberties *more geometrico.* These premises were not, of course, the only ones from which such morally dismal results were reached by these clear-headed and upright men; but they were the controlling ones. If merit or work or agreement, or any combination of the three, are made the final principles of distributive justice, it will not be hard to find plausible collateral premises from which to get such results. What then should a natural rights philosopher do with these maxims? Must he regard them as fifth-columnists? Or can he keep them as members of his working team, useful, if subordinate, principles of his equalitarian justice? Can this be done without making concessions to inequality which will divide his allegiance to equality?

(3) Finally, are natural rights "absolute," i.e., are their claims unexceptionable? If I have a natural right to a given benefit does it follow that I ought to be granted that benefit in all possible circumstances no matter how my other rights or those of others might be affected? Is this the meaning of the well-known statements that natural rights are "inalienable" and "imprescriptible"?

I believe that all these questions admit of reasonable answers which, when worked out fully, would amount to a revised theory of natural rights or, what is the same thing, a theory of human rights: I shall use the two expressions interchangeably. Progress has been made in this direction in recent years in a number of important essays. I shall borrow freely results reached by various contributors to this work, though without taking time to make explicit acknowledgments or register specific disagreements.

Let me begin with the answer to the third of the questions I raised. Are human rights absolute? All of these writers would say, "No." I am convinced that in this they are right, and am even prepared to add that neither is there anything explicitly contrary to this in that branch of the classical theory which is of greatest interest to us today: in Locke, for example. Locke has indeed been understood to mean that natural rights are absolute. But nowhere does Locke *say* this. Contrariwise he believes many things which imply the opposite. For example, he would certainly approve of imprisonment as a punishment for crime; and we hear him recommending that beggars be detained in houses of correction or impressed in the navy. Such constraints

he would have to reckon justified exceptions to that freedom of movement which all persons claim in virtue of their natural right to liberty. So too he would have to think of the death penalty for convicted criminals, or of a military order which would bring death to many of those obeying it, as justified exceptions to some men's natural right to life. Even the right to property—indeed, that special form of it which is upheld more zealously than any other right in the *Second Treatise,* one's right not to be deprived of property without consent— could not be unconditional; Locke would have to concede that it should be over-ruled, e.g., in a famine when stores of hoarded food are requisitioned by public authority. We would, therefore, improve the consistency of Locke's theory if we understood him to mean that natural rights are subject to justified exceptions. In any case, I shall adhere to his view here and, borrowing from current usage, shall speak of human rights as "prima facie" rights to mean that the claims of any of them may be over-ruled in special circumstances. Can one say this without giving away the radical difference which the traditional doctrine fixed between natural rights and all others? To this the answer would be that, though in this respect all rights are alike, the vital difference remains untouched: one need only be a man to have *prima facie* rights to life, liberty, welfare, and the like; but to be a man is not all one needs to have a *prima facie* right to the house he happens to own or the job he happens to hold. As for the "inalienability" and "imprescriptibility" of natural rights, we may understand them with this proviso to mean exactly what they say: that no man can alienate (i.e., sign away, transfer by contract) a *prima facie* natural right, his own or anyone else's; and that no people can lose *prima facie* natural rights by prescription, e.g., in virtue of the time-hallowed possession of despotic power over them by a royal dynasty.

II

Let me begin with the first on my list of maxims of distributive justice: "To each according to his need." Since needs are often unequal, this looks like a precept of unequal distribution. But this is wrong. It is in fact *the most perfect form of equal distribution.* To explain this let me take one of the best established rights in the natural law tradition: the right to the security of life and person. Believing that this is an equal right, what do we feel this means in cases of special need?

Suppose, for instance, New Yorker X gets a note from Murder, Inc., that looks like business. To allocate several policemen and plainclothesmen to guard him over the next few weeks at a cost a hundred times greater than the per capita cost of security services to other citizens during the same period, is surely *not* to make an exception to the equal distribution required by the equal right of all citizens to the security of their life and person; it is not done on the assumption that X has a greater right to security or a right to greater security. If the visitor from Mars drew this conclusion from the behavior of the police, he would be told that he was just mistaken. The greater allocation of community resources in X's favor, we would have to explain, is made precisely *because* X's security rights are equal to those of other people in New York. This means that X is entitled to the same level of police-made security as is maintained for other New Yorkers. Hence in these special circumstances, where his security level would drop to zero without extra support, he should be given this to bring his security level nearer the normal. I say "nearer," not "up to" the normal, because I am talking of New York as of 1961. If I were thinking of New York with an ideal municipal government, ideally supplied with police resources, I *would* say "up to the normal," because that is what equality of right would ideally mean. But as things are, perhaps the best that can be done for X without disrupting the general level of security maintained for all the other New Yorkers is to decrease his chances of being bumped off in a given week to, say, one to ten thousand, while those of ordinary citizens, with ordinary protection are, say, one to ten million—no small difference. Now if New York were more affluent, it would be able to buy more equality of security for its citizens (as well as more security): by getting more, and perhaps also better paid, policemen, it would be able to close the gap between security maintained for people in ordinary circumstances and that supplied in cases of special need, like that of X in his present jam. Here we stumble on something of considerable interest: that approximation to the goal of completely equal security benefits for all citizens is a function of two variables: first, and quite obviously, of the pattern of distribution of the resources; second, and less obviously, of their size. If the distributable resources are so meager that they are all used up to maintain a general level barely sufficient for ordinary needs, their reallocation to meet exceptional need will look too much like robbing Peter to pay Paul. In such conditions there is likely to be little, if any, provision for extremity of need and, what is more, the failure to meet the extremity will not be felt as a social injustice but as a calamity of fate. And since humanity has lived most of its life under conditions of general in-

digence, we can understand why it has been so slow to connect provision for special need with the notion of justice, and has so often made it a matter of charity; and why "to each according to his need" did not become popularized as a precept of justice until the first giant increase in the productive resources, and then only by men like Blanc and Marx, who projected an image of a super-affluent, machine-run society on the grid of an austerely equalitarian conception of justice.

So we can see why distribution according to personal need, far from conflicting with the equality of distribution required by a human right, is so linked with its very meaning that under ideal conditions equality of right would coincide with distribution according to personal need. Our visitor misunderstood the sudden mobilization of New York policemen in favor of Mr. X, because he failed to understand that it is benefits to persons, not allocation of resources as such, that are meant to be made equal; for then he would have seen at once that unequal distribution of resources would be required to equalize benefits in cases of unequal need. But if he saw this he might then ask, "But why do you want this sort of equality?" My answer would have to be: Because the human worth of all persons is equal, however unequal may be their merit. To the explanation of this proposition I shall devote the balance of this Section.

By "merit" I shall refer throughout this essay to all the kinds of valuable qualities or performances in respect of which persons may be graded. The concept will not be restricted to moral actions or dispositions. Thus wit, grace of manner, and technical skill count as meritorious qualities fully as much as sincerity, generosity, or courage. Any valuable human characteristic, or cluster of characteristics, will qualify, provided only it is "acquired," i.e., represents what its possessor has himself made of his natural endowments and environmental opportunities. Given the immense variety of individual differences, it will be commonly the case that of any two persons either may excel the other in respect of different kinds or sub-kinds or merit. Thus if A and B are both clever and brave men, A may be much the cleverer as a business man, B as a literary critic, and A may excel in physical, B in moral, courage. It should be clear from just this that to speak of "a person's merit" will be strictly senseless except insofar as this is an elliptical way of referring to that person's merits, i.e., to those specifiable qualities or activities in which he rates well. So if there is a value attaching to the person himself as an integral and unique individual, *this* value will not fall under merit or be reducible to it. For it is of the essence of merit, as here defined, to be a grading concept; and there is no way of grading individuals as such. We can only grade them with respect to their qualities, hence only by abstracting from their individuality. If A is valued for some meritorious quality, $m,$ his individuality does not enter into the valuation. As an individual he is then dispensable; his place could be taken without loss of value by any other individual with as good an m-rating. Nor would matters change by multiplying and diversifying the meritorious qualities with which A is endowed. No matter how enviable a package of well-rounded excellence A may represent, it would still follow that, if he is valued only for his merit, he is not being valued as an individual. To be sure individuals *may* be valued only for their merits. This happens all too commonly. A might be valued in just this way by $P,$ the president of his company, for whom $A,$ highly successful vice-president in charge of sales, amusing dinner-guest, and fine asset to the golf club, is simply high-grade equipment in various complexes of social machinery which P controls or patronizes. On the other hand, it is possible that, much as P prizes this conjunct of qualities $(M),$ he values A also as an individual. A may be his son, and he may be genuinely fond of him. If so, his affection will be for $A,$ not for his M-qualities. The latter P approves, admires, takes pride in, and the like. But his affection and good will are for $A,$ and *not only because,* or *insofar as,* A has the M-qualities. For P may be equally fond of another son who rates well below A in P's scoring system. Moreover, P's affection for $A,$ as distinct from his approval or admiration of him, need not fluctuate with the ups and downs in A's achievements. Perhaps A had some bad years after graduating from college, and it looked then as though his brilliant gifts would be wasted. It does not follow that P's love for A then lapsed or even ebbed. Constancy of affection in the face of variations of merit is one of the surest tests of whether or not a parent does love a child. If he feels fond of it only when it performs well, and turns coldly indifferent or hostile when its achievements slump, then his feeling for the child can scarcely be called *love.* There are many relations in which one's liking or esteem for a person are strictly conditional on his measuring up to certain standards. But convincing evidence that the relation is of this type is no evidence that the relation is one of parental love or any other kind of love. It does nothing to show that one has this feeling, or any feeling, for an *individual,* rather than for a placeholder of qualities one likes to see instantiated by somebody or other close about one.

Now if this concept of value attaching to a person's individual existence, over and above his merit—

"individual worth," let me call it—were applicable *only* in relations of personal love, it would be irrelevant for the analysis of justice. To serve our purpose its range of application must be coextensive with that of justice. It must hold in all human relations, including (or rather, especially in) the most impersonal of all, those to total strangers, fellow-citizens or fellow-men. I must show that the concept of individual worth does meet this condition.

Consider its role in our political community, taking the prescriptions of our laws for the treatment of persons as the index to our valuations. For merit (among other reasons) persons may be appointed or elected to public office or given employment by state agencies. For demerit they may lose licences, jobs, offices; they may be fined, jailed, or even put to death. But in a large variety of law-regulated actions directed to individuals, either by private persons or by organs of the state, the question of merit and demerit does not arise. The "equal protection of the laws" is due to persons not to meritorious ones, or to them in some degree above others. So too for the right to vote. One does not have it for being intelligent and public-spirited, or lose it for being lazy, ignorant, or viciously selfish. One is entitled to exercise it as long as, having registered, one manages to keep out of jail. This kind of arrangement would look like whimsy or worse, like sheer immoralism, if the only values recognized in our political community were those of merit. For obviously there is nothing compulsory about our political system; we could certainly devise, if we so wished, workable alternatives which would condition fundamental rights on certain kinds of merit. For example, we might have three categories of citizenship. The top one might be for those who meet high educational qualifications and give definite evidence of responsible civic interest, e.g., by active participation in political functions, tenure of public office, record of leadership in civic organizations and support to them, and the like. People in this A-category might have multiple votes in all elections and exclusive eligibility for the more important political offices; they might also be entitled to a higher level of protection by the police and to a variety of other privileges and immunities. At the other end there would be a C-category, disfranchised and legally underprivileged, for those who do not meet some lower educational test or have had a record of law-infraction or have been on the relief rolls for over three months. In between would be the B's with ordinary suffrage and intermediate legal status.

This "M-system" would be more complicated and cumbersome than ours. But something like it could certainly be made to work if we were enamoured of its peculiar scheme of values. Putting aside the question of efficiency, it gives us a picture of a community whose political valuations, conceived entirely in terms of merit, would never be grounded on individual worth, so that this notion would there be politically useless. For us, on the other hand, it is indispensable. We have to appeal to it when we try to make sense of the fact that our legal system accords to all citizens an identical status, carrying with it rights such as the *M*-system reserves to the *B*'s or the *A*'s, and some of which (like suffrage or freedom of speech) have been denied even to the nobility in some caste-systems of the past. This last comparison is worth pressing: it brings out the illuminating fact that in one fundamental respect our society is much more like a caste society (with a *unique* caste) than like the *M*-system. The latter has no place for a rank of dignity which descends on an individual by the purely existential circumstance (the "accident") of birth and remains his unalterably for life. To reproduce this feature of our system we would have to look not only to caste societies, but to extremely rigid ones, since most of them make some provision for elevation in rank for rare merit or degradation for extreme demerit. In our legal system no such thing can happen: even a criminal may not be sentenced to second-class citizenship. And the fact that first-class citizenship, having been made common, is no longer a mark of distinction does not trivialize the privileges it entails. It is the simple truth, not declamation, to speak of it, as I have done, as a "rank of dignity" in some ways comparable to that enjoyed by hereditary nobilities of the past. To see this one need only think of the position of groups in our society who have been cheated out of this status by the subversion of their constitutional rights. The difference in social position between Negroes and whites described in Dollard's classic is not smaller than that between, say, bourgeoisie and aristocracy in the *ancien régime* of France. It might well be greater.

Consider finally the role of the same value in the moral community. Here differences of merit are so conspicuous and pervasive that we might even be tempted to *define* the moral response to a person in terms of moral approval or disapproval of his acts or disposition, i.e., in terms of the response to his moral merit. But there are many kinds of moral response for which a person's merit is as irrelevant as is that of New Yorker *X* when he appeals to the police for help. If I see someone in danger of drowning I will not need to satisfy myself about his moral character before going to his aid. I owe assistance to any man in such circumstances,

not merely to good men. Nor is it only in rare and exceptional cases, as this example might suggest, that my obligations to others are independent of their moral merit. To be sincere, reliable, fair, kind, tolerant, unintrusive, modest in my relations with my fellows is not due them because they have made brilliant or even passing moral grades, but simply because they happen to be fellow-members of the moral community. It is not necessary to add, "members in good standing." The moral community is not a club from which members may be dropped for delinquency. Our morality does not provide for moral outcasts or half-castes. It does provide for punishment. But this takes place *within* the moral community and under its rules. It is for this reason that, for example, one has no right to be cruel to a cruel person. His offense against the moral law has not put him outside the law. He is still protected by its prohibition of cruelty—as much so as are kind persons. The pain inflicted on him as punishment for his offense does not close out the reserve of good will on the part of all others which is his birthright as a human being; it is a limited withdrawal from it. Capital punishment, if we believe in it, is no exception. The fact that a man has been condemned to death does not license his jailors to beat him or virtuous citizens to lynch him.

Here, then, as in the single-status political community, we acknowledge personal rights which are not proportioned to merit and could not be justified by merit. Their only justification could be the value which persons have simply because they are persons: their "intrinsic value as individual human beings," as Frankena calls it; the "infinite value" or the "sacredness" of their individuality, as others have called it. I shall speak of it as "individual human worth"; or "human worth," for short. What these expressions stand for is also expressed by saying that men are "ends in themselves." This latter concept is Kant's. Some of the kinks in his formulation of it can be straightened out by explaining it as follows: Everything other than a person can only have value *for* a person. This applies not only to physical objects, natural or manmade, which have only instrumental value, but also to those products of the human spirit which have also intrinsic, no less than extrinsic, value: an epic poem, a scientific theory, a legal system, a moral disposition. Even such things as these will have value only because they can be (a) experienced or felt to be valuable by human beings and (b) chosen by them from competing alternatives. Thus of everything without exception it will be true to say: if *x* is valuable and is not a person, then *x* will have value for some individual other than itself. Hence even a musical composition or a courageous deed, valued for their own sake, as "ends" not as means to anything else, will still fall into an entirely different category from that of the *valuers,* who do not need to be valued as "ends" by someone else in order to have value. In just this sense persons, and only persons, are "ends in themselves."

The two factors in terms of which I have described the value of the valuer—the capacities answering to (a) and (b) above—may not be exhaustive. But their conjunction offers a translation of "individual human worth" whose usefulness for working purposes will speak for itself. To (a) I might refer as "happiness," if I could use this term as Plato and Aristotle used *eudaimonia,* i.e., without the exclusively hedonistic connotations which have since been clamped on it. It will be less misleading to use "well-being" or "welfare" for what I intend here; that is, the enjoyment of value in all the forms in which it can be experienced by human beings. To (b) I shall refer as "freedom," bringing under this term not only conscious choices and deliberate decisions but also those subtler modulations and more spontaneous expressions of individual preference which could scarcely be called "choices" or "decisions" without some forcing of language. So understood, a person's well-being and freedom are aspects of his individual existence as unique and unrepeatable as is that existence itself: If A and B are listening to the same symphony with similar tastes and dispositions, we may speak of their enjoying the "same" good, or having the "same" enjoyment, and say that each has made the "same" choice for this way of spending his time and money. But here "same" will mean no more than "very similar;" the two enjoyments and choices, occurring in the consciousness of A and B respectively, are absolutely unique. So in translating "A's human worth" into "the worth of A's well-being and freedom" we are certainly meeting the condition that the former expression is to stand for whatever it is about A which, unlike his merit, has *individual* worth.

We are also meeting another condition: that the equality of human worth be justification, or ground, of equal human rights. I can best bring this out by reverting to the visitor from Mars who had asked a little earlier why we want equalization of security benefits. Let us conjure up circumstances in which his question would spring, not from idle curiosity, but from a strong conviction that this, or any other, right entailing such undiscriminating equality of benefits, would be entirely *unreasonable.* Suppose then that he hails from a strict meritarian community, which maintains the M

system in its political life and analogous patterns in other associations. And to make things simpler, let us also suppose that he is shown nothing in New York or elsewhere that is out of line with our formal professions of equality, so that he imagines us purer, more strenuous, equalitarians than we happen to be. The pattern of valuation he ascribes to us then seems to him fantastically topsy-turvy. He can hardly bring himself to believe that rational human beings should want equal personal rights, legal and moral, for their "riff-raff" and their elites. Yet neither can he explain away our conduct as pure automatism, a mere fugue of social habit. "These people, or some of them," he will be saying to himself, "must have some reasons for this incredible code. What could these be?" If we volunteered an answer couched in terms of human worth, he might find it hard to understand us. Such an answer, unglossed, would convey to him no more than that we recognize something which is highly and equally valuable in all persons, but has nothing to do with their merit, and constitutes the ground of their equal rights. But this might start him hunting—snark-hunting—for some special quality named by "human worth" as honesty is named by "honesty" and kindness by "kindness," wondering all the while how it could have happened that he and all his tribe have had no inkling of it, if all of them have always had it.

But now suppose that we avail ourselves of the aforesaid translation. We could then tell him: "To understand our code you should take into account how very different from yours is our own estimate of the relative worth of the welfare and freedom of different individuals. We agree with you that not all persons are capable of experiencing the same values. But there is a wide variety of cases in which persons are capable of this. Thus, to take a perfectly clear case, no matter how A and B might differ in taste and style of life, they would both crave relief from acute physical pain. In that case we would put the same value on giving this to either of them, regardless of the fact that A might be a talented, brilliantly successful person, B 'a mere nobody.' On this we would disagree sharply. You would weigh the welfare of members of the elite more highly than that of 'riff-raff,' as you call them. We would not. If A were a statesman, and giving him relief from pain enabled him to conclude an agreement that would benefit millions, while B, an unskilled laborer, was himself the sole beneficiary of the like relief, we would, of course, agree that the *instrumental* value of the two experiences would be vastly different—but not their *intrinsic* value. In all cases where human beings are capable of enjoying the same goods, we feel that the intrinsic value of their enjoyment is the same. In just this sense we hold that (1) *one man's well-being is as valuable as any other's*. And there is a parallel difference in our feeling for freedom. You value it only when exercised by good persons for good ends. We put no such strings on its value. We feel that choosing for oneself what one will do, believe, approve, say, see, read, worship, has its own intrinsic value, the same for all persons, and quite independently of the value of the things they happen to choose. Naturally, we hope that all of them will make the best possible use of their freedom of choice. But we value their exercise of that freedom, regardless of the outcome; and we value it equally for all. For us (2) *one man's freedom is as valuable as any other's*."

This sort of explanation, I submit, would put him in a position to resolve his dilemma. For just suppose that, taking this homily at face value, he came to think of us as believing (1) and (2). No matter how unreasonable he might think us he would feel it entirely reasonable that, since we do believe in equal *value* of human well-being and freedom, we should also believe in the *prima facie* equality of men's *right* to well-being and to freedom. He would see the former as a good reason for the latter; or, more formally, he could think of (1) and (2) respectively as the crucial premises in justification arguments whose respective conclusions would be: (3) One man's (*prima facie*) right to well-being is equal to that of any other, and (4) One man's (*prima facie*) right to freedom is equal to that of any other. Then, given (4), he could see how this would serve as the basis for a great variety of rights to specific kinds of freedom: freedom of movement, of association, of suffrage, of speech, of thought, of worship, of choice of employment, and the like. For each of these can be regarded as simply a specification of the general right to freedom, and would thus be covered by the justification of the latter. Moreover, given (3), he could see in it the basis for various welfare-rights, such as the right to education, medical care, work under decent conditions, relief in periods of unemployment, leisure, housing, etc. Thus to give him (1) and (2) as justification for (3) and (4) would be to give him a basis for every one of the rights which are mentioned in the most complete of currently authoritative declarations of human rights, that passed by the Assembly of the United Nations in 1948. Hence to tell him that we believe in the equal worth of individual freedom and happiness would be to answer, in terms he can understand, his question, "What is your reason for your equalitarian code?"

Nowhere in this defense of the translation of "equal human worth" into "equal worth of human well-being and freedom" have I claimed that the former can be *reduced* to the latter. I offered individual well-being and freedom simply as two things which do satisfy the conditions defined by individual human worth. Are there others? For the purposes of this essay this may be left an open question. For if there are, they would provide, at most, additional grounds for human rights. The ones I have specified are grounds enough. They are all I need for the analysis of equalitarian justice as, I trust, will appear directly.

III

I offer the following definition: An action is *just* if, and only if, it is prescribed exclusively by regard for the rights of all whom it affects substantially. This definition could be discussed at length. I shall make, and with the utmost brevity, just two general points by way of elucidation:

(a) The standard cases are clearly covered, e.g., that of the judge adjudicating a dispute. To perform justly this strictly judicial function he must (i) seek to determine with scrupulous care what, in these circumstances, are the rights of the litigants and of others, if any, who are substantially affected, and then (ii) render a verdict determined by regard for those rights and by nothing else. He may be unjust by failing at (i) through ignorance, carelessness, impatience, laziness, addiction to stereotypes of race or class, and the like; at (ii) by any sort of partiality, even if this is due to nothing so low as venality or prejudice, but perhaps even to humane and generous sentiments. Thus, if in the case before him an honest and upright man has trespassed on the rights of a well-known bully (perhaps only to protect one of the latter's victims), the judge will have no choice but to find for the bully: he must be "blind" to anything but the relevant rights when making up his verdict. This is the commonsense view of the matter, and it accords perfectly with what follows from the definition.

(b) The definition does not flout common usage by making "just" *interchangeable* with "right," and "unjust" with "wrong." Whenever the question of regard, or disregard, for substantially affected rights does not arise, the question of justice, or injustice, does not arise. We see a man wasting his property and talents in dissolute living. It would not occur to us to think of his conduct as unjust, unless we see it as having a substantial effect on somebody's rights, say, those of dependents: it is unfair or unjust *to* them. Again, whenever one is in no position to govern one's action by regard for rights, the question of justice, or injustice, does not arise. Two strangers are in immediate danger of drowning off the dock on which I stand. I am the only one present, and the best I can do is to save one while the other drowns. Each has a right to my help, but I cannot give it to both. Hence regard for rights does not prescribe what I am to do, and neither "just" nor "unjust" will apply: I am not unjust to the one who drowns, nor just to the one I save.

A major feature of my definition of "just" is that it makes the answer to "Is x just?" (where x is any action, decision, etc.) strictly dependent on the answer to another question: "What are the rights of those who are substantially affected by x?" The definition cannot, and does not pretend that it can, give the slightest help in answering the latter question, with but one exception: it does tell us that the substantially affected rights, whatever they may be, should all be impartially respected. Thus it does disclose one right, though a purely *formal* one: the right to have one's *other* rights respected as impartially as those of any other interested party. But what are these other rights? Are they equal or unequal? On this the definition is silent. It is thus completely neutral in the controversy between meritarians and equalitarians, and should prove equally acceptable to either party. Its neutralism should not be held against it. The words "just" and "unjust" are not the private property of the equalitarians; they may be used as conscientiously by those who reject, as by those who share, their special view of justice. We are not compelled to provide for this in our definitions; but there are obvious advantages in doing so. For we thereby offer our opponents common ground on which they too may stand while making their case. We allow Aristotle, for instance, to claim, without misusing language, that slavery and the disfranchisement of manual workers are just institutions. It allows us to rebut his claim, not by impugning its linguistic propriety, but by explaining that we affirm what his claim implicitly denies: that all human beings have the right to personal and political freedom.

It should now be plain to the reader why I have been so heavily preoccupied with the question of human rights throughout the first half of this essay, and content to write most of Section II without even mentioning the word "justice." I have done so precisely because my purpose in this essay is not to discuss justice in general, but equalitarian justice. As should now be obvious, had I tried to reason from the concept of justice to that of equalitarian justice I would have been reasoning in a circle. I did allude at the start to important historical and linguistic ties of justice with equality. But these, while perfectly relevant, are obviously not conclusive. They would be dismissed by a determined and clear-headed opponent, like Plato, as mere evidences of a widespread *mis*conception of justice. I am not suggesting that we should yield him this point or that, conversely, there is any good reason to think that he would come around to our view if we presented him with the argument of Section II (or a stronger one to the same effect). My contention is rather that we would be misrepresenting our view of justice if we were to give him the idea that it is susceptible of proof by that kind of historical and linguistic evidence. To explain our position to him so that, quite apart from his coming to agree with it, he would at least have the chance to *understand* it, one thing would matter above all: to show that we believe in human rights, and why.

That is why the weight of the argument in the preceding Section II fell so heavily on the notion of human worth, understood to mean nothing less than the equal worth of the happiness and freedom of all persons. Given this, we have equal welfare-rights and freedom-rights; and this puts us in a position to cover the full range of human rights which the natural rights tradition left so perplexingly indeterminate. I did not stop to argue for this contention when I made it in Section II, and will not do so now, for I have more important business ahead of me. I have not forgotten the task I set myself at the close of Section I, and wish to proceed to it as soon as possible. But before proceeding to this in Section IV, there is a major item of still unfinished business that must be attended to. It concerns a feature of equalitarian justice that must be made fully explicit, if only because it will play an important role in the argument that is to follow in Section IV.

Consider the following very simple rule of just distribution: *If A and B have sole and equal right to* x, *they have a joint right to the whole of* x. This rule (R_1) would be normally taken as axiomatic. Thus if *A* and *B* had sole and equal right to an estate, no executor bent on making a just settlement of their claims would think of giving away a part of the estate to some other person, *C*. But why not? Can it be shown that the consequent of R_1 does follow from its antecedent? It can. *Only* A *and* B *have any right to* x entails *anyone other than* A *or* B *has no right to* x and hence *C has no right to* x. Hence if some part of *x* were distributed to *C, it* would be going to someone who has no right to it. Such a distribution would not conform to our definition of "just:" it would not be the one prescribed by impartial regard for the relevant rights. Now what if the executor withheld some part of x from A and B, without giving it to a third party? But how could that happen? Did he perhaps abandon it in a deserted place? He has no right to do that with any property unless it happens to be *his own*. So if he did such a foolish thing with a part of the estate, he has acted as though *he* is the third party to whom this has been distributed, and most unjustly, since he has no right to it. But what if he actually destroyed a part, perhaps throwing it overboard in a strong-box stuffed with valuables to sink to the bottom of the ocean? This too he would have no right to do, unless this part of the property were already *his*. So this action would be as unjust as before and for the same reason. And there is no other possibility, unless a part of the estate were lost, or destroyed through some natural calamity, in which case the question of its being *withheld* by the executor from A and B would not arise. If he does withhold it, he would have to give it to some third party or else act as though he had already given it to himself, hence in either case to someone who has no right to x, hence unjustly. To act justly he must give the whole of it to those who have sole right to it.

Now let us think of an allied case. A man leaves a will containing many marks of his affection for his two sons and sole heirs and of his wish to benefit them. The terms of his will provide, *inter alia,* that a large industrial property is to be used, at the direction of trustees, to produce income for the sole and equal benefit of D and E, the income to be divided annually between them. Here the annual distribution of the income will fall directly under R_1. But another decision, in which D and E have as big a stake, will not: how the property is to be used to yield the desired income. Let L and M be the only known feasible dispositions of the property for this purpose between which the trustees must decide at a given time: each, let us say, would involve a five-year commitment, but L would assure the estate twice the income, security, etc. being the same. L is obviously a windfall for the estate, and the trustees are not likely to waste a second thought on M as a possibly just decision in the circumstances. Why not? Why is it that in fairness to D and E they *should* choose L? Not in virtue of R_1, since that does not apply here: L is not a whole of which M is a part. What the trustees must be invoking (or would be, if they were thinking out the basis of their decision) is an analogue to R_1, covering cases

such as this, where the right is not to an already existing object but to a future benefit which may be secured at any one of several possible levels: *if* D *and* E *have sole and equal right to benefit from* x, *they have a joint right to the benefit at the highest level at which it may be secured.* If we were asked to justify this rule (R_2), how would we go about it? If the trustees' reason for preferring M to L were to benefit a third party, C, the reasoning would be the same as before: since only D and E have the right to benefit from x, C has no such right; hence M cannot be the disposition prescribed by regard for the relevant rights. But what if the trustees were to prefer M, without aiming to benefit a third party? This possibility would be analogous to the case above in which R_1 was violated by the wilful loss or destruction of part of x. For a preference for M would be fully as injurious to D and E, and as unjust to them, as if the trustees had voted for L with the diabolical rider that half the annual income during the next five years was to be withheld from D and E and destroyed. The loss to D and E would be exactly the same, and the injustice would be the same: the trustees might have the right to forgo a benefit to *themselves* equivalent to the difference between L and M, but only if *they* had the right to this benefit in the first place. In choosing M over L they would be acting as though they did have this right, hence in clear violation of D's and E's *sole* right.

Now the validity of R_2 is obviously unaffected by the number of those who have sole and equal right to a benefit. It would hold for any number; hence for the whole of humanity, or any lesser part of it. Consider then the total benefit derivable by humanity from men's use of what we may call "the means of well-being," i.e., of their own bodies and minds and of the resources of the natural universe. Since men have an equal right to well-being (apart from special property-rights, and the like, with which we are not now concerned), they have an equal right to the means of well-being. And the right of humanity to these means is exclusive. We are, therefore, entitled to assert that *men have sole and equal right to benefit from the means of well-being.* From this we may conclude, in conformity with R_2 that *men are jointly entitled to this benefit at the highest level at which it may be secured.*

This conclusion affects importantly the concept of equalitarian justice. It implies that the fundamental and distinctive idea in its notion of just distribution is (i) not equal distribution of benefits, but (ii) their equal distribution at the highest obtainable level (i) has already been argued for in Frankena's essay when he considered, and rejected, Hourani's attractive formula, "Justice is equality, evident or disguised," as an over-simplification. But on Frankena's view neither can (ii) constitute the needed corrective. It is an obligation of beneficence, not of justice, he argues, "to promote the greatest possible good." He writes: "even if we allow . . . that society has an obligation to be beneficent, then we must insist that such beneficence, at least if it exceeds a certain minimum, is no part of social justice as such." Now there is no difference of opinion between us as to the importance of distinguishing sharply the concept of beneficence (or of benevolence) from that of equalitarian justice. But I submit that this can be done perfectly by adhering to the concept of equalitarian justice I have given here, and is in no way imperilled by my thesis here at (ii). To go back to the definition of "just" at the start: this leaves plenty of scope for acts which might be beneficent but *un*just, as, e.g., when A defrauds B to help C; or beneficent and *non*-just (neither just nor unjust: "just" does not apply), as when A helps one needy person, disregarding the claim of millions of others for the simple reason that he is in no position to help more than one out of all these millions. Conversely, neither would it follow from my theory of equalitarian justice that every just act, decision, practice, etc., will be beneficent. A large number will be non-beneficent (neither beneficent nor maleficent; "beneficent" will not apply): the repayment of debts, the rendering of ordinary judicial verdicts, or the enforcement of punishments. So *equalitarian justice* and *beneficence* will have different extensions, and their meanings will be as different as is that of *justice* on the present definition from that of *beneficence* on the usual view. Hence the concepts are entirely distinct, both intensionally and extensionally. But distinct concepts may, of course, overlap. And this is precisely what I maintain in the present case: (ii) above certainly falls under beneficence; but that, of itself, is no reason whatever why it *may* not *also* fall under equalitarian justice. That it does is what the foregoing argument for the validity of R_2 and its applicability to human rights, was designed to show.

One way of stating the thesis of that argument would be that equalitarian justice has a direct stake not only in equalizing the distribution of those goods whose enjoyment constitutes well-being, but also in promoting their creation. That it would have an indirect stake in the latter even if it were concerned *only* with equalizing their distribution could be argued independently by an obvious generalization of the point I made at the start of Section II, where I argued that a more affluent society could "buy more equality." The reasoning for and from R_2 provides a stronger and more general argument that *given any two levels of the production of good known to be possible in given circumstances, then,* other things being equal, *the higher should be preferred on grounds of justice.* "Good here, as throughout this essay, is a general expression for a class of which economic goods would be a sub-class. We may thus use an economic test-case of the underlined proposition: Suppose that the supreme policy-maker of the N's (whose economy resembles closely that of the U.S.A.) had to choose between two policies, P(L) and P(M), knowing that (a) the effect of P(M) would be to maintain throughout the next five years the current rate of annual increase of the gross national product (which is, say, 2.5 per cent), while that of P(L) would *double* that rate; (b) the pattern of distribution of the national income would remain the same; (c) the greater wealth produced under P(L) would not be offset by aggravation of the risk of war, cultural deterioration, corruption of morals, or of any other significant evil. (c) is, of course, a strong restriction; but, like (b), it is built into the hypothesis to ensure that the *only* appreciable difference between the two policies would be in the lesser, or fuller, utilization and expansion of the economic resources of the nation. This, and the artificiality of the whole model, by no means trivializes the contention that in such circumstances equalitarian justice would leave the policy-maker no choice but P(L). To say that beneficence (or benevolence) would leave him no other choice *would* be trivial: no one would care to dispute this. But the same thing said for equalitarian justice can be, and is being, disputed. This asserts that the N's have *rights* in this matter which the policy-maker would violate if he were to choose P(M)—as much so as the trustees in the example would violate the rights of D and E if they chose M. That the rights of the N's, unlike those of D and E, are moral, not legal, is immaterial: *only* the moral justice of the decision is here in view. The moral rights in question are those of the N's to well-being, hence to the means of well-being: to anything which would enrich their life, save it from pain, disease, drudgery, emptiness, ugliness. Given (a) in the hypothesis, an enormously larger quantity of such means would be made available to the N's under P(L) in the course of the five-year period; and given (b) their distribution would be no more unequal than that of the smaller volume of goods produced under P(M). Hence the N's have jointly a right to P(L). They have this for just the reasons which justify the inference from the antecedent of R_2 to its consequent. The crux of the inference is that since the N's, and only they, have a right to the benefits obtainable under either alternative, they have a right to that alternative which produces the greater benefit. Only (and at most) if the policy-maker had *himself* the right to the aggregate benefit represented by the difference between P(L) and P(M) would he have the right to frustrate the realization of that benefit. But he does not have that right. So if he were to choose P(M) he would violate the right of those who do. That is why that decision would be unjust.

Two more points:

(A) That not equality as such, but equality at the highest possible level, is the requirement of equalitarian justice may be argued as strongly in the case of the right to freedom. Thus if a legislature had before it two bills, B(L) and B(M), such that B(L) would provide for greater personal freedom than would B(M), then, other things remaining equal, they would be voting unjustly if they voted for the second: they would be violating the human right to freedom of those affected by the legislation. A vote for B(M) would be tantamount to a vote for the needless *restriction* of freedom. And since *freedom* is a personal (or individual) right, to equalize its restriction would be to aggravate, not to alleviate, its injustice. Would any of us feel that no injustice was suffered by Soviet citizens by the suppression of *Doctor Zhivago* if we were reliably informed that no one, not even Khrushchev, was exempted, and that the censors themselves had been foreign mercenaries?

(B) The conjunction of equalitarian justice and benevolence could have been argued at a still deeper level if we had gone down to the ultimate *reasons* for the equal right to well-being and freedom, i.e., to (1) and (2) at the close of Section II above. What could be a stronger expression of benevolence towards one's fellow-men, than to say that the well-being and freedom of every one of them is worth as much as one's own and that of those few persons one happens to love? At this level equalitarian justice is as deeply committed to two notions which it does not display in its title, benevolence and freedom, as to the notion of equality, which it does. It now remains to show how, given this threefold commitment, it can *also* recognize claims of *un*equal distribution.

IV

Why is it just to distribute good according to merit? I shall answer this for one distributable good which I shall call "praise," using this word to cover all direct expressions of admiration, appreciation, or approval of merit which are subject to voluntary control. This is an extended use of the word, but it has definite limits. Thus if A and B are competing for an office, the mere fact of C's appointing A is not to count as praise from C to A, no matter how emphatic be the approval of A's merit it is understood to imply. To qualify as praise something more direct or express would be needed, though not necessarily in verbal form. Thus C would not have to congratulate A on the appointment, or tell him he has the good qualities the job calls for; it would be enough to convey as much to him by one's demeanor or facial expression.

A man should not be praised for merit he does not have. Indiscriminate praise is a fake; and to fake praise in special cases is to cheapen it, and hence to violate the equal right of all persons to be praised in a sound currency, if they are to be praised at all. It does not follow from this, nor is it true, that merit has to be the necessary *and* sufficient condition of giving praise. At times we would not praise a person unless we felt he needed a special reassurance or encouragement. But far more frequently merit *is* sufficient. Take our ordinary response to a delightful conversationalist, for example. In the various subtle, but unmistakable, ways in which we manifest our approval we measure out to him sizeable quantities of what some economists, without intending to be humorous, call "psychic income." We know that to give this is to please him. But the question of his need of it is not a factor in our giving it, any more than the landlord's need is a factor in the tenant's payment of the rent. And this is what happens in the majority of cases. This is "the generally expected thing" when praise is given in our society, and this is what I shall call the practice of *praising for merit ("mp")* or *giving praise according to merit.* If we did not have *mp,* it would be understood that no person, or only some privileged persons (e.g., the monarch, the nobility, Aryans, members of the Communist Party, Platonic philosophers), have the right to praise any person they choose on the sole ground of his merit.

Mp is a "practice" in the somewhat technical sense this term has acquired in recent moral philosophy. For my present purpose two important points are involved here: (a) *mp* may be formulated in terms of a set of rules, conformity to which depends on voluntary compliance with (or, obedience to) the rules. Thus one of the rules would be, "Those in a position to praise both A and B should give more praise to A if his merit is the greater." One's compliance with this rule is not forced by the *fact* that A has the greater merit, nor by one's *belief* that he has. C might be well aware of the fact, yet lavish praise on *B,* cold-shouldering *A* (perhaps because he is fond of *B* and hates *A*). That the rule can be disobeyed in this and other ways proves that the usual compliance with it is voluntary. (b) In the absence of *mp,* actions which are now understood as praising for merit would be normally understood very differently even if they had, in all other respects, the same characteristics. Thus suppose that *mp* did not exist, while praising for need did. In such a society the conduct by *C* just described would be construed very differently. No one would take it as an unfavorable reflection on *A*'s merit, and *A* could not feel slighted by it; from *C*'s excessive praise for *B, A* would merely gather that *C* has an exaggerated idea of *B*'s need of encouragement. *Not* to be praised in that society would be itself a kind of tribute.

If this is what *mp* means, then the distribution of praise under this practice is bound to reflect to some degree inequalities in the distribution of merit. To live with *mp* is to live in a world in which some people will get this kind of "psychic income" in abundance, while others must subsist on miserable pittances of it. For this reason equalitarian justice would have no choice but to condemn *mp* as an inherently unjust practice, *if* equality in the distribution of good were its only concern. But from the account of it in Section III we know that it is also concerned that happiness and freedom be secured at the highest possible levels. Let us see what difference this makes.

But first let us take account of a matter of fact: that the effect of praising an achievement is generally to enhance the relevant creative effort. To say this is not to deny that sometimes praise has no effect and sometimes a bad effect. But if it were *generally* ineffective the argument I am about to make for it would fail. And *every* argument for it would fail if its normal effect were sufficiently bad—if, say, it were like that of alcohol on alcoholics. If it demoralized all, or most, people, praise would be as vile as flattery, or viler; only a few poisonous individuals would indulge in it. The actual facts are reassuringly different, in spite of occasional swelled heads. What happens for the most part is that in praising a meritorious performance we give its merit our backing. We thereby help the performer, giving him the incentive to attain again the same merit, or a higher one. We even help ourselves: by going on record in favor of the meritorious performance we are more likely to emulate it ourselves in the future. This being the case, the proponent of equalitarian justice cannot judge *mp* fairly unless he connects it with his interest in getting all human beings to be as creative as possible, i.e., to bring into existence, to the best of their

ability, those values which will enrich their own life and that of others. This gives him at once a strong initial interest in *mp* as a practice generating incentives to creative effort. And since *mp* can exist *alongside* of other incentive-generating practices (and always has in every known society), its presence in a given society represents a net addition (and a substantial one) to the aggregate stimuli to creative effort. A society with *mp,* therefore, would have a higher level of production of good than it would have without *mp.* But as has been argued in Section III,

> given any two levels of production of good known to be possible in given circumstances, then, other things being equal, the higher should be preferred on grounds of justice.

This would provide a utilitarian argument for the justice of *mp* (justifying it as a means to an end which justice approves), *if* the "other things being equal" clause can be made good.

To make up our minds on this "if," let us first be clear about the fact that *mp* as such does not require, or even favor, inequality in the distribution of any of the *other* goods (goods other than praise) whose creation it tends to enhance. How equally or unequally these are going to be distributed will depend on decisions which are entirely distinct from the decision to maintain *mp.* Thus it would be sheer confusion to think that there would be any incompatibility between deciding to distribute praise according to merit and economic goods according to need. The most starry-eyed equalitarian, intent on running his whole economy on the latter maxim, could afford to be as much of an enthusiast for *mp* as anyone else; indeed he would have good reason to be much more of one: having denied himself the usual economic incentives, he would have to work this one for all it was worth. As this example may suggest, *mp* fits a generally equalitarian society not only as well as a meritarian one, but better. But I do not wish to make anything of this last point. All that is needed for the present argument is that the practice of *mp* as such cannot be held *generally* responsible for inequalities in the distribution of goods in the society, but only for those inherent in its own operation, i.e., inequalities in the distribution of praise itself. The question then is whether *these* inequalities will be so repugnant to justice as to constitute offsetting factors against the tonic effect of *mp* on human productivity which our concept of justice approves. When we narrow down the question in this way I think it can be shown that they will not be repugnant to justice at all, and will not only leave "other things equal," but better than equal.

To simplify the problem to the utmost let us think of a purely economic society of two individuals, *A* and *B, A* being the more efficient producer. An angel is set over them, whose good will for each of them is boundless. If he could measure out to them well-being directly from some celestial storehouse, he would be giving vast and equal measures to each. Such direct munificence is unfortunately denied him. He has been told that whatever well-being is to come to *A* and *B* must reach them entirely through their own efforts; all the angel can do for them is to propose to them new practices. He now puts his mind on whether or not he should offer them *mp,* which they have hitherto done without. To isolate the probable effect of *mp* itself on their lives, he pegs the solution on two assumptions: (a) that they will operate it fairly (for if they did not, the results would not be an indication of the use of *mp,* but of its misuse); (b) the expected increment in their joint product is to be divided in the same ratio as at present (for there is nothing about *mp* to require any special ratio, hence any ratio different from the present). He then sees that, on these conditions, *A* and *B* have both much to gain from the new arrangement: the economic income of each will increase; and each will get some of the newly created "psychic income," though *A,* the more meritorious producer, will get more of this than *B.* If these were the only results of the change, the angel would have no reason to hesitate between leaving them in their present state or giving them *mp.* He would give it to them, and not because of having any preference, even the slightest, for the well-being of *A* over that of *B,* but precisely because he has the same desire to increase the happiness of both as much as possible in the circumstances of his choice, i.e., circumstances in which he must choose either for the *status quo* or for their present way of life as modified by *mp.*

But, of course, there may be another result from the change: the mere fact that *A* will be made happier than *B* (*A* can count on getting the larger share of the praise) may make *B* unhappy, and so much so that his unhappiness from just this source might be great enough to outbalance his gains and even (if we allow the angel some way of determining such things) *A*'s gains as well. This possibility could be quite enough to disrupt totally the angel's calculations. Whether or not *mp* will prove a blessing or a curse will now turn on how *B* takes it; and *B* knowing this could use it to blackmail the angel against even making the offer: *B* need only announce that he would make himself miserable enough to offset the expected gains. Fortunately the situation has a saving feature: *A* and *B* are moral beings. This

has not been stated; but is certainly implied in assumption (a), for only moral beings could operate this practice fairly. Our angel then can ask *B* to look at *mp* as a moral being should, hence with equal regard for *A*'s well-being as for his own. If he did so, *B* would not be made unhappy merely because *A* became happier than himself, that is to say, out of envy. To say this to *B* is not, alas, to assure him that he will react to the effects of the practice as a moral being should, thereby saving himself the misery of jealousy. No one can ensure this for *B* except (at most) *B* himself and by his own effort. All the angel can tell *B* is that he should make this effort; but that, in any case, *B* cannot bring up any unfavorable results due to *envy* as a reason against the *justice* of the proposed institution. To allow such reasons to count would ruin the prospects of giving a moral justification of any practice: by the same token unhappiness due to arrogance (i.e., to the demand for special privilege) would also count, and that would be the end of justice.

The upshot of the argument is simply this: *because* (not in spite) of his equal concern for the happiness of all persons, a proponent of equalitarian justice would have good reason to approve *mp,* given its stimulating effect on the creation of those goods whose enjoyment constitutes happiness, *unless* the effect were offset by others repugnant to his sense of justice. But there are no such effects. The fact that envious people are made unhappy by an institution is no evidence of its injustice.

This is not the only argument for *mp,* or even the strongest. There are two others which deserve at least as full a treatment, but fortunately do not require it. I shall make them in the most summary fashion to compensate for the unavoidable length of the one I have just finished. Both of them argue from the right to freedom.

(1) Praising for merit is something people like to do, and do spontaneously when they are left free to talk and laugh and applaud without restraints from political or clerical or domestic martinets. It is thus a direct expression of human freedom, and such a pervasive one that it spreads over every area of life, private or public. To try to suppress this practice would involve enormous inroads on personal liberty.

(2) Over and above its coincidence, for the reason just given, with one of the major *ends* of freedom (that of expressing without impediment one's actual feelings about one's fellows' character and conduct), it is also an indispensable *means* for another such end: that of diffusing widely among the population free choices

between competing values. It is like "consumer's vote" in a free economy: it gives the consumers of the values produced in a society a means of influencing the producers, and thus a share in determining which values are produced and in what proportions. Its obvious disadvantage is its lack of any facilities for aggregating and recording the results of individual decisions, either directly, as through elections, or indirectly, as through the market. But it has the advantage of being as equally distributed as the suffrage, while extending, and more flexibly, to even larger and more varied sets of choices than those of the market.

With this case for the justice of the practice of praising for merit thus laid out before us, let us take stock of what has been accomplished and how. I have taken the maxim, "to each according to his merit," as in need of justification, and have undertaken to derive it from a set of propositions which includes only equalitarian value-premises (those from which the equal right of human beings to well-being and freedom is derived) plus one or more factual premises. Since I limited the demonstration to the special proposition, "to each *praise* according to his merit," I needed such factual premises as that the general effect of so distributing praise enhances the production of value and offers a useful device for its control by the free responses of private individuals. From each of these we get an instrumental, or utilitarian, justification: we justify this way of distributing praise because it is a means to the advancement of those ends which are stated in our value-premises, such as the well-being and the freedom to which all persons have a severally equal and jointly exclusive right. We also get a collateral non-instrumental justification in terms of freedom: praising for merit is itself one of the forms in which persons choose to express their freedom. Since merit is unequal, to justify *mp* is to justify unequal rights in respect of praise. The whole argument then falls into the following form: Because persons have *equal* rights to well-being and to freedom, then, in the special circumstances of distributing praise for merit (those noticed in the factual premises of the argument) their right to this particular good is *un*equal. If we then think of the latter as an exception, or as a whole class of exceptions, to men's equal right to enjoyable good, we are in a position to justify the exception in the way in which I said earlier (at the close of Section I) exceptions to natural rights should be justified. The moral (as distinct from the factual) reasons given for this exception to the equal right to good have been only such reasons as were built into our concept of equalitarian justice and would be given

as the reasons for all our natural rights: men's joint and equal right to well-being and freedom at the highest obtainable level.

But apart from the theoretical import of this argument, it has useful practical implications. In telling us why we *may* justly distribute praise unequally according to merit, it tells us also what we may *not* do. In general it warns us against confusing merit with human worth, and against allowing merit to swamp human worth. It reminds us that terms like "superior" and "inferior," properly applicable to a person's merit, are inapplicable to the person: there can be strictly and literally superior or inferior poets, teachers, bankers, garage-mechanics, actresses, statesmen; but there can be strictly and literally no superior or inferior persons, individuals, men. From this it follows that when we praise a man we must not praise him *as* a man. His humanity is not a fit subject for praise. To think otherwise is to incur a "category mistake," and one fraught with grave moral consequences. For given men's sensitiveness to honor and dishonor, when merit is made the measure of their human dignity, their own sense of dignity tends to become distorted. If they are talented and successful, praise misdirected from their achievements to their person will foster the illusion that they are superior persons, belong to a higher moral caste, and may claim on moral grounds a privileged status for their own well-being and freedom. Conversely, if low achievement scores are not kept wholly distinct from personal worth, which does not register on any score, men may be made to feel that they are the human inferiors of others, that their own happiness or freedom has inferior worth. This would be a grave injustice. Any practice which tends to so weaken and confuse the personal self esteem of a group of persons—slavery, serfdom or, in our own time, racial segregation—may be morally condemned on this one ground, even if there were no other for indicting it. Some such ground is alluded to in the Court opinion in the decision which finally struck down segregation in the public schools. That verdict could be reached more directly and extended to every form of racial segregation by applying the ideas that have been sketched in this essay. If one thinks of human worth as the moral foundation of all rights, one will see that the equal honor of persons is presupposed by the unequal honor that may be given to unequal merit and, hence, that no practice which habitually humiliates persons can be defended by differences of merit, real or imagined.

Along similar lines I believe it may be argued that other differentials—in particular those of economic reward, economic power, and political power—can be justified on the terms of equalitarian justice. Given certain propositions which, if true, are true on empirical grounds, recording observable uniformities of human nature and conduct with which every moral philosophy must reckon, good *moral* reasons may be offered for inequalities of various kinds, which would be "just-making" reasons, the very same as those which would be offered for equalizing benefits of other kinds. And the very procedure which led to these results would contain built-in protections of human equality, limiting the differentials in income and in power by the very machinery which certifies their justice within the permissible range. To accomplish this would be to answer Plato's question, the one that started us off on this whole inquiry early in Section I. It would be to show him over what special form the three maxims of unequal distribution, "to each according to his merit, his work, and the agreements he has made," may be joined without theoretical inconsistency or moral compromise to the two maxims of equal distribution, "to each according to his need, and to his [human] worth."

READING 37

Equality As a Moral Ideal

Harry Frankfurt

Harry Frankfurt (1929–) is Professor of Philosophy at Princeton University and the author of several works in ethics, action theory, and social philosophy.

Some philosophers, like Ronald Dworkin and Thomas Nagel, seem to think that economic equality is an inherent value. It's just morally right that all people have the same amount of wealth. Frankfurt argues that there is nothing inherently good or morally important about equality, though sufficiency is morally important. People should have sufficient wealth to live a decent life. Moreover, preoccupation with economic equality can divert us from our morally defined goals, lead to envy, and contribute to moral disorientation and shallowness.

This reading is taken from *Ethics 98:* (1987), by permission of the University of Chicago Press; copyright © 1987 by the University of Chicago.

First Man: "How are your children?"
Second Man: "Compared to what?"

I

Economic egalitarianism is, as I shall construe it, the doctrine that it is desirable for everyone to have the same amounts of income and of wealth (for short, "money"). Hardly anyone would deny that there are situations in which it makes sense to tolerate deviations from this standard. It goes without saying, after all, that preventing or correcting such deviations may involve costs which—whether measured in economic terms or in terms of non-economic considerations—are by any reasonable measure unacceptable. Nonetheless, many people believe that economic equality has considerable moral value in itself. For this reason they often urge that efforts to approach the egalitarian ideal should be accorded—with all due consideration for the possible effects of such efforts in obstructing or in conducing to the achievement of other goods—a significant priority.

In my opinion, this is a mistake. Economic equality is not as such of particular moral importance. With respect to the distribution of economic assets, what is important from the point of view of morality *is* not that everyone should have *the same* but that each should have *enough*. If everyone had enough it would be of no moral consequence whether some had more than others. I shall refer to this alternative to egalitarianism—namely, that what is morally important with respect to money is for everyone to have enough—as "the doctrine of sufficiency."

The fact that economic equality is not in its own right a morally compelling social ideal is in no way, of course, a reason for regarding it as undesirable. My claim that equality in itself lacks moral importance does not entail that equality is to be avoided. Indeed, there may well be good reasons for governments or for individuals to deal with problems of economic distribution in accordance with an egalitarian standard, and to be concerned more with attempting to increase the extent to which people are economically equal than with efforts to regulate directly the extent to which the amounts of money people have are enough. Even if equality is not as such morally important, a commitment to an egalitarian social policy may be indispensable to promoting the enjoyment of significant goods besides equality, or to avoiding their impairment.

Moreover, it might turn out that the most feasible approach to the achievement of sufficiency would be by the pursuit of equality.

But despite the fact that an egalitarian distribution would not necessarily be objectionable, the error of believing that there are powerful moral reasons for caring about equality is far from innocuous. In fact, this belief tends to do significant harm. It is often argued as an objection to egalitarianism that there is a dangerous conflict between equality and liberty: if people are left to themselves inequalities of income and wealth inevitably arise, and therefore an egalitarian distribution of money can be achieved and maintained only at the cost of repression. Whatever may be the merit of this argument concerning the relationship between equality and liberty, economic egalitarianism engenders another conflict which is of even more fundamental moral significance.

To the extent that people are preoccupied with equality for its own sake, their readiness to be satisfied with any particular level of income or wealth is guided not by their own interests and needs but just by the magnitude of the economic benefits that are at the disposal of others. In this way egalitarianism distracts people from measuring the requirements to which their individual natures and their personal circumstances give rise. It encourages them instead to insist upon a level of economic support that is determined by a calculation in which the particular features of their own lives are irrelevant. How sizeable the economic assets of others are has nothing much to do, after all, with what kind of person someone is. A concern for economic equality, construed as desirable in itself, tends to divert a person's attention away from endeavoring to discover—within his experience of himself and of his life—what he himself really cares about and what will actually satisfy him, although this is the most basic and the most decisive task upon which an intelligent selection of economic goals depends. Exaggerating the moral importance of economic equality is harmful, in other words, because it is alienating.

To be sure, the circumstances of others may reveal interesting possibilities and provide data for useful judgments concerning what is normal or typical. Someone who is attempting to reach a confident and realistic appreciation of what to seek for himself may well find this helpful. It is not only in suggestive and preliminary ways like these, moreover, that the situations of other people may be pertinent to someone's efforts to decide what economic demands it is reasonable or important for him to make. The amount of money he needs may depend in a more direct way on the amounts others have. Money may bring power or prestige or other competitive advantages. A determination of how much money would be enough cannot intelligently be made by someone who is concerned with such things except on the basis of an estimate of the resources available to those with whose competition it may be necessary for him to contend. What is important from this point of view, however, is not the comparison of levels of affluence as such. The measurement of inequality is important only as it pertains contingently to other interests.

The mistaken belief that economic equality is important in itself leads people to detach the problem of formulating their economic ambitions from the problem of understanding what is most fundamentally significant to them. It influences them to take too seriously, as though it were a matter of great moral concern, a question that is inherently rather insignificant and not directly to the point: viz., how their economic status compares with the economic status of others. In this way the doctrine of equality contributes to the moral disorientation and shallowness of our time.

The prevalence of egalitarian thought is harmful in another respect as well. It not only tends to divert attention from considerations of greater moral importance than equality. It also diverts attention from the difficult but quite fundamental philosophical problems of understanding just what these considerations are and of elaborating, in appropriately comprehensive and perspicuous detail, a conceptual apparatus which would facilitate their exploration. Calculating the size of an equal share is plainly much easier than determining how much a person needs in order to have enough. In addition, the very concept of having an equal share is itself considerably more patent and accessible than the concept of having enough. It is far from self-evident, needless to say, precisely what the doctrine of sufficiency means and what applying it entails. But this is hardly a good reason for neglecting the doctrine or for adopting an incorrect doctrine in preference to it. Among my primary purposes in this essay is to suggest the importance of systematic inquiry into the analytical and theoretical issues raised by the concept of having enough, whose importance egalitarianism has masked.

II

There are a number of ways of attempting to establish the thesis that economic equality is important. Sometimes it is urged that the prevalence of fraternal relationships among the members of a society is a desirable goal and that equality is indispensable to it. Or it may be maintained that inequalities in the distribution of economic benefits are to be avoided because they lead invariably to undesirable discrepancies of other kinds—for example, in social status, in political influence, or in the abilities of people to make effective use of their various opportunities and entitlements. In both of these arguments, economic equality is endorsed because of its supposed importance in creating or preserving certain non-economic conditions. Such considerations may well provide convincing reasons for recommending equality as a desirable social good, or even for preferring egalitarianism as a policy over the alternatives to it. But both arguments construe equality as valuable derivatively, in virtue of its contingent connections to other things. In neither argument is there an attribution to equality of any unequivocally inherent moral value.

A rather different kind of argument for economic equality, which comes closer to construing the value of equality as independent of contingencies, is based upon the principle of diminishing marginal utility. According to this argument, equality is desirable because an egalitarian distribution of economic assets maximizes their aggregate utility. The argument presupposes: (a) for each individual the utility of money invariably diminishes at the margin; and (b) with respect to money, or with respect to the things money can buy, the utility functions of all individuals are the same. In other words, the utility provided by or derivable from an nth dollar is the same for everyone, and it is less than the utility for anyone of dollar $(n - 1)$. Unless (b) were true, a rich man might obtain greater utility than a poor man from an extra dollar. In that case an egalitarian distribution of economic goods would not maximize aggregate utility even if (a) were true. But given both (a) and (b), it follows that a marginal dollar always brings less utility to a rich person than to one who is less rich. And this entails that total utility must increase when inequality is reduced by giving a dollar to someone poorer than the person from whom it is taken.

In fact, however, both (a) and (b) are false. Suppose it is conceded, for the sake of the argument, that the maximization of aggregate utility is in its own right a morally important social goal. Even so, it cannot legitimately be inferred that an egalitarian distribution of money must therefore have similar moral importance. For in virtue of the falsity of (a) and (b), the argument linking economic equality to the maximization of aggregate utility is unsound.

So far as concerns (b), it is evident that the utility functions for money of different individuals are not even approximately alike. Some people suffer from physical, mental, or emotional weaknesses or incapacities that limit the satisfactions they are able to obtain. Moreover, even apart from the effects of specific disabilities, some people simply enjoy things more than other people do. Everyone knows that there are, at any given level of expenditure, large differences in the quantities of utility that different spenders derive.

So far as concerns (a), there are good reasons against expecting any consistent diminution in the marginal utility of money. The fact that the marginal utilities of certain goods do indeed tend to diminish is not a principle of reason. It is a psychological generalization, which is accounted for by such considerations as that people often tend after a time to become satiated with what they have been consuming and that the senses characteristically lose their freshness after repetitive stimulation. It is common knowledge that experiences of many kinds become increasingly routine and unrewarding as they are repeated.

It is questionable, however, whether this provides any reason at all for expecting a diminution in the marginal utility of *money*—that is, of anything that functions as a generic instrument of exchange. Even if the utility of everything money can buy were inevitably to diminish at the margin, the utility of money itself might nonetheless exhibit a different pattern. It is quite possible that money would be exempt from the phenomenon of unrelenting marginal decline because of its limitlessly protean versatility. As Blum and Kalven explain:

> In . . . analysing the question whether money has a declining utility it is . . . important to put to one side all analogies to the observation that particular commodities have a declining utility to their users. There is no need here to enter into the debate whether it is useful or necessary, in economic theory, to assume that commodities have a declining utility. Money is infinitely versatile. And even if all the things money can buy are subject to a law of diminishing utility, it does not follow that money itself is.

From the supposition that a person tends to lose more and more interest in what he is consuming as his consumption of it increases, it plainly cannot be inferred that he must also tend to lose interest in consumption itself or in the money that makes consumption possible. For there may always remain for him, no matter how tired he has become of what he has been doing, untried goods to be bought and fresh new pleasures to be enjoyed.

There are in any event many things of which people do not from the very outset immediately begin to tire. From certain goods, they actually derive more utility after sustained consumption than they derive at first. This is the situation whenever appreciating or enjoying or otherwise benefiting from something depends upon repeated trials, which serve as a kind of "warming up" process: for instance, when relatively little significant gratification is obtained from the item or experience in question until the individual has acquired a special taste for it, or has become addicted to it, or has begun in some other way to relate or respond to it profitably. The capacity for obtaining gratification is then smaller at earlier points in the sequence of consumption than at later points. In such cases marginal utility does not decline; it increases. Perhaps it is true of everything, without exception, that a person will ultimately lose interest in it. But even if in every utility curve there is a point at which the curve begins a steady and irreversible decline, it cannot be assumed that every segment of the curve has a downward slope.

III

When marginal utility diminishes, it does not do so on account of any deficiency in the marginal unit. It diminishes in virtue of the position of that unit as the latest in a sequence. The same is true when marginal utility increases: the marginal unit provides greater utility than its predecessors in virtue of the effect which the acquisition or consumption of those predecessors has brought about. Now when the sequence consists of units of money, what corresponds to the process of warming up—at least, in one pertinent and important feature—is *saving*. Accumulating money entails, as warming up does, generating a capacity to derive at some subsequent point in a sequence gratifications that cannot be derived earlier.

The fact that it may at times be especially worthwhile for a person to save money rather than to spend each dollar as it comes along is due in part to the incidence of what may be thought of as *utility thresholds.* Consider an item with the following characteristics: it is non-fungible, it is the source of a fresh and otherwise unobtainable type of satisfaction, and it is too expensive to be acquired except by saving up for it. The utility of the dollar that finally completes a program of

saving up for such an item may be greater than the utility of any dollar saved earlier in the program. That will be the case when the utility provided by the item is greater than the sum of the utilities that could be derived if the money saved were either spent as it came in or divided into parts and used to purchase other things. In a situation of this kind, the final dollar saved permits the crossing of a utility threshold.

It is sometimes argued that, for anyone who is rational in the sense that he seeks to maximize the utility generated by his expenditures, the marginal utility of money must necessarily diminish. Abba Lerner presents this argument as follows:

> The principle of diminishing marginal utility of income can be derived from the assumption that consumers spend their income in the way that maximizes the satisfaction they can derive from the good obtained. With a given income, all the things bought give a greater satisfaction for the money spent on them than any of the other things that could have been bought in their place but were not bought for this very reason. From this it follows that if income were greater the additional things that would be bought with the increment of income would be things that are rejected when income is smaller because they give less satisfaction; and if income were greater still, even less satisfactory things would be bought. The greater the income the less satisfactory are the additional things that can be bought with equal increases of income. That is all that is meant by the principle of the diminishing marginal utility of income.

Lerner invokes here a comparison between the utility of G(n)—the goods which the rational consumer actually buys with his income of n dollars—and "the other things that could have been bought in their place but were not." Given that he prefers to buy G(n) rather than the other things, which by hypothesis cost no more, the rational consumer must regard G(n) as offering greater satisfaction than the others can provide. From this Lerner infers that with an additional n dollars the consumer would be able to purchase only things with less utility than G(n); and he concludes that, in general, "the greater the income the less satisfactory are the additional things that can be bought with equal increases of income." This conclusion, he maintains, is tantamount to the principle of the diminishing marginal utility of income.

It seems apparent that Lerner's attempt to derive the principle in this way fails. One reason is that the amount of satisfaction a person can derive from a certain good may vary considerably according to whether or not he also possesses certain other goods. The satisfaction obtainable from a certain expenditure may therefore be greater if some other expenditure has already been made. Suppose that the cost of a serving of popcorn is the same as the cost of enough butter to make it delectable; and suppose that some rational consumer who adores buttered popcorn gets very little satisfaction from unbuttered popcorn, but that he nonetheless prefers it to butter alone. He will buy the popcorn in preference to the butter, accordingly, if he must buy one and cannot buy both. Suppose now that this person's income increases so that he can buy the butter too. Then he can have something he enjoys enormously: his incremental income makes it possible for him not merely to buy butter in addition to popcorn, but to enjoy buttered popcorn. The satisfaction he will derive by combining the popcorn and the butter may well be considerably greater than the sum of the satisfactions he can derive from the two goods taken separately. Here, again, is a threshold effect.

In a case of this sort, what the rational consumer buys with his incremental income is a good—G(i)—which, when his income was smaller, he had rejected in favor of G(n) because having it alone would have been less satisfying than having only G(n). Despite this, however, it is not true that the utility of the income he uses to buy G(i) is less than the utility of the income he used to buy G(n). When there is an opportunity to create a combination which is (like buttered popcorn) synergistic in the sense that adding one good to another increases the utility of each, the marginal utility of income may not decline even though the sequence of marginal items—taking each of these items by itself—does exhibit a pattern of declining utilities.

Lerner's argument is flawed in virtue of another consideration as well. Since he speaks of "the *additional* things that can be bought with equal increases of income," he evidently presumes that a rational consumer uses his first n dollars to purchase a certain good and that he uses any incremental income beyond that to buy something else. This leads Lerner to suppose that what the consumer buys when his income is increased by i dollars (where i is equal to or less than n) must be something which he could have bought and which he chose not to buy when his income was only n dollars. But this supposition is unwarranted. With an income of (n + i) dollars the consumer need not use his money to purchase both G(n) and G(i). He might use it to buy something which costs more than either

of these goods—something which was too expensive to be available to him at all before his income increased. The point is that if a rational consumer with an income of n dollars defers purchasing a certain good until his income increases, this does not necessarily mean that he "rejected" purchasing it when his income was smaller. The good in question may have been out of his reach at that time because it cost more than n dollars. His reason for postponing the purchase may have had nothing to do with comparative expectations of satisfaction or with preferences or priorities at all.

There are two possibilities to consider. Suppose on the one hand that, instead of purchasing G(n) when his income is n dollars, the rational consumer saves that money until he can add an additional i dollars to it and then purchases G(n + i). In this case it is quite evident that his deferral of the purchase of G(n + i) does not mean that he values it less than G(n). On the other hand, suppose that the rational consumer declines to save up for G(n + i) and that he spends all the money he has on G(n). In this case too it would be a mistake to construe his behavior as indicating a preference for G(n) over G(n + i). For the explanation of his refusal to save for G(n + i) may be merely that he regards doing so as pointless because he believes that he cannot reasonably expect to save enough to make a timely purchase of it.

The utility of G(n + i) may not only be greater than the utility either of G(n) or of G(i). It may also be greater than the sum of their utilities. That is, in acquiring G(n + i) the consumer may cross a utility threshold. The utility of the increment i to his income is then actually greater than the utility of the n dollars to which it is added, even though i equals or is less than n. In such a case, the income of the rational consumer does not exhibit diminishing marginal utility.

IV

The preceding discussion has established that an egalitarian distribution may fail to maximize aggregate utility. It can also easily be shown that, in virtue of the incidence of utility thresholds, there are conditions under which an egalitarian distribution actually minimizes aggregate utility. Thus suppose that there is enough of a certain resource (e.g., food or medicine) to enable some but not all members of a population to survive. Let us say that the size of the population is ten, that a person needs at least five units of the resource in question to live, and that forty units are available. If any members of this population are to survive, some must have more than others. An equal distribution, which gives each person four units, leads to the worst possible outcome: viz., everyone dies. Surely in this case it would be morally grotesque to insist upon equality! Nor would it be reasonable to maintain that, under the conditions specified, it is justifiable for some to be better off only when this is in the interests of the worst off. If the available resources are used to save eight people, the justification for doing this is manifestly not that it somehow benefits the two members of the population who are left to die.

An egalitarian distribution will almost certainly produce a net loss of aggregate utility whenever it entails that fewer individuals than otherwise will have, with respect to some necessity, enough to sustain life—in other words, whenever it requires a larger number of individuals to be below the threshold of survival. Of course, a loss of utility may also occur even when the circumstances involve a threshold that does not separate life and death. Allocating resources equally will reduce aggregate utility whenever it requires a number of individuals to be kept below *any* utility threshold without ensuring a compensating move above some threshold by a suitable number of others.

Under conditions of scarcity, then, an egalitarian distribution may be morally unacceptable. Another response to scarcity is to distribute the available resources in such a way that as many people as possible have enough, or, in other words, to maximize the incidence of sufficiency. This alternative is especially compelling when the amount of a scarce resource that constitutes enough coincides with the amount that is indispensable for avoiding some catastrophic harm—as in the example just considered, where falling below the threshold of enough food or enough medicine means death. But now suppose that there are available, in this example, not just forty units of the vital resource but forty-one. Then maximizing the incidence of sufficiency by providing enough for each of eight people leaves one unit unallocated. What should be done with this extra unit?

It has been shown above that it is a mistake to maintain that *where some people have less than enough, no one should have more than anyone else.* When resources are scarce, so that it is impossible for everyone to have enough, an egalitarian distribution may lead to disaster. Now there is another claim that might be made here, which may appear to be quite plausible, but which is also mistaken: *where some people have less than enough, no one should have more than enough.* If this claim were correct, then—in the example at hand—the extra unit should go to one of the two people who have nothing. But one additional unit of the resource in question will not improve the condition of a person who has none. By hypothesis, that person will die even with the additional unit. What he needs is not one unit, but five. It cannot be taken for granted that a person who has a certain amount of a vital resource is necessarily better off than a person who has a lesser amount, for the larger amount may still be too small to serve any useful purpose. Having the larger amount may even make a person worse off. Thus it is conceivable that while a dose of five units of some medication is therapeutic, a dose of one unit is not better than none but actually toxic. And while a person with one unit of food may live a bit longer than someone with no food whatever, perhaps it is worse to prolong the process of starvation for a short time than to terminate quickly the agony of starving to death.

The claim that no one should have more than enough while anyone has less than enough derives its plausibility, in part, from a presumption that is itself plausible but that is nonetheless false: to wit, giving resources to people who have less of them than enough necessarily means giving resources to people who need them and, therefore, making those people better off. It is indeed reasonable to assign a higher priority to improving the condition of those who are in need than to improving the condition of those who are not in need. But giving additional resources to people who have less than enough of those resources, and who are accordingly in need, may not actually improve the condition of these people at all. Those below a utility threshold are not necessarily benefited by additional resources that move them closer to the threshold. What is crucial for them is to attain the threshold. Merely moving closer to it may either fail to help them or be disadvantageous.

By no means do I wish to suggest, of course, that it is never or only rarely beneficial for those below a utility threshold to move closer to it. Certainly it may be beneficial, either because it increases the likelihood that the threshold will ultimately be attained or because, quite apart from the significance of the threshold, additional resources provide important increments of utility. After all, a collector may enjoy expanding his collection even if he knows that he has no chance of ever completing it. My point is only that additional resources do not necessarily benefit those who have less than enough. The additions may be too little to make any difference. It may be morally quite acceptable, accordingly, for some to have more than enough of certain resource even while others have less than enough of it.

V

Quite often, advocacy of egalitarianism is based less upon an argument than upon a purported moral intuition: economic inequality, considered as such, just seems wrong. It strikes many people as unmistakably apparent that, taken simply in itself, the enjoyment by some of greater economic benefits than are enjoyed by others is morally offensive. I suspect, however, that in many cases those who profess to have this intuition concerning manifestations of inequality are actually responding not to the inequality but to another feature of the situations they are confronting. What I believe they find intuitively to be morally objectionable, in the types of situations characteristically cited as instances of economic inequality, is not the fact that some of the individuals in those situations have *less* money than others but the fact that those with less have *too little*.

When we consider people who are substantially worse off than ourselves, we do very commonly find that we are morally disturbed by their circumstances. What directly touches us in cases of this kind, however, is not a quantitative discrepancy but a qualitative condition—not the fact that the economic resources of those who are worse off are *smaller in magnitude* than ours, but the different fact that these people are so *poor.* Mere differences in the amounts of money people have are not in themselves distressing. We tend to be quite unmoved, after all, by inequalities between the well-to-do and the rich; our awareness that the former are substantially worse off than the latter does not disturb us morally at all. And if we believe of some person that his life is richly fulfilling, that he himself is genuinely content with his economic situation, and that he suffers no resentments or sorrows which more money could assuage, we are not ordinarily much interested—from a moral point of view—in the question of how the amount of money he has compares with the amounts possessed by others. Economic discrepancies in cases of these sorts do not impress us in the least as matters of significant moral concern. The fact that some people have much less than others is morally undisturbing when it is clear that they have plenty.

It seems clear that egalitarianism and the doctrine of sufficiency are logically independent: considerations that support the one cannot be presumed to provide support also for the other. Yet proponents of egalitarianism frequently suppose that they have offered grounds for their position when in fact what they have offered is pertinent as support only for the doctrine of sufficiency. Thus they often, in attempting to gain acceptance for egalitarianism, call attention to disparities between the conditions of life characteristic of the rich and those characteristic of the poor. Now it is undeniable that contemplating such disparities does often elicit a conviction that it would be morally desirable to redistribute the available resources so as to improve the circumstances of the poor. And, of course, that would bring about a greater degree of economic equality. But the indisputability of the moral appeal of improving the condition of the poor by allocating to them resources taken from those who are well off does not even tend to show that egalitarianism is, as a moral ideal, similarly indisputable. To show of poverty that it is compellingly undesirable does nothing whatsoever to show the same of inequality. For what makes someone poor in the morally relevant sense—in which poverty is understood as a condition from which we naturally recoil—is not that his economic assets are simply of lesser magnitude than those of others.

A typical example of this confusion is provided by Ronald Dworkin. Dworkin characterizes the ideal of economic equality as requiring that "no citizen has less than an equal share of the community's resources just in order that others may have more of what he lacks."[1] But in support of his claim that the United States now falls short of this ideal, he refers to circumstances that are not primarily evidence of inequality but of poverty:

> It is, I think, apparent that the United States falls far short now [of the ideal of equality]. A substantial minority of Americans are chronically unemployed or earn wages below any realistic "poverty line" or are handicapped in various ways or burdened with special needs; and most of these people would do the work necessary to earn a decent living if they had the opportunity and capacity.

What mainly concerns Dworkin—what he actually considers to be morally important—is manifestly not that our society permits a situation in which a substantial minority of Americans have *smaller shares* than others of the resources which he apparently presumes should be available for all. His concern is, rather, that the members of this minority *do not earn decent livings.*

The force of Dworkin's complaint does not derive from the allegation that our society fails to provide some individuals with as much as others, but from a quite different allegation: viz., our society fails to provide each individual with "the opportunity to develop and lead a life he can regard as valuable both to himself and to [the community]". Dworkin is dismayed most fundamentally, not by evidence that the United States permits economic inequality, but by evidence that it fails to ensure that everyone has enough to lead "a life of choice and value"—in other words, that it fails to fulfill for all the ideal of sufficiency. What bothers him most immediately is not that certain quantitative relationships are widespread but that certain qualitative conditions prevail. He cares principally about the value of people's lives, but he mistakenly represents himself as caring principally about the relative magnitudes of their economic assets.

My suggestion that situations involving inequality are morally disturbing only to the extent that they violate the ideal of sufficiency is confirmed, it seems to me, by familiar discrepancies between the principles egalitarians profess and the way in which they commonly conduct their own lives. My point here is not that some egalitarians hypocritically accept high incomes and special opportunities for which, according to the moral theories they profess, there is no justification. It is that many egalitarians (including many academic proponents of the doctrine) are not truly concerned whether they are as well off economically as other people are. They believe that they themselves have roughly enough money for what is important to them, and they are therefore not terribly preoccupied with the fact that some people are considerably richer than they. Indeed, many egalitarians would consider it rather shabby or even reprehensible to care, with respect to their own lives, about economic comparisons of that sort. And, notwithstanding the implications of the doctrines to which they urge adherence, they would be appalled if their children grew up with such preoccupations.

VI

The fundamental error of egalitarianism lies in supposing that it is morally important whether one person has less than another regardless of how much either of them has. This error is due in part to the false assumption that someone who is economically worse off has more important unsatisfied needs than someone who is better off. In fact the morally significant needs of both individuals may be fully satisfied or equally unsatisfied. Whether one person has more money than another is a wholly extrinsic matter. It has to do with a rela-

tionship between the respective economic assets of the two people, which is not only independent of the amounts of their assets and of the amounts of satisfaction they can derive from them, but which is also independent of the attitudes of these people toward those levels of assets and of satisfaction. The economic comparison implies nothing concerning whether either of the people compared has any morally important unsatisfied needs at all, nor concerning whether either is content with what he has.

This defect in egalitarianism appears plainly in Thomas Nagel's development of the doctrine. According to Nagel:

> The essential feature of an egalitarian priority system is that it counts improvements to the welfare of the worse off as more urgent than improvements to the welfare of the better off. . . . What makes a system egalitarian is the priority it gives to the claims of those . . . at the bottom. . . . Each individual with a more urgent claim has priority . . . over each individual with a less urgent claim.[2]

And in discussing Rawls's Difference Principle, which he endorses, Nagel says the Difference Principle "establishes an order of priority among needs and gives preference to the most urgent." But the preference actually assigned by the Difference Principle is not in favor of those whose needs are most urgent; it is in favor of those who are identified as worst off. It is a mere assumption, which Nagel makes without providing any grounds for it whatever, that the worst off individuals have urgent needs. In most societies the people who are economically at the bottom are indeed extremely poor; and they do, as a matter of fact, have urgent needs. But this relationship between low economic status and urgent need is wholly contingent. It can be established only on the basis of empirical data. There is no necessary conceptual connection between a person's relative economic position and whether he has needs of any degree of urgency.

It is possible for those who are worse off not to have more urgent needs or claims than those who are better off, because it is possible for them to have no urgent needs or claims at all. The notion of "urgency" has to do with what is *important*. Trivial needs or interests, which have no significant bearing upon the quality of a person's life or upon his readiness to be content with it, cannot properly be construed as being urgent to any degree whatever or as supporting the sort of morally demanding claims to which genuine urgency gives rise. From the fact that a person is at the bottom of some economic order, moreover, it cannot even be inferred that he has *any* unsatisfied needs or claims. After all, it is possible for conditions at the bottom to be quite good; the fact that they are the worst does not in itself entail that they are bad, or that they are in any way incompatible with richly fulfilling and enjoyable lives.

Nagel maintains that what underlies the appeal of equality is an "ideal of acceptability to each individual." On his account, this ideal entails that a reasonable person should consider deviations from equality to be acceptable only if they are in his interest in the sense that he would be worse off without them. But a reasonable person might well regard an unequal distribution as entirely acceptable even though he did not presume that any other distribution would benefit him less. For he might believe that the unequal distribution provided him with quite enough; and he might reasonably be unequivocally content with that, with no concern for the possibility that some other arrangement would provide him with more. It is gratuitous to assume that every reasonable person must be seeking to maximize the benefits he can obtain, in a sense requiring that he be endlessly interested in or open to improving his life. A certain deviation from equality might not be *in* someone's interest, because it might be that he would in fact be better off without it. But as long as it does not *conflict* with his interest, by obstructing his opportunity to lead the sort of life that it is important for him to lead, the deviation from equality may be quite acceptable. To be wholly satisfied with a certain state of affairs, a reasonable person need not suppose that there is no other available state of affairs in which he would be better off.

Nagel illustrates his thesis concerning the moral appeal of equality by considering a family with two children, one of whom is "normal and quite happy" while the other "suffers from a painful handicap." If this family were to move to the city the handicapped child would benefit from medical and educational opportunities that are unavailable in the suburbs, but the healthy child would have less fun. If the family were to move to the suburbs, on the other hand, the handicapped child would be deprived but the healthy child would enjoy himself more. Nagel stipulates that the gain to the healthy child in moving to the suburbs would be greater than the gain to the handicapped child in moving to the city: in the city the healthy child would find life positively disagreeable, while the handicapped child would not become happy "but only less miserable."

Given these considerations, the egalitarian decision is to move to the city; for "it is more urgent to benefit the [handicapped] child even though the benefit we can give him is less than the benefit we can give the [healthy] child." Nagel explains that this judgment concerning the greater urgency of benefiting the handicapped child "depends on the worse off position of the [handicapped] child. An improvement in his situation is more important than an equal or somewhat greater improvement in the situation of the [normal] child." But it seems to me that Nagel's analysis of this matter is flawed by an error similar to the one that I attributed above to Dworkin. The fact that it is preferable to help the handicapped child is not due, as Nagel asserts, to the fact that this child is worse off than the other. It is due to the fact that this child, and not the other, suffers from a painful handicap. The handicapped child's claim is important because his condition is *bad*—significantly undesirable—and not merely because he is *less well off* than his sibling.

This does not imply, of course, that Nagel's evaluation of what the family should do is wrong. Rejecting egalitarianism certainly does not mean maintaining that it is always mandatory simply to maximize benefits, and that therefore the family should move to the suburbs because the normal child would gain more from that than the handicapped child would gain from a move to the city. However, the most cogent basis for Nagel's judgment in favor of the handicapped child has nothing to do with the alleged urgency of providing people with as much as others. It pertains rather to the urgency of the needs of people who do not have enough.

VII

What does it mean, in the present context, for a person to have enough? One thing it might mean is that any more would be too much: a larger amount would make the person's life unpleasant, or it would be harmful or in some other way unwelcome. This is often what people have in mind when they say such things as "I've had enough!" or "Enough of that!" The idea conveyed by statements like these is that *a limit has been reached* beyond which it is not desirable to proceed. On the other hand, the assertion that a person has enough may entail only that a *certain requirement or standard has been met* with no implication that a larger quantity would be bad. This is often what a person intends when he says something like "That should be enough." Statements such as this one characterize the indicated amount as sufficient while leaving open the possibility that a larger amount might also be acceptable.

In the doctrine of sufficiency the use of the notion of "enough" pertains to *meeting a standard* rather than to *reaching a limit*. To say that a person has enough money means that he is content, or that it is reasonable for him to be content, with having no more money than he has. And to say this is, in turn, to say something like the following: the person does not (or cannot reasonably) regard whatever (if anything) is unsatisfying or distressing about his life as due to his having too little money. In other words, if a person is (or ought reasonably to be) content with the amount of money he has, then insofar as he is or has reason to be unhappy with the way his life is going, he does not (or cannot reasonably) suppose that more money would—either as a sufficient or as a necessary condition—enable him to become (or to have reason to be) significantly less unhappy with it.

It is essential to understand that having enough money differs from merely having enough to get along, or enough to make life marginally tolerable. People are not generally content with living on the brink. The point of the doctrine of sufficiency is not that the only morally important distributional consideration with respect to money is whether people have enough to avoid economic misery. A person who might naturally and appropriately be said to have just barely enough does not, by the standard invoked in the doctrine of sufficiency, have enough at all.

There are two distinct kinds of circumstances in which the amount of money a person has is enough—that is, in which more money will not enable him to become significantly less unhappy. On the one hand, it may be that the person is suffering no substantial distress or dissatisfaction with his life. On the other hand, it may be that although the person is unhappy about how his life is going, the difficulties that account for his unhappiness would not be alleviated by more money. Circumstances of this second kind obtain when what is wrong with the person's life has to do with non-economic goods such as love, a sense that life is meaningful, satisfaction with one's own character, and so on. These are goods that money cannot buy; moreover, they are goods for which none of the things money can buy are even approximately adequate substitutes. Sometimes, to be sure, non-economic goods are obtainable or enjoyable only (or more easily) by someone who has a certain amount of money. But the person who is distressed with his life while content with his economic situation may already have that much money.

It is possible that someone who is content with the amount of money he has might also be content with an even larger amount of money. Since having enough money does not mean being at a limit beyond which more money would necessarily be undesirable, it would be a mistake to assume that for a person who already has enough the marginal utility of money must be either negative or zero. Although this person is by hypothesis not distressed about his life in virtue of any lack of things which more money would enable him to obtain, nonetheless it remains possible that he would enjoy having some of those things. They would not make him less unhappy, nor would they in any way alter his attitude toward his life or the degree of his contentment with it, but they might bring him pleasure. If that is so, then his life would in this respect be better with more money than without it. The marginal utility for him of money would accordingly remain positive.

To say that a person is content with the amount of money he has does not entail, then, that there would be no point whatever in his having more. Thus someone with enough money might be quite *willing* to accept incremental economic benefits. He might in fact be *pleased* to receive them. Indeed, from the supposition that a person is content with the amount of money he has it cannot even be inferred that he would not *prefer* to have more. And it is even possible that he would actually be prepared to *sacrifice* certain things that he values (for instance, a certain amount of leisure) for the sake of more money.

But how can all this be compatible with saying that the person is content with what he has? What *does* contentment with a given amount of money preclude, if it does not preclude being willing or being pleased or preferring to have more money or even being ready to make sacrifices for more? It precludes his having an *active interest* in getting more. A contented person regards having more money as *inessential* to his being satisfied with his life. The fact that he is content is quite consistent with his recognizing that his economic circumstances could be improved and that his life might as a consequence become better than it is. But this possibility is not important to him. He is simply not much interested in being better off, so far as money goes, than he is. His attention and interest are not vividly engaged by the benefits which would be available to him if he had more money. He is just not very responsive to their appeal. They do not arouse in him any particularly eager or restless concern, although he acknowledges that he would enjoy additional benefits if they were provided to him.

In any event, let us suppose that the level of satisfaction that his present economic circumstances enable him to attain is high enough to meet his expectations of life. This is not fundamentally a matter of how much utility or satisfaction his various activities and experiences provide. Rather, it is most decisively a matter of his attitude toward being provided with that much. The satisfying experiences a person has are one thing. Whether he is satisfied that his life includes just those satisfactions is another. Although it is possible that other feasible circumstances would provide him with greater amounts of satisfaction, it may be that he is wholly satisfied with the amounts of satisfaction that he now enjoys. Even if he knows that he could obtain a greater quantity of satisfaction overall, he does not experience the uneasiness or the ambition that would incline him to seek it. Some people feel that their lives are good enough, and it is not important to them whether their lives are as good as possible.

The fact that a person lacks an active interest in getting something does not mean, of course, that he prefers not to have it. This is why the contented person may without any incoherence accept or welcome improvements in his situation and why he may even be prepared to incur minor costs in order to improve it. The fact that he is contented means only that the possibility of improving his situation is not *important* to him. It only implies, in other words, that he does not resent his circumstances, that he is not anxious or determined to improve them, and that he does not go out of his way or take any significant initiatives to make them better.

It may seem that there can be no reasonable basis for accepting less satisfaction when one could have more, that therefore rationality itself entails maximizing, and hence that a person who refuses to maximize the quantity of satisfaction in his life is not being rational. Such a person cannot, of course, offer it as his reason for declining to pursue greater satisfaction that the costs of this pursuit are too high; for if that were his reason then, clearly, he would be attempting to maximize satisfaction after all. But what other good reason could he possibly have for passing up an opportunity for more satisfaction? In fact, he may have a very good reason for this: namely, *that he is satisfied with the amount of satisfaction he already has.* Being satisfied with the way things are is unmistakably an excellent reason for having no great interest in changing them. A person who is indeed satisfied with his life as it is can hardly be criticized, accordingly, on the grounds that he has no good reason for declining to make it better.

He might still be open to criticism on the grounds that he *should not* be satisfied—that it is somehow un-

reasonable, or unseemly, or in some other mode wrong for him to be satisfied with less satisfaction than he could have. On what basis, however, could *this* criticism be justified? Is there some decisive reason for insisting that a person ought to be so hard to satisfy? Suppose that a man deeply and happily loves a woman who is altogether worthy. We do not ordinarily criticize the man in such a case just because we think he might have done even better. Moreover, our sense that it would be inappropriate to criticize him for that reason need not be due simply to a belief that holding out for a more desirable or worthier woman might end up costing him more than it would be worth. Rather, it may reflect our recognition that the desire to be happy or content or satisfied with life is a desire for a satisfactory amount of satisfaction, and is not inherently tantamount to a desire that the quantity of satisfaction be maximized.

Being satisfied with a certain state of affairs is not equivalent to preferring it to all others. If a person is faced with a choice between less and more of something desirable, then no doubt it would be irrational for him to prefer less to more. But a person may be satisfied without having made any such comparisons at all. Nor is it necessarily irrational or unreasonable for a person to omit or to decline to make comparisons between his own state of affairs and possible alternatives. This is not only because making comparisons may be too costly. It is also because if someone is satisfied with the way things are, he may have no motive to consider how else they might be.

Contentment may be a function of excessive dullness or diffidence. The fact that a person is free both of resentment and of ambition may be due to his having a slavish character or to his vitality being muffled by a kind of negligent lassitude. It is possible for someone to be content merely, as it were, by default. But a person who is content with resources providing less utility than he could have may be neither irresponsible nor indolent nor deficient in imagination. On the contrary, his decision to be content with those resources— in other words, to adopt an attitude of willing acceptance toward the fact that he has just that much—may be based upon a conscientiously intelligent and penetrating evaluation of the circumstances of his life.

It is not essential for such an evaluation to include an *extrinsic* comparison of the person's circumstances with alternatives to which he might plausibly aspire, as it would have to do if contentment were reasonable only when based upon a judgment that the enjoyment of possible benefits has been maximized. If someone is less interested in whether his circumstances enable him to live as well as possible than in whether they enable him to live satisfyingly, he may appropriately devote his evaluation entirely to an *intrinsic* appraisal of his life. Then he may recognize that his circumstances lead him to be neither resentful nor regretful nor drawn to change and that, on the basis of his understanding of himself and of what is important to him, he accedes approvingly to his actual readiness to be content with the way things are. The situation in that case is not so much that he rejects the possibility of improving his circumstances because he thinks there is nothing genuinely to be gained by attempting to improve them. It is rather that this possibility, however feasible it may be, fails as a matter of fact to excite his active attention or to command from him any lively interest.

READING 38

Why the Emperor Has No Clothes: A Critique of Contemporary Egalitarianism

Louis P. Pojman

Louis Pojman is Professor of Philosophy at the United States Military Academy at West Point and editor of this book. He was a civil rights activist and minister of an interracial church in the 1960s. He has also taught at the University of Notre Dame, Brigham Young University, and the University of Mississippi. He is the author or editor of several books, including *Ethics: Discovering Right and Wrong; Life and Death: Grappling with the Moral Dilemmas of Our Time; Religious Belief and the Will; What Can We Know?* and *Global Environmental Ethics.*

In this article, Pojman examines several prominent contemporary arguments for equal human worth, the widely held theory on which equal human rights are based. He argues that none of them are sound. He shows that the idea of equal worth is rooted in a deeper metaphysic

than any of these secular theories support and that without such a metaphysical view of the nature and origins of humanity, the doctrine of equal human worth is, at best, a Noble Lie.

Parts of this reading were taken from "A Critique of Contemporary Egalitarianism," in *Faith and Philosophy* 8, no. 4 (October 1991) and "Are Human Rights Based on Equal Human Worth?" in *Philosophy and Phenomenological Research* 52, no. 3 (September 1992), but it appears here in this form for the first time. © L.P. Pojman 2001.

All human beings are born free and equal in dignity and rights. They are endowed with reason and conscience and should act towards one another in a spirit of brotherhood (United Nations' Universal Declaration of Human Rights, 1948).

Theories of equal human rights have experienced an exponential growth during the past thirty or forty years. From declarations of human rights, such as the United Nations' Universal Declaration of Human Rights [see Reading 50], to arguments about the rights of fetuses versus the rights of women, to claims and counterclaims about the rights of minorities to preferential hiring, the rights of animals to life and well-being, and the rights of trees to be preserved, the proliferation of rights claims affects every phase of our sociopolitical discourse. Hardly a month goes by without a new book appearing on the subject.[1]

As J. L. Mackie used to say, "Rights are pleasant. They allow us to make claims of others. Duties are onerous. They obligate us to others." Rights threaten to replace responsibility as the central focal point of moral theory. But this need not be the case. A rights theory balanced by a strong sense of the social good and individual responsibility may well be the best kind of moral-political theory we can have.

Virtually the only candidate for a rights theory today is egalitarianism, at least with regard to rational human beings. Although there are differences between contemporary egalitarian arguments, they all accept what Ronald Dworkin calls "the egalitarian plateau," the "deepest moral assumption" of our time, that each person is of equal intrinsic value, of "dignity" and thus ought to be treated with equal respect and be given equal rights.[2] The phrase, *dignity of the human person,* signifies, in the words of Jacques Maritain, that "the human person has the right to be respected, is the subject of rights, possesses rights. These are things which are owed to [a person] because of the very fact that he is a [person]."[3] Will Kymlicka states that "every plausible political theory has the same ultimate value, which is equality. They are all 'egalitarian theories.'"[4]

Ronald Green says that egalitarianism is the presupposition for morality itself, the precondition of moral discourse and the necessary first assumption of any moral system, whatever its resultant values.[5] Political theories as diverse as Robert Nozick's libertarianism, John Rawls's liberalism, Peter Singer's utilitarianism, and Kai Nielsen's Marxism all share the notion that each person matters and all persons matter equally.

What distinguishes most contemporary egalitarianism from earlier natural law models is its self-conscious secularism. There is no appeal to a God or a transcendental realm. Although Kant's doctrine of Ends ("Human beings qua rational have an inherent dignity and so ought to treat each other as ends and never merely as means.") is the touchstone of most egalitarians, they generally distance themselves from the metaphysical grounding of Kant's doctrine. In the words of Dworkin, contemporary egalitarianism is "metaphysically unambitious."[6] Yet it may well be that without some deeper metaphysical underpinnings equal rights theories fail to persuade thoughtful persons.

If a deconstructed Kant is the father of contemporary egalitarians, their enemies are Aristotle and Thomas Hobbes. Aristotle thought that humans were essentially unequal, relative to their ability to reason. Hobbes (*Leviathan*) rejected the notion of humans' having any intrinsic worth at all. "The value or worth of a man is, as of all other things, his price—that is to say, so much as would be given for the use of his power—and therefore is not absolute but a thing dependent on the need and judgment of another."

In this paper I examine the principal arguments for equal human rights given by contemporary egalitarians. Specifically, I explore the basis for attributing *equal worth* to all human beings or all minimally rational persons, since it is the doctrine of equal worth that undergirds most egalitarian theories of both rights and justice. In Part I, I argue that in their present form none of the arguments given for the doctrine of equal human worth are sound. In Part II, I suggest that the doctrine of equal human worth has its home in a deeper metaphysical system than secular egalitarians are able to embrace: non-natural systems, not necessarily religious, but typically so. My conclusion is that on the secularist's naturalistic assumptions, there is reason to give up egalitarianism altogether.

PART I. CONTEMPORARY SECULAR ARGUMENTS FOR EQUAL HUMAN WORTH

Ten arguments (or strategies) for equal human rights based on equal human worth appear in current philosophical literature. They are (1) the Presumption Argument, (2) the Properly Basic Belief Strategy, (3) the Existential Strategy, (4) the Libertarian Argument, (5) the Family Metaphor, (6) the Pragmatic Argument, (7) the Utilitarian Argument, (8) the Coherentist Argument, (9) the Rational Agency Argument, and (10) the Argument from Moral Personality. Let me briefly describe them and point out their deficiencies. I regret the cursory treatment of important theories, but my purpose is primarily to show how little attention has been paid to justifying the egalitarian plateau. Having until recently simply taken egalitarianism for granted, I now am puzzled by this idea or ideal and wonder whether it's simply a leftover from a religious world view now rejected by all of the philosophers discussed in this essay. At any rate, my discussion is meant to be exploratory and provocative, not the final word on the subject.

1. The Presumption of Equality Argument

R. S. Peters, Stanley Benn, Monroe Beardsley, E. F. Carritt, and James Rachels interpret equal worth in terms of equal consideration or impartiality and argue that there is a presumption in favor of treating people equally. "All persons are to be treated alike, unless there are good reasons for treating them differently."[7] But there are problems. First of all, this type of egalitarianism is unduly formal. It lacks a material criterion or metric to guide deliberation. One might as well say that "all sentient beings should be treated alike, unless there are good reasons for treating them differently." The formula only shifts the focus onto the idea of *good reasons*. We need to know by virtue of what material criterion people are to be treated equally or differently. What are the material criteria? Need, effort, contribution, intelligence, sentience, self-consciousness, or moral merit? And if there is more than one, how do we weight them in various circumstances? As far as I know, the problem of material criteria has not been solved.

Plato's hierarchical theory and Aristotle's aristocracy could accommodate this formal notion of equality (treating equals equally and unequals unequally), and even Hitler could have used it to justify his atrocities.

Inegalitarians simply claim that there is a good reason for unequal treatment of human beings. They are of unequal worth.

The presumption of equality argument reduces to the notion of impartiality (what R. M. Hare calls "universalizability") and is not really an egalitarian argument at all. It makes no restrictions upon what reasons may be given to warrant inequalities. It merely prescribes that we not act arbitrarily, but consistently. We should make our discriminations according to a proper standard, but doing so does not commit us to egalitarianism. For all rational action is governed by the idea of consistency.

Furthermore, there seems something arbitrary about the Presumption Argument. Why should we start off with a bias toward equality and not inequality? Why don't we have a principle presuming unequal treatment? "All persons are to be treated unequally unless there is some reason for treating them equally." Neither a presumption of equality nor one of inequality is necessary, though there may be pragmatic or utilitarian considerations that incline us to opt for a presumption of equality rather than inequality. We will consider those strategies later.

2. The Properly Basic Belief Strategy

Sometimes, no argument at all is given for the claim of equal human worth and the equal human rights that flow from it. Ronald Dworkin begins *Taking Rights Seriously* with a rejection of metaphysical assumptions.

> Individual rights are political trumps held by individuals. Individuals have rights when, for *some reason,* a collective goal is not a sufficient justification for denying them what they wish, as individuals, to have or to do, or not a sufficient justification for imposing some loss or injury upon them. That characterization of a right is, of course, formal in the sense that it does not indicate what rights people have or guarantee, indeed, that they have any. But it does not suppose that rights have some special metaphysical character, and the theory defended in these essays therefore departs from older theories of rights that do rely on that supposition. [P. xi, emphasis added.]

Nowhere in his book does Dworkin parse out the notion of "some reason" to override "collective goals." It is a given. The notion of equal human rights based on equal human worth simply becomes the assumption

that replaces earlier religious or Kantian metaphysical assumptions. Every plausible political theory is egalitarian in that it holds that all members of the community have a right to equal concern and respect. "The Deepest Moral Assumption: the assumption of a natural right of all men and women to an equality of concern and respect, a right they possess not in virtue of birth or characteristic or merit or excellence but simply as human beings with the capacity to make plans and give justice."[8] In other words, we don't need to argue for this thesis. In a series of lengthy articles on welfare and resource egalitarianism Dworkin simply assumes the ideal of equality: that "people matter and matter equally."

Dworkin's view seems similar to what Alvin Plantinga calls "a properly basic belief," a foundational belief which doesn't need any justification. But whatever merits this strategy has for religious beliefs, it seems unsatisfactory when employed to justify moral and political equality. At the very least, we should want to know why the capacity to "make plans and give justice" grants all and only humans equal concern and respect.

3. The Existential Strategy

Closely related to Dworkin's view is Kai Nielsen's "Radical Egalitarianism," which holds that the ideal of equal human life prospects is something to which we arbitrarily, that is, existentially, choose to commit ourselves. It enjoins treating equal life prospects as both a goal to be aimed at and a right to be claimed, but one cannot rationally justify these commitments.

> Instead of putting out, "All people are of equal worth regardless of merit" as some kind of mysterious truth-claim which appears in fact to be at best groundless and at worst false, would it not have been clearer and less evasive of the human-rights advocate simply to remark that he starts with a commitment on which he will not bend, namely a commitment to the treatment of all people as beings who are to have quite unforfeitably an equality of concern and respect? It is that sort of world that he or she most deeply desires and it is there that he stands pat. There are other equally intelligible and no doubt equally rational, moral points of view that do not contain such commitments. But it is with such a commitment that he takes his stand.[9]

Nielsen claims that it is "a great Kantian illusion" to think that one can or should justify our moral views through reason. These views are ultimate commitments, more basic than any of our other beliefs, so they are the grounds of belief which themselves cannot be justified, but must be chosen. That is where he distinguishes himself from Dworkin, who sees equality as a properly basic intuition.[10] Nielsen sees it as an existential and arbitrary choice. Nielsen continues:

> I do not know how anyone could show this belief to be true—to say nothing of showing it to be self-evident—or in any way prove it or show that if one is through and through rational, one must accept it. . . . A Nietzschean, a Benthamite, or even a classist amoralist who rejects it cannot thereby be shown to be irrational or even in any way necessarily to be diminished in his reason. It is a moral belief that I am committed to . . . [and which leads] to some . . . form of radical egalitarianism.[11]

In other words, equal human worth is a posit of secular faith, but a faith that seems to suffer from counter-examples: the apparent inequalities of abilities of every sort. Furthermore, many moral and political philosophers, myself included, believe that we can provide rational support for our moral and political beliefs. Nothing Nielsen says shows why we must resort to arbitrary existential leaps, but if this is all that can be said for egalitarianism, then the inegalitarian is quite safe. Since he or she doesn't choose to make the leap of faith into the religion of egalitarianism, we have a stand-off. But such a stand-off is hardly compelling grounds for demanding universal human rights based on equal human worth.

These first three types of egalitarianism can hardly be called arguments at all. Presumption arguments simply presume, properly basic beliefs stipulate, and existential choices do not claim rational justification. These theories already suppose egalitarian foundations. Let us turn now to more substantive efforts.

4. The Libertarian Argument

At the other end of the political spectrum from Nielsen's Socialism with a rich panoply of positive welfare rights is the Libertarian idea that there is only one natural right: the negative equal right not to be interfered with. Robert Nozick, like Dworkin, simply assumes such a natural right: "Individuals have rights, and there are things no persons or groups may do to them [without violating their rights]." But, unlike Dworkin, Nozick believes that only the minimal state, which protects the individual "against force, theft, fraud, [the breaking] of contracts, and so on, is justi-

fied."[12] An equal and absolute right to self-ownership gives people an absolute right to their justly acquired property. Tibor Machan formulates the Libertarian position in this way: "In short, a just human community is one that first and foremost protects the individual's right to life and liberty—the sovereignty of human individuals to act without aggressive intrusion from other human beings."[13]

On the face of it, after the rhetoric of absolute rights to property is deflated (Nozick wrongly supposes that the notion of self-ownership entails this absolute right), Libertarian arguments come down to little more than the back side of an ultra-minimalist morality, one which sets up as its single principle: Do no unnecessary harm. But this by itself doesn't even distinguish humans from animals. We shouldn't cause harm to anyone without a moral justification.

Machan separates himself from Libertarians like Nozick, who does not offer arguments for natural rights, and John Hospers, who is a metaphysical determinist and grounds his political Libertarianism in metaphysical Libertarianism. For Machan it is our ability to act freely (contra-causally) that separates humans from other animals and gives us value.

This seems a promising move, a departure from the mainstream rejection of metaphysics, but it has problems. The first is that the Libertarian (contra-causal) notion of freedom seems mysterious and hard to argue for. It seems to presuppose a notion of the self that is metaphysically richer than the physicalist version held by most compatibilists; though if we grant a transcendent notion of agency, the Libertarian notion will be more promising. However, it will probably not be secular in the usual meaning of that term (as disclaiming a notion of the spiritual or transcendent).

Second, even if the property of Libertarian free will is granted, if it has nothing to *choose*, it is of little practical value. By increasing a person's opportunities (through non-Libertarian institutions like public education and welfare economics) we enable free will to be exercised.

Third, it seems that people are unequally free. Some people deliberate with great ease and accuracy, while others become muddled in emotion. Some choose according to the best reasons available, while others suffer from weakness of will. Some plan their lives according to long-term goals and are able to execute those plans with consummate skill, while others are driven by circumstances, short-term goals, and impulse. So Libertarianism is not obviously egalitarian. Even if we all possess some free will, we do not possess it equally.

There seems no reason on Libertarian premises to value all humans equally. Here David Gauthier's Libertarian theory of "morals by agreement" is more consistent with a secular world view. People do not have inherent moral value. Indeed, there are no objective values. Values are simply subjective preferences of different individuals, and the "moral artifice" is a merely a convention which is mutually advantageous. We refrain from coercing or harming, not because people have inherent equal dignity, but because it is not mutually advantageous to do so.[14]

5. The Family Metaphor

Gregory Vlastos, in his celebrated article "Justice and Equality," [see Reading 36] appeals to the metaphor of a "loving family" to defend his egalitarianism. Vlastos has us imagine that we are visited by a Martian unfamiliar with our customs who asks us why we hold to the ideal of equal human rights. Vlastos replies, "Because the human worth of all persons is equal, however unequal may be their merit."[15]

> The moral community is not a club from which members may be dropped for delinquency. Our morality does not provide for moral outcasts or half-castes. It does provide for punishment. But this takes place within the moral community and under its rules. It is for this reason that, for example, one has no right to be cruel to a cruel person. His offence against the moral law has not put him outside the law. . . . The pain inflicted on him as punishment for his offence does not close out the reserve of goodwill on the part of all others which is his birthright as a human being; it is a limited withdrawal for it. . . . [The] only justification [of human rights is] the value which persons have simply because they are persons: their "intrinsic value as individual human beings," as Frankena calls it; the "infinite value" or the "sacredness" of their individuality, as others have called it.

Vlastos distinguishes gradable or meritorious traits from nongradable but valuable traits and says that talents, skills, character and personality belong to the gradable sort, but that our humanity is a nongradable value. Regarding human worth, all humans get equal grades. In this regard, human worth is like love. "Constancy of affection in the face of variations of merit is one of the surest tests of whether a parent does love a child." But the family metaphor, which is the closest Vlastos comes to providing an argument for his

position, needs further support. It is not obvious that all humans are related to each other as members of a family. If we're all brothers and sisters, who's the parent? By virtue of what property in human beings do we obtain value? Vlastos doesn't tell us. To the contrary, if we evolved from other animals, there is no more reason to think that we are siblings to all humans than to think that we are siblings to apes and gorillas.

Note that Vlastos offers as evidence for equal worth the fact that "no one has a right to be cruel to a cruel person." But surely these are not evidences for equality, for we shouldn't be cruel—without justification—to anyone, animal or human. Aristotle, certainly no egalitarian, regarded cruelty as a vice.

Nor does the gradable–nongradable distinction make a difference here. There are nongradable properties: all members of the set of books or cats may possess the nongradable property of being equally books or cats, but we can still grade members with respect to specific interests or standards and say from the point of view of aesthetic value some books and cats are better than others. Likewise, we may agree that all members of the species *Homo sapiens* equally are *Homo sapiens* but insist that within that type there are important differences which include differences in value. Some humans are highly moral, some moderately moral, and others immoral. Why not make the relevant metric morality rather than species-membership? The point is that Vlastos has not grounded his claim of *equal* worth, or any *worth* for that matter, and until he does, his idea of the family connection remains a mere metaphor.

Finally, one must wonder at the sacerdotal language used of human beings: "sacred," of "infinite value," "inviolability," and so forth. The religious tone is not accidental, but the lack of reference to religion is a serious omission.

Suppose one of Vlastos's Martians asks the egalitarian why he uses such language of mere animals. He invites Vlastos to consider Smith, a man of low morals and lower intelligence, who abuses his wife and children, who hates exercising and working, who prefers pushpin to Pushkin, and whose supreme joy it is to spend his days as a couch potato, drinking beer, while watching mud wrestling, violent sports, and soap operas on TV. He is an avid voyeur, devoted to child pornography. He is devoid of intellectual curiosity; eschews science, politics, and religion; and eats and drinks in a manner more befitting a pig than a person. Smith lacks wit, grace, humor, technical skill, ambition, courage, self-control, and wisdom. He is antisocial, morose, lazy; a freeloader who feels no guilt about living on welfare when he is perfectly able to work, has no social conscience, and barely avoids getting caught for his petty thievery. He has no talents, makes no social contribution, lacks a moral sense, and, from the perspective of the good of society, would be better off dead. But Smith is proud of one thing: that he is "sacred," of "infinite worth," of equal intrinsic value as Abraham Lincoln, Mother Teresa, Albert Schweitzer, the Dalai Lama, Jesus Christ, Mahatma Gandhi, and Albert Einstein. He is inviolable—and proud of it—despite any deficiency of merit. From the egalitarian perspective, despite appearances to the contrary, Smith is of equal intrinsic worth as the best citizen in his community. We could excuse the Martian if he exhibited amazement at this incredible doctrine.

6. The Pragmatic (or Useful Attitude) Argument

Joel Feinberg, who rejects Vlastos's essentialist position as unpromising, concedes that the notion of human worth is "not demonstrably justifiable." His support for the principle of equal human worth seems based on a combination of existential commitment and pragmatic concerns.

> "Human worth" itself is best understood to name no property in the way that "strength" names strength and "redness" names redness. In attributing human worth to everyone we may be ascribing no property or set of qualities, but rather expressing an attitude—the attitude of respect—towards the humanity in each man's person. That attitude follows naturally from regarding everyone from the "human point of view," but it is not grounded on anything more ultimate than itself, and it is not demonstrably justifiable.
>
> It can be argued further against the skeptics that a world with equal human rights is a *more just* world, a way of organizing society for which we would all opt if we were designing our institutions afresh in ignorance of the roles we might one day have to play in them. It is also a *less dangerous* world generally, and one with a *more elevated and civilized* tone. If none of this convinces the skeptic, we should turn our backs on him to examine more important problems.[16]

Feinberg may be correct in seeking to disentangle the concept of human worth from a property-view, but his position seems to have problems of its own. He needs to tell us *why* we should take the attitude of regarding everyone as equally worthy. What is this peculiar "human point of view" which supposedly grounds the notion of equal human worth? His pragmatic justification (i.e., that it will result in a less dangerous world and a more elevated and civilized tone) simply needs to be argued out, for it's not obvious that acting as if everyone were of equal worth would result in a less dangerous world than one in which we treated people according to some other criteria.

Feinberg's claim that a world with equal human rights based on equal worth "is a more just world" is simply question-begging, since it is exactly the notion of equal worth that is contested in the idea of justice. Formally, we are to treat equals equally and unequals unequally. Feinberg seems to be saying that justice consists in treating everyone as though they were equal whether or not they are.

But ignoring this and supposing that there were good utilitarian reasons to treat people as though they were of equal worth, we would still want to know whether we really were of equal worth. If the evidence is not forthcoming, then the thesis of equal worth will have all the earmarks of Plato's Noble Lie, ironically, asserting the very contrary of the original. Whereas for Plato the Noble Lie specified that we are to teach people that they are really unequal in order to produce social stability in an aristocratic society, in Feinberg's version of the Noble Lie we are to teach people that they are all equal in order to bring social stability to a democratic society.

Feinberg's final comment, "If none of this convinces the skeptic, we should turn our backs on him to examine more important problems," signals a flight from the battle, an admission that the Emperor has no clothes, for what could be more important than setting the foundations of sociopolitical philosophy?

7. The Utilitarian Argument for Human Equality

According to Jeremy Bentham, the founder of classical utilitarianism, "Each [is] to count as one and no one to count as more than one." This principle individuates persons (and sentient beings) as locuses of utility, and the Utility Principle enjoins us to take everyone's utility function into consideration in the process of producing the highest net utility possible. But if this is all that is said, the alleged egalitarianism is spurious, for it is the net utility that is aimed at, not equal distribution of welfare or resources (except perchance that such a distribution would actually coincide with maximal utility). My ten hedons (units of pleasure) count as much as yours, but what matters is the hedons, not you or I. While the initial measuring unit is the individual, the relevant goal is aggregative, ignoring any distribution pattern. If I can produce one hundred more hedons by inegalitarian distribution schemes than by egalitarian ones, I should use the inegalitarian ones.

Utilitarian egalitarians, such as R. M. Hare, respond that the doctrine of diminishing marginal utility leads to egalitarian distribution schemes, because with respect to many goods, including money, their utility diminishes at the margin.[17] For example, redistributing $10 from a millionaire to a hungry person will increase net utility, for the hungry person will be able to sustain his life by what is a mere trifle to the millionaire. The idea is that since people are relevantly similar, egalitarian redistribution of wealth will tend to maximize utility.

The interesting feature of utilitarianism is that it doesn't need a deep theory of human nature to promote its philosophy—all it needs is the thesis that humans are placeholders for hedons and dolors (units of suffering). So this may be a way to get around the problem of grounding the worth of the self in something metaphysical. But this is an illusion. First of all, utility functions apply as much to animals as to humans. If cats or rats get more pleasure than humans for $10 worth of food or an artificial stimulation machine, we should redistribute wealth in favor of animals. Of course, utilitarians like Peter Singer would accept such otherwise counterintuitive implications of their theory.

But, more important, the doctrine of diminishing marginal utility has severe restrictions. The utility of money or other good does not invariably diminish at the margin, and utility functions are not the same for all people. After a certain threshold point of subsistence needs, people's utility functions diverge radically. A monk needs far less than a corporate executive to meet his needs.

Furthermore, each unit of money (or whatever the good in question is) does not have the same function for each person. Some people, optimists and cheerful folk, are better converters of resources to utility than are pessimists and morose people. Some are Stoics who are able to handle adversity nobly and overcome it through resolute courage and wisdom. On the other hand, some people, grumpy, greedy, or masochistic, may misuse resources to enhance their suffering.

Finally, there is a synergistic effect which causes the unit that crosses the threshold to make the difference between great utility and little or none at all. Frankfurt illustrates this point.

Suppose that the cost of a serving of popcorn is the same as the cost of enough butter to make it delectable; and suppose that some rational consumer who adores buttered popcorn gets very little satisfaction from unbuttered popcorn, but that he nevertheless prefers it to butter alone. He will buy one and cannot buy both. Suppose now that this person's income increases so that he can buy the butter too. Then he can have something he enjoys enormously: his incremental income makes it possible for him not merely to buy butter in addition to popcorn, but to enjoy buttered popcorn. The satisfaction he will derive by combining the popcorn and the butter may well be considerably greater than the sum of the satisfactions he can derive from the two goods taken separately. Here again, is a threshold effect.[18] [See reading 39]

The Principle of Diminishing Marginal Utility is more a principle of utility than one of equality. Consider the following illustration from Frankfurt. Suppose ten people are starving and each one needs five units to survive. We have only 40 units of food. If we share it equally all will die, but if we distribute it unequally so that eight people get five units and two are left to die, we at least save eight people. Furthermore, suppose we have 41 units, the additional unit would not, on utilitarian grounds, go to one of the two who are dying, but to one of the surviving.

But there is an even deeper problem lurking in the background, and that is the problem of a justification of utility as the sole moral principle to guide our behavior. A problem arises when we apply the utilitarian calculus to competing interests. Suppose Aristotle needs slaves to do his manual labor so that he can carry on his philosophical contemplation. It is not in the slaves' interest to be slaves to Aristotle, but if we can maximize utility by subjugating the interests of the slaves to the interests of the whole group (treating the slaves kindly, of course), what becomes of the utilitarian's ideal of equal consideration of interests? Does he say to the slaves, "We considered your interests along with Aristotle's and the rest of society and concluded that on balance it's in all our interest that you stay slaves." Perhaps the same logic can be used to justify some of the harmful animal experiments that the utilitarian Peter Singer condemns in his book *Animal Liberation*. If this is so, it turns out that equal consideration of interests is simply a gloss for total utilitarian calculations in which individual rights are sacrificed for the good of the whole. We can still do the animal experiments if we anesthetize them first, so that they don't feel pain. But we may kill them and anyone else where net utility is expected.

Or suppose that I could create more utility by letting my children starve or go without books as I send my income to the starving people in Ethiopia or Bangladesh or West Virginia. I don't see any reason to follow utilitarian prescriptions here. If we don't find utilitarianism a compelling theory, we certainly won't be tempted to take the doctrine of diminishing marginal utility as an overriding principle—even if it did guarantee egalitarian results.

8. The Coherentist Argument

In an article titled "On Not Needing to Justify Equality," Kai Nielsen derives a defense of egalitarianism from John Rawls's and Norman Daniels's method of wide reflective equilibrium—a method which aims at providing a fit between our moral theory and particular moral judgments, which results in an overall coherent account of morality. Nielsen claims that the method can be used to show that the principle of equal human worth and equal treatment is justified as part of an overall coherent account of morality.[19]

If an egalitarianism rights theory is to succeed, my guess is that it will be a coherentist theory of the kind that Nielsen adumbrates. But, as things stand, there are two criticisms of Nielsen's argument. First, at best we have only a promissory note for a coherent secular system where equal worth plays a legitimate role. That is, no one has set forth a naturalistic account of morality where human worth, let alone equal human worth, doesn't have an unduly ad hoc appearance. Second, Coherentist justifications in general are subject to the criticism of not tying into reality. A Nazi world view, a religious fundamentalist theology, and Nielsen's Marxist egalitarianism, not to mention fairy tales, are all coherent and internally consistent; but no more than one of these mutually incompatible world views can be correct. Coherence is a necessary but not sufficient condition for justification. We want to know by which criteria we can distinguish between coherent theories. In scientific theory, building empirical observation and theoretical constraints do this sort of work. But it would seem that the empirical and theoretical data we have count against the notion of equal worth, so that the kind of justification needed for secular egalitarianism is wanting.

9. The Rational Agency Argument

The ninth attempt at getting a deeper argument for equal rights based on equal worth is found in the work of Alan Gewirth. In his book *Reason and Morality,* his essay "Epistemology of Human Rights," and elsewhere, Gewirth argues that we can infer equal human rights to freedom and well-being from the notion of rational agency.[20] A broad outline of the argument is as follows: Each rational agent must recognize that a measure of freedom and well-being is necessary for his or her exercise of rational agency. That is, each rational agent must will, if he is to will at all, that he possess that measure of freedom and well-being. Therefore anyone who holds that freedom and well-being are necessary for his exercise of rational agency is logically committed to holding that he has a prudential right to these goods. By the principle of universalizability we obtain the conclusion that all rational agents have a prima facie right to freedom and well-being.

But Gewirth's argument is invalid. From the premise that I need freedom and well-being in order to exercise my will nothing follows by itself concerning a right to freedom and well-being. From the fact that I assert a prudential right to some *x* does not give anyone else a sufficient reason to grant me that *x*.

But even if we can make sense of Gewirth's argument, this doesn't give us a notion of equal human worth, but merely minimal equal prima facie rights to freedom and well-being, which could be overridden for other reasons. Inegalitarians like Aristotle could accept this kind of equal right and argue that the prima facie right to minimal freedom of action should be overridden either when the actions are irrational or when a hierarchically structured society has need of slaves, in which case those who were best suited to this role would have their prima facie right to free action suitably constrained. In like manner, Utilitarians could accept Gewirthian equal prima facie rights and override them whenever greater utility was at stake. Gewirthian equal rights reduce to little more than recognizing that noninterference and well-being are values which we have a prima facie moral duty to promote whether in animals or angels, humans or Galacticans. They don't give us a set of thick natural rights.

Tom Nagel has set forth a version of Gewirth's Rational Agency Argument in his books *A View from Nowhere* and *Equality and Partiality* that may be more promising than Gewirth's own version in that it centers not on free action but on essential value viewed from an impersonal standpoint ("a view from nowhere").

> You cannot sustain an impersonal indifference to the things in your life which matter to you personally. . . . But since the impersonal standpoint does not single you out from anyone else, the same must be true of the value arising in other lives. If you matter impersonally, so does everyone. We can usefully think of the values that go into the construction of a political theory as being revealed in a series of four stages, each of which depends on a moral response to an issue posed by what was revealed at the previous stage. At the first stage, the basic insight that appears from the impersonal standpoint is that everyone's life matters, and no one is more important in virtue of [his] greater value for others. But at the baseline of value in the lives of individuals, from which all higher-order inequalities of value must derive, everyone counts the same. For a given quality of whatever it is that's good or bad—suffering or happiness or fulfillment or frustration—its intrinsic impersonal value doesn't depend on whose it is.[21]

The argument goes like this.

1. I cannot help but value myself as a subject of positive and negative experiences (e.g., suffering, happiness, fulfillment or frustration).
2. All other humans are relevantly similar to me, subjects of positive and negative experiences.
3. Therefore, I must, on pain of contradiction, ascribe equal value to all other human beings.

Although this looks more promising than Gewirth's argument, it too is defective. First of all, it is not necessary to value oneself primarily as a possessor of the capacity for positive and negative experiences. Why cannot I value myself because of a complex of specific properties—excellence of skill, ability to engage in complex deliberation, rationality, discipline and self-control, industriousness, high integrity, athletic ability, creative and artistic talent, or quickness of wit—without which I would not deem living worth the effort? I value myself more for actually *having* these properties than I do my *capacity* to suffer. These are what positively make up my happiness and give me a sense of worth—from the *impersonal* (i.e., impartial) point of view. If I were to lose any one of these properties, I, given my present identity, would value myself less than I do now. Should I lose enough of them my present self would view this future self as lacking pos-

itive value altogether, and my future self might well agree. Should I become immoral, insane, or desperately disease ridden, I would be valueless and I hope I would die as swiftly as possible. So it follows that I am under no obligation to value everyone, since not everyone is moral, rational, or healthy. There is no contradiction in failing to value the debauched Smith (section 5) or Rawls's blade-of-grass counter, the rapist or child molester, the retarded or the senile, since they lack the necessary qualities in question. Furthermore, I may value people *in degrees,* according to the extent that they exhibit the set of positive qualities.

So, letting these positive values be called "traits T," we need to revise the first premise to read: 1A. I cannot help but value myself as the possessor of a set of traits T.

But then 2 becomes false—all other human beings are *not* relevantly similar to me in this regard—so Nagel's conclusion does not follow. I do not contradict myself in failing to value people who lack the relevant qualities.

There is a second problem with Nagel's argument. It rests too heavily on the agent's judgment about himself. "If you matter impersonally, so does everyone." There are two ways to invalidate this conditional. The conditional won't go through if you don't value yourself. If I am sick of life and believe that I don't matter, then, on Nagel's premises, I have no reason to value anyone else. Second, I may deny the consequent and thereby reject the antecedent. I may come to believe that no one else does matter and then be forced to acknowledge that I don't matter either. We're all equal—equally worthless. If reflection has any force, Nagel's first premise (i.e., I cannot help but value myself as a subject of positive and negative experiences) seems false. People cease to value themselves when they lose the things which give life meaning.

Third, note the consequentialist tone of the last two sentences of Nagel's statement: "at the baseline of value in the lives of individuals, from which all higher-order inequalities of value must derive, everyone counts the same. For a given quantity of whatever it is that's good or bad—suffering or happiness or fulfillment or frustration—its intrinsic impersonal value doesn't depend on whose it is." We hear the echo of Bentham's "each one to count for one and no one for more than one" in this passage. But Nagel, like Bentham before him, cannot both be a maximizer *and* an egalitarian. If it is *happiness* that really is the good to be maximized or *suffering* to be minimized, then individuals are mere placeholders for these qualities, so that if we can maximize happiness (or minimize suffering) by subordinating some individuals to others, we should do so. If *A* can derive ten hedons by eliminating *B* and *C,* who together can obtain only eight hedons, it would be a good thing for *A* to kill *B* and *C*. If it turns out that a pig satisfied really is happier than Socrates dissatisfied, then we ought to value the pig's life more than Socrates', and if a lot of people are miserable and are making others miserable, we would improve the total happiness of the world by killing them.

I for one confess that I don't care whether cats thrive more than mice or whether all cats are equally prosperous. No one I know cares about this either. But from Nagel's impersonal "View from Nowhere," shouldn't we care as much about them, since cats and mice are subjects to positive and negative experiences—pleasures and suffering? How, on Nagel's premises, are humans—themselves animal—intrinsically better than cats and mice? I can appreciate it if a religious person responds that humans are endowed with the image of God, but Nagel, not being religious, can't use that response. Why should I care that all humans are equally happy anymore than I care whether all cats or mice are equally happy and as equally happy as humans? If the question is absurd, I'd like to know why. Do not misunderstand me, I don't want to harm anyone without moral justification, but I don't see any moral reason to treat all humans, let alone all animals, with equal respect.

10. The Argument from Moral Personality

No exposition of egalitarianism has had a greater influence on our generation than John Rawls's *A Theory of Justice,* which Robert Nisbet has called "the long awaited successor to Rousseau's *Social Contract . . .* the Rock on which the Church of Equality can properly be founded in our time."[22] Rawls sets forth a hypothetical contract theory in which the bargainers go behind a veil of ignorance in order to devise a set of fundamental agreements that are fair.

> First of all no one knows his place in society, his class position or social status; nor does he know his fortune in the distribution of natural assets and abilities, his intelligence and the like. Nor, again, does anyone know his conception of the good, the particulars of his rational plan of life, or even the special features of his psychology such as his aversion to risk or liability to optimism or pessimism.

More than this, I assume that the parties do not know the particular circumstances of their own society. That is, they do not know its economic or political situation, or the level of civilization and culture it has been able to achieve. The persons in the original position have no information as to which generation they belong. [See Reading 26.]

By denying individuals knowledge of their natural assets and social position Rawls prevents them from exploiting their advantages, thus transforming a decision under risk (where probabilities of outcomes are known) to a decision under uncertainty (where probabilities are not known). To the question, Why should the individual acknowledge the principles chosen as morally binding? Rawls would answer, "We should abide by these principles because we all chose them under fair conditions." That is, the rules and rights chosen by fair procedures are themselves fair, since these procedures take full account of our moral nature as equally capable of "doing justice." The two principles that would be chosen, Rawls argues, are (1) everyone will have an equal right to equal basic liberties, and (2) social and economic inequalities must satisfy two conditions: (a) they are to attach to positions open to all under conditions of fair equality of opportunity, and (b) they must serve the greatest advantage of the least advantaged members of society (the Difference Principle).

Michael Sandel has criticized Rawls's project as lacking a notion of intrinsic worth. "Rawls' principles do not mention moral desert because, strictly speaking, no one can be said to deserve anything. . . . On Rawls' view *people have no intrinsic worth,* [emphasis added] no worth that is intrinsic in the sense that it is theirs prior to or independent of . . . what just institutions attribute to them."[23]

Although Rawls sometimes lays himself open to this kind of charge, I think that Sandel is wrong here. What grounds Rawls's social contract is a Kantian humanism.

> Each person possesses an inviolability founded on justice that even the welfare of society as a whole cannot override. For this reason justice denies that the loss of freedom for some is made right by a greater good shared by others. It does not allow that the sacrifices imposed on a few are outweighed by the larger sum of advantages enjoyed by the many. Therefore, in a just society the liberties of equal citizenship are taken as settled; the rights secured by justice are not subject to political bargaining or the calculus of social interests.

At the center of Rawls's project is a respect for the individual as "inviolable," sacred, whose essential rights are inalienable. In Section 77 of *A Theory of Justice* this inviolability is grounded in our having "the capacity for moral personality," that is, the ability to enter into moral deliberation. "It is precisely the moral persons who are entitled to equal justice. Moral persons are distinguished by two features: first they are capable of having . . . a conception of the good; and second they are capable of having . . . a sense of justice. . . . One should observe that moral personality is here defined as a potentiality that is ordinarily realized in due course. It is this potentiality which brings the claims of justice into play."[24]

Members in the original position are not mere utilitarian containers of the good but Kantian "ends in themselves," who are worthy of "equal concern and respect." Rawls presupposes equal and positive worth at the very beginning of his project. The question is, Is this presupposition reasonable? Is Rawls's egalitarian starting point justified? I think not. Given the framework in which Rawls writes, there is no reason to suppose that we have intrinsic and equal value. Let me explain.

A standard criticism of *A Theory of Justice* is that it fails to take into account the conservative who, as would a gambler, would rather take his chances on a meritocratic or hierarchical society and so reject part or all of Rawls's second principle. I think that this objection is even stronger than has been made out, for it is not simply because the conservative is like a *gambler* that he will self-interestedly choose meritocracy, but rather because he deems it the essence of justice.

This point becomes highlighted when we examine Rawls's *threshold* principle. "Once a certain minimum is met, a person is entitled to equal liberty on a par with everyone else." This move seems ad hoc. There is no obvious reason why we should opt for tacit equal status (let alone inviolability) rather than an Aristotelian hierarchical structure based on differential ability to reason or deliberate. Even as some life plans are objectively better than others, so some people might well be considered worthier than others and treated accordingly.

Why would it be wrong to weight the votes behind the veil of ignorance according to criteria of assessment? For example, the deeply reflective with low time preferences would be given more votes than the less reflective with high time preferences. Those with high grades might get four or five votes, whereas the minimally reflective might get only one vote. Why have only one threshold between those who pass and those who fail the rationality test, as Rawls proposes? Why not have five or six thresholds?

With different layers of weighted votes one would still expect a benevolent society, but the difference principle might well be replaced by Harsanyi's average utility principle[25] or Frankfurt's sufficiency principle [see Reading 37], permitting hierarchical arrangements. Rawls's first principle (maximum liberty) and the first half of the second principle (equal opportunity) would very likely result in a hierarchical, elitist society.

Normally we think that each person has a right—based on freedom and moral worth (the very principles Rawls embraces)—to develop his or her capacities and talents and to extend his or her goals higher and higher. Suppose that I love to travel for both enjoyment and educational purposes. I use the knowledge I receive for education purposes, including writing books, for which I receive generous royalties. Even though I give more than average to charity, I still end up with vastly more wealth than the average person, and thus am enabled to buy more books, do more traveling, and enjoy the good things of life several times that of the average person. Presumably, I am violating the Equality Principle of having only as much of available resources (or welfare) as the average person. But this seems counterintuitive. In economics, the Pareto Principle of Optimality prescribes that an agent should maximize his own welfare so long as no one is thereby made (unjustly) worse off. Either the Pareto Principle is illegitimate and we are not allowed to advance our interests while others have less or the Equality Principle is mistaken and we may advance our interests even when it brings us to a position where we are far better off than others.

But we may go even further than the Pareto Principle. Even if my fulfilling my goals leaves others worse off, that still may not be wrong. Drawing on an illustration from Nozick, suppose that my marrying the most beautiful woman in my community leaves twenty rival suitors is abject despair, on the brink of suicide. Even though each of them is worse off, I am justified in using my superior talents to win my beloved and thus end up in a far better position than my despairing rivals. The situation is unequal, but not unjust.

What would Rawls say to these criticisms? Why does he hold on to a principle of equal intrinsic worth? The closest Rawls comes to addressing this question gets us back to his self-respect argument, discussed in section 8. Self-respect, according to Rawls, is a fundamental human need which his theory satisfies and which hierarchical arrangements fail to satisfy. But we have already seen that this answer is severely problematic. It is noteworthy that these matters are not addressed in one of Rawls's later books, *Political Liberalism.*

Counterevidence to Egalitarianism: The Empirical Consideration

Contrary to egalitarian claims, there is good reason to believe that humans are not of equal worth. Given empirical observation, it is hard to believe that humans are equal in any way at all. We all seem to have vastly different levels of abilities. Some, like Aristotle, Newton, Shakespeare, and Einstein are very intelligent; others are imbeciles and idiots. Some are wise like Socrates and Abraham Lincoln; others are very foolish. Some have great foresight and are able to defer gratification, while others can hardly assess their present circumstances, gamble away their future, succumb to immediate gratification, and generally go through life as through a fog. From the perspective of the moral point of view, it looks as if Einstein, Gandhi, and Mother Teresa have more value than Jack the Ripper and Adolf Hitler. If a research scientist with the cure for cancer is on the same raft with an ordinary person, there is no doubt about whom should be saved on the basis of functional value.

Take any capacity or ability you like—reason, a good will, the capacity to suffer, the ability to deliberate and choose freely, the ability to make moral decisions and carry them out, self-control, sense of humor, health, athletic or artistic ability—and it seems that humans (not to mention animals) differ in the degree to which they have those capacities and abilities.

Furthermore, given the purely secular version of the theory of evolution, there doesn't seem to be any reason to believe that the family metaphor, supposed by philosophers like Vlastos and the drafters of the United Nations' Declaration on Human Rights, has much evidence in its favor. If we're simply a product of blind evolutionary chance and necessity, it is hard to see where the family connection comes in. Who is the parent? In fact, given a naturalistic account of the origins of *Homo sapiens,* it is hard to see that humans have intrinsic value at all. If we are simply physicalist constructions, where does intrinsic value emerge?

Of course, most, if not all, of the egalitarians discussed above recognize this empirical consideration. The point is that the empirical problem seems to place its own burden of proof on any theory that would claim

that equal rights are based on equal human worth. As far as I can see, not one has countered the presumption of inequality.

PART II. THE METAPHYSICAL ORIGINS OF THE IDEA OF EQUAL WORTH: OUR JUDEO-CHRISTIAN TRADITION

The doctrine that all people are of equal worth, and thus endowed with inalienable rights, is rooted in our religious heritage. The language of human dignity and worth implies a great family in which a benevolent and sovereign Father binds together all his children in love and justice. The originators of rights language presupposed a theistic world view, and secular advocates of equal rights are, to cite Tolstoy, like children who see beautiful flowers, grab them, break them at their stems, and try to transplant them without their roots. The egalitarian assertions of the *United Nations' Universal Declaration of Human Rights* are similar to those of our *Declaration of Independence* with one important difference—God is left out of the former; but that makes all the difference. The posit of God (or some metaphysical idea which will support equal and positive worth) is not just an ugly appendage or a pious afterthought but a root necessary for the bloom of rights.

Although the thesis of equal human worth may not have been clearly recognized, let alone embraced, by ancient Israel or in all Jewish and Christian quarters, the Jewish prophetic tradition and much of the Christian tradition support it. In such texts as the first three chapters of Genesis, which speak of God's creating man and woman in His image, as "good"; in Malachi 2:10, where the prophet writes, "Have we not all one Father? Has not one God created us? Why then are we faithless to one another?"; and in Psalms 8:3–6, where the psalmist asks, "When I look at thy heavens, the work of thy fingers, the moon and the stars which thou has established: What is man that thou are mindful of him, or the son of man that thou does care for him?" and answers his own question, "Thou hast made him a little less than God, and dost crown him with glory and honor. Thou has given him dominion over the works of thy hands; thou has put all things under his feet." The prophets Amos, Micah, and Isaiah speak of God's concern as being universal and of a coming universal kingdom wherein all people will enjoy peace and prosperity.[26]

In the New Testament and in the early Christian church there are strains which point to the thesis that all humans are loved equally by God and are equally accountable to him for their actions. The moral law is revealed to each person, so that each will be judged according to his or her moral merit (Romans 2). Still, even the sinner is of incalculable worth; like a corroded and distorted coin of the royal mint, he or she still bears the King's image.

Of course, in itself theism is no guarantee of equal worth, for God could have created people unequal. The argument implicit in the Judeo-Christian tradition seems to be that God is the ultimate value and that humans derive their value by having been created in his image and likeness. To paraphrase the psalmist, we are a little lower than God, mini-gods, the Hebrew seems to suggest. With regard to possessing intrinsic value we all get equal grades.

There are two arguments for equal human worth which I find implicit in the Judeo-Christian tradition: the Essentialist Argument and the Argument from Grace. The Essentialist Argument goes like this: God created all humans with an equal amount of some property P, which constitutes high value. The property may be a natural or a nonnatural one. If it is a natural property, then conceivably we could discover it and act upon it without needing God to reveal it. If it is a nonnatural property, the only reason to suppose that we possess it is that our theory says we do. The fact that we cannot identify it constitutes some evidence against the theory itself, but if there are good reasons to accept the theory as a whole, one might be content to live humbly with this mystery. Since no empirical quality is had by all humans in the same quantity, the naturalistic picture seems foreclosed and the nonnatural one wins by default.

The second argument which I find in the Judeo-Christian tradition is the Argument from Grace. Strictly speaking it is not an egalitarian argument, if egalitarianism means that all persons have equal intrinsic worth. Here the actual value may be different in different people, but grace compensates the differences. It raises the worst off until they are equal with the best off. The Argument from Grace often makes use of the family metaphor, such as we find in Vlastos's work—only in this case the family has a parent. God is the Heavenly Father, and we are all family, brothers and sisters to one another. As our Father, God loves us each equally and unconditionally and wants us, his children, to love each other. Each person does matter and matter equally, not because of some innate property but simply by virtue of God's gracious love.

The meaning of the Sermon on the Mount, with its prescriptions to love even one's enemies, of the Parable of the Good Samaritan, which enjoins us to recognize people of despised groups as capable of moral grandeur, of the Parable of the Prodigal Son, which teaches us to forgive and restore lost causes, is that God's grace triumphs over human difference, both moral and nonmoral, and raises each of us to an equal pinnacle of sanctity and dignity.

The Argument from Grace is a version of the divine command theory of ethics, though it does not entail reducing all morality to divine commands. Some moral duties may be based on human nature, while the duty to equal concern for the welfare of all persons may be a product of God's command. That is, morality may be a combination of divine commands and rational discoveries.

These two arguments can stand separately or together in making a case for the thesis of equal human rights based on equal human worth. That is, it is the God-relationship that provides the metaphysical basis for this thesis, whether the equality comes in at creation or whether it is due to grace.

Of course, I do not mean to imply that the Judeo-Christian tradition is the only logical basis for a doctrine of equal worth. I am simply pointing to the historical origins of our perspective. One could opt for a Stoic pantheism which maintains that all humans have within them a part of God, the *logos spermatikos* (the divinely rational seed). We are all part of God, chips off the old divine block, as it were. Other religious traditions, such as the Islamic and Hindu, also have a notion of the divine origins and high worth of humanity. Perhaps a version of a Platonic system could do the trick as well.

The possibilities are frighteningly innumerable. My point is that you need some metaphysical explanation to ground the doctrine of equal worth, if it is to serve as a basis for equal human rights. It is not enough simply to assert, as philosophers like Dworkin do, that their egalitarian doctrines are "metaphysically unambitious." But, of course, there are severe epistemological difficulties with the kinds of metaphysical systems I have been discussing. My point has not been to defend religion. For purposes of this paper I am neutral on the question of whether any religion is true. Rather, my purpose is to show that we can't burn our bridges and still drive Mack trucks over them. But, if we can't return to religion, then it would seem perhaps we should abandon egalitarianism and devise political philosophies that reflect naturalistic assumptions, theories which are forthright in viewing humans as differentially talented animals who must get on together.

CONCLUSION

Secular egalitarian arguments for equal rights seem, at best, to be based on a posit of faith that all humans are of equal worth or that it is useful to regard them as such. They have not offered plausible reasons for their thesis, and, given the empirical consideration, inegalitarianism seems plausible. If my analysis of the subject is confirmed by fuller arguments, then there are only two choices for egalitarians and the rest of us: either secular inegalitarian moral political systems or religious (or comparable metaphysical) systems.

I have suggested that secular egalitarians have inherited a notion of inviolability or intrinsic human worth from a religious tradition which they no longer espouse. The question is whether the kind of democratic ideals that egalitarians espouse can do without a religious tradition. If they cannot, then egalitarians may be living off the borrowed interest of a religious metaphysic, which (in their eyes) has gone bankrupt. The question is: Where's the capital?

ACKNOWLEDGMENTS

I am indebted to Richard Arneson, Robert Audi, Donald Blackeley, Mane Hajdin, Tziporah Kasachkoff, Michael Levin, Paul Pojman, Steven Ross, William Rowe, Peter Simpson, and Robert Westmoreland for comments on previous versions of this paper.

READING 39
Liberty versus Equal Opportunity

James Fishkin

James Fishkin is Professor of Political science at the University of Texas and the author of several works in political philosophy.

In this interesting criticism of equal opportunity, Fishkin, drawing on examples such as the warrior class, argues that there is something contradictory about the notion of equal opportunity—at least in the form in which it is held by many contemporary liberals. For liberals seem to want three things in their policies: (1) positions assigned by merit in fair competition; (2) equal life chances for all citizens; and (3) family autonomy. Fishkin describes these ideals

(1) *Equality of Life Chances:* The prospects of children for eventual positions in the society should not vary in any systematic and significant manner with their arbitrary native characteristics.
(2) *Merit:* There should be widespread procedural fairness in the evaluation of qualifications for positions.
(3) *The Autonomy of the Family:* Consensual relations within a given family governing the development of its children should not be coercively interfered with except to ensure for the children the essential prerequisites for adult participation in the society.

and then argues that given the reality of unequal abilities in individuals and unequal conditions in families, a trilemma obtains. We can satisfy two but not all three of these principles. Suppose we aim at providing children with equal life chances and also decide to distribute positions by merit. Since children receive unequal benefits in families, we will have to abolish the family in order to realize this sort of equal opportunity. We would have to devise a system of collectivized child rearing similar to that described in Plato's *Republic* in order to offset the differential investments of families in their children.

According to Fishkin, this option will seem morally unacceptable to most of us. We look upon the family as one of those institutions necessary for human flourishing. We should be allowed to invest our resources in children, and the State should not penalize us for doing so.

Suppose you decide to limit your family to two children and invest all your resources into their education, and suppose your neighbors choose to have ten children and provide only minimal resources for them, spending their money on boats or gambling. If our theory of psychological development is correct and the early years make enormous differences in child development, there is no way that the State can make up the difference in life chances between the two sets of children. Short of abolishing the family or the practice of rewarding positions by merit, unequal life chances will result.

This reading is taken from "Liberty vs Equal Opportunity," *Social Philosophy & Policy* 5:1 (1978) 32–48, © Blackwell Publishers, Ltd.

1. INTRODUCTION

Liberalism has often been viewed as a continuing dialogue about the relative priorities between liberty and equality. When the version of equality under discussion requires equalization of outcomes, it is easy to see how the two ideals might conflict. But when the version of equality requires only equalization of opportunities, the conflict has been treated as greatly muted since the principle of equality seems so meager in its implications. However, when one looks carefully at various versions of equal opportunity and various versions of liberty, the conflict between them is, in fact, both dramatic and inescapable. Each version of the conflict poses hard choices which defy any *systematic* pattern granting priority to one of these basic values over the

other. In this essay, I will flesh out and argue for this picture of fundamental conflict, and then turn to some more general issues about the kinds of answers we should expect to the basic questions of liberal theory.

I will explore the conflicts between liberty and equal opportunity by focusing on three positions, each of which can be considered in terms of its corresponding account of liberty and equal opportunity. Charts 1 and 2 below illustrate the relation among these concepts. I will term the three positions Laissez Faire, Meritocracy, and Strong Equality. While these labels are in some respects arbitrary, the positions they represent will turn out, I believe, to be familiar ones even though they travel under various banners.

2. LAISSEZ-FAIRE

A good recent example of the laissez-faire position is the one Nozick takes in *Anarchy, State, and Utopia*. One of the more provocative examples in the book compares decisions to marry with decisions by prospective employers and employees:

> Suppose there are twenty-six women and twenty-six men each wanting to be married. For each sex, all of that sex agree on the same ranking of the twenty-six members of the opposite sex in terms of desirability as marriage partners: call them A to Z and A' to Z' respectively in decreasing preferential order. A and A' voluntarily choose to get married. . . . When B and B' marry, their choices are not made nonvoluntary merely by the fact that there is something else they each would rather do. . . . This contraction of the range of options continues down the line until we come to Z and Z', who each face a choice between marrying the other or remaining unmarried.

CHART 1: Notions of Negative Liberty

Bench mark for Harm includes:	Laissez-Faire	Meritocracy	Strong Equality
Lockean Rights	+	+	+
Right to Equal Consideration in Job Market	−	+	+
Right to Conditions for an Equal Life Chance	−	−	+

CHART 2: Notions of Equal Opportunity

Negative Liberty:	Laissez-Faire	Meritocracy	Strong Equality
Unfettered in Private Sphere	+	+	−
Unfettered in Public Sphere	+	−	−

Nozick explicitly develops his account of liberty in market exchanges on analogy with these mating decisions:

> Similar considerations apply to market exchanges between workers and owners of capital. Z is faced with working or starving; the choices and actions of all other persons do not add up to providing Z with some other options. . . . Does Z choose to work voluntarily? . . . Z does choose voluntarily if the other individuals A through Y each acted voluntarily and within their rights.

In both the market and the mating cases, "A person's choice among differing degrees of unpalatable alternatives is not rendered nonvoluntary by the fact that others voluntarily chose and acted within their rights in a way that did not provide him with a more palatable alternative." Others acting within their rights cannot, on this view, do me harm. If we think of harm in the core negative-liberty sense of people individually or collectively being able to do as they please so long as they do not harm or violate the rights of others (with rights violations being construed as harms for these purposes), then one can easily subsume both the right to marry and the right to get a job within the same conception of liberty and the same conception of justice. Nozick's slogan "From each as they choose, to each as they are chosen" works perfectly for the selection of mates under modern conditions. Nozick's extension of it to the market means only that the welfare state and other redistributive devices seem objectionable because they would prohibit capitalist acts between consenting adults.

Because A and A′ are fully within their rights to marry, we do not think of their action as harming B and B′ even though it does, obviously, limit their options. So far, the analogy between mating and employment retains some plausibility. However, there is also a crucial disanalogy, at least from the perspective of any advocate of equal opportunity.

In modern, secular, Western moral culture, we commonly think that members of the same ethnic group, race, or religion can, *if they choose,* select mates only from the same ethnic group, race, or religion. In fact, we commonly think they can marry more or less whomever they like. Those who would like to marry others who are similar in those respects are fully within their rights to do so; those who have other views are free to follow them as well.

In the job market, by contrast, if employers hire only members of the same ethnic group, race, or reli-

gion, we commonly view that not as an exercise of liberty but, rather, as an act of blatant discrimination. The laissez-faire view includes Lockean rights but not the right to equal consideration in the job market within the bench mark for relevant harms (see Chart 1). Another way of making this point is to say that negative liberty is completely unfettered in both the private and public spheres on the laissez-faire view (completely unfettered in that so long as no one is harmed in the relevant sense, people may do as they please in both areas). Nozick's analogy between the distribution of mates and that of jobs (or, more generally, of goods) is exemplified by the two pluses in the laissez-faire column in Chart 2. The two spheres are treated in the same way. But treating them in the same way trivializes equal opportunity in the job market because it eliminates any basis for complaints against discrimination and sheer arbitrariness. For this reason, the bench mark on harm compatible with meritocratic notions of equal opportunity can be thought of as the same as the laissez-faire notion—except for the incorporation of an additional right defining relevant harms, the right to equal consideration of one's qualifications in the job market.

Now it might be argued in defense of the laissez-faire view that rational employers will not discriminate; they will not hire less "qualified" people merely on the basis of irrelevant factors such as race, ethnicity, or religion. They will not do so because it will cost them something in terms of efficiency, productivity, or the like. There are two replies worth noting briefly. First, the rational behavior of economic actors is a theoretical idealization which some firms and some people approximate under some conditions, but fall far short of in others. There is no reason to assume that departures from rationality of this sort will not occur. Furthermore, within the laissez-faire theory, these actors are within their rights to be irrational, just as any prospective couple about to make an unwise decision to marry would also be within its rights to be irrational. (If, say, they were on any objective assessment really incompatible, they would still be within their rights to get married if they wished to do so.)

Second, statistical discrimination will, in fact, be rational for economic actors under some conditions. If members of a given group generally perform badly, then firms may decide to forgo the decision costs of individual evaluation and substitute group membership as a fairly reliable proxy for whatever individual factors they would have tested. If they do, they will be right most of the time, but at the cost of some serious injustices (in the meritocratic sense) to some individuals. Discrimination can be economically rational. The self-interest of economic actors is not sufficient protection if nondiscrimination is an important goal.

3. MERITOCRACY

The second position in Charts 1 and 2, meritocracy, is designed to rule out discrimination. Roughly, this position entails that there should be widespread procedural fairness in the evaluation of qualifications for positions. Qualifications must be job-relevant for the positions to be filled, and they must represent actual efforts of the individual, not merely group membership (shared, arbitrary native characteristics).

On the meritocratic position, an additional right has been added to the standard Lockean rights for determining the bench mark for harm. If I am discriminated against, then I am harmed in the sense that my right to equal consideration of my qualifications has been violated. This addition represents a sharp departure from the kind of negative liberty we presume in the private sphere. If Jane prefers John to Joseph as a mate, Joseph does not have grounds for complaint that his qualifications were not given equal consideration. Jane's preference is decisive, regardless of her reasons. But if Company X prefers John to Joseph as an employee, Joseph would have grounds for complaint if he could show that, because of his race or religion, a less qualified person (John) was hired instead. Under meritocracy, negative liberty is not unfettered in the public sphere as it is in the private, while under laissez-faire, the two spheres are treated in the same way (see Chart 2).

4. STRONG EQUALITY

From the standpoint of advocates of strong equality, meritocracy does not go far enough. I believe its limitations are nicely captured by an example which I adopt from Bernard Williams. Imagine a warrior society, one which, from generation to generation, has been dominated by a warrior class. At some point, advocates of equal opportunity are granted a reform. From now on, new membership in the warrior class will be determined by a competition which tests warrior skills. A procedurally fair competition is instituted, but the children of the present warriors triumph overwhelmingly. To make it simple, let us assume that children from the other classes are virtually on the verge of starvation, and children from the warrior class have been exceedingly well nourished. Hence, in the warrior's competition we might imagine three hundred–pound Sumo wrestlers vanquishing ninety-pound weaklings. While this competition is procedurally fair in that, we will assume, it really does select the best warriors, it does not embody an adequate ideal of equal opportunity. The Sumo wrestlers have been permitted to develop their talents under such favorable conditions, while the weaklings have developed theirs under such unfavorable conditions, that measuring the results of such overwhelmingly predictable (and manipulable) causal processes does not represent an equal opportunity for the less advantaged to compete. The causal conditions under which they prepare for the competition deny them an effective opportunity. This criticism holds despite the fact that, on meritocratic grounds, the competition may operate perfectly so as to select the best warriors—as those warriors have developed under such unequal conditions.

A principle which captures the injustice embodied in the warrior society is the criterion of equal life chances. According to this principle, I should not be able to enter a hospital ward of newborn infants and predict what strata they will eventually reach merely on the basis of their arbitrary native characteristics such as race, sex, ethnic origin, or family background. To the extent that I can reliably make such predictions about a society, it is subject to a serious kind of inequality of opportunity. Obviously, inequality of life chances would be compatible with strictly meritocratic assignment. The warrior society scenario, where family background perfectly predicts success in the competition, illustrates how one sort of equal opportunity is entirely separable from the other. By contrast, the position I label "Strong Equality" in Charts 1 and 2 is committed to both forms—meritocratic assignment and, in addition, equality of life chances.[1]

The difficulty with strong equality is that it is only realizable at an even more severe cost in liberty than that required for meritocracy. A clue as to the issues at stake can be found in the restriction of negative liberty by strong equality, not only in the public sphere but also in the private sphere (the two minuses in the last column in Chart 2). The liberty at stake in the private sphere turns out to be the autonomy of the family—the liberty of families, acting consensually, to benefit their children.

5. THE TRILEMMA

When family autonomy is combined with the two demanding components of equal opportunity considered thus far—meritocratic assignment and equal life chances—a pattern of conflicting and difficult choices emerges, a kind of dilemma with three corners which I term a "trilemma." It is a trilemma because realization of any two of these principles can realistically be expected to preclude the third. This pattern of conflict applies even under the most optimistic scenarios of ideal theory. If equal opportunity is to provide a coherent ideal which we should aspire to implement, then certain hard choices need to be faced. The options in this trilemma are pictured in Chart 3.

CHART 3: Options in the Trilemma

	Meritocracy	Reverse Discrimination	Strong Equality
Merit	+	−	+
Equal Life Chances	−	+	+
Family Autonomy	+	+	−

The trilemma of equal opportunity can be sketched quickly. Let us assume favorable and realistic conditions—only moderate scarcity, and good faith efforts at strict compliance with the principles we propose (both in the present and in the relevant recent past). However, to be realistic, let us also assume background conditions of inequality, both social and economic. The issue of equal opportunity—the rationing of chances for favored positions—would be beside the point if there were no favored positions, i.e., if there were strict equality of result throughout the society. Every modern developed country, whether capitalist or socialist, has substantially unequal payoffs to positions. The issue of equal opportunity within liberal theory is *how* people get assigned to those positions—by which I mean both their *prospects* for assignment and the *method* of assignment (whether, for example, meritocratic procedures are employed guaranteeing equal consideration of relevant claims).

The trilemma consists in a forced choice among three principles.

Merit: There should be widespread procedural fairness in the evaluation of qualifications[2] for positions.

Equality of Life Chances: The prospects of children for eventual positions in the society should not vary in any systematic and significant manner with their arbitrary native characteristics.[3]

The Autonomy of the Family: Consensual relations within a given family governing the development of its children should not be coercively interfered with except to ensure for the children the essential prerequisites for adult participation in the society.[4]

Given background conditions of inequality, implementing any two of these principles can reasonably be expected to preclude the third. For example, implementing the first and third undermines the second. The autonomy of the family protects the process whereby advantaged families differentially contribute to the development of their children. Given background conditions of inequality, children from the higher strata will have been systematically subjected to developmental opportunities which can reliably be expected to give them an advantage in the process of meritocratic competition. Under these conditions, the principle of merit—applied to talents as they have developed under such unequal conditions—becomes a mechanism for generating unequal life chances. Hence, the difficulty with the meritocratic option in Chart 3 is the denial of equal life chances.

Suppose one were to keep the autonomy of the family in place but attempt to equalize life chances. Fulfilling the second and third principles would require sacrifice of the first. Given background conditions of inequality, the differential developmental influences just mentioned will produce disproportionate talents and other qualifications among children in the higher strata. If they must be assigned to positions so as to equalize life chances, then they must be assigned regardless of these differential claims. Some process of "reverse discrimination" in favor of those from disadvantaged backgrounds would have to be applied systematically throughout the society if life chances were to be equalized (while also maintaining family autonomy). Hence, the difficulty with the second option in Chart 3, which I have labeled reverse discrimination, is the cost in merit.

Suppose one were to attempt to equalize life chances while maintaining the system of meritocratic assignment. Given background conditions of inequality, it is the autonomy of families that protects the process by which advantaged families differentially influence the development of talents and other qualifications in their children. Only if this process were interfered with in a systematic manner could both the principles of merit and of equal life chances be achieved. Perhaps a massive system of collectivized child rearing could be devised. Or perhaps a compulsory schooling system could be devised so as to even out home-inspired developmental advantages and prevent families from making any *differential* investments in human capital in their children, either through formal or informal processes. In any case, achieving both merit and equal life chances would require a systematic sacrifice in family autonomy. Hence, the difficulty with the third scenario, the strong equality position in Chart 3, is the sacrifice in family autonomy.

Implementation of any two of these principles precludes the third. While inevitable conflicts might be tolerated by systematic theorists in the nonideal world, these conflicts arise within ideal theory. This argument is directed at the aspiration to develop a rigorous solution even if it is limited to the ideal theory case. Given only moderate scarcity and strict compliance with the principles chosen, and given that there is no aftermath of injustice from the immediate past, we are applying these principles in our thought experiment to the best conditions that could realistically be imagined for a modern, large-scale society.

Of course, liberalism has long been regarded as an amalgam of liberty and equality. And liberals and libertarians have long been fearful of the sacrifices in liberty that would be required to achieve equality of result. Equality of opportunity, by contrast, has been regarded as a weakly reformist, tame principle which avoids such disturbing conflicts. However, even under the best conditions, it raises stark conflicts with the one area of liberty which touches most of our lives most directly. Once we take account of the family, equal opportunity is an extraordinarily radical principle, and achieving it would require sacrifices in liberty which most of us would regard as grossly illiberal.

The force of the trilemma argument depends on there being independent support for each of the principles. Merit makes a claim to procedural fairness. However, as Brian Barry has argued, procedural fairness is a thin value without what he calls "background fairness," and background fairness would be achieved by equality of life chances. Family autonomy can be rationalized within a broader private sphere of liberty; it protects the liberty of families, acting consensually, to benefit their children through developmental influences. The principle leaves plenty of room for the state to intervene when some sacrifice in the essential interests of the child is in question or when consensual re-

lations within the family have broken down (raising issues of child placement or children's rights). Without the core area of liberty defined by this narrow principle, the family would be unrecognizably different.

Hence, these principles are not demanding by themselves; they are demanding in combination. Each of the trilemma scenarios which fully implements two of the principles leads to drastic sacrifice of the third. To blithely assume that we can realize all three is to produce an incoherent scenario for equal opportunity, even under ideal conditions.

One reasonable, but unsystematic response to this pattern of conflict would be to trade off small increments of each principle without full realization of any. But this is to live without a systematic solution. The aspiration fueling the reconstruction of liberal theory has been that some single solution in clear focus can be defined for ideal conditions, and then policy can be organized so as to approach this vision asymptotically. But if trade-offs are inevitable, even for ideal theory, then we have ideals without an ideal, conflicting principles without a unifying vision.

6. POLICY IMPLICATIONS

My position is, first, that equal opportunity is a prime case for this result; second, that despite the lack of a systematic solution for ideal theory, there are significant policy prescriptions which can be derived without solving the priority relations among these principles; and third, that the lack of a systematic solution exemplifies the special difficulties facing liberalism in our contemporary culture.

Having sketched the first point, let us turn to the second: the issue of policy implications. There are two kinds of policy implications we can evaluate without having to solve the problem of priority relations among these three principles for ideal theory—without, in other words, employing the model of an asymptotic aspiration to a single unified and coherent ideal which we should, as best we can, approach through partial realization. The first kind of policy implication involves cases in which we can achieve a major *improvement* in the realization of one of these values without a major loss in any of the others (or in any other new values which the proposal impinges upon). The second kind of policy implication involves cases in which a proposal would impose a major *loss* in one of these values without any comparable gain in any of the other values (or in any new values which the proposal impinges upon).

The first kind of policy implication is exemplified by all those things we could do to improve equality of life chances, family autonomy, or meritocratic assignment. In the U.S. for example, we are far from the possibility frontier in achieving any of these values and, in some cases, we have moved further away rather than closer in recent years. We blithely tolerate the perpetuation of an urban underclass; a whole generation of urban youth is growing up with blighted life chances and with few opportunities to make it into the mainstream economy, and with few policy initiatives now focused on their problem. Family autonomy is protected for middle-class families, but poor families have far greater difficulty in forming and maintaining themselves intact. By neglecting job prospects among the poor, the Reagan administration has also affected the incentives for family formation, as well as the ability of poor families to provide essential prerequisites for child development and socialization. We are also far from achieving meritocratic assignment. Discrimination persists against blacks, Hispanics, women, and other minorities, including homosexuals. There is no justification for tolerating job discrimination on the basis of arbitrary factors which are irrelevant to the roles in question. In other words, despite Reagan's talk of protecting "the family" and of creating an "opportunity society," his policies have promoted middle-class families and middle-class opportunities at the expense of the disadvantaged.

The second kind of policy implication is exemplified by the major quick fix for the first set of problems—preferential treatment based *merely* on arbitrary native characteristics. When it is applied in competitive meritocratic contexts, this policy yields a major sacrifice in one of our values, meritocratic assignment, without a significant gain in either of the others. The difficulty is that preferential treatment, when it is based merely on arbitrary native characteristics, is mistargeted as a policy which could have any effect on equality of life chances. It is mistargeted because, in competitive meritocratic contexts (e.g., admissions to graduate and professional schools) there are strong institutional pressures to accept the most qualified applicants with the specified arbitrary native characteristics. Just as family background provides disproportionate opportunities to develop qualifications among advantaged white children, it does so among relatively advantaged minority children. This policy only serves to widen the gap between the urban underclass and the black middle class—despite the fact that it is typically justified as special consideration for those who are from disadvantaged backgrounds.

My objection does not apply to policies which apply preferential treatment to those who are actually from disadvantaged backgrounds. In that case, meritocratic assignment is sacrificed for a gain in equal life chances. Rather, my objection applies to programs which are applied *merely* on the basis of arbitrary native characteristics, so as to reward the most qualified members of the group (who will, as a statistical matter, tend to come from its more advantaged portions). Hence, the irony of the De Funis and Bakke cases. De Funis, a Sephardic Jew from a relatively poor background, was not admitted to the University of Washington Law School while most of the minority students admitted on the basis of preferential treatment were, apparently, from more advantaged backgrounds (or, at least, were the children of black professionals). On the other hand, the program at the University of California at Davis which the Court struck down in the Bakke case was unusual for having procedures in place to direct special consideration to those who actually came from economically disadvantaged backgrounds. Theoretically, the program which the Court struck down in *Bakke* was defensible within our framework, while the program on which it avoided making a decision in *De Funis* (providing preferential treatment for race as such) would not be.

We should mention one persistent counterargument to this conclusion about preferential treatment. Preferential treatment based merely on race (or on other arbitrary native characteristics) is sometimes supported not as a remedy for developmental disadvantages in the present, but as a form of *compensation* for injustices in the past. However, the mistargeting objection has force here as well, but with additional complications.

First, the list of groups which were historically victims of discrimination is much broader than the groups now demanding compensation. Consistent pursuit of this argument would produce a host of other ethnic claims—Irish, Polish, and Italian, Catholic as well as Jewish, in addition to the more familiar arguments made on behalf of Hispanics, Native Americans, and Orientals. This proliferation is not fanciful. The AntiDefamation League discovered one American law school which had no less than sixteen racial and ethnic categories for admissions classifications.[5]

Second, the very notion of compensation raises conceptual challenges—unacknowledged by its proponents—when it is applied to this kind of problem. An individual *X* is supposed to be compensated by returning him to the level of well-being he would have reached had some identifiable injustice in the past (against his forebears) not occurred. In tracing back through the generations, however, it soon becomes clear that X would usually not now exist were it not for the historical injustice. If we try to imagine the world which would have existed had the historical injustices not occurred, we cannot return X to the level he would have reached, because he would not have reached any level at all. For example, let us take the well-documented case of Kunta Kinte. If Kunta Kinte, Alex Haley's ancestor in *Roots,* had not been brutally kidnapped and sold as a slave, there is no likelihood that the author of *Roots* would have come to exist in the twentieth century. The mating and reproduction of each generation, in turn, depend on a host of contingencies. If the chain were to have been broken at any point, by a parent, grandparent, or great-grandparent, we would get a different result in this generation. If it were not for the initial injustice, Kunta Kinte's descendants might well have been native Africans, perhaps residents today of Juffure (Kunta Kinte's village in West Africa).

Hence, we cannot employ the straightforward notion of compensation (returning people to the level they would have reached had the injustice not occurred) when the injustice spans several generations. Perhaps some compelling version of the argument might be created which confronts this difficulty. Rather than deny this possibility I wish merely to claim that such an argument, if it were developed, should, at the least, accept my objection to mistargeting.

Compensation is not compatible with the mistargeting which results from preferential treatment applied *merely* to racial categories in competitive meritocratic contexts. Compensation cannot plausibly mean benefiting some blacks (who may be already well-off) for earlier injustices to *other* blacks—particularly when those who do *not,* by and large, benefit from the compensatory argument (the urban underclass) are experiencing extremely disadvantaged conditions. To take a provocative analogy, would it not have been outrageous if the German government, after World War II, had paid "compensation" to well-off American Jews, ignoring the orphans and other direct victims of the Holocaust? It would not have been compensation to benefit Jews indiscriminately or, even worse, to benefit disproportionately those who were untouched by the injustices at issue. For this reason, I conclude that the compensation argument does not alter the general conclusion about preferential treatment reached earlier. When it is directed at those who are themselves from disadvantaged backgrounds, it is admissible within our framework, for then the gain in equal life chances may balance the loss in strictly meritocratic assignment. But when, in competitive merito-

cratic contexts, it is applied merely on the basis of arbitrary native characteristics, then we have grounds for objecting to it.

7. THE LIMITS OF THEORY

Turning to our third general issue, I believe these arguments show that equal opportunity is a useful test case for contemporary liberalism. First, it provides an area of social choice where major substantive commitments of liberalism inevitably clash, even for ideal theory. Hence, it should affect our conception of the appropriate connections between ideal theory and the real world of policy prescriptions. It should discredit the model according to which we make asymptotic approaches to a single, unified, and coherent ideal. Rather, we have conflicting principles, any one of which, if given further emphasis, would take policy in a different direction. Even for the best of circumstances, we have to balance conflicting principles. We are left with ideals without an ideal.

Second, the intuitionism which results is not trivial in its implications. The two clearest routes to substantive implications—embracing substantial gains without a loss and rejecting substantial losses without a gain—yield significant results on the contemporary scene. They do not add up to a systematic theory, but they should assist us in rethinking important policies.

Third, these results reveal the vulnerable position in which liberalism finds itself within our contemporary moral culture. In my recent book on the psychology of moral reasoning, I classify moral reasoners according to the seven ethical positions listed across the top of Chart 4. The six ethical claims [explained in Chart 5] listed at the left can be combined, consistently, only into the seven possibilities listed across the top. There are, of course, many other possible ways of dividing up the terrain. But this particular map purports to be exhaustive in the sense that it captures the consistent possibilities on the issues which it classifies.

The focus of my study is an investigation into the rationales motivating adoption of any of the subjectivist positions (IV through VII). It turns out that the rationales for subjectivism all depend on failed absolutist expectations. It is the difficulty or unavailability of positions I or II—Absolutism or Rigorism—which appears to support the conclusion that the only possible alternative is subjectivism in the form of positions IV through VII. The arguments of ordinary reasoners rely on absolutist expectations which specify that principles

CHART 4: Seven Ethical Positions

	I	II	III	IV	V	VI	VII
			Minimal	*Subjective*			
	Absolutism	*Rigorism*	*Objectivism*	*Universalism*	*Relativism*	*Personalism*	*Amoralism*
The Absolutist Claim	+	–	–	–	–	–	–
The Inviolability Claim	+	+	–	–	–	–	–
The Objective Validity Claim	+	+	+	–	–	–	–
The Universalizability Claim	+	+	+	+	–	–	–
The Interpersonal Judgment Claim	+	+	+	+	+	–	–
The Judgment of Self Claim	+	+	+	+	+	+	–

CHART 5: Six Ethical Claims

Claim 1: One's judgments are *absolute,* i.e., their inviolable character is rationally unquestionable.

Claim 2: One's judgments are *inviolable,* i.e., it would be objectively wrong ever to violate (permit exceptions to) them.

Claim 3: One's judgments are *objectively valid,* i.e., their consistent application to everyone is supported by considerations that anyone should accept were he to view the problem from what is contended to be the appropriate moral perspective.

Claim 4: One's judgments apply *universalizably,* i.e., they apply consistently to everyone, so that relevantly similar cases are treated similarly.

Claim 5: One's judgments apply *interpersonally,* i.e., to others as well as to oneself.

Claim 6: One's judgments apply to oneself.

must be rationally unquestionable and must hold without exception, thereby ruling out the intuitionist balancing of a conflicting principles, in order to avoid subjectivism.

However, the main burden of our substantive argument here has been that positions I or II are not plausible interpretations of liberal theory—at least for the crucial issue of equal opportunity. Even for ideal theory, we cannot establish inviolable priority relations. Unless we abandon one of our initial, central commitments, we find ourselves faced with interminable conflicts even under the best conditions which could realistically be imagined for a modern industrial society. If we are correct in this substantive conclusion, this result is profoundly disappointing for liberal theoretical aspirations.

However, this result also poses a crucial challenge to the viability of liberalism as a form of moral culture. If my empirical study is correct, we live in a moral culture imbued with absolutist expectations. When those expectations for rationally unquestionable, inviolable, and complete principles are combined with the inevitable conflicts and indeterminacies of liberalism—even under the best conditions—liberal ideology becomes vulnerable to a legitimacy crisis. The ingredients are the clash between expectations and inevitable limits. The expectations define the assumption that, in our scheme, moral positions must either live up to the requirements of positions I or II or be relegated to the moral arbitrariness of IV, V, VI or VII. The thrust of our

substantive analysis has been that the best liberalism can reasonably aspire to achieve is position III. In this middle ground position, liberalism lays claim to valid principles but embraces their conflicting and controversial character. At this position, principles are not arbitrary, but neither are they inviolable or beyond reasonable question—as at positions I or II. The inevitability of moral conflict about equal opportunity makes it a good substantive case for the general problem confronting liberalism.

Either we must learn to expect less, or liberalism undermines itself as a coherent moral ideology; it undermines itself by robbing itself of moral legitimacy, of claims to moral validity. It seems to lead to the unavoidable conclusion that all value judgments are arbitrary, a matter of mere personal taste—including all value judgments which can be made on behalf of the liberal state itself. Balancing conflicting principles is widely seen in our culture as a kind of nonanswer, just as intuitionism is seen as a nontheory. The difficulty facing liberalism arises if we are right about the limits of liberal theory and if we accept the absolutist expectations. I reject the latter step. My solution is to jettison the absolutist expectations and to embrace, by contrast, a limited liberalism, one which confines itself to position III in my scheme. As a matter of public ideology this requires a revision of expectations, a revision of moral culture. As for equal opportunity, we do not need a *systematic* theory and the demand for one is a part of the problem.

READING 40

A Liberal Defense of Equality of Opportunity

William Galston

For Galston's biography, see Reading 34. In this reading, Galston discusses four bases for arguments in favor of equal opportunity: *efficiency, desert,* the opportunity to *develop one's talents* to the utmost, and *personal satisfaction.*

This reading is taken from *Justice and Equality: Here and Now,* ed. Frank S. Lucash. Copyright © 1986 by Cornell University; used by permission of the publisher, Cornell University Press.

I

Every society embodies a conception of justice. The modern liberal society is no exception. Two principles are of particular importance. First, goods and services that fall within the sphere of basic needs are to be distributed on the basis of need, and the needs of all individuals are to be regarded as equally important. Second, many opportunities outside the sphere of need are to be allocated to individuals through a competition in which all have a fair chance to participate.

The latter principle entered American political thought under the rubric of "equality of opportunity." Much of American social history can be interpreted as a struggle between those who wished to widen the scope of its application and those who sought to restrict it. Typically, its proponents have promoted *formal* equality of opportunity by attacking religious, racial, sexual, and other barriers to open competition among individuals. And they have promoted *substantive* equality of opportunity by broadening access to the institutions that develop socially valued talents.

Recently, equality of opportunity has come under renewed attack. Conservatives charge that it fosters excessive public intervention in essentially private or voluntary relations. Radicals point with scorn to the competitive selfishness it fosters and to the unequal outcomes it permits. In the face of such assaults, liberals seem bewildered and defensive.

In this paper I want to sketch the grounds on which I believe equality of opportunity can be defended, and on that basis reply to the strictures of its critics. In the course of doing so I shall revise the generally accepted understanding of this principle in several respects. As I interpret it, equality of opportunity is less juridical and more teleological than is commonly supposed. It rests on an understanding of human equality more substantive than "equality of concern and respect." It is broader than the traditional concept of meritocracy. And it is embedded in a larger vision of a good society.

My argument proceeds in four steps. First, I shall examine in summary fashion some propositions that provide the philosophical foundation for equality of opportunity. Next I shall explore the strengths and limits of four kinds of arguments commonly offered in defense of this principle. Third, I shall discuss some difficulties that attend the translation of the abstract principle into concrete social practices. Finally, I shall briefly respond to three recent critics of equality of opportunity.

II

Let me begin my foundational argument with two propositions about individuals. Proposition 1: *All judgments concerning justice and injustice are ultimately relative to individuals* who are benefited or harmed, honored or dishonored in the distribution of contested goods. When we say that a group has been treated unjustly, we mean that the individuals comprising that group have been so treated. It would make no sense to say that every member of a group has been treated justly but that nevertheless the group has been treated unjustly. Membership in the group does not constitute an additional basis of entitlement beyond individual circumstances.

The insistence on the individual as the benchmark of justice is essential to the principle of equality of opportunity and to liberal theory as a whole. Not surprisingly, this premise has been sharply questioned. Communitarian critics of liberalism contend that the physical boundaries of individuals do not correspond to the social unities from which we ought to take our bearings. We become human only in society, they argue. Our language, our customs, our ambitions—everything that defines us is formed in social interchange. To be human is to participate in activities that are essentially social and relational. We are inextricably fused with others through that participation. It is impossible to say "I" without meaning "we."

This argument is, I believe, a non sequitur. While the formative power of society is surely decisive, it is nevertheless *individuals* that are being shaped. I may share everything with others. But it is *I* that shares them—an independent consciousness, a separate locus of pleasure and pain, a demarcated being with interests to be advanced or suppressed. My interpretation of my own good may be socially determined, but it is still *my* good, and it may well not be fully congruent with the good of others. Thus, as we counter the hyperindividualism of those who deny the existence of any social bonds with or moral obligations to others, it is important not to fall into the hyperorganicism that denies the ineradicable separateness of our individual existences.[1]

I turn now to my second proposition: *All principles of justice—including liberal principles—rest on some view of the good life for individuals.* It is now widely believed that principles of justice need not rest on this foundation, and that liberalism is precisely the theory that rests on the studied refusal to specify the human good. This is the premise underlying John Rawls's so-called priority of the right over the good, as well as the neutrality thesis of Ronald Dworkin and Bruce Ackerman.[2] But it is mistaken. Let me cite just one reason why.

Every principle of justice is intended to guide human conduct. Confronted with such a principle, the skeptic is entitled to ask, "Why should I be just?" It certainly won't do to reply, "Be just because the moral point of view requires it." A well-formed answer, I suggest, must link justice to intelligible motives for action. That is, it must invoke some conception of the good as the end of action—happiness, perfection, moral freedom, or the like. Even the strong claim that justice is a requirement of reason derives its hortatory force from the assumed goodness of the rational life.[3]

Some views of the human good argue for a *summum bonum*—one best way of life on the basis of which all others can be judged and rank-ordered. It may well be possible to defend such a view. For my present purposes, however, a more latitudinarian approach will suffice, along the following lines.

Every human being is born with a wide range of potential talents. Some ought not to be encouraged—a capacity for ingenious and guiltless cruelty, for example. Among the capacities of an individual that are in some sense worth developing, a small subset are comprehensive enough to serve as organizing principles for an entire life. The fullest possible development of one or more of these capacities is an important element of the good life for that individual.

Experience teaches us that individuals vary widely. Each of us is naturally gifted along some dimensions and inept along others. Some are naturally good at many things, others at few. Experience also suggests that talents vary qualitatively. Some are common and rudimentary, others are rare and highly prized.

Here I want to propose a notion of human equality that is essential to equality of opportunity as I understand it. I want to suggest that in spite of profound differences among individuals, the full development of each individual—however great or limited his or her natural capacities—is equal in moral weight to that of every other. For any individuals A and B, a policy that leads to the full development of A and partial development of B is, *ceteris paribus,* equal in value to a policy that fully develops B while restricting A's development to the same degree. Thus a policy that neglects the educable retarded so that they do not learn how to care for themselves and must be institutionalized is, considered in itself, as bad as one that reduces extraordinary gifts to mere normality.

On one level, this proposal runs counter to our moral intuitions. It seems hard to deny that the full realization of high capacities is preferable to the full development of lower, more limited capacities. But this consideration is not decisive.

We would of course prefer a world in which everyone's innate capacities were more extensive than they are at present, and we would choose to be (say) mathematically talented rather than congenitally retarded. Accordingly, we would prefer *for ourselves* the full development of more extensive capacities to the full development of lesser ones. But it does not follow that whenever the developmental interests of different individuals come into conflict, the development of higher or more extensive capacities is to be given priority. A policy that focuses exclusively on the intrinsic worth of our capacities treats the characteristics of separate individuals as an artificial, disembodied unity, ignoring the fact that they have no existence apart from the individuals in whom they inhere.

It may be argued, nonetheless, that there is something more horrible about the incomplete development of great capacities than about the waste of lesser gifts. Perhaps so. But one might say with equal justice that it is more horrible for someone who can be taught to speak to be condemned to a life of inarticulate quasi-animality than it is for someone who could have been a great mathematician to lead an ordinary life. Our intuitions about the relative desirability of the best cases are more or less counterbalanced by the relative unacceptability of the worst.

I can now offer a partial definition of a good society. In such a society, the range of social possibilities will equal the range of human possibilities. Each worthy capacity, that is, will find a place within it. No one will be compelled to flee elsewhere in search of opportunities for development, the way ambitious young people had to flee farms and small towns in nineteenth-century societies. Further, each worthy capacities will be treated fairly in the allocation of resources available for individual development within that society.

These criteria, I suggest, are more fully satisfied in a liberal society than in any other. Historically, liberal societies have come closer than any others to achieving the universality that excludes no talent or virtue. The development of great gifts encounters few material or political impediments. The development of ordinary gifts is spurred by education and training open to all. Warriors, statesmen, poets, philosophers, men and women of devoted piety—all are welcomed and accommodated. The fundamental argument for a diverse society is not—as some believe—that our reason is incompetent to judge among possible ways of life. It is rather that the human good is not one thing but many things.

Although the principle of equality of opportunity is embedded in this kind of society, it is nonetheless commonly thought to presuppose a sharp distinction between the natural endowments of individuals and their social environment. The life chances of individuals, it is argued, should not be determined by such factors as race, economic class, and family background. To the extent that these factors do tend to affect the development and exercise of individual talents, it is the task of social policy to alleviate their force. If malnutrition stunts mental and physical development, then poor children must be fed by the community. If social deprivation leaves some children irreparably behind before they start first grade, then compensatory preschool programs are essential.

The proposition that natural but not social differences should affect individual life chances raises a number of difficult problems. To begin with, natural differences are usually viewed as genetic endowments not subject to external intervention. But increasingly, natural endowments are malleable, and the time may not be far off when they can be more predictably altered than can social circumstances. This eventuality will transform not only the distinction between the natural and the social

but also its normative consequences. To that extent that, for example, modern techniques can overcome genetic defects or even determine genetic endowments, disputes will arise among families over access to these scarce and expensive techniques. Before the opportunity to develop one's capacities will come the opportunity to have certain capacities to develop. At this point—as Bernard Williams rightly suggests—equality of opportunity will merge into broader issues of absolute equality and the morality of genetic intervention.[4]

Assuming that we are still some time away from the obliteration of the naturally given, we can still ask why differences of social background are thought to be impermissible determinants of social outcomes and, conversely, why natural differences are thought to be appropriate determinants.

Why shouldn't the chief's eldest child be the next chief? This question is seldom asked because it seems absurd to us. We take it for granted that a competitive system ought to winnow out the candidate "best qualified" and that family membership is utterly irrelevant to this selection. But of course it need not be. If the tribe is held together by shared loyalty based in part on family sentiments, the chief's child may be uniquely qualified. Descent may be an important ingredient of social legitimacy and therefore an important claim to rule, especially when other sources of legitimacy have been weakened. Contemporary Lebanon, where sons gain power from fathers and assume their murdered brothers' burdens, typifies this sort of society.

Underlying the usual distinction between social and natural differences is the moral intuition that social outcomes should be determined by factors over which individuals have control. But the wealth and social standing of one's family are facts over which individuals cannot exercise control, and therefore they shouldn't matter.

The difficulty with this argument is that individuals don't control their natural endowments any more than they do their ancestry. The requirement that the basis on which we make claims must somehow be generated through our own efforts amounts to a nullification of the very procedure of claiming *anything*.

The costs of this conclusion are very high. Every conception of justice presupposes the distinction between valid and invalid claims, which in turn rests on some facts about individuals. There can be no theory of justice without some notion of individual desert, and no notion of individual desert that doesn't eventually come to rest on some "undeserved" characteristics of individuals.

Some may wish to conclude that the cause of justice is lost. I disagree, because I reject the premise of the preceding argument. The world's fastest sprinter doesn't "deserve" his natural endowment of speed, but surely he deserves to win the race established to measure and honor this excellence. There is nothing in principle wrong with a conception of individual desert that rests on the possession of natural gifts.

I would conclude, rather, that the normative distinction between social facts and natural endowments is not so sharp as most interpretations of equality of opportunity presuppose. This distinction provided the historical impetus for the development of the principle: the triumph of meritocratic over patriarchal and hereditary norms is an oft-told tale. But philosophically, the social/natural distinction must be reinterpreted as the distinction between relevant and irrelevant reasons for treating individuals in certain manners.

To further this reinterpretation, I want to examine four ways in which equality of opportunity can be defended.

III

First—and most obviously—equality of opportunity can be justified as a principle of *efficiency*. Whatever the goals of a community may be, they are most likely to be achieved when the individuals most capable of performing the tasks that promote those goals are allowed to do so. Such efficiency, it may be argued, requires a system that allows individuals to declare their candidacy for positions they prefer and then selects the ablest. From this standpoint, equality of opportunity is a dictate of instrumental rationality, a measure of collective devotion to social goals.

But a complication crops up immediately. Competition among individuals to fill social roles may not produce aggregate efficiency, even if the most talented is chosen to fill each individual role.

To see why, consider a two-person society with two tasks. Suppose that person *A* can perform both tasks better than person *B* and is by an absolute measure better at the first task than at the second. If *A* is only slightly better than *B* at the first but much better at the second, it is more productive for the society as a whole to allocate the first task to *B,* even though *A* will then not be doing what he does best.

In actual societies, the differential rewards attached to tasks can produce comparable distortions. If (say)

lawyers are paid much more than teachers, the talent pool from which lawyers are selected is likely to be better stocked. Teachers will then tend to be mediocre, even if the best are selected from among the candidates who present themselves. This circumstance may well impose aggregate costs on society, at least in the long run.

These difficulties arise for two reasons. First, applying equality of opportunity to a society characterized by division of labor produces a set of individual competitions whose aggregate results will fall short of the best that society could achieve through more centralized coordination among these contests. Second, equality of opportunity embodies an element of individual liberty. Individuals can choose neither the rules of various competitions nor their outcomes. But they can choose which game to play. The fact that society as a whole will benefit if I perform a certain task does not mean that I can be coerced to perform it. Within limits, I can choose which talents to develop and exercise, and I can refuse to enter specific competitions, even if I would surely emerge victorious. "From each according to his ability" is not the principle of a liberal society, for the simple reason that the individual is regarded as the owner of his or her capacities. Equality of opportunity is a meritocratic principle, but it is applied to competitions among self-selected individuals.

I do not wish to suggest that this liberty is anything like absolute. Duties to other individuals, particularly family members who have made sacrifices on my behalf, may require me to develop and exercise certain abilities. Similarly, duties to my country may require me to become a first-rate general or physicist, if I am capable of doing so. But after all such duties are taken into account, there will still be a range of choice into which a liberal society should not intrude. This will always be a barrier to the single-minded pursuit of efficiency, and to the use of coercive meritocracy to achieve it.

The second justification of equality of opportunity focuses on the notion of *desert*. For each social position, it is argued, a certain range of personal qualities may be considered relevant. Individuals who possess these qualities to an outstanding degree deserve those positions. A fair competition guided by equality of opportunity will allow exemplary individuals to be identified and rewarded.

Many critics have objected to this line of reasoning. It is a mistake, they argue, to regard social positions as prizes. In athletic competition, first prize goes to the one who has performed best. It would be inappropriate to take future performance into account or to regard present performance in the context of future possibilities. The award of the prize looks only backward to what has already happened. The prize winner has established desert through completed performance. In the case of social positions, on the other hand, the past is of interest primarily as an index of future performance. The alleged criterion of desert is thus reducible to considerations of efficiency.

This critique contains elements of truth, but I believe that the sharp contrast it suggests is overdrawn. After all, societies do not just declare the existence of certain tasks to be performed. They also make known, at least in general terms, the kinds of abilities that will count as qualifications to perform these tasks. Relying on this shared public understanding, young people strive to acquire and display these abilities. If they succeed in doing so, they have earned the right to occupy the corresponding positions. They deserve them. It would therefore be wrong to breach these legitimate expectations, just as it would be wrong to tell the victorious runner, "Sorry. We know you crossed the finish line first, but we've decided to give the prize to the runner who stopped to help a fallen teammate."

To be sure, circumstances may prevent society from honoring legitimate desert claims. Individuals may spend years preparing themselves for certain occupations, only to find that economic or demographic changes have rendered their skills outmoded. Socially established expectations cannot be risk-free—a fact that security-seeking young people are not always quick to grasp. But this fact does not distinguish social competition from athletic competition. The Americans who worked so hard for the 1980 Olympic Games, only to be denied the right to compete, were deeply disappointed, but they could not maintain that they had been treated unjustly.

In short, no clear line can be drawn between tasks and prizes. Many tasks *are* prizes—opportunities to perform activities that are intrinsically or socially valuable. These prizes are of a special character—forward-looking rather than complete in themselves—and this gives rise to legitimate disagreement about the criteria that should govern their distribution. There is no science that permits completely reliable inferences from past to future performance in any occupation. But once criteria, however flawed, have been laid down, they create a context within which claims of desert can be established and must be honored if possible. Performance criteria may be altered, but only after ex-

isting claims have been discharged, and only in a manner that gives all individuals the fairest possible chance to redirect their efforts.

A third kind of justification of equality of opportunity focuses on *personal development.* When a society devotes resources to education and training, when it encourages individuals to believe that their life chances will be significantly related to their accomplishments, and when it provides an attractive array of choices, there is good reason to believe that individuals will be moved to develop some portion of their innate capacities. Thus, it may be argued, equality of opportunity is the principle of task allocation most conducive to a crucial element of the human good.

I accept this argument. But it has significant limitations. It ignores, for example, ways in which individuals may benefit from performing certain tasks even if they are less competent to do so than others. If an apprentice is not permitted to perform the activities of his craft, he cannot increase his competence. In this process, the master craftsman must be willing to accept errors and inefficiencies. This is true even if the learner can never achieve the full competence of the best practitioner. Even individuals of mediocre talents can increase their knowledge, skill, and self-confidence when they are allowed to discharge demanding responsibilities. Thus developmental considerations may suggest rotating some tasks fairly widely rather than restricting them to the most able.

In addition, most individuals can achieve excellence in specific demanding tasks only when they concentrate on mastering that task to the exclusion of all others. Equality of opportunity is thus linked to the division of labor, to specialization, and to the principle of "one person, one job." An argument of considerable antiquity questions the human consequences of this principle. Perhaps it is better for individuals to be minimally competent and developed in many areas rather than allowing most of their capacities to lie fallow. Perhaps a system of task assignment that deemphasized competence in favor of variety would be preferable.

These considerations raise a broader issue. Human activities have both external and internal dimensions. On the one hand, they effect changes in the natural world and in the lives of others. On the other hand, they alter—develop, stunt, pervert—the character and talent of those who perform them. Neither dimension can be given pride of place; neither can be ignored.

Without a measure of physical security and material well-being, no society can afford to devote resources to individual development or to exempt individuals from material production for any portion of their lives. In societies living at the margin, child labor is a necessity and scholarly leisure is an unaffordable luxury. But structuring a social and economic system to promote productive efficiency is justified only by physical needs and by the material preconditions of development itself. Thus a fundamental perversion occurs when the subordination of development to production continues beyond that point. A wealthy community that determines the worth of all activities by the extent to which they add to its wealth has forgotten what wealth is for. A system of training, education, and culture wholly subservient to the system of production denies the fuller humanity of its participants.

For these reasons, I suggest, a prosperous society must carefully consider not only how it allocates its tasks but also how it defines and organizes the tasks it allocates. The very concern for individual development that makes equality of opportunity so attractive leads beyond that principle to basic questions of social structure.

Finally, equality of opportunity may be defended on the grounds that it is conducive to *personal satisfaction*. Within the limits of competence, individuals are permitted to choose their lives' central activity, and they are likely to spend much of their time in occupations they are competent to perform. No system can guarantee satisfaction, of course. But one that reduces to a minimum the compulsory elements of labor and allows individuals to feel competent in the course of their labor will come closer than any alternative.

While this argument is probably correct, it is important to keep its limits in mind. To begin with, the satisfaction derived from an activity is not always proportional to our ability to perform it. We may want to do what we cannot do very well, and we may obtain more pleasure from doing what we regard as a higher task in a mediocre manner than from doing a lower task very well. In addition, in a system fully governed by equality of opportunity, there would be no external causes of failure and no alternative to self-reproach for the inability to achieve personal ambitions.

An equal opportunity system stimulates many to strive for what they cannot attain. By broadening horizons, it may well increase frustration. Of course, this is not necessarily a bad thing. Such a system does induce many who can excel to develop themselves more fully. It is not clear that a system that increases both achievement and frustration is inferior to one that increases the subjective satisfaction of the less talented only by decreasing the motivation of the more talented to realize

their abilities. And many people not capable of the highest accomplishments will nevertheless develop and achieve more in a context that infuses them with a desire to excel. A permanent gap between what we are and what we want to be need not be debilitating. On the contrary, it can be a barrier to complacency, a source of modesty, an incentive for self-discipline, and a ground of genuine respect for excellence.

IV

I remarked at the outset that the principle of equality of opportunity gains both content and justification from the society in which it is embedded. There are, I believe, four major dimensions along which this abstract principle is rendered socially concrete: first, the range of possibilities available within a society; second, the manner in which these activities are delimited and organized; third, the criteria governing the assignment of individuals to particular activities; and finally, the manner in which activities are connected to external goods such as money, power, and status.

I need not add much to the previous discussion of possibilities. A good society is maximally inclusive, allowing the greatest possible scope for the development and exercise of worthy talents.

Opportunities for development are affected not just by the kinds of activities that take place within a society but also by their manner of organization. Consider the provision of health care. At present in the United States, doctors, nurses, orderlies, and administrators perform specific ranges of activities, linked to one another by rigid lines of authority. It is possible— and probably desirable—to redraw these boundaries of specialization. Nurses, for example, could well be given more responsibility for tasks now performed by doctors, particularly in areas where judgment, experience, and sensitivity to the needs of specific individuals are more significant than are high levels of technical training. Similarly, it is possible to reorganize the process of production. At some plants, small groups of workers collectively produce entire automobiles, performing the required operations sequentially in the group's own area rather than along an assembly line. Proposals to expand managerial decision making to include production workers have been tried out in a number of European countries.

Behind all such suggestions lies the belief that the existing organization of social tasks rests more on habit and special privilege than on an impartial analysis of social or individual benefit. Occupational hierarchies in which all creativity and authority are confined to a few tasks while all the rest enforce routine drudgery are typically justified on the grounds of efficiency. Maintaining a certain quality and quantity of goods and services is said to demand this kind of hierarchy. In general, there is little evidence to support this proposition and much to question it. Besides, as we have seen, there are other things to consider—in particular, the effect of tasks on the development and satisfaction of the individuals who perform them. Equal opportunity requires an appropriate balance between the preconditions of productive efficiency and the internal consequences of tasks—a balance that may well depend on a far-reaching reorganization of social tasks.

Let me assume that a society has actually reached agreement on such a balance. The assignment of individuals to the tasks embodied in that agreement will remain controversial, because criteria of assignment are open to reasonable dispute. Some considerations are clearly irrelevant. Barring aberrant background circumstances, such factors as the color of one's hair or eyes should have no bearing on one's chances of becoming a doctor, because they have no bearing on one's capacity to practice the medical art. But beyond such obvious cases, there is disagreement about the nature of the good doctor. In the prevailing view the good doctor is one who is capable of mastering a wide variety of techniques and employing them appropriately. But dissenters suggest that moral criteria should be given equal weight: the good doctor cares more about her patients' welfare than about her own material advancement, gives great weight to need in distributing her services, never loses sight of the humanity of her patients. Still others believe that the willingness to practice where medical needs are greatest is crucial. They urge that great weight be given to the likelihood—or the promise—that a prospective doctor will provide health care to rural areas, small towns, urban ghettos, or other localities lacking adequate care. From this standpoint, otherwise dubious criteria such as geographical origin or even race might become very important.

This dispute cannot be resolved in the abstract. The relative weight accorded the technical, moral, and personal dimensions will vary with the needs and circumstances of particular societies. It will also vary among specialties within professions. In the selection of brain surgeons, technical mastery is probably paramount. For pediatricians, human understanding is far more important. Whatever the criteria, they must be made as explicit as possible, so that individuals can make informed commitments to courses of training and preparation. Those who control the selection are not free to vary publicly declared criteria once they have engendered legitimate expectations.

I turn now to the connection between activities and external goods. Here my point is simple. A fair competition may demonstrate my qualification for a particular occupation. But the talents that so qualify me do not entitle me to whatever external rewards happen to be attached to that occupation. I may nevertheless be entitled to them, but an independent line of argument is needed to establish that fact. So, for example, in accordance with public criteria, my technical competence may entitle me to a position as a brain surgeon. It does not follow that I am entitled to half a million dollars a year. Even if we grant what is patently counterfactual in the case of doctors—that compensation is determined by the market—the principle of task assignment in accordance with talents does not commit us to respect market outcomes. Indeed, the kind of competition inherent in a system of equal opportunity bears no clear relation to the competition characteristic of the market.

This distinction has an important consequence. Many thinkers oppose meritocratic systems on the ground that there is no reason why differences of talent should generate or legitimate vast differences in material rewards. They are quite right. But this is not an objection to meritocracy as such. It is an objection to the way society assigns *rewards* to tasks, not to the way it assigns *individuals* to tasks.

Indeed, one could argue that current salary inequalities should be reversed. Most highly paid jobs in our society are regarded as intrinsically desirable by the people who perform them. In moments of candor, most business executives, doctors, lawyers, generals, and college professors admit that they would want to continue in their professions even at considerably lower income levels. The incomes generally associated with such occupations cannot then be justified as socially necessary incentives.

There are, however, some rewards that are intrinsically related to tasks themselves. The most obvious is the gratification obtained from performing them. Another is status. Although I cannot prove it, it seems likely that there is a hierarchy of respect and prestige independent of income, correlated with what is regarded as the intrinsic worth of activities. Tasks involving extraordinary traits of mind and character or the ability to direct the activities of others are widely prized.

Finally, certain activities may entail legitimate claims to some measure of power and authority. As Aristotle pointed out, there are inherent hierarchical relations among specialized functions. The architect guides the work of the bricklayer and the plasterer. Moreover, if members of a community have agreed on a goal, knowledge that conduces to the achievement of that goal provides a rational basis for authority. If everyone wishes to cross the ocean and arrive at a common destination, then the skilled navigator has a rational claim to the right to give orders. But the navigator's proper authority is limited in both extent and time. It does not regulate the community's nonnavigational activities, and it vanishes when all reach their destination.

V

At the outset of this paper I said that I would employ my analysis of equality of opportunity to reply to its critics, radical and conservative. I wish, in conclusion, to touch on three arguments that are frequently brought against equality of opportunity.

The first objection is the *libertarian,* raised in its purest form by Robert Nozick. According to Nozick, equality of opportunity understates the individualistic character of human existence. Life is not a race with a starting line, a finish line, a clearly designated judge, and a complex of attributes to be measured. Rather, there are only individuals, agreeing to give to and receive from each other.

I believe that this contention overlooks important social facts. Within every community, certain kinds of abilities are generally prized. Being excluded from an equal chance to develop them means that one is unlikely to have much of value to exchange with others: consider the problem of hard-core unemployment when the demand for unskilled labor is declining. To be sure, there is more than one social contest, but the number is limited. In a society in which rising educational credentials are demanded even for routine tasks, exclusion from the competition for education and training—or inclusion on terms that amount to a handicap—will make it very difficult to enter the system of exchange. Equality of opportunity acknowledges these prerequisites to full participation in social competition, and it therefore legitimates at least some of the social interventions needed to permit full participation.

The second objection is the *communitarian.* According to this view, advanced by John Schaar

among others, even the most perfect competition is insufficient, because competition is a defective mode of existence. It sets human beings apart from each other and pits them against one another, in an essentially destructive struggle.[5]

Certainly an equal opportunity system contains some competitive elements. But not all forms of competition are bad. Some competition brings human beings closer together, into communities of shared endeavor and mutual respect. Consider the embrace of two exhausted boxers at the end of a match, or even the spontaneous bond between Anwar Sadat and Golda Meir at their first face-to-face encounter. Moreover, competition can be mutually beneficial. Scientific competition may produce simultaneous discoveries, neither of which would have occurred without the presence of the competitor; gymnastic competition may inspire two perfect performances. And finally, the traditional antithesis between competition and community is too simple. Community rests on some agreement. A competitive system can be a form of community if most participants are willing to accept the principle of competition.

The third objection to equality of opportunity is the *democratic.* According to this objection—articulated by Michael Walzer, among others—equality of opportunity is at best a limited principle because it cannot apply to the sphere of politics. Technical expertise may confer a limited authority. But because there is no rationally binding conception of the good, there is no technique for selecting the ends of political life. Political power does not look *up* to Platonic ideas, but rather *around* to prevailing opinions: "The proper exercise of power is nothing more than the direction of the city in accordance with the civic consciousness or public spirit of the citizens."[6]

I do not believe that any contemporary political thinker has adequately defended the crucial premise of this argument: that no rational theory of political ends is available. But let me set this question to one side and focus briefly on what it means to direct a community in accordance with its own self-understanding.

At one juncture Walzer notes that a majority of citizens "might well misunderstand the logic of their own institutions or fail to apply consistently the principles they professed to hold." There may, then, be a kind of expertise in the understanding of civic consciousness that cuts against simply majoritarian institutions and democratic procedures. In *Brown v. Board of Education,* for example, the U.S. Supreme Court rendered a decision that would certainly have been rejected by majority vote at the time, but that was ultimately accepted as the authoritative interpretation of American principles.

More broadly: I would argue there are distinctive political excellences and virtues; they are necessary for the success of all political orders, including democracies; and they do constitute one claim—though not the only claim—to political authority, because they contribute to needed cooperation and to the achievement of shared purposes. Without them, a political community will lose its bearings and its self-confidence. It would be very fortunate if these virtues were widely distributed. But experience suggests that the percentage of individuals who possess them to any significant degree within a given community will be small.

This does not necessarily mean that democracy is based on a mistake. As Jefferson saw, the problem of democracy is to achieve some convergence of participation, consent, and excellence. He believed that this problem is soluble—in part through social and political institutions that single out the natural *aristoi*, develop their special gifts, and reliably promote them to high office. From this standpoint, the purpose of elections is not just to register opinion but also to identify excellence. Indeed, the test of an electoral system is its propensity to confer the mantle of leadership on those most worthy to lead. Properly understood, the distribution of power in democracies is not wholly distinct from, but rather partly governed by, the merit-based principle of equal opportunity.

READING 41

The Case for Affirmative Action

Albert Mosley

Albert Mosley is Professor of Philosophy at Smith College and the author of several works on African and African American philosophy. In this essay, he argues that governments have a strong prima facie obligation to recompense groups and individuals for liabilities they have suffered due to the oppressive behavior of the government. He develops a backward-looking argument of restitu-

tion to those unjustly oppressed as well as a forward-looking argument that aims at rectifying present injustice.

This reading is taken from *Affirmative Action: Social Justice or Unfair Preference,* by Albert Mosley and Nicholas Capaldi (Lanham, Maryland: Rowman & Littlefield, 1997), by permission. notes edited.

There are many interests that governments pursue—maximization of social production; equitable distribution of rights, opportunities, and services; social safety and cohesion; restitution—and those interests may conflict in various situations. In particular, governments as well as their constituents have a *prima facie* obligation to satisfy the liabilities they incur. One such liability derives from past and present unjust exclusionary acts depriving minorities and women of opportunities and amenities made available to other groups.

BACKWARD-LOOKING JUSTIFICATIONS OF AFFIRMATIVE ACTION

"Backward looking" arguments defend affirmative action as a matter of *corrective justice,* where paradigmatically the harm doer is to make restitution to the harmed so as to put the harmed in the position the harmed most likely would have occupied had the harm not occurred. An important part of making restitution is the acknowledgment it provides that the actions causing injury were unjust and such actions will be curtailed and corrected. In this regard Bernard Boxill writes:

> Without the acknowledgment of error, the injurer implies that the injured has been treated in a manner that befits him. . . . In such a case, even if the unjust party repairs the damage he has caused . . . nothing can be demanded on legal or moral grounds, and the repairs made are gratuitous. . . . Justice requires that we acknowledge that this treatment of others can be required of us; thus, where an unjust injury has occurred, the injurer reaffirms his belief in the other's equality by conceding that repair can be demanded of him, and the injured rejects the allegation of his inferiority . . . by demanding reparation.[1]

This view is based on the idea that restitution is a basic moral principle that creates obligations that are just as strong as the obligations to maximize wealth and distribute it fairly. If x has deprived y of opportunities y had a right not to be deprived of in this manner, then x is obligated to return y to the position y would have occupied had x not intervened; x has this obligation irrespective of other obligations x may have. This can be illustrated another way as follows: Suppose y is deprived of t by x and we determine retroactively that y had a right to t. Then x has an obligation to return t to y or provide y with something else of equal value to t. In other words, x has an obligation to correct his or her effect on y, and restore y's losses.

A slightly different case illustrates a further point. Suppose x deprives y of the use of y's car for a day without y's consent and suppose further that x's use of the car produces $100 while y's use of the car would have produced only $50. In so far as an act is justified if it increases social utility, x is justified in having taken y's car. At most, x need only provide y with the value ($50) that y would have received if x had not taken the car. If y would not have used the car at all, presumably x would owe y only the depreciated value of the car resulting from its extra use. But though x increases social utility, x also deprives y of the exclusive use of y's private property. And to the extent that we consider the right of exclusive use important, it is wrong for x to profit from benefits that derive from x's enrichment through a violation of y's rights.

A further application of this principle involves the case where x is not a person but an entity, like a government or a business. If y was unjustly deprived of employment when firm F hired z instead of y because z was White and y Black, then y has a right to be made whole, that is, brought to the position he/she would have achieved had that deprivation not occurred. Typically, this involves giving y a position at least as good as the one he/she would have acquired originally and issuing back pay in the amount that y would have received had he/she been hired at the time of the initial attempt.

Most critics of preferential treatment acknowledge the applicability of principles of restitution to individuals in specific instances of discrimination. The strongest case is where y was as or more qualified than z in the initial competition, but the position was given to z because y was Black and z was White. Subsequently, y may not be as qualified for an equivalent position as some new candidate z', but is given preference because of the past act of discrimination by F that deprived y of the position he or she otherwise would have received.

Some critics have suggested that, in such cases, z' is being treated unfairly. For z', as the most qualified applicant, has a right not to be excluded from the position in question purely on the basis of race; and y has a right to restitution for having unjustly been denied the position in the past. But the dilemma is one in appearance only. For having unjustly excluded y in the past, the current position that z' has applied for is not one that F is free to offer to the public. It is a position that is already owed to y, and is not available for open competition. Judith Jarvis Thompson makes a similar point:

> Suppose two candidates [A and B] for a civil service job have equally good test scores, but there is only one job available. We could decide between them by coin-tossing. But in fact we do allow for declaring for A straightway, where A is a veteran, and B is not. It may be that B is a non-veteran through no fault of his. . . . Yet the fact is that B is not a veteran and A is. On the assumption that the veteran has served his country, the country owes him something. And it is plain that giving him preference is not an unjust way in which part of that debt of gratitude can be paid.[2]

In a similar way, individual Blacks who have suffered from acts of unjust discrimination are owed something by the perpetrator(s) of such acts, and this debt takes precedence over the perpetrator's right to use his or her options to hire the most qualified person for the position in question.

Many White males have developed expectations about the likelihood of their being selected for educational, employment, and entrepreneurial opportunities that are realistic only because of the general exclusion of women and non-Whites as competitors for such positions. Individuals enjoying inflated odds of obtaining such opportunities because of racist and sexist practices are recipients of an "unjust enrichment."

Redistributing opportunities would clearly curtail benefits that many have come to expect. And given the frustration of their traditional expectations, it is understandable that they would feel resentment. But blocking traditional expectations is not unjust if those expectations conflict with the equally important moral duties of restitution and just distribution. It is a question, not of "is," but of "ought": not "Do those with decreased opportunities as a result of affirmative action feel resentment?" but "Should those with decreased opportunities as a result of affirmative action feel resentment?"

White males who are affected by such redistributions may be innocent in the sense that they have not practiced overt acts of racial discrimination, have developed reasonable expectations based on the status quo, and have exerted efforts that, given the status quo, would normally have resulted in their achieving certain rewards. Their life plans and interests are thus thwarted despite their having met all of the standards "normally" required for the achievement of their goals. Clearly, disappointment is not unnatural or irrational. Nonetheless, the resentment is not sufficiently justified if the competing moral claims of restitution and fair distribution have equal or even greater weight.

Since Title VII protects bona fide seniority plans, it forces the burden of rectification to be borne by Whites who are entering the labor force rather than Whites who are the direct beneficiaries of past discriminatory practices. Given this limitation placed on affirmative action remedies, the burden of social restitution may, in many cases, be borne by those who were not directly involved in past discriminatory practices. But it is generally not true that those burdened have not benefited at all from past discriminatory practices. For the latent effects of acts of invidious racial discrimination have plausibly bolstered and encouraged the efforts of Whites in roughly the same proportion as they have inhibited and discouraged the efforts of Blacks. Such considerations are also applicable to cases where F discriminated against y in favor of z, but the make-whole remedy involves providing compensation to y′ rather than y. This suggests that y′ is an *undeserving beneficiary* of the preferential treatment meant to compensate for the unjust discrimination against y, just as z′ above appeared to be the innocent victim forced to bear the burden that z benefited from. Many critics have argued that this misappropriation of benefits and burdens demonstrates the unfairness of compensation to groups rather than individuals. But it is important that the context and rationale for such remedies be appreciated.

In cases of "egregious" racial discrimination, not only is it true that F discriminated against a particular Black person y, but F's discrimination advertised a general disposition to discriminate against another Black person who might seek such positions. The specific effect of F's unjust discrimination was that y was refused a position he or she would otherwise have received. The latent (or dispositional) effect of F's unjust discrimination was that many Blacks who otherwise would have sought such positions were discouraged from doing so. Thus, even if the specific y actually discrimi-

nated against can no longer be compensated, F has an obligation to take affirmative action to communicate to Blacks as a group that such positions are indeed open to them. After being found in violation of laws prohibiting racial discrimination, many agencies have disclaimed further discrimination while in fact continuing to discriminate. In such cases, the courts have required the discriminating agencies to actually hire and/or promote Blacks who may not be as qualified as some current White applicants until Blacks approach the proportion in F's labor force they in all likelihood would have achieved had F's unjust discriminatory acts not deterred them.

Of course, what this proportion would have been is a matter of speculation. It may have been less than the proportion of Blacks available in the relevant labor pool from which applicants are drawn if factors other than racial discrimination act to depress the merit of such applicants. This point is made again and again by critics. Some, such as Thomas Sowell, argue that cultural factors often mitigate against Blacks' meriting representation in a particular labor force in proportion to their presence in the pool of candidates looking for jobs or seeking promotions. Others, such as Michael Levin, argue that cognitive deficits limit Blacks from being hired and promoted at a rate proportionate to their presence in the relevant labor pool. What such critics reject is the assumption that, were it not for pervasive discrimination and overexploitation, Blacks would be equally represented in the positions in question. What is scarcely considered is the possibility that, were it not for racist exclusions, Blacks might be over rather than under represented in competitive positions.

Establishing Blacks' presence at a level commensurate with their proportion in the relevant labor market need not be seen as an attempt to actualize some valid prediction. Rather, given the impossibility of determining what level of representation Blacks would have achieved were it not for racist discrimination, the assumption of proportional representation is the only *fair* assumption to make. This is not to argue that Blacks should be maintained in such positions, but their contrived exclusion merits an equally contrived rectification.

Racist acts excluding Blacks affected particular individuals but were directed at affecting the behavior of the group of all those similar to the victim. Likewise, the benefits of affirmative action policies should not be conceived as limited in their effects to the specific individuals receiving them. Rather, those benefits should be conceived as extending to all those identified with the recipient, sending the message that opportunities are indeed available to qualified Black candidates who would have been excluded in the past.

Reflecting the view of many critics of preferential treatment, Robert Fullinwider writes:

> Surely the most harmed by past employment discrimination are those Black men and women over fifty years of age who were denied an adequate education, kept out of the unions, legally excluded from many jobs, who have lived in poverty or close to it, and whose income-producing days are nearly at an end. Preferential hiring programs will have virtually no effect on these people at all. Thus, preferential hiring will tend not to benefit those most deserving of compensation.[3]

Because of the failure to appreciate the latent effects of discriminatory acts, this conclusion is flawed in two important respects. First, it limits the effect of specific acts of discrimination to the specific individuals involved. But the effect on the individual that is the specific object of a racist exclusion is not the only effect of that act, and may not be the effect that is most injurious or long term. For an invidious act affects not only y, but also y's family and friends. And it may well be that the greatest injury is, not to y, but to those who are deprived of sharing not only the specific benefits denied y, but also the motivation to seek (as y did) educational and employment opportunities they believe they would be excluded from (as y was).

Second, the conclusion that "preferential hiring will tend not to benefit those most deserving of compensation" fails to appreciate the extent that helping one member of a group may contribute indirectly to helping other members of that group. Clearly, admitting y′ to medical school to compensate for not having admitted y in the past may nonetheless benefit y by increasing y's chance of obtaining medical services that otherwise might not be available.

We should conceive of the purpose of preferential treatment as being to benefit, not only the specific individuals directly affected by past racist acts, but also those counterfactually indicated in such acts. Affirmative action communicates not only to the specific Blacks and Whites involved in a particular episode, but to all Blacks and Whites that invidious racial discrimination is no longer the order of the day. Unless this is recognized, the purpose of preferential treatment will not be understood. . . .

There are many factors that influence individual prospective employers in choosing between candidates—the way they dress, their posture and demeanor, their choice of cologne, hairstyle, personal relationship to the employer—and many if not most may be totally irrelevant to the person's ability to perform the job in question. But it is not always immoral to choose a candidate based on factors irrelevant to [his] ability to perform, as in the case of hiring a person because he or she is a close relative. In any case, it would be impossible to identify all such factors and legislate against them.

Civil rights legislation prohibits using factors that historically have been used systematically to exclude certain groups of individuals from opportunities generally available to members of other groups. Thus, the disabled have systematically been excluded relative to the physically normal, women excluded relative to men, Blacks excluded relative to Whites, Muslims and Jews excluded relative to Christians, and so on.

We can expect many individuals equal with respect to their productive capacity to have been treated unequally by the market because of random factors that influence the choices of decision makers for available opportunities. Within both excluded and preferred groups, there will be some who are better off than others, based on random factors that have influenced their economic destiny. But it is only at the level of the group that systematic as opposed to random factors can be distinguished. Economist Lester Thurow estimates that "70 to 80 percent of the variance in individual earnings is caused by factors that are not within the control of even perfect governmental economic policies," and he concludes: "The economy will treat different individuals unequally no matter what we do. Only groups can be treated equally."

Because of a history of racist exclusion from educational, employment, and investment opportunities, Blacks generally have a lower ratio of relevant job-related skills and attitudes than Whites. Eliminating racism would do nothing to eliminate this deficit in human capital, which in itself is sufficient to ground a continuing prejudice against Blacks.

As Owen Fiss has argued, preferential treatment for a disadvantaged group provides members of that group with positions of power, prestige, and influence that they would otherwise not attain in the near future. Such positions empower both the individuals awarded those positions as well as the group they identify with and are identified with by others. Individuals awarded such positions serve as models that others within their group may aspire to, and (more often than not) provide the group with a source of defense and advocacy that improves the status of the group.

Fiss acknowledges, as many critics have stressed, that preferential treatment might encourage claims that Blacks do not have the ability to make it on their own, thereby perpetuating the myth of Black inferiority. But I do not see this as a serious problem. For the assumption of Black inferiority is used to explain both why Blacks do not occupy prestigious positions when they are in fact absent from such positions and why they do occupy them when they are in fact present in such positions. The assumption of Black inferiority exists with either option, and Blacks who do occupy positions they would likely not occupy but for affirmative action are not losing credibility they otherwise might have. On the other hand, Blacks who do occupy such positions and perform at or above expectation do gain a credibility they otherwise would not have.

An enduring legacy of racism (and sexism) is the presumption that Blacks (and women) are generally less competent and undeserving of nonmenial opportunities. Thus, the issue is not whether Blacks will be considered incompetent, but whether the effects of that assumption will continue. "The ethical issue is whether the position of perpetual subordination is going to be brought to an end for our disadvantaged groups, and if so, at what speed and at what cost." . . . [Owen Fiss]

I believe that government perpetrates the injuries of slavery—and segregation if it initiates no effort to correct for those injuries. Refusing to act when action is called for can be as great a source of injury as inappropriate intervention. It does no good to cite a statute of limitations, since demands for restitution have been made continuously since slavery was abolished. The Freedmen's Bureau was initially conceived as a means of providing freed slaves with the education and capital necessary to make them at least self-sufficient. But these amenities were withdrawn in favor of a system that perpetuated the subordination of freed slaves through political exclusion, inadequate educational facilities, job reservations, and housing segregation. . . .

In response to the claim that Blacks are owed restitution for the injuries suffered under slavery, segregation, and other racially exclusionary practices, some critics have objected that contemporary Whites should not be required to accept responsibility for something they had no choice in. Whatever benefits they may have received, they had no choice in receiving. And since a person or party can be held morally responsible only for something that they could have done or avoided doing, it is unjust to require restitution from those least responsible for the injuries inflicted by seg-

regation and racism. As one critic puts it, "it is morally absurd to penalize [someone] for an evil that he could not have prevented." [Paul Hoffman]

But the morally relevant issue is not whether the beneficiaries of unjust acts are responsible for the unjust acts, but whether the beneficiaries sincerely attempt to make restitution for their continuing enrichment from such acts. Certainly, contemporary Whites are not responsible for many of the current injuries suffered by Blacks. But they are responsible for continuing to profit from benefits that derive from such injuries. Continuing to benefit from acts of injustice creates a liability to make restitution for them, at least to the degree of relinquishing the undeserved benefits.

Another objection to preferential treatment as a form of restitution derives from the principle, central to corrective justice, that those most responsible for harm should bear the primary cost of restitution and those most harmed should receive the greatest share of the restitution. However, while older Whites are most likely to be responsible for the injuries of racism, it is young Whites seeking educational and employment positions who are forced to bear the primary cost of restitution. Likewise, while it is older Blacks with the least education and training who bear the greatest injuries from the legacy of slavery and segregation, it is young Blacks with the highest qualifications who are the beneficiaries of preferential treatment.

But again, there is little need to quibble with the fact that older White workers are the direct beneficiaries of past racist exclusions, and are now granted a strong measure of protection by seniority systems in recognition of their subsequent investment of time, energy, and effort in those positions. But young Whites are the indirect beneficiaries of past racist acts and the direct beneficiaries of current ones. Institutional racism gives young Whites a decided advantage over young Blacks because they have generally received better educational and entrepreneurial opportunities, and because they are less subject to stigmatized stereotypes.

Prior to affirmative action, Blacks were penalized in direct proportion to their level of qualification. Those with higher levels of qualifications were typically subjected to greater prejudice and higher rates of exclusion from opportunities to develop and profit from those qualifications. Among Blacks harmed most by racism would thus be individuals with maximum potential who were prevented by racist exclusions from developing that potential into even minimal qualifications. However, the fact that preferential treatment does not reach Blacks who have been most harmed by racism is no criticism for helping those less harmed. One does not condemn aspirin as a remedy for headaches because it does not also remedy migraines. . . .

FORWARD-LOOKING JUSTIFICATIONS OF AFFIRMATIVE ACTION

While [Glenn] Loury defends a form of reparation for Blacks but rejects preferential treatment, others have defended preferential treatment but denied that it should be viewed as a form of reparation. This latter group rejects "backward-looking" justifications of affirmative action and defends it instead on "forward-looking" grounds that include distributive justice, minimizing subordination, and maximizing social utility.

Thus, Ronald Fiscus argues that backward-looking arguments have distorted the proper justification for affirmative action policies. Backward-looking arguments depend on the paradigm of traditional tort cases, where a specific individual x has deprived another individual y of a specific good t through an identifiable act a, and x is required to restore y to the position y would have had, had a not occurred. But typically, preferential treatment requires that x' (rather than x) restore y' (instead of y) with a good t' that y' supposedly would have achieved had y not been deprived of t by x. The displacement of perpetrator (x' for x) and victim (y' for y) gives rise to the problem of (1) White males who are innocent of acts having caused harm nonetheless being forced to provide restitution for such acts; and (2) Blacks who were not directly harmed by those acts nonetheless becoming the principal beneficiaries of restitution for those acts.

For many, the backward-looking justification for affirmative action makes it seem that innocent White males are forced to bear the principle burden for correcting the wrongs of the past, and that the least harmed Blacks are the undeserving beneficiaries of their unjust sacrifice. This is clearly the sense expressed in Justice Scalia's opposition to affirmative action:

My father came to this country when he was a teenager. Not only had he never profited from the sweat of any Black man's brow, I don't think he had ever seen a Black man. There are, of course many White ethnic groups that came to this country in great numbers relatively late in its history—Italians, Jews, Poles—who not only took no part in, and derived no profit from, the major historic suppression of the currently acknowledged minor-

ity groups, but were, in fact, themselves the object of discrimination by the dominant Anglo-Saxon majority. To be sure, in relatively recent years some or all of these groups have been the beneficiaries of discrimination against Blacks, or have themselves practiced discrimination, but to compare their racial debt . . . with that of those who plied the slave trade, and who maintained a formal caste system for many years thereafter, is to confuse a mountain with a molehill. Yet curiously enough, we find that in the system of restorative justice established by the Wisdoms and the Powells and the Whites, it is precisely these groups that do most of the restoring. It is they who, to a disproportionate degree, are the competitors with the urban Blacks and Hispanics for jobs, housing, education.

Similarly Judge Richard Posner writes:

The members of the minority group who receive preferential treatment will often be those who have not been the victims of discrimination while the nonminority people excluded because of preferences are unlikely to have perpetrated, or to have in any demonstrable sense benefited from, the discrimination.

Fiscus argues that the backward-looking argument reinforces the perception that preferential treatment is unfair to innocent White males, and so long as this is the case, both the courts and the public are likely to oppose strong affirmative action policies such as quotas, set-asides, and other preferential treatment policies.

In contrast, Fiscus recommends that preferential treatment be justified in terms of distributive justice, which as a matter of equal protection, "requires that individuals be awarded the positions, advantages, or benefits they would have been awarded under fair conditions," that is, conditions under which racist exclusion would not have precluded Blacks from attaining "their deserved proportion of the society's important benefits." Conversely, "distributive justice also holds that individuals or groups may not claim positions, advantages, or benefits that they would not have been awarded under fair conditions." These conditions jointly prohibit White males from claiming an unreasonable share of social benefits and protect White males from having to bear an unreasonable share of the redistributive burden.

Fiscus takes the position that any deviation between Blacks and Whites from strict proportionality in the distribution of current goods is evidence of racism. Thus, if Blacks were 20 percent of a particular population but held no positions in the police or fire departments, that is indicative of past and present racial discrimination. While discrimination exists with respect to many characteristics other than race (i.e., height and attractiveness), the Fourteenth Amendment prohibits such in the case of race. As such, deviation in the distribution of goods with respect to groups defined by race are subject to legal review, unlike deviations in the distribution of goods with respect to groups defined by attractiveness.

Because the Equal Protection Clause of the Fourteenth Amendment protects citizens from statistical discrimination on the basis of race, the use of race as the principal reason for excluding certain citizens from benefits made available to other citizens is a violation of that person's constitutional rights. This was one basis for Bakke's suit against the UC Davis medical school's 16 percent minority set-aside for medical school admission. There were eighty-four seats out of the one hundred admission slots that he was eligible to fill, and he was excluded from competing for the other sixteen slots because of his race. On the basis of the standard criteria (GPA, MCAT scores, etc.), Bakke argued that he would have been admitted before any of the Black applicants admitted under the minority set-aside. He therefore claimed that he was being excluded from the additional places available because he was White.

Currently, Blacks have approximately 3.25 times fewer physicians than would be expected given their numbers in the population. Native Americans have 7 times fewer physicians than what would have been expected if intelligent, well-trained, and motivated Native Americans had tried to become physicians at the same rate as did European Americans.

For Fiscus, the underrepresentation of African and Native Americans among physicians and the maldistribution of medical resources to minority communities is clearly the effect of generations of racist exclusions. Because of stereotypes portraying them as the product of cognitive deficiencies, unstable families, bad habits, and inadequate educations, Blacks and Native Americans seeking to obtain educational, employment, and investment opportunities have traditionally been perceived to be less prepared than their White competitors. Not only are qualified members of the oppressed group harmed by this prejudice, but even more harmed are the many who would have been qualified but for injuries induced by racial prejudice.

For Fiscus, individuals of different races would have been as equally distributed in the social body as the molecules of a gas in a container and he identifies the belief in the inherent equality of races with the Equal Protection Clause of the Fourteenth Amendment.

In a world without racism, minorities would be represented among the top one hundred medical school applicants at UC Davis in the same proportion as they were in the general population. Accordingly, because Bakke did not score among the top eighty-four Whites, he would not have qualified for admission. Thus, he had no right to the position he was contesting, and indeed if he were given such a position in lieu of awarding it to a minority, Bakke would be much like a person who had received stolen goods. "Individuals who have not personally harmed minorities may nevertheless be prevented from reaping the benefits of the harm inflicted by the society at large."

Justice O'Connor has voiced skepticism toward the assumption that members of different races would "gravitate with mathematical exactitude to each employer or union absent unlawful discrimination." She considers it sheer speculation as to "how many minority students would have been admitted to the medical school at Davis absent past discrimination in educational opportunities." I likewise consider it speculative to assume that races would be represented in every area in proportion to their proportion of the general population. But because it is impossible to reasonably predict what that distribution would have been absent racial discrimination, it is not mere speculation but morally fair practice to assume that it would have been the same as the proportion in the general population. Given the fact of legally sanctioned invidious racism against Blacks in U.S. history, the burden of proof should not be on the oppressed group to prove that it would be represented at a level proportionate to its presence in the general population. Rather, the burden of proof should be on the majority to show why its overrepresentation among the most well off is not the result of unfair competition imposed by racism. We are morally obligated to assume proportional representation until there are more plausible reasons than racism for assuming otherwise.

Like Fiscus, I believe that races are equal, but that need not imply that they are identical in all relevant respects. Belief in racial equality requires us to acknowledge that racial differences, if they exist, should be allowed opportunities for cultivation free of racist restrictions. Only when opportunities are openly available can natural distributions based on natural differences be determined. In a situation not skewed by racism, Blacks might be more concentrated in certain areas and less concentrated in others. But to accept as the norm that they would be concentrated in the lower echelons of most areas, if represented at all, is racist. Because of the universality of prejudice against Blacks, gross disparities in proportional representation should alert us to the probability that it is caused by racist restrictions rather than racialist differences or personal preferences.

Thus, it should be the responsibility of the Alabama Department of Public Safety to show why no Blacks were members of its highway patrol as of 1970, even though Blacks were 25 percent of the relevant workforce in Alabama. It should be the responsibility of the company and the union to explain why there were no Blacks with seniority in the union at the Kaiser plant in Louisiana, although Blacks made up 39 percent of the surrounding population. Likewise, it should be the responsibility of the union to explain why no Blacks had been admitted to the Sheet Metal Workers' Union in New York City although minorities were 29 percent of the available workforce. If no alternative explanations are more plausible, then the assumption that the disparity in representation is the result of racism should stand.

The question should not be whether White males are innocent or guilty of racism or sexism, but whether they have a right to inflated odds of obtaining benefits relative to minorities and women. A White male is innocent only up to the point where he takes advantage of "a benefit he would not qualify for without the accumulated effects of racism. At that point he becomes an accomplice in, and a beneficiary of, society's racism. He becomes the recipient of stolen goods." [Ronald J. Fiscus]

While Justice Scalia dismisses the racism that may have been practiced by Italians, Irish, and other immigrant groups as insignificant compared to the racism practiced under slavery, it is plausible that racism after slavery was more instrumental in creating the situation that affirmative action was meant to relieve than racism during slavery.

While many European immigrant groups were no more literate than Blacks who were already in America, they were nonetheless granted state support in acquiring property (the Homestead Acts, the FHA, urban renewal), education (the Morrill Act, segregated schools), and jobs (NLRB and governmental support for racist unions) that Blacks were denied. Unions, municipalities, and lending institutions used legally sanctioned means to exclude Blacks from employment, educational, and investment opportunities made available to European immigrants. While union members benefited from government interventions in the labor market as a result of legislation such as the Wagner Act, the National Apprenticeship Act, and the Davis-Bacon Act, they actively practiced nepotism and ethnic preferences in the award of jobs and training. . . .

In aiming at proportionality, not as a natural outcome but as a condition necessary to determine natural outcomes, the rights of innocent White males are not being sacrificed for the greater good of increasing the participation of minorities and women. The good of a more diverse society should not be conceived of as justifying the sacrifice of a "randomly chosen" subset of White males currently seeking educational, employment, and entrepreneurial opportunities. Rather, White males are being forced to relinquish benefits that are ill gotten, benefits they would likely not have received in a racially fair world. . . .

A central question in the debate over affirmative action is the extent to which racial classifications are important in accomplishing the goal of relieving the subordinate status of minorities and women. Given the aim of improving safety in transportation, classifying people in terms of their race is rationally irrelevant, while classifying them in terms of their driving competency, visual acuity, and maturity is essential. On the other hand, given the aim of improving health care in Black neighborhoods, classifying applicants for medical school in terms of their race is, in addition to their academic and clinical abilities, a very relevant factor.

To illustrate, African Americans, Hispanics, and Native Americans make up 22 percent of the population but represent only 10 percent of entering medical students and 7 percent of practicing physicians. A number of studies have shown that underrepresented minority physicians are more likely than their majority counterparts to care for poor patients and patients of similar ethnicity. Indeed, "each ethnic group of patients was more likely to be cared for by a physician of their own ethnic background than by a physician of another ethnic background."[4] This suggests that sociocultural factors such as language, physical identity, personal background, and experiences are relevant factors in determining the kinds of communities in which a physician will establish a practice. If this is the case, then the race of a medical school applicant would be an important factor in providing medical services to certain underrepresented communities. Thus, while there might be some purposes for which race is irrelevant, there might be other purposes in which race is important (though perhaps not necessary) for achieving the end in view. The remedy targets Blacks as a group because racially discriminatory practices were directed against Blacks as a group.[5]

Some argue that characteristics such as race, sex, and social background are morally irrelevant because an individual has no choice as to whether such attributes shall attach to him or her. But an individual has no choice about whether he or she will be born with a high IQ or not. Yet, we do not advocate eliminating intellectual potential as a criterion for receiving scarce educational opportunities. Individuals with high IQ are valued because we believe that such individuals play an important role in increasing aggregate wealth. To the extent that we want our society to be a productive one, we allocate special places to such individuals.

A similar rationale holds in the case of race. To the extent that we want our society to be not only productive, but also just, to that extent it is important to demonstrate a concern for those who face decreased opportunities because of racism. Preferential treatment programs are meant to offset the disadvantages imposed by racism so that Blacks are not forced to bear the principal costs of that error.

It is commonly objected that proportionate representation achieved in this manner is artificial. But barriers that exclude Blacks from educational, employment, and entrepreneurial opportunities impose and maintain an artificial underrepresentation. To condemn policies meant to correct for racial barriers as themselves erecting barriers is to ignore the difference between action and reaction, cause and effect, aggression and self-defense. Even a critic of affirmative action such as Robert Fullinwider admits that "If equal opportunity is looked at as some kind of equilibrium, then we can see nothing amiss about tampering with a situation that has got into disequilibrium. We add and subtract weights here and there until equilibrium is restored." Clearly, granting preferential treatment to individuals who suffer the present burdens of discrimination is exactly the kind of tampering that is appropriate.

CONCLUSION

Racism was directed against Blacks whether they were talented, average, or mediocre, and attenuating the effects of racism requires distributing remedies similarly. Affirmative action policies compensate for the harms of racism (overt and institutional) through antidiscrimination laws and preferential policies. Prohibiting the benign use of race as a factor in the award of educational, employment and business opportunities would eliminate compensation for past and present racism

and reinforce the moral validity of the status quo, with Blacks overrepresented among the least well off and underrepresented among the most well off.

It has become popular to use affirmative action as a scapegoat for the increased vulnerability of the White working class. But it should be recognized that the civil rights revolution (in general) and affirmative action (in particular) [have] been beneficial, not just to Blacks, but also to Whites (e.g., women, the disabled, the elderly) who otherwise would be substantially more vulnerable than they are now.

Affirmative action is directed toward empowering those groups that have been adversely affected by past and present exclusionary practices. Initiatives to abolish preferential treatment would inflict a grave injustice on African Americans, for they signal a reluctance to acknowledge that the plight of African Americans is the result of institutional practices that require institutional responses.

READING 42

The Case Against Affirmative Action

Louis P. Pojman

For Pojman's biography, see Reading 38. In this essay he sets forth eight arguments against Strong Affirmative Action, which he defines as preferential treatment, discriminating in favor of members of underrepresented groups that have been treated unjustly in the past and against innocent people. He distinguishes this from Weak Affirmative Action, which simply seeks to promote equal opportunity to the goods and offices of a society. Pojman does not argue against this policy, but against Strong Affirmative Action, attempting to show that *two wrongs don't make a right*. Strong Affirmative Action, as it is applied against Whites and Asians is racist. It is a form of racial profiling. When it is applied against White and Asian males, it is both racist and sexist. It is the dominant form of Affirmative Action in contemporary university admissions and hiring programs.

An earlier version of this article appeared in the *International Journal of Applied Philosophy,* 12 (1998). Copyright © 2000 Louis P. Pojman.

"A ruler who appoints any man to an office, when there is in his dominion another man better qualified for it, sins against God and against the State." (The Koran)

"Each person possesses an inviolability founded on justice that even the welfare of society cannot override." (John Rawls, *A Theory of Justice*)

Hardly a week goes by but that the subject of affirmative action does not come up. Whether in the form of preferential hiring, nontraditional casting, quotas, "goals and time tables," minority scholarships, race-norming, reverse discrimination, or employment of members of underutilized groups, the issue confronts us as a terribly perplexing problem. Affirmative action was one of the issues that divided the Democratic and Republican parties during the 1996 election, the Democrats supporting it ("Mend it don't end it") and the Republicans opposing it ("affirmative action is reverse racism"). During the November 7, 1996, general election, California voters by a 55 percent to 45 percent vote approved Proposition 209 (called the "California Civil Rights Initiative"), which made it illegal to discriminate on the basis of race or gender, hence ending affirmative action in public institutions in California. The U.S. Supreme Court subsequently refused to rule on the appeal that followed, thus leaving it to the individual states to decide how they will deal with this issue. Both sides reorganized for a renewed battle, and during the 2000 presidential election campaigns both the Democrat and the Republican party leaders endorsed affirmative action.[1] Not long before, the European Union's High Court of Justice in Luxembourg had approved affirmative action programs giving women preferential treatment in the European Union countries (November 11, 1997).

Let us agree that despite the evidences of a booming economy, the poor are suffering grievously, with children being born into desperate material and psychological poverty, for whom the ideal of "equal opportunity for all," as eloquently set forth by William Galston in his essay [Reading 40], is a cruel joke. Many feel that the federal government has abandoned its guarantee to provide the minimum necessities for each American, so that the pace of this tragedy seems to be accelerating daily. Add to this the fact that in our country African Americans have a legacy of slavery and unjust discrimination to contend with and we have the makings of an inferno and, perhaps, in the worse case scenario, the downfall of a nation. What is the answer to our national problem? Is it increased welfare? More job training? More support for education? Required licensing of parents to have children? A negative income tax? More support for families or for mothers with small children? All of these have merit and should be part of the national debate. But, my thesis is, however tragic the situation may be (and we may disagree on just how tragic it is), one policy is *not* a legitimate part of the solution, and that is *unjust reverse discrimination* against young white males or any other group of people (e.g., white women, Asians, Jews, or Mormons). Strong Affirmative Action, which implicitly advocates reverse discrimination, while no doubt well intentioned, is morally heinous, asserting, by implication, that *two wrongs make a right.*

The *Two Wrongs Make a Right Thesis* goes like this: Because *some* whites once enslaved some blacks, the descendants of those slaves, some of whom may now enjoy high incomes and social status, have a right to opportunities and offices over better-qualified whites who had nothing to do with either slavery or the oppression of blacks and who may even have suffered hardship comparable to those of poor blacks. In addition, Strong Affirmative Action creates a new Hierarchy of the Oppressed: blacks get primary preferential treatment, women second, Native Americans third, Hispanics fourth, the handicapped fifth, and so on until white and, sometimes, Asian males, no matter how needy or well qualified, must accept the leftovers. Naturally, individuals in whom oppressed classes are combined (e.g., a one-eyed, black Hispanic female) trump all single-classification individuals. The Equal Protection Clause of the Fourteenth Amendment becomes reinterpreted as "Equal protection for all equals, but some equals are more equal than others."

Before analyzing arguments concerning affirmative action, I must define my terms. Let SAA represent Strong Affirmative Action and WAA stand for Weak Affirmative Action.

WAA: A policy that attempts to increase the opportunities for members of underrepresented or historically disadvantaged groups implemented on the basis of the desire to equalize opportunity, achieve some other valuable result (e.g., role modeling or diversity), or satisfy the demands of compensatory justice, where such policies do not include giving preference to less-qualified candidates.

SAA: A policy that gives some preference to less-qualified candidates on the basis of the desire to equalize results or opportunity, achieve some other valuable result (e.g., role modeling or diversity), or satisfy the demands of compensatory justice.

By *Weak Affirmative Action* I mean policies that will increase the opportunities of disadvantaged people to attain social goods and offices. It includes the dismantling of segregated institutions, widespread advertisement to groups not previously represented in certain privileged positions, special scholarships for the disadvantaged classes (e.g., the poor, regardless of race or gender), and even using diversity or underrepresentation of groups or a history of past discrimination as a tie breaker when candidates for these goods and offices are relatively equal. The goal of Weak Affirmative Action is *equal opportunity* to compete, not *equal results*. We seek to provide each citizen, regardless of race or gender, a fair chance to the most favored positions in society. There is no more moral requirement to guarantee that 12 percent of professors at American universities are black than to guarantee that 85 percent of the players in the National Basketball Association are white.

By *Strong Affirmative Action* I mean preferential treatment on the basis of race, ethnicity, or gender (or some other morally irrelevant criterion), discriminating in favor of underrepresented groups against overrepresented groups, aiming at roughly equal results. Strong Affirmative Action is reverse discrimination. It says it is right to do wrong to correct a wrong. It is the policy that is currently being promoted under the name of *Affirmative Action,* so I will use that term, or AA for short, throughout this essay to stand for this version of affirmative action. I will not argue for or against the principle of Weak Affirmative Action. Indeed, I think it has considerable moral weight. Strong Affirmative Action has none, or so I will argue. But it is this type of AA that is the dominant form in college admissions and university hiring, the two areas with which I am most familiar.

In what follows I will mainly concentrate on affirmative action policies with regard to race, but the arguments can be extended to cover ethnicity and gender. I think that if a case for affirmative action can be made it will be as a corrective to racial oppression. I will examine eight arguments regarding affirmative action.

The first five will be *negative,* attempting to show that the best arguments for affirmative action fail. The last three will be *positive* arguments for policies opposing affirmative action.

I. A CRITIQUE OF ARGUMENTS FOR AFFIRMATIVE ACTION

1. The Need for Role Models Argument

The role model argument is straightforward. We all have need of role models, and it helps to know that others like us can be successful. We learn and are encouraged to strive for excellence by emulating our heroes and "our kind of people" who have succeeded.

In the first place it's not clear that role models of one's own racial or sexual type are necessary (let alone sufficient) for success. One of my heroes was Gandhi, an Indian Hindu; another was my grade school science teacher, Miss DeVoe; and another, Martin Luther King Jr., behind whom I marched in civil rights demonstrations. More important than having role models of one's "own type" is having genuinely good people, of whatever race or gender, to emulate. Our common humanity should be a sufficient basis for us to see the possibility of success in people of virtue and merit. To yield to the demand, however tempting it may be to do so, for "role models just like us" is to treat people like means not ends. It is a policy of disrespect for the individual as a person. It elevates morally irrelevant particularity over relevant traits, such as ability and integrity. We don't need people exactly like us to find inspiration. As Steve Allen once quipped, "If I had to follow a role model exactly, I would have become a nun."

Furthermore, even if it is of some help to people with low self-esteem to gain encouragement from seeing others of their particular kind in successful positions, it is doubtful whether this need is a sufficient reason to justify preferential hiring or reverse discrimination. What good is a role model who is inferior to other professors or physicians or business personnel? The best way to create role models is to promote people not because of race or gender but because they are the best qualified for the job. It is the violation of this fact that is largely responsible for the widespread whisper in the medical field (at least in New York State) that you should "never go to a black physician under 40" (referring to the fact that AA has affected the medical system during the past twenty years). Fight the feeling however hard I try, I cannot help wondering on seeing a black or a woman in a position of honor, "Is she in this position because she merits it or because of Affirmative Action?" Where Affirmative Action is the policy, the "figment of pigment" creates a stigma of undeservedness, whether or not it is deserved.[2]

Finally, entertain this thought experiment. Suppose we discovered that tall handsome white males somehow made the best role models for the most people, especially poor people. Suppose even large numbers of minority people somehow found inspiration in their sight. Would we be justified in hiring tall handsome white males over better qualified short Hispanic women?

2. The Compensation Argument

The compensation argument goes like this: Blacks have been wronged and severely harmed by whites. Therefore white society should compensate blacks for the injury caused them. Reverse discrimination in terms of preferential hiring, contracts, and scholarships is a fitting way to compensate for the past wrongs.[3]

This argument actually involves a distorted notion of compensation. Normally, we think of compensation as owed by a specific person A to another person B whom A has wronged in a specific way C. For example, if I have stolen your car and used it for a period of time to make business profits that would have gone to you, it is not enough that I return your car. I must pay you an amount reflecting your loss and my ability to pay. If I have made only $5,000 and have only $10,000 in assets, it will not be possible for you to collect $20,000 in damages—even though that is the amount of loss you have incurred.

Sometimes compensation is extended to groups of people who have been unjustly harmed by the greater society. For example, the U.S. government has compensated the Japanese Americans who were interred during World War II, and the West German government has paid reparations to the survivors of Nazi concentration camps. But here a specific group of people have been identified who were wronged in an identifiable way by the government of the nation in question.

On the face of it, demands by blacks for compensation do not fit the usual pattern. Perhaps Southern states with Jim Crow laws could be accused of unjustly harming blacks, but it is hard to see that the U.S. government was involved in doing so. Much of the harm done to blacks was the result of private discrimination,

not state action. So the Germany/U.S. analogy doesn't hold. Furthermore, it is not clear that all blacks were harmed in the same way or whether some were *unjustly* harmed or harmed more than poor whites and others (e.g., short people). Most "blacks" are partially Caucasian or Native American, mulattos or quadroons, so that, even if we accepted some form of the compensation argument, determining how much compensation each "black" is owed would be a Herculean task. If compensation is to be paid by the descendants of those who participated in slavery, then the present members of the nations of West Africa, whose ancestors sold their own people into slavery, should bear a large part of the burden. Finally, even if identifiable blacks were harmed by identifiable social practices, it is not clear that most forms of Affirmative Action are appropriate to restore the situation. The usual practice of a financial payment seems more appropriate than giving a high-level job to someone unqualified or only minimally qualified, who, speculatively, might have been better qualified had he not been subject to racial discrimination. If John is the star tailback of our college team and has a promising professional future, and I accidentally (but culpably) drive my pickup truck over his legs, and so cripple him, John may be due compensation, but he is not due the tailback spot on the football team.

Still, there may be something intuitively compelling about compensating members of an oppressed group who are minimally qualified. Suppose that the Hatfields and the McCoys are enemy clans and some youths from the Hatfields go over and steal diamonds and gold from the McCoys, distributing it within the Hatfield economy. Even though we do not know which Hatfield youths did the stealing, we would want to restore the wealth, as far as possible, to the McCoys. One way might be to tax the Hatfields, but another might be to give preferential treatment in terms of scholarships and training programs and hiring to the McCoys.

This is perhaps the strongest argument for Affirmative Action, and it may well justify some weaker versions, but it is doubtful whether the compensation argument is sufficient to justify strong versions with quotas and "goals and timetables" (really a euphemism for *quotas*) in skilled positions. There are at least two reasons for this. First, we have no way of knowing how many people of any given group would have achieved some given level of competence had the world been different. This is especially relevant if my objections to the equal results argument (see section 5) are correct. Second, the normal criterion of competence is a strong prima facie consideration when the most important positions are at stake. There are three reasons for this: (1) Treating people according to their merits respects them as persons, as ends in themselves, rather than as means to social ends. In the words of John Rawls, "Each person possesses an inviolability founded on justice that even the welfare of society cannot override."[4] If we believe that individuals possess a dignity which deserves to be respected, then we ought to treat each individual on the basis of his or her merits, not as a mere instrument for social policy. (2) Society has given people expectations that if they attain certain levels of excellence they will be awarded appropriately. (3) Filling the most important positions with the best qualified is the best way to ensure efficiency in job-related areas and in society in general. These reasons are not absolutes. They can be overridden.[5] But there is a strong presumption in their favor so that a burden of proof rests with those who would override them.

At this point we get into the problem of whether innocent nonblacks should have to pay a penalty in terms of preferential hiring of blacks. We turn to that argument.

3. The Argument for Compensation from Those Who Innocently Benefited from Past Injustice

Young white males as innocent beneficiaries of unjust discrimination against blacks and women have no grounds for complaint when society seeks to level the tilted field. They may be innocent of oppressing blacks, other minorities, and women, but they have unjustly benefited from that oppression or discrimination. So it is perfectly proper that less qualified women and blacks be hired before them.

The operative principle is: He who knowingly and willingly benefits from a wrong must help pay for the wrong. Judith Jarvis Thompson puts it this way. "Many [white males] have been direct beneficiaries of policies which have down-graded blacks and women . . . and even those who did not directly benefit . . . had, at any rate, the advantage in the competition which comes of the confidence in one's full membership [in the community], and of one's right being recognized as a matter of course."[6] That is, white males obtain advantages in self-respect and self-confidence deriving from a racist-sexist system which denies these to blacks and women.

Here is my response to this argument: As I noted in section 2, compensation is normally individual and specific. If A harms B regarding x, B has a right to compensation from A in regard to x. If A steals B's car and wrecks it, A has an obligation to compensate B for the stolen car, but A's son has no obligation to compensate B. Furthermore, if A dies or disappears, B has no moral right to claim that society compensate him for the stolen car—though if he has insurance, he can make such a claim to the insurance company. Sometimes a wrong cannot be compensated, and we just have to make the best of an imperfect world.

Suppose my parents, divining that I would grow up to have an unsurpassable desire to be a basketball player, bought an expensive growth hormone for me. Unfortunately, a neighbor stole it and gave it to little Michael, who gained the extra 13 inches—my 13 inches—and shot up to an enviable 6 feet 6 inches. Michael, better known as Michael Jordan, would have been a runt like me but for his luck. As it is he profited from the injustice and excelled in basketball, as I would have done had I had my proper dose.

Do I have a right to the millions of dollars that Jordan—the innocent beneficiary of my unjustly obtained growth hormone—made as a professional basketball player? I have a right to something from the neighbor who stole the hormone, and it might be kind of Jordan to give me free tickets to the Bull's basketball games, and perhaps I should be remembered in his will. As far as I can see, however, he does not *owe* me anything, either legally or morally.

Suppose further that Michael Jordan and I are in high school together and we are both qualified to play basketball, only he is far better than me. Do I deserve to start in his position because I would have been as good as he is had someone not cheated me as a child? Again, I think not. But if being the lucky beneficiary of wrongdoing does not entail that Jordan (or the coach) owes me anything in regard to basketball, why should it be a reason to engage in preferential hiring in academic positions or highly coveted jobs? If minimal qualifications are not adequate to override excellence in basketball, even when the minimality is a consequence of wrongdoing, why should they be adequate in other areas?

4. The Diversity Argument

It is important that we learn to live in a pluralistic world, learning to get along with those of other races and cultures, so we should have fully integrated schools and employment situations. We live in a shrinking world and need to appreciate each other's culture and specific way of looking at life. Diversity is an important symbol and educative device. As Barbara Bergmann argues, "Diversity has positive value in many situations, but in some its value is crucial. To give an obvious example, a racially diverse community needs a racially diverse police force if the police are to gain the trust of all parts of the community and if one part of the community is not to feel dominated by the other part."[7] Thus preferential treatment is warranted to perform this role in society.

Once again, there is some truth in these concerns. Diversity of ideas challenges us to scrutinize our own values and beliefs, and diverse customs have aesthetic and moral value, helping us to appreciate the novelty and beauty in life. Diversity may expand our moral horizons. But, again, although we can admit the value of diversity, it hardly seems adequate to override the moral requirement to treat each person with equal respect. *Diversity for diversity's sake is moral promiscuity,* since it obfuscates rational distinctions, undermines the moral principle of treating individuals as ends, treating them, instead, as mere means (to the goals of social engineering), and, furthermore, unless those hired are highly qualified, the diversity factor threatens to become a fetish. Each person is a unique individual, different from every other. Perhaps it is a sad commentary of our shallow conformist society that we are turning out look-alike, act-alike, Barbie dolls, instead of eccentric gems who cannot be put into a mold, who stand out, offering their own unique contribution. It's not diversity of race or gender that is important but diversity of ideas, of perspective and personality. At the same time we want a uniformity in some areas. We want a highly unified commitment to the moral point of view, to tolerance of individual difference, and to the goals of a democratic society. The motto of the Unitarian Church is, "We don't have to think alike to love alike." That seems a worthy motto for a culturally diverse society, where difference is accepted, but it depends on considerable cooperation.

There may be times when diversity may seem to be "crucial" to the well-being of a diverse community, such as a diverse police force. Suppose that white policemen overreact to young black males and the latter group then comes to distrust white policemen. Hiring more less-qualified black policemen, who would relate better to these youth, may have overall utilitarian value. But such a move, while we might make it as a lesser evil, could have serious consequences in allowing the demographic prejudices to dictate social policy. A better strategy would be to hire the best police, that is, those who can perform in a disciplined, intelligent manner, regardless of their race. A white policeman must be able to arrest a black burglar, even as a black policeman must be able to arrest a white rapist. The quality of the police man or woman, not his or her race or gender, is what counts.

On the other hand, if the black policeman, though lacking certain formal skills of the white policeman, really is able to do a better job in the black community, this might constitute a case of merit, not affirmative action. This is similar to the legitimacy of hiring Chinese men to act as undercover agents in Chinatown.[8]

5. The Equal Results Argument

Some philosophers and social scientists hold that human nature is roughly identical, so that on a fair playing field the same proportion from every race and ethnic group and both genders would attain to the highest positions in every area of endeavor. It would follow that any inequality of results itself is evidence for inequality of opportunity.

> History is important when considering governmental rules like Test 21 because low scores by blacks can be traced in large measure to the legacy of slavery and racism: segregation, poor schooling, exclusion from trade unions, malnutrition, and poverty have all played their roles. Unless one assumes that blacks are naturally less able to pass the test, the conclusion must be that the results are themselves socially and legally constructed, not a mere given for which law and society can claim no responsibility.
>
> The conclusion seems to be that genuine equality eventually requires equal results. Obviously blacks have been treated unequally throughout U.S. history, and just as obviously the economic and psychological effects of that inequality linger to this day, showing up in lower income and poorer performance in school and on tests than whites achieve. Since we have no reason to believe that differences in performance can be explained by factors other than history, equal results are a good benchmark by which to measure progress made toward genuine equality.[9]

Sterling Harwood seems to support a similar theory when he writes, "When will [AA] end? When will affirmative action stop compensating blacks? As soon as the unfair advantage is gone, affirmative action will stop. The elimination of the unfair advantage can be determined by showing that the percentage of blacks hired and admitted at least roughly equaled the percentage of blacks in the population."[10]

Albert G. Mosley develops a similar argument. "Establishing Blacks' presence at a level commensurate with their proportion in the relevant labor market need not be seen as an attempt to actualize some valid prediction. Rather, given the impossibility of determining what level of representation Blacks would have achieved were it not for racial discrimination, the assumption of proportional representation is the only *fair* assumption to make. This is not to argue that Blacks should be maintained in such positions, but their contrived exclusion merits equally contrived rectification."[11] [See also Reading 41.] The result of a just society should be equal numbers in proportion to each group in the work force.

However, Arthur, Harwood, and Mosley fail even to consider studies that suggest that there are innate differences between races, sexes, and groups. If there are genetic differences in intelligence and temperament within families, why should we not expect such differences between racial groups and the two genders? Why should the evidence for this be completely discounted?

Mosley's reasoning is as follows: Since we don't know for certain whether groups proportionately differ in talent, we should presume that they are equal in every respect. So we should presume that if we were living in a just society, there would be roughly proportionate representation in every field (e.g., equal representation of doctors, lawyers, professors, carpenters, airplane pilots, basketball players, and criminals). Hence, it is only fair—productive of justice—to aim at proportionate representation in these fields.

But the logic is flawed. Under a situation of ignorance we should not presume equality or inequality of representation—but should conclude that we *don't know* what the results would be in a just society. Ignorance doesn't favor equal group representation any more than it favors unequal group representation. It is neutral between them.

Consider this analogy. Suppose that you are the owner of a National Basketball Association team. Suppose, also, that I and other frustrated white basketball players bring a class-action suit against you and all the other owners, claiming that you have subtly and systematically discriminated against white and Asian basketball players, who make up less than 20 percent of the NBA players. When you respond to our charges that you and your owners are just responding to individual merit, we respond that the discrimination is a function of deep prejudice against white athletes, especially basketball players, who are discouraged in every way from competing on fair terms with blacks, who dominate the NBA. You probably wish that the matter of unequal results had not been brought up in the first place, but now that it has been, are you not in your rights to defend yourself by producing evidence showing that *average* physiological differences exist between blacks and whites and Asians, so that we should not presume unjust discrimination?

Similarly, the doctrine of equal results opens the door to a debate over average ability in ethnic, racial, and gender groups. The proponent of equal or fair opportunity would just as soon downplay this feature in favor of judging people as individuals by their merit (hard though that may be). But if the proponent of AA insists on the Equal Results Thesis, we are obliged to examine the Equal Abilities Thesis, on which it is based—the thesis that various ethnic and gender groups all have the same distribution of talent on the relevant characteristic.

With regard to cognitive skills we must consult the best evidence we have on average group differences. We need to compare average IQ scores, SAT scores, standard personality testing, success in academic and professional areas, and the like. If the evidence shows that group differences are nonexistent, the AA proponent may win, but if the evidence turns out to be against the Equal Abilities Thesis, the AA proponent loses. Consider for a start (1) that the average white and Asian scores are 195 points higher than black scores on the SAT tests, (2) that on virtually all IQ tests for the past seven or eight decades the average black IQ is 85, whereas the average white and Asian IQ is over 100, and (3) that the mean IQ score for university teachers and physicians is 114 and for professional scientists it is 143, so, on the basis of these averages, one would expect fewer blacks than whites or Asians in these professions.[12] The results of average GRE, LSAT, MCAT scores show similar patterns of significant average racial difference. The black scholar Glenn Loury notes, "In 1990 black high school seniors from families with annual incomes of $70,000 or more scored an average of 855 on the SAT, compared with average scores of 855 and 879 respectively for Asian-American and white seniors whose families had incomes between $10,000 and $20,000 per year."[13]

When such statistics are discussed, many people feel uncomfortable and want to drop the subject. Perhaps these statistics are misleading, but then we need to look carefully at the total evidence. The proponent of equal opportunity would urge us to get beyond racial and gender criteria in assignment of offices and opportunities and treat each person, not as an *average* white or black or female or male, but as a *person* judged on his or her own merits.

Furthermore, on the logic of Mosley and company, we should take aggressive AA against Asians and Jews since they are overrepresented in science, technology, and medicine, and we should presume that Asians and Jews are no more talented than average. So that each group receives its fair share, we should ensure that 12 percent of the philosophers in the United States are black, reduce the percentage of Jews from an estimated 15 percent to 2 percent—firing about 1,300 Jewish philosophers. The fact that Asians are producing 50 percent of Ph.D.s in science and math in this country and blacks less than 1 percent clearly shows, on this reasoning, that we are providing special secret advantages to Asians. By this logic, we should reduce the quota of blacks in the NBA to 12 percent.

But why does society have to enter into this results game in the first place? Why do we have to decide whether all difference is environmental or genetic? Perhaps we should simply admit that we lack sufficient evidence to pronounce on these issues with any certainty—but if we do lack evidence, should we not be more modest in insisting on equal results? Here's a thought experiment. Take two families of different racial groups, Green and Blue. The Greens decide to have only two children, to spend all their resources on them, and to give them the best education. The two Green kids respond well and end up with achievement test scores in the ninety-ninth percentile. The Blues fail to practice family planning and have fifteen children. They can afford only two children. Now they need help to support their large family. Why does society have to step in and help them? Society did not force them to have fifteen children. Suppose that the achievement test scores of the fifteen children fall below the twenty-fifth percentile. They cannot compete with the Greens. But now enters AA. It says that it is society's fault that the Blue children are not as able as the Greens and that the Greens must pay extra taxes to enable the Blues to compete. No restraints are put on the Blues regarding family size. This seems unfair to the Greens. Should the Green children be made to bear responsibility for the consequences of the Blues' voluntary behavior?[14]

My point is simply that philosophers like Arthur, Harwood, and Mosley need to cast their net wider and recognize that demographics and child-bearing and rearing practices are crucial factors in achievement. People have to take some responsibility for their actions. The equal results argument (or axiom) misses a greater part of the picture.

So much for a critique of the major arguments for Affirmative Action. I now turn to three positive arguments for why AA is wrong.

II. ARGUMENTS AGAINST AFFIRMATIVE ACTION

6. Affirmative Action Requires Discrimination Against a Different Group

Weak Affirmative Action weakly discriminates against new minorities, mostly innocent young white males, and Strong Affirmative Action strongly discriminates against these new minorities. As I argued in Section I.4, this discrimination is unwarranted, since, even if some compensation to blacks were indicated, it would be unfair to make innocent young white males bear the whole brunt of the payments. Albert Mosley has asserted that my arguments against AA are straw men, because the Strong AA I'm arguing against almost never happens and isn't really defended.[15] Recently I had this experience. I knew a brilliant philosopher who had outstanding publications in first-level journals and was having difficulty getting a tenure-track position. For the first time in my life I offered to make a phone call on his behalf to a university to which he had applied. When I got the Chair of the Search Committee, he offered that the committee was under instructions from the administration to hire a woman or a black. They had one of each on their short-list, so they weren't even considering the applications of white males. At my urging he retrieved my friend's file, and said, "This fellow looks far superior to the two candidates we're interviewing, but there's nothing I can do about it."

Early in my career I was invited for an interview for a position at a prominent university. Because my references and dossier showed that I had been a Black Studies major, had been the minister of a predominately black church in Bedford-Stuyvesant, and had publications on civil rights, the search committee assumed that I was black and would serve as their representative black. Consternation on the faces of the members of the search committee greeted me during my embarrassing interview. Being only another white philosopher, I didn't get the job, which went to a more qualified white male. I discovered that there were many candidates more qualified than myself, but since the search committee was operating under affirmative action guidelines, I was the only candidate they had seriously considered until the Great Awakening. Cases like this come to my attention regularly. In fact, it is poor white youths who become the new pariahs on the job market. The children of the wealthy have no trouble getting into the best private grammar schools and, on the basis of superior early education, into the best universities, graduate schools, and managerial and professional positions. Affirmative Action simply shifts injustice, setting blacks, Hispanics, Native Americans, Asians, and women against young white males, especially ethnic and poor white males. It makes no more sense to discriminate in favor of a rich black or female who had the opportunity of the best family and education available against a poor white than it does to discriminate in favor of white males against blacks or women. It does little to rectify the goal of providing equal opportunity to all.

At the end of his essay supporting AA, Albert Mosley points out that other groups besides blacks have been benefited by AA, "women, the disabled, the elderly."[16] He's correct in including the elderly, for through powerful lobbies, such as the AARP, they do get special benefits, including Medicare, and may sue on the grounds of being discriminated against due to agism, prejudice against older people. Might this not be a reason to reconsider Affirmative Action? Consider the sheer rough percentages of those who qualify for Affirmative Action programs.

Group	Percentage of U.S. Population Who Qualify for AA
1. Women	52
2. Blacks	12
3. Hispanics	9
4. Native Americans	2
5. Asians	4
6. Physically disabled	10
7. Welfare recipients	6
8. The elderly	25% (estimated adults over 60)
9. Italians (in New York City)	10%
Total	130%

The elderly can bring litigation on the grounds of agism, receive entitlements in terms of Social Security and Medicare, and have the AARP lobbying on their behalf. Recently, it has been proposed that homosexuals be included in oppressed groups deserving Affirmative Action.[17] At Northeastern University in 1996 the faculty governing body voted to grant homosexuals Affirmative Action status. How many more percentage points would this add? Several authors have advocated putting all poor people on the list.[18] And if we took handicaps seriously would we not add ugly people, obese people, and, especially, short people, for which there is ample evidence of discrimination? How about left-handed people (about 9 percent of the population)—they can't play shortstop or third base and have to put up with a right-handed–biased world. The only group not on the list is white males. Are they, especially healthy, middle-class young white males, becoming the new "oppressed class"? Should we add them to our list?

Respect for persons entails that we treat each person as an end in him- or herself, not simply as a means to be used for social purposes. What is wrong about discrimination against blacks is that it fails to treat black people as individuals, judging them by their skin color rather than their merit. What is wrong about discrimination against women is that it fails to treat them as individuals, judging them by their gender, not their merit. What is equally wrong about Affirmative Action is that it fails to treat white males with dignity as individuals, judging them by *both their race and gender,* instead of their merit. Affirmative Action, as presently practiced, *is both racist and sexist.*

Along these same lines, note how indignant members of minority groups become at instances of racial profiling. Innocent black males are often stopped and inconvenienced by policemen simply because black males are overrepresented in some classes of crime. We can appreciate their resentment. But how is this different from Affirmative Action which discriminates against innocent white young people simply because they're members of a group that is overrepresented in college or high-profile professions?

7. Affirmative Action Encourages Mediocrity and Incompetence

A few years ago Jesse Jackson joined protesters at Harvard Law School in demanding that the Law School faculty hire black women. Jackson dismissed Dean of the Law School, Robert C. Clark's standard of choosing the best qualified person for the job as "Cultural anemia." "We cannot just define who is qualified in the most narrow vertical academic terms," he said. "Most people in the world are yellow, brown, black, poor, non-Christian and don't speak English, and they can't wait for some white males with archaic rules to appraise them.[19] It might be noted that if Jackson is correct about the depth of cultural decadence at Harvard, blacks might be well advised to form and support their own more vital law schools and leave places like Harvard to their archaism.

At several universities, the administration has forced departments to hire members of minorities even when far superior nonminority candidates were available. Stories of the bad effects of Affirmative Action abound. The philosopher Sidney Hook writes that "at one Ivy League university, representatives of the Regional HEW demanded an explanation of why there were no women or minority students in the Graduate Department of Religious Studies. They were told that a reading knowledge of Hebrew and Greek was presupposed. Whereupon the representatives of HEW advised orally: 'Then end those old-fashioned programs that require irrelevant languages. And start up programs on relevant things which minority group students can study without learning languages.'"[20] Nicholas Capaldi notes that the staff of HEW itself was one-half women, three-fifths members of minorities, and one-half black—a clear case of racial overrepresentation.

In 1972 officials at Stanford University discovered a proposal for the government to monitor curricula in higher education: the "Summary Statement . . . Sex Discrimination Proposed HEW Regulation to Effectuate Title IX of the Education Amendment of 1972" to "establish and use internal procedures for reviewing curricula, designed both to ensure that they do not reflect discrimination on the basis of sex and to resolve complaints concerning allegations of such discrimination, pursuant to procedural standards to be prescribed by the Director of the office of Civil Rights." Fortunately, Secretary of HEW Caspar Weinberger discovered the intrusion and assured Stanford University that he would never approve of it.[21]

Government programs of enforced preferential treatment tend to focus on the lowest possible common denominator. Witness the 1974 HEW Revised Order No. 14 on Affirmative Action expectations for preferential hiring: "Neither minorities nor female employees should be required to possess higher qualifica-

tions than those of the lowest qualified incumbents." Furthermore, no test may be given to candidates unless it is *proved* to be relevant to the job.

> No standard or criteria which have, by intent or effect, worked to exclude women or minorities as a class can be utilized, unless the institution can demonstrate the necessity of such standard to the performance of the job in question.
>
> Whenever a validity study is called for . . . the user should include . . . an investigation of suitable alternative selection procedures and suitable alternative methods of using the selection procedure which have as little adverse impact as possible. . . . Whenever the user is shown an alternative selection procedure with evidence of less adverse impact and substantial evidence of validity for the same job in similar circumstances, the user should investigate it to determine the appropriateness of using or validating it in accord with these guidelines.[22]

But if we are going this far in allowing for mediocrity, why not race-norm in grading and SAT scores and other standardized tests? We could make a grade of 80 a B− for a white or Asian, a B+ for an Hispanic, and an A for a black. This seems in line with the logic of Affirmative Action.

At the same time Americans are wondering why standards in our country are falling and the Japanese and Koreans are getting ahead. Affirmative Action with its twin idols, Sufficiency and Diversity, is the enemy of excellence. I will develop this thought in section 8.

8. An Argument from the Principle of Merit

Traditionally, we have believed that the highest positions in society should be awarded to those who are best qualified. The Koran states that "a ruler who appoints any man to an office, when there is in his dominion another man better qualified for it, sins against God and against the State." Rewarding excellence both seems just to the individuals in the competition and makes for efficiency. Note that one of the most successful acts of racial integration, the Brooklyn Dodgers' recruitment of Jackie Robinson in the late 1940s, was done in just this way, according to merit. If Robinson had been brought into the major league as a mediocre player or had batted .200 he would have been scorned and sent back to the minors where he belonged.

As I mentioned earlier, merit is not an absolute value, but there are strong *prima facie* reasons for awarding positions on its basis, and it should enjoy a weighty presumption in our social practices.

In a celebrated article, Ronald Dworkin says that "Bakke had no case" because society did not owe Bakke anything. That may be, but then why does it owe anyone anything? Dworkin puts the matter in utility terms, but if that is the case, society may owe Bakke a place at the University of California–Davis, for it seems a reasonable rule-utilitarian principle that achievement should be rewarded in society. We generally want the best to have the best positions, the best qualified candidate to win the political office, the most brilliant and competent scientist to be chosen for the most challenging research project, the best qualified pilots to become commercial pilots, the best soldiers to become generals. Only when little is at stake do we weaken the standards and content ourselves with sufficiency (rather than excellence)—there are plenty of jobs that require only "sufficiency" rather than excellence. Perhaps we have even come to feel that medicine or law or university professorships are so routine that they can be performed by minimally qualified people—in which case AA has a place.

Note! No one is calling for quotas or proportional representation of *underutilized* groups in the National Basketball Association, where blacks make up 80 percent of the players. But, surely, if merit and merit alone reigns in sports, should it not be valued at least as much in education and industry?

The case for meritocracy has two pillars. One pillar is a deontological argument which holds that we ought to treat people as ends and not merely means. By giving people what they deserve as *individuals,* rather than as members of *groups,* we show respect for their inherent worth. If you and I take a test, and you get 95 percent of the answers correct and I get only 50 percent correct, it would be unfair to you to give both of us the same grade, say an A, and even more unfair to give me a higher grade, A+, than your B+. Although I have heard of cases in which teachers have been instructed to "race norm" in grading (giving blacks and Hispanics higher grades for the same numerical scores), most proponents of AA stop short of advocating such a practice. But, I would ask them, what's really the difference between taking the overall average of a white and a black and "race norming" that average? If teachers shouldn't do it, why should administrators?

The second pillar for meritocracy is utilitarian. In the end, we will be better off by honoring excellence.

We want the best leaders, teachers, policemen, physicians, generals, lawyers, and airplane pilots that we can possibly produce in society. So our program should be to promote equal opportunity, as much as is feasible in a free market economy, and reward people according to their individual merit.

CONCLUSION

Let me sum up my discussion. The goal of the Civil Rights Movement and of moral people everywhere has been justice for all, including equal opportunity. The question is how best to get there. Civil Rights legislation removed the legal barriers, opening the way toward equal opportunity, but it did not tackle the deeper causes that produce differential results. Weak Affirmative Action aims at encouraging minorities to strive for the highest positions without unduly jeopardizing the rights of majorities. The problem of Weak AA is that it easily slides into Strong AA, where quotas, "goals and timetables," and "equal results"—in a word, reverse discrimination—prevail and are forced onto groups, thus promoting mediocrity, inefficiency, and resentment. Furthermore, Affirmative Action aims at the higher levels of society—universities and skilled jobs—but if we want to improve our society, the best way to do it is to concentrate on families, children, early education, and the like, so that all are prepared to avail themselves of opportunity. Affirmative Action, on the one hand, is too much, too soon and on the other hand, too little, too late.

I have not had space to consider all the objections to my position or discuss the issue of freedom of association which, I think, should be given much scope in private but not in public institutions. Barbara Bergmann[23] and others argue that we already allow preferential treatment for athletes and veterans, especially in university admissions, so, being consistent, we should provide it for women and minorities. My response is that I am against giving athletic scholarships; I regard scholarships to veterans as a part of a contractual relationship, a reward for service to one's country. But I distinguish entrance programs from actual employment. I don't think that veterans should be afforded special privilege in hiring practices, unless it be as a tie breaker.

I should also mention that my arguments from merit and respect apply more specifically to public institutions than to private ones, where issues of property rights and freedom of association carry more weight. If a university unfairly discriminated against blacks or women, it would soon find its federal funds withdrawn. But it can discriminate against better qualified whites and Asians and enjoy full support. It does not seem fair or, I have argued, morally justifiable.

In addition to the arguments I have offered, Affirmative Action, rather than uniting people of good-will in the common cause of justice, tends to balkanize us into segregationist thinking. Professor Derrick Bell of Harvard Law School said that the African American U.S. Supreme Court Judge Clarence Thomas, who opposes Affirmative Action, "doesn't think black."[24] Does Bell really claim that there is a standard and proper "black" (and presumably a white) way of thinking? Ideologues like Bell, whether radical blacks like himself or Nazis who advocate "think Aryan," all represent the same thing: cynicism about rational debate, the very antithesis of the quest for impartial truth and justice. People who have believe in using reason to resolve our differences will oppose this kind of balkanization of the races.

Finally, ask yourself: In general, have individuals of any group ever succeeded in the long run by being given special privilege? Hasn't the American way (indeed the way of every successful culture) been equal opportunity, keeping the standards high and encouraging individuals to work hard, to take responsibility for their actions, and eventually reaching such a high level of excellence that we can't help admiring them? It could be argued, as Thomas Sowell does, that AA has actually hindered many blacks in their journey toward success.

Martin Luther said that humanity is like a man mounting a horse who always tends to fall off on the other side of the horse. This seems to be the case with Affirmative Action. Attempting to redress the discriminatory inequities of our history, our well-intentioned social engineers now engage in new forms of discriminatory inequity and thereby think that they have successfully mounted the horse of racial harmony. They have only fallen off on the other side.

ACKNOWLEDGMENTS

I am indebted to Stephen Kershnar, Tziporah Kasachkoff, John Kleinig, Michael Levin, Elliot Cohen, Bill Shaw, Stephen Nathanson, Mylan Engel, and Wallace Matson for comments on earlier drafts of this paper.

READING 43

Diversity

George Sher

George Sher is Professor of Philosophy at Rice University and the author of several works in ethics and political philosophy, including *Desert* (1987). In this reading Sher explores some forms of the argument that preferential treatment is needed to increase diversity and shows that the alleged advantages of these arguments are illusory.

This reading is taken from *Approximate Justice: Studies in Non-Ideal Theory* (Lanham, Maryland. Rowman and Littlefield, 1997), by permission.

I

Justifications of preferential treatment come in two main types. Arguments of one type—often called backward-looking—make essential reference to the discrimination and injustice that blacks, women, and members of certain other groups have suffered in the past. These arguments urge that current group members be given preference in employment or admission to educational institutions to make amends for or rectify the effects of such wrongdoing—to put things right or, as far as possible, "make the victims whole." By contrast, the other type of justification—often called *forward-looking*—makes *no* essential reference to past wrongdoing, but instead defends preferential treatment entirely as a means to some *desirable future goal*. Even when the goal is to eliminate inequalities or disadvantages that *were in fact* caused by past wrongdoing, the reason for eliminating them is not *that* they were caused by past wrongdoing. Rather, their continued existence is said to violate some purely *non*-historical principle or ideal—for example, the principle of utility or some ideal of equality.

Of the two types of argument, the forward-looking type is often viewed as more straightforward. Those who look exclusively to the future are spared both the daunting task of documenting the effects of past injustice on specific individuals and the even more difficult task of specifying *how much* better off any given individual would now be in its absence. In a more theoretical vein, they need not answer the troublesome question of whether (and if so why) we must compensate persons who would not even have existed, and so *a fortiori* would not be better off, if historical wrongs such as slavery had not taken place; and neither need they specify how many generations must elapse before claims to compensation lose their force. Perhaps for these reasons, defenders of preferential treatment seem increasingly inclined to eschew the backward-looking approach and to cast their lot with forward-looking arguments.

It seems to me, however, that this strategy is badly misguided for two distinct but related reasons: first, because the forward-looking defenses of preferential treatment are only superficially less problematic than their backward-looking counterparts, and, second, because the most promising way of rectifying their inadequacies is to reintroduce precisely the sorts of reference to the past that their proponents have sought to avoid. Although a full elaboration of these claims is beyond my scope, I can at least illustrate them with a few observations about the utilitarian variant of the forward-looking approach.

For no less than any backward-looking defender of preferential treatment, a utilitarian defender must answer some hard questions of both an empirical and a theoretical nature. On the empirical side, he must explain why it is reasonable to expect the benefits of preferential treatment to outweigh its costs. The costs that are often cited include the losses of efficiency that occur when less-than-best-qualified applicants are chosen, the hostility and suspicion of the bypassed candidates who believe—rightly or wrongly—that their efforts and accomplishments have been ignored, the more subtle effects of preference on those who believe they have received it, and the damaging balkanization of public life that many consider to flow from policies centered on group membership. To show that these costs are less weighty than some equally heterogenous collection of benefits, one would need an integrative argument of a type that no one has even begun to provide. In addition, on the more theoretical side, a utilitarian must explain why, if we are obligated or permitted to discriminate in favor of minorities and women when doing so would maximize utility, we are not similarly obligated or permitted to discriminate *against* the members of these groups when doing *that* would maximize utility. Although a good deal has been written about each topic, I think it is fair to say that the empirical situation remains too complex to assess with any confidence and that the theoretical challenge has not been convincingly met.

These observations suggest that the apparently greater simplicity of at least the utilitarian version of the forward-looking approach is largely illusory. But in addition, they lend credence to two further and even more important points, one concerning the underlying structure of the utilitarian argument, the other concerning the thinking of those who advance it.

The further point about the argument's structure is that anyone who defends preferential treatment on the grounds that it maximizes utility, yet insists that mere utility can never justify outright racial or sexual discrimination, is committed to the view that blacks and women differ from white males in some morally important dimension. Because intrinsic differences do not seem relevant, the crucial difference seems apt to lie in the histories of the respective groups; and the most pertinent historical facts are of course those of discrimination and injustice. Thus, if selecting a less-than-best-qualified applicant is to be an acceptable way of promoting utility when the chosen applicant is black or female but not when that applicant is a white male, the reason is very likely to be that blacks and women, but not white males, were often treated unjustly in the past.

The other further point that needs to be made is simply that this reasoning is very likely to have shaped many people's actual beliefs. When someone rejects all forms of racial and sexual discrimination but defends preferential treatment on utilitarian grounds—and, we may add, when someone rejects racial and sexual discrimination but defends preferential treatment on *egalitarian* grounds—the best explanation of his willingness to set aside his usual merit-based standards is that he takes the exception to be warranted by the pressing need to rectify the continuing effects of past injustice. Also, given both the salience of that injustice and the moral passion with which defenders of preferential treatment often press their case, I suspect that many who defend that practice on utilitarian grounds are moved less by their high degree of confidence in its favorable cost-benefit ratio than by the quite different thought that it is especially important to benefit members of groups whose disadvantages were wrongfully inflicted. And, along similar lines, I strongly suspect that the reason many favor preferential treatment to mitigate inequalities that follow racial and sexual lines, yet are quite willing to tolerate many other inequalities (including the very inequalities of reward that make some positions worth distributing preferentially), is precisely that they view only the former inequalities as having resulted from previous wrongdoing.

My topic here, however, is neither the general contrast between the forward- and backward-looking defenses of preferential treatment nor the prospects for mounting a successful utilitarian or egalitarian defense. Instead, I mention these matters only to frame what I want to say about a different forward-looking defense that has recently come to the fore. This new defense is, of course, the one I mentioned at the outset—the argument that preferential treatment is justified by the need to promote racial, sexual, and ethnic diversity in such crucial sectors of our society as the academy and the workplace. A bit more precisely, it is the argument that preferential treatment is justified when, and because, it moves us closer to a situation in which the holders of every (desirable) type of job and position include representatives of all racial, sexual, and ethnic groups in rough proportion to their overall numbers.

The rhetoric of this new argument is all around us. Its ideal of diversity informs such phrases as "underrepresented group," and is also implicit in President Clinton's call for a cabinet that "looks like America." Yet just because the diversity argument is generally advanced by politicians and others with political agendas—bureaucrats, academic administrators, and the like—it is seldom formulated with much precision or care. Thus, before we can hope to assess its claims, we must get clearer about what these are. That means asking both why diversity should be conceived primarily in racial, sexual, and ethnic terms and why diversity as so conceived is morally important. To these questions, I now turn.

II

Why is racial, sexual, and ethnic diversity morally important? It is a measure of how entrenched this ideal has become that the very question has a heretical sound. However, like many other heresies, this one is all the more worth committing because it challenges a rarely examined orthodoxy.

I can envision four possible ways of arguing that racial, sexual, and ethnic diversity is morally important. To show this, someone might argue that such diversity is either (1) a requirement of justice or (2) intrinsically valuable or (3) conducive to the general welfare or (4) conducive to some value *other* than well-being. However, as we will see, each version of the diversity argument remains vulnerable to essentially the same objection that I advanced against the other forward-looking defenses of preferential treatment—

namely, that when we ask why the argument focuses only on certain groups, we are invariably thrown back on the injustice or discrimination that their past members have suffered.

Consider first the claim that diversity is a requirement of justice. To defend this claim, one must first specify the relevant conception of justice and then show why it requires that every desirable job and position be distributed among all racial, sexual, and ethnic groups in rough proportion to their numbers. Although there are obviously many ways of filling in the blanks, I shall consider only two that I think may actually exert some influence. Of these two proposals, one construes racial, sexual, and ethnic groups as morally fundamental entities with claims of justice of their own, while the other takes these groups to be only derivatively relevant.

Suppose, first, that racial, sexual, and ethnic groups do themselves have claims of justice; and suppose, further, that the best theory of justice is egalitarian. In that case, the best theory of justice will require that all racial, sexual, and ethnic groups be made roughly equally well off. Because such groups are not organized entities, and so are incapable either of having experiences or of pursuing goals, their well-being cannot reside either in the quality of their subjective states or in their success in achieving their goals. Instead, each group's well-being must be a function of the well-being of its individual members, which in turn can be expected to vary with the members' income and social standing. Because these connections hold, any society that wishes to implement a conception of justice that requires that all racial, sexual, and ethnic groups be made equally well off may indeed have to distribute all desirable jobs and positions among all relevant groups in rough proportion to their numbers.

Here, then, is one way of grounding the case for racial, sexual, and ethnic diversity in a broader conception of justice. But should we accept this argument? Elsewhere, I have contended that racial, sexual, and ethnic groups are in fact *un*likely to have independent claims of justice; I also doubt that the best theory of justice is straightforwardly egalitarian. However, in the current discussion, I shall simply grant both premises and focus only on the argument's further assumption that not all groups, but only some subset that includes racial, sexual, and ethnic groups, have independent claims of justice.

Why, exactly, must the argument make this further assumption? One answer is simply that if enough other groups *did* have independent claims of justice, then even distributing every desirable position among all racial, sexual, and ethnic groups in exact proportion to their numbers would at best eliminate only a small fraction of a society's unjust inequalities. However, while this answer is not wrong, it does not go far enough. The more decisive answer is that if enough other groups also had independent claims of justice, then no increase in a society's diversity could possibly bring *any* increase in its overall justice.

To see why this is so, consider a simple case. Letting "B1," "B2," etc., designate individual blacks, "W1," "W2," etc., designate individual whites, and "D" and "U" designate desirable and undesirable positions, suppose the initial distribution of desirable and undesirable positions among blacks and whites within a society is

B1U, B2U, B3U, B4U

W1D, W2D, W3D, W4D

Suppose, further, that as a result of a campaign to increase racial diversity, this distribution is changed to

B1D, B2D, B3U, B4U

W1U, W2U, W3D, W4D

After this change, the society may appear to be at least marginally more just, since whatever inequalities remain, at least one significant inequality—the one that initially obtained between blacks and whites—has now been eliminated.

Yet if enough other groups also have moral standing, then the gain in racial diversity will mean *no* overall increase in the society's justice; for the new equality between the groups of blacks and whites will be precisely matched by a new *in*equality between the mixed groups [W1, W2, B3, B4] and [B1, B2, W3, W4]. Before the campaign to increase diversity, the distribution of desirable and undesirable positions between the two mixed groups was

W1D, W2D, B3U, B4U

B1U, B2U, W3D, W4D

Afterwards, it is

W1U, W2U, B3U, B4U

B1D, B2D, W3D, W4D

Because the first mixed group has thus gone from having half of the society's desirable positions to having none while the second has gone from having half to having all, the loss of equality between these groups

will exactly offset the gain in equality between blacks and whites. Assuming that all four groups are equally significant, the society's overall level of equality, and so too its degree of justice, will therefore be unaffected by its increased racial diversity. Thus, if anyone wants to argue that racial, sexual, and ethnic diversity *is* a requirement of justice among groups, he must deny that mixed groups such as [W1, W2, B3, B4] and [B1, B2, W3, W4] have the same moral status as natural groups such as [B1, B2, B3, B4] and [W1, W2, W3, W4].

But on what basis could someone deny this? One obvious difference between racial and mixed groups is that skin color and other traits associated with race (and, by extension, sex and ethnicity) are salient in a way that the membership in a mixed group is not. However, this will not yield the desired conclusion because the mere fact that a trait is salient does not endow it with any special moral status. Nor, despite what some have said, can it plausibly be argued that racial, sexual, and ethnic groups are more significant than others because their members identify far more with the fortunes and accomplishments of other group members (and with the fortunes of the group itself) than do the members of most other groups. Here again, the problem is not that this premise is false—it plainly contains much truth—but rather that it does not yield the desired conclusion. For, at least offhand, what really follows from a high degree of mutual identification within a group is not that the group *itself* has any special moral standing, but only that the well-being of each member is connected to the well-being of many other members in a rather distinctive way.

There are, of course, many other possible ways of arguing that mixed groups lack the moral status of racial, sexual, and ethnic groups. Thus, the mere fact that the cited arguments fail is hardly decisive. Still, in the absence of any better argument, the best explanation of the impulse to single out certain racial, sexual, and ethnic groups is again that it reflects a desire to make amends for (or rectify the lingering effects of) the discrimination that their past members have suffered. As Paul Taylor has put it, the guiding thought appears to be that the relevant groups were "as it were, *created* by the original unjust practice[s]."[1] I think, in fact, that this way of formulating the moral importance of past injustice is highly misleading, but I shall not argue that point here. Instead, in keeping with my broader theme, I shall simply observe that if anyone *were* to elaborate the diversity argument in these terms, he would be abandoning all pretense that his argument is purely forward-looking.

III

What, next, of the suggestion that racial, sexual, and ethnic diversity is a requirement of justice for individuals? Unlike its predecessor, this suggestion does not presuppose a problematic moral ontology. Yet just because the suggestion does not construe groups as morally fundamental, it raises a difficult new question—namely, why should justice for individuals call for *any* special distribution of positions among groups?

Although this question, too, can be answered in various ways, I shall consider only the single answer that I think proponents of diversity would be most likely to give. Put most briefly, that answer is, first, that the operative principle of justice is one of equality of opportunity, and, second, that a lack of racial, sexual, and ethnic diversity is significant precisely because it shows that opportunities remain *un*equal. Even though legal barriers are a thing of the past, the fact that relatively few blacks, women, and members of other minorities hold well-paying, authoritative positions is often viewed as compelling evidence that the members of these groups have lacked, and continue to lack, equal opportunity. That in turn may be thought to show that using preferential treatment to bring about their representation within desirable professions in proportion to their numbers is justified by the fact that it will make opportunities *more* equal.

But, whatever else is true, the last step of this argument is surely questionable; for if a given group is now "underrepresented" within a profession, then bringing its representation into proportion with its numbers in the general population will require that it be *over*represented in the profession's new hires. For example, if group G comprises 20 percent of the overall population but only 10 percent of profession P, then any attempt to diversify P will require that *more* than 20 percent of P's *new* members be Gs. Thus, assuming that genuine equality of opportunity exists only when each group that comprises n percent of the population wins n percent of the competitions for each type of position—and this, of course, is precisely the assumption that is needed to support the inference that opportunities for Gs have been unequal up to now—the hiring of Gs at a rate greater than 20 percent must entail the denial of equal opportunity to at least some current non-Gs. When preferential treatment is used to promote the proportional representation of all racial, sexual, and ethnic groups, its immediate effect is therefore not to make opportunities more equal, but only to compound any earlier inequalities that may have existed.

This observation does not show that such uses of preferential treatment cannot make opportunities more equal; but it does show that any relevant gains must be long-term rather than immediate. The point must be not that opportunities will be more equal *when* the preferential treatment is used, but rather that they will be more equal *afterwards*. This will be true (the argument must run) because the proportional distribution of desirable positions among all racial, sexual, and ethnic groups will convey to the members of previously excluded groups the message that people like them can successfully acquire and hold such positions, and that in turn will raise the aspirations of many. Because this reasoning appeals to the effects of diversity upon the motivation of future group members, it is, in essence, a variant of the familiar "role model" argument.

But motivation is a dangerous topic for someone who seeks to link diversity to equal opportunity to introduce; for if he is willing to say that the *future* distribution of desirable positions among different groups will be affected by the motivation as well as the skills of their members, then he can hardly deny that the *current* distribution of desirable positions is likely to have been similarly affected. Thus, in particular, he must acknowledge that if a given group is underrepresented within a profession, at least some, and perhaps much, of its underrepresentation is probably traceable to its members' attitudes and choices. This complicates what was initially proffered as a straightforward inference from "some groups are underrepresented in desirable positions" to "the members of those groups have not had equal opportunities to compete;" for a group's underrepresentation within a given field will *not* reflect a lack of equal opportunity if the majority of its members have freely chosen to pursue a different path.

It would, of course, be foolish to suppose either that all preferences have been innocently acquired or that all choices have been freely made. Someone whose low aspirations were determined by a culture forged in oppression has been harmed by that oppression as definitely, if not as directly, as the grandparents who were simply not allowed to work or learn. Thus, if the choices that led to a group's underrepresentation within a profession were expressions of such attitudes, it may be true both that the group's underrepresentation is largely a reflection of its members' choices *and* that the members who made the choices were denied equal opportunity.

But, once again, it is precisely the role of past injustice that makes this suggestion compelling. If the culture that causes the members of a group to acquire counterproductive preferences is itself an effect of past wrongdoing—if, for instance, that culture is an adaptive response to generations of slavery, discrimination, and Jim Crow laws—then we will quite naturally classify those preferences among the mechanisms through which the opportunities of the current group members are kept unequal. But if, instead, the preferences responsible for a group's underrepresentation are manifestations of an innate disposition of the kind that the maternal urge is sometimes said to exemplify—if, as some have claimed, female biology is (statistical) destiny—then the claim that the group's members lack equal opportunity will have no force. Thus, in this context, too, what at first looks like a purely forward-looking defense of preferential treatment turns out, on closer examination, to have an important backward-looking component.

If all preferences and attitudes were either innate or else the results of past wrongdoing, we could end this part of our discussion here. However, in fact, these alternatives are not exhaustive. Many people have acquired their current attitudes from cultures that did *not* evolve in response to wrongdoing or oppression; and such attitudes, too, can lead the relevant groups to be underrepresented within professions. It may be, for example, that the reason relatively few members of a given group have pursued careers that require academic success or extended training is simply that the group's culture, which was shaped by its earlier agrarian lifestyle, does not attach much value to education. If internalizing this attitude also counts as being denied equal opportunity, and if increasing the group's presence within various professions would help eventually to dispel the attitude, then using preferential treatment to promote such diversity may indeed be justified on purely forward-looking grounds.

How significant is this challenge to my thesis that every ostensibly forward-looking defense of diversity has a backward-looking core? That depends, I think, on the answers to several further questions. It depends, most obviously, on whether equal opportunity *does* require that no one be brought up in a culture that instills attitudes unconducive to success in the modern world; but it depends, as well, on whether equal opportunity trumps respect for ancestral cultures; whether increasing diversity would effectively diminish the transmission of counterproductive attitudes; and whether, even if it would, we can more effectively alter these attitudes in some other way (or can simply wait until they are transformed in the American melting pot as were the attitudes of previous generations of immigrants). I suspect that a careful investigation of these questions would at least mitigate if not eliminate the challenge to

my thesis; but I cannot undertake that investigation here. Thus, pending further discussion, this issue must simply remain unresolved.

IV

So far, I have discussed only the first of the four possible arguments for racial, sexual, and ethnic diversity. That argument, which construes such diversity as a requirement of justice, predictably raised a variety of complications. By contrast, the second and third arguments—that diversity is intrinsically valuable and that it is conducive to the general welfare—raise fewer new issues and so can be dealt with much more quickly.

The challenge to someone who holds that racial, sexual, and ethnic diversity is *intrinsically* valuable is to provide some justification of this claim that goes beyond the bare fact that he believes it. He cannot simply assert that the claim is self-evident because such assertions are equally available to his opponents; yet once we ask what else can be said, we almost immediately run out of argument. I say "almost immediately" because many of the metaphors that are commonly used in this connection—for example, descriptions of a diverse society as a tapestry or a "gorgeous mosaic"—can themselves be viewed as arguments that the relevant intrinsic values are familiar aesthetic ones. However, I hope it goes without saying that the aesthetic appeal of a given pattern of distribution is not a proper basis for any decision about social policy.

Because the appeal to intrinsic value is essentially a nonargument, I cannot pinpoint the exact place at which it goes historical. Yet just because that appeal has so little to recommend it, the best explanation of whatever influence it has—and, though I cannot prove it, I think it does have some influence—is again that it provides cover for a policy whose real aim is to benefit members of unjustly disadvantaged groups.

The third possible argument for diversity—that it is conducive to the general welfare— is very different; for unlike the appeal to intrinsic value, this argument can be developed in various ways. One obvious possibility is to exploit our earlier observation that the members of many racial, sexual, and ethnic groups identify strongly with the fortunes and accomplishments of other group members; for given this mutual identification, increasing diversity will benefit not only those group members who actually gain prestigious, well-paying positions, but also the many others who take pride and pleasure in their success. Alternatively or in addition, it can be argued that working closely with members of unfamiliar groups breaks down barriers and disrupts stereotypes, and that increasing racial, sexual, and ethnic diversity will therefore increase overall well-being by fostering understanding and harmony.

Because diversity yields these and other benefits, there is an obvious case for the use of preferential treatment to promote it. However, when the issue is framed in these terms, the diversity argument is no longer an alternative to a utilitarian defense of preferential treatment, but rather is itself such a defense. Despite its interposition of diversity, its essential message is precisely that preferential treatment is justified by its beneficial consequences. Thus, if my conjecture about the other utilitiarian defenses was correct—if the disparity between the difficulties they confront and the confidence with which they are advanced suggests that their proponents' real impulse is compensatory—then that conjecture must apply here too.

V

That leaves only the fourth argument for diversity's importance—the argument that it promotes some value *other* than well-being. Although there are many nonwelfarist values to which appeal might theoretically be made, the only live version of this argument is one that appeals to the intellectual values of the academy.

That increasing racial, sexual, and ethnic diversity will advance the academic enterprise is an article of faith among many academics. Neil Rudenstine, the president of Harvard, expressed the conventional wisdom this way: "A diverse educational environment challenges [students] to explore ideas and arguments at a deeper level—to see issues from various sides, to rethink their own premises, to achieve the kind of understanding that comes only from testing their own hypotheses against those of people with other views."[2] Although these claims obviously do not support all forms of preferential treatment—they are, for example, irrelevant both to nonacademic hiring and to contractual "set-asides"—they do purport to justify, through an appeal to values internal to the academy's own mission, both preferential admission to many educational institutions and preferential hiring across the curricular spectrum.

Like many of the other arguments we have considered, this one can itself be fleshed out in various ways. Some of its proponents, including Rudenstine

himself, stress the value *to students* of exposure to different perspectives, while others stress the value of diversity in research. Of those who focus on research, some argue that including hitherto excluded groups will open up new areas of investigation, while others emphasize the value of diverse challenges to all hypotheses, including, or especially, hypotheses in traditional, well-worked areas. Of those who emphasize challenges to hypotheses, some stress the importance of confronting all hypotheses with the broadest possible range of potentially falsifying tests, while others focus on exposing the hidden biases of investigators. Because the appeal to diversity's contribution to intellectual inquiry is so protean, I cannot work systematically through its variants, but will pose only a single question that applies to each. That question, predictably enough, is why we should single out the contributions of any small set of groups such as those on the official Affirmative Action list.

For even if diversity yields every one of the intellectual benefits that are claimed for it, why should we benefit most when the scholarly community contains substantial numbers of blacks, women, Hispanics, (American) Indians, Aleuts, and Chinese-Americans? Why not focus instead, or in addition, on Americans of Eastern European, Arabic, or (Asian) Indian extraction? For that matter, can't we achieve even greater benefit by extending preference to *native* Africans, Asians, Arabs, and Europeans? And why understand diversity only in terms of gender, ethnicity, and national origin? Why should a population that is diverse in this dimension provide any more educational or scholarly benefit than one that is ethnically homogeneous but includes suitable numbers of gays, religious fundamentalists, the young, the old, the handicapped, ex-military officers, conservatives, Marxists, Mormons, and blue-collar workers? These groups, too, have characteristic concerns, types of experience, and outlooks on the world. Thus, why not also monitor the degree to which *they* are represented in academic circles? Why not also give *them* preference when they are not represented in proportion to their numbers? And why, to realize the benefits of the female perspective, must we further increase the number of women when the academy already contains far more women than members of many other groups with distinct perspectives?

The most salient feature of the groups on the official list is of course the discrimination they have suffered. This may not entirely explain why just these groups are included—that may in part be traceable to the play of political forces—but it does explain the prominence of such core groups as blacks and women. This strongly suggests that the current argument is also covertly backward-looking. However, before we can draw this conclusion, we must consider an important alternative—namely, that the real reason for concentrating on previously oppressed groups is not that their members alone are owed compensation, but rather that beliefs and attitudes shaped by oppression are better suited than others to advance educational or scholarly aims.

For although we obviously cannot assume that all the members of any group think alike, a history of discrimination may indeed affect the way many of a group's members tend to view the world. In addition to the already-noted high degree of collective identification, the perspective of the oppressed is often said to include a keen awareness of the motives, prejudices, and hidden agendas of others, a heightened sense of the oppressive effects of even seemingly benign social structures, and a strong commitment to social change. As a corollary, that perspective may include a degree of antagonism toward received opinion and a certain impatience with abstraction. Thus, the question that remains to be addressed is whether, and if so how, any of these beliefs, attitudes, or traits might make a special contribution to education or research.

Here it is important to distinguish between the educational or scholarly value of *learning about* the perspective of the oppressed and the educational or scholarly value of *actually taking* that perspective. This distinction is important because some who urge wide exposure to the relevant beliefs, attitudes, etc., do appear to believe that what matters is simply learning about them. That, at any rate, is one natural interpretation of the common claim that diversity is important because it acquaints nonminority students with the hardships and obstacles that many members of minority groups confront daily, and because it teaches nonminority students that many members of these groups consider themselves disenfranchised and do not trust social institutions whose necessity and justice others take for granted. Yet while such knowledge may contribute significantly to mutual understanding and social harmony, the beliefs, attitudes, traits, and experiences that are characteristic of oppressed groups are in the end only one class of facts among innumerable others. Considered simply as objects of study—and that is how we must consider them if the current argument is not to be yet another tributary of the great utilitarian river—the beliefs, attitudes, traits, and experiences of the oppressed are no more important than those of the

nonoppressed, which in turn are no more important than indefinitely many other possible objects of inquiry.

Thus, to give their variant of the argument a fighting chance, those who attach special educational and scholarly value to the perspective of the oppressed must take the other path. They must locate its special educational or scholarly value not in anyone's *coming to know* that oppressed groups hold certain beliefs, attitudes, etc., but rather in the contribution of those beliefs and attitudes to the acquisition of *other* knowledge. Their argument must be that this perspective uniquely enhances our collective ability to pose or resolve questions across much of the intellectual spectrum. To show that the perspective of the oppressed generates new lines of inquiry, friends of diversity often cite the tendency of women to pursue scientific research with humanitarian rather than militaristic applications and the contributions that various minorities have made to history and other fields by studying their own past and present. To show that this perspective contributes to the investigation of established topics, they point out that black and female investigators tend to be specially attuned to the inclusion of blacks and women in experimental control groups, that black students bring to the study of law a well-founded mistrust of the police, and that enhanced sensitivity to power relations has opened up fruitful new ways of interpreting literary texts.

We certainly must agree that the beliefs, attitudes, and traits of oppressed groups have made important contributions to the way academic questions are now formulated and addressed. However, what friends of diversity must show is not merely that these beliefs, attitudes, and traits make *some* significant contribution to effective inquiry, but that they are *more* conducive to it, all things considered, than any of the alternative mixtures that would emerge if there were no Affirmative Action or if preference were given to other sorts of groups. To see what is wrong with this stronger conclusion, we need only revisit the argument's two main claims, that the members of oppressed groups are likely to pose novel questions and that they are likely to bring novel perspectives to familiar ones.

For, first, oppressed groups are hardly the only ones whose concerns and interests can be expected to channel research in some directions rather than others. Just as the recent influx of blacks, Hispanics, and women has led to a variety of new scientific, historical, and literary projects, and to various new interpretive strategies, so would any comparable influx of (say)

Baptists, Muslims, Marxists, or vegetarians. More subtly, any admissions policy that self-consciously sought out persons with certain traits of intellect or character would also greatly influence what people study and how they study it. The academic agenda would evolve in one way if students and faculty were selected primarily for (say) altruism, in another if they were selected for intellectual honesty, and in yet others if they were selected for dogged persistence, intellectual playfulness, or literary imagination and a flair for language. Indeed, even without any such attempt to depart from traditional merit-based selection criteria, the endless play of human creativity can be expected to ensure continuing novelty in the projects and approaches that find adherents. The history of intellectual inquiry prior to Affirmative Action is hardly a chronicle of stagnation.

Nor, second, are the beliefs, attitudes, and traits of the oppressed any more likely to be helpful in *answering* intellectual questions than any number of others. There are, to be sure, many contexts in which antagonism toward received opinion, impatience with useless abstraction, and a desire to unearth or vindicate the contributions of a particular group do make important contributions to the solution of a problem—but in many other contexts, these traits and attitudes are distracting and counterproductive. They are, for example, more likely to be a hindrance than a help if one is trying to construct a mathematical proof, evaluate the properties of a new chemical compound, understand how neurotransmitters work, or write a computer program. Where such tasks are concerned, the biases of others are irrelevant unless they issue in bad inferences or dishonesty in handling data—flaws which the standard techniques of review and replication seem well suited to discover. Neither skepticism about others' motives nor a deep commitment to social change seems likely to generate many potentially falsifying hypotheses.

My own view is that we will make the most progress if we simply stock the academy with persons who display the traditional academic excellences to the highest degree. The students and faculty members who are most likely to help us progress toward true beliefs, powerful explanations, deep understanding, and a synoptic world-view are just the ones with the greatest analytical ability, the most imagination, the best memory, and the strongest desire to pursue the truth wherever it leads. However, while these are things that I deeply believe, my argument does not require any premise this strong. Instead, it requires only the much weaker premise that indefinitely many traits of intellect or character are sometimes useful in advancing cognitive

or pedagogical aims, and that we have no reason to expect the beliefs and attitudes of the oppressed to be preeminent among these.

This reasoning of course presupposes that the aims of the academy *are* to be understood in terms of truth, understanding, explanation, and the rest. If they are not—if, for example, the basic aim is instead to promote social change—then the case for favoring the beliefs and attitudes of the oppressed may well be stronger. However, if someone does take the basic aim to be social change, and if he urges the hiring and admission of more members of oppressed groups to expedite the desired changes, then he will no longer be appealing to the very academic values that even his opponents share. He will, instead, be mounting an appeal to some further conception of social justice—one whose evaluation must await its more precise articulation. Thus, pending further discussion, my main thesis—that every major defense of diversity is either incomplete or backward-looking—remains intact. . . .

READING 44

Is Inheritance Immoral?

Sterling Harwood

Sterling Harwood earned his law degree from Cornell Law School and his Ph.D. in philosophy from Cornell University. He has taught at Cornell, Illinois State University, Hobart and William Smith Colleges, San Jose State University, San Jose City College, and Chabot College. He currently teaches at the University of Phoenix in Arizona, and practices law primarily in the fields of immigration, family law, and criminal law. His work includes authoring *Judicial Activism: A Restrained Defense* and editing *Business As Ethical* and *Business As Usual*. His answer to the title question is "Yes, when it is too much of a good thing at the expense of others' equality of opportunity."

This paper was commissioned for this book and appears here in print for the first time.

"We're a world . . . of filthy streets and clean houses, poor schools and expensive television. . . . Nothing so denies a person liberty as the total absence of money." John Kenneth Galbraith ("The Progressive Interview," The Progressive, Oct. 2000, p. 38).

Inheritance taxes are unpopular. For example, 60 percent of Americans favor repealing the estate tax. However, only 2 percent of Americans who died last year had estates that paid the estate tax.[1] I shall argue that a properly structured inheritance tax on the estate of the deceased should not be unpopular or opposed. I shall argue that an inheritance tax is a major and morally permissible tool to help deal with serious inequalities of opportunity, and thus injustices, in America. Here are facts about American inequality and inheritance of the family fortune (inheritance, for short). The top 1 percent of American income recipients receive so much income that they pay about 33 percent of all yearly income taxes.[2] Two percent of families own 28 percent of net family wealth, and 10 percent of families own 57 percent of net family wealth.[3] The richest 20 percent of Americans own 80 percent of private wealth, while the poorest 20 percent own only 0.2 percent. Twenty percent of families receive 57.3 percent of all family income, while the bottom 20 percent receives only 7.2 percent of all family income.[4] Seventy-five percent of unemployed Americans receive no unemployment benefits. Sixty percent of families living below the poverty line have at least one member employed.[5]

The average homeless person lives seven years on the street.[6] In 1987 Chrysler paid Lee Iacocca an hourly wage of $8,608 (the equivalent of $17,216,000 a year assuming 40 hours a week for 50 weeks and two weeks of vacation), while 33 percent of American workers earning hourly wages made less than $5 an hour.[7] Today, $17 million is the average "annual salary Carlos Delgado will receive in a four-year contract with the Toronto Blue Jays, as baseball's highest-paid player."[8] By contrast, the "janitors who sweep and mop the most prestigious supermarkets in the city [of Los Angeles] are sometimes being paid as little as $275 for a soul-crushing fifty-six-hour workweek."[9] Vice-President Dick "Cheney made several fortunes from his helmsmanship at Halliburton: According to Reuters, he was paid nearly $2 million in compensation in 1999 (down from $4.4 million the previous year) and given stock options worth from $7.4 million to $18.8 million (depending on the stock's future performance). This is on top of the $45.5 million in stock that Cheney owns as the company's largest shareholder, plus another $12.5 million in exercisable stock options."[10] CEO Vinny Smith of Quest Software is worth $1.9 billion at age 36—and he is only #9 on Forbes Magazine's list of the 40 wealthiest Americans under 40.[11] The average age of the 40 is 35 and the average net worth of the 40 is $1.84 billion.[12] Michael Dell of Dell Computers is the wealthiest American under 40—he's worth $17.08 billion at age 35.[13]

By contrast, 15 percent of Americans under age 65 have no health insurance. Forty percent of children in New York City live below the poverty line. From 1980 to 1987 the number of millionaires increased 145 percent.[14] Before 1981 the average tax on an estate bequeathed was 0.2 percent, including 0.8 percent for estates worth over $500,000.[15] The current law imposes no federal tax on any estate worth less than $600,000. Some prime states for retirement (for example, Florida) have no inheritance tax. Some states (for example, New Hampshire) have no income tax.

The foregoing facts would be morally questionable even if women and racial minorities participated equally at each level of wealth, but they do not. According to Working Women magazine, the average working woman makes only 79.5 percent of what the average working man makes. Sixty percent of those earning minimum wage are women. (Sen. Harry Reid, D-NV, speaking on CNN "Capital Gang," airdate July 1, 2000). At least 46.7 percent of black children live below the poverty line.[16] At least 18.3 percent of black, but only 7.4 percent of white, high school graduates over 16 are unemployed.[17] At least 23.6 percent of black high school graduates, but only 16.3 percent of white high school dropouts, under age 25 are unemployed. Ninety-seven percent of coronary bypass operations are performed on whites.[18]

In 1983, median income for black families was only 56 percent of that of white families. At least 32.4 percent of black families, and 9.7 percent of white families are below the poverty level.[19] Savings and loans nationally reject black applicants for home loans twice as often as they reject whites.[20] At least 92.8 percent of the board members of the Fortune 1000 companies are white and male. A woman's change in standard of living after divorce is a decrease of 73 percent, while a man's average change is an increase of 43 percent. Twenty-four percent of mothers fail to receive their court-ordered child support. The market value of labor performed annually by the average housewife is over $40,000.[21] Given the inequality shown above, we should ask if we may do better. We have progressive income taxes, affirmative action, and welfare programs; but inequality persists even with these three types of redistributive programs. These redistributive programs are unreliable for at least five reasons. First, loopholes notoriously riddle the progressivity of income taxes. Second, many who need help from welfare programs lack the literacy or self-confidence to know or successfully pursue the help for which they are eligible. Third, the Clinton administration has pursued its "New Democrat" policies of the Democratic Leadership Council to ally with a Republican Congress to "change welfare as we know it" by putting a time limit on the receipt of welfare payments as one trains for entering the workplace. The time limit, the quality of the training, and the vagaries of the workplace and marketplace make such programs less reliable than other alternatives.

Regarding tax loopholes, 579 Americans declared over $200,000 in income in 1983 yet paid no taxes.[22] Since 1977, the amount in federal taxes paid by the richest 1 percent of families decreased by $44,440, while the amount for the remaining 99 percent of Americans increased by $212.[23] A family of four living at poverty level paid 1.9 percent in federal taxes in 1980, but 10.4 percent in 1986.[24] Tax loopholes often result from lobbying and political campaign contributions, obviously, since money talks in politics and since money is the lifeblood of American politics. For example, "two-thirds of the [Republican] party's $137 million in unrestricted 'soft' money has been provided by just 739 contributors, many using disguised identities. Delivering at least $250,000 each were 150 Republican 'Regents'—about a hundred individuals and fifty corporations."[25]

Fourth, the Supreme Court and other organs of government are now putting severe limits on affirmative action. The *Bakke* decision banned almost all quotas as long ago as 1978, though one would never know it by how often politicians compaign against quotas. The *Weber* decision allowed quotas only in a narrow case where both management and union leaders agreed to have quotas. The *Croson* case has limited the use of statistics and history as the basis for affirmative action. Prop 209 in California has banned much affirmative action.

Fifth, welfare programs are too imperfect. For example, "a parent with one child loses all benefits on a wage of $6.26 an hour" in the Minnesota Family Investment Program (MFIP). There is reason to believe that Minnesota is one of the more liberal states. For example, Minnesota has voted Democratic in every presidential election stretching as far back as 24 years to 1976. "Even though federal law requires that food stamps be given according to need, MFIP now gives all recipients the average amount, so that more than half of families get less than before—as much as $80 a month less."[26] Further, in 1985 $43.6 billion in federal tax revenues were lost in homeowner deductions (including those for second homes), while only $12.3 billion was spent in federal subsidies for housing the poor.[27] So we have socialism for the rich and richer, subsidizing homeowners more than providing shelter for the poor. One result is that the average price of a home in Santa Clara County, California is over $435,000. Similarly, Cyndy Kulp, head of the Colorado Springs Housing Advocacy Coalition, claims "the average price for a new home in Colorado is $220,000, or twenty times what a minimum wage worker will earn in a year."[28] Here is another result. Zip Code 90210 is in California and runs from "Wilshire Boulevard, up the glittering gulch of Rodeo Drive, past the slinky curves of Sunset and snaking up leafy Colwater and Benedict canyons to the legendary top-of-the-hill stretch of Mulholland Drive." The area of Zip Code 90059 is "barely a half-hour drive south" of the area of Zip Code 90210. In [Zip Code] "90210, 84 percent of the inhabitants are white and 50 percent of them have four years or more of college. In [Zip Code] 90059, [South Central Los Angeles], 0.00 percent are white (48 percent are black, 51 percent Latino) and only 5 percent have four years or more of college; 53 percent haven't completed high school. In 90210, the median home value is $501,000; in 90059, it's about $100,000—still only $20,000 or so under the national median, reflecting LA's inflated housing market." Let's not forget renters. "Housing costs in LA are high enough that there are more renters than homeowners. More than 40 percent of those renters pay more than one-third of their monthly income for housing. A third of adults haven't completed high school. An almost equal number, 1.8 million people, are illiterate. A third live in poverty. Thirty percent of adults and 25 percent of children have no health insurance. If you include those families subsisting on the remnants of the 're-formed' welfare system and those receiving food stamps, about 20 percent of America's welfare case-load lives in Los Angeles County."[29] Further, as we saw above, 75 percent of the unemployed have no unemployment insurance benefits, and 15 percent of Americans have no health insurance, etc. So we need to do better.

I advocate reform, rather than abolition, of inheritance merely as one of many important and justified ways we may permissibly attack inequality and its underlying causes. I urge reform rather than abolition of inheritance because I am prepared to grant that parents do have a legitimate and admirable interest—even duty—in trying to ensure that their children enter society fully without unfair disadvantages. . . . So the inheritance tax should aim for that goal. Inheritance earmarked for education should be exempt from tax. Further, moderate amounts for each child's food, clothing, and shelter should be exempt. However, the current $600,000 federal exemption, regardless of how few will inherit or how rich the legatees already are, is too extreme to justify. Further, any state's unlimited exemption is maximally extreme and impossible to justify. For example, investing $600,000 in a 5 percent tax-free municipal bond would earn one $30,000 tax free every year for life, without even touching the principal of $600,000. Of course, $30,000 is higher than the average American's income. For example, average incomes vary state by state from a low of $15,838 in Mississippi to a high of $29,402 in Connecticut (and $31,136 in the District of Columbia) (the U.S. Dept. of Commerce, 1993).

I grant that each spouse has an interest and duty in seeing that, upon his or her death, the other spouse avoids plunging into poverty. So the government should exempt inheritance guaranteeing the national median income during a transition period (between death of the spouse and finding, if he or she lacks, steady employment paying at least the national average). Further, all inheritance earmarked for medical expenses of the spouse and children should be exempt. Inheritance beyond that which promotes the goal stated above should be taxed at nearly 100 percent. We will need details such as a legatee's right of first refusal to buy items to be taxed at 100 percent, and a savings clause to phase the system in gradually in order to avoid financial shocks. However, we need no more details here to show my main point that we must make fundamental reforms.

One might ask: What should the government do with the money from the inheritance tax? The spending should combat inequality of opportunity. We could provide moderate health insurance for those now lacking it. We could guarantee tuition to qualified applicants who cannot afford it. We could spend some on projects that benefit all citizens roughly equally (for example, reducing pollution or global warming; but quite independently of how we spend the money, part of the goal of promoting equality of opportunity will already have been served by simply taxing inheritances so they are unable to perpetuate significant financial advantages based on irrelevancies such as parentage, race, or sex.

I wish to consider three objections to my view. First, one may object that I seek equality of outcome in the name of equality of opportunity, and that equality of outcome will weaken incentives to produce and thus lower productivity. My first reply is that the two forms of equality are hardly as sharply distinct as many would have us believe. To the extent that one has inferior resources (lacking equality of outcome so far), one will lack opportunities to compete equally in business. My second reply is that the objection underestimates greed and socialization. Ours is an acquisitive society, and those motivated or socialized to acquire much wealth cannot or will not just turn off their drives and personalities once they reach some tax bracket, especially when inheritance tax scarcely prevents them from enjoying their wealth at any time during their lives. For example, many of the Silicon Valley millionaires are still working full-time. My third reply is that the objection simply assumes that those who turn off their drives and produce less will not be adequately replaced in a competitive market. There is no evidence for this assumption. Further, the government can easily use some revenue from inheritance taxes to subsidize small businesses to enhance competition and replacement. Finally, we can try the tax and end or modify it if it causes production to decline too much.

Second, one may object that I seek egalitarian justice by violating meritocratic justice. One may argue that the rich deserve their wealth because they have been so meritorious in contributing to our society. However, 67 percent of the wealth of the ultra-rich, which this objection implies are the most deserving and meritorious contributors, was itself unearned gain through inheritance.[30] Having rich parents is hardly a social contribution meriting reward. Inheritance is determined by an accident of birth beyond one's control. Further, in capitalism there is, commonsensically, a strong tendency—if left unchecked by government—for the rich to get richer and the poor to get poorer. The rich use their superior resources (for example, more efficient machines and better credit) to force their business rivals out of business. Superior resources allow the rich to weather bad periods (for example, droughts and recessions) that cripple or bankrupt their competitors. So initial inheritances, however unearned, strongly tend to magnify one's wealth, which is less deserved than that of those who work harder with less to earn wealth.

Third, one may object that getting perfect equality is impossible, so we should avoid even trying to combat the inequality of opportunity we now have. For example, some people are born, or naturally develop to become, more attractive than others. Further, it is not feasible to run around compensating people for having sub-par natural beauty. However, this objection denies the commonsense truth that half a loaf is better than none. We should take what equality we can get. Ending all inequality is indeed impossible, but we should rectify many of the most egregious and correctible inequalities of opportunity. The objection wants us to quit prematurely in the fight against inequality of opportunity.

Fourth, to anticipate one last objection, I can hear the conservative refrain often echoed throughout the supposedly liberal media: that we are unwisely trusting government rather than the people. But this is a false dichotomy, for American government is of, by, and for the people. The government is composed of people. I propose using the democratic process to increase the inheritance tax as outlined above.

I conclude that inheritance, as currently structured, is immoral. American inequality is too great and too dependent on irrelevancies such as parentage, race, and sex, to justify a complete federal tax exemption for estates under $600,000, much less a state tax exemption on all estates. However, inheritance can be moral. Parents have a legitimate interest, even duty, to try to make at least moderate provisions for their children. Further, spouses have duties to provide for one another in the event of death during the marriage. So I advocate fundamental reform, rather than abolition, of inheritance. Given the enormity—and the racist and sexist nature—of American inequality of opportunity, justice requires fundamental reforms in inheritance.

END NOTES

Introduction

[1] Gracchus Babeuf, quoted in Steven Lukes, "Socialism and Equality," *Dissent* 22 (1975): 155.

[2] Thomas Nagel, "Equality," in his book *Mortal Questions* (Cambridge University Press, 1979).

[3] Christopher Jencks, *Inequality: A Reassessment of the Effect of the Family and Schooling in America* (New York: Basic Books, 1972), p. 73.

[4] Richard Watson, "World Hunger and Equality," in *World Hunger and Moral Obligation,* ed. John Arthur and Hugh LaFollette (Englewood Cliffs, N.J.: Prentice Hall, 1978).

[5] Quoted in George Abernethy, ed., *The Idea of Equality* (Richmond, Va.: John Know Press, 1959), p. 101.

[6] de Tocqueville, *Democracy in America,* op. cit., p. 57.

[7] Onora O'Neill, "How Do We Know When Opportunities Are Equal?" in *Feminism and Philosophy,* ed. Mary Vetterling-Braggin, Frederick Elliston, and Jane English (Littlefield, Adams, & Co., 1977).

[8] John Schaar, "Equal Opportunity and Beyond," in *Equality: Selected Readings,* ed. Louis Pojman and Robert Westmoreland (Oxford University Press, 1997).

Frankfurt

[1] Ronald Dworkin, *A Matter of Principle* (Harvard University Press, 1985), pp. 206–212.

[2] Thomas Nagel, *Mortal Questions* (Cambridge University Press, 1979), p. 118.

Pojman

[1] Among the most prominent recent works on equal human rights are John Baker, *Arguing for Equality* (Verso, 1987); Maurice Cranston, *What Are Human Rights?* (Taplinger, 1973); J. Finnis, *Natural Law and Natural Rights* (Clarendon Press, 1980); Alan Gewirth, *Human Rights* (University of Chicago; 1982); Ronald Dworkin, *Taking Rights Seriously* (Harvard University, 1977); Will Kymlicka, *Contemporary Political Philosophy: An Introduction* (Oxford University, 1990); Rex Martin, *Rawls and Rights* (University of Kansas, 1985); Tibor Machan, *Individual Rights* (Open Court, 1989); James Nickel, *Making Sense of Human Rights* (University of California, 1987); Ellen Frankl Paul, Fred Miller, and Jeffrey Paul, eds., *Human Rights* (Basil Blackwell, 1984); Robert Nozick, *Anarchy, State and Utopia* (Basic Books, 1974); John Rawls, *A Theory of Justice* (Harvard, 1971); Jeremy Waldron, ed., *Theories of Rights* (Oxford University, 1984); Carl Wellman, *A Theory of Rights* (Rowman and Allenheld, 1985) and Morton E. Winston, ed., *The Philosophy of Human Rights* (Wadsworth, 1989).

[2] Ronald Dworkin, "The Original Position," *University of Chicago Law Review,* 40, no. 3 (Spring 1973): 532.

[3] Jacques Maritain, *The Rights of Man,* (London, 1944), p. 37.

[4] Will Kymlicka, *Contemporary Political Philosophy*, p. 4. Inegalitarianism is often dismissed as a crackpot idea that no self-respecting person would seriously consider. In another work, as though to apply the coup de grace to inegalitarianism, Kymlicka notes, "Some theories, like Nazism, deny that each person matters equally. But such theories do not merit serious consideration" (*Liberalism, Community and Culture* [Oxford University Press, 1989], p. 40). In *The End of Equality* (New York: Basic Books, 1992), Mickey Kaus writes, "I confess I had forgotten that social inegalitarians still existed in this country. Since writing the book I have encountered a few lively specimens. Still, I have confidence that they remain a small minority" (p. viii).

[5]Ronald Green, *Morality and Religion* (Oxford University Press, 1988), p. 140. I have challenged Green's idea of moral equality in my article "Equality: The Concept and Its Conceptions," in *Behavior and Philosophy*.

[6]Dworkin, "The Original Position," p. 532.

[7]R. S. Peters and S. I. Benn, *Social Principles and the Democratic State* (London, England: George Allen and Unwin, 1959), ch. 5; R. S. Peters, "Equality and Education," S. I. Benn and R. S. Peters," "Justice and Equality," and Monroe Beardsley, "Equality and Obedience to Law," all in *The Concept of Equality*, W. T. Blackstone, ed. (Burgess Publishing Company, 1960). Benn and Peters recognize the negative character of their definition and appeal to the principle of relevance to fill in the positive content (*Social Principles and the Democratic State,* p. 111f). E. F. Carritt in *Ethical and Political Thinking* (Oxford England, Oxford University Press 1947), pp. 156f, writes, "Equality of consideration is the only thing to the whole of which men have a right, [and] it is just to treat men as equal until some reason, other than preference, such as need, capacity, or desert, has been shown to the contrary."

[8]Ronald Dworkin, *Taking Rights Seriously* (Harvard University Press, 1977), p. 184. In his response to Jan Narveson's request for a supporting argument, Dworkin concedes that he has no argument to convince the skeptic regarding the "egalitarian plateau" but argues that rejecting it has such unwelcome consequences (such as class and caste systems) that we are justified in accepting it. In addition, Dworkin correctly states that we *deeply* value our lives and do so before imputing moral criteria, but he is wrong if he thinks that valuing our lives must be the basis of political and social arrangements. It is a large step from (1) "I matter most to myself" and "everyone else matters most to him or herself" to (2) everyone should matter *equally* to the State, for when we enter into society, we bring in contractual or utilitarian considerations, or both, which have normative features of their own. And these normative features may well specify that some interests count more than others, that virtue be rewarded differentially, and that some individual contributions or abilities be valued over others.

[9]Kai Nielsen, *Equality and Liberty: A Defense of Radical Egalitarianism* (Totowa, N.J.: Rowman and Allenheld, 1985), p. 23.

[10]Nielsen elsewhere speaks of his view that vast discrepancies in life prospects should be corrected as a "very basic considered judgment (moral intuition)," making his view identical with Dworkin's (*Taking Rights Seriously,* p. 8). Nielsen may differ from Dworkin only in emphasizing the role of choice in adopting his intuition. The question remains: What is the basis of the intuition that equality is intrinsically a good thing? Is it a natural intuition constitutive of the human condition, so that those who lack it are fundamentally deficient? Is it the product of a religious system which holds that all humans are made in the image of God with infinite value? Is it an aesthetic principle—similar to a sense of symmetry or unity? If for a secularist it is bad that humans are unequal in ability, why is it not bad that humans and apes or dogs or mice are of unequal ability?

[11]Nielsen, *Equality and Liberty,* p. 95.

[12]Nozick, in *Anarchy, State and Utopia* (New York: Basic Books, 1974), p. ix. In this regard Jeffrie Murphy points out that Nozick's Lockean theory of original acquisition of property fails because it omits the theological assumptions that supported Locke's own theory. Nozick seeks to prevent hoarding by property first-comers, so he invokes "The Lockean Proviso" that there be "enough and as good left in common for others." His Lockean justification is that no one's position is worsened. But what Nozick fails to explain is why anyone should care whether anyone else's position is worsened. As Murphy says, "If nature is unowned and I am bound, why may I not simply say, 'Lucky me I got it all first and unlucky you who came too late'—and let it go at that? What right do you have with respect to unowned and morally virgin nature?" (Jeffrie Murphy, "Afterword: Constitutionalism, Moral Skepticism, and Religious Belief," in *Constitutionalism,* ed. Alan Rosenbaum [Greenwood Press, 1988], p. 247).

[13]Tibor Machan, *Individuals and Their Rights* (Open Court, 1989), p. xxiv. For Machan's views on freedom of the will, see pp. 14f.

[14]David Gauthier, *Morals by Agreement* (Oxford University Press, 1986), pp. 55ff, 222. Gauthier seems to hold the Hobbesian idea that people are more or less equal in their ability to harm others, in their vulnerability to being harmed, and in their bargaining power, but I doubt this very much. The strong and clever can do more damage to others and have more to bring to the bargaining table.

[15]Gregory Vlastos, "Justice and Equality," *Social Justice,* ed. Richard Brandt (Prentice Hall, 1962). Reprinted in this volume.

[16]Joel Feinberg, *Social Philosophy* (Englewood Cliffs, N.J.: Prentice Hall, 1973), pp. 93f.

[17]R. M. Hare, "Justice and Equality," in *Justice and Economic Distribution,* ed. John Arthur and William H. Shaw (Englewood Cliffs, N.J.: Prentice Hall, 1978). Thomas Nagel, "Equality," in *Mortal Questions* (Cambridge University Press, 1979), also holds such a position, though he is not a utilitarian.

[18]For a cogent criticism of the uses of the doctrine of diminishing marginal utility for egalitarian purposes, see Harry Frankfurt, "Equality As a Moral Ideal," *Ethics* 98 (1987). My work is indebted to Frankfurt.

[19]Kai Nielsen, "On Not Needing to Justify Equality," *International Studies in Philosophy,* 20, no. 3 (1988): 55–71.

[20]Alan Gewirth, *Reason and Morality* (University of Chicago Press, 1978); "Epistemology of Human Rights," in *Human Rights,* ed. Ellen Frankl Paul, Fred Miller, and Jeffrey Paul (New York: Basil Blackwell, 1984); and *Human Rights: Essays on Justification and Applications* (University of Chicago Press, 1982).

[21]Tom Nagel, *A View from Nowhere* (Oxford University Press, 1986) and *Equality and Impartiality* (Oxford University Press, 1991), p. 11.

[22]Robert Nisbet, "The Pursuit of Equality," *Public Interest,* 35 (1974): 103–120.

[23]Michael Sandel, *Liberalism and the Limits of Justice* (Cambridge University Press, 1982), p. 88.

[24]John Rawls, *A Theory of Justice,* pp. 3f., 505, 506.

[25]John Harsanyi, *Essays in Ethics, Social Behavior and Scientific Explanation* (Reidel, 1976).

[26]See for example Isaiah 2; 19:21–25; 60:1–5; Micah 4 and Revelations 21 and 22. See Lenn Evan Goodman's "Equality and Human Rights: The Lockean and Judaic Views" in *Judaism* (1984) for an interpretation similar to my own.

Fishkin

[1]Rawls's principle of fair equality of opportunity approximates strong equality, but without confronting the implications for family autonomy. See John Rawls, *A Theory of Justice* (Harvard University Press, 1971), especially pp. 73–74.

[2]By "qualifications" I mean criteria that are job-related in that they can fairly be interpreted as indicators of competence or motivation for an individual's performance in a given position. Education, job history, fairly administered test results, or other tokens of ability or effort might all be included. Inferences that because one is a member of a group which generally does poorly, one is unlikely to do well would not be included within my account of qualifications. Such inferences would constitute statistical discrimination.

[3]By a "native characteristic," I mean any factor knowable at birth that could be employed to differentiate adult persons of at least normal health and endowment. These characteristics are not necessarily unalterable, as cases of sex change illustrate dramatically. A native characteristic will be considered arbitrary unless it predicts the development of qualifications to a high degree among children who have been subjected to equal developmental conditions. Race, sex, ethnic origin and family background are considered arbitrary here.

[4]By "essential prerequisites," I mean the physical and psychological health of the child and his or her knowledge of those social conventions necessary for participation in adult society. Literacy, the routines of citizenship, and other familiar elements of secondary education would count among the essential prerequisites.

[5]See Anti-Defamation League of B'Nai B'rith, "A Study of Post-Bakke Admissions Policies in Medical, Dental and Law Schools," *Rights*, 10, no. 1 (Summer 1979), pp. 11–12.

Galston

[1]For the best example of what I call "hyperindividualism," see Robert Nozick, *Anarchy, State, and Utopia* (New York: Basic Books, 1974), pp. 30–33.

[2]John Rawls, *A Theory of Justice* (Harvard University Press, 1971); Ronald Dworkin, "Liberalism," in Stuart Hampshire, ed., *Public and Private Morality* (Cambridge University Press, 1978); Bruce Ackerman, *Social Justice in the Liberal State* (Yale University Press, 1980).

[3]For a fuller discussion, see William Galston, *Justice and the Human Good* (University of Chicago Press, 1980), pp. 55–56, 279–280; and "Defending Liberalism," *American Political Science Review* 76 (1982): 621–629.

[4]Bernard Williams, "The Idea of Equality."

[5]John Schaar, "Equality of Opportunity and Beyond," in J. Roland Pennock and John W. Chapman, eds., *Nomos 9: Equality* (New York: Atherton, 1967).

[6]Michael Walzer, *Spheres of Justice: A Defense of Pluralism and Equality* (New York: Basic Books, 1983), p. 287.

Mosley

[1]Bernard Boxill, "The Morality of Reparation" in *Social Theory and Practice*, 2, no. 1, Spring 1972: 118–119.

[2]Judith Jarvis Thompson, *Philosophy and Public Affairs 2*, (Summer 1973): 379–380.

[3]Robert Fullinwider, *The Reverse Discrimination Controversy: A Moral and Legal Analysis* Lanham, MD: Rowman and Littlefield, 1980, p. 55; also Alan Goldman, "Reparations to Individuals or Groups?" *Analysis* 35, April 1975: 168–170.

[4]Gang Xu, Sylvia Fields, et al. "The Relationship between the Ethnicity of Generalist Physicians and Their Care for Underserved Populations," Ohio University College of Osteopathic Medicine, Ohio, 10.

[5]Remedial action based on the imbalance between blacks in the available work force and their presence in skilled jobs categories presumes that imbalance is caused by social discrimination. This assumption has been challenged by many who cite cultural and cognitive factors that might equally be the cause of such imbalances. See Thomas Sowell, *Markets and Minorities,* New York: Basic Books, 1981; Richard Hernstein and Charles Murray, *The Bell Curve,* New York: The Free Press, 1994. See also Christopher Jenks, *Rethinking Social Policy,* NY: Harper, 1993.

Pojman

[1]Both George W. Bush and Albert Gore have spoken in favor of Affirmative Action. Gore's vice president choice, Joel Lieberman, had strongly opposed Affirmative Action as reverse discrimination in the Senate, but, during the Democratic Convention in 2000, upon meeting with Jesse Jackson and the Black Caucus, he did an about-face and maintained that he had always supported Affirmative Action.

[2]This argument is related to the *Need of Breaking Stereotypes Argument.* Society may simply need to know that there are talented blacks and women, so that it does not automatically assign them lesser respect or status. The right response is that hiring less qualified people is neither fair to those better qualified who are passed over nor an effective way to remove inaccurate stereotypes. If high competence is accepted as the criterion for hiring, then it is unjust to override it for purposes of social engineering. Furthermore, if blacks and women are known to hold high positions simply because of reverse discrimination, they will still lack the respect due to those of their rank.

[3]For a good discussion of this argument see Boxill, "The Morality of Reparation" in *Social Theory and Practice* 2: no. 1 (1972) and Mosley, *op. cit.,* pp. 23–27.

[4]John Rawls, *A Theory of Justice* (Harvard University Press, 1971), p. 3.

[5]Merit sometimes may be justifiably overridden by need, as when parents choose to spend extra earnings on special education for their disabled child rather than for their gifted child. Sometimes we may override merit for utilitarian purposes. For example, suppose you are the best shortstop on a baseball team but are also the best catcher. You'd rather play shortstop, but the manager decides to put you at catcher because your friend can do an adequate job at short, but no one else is adequate at catcher. It's permissible for you to be assigned the job of catcher. Probably, some expression of appreciation would be due you.

[6]Judith Jarvis Thompson, "Preferential Hiring," in Marshall Cohen, Thomas Nagel, and Thomas Scanlon, eds., *Equality and Preferential Treatment* (Princeton University Press, 1977).

[7]Barbara Bergmann, *In Defense of Affirmative Action* (New York: Basic Books, 1996), pp. 9–10.

[8]Stephen Kershnar pointed this out in written comments (Dec. 22, 1997).

[9]John Arthur, *The Unfinished Constitution* (Belmont, Calif: Wadsworth Publishing, 1990), p. 238.

[10]Sterling Harwood, "The Justice of Affirmative Action," in Yearger Hudson and C. Peden, eds., *The "Bill of Rights" Bicentennial Reflections* (Lewiston, N.Y.: Edwin Mellen, 1996).

[11]Albert G. Mosley and Nicholas Capaldi, *Affirmative Action: Social Justice or Unfair Preference?* (Rowman & Littlefield, 1996), p. 28. Bernard Boxill, *Blacks and Social Justice* (Rowman & Littlefield, Lanham, Maryland, 1984), whom Mosley quotes in his article, also defends this position.

[12]Larry Hedges and Amy Nowell, "Sex Differences in Mental Test Scores, Variability, and Numbers of High-Scoring Individuals," *Science,* 269 (July 1995): 41–45. See Phillip E. Vernon's summary of the literature in *Intelligence: Heredity and Environment* (New York, 1979); Yves Christen, "Sex Differences in the Human Brain," in Nicholas Davidson, ed., *Gender Sanity* (Rowman & Littlefield, 1989); and T. Bouchard, et al., "Sources of Human Psychological Differences: The Minnesota Studies of Twins Reared Apart," *Science,* 250 (1990); Richard Hernstein and Charles Murray, *The Bell Curve* (New York: Free Press, 1994); and Michael E. Levin, *Why Race Matters* (Westport, Conn.: Praeger, 1997) for support for the thesis of racial and gender differences. Although these matters are controversial, the evidence for average differences must be carefully considered before we accept the equal outcomes thesis. Arianna Stassinopoulos sums up a large body of research on gender difference this way:

> Men are less average than women. They are the geniuses and the idiots, the giants and the dwarfs. The greater variability of men cannot possibly be explained on environmental grounds, as a simple difference in averages might be. If women are not found in the top positions in society in the same proportions as men because, as Women's Lib claims, they are treated as mentally inferior to men and become so, why are there so many more male idiots? Why are the remedial classes in schools full of boys? Why are the inmates of hospitals for

the mentally subnormal predominantly male? The reason why Women's Lib does not mention this conspicuous difference between the sexes is that it can only be explained on purely biological grounds. (*The Female Woman* [Davis-Poynter, 1973], pp. 28f.)

[13]Note, we are speaking about statistical averages. There are ample brilliant, as well as retarded, people in each group. See Levin, *Why Race Matters;* Hernstein and Murray, *The Bell Curve;* Doreen Kimura, "Sex Differences in the Brain," *Scientific American* (September 1992); and Hedges and Nowell, "Sex Differences in Mental Test Scores, Variability, and Numbers of High-Scoring Individuals."

[14]Iddo Landau ("Are You Entitled to Affirmative Action?" *Applied Philosophy,* 11 [Winter/Spring 1997]) and Richard Kahlenberg, ("Class Not Race," *New Republic* [April 3, 1995]) advocate affirmative action on the basis of class or low income, not race or gender. I think this is an improvement, depending on how it is implemented, but it ignores family responsibility.

[15]Albert Mosley, "Pojman's Strawman Arguments Against Affirmative Action," *International Journal of Applied Philosophy* 12, no. 2 (1998). See my response in that same issue. The Center for Equal Opportunity has documented that many state and private universities use race-norming criteria in admissions, generally admitting blacks with SAT scores 200 or more points lower than whites and Asians. The practice has been defended by several writers, including William Bowen and Derek Bok in *The Shape of the River* (Princeton University Press, 1998).

[16]Albert Mosley, "Affirmative Action: Pro," in Mosley and Capaldi, *Affirmative Action,* p. 53.

[17]J. Sartorelli, "The Nature of Affirmative Action, Anti-Gay Oppression, and the Alleviation of Enduring Harm," *International Journal of Applied Philosophy,* 11, no. 2 (1997).

[18]For example, I. Landau, "Are You Entitled to Affirmative Action?" and R. Kahlenberg, "Class Not Race."

[19]*New York Times,* May 10, 1990.

[20]Quoted by Nicholas Capaldi, *Out of Order: Affirmative Action and the Crisis of Doctrinaire Liberalism* (Buffalo, N.Y.: Prometheus, 1985).

[21]Capaldi, *Out of Order,* p. 95.

[22]Capaldi, *Out of Order,* p. 95. Michael Levin begins his book *Feminism and Freedom* (Transaction Press: New Brunswick, New Jersey, 1987) with federal court case *Beckman v. NYFD,* in which eighty-eight women who failed the New York City Fire Department's entrance exam in 1977 filed a class-action sex discrimination suit. The court found that the physical strength component of the test was not job-related, and thus was a violation of Title VII of the Civil Rights Act, and ordered the city to hire forty-nine of the women. It further ordered the fire department to devise a special, less-demanding physical strength exam for women. Following EEOC guidelines, if the passing rate for women is less than 80 percent of the passing rate for men, the test is presumed invalid.

[23]Bergmann, *In Defense of Affirmative Action,* pp. 122–125.

[24]See L. Gordon Crovitz, "Borking Begins, But Mudballs Bounce Off Judge Thomas," *Wall Street Journal,* July 17, 1991. Did you notice the irony in this mudslinging at Judge Thomas? The same blacks and whites who opposed Judge Thomas, as not the best person for the job, were themselves the strongest proponents of Affirmative Action, which embraces the tenet that minimally qualified blacks and women should get jobs over white males.

Sher

[1]Paul W. Taylor, "Reverse Discrimination and Compensatory Justice," in Steven M. Cahn, editor, *The Affirmative Action Debate* (New York: Routledge, 1995), p. 14.

[2]Neil L. Rudenstine, "Why a Diverse Student Body Is So Important," *Chronicle of Higher Education,* April 19, 1996 p. Bl.

Harwood

[1]Harper's, Sept. 2000, p. 9.

[2]Internal Revenue Service Website.

[3]R. Avery, G. Elliehausen, G. Canner, and T. Gustafson, "Survey of Consumer Finances, 1983: Second Report," *Res. Bull.* (1984) 865.

[4]Lester Thurow, "Tax Wealth, Not Income," *New York Times Magazine,* April 11, 1976, p. 33.

[5]*Harper's Index Book,* p. 51.

[6]Ibid., p. 86.

[7]*Harper's,* July 1988, p. 15.

[8]*Time,* Oct. 30, 2000, p. 31.

[9]Marc Cooper, "The Two Worlds of Los Angeles," *The Nation,* August 21–28, 2000, p. 18.

[10]Doug Ireland, "Tricky Dick," *The Nation,* Aug. 21–28, 2000.

[11]Ahmad Diba and Noshua Watson, "America's Forty Richest Under 40," *Forbes,* Sept. 18, 2000, p. 100.

[12]Eryn Brown, "So Rich So Young: But Are They Really Happy?" *Forbes,* Sept. 18, 2000, p. 104.

[13]Diba and Watson, p. 115.

[14]*Harper's Index Book,* pp. 57, 3, 1.

[15]D. W. Haslett, "Is Inheritance Justified?" *Phil. & Pub. Affairs* 15 122–155 (1986), p. 124.

[16]*Harper's Index Book,* p. 14.

[17]U.S. Dept. of Commerce, Bureau of the Census, *Statistical Abstract of the U.S. 1985,* p. 407, hereinafter: Census.

[18]*Harper's Index Book,* pp. 24, 10.

[19]Census, p. 446.

[20]*Atlanta Journal-Constitution,* Jan. 22, 1989.

[21]*Harper's Index Book,* pp. 15, 16, 72, 58.

[22]*Harper's Index Book,* p. 9.

[23]*Harper's,* April 1989, p. 17.

[24]*Harper's,* March 1989, p. 11.

[25]Eric Alterman, "Your Show of Show," *The Nation,* August 21–28, 2000, p. 13.

[26]Katha Pollitt, "The Politics of Personal Responsibility," *The Nation,* August 21–28, 2000, p. 12.

[27]*Harper's Index Book,* p. 24.

[28]*The Progressive,* Oct. 2000, p. 27.

[29]Cooper, "The Two Worlds of Los Angeles," *The Nation,* August 21/28, 2000, pp. 15, 16.

[30]John A. Brittain, *Inheritance and the Inequality of National Wealth* (Brookings Institution, 1978), p. 991.

CHAPTER VII

Rights

We hold these truths to be self-evident that all men are created equal; that they are endowed by their Creator with certain inalienable rights; that among these are life, liberty and the pursuit of happiness.
(Declaration of Independence of the United States of America, July 4, 1776)

Human rights have been the centerpiece of political theory for over two centuries. They were the justification for the American and French revolutions in the eighteenth century and for a succession of revolutions for political independence in the nineteenth and twentieth centuries, as well as the motivation for the civil rights movement in the 1960s and the women's movement in the 1970s.

Natural rights are said to be the moral basis of positive law and the grounds for welfare rights and foreign aid, but the exact set of such universal rights varies. The United Nations Universal Declaration of Human Rights (Reading 50) includes free education and paid holidays. Other groups extend rights to animals, to corporations, and to forests. Nevertheless, almost all rights systems grant human beings the rights of life, liberty, property, and the pursuit of happiness.

Rights are important to our lives. We are ready to defend them, to demand their recognition and enforcement, and to complain of injustice when they are not complied with. We use them as vital premises in arguments that proscribe courses of action (for example, "Please stop smoking in this public place, for we nonsmokers have a right to clean air"). Eventually, when we receive no redress for violations of our rights, we even consider civil disobedience.

It is because of their importance that we need to ask: What precisely are rights? Where do rights come from? Are there any natural rights, rights that do not depend on social contract, prior moral duties, utilitarian outcomes, or ideals?

Although there is a great deal of variation in defining "rights" in the literature, for our purposes we can say that a right is a claim against others that at the same time includes a liberty on one's own behalf.[1] J. L. Mackie captures this combination when he writes, "A right, in the most important sense, is a conjunction of a freedom and a claim-right. That is, if someone, A, has the moral right to do X, not only is he entitled to do X if he chooses—he is not morally required not to do X—but he is also protected in his doing of X—others are morally required not to interfere or prevent him."[2] Rights are typically relational in that we have them against other people: If I have a right against you regarding X, you have a duty to me regarding X. For example, if you have promised to pay me $10 for cutting your lawn and I have done so, I have a right to that $10 and you have a duty to pay me.

Rights give us special advantage. If you have a right, then others require special justification for overriding or limiting your right; and conversely, if you have a right, you have a justification for limiting the freedom of others in regard to exercising that right.

Next we should distinguish among the basic types of rights that we will encounter in this chapter:

1. Natural rights. Those rights, if any, that humans (or other beings) have simply by nature of what

they are. According to the U.S. Declaration of Independence, God bestows these rights upon us.

2. Human rights. This is an ambiguous term. Sometimes it means "natural rights," at other times it means rights that humans have, and at still other times it means moral rights.

3. Moral rights. Those rights that are justified by a given moral system. They may be derivative of duties or ideals or utilitarian outcomes.

4. Positive rights. Those rights that society affords its members, including legal rights, such as the right of a woman to have an abortion or the right to vote.

5. Prima facie rights. Presumptive rights that may not necessarily be an actual right in a given situation. My right to hear loud music may be overridden by your right to peace and quiet.[3]

6. Absolute rights. Rights that cannot be overridden. For example, for those who hold that justice is an absolute right, my right to fair treatment may not be overridden by utilitarian considerations.

Many take natural rights for granted. In his book *Taking Rights Seriously,* even so capable a philosopher as Ronald Dworkin simply assumes that we have rights without argument:

> Some philosophers, of course, reject the idea that citizens have rights apart from what the law happens to give them. Bentham thought that the idea of moral rights was "nonsense on stilts." But that view has never been part of our orthodox political theory, and politicians of both parties appeal to the rights of the people to justify a great part of what they want to do. I shall not be concerned, in this essay, to defend the thesis that citizens have moral rights against their governments.[4]

This attitude seems philosophically unsatisfying. We want to know what the nature of rights is, whether we have any human rights, and what they are. We want, as philosophical beings, to have a justification for our rights claims. Consider, for instance, two claims: (1) "I have a right to smoke wherever I please," and (2) "I have a right to be treated justly." What distinguishes (2) from (1)? Why accept (2), but not (1), as a valid right? Are all rights simply legal rights? Or are rights simply relative to cultural tastes? Consider Arthur Danto's view that they are simply what our peers will let us get away with:

> In the afterwash of 1968, I found myself a member of a group charged with working out discipli-

nary procedures for acts against my university. It was an exemplary group from the perspective of representation so urgent at the time: administrators, tenured and nontenured faculty, graduate and undergraduate students, men and women, whites and blacks. We all wondered, nevertheless, what right we had to do what was asked of us, and a good bit of time went into expressing our insecurities. Finally, a man from the law school said, with the tried patience of someone required to explain what should be plain as day and in a tone of voice I can still hear: "This is the way it is with rights. You want'em, so you say you got'em, and if nobody says you don't then you do." In the end he was right. We worked a code out which nobody liked, but in debating it the community acknowledged the rights.[5]

But apply this idea to Gangster Gus, who extorts "protection" money from all the local businesses, claiming that he has a right to do so. When challenged, he quotes Danto's colleague: "This is the way it is with rights. You want'em, so you say you got'em, and if nobody says you don't then you do." He might just as well have said, "Might makes right." We should be able to do better than this or else drop rights language altogether.

We must first consider what is meant by natural rights and by what is often used as its synonym, human rights. By a *natural right* we mean a right that is ours simply by the nature of things, independent of any other reason or moral duty or ideal. This notion, which may be traced back to the Stoics and was explicit in the late Middle Ages, became prominent in the seventeenth century with the works of Hugo Grotius (1583–1645) and John Locke. For Locke (see Reading 3), humans possess rights by nature (namely, life, liberty, and property) that society must recognize if it is to be legitimate. They are bestowed on us by God. Because these rights are a gift of God, they are "inalienable" or "imprescriptible;" that is, we do not give them to people, nor can we take them away or even give our own rights away (for example, we cannot give away our right to freedom by selling ourselves into slavery). They become the proper basis of all specific rights, such as the right to vote, to be protected by the law, to sell property, to work, and to be educated. Let us call this position the natural law theory of rights. Here is a contemporary expression of this theory:

> The human person possesses rights because of the very fact that it is a person, a whole, master of it-

self and of its acts, and which consequently is not merely a means to an end, but an end, an end which must be treated as such. The dignity of the human person? The expression means nothing if it does not signify that by virtue of natural law, the human person has the right to be respected, is the subject of rights, possesses rights. These are things which are owed to man because of the very fact that he is man.[6]

Most philosophers who deny natural rights do not deny that we have rights. They simply deny that they are in the nature of things, as the natural law theorists affirm. As Jeremy Bentham put it in 1843, "Natural rights is . . . nonsense upon stilts. . . . Right is a child of law; from real laws come real rights, but from imaginary law, from 'laws of nature,' come imaginary rights. . . . A natural right is a son that never had a father."[7] These antinaturalists state that all rights are derivable from something else, such as law, moral duty, utilitarian outcomes, or ideals. Let us look at each of these possibilities.

1. Some philosophers, including the legal positivists John Austin, Jeremy Bentham, and, Alasdair MacIntyre (Reading 47), argue that all rights (as well as their correlative duties) are institutional in the way that legal rights are. We referred to these earlier as positive rights, those actually recognized by organized society. As MacIntyre (Reading 47) writes: "[C]laims to the possession of rights . . . presuppose the existence of a socially established set of rules. Such sets of rules only come into existence at particular historical periods under particular social circumstances. They are in no way universal features of the human condition. . . . [T]he existence of particular types of social institution or practice is a necessary condition for the notion of a claim to the possession of a right."

2. Duty-based (deontological) ethical theories, such as those of Kant, W. D. Ross, or William Frankena, hold that rights are simply entailments of moral obligations. Since I have a duty to pay you back the money I borrowed, you have a corresponding right to the money. However, some duties do not generate rights. For example, I have a duty to share my abundance with the poor and needy, but no one poor and needy person has a right to it. If you are poor, you cannot properly demand $50 from me, for there may be others equally poor to whom I choose to give the money. It is duty that is primary to the moral system, and rights are but correlates to duties. To have a right means simply that one is the beneficiary of someone else's duty. For this

reason, it is misleading to speak of human rights as a separate subject apart from a duty-based moral system.

3. Goal-based theories, such as the utilitarianism of John Stuart Mill, argue that rights are derivable from our understanding of utility. We will all be happier if we have certain of our interests protected, especially our interest in noninterference.

4. A variation on this theme is the view of Kurt Baier and Richard Brandt that rights are those claims and liberties that would be included in an ideal moral system, which need not be a utilitarian one. They are moral features that should be assigned to us even though they may be missing. Hence, we may assert that blacks had a right to freedom from slavery before the Emancipation Proclamation, even though the majority of people in the southern United States, as well as the law, failed to recognize that right. It is in this light that we may interpret the rights enumerated in the United Nations Universal Declaration of Human Rights (Reading 50), such as the right to free education and paid holidays. These are ideals that we should strive to realize.

To philosophers who hold to natural rights, these antinaturalist views seem like a profanation of rights, an undermining of rights' power and presence. In order to counter this tendency to treat rights as second-class citizens in our moral repertoire, Joel Feinberg, in Reading 45, imagines a place, Nowheresville, that has all the benefits of a good society except rights. Feinberg argues that because Nowheresville people cannot make moral claims, which are logically connected with rights, they are deprived of a certain self-respect and dignity. "To respect a person . . . , or to think of him as possessed of human dignity, simply *is* to think of him as a potential maker of claims." As such, rights are necessary to an adequate moral theory.

In Reading 46, Alan Gewirth goes further than Feinberg, arguing that rights are the basis of morality and can be proved rationally. He constructs an argument showing that there are universal human rights. His argument is succinct and precise. It constitutes a challenge to antinatural rights philosophers to show where his argument goes wrong.

In Reading 47, Alasdair MacIntyre takes up the challenge. He criticizes rights-based moral theories and analyzes Gewirth's defense of human rights.

In order to provide a concrete example of the way rights language is used in our world, I have included a copy of the United Nations Universal Declaration of Human Rights (Reading 50).

READING 45

The Nature and Value of Rights

Joel Feinberg

For Feinberg's biography, see Reading 17. In this essay, Feinberg begins with a thought experiment in which he asks you to imagine Nowheresville, a world very much like our own. Although it has all the other benefits a good society could offer, including moral duties and benevolence, Nowheresville is still missing something important—rights. The people of Nowheresville cannot make moral claims or righteous demands when they are discriminated against, and in this way they are deprived of a certain self-respect and dignity. Rights are valid moral claims that give us inherent dignity, and as such they are necessary to an adequate moral theory.

This reading is taken from *The Journal of Value Inquiry* 4 (1970).

1

I would like to begin by conducting a thought experiment. Try to imagine Nowheresville—a world very much like our own except that no one, or hardly any one (the qualification is not important), has *rights*. If this flaw makes Nowheresville too ugly to hold very long in contemplation, we can make it as pretty as we wish in other moral respects. We can, for example, make the human beings in it as attractive and virtuous as possible without taxing our conceptions of the limits of human nature. In particular, let the virtues of moral sensibility flourish. Fill this imagined world with as much benevolence, compassion, sympathy, and pity as it will conveniently hold without strain. Now we can imagine men helping one another from compassionate motives merely, quite as much or even more than they do in our actual world from a variety of more complicated motives.

This picture, pleasant as it is in some respects, would hardly have satisfied Immanuel Kant. Benevolently motivated actions do good, Kant admitted, and therefore are better, *ceteris paribus*, than

malevolently motivated actions; but no action can have supreme kind of worth—what Kant called "moral worth"—unless its whole motivating power derives from the thought that it is *required by duty*. Accordingly, let us try to make Nowheresville more appealing to Kant by introducing the idea of duty into it, and letting the sense of duty be a sufficient motive for many beneficent and honorable actions. But doesn't this bring our original thought experiment to an abortive conclusion? If duties are permitted entry into Nowheresville, are not rights necessarily smuggled in along with them?

The question is well-asked, and requires here a brief digression so that we might consider the so-called "doctrine of the logical correlativity of rights and duties." This is the doctrine that (i) all duties entail other people's rights and (ii) all rights entail other people's duties. Only the first part of the doctrine, the alleged entailment from duties to rights, need concern us here. Is this part of the doctrine correct? It should not be surprising that my answer is: "In a sense yes and in a sense no." Etymologically, the word "duty" is associated with actions that are *due* someone else, the payments of debts *to* creditors, the keeping of agreements with promises, the payment of club dues, or legal fees, or tariff levies to appropriate authorities or their representatives. In this original sense of "duty," all duties are correlated with the rights of those *to* whom the duty is owed. On the other hand, there seem to be numerous classes of duties, both of a legal and non-legal kind, that are *not* logically correlated with the rights of other persons. This seems to be a consequence of the fact that the word "duty" has come to be used for *any* action understood to be *required*, whether by the rights of others, or by law, or by higher authority, or by conscience, or whatever. When the notion of requirement is in clear focus it is likely to seem the only element in the idea of duty that is essential, and the other component notion—that a duty is something *due* someone else—drops off. Thus, in this widespread but derivative usage, "duty" tends to be used for any action we *must* (for whatever reason) do. It comes, in short, to be a term of moral modality merely; and it is no wonder that the first thesis of the logical correlativity doctrine often fails.

Let us then introduce duties into Nowheresville, but only in the sense of actions that are, or believed to be, morally mandatory, but not in the older sense of actions that are due others and can be claimed by others as their right. Nowheresville now can have duties of the sort imposed by positive law. A legal duty is not something we are implored or advised to do merely; it is something the law, or an authority under the law, *requires* us to do whether we want to or not, under pain of penalty. When traffic lights turn red, however, there is no determinate person who can plausibly be said to claim our stopping as his due, so that the motorist owes it to *him* to stop, in the way a debtor owes it to his creditor to pay. In our own actual world, of course, we sometimes owe it to our *fellow motorists* to stop; but that kind of right-correlated duty does not exist in Nowheresville. There, motorists "owe" obedience to the Law, but they owe nothing to one another. When they collide, no matter who is at fault, no one is accountable to anyone else, and no one has any sound grievance or "right to complain."

When we leave legal contexts to consider moral obligations and other extra-legal duties, a greater variety of duties-without-correlative-rights present themselves. Duties of charity, for example, require us to contribute to one or another of a large number of eligible recipients, no one of whom can claim our contribution from us as his due. Charitable contributions are more like gratuitous services, favours, and gifts than like repayments of debts or reparations; and yet we do have duties to be charitable. Many persons, moreover, in our actual world believe that they are required by their own consciences to do more than that "duty" that *can* be demanded of them by their prospective beneficiaries. I have quoted elsewhere the citation from H. B. Acton of a character in a Malraux novel who "gave all his supply of poison to his fellow prisoners to enable them by suicide to escape the burning alive which was to be their fate and his." This man, Acton adds, "probably did not think that [the others] had more of a right to the poison than he had, though he thought it his duty to give it to them."[1] I am sure that there are many actual examples, less dramatically heroic than this fictitious one, of persons who believe, rightly or wrongly, that they *must do* something (hence the word "duty") for another person in excess of what that person can appropriately demand of him (hence the absence of "right").

Now the digression is over and we can return to Nowheresville and summarize what we have put in it thus far. We now find spontaneous benevolence in somewhat larger degree than in our actual world, and also the acknowledged existence of duties of obedience, duties of charity, and duties imposed by exacting private consciences, and also, let us suppose, a degree of conscientiousness in respect to those duties somewhat in excess of what is to be found in our actual world. I doubt that Kant would be fully satisfied with

Nowheresville even now that duty and respect for law and authority have been added to it; but I feel certain that he would regard their addition at least as an improvement. I will now introduce two further moral practices into Nowheresville that will make the world very little more appealing to Kant, but will make it appear more familiar to us. These are the practices connected with the notions of *personal desert* and what I call a *sovereign monopoly of rights*.

When a person is said to deserve something good from us what is meant in part is that there would be a certain propriety in our giving that good thing to him in virtue of the kind of person he is, perhaps, or more likely, in virtue of some specific thing he has done. The propriety involved here is a much weaker kind than that which derives from our having promised him the good thing or from his having qualified for it by satisfying the well-advertised conditions of some public rule. In the latter case he could be said not merely to deserve the good thing but also to have a *right* to it, that is to be in a position to demand it as his due; and of course we will not have that sort of thing in Nowheresville. That weaker kind of propriety which is mere desert is simply a kind of *fittingness* between one party's character or action and another party's favorable response, much like that between humor and laughter, or good performance and applause.

The following seems to be the origin of the idea of deserving good or bad treatment from others: A master or lord was under no obligation to reward his servant for especially good service; still a master might naturally feel that there would be a special fittingness in giving a gratuitous reward as a grateful response to the good service (or conversely imposing a penalty for bad service). Such an act while surely fitting and proper was entirely supererogatory. The fitting response in turn from the rewarded servant should be gratitude. If the deserved reward had not been given him he should have had no complaint, since he only *deserved* the reward, as opposed to having a *right* to it, or a ground for claiming it as his due.

The idea of desert has evolved a good bit away from its beginnings by now, but nevertheless, it seems clearly to be one of those words J. L. Austin said "never entirely forget their pasts."[2] Today servants qualify for their wages by doing their agreed upon chores, no more and no less. If their wages are not forthcoming, their contractual rights have been violated and they can make legal claim to the money that is their due. If they do less than they agreed to do, however, their employers may "dock" them, by paying them proportionately less than the agreed upon fee. This is all a matter of right. But if the servant does a splendid job, above and beyond his minimal contractual duties, the employer is under no further obligation to reward him, for this was not agreed upon, even tacitly, in advance. The additional service was all the servant's idea and done entirely on his own. Nevertheless, the morally sensitive employer may feel that it would be exceptionally appropriate for him to respond, freely on *his* own, to the servant's meritorious service, with a reward. The employee cannot demand it as his due, but he will happily accept it, with gratitude, as a fitting response to his desert.

In our age of organized labor, even this picture is now archaic; for almost every kind of exchange of service is governed by hard bargained contracts so that even bonuses can sometimes be demanded as a matter of right, and nothing is given for nothing on either side of the bargaining table. And perhaps that is a good thing; for consider an anachronistic instance of the earlier kind of practice that survives, at least as a matter of form, in the quaint old practice of "tipping." The tip was originally conceived as a reward that has to be earned by "zealous service." It is not something to be taken for granted as a standard response to *any* service. That is to say that its payment is a *"gratuity,"* not a discharge of obligation, but something given apart from, or in addition to, anything the recipient can expect as a matter of right. That is what tipping originally meant at any rate, and tips are still referred to as "gratuities" in the tax forms. But try to explain all that to a New York cab driver! If he has *earned* his gratuity, by God, he has it coming, and there had better be sufficient acknowledgement of his desert or he'll give you a piece of his mind! I'm not generally prone to defend New York cab drivers, but they do have a point here. There is the making of a paradox in the queerly unstable concept of an "earned gratuity." One can understand how "desert" in the weak sense of "propriety" or "mere fittingness" tends to generate a stronger sense in which desert is itself the ground for a claim of right.

In Nowheresville, nevertheless, we will have only the original weak kind of desert. Indeed, it will be impossible to keep this idea out if we allow such practices as teachers grading students, judges awarding prizes, and servants serving benevolent but class-conscious masters. Nowheresville is a reasonably good world in many ways, and its teachers, judges, and masters will generally try to give students, contestants, and servants the grades, prizes, and rewards they deserve. For this the recipients will be grateful; but they will never think

to complain, or even feel aggrieved, when expected responses to desert fail. The masters, judges, and teachers don't *have* to do good things, after all, for *anyone.* One should be happy that they *ever* treat us well, and not grumble over their occasional lapses. Their hoped for responses, after all, are *gratuities,* and there is no wrong in the omission of what is merely gratuitous. Such is the response of persons who have no concept of *rights,* even persons who are proud of their own deserts.

Surely, one might ask, rights have to come in somewhere, if we are to have even moderately complex forms of social organization. Without rules that confer rights and impose obligations, how can we have ownership of property, bargains and deals, promises and contracts, appointments and loans, marriages and partnerships? Very well, let us introduce all of these social and economic practices into Nowheresville, but *with one big twist.* With them I should like to introduce the curious notion of a "sovereign right-monopoly." You will recall that the subjects in Hobbes's *Leviathan* had no rights whatever against their sovereign. He could do as he liked with them, even gratuitously harm them, but this gave them no valid grievance against him. The sovereign, to be sure, had a certain duty to treat his subjects well, but this duty was owed not to the subjects directly, but to God, just as we might have a duty to a person to treat his property well, but of course no duty to the property itself but only to its owner. Thus, while the sovereign was quite capable of *harming* his subjects, he could commit no wrong against them that they could complain about, since they had no prior claims against his conduct. The only party *wronged* by the sovereign's mistreatment of his subjects was God, the supreme lawmaker. Thus, in repenting cruelty to his subjects, the sovereign might say to God, as David did after killing Uriah, "to Thee only have I sinned" [2 Sam. II].

Even in *Leviathan,* however, ordinary people had ordinary rights *against one another.* They played roles, occupied offices, made agreements, and signed contracts. In a genuine "sovereign right-monopoly," as I shall be using that phrase, they will do all those things too, and thus incur genuine obligations toward one another; but the obligations (here is the twist) will not be owed directly *to* promisees, creditors, parents, and the like, but rather to God alone, or to the members of some elite, or to a single sovereign under God. Hence, the rights correlative to the obligations that derive from these transactions are all owned by some "outside" authority.

As far as I know, no philosopher has ever suggested that even our role and contract obligations (in this, our actual world) are all owed directly to a divine intermediary, but some theologians have approached such extreme moral occasionalism. I have in mind the familiar phrase in certain widely distributed religious tracts that "it takes three to marry," which suggests that marital vows are not made between bride and groom directly but between each spouse and God, so that if one breaks his vow, the other cannot rightly complain of being wronged, since only God could have claimed performance of the marital duties as his *own* due; and hence God alone had a claim-right violated by the nonperformance. If John breaks his vow to God, he might then properly repent in the words of David: "To Thee only have I sinned."

In our actual world, very few spouses conceive of their mutual obligations in this way; but their small children, at a certain stage in their moral upbringing, are likely to feel precisely this way toward *their* mutual obligations. If Billy kicks Bobby and is punished by Daddy, he may come to feel contrition for his naughtiness induced by his painful estrangement from the loved parent. He may then be happy to make amends and sincere apology to *Daddy;* but when Daddy insists that he apologize to his wronged brother, that is another story. A direct apology to Billy would be a tacit recognition of Billy's status as a right-holder against him, someone he can wrong as well as harm, and someone to whom he is directly accountable for his wrongs. This is a status Bobby will happily accord Daddy; but it would imply a respect for Billy that he does not presently feel, so he bitterly resents according it to him. On the "three-to-marry" model, the relations between each spouse and God would be like those between Bobby and Daddy; respect for the other spouse as an independent claimant would not even be necessary; and where present, of course, never sufficient.

The advocates of the "three-to-marry" model who conceive it either as a description of our actual institution of marriage or a recommendation of what marriage ought to be, may wish to escape this embarrassment by granting rights to spouses in capacities other than as promisees. They may wish to say, for example, that when John promises God that he will be faithful to Mary, a right is thus conferred not only on God as promisee but also on Mary herself as third-party beneficiary, just as when John contracts with an insurance company and names Mary as his intended beneficiary, she has a right to the accumulated funds after John's death, even though the insurance company made no

promise to her. But this seems to be an unnecessarily cumbersome complication contributing nothing to our understanding of the marriage bond. The life insurance transaction is necessarily a three-party relation, involving occupants of three distinct offices, no two of whom alone could do the whole job. The transaction, after all, is defined as the purchase by the customer (first office) from the vendor (second office) of protection for a beneficiary (third office) against the customer's untimely death. Marriage, on the other hand, in this our actual world, appears to be a binary relation between a husband and wife, and even though third parties such as children, neighbors, psychiatrists, and priests may sometimes be helpful and even causally necessary for the survival of the relation, they are not logically necessary to our *conception* of the relation, and indeed many married couples do quite well without them. Still I am not now purporting to describe our actual world, but rather trying to contrast it with a counterpart world of the imagination. In *that* world, it takes three to make almost *any* moral relation and all rights are owned by God or some sovereign under God.

There will, of course, be delegated authorities in the imaginary world, empowered to give commands to their underlings and to punish them for their disobedience. But the commands are all given in the name of the right-monopoly who in turn are the only persons to whom obligations are owed. Hence, even intermediate superiors do not have claim-rights against their subordinates but only legal *powers* to create obligations in the subordinates *to* the monopolistic right-holders, and also the legal *privilege* to impose penalties in the name of that monopoly.

2

So much for the imaginary "world without rights." If some of the moral concepts and practices I have allowed into that world do not sit well with one another, no matter. Imagine Nowheresville with all of these practices if you can, or with any harmonious subset of them, if you prefer. The important thing is not what I've let into it, but what I have kept out. The remainder of this paper will be devoted to an analysis of what precisely a world is missing when it does not contain rights and why that absence is morally important.

The most conspicuous difference, I think, between the Nowheresvillians and ourselves has something to do with the activity of *claiming*. Nowheresvillians, even when they are discriminated against invidiously, or left without the things they need, or otherwise badly treated, do not think to leap to their feet and make righteous demands against one another though they may not hesitate to resort to force and trickery to get what they want. They have no notion of rights, so they do not have a notion of what is their due; hence they do not claim before they take. The conceptual linkage between personal rights and claiming has long been noticed by legal writers and is reflected in the standard usage in which "claim-rights" are distinguished from other mere liberties, immunities, and powers, also sometimes called "rights," with which they are easily confused. When a person has a legal claim-right to *X*, it must be the case (i) that he is at liberty in respect to *X*, i.e., that he has no duty to refrain from or relinquish *X*, and also (ii) that his liberty is the ground of other people's *duties* to grant him *X* or not to interfere with him in respect to *X*. Thus, in the sense of claim-rights, it is true by definition that rights logically entail other people's duties. The paradigmatic examples of such rights are the creditor's right to be paid a debt by his debtor, and the landowner's right not to be interfered with by anyone in the exclusive occupancy of his land. The creditor's right against his debtor, for example, and the debtor's duty to his creditor, are precisely the same relation seen from two different vantage points, as inextricably linked as the two sides of the same coin.

And yet, this is not quite an accurate account of the matter, for it fails to do justice to the way claim-rights are somehow prior to, or more basic than, the duties with which they are necessarily correlated. If Nip has a claim-right against Tuck, it is because of this fact that Tuck has a duty to Nip. It is only because something from Tuck is *due* Nip (directional element) that there is something Tuck *must do* (modal element). This is a relation, moreover, in which Tuck is bound and Nip is free. Nip not only *has* a right, but he can choose whether or not to exercise it, whether to claim it, whether to register complaints upon its infringement, even whether to release Tuck from his duty, and forget the whole thing. If the personal claim-right is also backed up by criminal sanctions, however, Tuck may yet have a duty of obedience to the law from which no one, not even Nip, may release him. He would even have such duties if he lived in Nowheresville; but duties subject to acts of claiming, duties derivative from and contingent upon the personal rights of others, are unknown and undreamed of in Nowheresville.

Many philosophical writers have simply identified rights with claims. The dictionaries tend to define

"claims," in turn as "assertions of right," a dizzying piece of circularity that led one philosopher [H. B. Acton] to complain—"We go in search of rights and are directed to claims, and then back again to rights in bureaucratic futility." What then is the relation between a claim and a right?

As we shall see, a right *is* a kind of claim, and a claim is "an assertion of right," so that a formal definition of either notion in terms of the other will not get us very far. Thus if a "formal definition" of the usual philosophical sort is what we are after, the game is over before it has begun, and we can say that the concept of a right is a "simple, undefinable, unanalysable primitive." Here as elsewhere in philosophy this will have the effect of making the commonplace seem unnecessarily mysterious. We would be better advised, I think, not to attempt definition of either "right" or "claim," but rather to use the idea of a claim in informal elucidation of the idea of a right. This is made possible by the fact that *claiming* is an elaborate sort of rule-governed *activity*. A claim is that which is claimed, the object of the act of claiming. . . . If we concentrate on the whole activity of claiming, which is public, familiar, and open to our observation, rather than on its upshot alone, we may learn more about the generic nature of rights than we could ever hope to learn from a formal definition, even if one were possible. Moreover, certain facts about rights more easily, if not solely, expressible in the language of claims and claiming are essential to a full understanding not only of what rights are, but also why they are so vitally important.

Let us begin then by distinguishing between: (i) making claim to . . . , (ii) claiming that . . . , and (iii) having a claim. One sort of thing we may be doing when we claim is to *make claim to something*. This is "to petition or seek by virtue of supposed right; to demand as due." Sometimes this is done by an acknowledged right-holder when he serves notice that he now wants turned over to him that which has already been acknowledged to be his, something borrowed, say, or improperly taken from him. This is often done by turning in a chit, a receipt, an I.O.U., a check, an insurance policy, or a deed, that is, a *title* to something currently in the possession of someone else. On other occasions, making claim is making application for titles or rights themselves, as when a mining prospector stakes a claim to mineral rights, or a householder to a tract of land in the public domain, or an inventor to his patent rights. In the one kind of case, to make claim is to exercise rights one already has by presenting title; in the other kind of case it is to apply for the title itself, by showing that one has satisfied the conditions specified by a rule for the ownership of title and therefore that one can demand it as one's due.

Generally speaking, only the person who has a title or who has qualified for it, or someone speaking in his name, can make claim to something as a matter of right. It is an important fact about rights (or claims), then, that they can be claimed only by those who have them. Anyone can claim, of course, *that* this umbrella is yours, but only you or your representative can actually claim the umbrella. If Smith owes Jones five dollars, only Jones can claim the five dollars as his own, though any bystander can *claim that* it belongs to Jones. One important difference then between *making legal claim to* and *claiming that* is that the former is a legal performance with direct legal consequences whereas the latter is often a mere piece of descriptive commentary with no legal force. Legally speaking, *making claim to* can itself make things happen. This sense of "claiming," then, might well be called "the performative sense." The legal power to claim (performatively) one's right or the things to which one has a right seems to be essential to the very notion of a right. A right to which one could not make claim (i.e., not even for recognition) would be a very "imperfect" right indeed!

Claiming that one has a right (what we can call "propositional claiming" as opposed to "performative claiming") is another sort of thing one can do with language, but it is not the sort of doing that characteristically has legal consequences. To claim that one has rights is to make an assertion that one has them, and to make it in such a manner as to demand or insist that they be recognized. In this sense of "claim" many things in addition to rights can be claimed, that is, many other kinds of proposition can be asserted in the claiming way. I can claim, for example, that you, he, or she has certain rights, or that Julius Caesar once had certain rights; or I can claim that certain statements are true, or that I have certain skills, or accomplishments, or virtually anything at all. I can claim that the earth is flat. What is essential to *claiming that* is the manner of assertion. One can assert without even caring very much whether anyone is listening, but part of the point of propositional claiming is to *make sure* people listen. When I claim to others that I know something, for example, I am not merely asserting it, but rather "obtruding my putative knowledge upon their attention, demanding that it be recognized, that appropriate notice be taken of it by those concerned."[3] Not every truth is properly assertable, much less claimable, in every context. To claim that something is the case in circum-

stances that justify no more than calm assertion is to behave like a boor. (This kind of boorishness, I might add, is probably less common in Nowheresville.) But not to claim in the appropriate circumstances that one has a right is to be spiritless or foolish. A list of "appropriate circumstances" would include occasions when one is challenged, when one's possession is denied, or seems insufficiently acknowledged or appreciated; and of course even in these circumstances, the claiming should be done only with an appropriate degree of vehemence.

Even if there are conceivable circumstances in which one would admit rights diffidently, there is no doubt that their characteristic use and that for which they are distinctively well suited, is to be claimed, demanded, affirmed, insisted upon. They are especially sturdy objects to "stand upon," a most useful sort of moral furniture. Having rights, of course, makes claiming possible; but it is claiming that gives rights their special moral significance. This feature of rights is connected in a way with the customary rhetoric about what it is to be a human being. Having rights enables us to "stand up like men," to look others in the eye, and to feel in some fundamental way the equal of anyone. To think of oneself as the holder of rights is not to be unduly but properly proud, to have that minimal self-respect that is necessary to be worthy of the love and esteem of others. Indeed, respect for persons (this is an intriguing idea) may simply be respect for their rights, so that there cannot be the one without the other; and what is called "human dignity" may simply be the recognizable capacity to assert claims. To respect a person then, or to think of him as possessed of human dignity, simply *is* to think of him as a potential maker of claims. Not all of this can be packed into a definition of "rights;" but these are *facts* about the possession of rights that argue well their supreme moral importance. More than anything else I am going to say, these facts explain what is wrong with Nowheresville.

We come now to the third interesting employment of the claiming vocabulary, that involving not the verb "to claim" but the substantive "a claim." What is to *have a claim* and how is this related to rights? I would like to suggest that *having a claim consists in being in a position to claim, that is, to make claim to* or *claim that.* If this suggestion is correct it shows the primacy of the verbal over the nominative forms. It links claims to a kind of activity and obviates the temptation to think of claims as *things,* on the model of coins, pencils, and other material possessions which we can carry in our hip pockets. To be sure, we often make or establish our claims by presenting titles, and these typically have the form of receipts, tickets, certificates, and other pieces of paper or parchment. The title, however, is not the same thing as the claim; rather it is the evidence that establishes the claim as valid. On this analysis, one might have a claim without ever claiming that to which one is entitled, or without even knowing that one has the claim; for one might simply be ignorant of the fact that one is in a position to claim; or one might be unwilling to exploit that position for one reason or another, including fear that the legal machinery is broken down or corrupt and will not enforce one's claim despite its validity.

Nearly all writers maintain that there is some intimate connection between having a claim and having a right. Some identify right and claim without qualification; some define "right" as justified or justifiable claim, others as recognized claim, still others as valid claim. My own preference is for the latter definition. Some writers, however, reject the identification of rights with valid claims on the ground that all claims as such are valid, so that the expression "valid claim" is redundant. These writers, therefore, would identify rights with claims *simpliciter*. But this is a very simple confusion. All claims, to be sure, are *put forward* as justified, whether they are justified in fact or not. A claim conceded even by its maker to have no validity is not a claim at all, but a mere demand. The highwayman, for example, *demands* his victim's money; but he hardly makes claim to it as rightfully his own.

But it does not follow from this sound point that it is redundant to qualify claims as justified (or as I prefer, valid) in the definition of a right; for it remains true that not all claims put forward as valid really are valid; and only the valid ones can be acknowledged as rights.

If having a valid claim is not redundant, i.e. if it is not redundant to pronounce *another's* claim valid, there must be such a thing as having a claim that is not valid. What would this be like? One might accumulate just enough evidence to argue with relevance and cogency that one has a right (or ought to be granted a right), although one's case might not be overwhelmingly conclusive. In such a case, one might have strong enough argument to be entitled to a hearing and given fair consideration. When one is in this position, it might be said that one "has a claim" that deserves to be weighed carefully. Nevertheless, the balance of reasons may turn out to militate against recognition of the claim, so that the claim, which one admittedly had, and perhaps still does, is not a valid claim or right. "Having a claim" in this sense is an expression very much like the legal phrase "having a *prima facie* case." A plaintiff estab-

lishes a *prima facie* case for the defendant's liability when he establishes grounds that will be sufficient for liability unless outweighed by reasons of a different sort that may be offered by the defendant. Similarly, in the criminal law, a grand jury returns an indictment when it thinks that the prosecution has sufficient evidence to be taken seriously and given a fair hearing, whatever countervailing reasons may eventually be offered on the other side. That initial evidence, serious but not conclusive, is also sometimes called a *prima facie* case. In a parallel "*prima facie* sense" of "claim," having a claim to X is not (yet) the same as having a right to X, but is rather having a case of at least minimal plausibility that one has a right to X, a case that does establish a right, not to X, but to a fair hearing and consideration. Claims, so conceived, differ in degree: some are stronger than others. Rights, on the other hand, do not differ in degree; no one right is more of a right than another.[4]

Another reason for not identifying rights with claims *simply* is that there is a well-established usage in international law that makes a theoretically interesting distinction between claims and rights. Statesmen are sometimes led to speak of "claims" when they are concerned with the natural needs of deprived human beings in conditions of scarcity. Young orphans *need* good upbringings, balanced diets, education, and technical training everywhere in the world; but unfortunately there are many places where these goods are in such short supply that it is impossible to provision all who need them. If we persist, nevertheless, in speaking of these needs as constituting rights and not merely claims, we are committed to the conception of a right which is an entitlement *to* some good, but not a valid claim *against* any particular individual; for in conditions of scarcity there may be no determinate individuals who can plausibly be said to have a duty to provide the missing goods to those in need. J. E. S. Fawcett therefore prefers to keep the distinction between claims and rights firmly in mind. "Claims," he writes, "are needs and demands in movement, and there is a continuous transformation, as a society advances [towards greater abundance] of economic and social claims into civil and political rights . . . and not all countries or all claims are by any means at the same stage in the process."[5] The manifesto writers on the other side who seem to identify needs, or at least basic needs, with what they call "human rights," are more properly described, I think, as urging upon the world community the moral principle that *all* basic human needs ought to be recognized as *claims* (in the customary *prima facie* sense) worthy of sympathy and serious consideration right now, even though, in many cases, they cannot yet plausibly be treated as *valid* claims, that is, as grounds of any other people's duties. This way of talking avoids the anomaly of ascribing to all human beings now, even those in pre-industrial societies, such "economic and social rights" as "periodic holidays with pay" [Reading 50].

Still for all of that, I have a certain sympathy with the manifesto writers, and I am even willing to speak of a special "manifesto sense" of "right," in which a right need not be correlated with another's duty. Natural needs are real claims if only upon hypothetical future beings not yet in existence. I accept the moral principle that to have an unfulfilled need is to have a kind of claim against the world, even if against no one in particular. A natural need for some good as such, like a natural desert, is always a reason in support of a claim to that good. A person in need, then, is always "in a position" to make a claim, even when there is no one in the corresponding position to do anything about it. Such claims, based on need alone, are "permanent possibilities of rights," the natural seed from which rights grow. When manifesto writers speak of them as if already actual rights, they are easily forgiven, for this is but a powerful way of expressing the conviction that they ought to be recognized by states here and now as potential rights and consequently as determinants of *present* aspirations and guides to *present* policies. That usage, I think, is a valid exercise of rhetorical license.

I prefer to characterize rights as valid claims rather than justified ones, because I suspect that justification is rather too broad a qualification. "Validity," as I understand it, is justification of a peculiar and narrow kind, namely justification within a system of rules. A man has a legal right when the official recognition of his claim (as valid) is called for by the governing rules. This definition, of course, hardly applies to moral rights, but that is not because the genus of which moral rights are a species is something other than *claims*. A man has a moral right when he has a claim the recognition of which is called for—not (necessarily) by legal rules—but by moral principles, or the principles of an enlightened conscience.

There is one final kind of attack on the generic identification of rights with claims, and it has been launched with great spirit in a recent article by H. J. McCloskey, who holds that rights are not essentially claims at all, but rather entitlements. The springboard of his argument is his insistence that rights in their essential character are always *rights to*, not *rights against:*

My right to life is not a right against anyone. It is my right and by virtue of it, it is normally permissible for me to sustain my life in the face of obstacles. It does give rise to rights against others *in the sense* that others have or may come to have duties to refrain from killing me, but it is essentially a right of mine, not an infinite list of claims, hypothetical and actual, against an infinite number of actual, potential, and as yet nonexistent human beings. . . . Similarly, the right of the tennis club member to play on the club courts is a right to play, not a right against some vague group of potential or possible obstructors.[6]

The argument seems to be that since rights are essentially rights *to,* whereas claims are essentially claims *against,* rights cannot be claims, though they can be grounds for claims. The argument is doubly defective though. First of all, contrary to McCloskey, rights (at least legal claim-rights) *are* held *against* others. McCloskey admits this in the case of *in personam* rights (what he calls "special rights") but denies it in the case of *in rem* rights (which he calls "general rights"):

Special rights are sometimes against specific individuals or institutions—e.g., rights created by promises, contracts, etc., . . . but these differ from . . . characteristic . . . general rights where the right is simply a right to.

As far as I can tell the only reason McCloskey gives for denying that *in rem* rights are against others is that those against whom they would have to hold make up an enormously multitudinous and "vague" group, including hypothetical people not yet even in existence. Many others have found this a paradoxical consequence of the notion of *in rem* rights, but I see nothing troublesome in it. If a general rule gives me a right of non-interference in a certain respect against everybody, then there are literally hundreds of millions of people who have a duty toward me in that respect; and if the same general rule gives the same right to everyone else, then it imposes on me literally hundreds of millions of duties—or duties towards hundreds of millions of people. I see nothing paradoxical about this, however. The duties, after all, are negative; and I can discharge all of them at a stroke simply by minding my own business. And if all human beings make up one moral community and there are hundreds of millions of human beings, we should expect there to be hundreds of millions of moral relations holding between them.

McCloskey's other premise is even more obviously defective. There is no good reason to think that all *claims* are "essentially" *against,* rather than *to.* Indeed most of the discussion of claims above has been of claims *to,* and we have seen, the law finds it useful to recognize claims *to* (or "mere claims") that are not yet qualified to be claims *against,* or rights (except in a "manifesto sense" of "rights").

Whether we are speaking of claims or rights, however, we must notice that they seem to have two dimensions, as indicated by the prepositions "to" and "against," and it is quite natural to wonder whether either of these dimensions is somehow more fundamental or essential than the other. All rights seem to merge *entitlements to* do, have, omit, or be something with *claims against* others to act or refrain from acting in certain ways. In some statements of rights the entitlement is perfectly determinate (e.g., *to* play tennis) and the claim vague (e.g., *against* "some vague group of potential or possible obstructors"); but in other cases the object of the claim is clear and determinate (e.g., *against* one's parents), and the entitlement general and indeterminate (e.g., to be given a proper upbringing). If we mean by "entitlement" that *to* which one has a right and by "claim" something directed at those against whom the right holds (as McCloskey apparently does), then we can say that all claim-rights necessarily involve both, though in individual cases the one element or the other may be in sharper focus.

In brief conclusion: To have a right is to have a claim against someone whose recognition as valid is called for by some set of governing rules or moral principles. To have a *claim* in turn, is to have a case meriting consideration, that is, to have reasons or grounds that put one in a position to engage in performative and propositional claiming. The activity of claiming, finally, as much as any other thing, makes for self-respect and respect for others, gives a sense to the notion of personal dignity, and distinguishes this otherwise morally flawed world from the even worse world of Nowheresville.

READING 46

The Epistemology of Human Rights

Alan Gewirth

Alan Gewirth is Professor Emeritus of Philosophy at the University of Chicago and the author of *Reason and Morality* and several essays in moral theory. He be-lieves that rights are the basis of morality and can be proved rationally. After clearly defining human rights ("rights which all persons equally have simply insofar as they are human") and critically surveying previous attempts to justify the belief in the existence of these rights, Gewirth sets forth an argument that claims to demonstrate that such rights exist. Starting from the premise that "I do X for end or purpose E," which entails "E is good," he constructs an argument showing that on the basis of "generic features" of action, freedom, and purposiveness, we can conclude that there are universal human rights.

This reading is taken from *Human Rights,* eds. E. Paul, F. Miller & J. Paul (Blackwell, 1984).

Human rights are rights which all persons equally have simply insofar as they are human. But are there any such rights? How, if at all, do we know that there are?

It is with this question of knowledge, and the related question of existence, that I want to deal in this paper.

I. CONCEPTUAL QUESTIONS

The attempt to answer each of these questions, however, at once raises further, more directly conceptual questions. In what sense may human rights be said to exist? What does it mean to say that there *are* such rights or that persons have them? This question, in turn, raises a question about the nature of human rights. What is the meaning of the expression "human rights?"

Within the limits of the present paper I cannot hope to deal adequately with the controversial issues raised by these conceptual questions. But we may make at least a relevant beginning by noting that, in terms of Hohfeld's famous classification of four different kinds of rights,[1] the human rights are primarily claim-rights, in that they entail correlative duties of other persons or groups to act or to refrain from acting in ways required for the right-holders' having that to which they have rights.

It will help our understanding of this and other aspects of human rights if we note that the full structure of a claim-right is given by the following formula:

A has a right to X against B by virtue of Y.

There are five main elements here: first, the *Subject* (A) of the right, the person or persons who have the right; second, the *Nature* of the right; third, the *Object* (X) of the right, what it is a right to; fourth, the *Respondent* (B) of the right, the person or persons who have the correlative duty; fifth, the *Justifying Basis* or *Ground* (Y) of the right. (I capitalize each of these elements for the sake of emphasis and for easier recognition in what follows.)

Let us now briefly analyze the human rights in terms of these five elements. Each element involves controversial questions about the interpretation of human rights, but for the present purposes I shall have to be content with a brief summary. The Subjects of the human rights are all human beings equally. The Respondents of the human rights are also all human beings, although in certain respects governments have special duties to secure the rights. The Objects of the human rights, what they are rights to, are certain especially important kinds of goods. I shall subsequently argue that these goods consist in the necessary conditions of human action, and that it is for this reason that the human rights are supremely mandatory. It is also largely because the human rights have these Objects that they are uniquely and centrally important among all moral concepts, since no morality, together with the goods, virtues, and rules emphasized in diverse moralities, is possible without the necessary goods of action that are the Objects of human rights.

Let us, now, turn to the Nature of human rights, which was one of the conceptual questions I raised at the outset. This Nature is often expressed by formulations that are common to all claim-rights: that rights are entitlements, or justified claims, or the moral property of individuals. While recognizing some merit in each of these formulations, I wish to suggest another that is at once more comprehensive and more specifically tied to human rights. Such rights are *personally oriented, normatively necessary moral requirements.* Let me briefly elucidate the point of each part of this definition. The point of calling the human rights *personally oriented* is to bring out that they are requirements that are owed to distinct Subjects or individuals for the good of those individuals. This feature distinguishes human rights from utilitarian and collectivist norms where rights, if upheld at all, are consequential upon or instrumental to the fulfillment of aggregative or collective goals. The point of saying that the rights are *normatively necessary* is to indicate that compliance with them is morally mandatory. Such mandatoriness distinguishes the human rights from virtues and other goods whose moral status may be supererogatory,

such as generosity or charity. Finally, in saying that the human rights are *moral requirements,* I wish to indicate three distinct but related aspects of human rights: they are requirements, first, in the sense of necessary needs; second, in the sense of justified entitlements; and third, in the sense of claims or demands made on or addressed to other persons. These three aspects involve the relations, respectively, between the Subjects and the Objects of the rights, between the Objects and their Justifying Basis, and between the Subjects and their Respondents.

What has been said so far, then, is that the Nature of human rights consists in personally oriented, normatively necessary moral requirements that every human have the necessary goods of action. From this it follows that the Justifying Basis or Ground of human rights is a normative moral principle that serves to prove or establish that every human morally ought, as a matter of normative necessity, to have the necessary goods as something to which he is personally entitled, which he can claim from others as his due.

These considerations have a direct bearing on one of the other conceptual questions I raised at the outset, about what it means for human rights to exist. The existence in question is not, in any straightforward way, empirical. Although Thomas Jefferson wrote that all humans "are endowed by their Creator with certain inalienable rights," it is not the case that humans are born having rights in the sense in which they are born having legs. At least, their having legs is empirically verifiable, but this is not the case with their having moral rights. The having or existence of human rights consists in the first instance not in the having of certain physical or mental attributes, but rather in certain justified moral requirements, in the three senses of "requirement" mentioned above.

There is, indeed, a sense in which the existence of human rights may be construed as consisting in certain positive institutional conditions. In this sense, human rights exist, or persons have human rights, when and insofar as there is social recognition and legal enforcement of all persons' equal entitlement to the aforementioned Objects, i.e., the necessary goods of action. But this positivist interpretation of the existence of human rights is posterior to a normative moral interpretation, since, as we have seen, the rights are in the first instance justified moral requirements. In the phrase, "there are human rights," "there are" is ambiguous as between positive and normative meanings. In the sense of "existence" that is relevant here, the existence of human rights is independent of whether they are guaranteed or enforced by legal codes or are socially recognized. For if the existence of human rights depended on such recognition or enforcement, it would follow that there were no human rights prior to or independent of these positive enactments.

The primary relevant sense of the existence of human rights, then, is the normatively moral justificatory one. In this sense, for human rights to exist, or for all persons to have human rights, means that there are conclusive moral reasons that justify or ground the moral requirements that constitute the Nature of human rights, such that every human can justifiably claim or demand, against all other humans or, in relevant cases, against governments, that he have or possess the necessary conditions of human action.

From this it follows that the epistemological question I raised at the outset is crucial to answering the ontological question of whether there are any human rights. That human rights exist, or that persons have human rights, is a proposition whose truth depends on the possibility, in principle, of constructing a body of moral justificatory argument from which that proposition follows as a logical consequence. This consideration also entails the epistemological point that to know or ascertain whether there are human rights requires not the scrutiny of legal codes or the empirical observation of social conditions but rather the ability, in principle, to construct such a moral argument.

The qualification "in principle" must be emphasized here. I am not saying that the very existence of human rights as a certain kind of morally justified norm is contingent on the actual success of this or that philosophical justificatory exercise. The existence of human rights depends on the existence of certain moral justificatory reasons; but these reasons may exist even if they are not explicitly ascertained. Because of this, it is correct to say that all persons had human rights even in ancient Greece, whose leading philosophers did not develop the relevant reasons. Thus, the existence of moral reasons is in important respects something that is discovered rather than invented. The failure of this or that attempt at discovery does not, of itself, entail that there is nothing there *to be* discovered.

The epistemological structure suggested by these considerations is unilinear and foundationalist, since the existence of human rights is held to follow from justificatory moral reasons and ultimately from a supreme moral principle. An alternative, coherentist structure would involve that the existence of human rights is not to be established in any such unilinear way but rather by a sequence of interrelated reasons that may themselves include judgments about the existence

of human rights. This latter structure, however, besides being more complicated, may be convicted of vicious circularity, including the difficulty that it may not serve to convince those who on purportedly rational grounds have denied the existence of human rights. I shall deal below with some further aspects of this question.

There have, of course, been philosophers, such as Bentham and Marx, who on various other grounds have denied the very possibility of constructing a moral justificatory argument for human rights. Hence, they have denied that human rights exist in what I have said is the primary sense of such existence. Among the grounds they have given for this denial is the moral one that human rights are excessively individualistic or egoistic, so that their espousal leads, in Bentham's words, to overriding what is "conducive to the happiness of society,"[2] and, in Marx's words, to separating man from the values of "community" and "degrading the sphere in which man functions as a species-being."[3] I shall not deal further with these criticisms here, except to note that they involve the epistemological question of whether a rational justification can be given of a moral principle that holds that all persons equally have certain moral rights. Such a principle should be able to accommodate the social emphasis of thinkers like Bentham and Marx while avoiding their excesses.

In the remainder of this paper, then, I want to do two main things. First, I shall conduct a brief critical examination of some of the main recent attempts on the part of moral philosophers to work out an affirmative answer to the epistemological question of whether the existence of human rights can be known, proved, or established. In criticizing each of these attempted answers, I shall elicit certain conditions that must be satisfied by a successful answer to the question. Second, I shall give my own answer and shall indicate why I think it fulfills these conditions.

II. PRIOR ATTEMPTS AT JUSTIFICATION: CONDITIONS FOR SUCCESS

Before considering the answers given by other philosophers, we should note that arguments for human rights are sometimes identical with arguments for distributive justice, or at least are presented in the context of arguments for distributive justice. The reason for this is that the concepts of rights and of distributive justice are closely related. One of the most traditional definitions of justice is that it consists in giving each person his due, and this is largely equivalent to giving each person what he has a right to. Hence, rights are the substantive content of what, according to many conceptions of justice, ought to be distributed to persons. The universality of human rights is further brought out in the definition's reference to "each person." This definition as such, however, does not include the additional, formal idea of the *equal* distribution of rights. But many traditional conceptions of justice do, of course, incorporate this further element of equality.

The answers I shall consider to the epistemological question of human rights will also coincide in part, then, with answers that have been given in arguments for egalitarian justice, which involve especially that all persons have a right to be treated equally in certain basic respects.

One traditional answer is intuitionist. Thus, Thomas Jefferson held it to be "self-evident" that all humans equally have certain rights, and Robert Nozick has peremptorily asserted that "individuals have rights." Such assertion is not, of course, an argument for the existence of human rights; it would not serve at all to convince the many persons throughout history who have had different intuitions on this question. Hence, this answer fails to satisfy *the condition of providing an argument.*

The remaining answers to be considered do provide arguments of various sorts. One argument is "formal." It holds that all persons ought to be treated alike unless there is some good reason for treating them differently. The "ought" contained in this principle is held to entail that all persons have a *right* to be treated alike, and hence to be treated as equals. This in turn is held to entail that all persons have rights to equal consideration. This principle is based on the still more general principle that cases which are of the same kind ought to be treated in the same way, and being human is held to be such a kind.

The formal principle raises many difficult problems of interpretation. In particular, it leaves unspecified what constitutes a "good reason" for treating persons differently, that is, what sub-kinds are relevant to differential treatment; and, of course, very many differences, including intelligence, sex, religion, color, economic class, have been held to be thus relevant. The principle, then, can eventuate not only in egalitarianism but also in drastic inegalitarianism of many different sorts. Hence, the argument fails to satisfy what I shall call *the condition of determinacy,* since it may serve to justify mutually opposed allocations of rights.

The next three answers I shall consider bring in certain contents. One is the argument of Joel Feinberg, who sets forth the "interest principle" that "the sorts of things who *can* have rights are precisely those who have (or can have) interests." Now, waiving the murkiness of the concept of "interests," I think this principle is true as far as it goes; but it does not, of itself, go far enough to provide an adequate basis for human rights. Feinberg's arguments for the principle establish at most that it gives a necessary rather than a sufficient condition for having rights. More generally, he does not show just how the having of interests serves to ground the having of rights. Surely, not every case of having an interest is a case of having a right to the satisfaction of the interest. Hence, the argument does not fulfill what I shall call *the condition of sufficiency,* of providing a sufficient ground for the ascription of rights. Moreover, since animals may have interests and humans may have unequal interests, the "interest principle" does not justify either rights that belong only to humans or rights that belong to all humans equally. Hence the argument does not satisfy *the condition of adequate egalitarian premises,* since it does not establish *equality* of rights among all humans.

Another answer that tries to base human rights on human needs or interests was given by William Frankena. He held that humans "are capable of enjoying a good life in a sense in which other animals are not. . . . As I see it, it is the fact that all men are similarly capable of enjoying a good life in this sense that justifies the *prima facie* requirement that they be treated as equals." The sense in question is one which Frankena identifies as "the happy or satisfactory life."

It will be noted that this argument moves from an "is" ("the fact that all men are similarly capable . . .") to an "ought" ("the requirement that they be treated as equals"). The argument does not fulfill *the condition of logical derivability of "ought" from "is."* For it fails to show how the factual similarity adduced by Frankena justifies the normative egalitarian obligation he upholds. One might accept the factual antecedent and yet deny the normative consequent, on the ground, for example, that the value of some person's happiness or goodness of life is greatly superior to that of other persons, so that their rights to happiness or to certain modes of treatment are not equal. In addition, the argument may also fail to satisfy the condition of justified egalitarian premises, for it still remains to be shown that all humans are equal (or even sufficiently similar) in their capacity for enjoying happiness in the sense intended by Frankena.

His argument, also, does not satisfy *the condition of a rational justification of the criterion of relevance.* It fails to show why the factual characteristics in respect of which humans are *equal* or *similar* are decisively relevant to how they ought to be treated, as against those factual characteristics in respect of which humans are *unequal* or *dissimilar,* such as the capacity to reason or to attain command over others or to control their appetites or to produce valued commodities or to work toward long-range goals, and so forth. Hence, the degree to which some factual characteristic is distributed among persons cannot of itself be the justifying ground for the allocation of rights.

A more direct way of deriving rights from needs is to *define* human rights as justified claims to the fulfillment of important needs. This, in effect, is what is done by Susan Moller Okin when she defines a human right as "a claim to something (whether a freedom, a good, or a benefit) of crucial importance for human life." She lists three kinds of important human needs—to basic physical goods, to physical security, to being treated with respect. She then says, "Using the definition of human rights given above . . . we can logically infer three fundamental human rights from these three needs."

This definitional way of inferring the existence of human rights suffers from at least two difficulties. First, just because human rights are *defined* as claims to important goods, this does not prove that anyone *has* such claims, in the sense that these claims *ought* to be fulfilled. Since human rights, as claim-rights, entail correlative duties, how does the *definition* of human rights as claims to the fulfillment of important needs serve to ground the substantive assertion that persons have duties to fulfill these needs? Why should any person who is reluctant to accept this duty regard Okin's definition as a sufficient justifying ground? Her argument, then, does not fulfill *the condition of rationally necessary acceptability to all rational persons.*

A related difficulty is that Okin's definition takes sides on controverted substantive issues about human rights. Some philosophers have held, for example, that the only human rights are the rights to freedom, which require only duties of noninterference on the part of Respondents. Why, then, should they accept Okin's definition as a basis for the positive duties she attributes to Respondents? For this reason, her argument does not satisfy *the condition of an adequate account of the Objects of rights.*

Let us next consider a fifth answer to the epistemological question. This is H. L. A. Hart's famous pre-

suppositional argument. He says: "If there are any moral rights at all, it follows that there is at least one natural right, the equal right of all men to be free" [see Reading 49]. His point is that all special moral rights are grounded either in Respondents' freely choosing to create their obligations or in the fairness of having an equal distribution of freedom among persons who subject themselves to mutual restrictions. Hence, Hart's argument for the equal natural right of all humans to freedom is that this right is presupposed by all or at least some of the most important special moral rights.

This argument suffers from at least three difficulties. First, it does not satisfy what I shall call *the condition of justified premises.* Hart has not adequately established that there *are* the special moral rights that figure in the antecedent of his initial statement. He appeals especially to the rights created by promises. But it is not self-evident that an act of saying, "I promise," taken by itself, generates any rights or duties. If there is indeed such generation, it is because there is presupposed a background institution defined by certain rules. Hence, there must be a prior justification of this institution as authorizing the generation of valid rights and duties. Here, however, Hart's argument fails to satisfy the condition of determinacy. For there may be morally wrong institutions, so that even though they are constituted by certain rules, these do not authorize valid rights and duties. Hart, however, has not provided this more general justification of the institutions he invokes. Hence, since his implicit appeal to institutions may yield morally wrong as well as morally right results, his premise is not morally determinate.

A further difficulty of Hart's argument is that, like Feinberg's argument, it does not fulfill the condition of justified egalitarian premises. If special moral rights are to be used to show that there is an *equal* right of *all* men to be free, then such universal equality must be found in the special rights themselves. But Hart has not shown that all men equally derive rights from the transactions of promising, consenting, and imposing mutual restrictions. He presupposes, without any justificatory argument, the very egalitarianism he seeks to establish. A believer in basic human inequality, such as Nietzsche, would deny that all men are equal with regard to the special rights. Hence, Hart's argument does not establish the egalitarian universalism he upholds.

A sixth argument for equality of rights is the procedural one given in Rawls's famous theory of justice. He justifies this equality by arguing that if the constitutional structure of a society were to be chosen by persons who are "in an initial position of equality" and who choose from behind a "veil of ignorance" of all their particular qualities, the principles of justice they would choose would provide that each person must have certain basic, equal rights [see Reading 26].

Amid its many complexities, this by now familiar argument fails to satisfy three important conditions. One is *the condition of truth*: persons are not in fact equal in power and ability, nor are they ignorant of all their particular qualities. Hence, to assume that they are (in some sort of "original position"), and to base on this equality and ignorance one's ascription of equal rights, is to argue from a false premise. In making this point I do not overlook that arguments based on counterfactual assumptions may be cogent and even powerful. But the cogency of Rawls's assumptions is reduced because of their exceptional extensiveness and the direct use he makes of them to justify an egalitarian conclusion. His argument also fails to satisfy the condition of rationally necessary acceptability to all rational persons, to which I have previously referred. For the total ignorance of particulars that Rawls ascribes to his equal persons has no independent rational justification. Hence, no reason is given as to why actual rational persons, who know their particular characteristics, should accept the equality of rights that is based on their assumed ignorance. In addition, Rawls's argument does not satisfy *the condition of non-circularity,* since he attains his egalitarian result only by putting into his premises an equality (of power and ignorance) which cannot itself be justified.

The seventh and final argument for equal human rights that I shall consider here is based on the doctrine that all humans are equal in dignity or worth. Thus the United Nations Universal Declaration on Human Rights [see Reading 50], in its first Article, says: "All human beings are born free and equal in dignity and rights." It is important to consider what is meant here by "dignity." Presumably, dignity is not an "empirical" characteristic in the way the having of interests or the capacity for feeling physical pain is empirically ascertainable. The sense of "dignity" in which all humans are said to have equal dignity is not the same as that in which it may be said of some person that he lacks dignity or that he behaves without dignity, where what is meant is that he is lacking in decorum, is too raucous or obsequious, or is not "dignified." This kind of dignity is one that humans may occurrently exhibit, lack, or lose, whereas the dignity in which all humans are said to be equal is a characteristic that belongs permanently and inherently to every human as such.

One difficulty with the attempt to derive human rights from such inherent dignity is that the two expressions, "A has human rights" and "A has inherent dignity" may seem to be equivalent, so that the latter simply reduplicates the former. Thus, for example, Jacques Maritain wrote: "The dignity of the human person? The expression means nothing if it does not signify that by virtue of natural law, the human person has the right to be respected, is the subject of rights, possesses rights." If, however, the two expressions are thus equivalent in meaning, the attribution of dignity adds nothing substantial to the attribution of rights, and someone who is doubtful about the latter attribution will be equally doubtful about the former. Thus, the argument for rights based on inherent dignity, so far, does not satisfy the condition of non-circularity.

It is essential, then, to consider whether the attribution of inherent dignity can have a status independent of and logically prior to the attribution of rights. An important doctrine of this sort was set forth by Kant, who based his attribution of dignity (*Würde*) to the rational being on his autonomy or freedom, his capacity for self-legislation, for acting according to laws he gives to himself. Now, Kant held that such autonomy is not an empirical characteristic since it applies only to rational beings as things-in-themselves and, hence, as not subject to the deterministic laws of natural phenomena. This doctrine, however, involves all the difficulties of the distinction between phenomena and noumena, including the cognitive non-ascertainability of the latter. Hence, the Kantian derivation of rights from inherent dignity does not satisfy *the condition of empirical reference* as regards the characteristics of humans to which one appeals.

There is more to be said on this matter of the relation of human rights to human dignity, but I shall be able to make my view of this relation clearer after I have set forth my own positive doctrine.

This concludes my examination of seven recent attempts to give justificatory arguments for equal human rights. The examination has indicated that a successful argument must satisfy at least twelve conditions: providing an argument, determinacy, sufficiency, adequate egalitarian premises, logical derivability of "ought" from "is," rational justification of the criterion of relevance, rationally necessary acceptability to all rational persons, adequate account of the Objects of rights, justified premises, truth, non-circularity, and empirical reference.

III. THE JUSTIFICATORY ARGUMENT FOR HUMAN RIGHTS

I now wish to present my own answer to the justificatory or epistemological question of human rights. It will be recalled that the Justifying Basis or Ground of human rights must be a normative moral principle that serves to prove or establish that every person morally ought to have the necessary goods of action as something to which he or she is entitled. The epistemological question, hence, comes down to whether such a moral principle can be rationally justified.

It is important to note that not all moral principles will serve for this purpose. Utilitarian, organicist, and elitist moral principles either do not justify any moral rights at all, or justify them only as ancillary to and contingent upon various collective goals, or do make rights primary but not as equally distributed among all humans. Hence, it will be necessary to show how the moral principle that justifies equal human rights is superior, in point of rational cogency, to these other kinds of moral principles.

Now, there are well-known difficulties in the attempt to provide a rational justification of any moral principle. Obviously, given some high-level moral principle, we can morally justify some specific moral rule or particular moral judgment or action by showing how its rightness follows from the principle. But how can we justify the basic principle itself? Here, by definition, there is no higher or more general moral principle to be appealed to as an independent variable. Is it the case, then, that justification comes to a stop here? This would mean that we cannot rationally adjudicate between *conflicting* moral principles and ways of life and society, such as those epitomized, for example, by Kant's categorical imperative, Bentham's utilitarianism, Kierkegaard's theological primacy, Stirner's egoism, Nietzsche's exaltation of the superman, Spencer's doctrine of the survival of the fittest, and so on.

The Problem of the Independent Variable

One of the central problems here is that of the independent variable. Principles serve as independent variables for justifying lower-level rules and judgments; but what is the independent variable for justifying principles themselves? Another way to bring out this problem in relation to morality is to contrast particular empirical statements and particular moral judgments.

Consider, on the one hand, such a statement as "Mrs. Jones *is* having an abortion," and, on the other hand, "Mrs. Jones *ought* to have an abortion." We know, at least in principle, how to go about checking the truth of the first statement, namely, by referring to certain empirical facts that serve as the independent variables for the statement to be checked against. But how do we go about checking the truth of the second statement, that Mrs. Jones *ought* to have an abortion? Indeed, what would it *mean* for the second statement to be true? What is the independent variable for *it* to be checked against? For the first statement to be true means that it corresponds to certain empirical facts. But with regard to a judgment like "Mrs. Jones *ought* to have an abortion," what facts would *it* have to correspond to in order to be true? Is there any moral *"ought"* in the world, in the way in which the factual *"is"* is in the world, serving as the independent variable for testing or confirming the relevant statements? If not, then is the moral judgment in no sense either true or false?

The problem we have reached, then, is whether there is any non-question-begging answer to the problem of the independent variable in morality. I now want to suggest that there is. To see this, we must recall that all moral precepts, regardless of their greatly varying contents, are concerned with how persons ought to *act* toward one another. Think, for example, of the Golden Rule: "*Do* unto others as you would have them do unto you." Think also of Kant's categorical imperative: "*Act* in such a way that the maxim of your action can be a universal law." Similarly, Bentham tells us to *act* so as to maximize utility; Nietzsche tells us to *act* in accord with the ideals of the superman; Marx tells us to *act* in accord with the interests of the proletariat; Kierkegaard tells us to *act* as God commands, and so forth.

The independent variable of all morality, then, is human *action*. This independent variable cuts across the distinctions between secular and religious moralities, between egalitarian and elitist moralities, between deontological and teleological moralities, and so forth.

But how does this independent variable of action help us to resolve the difficulties of moral justification? Surely we can't take the various rival moral principles and justify one of them as against the others simply by checking it against the fact of human action. Moreover, since if action is to be genuinely the non-question-begging independent variable of morality, it must fit *all* moral principles, how does action enable us to justify *one* moral principle *as against* its rivals?

The answer to these questions is given by the fact that action has what I have called a *normative structure,* in that, logically implicit in action, there are certain evaluative and deontic judgments, certain judgments about goods and rights made by agents; and when these judgments are subjected to certain morally neutral rational requirements, they entail a certain supreme moral principle. Hence, if any agent denies the principle, he can be shown to have contradicted himself, so that his denial, and the actions stemming from it, cannot be rationally justifiable. Thus, together with action, the most basic kind of reason, deductive rationality, also serves as an independent variable for the justification of the supreme principle of morality.

Why Action Gives the Principle a Rationally Necessary Acceptability

It is important to note that because the principle is grounded in the generic features of action, it has a certain kind of *material necessity*. It will be recalled that some of the justificatory arguments for rights examined above failed because they did not satisfy the condition that they be acceptable to all rational persons as a matter of rational necessity. For example, why must any rational person accept Rawls's starting point in the "veil of ignorance"? Why, for that matter, is it rationally necessary for any rational person to accept the Golden Rule or any other moral principle that has hitherto been propounded?

The condition of rationally necessary acceptability is fulfilled, however, when the independent variable of the argument is placed in the generic features of action. For this involves that, simply by virtue of being an agent, one logically must accept the argument and its conclusion that all persons equally have certain moral rights. Now, being an actual or prospective agent is not an optional or variable condition for any person, except in the sense that he may choose to commit suicide or, perhaps, to sell himself into slavery; and even then the steps he intentionally takes toward these goals involve agency on his part. Hence, if there are moral rights and duties that logically accrue to every person simply by virtue of being an actual or prospective agent, the argument that traces this logical sequence will necessarily be rationally acceptable to every agent: he will have to accept the argument on pain of self-contradiction.

There is a sense in which this grounding of the moral principle in action involves a foundationalist conception of justification. For, as we shall see, the argument begins with a statement attributable to any agent, that he performs some purposive action. This statement is based on the agent's direct awareness of what he is doing, and it leads, in a unilinear sequence, to his statement that he and all other agents have certain rights and correlative duties. I need not be concerned, in the present context, with further epistemological issues about the certainty or trustworthiness of the rational agent's direct awareness or about any presumed "data" on which this awareness might be based.

The argument's unilinearity, with its concomitant avoidance of circularity, is an important asset. In this regard, the justificatory procedure I shall follow does not have the defects of Rawls's method of "reflective equilibrium," according to which "considered" moral judgments and general moral principles are reciprocally tested against and adjusted to one another. There are at least two difficulties with this method. First, the "considered moral judgments" of one person or group may differ markedly from those of another person or group, so that they do not provide a firm or consistent basis for justifying a moral principle. Second, the argument is circular since the principle is justified by the very judgments that it is in turn adduced to justify.

My argument, in contrast, begins not from variable moral judgments but from statements that must be accepted by every agent because they derive from the generic features of purposive action. Hence, my argument is not "foundationalist" in the sense that it begins from *moral* or *evaluative* statements that are taken to be self-justifying or self-evident. The present argument is one in which statements about actions, and not statements about values or duties, are taken as the basic starting point. And these statements entail, in a noncircular sequence, certain judgments about the existence of human rights.

The Argument for Equal Human Rights

I shall, now, give a brief outline of the rational line of argument that goes from action, through its normative structure, to the supreme principle of morality, and thence to equal human rights. In my book *Reason and Morality,* I have presented a full statement of the argument, so that for present purposes I shall stress only certain main points.

To begin with, we must note certain salient characteristics of action. In ordinary as well as scientific language, the word "action" is used in many different senses: we talk, for example, about physical action at a distance, about the action of the liver, and so forth. But the meaning of "action" that is relevant here is that which is the common object of all moral and other practical precepts, such as the examples I gave before. Moral and other practical precepts, as we have seen, tell persons to *act* in many different ways. But amid these differences, the precepts all assume that the persons addressed by them can control their behaviour by their unforced choice with a view to achieving whatever the precepts require. All actions as envisaged by moral and other practical precepts, then, have two *generic features*. One is *voluntariness* or *freedom,* in that the agents control or can control their behavior by their unforced choice while having knowledge of relevant circumstances. The other generic feature is *purposiveness* or *intentionality,* in that the agents aim to attain some end or goal which constitutes their reason for acting; this goal may consist either in the action itself or in something to be achieved by the action.

Now, let us take an agent A, defined as an actual or prospective performer of actions in the sense just indicated. When he performs an action, he can be described as saying or thinking:

(1) "I do X for end or purpose E."

Since E is something he unforcedly chooses to attain, he thinks E has sufficient value to merit his moving from quiescence to action in order to attain it. Hence, from his standpoint, (1) entails

(2) "E is good."

Note that (2) is here presented in quotation marks, as something said or thought by the agent A. The kind of goodness he here attributes to E need not be moral goodness; its criterion varies with whatever purpose E the agent may have in doing X. But what it shows already is that, in the context of action, the "Fact-Value gap" is already bridged, for by the very *fact* of engaging in action, every agent must implicitly accept for himself a certain *value*-judgment about the value or goodness of the purposes for which he acts.

Now, in order to act for E, which he regards as good, the agent A must have the proximate necessary conditions of action. These conditions are closely related to the generic features of action that I mentioned before. You will recall that these generic features are voluntariness or freedom and purposiveness or intentionality. But when purposiveness is extended to the general conditions required for success in achieving one's purposes, it becomes a more extensive condition

which I shall call *well-being.* Viewed from the standpoint of action, then, well-being consists in having the various substantive conditions and abilities, ranging from life and physical integrity to self-esteem and education, that are required if a person is to act either at all or with general chances of success in achieving the purposes for which he acts. So freedom and well-being are the necessary conditions of action and of successful action in general. Hence, from the agent's standpoint, from (2) "E is good" there follows

(3) "My freedom and well-being are necessary goods."

This may also be put as

(4) "I must have freedom and well-being."

where this "must" is a practical-prescriptive requirement, expressed by the agent, as to his having the necessary conditions of his action.

Now from (4) there follows

(5) "I have rights to freedom and well-being."

To show that (5) follows from (4), let us suppose that the agent were to deny (5). In that case, because of the correlativity of rights and strict "oughts," he would also have to deny

(6) "All other persons ought at least to refrain from removing or interfering with my freedom and well-being."

By denying (6), he must accept

(7) "It is not the case that all other persons ought at least to refrain from removing or interfering with my freedom and well-being."

By accepting (7), he must also accept

(8) "Other persons may (i.e., it is permissible that other persons) remove or interfere with my freedom and well-being."

And by accepting (8), he must accept

(9) "I may not (i.e., it is permissible that I not) have freedom and well-being."

But (9) contradicts (4), which said "I must have freedom and well-being." Since every agent must accept (4), he must reject (9). And since (9) follows from the denial of (5), "I have rights to freedom and well-being," every agent must also reject that denial. Hence, every agent logically must accept (5) "I have rights to freedom and well-being."

What I have shown so far, then, is that the concept of a right, as a justified claim or entitlement, is logically involved in all action as a concept that signifies for every agent his claim and requirement that he have, and at least not be prevented from having, the necessary conditions that enable him to act in pursuit of his purposes. I shall sometimes refer to these rights as *generic rights,* since they are rights that the generic features of action and of successful action characterize one's behavior.

It must be noted, however, that, so far, the criterion of these rights that every agent must claim for himself is only prudential, not moral, in that the criterion consists for each agent in his own needs of agency in pursuit of his own purposes. Even though the right-claim is addressed to all other persons as a correlative "ought"-judgment, still its justifying criterion for each agent consists in the necessary conditions of his own action.

To see how this prudential right-claim also becomes a moral right, we must go through some further steps. Now, the sufficient as well as necessary reason or justifying condition for which every agent must hold that he has rights to freedom and well-being is that he is a prospective purposive agent. Hence, he must accept

(10) "I have rights to freedom and well-being because I am a prospective purposive agent,"

where this "because" signifies a sufficient as well as a necessary justifying condition.

Suppose some agent were to reject (10), and were to insist, instead, that the only reason he has the generic rights is that he has some more restrictive characteristic R. Examples of R would include: being an American, being a professor, being an *Übermensch,* being male, being a capitalist or a proletarian, being white, being named "Wordsworth Donisthorpe," and so forth. Thus, the agent would be saying

(11) "I have rights to freedom and well-being *only* because I am R,"

where "R" is something more restrictive than being a prospective purposive agent.

Such an agent, however, would contradict himself. For he would then be in the position of saying that if he did *not* have R, he would *not* have the generic rights, so that he would have to accept

(12) "I do not have rights to freedom and well-being."

But we saw before that, as an agent, he *must* hold that he has rights to freedom and well-being. Hence, he

must drop his view that R alone is the sufficient justifying condition of his having the generic rights, so that he must accept that simply being a prospective purposive agent is a sufficient as well as a necessary justifying condition of his having rights to freedom and well-being. Hence, he must accept (10).

Now by virtue of accepting (10), the agent must also accept

(13) "All prospective purposive agents have rights to freedom and well-being."

(13) follows from (10) because of the principle of universalization. If some predicate P belongs to some subject S because that subject has some general quality Q (where this "because" signifies a sufficient reason), then that predicate logically must belong to every subject that has Q. Hence, since the predicate of having the generic rights belongs to the original agent because he is a prospective purposive agent, he logically must admit that every purposive agent has the generic rights.

At this point the rights become moral ones, and not only prudential, on that meaning of "moral" where it has both the formal component of setting forth practical requirements that are categorically obligatory, and the material component that those requirements involve taking favorable account of the interests of persons other than or in addition to the agent or the speaker. When the original agent now says that *all* prospective purposive agents have rights to freedom and well-being, he is logically committed to respecting and hence taking favorable account of the interests of all other persons with regard to their also having the necessary goods or conditions of action.

Since all other persons are actual or potential recipients of his action, every agent is logically committed to accepting

(14) "I ought to act in accord with the generic rights of my recipients as well as of myself."

This requirement can also be expressed as the general moral principle:

(15) "Act in accord with the generic rights of your recipients as well as of yourself."

I shall call this the Principle of Generic Consistency (*PGC),* since it combines the formal consideration of consistency with the material consideration of the generic features and rights of action. As we have seen, every agent, on pain of contradiction and hence of irrationality, must accept this principle as governing all his interpersonal actions.

This, then, completes my argument for equal human rights. Its central point can be summarized in two main parts. In the first part (steps 1 to 9), I have argued that every agent logically must hold or accept that he has rights to freedom and well-being as the necessary conditions of his action, as conditions that he *must* have; for if he denies that he has these rights, then he must accept that other persons may remove or interfere with his freedom and well-being, so that he *may not* have them; but this would contradict his belief that he *must* have them. In the second part (steps 10 to 14), I have argued that the agent logically must accept that all other prospective purposive agents have the same rights to freedom and well-being as he claims for himself.

Since all humans are actual, prospective, or potential agents, the rights in question belong equally to all humans. Thus, the argument fulfills the specifications for human rights that I mentioned at the outset: that both the Subjects and the Respondents of the rights are all human equally, that the Objects of the rights are the necessary goods of human action, and that the Justifying Basis of the rights is a valid moral principle.

How the Argument Fulfills the Conditions of Justification

It will also be recalled that in my critique of previous attempts to answer the epistemological question of human rights I listed twelve conditions that the attempts had collectively failed to satisfy. I do not have the time now to do any more than to indicate very briefly how my own argument satisfies each of these conditions. The condition of providing an argument is obviously satisfied. The remaining eleven conditions, which concern the requirements for a successful argument justifying or proving the existence of human rights, may be divided into four groups. First, the conditions of justified premises, truth, and empirical reference are fulfilled by my argument because I begin from actual, empirically discriminable agents who pursue their purposes and know the relevant circumstances of their action. Second, the argument also fulfills the conditions of adequate egalitarian premises and rational justification of the criterion of relevance, because the agents are equal as having purposes and it is this having of purposes which has been shown to be relevant to their claiming of rights. Third, the argument has fulfilled the conditions of non-circularity and logical derivability of "ought" from "is," because it has shown how the claiming of rights with their correlative "ought"

logically follows from being a purposive agent, while at the same time such agency has not been defined in terms of claiming or having rights. Fourth, the argument fulfills the remaining conditions of determinacy, sufficiency, rationally necessary acceptability to all rational persons, and adequate account of the Objects of rights. For the argument has shown how every agent's needs for the necessary goods of action provide a sufficient basis for his claiming rights to their fulfillment; and the opposites of these rights are not derivable from the argument in question. Moreover—and the importance of this must again be stressed—the argument is necessarily acceptable to all rational persons *qua* agents because it is logically grounded in the generic features that characterize all actions and agents.

Some Objections to the Argument

Many questions may be raised about this argument. They include objections made on behalf of egoists, amoralists, "fanatics," radical social critics, and historians, as well as charges that the idea of prudential rights (as found in step (5) above) makes no sense and that the argument's egalitarian conclusion is not in fact justified. I have dealt with these objections elsewhere.

I wish, now, to consider two further objections against the first nine steps of my argument as given above. These steps culminate in the assertion that every agent logically must hold or accept that he has rights to freedom and well-being as the necessary conditions of his action. One objection bears on the Objects of these rights. My argument moves from step (4), "I must have freedom and well-being," to step (5), "I have rights to freedom and well-being." The argument is that if the agent denies (5) then he also has to deny (4). It may be objected, however, that this argument entails that whenever some person holds that he must have something X, he also has to hold that he has a right to X. But this, to put it mildly, is implausible. If someone thinks that he *must* have a ten-speed bicycle, or the love of some woman, it surely does not follow that he thinks, let alone has to think, that he has a *right* to these Objects.

My reply to this objection is that it overlooks an important restriction. My argument is confined to *necessary contents*—to what is necessarily connected with being an agent, and hence to the necessary goods of action. Hence the argument excludes the kinds of *contingent reasons* that figure in the objection. Persons do, of course, desire many particular things, and they may even feel that they *must* have some of these. But there is a difference between a "must" that is concerned with Objects that are, strictly speaking, dispensable, and a "must" whose Objects are the necessary conditions of action. The latter Objects, unlike the former, have an ineluctableness within the context of action that reflects the rational necessity to which the argument must be confined if its culminating obligatoriness is to be justified. I shall deal with this further below, in connection with the dialectically necessary method.

A second objection bears on the Subjects of the rights. In my argument above I held that if the agent denies (5), "I have rights to freedom and well-being," then, because of the correlativity of rights and strict "oughts," he must also deny (6), "All other persons ought at least to refrain from removing or interfering with my freedom and well-being." I, then, showed that the denial of (6) entails a statement (9) which contradicts another statement (4) which every agent must accept, so that to avoid self-contradiction every agent must accept (5). It may be objected, however, that a statement like (6) may be accepted on grounds other than the acceptance of a rights-statement like (5). The grounds may be utilitarian or of some other non-rights sort. Consider, for example, (6a), "All persons ought to refrain from removing or interfering with the well-being of trees (or animals, or fine old buildings)." One may accept this without having to accept (5a), "Trees (or animals, or fine old buildings) have rights to well-being." In other words, one may accept that one ought not to harm certain entities without accepting that these entities have *rights* to non-harm. But since my argument above depended on the logical equivalence between a statement (5) that upholds rights and a statement (6) that upholds the "ought" of not harming, the objection is that the need to accept (6) does not entail the need to accept (5). If it did, we should have to accept that trees, animals, and even old buildings have rights.

My answer to this objection is that it misconstrues the criterion of the "ought" in (6). This "ought" is not upheld on general utilitarian grounds or on other general grounds not primarily related to its beneficiary. Rather, it is upheld as signifying something that is due or owed to the beneficiary, something to which he is entitled by virtue of its being required for all his purposive actions. Thus the "ought" in (6) has a specificity and stringency which are not captured in (6a). Hence, my argument does not entail that entities other than human purposive agents have rights, since its "ought" involves the more specific requirement of something that is owed or due.

This more specific "ought" can pertain only to human purposive agents as its beneficiaries. And such a strict "ought," unlike other "oughts" that are looser or less specific, is correlative with a rights-judgment.

READING 47

A Critique of Gewirth's Argument and the Notion of Rights

Alasdair MacIntyre

For MacIntyre's biography, see Reading 28. In this selection from *After Virtue,* MacIntyre criticizes rights-based moral theories—much in the spirit of Bentham—as nonsense on stilts. Natural rights no more exist than do unicorns and witches. He then analyzes Gewirth's rationalistic version of a defense of human rights and argues that Gewirth has committed the logical mistake of deriving a right from a need.

This reading is taken from *After Virtue* (University of Notre Dame Press, 1981).

[. . . Analytic philosophers revived the Kantian project demonstrating that the] authority and objectivity of moral rules [are] precisely that authority and objectivity which belong to the exercise of reason. Hence their central project was, indeed is, that of showing that any rational agent is logically committed to the rules of morality in virtue of his or her rationality.

The example which I have chosen is that made by Alan Gewirth in *Reason and Morality* (1978). I choose Gewirth's book because it is not only one of the most recent of such attempts, but also because it deals carefully and scrupulously with objections and criticisms that have been made of earlier writers. Moreover Gewirth adopts what is at once a clear and a strict view of what reason is: in order to be admitted as a principle of practical reason, a principle must be analytic; and in order for a conclusion to follow from premises of practical reason, it must be demonstrably entailed by those premises. There is none of the looseness and vagueness about what constitutes "a good reason" which had weakened some earlier analytic attempts to exhibit morality as rational.

The key sentence of Gewirth's book is: "Since the agent regards as necessary goods the freedom and well-being that constitute the generic features of his successful action, he logically must also hold that he has rights to these generic features and he implicitly makes a corresponding rights-claim" [see Reading 46]. Gewirth's argument may be spelled out as follows. Every rational agent has to recognise a certain measure of freedom and well-being as prerequisites for his exercise of rational agency. Therefore each rational agent must will, if he is to will at all, that he possess that measure of these goods. This is what Gewirth means when he writes in the sentence quoted of "necessary goods." And there is clearly no reason to quarrel with Gewirth's argument so far. It turns out to be the next step that is at once crucial and questionable.

Gewirth argues that anyone who holds that the prerequisites for his exercise of rational agency are necessary goods is logically committed to holding also that he has a right to these goods. But quite clearly the introduction of the concept of a right needs justification both because it is at this point a concept quite new to Gewirth's argument *and* because of the special character of the concept of a right.

It is first of all clear that the claim that I have a right to do or have something is a quite different type of claim from the claim that I need or want or will be benefited by something. From the first—if it is the only relevant consideration—it follows that others ought not to interfere with my attempts to do or have whatever it is, whether it is for my own good or not. From the second it does not. And it makes no difference what kind of good or benefit is at issue.

Another way of understanding what has gone wrong with Gewirth's argument is to understand why this step is so essential to his argument. It is of course true that if I claim a right in virtue of my possession of certain characteristics, then I am logically committed to holding that anyone else with the same characteristics also possess this right. But it is just this property of necessary universalisability that does not belong to claims about either the possession of or the need or desire for a good, even a universally necessary good.

One reason why claims about goods necessary for rational agency are so different from claims to the possession of rights is that the latter in fact presuppose, as the former do not, the existence of a socially established set of rules. Such sets of rules only come into existence at particular historical periods under particular social circumstances. They are in no way universal features of the human condition. Gewirth readily acknowledges that expressions such as "a right" in English and cognate terms in English and other languages only appeared at a relatively late point in the history of the language toward the close of the Middle Ages. But he argues that the existence of such expressions is not a necessary condition for the embodiment of the concept of a right in forms of human behaviour; and in this at least he is clearly right. But the objection that Gewirth has to meet is precisely that those forms of human behaviour which presuppose notions of some ground to entitlement, such as the notion of a right, always have a highly specific and socially local character, and that the existence of particular types of social institution or practice is a necessary condition for the notion of a claim to the possession of a right being an intelligible type of human performance. (As a matter of historical fact such types of social institution or practice have not existed universally in human societies.) Lacking any such social form, the making of a claim to a right would be like presenting a check for payment in a social order that lacked the institution of money. Thus Gewirth has illicitly smuggled into his argument a conception which does not in any way belong, as it must do if his case is to succeed, to the minimal characterization of a rational agent.

By "rights" I do not mean those rights conferred by positive law or custom on specified classes of people; I mean those rights which are alleged to belong to human beings as such and which are cited as a reason for holding that people ought not to be interfered with in their pursuit of life, liberty and happiness. They are the rights which were spoken of in the eighteenth century as natural rights or as the rights of man. Characteristically in that century they were defined negatively, precisely as rights *not* to be interfered with. But sometimes in that century and much more often in our own, positive rights—rights to due process, to education or to employment are examples—are added to the list. The expression "human rights" is now commoner than either of the eighteenth-century expressions. But whether negative or positive and however named they are supposed to attach equally to all individuals, whatever their sex, race, religion, talents or deserts, and to provide a ground or a variety of particular moral stances.

It would of course be a little odd that there should be such rights attaching to human beings simply *qua* human beings in light of the fact, which I alluded to in my discussion of Gewirth's argument, that there is no expression in any ancient or medieval language correctly translated by our expression "a right" until near the close of the Middle Ages: the concept lacks any means of expression in Hebrew, Greek, Latin or Arabic, classical or medieval, before about 1400, let alone in Old English, or in Japanese even as late as the mid-nineteenth century. From this it does not of course follow that there are no natural or human rights; it only follows that no one could have known that there were. And this at least raises certain questions. But we do not need to be distracted into answering them, for the truth is plain: there are no such rights, and belief in them is one with belief in witches and in unicorns.

The best reason for asserting so bluntly that there are no such rights is indeed of precisely the same type as the best reason which we possess for asserting that there are no witches and the best reason which we possess for asserting that there are no unicorns: every attempt to give good reasons for believing that there *are* such rights has failed. The eighteenth-century philosophical defenders of natural rights sometimes suggest that the assertions which state that men possess them are self-evident truths; but we know that there are no self-evident truths. Twentieth-century moral philosophers have sometimes appealed to their and our intuitions; but one of the things that we ought to have learned from the history of moral philosophy is that the introduction of the word "intuition" by a moral philosopher is always a signal that something has gone badly wrong with an argument. In the United Nations Declaration of Human Rights of 194[8] what has since become the normal U.N. practice of not giving good reasons for *any* assertions whatsoever is followed with great rigour. And the latest defender of such rights, Ronald Dworkin (*Taking Rights Seriously*) concedes that the existence of such rights cannot be demonstrated, but remarks on this point simply that it does not follow from the fact that a statement cannot be demonstrated that it is not true. Which is true, but could equally be used to defend claims about unicorns and witches.

Natural or human rights then are fictions—just as is utility—but fictions with highly specific properties. In order to identify them it is worth noticing briefly once more the other moral fiction which emerges from the eighteenth century's attempts to reconstruct morality, the concept of utility. When Bentham first turned "utility" into a quasi-technical term, he did so, as I have already noticed, in a way that was designed to make plausible the notion of summing individual

prospects of pleasure and pain. But, as John Stuart Mill and other utilitarians expanded their notion of the variety of aims which human beings pursue and value, the notion of its being possible to sum all those experiences and activities which give satisfaction became increasingly implausible for reasons which I suggested earlier. The objects of natural and educated human desire are irreducibly heterogeneous and the notion of summing them either for individuals or for some population has no clear sense. But if utility is thus not a clear concept, then to use it as if it is, to employ it as if it could provide us with a rational criterion, is indeed to resort to a fiction.

A central characteristic of moral fictions which comes clearly into view when we juxtapose the concept of utility to that of rights is now identifiable: they purport to provide us with an objective and impersonal criterion, but they do not. And for this reason alone there would have to be a gap between their purported meaning and the uses to which they are actually put. Moreover we can now understand a little better how the phenomenon of incommensurable premises in modern moral debate arises. The concept of rights was generated to serve one set of purposes as part of the social invention of the autonomous moral agent; the concept of utility was devised for quite another set of purposes. And both were elaborated in a situation in which substitute artifacts for the concepts of an older and more traditional morality were required, substitutes that had to have a radically innovative character if they were to give even an appearance of performing their new social functions. Hence when claims invoking rights are matched against claims appealing to utility or when either or both are matched against claims based on some traditional concept of justice, it is not surprising that there is no rational way of deciding which type of claim is to be given priority or how one is to be weighed against the other. Moral incommensurability is itself the product of a particular historical conjunction.

This provides us with an insight important for understanding the politics of modern societies. For what I described earlier as the culture of bureaucratic individualism results in their characteristic overt political debates being between an individualism which makes its claims in terms of rights and forms of bureaucratic organisation which make their claims in terms of utility. But if the concept of rights and that of utility are a matching pair of incommensurable fictions, it will be the case that the moral idiom employed can at best provide a semblance of rationality for the modern political process, but not its reality. The mock rationality of the debate conceals the arbitrariness of the will and power at work in its resolution.

READING 48

Wrong Rights

Elizabeth Wolgast

Elizabeth Wolgast is Professor of Philosophy at California State University–Heyward and the author of *Equality and the Rights of Women* (1980) and *The Grammar of Justice,* from which this selection is taken.

Wolgast argues that, although rights are valuable tools for some moral purposes, they are not always so. Sometimes they can be unkind weapons to coerce others to do our bidding and they often overly emphasize an atomistic view of human nature, neglecting our common humanity as fellow sufferers who need concern and respect, not abstract rights. She illustrates her thesis by examples from medical ethics.

This reading is taken from *Hypatia,* 1987 by permission of Indiana University Press.

If the basic units of society are discrete and autonomous individuals, that fact must determine the way they should be treated. Thus it is a natural step from atomism to the concept of individual rights, rights that will attach to each individual regardless of his or her characteristics. As persons are independent, so their rights will be defined in a framework of independence. And as the indistinguishable atoms are equal, so their rights need to be equal. The concept of individual rights is a natural adjunct to atomism.

The language of rights is also a way of looking at wrongs, a conceptual grid, a schema. It both gives us a sense of *how* wrongs are wrong and points to the way to address them, that is, by establishing a right. Although it is a powerful and useful tool, still the schema of rights is sometimes unfit for the uses we make of it. It can bind us to a senseless stance, stereotype our reasoning, and lead to remedies that are grotesque. Our commitment to this language is deep, however; even in the face of bizarre consequences we hold it fast and view the consequent problems as demands for further rights. Thus our reasoning often goes on in an enclosed framework of rights, a framework from which counterexamples are excluded *a priori.* What does this commitment to rights mean to us, and how can it be sensibly limited?

I

Rights are often spoken of in the language of possessions. They are, Richard Wasserstrom writes, "distinctive moral 'commodities,'"[1] H. L. A. Hart spells out the metaphor: "Rights are typically conceived of as *possessed* or *owned by* or *belonging to* individuals, and these expressions reflect the conception of moral rules as not only prescribing conduct but as forming a kind of moral property of individuals to which they are as individuals entitled; only when rules are conceived in this way can we speak of *rights* and *wrongs* as well as right and wrong actions." [See Reading 49.] The idea of rights as moral property, as belonging to individuals the way property does, is an important aspect of the concept of rights. It focuses attention on the person to whom something is due, just as property law focuses attention on the possessor of property. The individual person with his needs and desires is the central motif.

This perspective is in contrast with one that focuses on the misdeeds of the offender, that condemns the misdeeds and castigates the doer. Instead of condemning, our perspective asserts something positive, namely, that a certain kind of thing—a *right*—exists. But what kind of thing is this, and how can we prove its existence? The answers given in response to this question are often vague, and they commonly lead to talk of "natural" rights as necessary features of human existence. In the end we have something that sounds like a moral metaphysics. What is it that the possessor of a right holds? David Lyons explains:

> When A in particular, holds a certain right *against B, A* is a *claimant* against B. A "claimant" is one empowered to press or waive a claim against someone with a corresponding duty or obligation. He can, if he wishes, release the other from his obligation and cancel it, or he can insist upon its performance. . . . A claimant is thus one to whom the performance of a duty or obligation is *owed*—he is the one who holds the claim against the other and who is entitled to administer the claim as he chooses.[2]

Lyons describes an important feature of the language of rights: the power it puts in the hands of the owner to press his right against someone or some agency. Rights are there to be *claimed*—asserted, demanded, pressed—or, on the other hand, waived. What the claimant is entitled to press for is no doubt a benefit; rights are generally associated with benefits, if only the benefit of being able to do something one doesn't want to do. But a right can be distinguished from a benefit in that a beneficiary often need not do anything; the role can be described as passive, you might say, while a rightholder can choose to claim his right or not; his right enables him to act in a certain way or to decline to do so.

Thus a right puts its possessor in an assertive position in which he may claim something, and to claim something is to claim it against another. So a right to a free education may be claimed by any child *against* the state, the right to vote may be asserted by any citizen *against* anyone who would interfere, the right of habeas corpus may be demanded *against* the court by anyone charged with a crime, and so on. But these rights differ quite a bit from benefits, since a gift generally doesn't need to be claimed, and the giver doesn't owe it if it is.

II

Rights put the rightholder in the driver's seat; a rightholder may be seen as active while the recipient of a benefit is passive. Joel Feinberg captures the difference by comparing a world with rights to a world without them. He imagines "Nowheresville," a world without rights, and asks "what precisely [such] a world is missing . . . and why that absence is morally important." The crucial thing absent, he argues, is the activity of claiming: "Nowheresvillians, even when they are discriminated against invidiously, or left without the things they need, or otherwise badly treated, do not think to leap to their feet and make righteous demands against one another. . . . They do not have a notion of what is their due" [see Reading 45]. Claiming depends on a prior right to claim, and although a right may be waived, rights' "characteristic use, and that for which they are distinctively well suited, is to be claimed, demanded, affirmed, insisted upon."

Why do rights have such crucial moral importance? Feinberg answers that it is precisely the feature of claiming that "gives rights their special moral significance." It is "connected . . . with the customary rhetoric

about what it is to be a human being. Having rights enables us to 'stand up like men,' to look others in the eye, and to feel in some fundamental way the equal of anyone. To think of oneself as a holder of rights is not to be unduly but properly proud . . . and what is called 'human dignity' may simply be the recognizable capacity to assert claims." People need to think of themselves as equal to others and thus able to claim their rights against others: that is a large part of what it is to be in the fullest sense a person. Nothing is more appropriate to a person than the possession of individual rights, rights that by their nature are given equally to everyone. In Feinberg's view the claiming of these possessions has a moral value of its own: "the activity of claiming . . . as much as any other thing, makes for self-respect and respect for others [and] gives a sense to the notion of personal dignity" [see Reading 45].

The language in which Feinberg praises rights is recognizably atomistic. He thinks of individuals as independent units whose self-respect is of prime importance to them *as* separate entities. Further, their capacity to claim rights is an important part of their active pursuit of their own interests. In such ways the language of rights both confirms the main features of the atomistic model and relies on its implicit values.

My claim is that such a conception of individuals and their rights may not be an effective means of addressing some injustices.

III

Consider the issue of the maltreatment of patients by doctors and medical staff in hospitals. In a hospital a patient is entirely at the mercy of medical people, whose expertise and positions give them great power, and so they are vulnerable to abuses of that power. The patient who is weak and frightened is by definition dependent on the staff; and they, in virtue of their practical knowledge and ability, are in the position of his rescuers—can instruct him and help him to survive. Abuse of such power and authority is, in view of the patient's helplessness, a frightening possibility.

Michel Foucault argues that with the development of clinics and the opportunities they offer to study disease, a new doctor–patient relationship develops. In this impersonal, scientific context the doctor becomes an expert in diseases, and "if one wishes to know the illness from which he is suffering, one must abstract the individual, with his particular qualities." The doctor must look through the patient at the disease.

On the one side of the patient is the family, whose "gentle, spontaneous care, expressive of love and a common desire for a cure, assists nature in its struggle against the illness;" on the other side is the hospital doctor, who "sees only distorted, altered diseases, a whole teratology of the pathological." The traditional family doctor, in contrast, cannot have the clinical detachment of the hospital doctor, but in his practice "must necessarily be respectful" of the patient.[3] Foucault's account provides a plausible explanation of how the problem of disrespectful treatment of patients in a modern hospital comes about; it is a natural, logical development. Inevitably, too, the search for knowledge and the holding of power go hand in hand, and as the doctor seeks knowledge of a scientific kind, his patient becomes increasingly an object under his control, and less and less someone to be dealt with in personal terms.

Here's the problem, then. The patient is weak, frightened, helpless, but needs to be treated in many ways as a normal person—needs to be respected, even in his wishes regarding treatment, and ultimately perhaps in his wish to die or to be sent home uncured. The issue may be addressed in various ways, but the most common way of dealing with it is to say that the patient has a *right* to respectful and considerate treatment, a right to have his wishes in regard to his treatment respected, a right to be informed about the character of his treatment, and so on. To force upon him decisions he might not accept if he weren't ill and dependent is then to subject him to a kind of domination. It is as if the patient could be mistreated *because he is ill,* and that thought recalls Samuel Butler's grotesque society Erewhon, where illness is a crime demanding punishment. There a judge trying a case of pulmonary congestion pronounces, "You may say that it is your misfortune to be criminal; I answer that it is your crime to be unfortunate."[4]

In the wake of protests over mistreatment of patients, the American Hospital Association instituted a code of patients' rights which has been widely adopted in this country. The first of these rights is "the right to considerate and respectful care," the fourth is the "right to refuse treatment to the extent permitted by law and to be informed of the medical consequences of his action," the eighth is the patient's "right to obtain information as to the existence of any professional relationships among individuals . . . who are treating him." Yet at the end we are told: "No catalog of rights can guarantee for the patient the kind of treatment he has a right to expect. . . . All [the hospital's various] activities must be conducted with an overriding concern for the patient, and above all, the recognition of his dignity as a human being."[5] Nonetheless, these rights are posted prominently in the hospital so that both patients and staff will be reminded of them as they go about their routines.

Now what can be wrong with this way of dealing with patient care? First, these rights, like the right not to be beaten by your spouse, call to mind the abuses they were designed to mitigate. They imply that hospital personnel are commonly guilty of unethical or insensitive conduct; otherwise there would be no need to protect patients against abuse. Second, the institution of rights focuses on a patient as complainant. As we have seen, the language of rights gives the rightholder a license to protest under certain circumstances; that is part of the language and the reason it's connected with self-respect. But as we have also remarked, the patient is not in a good position to exercise such rights. In his weakened condition, under medication, who is he to complain? Giving him rights puts him in the role of an assertive and able individual, but this role is inconsistent with being ill.

Someone who presses a claim and demands respect for his rights does so from the stance of a peer vis-à-vis the one complained against, as Feinberg says; but the doctor–patient relationship is not one of peers. As one writer observes, "Strong statements of patient rights imply a parity between physician and patient not usually possible in the situations under which . . . physician–patient relationships are developed." The patient needs the doctor; the doctor doesn't in the same way need him. Moreover, the patient "often enters into the arms of medicine as one might enter passionately into the arms of a lover—with great haste and need, but little forethought;" thus by definition a cool consideration of his situation is excluded. Once recovered and out of the hospital, *then* the patient can exercise his rights—take the doctor and hospital administrator to court and sue for damages. But this remedy is no remedy at all. What a sick and dependent person needs is responsible treatment from others *while he is unable to press claims against anyone.*

How then ought the problem to be addressed? The moral difficulty comes to roost in the doctor–patient or staff–patient relationship: something isn't right there. As the Patient's Bill of Rights asserts, a doctor has to treat his patients with respect and concern, for that is his responsibility and part of his professional role. If he fails to do so, he is not a good doctor, no matter how knowledgeable he is. Then why is a set of rights given to the patient? It's the doctor who needs to be reminded of his charge, and that's where the focus ought to be, logically—on the doctor and his or her responsibility.

The doctor who sees the disease as the object of his interest, and sees the patient's idiosyncrasies as distractions from the pure case he wants to understand, is surely dehumanizing the patient. Foucault speaks of this outlook as a botanical view of medicine, for it is similar to the view found in botany, as well as in mechanics and physics. Moreover, if we regard medicine as a science, it is difficult to see why a doctor *should* take the patient seriously *as a person.* Such a view isn't *objective;* that isn't the way a physical scientist would view his subject. Humanity, sympathy, and sensitivity have no place in physical science. The problem of patient treatment, then, is connected with the way medicine is conceived, its claim to be a science, and its place in the community.

An obvious way to address the issue of disrespectful treatment of patients would be to approach the medical community with exactly this concern, a concern that pertains potentially to everyone. One can imagine penalties being imposed when an ethical code is violated. Medical practice might be monitored by people outside of the medical brotherhood. Various legal and institutional ways could be devised to deal with the problem; we don't need to decide here which ones would be the most practical.

There are barriers to this approach, however. In the atomistic model, connections of responsibility and dependency don't appear; there aren't any. In the same way that molecular theory cannot allow that some molecules take care of others or defer to them, independent autonomous beings cannot be connected. The language of rights reflects this atomistic fact, that relations of individuals to one another are relations between entities who are peers. And as we saw, these peer relations give rise to contracts in which both parties pursue their self-interests. Looking at the doctor–patient relation in this light, we see that there's no room for—no representation of—the doctor's *responsibility for the patient.* There is similarly no room in the model for anyone's responsibility for another; everyone is responsible for himself and that's all. Thus we are blocked from dealing with the problem in terms of the medical professional's responsibility for patients. Atomism prefers to give the patient rights.

But it doesn't make sense to do what we do in this case, to put the burden of straightening out the problem of medical negligence and disrespect on the shoulders of those already unable to handle the practical details of life—to say to such people, "Here are your rights; now you may press a claim against the doctor in whose care you placed yourself or waive your right, just as you please." The relationship between doctor and patient is appropriately one of trust, while this remedy implies the absence of trust.

It is no solution to assume that a patient has a healthy person to speak for him and press his rights. For even when such a person exists, the patient's dependency may still prevent his taking action against those who are supposed to care for him. When he is well (if he recovers), he and his representative can then bring suit against the doctor or whoever. But here again the right he possesses is a right appropriate to a well person, not a sick one. I conclude that the conception of patients' rights is irrational and impractical. . . .

IV

Another class of wrong rights affects women and the connections between them and their children. Consider the "equal rights" guaranteed to women who have committed substantial parts of their lives to raising a family and managing a home, and who then need work. The theory says that they have equal rights to a job, an equal opportunity in a free, competitive labor market. The image operating here is that of similar units—men and women of all ages—similarly situated, and in that case fair treatment would be identical treatment of them all. A woman is discriminated against and pays a penalty for her sex only if she is denied a job *when other factors are equal.* But if we suppose her situation to be as I have described it, then other factors are not equal. The model and its assumptions beg the essential question, namely, how she should be treated given that her situation is not like a man's. Affirmative action programs and a ban on "age discrimination" are stopgap efforts that inherently conflict with the model and bow in apology for the offense. They rest on the factors that distinguish people from one another, while in the model any distinctions of treatment are discriminatory and thus unfair. Thus there is no theoretical solution to the problem. Measures that make reasonable moral sense are theoretically excluded.

Consider another issue, the debate over the constitutionality of mandated maternity leaves. The model requires this benefit to be couched in the language of equality; otherwise it appears as discriminatory against men. In order to avoid making a distinction between men and women, we assimilate maternity leaves to a disability or sickness leave, comparable to a leave one takes for the flu. When the benefit is thus clothed in sex-neutral terms, the question arises whether or not a right to maternity leave is an "equal right." The argument then turns on the importance of men's immunity to pregnancy. In such famous cases as *Miller-Wohl* and *California Federal Savings,*[6] the issue is exactly this: If a maternity leave is an equal right, it may be fair; otherwise it provides to women a benefit that is unavailable to men, and therefore it is unconstitutional under Title V of the Civil Rights Act. Thus the very document that was meant to ensure fairness in employment and education is used to frustrate a policy to accommodate the most fundamental process of human life, reproduction.

The reasoning that ensues from a concept of fairness defined as equality among autonomous agents is often strange. It is seriously asked, for instance, whether men have an equal maternity right because they could have such a leave *if they should become pregnant.* What a strange question—and how can a reasonable person answer? One legal writer discusses the *Miller-Wohl* case in these terms: "The equal treatment proponents . . . are thinking metaphysically. They approach the question [of the legality of maternity leave legislation] . . . by asking whether or not the statute conforms to a particular legal construct, i.e., the equal treatment principle. They focus the debate on legal theoretical levels, rather than starting with an analysis of the concrete material problems of women in the workforce."[7]

Realistically, maternity leaves are needed because childbirth is exhausting and because a newborn baby and its mother need care. In part it is the child's needs that dictate that its mother shouldn't work full time just after its birth. But if we introduce the mother–child complex into the argument, we lose the framework of individual rights. And how else can we deal with the issue?

If we consider the central position of a baby in birth, we may decide that the baby has the principal right. But the issue is obscure: first we need to know if the baby is an individual who can possess rights, and then we have the harder question of whether that individual can have a right to its mother's maternity leave. On the face of it, that notion makes no sense. A right, as we have seen, attaches directly to a person; one person can't have a right *for* another. Moreover, involving the child in the maternal right won't work because it isn't born during the last weeks of pregnancy, when, just because its birth is imminent, the mother needs extra rest and leave from work.

The language of individual rights makes this issue into a puzzle in which by ingenious distortion we force something into a form that's essentially alien to it. How many people are involved in childbirth and do they each have a right, or together have a joint right, to maternity leave? And how does this complex of mother-and-baby compare with the less complicated case of a man? If both sexes are equal, which sex sets the standard? And if we are talking of disabilities, [not] abilities, what kind of "disability" is it that leads to the birth of a child and a subsequent commitment to its care? The model gives no answers. Common sense would say that pregnancy isn't an illness but a strenuous productive period culminating in new responsibilities for a creature whose existence is fragile and who requires care to survive. But the model can't admit this description. The dignity of a rightholder brings no dignity to the condition of pregnancy or the occasion of childbirth.

The argument that a right to a maternity leave is a special and unfair right of women unless it is extended and adapted to men is a consequence of individualism and the language of equal rights. In this case it puts men in the position of jealous siblings, watching for any sign of partiality shown to others. They are in the position of competing with pregnant women for favorable treatment, and in this stance they show a blind disregard for the realities of childbirth.

The debate about abortion also shows the inadequacies of a theory of rights in regard to reproduction. It is a subject of serious debate whether the fetus is an autonomous individual with equal rights. If so, then it has all the rights of any person and should be able to claim its rights against its mother-to-be. But how can we imagine such a thing?

The fetus's need for its mother is more total and unqualified than that of an infant for its parents. But if a fetus isn't a person, what else can it be? Some people have proposed to deal with it as a kind of property, as belonging to the mother as part of her body. To be sure, we sometimes speak this way of a foot or a kidney, and even of self-respect and reputation. But a fetus *isn't* like a body part or reputation. It is a potential baby, which is to say a potential human being, and its birth is not like an amputation or organ removal but is the advent of a new member (albeit immature) into the community.

Either way of representing a fetus, as a person or as property, is fraught with difficulties. On the one hand we make too much of it, granting it rights that cannot apply to its case, and on the other we make too little of it, treating it as property whose owner can dispose of it any way she likes, for the point and virtue of ownership is one's right to do what one wants with one's property.

There are certainly two sides to the question of whether abortions should be restricted and what restrictions should be imposed; that's understandable. What is strange is the way we are forced to *present* the two sides, forced to caricature both the pregnant woman and the fetus. We are forced to caricature them by our commitment to fit the issue into a grid that has room only for individuals who are autonomous, have property, and make contracts. But the reasoning is bizarre.

Imagine a Martian who has come to study us and make sense of our society. He hears arguments about whether the fetus is a person (in the full and legal sense) or a bit of property (in the tort-law sense). Wouldn't he consider us morally undeveloped or mentally handicapped? A human fetus is not like anything except another fetus, conceptually more like a rabbit fetus or a racoon fetus or an elephant fetus than like a fully developed human. It is a stage in a process by which an infant comes into a community—a community of rabbits or racoons or elephants or humans. Apart from this framework it's indefinable. It would be best to say, then, that a fetus is *sui generis,* its own kind of thing, and so irreducible to something else.

What is wrong with us, the Martian wonders, that we don't see this and persist in arguing about fetal personhood and fetal rights? But basically what is wrong here is the grid we press upon the facts of reproduction.

V

One major problem with the model, as we have seen, is that it cannot show the variety of relationships in which people take responsibility and care for one another, some relationships of family, some of profession, some of simple concern. Its tendency to assimilate all relationships to that of independent, free, and self-interested persons also becomes a limitation in economic theory, as James Coleman observes. "Classical economic theory always assumes that the individual will act in his interest; but it never examines carefully the entity to which 'his' refers. Often, as when households are taken as the unit for income and consumption, it is implicitly assumed that 'the family' or 'the household' is this entity whose interest is being maximized. Yet this is without theoretical foundation, merely a convenient but slipshod device."[8] The "household" is a convenient device for preserving the outlines of atomism. But treating a family—which consists of

more than one person—as a single individual "acting in its own interest" is at the same time at odds with the assumptions of atomism. The term *household* preserves the surface of atomism by making it a fictional person.

Rawls makes a similar adjustment, explaining that "the term 'person' is to be construed variously. . . . On some occasions it will mean human individuals, but in others it may refer to . . . business firms, churches, teams," and of course families. Each of these units is then regarded as a rational and self-interested entity. [See Reading 26.] How else can we conceive of families? As a voluntary association of autonomous persons? That notion doesn't square with the facts.

When autonomous persons enter into an agreement, each party agrees to make some concessions in return for advantages to himself: mutual self-interest is the explanatory factor in all bonds. Milton Friedman emphasizes its exclusive power: "If an exchange between two parties is voluntary, it will not take place unless both believe they will benefit from it." Thus it is that "economic order can emerge as the unintended consequence of the actions of many people, each seeking his own interest."

Apply this picture to the sick person, who needs help, and to the doctor, who has what Friedman calls his "personal capacity" to sell. According to Friedman, the doctor's only motive in helping the patient is his own interest, although he concedes that this interest can be defined as more than "myopic selfishness." "It is whatever it is that interests the participants, whatever they value, whatever goals they pursue. The scientist . . . the missionary . . . the philanthropist . . . are all pursuing their interests, as they see them, as they judge them by their own values."[9] The doctor may or may not be acting selfishly; he may have a personal interest in the patient's health. There's no room for a distinction, in Friedman's theory, between the good doctor and the clever mercenary one. None has any *responsibility* to concern himself with anyone else's health.

Plato thought the distinction between good and bad doctors was clear enough. In the *Republic* he has Socrates ask Thrasymachus, "But tell me, your physician in the precise sense . . . is he a money-maker, an earner of fees, or a healer of the sick? And remember to speak of the physician who is really such." Later he asks: "Then medicine . . . does not consider the advantage of medicine but of the body?" He concludes: "Can we deny, then . . . that neither does any physician insofar as he is a physician seek or enjoin the advantage of the physician but that of the patient? For we have agreed that the physician, 'precisely' speaking, is a ruler and governor of bodies and not a money-maker."[10]

Now if the doctor–patient relationship is a contract, and a sick person must approach a doctor who is motivated by his own gain, the contract is grossly unfair and susceptible to a multitude of exploitations, and therefore probably invalid. H. Tristram Engelhardt describes the initial approach like this: "The physician–patient relationship is likely to be assumed under circumstances that compromise the integrity of the patient. . . . At the very moments when much must be decided by the ill or dying person, he is often least able to decide with full competence. Disease not only places the patient at a general disadvantage . . . it also makes the patient dependent upon the physician."[11]

Here there is a relation governed by dependency, not autonomy, one in which most of the power and the clear options are on the side of the doctor. The patient is a poor example of the rational consumer. Given the doctor's motive and ability to get the best of him, it might be most rational in all self-interest for a patient not to approach him.

The best attitude of a sick person toward his doctor is trust, it is often remarked. The attitude intended is not trust that the doctor will fulfill a contract whose terms are unspecified, but trust in the doctor's concern. Without that sort of trust a doctor becomes a hired physiological consultant.

VI

A deeper question about the language of rights needs to be raised: Why, whenever we deal with a wrongful act or practice, do we feel impelled to refer to some right or other? Besides the influence of atomism, we think of a right as a justification for condemning something as wrong. Feinberg, for instance, says that claim rights are prior to and thus more basic than the duties with which they are correlated. Thus they give a foundation for the demand that someone do or refrain from doing something and justify condemnation by showing the action as a violation of a (prior) right.

In practice the reasoning works like this. Burglary is wrong, everyone agrees; but what justifies us in calling it wrong? Some answer must exist, and one reasonable possibility is that it's wrong because a person has a right not to be burglarized, not to have his property invaded, abused, or stolen. Similarly we say that mugging is wrong, and then defend this judgment by arguing that it is wrong because a person has a right to walk down the street safely. Along these lines, murder is wrong because a person has a right to life; slander is

wrong because a person has a right to be treated with respect; and so on. Rights proliferate as we seek justifications for every variety of things condemnable as wrong.

If justifications are needed, then the invocation of rights may make sense, but are such justifications necessary? Isn't murder simply wrong, wrong in itself? A commonsense answer might be yes—why should one need to justify such an obvious judgment? And if we reflect on the logical path that brought us here, we see that it is our conviction that we are justified in calling murder wrong that makes us sure that something must *justify* our judgment. We are of course justified; but does our justification imply that some separate justification lies behind it? What would happen if none did?

Murder's wrongness can be contrasted with the wrongness of something stipulated by a rule, such as moving a castle diagonally in chess. There a justification for the wrongness of the move clearly exists, that is, the rule that governs the way castles can move. And the wrongness of nonperformance of a contract has a justification, namely, that the contract specifies that one will do such-and-such. But in the case of some serious moral offenses it is less clear that analogous justifications exist. As Wittgenstein said of justifications of beliefs, "the chain of reasons has an end" and "at some point one has to pass from explanation to mere description."[12] Calling murder wrong is here like calling a certain color red, that is, what justifies us in using these terms is that the word means what it does. We are justified, but being justified is not the same as having a justification.

We have no particular reason to think that we need to invoke a right before we can call murder wrong. The "right to life" is unnecessary, and by eschewing it we avoid the curious consequence that death, which negates life, is wrong. We also acquire an important general benefit. When we leave rights aside, our view of murder takes on a different appearance, just as the mistreatment of patients looks different when we stop focusing on patients' rights. Saying that Smith is wrong in murdering Jones because the murder violates Jones's right to life puts the focus on Jones and his rights, even makes it appear that there is something that Jones can do with this right after the fact, which is nonsense. What really concerns us in such a case is what Smith did; *his* action belongs in the center of our perspective, his culpability, not the violation of Jones's now-useless right. Seen this way, an emphasis on individual rights serves to obscure the focus of moral objection to killing rather than giving the objection a firm foundation.

Without doubt rights have an important place in our legal and political system and they often do give reasons for condemning actions that would be permissible without them. But since they are justifications in some instances—the right to vote, for example, justifies us in calling a poll tax wrong or unjust—we are led to think that they are always valuable, that without them our censure of wrongs is weakened and the substance of condemnation is in jeopardy. This conclusion is mistaken. Rights sometimes supply a justification, but sometimes they supply only the appearance or form of one. We should recognize that sometimes they are superfluous.

The corrective to the tendency to invoke rights as justifications is the realization that we know some things to be wrong more securely and fundamentally than we know what rights people have or ought to have. In discussing our demands for justifications for beliefs, Wittgenstein observed that "it is so difficult to find the *beginning*. Or, better: it is difficult to begin at the beginning. And not try to go further back."[13] We may distort our subject if we try always to find something deeper, look for another and another reason. There has to be an end to justifications, and with murder and lying and cheating we have hit bedrock.

This tendency to seek justifications has another, more unfortunate side. The notion that one really needs a justification for the wrongness of murder implies that one isn't sure that murder is wrong, and that its wrongness depends on the adequacy of some further proof. But in that case, one's moral judgment in regard to murder is uncertain, and if it is uncertain about murder, then a great deal of moral understanding is missing. In that event, it's unclear how the demand could be satisfied. Uncertainty about something so basic may put the questioner beyond the framework in which moral justifications are meaningfully asked for and given, and beyond that framework is a no-man's-land often identified with skepticism. The demand for justification thus threatens to weaken rather than support the structure of moral thinking. The move cannot do any good here.

I conclude that rights and their invocation are often important and valuable. The right to performance of contract and the right to vote and the right to assemble are all embodied in protective legislation and certainly justify court action against anyone who would prevent exercise of them. But three kinds of problems can arise when rights are invoked too freely. The first concerns their application to people who are not in a position to exercise them. There the invocation of a right is often a means of avoiding placing responsibility on someone in a position of strength and control. In such a case our moral focus is wrong. The second problem has to do with people in situations and connections that vitiate assumptions in other ways, as the situations of women and fetuses do. The third has to do with justifying the condemnation of offenses whose moral wrongness is perfectly clear and unequivocal. The invocation of a right does not automatically fortify a conviction but may echo a doubt, and in some cases the doubt, once raised, cannot be put to rest, not by the invocation of a right or by any other means.

Rights have their place, but their place is limited. They don't provide a moral panacea, a handy set of justifications to be called on when justification is desired. They need to be used with judgment and restraint, without a blanket commitment to the atomistic vision.

READING 49

Are There Any Natural Rights?

H. L. A. Hart

For Hart's biography, see Reading 31. In this essay Hart argues that, if there are any natural rights, rights not created by society, but universal and objective, they must include the equal right to liberty. This article is important because it sets forth the fairness argument for political obligation, developed by John Rawls (see Reading 13).

This reading is taken from "Are There Any Natural Rights?" *Philosophical Review* 64 (1955).

I shall advance the thesis that if there are any moral rights at all, it follows that there is at least one natural right, the equal right of all men to be free. By saying that there is this right, I mean that in the absence of certain special conditions which are consistent with the right being an equal right, any adult human being capable of choice (1) has the right to forbearance on the part of all others from the use of coercion or restraint against him save to hinder coercion or restraint and (2) is at liberty to do (i.e., is under no obligation to abstain from) any action which is not one coercing or restraining or designed to injure other persons.

I have two reasons for describing the equal rights of all men to be free as a *natural* right; both of them were always emphasized by the classical theorists of natural rights. (1) This right is one which all men have if they are capable of choice: they have it *qua* men and not only if they are members of some society or stand in some special relation to each other. (2) This right is not created or conferred by men's voluntary action: other moral rights are. Of course, it is quite obvious that my thesis is not as ambitious as the traditional theories of natural rights; for although on my view all men are *equally* entitled to be free in the sense explained, no man has an absolute or unconditional right to do or not to do any particular thing or to be treated in any particular way; coercion or restraint of any action may be justified in special conditions consistently with the general principle. So my argument will not show that men have any right (save the equal right of all to be free) which is "absolute," "indefeasible," or "imprescriptible." This may for many reduce the importance of my contention, but I think that the principle that all men have an equal right to be free, meagre as it may seem, is probably all that the political philosophers of the liberal tradition need have claimed to support any programme of action even if they have claimed more. But my contention that there is this one natural right may appear unsatisfying in another respect; it is only the conditional assertion that *if* there are any moral rights then there must be this one natural right. Perhaps few would now deny, as some have, that there are moral rights; for the point of that denial was usually to object to some philosophical claim as to the "ontological status" of rights, and this objection is now expressed not as a denial that there are any moral rights but as a denial of some assumed logical similarity between sentences used to assert the existence of rights and other kinds of sentences. But it is still important to remember that there may be codes of conduct quite properly termed moral codes (though we can of course say they are "imperfect") which do not employ the notion of *a* right, and there is nothing contradictory or otherwise absurd in a code or morality consisting wholly of prescriptions or in a code which prescribed only what should be done for the realization of happiness or some ideal of personal perfection. Human actions in such systems would be evaluated or criticized as compliances with prescriptions or as *good* or *bad, right* or *wrong, wise* or *foolish, fitting* or *unfitting,* but no one in such a system would have, exercise, or claim rights, or violate or infringe them. So those who lived by such systems could not of course be committed to the recog-

nition of the equal right of all to be free; nor, I think (and this is one respect in which the notion of a right differs from other moral notions), could any parallel argument be constructed to show that, from the bare fact that actions were recognized as ones which ought or ought not to be done, as right, wrong, good, or bad, it followed that some specific kind of conduct fell under these categories.

I

(A) Lawyers have for their own purposes carried the dissection of the notion of a legal right some distance, and some of their results are of value in the elucidation of statements of the form "X has a right to . . ." outside legal contexts. There is of course no simple identification to be made between moral and legal rights, but there is an intimate connection between the two, and this itself is one feature which distinguishes a moral right from other fundamental moral concepts. It is not merely that as a matter of fact men speak of their moral rights mainly when advocating their incorporation in a legal system, but that the concept of a right belongs to that branch of morality which is specifically concerned to determine when one person's freedom may be limited by another's[1] and so to determine what actions may appropriately be made the subject of coercive legal rules. The words *"droit," "diritto,"* and *"Recht,"* used by continental jurists, have no simple English translation and seem to English jurists to hover uncertainly between law and morals, but they do in fact mark off an area of morality (the morality of law) which has special characteristics. It is occupied by the concepts of justice, fairness, rights, and obligation (if this last is not used as it is by many moral philosophers as an obscuring general label to cover every action that morally we ought to do or forbear from doing). The most important common characteristic of this group of moral concepts is that there is no incongruity, but a special congruity in the use of force or the threat of force to secure that what is just or fair or someone's right to have done shall in fact be done; for it is in just these circumstances that coercion of another human being is legitimate. Kant, in the *Rechtslehre,* discusses the obligations which arise in this branch of morality under the title of *officia juris,* "which do not require that respect for duty shall be of itself the determining principle of the will," and contrasts them with *officia virtutis,* which have no moral worth unless done for the sake of the moral principle. His point is, I think, that we must distinguish from the rest of morality those principles regulating the proper distribution of human freedom which alone make it morally legitimate for one human being to determine by his choice how another should act; and a certain specific moral value is secured (to be distinguished from moral virtue in which the goodwill is manifested) if human relationships are conducted in accordance with these principles even though coercion has to be used to secure this, for only if these principles are regarded will freedom be distributed among human beings as it should be. And it is I think a very important feature of a moral right that the possessor of it is conceived as having a moral justification for limiting the freedom of another and that he has this justification not because the action he is entitled to require of another has some moral quality but simply because in the circumstances a certain distribution of human freedom will be maintained if he by his choice is allowed to determine how that other shall act.

(B) I can best exhibit this feature of a moral right by reconsidering the question whether moral rights and "duties"[2] are correlative. The contention that they are means, presumably, that every statement of the form "X has a right to . . ." entails and is entailed by "Y has a duty (not) to . . . ," and at this stage we must not assume that the values of the name-variables "X" and "Y" must be different persons. Now there is certainly one sense of "a right" (which I have already mentioned) such that it does not follow from X's having a right that X or someone else has any duty. Jurists have isolated rights in this sense and have referred to them as "liberties" just to distinguish them from rights in the centrally important sense of "right" which has "duty" as a correlative. The former sense of "right" is needed to describe those areas of social life where competition is at least morally unobjectionable. Two people walking along both see a ten-dollar bill in the road twenty yards away, and there is no clue as to the owner. Neither of the two are under a "duty" to allow the other to pick it up; each has in this sense a right to pick it up. Of course there may be many things which each has a "duty" not to do in the course of the race to the spot—neither may kill or wound the other—and corresponding to these "duties" there are rights to forbearances. The moral propriety of all economic competition implies this minimum sense of "a right" in which to say that "X has a right to" means merely that X is under no "duty" not to. Hobbes saw that the expression "a right" could have this sense but he was wrong if he thought that there is no sense in which it does follow from X having a right that Y has a duty or at any rate an obligation.

(C) More important for our purpose is the question whether for all moral "duties" there are correlative moral rights, because those who have given an affirmative answer to this question have usually assumed wihout adequate scrutiny that to have a right is simply to be capable of benefiting by the performance of a "duty," whereas in fact this is not a sufficient condition (and probably not a necessary condition) of having a right. Thus animals and babies who stand to benefit by our performance of our "duty" not to ill-treat them are said *therefore* to have rights to proper treatment. The full consequence of this reasoning is not usually followed out; most have shrunk from saying that we have rights against ourselves because we stand to benefit from our performance of our "duty" to keep ourselves alive or develop our talents. But the moral situation which arises from a promise (where the legal-sounding terminology of rights and obligations is most appropriate) illustrates most clearly that the notion of having a right and that of benefiting by the performance of a "duty" are not identical. X promises Y in return for some favour that he will look after Y's aged mother in his absence. Rights arise out of this transaction, but it is surely Y to whom the promise has been made and not his mother who *has* or *possesses* these rights. Certainly Y's mother is a person concerning whom X has an obligation and a person who will benefit by its performance, but the person *to whom* he has an obligation to look after her is Y. This is something *due to* or *owed to* Y, so it is Y, not his mother, whose right X will disregard and to whom X will have done *wrong* if he fails to keep his promise, though the mother may be physically injured. And it is Y who has a moral *claim* upon X; is *entitled* to have his mother looked after, and who can *waive* the claim and *release* Y from the obligation. Y is, in other words, morally in a position to determine by his choice how X shall act and in this way to limit X's freedom of choice; and it is this fact, not the fact that he stands to benefit, that makes it appropriate to say that he has a *right*. Of course often the person to whom a promise has been made will be the only person who stands to benefit by its performance, but this does not justify the identification of "having a right" with "benefiting by the performance of a duty." It is important for the whole logic of rights that, while the person who stands to benefit by the performance of a duty is discovered by considering what will happen if the duty is not performed, the person who has a right (to whom performance is *owed* or *due*) is discovered by examining the transaction or antecedent situation or relations of the parties out of which the "duty" arises.

These considerations should incline us not to extend to animals and babies whom it is wrong to ill-treat the notion of a right to proper treatment, for the moral situation can be simply and adequately described here by saying that it is wrong or that we ought not to ill-treat them or, in the philosopher's generalized sense of "duty," that we have a duty not to ill-treat them. If common usage sanctions talk of the rights of animals or babies it makes an idle use of the expression "a right," which will confuse the situation with other different moral situations where the expression "a right" has a specific force and cannot be replaced by the other moral expressions which I have mentioned. Perhaps some clarity on this matter is to be gained by considering the force of the preposition "to" in the expression "having a duty to Y" or "being under an obligation to Y" (where "Y" is the name of a person); for it is significantly different from the meaning of "to" in "doing something to Y" or "doing harm to Y," where it indicates the person affected by some action. In the first pair of expressions, "to" obviously does not have this force, but indicates the person to whom the person morally bound is bound. This is an intelligible development of the figure of a bond (*vinculum juris: obligare*); the precise figure is not that of two persons bound by a chain, but of one person bound, the other end of the chain lying in the hands of another to use if he chooses. So it appears absurd to speak of having duties or owing obligations to ourselves—of course we may have "duties" not to do harm to ourselves, but what could be meant (once the distinction between these different meanings of "to" has been grasped) by insisting that we have duties or obligations *to* ourselves not to do harm to ourselves?

(D) The essential connection between the notion of a right and the justified limitation of one person's freedom by another may be thrown into relief if we consider codes of behaviour which do not purport to confer rights but only to prescribe what shall be done. Most natural law thinkers down to Hooker conceived of natural law in this way: there were natural duties compliance with which would certainly benefit man—things to be done to achieve man's natural end—but not natural rights. And there are of course many types of codes of behaviour which only prescribe what is to be done, e.g., those regulating certain ceremonies. It would be absurd to regard these codes as conferring rights, but illuminating to contrast them with rules of games, which often create rights, though not, of course, moral rights. But even a code which is plainly a moral code need not establish rights; the Decalogue is per-

haps the most important example. Of course, quite apart from heavenly rewards human beings stand to benefit by general obedience to the Ten Commandments: disobedience is wrong and will certainly harm individuals. But it would be a surprising interpretation of them that treated them as conferring rights. In such an interpretation obedience to the Ten Commandments would have to be conceived as due to or owed to individuals, not merely to God, and disobedience not merely as wrong but as *a wrong to* (as well as harm to) individuals. The Commandments would cease to read like penal statutes designed only to rule out certain types of behaviour and would have to be thought of as rules placed at the disposal of individuals and regulating the extent to which *they* may demand certain behaviour from others. Rights are typically conceived of as *possessed* or *owned by* or *belonging to* individuals, and these expressions reflect the conception of moral rules as not only prescribing conduct but as forming a kind of moral property of individuals to which they are as individuals entitled; only when rules are conceived in this way can we speak of *rights* and *wrongs* as well as right and wrong actions.

II

So far I have sought to establish that to have a right entails having a moral justification for limiting the freedom of another person and for determining how he should act; it is now important to see that the moral justification must be of a special kind if it is to constitute a right, and this will emerge most clearly from an examination of the circumstances in which rights are asserted with the typical expression "I have a right to . . .". It is I think the case that this form of words is used in two main types of situations: (A) when the claimant has some special justification for interference with another's freedom which other persons do not have ("*I* have a right to be paid what you promised for my services"); (B) when the claimant is concerned to resist or object to some interference by another person as having no justification ("*I* have a right to say what I think").

(A) *Special rights.* When rights arise out of special transactions between individuals or out of some special relationship in which they stand to each other, both the persons who have the right and those who have the corresponding obligation are limited to the parties to the special transaction or relationship. I call such rights special rights to distinguish them from those moral rights which are thought of as rights against (i.e., as imposing obligations upon) everyone, such as those that are asserted when some unjustified interference is made or threatened as in (B) above.

(i) The most obvious cases of special rights are those that arise from promises. By promising to do or not to do something, we voluntarily incur obligations and create or confer rights on those to whom we promise; we alter the existing moral independence of the parties' freedom of choice in relation to some action and create a new moral relationship between them, so that it becomes morally legitimate for the person to whom the promise is given to determine how the promisor shall act. The promisee has a temporary authority or sovereignty in relation to some specific matter over the other's will which we express by saying that the promisor is under an obligation *to* the promisee to do what he has promised. To some philosophers the notion that moral phenomena—rights and duties or obligations—can be brought into existence by the voluntary action of individuals has appeared utterly mysterious; but this I think has been so because they have not clearly seen how special the moral notions of a right and an obligation are, nor how peculiarly they are connected with the distribution of freedom of choice; it would indeed be mysterious if we could make actions morally good or bad by voluntary choice. The simplest case of promising illustrates two points characteristic of all special rights: (1) the right and obligation arise not because the promised action has itself any particular moral quality, but just because of the voluntary transaction between the parties; (2) the identity of the parties concerned is vital—only *this* person (the promisee) has the moral justification for determining how the promisor shall act. It is *his* right; only in relation to him is the promisor's freedom of choice diminished, so that if he chooses to release the promisor no one else can complain.

(ii) But a promise is not the only kind of transaction whereby rights are conferred. They may be *accorded* by a person consenting or authorizing another to interfere in matters which but for his consent or authorization he would be free to determine for himself. If I consent to your taking precautions for my health and happiness or authorize you to look after my interests, then you have a right which others have not, and I cannot complain of your interference if it is within the sphere of your authority. This is what is meant by a person surrendering his rights to another; and again the typical characteristics of a right are present in this situation: the person authorized has the right to inter-

fere not because of its intrinsic character but because *these* persons have stood in *this* relationship. No one else (not similarly authorized) has any *right* to interfere in theory even if the person authorized does not exercise his right.

(iii) Special rights are not only those created by the deliberate choice of the party on whom the obligation falls, as they are when they are accorded or spring from promises, and not all obligations to other persons are deliberately incurred, though I think it is true of all special rights that they arise from previous voluntary actions. A third very important source of special rights and obligations which we recognize in many spheres of life is what may be termed mutuality of restrictions, and I think political obligation is intelligible only if we see what precisely this is and how it differs from other right-creating transactions (consent, promising) to which philosophers have assimilated it. In its bare schematic outline it is this: when a number of persons conduct any joint enterprise according to rules and thus restrict their liberty, those who have submitted to these restrictions when required have a right to a similar submission from those who have benefited by their submission. The rules may provide that officials should have authority to enforce obedience and make further rules, and this will create a structure of legal rights and duties, but the moral obligation to obey the rules in such circumstances is *due to* the co-operating members of the society, and they have the correlative moral right to obedience. In social situations of this sort (of which political society is the most complex example) the obligation to obey the rules is something distinct from whatever other moral reasons there may be for obedience in terms of good consequences (e.g., the prevention of suffering); the obligation is due to the co-operating members of the society as such and not because they are human beings on whom it would be wrong to inflict suffering. The utilitarian explanation of political obligation fails to take account of this feature of the situation both in its simple version that the obligation exists because and only if the direct consequences of a particular act of disobedience are worse than obedience, and also in its more sophisticated version that the obligation exists even when this is not so, if disobedience increases the probability that the law in question or other laws will be disobeyed on other occasions when the direct consequences of obedience are better than those of disobedience.

Of course to say that there is such a moral obligation upon those who have benefited by the submission of other members of society to restrictive rules to obey these rules in their turn does not entail either that this is the only kind of moral reason for obedience or that there can be no cases where disobedience will be morally justified. There is no contradiction or other impropriety in saying "I have an obligation to do X, someone has a right to ask me to, but I now see I ought not to do it." It will in painful situations sometimes be the lesser of two moral evils to disregard what really are people's rights and not perform our obligations to them. This seems to me particularly obvious from the case of promises: I may promise to do something and thereby incur an obligation just because that is one way in which obligations (to be distinguished from other forms of moral reasons for acting) are created; reflection may show that it would in the circumstances be wrong to keep this promise because of the suffering it might cause, and we can express this by saying "*I ought not to do it though I have an obligation to him to do it*" just because the italicized expression are not synonyms but come from different dimensions of morality. The attempt to explain this situation by saying that our real obligation here is to avoid the suffering and that there is only a *prima facie* obligation to keep the promise seems to me to confuse two quite different kinds of moral reason, and in practice such a terminology obscures the precise character of what is at stake when "for some greater good" we infringe people's rights or do not perform our obligations to them.

The social-contract theorists rightly fastened on the fact that the obligation to obey the law is not merely a special case of benevolence (direct or indirect), but something which arises between members of a particular political society out of their mutual relationship. Their mistake was to identify *this* right-creating situation of mutual restrictions with the paradigm case of promising; there are of course important similarities, and these are just the points which all special rights have in common, viz., that they arise out of special relationships between human beings and not out of the character of the action to be done or its effects.

(iv) There remains a type of situation which may be thought of as creating rights and obligations: where the parties have a special natural relationship, as in the case of parent and child. The parent's moral right to obedience from his child would I suppose now be thought to terminate when the child reaches the age "of discretion," but the case is worth mentioning because some political philosophies have had recourse to analogies with this case as an explanation of political obligation, and also because even this case has some of the features we have distinguished in special rights, viz.,

the right arises out of the special relationship of the parties (though it is in this case a natural relationship) and not out of the character of the actions to the performance of which there is a right.

(v) To be distinguished from special rights, of course, are special liberties, where, exceptionally, one person is *exempted* from obligations to which most are subject but does not thereby acquire a *right* to which there is a correlative obligation. If you catch me reading your brother's diary, you say, "You have no right to read it." I say, "I have a right to read it—your brother said I might unless he told me not to, and he has not told me not to." Here I have been specially *licensed* by your brother who had a right to require me not to read his diary, so I am exempted from the moral obligation not to read it. Cases where *rights,* not liberties, are accorded to manage or interfere with another person's affairs are those where the licence is not revocable at will by the person according the right.

(B) *General rights.* In contrast with special rights, which constitute a justification peculiar to the holder of the right for interfering with another's freedom, are general rights, which are asserted defensively, when some unjustified interference is anticipated or threatened, in order to point out that the interference is unjustified. "I have the right to say what I think."[3] "I have the right to worship as I please." Such rights share two important characteristics with special rights. (1) To have them is to have moral justification for determining how another shall act, viz., that he shall not interfere.[4] (2) The moral justification does not arise from the character of the particular action to the performance of which the claimant has a right; what justifies the claim is simply—there being no special relation between him and those who are threatening to interfere to justify that interference—that this is a particular exemplification of the equal right to be free. But there are of course striking differences between such defensive general rights and special rights. (1) General rights do not arise out of any special relationship or transaction between men. (2) They are not rights which are peculiar to those who have them but are rights which all men capable of choice have in the absence of those special conditions which give rise to special rights. (3) General rights have as correlatives obligations not to interfere to which everyone else is subject and not merely the parties to some special relationship or transaction, though of course they will often be asserted when some particular persons threaten to interfere as a moral objection to the interference. To assert a general right is to claim in relation to some particular action the equal right of all men to be free in the absence of any of those special conditions which constitute a special right to limit another's freedom; to assert a special right is to assert in relation to some particular action a right constituted by such special conditions to limit another's freedom. The assertion of general rights directly invokes the principle that all men equally have the right to be free; the assertion of a special right (as I attempt to show in Section III) invokes it indirectly.

III

It is, I hope, clear that unless it is recognized that interference with another's freedom requires a moral justification the notion of a right could have no place in morals; for to assert a right is to assert that there is such a justification. The characteristic function in moral discourse of those sentences in which the meaning of the expression "a right" is to be found—"I have a right to . . .", "You have no right to . . .", "What right have you to . . . ?"—is to bring to bear on interferences with another's freedom, or on claims to interfere, a type of moral evaluation or criticism specially appropriate to interference with freedom and characteristically different from, the moral criticism of actions made with the use of expressions like "right," "wrong," "good," and "bad." And this is only one of many different types of moral ground for saying "You ought . . ." or "You ought not . . .". The use of the expression "What right have you to . . . ?" shows this more clearly, perhaps, than the others; for we use it, just at the point where interference is actual or threatened, to call for the moral *title* of the person addressed to interfere; and we do this often without any suggestion at all that what he proposes to do is otherwise wrong and sometimes with the implication that the same interference on the part of another person would be unobjectionable.

But though our use in moral discourse of "a right" does presuppose the recognition that interference with another's freedom requires a moral justification, this would not itself suffice to establish, except in a sense easily trivialized, that in the recognition of moral rights there is implied the recognition that all men have a right to equal freedom; for unless there is some restriction inherent in the meaning of "a right" on the type of moral justification for interference which can constitute a right, the principle could be made wholly vacuous. It would, for example, be possible to adopt the principle and then assert that some characteristic

or behaviour of some human beings (that they are improvident, or atheists, or Jews, or Negroes) constitutes a moral justification for interfering with their freedom; *any* differences between men could, so far as my argument has yet gone, be treated as a moral justification for interference and so constitute a right, so that the equal right of all men to be free would be compatible with gross inequality. It may well be that the expression "moral" itself imports some restriction on what can constitute a moral justification for interference which would avoid this consequence, but I cannot myself yet show that this is so. It is, on the other hand, clear to me that the moral justification for interference which is to constitute a *right* to interfere (as distinct from merely making it morally good or desirable to interfere) is restricted to certain special conditions and that this is inherent in the meaning of "a right" (unless this is used so loosely that it could be replaced by the other moral expressions mentioned). Claims to interfere with another's freedom based on the general character of the activities interfered with (e.g., the folly or cruelty of "native" practices) or the general character of the parties ("We are Germans. They are Jews.") even when well founded are not matters of moral right or obligation. Submission in such cases even where proper is not *due to* or *owed to* the individuals who interfere; it would be equally proper whoever of the same class of persons interfered. Hence other elements in our moral vocabulary suffice to describe this case, and it is confusing here to talk of rights. We saw in Section II that the types of justification for interference involved in special rights was independent of the character of the action to the performance of which there was a right but depended upon certain previous transactions and relations between individuals (such as promises, consent, authorization, submission to mutual restrictions). Two questions here suggest themselves: (1) On what intelligible principle could these bare forms of promising, consenting, submission to mutual restrictions, be either necessary or sufficient, irrespective of their content, to justify interference with another's freedom? (2) What characteristics have these types of transaction or relationship in common? The answer to both these questions is I think this: if we justify interference on such grounds as we give when we claim a moral right, we are in fact indirectly invoking as our justification the principle that all men have an equal right to be free. For we are in fact saying in the case of promises and consents or authorizations that this claim to interfere with another's freedom is justified because he has, in exercise of his equal right to be free, freely chosen to create this claim; and in the case of mutual restrictions we are in fact saying that this claim to interfere with another's freedom is justified because it is fair; and it is fair because only so will there be an equal distribution of restrictions and so of freedom among this group of men. So in the case of special rights as well as of general rights recognition of them implies the recognition of the equal right of all men to be free.

READING 50

Universal Declaration of Human Rights

United Nations

The Universal Declaration of Human Rights was adopted on December 10, 1948, by the General Assembly of the United Nations at the Palais de Chaillot, Paris.

Whereas Member States have pledged themselves to achieve, in co-operation with the United Nations, the promotion of universal respect for and observance of human rights and fundamental freedoms.

Whereas a common understanding of these rights and freedoms is of the greatest importance for the full realisation of this pledge,

Now, therefore, the General Assembly, Proclaim this Universal Declaration of Human Rights as a common standard of achievement for all peoples and all nations, to the end that every individual and every organ of society, keeping this Declaration constantly in mind, shall strive by teaching and education to promote respect for these rights and freedoms and by progressive measures, national and international, to secure their universal and effective recognition and observance, both among the peoples of Member States themselves and among the peoples of territories under their jurisdiction.

ARTICLE 1

All human beings are born free and equal in dignity and rights. They are endowed with reason and conscience and should act towards one another in a spirit of brotherhood.

ARTICLE 2

1. Everyone is entitled to all the rights and freedoms set forth in this Declaration, without distinction of any kind, such as race, color, sex, language, religion, political or other opinion, national or social origin, property, birth or other status.

2. Furthermore, no distinction shall be made on the basis of the political, jurisdictional or international status of the country or territory to which a person belongs, whether it be independent, trust, non-self-governing or under any other limitation of sovereignty.

ARTICLE 3

Everyone has the right to life, liberty and security of person.

ARTICLE 4

No one shall be held in slavery or servitude; slavery and the slave trade shall be prohibited in all their forms.

ARTICLE 5

No one shall be subjected to torture or to cruel, inhuman or degrading treatment or punishment.

ARTICLE 6

Everyone has the right to recognition everywhere as a person before the law.

ARTICLE 7

All are equal before the law and are entitled without any discrimination to equal protection of the law. All are entitled to equal protection against any discrimination in violation of this Declaration and against any incitement to such discrimination.

ARTICLE 8

Everyone has the right to an effective remedy by the competent national tribunals for acts violating the fundamental rights granted him by the constitution or by law.

ARTICLE 9

No one shall be subjected to arbitrary arrest, detention or exile.

ARTICLE 10

Everyone is entitled in full equality to a fair and public hearing by an independent and impartial tribunal, in the determination of his rights and obligations and of any criminal charge against him.

ARTICLE 11

1. Everyone charged with a penal offence has the right to be presumed innocent until proved guilty according to law in a public trial at which he has had all the guarantees necessary to his defence.

2. No one shall be held guilty of any penal offence on account of any act or omission which did not constitute a penal offence, under national or international law, at the time when it was committed. Nor shall a heavier penalty be imposed than the one that was applicable at the time the penal offence was committed.

ARTICLE 12

No one shall be subjected to arbitrary interference with his privacy, family, home or correspondence, nor to attacks upon his honour and reputation. Everyone has the right to the protection of the law against such interference or attacks.

ARTICLE 13

1. Everyone has the right to freedom of movement and residence within the borders of each State.

2. Everyone has the right to leave any country, including his own, and to return to his country.

ARTICLE 14

1. Everyone has the right to seek and to enjoy in other countries asylum from persecution.

2. This right may not be invoked in the case of prosecutions genuinely arising from nonpolitical crimes or from acts contrary to the purposes and principles of the United Nations.

ARTICLE 15

1. Everyone has the right to a nationality.

2. No one shall be arbitrarily deprived of his nationality nor denied the right to change his nationality.

ARTICLE 16

1. Men and women of full age, without any limitation due to race, nationality or religion, have the right to marry and to found a family. They are entitled to equal rights as to marriage, during marriage and at its dissolution.

2. Marriage shall be entered into only with the free and full consent of the intending spouses.

3. The family is the natural and fundamental group unit of society and is entitled to protection by society and the State.

ARTICLE 17

1. Everyone has the right to own property alone as well as in association with others.

2. No one shall be arbitrarily deprived of his property.

ARTICLE 18

Everyone has the right to freedom of thought, conscience and religion; this right includes freedom to change his religion or belief, and freedom, either alone or in community with others and in public or private, to manifest his religion or belief in teaching, practice, worship and observance.

ARTICLE 19

Everyone has the right to freedom of opinion and expression; this right includes freedom to hold opinions without interference and to seek, receive and impart information and ideas through any media and regardless of frontiers.

ARTICLE 20

1. Everyone has the right to freedom of peaceful assembly and association.

2. No one may be compelled to belong to an association.

ARTICLE 21

1. Everyone has the right to take part in the government of his country, directly or through freely chosen representatives.

2. Everyone has the right of equal access to public service in his country.

3. The will of the people shall be the basis of the authority of government; this will shall be expressed in periodic and genuine elections which shall be by universal and equal suffrage and shall be held by secret vote or by equivalent free voting procedures.

ARTICLE 22

Everyone, as a member of society, has the right to social security and is entitled to realisation, through national effort and international cooperation and in accordance with the organisation and resources of each State, of the economic, social and cultural rights indispensable for his dignity and the free development of his personality.

ARTICLE 23

1. Everyone has the right to work, to free choice of employment, to just and favorable conditions of work and to protection against unemployment.

2. Everyone, without any discrimination, has the right to equal pay for equal work.

3. Everyone who works has the right to just and favorable remuneration ensuring for himself and his family an existence worthy of human dignity, and supplemented, if necessary, by other means of social protection.

4. Everyone has the right to form and to join trade unions for the protection of his interests.

ARTICLE 24

Everyone has the right to rest and leisure, including reasonable limitation of working hours and periodic holidays with pay.

ARTICLE 25

1. Everyone has the right to a standard of living adequate for the health and well-being of himself and of his family, including food, clothing, housing and medical care and necessary social services, and the right to security in the event of unemployment, sickness, disability, widowhood, old age or other lack of livelihood in circumstances beyond his control.

2. Motherhood and childhood are entitled to special care and assistance. All children, whether born in or out of wedlock, shall enjoy the same social protection.

ARTICLE 26

1. Everyone has the right to education. Education shall be free, at least in the elementary and fundamental stages. Elementary education shall be compulsory. Technical and professional education shall be made generally available and higher education shall be equally accessible to all on the basis of merit.

2. Education shall be directed to the full development of the human personality and to the strengthening of respect for human rights and fundamental freedoms. It shall promote understanding, tolerance and friendship among all nations, racial or religious groups, and shall further the activities of the United Nations for the maintenance of peace.

3. Parents have a prior right to choose the kind of education that shall be given to their children.

ARTICLE 27

1. Everyone has the right freely to participate in the cultural life of the community, to enjoy the arts and to share in scientific advancement and its benefits.

2. Everyone has the right to the protection of the moral and material interests resulting from any scientific, literary or artistic production of which he is the author.

ARTICLE 28

Everyone is entitled to a social and international order in which the rights and freedoms set forth in this Declaration can be fully realised.

ARTICLE 29

1. Everyone has duties to the community in which alone the free and full development of his personality is possible.

2. In the exercise of his rights and freedoms, everyone shall be subject only to such limitations as are determined by law solely for the purpose of securing due recognition and respect for the rights and freedoms of others and of meeting the just requirements of morality, public order and the general welfare in a democratic society.

3. These rights and freedoms may in no case be exercised contrary to the purposes and principles of the United Nations.

ARTICLE 30

Nothing in this Declaration may be interpreted as implying for any State, group or person any right to engage in any activity or to perform any act aimed at the destruction of any of the rights and freedoms set forth herein.

END NOTES

Introduction

[1]For a more comprehensive treatment of the nature of a right, see Carl Wellman, *A Theory of Rights* (Rowman and Allanheld, 1985), chapter 2; and James Nickel, *Making Sense of Human Rights*

(University of California Press, 1987), chapter 2. Wellman develops Wesley Hohfeld's fourfold meaning of a right in terms of claim, liberty, power, and immunity.

[2]J. L. Mackie, "Can There Be a Rights-Based Moral Theory?" *Midwest Studies in Philosophy* 3 (1978).

[3]We need to distinguish a "prima facie right" from some acts' being "prima facie the right thing to do." A person may have a prima facie right to be a miser, but it may not be the morally right thing to do.

[4]Ronald Dworkin, *Taking Rights Seriously* (Harvard University Press, 1977), p. 184.

[5]Arthur Danto, "Constructing an Epistemology of Human Rights: A Pseudo Problem?" in *Human Rights,* ed. E. Paul, F. Miller, and J. Paul (New York: Blackwell, 1984), p. 30.

[6]Jacques Maritain, *The Rights of Man* (London: Charles Scribner's, 1944), p. 37.

[7]Jeremy Bentham, "Anarchical Fallacies," in *The Works of Jeremy Bentham,* vol. 2, ed. John Bowring, 1843.

Feinberg

[1]H. B. Acton, "Symposium of 'Rights'," *Proceedings of the Aristotelian Society,* Supplementary Volume 24 (1950): 107–108.

[2]J. L. Austin, "A Plea for Excuses," *Proceedings of the Aristotelian Society,* 57 (1956–57).

[3]G. J. Warnock, "Claims to Knowledge," *Proceedings of the Aristotelian Society,* Supplementary Volume 36 (1962): 21.

[4]This is the important difference between rights and mere claims. It is analogous to the difference between *evidence* of guilt (subject to degrees of cogency) and conviction of guilt (which is all or nothing). One can "have evidence" that is not conclusive just as one can "have a claim" that is not valid. "Prima-facieness" is built into the sense of "claim," but the notion of a "prima-facie right" makes little sense.

[5]J. E. S. Fawcett, "The International Protection of Human Rights," in D. D. Raphael, ed. *Political Theory and the Rights of Man* (Indiana University Press, 1967), pp. 125, 128.

[6]H. J. McCloskey, "Rights," *Philosophical Quarterly* 15 (1965): 118.

Gewirth

[1]Wesley N. Hohfeld, *Fundamental Legal Conceptions* (Yale University Press, 1964), 36ff.

[2]Jeremy Bentham, *A Critical Examination of the Declaration of Rights,* in B. Parekh, ed., *Bentham's Political Thought* (New York: Barnes and Noble, 1973), 271.

[3]Karl Marx, *On the Jewish Question,* in R. C. Tucker, ed., *The Marx-Engels Reader,* 2nd ed. (New York: W. W. Norton, 1978), 43.

Wolgast

[1]Richard Wasserstrom, "Rights, Human Rights, and Racial Discrimination," in *Rights,* ed. David Lyons (Belmont, Calif.: Wadsworth, 1979), p. 48.

[2]David Lyons, "Rights, Claimants, and Beneficiaries," in *Rights,* ed. Lyons, p. 60.

[3]Michel Foucault, *The Birth of the Clinic,* trans. A. M. Sheridan Smith (New York: Random House, 1975), pp. 14, 17.

[4]Samuel Butler, *Erewhon* (New York: Random House, 1927), p. 110.

[5]American Hospital Association, "Statement on a Patient's Bill of Rights," *Hospitals* 4 (February 16, 1973).

[6]Miller-Wohl Co. v. Commissioner of Labor and Industry, State of Montana, 575 F. Supp. 1264 (D. Mont. 1981); California Federal Savings & Loan v. Guerra, 55 U.S. Law Week 4077 (1987).

[7]Linda Krieger and Patricia Cooney, "The Miller-Wohl Controversy: Equal Treatment, Positive Action, and the Meaning of Women's Equality," *Golden Gate University Law Review* 13 (Summer 1983): 566.

[8]James Coleman, *Papers on Non-Marketing Decision-Making,* quoted in Howard Margolis, *Selfishness, Altruism, and Rationality: A Theory of Social Choice* (Cambridge University Press, 1982), p. 1.

[9]Friedman, *Free to Choose,* pp. 13–14, 27.

[10]Plato, *Republic,* trans. Paul Shorey, in *The Collected Dialogues of Plato,* ed. Edith Hamilton and Huntington Cairns (Princeton University Press, 1961), V, 341c–342d.

[11]Engelhardt, "Rights and Responsibilities of Patients and Physicians," p. 133.

[12]Ludwig Wittgenstein, *The Blue and Brown Books* (New York: Harper, 1958), p. 143, and *On Certainty,* ed. G. E. M. Anscombe and G. H. von Wright, trans. Denis Paul and Anscombe (New York: Harper & Row, 1969), 189.

[13]Wittgenstein, *On Certainty,* 471.

Hart

[1]Here and subsequently I use "interfere with another's freedom," "limit another's freedom," "determine how another shall act," to mean either the use of coercion or demanding that a person shall do or not do some action. The connection between these two types of "interference" is too complex for discussion here; I think it is enough for present purposes to point out that having a justification for demanding that a person shall or shall not do some action is a necessary though not a sufficient condition for justifying coercion.

[2]I write "duties" here because one factor obscuring the nature of a right is the philosophical use of "duty" and "obligation" for all cases where there are moral reasons for saying an action ought to be done or not done. In fact "duty," "obligation," "right," and "good" come from different segments of morality, concern different types of conduct, and make different types of moral criticism or evaluation. Most important are the points (1) that obligations may be voluntarily incurred or created, (2) that they are *owed* to special persons (who have rights), (3) that they do not arise out of the character of the actions which are obligatory but out of the relationship of the parties. Language roughly though not consistently confines the use of "having an obligation" to such cases.

[3]In speech the difference between general and special rights is often marked by stressing the pronoun where a special right is claimed or where the special right is denied. "You have no right to stop him reading that book" refers to the reader's general right. "*You* have no right to stop him reading that book" denies that the person addressed has a special right to interfere though others may have.

[4]Strictly, in the assertion of a general right both the *right* to forbearance from coercion and the *liberty* to do the specified action are asserted, the first in the face of actual or threatened coercion, the second as an objection to an actual or anticipated demand that the action should not be done. The first has as its correlative an obligation upon everyone to forbear from coercion. The second, the absence in any one of a justification for such a demand.

CHAPTER VIII

National Sovereignty, Patriotism, and International Government

If anarchy is the first challenge to government in general, driving the State to justify itself, anarchy poses an ultimate challenge on the global scene among the collection of governments. Even as each government is threatened internally by destruction when law, order, and reliable expectations are absent, the world itself is threatened by lawlessness as each nation tends to act on the global scene in a manner analogous to the individual in a state of anarchy (Hobbes's state of nature, where "life is solitary, poor, nasty, brutish and short"). Consider nations on the international playing field. Any nation, so long as it is strong enough, can make a promise when it is advantageous to do so and break it with impunity when it is advantageous to do so. Treaties are essentially unenforceable, and laws without binding sanctions are mere documents of convenience. Essentially, Might makes Right! And War, whether cold or hot, the constant companion of every corporate body. Whereas the State can enforce its laws and treaties among its members, no international entity exists that can enforce laws and treaties among its members. In international affairs we are in a Hobbesian state of nature, a state of war (a "war of all against all"), not necessarily hot, but where the threat of aggression and violence is imminent.

The history of Western Europe in the nineteenth and twentieth centuries amply illustrates this thesis, that nations break treaties and aggress others when they perceive it is in their interest to do so. For example, Germany invaded France in 1870, seeking to add territory to its state; Germany and its allies attacked Belgium and France in 1914 because of the absence of an arbiter of disputes; and Germany broke the Treaty of Versailles and invaded Czechoslovakia in 1939 and,

thereafter, Poland, Belgium, and France, and it broke the Ribbentrop Treaty, invading Russia, in 1941, doing so in the name of *lebensraum,* the need for more land. When we look at the contemporary situation, the ethnic violence in Kosovo and Bosnia, the struggles in Israel between Palestinians and Israelis, Basques separatism in Spain, the terrorism and internecine violence in Northern Ireland, and the Island of Timor, the struggles in Chechnya—all instances of nationalism, demanding a separate state.

It is obvious that a global judicial law creating and enforcing institutions is desirable to promote peace, ensure compliance with contracts and treaties, and prevent international anarchy by promoting orderly processes, international morality, and reliable expectations. A universal set of laws with fixed penalties that is impartially enforced by a central policelike agency could be a catalyst for peace, the protection of human rights, and environmental wholeness. This last function is a modern one, having to do with the fact that air and water pollution tend to spread, impervious to political boundaries. For example, contaminated air from the nuclear explosion at Chernobyl wafted westward to Sweden and Switzerland. Greenhouse gases that originate in specific locales have global effects, changing climate patterns throughout the world. Recent international conferences on global warming and environmental policy, such as the Kyoto Accords in 1998 which failed to reach universal agreements with strong sanctions, demonstrate the need for a global entity with authority and power to enforce international treaties.

Add to these factors the facts of an increasingly global economy, international transportation and communication (from the airplane to the Internet), and the growing global consciousness (CNN and other news networks beam the latest Asian uprising or African coup into our living rooms, sometimes before our government is aware of it). Combine all of these factors, and we get a picture of the growing pressures for the eroding of national boundaries in favor of Globalism, an International Government.

A *prima facie* case exists for International Government or, at least, for a sovereign entity to enforce international laws, to safeguard the rights of individuals and individual nations against unjust incursions and exploitation. But such a cosmopolitan institution threatens the very existence of the traditional nation-state, so much a part of our world since the eighteenth century. If our ultimate allegiance is to a super global State, then what is the role of the nation? Does it have moral legitimacy?

Many philosophers would say, No, the nation lacks any ultimate moral justification. It is, at best, a temporary and necessary evil, organizing people in restricted manners until the principle of universal humanity can take hold on our collective consciousness. The principle of special allegiance to the individual state is no more justified than giving special privilege to one's race or gender or ethnic group. We must transcend this immoral *nationalism,* with its atavistic rituals, its narrow patriotism, and replace it with a universal loyalty. There is a duty to become moral *cosmopolitans,* committed to the well-being and rights of every human being, regardless of country of origin. There are practical obstacles to overcome, as well as moral ones, so that we cannot immediately move into an international allegiance, but this should be our goal. Moral cosmopolitanism, treating each person as a moral equal, leads to institutional cosmopolitanism. The benefits of World Government are greater prospects of peace, enforcement of treaties and contracts, fluid trade and economic relations, and the allocation of resources according to need and desert, rather than according to purely the luck of being born in a resource-rich country or family.

On the other hand, some philosophers reject cosmopolitanism and argue for the legitimacy of the nation-state. For moral and practical reasons the nation-state is the legitimate center of political authority and obligation. These philosophers point out that people need to identify with particular groups, cultures, and geographical places in order to lead meaningful lives. These identifications contribute to our personal identity, constituting who we are. We may divide these nationalists into two groups: *hard* nationalists and *soft* nationalists. Hard nationalists hold that the nation is al-

together justified as the ultimate locus of political obligation, so that internationalism is simply confused or immoral. Even as we have a natural duty to prefer our family to other people and strangers, we have a duty to prefer our nation, to be patriotic. Nationalistic concerns override all other loyalties or obligations. Soft nationalists maintain that although we do have some obligations to people everywhere and that we need some adjudicating overseer to enforce treaties and prevent war, these obligations and this need do not completely override the need for nation-states. They agree with hard nationalists that we do have special obligations to our own country, but just as the needs or rights of others may sometimes override our familial obligations, our nationalistic obligations may be overridden at times by obligations to humankind at large or to people not citizens of our nation.

Soft nationalists are open to the possibility of World Government, recognizing the ideals thereby attained, but they also are troubled by the problems of ensuring local autonomy and preventing unwieldy bureaucracy and tyranny. However, suppose we can attain an efficient World Government, a sort of United Nations with authority and power. Then, the soft nationalists maintain, nations will still have local jurisdiction, much as the individual states do within the United States. We will still have special obligations to people in our own states, relating to them in special moral ways, while, at the same time, sharing our resources with people throughout the world.

In Reading 51, by the Russian count and writer Leo Tolstoy, patriotism is seen as a kind of corporate insanity, the very antithesis of reasoned deliberation and sober living. Tolstoy urges us to think globally, to recognize the brotherhood of all people.

In Reading 52, Alasdair MacIntyre argues that the idea of patriotism has meaning within a communal understanding of morality, which it lacks in contemporary liberalism. MacIntyre points out that although the morality of patriotism may endanger the objectivity of ethics, liberal morality has the problem of dislocating morality from those features of life that are necessary for the full flourishing of the moral individual and the moral life.

The basic arguments for a World Government are set forth in Reading 53 by the French philosopher Jacques Maritain, who outlines the main idea and considers objections. The basic alternatives, given our global economic interdependence, are world government or anarchy, which leads to war, including an annihilating nuclear war. If we are to resolve national conflicts of interest peacefully, we will need an impartial arbiter to adjudicate our differences, and this arbiter must have authority to carry out its will. As such, nation-states must give up their sovereignty (the sole power to govern their internal and external affairs), while still possessing autonomy (their ability to determine their internal relations by use of rational discourse). Maritain notes that natural law philosophers like Thomas Aquinas and the leaders of the Roman Catholic Church have always endorsed World Government, based on our common humanity. Maritain defends a secular version of natural law, based on freedom and reason, which will, he argues, eventually lead humankind to choose international government in place of the outworn nation-state.

In Reading 54, Avishai Margalit and Joseph Raz defend the idea of the nation-state by setting forth the necessary criteria, a morally sophisticated nationalism. Reading 55, by Brian Barry, defends a very different, hypothetical contractarian view of international relations, based on liberal principles of justice, such as equality of interests, responsibility, priority of vital needs, and mutual advantage, in developing a cosmopolitan theory of justice. In Reading 56, Allen Buchanan sets forth the conditions for morally justified secession of nations from larger ruling states. In Reading 57, Andrew Valls argues that, from the perspective of just war theory, terrorism can be sometimes justified.

READING 51

Against the Insane Superstition of Patriotism

Leo Tolstoy

Leo Nicolayevich Tolstoy (1828–1910) was born to a Russian noble family and became one of the greatest Russian writers of all time. Among his most famous novels are *War and Peace* and *Anna Karenina*. He was a deeply spiritual, Christian anarchist, whose religious writings, especially *What I Believe*, were condemned by the Russian Orthodox Church as heretical and were banned. Tolstoy was excommunicated in 1901. During the last years of his life, he liberated his peasants, gave them most of his possessions, and lived like a peasant himself.

In this little known essay, written in the 1890s, Tolstoy condemns the idea of patriotism as a superstitious and dangerous emotion, tending to produce war and xenophobic behavior. It falsely supposes that one's own nation is superior to all others, so that it is always justified in settling grievances violently by use of force. But moral people, especially Christians who follow Christ in his glorification of peace, should eschew such folly, which promises only death and destruction. Instead they should commit themselves to universal peace and brotherhood. Tolstoy begins this essay by recounting two contemporary celebrations of the Franco-Russian Alliance in Kronstadt, Russia, and Toulon, France, both aimed at cementing their alliance and conducting hostile maneuvers against Germany. Tolstoy comments that such mass hysteria and misplaced loyalty are with the assistance of the media and educational system promoted by the leaders of nations in order to ensure that canon fodder, the common people, is available for their future self-aggrandizing adventures. But a moral conscience must condemn such evil and work for a cosmopolitan outlook, wherein all human life is viewed as sacred.

This reading is taken from *Leo Tolstoy's Writings on Civil Disobedience and Nonviolence*, trans. Aylmer Maude (London: Peter Owens Co., 1899).

The Franco-Russian festivities which took place in October, 1894, in France made me, and others, no doubt, as well, first amused, then astonished, then indignant—feelings which I wished to express in a short article.

But while studying further the chief causes of this strange phenomenon, I arrived at the reflections which I here offer to the reader.

The Russian and French peoples have been living for many centuries with a knowledge of each other—entering sometimes into friendly, more often, unfortunately, into very unfriendly, relations at the instigation of their respective governments—when suddenly, because two years ago a French squadron came to Kronstadt, and its officers, having landed, eaten much, and drunk a variety of wine in various places, heard and made many false and foolish speeches; and because last year a Russian squadron arrived at Toulon, and its officers, having gone to Paris and there eaten and drunk copiously, heard and made a still greater number of silly and untruthful speeches—it came to pass that not only those who ate, drank, and spoke, but every one who was present, and even those who merely heard or read in the papers of these proceedings—all these millions of French and Russians—imagined suddenly that in some especial fashion they were enamored of each other; that is, that all the French love all the Russians, and all the Russians all the French.

These sentiments were expressed in France last October in the most unheard-of ways.

The following description of these proceedings appeared in the *Village Review,* a paper which collects its information from the daily press:—

"When the French and Russian squadrons met they greeted each other with salvos of artillery, and with ardent and enthusiastic cries of 'Hurrah!' 'Long live Russia!' 'Long live France!'

"To all this uproar the naval bands (there were orchestras also on most of the hired steamboats) contributed, the Russian playing 'God save the Tsar,' and the French the 'Marseillaise,' the public upon the steamboats waving their hats, flags, handkerchiefs, and nosegays. Many barges were loaded entirely with men and women of the working-class with their children, waving nosegays and shouting 'Long live Russia!' with all their might. Our sailors, in view of such national enthusiasm, could not restrain their tears.

"In the harbor all the French men-of-war present were ranged in two divisions, and our fleet passed between them, the admiral's vessel leading. A splendid moment was approaching.

"A salute of fifteen guns was fired from the Russian flagship in honor of the French fleet, and the French flagship replied with thirty. The Russian National Hymn pealed from the French lines; French sailors mounted their masts and rigging; vociferations of welcome poured uninterruptedly from both fleets, and from the surrounding vessels. The sailors waved their caps, the spectators their hats and handkerchiefs, in honor of the beloved guests. From all sides, sea and shore, thundered the universal shout, 'Long live Russia!' 'Long live France!'

"According to the custom in naval visits, Admiral Avellan and the officers of his staff came on shore in order to pay their respects to the local authorities.

"At the landing-stage they were met by the French naval staff and the senior officials of the port of Toulon.

"Friendly greetings followed, accompanied by the thunder of artillery and the pealing of bells. The naval band played the Russian National Hymn, 'God save the Tsar,' which was received with a roar from the spectators of 'Long live the Tsar!' 'Long live Russia!'

"The shouting swelled into one mighty din, which drowned the music and even the cannonade. Those present declare that the enthusiasm of the huge crowd of people attained at that moment its utmost height, and that it would be impossible to express in words the feelings which overflowed the hearts of all upon the scene.

"Admiral Avellan, with uncovered head, and accompanied by the French and Russian officers, then drove to the naval administration buildings, where he was received by the French Minister of Marine.

"In welcoming the admiral, the minister said, 'Kronstadt and Toulon have severally witnessed the sympathy which exists between the French and the Russian peoples. Everywhere you will be received as the most welcome of friends.'

"'Our government and all France greet you and your comrades on your arrival as the representatives of a great and honorable nation.'

"The admiral replied that he was unable to find language to express his feelings. 'The Russian fleet, and all Russia,' he said, 'will be grateful to you for this reception.'

"After some further speeches, the admiral again, in taking leave of the minister, thanked him for his reception, and added, 'I cannot leave you without pronouncing the words which are written in the hearts of every Russian: 'Long live France!' " (*Siel'sky Vyestnik,* 1893, No. 41.)

Such was the reception at Toulon. In Paris the welcome and the festivities were still more extraordinary.

The following is a description, taken from the papers, of the reception in Paris:—

"All eyes are directed toward the Boulevard des Italiens, whence the Russian sailors are expected to emerge. At length, far away, the roar of a whole hurricane of shouts and cheers is heard. The roar grows louder, more distinct. The hurricane is evidently approaching. The crowd surges in the Place. The police press forward to clear the route to the Cercle Militaire, but the task is not easy. Among the spectators the pushing and scrambling baffles description. . . . At last the head of the cortège appears in the Place. At once arises a deafening shout of 'Vive la Russie! Vivent les Russes!'

"All heads are uncovered; spectators fill the windows and balconies, they even cover the housetops, waving handkerchiefs, flags, hats, cheering enthusiastically, and flinging clouds of tricolor cockades from the upper windows. A sea of handkerchiefs, hats, and flags waves over the heads of the crowd below; a hundred thousand voices shout frantically, 'Vive la Russie! Vivent les Russes;' the throng make wild efforts to catch a glimpse of the dear guests, and try in every possible way to express their enthusiasm."

Another correspondent writes that the rapture of the crowd was like a delirium. A Russian journalist who was in Paris at the time thus describes the entry of the Russian marines:—

"It may truthfully be said that this event is of universal importance, astounding, sufficiently touching to produce tears, an elevating influence on the soul, making it throb with *that love which sees in men brothers, which hates blood, and violence, and the snatching of children from a beloved mother*. I have been in a kind of torpor for the last few hours. It seemed almost overpoweringly strange to stand in the terminus of the Lyons Railway, amid the representatives of the French government, in their uniforms embroidered with gold, amongst the municipal authorities in full dress, and to hear cries of 'Vive la Russie!' 'Vive le Tsar!' and our national anthem played again and again.

"Where am I? I reflected. What has happened? What magic current has united all these feelings, these aspirations, into one stream? Is not this the sensible presence of the God of love and of fraternity, the presence of the loftiest ideal descending in His supremest moments upon man?

"My soul is so full of something beautiful, pure, and elevated that my pen is unable to express it. Words are weak in comparison with what I saw and felt. It was not rapture, the word is too commonplace; it was better than rapture. More picturesque, deeper, happier, more various. It is impossible to describe what took place at the Cercle Militaire when Admiral Avellan appeared on the balcony of the second story. Words here are of no avail. During the 'Te Deum,' while the choir in the church was singing, 'O Lord, save Thy people,' through the open door were blown the triumphal strains of the 'Marseillaise,' played by the brass bands in the street.

"It produced an astounding, an inexpressible impression." (*Novoye Vremya* (New Time), Oct. 1893.) . . .

"We love each other; we love peace. Kronstadt-Toulon!" What more can be said, especially to the sound of glorious music, performing at one and the same time two national anthems—one glorifying the Tsar and praying for him all possible good fortune, the other cursing all tsars and promising them destruction?

Those that expressed their sentiments of love especially well on these occasions received orders and rewards. Others, either for the same reason or from the exuberance of the feelings of the givers, were presented with articles of the strangest and most unexpected kind. The French fleet presented the Tsar with a sort of golden book in which, it seems, nothing was written—or, at least, nothing of any concern; and the Russian admiral received an aluminium plow covered with flowers, and many other trifles equally astonishing.

Moreover, all these strange acts were accompanied by still stranger religious ceremonies and public services such as one might suppose Frenchmen had long since become unaccustomed to.

Since the time of the Concordat scarcely so many prayers can have been offered as during this short period. All the French suddenly became extraordinarily religious, and carefully deposited in the rooms of the Russian mariners the very images which a short time previously they had as carefully removed from their schools as harmful tools of superstition; and they said prayers incessantly. The cardinals and bishops everywhere enjoined devotions, and themselves offered some of the strangest of prayers. Thus a bishop at Toulon, at the launch of a certain ironclad, addressed the God of Peace, letting it, however, at the same time be felt that he could communicate as readily, if the necessity arose, with the God of War. . . .

The canon of Arrare conveyed to the most reverend protopresbyter of the court clergy the assurance that a deep affection toward Russia, his imperial majesty the Emperor Alexander III, and all the imperial family, exists in the hearts of all the French cardinals and bishops, and that the French and Russian clergy profess almost a similar faith, and alike worship the Holy Virgin. To this the most reverend protopresbyter replied that the prayers of the French clergy for the imperial family were joyously echoed by the hearts of all the Russian people, lovingly attached to the Tsar, and that as the Russian nation also worships the Holy Virgin, France may count upon it in life and death. The same kind of messages were sent by various generals, telegraph clerks, and dealers in groceries.

Every one sent congratulations to every one else, and thanked some one for something.

The excitement was so great that some extraordinary things were done; and yet no one remarked their strangeness, but on the contrary every one approved of them, was charmed with them, and as if afraid of being left behind, made haste to accomplish something of a similar kind in order not to be outdone by the rest.

If at times protests, pronounced or even written and printed, against this madness made their appearance, proving its unreasonableness, they were either hushed up or concealed.

Not to mention the millions of working-days spent in these festivities; the widespread drunkenness of all who took part in them, involving even those in command; not to speak of the senselessness of the speeches which were made,—the most insane and ruthless deeds were committed, and no one paid them any attention.

For instance, several score of people were crushed to death, and no one found it necessary to record the fact.

One correspondent wrote that he had been informed at a ball that there was scarcely a woman in Paris who would not have been ready to forget her duties to satisfy the desire of any of the Russian sailors.

And all this passed unremarked as something quite in the order of things. There were also cases of unmistakable insanity brought about by the excitement.

Thus one woman, having put on a dress composed of the colors of the Franco-Russian flags, awaited on a bridge the arrival of the Russian sailors, and shouting "Vive la Russie," threw herself into the river, and was drowned.

In general the women on all these occasions played the leading part, and even directed the men. Besides the throwing of flowers and various little ribbons and the presenting of gifts and addresses, the French women in the streets threw themselves into the arms of the Russian sailors and kissed them.

Some women brought their children, for some reason or other, to be kissed, and when the Russian sailors had granted this request, all present were transported with joy and shed tears.

This strange excitement was so contagious that, as one correspondent relates, a Russian sailor who appeared to be in perfect health, after having witnessed these exciting scenes for a fortnight, jumped overboard in the middle of the day, and swam about, crying "Long live France." When pulled out of the water, and questioned as to his conduct, he replied that he had vowed to swim round his ship in honor of France.

Thus the unthwarted excitement grew and grew, like a ball of snow, and finally attained such dimensions that not alone those on the spot, or merely nervously predisposed persons, but strong, healthy men were affected by the general strain and were betrayed into an abnormal condition of mind.

I remember even that whilst reading distractedly a description of these festivities, I was suddenly overcome by strong emotion, and was almost on the verge of tears, having to check with an effort this expression of my feelings.

A professor of psychiatry, Sikorsky by name, not long ago described in the *Kief University Review* what he calls the psychopathic epidemic of Malevanshchina, which he studied in the district of Vasilkof. The essence of this epidemic, according to Sikorsky, was that the peasants of certain villages, under the influence of their leader, Malevanni, became convinced that the end of the world was at hand; in consequence of which they changed their mode of life, began to dispose of their property, to wear gay clothing, to eat and drink of the best, and ceased to work. The professor considered this condition abnormal. He says:

"Their remarkable good humor often attained to exaltation, a condition of gaiety lacking all external motives. They were sentimentally inclined, polite to excess, talkative, excitable, tears of happiness being readily summoned to their eyes, and disappearing without leaving a trace. They sold the necessities of life in order to buy parasols, silk handkerchiefs, and similar articles, which, however, they only wore as ornaments. They ate a great quantity of sweets. Their condition of mind was always joyous, they led a perfectly idle life, visiting one another and walking about together. . . . When chided for the insanity of their conduct and their idleness, they replied invariably with the same phrase: 'If it pleases me, I will work; if it does not, why compel myself to?'"

The learned professor regards the condition of these people as a well-defined psychopathic epidemic, and in advising the government to adopt measures to prevent its extension, concludes, "Malevanshchina is the cry of a sick population, a prayer for deliverance from drunkenness, and for improved educational and sanitary conditions."

But if malevanshchina is the cry of a sick population for deliverance from inebriety and from pernicious social conditions, what a terrible clamor of a sick people, and what a petition for a rescue from the effects of wine and of a false social existence, is this new disease which appeared in Paris with such fearful suddenness, infecting the greater part of the urban population of France, and almost the entire governmental, privileged, and civilized classes of Russia?

But if we admit that danger exists in the psychical conditions of malevanshchina, and that the government did well in following the professor's advice, by confining some of the leaders of the malevanshchina in asylums and monasteries, and by banishing others into distant places; how much more dangerous must we consider this new epidemic which has appeared in Toulon and Paris, and spread thence throughout Russia and France, and how much more needful is it that society—if the government refuse to interfere—should take decisive measures to prevent the epidemic from spreading?

The analogy between the two diseases is complete. The same remarkable good humor, passing into a vague and joyous ecstasy, the same sentimental, exaggerated politeness, loquacity, emotional weeping, without reason for its commencement or cessation, the same festal mood, the same promenading and paying calls, the same wearing of gorgeous clothes and fancy for choice food, the same misty and senseless speeches, the same indolence, the same singing and music, the same direction on the part of the women, the same clownish state of *attitudes passionnées,* which Sikorsky observed, and which corresponds, as I understand it, with the various unnatural physical attitudes adopted by people during triumphal receptions, acclamations, and after-dinner speeches.

The resemblance is absolute. The difference, an enormous one for the society in which these things take place, is merely that in one case it is the madness of a few scores of poor peaceful country people who, living on their own small earnings, cannot do any violence to their neighbors, and infect others only by personal and vocal communication of their condition; whereas in the other case it is the madness of millions of people who possess immense sums of money and means of violence—rifles, cannon, fortresses, ironclads, melinite, dynamite—and having, moreover, at their disposal the most effective means for communicating their insanity: the post, telegraph, telephone, the entire press, and every class of magazine, which print the infection with the utmost haste, and distribute it throughout the world.

Another difference is that the former not only remain sober, but abstain from all intoxicating drinks, while the latter are in a constant state of semi-drunkenness which they do their best to foster.

Hence for the society in which such epidemics take place, the difference between that at Kief, when, according to Sikorsky, no violence nor manslaughter was recorded, and that of Paris, where in one procession more than twenty women were crushed to death, is equivalent to that between the falling of a small piece of smoldering coal from the fireplace upon the floor, and a fire which has already obtained possession of the floors and walls of the house.

At its worst the result of the epidemic at Kief will be that the peasants of a millionth part of Russia may spend the earnings of their own labor, and be unable to meet the government taxes; but the consequences of the Paris-Toulon epidemic, which has affected people who have great power, immense sums of money, weapons of violence, and means for the propagation of their insanity, may and must be terrible. . . .

In many of the articles describing the festivities a naïve satisfaction is clearly expressed that no one during them alluded to what it was determined, by silent consent, to hide from everybody, and that only one incautious fellow, who was immediately removed by the police, voiced what all had in their minds by shouting, *"A bas l'Allemagne!"*—Down with Germany!

In the same way children are often so delighted at being able to conceal an escapade that their very high spirits betray them.

Why, indeed, be so glad that no one said anything about war, if the subject were not uppermost in our minds?

No one is thinking of war; only milliards are being spent upon preparations for it, and millions of men are under arms in France and Russia.

"But all this is done to insure peace." . . .

But if such be the case, why are the military advantages of a Franco-Russian alliance in the event of a war with Germany not only explained in every paper and magazine published for a so-called educated people, but also in the *Village Messenger,* a paper published for the people by the Russian government? Why is it inculcated to this unfortunate people, cheated by its own government, that "to be in friendly relations with France is profitable to Russia, because if, unexpectedly, the before-mentioned states (Germany, Austria, and Italy) made up their minds to declare war with Russia, then though with God's help she might be able to withstand them by herself, and defeat even so considerable an alliance, the feat would not be an easy one, and great sacrifices and losses would be entailed by success." (*Siel'sky Viestnik,* 1893, No. 43.)

And why in all French schools is history taught from the primer of M. Lavisse (twenty-first edition, 1889,) in which the following is inserted:—

"Since the insurrection of the Commune was put down France has had no further troubles. The day following the war she again resumed work. She paid Germany without difficulty the enormous war indemnity of five milliards.

"But France lost her military renown during the war of 1870. She lost part of her territory. More than fifteen thousand inhabitants of our departments of the Upper Rhine, Lower Rhine, and the Moselle who were good Frenchmen have been compelled to become Germans. But they are not resigned to their fate. They detest Germany; they continue to hope that they may once more be Frenchmen.

"But Germany appreciates its victory, and it is a great country, all the inhabitants of which sincerely love their fatherland, and whose soldiers are brave and well disciplined. In order to recover from Germany what she took from us we must be good citizens and soldiers. It is to make you good soldiers that your teachers instruct you in the history of France.

"The history of France proves that in our country the sons have always avenged the disasters of their fathers.

"Frenchmen in the time of Charles VII, avenged the defeat of their fathers at Crécy, at Poitiers, at Agincourt.

"It is for you, boys being educated in our schools, to avenge the defeat of your fathers at Sedan and at Metz.

"It is your duty—the great duty of your life. You must ever bear that in mind."

At the foot of the page is a series of questions upon the preceding paragraphs. The questions are the following:—

"What has France lost by losing part of her territory?"

"How many Frenchmen have become Germans by the loss of this territory?"

"Do these Frenchmen love Germany?"

"What must we do to recover some day what Germany has taken from us?"

In addition to these there are certain "Reflections on Book VII," where it is said that "the children of France must not forget her defeat of 1870;" that they must bear on their hearts "the burden of this remembrance," but that "this memory must not discourage them, on the contrary, it must excite their courage." . . .

"But nothing of the kind exists; we have no bellicose intentions," it is replied. "All that has happened is the expression of mutual sympathy between two nations. What can be amiss in the triumphal and honorable reception of the representatives of a friendly nation by the representatives of another nation? What can be wrong in this, even if we admit that the alliance is significant of a protection from a dangerous neighbor who threatens Europe with war?"

It is wrong, because it is false—a most evident and insolent falsehood, inexcusable, iniquitous.

It is false, this suddenly begotten love of Russians for French and French for Russians. And it is false, this insinuation of our dislike to the Germans, and our distrust of them. And more false still is it that the aim of all these indecent and insane orgies is supposed to be the preservation of the peace of Europe.

We are all aware that we neither felt before, nor have felt since, any special love for the French, or any animosity toward the Germans.

We are told that Germany has projects against Russia, that the Triple Alliance threatens to destroy our peace and that of Europe, and that our alliance with France will secure an equal balance of power and be a guarantee of peace. But the assertion is so manifestly stupid that I am ashamed to refute it seriously. For this to be so—that is, for the alliance to guarantee peace— it would be necessary to make the Powers mathematically equal. If the preponderance were on the side of the Franco-Russian alliance, the danger would be the same, or even greater, because if Wilhelm, who is at the head of the Triple Alliance, is a menace to peace, France, who cannot be reconciled to the loss of her provinces, would be a still greater menace. The Triple Alliance was called an alliance of peace, whereas for us it proved an alliance of war. Just so now the Franco-Russian alliance can only be viewed truly as an alliance for war.

Moreover, if peace depends upon an even balance of power, how are those units to be defined between which the balance is to be established?

England asserts that the Franco-Russian alliance is a menace to her security, which necessitates a new alliance on her part. And into precisely how many units is Europe to be divided that this even balance may be attained?

Indeed, if there be such a necessity for equilibrium, then in every society of men a man stronger than his fellows is already dangerous, and the rest must join defensive alliances in order to resist him.

It is asked, "What is wrong in France and Russia expressing their mutual sympathies for the preservation of peace?" The expression is wrong because it is false, and a falsehood once pronounced never ends harmlessly.

The devil was a murderer and the father of lies. Falsehood always leads to murder: and most of all in such a case as this.

Just what is now taking place occurred before our last Turkish war, when a sudden love on our part was supposed to have been awakened toward certain

Slavonic brethren none had heard of for centuries; though French, Germans, and English always have been, and are, incomparably nearer and dearer to us than a few Bulgarians, Servians, or Montenegrins. And on that occasion just the same enthusiasm, receptions, and solemnities were to be observed, blown into existence by men like Aksakof and Katkof, who are already mentioned in Paris as model patriots. Then, as now, the suddenly begotten love of Russ for Slav was only a thing of words.

Then in Moscow as now in Paris, when the affair began, people ate, drank, talked nonsense to one another, were much affected by their noble feelings, spoke of union and of peace, passing over in silence the main business—the project against Turkey.

The press goaded on the excitement, and by degrees the government took a hand in the game. Servia revolted. Diplomatic notes began to circulate and semiofficial articles to appear. The press lied, invented, and fumed more and more, and in the end Alexander II, who really did not desire war, was obliged to consent to it; and what we know took place, the loss of hundreds of thousands of innocent men, and the brutalizing and befooling of millions.

What took place at Paris and Toulon, and has since been fomented by the press, is evidently leading to a like or a worse calamity.

At first, in the same manner, to the strains of the "Marseillaise" and "God save the Tsar," certain generals and ministers drink to France and Russia in honor of various regiments and fleets; the press publishes its falsehoods; idle crowds of wealthy people, not knowing how to apply their strength and time, chatter patriotic speeches, stirring up animosity against Germany; and in the end, however peaceful Alexander III may be, circumstances will so combine that he will be unable to avoid war, which will be demanded by all who surround him, by the press, and, as always seems in such cases, by the entire public opinion of the nation. And before we can look round, the usual ominous absurd proclamation will appear in the papers:—

"We, by God's grace, the autocratic great Emperor of all Russia, King of Poland, Grand Duke of Finland, etc., etc., proclaim to all our true subjects, that, for the welfare of these our beloved subjects, bequeathed by God into our care, we have found it our duty before God to send them to slaughter. God be with us."

The bells will peal, long-haired men will dress in golden sacks and pray for successful slaughter. And the old story will begin again, the awful customary acts.

The editors of the daily press, happy in the receipt of an increased income, will begin virulently to stir men up to hatred and manslaughter in the name of patriotism. Manufacturers, merchants, contractors for military stores will hurry joyously about their business, in the hope of double receipts.

All sorts of government functionaries will buzz about, foreseeing a possibility of purloining something more than usual. The military authorities will hurry hither and thither, drawing double pay and rations, and with the expectation of receiving for the slaughter of other men various silly little ornaments which they so highly prize, as ribbons, crosses, orders, and stars. Idle ladies and gentlemen will make a great fuss, entering their names in advance for the Red Cross Society, and ready to bind up the wounds of those whom their husbands and brothers will mutilate, and they will imagine that in so doing they are performing a most Christian work.

And, smothering despair within their souls by songs, licentiousness, and wine, men will trail along, torn from peaceful labor, from their wives, mothers, and children,—hundreds of thousands of simpleminded, good-natured men with murderous weapons in their hands—anywhere they may be driven.

They will march, freeze, hunger, suffer sickness, and die from it, or finally come to some place where they will be slain by thousands, or kill thousands themselves with no reason—men whom they have never seen before, and who neither have done nor could do them any mischief.

And when the number of sick, wounded, and killed becomes so great that there are not hands enough left to pick them up, and when the air is so infected with the putrefying scent of the "food for cannon" that even the authorities find it disagreeable, a truce will be made, the wounded will be picked up anyhow, the sick will be brought in and huddled together in heaps, the killed will be covered with earth and lime, and once more all the crowd of deluded men will be led on and on till those who have devised the project weary of it, or till those who thought to find it profitable receive their spoil.

And so once more men will be made savage, fierce, and brutal, and love will wane in the world, and the Christianizing of mankind, which has already begun, will lapse for scores and hundreds of years. And so once more the men who reaped profit from it all will assert with assurance that since there has been a war there must needs have been one, and that other wars must follow, and they will again prepare future generations for a continuance of slaughter, depraving them from their childhood. . . .

About four years ago the first swallow of this Toulon spring, a well-known French agitator for a war with Germany, came to Russia to prepare the way for the Franco-Russian alliance, and paid a visit to us in the country. He came to us when we were all engaged cutting the hay crop, and when we had come in to lunch and made our guest's acquaintance, he began at once to tell us how he had fought, been taken prisoner, made his escape, and finally pledged himself as a patriot—a fact of which he was evidently proud—never to cease agitating for a war with Germany until the boundaries and glory of France had been reëstablished.

All our guest's arguments as to the necessity of an alliance of France with Russia in order to reconstruct the former boundary, power, and glory of his country, and to assure our security against the evil intentions of Germany, had no success in our circle.

To his arguments that France could never settle down until she had recaptured her lost provinces, we replied that neither could Russia be at rest till she had been avenged for Jena, and that if the *revanche* of France should happen to be successful, Germany in her turn would desire revenge, and so on without end.

To his arguments that it was the duty of France to recover the sons that had been snatched from her, we replied that the condition of the majority of the working population of Alsace-Lorraine under the rule of Germany had probably suffered no change for the worse since the days when it was ruled by France, and the fact that some of the Alsatians preferred to be registered as Frenchmen and not as Germans, and that he, our guest, wished to reëstablish the fame of the French arms, was no reason to renew the awful calamities which a war would cause, or even to sacrifice a single human life.

To his arguments that it was very well for us to talk like that, who had never endured what France had, and that we would speak very differently if the Baltic provinces, or Poland, were to be taken from us, we replied that, even from the imperial standpoint, the loss of the Baltic provinces or Poland could in no wise be considered as a calamity, but rather as an advantage, as it would decrease the necessity of armed forces and State expenses; and that from the Christian point of view one can never admit the justice of war, as war demands murder; while Christianity not only prohibits all killing, but demands of us the betterment of all men, regarding all men as brothers, without distinction of nationalities.

A Christian nation, we said, which engages in war, ought, in order to be logical, not only to take down the cross from its church steeples, turn the churches to some other use, give the clergy other duties, having first prohibited the preaching of the Gospel, but also ought to abandon all the requirements of morality which flow from the Christian law.

"*C'est à prendre ou à laisser,*" we said. Until Christianity be abolished it is only possible to attract mankind toward war by cunning and fraud, as now practised. We who see this fraud and cunning cannot give way to it.

Since, during this conversation, there was no music or champagne, or anything to confuse our senses, our guest merely shrugged his shoulders, and, with the amiability of a Frenchman, said he was very grateful for the cordial welcome he had experienced in our house, but was sorry that his views were not as well received.

After this conversation we went out into the hayfield, where our guest, hoping to find the peasants more in sympathy with his ideas, asked me to translate to an old, sickly muzhik, Prokophy by name—who, though suffering from severe hernia, was still working energetically, mowing with us—his plan for putting pressure on Germany from both sides, the Russian and the French.

The Frenchman explained this to him graphically, by pressing with his white fingers on either side of the mower's coarse shirt, which was damp with perspiration.

I well remember Prokophy's good-humored smile of astonishment when I explained the meaning of the Frenchman's words and action. He evidently took the proposal to squeeze the Germans as a joke, not conceiving that a full-grown and educated man would quietly and soberly speak of war as being desirable.

"Well, but, if we squeeze him from both sides," he answered, smiling, giving one pleasantry for another, as he supposed, "he will be fixed too fast to move. We shall have to let him out somewhere."

I translated this answer to my guest.

"Tell him we love the Russians," he said.

These words astonished Prokophy even more than the proposal to squeeze the Germans, and awoke in him a certain feeling of suspicion.

"Whence does he come?" he inquired.

I replied that he was a wealthy Frenchman.

"And what business has brought him here?" he asked.

When I replied that the Frenchman had come in the hope of persuading the Russians to enter into an alliance with the French in the event of a war with Germany, Prokophy was clearly entirely displeased, and, turning to the women who were sitting close by on a cock of hay, called out to them, in an angry voice, which unwittingly displayed the feelings which had been aroused in him, to go and stack the rest of the hay.

"Well, you crows," he cried, "you are all asleep! Go and stack! A nice time for squeezing the Germans! Look there, the hay has not been turned yet, and it looks as if we might have to begin on the corn on Wednesday." And then, as if afraid of having offended our visitor, he added, smiling good-naturedly and showing his worn teeth, "Better come and work with us, and bring the Germans too. And when we have finished we will have some feasting, and make the Germans join us. They are men like ourselves."

And so saying Prokophy took his sinewy hand from the fork of the rake on which he had been leaning, lifted it on to his shoulder, and went to join the women.

"Oh, le brave homme!" exclaimed the polite Frenchman, laughing. And thus was concluded for the time his diplomatic mission to the Russian people.

The different aspects of these two men—one shining with freshness and high spirits, dressed in a coat of the latest cut, displaying with his white hands, which had never known labor, how the Germans should be squeezed; the other coarse, with haydust in his hair, shrunken with hard work, sunburnt, always weary, and, notwithstanding his severe complaint, always at work: Prokophy, with his fingers swollen with toil, in his large home-made trousers, worn-out shoes, and a great heap of hay upon his shoulders, moving slowly along with that careful economy of stride common to all workingmen—the different aspects of these two men made much clear to me at the time, which has come back to me vividly since the Toulon-Paris festivities.

One of them represented the class fed and maintained by the people's labor, who in return use up that people as "food for cannon;" while the other was that very "food for cannon" which feeds and maintains those who afterwards so dispose of it. . . .

It is assumed that patriotism is, to start with, a sentiment natural to all men, and that, secondly, it is so highly moral a sentiment that it should be induced in all who have it not.

But neither one nor the other is true. I have lived half-a-century amid the Russian people, and in the great mass of laborers, during that period, I have never once seen or heard any manifestation or expression of this sentiment of patriotism, unless one should count those patriotic phrases which are learned by heart in the army, and repeated from books by the more superficial and degraded of the populace. I have never heard from the people any expression of patriotism, but, on the contrary, I have often listened to expressions of indifference, and even contempt, for any kind of patriotism, by the most venerable and serious of working-folk. I have observed the same thing amongst the laboring classes of other nations, and have received confirmation from educated Frenchmen, Germans, and Englishmen, from observation of their respective working-classes.

The working-classes are too much occupied supporting the lives of themselves and of their families, a duty which engrosses all their attention, to be able to take an interest in those political questions which are the chief motives of patriotism. . . .

An old friend of mine, who passed the winters alone in the country while his wife, whom he visited from time to time, lived in Paris, often conversed during the long autumn evening with his steward, an illiterate but shrewd and venerable peasant, who used to come to him in the evening to receive his orders; and my friend once mentioned amongst other things the advantages of the French system of government compared with our own. The occasion was a short time previous to the last Polish insurrection and the intervention of the French government in our affairs. At that time the patriotic Russian press was burning with indignation at this interference, and so excited the ruling classes that our political relations became very strained, and there were rumors of an approaching war with France.

My friend, having read the papers, explained to this peasant the misunderstanding between France and Russia; and coming under the influence of the journal, and being an old military man, said that were war to be declared he would reënter the army and fight with France. At that time a *revanche* against the French for Sevastopol was considered a necessity by patriotic Russians.

"Why should we fight with them?" asked the peasant.

"Why, how can we permit France to dictate to us?"

"Well, you said yourself that they were better governed than we," replied the peasant quite seriously; "let them arrange things as well in Russia."

And my friend told me that he was so taken aback by this argument that he did not know what to reply, and burst into laughter, as one who has just awakened from a delusive dream.

The same argument may be heard from every Russian workman if he has not come under the hypnotic influence of the government. People speak of the Russian's love for his faith, Tsar, and country; and yet a single community of peasants could not be found in Russia which would hesitate one moment had they to choose of two places for emigration—one in Russia, under the "Father-Tsar" (as he is termed only in books), and the holy orthodox faith of his idolized country, but with less or worse land; and the other without the "White-father-Tsar," and without the orthodox faith, somewhere outside Russia, in Prussia, China, Turkey, Austria, only with more and better land—the choice would be in favor of the latter, as we have often had opportunity to observe.

The question as to who shall govern him (and he knows that under any government he will be equally robbed) is for the Russian peasant of infinitely less significance than the question (setting aside even the matter of water), Is the clay soft and will cabbage thrive in it?

But it might be supposed that this indifference on the part of Russians arises from the fact that any government under which they might live would be an improvement on their own, because in Europe there is none worse. But that is not so; for as far as I can judge, one may witness the same indifference among English, Dutch, and German peasants emigrating to America, and among the various nationalities which have emigrated to Russia.

Passing from the control of one European government to another—from Turkish to Austrian, or from French to German—alters so slightly the position of the genuine working-classes, that in no case would the change excite any discontent, if only it be not effected artificially by the government and the ruling classes. . . .

What is called patriotism in our time is, on the one hand, only a certain disposition of mind, constantly produced and sustained in the minds of the people in a direction desired by the existing government, by schools, religion, and a subsidized press; and on the other hand it is a temporary excitement of the lowest stratum, morally and intellectually, of the people, produced by special means by the ruling classes, and finally acclaimed as the permanent expression of the people's will.

The patriotism of states oppressed by a foreign power presents no exception. It is equally unnatural to the working masses, and artificially induced by the higher classes.

"But if the common people have no sentiment of patriotism, it is because they have not yet developed this elevated feeling natural to every educated man. If they do not possess this nobility of sentiment, it must be cultivated in them. And this the government does."

So say, generally, the ruling classes, with such assurance that patriotism is a noble feeling, that the simple populace, who are ignorant of it, think themselves, in consequence, at fault, and try to persuade themselves that they really possess it, or at least pretend to have it.

But what is this elevated sentiment which, according to the opinion of the ruling classes, must be educated in the people?

The sentiment, in its simplest definition, is merely the preference for one's own country or nation above the country or nation of any one else; a sentiment perfectly expressed in the German patriotic song, "Deutschland, Deutschland über Alles," in which one need only substitute for the first two words, "Russland," "Frankreich," "Italien," or the name of any other country, to obtain a formula of the elevated sentiment of patriotism for that country.

It is quite possible that governments regard this sentiment as both useful and desirable, and of service to the unity of the State; but one must see that this sentiment is by no means elevated, but, on the contrary, very stupid and immoral. Stupid, because if every country were to consider itself superior to others, it is evident that all but one would be in error; and immoral because it leads all who possess it to aim at benefiting their own country or nation at the expense of every other—an inclination exactly at variance with the fundamental moral law, which all admit, "Do not unto others as you would not wish them to do unto you."

Patriotism may have been a virtue in the ancient world when it compelled men to serve the highest idea of those days—the fatherland. But how can patriotism be a virtue in these days when it requires of men an ideal exactly opposite to that of our religion and morality—an admission, not of the equality and fraternity of all men, but of the dominance of one country or nation over all others? But not only is this sentiment no virtue in our times, but it is indubitably a vice; for this sentiment of patriotism cannot now exist, because there is neither material nor moral foundation for its conception.

Patriotism might have had some meaning in the ancient world, when every nation was more or less uniform in composition, professing one national faith, and subject to the unrestrained authority of its great and adored sovereign, representing, as it were, an island, in an ocean of barbarians who sought to overflow it.

It is conceivable that in such circumstances patriotism—the desire of protection from barbarian assault, ready not only to destroy the social order, but threatening it with plunder, slaughter, captivity, slavery, and the violation of its women—was a natural feeling; and it is conceivable that men, in order to defend themselves and their fellow-countrymen, might prefer their own nation to any other, and cherish a feeling of hatred toward the surrounding barbarians, and destroy them for self-protection.

But what significance can this feeling have in these Christian days?

On what grounds and for what reason can a man of our time follow this example—a Russian, for instance, kill Frenchmen; or a Frenchman, Germans—when he is well aware, however uneducated he may be, that the men of the country or nation against whom his patriotic animosity is excited are no barbarians, but men, Christians like himself, often of the same faith as himself, and, like him, desirous of peace and the peaceful interchange of labor; and besides, bound to him, for the most part, either by the interest of a common effort, or by mercantile or spiritual endeavors, or even by both? So that very often people of one country are nearer and more needful to their neighbors than are these latter to one another, as in the case of laborers in the service of foreign employers of labor, of commercial houses, scientists, and the followers of art.

Moreover, the very conditions of life are now so changed, that what we call fatherland, what we are asked to distinguish from everything else, has ceased to be clearly defined, as it was with the ancients, when men of the same country were of one nationality, one state, and one religion.

The patriotism of an Egyptian, a Jew, a Greek is comprehensible, for in defending his country he defended his religion, his nationality, his fatherland, and his state.

But in what terms can one express to-day the patriotism of an Irishman in the United States, who by his religion belongs to Rome, by his nationality to Ireland, by his citizenship to the United States? In the same position is a Bohemian in Austria, a Pole in Russia, Prussia, or Austria; a Hindu in England; a Tartar or Armenian in Russia or Turkey. Not to mention the peo-

ple of these particular conquered nations, the people of the most homogeneous countries; Russia, France, Prussia, can no longer possess the sentiment of patriotism which was natural to the ancients, because very often the chief interest of their lives—of the family, for instance, where a man is married to a woman of another nationality; commercial, where his capital is invested abroad; spiritual, scientific, or artistic—are no longer contained within the limits of his country, but outside it, in the very state, perhaps, against which his patriotic animosity is being excited.

But patriotism is chiefly impossible to-day because, however much we may have endeavored during eighteen hundred years to conceal the meaning of Christianity, it has nevertheless leaked into our lives, and controls them to such an extent that the dullest and most unrefined of men must see today the complete incompatibility of patriotism with the moral law by which we live.

Patriotism was a necessity in the formation and consolidation of powerful states composed of different nationalities and acting in mutual defense against barbarians. But as soon as Christian enlightenment transformed these states from within, giving to all an equal standing, patriotism became not only needless, but the sole impediment to a union between nations for which, by reason of their Christian consciousness, they were prepared.

Patriotism today is the cruel tradition of an outlived period, which exists not merely by its inertia, but because the governments and ruling classes, aware that not their power only, but their very existence, depends upon it, persistently excite and maintain it among the people, both by cunning and violence.

Patriotism today is like a scaffolding which was needful once to raise the walls of the building, but which, though it presents the only obstacle to the house being inhabited, is none the less retained, because its existence is of profit to certain persons.

For a long while there has not been and cannot be any reason for dissension between Christian nations. It is even impossible to imagine, how and for what, Russian and German workmen, peacefully and conjointly working on the frontiers or in the capitals, should quarrel. And much less easily can one imagine animosity between some Kazan peasant who supplies Germans with wheat, and a German who supplies him with scythes and machines.

It is the same between French, German, and Italian workmen. And it would be even ridiculous to speak of the possibility of a quarrel between men of science, art, and letters of different nationalities, who have the same objects of common interest independent of nationalities or of governments.

But the various governments cannot leave the nations in peace, because the chief, if not the sole, justification for the existence of governments is the pacification of nations, and the settlement of their hostile relationships. Hence governments evoke such hostile relationships under the aspect of patriotism, in order to exhibit their powers of pacification. Somewhat like a gipsy who, having put some pepper under a horse's tail and beaten it in its stall, brings it out, and hanging on to the reins, pretends that he can hardly control the excited animal.

We are told that governments are very careful to maintain peace between nations. But how do they maintain it? People live on the Rhine in peaceful communication with one another. Suddenly, owing to certain quarrels and intrigues between kings and emperors, a war commences; and we learn that the French government has considered it necessary to regard this peaceful people as Frenchmen. Centuries pass, the population has become accustomed to their position, when animosity again begins amongst the governments of the great nations, and a war is started upon the most empty pretext, because the German government considers it necessary to regard this population as Germans: and between all Frenchmen and Germans is kindled a mutual feeling of ill-will.

Or else Germans and Russians live in friendly fashion on their frontiers, pacifically exchanging the results of their labor; when all of a sudden those same institutions, which only exist to maintain the peace of nations, begin to quarrel, are guilty of one stupidity after another, and finally are unable to invent anything better than a most childish method of self-punishment in order to have their own way, and do a bad turn to their opponent—which in this case is especially easy, as those who arrange a war of tariffs are not the sufferers from it; it is others who suffer—and so arrange such a war of tariffs as took place not long ago between Russia and Germany. And so between Russians and Germans a feeling of animosity is fostered, which is still more inflamed by the Franco-Russian festivities, and may lead at one moment or another to a bloody war.

I have mentioned these last two examples of the influence of a government over the people used to excite their animosity against another people, because they have occurred in our times: but in all history there is no war which was not hatched by the governments,

the governments alone, independent of the interests of the people, to whom war is always pernicious even when successful.

The government assures the people that they are in danger from the invasion of another nation, or from foes in their midst, and that the only way to escape this danger is by the slavish obedience of the people to their government. This fact is seen most prominently during revolutions and dictatorships, but it exists always and everywhere that the power of the government exists. Every government explains its existence, and justifies its deeds of violence, by the argument that if it did not exist the condition of things would be very much worse. After assuring the people of its danger the government subordinates it to control, and when in this condition compels it to attack some other nation. And thus the assurance of the government is corroborated in the eyes of the people, as to the danger of attack from other nations.

"Divide et impera."

Patriotism in its simplest, clearest, and most indubitable signification is nothing else but a means of obtaining for the rulers their ambitions and covetous desires, and for the ruled the abdication of human dignity, reason, and conscience, and a slavish enthralment to those in power. And as such it is recommended wherever it is preached.

Patriotism is slavery.

Those who preach peace by arbitration argue thus: Two animals cannot divide their prey otherwise than by fighting; as also is the case with children, savages, and savage nations. But reasonable people settle their differences by argument, persuasion, and by referring the decision of the question to other impartial and reasonable persons. So the nations should act today. This argument seems quite correct. The nations of our time have reached the period of reasonableness, have no animosity toward one another, and might decide their differences in a peaceful fashion. But this argument applies only so far as it has reference to the people, and only to the people who are not under the control of a government. But the people that subordinate themselves to a government cannot be reasonable, because the subordination is in itself a sign of a want of reason.

How can we speak of the reasonableness of men who promise in advance to accomplish everything, including murder, that the government—that is, certain men who have attained a certain position—may command? Men who can accept such obligations, and resignedly subordinate themselves to anything that may be prescribed by persons unknown to them in

Petersburg, Vienna, Berlin, Paris, cannot be considered reasonable; and the government, that is, those who are in possession of such power, can still less be considered reasonable, and cannot but misuse it, and become dazed by such insane and dreadful power.

This is why peace between nations cannot be attained by reasonable means, by conversations, by arbitration, as long as the subordination of the people to the government continues, a condition always unreasonable and always pernicious.

But the subordination of people to governments will exist as long as patriotism exists, because all governmental authority is founded upon patriotism, that is, upon the readiness of people to subordinate themselves to authority in order to defend their nation, country, or state from dangers which are supposed to threaten. . . .

It is dreadful to say so, but there is not, nor has there been, any conjoint violence of one people against another which was not accomplished in the name of patriotism. In its name the Russians fought the French, and the French the Russians; in its name Russians and French are preparing to fight the Germans, and the Germans to wage war on two frontiers. And such is the case not only with wars. In the name of patriotism the Russians stifle the Poles, the Germans persecute the Slavonians, the men of the Commune killed those of Versailles, and those of Versailles the men of the Commune.

It would seem that, owing to the spread of education, of speedier locomotion, of greater intercourse between different nations, to the widening of literature, and chiefly to the decrease of danger from other nations, the fraud of patriotism ought daily to become more difficult and at length impossible to practise.

But the truth is that these very means of general external education, facilitated locomotion and intercourse, and especially the spread of literature, being captured and constantly more and more controlled by government, confer on the latter such possibilities of exciting a feeling of mutual animosity between nations, that in degree as the uselessness and harmfulness of patriotism have become manifest, so also has increased the power of the government and ruling class to excite patriotism among the people.

The difference between that which was and that which is consists solely in the fact that now a much larger number of men participate in the advantages which patriotism confers on the upper classes, hence a much larger number of men are employed in spreading and sustaining this astounding superstition.

The more difficult the government finds it to retain its power, the more numerous are the men who share it.

In former times a small band of rulers held the reins of power, emperors, kings, dukes, their soldiers and assistants; whereas now the power and its profits are shared not only by government officials and by the clergy, but by capitalists—great and small, landowners, bankers, members of Parliament, professors, village officials, men of science, and even artists, but particularly by authors and journalists.

And all these people, consciously or unconsciously, spread the deceit of patriotism, which is indispensable to them if the profits of their position are to be preserved.

And the fraud, thanks to the means for its propagation, and to the participation in it of a much larger number of people, having become more powerful, is continued so successfully, that, notwithstanding the increased difficulty of deceiving, the extent to which the people are deceived is the same as ever.

A hundred years ago the uneducated classes, who had no idea of what composed their government, or by what nations they were surrounded, blindly obeyed the local government officials and nobles by whom they were enslaved, and it was sufficient for the government, by bribes and rewards, to remain on good terms with these nobles and officials, in order to squeeze from the people all that was required.

Whereas now, when the people can, for the most part, read, know more or less of what their government consists, and what nations surround them; when working-men constantly and easily move from place to place, bringing back information of what is happening in the world—the simple demand that the orders of the government must be accomplished is not sufficient; it is needful as well to cloud those true ideas about life which the people have, and to inculcate unnatural ideas as to the condition of their existence, and the relationship to it of other nations.

And so, thanks to the development of literature, reading, and the facilities of travel, governments which have their agents everywhere, by means of statutes, sermons, schools, and the press, inculcate everywhere upon the people the most barbarous and erroneous ideas as to their advantages, the relationship of nations, their qualities and intentions; and the people, so crushed by labor that they have neither the time nor the power to understand the significance or test the truth of the ideas which are forced upon them or of the demands made upon them in the name of their welfare, put themselves unmurmuringly under the yoke.

Whereas working-men who have freed themselves from unremitting labor and become educated, and who have, therefore, it might be supposed, the power of seeing through the fraud which is practised upon them, are subjected to such a coercion of threats, bribes, and all the hypnotic influence of governments, that, almost without exception, they desert to the side of the government, and by entering some well-paid and profitable employment, as priest, schoolmaster, officer, or functionary, become participators in spreading the deceit which is destroying their comrades.

It is as if nets were laid at the entrances to education, in which those who by some means or other escape from the masses bowed down by labor, are inevitably caught.

At first, when one understands the cruelty of all this deceit, one feels indignant in spite of oneself against those who from personal ambition or greedy advantage propagate this cruel fraud which destroys the souls as well as the bodies of men, and one feels inclined to accuse them of a sly craftiness; but the fact is that they are deceitful with no wish to deceive, but because they cannot be otherwise. And they deceive, not like Machiavellians, but with no consciousness of their deceit, and usually with the naïve assurance that they are doing something excellent and elevated, a view in which they are persistently encouraged by the sympathy and approval of all who surround them. . . .

Thus emperors, kings, and their ministers, with all their coronations, manœuvers, reviews, visiting one another, dressing up in various uniforms, going from place to place, and deliberating with serious faces as to how they may keep peace between nations supposed to be inimical to each other—nations who would never dream of quarreling—feel quite sure that what they are doing is very reasonable and useful.

In the same way the various ministers, diplomatists, and functionaries—dressed up in uniforms, with all sorts of ribbons and crosses, writing and docketing with great care, upon the best paper, their hazy, involved, altogether needless communications, advices, projects—are quite assured that, without their activity, the entire existence of nations would halt or become deranged.

In the same manner military men, got up in ridiculous costumes, arguing seriously with what rifle or cannon men can be most expeditiously destroyed, are quite certain that their field-days and reviews are most important and essential to the people.

So likewise the priests, journalists, writers of patriotic songs and class-books, who preach patriotism and receive liberal remuneration, are equally satisfied.

And no doubt the organizers of festivities—like the Franco-Russian fêtes—are sincerely affected while pronouncing their patriotic speeches and toasts.

All these people do what they are doing unconsciously, because they must, all their life being founded upon deceit, and because they know not how to do anything else; and coincidently these same acts call forth the sympathy and approbation of all the people amongst whom they are done. Moreover, being all linked together, they approve and justify one another's acts—emperors and kings those of the soldiers, functionaries, and clergymen; and soldiers, functionaries, and clergymen the acts of emperors and kings, while the populace, and especially the town populace, seeing nothing comprehensible in what is done by all these men, unwittingly ascribe to them a special, almost a supernatural, significance.

The people see, for instance, that a triumphal arch is erected; that men bedeck themselves with crowns, uniforms, robes; that fireworks are let off, cannons fired, bells rung, regiments paraded with their bands; that papers and telegrams and messengers fly from place to place, and that strangely arrayed men are busily engaged in hurrying from place to place and much is said and written; and the throng being unable to believe that all this is done (as is indeed the case) without the slightest necessity, attribute to it all a special mysterious significance, and gaze with shouts and hilarity or with silent awe. And on the other hand, this hilarity or silent awe confirms the assurance of those people who are responsible for all these foolish deeds.

Thus, for instance, not long ago, Wilhelm II ordered a new throne for himself, with some special kind of ornamentation, and having dressed up in a white uniform, with a cuirass, tight breeches, and a helmet with a bird on the top, and enveloped himself in a red mantle, came out to his subjects, and sat down on this new throne, perfectly assured that his act was most necessary and important; and his subjects not only saw nothing ridiculous in it, but thought the sight most imposing.

For some time the power of the government over the people has not been maintained by force, as was the case when one nation conquered another and ruled it by force of arms, or when the rulers of an unarmed people had separate legions of janizaries or guards.

The power of the government has for some time been maintained by what is termed public opinion.

A public opinion exists that patriotism is a fine moral sentiment, and that it is right and our duty to regard one's own nation, one's own state, as the best in the world; and flowing naturally from this public opinion is another, namely, that it is right and our duty to acquiesce in the control of a government over ourselves, to subordinate ourselves to it, to serve in the army and submit ourselves to discipline, to give our earnings to the government in the form of taxes, to submit to the decisions of the law-courts, and to consider the edicts of the government as divinely right. And when such public opinion exists, a strong governmental power is formed possessing milliards of money, an organized mechanism of administration, the postal service, telegraphs, telephones, disciplined armies, law-courts, police, submissive clergy, schools, even the press; and this power maintains in the people the public opinion which it finds necessary.

The power of the government is maintained by public opinion, and with this power the government, by means of its organs—its officials, law-courts, schools, churches, even the press—can always maintain the public opinion which they need. Public opinion produces the power, and the power produces public opinion. And there appears to be no escape from this position.

Nor indeed would there be, if public opinion were something fixed, unchangeable, and governments were able to manufacture the public opinion they needed.

But, fortunately, such is not the case; and public opinion is not, to begin with, permanent, unchangeable, stationary; but, on the contrary, is constantly changing, moving with the advance of humanity; and public opinion not only cannot be produced at will by a government, but is that which produces governments and gives them power, or deprives them of it. . . .

. . . [W]e need only take public opinion in its relation to the life of mankind to see that, as with the day or the year, it is never stagnant, but always proceeds along the way by which all humanity advances, as, notwithstanding delays and hesitations, the day or the spring advances by the same path as the sun. . . .

The nature of public opinion is a constant and irresistible movement. If it appears to us to be stationary it is because there are always some who have utilized a certain phase of public opinion for their own profit, and who, in consequence, use every effort to give it an appearance of permanence, and to conceal the manifestations of real opinion, which is already alive, though not yet perfectly expressed, in the consciousness of men. And such people, who adhere to the outworn opinion and conceal the new one, are at the present time those who compose governments and ruling classes, and who preach patriotism as an indispensable condition of human life.

The means which these people can control are immense; but as public opinion is constantly pouring in upon them their efforts must in the end be in vain: the old falls into decrepitude, the new grows.

The longer the manifestation of nascent public opinion is restrained, the more it accumulates, the more energetically will it burst forth.

Governments and ruling classes try with all their strength to conserve that old public opinion of patriotism upon which their power rests, and to smother the expression of the new, which would destroy it.

But to preserve the old and to check the new is possible only up to a certain point; just as, only to a certain extent, is it possible to check running water with a dam.

However much governments may try to arouse in the people a public opinion, of the past, unnatural to them, as to the merit and virtue of patriotism, those of our day believe in patriotism no longer, but espouse more and more the solidarity and brotherhood of nations.

Patriotism promises men nothing but a terrible future, but the brotherhood of nations represents an ideal which is becoming ever more intelligible and more desirable to humanity. Hence the progress of mankind from the old outworn opinion to the new must inevitably take place. This progression is as inevitable as the falling in the spring of the last dry leaves and the appearance of the new from swollen buds.

And the longer this transition is delayed, the more inevitable it becomes, and the more evident its necessity.

And indeed, one has only to remember what we profess, both as Christians and merely as men of our day, those fundamental moralities by which we are directed in our social, family, and personal existence, and the position in which we place ourselves in the name of patriotism, in order to see what a degree of contradiction we have placed between our conscience and what, thanks to an energetic government influence in this direction, we regard as our public opinion.

One has only thoughtfully to examine the most ordinary demands of patriotism, which are expected of us as the most simple and natural affair, in order to understand to what extent these requirements are at variance with that real public opinion which we already share. We all regard ourselves as free, educated, humane men, or even as Christians, and yet we are all in such a position that were Wilhelm tomorrow to take offense against Alexander, or Mr. N. to write a lively article on the Eastern Question, or Prince So-and-so to plunder some Bulgarians or Servians, or some queen or empress to be put out by something or other, all we educated humane Christians must go and kill people of whom we have no knowledge, and toward whom we are as amicably disposed as to the rest of the world. . . .

If people would only speak what they think, and not what they do not think, all the superstitions emanating from patriotism would at once drop away with the cruel feelings and violence founded upon it. The hatred and animosity between nations and peoples, fanned by their governments, would cease; the extolling of military heroism, that is of murder, would be at an end; and, what is of most importance, respect for authorities, abandonment to them of the fruits of one's labor, and subordination to them, would cease, since there is no other reason for them but patriotism.

And if merely this were to take place, that vast mass of feeble people who are controlled by externals would sway at once to the side of the new public opinion, which should reign henceforth in place of the old.

Let the government keep the schools, Church, press, its milliards of money and millions of armed men transformed into machines: all this apparently terrible organization of brute force is as nothing compared to the consciousness of truth, which surges in the soul of one man who knows the power of truth, which is communicated from him to a second and a third, as one candle lights an innumerable quantity of others.

The light needs only to be kindled, and, like wax in the face of fire, this organization, which seems so powerful, will melt, and be consumed.

Only let men understand the vast power which is given them in the word which expresses truth; only let them refuse to sell their birthright for a mess of pottage; only let people use their power—and their rulers will not dare, as now, to threaten men with universal slaughter, to which, at their discretion, they may or may not subject them, nor dare before the eyes of a peaceful populace to hold reviews and manœuvers of disciplined murderers; nor would the governments dare for their own profit and the advantage of their assistance to arrange and derange custom-house agreements, nor to collect from the people those millions of rubles which they distribute among their assistants, and by the help of which their murders are planned.

And such a transformation is not only possible, but it is as impossible that it should not be accomplished as that a lifeless, decaying tree should not fall, and a younger take its place.

"Peace I leave with you; my peace I give unto you: not as the world giveth, give I unto you. Let not your heart be troubled, neither let it be afraid," said Christ. And this peace is indeed among us, and depends on us for its attainment.

If only the hearts of individuals would not be troubled by the seductions with which they are hourly seduced, nor afraid of those imaginary terrors by which they are intimidated; if people only knew wherein their chiefest, all-conquering power consists—a peace which men have always desired, not the peace attainable by diplomatic negotiations, imperial or kingly progresses, dinners, speeches, fortresses, cannon, dynamite, and melinite, by the exhaustion of the people under taxes, and the abduction from labor of the flower of the population, but the peace attainable by a voluntary profession of the truth by every man, would long ago have been established in our midst.

READING 52

Is Patriotism a Virtue?

Alasdair MacIntyre

For MacIntyre's biography, see Reading 28. In this essay MacIntyre contrasts two opposing moral theories: liberal morality and communitarian morality ("the morality of patriotism"). The former adopts the impersonal, impartial point of view in order to reach a universal objective set of rules; the latter roots morality in a particular social community, which grounds and sustains the moral life. The danger of communitarian ethics is that it may degenerate into moral relativism, but the danger of liberal morality is that it tends to alienate the individual from those features of the moral life that sustain and motivate moral living.

This reading is taken from the Lindley Lecture, University of Kansas (1984). Copyright © 1984 by the University of Kansas. Reprinted by permission.

I

One of the central tasks of the moral philosopher is to articulate the convictions of the society in which he or she lives so that these convictions may become available for rational scrutiny. This task is all the more urgent when a variety of conflicting and incompatible beliefs are held within one and the same community, either by rival groups who differ on key moral questions or by one and the same set of individuals who find within themselves competing moral allegiances. In either of these types of case the first task of the moral philosopher is to render explicit what is at issue in the various disagreements and it is a task of this kind that I have set myself in this lecture.

For it is quite clear that there are large disagreements about patriotism in our society. And although it would be a mistake to suppose that there are only two clear, simple and mutually opposed sets of beliefs about patriotism, it is at least plausible to suggest that the range of conflicting views can be placed on a spectrum with two poles. At one end is the view, taken for granted by almost everyone in the nineteenth century, a commonplace in the literary culture of the McGuffey readers, that "patriotism" names a virtue. At the other end is the contrasting view, expressed with sometimes shocking clarity in the nineteen sixties, that "patriotism" names a vice. It would be misleading for me to suggest that I am going to be able to offer good reasons for taking one of these views rather than the other. What I do hope to achieve is a clarification of the issues that divide them.

A necessary first step . . . is to distinguish patriotism properly so-called from two other sets of attitudes that are all too easily assimilated to it. The first is that exhibited by those who are protagonists of their own nation's causes because and only because, so they assert, it is their nation which is *the* champion of some great moral ideal. In the Great War of 1914–18 Max Weber claimed that Imperial Germany should be supported because its was the cause of *Kultur,* while Emile Durkheim claimed with equal vehemence that France should be supported because its was the cause of *civilisation.* And here and now there are those American politicians who claim that the United States deserves our allegiance because it champions the goods of freedom against the evils of communism. What distinguishes their attitude from patriotism is twofold: first it is the ideal and not the nation which is the primary object of their regard; and secondly insofar as their regard for the ideal provides good reasons for allegiance to

their country, it provides good reasons for anyone at all to uphold their country's cause, irrespective of their nationality or citizenship.

Patriotism by contrast is defined in terms of a kind of loyalty to a particular nation which only those possessing that particular nationality can exhibit. Only Frenchmen can be patriotic about France, while anyone can make the cause of *civilisation* their own. But it would be all too easy in noticing this to fail to make a second equally important distinction. Patriotism is not to be confused with a mindless loyalty to one's own particular nation which has no regard at all for the characteristics of that particular nation. Patriotism does generally and characteristically involve a peculiar regard not just for one's own nation, but for the particular characteristics and merits and achievements of one's own nation. These latter are indeed valued *as* merits and achievements and their character as merits and achievements provides reasons supportive of the patriot's attitudes. But the patriot does not value in the same way precisely similar merits and achievements when they are the merits and achievements of some nation other than his or hers. For he or she—at least in the role of patriot—values them not just as merits and achievements, but as the merits and achievements of this particular nation. . . .

The particularity of the relationship is essential and ineliminable, and in identifying it as such we have already specified one central problem. What *is* the relationship between patriotism as such, the regard for this particular nation, and the regard which the patriot has for the merits and achievements of his or her nation and for the benefits which he or she has received? The answer to this question must be delayed for it will turn out to depend upon the answer to an apparently even more fundamental question, one that can best be framed in terms of the thesis that, if patriotism is understood as I have understood it, then "patriotism" is not merely not the name of a virtue, but must be the name of a vice, since patriotism thus understood and morality are incompatible.

II

The presupposition of this thesis is an account of morality which has enjoyed high prestige in our culture. According to that account to judge from a moral standpoint is to judge impersonally. It is to judge as any rational person would judge, independently of his or her interests, affections and social position. And to act morally is to act in accordance with such impersonal judgments. Thus to think and to act morally involves the moral agent in abstracting him or herself from all social particularity and partiality. The potential conflict between morality so understood and patriotism is at once clear. For patriotism requires me to exhibit peculiar devotion to my nation and you to yours. It requires me to regard such contingent social facts as where I was born and what government ruled over that place at that time, who my parents were, who my great-great-grandparents were and so on, as deciding for me the question of what virtuous action is—at least insofar as it is the virtue of patriotism which is in question. Hence the moral standpoint and the patriotic standpoint are systematically incompatible.

Yet although this is so, it might be argued that the two standpoints need not be in conflict. For patriotism and all other such particular loyalties can be restricted in their scope so that their exercise is always within the confines imposed by morality. Patriotism need be regarded as nothing more than a perfectly proper devotion to one's own nation which must never be allowed to violate the constraints set by the impersonal moral standpoint. This is indeed the kind of patriotism professed by certain liberal moralists who are often indignant when it is suggested by their critics that they are not patriotic. To those critics, however, patriotism thus limited in its scope appears to be emasculated, and it does so because in some of the most important situations of actual social life either the patriotic standpoint comes into serious conflict with the standpoint of a genuinely impersonal morality or it amounts to no more than a set of practically empty slogans. What kinds of circumstances are these? They are at least twofold.

The first kind arises from scarcity of essential resources, often historically from the scarcity of land suitable for cultivation and pasture, and perhaps in our own time from that of fossil fuels. What your community requires as the material prerequisites for your survival as a distinctive community and your growth into a distinctive nation may be exclusive use of the same or some of the same natural resources as my community requires for its survival and growth into a distinctive nation. When such a conflict arises, the standpoint of impersonal morality requires an allocation of goods such that each individual person counts for one and no more than one, while the patriotic standpoint requires that I strive to further the interests of my community and you strive to further those of yours, and certainly where the survival of one community is at stake, and sometimes perhaps even when only large interests of

one community are at stake, patriotism entails a willingness to go to war on one's community's behalf.

The second type of conflict-engendering circumstance arises from differences between communities about the right way for each to live. Not only competition for scarce natural resources, but incompatibilities arising from such conflict-engendering beliefs may lead to situations in which once again the liberal moral standpoint and the patriotic standpoint are radically at odds. The administration of the *pax Romana* from time to time required the Roman *imperium* to set its frontiers at the point at which they could be most easily secured, so that the burden of supporting the legions would be reconcilable with the administration of Roman law. And the British empire was no different in its time. But this required infringing upon the territory and the independence of barbarian border peoples. A variety of such peoples—Scottish Gaels, Iroquois Indians, Bedouin—have regarded raiding the territory of their traditional enemies living within the confines of such large empires as an essential constituent of the good life; whereas the settled urban or agricultural communities which provided the target for their depredations have regarded the subjugation of such peoples and their reeducation into peaceful pursuits as one of their central responsibilities. And on such issues once again the impersonal moral standpoint and that of patriotism cannot be reconciled.

For the impersonal moral standpoint, understood as the philosophical protagonists of modern liberalism have understood it, requires neutrality not only between rival and competing interests, but also between rival and competing sets of beliefs about the best way for human beings to live. Each individual is to be left free to pursue in his or her own way that way of life which he or she judges to be best; while morality by contrast consists of rules which, just because they are such that any rational person, independently of his or her interests or point of view on the best way for human beings to live, would assent to them, are equally binding on all persons. Hence in conflicts between nations or other communities over ways of life, the standpoint of morality will once again be that of an impersonal arbiter, adjudicating in ways that give equal weight to each individual person's needs, desires, beliefs about the good and the like, while the patriot is once again required to be partisan.

Notice that in speaking of the standpoint of liberal impersonal morality in the way in which I have done I have been describing a standpoint whose truth is both presupposed by the political actions and utterances of

a great many people in our society and explicitly articulated and defended by most modern moral philosophers; and that it has at the level of moral philosophy
a number of distinct versions—some with a Kantian
flavour, some utilitarian, some contractarian. I do not
mean to suggest that the disagreements between these
positions are unimportant. Nonetheless the five central
positions that I have ascribed to that standpoint appear
in all these various philosophical guises: first, that
morality is constituted by rules to which any rational
person would under certain ideal conditions give assent; secondly, that those rules impose constraints upon
and are neutral between rival and competing interests—
morality itself is not the expression of any particular
interest; thirdly, that those rules are also neutral between rival and competing sets of beliefs about what
the best way for human beings to live is; fourthly, that
the units which provide the subject-matter of morality
as well as its agents are individual human beings and
that in moral evaluations each individual is to count for
one and nobody for more than one; and fifthly, that the
standpoint of the moral agent constituted by allegiance
to these rules is one and the same for all moral agents
and as such is independent of all social particularity.
What morality provides are standards by which all actual social structures may be brought to judgment from
a standpoint independent of all of them. It is morality
so understood allegiance to which is not only incompatible with treating patriotism as a virtue, but which
requires that patriotism—at least in any substantial
version—be treated as a vice.

But is this the only possible way to understand
morality? As a matter of history, the answer is clearly
"No." This understanding of morality invaded post
Renascence Western culture at a particular point in
time as the moral counterpart to political liberalism and
social individualism, and its polemical stances reflect
its history of emergence from the conflicts which those
movements engendered and themselves presuppose alternatives against which those polemical stances were
and are directed. Let me therefore turn to considering
one of those alternative accounts of morality, whose
peculiar interest lies in the place that it has to assign to
patriotism.

III

According to the liberal account of morality *where* and
from whom I learn the principles of morality are and
must be irrelevant both to the question of what the con-

tent of morality is and to that of the nature of my commitment to it, as irrelevant as *where* and *from whom* I
learn the principles and precepts of mathematics are to
the content of mathematics and the nature of my commitment to mathematical truths. By contrast on the alternative account of morality which I am going to
sketch, the questions of *where* and *from whom* I learn
my morality turn out to be crucial for both the content
and the nature of moral commitment.

On this view it is an essential characteristic of the
morality which each of us acquires that it is learned
from, in and through the way of life of some particular community. Of course the moral rules elaborated in
one particular historical community will often resemble and sometimes be identical with the rules to which
allegiance is given in other particular communities, especially in communities with a shared history or which
appeal to the same canonical texts. But there will characteristically be *some* distinctive features of the set of
rules considered as a whole, and those distinctive features will often arise from the way in which members
of that particular community responded to some earlier
situation or series of situations in which particular features of difficult cases led to one or more rules being
put in question and reformulated or understood in some
new way. Moreover the form of the rules of morality
as taught and apprehended will be intimately connected
with specific institutional arrangements. The moralities
of different societies may agree in having a precept en-
joining that a child should honor his or her parents, but
what it is so to honor and indeed what a father is and
what a mother is will vary greatly between different social orders. So that what I learn as a guide to my actions and as a standard for evaluating them is never
morality as such, but always the highly specific morality of some highly specific social order.

To this the reply by the protagonists of modern
liberal morality might well be: doubtless this is how a
comprehension of the rules of morality is first acquired.
But what allows such specific rules, framed in terms of
particular social institutions, to be accounted moral
rules at all is the fact they are nothing other than applications of universal and general moral rules, and individuals acquire genuine morality only because and
insofar as they progress from particularised socially
specific applications of universal and general moral
rules to comprehending them as universal and general.
To learn to understand oneself as a moral agent just is
to learn to free oneself from social particularity and to
adopt a standpoint independent of any particular set of
social institutions, and the fact that everyone or almost

everyone has to learn to do this by starting out from a standpoint deeply infected by social particularity and partiality goes no way towards providing an alternative account of morality. But to this reply a three-fold rejoinder can be made.

First, it is not just that I first apprehend the rules of morality in some socially specific and particularised form. It is also and correlatively that the goods by reference to which and for the sake of which any set of rules must be justified are also going to be goods that are socially specific and particular. For central to those goods is the enjoyment of one particular kind of social life, lived out through a particular set of social relationships and thus what I enjoy is the good of *this* particular social life inhabited by me and I enjoy *it* as what *it* is. It may well be that it follows that I would enjoy and benefit equally from similar forms of social life in other communities; but this hypothetical truth in no way diminishes the importance of the contention that my goods are as a matter of fact found *here,* among *these* particular people, in *these* particular relationships. Goods are never encountered except as thus particularised. Hence the abstract general claim, that rules of a certain kind are justified by being productive of and constitutive of goods of a certain kind, is true only if these and these and these particular sets of rules incarnated in the practices of these and these and these particular communities are productive of or constitutive of these and these and these particular goods enjoyed at certain particular times and places by certain specifiable individuals.

It follows that *I* find *my* justification for allegiance to these rules of morality in *my* particular community; deprived of the life of that community, *I* would have no reason to be moral. But this is not all. To obey the rules of morality is characteristically and generally a hard task for human beings. Indeed were it not so, our need for morality would not be what it is. It is because we are continually liable to be blinded by immediate desire, to be distracted from our responsibilities, to lapse into backsliding and because even the best of us may at times encounter quite unusual temptations that it is important to morality that *I* can only be a moral agent because *we* are moral agents, that I need those around me to reinforce my moral strengths and assist in remedying my moral weaknesses. It is in general only within a community that individuals become capable of morality, are sustained in their morality and are constituted as moral agents by the way in which other people regard them and what is owed to and by them as well as by the way in which they regard themselves. In requiring much from me morally the other members of my community express a kind of respect for me that has nothing to do with expectations of benefit; and those of whom nothing or little is required in respect of morality are treated with a lack of respect which is, if repeated often enough, damaging to the moral capacities of those individuals. Of course, lonely moral heroism is sometimes required and sometimes achieved. But we must not treat this exceptional type of case as though it were typical. And once we recognize that typically moral agency and continuing moral capacity are engendered and sustained in essential ways by particular institutionalised social ties in particular social groups, it will be difficult to counterpose allegiance to a particular society and allegiance to morality in the way in which the protagonists of liberal morality do.

Indeed the case for treating patriotism as a virtue is now clear. *If* first of all it is the case that I can only apprehend the rules of morality in the version in which they are incarnated in some specific community; and *if* secondly it is the case that the justification of morality must be in terms of particular goods enjoyed within the life of particular communities; and *if* thirdly it is the case that I am characteristically brought into being and maintained as a moral agent only through the particular kinds of moral sustenance afforded by my community, *then* it is clear that deprived of this community, I am unlikely to flourish as a moral agent. Hence my allegiance to the community and what it requires of me— even to the point of requiring me to die to sustain its life—could not meaningfully be contrasted with or counterposed to what morality required of me. Detached from my community, I will be apt to lose my hold upon all genuine standards of judgment. Loyalty to that community, to the hierarchy of particular kinship, particular local community and particular natural community, is on this view a prerequisite for morality. So patriotism and those loyalties cognate to it are not just virtues but central virtues. Everything however turns on the truth or falsity of the claims advanced in the three preceding if-clauses. And the argument so far affords us no resources for delivering a verdict upon that truth or falsity. Nonetheless some progress has been achieved, and not only because the terms of the debate have become clearer. For it has also become clear that this dispute is not adequately characterised if it is understood simply as a disagreement between two rival accounts of morality, as if there were some independently identifiable phenomenon situated somehow or other in the social world waiting to be described more or less accurately by the contending parties. What we have here are two rival and incompatible moralities, each of which is viewed from within by its adherents as morality-as-such, each of which makes its exclusive claim to our allegiance. How are we to evaluate such claims?

One way to begin is to be learned from Aristotle. Since we possess no stock of clear and distinct first principles or any other such epistemological resource which would provide us with a neutral and independent standard for judging between them, we shall do well to proceed dialectically. And one useful dialectical strategy is to focus attention on those accusations which the adherents of each bring against the rival position which the adherents of that rival position treat as of central importance to rebut. For this will afford at least one indication of the issues about the importance of which both sides agree and about the characterisation of which their very recognition of disagreement suggests that there must also be some shared beliefs. In what areas do such issues arise?

IV

One such area is defined by a charge which it seems reasonable at least *prima facie* for the protagonists of patriotism to bring against morality. The morality for which patriotism is a virtue offers a form of rational justification for moral rules and precepts whose structure is clear and rationally defensible. The rules of morality are justifiable if and only if they are productive of and partially constitutive of a form of shared social life whose goods are directly enjoyed by those inhabiting the particular communities whose social life is of that kind. Hence *qua* member of this or that particular community I can appreciate the justification for what morality requires of me from within the social roles that I live out in my community. By contrast, it may be argued, liberal morality requires of me to assume an abstract and artificial—perhaps even an impossible—stance, that of a rational being as such, responding to the requirements of morality not *qua* parent or farmer or quarterback, but *qua* rational agent who has abstracted him or herself from all social particularity, who has become not merely Adam Smith's impartial spectator, but a correspondingly impartial actor, and one who in his impartiality is doomed to rootlessness, to be a citizen of nowhere. How can I justify to myself performing this act of abstraction and detachment?

The liberal answer is clear: such abstraction and detachment is defensible, because it is a necessary condition of moral freedom, of emancipation from the bondage of the social, political and economic *status quo*. For unless I can stand back from every and any feature of that *status quo,* including the roles within it which I myself presently inhabit, I will be unable to view it critically and to decide for myself what stance it is rational and right for me to adopt towards it. This does not preclude that the outcome for such a critical evaluation may not be an endorsement of all or some of the existing social order; but even such an endorsement will only be free and rational if I have made it for myself in this way. (Making just such an endorsement of much of the economic *status quo* is the distinguishing mark of the contemporary conservative liberal, such as Milton Friedman, who is as much a liberal as the liberal liberal who finds much of the *status quo* wanting—such as J. K. Galbraith or Edward Kennedy—or the radical liberal.) Thus liberal morality does after all appeal to an overriding good, the good of this particular kind of emancipating freedom. And in the name of this good it is able not only to respond to the question about how the rules of morality are to be justified, but also to frame a plausible and potentially damaging objection to the morality of patriotism.

It is of the essence of the morality of liberalism that no limitations are or can be set upon the criticism of the social *status quo*. No institution, no practice, no loyalty can be immune from being put in question and perhaps rejected. Conversely the morality of patriotism is one which precisely because it is framed in terms of the membership of some particular social community with some particular social, political and economic structure, must exempt at least some fundamental structures of that community's life from criticism. Because patriotism has to be a loyalty that is in some respects unconditional, so in just those respects rational criticism is ruled out. But if so the adherents of the morality of patriotism have condemned themselves to a fundamentally irrational attitude—since to refuse to examine some of one's fundamental beliefs and attitudes is to insist on accepting them, whether they are rationally justifiable or not, which is irrational—and have imprisoned themselves within that irrationality. What answer can the adherents of the morality of patriotism make to this kind of accusation? The reply must be threefold.

When the liberal moralist claims that the patriot is bound to treat his or her nation's projects and practices in some measure uncritically, the claim is not only that at any one time certain of these projects and practices will be being treated uncritically; it is that some at least must be permanently exempted from criticism. The patriot is in no position to deny this; but what is crucial to the patriot's case is to identify clearly precisely what it is that is thus exempted. . . . What then is exempted? The answer is: the nation conceived *as a project,* a project somehow or other brought to birth in the past and carried on so that a morally distinctive community was brought into being which embodied a claim to political autonomy in its various organized and institutionalised expressions. Thus one can be patriotic towards a nation whose political independence is yet to come—as Garibaldi was; or towards a nation which once was and perhaps might be again—like the Polish patriots of the 1860s. What the patriot is committed to is a particular way of linking a past which has conferred a distinctive moral and political identity upon him or her with a future for the project which is his or her nation which it is his or her responsibility to bring into being. Only this allegiance is unconditional and allegiance to particular governments or forms of government or particular leaders will be entirely conditional upon their being devoted to furthering that project rather than frustrating or destroying it. Hence there is nothing inconsistent in a patriot's being deeply opposed to his country's contemporary rulers, as Péguy was, or plotting their overthrow as Adam von Trott did.

Yet although this may go part of the way towards answering the charge of the liberal moralist that the patriot must in certain areas be completely uncritical and therefore irrationalist, it certainly does not go all the way. For everything that I have said on behalf of the morality of patriotism is compatible with it being the case that on occasion patriotism might require me to support and work for the success of some enterprise of my nation as crucial to its overall project crucial perhaps to its survival, when the success of that enterprise would not be in the best interests of mankind, evaluated from an impartial and an impersonal standpoint. The case of Adam von Trott is very much to the point.

Adam von Trott was a German patriot who was executed after the unsuccessful assassination attempt against Hitler's life in 1944. Trott deliberately chose to work inside Germany with the minuscule, but highly placed, conservative opposition to the Nazis with the aim of replacing Hitler from within, rather than to work for an overthrow of Nazi Germany which would result in the destruction of the Germany brought to birth in 1871. But to do this he had to appear to be identified with the cause of Nazi Germany and so strengthened

not only his country's cause, as was his intention, but also as an unavoidable consequence the cause of the Nazis. This kind of example is a particularly telling one, because the claim that such and such a course of action is "to the best interests of mankind" is usually at best disputable, at worst cloudy rhetoric. But there are a very few causes in which so much was at stake—and that this is generally much clearer in retrospect than it was at the time does not alter that fact—that the phrase has clear application: the overthrow of Nazi Germany was one of them.

How ought the patriot then to respond? Perhaps in two ways. The first begins by reemphasising that from the fact that the particularist morality of the patriot is rooted in a particular community and inextricably bound up with the social life of that community, it does not follow that it cannot provide rational grounds for repudiating many features of that country's present organized social life. The conception of justice engendered by the notion of citizenship within a particular community may provide standards by which particular political institutions are found wanting: when Nazi anti-Semitism encountered the phenomena of German Jewish ex-soldiers who had won the Iron Cross, it had to repudiate German particularist standards of excellence (for the award of the Iron Cross symbolised a recognition of devotion to Germany). Moreover the conception of one's own nation having a special mission does not necessitate that this mission may not involve the extension of a justice originally at home only in the particular institutions of the homeland. And clearly particular governments or agencies of government may defect and may be understood to have defected from this mission so radically that the patriot may find that a point comes when he or she has to choose between the claims of the project which constitutes his or her nation and the claims of the morality that he or she has learnt as a member of the community whose life is informed by that project. Yes, the liberal critic of patriotism will respond, this indeed *may* happen; but it may not and it often will not. Patriotism turns out to be a permanent source of moral danger. And this claim, I take it, cannot in fact be successfully rebutted.

A second possible, but very different type of answer on behalf of the patriot would run as follows. I argued earlier that the kind of regard for one's own country which would be compatible with a liberal morality of impersonality and impartiality would be too insubstantial, would be under too many constraints, to be regarded as a version of patriotism in the traditional sense. But it does not follow that some version of traditional patriotism may not be compatible with some other morality of universal moral law, which sets limits to and provides both sanction for and correction of the particularist morality of the patriot. Whether this is so or not is too large and too distinct a question to pursue in this present paper. But we ought to note that even if it is so—and all those who have been both patriots and Christians *or* patriots and believers in Thomistic natural law *or* patriots and believers in the Rights of Man have been committed to claiming that it is so—this would not diminish in any way the force of the liberal claim that patriotism is a morally dangerous phenomenon.

That the rational protagonist of the morality of patriotism is compelled, if my argument is correct, to concede this does not mean that there is not more to be said in the debate. And what needs to be said is that the liberal morality of impartiality and impersonality turns out also to be a morally dangerous phenomenon in an interestingly corresponding way. For suppose the bonds of patriotism to be dissolved: would liberal morality be able to provide anything adequately substantial in its place? What the morality of patriotism at its best provides is a clear account of and justification for the particular bonds and loyalties which form so much of the substance of the moral life. It does so by underlining the moral importance of the different members of a group acknowledging a shared history. Each one of us to some degree or other understands his or her life as an enacted narrative; and because of our relationships with others we have to understand ourselves as characters in the enacted narratives of other people's lives. Moreover the story of each of our lives is characteristically embedded in the story of one or more larger units. I understand the story of my life in such a way that it is part of the history of my family or of this farm or of this university or of this countryside; and I understand the story of the lives of other individuals around me as embedded in the same larger stories, so that I and they share a common stake in the outcome of that story and in what sort of story it both is and is to be: tragic, heroic, comic.

A central contention of the morality of patriotism is that I will obliterate and lose a central dimension of the moral life if I do not understand the enacted narrative of my own individual life as embedded in the history of my country. For if I do not so understand it I will not understand what I owe to others or what others owe to me, for what crimes of my nation I am bound to make reparation, for what benefits to my nation I am bound to feel gratitude. Understanding what is owed to and by me and understanding the history of the communities of which I am a part is on this view one and the same thing.

It is worth stressing that one consequence of this is that patriotism, in the sense in which I am understanding it in this paper, is only possible in certain types of national community under certain conditions. A national community, for example, which systematically disowned its own true history or substituted a largely fictitious history for it or a national community in which the bonds deriving from history were in no way the real bonds of the community (having been replaced for example by the bonds of reciprocal self-interest) would be one towards which patriotism would be—from any point of view—an irrational attitude. For precisely the same reasons that a family whose members all came to regard membership in that family as governed only by reciprocal self-interest would no longer be a family in the traditional sense, so a nation whose members took up a similar attitude would no longer be a nation and this would provide adequate grounds for holding that the project which constituted that nation had simply collapsed. Since all modern bureaucratic states tend towards reducing national communities to this condition, all such states tend towards a condition in which any genuine morality of patriotism would have no place and what paraded itself as patriotism would be an unjustifiable simulacrum.

Why would this matter? In modern communities in which membership is understood only or primarily in terms of reciprocal self-interest, only two resources are generally available when destructive conflicts of interest threaten such reciprocity. One is the arbitrary imposition of some solution by force; the other is appeal to the neutral, impartial and impersonal standards of liberal morality. The importance of this resource is scarcely to be underrated; but how much of a resource is it? The problem is that some motivation has to be provided for allegiance to the standards of impartiality and impersonality which both has rational justification and can outweigh the considerations provided by interest. Since any large need for such allegiance arises precisely and only when and insofar as the possibility of appeals to reciprocity in interests has broken down, such reciprocity can no longer provide the relevant kind of motivation. And it is difficult to identify anything that can take its place. The appeal to moral agents *qua* rational beings to place their allegiance to impersonal rationality above that to their interests has, just because it is an appeal to rationality, to furnish an adequate reason for so doing. And this is a point at which liberal accounts of morality are notoriously vulnerable. This vulnerability becomes a manifest practical liability at one key point in the social order.

Every political community except in the most exceptional conditions requires standing armed forces for its minimal security. Of the members of these armed forces it must require both that they be prepared to sacrifice their own lives for the sake of the community's security and that their willingness to do so be not contingent upon their own individual evaluation of the rightness or wrongness of their country's cause on some specific issue, measured by some standard that is neutral and impartial relative to the interests of their own community and the interests of other communities. And, that is to say, good soldiers may not be liberals and must indeed embody in their actions a good deal at least of the morality of patriotism. So the political survival of any polity in which liberal morality had secured large-scale allegiance would depend upon there still being enough young men and women who rejected that liberal morality. And in this sense liberal morality tends towards the dissolution of social bonds.

Hence the charge that the morality of patriotism can successfully bring against liberal morality is the mirror-image of that which liberal morality can successfully urge against the morality of patriotism. For while the liberal moralist was able to conclude that patriotism is a permanent source of moral danger because of the way it places our ties to our nation beyond rational criticism, the moralist who defends patriotism is able to conclude that liberal morality is a permanent source of moral danger because of the way it renders our social and moral ties too open to dissolution by rational criticism. And each party is in fact in the right against the other.

V

. . . Hegel employs a useful distinction which he marks by his use of words *Sittlichkeit* and *Moralität*. *Sittlichkeit* is the customary morality of each particular society, pretending to be no more than this. *Moralität* reigns in the realm of rational universal, impersonal morality, of liberal morality, as I have defined it. What those immigrants were taught in effect was that they had left behind countries and cultures where *Sittlichkeit* and *Moralität* were certainly distinct and often opposed and arrived in a country and a culture whose *Sittlickeit* just is *Moralität*. And thus for many Americans the

cause of America, understood as the object of patriotic regard, and the cause of morality, understood as the liberal moralist understands it, came to be identified. The history of this identification could not be other than a history of confusion and incoherence, if the argument which I have constructed in this lecture is correct. For a morality of particularist ties and solidarities has been conflated with a morality of universal, impersonal and impartial principles in a way that can never be carried through without incoherence.

One test therefore of whether the argument that I have constructed has or has not empirical application and practical significance would be to discover whether it is or is not genuinely illuminating to write the political and social history of modern America as in key part the living out of a central conceptual confusion, a confusion perhaps required for the survival of a large-scale modern polity which has to exhibit itself as liberal in many institutional settings, but which also has to be able to engage the patriotic regard of enough of its citizens, if it is to continue functioning effectively. To determine whether that is or is not true would be to risk discovering that we inhabit a kind of polity whose moral order requires systematic incoherence in the form of public allegiance to mutually inconsistent sets of principles. But that is a task which—happily—lies beyond the scope of this lecture.

READING 53

The Problem of World Government

Jacques Maritain

Jacques Maritain (1882–1973), distinguished French Roman Catholic philosopher, was Professor of Philosophy at the Institute Catholique de Paris, as well as at Columbia and Princeton Universities. He was the author of more than fifty books. He also served as French Ambassador to the Vatican from 1945 to 1948.

In this essay from his book *Man and the State*, Maritain argues for a world government through which peace and justice will be guaranteed. Given the possibility of nations destroying each other through atomic weapons, an international authority is necessary to ensure peace. He argues that it is the false Hegelian hypostatization of the abstract idea of the State that has misled philosophers into treating the nation-state with such reverence, as a Supraperson, when it is merely an abstraction with concrete powers. Hobbes's *Leviathan* is a pre-Hegelian example of this fallacy. The traditional nation-state no longer serves a viable purpose and will have to give up its sovereignty in favor of an international government. He defends his proposal via the idea of a universal natural law, which he believes to be inherent in all human beings and which can be recognized by all rational beings. Maritain does not expect a world government to become a reality in our time, but it must eventually occur if we are to flourish in peace and prosperity.

This reading is taken from *Man and the State* (Catholic University Press, 1950), by permission.

I. THE ALTERNATIVE

In 1944, Mr. Mortimer Adler published a book entitled *How to Think About War and Peace,* in which he advocated in a conclusive manner World Government as the only means of ensuring peace. This book was written just on the eve of the advent of what they now call the atomic age;—that's a proof that philosophers do not need to be stimulated by the atomic bomb in order to think. Yet the advent of the atomic bomb is a strong invitation to think, directed both to the States, which, having no soul of their own, find it a harder matter to think than mechanical brains do, and to the peoples, which, as long as they are not atomized, still have human brains.

The problem of World Government—I would prefer to say, of a genuinely political organization of the world—is the problem of lasting peace. And in a sense we might say that the problem of lasting peace is simply the problem of peace, meaning that mankind is confronted today with the alternative: either lasting peace or a serious risk of total destruction.

I need not emphasize the reality and significance of this alternative, which results from the fact that mod-

ern wars are world wars, and total wars, involving the whole of human existence, with regard to the deepest structures of social life as well as to the extent of the population mobilized by war, and threatened by it, in every nation.

What I should like is rather to seek for the reasons for this alternative.

The basic fact is the henceforth unquestionable interdependence of nations, a fact which is not a token of peace, as people for a moment believed in their wishful thinking, but rather a token of war: why? because that interdependence of nations is essentially an economic interdependence, not a politically agreed-upon, willed, and built up interdependence, in other words, because it has come to exist by virtue of a merely technical or material process, not by virtue of a simultaneous genuinely political or rational process.

Quoting a statement of Mr. Emery Reves, Mortimer Adler, in his chapter on *The Economic Community,* points out that "the technical developments which render the world smaller, and its parts more interdependent, can have two consequences: '1) a political and economic rapprochement, or 2) fights and quarrels more devastating than ever, precisely because of the proximity of men to each other. Which one of these two possibilities will occur depends on matters essentially nontechnical.'" And he rightly adds: "Both will occur within the next great historic epoch, but the second before the first."[1]

An essentially *economic* interdependence, without any corresponding fundamental recasting of the *moral* and *political* structures of human existence, can but impose by material necessity a partial and fragmentary, growing bit by bit, political interdependence which is reluctantly and hatefully accepted, because it runs against the grain of nature as long as nations live on the assumption of their full political autonomy. In the framework and against the background of that assumed full political autonomy of nations, an essentially economic interdependence can but exasperate the rival needs and prides of nations; and the industrial progress only accelerates the process, as Professor John Nef has shown in his book *La Route de la guerre totale.*[2] Thus it is that we have the privilege of contemplating today a world more and more economically one, and more and more divided by the pathological claims of opposed nationalisms.

At this point we may make two remarks. In the first place, both economic life and political life depend on *nature* and *reason,* I mean *nature* as dominated by material forces and laws and by deterministic evolution, even when the human mind interferes in the process with its technical discoveries—and on *reason* as concerned with the ends of human existence and the realm of freedom and morality, and as freely establishing, in consonance with Natural Law, an order of human relations. In the second place, it is nature and matter that have the upper hand in the economic process; and it is reason and freedom that have the upper hand in the political, the genuinely political process.

As a result, it is permissible to say that the spectacle we are contemplating today is but an instance of that unfortunate law that in human history matter goes faster than the spirit. The human intellect is always getting winded in catching up with the advance of matter. It is probable that with the discovery of fire the caveman had to face predicaments not unlike those which our civilization is facing now. The question is whether human conscience and moral intelligence, teamed with the effort of creative energies, will be able to make the Machine a positive force in the service of mankind—in other words, to impose on man's instinctive greed, with its unsurpassable technical equipment, a collective reason grown stronger than instinct—without a period of trial and error more terrible to our kind than the prehistoric eras.

Now the preceding considerations are not enough. Another factor must be considered, which plays a far-reaching part in the development of that alternative: *either lasting peace or a serious risk of total destruction,* the reasons for which we are seeking.

This factor is the modern State, with its false pretense to be a person, a superhuman person, and to enjoy, as a result, a right of absolute sovereignty.

In a remarkable essay, entitled "The Modern State a Danger for Peace," the Belgian jurist Fernand de Visscher offers this primary fact for our consideration: the fundamental amorality of the foreign policy of modern States; a fundamental amorality whose unique rule and principle is the *raison d'État,* which raises the particular interest of a State to a supreme law of its activity, especially as to its relations with the other States. And the same author goes on to explain that the root of this evil is the false assumption that the State is a person, a supreme person, which consequently has its supreme justification, supreme reason for being and supreme end in itself, and possesses a supreme right to its own preservation and growth in power by any means whatever.

This false assumption has been previously discussed. Mr. de Visscher calls it a political "heresy," and thinks that it derives from a fatal misunderstanding, by virtue of which a mere metaphor, technically useful in the language of jurists—the notion of "juridical personality"—has been mistaken for a reality, and has given birth in this way to "one of the most baneful myths of our times." As we have seen, such a myth has much deeper roots, I would say Hegelian roots. Hegel did not invent, he gave full metaphysical expression to the idea of the State as a superhuman person. The modern States were Hegelian in practice long before Hegel and his theory. The modern State, heir of the kings of old, has conceived of itself as a person superior to the body politic, and either dominating the body politic from above or absorbing the body politic in itself. Now, since the State in actual fact is not a person, but a mere impersonal mechanism of abstract laws and concrete power, it is this impersonal mechanism which will become suprahuman, when that vicious idea comes to develop its whole potentialities; and as a result the natural order of things will be turned upside down: the State will be no longer in the service of men, men will be in the service of the peculiar ends of the State.

Let us not forget, moreover, that this trend toward supreme domination and supreme amorality, which has fully developed and is in full swing in the totalitarian States, is by no means inherent in the State in its real nature and its true and necessary functions, but depends on a perverted notion which preys upon the modern State, and of which democracy, if it is to survive, will get clear.

Let us also observe with de Visscher that this trend of modern States toward supreme domination and supreme amorality, which runs against the nature of the genuinely democratic State and can but impair its most beneficial initiatives, is constantly thwarted, in democratic nations, as concerns especially the *internal or domestic* activity of the State. Because in democratic nations the basic idea of justice, law, and common welfare, on which the State itself is grounded, the rights and freedom of the citizens, the constitution and the free institutions of the body politic, the control exercised by the assemblies of the representatives of the people, the pressure of public opinion, the freedom of expression, freedom of teaching and freedom of the press, tend of themselves to check the vicious trend in question and keep, somehow or other, the State within its proper and natural limits.

But as concerns the *external or foreign* activity of the State, that is, its relations with the other States, there is nothing to check the trend of modern States—to the extent to which they are infected with the Hegelian virus—toward supreme domination and supreme amorality, nothing except the opposite force of the other States. For there is no more powerful control, no organized international public opinion, to which these States can be submitted. And as to the superior law of justice, they deem it to be embodied in their own supreme interests. I by no means disregard the work which international institutions like the late League of Nations or the present United Nations Organization were or are performing in order to remedy that situation. Yet this work cannot touch the root of the evil, and remains inevitably precarious and subsidiary, from the very fact that such institutions are organs created and put into action by the sovereign States, whose decisions they can only register. As a matter of fact, modern States, with respect to international relations, are acting in a kind of vacuum, as supreme and adamantine, transcendent, absolute entities. While the modern State grows inevitably stronger as regards its supervision over national life, and the powers with which it is armed more and more dangerous for the peace of nations, at the same time the external relations of foreign policy between nations are strictly reduced to relations between those supreme entities in their harsh mutual competition, with an only remote participation of the people—their human aspirations and their human wills—in the course of fateful events developing above them in an unattainable Jovian heaven.

II. DISCARDING THE SO-CALLED SOVEREIGNTY OF THE STATE

From all that I have said it appears that the two main obstacles to the establishment of a lasting peace are, first, the so-called absolute sovereignty of modern States; second, the impact of the economic interdependence of all nations upon our present irrational stage of political evolution, in which no world political organization corresponds to world material unification.

As concerns the so-called absolute sovereignty of modern States, I am not unaware of the fact that we may use, and we often use, the expression "sovereignty of the State" to mean a genuine political concept, namely the full independence or autonomy of the body politic. Unfortunately, "sovereignty of the State" is exactly the wrong expression for that concept, because the subject involved is not the State but the body politic, and because the body politic itself is not genuinely sovereign. The right name is autonomy. No less unfortu-

nately, this very autonomy of the body politic no longer exists in full: as a matter of fact, the nations are no longer autonomous in their economic life; they are even only half autonomous in their political life, because their political life is impaired by the lasting threat of war and interfered with, in domestic affairs, by the ideology and pressure of other nations. Now I say that it is not enough to remark that modern bodies politic have ceased in actual fact to be "sovereign" in that improper sense which means full autonomy. It is also not enough to request from sovereign States limitations and partial surrenders of their sovereignty, as if it were only a matter of making more or less restricted in its extension a privilege genuinely and really inherent in the State, and as if, moreover, sovereignty could be limited in its own sphere.

That is not enough. We must come down to the roots, that is, we must get rid of the Hegelian or pseudo-Hegelian concept of the State as a person, a suprahuman person, and understand that the State is only a *part* (a topmost part, but a part) and an *instrumental agency* in the body politic,—thus bringing the State back to its true, normal, and necessary functions as well as to its genuine dignity. And we must realize that the State is not and has never been sovereign, because sovereignty means a *natural* right (which does not belong to the State but to the body politic as perfect society) to a supreme power and independence which are supreme *separately from* and *above* the whole that the sovereign rules (and of which neither the State nor the body politic is possessed). If the State were sovereign, in the genuine sense of this word, it could never surrender its sovereignty, nor even have it restricted. Whereas the body politic, which is not sovereign, but has a right to full autonomy, can freely surrender this right if it recognizes that it is no longer a perfect society, and decides to enter a larger, truly perfect political society.

III. NECESSITY FOR A WORLD POLITICAL SOCIETY

As concerns the second main obstacle to the establishment of a lasting peace, namely the present state of political *inorganization* of the world, well, here we are getting to the core of the problem we have to discuss.

If we place ourselves in the perspective of rational necessities, neglecting for a moment the factual entanglements of history, and if we transfer ourselves to the final conclusions made clear by the logical requirements of the issue, then we shall see how cogently the advocates of World Government, or of a *one world* politically organized, make out their case.

Suffice it briefly to recall the arguments they have developed to substantiate their contention.

Distinguishing from the various causes which are incitations to war (and which are epitomized in human nature and its need for material goods) the basic structural condition presupposed by war, Mr. Mortimer Adler states that "the only cause of war is anarchy," that is, "the condition of those who try to live together without government." "Anarchy occurs wherever men or nations try to live together without each surrendering their sovereignty."[3] As a result, if a time arrives in which war is made impossible, this will be a time in which anarchy between nations has been suppressed, in other words, a time in which world government has been established.

In a similar line of reasoning, Mr. Stringfellow Barr, having described *The Pilgrimage of Western Man,* writes: "The problem which confronted the generation of Armistice Two, the first generation of the Atomic Age, was clearly the oldest political problem of all: how to find government for a community that lacked it, even if each fraction of the community already lived under a government of its own. It had been solved by tribes that had merged to form a village, by villages that had merged to form city-states like those of Renaissance Italy, by city-states that had merged to form empires or to form sovereign nation-states. Now it was nation-states, not villages, that were the governed fractions of an ungoverned community. What was terribly new about the problem was that this time the community was world-wide, bound together for weal or woe by modern science, modern technology, and the clamorous needs of modern industry." Thus man today, broadening his imagination, has to grasp with respect to a whole planet the force of the argument of Alexander Hamilton in the first of the *Federalist Papers,* that is to say, as Stringfellow Barr puts it, "that the price of peace is justice, the price of justice is law, that the price of law is government, and that government must apply law to men and women, not merely to subordinate governments."[4]

Finally Chancellor Hutchins has admirably shown, in his lecture on *St. Thomas and the World State,*[5] that the concept of a pluralist world-wide political society perfectly squares with the basic principles of Thomas Aquinas's political philosophy. For Thomas Aquinas as well as for Aristotle, self-sufficiency (I do not say total self-sufficiency, I say real, if relative, self-sufficiency), self-sufficiency is the essential property of *perfect society*, which is the goal to which the evolution of political forms in mankind tends; and the primary good ensured by a perfect society—a good which is one indeed with its very unity and life—is its own internal and external peace. As a result, when neither peace nor self-sufficiency can be achieved by a particular form of society, like the city, it is no longer that particular form, but a broader one, for instance the kingdom, which is perfect society. Hence we are entitled to conclude, following the same line of argumentation: when neither peace nor self-sufficiency can be achieved by particular kingdoms, nations, or states, they are no longer perfect societies, and it is a broader society, defined by its capacity to achieve self-sufficiency and peace—therefore, in actual fact, with reference to our historical age, the international community politically organized—which is to become perfect society.

According to the same principles, it was on a merely moral ground, reinforced as far as possible by legal and customary bonds born of mutual agreement, in other words, it was by virtue of *natural law* and *jus gentium* or the common law of civilization, that kingdoms and States, as long as they answered in an approximate yet sufficient manner the concept of perfect society, had to fulfil their obligations toward that "community of the whole world," that international society whose existence and dignity have always been affirmed by Christian doctors and jurists, as well as by the common consciousness of mankind. And God knows how the obligations in question were fulfilled in the absence of the sword of the law. But when the particular bodies politic, our so-called national States, grown incapable of achieving self-sufficiency and assuring peace, definitely recede from the concept of perfect society, then the picture necessarily changes: since it is the international society which must become henceforth the perfect society, it is not only on a *moral,* but on a fully *juridical* ground that the obligations of the particular bodies politic, once they have become parts of a politically organized whole, will have to fulfil their obligations toward this whole: not only by virtue of *natural law* and *jus gentium,* but also by virtue of the *positive laws* which the politically organized world society will establish and which its government will enforce.

In the transitional period, or as long as a world government has not yet been founded by the only normal and genuine process of generation of political societies, that is, through the exercise of freedom, reason, and human virtues, it is obvious, as Mr. Hutchins points out, that the foundation of a World State by force, as well as any attempt by one State forcibly to impose its will upon another, should be opposed as contrary to Natural Law. As long as a pluralist world political society has not yet been founded, the particular bodies politic shaped by history remain the only political units in which the concept of perfect society, though they are now falling short of it, has been carried into effect: be they great or small, powerful or weak, they keep their right to full independence, as well as that right to make war and peace which is inherent in perfect society, and in the exercise of which moral law demands of them today more self-restraint than ever.

Yet the final aim is clearly determined. Once the perfect society required by our historical age, that is the world political society, has been brought into being, it will be bound in justice to respect to the greatest possible extent the freedoms—essential to the common good of the world—of those invaluable vessels of political, moral, and cultural life which will be its parts; but the particular States will have surrendered their full independence,—much more indeed in their external than in their internal sphere of activity, and the World State will have to enjoy, within the strict limits and the well-balanced modalities proper to such a completely new creation of human reason, the powers naturally required by a perfect society: legislative power, executive power, judicial power, with the coercive power necessary to enforce the law. . . .

A good many objections have been raised, of course, to the idea of a World Government. I should like only to allude to the most conspicuous one, which insists that the idea is fine and beautiful, but utterly impossible of realization, and therefore most dangerous, for it runs the risk of diverting toward a brilliant utopia efforts which should be directed toward more humble but possible achievements. The reply is that if the idea is grounded, as we believe, on true and sound political philosophy, it cannot be impossible *in itself.* Therefore it is up to human intelligence and energy to make it, in the long run, not impossible *with respect to* the enormous yet contingent obstacles and impediments that the sociological and historical conditions which lie heavy on mankind have piled up against it.

At this point I must confess that in my capacity as an Aristotelian I am not much of an idealist. If the idea of a world political society were only a beautiful idea,

I would not care much for it. I hold it to be a great idea, but also a sound and right idea. Yet the greater an idea is with respect to the weakness and entanglements of the human condition, the more cautious one must be in handling it. And the more attentive one must be in *not* demanding its immediate realization (a warning which, if I may be allowed to say, sounds especially distasteful in a generous country where good ideas are looked upon as something to be immediately applied and seem worthy of interest only to that extent). It would not be good, either for the cause of the idea or for the cause of peace, to use the idea of World Government as a weapon against the limited and precarious international agencies which for the time being are the only existing political means at the disposal of men to protract the truce among nations. Moreover the supporters of the concept of World Government perfectly know— Mr. Mortimer Adler has especially stressed that aspect of the question—that this concept can be brought into being only after many years of struggle and effort. They know, therefore, that their solution for a future perpetual peace has surely no more efficacy for the precarious peace to be ensured today than the work of the agencies to which I just alluded. The pros and cons, in the issue of World Government, do not concern our day, but the generations to come.

IV. FULLY POLITICAL VS. MERELY GOVERNMENTAL THEORY

So far I have dealt with the most general aspects of the problem. Perhaps I could be tempted to end my essay here; so at least I would spare the patience of the reader. Yet further consideration seems to me to be needed. My discussion is not finished, and this chapter has to set forth a new series of considerations.

The reason for this is that the problem has been posed in terms of its ultimate solution, and in terms of world government,—therefore, first of all in terms of *State* and *government.* Now, if we remember the distinction, emphasized in the first chapter of this book, between *state* and *body politic,* we shall see that the very idea of world government can be conceived in two opposite ways. The question, therefore, is: in which way should a sound political philosophy conceive of world government? A first possible manner of conceiving world government would reduce the whole matter to the *sole and exclusive* consideration of the *state and government*. Let us call it the *merely governmental* theory of world organization. The second possible manner of conceiving world government envisages the matter under the universal or integral consideration of the *body politic* or *political society*. Let us call it the *fully political* theory of world organization.

I think that the *fully political* theory is the good one, and that a *merely governmental* theory would be wrong and disastrous. I do not know of anybody having ever taken a stand in its behalf. But sins of omission are to be avoided like the others. My point is that it is necessary to clarify the issue, in order to brush aside any possibility of mistaking one theory for the other, and to get rid of misunderstandings quite detrimental to the very idea of world political organization.

Let me emphasize once again that the basic political reality is not the State, but the body politic with its multifarious institutions, the multiple communities which it involves, and the moral community which grows out of it. The body politic is the people organized under just laws. The State is the particular agency which specializes in matters dealing with the common good of the body politic, it is therefore the topmost political agency, but the State is a part, not a whole, and its functions are merely instrumental: it is for the body politic and for the people that it sees to the public order, enforces laws, possesses power; and being a part in the service of the people, it must be controlled by the people.

What is called in French *le gouvernement,* and here the Administration or the administrative officials, that is, the men who are in charge of the common good, are part both of the body politic and of the State; but because they are the head of the people, and deputies for the people with respect to whom they exercise a vicarious function, and by whom, in a democratic régime, they are chosen, their governing function is rooted in the body politic, not in the State; it is not because their function is rooted in the State that they are part of the body politic; it is because their function is rooted in the body politic that they are part of the State.

Since that is how things are, we might better say, as I observed at the start, the *Problem of the World's Political Organization* than the *Problem of World Government*. The whole issue is not simply *World Government*. It is *World Political Society*.

What I just called a *merely governmental* theory would consider the whole thing, Existence and Nature

of World Government, as well as Passage from the present state of affairs to the World Government, in the perspective of the State and government *separately* from that of the body politic. As a result, we would have to contemplate a process developed artificially, and against the grain of nature, resulting in a State without a body politic or a political society of its own, a world brain without a world body; and the World Government would be an absolute Super-state, or a superior State deprived of body politic and merely *superimposed* on and interfering with the life of the particular States—even though it were born of popular election and representation. For this procedure is of course the only authentic one—it is not through delegation from the various governments, it is through the free suffrage of men and women that the World State is to be founded and maintained—but this necessary procedure is a merely technical or juridical one and would be entirely insufficient to change in any way the fact that I am pointing out.

Just, then, as the ambition to become a sovereign person was transferred from the Holy Germanic Emperor to the kings—at the time when the French kings refused obedience to the Holy Empire—and from the kings to the States, so this same ambition would be transferred from the States to the World Superstate. So that by a tragic inconsistency, while putting an end to the modern myth of the State as regards all the particular States, men would again find this myth, the myth of the State as person and sovereign person and suprahuman person, enthroned at the top of the universe. All the consequences involved in the Hegelian conception of the State could then spread over humanity with irresistible power.

The quest of such a Superstate capping the nations is nothing else, in fact, than the quest of the old utopia of a universal Empire. This utopia was pursued in past ages in the form of the Empire of one single nation over all others. The pursuit, in the modern age, of an absolute World Superstate would be the pursuit of a democratic multinational Empire, which would be no better than the others. . . .

What I have just characterized as a merely governmental theory of world government is the exact opposite of what all of us who support the idea of world government are thinking, and, in particular, of the political philosophy of the Chicago plan's authors.[6] But other people may come along, and be in a hurry, and be mistaken. And the more we insist on the right way, the more we must be aware of, and point out, the dangers of the wrong one. A *merely governmental* theory of world organization would go the wrong way, because from the very start it would pursue the analogy between *State with respect to individuals* and *World State with respect to particular States* in the mere perspective of the topmost power.

The *fully political* theory of world organization goes the right way, because it pursues the same analogy in the perspective of the basic requirements of political life and freedom. As Adler and Hutchins have repeatedly pointed out, the problem is to raise international community to the condition of a perfect society, or of a politically organized international society.

At this point I should like to make a few remarks on the comparison which suggests itself, and which, quoting Mr. Stringfellow Barr, I used in the first part of this chapter, between the passage from the tribe to the village, from the village to the city, from the city to the kingdom or to the modern political society, and the passage from our present political society to a world political society. The processes in question are only analogical, of course, and took place in multiple and exceedingly various fashions. Mr. Max Ascoli has sharply criticized that comparison,[7] and accused of utter naïveté the notion that our present political societies, ripened by history, could or should develop into a world political society by a so-to-speak mechanical process of broadening in extension. This criticism, in my opinion, applies to the manner in which things would be conceived in a merely governmental theory. It does not apply to the manner in which things are conceived in the fully political theory of world organization.

From another point of view, Henri Bergson, distinguishing *closed societies,* which are temporal and terrestrial, from *open society,* which is spiritual, insisted that that kind of friendship which unites members of the village or the city can broaden from a closed society to another, larger, closed society, but that when it comes to love for all men, then it is a question of passing from one order to another; from the realm of closed societies to the realm, infinitely different, of open and spiritual society, in which man is united with that very Love which has created the world.[8] All that is true. But here also the mere consideration of extension is only accidental. If men are to pass from our present political societies to a world political society, they will pass to a larger *closed* society, as large as the whole company of nations, and civic friendship will have to broaden in the same manner. Civic friendship will still remain infinitely different from charity, just as the world society will remain infinitely different from the Kingdom of God.

Yet these remarks make us aware of a crucial point. The passage of which we are speaking implies a change not only in the dimension of extension, but first of all in the dimension of depth: a change in the inner structures of man's morality and sociality.

In the past epochs of history the will of men to live together, which is basic in the formation of political societies, was as a rule—with the splendid exception of this country—brought into being by any kind of means, save freedom. It has been enforced even by war; for, it is sad to say, wars have been the most general means—because they are the most primitive and brutal—of mixing and brewing peoples together and forcing them to know each other and to live with one another, conqueror and conquered, in the same place, and in the long run to develop between each other a kind of unhappy congeniality. Later on civic friendship could occur.

That time is past, at least as concerns democratic principles and the requirements of justice. Now, if a world political society is some day founded, it will be by means of freedom. *It is by means of freedom that the peoples of the earth will have been brought to a common will to live together.* This simple sentence makes us measure the magnitude of the moral revolution—the *real* revolution now proposed to the hopes and virtues of mankind—on the necessity for which Mr. Mortimer Adler laid stress in his book.

Living together does not mean occupying the same place in space. It does not mean, either, being subjected to the same physical or external conditions or pressures or to the same pattern of life; it does not mean *Zusammenmarschieren*. Living together means sharing as men, not as beasts, that is, with basic free acceptance, in certain common sufferings and in a certain common task.

The reason for which men will to live together is a positive, creative reason. It is not because they fear some danger that men will to live together. Fear of war is not and never has been the reason for which men have wanted to form a political society. Men want to live together and form a political society for a given task to be undertaken in common. When men will have a will to live together in a world-wide society, it will be because they will have a will to achieve a world-wide common task. What task indeed? The conquest of freedom. The point is to have men become aware of that task, and of the fact that it is worthy of self-sacrifice.

Given the human condition, the most significant synonym of *living together* is *suffering together*. When men form a political society, they do not want to share in common suffering out of love for each other. They want to accept common suffering out of love for the common task and the common good. The will to achieve a world-wide common task must therefore be strong enough to entail a will to share in certain common sufferings made inevitable by that task, and by the common good of a world-wide society. What sufferings indeed? Sufferings due to solidarity. Suffice it to observe that the very existence of a world-wide society will inevitably imply deep changes in the social and economic structures of the national and international life of peoples, and a serious repercussion of these changes on the free business of a number of individuals, who are not the most numerous in the world, but the most attached to profit-making. The very existence of a world-wide society will also inevitably imply a certain—relative no doubt, yet quite serious and appreciable—equalization of the standards of life of all individuals. Let us put it in crude terms: perhaps, if the issue were made sufficiently clear to them, people in occidental nations would be ready to accept, for the sake of peace and of a world political organization ensuring lasting peace, a serious lowering of their standards of life in order to provide people on the other side of the iron curtain with an equivalent raising of their standards of life. Yet this would suppose a kind of moral heroism, for which, I deem, we are badly prepared. People are unhappy, and it will be necessary for them to confront new obligations and sacrifices, connected with the life of other men at the other end of the world, in order to promote in the long run peace, happiness, and freedom for all.

We can meditate in this connection on two far-reaching sentences of Mr. John Nef: "Science and machinery," he wrote, "have enabled humanity to command the material resources of the planet in ways which have made world government indispensable. At the same time science and machinery are depriving individuals and societies of the vision and of the control over themselves, which alone might make world government human and worth having."[9] And: "The price of peace is the renunciation, to a large extent, of success as the principal driving force in thought, work and politics."[10] The matter is nothing less than having science perfected by wisdom, and the criterion of success superseded by the criterion of good and devotion to the good.

One body politic is *one* organized people. Of course the unity of a world body politic would be quite different from the unity which characterizes kingdoms or nations, and to which our thought is accustomed. It would be not even a federal unity, but rather, let me say, a *pluralist unity,* taking place only through the lasting diversity of the particular bodies politic, and fostering that diversity. The fact remains that when we say that the community of nations must form *one* body politic, even taking into account the qualifications to which such a unity would be subject, we are saying that the community of peoples must form *one* people, even taking into account the qualifications to which such a pluralist unity would be subject. That means that among all peoples the sense of the common good of that *one people* should develop, and supersede the sense of the common good peculiar to each body politic. A sense of civic friendship as large as that one people should also and simultaneously develop, since civic love or friendship is the very soul or animating form of every political society. To insist that this sense of a world-wide civic friendship and a world-wide common good is a prerequisite condition for the foundation of a world political society would be putting the cart before the horse. Yet some beginnings should actually take shape in the peoples; moreover the sense of the common good of the community of peoples, with the mood of good will and fellow-feeling it implies, is implicitly and virtually involved in the freely developed will to live together, which *is* the basic condition prerequired for the foundation of a world political society coming into existence by means of freedom. . . .

V. A SUPRA-NATIONAL ADVISORY COUNCIL

As to practical application, a conclusion follows from all the preceding considerations: namely, that the passage to a world political society presupposes a will to live together developed in all the peoples, especially all great peoples in the world; any effort to found a World State in the absence of such a universal basis, thus creating a half-universality to be extended progressively to the whole, would, I am afraid, invite war rather than peace.

A second conclusion is that the passage to a one world politically organized can only occur after a long time. I know that time is relative, not only in the sense that a long time with respect to our experience is a short time with respect to history, but also in the sense that time runs faster in proportion as human history goes on. Nevertheless the period of maturation will seem very long to our unhappy race.

It is regrettable that perpetual peace cannot be established immediately after the discovery of the atomic bomb. This is no more regrettable than the fact that it *was necessary* to discover the atomic bomb; this is no more regrettable than the fact that, twenty centuries after the good tidings in Bethlehem, mankind is still in a prehistoric age with regard to the application of the Gospel in actual life. Now the business of human history is not in a stage of free creative development, rather it reckons up its losses; we are paying century-old historical debts. Ancient Israel, in such moments, turned to God in self-accusation and hope. We are more proud, and less hopeful. I have often expressed the opinion that our major problems cannot be decisively settled before the time of great crisis and great reconciliation announced by St. Paul.

Yet the creative process, visibly or invisibly, is always at work in history; and the saddest periods are often the most fecund ones. If nations have still to extricate themselves, in a most precarious and far from brilliant way, from the dangers of universal destruction, and if the foundation of a politically organized community of the world is only to be expected in a distant future, this is but reason to hope for that foundation more strongly, and to undertake, right now, with greater energy, the task of preparing it, and of awakening common consciousness to the imperative necessity of moving toward it.

This task, as we well know, has already been undertaken by the most courageous and far-seeing pioneers—in Chicago especially it was undertaken six days after the first atomic bomb dropped on Hiroshima. Such a task will obviously develop first of all as a deep and continuing task of education and enlightenment, discussion and study. It will also develop through the efforts, limited as they may be, of the diverse cooperative agencies of the United Nations, and through all the various efforts that have been started everywhere to promote the federal idea, and which are especially valuable, in my opinion, when they tend to well defined objectives actually achievable in one partial field or another, and are on their guard, at the same time, against the risk of only creating new and larger patterns for the world competition they are trying to eliminate.

But is there no means whatever of inserting in the present structure of the world a germ, however small it may be, or a first beginning, however weak it may be, which would have a chance of proving useful, if, some day, better times make possible the *political preparation* for the foundation of a world political society? Everyone's imagination can exert itself in this regard. Well, at this point may I also be permitted to make, in the most tentative way, a suggestion of my own?

My own suggestion is that a new superior agency, which would be deprived of any *power* whatsoever, but endowed with unquestionable *moral authority,* would perhaps have a chance of being accepted by the States, and would also have a chance of becoming the first beginning of which I just spoke.

Let us suppose a kind of world council whose function would be only a function of ethical and political wisdom, and which would be made up of the highest and most experienced authorities in moral and juridical sciences. Let us suppose that the members of this supreme advisory council would be picked from the nations of the world according to some equitable method of apportionment, and would be directly elected by the people of all nations, among men previously proposed by the highest institutions and the governments of every State. But let us suppose that, once elected, they would lose their national citizenship and would be given world citizenship, so as to become independent of any government and completely free in the exercise of their spiritual responsibility.

Let us suppose that they would be materially disarmed, without any other means of action than their own pronouncements, and only protected by the mutual commitments of the States. And let us suppose that they would be deprived of any powers, even, in contradistinction to the present International Court of Justice, of any judicial power. No government could appeal to them to make any decision, they would have no juridical connection with the United Nations, they would be simply free to tell the governments and the nations what they held to be just.

In proportion as such a supreme advisory council acted in a really wise, independent, and firm manner, and resisted the pressures exerted upon it, its moral authority would grow stronger, as well as its influence on public opinion. It would give a voice to the conscience of the peoples.

I think that being really a world institution, shielded by its constitution from the interference of any government; being, at the same time, deprived of powers; and exercising a merely moral function, it would have a chance of disarming the fears—fears of manoeuvres, of encirclement, of loss of prestige, etc.—which spoil the activities of international organizations; as a result, and taking into account the lip service which even the most cynical governments deem it necessary to pay to the moral factor, I think that some day, perhaps after new ordeals shall have made the situation more desperate, the idea of such a supreme advisory council could perhaps have a chance of being accepted by all States and governments.

What makes me fond of that idea is the fact that by this means a possibility could be offered for the coming into being of something indispensable and badly needed—namely an organized international opinion.

It is also the fact that, by this means, people could be enlightened and helped with regard to the most intricate temporal problems which concern the common good of the world, and on which, in democratic nations, they have to make a decision. Some of such problems are even of a nature to put their consciences on the rack—I am thinking especially of the problem of just war. People know that participating in an unjust war is sharing in homicide. They are told, on the other hand, that things have become so obscure and entangled that they lack competence to bear judgment on each particular case: am I bound, then, to share in what is *perhaps* a crime, because my government is a better judge than I on the matter, even if I were a German at the time of the Hitlerian war? On the opposite side, systematic conscientious objection is a tragic illusion, no less harmful to justice than blind obedience. The old standards with respect to which a war was to be considered just or unjust are outworn, and nevertheless the fact of giving up the distinction between the just and the unjust, in the case of war as in any other case, would boil down to a simple abdication of moral reason. It would be good if, in given and especially serious international conjunctures, a senate of wise men were to tell people where, in their opinion, the road to justice was.

But first and foremost, if such a senate of wise men existed, it would be the first token of the possibility of a really supranational world organization, and it would foster in the consciousness of the peoples that great movement of intelligence and will on which depends the genuine and constructive revolution needed by our historical age, the foundation of a world community politically organized.

I am afraid that in expressing at the end of this chapter a practical suggestion of my own, I have perhaps yielded to the old temptation of philosophers, who would have reason, through the instrumentality of certain wise men, be accepted as an authority in human affairs. After all, this would be less serious an illusion, I suppose,—and in any case a less frequent one—than

the conviction treasured by so many fatalists, that any reliance on reason has to be carefully avoided in the conduct of *Man, and the State.*

READING 54

National Self-Determination

Avishai Margalit and Joseph Raz

Avishai Margalit is Professor of Philosophy at the Hebrew University of Jerusalem, and **Joseph Raz** is Professor of Law at Oxford University. Both are highly respected scholars. Raz's book *The Morality of Freedom* has been widely acclaimed. In this reading, Margalit and Raz examine the question of when, if ever, ethnic nationalities have a legitimate moral claim to self-determination. They argue for a set of necessary conditions and suggest ways of arbitrating between conflicts of interest between competing groups.

This reading is taken from the *Journal of Philosophy* 87 (1990), by permission.

I. ISOLATING THE ISSUE

The core content of the claim to be examined is that there is a right to determine whether a certain territory shall become, or remain, a separate state (and possibly also whether it should enjoy autonomy within a larger state). The idea of national self-determination or (as we shall refer to it in order to avoid confusion) the idea of self-government encompasses much more. The value of national self-government is the value of entrusting the general political power over a group and its members to the group. If self-government is valuable then it is valuable that whatever is a proper matter for political decision should be subject to the political decision of the group in all matters concerning the group and its members. The idea of national self-government, in other words, speaks of groups determining the character of their social and economic environment, their fortunes, the course of their development, and the fortunes of their members by their own actions, i.e., by the action of those groups, inasmuch as these are matters which are properly within the realm of political action. Given the current international state system, in which political power rests, in the main, with sovereign states, the right to determine whether a territory should be an independent state is quite naturally regarded as the main instrument for realizing the ideal of self-determination. Consideration of this right usually dominates all discussions of national self-determination. To examine the justification of the right is the ultimate purpose of this article. But we shall continuously draw attention to the fact that, as we shall try to show, the right of self-determination so understood is not ultimate, but is grounded in the wider value of national self-government, which is itself to be only instrumentally justified.

The next section deals with the nature of the groups that might be the subject of such a right. Section III considers what value, if any, is served by the enjoyment of political independence by such groups. Section IV examines the case for conceding that there is a moral right to self-determination. This examination may lead to revising our understanding of the content of the right. It may reveal that moral considerations justify only a narrower right, or that the argument that justifies the right warrants giving it a wider scope. But the core as identified here will provide the working base from which to launch the inquiry.

Before we start, a few words about this way of identifying the problem may be in place. In two ways the chosen focus of our examination is narrower than many discussions of self-determination in international relations. First, we disregard the claims made, typically by third-world countries, in the name of self-determination, against the economic domination of multinational companies, the World Bank, or against powerful regional or world powers. The considerations canvassed in this paper are relevant to such issues, but fall short of directly tackling them. To be complete, a discussion of a right must examine both its grounds and its consequences. This paper is concerned mostly with the grounds for the right of self-determination. It asks the question: Who has the right and under what conditions is it to be exercised? It does not go into the question of the consequences of the right beyond the assumption, already stated, that it is a right that a territory be a self-governing state. A good deal of the current turmoil in international law, and international relations, has to do with the exploration of that last notion. What is entailed by the fact that a state is a sovereign, self-governing, entity? The claims that economic domination violate the right to self-determination belong to

that discussion. The conclusions of this paper provide part of the grounds by which such claims are to be settled. But we do not propose to pursue this question here.

Second, claims of self-determination are invariably raised whenever one state invades and occupies another, or a territory belonging to another. Yet it is important to distinguish between the wrongness of military invasion or occupation, and the rights available against it, and the right (whatever it may turn out to be) to self-determination. In a word, the latter is a source of title, whereas the former is a possessory right based largely on public-order considerations. Any legal system, international law not excluded, recognizes certain ways as legitimate ways of solving disputes, and outlaws others. Subject to the exceptions of legitimate self-defense and self-help, the use of violence is forbidden. Violation of that prohibition gives rise to a right to have the *status quo ante* restored, before the deeper sources of the dispute between the parties are examined; that is, regardless of the soundness of one's title to a territory, one may not use force to occupy it. This is why the right to recover a territory lost by force is a possessory right. It does not depend on the ultimate soundness of one's title, and that is why it was said to be based on public-order considerations. A large part of its justification is in the need to establish that the proper means of dispute resolution be the only ones resorted to.

Not surprisingly, invocation of this possessory right is, however, accompanied by a claim of good title (the merits of which are not immediately relevant). The underlying title is often the right to self-determination. Hence the temptation to confuse the two. But notice that, apart from the different justificatory foundations, the two are far from identical in consequence. They merely overlap. The claims of a people who have been for many years ruled by another cannot be based on the possessory right that applies only against a recent occupier. On the other hand, the occupation of portions of Antarctica, or of some uninhabited island, do violate the possessory right, but not the right of self-determination. The latter is that of the inhabitants, and does not apply when there are no inhabitants.

II. GROUPS

Assuming that self-determination is enjoyed by groups, what groups qualify? Given that the right is normally attributed to peoples or nations, it is tempting to give that as the answer and concentrate on characterizing "peoples" or "nations." The drawbacks of this approach are two: it assumes too much and it poses problems that may not require a solution.

It is far from clear that peoples or nations rather than tribes, ethnic groups, linguistic, religious, or geographical groups are the relevant reference group. What is it that makes peoples particularly suited to self-determination? The right concerns determination whether a certain territory shall be self-governing or not. It appears to affect most directly the residents of a territory, and their neighbors. If anyone, then residents of geographical regions seem intuitively to be the proper bearers of the right. Saying this does not get us very far. It does not help in identifying the residents of which regions should qualify. To be sure, this is the crucial question. But even posing it in this way shows that the answer, "the largest regions inhabited by one people or nation," is far from being the obvious answer.

We have some understanding of the benefits self-government might bring. We need to rely on this in looking for the characteristics that make groups suitable recipients of those benefits. We want, in other words, to identify groups by those characteristics which are relevant to the justification of the right. If it turns out that those do not apply to peoples or nations, we shall have shown that the right to self-determination is misconceived and, as recognized in international law, unjustified. Alternatively, the groups identified may encompass peoples (or some peoples) as well as other groups. This will provide a powerful case for redrawing the boundaries of the right. Either way we shall be saved much argument concerning the characterization of nations which, interesting as it is in itself, is irrelevant to our purpose.

Having said that, it may be useful to take nations and peoples as the obvious candidates for the right. We need not worry about their defining characteristics. But we may gain insight by comparing them with groups, e.g., the fiction-reading public, or Tottenham Football Club supporters, which obviously do not enjoy such a right. Reflection on such examples suggests six characteristics that in combination are relevant to a case for self-determination.

1. The group has a common character and a common culture that encompass many, varied and important aspects of life, a culture that defines or marks a variety of forms or styles of life, types of activities, occupations, pursuits, and relationships. With national groups we expect to find national cuisines, distinctive

architectural styles, a common language, distinctive literary and artistic traditions, national music, customs, dress, ceremonies and holidays, etc. None of these is necessary. They are but typical examples of the features that characterize peoples and other groups that are serious candidates for the right to self-determination. They have pervasive cultures, and their identity is determined at least in part by their culture. They possess cultural traditions that penetrate beyond a single or a few areas of human life, and display themselves in a whole range of areas, including many which are of great importance for the well-being of individuals.

2. The correlative of the first feature is that people growing up among members of the group will acquire the group culture, will be marked by its character. Their tastes and their options will be affected by that culture to a significant degree. The types of careers open to one, the leisure activities one learned to appreciate and is therefore able to choose from, the customs and habits that define and color relations with strangers and with friends, patterns of expectations and attitudes between spouses and among other members of the family, features of lifestyles with which one is capable of empathizing and for which one may therefore develop a taste—all these will be marked by the group culture.

They need not be indelibly marked. People may migrate to other environments, shed their previous culture, and acquire a new one. It is a painful and slow process, success in which is rarely complete. But it is possible, just as it is possible that socialization will fail and one will fail to be marked by the culture of one's environment, except negatively, to reject it. The point made is merely the modest one that, given the pervasive nature of the culture of the groups we are seeking to identify, their influence on individuals who grow up in their midst is profound and far-reaching. The point needs to be made in order to connect concern with the prosperity of the group with concern for the well-being of individuals. This tie between the individual and the collective is at the heart of the case for self-determination.

As one would expect, the tie does not necessarily extend to all members of the group, and failure of socialization is not the only reason. The group culture affects those who grow up among its members, be they members or not. But to say this is no more than to point to various anomalies and dilemmas that may arise. Most people live in groups of these kinds, so that those who belong to none are denied full access to the opportunities that are shaped in part by the group's culture. They are made to feel estranged and their chances to have a rewarding life are seriously damaged. The same is true of people who grow up among members of a group so that they absorb its culture, but are then denied access to it because they are denied full membership of the group.

Nothing in the above presupposes that groups of the kind we are exploring are geographically concentrated, let alone that their members are the only inhabitants of any region. Rather, by drawing on the transmission of the group culture through the socialization of the young, these comments emphasize the historical nature of the groups with which we are concerned. Given that they are identified by a common culture, at least in part, they also share a history, for it is through a shared history that cultures develop and are transmitted.

3. Membership in the group is, in part, a matter of mutual recognition. Typically, one belongs to such groups if, among other conditions, one is recognized by other members of the group as belonging to it. The other conditions (which may be the accident of birth or the sharing of the group culture, etc.) are normally the grounds cited as reasons for such recognition. But those who meet those other conditions and are yet rejected by the group are at best marginal or problematic members of it. The groups concerned are not formal institutionalized groups, with formal procedures of admission. Membership in them is a matter of informal acknowledgment of belonging by others generally, and by other members specifically. The fiction-reading public fails our previous tests. It is not identified by its sharing a wide-ranging pervasive culture. It also fails the third test. To belong to the fiction-reading public all we have to do is to read fiction. It does not matter whether others recognize us as fiction-reading.

4. The third feature prepares the way for, and usually goes hand in hand with, the importance of membership for one's self-identification. Consider the fiction-reading public again. It is a historically significant group. Historians may study the evolution of the fiction-reading public, how it spread from women to men, from one class to others, from reading aloud in small groups to silent reading, from reliance on libraries to book buying, etc.; how it is regarded as important to one's qualification as a cultured person in one country, but not in another; how it furnishes a common topic of conversation in some classes but not in others; how belonging to the group is a mark of political awareness in some countries, while being a sign of escapist retreat from social concerns in another.

Such studies will show, however, that it is only in some societies that the existence of these features of the fiction-reading public is widely known. For the most part, one can belong to the group without being aware that one is a typical reader, that one's profile is that of most readers. Sometimes this is a result of a mistaken group image being current in that society. Our concern is rather with those cases where the society lacks any very distinct image of that group. This indicates that, in such societies, membership of that group does not have a highly visible social profile. It is not one of the facts by which people pigeonhole each other. One need not be aware who, among people one knows, friends, acquaintances, shopkeepers one patronizes, one's doctor, etc., shares the habit. In such societies, membership of the fiction-reading public is not highly visible; that is, it is not one of the things one will normally know about people one has contact with, one of the things that identify "who they are." But it happens in some countries that membership of the reading public becomes a highly visible mark of belonging to a social group, to the intelligentsia, etc. In such countries, talk of the recently published novel becomes a means of mutual recognition.

One of the most significant facts differentiating various football cultures is whether they are cultures of self-recognition: whether identification as a fan or supporter of this club or that is one of the features that are among the main markers of people in the society. The same is true of occupational groups. In some countries, membership is highly visible and is among the primary means of pigeon-holing people, of establishing "who they are;" in others, it is not.

Our concern is with groups, membership of which has a high social profile, that is, groups, membership of which is one of the primary facts by which people are identified, and which form expectations as to what they are like, groups membership of which is one of the primary clues for people generally in interpreting the conduct of others. Since our perceptions of ourselves are in large measure determined by how we expect others to perceive us, it follows that membership of such groups is an important identifying feature for each about himself. These are groups, members of which are aware of their membership and typically regard it as an important clue in understanding who they are, in interpreting their actions and reactions, in understanding their tastes and their manner.

5. Membership is a matter of belonging, not of achievement. One does not have to prove oneself, or to excel in anything, in order to belong and to be accepted

as a full member. To the extent that membership normally involves recognition by others as a member, that recognition is not conditional on meeting qualifications that indicate any accomplishment. To be a good Irishman, it is true, is an achievement. But to be an Irishman is not. Qualification for membership is usually determined by nonvoluntary criteria. One cannot choose to belong. One belongs because of who one is. One can come to belong to such groups, but only by changing, e.g., by adopting their culture, changing one's tastes and habits accordingly—a very slow process indeed. The fact that these are groups, membership of which is a matter of belonging and not of accomplishment, makes them suitable for their role as primary foci of identification. Identification is more secure, less liable to be threatened, if it does not depend on accomplishment. Although accomplishments play their role in people's sense of their own identity, it would seem that at the most fundamental level our sense of our own identity depends on criteria of belonging rather than on those of accomplishment. Secure identification at that level is particularly important to one's well-being.

6. The groups concerned are not small face-to-face groups, members of which are generally known to all other members. They are anonymous groups where mutual recognition is secured by the possession of general characteristics. The exclusion of small groups from consideration is not merely *ad hoc*. Small groups that are based on personal familiarity of all with all are markedly different in the character of their relationships and interactions from anonymous groups. For example, given the importance of mutual recognition to members of these groups, they tend to develop conventional means of identification, such as the use of symbolic objects, participation in group ceremonies, special group manners, or special vocabulary, which help quickly to identify who is "one of us" and who is not.

The various features we listed do not entail each other but they tend to go together. It is not surprising that groups with pervasive cultures will be important in determining the main options and opportunities of their members, or that they will become focal points of identification, etc. The way things are in our world, just about everyone belongs to such a group, and not necessarily to one only. Membership is not exclusive and many people belong to several groups that answer to our description. Some of them are rather like national groups, e.g., tribes or ethnic groups. Others are very different. Some religious groups meet our conditions, as do social classes, and some racial groups. Not all religions or racial groups did develop rich and pervasive cultures. But some did and those qualify.

III. THE VALUE OF SELF-GOVERNMENT

(A) *The Value of Encompassing Groups.* The description of the relevant groups in the preceding section may well disappoint the reader. Some will be disappointed by the imprecise nature of the criteria provided. This would be unjustified. The criteria are not meant to provide operational legal definitions. As such they clearly would not do. Their purpose is to pick on the features of groups which may explain the value of self-determination. As already mentioned, the key to the explanation is in the importance of these groups to the well-being of their members. This thought guided the selection of the features. They are meant to assist in identifying that link. It is not really surprising that they are all vague matters of degree, admitting of many variants and many nuances. One is tempted to say "that's life." It does not come in neatly parceled parts. While striving to identify the features that matter, we have to recognize that they come in many shapes, in many shades, and in many degrees rife with impurities in their concrete mixing.

A more justified source of disappointment is the suspicion that we have cast the net too wide. Social classes clearly do not have a right to self-determination. If they meet the above conditions then those conditions are at best incomplete. Here we can only crave the reader's patience. We tried to identify the features of groups which help explain the value of self-determination. These may apply not only beyond the sphere in which the right is commonly recognized. They may apply to groups that really should not possesses it for other reasons yet to be explored.

The defining properties of the groups we identified are of two kinds. On the one hand, they pick out groups with pervasive cultures; on the other, they focus on groups, membership of which is important to one's self-identity. This combination makes such groups suitable candidates for self-rule. Let us call groups manifesting the six features *encompassing groups*. Individuals find in them a culture which shapes to a large degree their tastes and opportunities, and which provides an anchor for their self-identification and the safety of effortless secure belonging.

Individual well-being depends on the successful pursuit of worthwhile goals and relationships. Goals and relationships are culturally determined. Being social animals means not merely that the means for the satisfaction of people's goals are more readily available within society. More crucially it means that those goals themselves are (when one reaches beyond what is strictly necessary for biological survival) the creatures of society, the products of culture. Family relations, all other social relations between people, careers, leisure activities, the arts, sciences, and other obvious products of "high culture" are the fruits of society. They all depend for their existence on the sharing of patterns of expectations, on traditions preserving implicit knowledge of how to do what, of tacit conventions regarding what is part of this or that enterprise and what is not, what is appropriate and what is not, what is valuable and what is not. Familiarity with a culture determines the boundaries of the imaginable. Sharing in a culture, being part of it, determines the limits of the feasible.

It may be no more than a brute fact that our world is organized in a large measure around groups with pervasive cultures. But it is a fact with far-reaching consequences. It means, in the first place, that membership of such groups is of great importance to individual well-being, for it greatly affects one's opportunities, one's ability to engage in the relationships and pursuits marked by the culture. Secondly, it means that the prosperity of the culture is important to the well-being of its members. If the culture is decaying, or if it is persecuted or discriminated against, the options and opportunities open to its members will shrink, become less attractive, and their pursuit less likely to be successful.

It may be no more than a brute fact that people's sense of their own identity is bound up with their sense of belonging to encompassing groups and that their self-respect is affected by the esteem in which these groups are held. But these facts, too, have important consequences. They mean that individual dignity and self-respect require that the groups, membership of which contributes to one's sense of identity, be generally respected and not be made a subject of ridicule, hatred, discrimination, or persecution.

All this is mere common sense, and is meant to be hedged and qualified in the way our common understanding of these matters is. Of course, strangers can participate in activities marked by a culture. They are handicapped, but not always very seriously. Of course, there are other determinants of one's opportunities, and

of one's sense of self-respect. Membership of an encompassing group is but one factor. Finally, one should mention that groups and their culture may be pernicious, based on exploitation of people, be they their members or not, or on the denigration and persecution of other groups. If so, then the case for their protection and flourishing is weakened, and may disappear altogether.

Having regard for this reservation, the case for holding the prosperity of encompassing groups as vital for the prosperity of their members is a powerful one. Group interests cannot be reduced to individual interests. It makes sense to talk of a group's prospering or declining, of actions and policies as serving the group's interest or harming it, without having to [couch] this in terms of individual interests. The group may flourish if its culture prospers, but this need not mean that the lot of its members or of anyone else has improved. It is in the interest of the group to be held in high regard by others, but it does not follow that, if an American moon landing increases the world's admiration for the United States, Americans necessarily benefit from this. Group interests are conceptually connected to the interests of their members but such connections are nonreductive and generally indirect. For example, it is possible that what enhances the interest of the group provides opportunities for improvement for its members, or that it increases the chance that they will benefit.

This relative independence of group interest is compatible with the view that informs this article: that the moral importance of the group's interest depends on its value to individuals. A large decline in the fortunes of the group may, e.g., be of little consequence to its members. There is no *a priori* way of correlating group interest with that of its members or of other individuals. It depends on the circumstances of different groups at different times. One clear consequence of the fact that the moral significance of a group's interest is in its service to individuals is the fact that it will depend, in part, on the size of the group. The fortunes of a larger group may be material to the well-being of a larger number of people. Other things being equal, numbers matter.

(B) *The Instrumental Case.* Does the interest of members in the prosperity of the group establish a right to self-determination? Certainly not, at least not yet, not without further argument. For one thing we have yet to see any connection between the prosperity of encompassing groups and their political independence. The easiest connection to establish under certain conditions is an instrumental one. Sometimes the prosperity of the group and its self-respect are aided by, sometimes they may be impossible to secure without, the group's enjoying political sovereignty over its own affairs. Sovereignty enables the group to conduct its own affairs in a way conducive to its prosperity. There is no need to elaborate the point. It depends on historical conditions. Hence the prominence of a history of persecution in most debates concerning self-determination. But a history of persecution is neither a necessary nor a sufficient condition for the instrumental case for self-government. It is not a necessary condition, because persecution is not the only reason why the groups may suffer without independence. Suffering can be the result of neglect or ignorance of or indifference to the prosperity of a minority group by the majority. Such attitudes may be so well entrenched that there is no realistic prospect of changing them.

Persecution is not a sufficient condition, for there may be other ways to fight and overcome persecution and because whatever the advantages of independence it may, in the circumstances, lead to economic decline, cultural decay, or social disorder, which only make their members worse off. Besides, as mentioned above, pernicious groups may not deserve protection, especially if it will help them to pursue repressive practices with impunity. Finally, there are the interests of nonmembers to be considered. In short, the instrumental argument (as well as others) for self-government is sensitive to counterarguments pointing to its drawbacks, its cost in terms of human well-being, possible violations of human rights, etc.

We shall return to these issues below. First, let us consider the claim that the instrumental argument trivializes the case for self-government by overlooking its intrinsic value. Of the various arguments for the intrinsic value of self-government which have been and can be advanced, we examine one which seems the most promising.

(C) *An Argument for the Intrinsic Value of Self-government.* The argument is based on an extension of individual autonomy or of self-expression (if that is regarded as independently valuable). The argument unravels in stages: (1) people's membership of encompassing groups is an important aspect of their personality, and their well-being depends on giving it full expression; (2) expression of membership essentially includes manifestation of membership in the open, public life of the community; (3) this requires

expressing one's membership in political activities within the community. The political is an essential arena of community life, and consequently of individual well-being; (4) therefore, self-government is inherently valuable; it is required to provide the group with a political dimension.

The first premise is unexceptionable. So is the second, though an ambiguity might be detected in the way it is often understood. Two elements need separating. First, given the importance of membership to one's well-being, it is vital that the dignity of the group be preserved. This depends, in part, on public manifestations of respect for the group and its culture, and on the absence of ridicule of the group, etc., from the public life of the society of which one is a member. One should not have to identify with or feel loyalty to a group that denigrates an encompassing group to which one belongs. Indeed, one should not have to live in an environment in which such attitudes are part of the common culture. Second, an aspect of well-being is an ability to express publicly one's identification with the group and to participate openly in its public culture. An encompassing group is centered on mutual recognition and is inevitably a group with a public culture. One cannot enjoy the benefits of membership without participation in its public culture, without public participation in its culture.

Both elements are of great importance. Both indicate the vital role played by public manifestations of group culture and group membership among the conditions of individual well-being. To the extent that a person's well-being is bound up with his identity as a member of an encompassing group it has an important public dimension. But that dimension is not necessarily political in the conventional narrow sense of the term. Even where it is, its political expression does not require a political organization whose boundaries coincide with those of the group. One may be politically active in a multinational, multicultural polity. . . .

(D) *The Subjective Element.* In an indirect way, the attempt to argue for the intrinsic value of self-government does point to the danger of misinterpreting the instrumental approach to the question. First, the argument does not deny the intrinsic value of the existence of the political option as a venue for activity and self-expression to all (adult) members of society. We are not advocating a purely instrumentalist view of politics generally. The intrinsic value to individuals of the political option does not require expression in polities whose boundaries coincide with those of encompassing groups. That is the only point argued for above.

Second, the pragmatic, instrumentalist character of the approach advocated here should not be identified with an aggregating impersonal consequentialism. Some people tend to associate any instrumentalist approach with images of a bureaucracy trading off the interest of one person against that of another on the basis of some cost-benefit analysis designed to maximize overall satisfaction; a bureaucracy, moreover, in charge of determining for people what is really good for them, regardless of their own views of the matter. Nothing of the kind should be countenanced. Of course, conflicts among people's interests do arise, and call for rational resolution that is likely to involve sacrificing some interests of some people for the sake of others. Such conflicts, however, admit of a large degree of indeterminacy, and many alternative resolutions may be plausible or rational. In such contexts, talking of maximization, with its connotations of comparability of all options, is entirely out of place.

Furthermore, nothing in the instrumentalist and pragmatic nature of our approach should be allowed to disguise its sensitivity to subjective elements, its responsiveness to the perceptions and sensibilities of the people concerned. To a considerable extent, what matters is how well people feel in their environment: Do they feel at home in it or are they alienated from it? Do they feel respected or humiliated? etc. This leads to a delicate balance between "objective" factors and subjective perceptions. On the one hand, when prospects for the future are concerned, subjective perceptions of danger and likely persecution, etc., are not necessarily to be trusted. These are objective issues on which the opinion of independent spectators may be more reliable than that of those directly involved. On the other hand, the factual issue facing the independent spectators is how people will respond to their conditions, what will be their perceptions, their attitudes to their environment, to their neighbors, etc. Even a group that is not persecuted may suffer many of the ills of real persecution if it feels persecuted. That its perceptions are mistaken or exaggerated is important in pointing to the possibility of a different cure: removing the mistaken perception. But that is not always possible, and up to a point in matters of respect, identification, and dignity, subjective responses, justified or not, are the ultimate reality so far as the well-being of those who have them is concerned.

IV. A RIGHT TO SELF-DETERMINATION

It may seem that the case for self-government establishes a right to self-determination. That is, it establishes the reasons for the right sort of group, an encompassing group, to determine that a territory shall be self-governing. But things are not that simple. The case for self-government shows that sometimes, under certain conditions, it is best that the political unit be roughly an encompassing group. A group's right to self-determination is its right to determine that a territory be self-governing, regardless of whether the case for self-government, based on its benefits, is established or not. In other words, the right to self-determination answers the question "who is to decide?" not "what is the best decision?" In exercising the right, the group should act responsibly in light of all the considerations we mentioned so far. It should, in particular, consider not only the interests of its members but those of others who may be affected by its decision. But if it has the right to decide, its decision is binding even if it is wrong, even if the case for self-government is not made.

The problem in conceding the existence of such a right is, of course, not the possibility that a group that would best be self-governing does not wish to be so. Given the strong subjectivist element in the instrumentalist argument, such reluctance to assume independence would suggest that the case for its being self-governing is much weakened. The problem is that the case for self-government is hedged by considerations of the interest of people other than members of the groups, and by the other interests of members of the groups, i.e., other than their interests as members of the groups. These include their fundamental individual interests which should be respected, e.g., by a group whose culture oppresses women or racial minorities. These considerations raise the question whether encompassing groups are the most suitable bodies to decide about the case for self-government. Can they be entrusted with the decision in a matter in which their group interests are in conflict with other interests of members of the group as well as with the interests of other people? At the very least this suggests that the right must be qualified and hedged to protect other interests.

More fundamental still is the question of how the right of self-determination fits within our general conception of democratic decision making. We are used to a two-level structure of argument concerning social issues, such as just taxation, the provision of public education, etc. First, we explore the principles that should govern the matter at issue. Second, we devise a form of democratic procedure for determining what shall be done. The first level answers the question "what should be done?" The second responds to the question "who should decide?"

On a simple majoritarian view, the issue of self-government seems to defy a democratic decision procedure. The question is "what is the relevant democratic unit?" and that question cannot be democratically decided, at least not entirely so. In fact, of course, we are not simple majoritarians. We adopt a whole range of democratic procedures such as constitution-making privileged majorities, ordinary legislative processes, plebiscites, administrative processes, and decisions by special agencies under conditions of public accountability and indirect democratic control. We match various democratic processes with various social and political problems. This means that there is no universal democratic formula serving as the universal answer to "who decides?" questions. Rather, we operate a mixed principled-democratic system in which principles, whose credentials do not derive entirely from their democratic backing, determine what form of a democratic procedure is suited for what problem. Within this mixed principled-democratic framework, the right to self-determination fits as just another qualified democratic process suited to its object.

What are the principles involved? It is tempting to see here a principle giving the part veto over the issue of membership in a larger whole. To form a new political unit, or to remain part of an existing one, all component parts should agree. To break up a political unit, or to foil the creation of a new one, all that is required is the will of the group that wants to secede or to stay out. This principle derives its appeal from its voluntaristic aura. It seems to regard the justification of all political units as based on consent. But this is an undesirable illusion. It is undesirable since, as was explained above regarding encompassing groups, the more important human groupings need to be based on shared history, and on criteria of nonvoluntaristic (or at least not wholly contractarian) membership to have the value that they have. The principle presents no more than an illusion of a contractarian principle since it refers to groups, not to individuals. But the whole contractarian ethos derives its appeal from the claim that each individual's consent is a condition of the legitimacy of political units. Beyond all that, the principle simply begs the question that it is meant to answer,

namely, what are the parts? Which groupings have the veto and which do not? Can the group of all the people whose surnames begin with a *g* and end with an *e* count for these purposes? Do they have the veto on membership in a larger political unit?

The right to self-determination derives from the value of membership in encompassing groups. It is a group right, deriving from the value of a collective good, and as such opposed in spirit to contractarian-individualistic approaches to politics or to individual well-being. It rests on an appreciation of the great importance that membership in and identification with encompassing groups has in the life of individuals, and the importance of the prosperity and self-respect of such groups to the well-being of their members. That importance makes it reasonable to let the encompassing group that forms a substantial majority in a territory have the right to determine whether that territory shall form an independent state in order to protect the culture and self-respect of the group, provided that the new state is likely to respect the fundamental interests of its inhabitants, and provided that measures are adopted to prevent its creation from gravely damaging the just interests of other countries. This statement of the argument for the right requires elaboration.

(1) The argument is an instrumental one. It says, essentially, that members of a group are best placed to judge whether their group's prosperity will be jeopardized if it does not enjoy political independence. It is in keeping with the view that, even though participation in politics may have intrinsic value to individuals, the shape and boundaries of political units are to be determined by their service to individual well-being, i.e., by their instrumental value. In our world, encompassing groups that do not enjoy self-government are not infrequently persecuted, despised, or neglected. Given the importance of their prosperity and self-respect to the well-being of their members, it seems reasonable to entrust their members with the right to determine whether the groups should be self-governing. They may sacrifice their economic or other interests for the sake of group self-respect and prosperity. But such a sacrifice is, given the circumstances of this world, often not unreasonable.

One may ask why should such matters not be entrusted to international adjudication by an international court, or some other international agency. Instead of groups having a right to self-determination which makes them judges in their own cause, the case for a group becoming self-governing should be entrusted to the judgment of an impartial tribunal. This would have been a far superior solution to the question "who is to decide?" Unfortunately, there simply does not exist any international machinery of enforcement that can be relied upon in preference to a right of self-determination as the right of self-help, nor is there any prospect of one coming into existence in the near future. In the present structure of international relations, the most promising arrangement is one that recognizes group rights to self-determination and entrusts international bodies with the duty to help bring about its realization, and to see to it that the limits and preconditions of the right are observed (these are enumerated in the points two to five below).

(2) The right belongs to the group. But how should it be exercised? Not necessarily by a simple majority vote. Given the long-term and irreversible nature of the decision (remember that while independence is up to the group, merger or union is not), the wish for a state must be shared by an overwhelming majority, reflecting deep-seated beliefs and feelings of an enduring nature, and not mere temporary popularity. The precise institutional requirements for the exercise of the right are issues that transcend the topic of this paper. They are liable to vary with the circumstances of different national and ethnic groups. Whatever they are, they should reflect the above principle.

(3) The right is over a territory. This simply reflects the territorial organization of our political world. The requirement that the group be a substantial majority of the territory stems from further considerations aimed at balancing the interest in self-government against the interests of nonmembers. First, it is designed to ensure that self-government for a territory does not generate a problem as great as it is meant to solve, by ensuring that the independence will not generate a large-scale new minority problem. That risk cannot be altogether avoided. As was remarked before, numbers count in the end.

A further factual assumption underlying this condition is that people are, even today, most directly affected by the goings-on in their region. It is true that one's economic conditions are affected by the economic activities in far away places. This, however, is more and more true of the international system generally. The ideal of economic autarchy died a natural death. (Correspondingly, the condition of economic viability which used to figure in theories of the states in international relations has little role in the modern world.) What can be secured and protected, and what vitally matters to the quality of life, is its texture as determined by the local culture and custom, the nature of

the physical environment, etc. Hence the right is given only to a group that is the majority in a territory. The case for self-government applies to groups that are not in the majority anywhere, but they do not have the right to self-determination anywhere. Their members, like other people, may have a right to immigration on an individual basis to a territory of their choice. But their case is governed by general principles of freedom of movement and the sovereign rights of existing states. This means that their communal interests remain an important consideration to be borne in mind by the decision makers, but they have no right, i.e., the decision is not up to them.

Do historical ties make a difference? Not to the right if voluntarily abandoned. Suppose that the group was unjustly removed from the country. In that case, the general principle of restitution applies, and the group has a right to self-determination and control over the territory it was expelled from, subject to the general principle of prescription. Prescription protects the interests of the current inhabitants. It is based on several deep-seated concerns. It is meant to prevent the revival of abandoned claims, and to protect those who are not personally to blame from having their life unsettled by claims of ancient wrongs, on the ground that their case now is as good as that of the wronged people or their descendants. Prescription, therefore, may lose the expelled group the right even though its members continue to suffer the effects of the past wrong. Their interest is a consideration to be borne in mind in decisions concerning immigration policies, and the like, but because of prescription they lost the right to self-determination. The outcome is not up to them to decide.

(4) The right is conditional on its being exercised for the right reasons, i.e., to secure conditions necessary for the prosperity and self-respect of the group. This is a major protection against abuse. Katanga cannot claim a right to self-determination as a way of securing its exclusive control over uranium mines within its territory. This condition does not negate the nature of a right. The group is still entrusted with the right to decide, and its decision is binding even if wrong, even if the case for self-government does not obtain, provided the reasons that motivate the group's decision are of the right kind.

(5) Finally, there are the two broad safeguards on which the exercise of the right is conditional. First, that the group is likely to respect the basic rights of its inhabitants, so that its establishment will do good rather than add to the ills of this world. Secondly, since the

establishment of the new state may fundamentally endanger the interests of inhabitants of other countries, its exercise is conditional on measures being taken to prevent or minimize the occurrence of substantial damage of this kind. Such measures, which will vary greatly from case to case, include free-trade agreements, port facilities, granting of air routes, demilitarization of certain regions, etc.

Two kinds of interests do not call for special protection. One is the interest of a people to regard themselves as part of a larger rather than a smaller grouping or country. The English may have an interest in being part of Great Britain, rather than mere Englanders. But that interest can be justly satisfied only with the willing co-operation of, e.g., the Scots. If the other conditions for Scottish independence are met, this interest of the English should not stand in its way. Secondly, unjust economic gains, the product of colonial or other forms of exploitation of one group by another, may be denied to the exploiting group without hesitation or compensation (barring arrangements for a transitory period). But where secession and independence will gravely affect other and legitimate interests of other countries, such interests should be protected by creating free-trade zones, demilitarized areas, etc.

(6) A right in one person is sufficient ground to hold some other person(s) to be under a duty. What duties arise out of the right to self-determination? How is this matter to be settled? As the previous discussion makes clear, the right of self-determination is instrumentally justified, as the method of implementing the case for self-government, which itself is based on the fact that in many circumstances self-government is necessary for the prosperity and dignity of encompassing groups. Hence, in fixing the limits of the right, one has to bear in mind the existing system of international politics, and show that, given other elements in that system, certain duties can be derived from the right to self-determination, whereas others cannot. The first and most important duty arising out of the right is the duty not to impede the exercise of the right, i.e., not to impede groups in their attempts to decide whether appropriate territories should be independent, so long as they do so within the limits of the right. This duty affects in practice first and foremost the state that governs the territory concerned and its inhabitants.

There may be other duties following from the right of self-determination. In particular, there may be a duty on the state governing the territory to provide aid in exercising the right, and a duty on other states to aid the relevant group in realizing its right, and thus to oppose the state governing the territory if it impedes its implementation. But the extent of these duties must be subject to the general principles of international morality, which indicate what methods may and may not be used in pursuit of worthwhile goals and in preventing the violation of rights. As indicated at the outset, the examination of the details of such implications of the right is beyond the scope of this article.

This brings to an end our consideration of the outlines of the case for a right to self-determination and its limits. It is an argument that proceeds in several stages from fundamental moral concerns to the ways in which they can be best implemented, given the way our world is organized. The argument is meant to present the normal justification for the right. It does not claim that there could not be alternative justifications. But it does claim to be the central case, which alternatives presuppose or of which they are variations.

Two conclusions emerge from this discussion. On the one hand, the right to self-determination is neither absolute nor unconditional. It affects important and diverse interests of many people, from those who will be citizens of the new state, if it comes into being, to others far away from it. Those who may benefit from self-government cannot insist on it at all costs. Their interests have to be considered along those of others. On the other hand, the interests of members of an encompassing group in the self-respect and prosperity of the group are among the most vital human interests. Given their importance, their satisfaction is justified even at a considerable cost to other interests. Furthermore, given the absence of effective enforcement machinery in the international arena, the interest in group prosperity justifies entrusting the decision concerning self-government to the hands of an encompassing group that constitutes the vast majority of the population in the relevant territory, provided other vital interests are protected.

READING 55

International Society from a Cosmopolitan Perspective

Brian Barry

Brian Barry is Professor of Political Science at the London School of Economics and a former editor of *Ethics*. He is the author of several works, including *Political Argument* and *The Liberal Theory of Justice*.

Barry sets forth the basic ideas of a hypothetical contractarian view of moral cosmopolitanism. It is impartial and universal, based on four principles that people could not reasonably reject. It allows for special obligations to family, friends, and country but not *because* they are family, friends, or country. It rules out discrimination on the basis of class, race, or nations. It includes the interests of future people. His four principles are:

1. Fundamental human equality, meaning, at least, equal opportunity to obtain life's benefits.
2. Personal responsibility and compensation. People are to be held accountable for their voluntary choices.
3. Priority of vital interests. Basic needs have a priority over nonbasic needs.
4. Mutual advantage. This is the utilitarian aspect of the proposal, including the Pareto Principle, that when a policy redounds to the general good, it should be incorporated. But it also includes a principle of the Priority of worst off.

Barry's conclusion is that the implications of these principles for International Society would result in taxing the rich nations in order to redistribute wealth to the poor. Toward the end of his article, he discusses how this system might come about.

This reading is taken from *International Society*, ed. David Mapel and Terry Nardin (Princeton University Press, 1999), by permission.

THE COSMOPOLITAN IDEA

Now that the Ethikon enterprise has been going for some time, we can begin to reap the rewards of continuity. Instead of offering my own definition of cos-

mopolitanism, I shall therefore take over the definition put forward by Charles Beitz in an earlier Ethikon book, *Political Restructuring in Europe*. According to Beitz, the two essential elements defining a cosmopolitan view are that it is inclusive and nonperspectival. "If local viewpoints can be said to be partial, then a cosmopolitan viewpoint is impartial." What I am concerned with here is what Beitz calls "moral cosmopolitanism," of which he says that "it applies to the whole world the maxim that answers to questions about what we should do, or what institutions we should establish, should be based on an impartial consideration of the claims of each person who would be affected by our choices."

Beitz distinguishes this moral cosmopolitanism from what he calls "institutional cosmopolitanism." It is important to recognize that moral cosmopolitanism leaves open the question of the ideal constitution of international society. Institutional cosmopolitanism is one answer to that question, or more precisely a family of answers. Thus, institutional cosmopolitanism "pertains to the way political institutions should be set up—to the political constitution of the world, so to speak. . . . Although the details may vary, the distinctive common feature is some ideal of world political organization in which states and state-like units have significantly diminished authority in comparison with the status quo and supranational institutions have more."

As Beitz says, "There is no necessary link between moral and institutional cosmopolitanism."[1] Thus, one may be a moral cosmopolitan without believing that its precepts would best be satisfied by institutions of the kind commended by institutional cosmopolitanism. At the level of domestic politics, it is quite consistent to start from a utilitarian position and then argue for a minimum state. Similarly, there is no inconsistency in counting the interests of everyone in the world equally and concluding that those interests will tend to be best advanced by a state-centered system with only weak international authority. Whether or not this is thought to be so will depend on what one takes the main interests of human beings to be and on the way in which one thinks the world works.

Conversely, one may support the policy conclusions embodied in institutional cosmopolitanism on a basis other than that of moral cosmopolitanism. Beitz himself says that "it is hard to think of anyone who has defended institutional cosmopolitanism on other than cosmopolitan moral grounds."[2] But it is easy to see that the case for a strengthening of international authority vis-à-vis states can plausibly be derived from Hobbesian premises under contemporary conditions. Warfare between countries now has a potential for almost unlimited destruction, and only concerted action can address global problems such as ozone depletion, the "greenhouse effect," and pollution of the oceans. I believe, therefore, that universal self-interest would support a shift toward institutional cosmopolitanism, as Beitz defines it. In addition, I believe that moral cosmopolitanism leads to the endorsement of international redistribution of a kind that Hobbesian premises do not appear to underwrite. My reasons for thinking this will appear later.

The general point I have made about moral cosmopolitanism is also made in this book for all the other approaches surveyed. That is to say, there is no automatic move from the ethical premises to any particular conclusion about the ideal world constitution. Where moral cosmopolitanism shows itself to be more distinctive is in its denial that membership of a society is of deep moral significance when the claims that people can legitimately make on one another are assessed. This differentiates it sharply from, for example, the kind of contractarian view advanced in this book by John Charvet, within which the bounds of society are also the bounds of justice.

I should explain what I mean by saying that membership of a society does not have *deep* moral significance. We can in a variety of ways acquire obligations that we owe to some people and not to others. There is no reason for doubting that the members of a politically constituted society can acquire obligations to one another that they do not owe to others. What moral cosmopolitanism insists on, however, is that it should be possible to justify this special treatment on grounds that can in principle be accepted by those excluded. A standard way of doing this is, of course, to point out that those who are excluded can and do acquire special obligations to members of their own societies in exactly the same way. The point has been put well by Thomas Hill, Jr., in the following way:

> All the impartiality thesis says is that, if and when one raises questions regarding fundamental moral standards, the court of appeal that one addresses is a court in which no particular individual, group, or country has *special* standing. Before that court, declaring "I like it," "It serves *my* country," and the like, is not decisive; principles must be defensible to anyone looking at the matter apart from his or her special attachments, from a larger, human perspective.[3]

SOME COSMOPOLITAN PRINCIPLES

At the heart of moral cosmopolitanism is the idea that human beings are in some fundamental sense equal. All claims are to be weighed in the same balance. But how is this balancing to be carried out? An answer that naturally presents itself is that we reduce all claims to interests and then resolve conflicts of interest by saying that the outcome that most satisfies interests (the one in which the greatest sum of interest satisfaction obtains) is the best. If "interests" are given a subjective interpretation this is the utilitarian prescription. It is objectionable on two grounds. First, it is not true that all claims can be expressed in a single currency: claims are irreducibly heterogeneous in their nature. And, second, the formula is indifferent to issues of distribution. Nobody has any good reason for accepting that he or she should do very badly merely because this is the most effective means of maximizing some aggregate good, however defined.

Rather than canvassing a number of alternatives, let me simply present what seems to me the best way of giving content to the idea of impartial treatment that underlies moral cosmopolitanism. Following an idea put forward by T. M. Scanlon, I propose that we should ask of any rule or principle whether or not it could reasonably be rejected by somebody who was motivated by "the desire to find principles which others similarly motivated could not reasonably reject."[4] We thus posit a hypothetical negotiating situation marked by equality (since everybody stands on an equal footing and is equipped with a veto to protect interests that cannot reasonably be denied) and freedom (since nobody can coerce anybody else into accepting an agreement by the exercise of superior power). Principles of justice are those principles that would emerge from a process taking this form.

We may envisage a variety of different sets of people making choices in such a hypothetical situation. By far the most effort has gone into the case in which the choice is made by people who are members of the same politically organized society. But for the present purpose I want to focus on the case in which the choice is made by all the people in the world, since it is quite possible to imagine a world in which each country is internally just but the system as a whole is extremely unjust. On the criterion of justice proposed here, this would be so if the rules governing relations between countries could reasonably be rejected by some people.

It seems clear that the premise of fundamental human equality applies without regard to time as well as without regard to place. There is no good moral reason for saying that the interests of people who will live in the future should be given less (or more) weight than the interests of those alive now simply because they come later in time. I do not, however, believe that it is useful to extend the idea of a hypothetical choosing situation to encompass relations between generations, mainly because asking how we would negotiate with people as yet unborn (especially those in the distant future) creates gratuitous problems. The point here is that, where the parties are contemporaries, the problem posed is closely related to a kind of which we have experience. Indeed, we can hope to learn from actual cases of agreement (relatively consensual policies in countries, or payment schemes in large organizations, for example), making adjustments to compensate for deviations from equal power relations. It does not follow, however, that we are without recourse to anything except a direct appeal to the idea of fundamental equality in regard to future generations. We can take the principles that would be agreed upon by contemporaries and ask if there is any reason why they should not be extrapolated to relations between different generations, perhaps being appropriately modified to cope with the special features of those relations. My belief is that this procedure will provide all we need in the way of guidance beyond the idea of fundamental equality itself.

Following Rawls, I shall take justice to be the highest-order organizing concept within political philosophy. The following are, I wish to maintain, four principles of justice. I shall say a little (but only a little) in defense of each as I go along. A point to be made about all of them together is that they meet the two objections to utilitarianism: their subject-matter is heterogeneous and they are sensitive to questions of distribution.

First principle: the presumption of equality. All inequalities of rights, opportunities, and resources have to be justifiable in ways that cannot reasonably be rejected by those who get least.

This principle does not immediately generate specific conclusions. But it is important in directing attention toward those who have the best *prima facie* reasons for rejecting some proposal. It emphasizes that any inequality must make sense to them. As it stands, it may appear a very weak principle, and it is undeniably lacking in content. In spite of this, what impresses me is how many relations of inequality at all levels

cannot meet its demands. These relations are maintained by unequal power relationships, or (not quite the same thing) by inertia, forming part of a pattern which it would not be advantageous to anyone acting alone to disturb. Thus, those disadvantaged by an inequality may well choose to act in ways that sustain it, even though they would reject it in a hypothetical ideal-choice situation.

There is a temptation (succumbed to by Rawls in some contexts) to drive the principle of the presumption of equality toward closure by specifying that the *only* justification for an inequality is that the minimum is as high as is feasible. I do not accept this because it would be inconsistent with the second principle. For this, as will be seen, has the implication that those who do worst from an inequality may under certain conditions accept reasonably that those who do better deserve to do better.

At the same time, I wish to ensure that the idea of the priority of the worst-off retains some critical force. I therefore add an *anti-aggregation* rider: aggregate gains by "winners" do not constitute a justification to "losers." This simply makes explicit the point that, from the perspective of the losers, the argument that there will be a net gain is not a sufficient ground for withdrawing a veto.

Second principle: personal responsibility and compensation. It is *prima facie* acceptable for people to fare differently if the difference arises from a voluntary choice on their part; conversely, victims of misfortunes that they could not have prevented have a *prima facie* valid claim for compensation or redress.

The first clause embodies the basic idea that human agency must be respected. It is an essential aspect of a fully human life that one's decisions should have some impact on the world, and that can happen only if what they do makes a difference to what actually happens. There is a great deal of evidence, both from surveys of opinion and from studies of freely accepted inequalities, to support the notion that the first clause would emerge from a hypothetical choice situation. What the formulation leaves open is, of course, the conditions under which a choice counts as being voluntary. The clause about personal responsibility sets the terms of the debate, however, and, I believe, imposes definite limits on the range of reasonable disagreement.

The second clause is the obverse of the first. It may be said to embody what Richard Arneson has described as "the intuition that when people's lives go badly through no fault or voluntary choice of their own, it is morally incumbent on others to offer aid to the disadvantaged so long as the cost of providing aid is not excessive".[5] I should, however, wish to approach the proviso at the end of this statement with some care. What makes the cost "excessive"? Not, I think, simply that the cost is high: if the loss is great, the cost is liable to be high, but that does not affect the force of the claim. The valid form of the proviso is, I suggest, that the obligation is weakened or in extreme cases extinguished altogether if the cost of providing the aid is greatly disproportional to the benefit gained by the recipient(s).

We may combine the two parts of this principle to obtain a somewhat more precise version of the doctrine of compensation. Suppose that people fare badly not as a result of their voluntary choices but as a result of unpreventable misfortune. Then, we may say, they can legitimately demand that (1) where "nature" is the cause, the more fortunate should contribute to a scheme of compensation; and (2) where the voluntary act of some person (or persons) is the cause, redress should be looked for in the first instance from that source.

Third principle: priority of vital interests. In the absence of some compelling consideration to the contrary, the vital interests of each person should be protected in preference to the nonvital interests of anyone. Vital interests include security from physical harm, nutrition adequate for the maintenance of health, clean drinking water and sanitary arrangements, clothing and shelter appropriate to the climate, medical care, and education to a level sufficient to function effectively within one's society.

It should be observed that this principle expresses priorities not in terms of persons (as the first principle did) but in terms of types of claim. The idea underlying it is that there are certain minimum requirements of living a good life that can be acknowledged to be such by almost everyone, whatever his or her own particular conception of the good may be. If the second principle is related to the idea of desert, this third principle is related to that of need. Thus, the second and third principles capture what are the commonly accepted bases for moral claims. The first principle is concerned with a third basis—the allocation of rights.

Fourth principle: mutual advantage. Whenever it would be to the prospective advantage of everyone to depart from the application of the above principles (compared with the results of applying them), it is permissible to do so. Where more than one arrangement has this property, the one to be preferred is that which maximizes the gain of those who gain least from the departure.

This principle is one of collective rationality: it endorses Pareto improvements over the baseline set by the operation of the other three principles. The second half of it provides a way of choosing between potential Pareto improvements and incorporates the idea of "the priority of the worst off." It should be observed, however, that the identity of the "worst off" here is not the same as it was in the anti-aggregation proviso. Here the worst off are defined in relation to the baseline created by applying the other principles. Those who stand to gain least by applying the fourth one may not be those who were the worst off from the application of the other three.

Read carelessly, the fourth principle may look as if it renders the others nugatory and simply gets us back to utilitarianism. It is important to recognize that this is not so. The other three principles retain their integrity. They can be supplemented by the fourth principle but they cannot be displaced by it. For those who like the vocabulary, we may say that the first three principles jointly have lexicographic priority over the fourth. This, of course, leaves us without a formula for resolving conflicts among the first three principles, but who said that ethical problems should be easy?

JUSTICE DENIED

The principles of justice I have put forward are intended to function as guides to debate: they should be capable of specifying kinds of argument that can be accepted as valid while ruling out other considerations that might be put forward. This structuring of moral discourse is what I believe principles should do. Clearly, for the full development of a theory of justice we would need to see how the principles put forward here work together to produce some conclusions about the kinds of institution they underwrite. In the space at my disposal, I have no hope of doing that. What I shall focus on, in keeping with the topic of this chapter, are the largest-scale global implications, extended into the distant future.

The most striking feature of the world as it exists at present, if we line it up against the principles of justice, is the extent to which the third principle is violated. Probably half the total world population lacks the material conditions that are necessary for the satisfaction of their vital interests. Even in Latin America, which is on the average considerably wealthier than Africa, the Indian subcontinent, and China, half the total population was estimated by a United Nations agency to have "unmet basic needs" in 1986.[6] These conditions coexist—in contravention of the principle of the priority of vital interests—with over a quarter of the world's population living at material standards vastly in excess of anything required to meet their basic needs.

A second observation is that there is no tendency toward an equalization of average incomes between rich and poor countries. On the contrary, the richest countries are continuing to increase their affluence (if slowly), while many poor countries have actually become poorer in the past decade, especially as a result of debt repayments. (On balance, poor countries now make net transfers to rich ones.) Moreover, within poor countries, the burden of the "adjustment" imposed by the IMF and the World Bank falls mainly on the poor, who are hit by increased unemployment and the disappearance of basic public services.

It is, of course, conceivable that the *prima facie* injustice arising from the wholesale violation of the third principle is nullified by the application of one or more of the other principles. There are two candidates: the second and the fourth. Under the second, it might be argued that the plight of those whose vital interests are not being met is entirely their own fault. This is immensely implausible. Insofar as natural resources make some countries better off than others, this is clearly a matter of pure good fortune. The inhabitants of the wealthier countries can claim some credit for maintaining their economic capital, social capital (institutions that work to provide a framework for prosperity), and human capital (a well-educated workforce). But even then much is inherited from previous generations. Within poor countries it is pure fantasy to suppose that the children of landless laborers in the country or dwellers in *favelas* or shanty-towns round the cities could all by sheer personal effort raise themselves in one generation to a position in which their vital interests would be fulfilled.

The other weapon of the apologists for the justice of the status quo is the fourth principle: any attempt to improve the lot of the worst off by redistributive measures, it is sometimes claimed, would have such an inhibiting effect on the efforts of the better off that in the end everybody would be worse off than they would be under a policy of leaving the outcome to market forces. Looking at the inequalities in many poor countries and in the world as a whole, this would be hard to believe, even if indefinite increases in global production were feasible. But they are not, and this has profound implications for the fourth principle. Recall that in the pre-

vious section I said that the interests of those who live in the future must be given as much weight as the interests of those who live in the present. This means (under principle two) that we cannot justly leave them worse off than we are, since this would not reflect a voluntary choice on their part. It also implies (under principle three) that we cannot give our own pursuit of our goals priority over their vital interests.

There is, manifestly, a range of views about what this would entail. But the general form of the question is clear: unless it blows itself up or destroys its environment, there is no reason why the human race should not continue to inhabit the globe for hundreds of thousands of years to come (as against about ten thousand since the beginnings of civilization). We cannot know how people in the future will live or what inventions and discoveries they will make. But we know that they will need an inhabitable planet, with such amenities as an ozone layer, land that is neither desert nor eroded, relative freedom from air and water pollution, and a diversity of species. This requires that the current generation should not leave its successors with conditions that are worse in these respects, or if this is impossible that the current generation at least moves as far toward "substainability" as is feasible. What is crucial is that the capacity of the planet to regenerate depleted natural resources and render toxic wastes harmless (metals such as mercury, lead, and cadmium, and nuclear waste, for example) is strictly limited. Some people say that we need not worry about any of this because people in the future *may* come up with some "technological fix" that will solve all the problems. This, however, is scarcely consistent with taking seriously the interests of future generations, since if we acted on the optimistic assumption and it turned out to be wrong the consequences would be catastrophic.

There is apparently little disagreement among those who accept this general diagnosis that current production levels globally are unsustainable. The only question is how far they would have to be reduced to become sustainable. A widely held view is that the world left the path of sustainability in the early 1950s. To the extent that processes of production are modified to use fewer natural resources and create less pollution, we can avoid the conclusion that production levels must go back to those prevalent in the early 1950s, but they would still have to be reduced substantially. Even if sustainability entails only freezing total production, this is enough to demand a fundamental reorientation of virtually all thinking in the last fifty years (and most of that in the preceding hundred) about distributive justice. For a common theme running through the work of thinkers on both the left and the right of the political spectrum has been that production is not a zero-sum game. What unites these thinkers is the "productivist" premise that "a rising tide lifts all boats." Inequalities of income are therefore of no moment in themselves. Only simple-minded people, according to the conventional wisdom, believe that the poor are poor because the rich are rich; on the contrary, the poor are as well off as they are only because the rich are rich. Inequality increases the size of the cake, so that even those with the smallest slices get more.

If we drop the presupposition of an indefinitely expandable cake, the older idea that the poor are poor because the rich are rich comes into its own again. Let us suppose that we are at the sustainable maximum, and that it would be possible to stay at this maximum while shifting income from rich to poor. Then it does become true that anyone with a large slice of the cake is directly responsible for somebody else having a small one. Internationally it means that poor countries can expand production (within the limits of global sustainability) only if the rich countries cut back to make room.

This would be true even if sustainability demanded only that total production level out at its current volume. Now suppose (as seems to me more plausible) that long-run sustainability entails a substantial overall reduction in what is produced. Then further implications can be derived. Thus, the rationale (widely acted on in all western European countries in the past decade) for cutting high marginal rates of taxation—that the incentive effect of letting high earners keep more increases economic growth—has to go into reverse. Since, however, the evidence suggests that reducing marginal tax rates from their previous levels has had negligible effects on effort, it seems likely that post-tax earnings could be almost equalized before production fell by a substantial amount. The limits on equalization would perhaps lie rather in those imposed by the second principle, which permits the consequences of voluntary choice to be reflected in outcomes. People who are particularly keen to make more money should be able to do so by working at a job within their capabilities involving longer or less convenient hours or more unpleasant conditions than other jobs open to people with their capabilities. It should be observed, however, that the second principle does not legitimize inequalities that do not result from choice, and I believe that it would not therefore underwrite the vast majority of existing earned income inequalities. The only ones it would support would be of an essentially compensatory nature.

A parallel argument may be made about transfers from one country to another. Even if unlimited expansion of production were feasible, it would be grossly implausible to maintain that even a low level of transfer from rich to poor countries would hamper production in the rich countries so much that in the long run everyone would lose. There seems to me no real case for thinking that production in rich countries would necessarily be reduced at all by some modest level of transfer. Even if it were, poor countries would still be better off with transfers. For unless some of the increased wealth of the rich countries is deliberately channeled to poor countries, there does not appear to be any mechanism that automatically results in the increased wealth of the rich countries creating more in the poor ones. There is certainly one force moving in the other direction, which is that technological progress tends to make the rich countries less and less dependent on the raw materials (jute and sisal, for example) that are the export staples of some poor countries.

Now suppose that global production will have to be reduced if pollution and resource depletion are not to place an unfair burden on future generations. In this case, any inhibiting effect on production of the extra taxation imposed on rich countries by international redistribution becomes a positive advantage. Assuming that aggregate global output needs to come down substantially, I should be very surprised if that goal could be accomplished solely through the drag on production in the rich countries imposed by international transfers. Governments in rich countries would still have to introduce deliberate measures to curb the propensity of their economies to produce more than is compatible with long-run sustainability.

MORAL COSMOPOLITANISM AND INTERNATIONAL REDISTRIBUTION

Moral cosmopolitanism is, in essence, an individualistic doctrine in that it focuses on how individuals fare. This does not mean that it slights the importance of families, communities, and countries. But it treats their value as derivative: they are of value to exactly the extent that they contribute to the welfare of individuals (both those within the group and those outside it, weighting their interests equally).

This moral individualism, taken together with the considerations advanced in the previous section, leads to a radical conclusion. The demands of cosmopolitanism would, I suggest, be best satisfied in a world in which rich people wherever they lived would be taxed for the benefit of poor people wherever they lived. On the revenue-raising side, the model would be that of the United States, where the federal government imposes a federal income tax, leaving the states to raise whatever taxes (including income taxes) they like. The expenditure side is rather more messy. I believe that a large proportion of the payout would have to be to individuals, either in the form of a universal unconditional basic income or an income dependent on status (youth, age, sickness and disability, unemployment). But it would clearly be advantageous for some of the resources to go to the improvement of communal facilities in areas where the most deprived people are concentrated.

As I have already said, the units within the federation (states in the U.S., countries within a world federation) would be able to raise their own taxes in addition and spend them as they wished. Nevertheless, it is clear that any such system would constitute a considerable derogation of state sovereignty. (It may be recalled that in the U.S. the introduction of a federal income tax required a constitutional amendment.) It seems to me that the least one can say is that any such scheme would be unimaginable unless it had been preceded by a long period in which transfers of a systematic kind between countries had become a well-established practice. On this alternative understanding, "international redistribution" means redistribution among countries. This immediately raises problems, since an unconditional transfer to a poor country may not benefit any poor people within that country. If, for example, the money having been raised by a broad-based tax in a relatively wealthy country goes straight into the Swiss bank accounts of the ruling elite, the net result will be predominantly a shift of resources from those in the middle to the very wealthy. Any system open to such abuse would fail to generate support from the contributors, and reasonably enough.

I do not wish to slight the importance of these problems. They are, however, best regarded as falling within the scope of a more general issue. This can be stated as follows: given a world that is made up of states, what is the morally permissible range of diversity among them? . . . In the rest of this [section], I shall leave on one side the question of the way in which the money is to be spent within countries and focus on the mechanism of transfer between countries.

We are looking for an alternative to a system in which an international authority levies taxes directly on individuals. The simplest alternative is to assess countries for contributions according to their gross national product at some standard rate (for example, one percent) provided their average income per head is above some level (roughly, that of the OECD countries). One percent is an amount that would scarcely be noticed, but it is vastly in excess of the amounts currently transferred and would make a large difference. I do not doubt that moral cosmopolitanism calls for more, but the point is that even that amount would represent a real transformation in the level of international transfers.

A scheme in which the levy is proportional to GNP, above some cutoff point of average income, is the simplest, as I have said. It would, obviously, be possible to make it more fancy by introducing an element of progressivity, so that (within the set of contributors) richer countries paid a larger amount in proportion to their GNP. There is no need to pursue such refinements here. The essential feature common to all is that each state would be assessed by some international authority according to some schedule and it would then be up to the state to determine how the money was to be raised—whether by direct or indirect taxes, for example. An example of such a system that is effective is the system prevailing within the European Union whereby constituent countries have to provide a sum each year, part of which is disbursed (as "solidarity" funds) to the poorer regions.

The case for taking something like income per head as the basis of assessment is twofold. The first is that if you want to raise money you had better go where the money is. In terms of classical taxation theory, the criterion is "ability to pay." In terms of the principles of justice set out earlier, it is that a rich country can afford to collect the money demanded without jeopardizing the vital interests of anybody in it. (Of course, this says only that it has the ability to do so. It may actually raise the money in a way that is detrimental to the interests of the worst-off members of the society. This is the obverse of the problem that the proceeds may go to the rich in the recipient society.) There is a second argument as well, and this is that income per head is a proxy for the use of natural resources and the degradation of the global environment. It is not, it must be admitted, precise: the United States, for example, is much more profligate in the resources it expends for a given unit of production than other countries at a roughly similar economic level. Nevertheless, there is enough of a correlation to add support to the case derived from ability to pay.

This argument, however, suggests an alternative way of raising money for an international redistributive authority: a system of user fees (as an alternative to a rationing scheme that would create windfall gains) and taxes on the infliction of global environmental damage. The object here would be two-fold. In part it would be driven by considerations of equity: those who make use of inherently limited facilities should pay, and those who impose burdens on the rest of the world should compensate for the damage they cause. But it would also work to modify behavior by providing an incentive to economize on scarce resources, and to reduce pollution.

Some recently proposed ideas are a surcharge on air tickets, a charge on ocean maritime transport, a special fee for maritime dumping of waste, parking fees for geostationary satellites, charges for the use of the electromagnetic spectrum, and charges for fishing rights in certain areas.[7] A more ambitious extension would include a "carbon tax" on emissions contributing to global warming, and a tax on the production of the CFCs that deplete the ozone layer. The author of this proposal does not discuss how the charges would actually be collected. Ideally, they would be gathered directly from the users or polluters. Only this would ensure that the cost entered into their calculations. It appears to me, however, that many charges would, as a practical matter, have to be levied against governments. The alternative would require an international corps of collectors of fees and taxes that would constitute the same infringement of sovereignty as a corps of international income tax inspectors. The result of assessing governments is that it would be possible for a country to pay its "carbon tax" by, in turn, assessing taxpayers at large rather than by imposing, say, a levy on the burning of coal and petroleum. There is, however, no way in which such slippage can be prevented. What can at least be said is that the system of fees and taxes would put some pressure on governments to reduce their liability.

It is worth noticing that this kind of indirect taxation has a different status vis-à-vis the taxation of individual incomes from a levy based on GNP per head. Both of the rationales for taxing national income would be better served by taxing individual income: ability to pay would be more sensitively captured by taxing individuals, and individual income acts as a proxy for resource use wherever the person with the income lives. The fees and taxes I have just been proposing, however, would be desirable regardless of the way in which the direct tax element might be collected. How much it could be expected to raise would depend entirely on the rates set and the scope of the tax net. Adding a

"carbon tax" could make it substantial. I believe, though, that direct taxation based on "ability to pay" is inevitably going to be required. For the indirect taxes would fall on poor countries as well as rich ones. No doubt by the nature of the case rich countries will pay the bulk, but poor countries pursuing "dirty" industrialization (for example China) will also have to pay. So they should: the whole point is to attach a realistic cost to their conduct. But the scheme as a whole can be acceptable only if there is also an element of straight transfer from rich to poor countries.

It may well be said that it is slightly absurd for me to pass over the idea of an international tax-collecting corps on the ground that it is politically infeasible when everything else I am advocating is politically infeasible. Let me begin a response by saying that it still makes good sense to say that one proposal is much *more* politically infeasible than another, even if both seem a long way off adoption. Turning to the question of feasibility head on, I suggest that we should divide it into two. What is commonly seen as the major problem is that of coercing recalcitrant states to play their part. I think the seriousness of this problem can be exaggerated. The European Union collects from its member states because that is the price of staying in, and there are perceived to be advantages in not being excluded. There is no suggestion that troops would be sent to storm the treasury of a nonpaying member. Similarly, the World Trade Organization has the authority to rule on violations, and has at its disposal the sanctions of expulsion or, short of that, denial of certain advantages available to adherents. Generalizing from this, the relatively wealthy countries (the only ones that concern us in this context) belong to a whole network of international agreements, and if the assessed contribution to the fund for international redistribution were the price for remaining a member in good standing, it would be worth paying.

The real problem is not so much coercing backsliders as setting up the scheme in the first place. I do not underestimate the scale of this problem, but I want to emphasize that the kind of political will required to create such a scheme will have to stem from moral motivation. Hobbesian reasoning, as I suggested at the beginning of this chapter, will go quite a way, but it will not underwrite international redistribution. Attempts are, of course, made regularly to argue that it is in the self-interest of rich countries to transfer resources to poor ones. I have the strong impression, however, that those who make such arguments are themselves led to the conclusion by cosmopolitan moral considerations.

It is therefore hardly surprising that their arguments fail to convince. All I can suggest here, then, is that, unless the moral case is made, we can be sure nothing good will happen. The more the case is made, the better the chance. . . .

INTRANATIONAL INJUSTICE AND INTERNATIONAL REDISTRIBUTION

My primary focus in this chapter is on the distribution of income, and I want in this final section to return to it. Here, the range of legitimate variation is inherently limited, since the principles of justice bear directly on the distribution of income. The great majority of existing countries have a degree of inequality greatly in excess of that which could reasonably be justified under the principles of justice set out here. How does this affect the case for international redistribution, whether conceived as transfers from rich to poor individuals (regardless of location) or as transfers from rich to poor countries?

The answer is perhaps surprising. Take first a scheme in which an international authority collected income taxes from relatively wealthy individuals and gave money to relatively poor individuals. (Some proportion of the money might go to such things as schools and hospitals or water and sewerage systems designed to benefit poor people collectively.) The contributors to the scheme could afford to take a quite relaxed attitude to the distribution of income within recipient countries both before and after the transfers had been made. So long as governments in the recipient countries did not use their taxing powers to take away the benefits gained by the poor, it could be said that at any rate the scheme was working in that resources were being transferred from rich to poor individuals.

Now think about a scheme in which the governments of relatively rich countries transfer resources in some systematic way to the governments of relatively poor countries. Here the distribution of income within the recipient countries becomes a matter of legitimate concern. There are two reasons for this. The first is that the whole notion of the transferred resources going to the poor is now less than transparent. The only way of determining that the results of whatever the government does can be said to constitute a transfer of the money to the poor is to ask if the poor have collectively benefited to the extent of the money provided. This requires close attention to the actual distribution of income and a comparison between it and what the distribution might be hypothesized to have been in its absence.

The second point is rather more subtle. We can best approach it by observing that the individualistic scheme treats national boundaries as having no significance (for this purpose, anyway). In contrast to this, any scheme that makes countries the units of redistribution immediately throws an emphasis on the internal distribution of income. Suppose that the distribution of income in a poor country is extremely unjust (as it actually is in virtually all cases). What implications, if any, does this have for the obligations of those in rich countries to pay taxes in order to provide the resources for transfers to be made to poor countries?

I have already mentioned one case: that in which not only is the distribution of internally generated income unjust but also any additional income from outside would be appropriated by the ruling elite. Here there can be no morally compelling reason for making transfers. There is, instead, a case for international intervention to displace the government and, if necessary, place the country under international trusteeship until more adequate institutions can be created. This intervention will have to be military rather than taking the form of economic sanctions. For (as the examples of Haiti and Iraq illustrate) a government can ensure that the worst burden of economic sanctions falls upon the poorest, and there is no reason to suppose that a government that had already proved itself indifferent to the suffering of its poorest citizens would be motivated to reform by the prospect of their plight becoming even worse as a result of economic sanctions.

The wisdom of military intervention can be challenged, and recent United Nations efforts (in the Horn of Africa, for example) are scarcely encouraging. I cannot here enter into that argument. I assert only the principle that cosmopolitan morality cannot object to intervention under the circumstances I have outlined except on grounds of inefficacy or counterproductiveness. For whatever can be said in favor of state autonomy as a contribution to the well-being of the citizens holds only contingently. Any government which is little more than a gang of looters (as in much of sub-Saharan Africa) forfeits any respect for its independence. If it can be toppled without making things worse, that has to be a (relatively) just outcome.

Bypassing cases in which the poor gain some from international transfers but less than by the amount of the transfers, let us consider now a case in which all the benefit of the transfers goes to those who should justly receive it. It might be suggested that this still does not create an obligation to make the transfer. To put the case in its strongest form, suppose that many people in the country are failing to have their vital needs met, but that there is an economically (though not politically) feasible internal redistribution of income that would enable everybody's vital needs to be met. (This is, in the nature of the case, going to be true only if the average income per capita of countries entitled to be recipients is set quite high. Brazil might then be a candidate.) It could be said then that justice begins at home: why should people elsewhere make sacrifices that would not be called for if the rich in the poor country were to behave justly?

We are here, as so often in matters of justice, confronted with the problem of the second best. If some people are not doing their bit, does that mean that others do not have to step in? If they do not, the vital needs of the poor in poor countries will continue to go unmet. If they act, vital needs will be met and the cost will be spread over hundreds of millions of people. It seems an inescapable conclusion that justice will be advanced by making the transfer. This is especially clear in the (normal) case in which even a just internal distribution would leave a need for international transfers. It would surely be unconscionable to use the lack of internal redistribution as an excuse for not acting. This is not to say that efforts should not be made to provide the government of the recipient country with strong incentives to do its bit for its poorer citizens. It would be reasonable to deny the country any development aid, for example, and this might well have some effect on the willingness of the better-off members of society to accept a measure of internal redistribution.

The obligation on rich countries to transfer resources to internally unjust poor countries might under certain conditions be challenged in another way. Imagine a country in which everyone accepts the unjust internal inequality. Can the victims of this injustice reasonably demand that their material position be improved by transfers from outside the country if they have no complaint against it themselves? . . .

The best case would be a democracy in which a majority persistently voted for parties that did little or nothing when in government to make the distribution of income more just. The electoral success in India since independence of either the Congress Party or parties economically to its right might be advanced as a case in point, given that neither has done anything significant to tackle the maldistribution of wealth and income that the new state inherited. The argument is weak, however, even in this most favorable case. Suppose we were to accept that majority support for the status quo implied majority acceptance of the justice of status quo, a majority is far from the consensus that the argument needs. But there is no reason to make that deduction. As Gunnar Myrdal observed many years ago, India is a "soft state," marked by lack of administrative effectiveness, and in particular the cooptation of officials by the wealthy and powerful in each locality.[8] An attitude of passive resignation on the part of the poor in the face of the failure and subversion of tax and land reform legislation is therefore scarcely to be wondered at. It cannot plausibly be deduced from passivity that they accept the moral legitimacy of the status quo.

This reply, of course, brings us back to the question of the efficacy of international transfers. If the administration of a state is so liable to derailment by powerful interests that its internal efforts at reform are hijacked, what are the prospects of external funds going to the poor rather than being misappropriated? I can only repeat in conclusion that there is no case from cosmopolitan justice for making transfers unless they do get to the people for whom they are intended. But in a second-best world, that does not provide any reason for not making transfers in the remaining cases. The outcome is more just if that is done than it would otherwise be. Needless to say, it is a question of immense practical importance how great a limitation on the scope of international redistribution this proviso imposes. But the answer to that question does not affect the validity of the idea that transfers should be made where they are called for by the principles of justice and will be efficacious in making the situation more just.

READING 56

Secession and Nationalism

Alan Buchanan

Alan Buchanan is Professor of Philosophy at the University of Arizona and the author of several works in political philosophy.

In this essay, Buchanan sets forth the moral case for secession. For secession to be morally justified, certain conditions must be met, but if they are met, then we should support this radical move. He also discusses the justification for forcibly resisting secession, when the necessary conditions are not met.

This reading is taken from *A Companion to Contemporary Political Philosophy,* ed. Robert Goodin and Philip Pettit (New York: Blackwell, 1995), by permission of the publisher.

SECESSION, AUTONOMY AND THE MODERN STATE

From Croatia to Azerbaijan to Quebec, secessionist movements are breaking states apart. In some cases, as with Lithuania, a formerly subordinate unit seeks to become and remain a fully sovereign state in its own right. In others, such as Ukraine, one of the first exercises of new-found sovereignty is to forge ties with other units to create new forms of political association—ties which immediately limit the sovereignty of their components. These momentous events call into question not only the legitimacy of particular states and their boundaries, but also the nature of sovereignty and the purposes of political association.

Less publicized and less dramatic movements for greater self-determination of groups within the framework of existing states are also becoming pervasive. The indigenous peoples' rights movement, pursued with vigour in the United Nations and other arenas of international law, embraces Indians in North, Central and South America, Southeast Asian Hill Tribes, the Saami (Lapps) in a number of countries touched by the Arctic Circle, and Native Hawaiians, among others. Self-determination movements among Flemings in Belgium and Scots in the United Kingdom appear to be building as well. In most of these cases the groups in question do not seek full sovereignty, but rather greater autonomy through the achievement of limited rights of self-government as distinct subunits within the state.

The proper analysis of the concept of sovereignty is, of course, a matter of dispute. However, the root idea is that of a supreme authority—one whose powers are unrestricted by those of other entities. It is useful to distinguish between *internal* and *external* sovereignty. Internal sovereignty is the state's supremacy with respect to all affairs within its borders. External sovereignty is the state's supremacy with respect to its relations with other political units beyond its borders;

in particular, its right to the integrity of its territory, and to control crossings of its borders, as well as the right to enter as an independent party into economic agreements or military alliances or treaties with other states.

No state enjoys literally unrestricted external sovereignty. International law imposes a number of restrictions on every state's dealings with other states, the most fundamental of which is that each is to recognize the others' territorial integrity. In addition, virtually all modern states acknowledge (in principle if not in practice) that their internal sovereignty is limited by *individual rights,* in particular the human rights recognized in international law.

Autonomy movements seek to impose further limitations on internal sovereignty through the recognition of various *group rights.* These include not only so-called minority cultural rights, such as the right to speak one's own language or to wear cultural dress, but also collective property rights for the group, rights of internal self-government, and in some cases rights to participate in joint decision-making concerning the development and exploitation of resources in the area occupied by the group.

Autonomy movements may appear to be less radical than outright bids for secession. After all, what they demand is not the dismemberment of the state into two or more new states, but only a reallocation of certain powers within the state. This appearance, however, is misleading. If a state recognizes substantial powers of self-determination for groups within its borders, it thereby acknowledges limits on its own sovereignty. And if the modern state is defined as a political authority which (credibly) claims full sovereignty over the entire area within its borders, then a state that recognizes rights of self-determination for minorities within its borders thereby transforms itself into something less than a fully sovereign state. (For example, American Indian law in conferring significant powers of self-government upon Indian tribes, uses the term "Indian Nation," and is increasingly regarded as approaching the status of *inter*national law.

Thus, secession movements only threaten the myth of the permanence of the state; autonomy movements assault the concept of state sovereignty itself. Successful and frequent secession would certainly shatter the international order; but it would not challenge the basic conceptual framework that has governed international law for over 300 years, since the rise of the modern state. What is fundamental to that framework is the assumption that international law concerns relations among sovereign states. If successful, autonomy movements within existing states may make the case of sovereign states the exception rather than the rule.

Even though secession is in this sense a phenomenon which the traditional framework of international law and relations can in principle accommodate, it is the most extreme and radical response to the problems of group conflict within the state. For this reason, a consideration of the case for and against secession puts the moral issues of group conflict in bold relief. In what follows, we will explore the morality of secession, while bearing in mind that it is only the most extreme point on a continuum of phenomena involving the struggles of groups within existing political units to gain greater autonomy.

NATIONALISM AND THE JUSTIFICATION OF SECESSION

Some see the spate of secessionist movements now appearing around the globe as the expression of an unpredicted and profoundly disturbing resurgence of *nationalism,* which many rightly regard as one of the most dangerous phenomena of the modern era. And indeed one of the most familiar and stirring justifications offered for secession appeals to *the right of self-determination for "peoples,"* interpreted such that it is equivalent to what is sometimes called the *normative nationalist principle*. It is also one of the least plausible justifications.

The normative nationalist principle states that every "people" is entitled to its own state, that is, that political and cultural (or ethnic) boundaries must coincide. In other words, according to the normative nationalist principle, the right of self-determination is to be understood in a very strong way, as requiring complete political independence—that is, full sovereignty.

An immediate difficulty, of course, is the meaning of "peoples." Presumably a "people" is a distinct ethnic group, the identifying marks of which are a common language, shared tradition and a common culture. Each of these criteria has its own difficulties. The question of what count as different dialects of the same language, as opposed to two or more distinct languages, raises complex theoretical and metatheoretical issues in linguistics. The histories of many groups exhibit frequent discontinuities, infusion of new cultural elements from outside, and alternating degrees of assimilation to and separation from other groups.

More disturbingly, if "people" is interpreted broadly enough, then the normative nationalist principle denies the legitimacy of any state containing more than one cultural group (unless all "peoples" within it freely waive their rights to their own states). Yet cultural pluralism is often taken to be a distinguishing feature of the modern state, or at least of the modern liberal state. Moreover, if the number of ethnic or cultural groups or peoples is not fixed but may increase, then the normative nationalist principle is a recipe for limitless political fragmentation.

Nor is this all. Even aside from the instability and economic costs of the repeated fragmentation which it endorses, there is a more serious objection to the normative nationalist principle, forcefully formulated by Ernest Gellner.

> To put it in the simplest terms: there is a very large number of potential nations on earth. Our planet also contains room for a certain number of independent or autonomous political units. On any reasonable calculation, the former number (of potential nations) is probably much, much larger than that of possible viable states. If this argument or calculation is correct, not all nationalisms can be satisfied, at any rate not at the same time. The satisfaction of some spells the frustration of others. This argument is furthered and immeasurably strengthened by the fact that very many of the potential nations of this world live, or until recently have lived, not in compact territorial units but intermixed with each other in complex patterns. It follows that a territorial political unit can only become ethnically homogenous, in such cases if it either kills, or expels, or assimilates all non-nationals.

With arch understatement, Gellner concludes that the unwillingness of people to suffer such fates "may make the implementation of the nationalist principle difficult." Thus, to say that the normative nationalist principle must be rejected because it is too *impractical* or *economically costly* would be grossly misleading. It ought to be abandoned because the *moral costs,* of even attempting to implement it would be prohibitive.

It is important to see that this criticism of the principle of self-determination is decisive *only* against the strong version of that principle that makes it equivalent to the normative nationalist principle, which states that each people (or ethnic group) is to have its own fully sovereign state. For the objection focuses on the unacceptable implications of granting a right of self-determination to all *"peoples" on the assumption that self-determination means complete political independence, that is, full sovereignty.*

However, as we have already suggested, the notion of self-determination is vague or, rather, multiply ambiguous, inasmuch as there are numerous forms and a range of degrees of political independence or autonomy that a group might attain. Instead of asserting an ambiguous *right* to self-determination, it might be better to acknowledge that many if not most groups have a *legitimate interest* in self-determination and that this interest can best be served in different circumstances by a range of more specific rights or combinations of rights, including a number of distinct group rights to varying forms and degrees of political autonomy, with the right to secede being only the most extreme of these.

I have argued elsewhere that there is a moral right to secede, though it is a highly qualified, limited right. It is not a right which all "peoples" or ethnic or cultural groups have simply by virtue of their being distinct groups. Instead, only those groups whose predicament satisfies the conditions laid out in any of several sound justifications for secession have this right. In this sense the right to secede, as I conceive it, is not a general right of groups, but rather a special or selective right that obtains only under certain conditions.

Among the strongest justifications that can be given for the claim that a group has a right to secede under certain circumstances are (1) the argument from the rectification of past unjust takings; (2) the self-defence argument; and (3) the argument from discriminatory redistribution. Since secession involves the taking of territory, not just the severing of bonds of political obligation, each prosecession argument must be construed as including the establishment of a valid claim to the territory on the part of the seceding group.

Rectifying Past Unjust Takings

This first justification is the simplest and most intuitively appealing argument for secession. It has obvious application to many actual secessionist movements, including some of those which completed the dissolution of the Soviet Union. The claim is that a region has a right to secede if it was unjustly incorporated into the larger unit from which its members seek to separate.

The argument's power stems from the assumption that secession is simply the reappropriation, by the legitimate owner, of stolen property. The right to secede, under these circumstances, is just the right to reclaim what is one's own. This simple interpretation is most plausible, of course, in situations in which the people attempting to secede are literally the same people who held legitimate title to the territory at the time of the unjust annexation, or at least are the indisputable descendants of those people (their legitimate political heirs, so to speak). But matters are considerably more complex if the seceding group is not closely or clearly related to the group whose territory was unjustly taken, or if the group that was wrongly dispossessed did not itself have clear, unambiguous title to it. But at least in the paradigm case, the argument from rectificatory justice is a convincing argument for a moral right to secede. The right of the Baltic Republics to secede from the Soviet Union, which forcibly and unjustly annexed them in 1940, is well supported by this first justification.

It is one thing to say that a group has the right to secede because in so doing they will simply be reclaiming what was unjustly taken from them. The *terms* of secession are another question. In some cases secession will adversely affect individuals who had no part in the unjust acquisition of the territory. Whether, or under what conditions, they are owed compensation or other special consideration is a complex matter.

The Self-defence Argument

The common law, common-sense morality and the great majority of ethical systems, religious and secular, acknowledge a right of self-defence against an aggressor who threatens lethal force. For good reason this is not thought to be an unlimited right. Among the more obvious restrictions on it are (1) that only that degree of force necessary to avert the threat be used, and (2) that the attack against which one defends oneself not be provoked by one's own actions. If such restrictions are acknowledged, the assertion that there is a right of self-defence is highly plausible. Each of these restrictions is pertinent to the right of groups to defend themselves. There are two quite different types of situations in which a group might invoke the right of self-defence to justify secession.

In the first, a group wishes to secede from a state in order to protect its members from extermination by that state itself. Under such conditions the group may either attempt to overthrow the government, that is, to engage in revolution; or, if strategy requires it, the group may secede in order to organize a defensible territory, forcibly appropriating the needed territory from the aggressor, creating the political and military machinery required for its survival, and seeking recognition and aid from other sovereign states and international bodies. Whatever moral title to the seceding territory the aggressor state previously held is *invalidated* by the gross injustice of its genocidal efforts. Or, at the very least, we can say that whatever legitimate claims to the seceding territory the state had are *outweighed* by the claims of its innocent victims. We may think of the aggressor's right to the territory, in the former case, as dissolving in the acid of his own iniquities, and, in the latter, as being pushed down in the scales of the balance by the greater weight of the victim's right of self-defence. Whether we say that the evil state's right to territory is invalidated (and disappears entirely) or merely is outweighed, it is clear enough that in these circumstances its claim to the territory should not be an insurmountable bar to the victim group's seceding, if this is the only way to avoid its wrongful destruction. Unfortunately, this type of case is far from fanciful. One of the strongest arguments for recognizing an independent Kurdish state, for example, is that only this status, with the control over territory it includes, will ensure the survival of this group in the face of genocidal threats from Turkey, Iran and Iraq.

There is a second situation in which secessionists might invoke the right of self-defence, but in a more controversial manner. They could argue that in order to defend itself against a lethal aggressor a group may secede from a state that is not itself that aggressor. This amounts to the claim that the need to defend itself against genocide can *generate* a claim to territory of sufficient moral weight to override the claims of those who until now held valid title to it and who, unlike the aggressor in the first version of the argument, have not forfeited their claim to it by lethal aggression.

Suppose the year is 1939. Germany has inaugurated a policy of genocide against the Jews. Jewish pleas to the democracies for protection have fallen on deaf ears (in part because the Jews are not regarded as a *nation*—nationhood carrying a strong presumption of territory, which they do not possess). Leaders of Jewish populations in Germany, Eastern Europe and the Soviet Union agree that the only hope for the survival of their people is to create a Jewish state, a sovereign territory to serve as a last refuge for European Jewry. Suppose further that the logical choice for its location—the only choice with the prospect of any success in saving large numbers of Jews—is a portion of Poland. Polish Jews, who are not being protected from the Nazis by the government of Poland, therefore occupy a portion of Poland and invite other Jews to join

them there in a Jewish sanctuary state. They do not expel non-Jewish Poles who already reside in that area but, instead, treat them as equal citizens. (From 1941 until 1945 something like this actually occurred on a smaller scale. Jewish partisans, who proved to be heroic and ferocious fighters, occupied and defended an area in the forests of Poland, in effect creating their own mini-state, for purposes of defending themselves and others from annihilation by the Germans.)

The force of this second application of the self-defence argument derives in part from the assumption that the Polish Jews who create the sanctuary state *are not being protected by their own state, Poland*. The idea is that a *state's authority over territory is based at least in part in its providing protection to all its citizens*—and that its retaining that authority is conditional on its continuing to do so. In the circumstances described, the Polish state is not providing protection to its Jewish citizens, and this fact voids the state's title to the territory in question. The Jews may rightly claim the territory, if doing so is necessary for their protection against extermination.

Escaping Discriminatory Redistribution

The idea here is that a group may secede if this is the only way for them to escape discriminatory redistribution. Discriminatory redistribution, also called regional exploitation and internal colonization, occurs whenever the state implements economic policies that systematically work to the disadvantage of some groups, while benefiting others, in morally arbitrary ways. A clear example of discriminatory redistribution would be the state imposing higher taxes on one group while spending less on it, or placing economic restrictions on one region, without any sound moral justification for this unequal treatment.

Charges of discriminatory redistribution abound in actual secessionist movements. Indeed, it would be hard to find cases in which this charge does not play a central role in justifications for secession, even though other reasons are often given as well. Here are only a few illustrations:

1. American Southerners complained that the federal tariff laws were discriminatory in intent and effect—that they served to foster the growth of infant industries in the North by protecting them from European and especially British competition, at the expense of the South's import-dependent

economy. The Southern statesman John C. Calhoun and others argued that the amount of money the South was contributing to the federal government, once the effects of the tariff were taken into account, far exceeded what that region was receiving from it.

2. Basque secessionists have noted that the percentage of total tax revenues in Spain paid by those in their region is more than three times the percentage of state expenditures there (a popular Basque protest song expresses this point vividly, saying that "the cow of the state has its mouth in the Basque country but its udder elsewhere").

3. Biafra, which unsuccessfully attempted to become independent from Nigeria in 1967, while containing only 22 per cent of the Nigerian population, contributed 38 per cent of total revenues, and received back from the government only 14 per cent of those revenues.

4. Secessionists in the Baltic Republics and in Soviet Central Asia protested that the government in Moscow for many years implemented economic policies that benefited the rest of the country at the expense of staggering environmental damage in their regions. To support this allegation of discriminatory redistribution, they cited reports of abnormally high rates of birth defects in Estonia, Latvia and Lithuania, apparently due to chemical pollutants from the heavy industry which Soviet economic policy concentrated there, and contamination of ground water in Central Asia due to massive use of pesticides and herbicides at the order of planners in Moscow whose goal it was to make that area a major cotton producer.

An implicit premise of the argument from discriminatory redistribution is that *failure to satisfy this fundamental condition of non-discrimination voids the state's claim to the territory in which the victims reside,* whereas the fact that they have no other recourse to avoid this fundamental injustice *gives them a valid title to it.* This premise forges the needed connection between the grounds for seceding (discriminatory redistribution) and the territorial claim that every sound justification for secession must include (since secession involves the taking of territory). One good reason for accepting this premise is that it explains our intuitions about the justifiability of secession in certain central and relatively uncontroversial cases.

In other words, unless this premise is acceptable, the argument from discriminatory redistribution is not sound; and unless the argument from discriminatory redistribution is sound, it is hard to see how secession is justifiable in certain cases in which there is widespread agreement that it is justified. Consider, for example, the secession of the thirteen American Colonies from the British Empire. (Strictly speaking this was secession, not revolution. The aim of the American colonists was not to overthrow the British government, but only to remove a part of the North American territory from the Empire.) The chief justification for American independence was discriminatory redistribution: Britain's mercantilist policies systematically worked to the disadvantage of the colonies for the benefit of the mother country. Lacking representation in the British Parliament, the colonists reasonably concluded that this injustice would persist. It seems, then, that if the American "Revolution" was justified, then there are cases in which the state's persistence in the injustice of discriminatory redistribution, together with the lack of alternatives to secession for remedying it, *generates* a valid claim to territory on the part of the secessionists.

The force of the argument from discriminatory redistribution does not rest solely, however, on brute moral intuitions about particular cases such as that of American independence. We can *explain* our responses to such cases by a simple but powerful principle: the legitimacy of the state—including its rightful jurisdiction over territory—depends upon its providing a framework for co-operation that does not systematically discriminate against any group.

The self-defence argument and the argument from discriminatory redistribution share an underlying assumption, namely, that the justification for a state's control over territory is at least in part *functional.* Generally speaking, what entitles a state to exercise exclusive jurisdiction ("territorial sovereignty") over a territory is the state's provision of a regime that enforces basic rights in a nondiscriminatory way. If the state fails to fulfil these legitimating jurisdictional functions with respect to a group, and if there is no other way for the group to protect itself from the ensuing injustices, then it can rightfully claim the jurisdictional authority for itself.

Attempts to justify secession on grounds of discriminatory redistribution are more complicated than might first appear. The mere fact that there is a net flow of revenue out of one region does not show that discriminatory redistribution is occurring. Instead, the state may simply be implementing policies designed to satisfy the demands of *distributive justice.* (Theories of distributive justice attempt to formulate and defend principles that specify the proper distribution of the burdens and benefits of social co-operation.) The problem is that distributive justice is a highly controversial matter and that different theories will yield different and in some cases directly opposing assessments of distributive patterns across regions of a country. A policy which redistributes wealth from one region to others may be a case of discriminatory redistribution according to one theory of distributive justice, but a case of just redistribution according to another. Even if there is fairly widespread agreement that the better-off owe *something* to the worse-off, there can be and is disagreement as to *how much* is owed. To this extent, the theory of secession is derivative upon the theory of distributive justice and subject to its uncertainties.

JUSTIFICATIONS FOR FORCIBLE RESISTANCE TO SECESSION

An adequate moral theory of secession must consider not only arguments to justify secession but justifications for resisting it as well. Here I will concentrate on only two of the more influential and plausible of the latter.

Avoiding Anarchy

From Lincoln to Gorbachev, leaders of states have opposed secession, warning that recognition of a right to secede would result in chaos. The *reductio ad absurdum* of the right to secede is the prospect of the most extreme anarchy: not every man's home his castle; rather, every man's yard his country. Even if political fragmentation stops short of this, recognition of a right to secede is likely to produce more fragmentation than is tolerable.

This argument would be much more plausible if recognizing a right to secede meant recognizing an *unlimited* right to secede. But as we have argued, the right to secede is a special or selective right that exists only when one or more of a limited set of justifying conditions is satisfied; it is not a general right of all peoples. Nor, as we have also seen, can it reasonably be understood to be included in or derivable from an alleged right of all peoples to self-determination. At most, the threat of anarchy could create a rebuttable presumption against secession, so that secessionists would, generally speaking, have to make a case for seceding.

The theory of the right to secede sketched above can be seen as including such a presumption: a sound justification for secession is to include a justification for the secessionists' claim to the territory. In a sense, this requirement constitutes a presumption in favour of the status quo and to that extent addresses the worry about anarchy. And since, as I have also noted, secession involves not only the severing of bonds of political obligation but also the taking of territory, this requirement seems reasonable.

Some might argue that by requiring secessionists to offer grounds for their claim to the territory, the theory proposed here stacks the deck against them. Especially from the standpoint of liberal political philosophy, which prizes liberty and self-determination, why should there not be a presumption that secession is justified, or at the very least, why should not secessionists and anti-secessionists start out on level ground in the process of justification?

There are, I believe, two sound reasons for a presumption that secessionists must make a case for taking the territory. First, a moral theory of secession should be viewed as a branch of *institutional ethics*. One relevant consideration for evaluating proposed principles for institutional ethics is the consequences of their general acceptance. So long as it is recognized that the presumption against secession can be rebutted by any of the arguments stated above in favour of a right to secede, such a presumption seems superior to the alternatives. Given the gravity of secession—and the predictable and unpredictable disruptions and violence which it may produce—legitimate interests in the stability of the international order speak in favour of the presumption.

Another consideration in favour of assigning the burden of argument where I have is that such a presumption—which gives some weight to the status quo—is much more likely to contribute to general acceptance of a right to secede in the international community. Other things being equal, a moral theory which is more likely to gain acceptance is to be preferred, especially if it is a theory of how institutions, in this case, the institutions of international law and diplomacy, ought to operate. It is often remarked that the one principle of international law that has gained almost universal acceptance is a strong presumption against violations of the territorial integrity of existing states. Requiring that secessionists be able to justify secession and in such a way as to establish their claim to the territory in question, serves to give appropriate weight to this fundamental principle, while at the same time recognizing that the state's claim to control over its territory is not absolute and can be overridden under certain conditions.

Avoiding Strategic Bargaining That Undermines Majority Rule

It could be argued that if the right to secede is recognized, then a minority may use the threat of secession to undermine majority rule. In conditions in which the majority views secession a prohibitive cost, a group's threat to secede can function as a veto over the majority's decisions. Consideration of this risk might lead one to conclude that the only adequate way to protect democracy is to refuse to acknowledge a right to secede.

However, as we have seen, there can be compelling justifications for secession under certain conditions. Accordingly, a more appropriate response than denying the right to secede is to devise constitutional mechanisms or processes of international law that give some weight both to legitimate interests in secession and to the equally legitimate interest in preserving the integrity of majority rule (and in political stability). The most obvious way to do this would be to allow secession under certain circumstances, but to minimize the risk of strategic bargaining with the threat of secession by erecting inconvenient but surmountable procedural hurdles to secession. For example a constitution might recognize a right to secede, but require a strong majority—say three-quarters—of those in the potentially seceding area to endorse secession in a referendum. This type of hurdle is the analogue of an obstacle to constitutional amendment which the U.S. Constitution's Amendment Clause itself establishes: any proposed amendment must receive a two-thirds vote in Congress and be ratified by three-quarters of the states.

The purpose of allowing amendment while erecting these two strong (that is, non-simple) majority requirements is to strike an appropriate balance between two legitimate interests: the interest in providing flexibility for needed change and the interest in securing stability. Similarly, the point of erecting inconvenient but surmountable barriers to secession (either in a constitution or in international law) would be not to make secession impossible but to avoid making it too easy. A second approach would be to levy special exit costs, a secession tax. Once these possibilities are recognized, the objection that acknowledgment of a right to secede necessarily undermines democracy is seen to be less than compelling.

SECESSION AND THE PROBLEM OF GROUP CONFLICT IN THE MODERN STATE

Secession is only the most extreme—and in some cases the least desirable—response to problems of group conflict. A comprehensive moral theory of international relations would include an account of the scope and limits of the right to secede; but it would also formulate and support principles to guide the establishment of a wider range of rights of self-determination. Such a theory, if it gained wide acceptance, would undoubtedly produce fundamental changes in our conceptions of the state, of sovereignty, and of the basic categories of international law.

READING 57

Can Terrorism Be Justified?

Andrew Valls

Andrew Valls is assistant Professor of Political science at Morehouse College and the author or editor of several works in political philosophy. In this essay Valls uses the criteria of just war theory to examine the question of whether terrorism can be morally justified. Just war theory originated in the Middle Ages as Christian theologians, such as Augustine and Thomas Aquinas, sought to determine under what conditions it would be morally right to engage in State violence, war. Just war theory inquires into (1) the possible moral grounds for going to war *(jus ad bellum)* and (2) the manner in which a just war must be carried out or fought *(jus in bello)*. Valls's discussion of terrorism in the light of just war theory challenges many of the public's attitudes toward terrorism.

This reading is taken from *Ethics in International Affairs*, ed. Andrew Valls (Rowman & Littlefield, 2000), by permission.

As the chapters in the previous section amply demonstrate, just war theory, despite its ambiguities, provides a rich framework with which to assess the morality of war. But interstate war is only the most conventional form of political violence. The question arises, Is it the only form of political violence that may ever be justified? If not, how are we to assess the morality of other cases of political violence, particularly those involving nonstate actors? In short, does just war theory apply to terrorism, and, if so, can terrorism satisfy its criteria?

In the public and scholarly reactions to political violence, a double standard often is at work. When violence is committed by states, our assessment tends to be quite permissive, giving states a great benefit of the doubt about the propriety of their violent acts. However, when the violence is committed by nonstate actors, we often react with horror, and the condemnations cannot come fast enough. Hence, terrorism is almost universally condemned, whereas violence by states, even when war has not been declared, is seen as legitimate, if not always fully justified. This difference in assessments remains when innocent civilians are killed in both cases and sometimes when such killing is deliberate. Even as thoughtful a commentator as Michael Walzer, for example, seems to employ this double standard. In his *Just and Unjust Wars*, Walzer considers whether "soldiers and statesmen [can] override the rights of innocent people for the sake of their own political community" and answers "affirmatively, though not without hesitation and worry."[1] Walzer goes on to discuss a case in point, the Allied bombing of German cities during World War II, arguing that, despite the many civilians who deliberately were killed, the bombing was justified. However, later in the book, Walzer rejects out of hand the possibility that terrorism might sometimes be justified, on the grounds that it involves the deliberate killing of innocents. He never considers the possibility that stateless communities might confront the same "supreme emergency" that justified, in his view, the bombing of innocent German civilians. I will have more to say about Walzer's position below, but for now I wish to point out that, on the face of it at least, his position seems quite inconsistent.

From a philosophical point of view, this double standard cannot be sustained. As Coady[2] argues, consistency requires that we apply the same standards to both kinds of political violence, state and nonstate. Of course, it may turn out that there are simply some criteria that states can satisfy that nonstate actors cannot, so that the same standard applied to both inevitably leads to different conclusions. There may be morally relevant features of states that make their use of violence legitimate and its use by others illegitimate. However, I will argue that this is not the case. I argue that, on the most plausible account of just war theory, taking into account the ultimate moral basis of its criteria, violence undertaken by nonstate actors can, in principle, satisfy the requirements of a just war.

To advance this view, I examine each criterion of just war theory in turn, arguing in each case that terrorism committed by nonstate actors can satisfy the criterion. The most controversial parts of my argument will no doubt be those regarding just cause, legitimate authority, and discrimination, so I devote more attention to these than to the others. I argue that, once we properly understand the moral basis for each of these criteria, it is clear that some nonstate groups may have the same right as states to commit violence and that they are just as capable of committing that violence within the constraints imposed by just war theory. My conclusion, then, is that if just war theory can justify violence committed by states, then terrorism committed by nonstate actors can also, under certain circumstances, be justified by it as well. But before commencing the substantive argument, I must attend to some preliminary matters concerning the definition of *terrorism*.

DEFINITIONAL ISSUES

There is little agreement on the question of how *terrorism* is best defined. In the political arena, of course, the word is used by political actors for political purposes, usually to paint their opponents as monsters. Scholars, on the other hand, have at least attempted to arrive at a more detached position, seeking a definition that captures the essence of terrorism. However, there is reason, in addition to the lack of consensus, to doubt whether much progress has been made.

Most definitions of terrorism suffer from at least one of two difficulties. First, they often define terrorism as murder or otherwise characterize it as intrinsically wrong and unjustifiable. The trouble with this approach is that it prejudges the substantive moral issue by a definitional consideration. I agree with Teichman, who writes that "we ought not to begin by *defining* terrorism as a bad thing."[3] Moral conclusions should follow from moral reasoning, grappling with the moral issues themselves. To decide a normative issue by definitional considerations, then, ends the discussion before it begins.

The second shortcoming that many definitions of terrorism exhibit is being too revisionist of its meaning in ordinary language. As I have noted, the word is often used as a political weapon, so ordinary language will not settle the issue. Teichman again is correct that any definition will necessarily be stipulative to some extent. But ordinary language does, nevertheless, impose some constraints on the stipulative definition that we can accept. For example, Carl Wellman defines *terrorism* as "the use or attempted use of terror as a means of coercion"[4] and draws the conclusion that when he instills terror in his students with threats of grade penalties on late papers, he commits terrorism. Clearly this is not what most of us have in mind when we speak of terrorism, so Wellman's definition, even if taken as stipulative, is difficult to accept.

Some definitions of terrorism suffer from both of these shortcomings to some degree. For example, those that maintain that terrorism is necessarily random or indiscriminate seem both to depart markedly from ordinary usage—there are lots of acts we call terrorist that specifically target military facilities and personnel—and thereby to prejudge the moral issue. (I will argue below that terrorism need not be indiscriminate at all.) The same can be said of definitions that insist that the aim of terrorism must be to terrorize, that it targets some to threaten many more. As Virginia Held has argued, "We should probably not construe either the intention to spread fear or the intention to kill noncombatants as necessary for an act of political violence to be an act of terrorism."[5] Annette Baier adds that "the terrorist may be ill named" because what she sometimes wants is not to terrorize but "the shocked attention of her audience population."[6]

With all of this disagreement, it would perhaps be desirable to avoid the use of the term *terrorism* altogether and simply to speak instead of political violence. I would be sympathetic to this position were it not for the fact that *terrorism* is already too much a part of our political vocabulary to be avoided. Still, we can with great plausibility simply define *terrorism* as a form of political violence, as Held does: "I [see] terrorism as a form of violence to achieve political goals, where creating fear is usually high among the intended effects."[7] This is a promising approach, though I would drop as nonessential the stipulation that terrorism is usually intended to spread fear. In addition, I would make two stipulations of my own. First, "violence" can include damage to property as well as harm to people. Blowing up a power plant can surely be an act of terrorism, even if no one is injured. Second, for the pur-

poses of this chapter, I am interested in violence committed by nonstate actors. I do not thereby deny the existence of state terrorism. However, for the purposes of my present argument, I assume that when a state commits terrorism against its own citizens, this is a matter for domestic justice, and that when it commits violence outside of its own borders, just war theory can, fairly easily, be extended to cover these cases. The problem for international ethics that I wish to address here is whether just war theory can be extended to nonstate actors. So my stipulative definition of *terrorism* in this chapter is simply that it is violence committed by nonstate actors against persons or property for political purposes. This definition appears to leave open the normative issues involved and to be reasonably consistent with ordinary language.

JUS AD BELLUM

It is somewhat misleading to speak of just war *theory,* for it is not a single theory but, rather, a tradition within which there is a range of interpretation. That is, just war theory is best thought of as providing a framework for discussion about whether a war is just, rather than as providing a set of unambiguous criteria that are easily applied. In what follows I rely on what I believe is the most plausible and normatively appealing version of just war theory. . . . I begin with the *jus ad bellum* criteria, concerning the justice of going to war, and then turn to *jus in bello* criteria, which apply to the conduct of the war.

Just Cause

A just cause for a war is usually a defensive one. That is, a state is taken to have a just cause when it defends itself against aggression, where *aggression* means the violation or the imminent threat of the violation of its territorial integrity or political independence. So the just cause provision of just war theory holds, roughly, that the state has a right to defend itself against the aggression of other states.

But on what is this right of the state based? Most students of international ethics maintain that any right that a state enjoys is ultimately based on the rights of its citizens. States in and of themselves have value only to the extent that they serve some good for the latter. The moral status of the state is therefore derivative, not foundational, and it is derivative of the rights of the individuals within it. This, it seems, is the dominant (liberal) view, and only an exceedingly statist perspective would dispute it.

The right that is usually cited as being the ground for the state's right to defend itself is the right of self-determination. The state is the manifestation of, as well as the arena for, the right of a people to determine itself. It is because aggression threatens the common life of the people within a state, as well as threatening other goods they hold dear, that the state can defend its territory and independence. This is clear, for example, from Walzer's discussion of intervention. Drawing on John Stuart Mill, Walzer argues that states generally ought not to intervene in the affairs of other states because to do so would be to violate the right of self-determination of the community within the state. However, once the right of self-determination is recognized, its implications go beyond a right against intervention or a right of defense. Walzer makes this clear as well, as his discussion of Mill's argument for non-intervention is followed immediately by exceptions to the rule, one of which is secession. When a secessionist movement has demonstrated that it represents the will of its people, other states may intervene to aid the secession because, in this case, secession reflects the self-determination of that people.

In the twenty years since Walzer presented this argument, a great deal of work has been done on nationalism, self-determination, and secession. Despite the range of views that has developed, it is fair to say that something of an overlapping consensus has formed, namely, that under certain circumstances, certain kinds of groups enjoy a right of self-determination that entitles them to their own state or at least to some autonomy in a federal arrangement within an existing state. The debate is mostly over what these circumstances are and what kinds of groups enjoy the right. For example, Alan Buchanan . . . argues that the circumstances must include a historical injustice before a group is entitled to secede [see Reading 56]. Others are more permissive. Christopher Wellman and Daniel Philpott argue that past injustice is not required to entitle a group to secession and, indeed, that any group within a territory may secede, even if it is not plausibly seen as constituting a nation.[8]

The modal position in the debate is, perhaps, somewhere between these positions, holding that certain groups, even absent a history of injustice, have a right to self-determination but that this applies not to just any group but only to "peoples" or "nations." This is essentially the position taken by Kymlicka, Tamir,

Miller, and Margalit and Raz [see Reading 54]. There are, of course, important differences among these authors. Kymlicka argues that groups with "societal cultures" have a right to self-government but not necessarily secession. Margalit and Raz advance a similar argument, and their notion of an "encompassing group" is very close to Kymlicka's "societal culture." Tamir emphasizes that, in her view, the right to self-determination is a cultural right, not a political one and does not necessarily support a right to political independence. Miller does interpret the right of self-determination as a right to a state, but he hesitates to call it a right, for it may not always be achievable due to the legitimate claims of others. (His concern would perhaps be alleviated by following Philpott in speaking of a "prima facie" right.)

For the purposes of my present argument, I need not enter this important debate but only point out that any one of these views can support the weak claim I wish to make. The claim is that under some circumstances, some groups enjoy a right to self-determination. The circumstances may include—or, following Buchanan, even be limited to—cases of injustice toward the group, or, in a more permissive view, it may not. This right may be enjoyed only by nations or by any group within a territory. It may be that the right of self-determination does not automatically ground a right to political independence, but if some form of self-determination cannot be realized within an existing state, then it can, under these circumstances, ground such a right. For the sake of simplicity, in the discussion that follows I refer to nations or peoples as having a right of self-determination, but this does not commit me to the view that other kinds of groups do not enjoy this right. Similarly, I will sometimes fail to distinguish between a right of self-determination and a right to a state, despite realizing that the former does not necessarily entail the latter. I will assume that in some cases—say, when a federal arrangement cannot be worked out—one can ground the right to a state on the right to self-determination.

My conclusion about the just cause requirement is obvious. Groups other than those constituted by the state in which they live can have a just cause to defend their right of self-determination. While just war theory relies on the rights of the citizens to ground the right of a state to defend itself, other communities within a state may have that same right. When the communal life of a nation is seriously threatened by a state, that nation has a just cause to defend itself. In the case in which the whole nation is within a single state, this can justify secession. In a case in which the community is stateless, as with colonial rule, it is probably less accurate to speak of secession than national liberation.

This is not a radical conclusion. Indeed, it is recognized and endorsed by the United Nations, as Khatchadourian points out: "The UN definition of 'just cause' recognizes the rights of peoples as well as states," and in Article 7 of the definition of *aggression,* the United Nations refers to "the right to self-determination, freedom, and independence, as derived from the Charter, of *peoples* forcibly deprived of that right."[9] So both morally and legally, "peoples" or "nations" enjoy a right to self-determination. When that right is frustrated, such peoples, I have argued, have the same just cause that states have when the self-determination of their citizens is threatened.

Legitimate Authority

The legitimate authority requirement is usually interpreted to mean that only states can go to war justly. It rules out private groups waging private wars and claiming them to be just. The state has a monopoly on the legitimate use of force, so it is a necessary condition for a just war that it be undertaken by the entity that is uniquely authorized to wield the sword. To allow other entities, groups, or agencies to undertake violence would be to invite chaos. Such violence is seen as merely private violence, crime.

The equation of legitimate authority with states has, however, been criticized by a number of philosophers—and with good reason. Gilbert has argued that "the equation of proper authority with a lawful claim to it should be resisted."[10] Tony Coates has argued at some length and quite persuasively that to equate legitimate authority with state sovereignty is to rob the requirement of the moral force that it historically has had. The result is that the principle has become too permissive by assuming that any de facto state may wage war. This requirement, then, is too easily and quickly "checked off:" If a war is waged by a state, this requirement is satisfied. This interpretation has meant that "the criterion of legitimate authority has become the most neglected of all the criteria that have been traditionally employed in the moral assessment of war."[11] Contrary to this tendency in recent just war thinking, Coates argues that we must subject to close scrutiny a given state's claim to represent the interests and rights of its people.

When we reject the view that all states are legitimate authorities, we may also ask if some nonstates may be legitimate authorities. The considerations just adduced suggest that being a state is not sufficient for being a legitimate authority. Perhaps it is not necessary either. What matters is the plausibility of the claim to represent the interests and rights of a people. I would like to argue that some nonstate entities or organizations may present a very plausible case for being a people's representative. Surely it is sufficient for this that the organization is widely seen as their representative by the members of the nation itself. If an organization claims to act on behalf of a people and is widely seen by that people as legitimately doing so, then the rest of us should look on that organization as the legitimate authority of the people for the purposes of assessing its entitlement to engage in violence on their behalf.

The alternative view, that only states may be legitimate authorities, "leads to political quietism [and is] conservative and uncritical."[12] Once we acknowledge that stateless peoples may have the right to self-determination, it would render that right otiose to deny that the right could be defended and vindicated by some nonstate entity. As Dugard has pointed out, in the case of colonial domination, there is no victim state, though there is a victim people.[13] If we are to grant that a colonized people has a right to self-determination, it seems that we must grant that a nonstate organization—a would-be state, perhaps—can act as a legitimate authority and justly engage in violence on behalf of the people. Examples are not difficult to find. Coates cites the Kurds and the Marsh Arabs in Iraq and asks, "Must such persecuted communities be denied the right of collective self-defense simply because, through some historical accident, they lack the formal character of states?"

It must be emphasized that the position advocated here requires that the organization not only claim representative status but be perceived to enjoy that status by the people it claims to represent. This is a rather conservative requirement because it rules out "vanguard" organizations that claim representative status despite lack of support among the people themselves. The position defended here is also more stringent than that suggested by Wilkins, who writes that it might "be enough for a terrorist movement simply to claim to represent the aspirations or the moral rights of a people." While I agree that "moral authority may be all that matters,"[14] I would argue that moral authority requires not merely claiming to represent a people but also being seen by the people themselves as their representative.

How do we know whether this is the case? No single answer can be given here. Certainly the standard should not be higher than that used for states. In the case of states, for example, elections are not required for legitimacy, as understood in just war theory. There are many members of the international community in good standing that are not democratic regimes, authorized by elections. In the case of nonstate entities, no doubt a number of factors will weigh in, either for or against the claim to representativeness, and, in the absence of legal procedures (or public opinion polls), we may have to make an all-things-considered judgment. No doubt there will be some disagreement in particular cases, but all that is required for the present argument is that, in principle, nonstate organizations may enjoy the moral status of legitimate authorities.

Right Intention

If a national group can have a just cause, and if a nonstate entity can be a legitimate authority to engage in violence on behalf of that group, it seems unproblematic that those engaging in violence can be rightly motivated by that just cause. Hence, if just cause and legitimate authority can be satisfied, there seems to be no reason to think that the requirement of right intention cannot be satisfied. This is not to say, of course, that if the first two are satisfied, the latter is as well, but only that if the first two requirements are met, the latter can be. All that it requires is that the relevant actors be motivated by the just cause and not some other end.

Last Resort

Can terrorist violence, undertaken by the representatives of a stateless nation to vindicate their right of self-determination, be a last resort? Some have doubted that it can. For example, Walzer refers to the claim of last resort as one of the "excuses" sometimes offered for terrorism. He suggests that terrorism is usually a first resort, not a last one, and that to truly be a last resort, "one must indeed try everything (which is a lot of things), and not just once. . . . Politics is an art of repetition."[15] Terrorists, according to Walzer, often claim that their resort to violence is a last resort but in fact it never is and never can be.

Two problems arise concerning Walzer's position. First, related to the definitional issues discussed above and taken up again below when discrimination is treated, Walzer takes terrorism to be "an attack upon the innocent," and he "take[s] the principle for granted: that every act of terrorism is a wrongful act." Given the understanding of terrorism as murder, it can never be a justified last resort. But as Fullinwider argues in his response to Walzer, it is puzzling both that Walzer construes terrorism this way, for not all terrorism is random murder, and that Walzer simply takes it for granted that nothing can justify terrorism. Walzer's position is undermined by a prejudicial definition of *terrorism* that begs the substantive moral questions, reflected in the fact that he characterizes arguments in defense of terrorism as mere "excuses."

The second problem is that again Walzer appears to use a double standard. While he does not say so explicitly in the paper under discussion, Walzer elsewhere clearly endorses the resort to war by states. Here, however, he argues that, because "politics is an art of repetition," the last resort is never arrived at for nonstate actors contemplating violence. But why is it that the territorial integrity and political independence of, say, Britain, justify the resort to violence—even violence that targets civilians—but the right of self-determination of a stateless nation never does? Why can states arrive at last resort, while stateless nations cannot? Walzer never provides an answer to this question.

The fact is that judgment is called for by all political actors contemplating violence, and among the judgments that must be made is whether last resort has been [reached]. This is a judgment about whether all reasonable nonviolent measures have been tried, been tried a reasonable number of times, and been given a reasonable amount of time to work. There will always be room for argument about what *reasonable* means here, what it requires in a particular case, but I see no justification for employing a double standard for what it means, one for states, another for nonstate actors. If states may reach the point of deciding that all nonviolent measures have failed, then so too can nonstate actors.

Probability of Success

Whether terrorism ever has any probability of success, or enough probability of success to justify embarking on a terrorist campaign, depends on a number of factors, including the time horizon one has in mind. Whether one considers the case of state actors deciding to embark on a war or nonstate actors embarking on terrorism, a prospective judgment is required, and prospective judgments are liable to miscalculations and incorrect estimations of many factors. Still, one must make a judgment, and if one judges that the end has little chance of being achieved through violence, the probability of success criterion requires that the violence not be commenced.

Does terrorism ever have any probability of success? There are differing views of the historical record on this question. For example, Walzer thinks not. He writes, "No nation that I know of owes its freedom to a campaign of random murder."[16] Again, we find that Walzer's analysis is hindered by his conception of what terrorism is, and so it is of little help to us here. To those who have a less loaded notion of terrorism, the evidence appears more ambiguous. Held provides a brief, well-balanced discussion of the issue. She cites authors who have argued on both sides of the question, including one who uses the bombing of the U.S. Marines' barracks in Beirut in 1982 (which prompted an American withdrawal) as an example of a successful terrorist attack. Held concludes that "it may be impossible to predict whether an act of terrorism will in fact have its intended effect" but notes that in this it is no different from other prospective judgments.[17] Similarly, Teichman concludes that the historical evidence on the effectiveness of terrorism is "both ambiguous and incomplete."[18] And Baier suggests that, at the least, "the prospects for the success of a cause do not seem in the past to have been reduced by resort to unauthorized force, by violent demonstrations that cost some innocent lives."[19] Finally, Wilkins believes that some terrorist campaigns have indeed accomplished their goal of national independence and cites Algeria and Kenya as examples.[20]

I am not in a position to judge all of the historical evidence that may be relevant to this issue. However, it seems clear that we cannot say that it is never the case that terrorism has some prospect of success. Perhaps in most cases—the vast majority of them, even—there is little hope of success. Still, we cannot rule out that terrorism can satisfy the probability of success criterion.

Proportionality

The proportionality criterion within *jus ad bellum* also requires a prospective judgment—whether the overall costs of the violent conflict will be outweighed by the overall benefits. In addition to the difficulties inherent in prospective judgments, this criterion is problematic in that it seems to require us to measure the value of costs and benefits that may not be amenable to measurement and seems to assume that all goods are commensurable, that their value can be compared. As a result, there is probably no way to make these kinds of judgments with any great degree of precision.

Still, it seems clear that terrorism can satisfy this criterion at least as well as conventional war. Given the large scale of destruction that often characterizes modern warfare, and given that some very destructive wars are almost universally considered just, it appears that just war theory can countenance a great deal of violence if the end is of sufficient value. If modern warfare is sometimes justified, terrorism, in which the violence is usually on a far smaller scale, can be justified as well. This is especially clear if the end of the violence is the same or similar in both cases, such as when a nation wishes to vindicate its right to self-determination.

JUS IN BELLO

Even if terrorism can meet all the criteria of *jus ad bellum,* it may not be able to meet those of *jus in bello,* for terrorism is often condemned, not so much for who carries it out and why but for how it is carried out. Arguing that it can satisfy the requirements of *jus in bello,* then, may be the greatest challenge facing my argument.

Proportionality

The challenge, however, does not come from the proportionality requirement of *jus in bello.* Like its counterpart in *jus ad bellum,* the criterion requires proportionality between the costs of an action and the benefits to be achieved, but now the requirement is applied to particular acts within the war. It forbids, then, conducting the war in such a way that it involves inordinate costs, costs that are disproportionate to the gains.

Again, there seems to be no reason to believe that terrorist acts could not satisfy this requirement. Given that the scale of the death and destruction usually involved in terrorist acts pales in comparison with that involved in wars commonly thought to be just, it would seem that terrorism would satisfy this requirement more easily than war (assuming that the goods to be achieved are not dissimilar). So if the means of terrorism is what places it beyond the moral pale for many people, it is probably not because of its disproportionality.

Discrimination

The principle of discrimination holds that in waging a war we must distinguish between legitimate and illegitimate targets of attack. The usual way of making this distinction is to classify persons according to their status as combatants and noncombatants and to maintain that only combatants may be attacked. However, there is some disagreement as to the moral basis of this distinction, which creates disagreement as to where exactly this line should be drawn. While usually based on the notion of moral innocence, noncombatant status, it can be argued, has little to do with innocence, for often combatants are conscripts, while those truly responsible for aggression are usually not liable (practically, not morally) to attack. Moreover, many who provide essential support to the war effort are not combatants.

For the moment, though, let us accept the conventional view that discrimination requires that violence be directed at military targets. Assuming the line can be clearly drawn, two points can be made about terrorism and discrimination. The first is that, *a priori,* it is possible for terrorism to discriminate and still be terrorism. This follows from the argument presented above that, as a matter of definition, it is implausible to define terrorism as intrinsically indiscriminate. Those who define terrorism as random or indiscriminate will disagree and maintain that "discriminate terrorism" is an oxymoron, a conceptual impossibility. Here I can only repeat that this position departs substantially from ordinary language and does so in a way that prejudges the moral issues involved. However, if my argument above does not convince on this question, there is little more to be said here.

Luckily, the issue is not a purely *a priori* one. The fact is that terrorists, or at least those called terrorists by almost everyone, in fact do often discriminate. One example, cited on page 569, is the bombing of the barracks in Beirut, which killed some 240 American soldiers. Whatever one wants to say to condemn the attack, one cannot say that it was indiscriminate. Fullinwider cites the example of the kidnapping, trial, and killing of Aldo Moro by the Italian Red Brigades in 1978 and argues that, whatever else one might want to say about it, "there was nothing indiscriminate about the taking of Aldo Moro."[21] Coady cites another example, that of an American diplomat in Uruguay who was targeted and killed in 1970 because of the assistance he was providing to the authoritarian regime. These may be the exceptions rather than the rule, but it clearly is not accurate to say that terrorists—and there was never any doubt that these were acts of terrorism—never discriminate.

It might be useful to look, one last time, at Walzer's position on this issue because, from the point of view I have developed, he errs on both the conceptual and the empirical question. Walzer maintains that "terrorism in the strict sense, the random murder of innocent people, emerged . . . only in the period after World War II."[22] Previously, nonstate actors, especially revo-

lutionaries, who committed violence did discriminate. Walzer gives several examples of this in which Russian revolutionaries, the Irish Republican Army, and the Stern Gang in the Middle East went to great lengths to not kill civilians. He also notes that these people were called terrorists. Yet he refuses to say that they *were* terrorists, insisting instead that they were not, really, and using scare quotes when he himself calls them terrorists. This is tortured analysis indeed. Why not simply acknowledge that these earlier terrorists were indeed terrorists while also maintaining, if evidence supports it, that today more terrorists are more indiscriminate than in the past? I suspect that Walzer and I would agree in our moral assessment of particular acts. Our main difference is that he believes that calling an act terrorism (without the scare quotes) settles the question.

All of this is consistent with the assumption that a clear line can be drawn between combatants and noncombatants. However, the more reasonable view may be that combatancy status, and therefore liability to attack, are matters of degree. This is suggested by Holmes,[23] and though Holmes writes as a pacifist critic of just war theory, his suggestion is one that just war theorists may nevertheless want to endorse. Holmes conceives of a spectrum along which we can place classes of individuals, according to their degree of responsibility for an aggressive war. At one end he would place political leaders who undertake the aggression, followed by soldiers, contributors to the war, supporters, and, finally, at the other end of the spectrum, noncontributors and nonsupporters. This view does indeed better capture our moral intuitions about liability to attack and avoids debates (which are probably not resolvable) about where the absolute line between combatants and noncombatants is to be drawn.

If correct, this view further complicates the question of whether and when terrorism discriminates. It means we must speak of more and less discriminate violence, and it forces us to ask questions like. To what *extent* were the targets of violence implicated in unjust aggression? Children, for example, would be clearly off-limits, but nonmilitary adults who actively take part in frustrating a people's right to self-determination may not be. With terrorism, as with war, the question to ask may not be, Was the act discriminate, yes or no? but, rather, How discriminate was the violence? Our judgment on this matter, and hence our moral appraisal of the violence, is likely to be more nuanced if we ask the latter question than if we assume that a simple yes or no settles the matter. After all, is our judgment really the same—and ought it be—when a school bus is attacked as when gun-toting citizens are attacked? Terrorism, it seems, can be more discriminate or less so, and our judgments ought to reflect the important matters of degree involved.

One final issue is worth mentioning, if only briefly. Even if one were to grant that terrorism necessarily involves the killing of innocents, this alone does not place it beyond the scope of just war theory, for innocents may be killed in a just war. All that just war theory requires is that innocents not be *targeted*. The basis for this position is the principle of double effect, which holds, roughly, that innocents may be killed as long as their deaths are not the intended effects of violence but, rather, the unintended (though perhaps fully foreseen) side effects of violence. So the most that can be said against my position, even granting that terrorism involves the killing of innocents, is that the difference between (just) war and terrorism is that in the former innocents are not targeted but (routinely) killed while in the latter they are targeted and killed. Whether this is a crucial distinction is a question that would require us to go too far afield at this point. Perhaps it is enough to say that if there are reasons to reject the principle of double effect, . . . there is all the more basis to think that terrorism and war are not so morally different from each other.

CONCLUSION

I have argued that terrorism, understood as political violence committed by nonstate actors, can be assessed from the point of view of just war theory and that terrorist acts can indeed satisfy the theory's criteria. Though stateless, some groups can nevertheless have a just cause when their right to self-determination is frustrated. Under such circumstances, a representative organization can be a morally legitimate authority to carry out violence as a last resort to defend the group's rights. Such violence must conform to the other criteria, especially discrimination, but terrorism, I have argued, can do so.

The argument has taken place entirely within the just war tradition but can be endorsed from other perspectives as well. For example, Annette Baier, though no just war theorist, comes to a very similar conclusion:

> It is fairly easy to say that the clearer it is that the terrorist group's case is *not* being listened to in decision making affecting it and that the less violent

ways to get attention have been tried in vain, the more excuse the terrorist has; that his case is better the more plausible his claim to represent his group's sense of injustice or wrong, not just his own; that the more limited, the less indiscriminate, his violence, the less outrage will we feel for his inhumanity. Those are not daring conclusions.[24]

Indeed they are not daring conclusions, and mine certainly are not. I have avoided consequentialist arguments that might, on utilitarian grounds, justify violence for the greater good to be achieved. I have not endorsed the notion of collective guilt, which, in my view, goes too far in eroding the distinction between combatants and noncombatants. My argument would not support the violence of a vanguard party, committing violence in the hope of winning the support of those it claims to already represent. Hence, the argument presented here places real, stringent moral limits on violence committed by nonstate actors.

Indeed, placing limits on violence is what just war theory is all about. As Coates argues, the main purpose of just war theory is to constrain violence. Coates emphasizes that just war theory should not convince perpetrators of violence of their own righteousness but, rather, is meant to instill a sense of limits and restraint. If we assume that terrorism is beyond the pale, however, we deprive ourselves of the capacity to impose some moral limits. If terrorists are monsters, then there is no reasoning with them. However, if we take their claims seriously, if we assess their violence by the same standards used to assess the violence of states, we at least have a chance that just war theory will impose some restraint on them, as it does (or at least is supposed to) with states.

It is important to be clear about what I have not argued here. I have not defended terrorism in general, nor certainly have I defended any particular act of violence. It follows from my argument not that terrorism can be justified but that if war can be justified, then terrorism can be as well. I wish to emphasize the conditional nature of the conclusion. I have not established just war theory as the best or the only framework within which to think about the moral issues raised by political violence. Instead I have relied on it because it is the most developed and widely used in thinking about violence carried out by states. I have done so because the double standard that is often used in assessing violence committed by states and nonstate actors seems indefensible. Applying just war theory to both, I believe, is a plausible way to bring both kinds of violence under one standard.

I have little doubt that most terrorist acts do not satisfy all of the criteria of just war theory and that many of them fall far short. In such cases we are well justified in condemning them. But the condemnation must follow, not precede, examination of the case and is not settled by calling the act terrorism and its perpetrators terrorists. I agree with Fullinwider that, while terrorism often fails to be morally justified, "this failure is contingent, not necessary. We cannot define terrorism into a moral corner where we do not have to worry any more about justification."[25] Furthermore, failure to satisfy the requirements of just war theory is not unique to acts of terrorism. The same could be said of wars themselves. How many wars, after all, are undertaken and waged within the constraints imposed by the theory?

The conditional nature of the conclusion, if the above argument is sound, forces a choice. Either both interstate war and terrorism can be justified or neither can be. For my part, I must confess to being sorely tempted by the latter position, that neither war nor terrorism can be justified. This temptation is bolstered by pacifist arguments that the killing of innocents is a perfectly predictable effect of modern warfare, the implication of which is that no modern war can be just. That is, even if we can imagine a modern just war, it is not a realistic possibility. Though the pacifist position is tempting, it also seems clear that some evils are great enough to require a response, even a violent response. And once we grant that states may respond violently, there seems no principled reason to deny that same right to certain nonstate groups that enjoy a right to self-determination.

END NOTES

Maritain

[1] Mortimer J. Adler, *How to Think about War and Peace* (New York: Simon & Schuster, 1944), pp. 228–29. Mr. Emery Reves's quotation is taken from his *Democratic Manifesto.*

[2] John U. Nef, *La Route de la guerre totale* (Paris: Armand Colin, 1949).

[3] Adler, *op. cit.,* p. 69.

[4] *The Pilgrimage of Western Man* (New York: Harcourt, Brace & Co., 1949), p. 341.

[5] Robert M. Hutchins, *St. Thomas and the World State* (Aquinas Lecture, 1949 [Milwaukee: Marquette University Press, 1949]). "Perfect society" does not mean a society without defect, but a society which has reached full formation.

[6] *The Preliminary Draft for a World Constitution,* known as the Chicago Plan, by the Committee to Frame a World Constitution: Robert M. Hutchins, G. A. Borgese, Mortimer J. Adler, Stringfellow Barr, Albert Guérard, Harold A. Innis, Erich Kahler, Wilber G. Katz, Charles H. McIlwain, Robert Redfield, and Rexford G. Tugwell. The "Preliminary Draft" was printed in the March, 1948, issue of the monthly *Common Cause* (University of Chicago).

[7] Max Ascoli, *The Power of Freedom* (New York: Farrar, Straus, 1949), Part III, chap. iv.

[8] Henri Bergson, *Les deux sources de la morale et de la religion* (Paris: Alcan, 1932), chap. iv.

[9] From a chapter, "Renewal (1950)," in a still unpublished book, "French Civilization and Universal Community."

[10] Nef, *La Route de la guerre totale,* p. 161.

Barry

[1] Charles R. Beitz, "Cosmopolitan Liberalism and the States System," in Chris Brown, ed., *Political Restructuring in Europe: Ethical Perspectives* (London: Routledge, 1994), 123–36, quotations at 124, 125, 126.

[2] Beitz, "Cosmopolitan Liberalism," 126.

[3] Thomas E. Hill, Jr., "The Importance of Autonomy," in Eva Kittay and Diane Meyers, eds., *Women and Moral Theory* (Totowa, NJ: Rowman and Allanheld, 1987), 132.

[4] T. M. Scanlon, "Contractualism and Utilitarianism," in Amartya Sen and Bernard Williams, eds., *Utilitarianism and Beyond* (Cambridge: Cambridge University Press, 1982), 103–28, quotation at 116, n. 2.

[5] Richard Arneson, "Property Rights in Persons," *Social Philosophy and Policy* 9 (1992): 201–30, at 209.

[6] Eduardo S. Bustelo, "Social Policies in Times of Cholera," paper presented to the IPSA World Congress, Buenos Aires, August 1991, 25, table 3.

[7] I. G. Patel, "Global Economic Governance: Some Thoughts on Our Current Discontents," Centre for the Study of Global Governance, London School of Economics, 1994.

[8] Gunnar Myrdal, "The 'Soft State' in Underdeveloped Countries," in P. Streeten, ed., *Unfashionable Economics: Essays in Honour of Lord Balogh* (London: Weidenfeld and Nicolson, 1970), 227–43.

Valls

[1] Walzer, Michael. 1992 [1979]. *Just and Unjust Wars: A Moral Argument with Historical Illustrations,* 2nd Edition. New York: Basic Books, p. 254.

[2] Coady, C.A.J. 1985. The Morality of Terrorism, *Philosophy* 60: 47–69.

[3] Teichman, Jenny. 1989. How to Define Terrorism. *Philosophy* 64: 505–17.

[4] Wellman, Carl. 1979. On Terrorism Itself. *Journal of Value Inquiry* 13: 250–58.

[5] Held, Virginia. 1991. Terrorism, Rights, and Political Goals. In *Violence, Terrorism, and Justice,* ed. R. G. Frey and Christopher W. Morris. Cambridge: Cambridge University Press.

[6]Baier, Annette. 1994. Violent Demonstrations. In *Moral Prejudices: Essays on Ethics*. Cambridge: Harvard University Press.

[7]Held, op. cite, p. 64.

[8]Wellman, Christopher H. 1995. A Defense of Secession and Political Self-Determination. *Philosophy and Public Affairs* 24: 142–71.

[8]Tamir, Yael. 1993. *Liberal Nationalism*. Princeton: Princeton University Press

[8a]Kymlicka, Will. 1995. *Multicultural Citizenship: A Liberal Theory of Minority Rights*. Oxford: Clarendon Press.

[8b]Philpott, Daniel. 1995. In Defense of Self-Determination. *Ethics* 105: 352–85.

[8c]Miller, David. 1995. *On Nationality*. Oxford: Oxford University Press.

[9]Khatchadourian, Haig. 1998. *The Morality of Terrorism*. New York: Peter Lang, p. 41.

[10]Gilbert, Paul. 1994. *Terrorism, Security, and Nationality: An Introductory Study in Applied Political Philosophy*. New York: Routledge, p. 29.

[11]Coates, Anthony J. 1997. *The Ethics of War*. Manchester: Manchester University Press.

[12]Ibid, p. 128.

[13]Dugard, John. 1982. International Terrorism and the Just War. In *The Morality of Terrorism: Religious and Secular Justifications,* ed. David C. Rapoport and Yonah Alexander. New York: Pergamon Books, p. 83.

[14]Wilkins, Burleigh Taylor. 1992. *Terrorism and Collective Responsibility*. New York: Routledge, p. 71–72.

[15]Walzer, Michael. 1988. Terrorism: A Critique of Excuses. In *Problems of International Justice,* ed. Steven Luper-Foy. Boulder: Westview Press, p. 238.

[16]Walzer, Ibid, p. 240.

[17]Held, op. cite.

[18]Teichman, op. cite, p. 517.

[19]Baier, op. cite, p. 208.

[20]Wilkins, op. cite, p. 39.

[21]Fullinwider, Robert K. 1988. Understanding Terrorism. In *Problems of International Justice,* ed. Steven Luper-Foy. Boulder: Westview Press

[22]Walzer, op. cite, p. 198.

[23]Holmes, Robert L. 1989. *On War and Morality*. Princeton: Princeton University Press, p. 187.

[24]Baier, op. cite., p. 217.

[25]Op. cite., p. 257.

Bibliography

General Introduction and Chapter I

Arthur, John. *The Unfinished Constitution*. Belmont, Calif.: Wadsworth Publishing, 1989.

Barker, Ernest. *Social and Political Thought*. Oxford University Press, 1946.

Barry, Brian. *Political Argument*. London and New York: Routledge & Kegan Paul, 1965.

Benn, Stanley I., and R. S. Peters. *The Principles of Political Thought*. New York: The Free Press, 1995.

Bowie, Norman, and Robert Simon. *The Individual and the Social Order*. Englewood Cliffs, N.J.: Prentice Hall, 1986.

Brown, Alan. *Modern Political Philosophy*. New York: Penguin, 1986.

Burke, Edmond. *Reflections on the Revolution in France*. Penguin, 1970.

Carritt, E. F. *Ethical and Political Thinking*. Oxford University Press, 1947.

Cohen, Marshall, and Nicole Freeman, eds., *Princeton Readings in Political Thought*. Princeton University Press, 1996.

Feinberg, Joel. *Social Philosophy*. Englewood Cliffs, N.J.: Prentice Hall, 1973.

Hampton, Jean. *Hobbes and the Social Contract Tradition*. Cambridge University Press, 1986.

Hume, David. *Essays Moral, Political and Literary*. Oxford University Press, 1960.

Jacobs, Lesley. *An Introduction to Modern Political Philosophy*. Englewood Cliffs, N.J.: Prentice Hall, 1997.

Kavka, Gregory. *Hobbesian Moral and Political Philosophy*. Princeton University Press, 1986.

Klosko, George. *History of Political Theory*. 2 vols. Fort Worth, Texas: Harcourt, 1995.

Kymlicka, Will. *Contemporary Political Thought*. Oxford University Press, 1990.

Locke, John. *Two Treatises of Government*. Cambridge University Press, 1988.

Lucas, J. R. *The Principles of Politics*. Oxford, England: Clarendon Press, 1984.

Machiavelli, Niccolò. *The Prince and the Discourses*. New York: Modern Library, 1950.

Marx, Karl. *Karl Marx: Selected Writing*. Edited by D. McLellan. Oxford University Press, 1978.

Mill, John Stuart. *On Liberty*. 1859. Indianapolis, Indiana: Bobbs-Merrill, 1956.

Miller, David. *Social Justice*. Oxford University Press, 1989.

Rousseau, Jean-Jacques. *Basic Political Writings*. Indianapolis, Indiana: Hackett, 1987.

Simmons, A. J. *The Lockean Theory of Rights*. Princeton University Press, 1992.

Skinner, Q. *Machiavelli*. Oxford University Press, 1981.

Skoble, Aeon, and Tibor Machan, eds. *Political Philosophy: The Essential Selections*. Englewood Cliffs, N.J.: Prentice Hall, 1999.

Sterba, James P. *Contemporary Social and Political Philosophy*. Belmont, Calif.: Wadsworth Publishing, 1995.

Sterba, James P., ed. *Justice: Alternative Political Perspectives*. Belmont, Calif.: Wadsworth Publishing, 1992.

Taylor, Richard. *Freedom, Anarchy, and Law*. 2nd ed. Amherst, N.Y.: Prometheus Books, 1982.

Thomas, Geoffrey. *Introduction to Political Philosophy*. London: Duckworth, 1999.

Wollstonecraft, Mary. *A Vindication of the Rights of Women*. edited by Mary Warnock. London, England: J.M. Dent Ltd., Everyman's Library, 1986.

Chapter II

Barker, Ernest. *Principles of Social and Political Theory*. Oxford University Press, 1951.

Copp, David. *Morality, Normativity, and Society*. Oxford University Press, 1995.

Kropotkin, Peter. *Mutual Aid*. William Heinemann, 1902.

Narveson, Jan F., ed. *For and Against the State*. Lanham, Md.: Rowman & Littlefield, 1996.

Plamenatz, J. P. *Consent, Freedom and Political Obligation*. Oxford University Press, 1968.

Quinton, Anthony, ed. *Political Philosophy*. Oxford University Press, 1967.

Raphael, D. D. *Problems of Political Philosophy*. New York: Macmillan, 1970.

Raz, Joseph. *The Morality of Freedom*. Oxford University Press, 1986.

Simmons, A. J. *Moral Principles and Political Obligation*. Princeton University Press, 1979.

Strauss, L. *The City and Man*. Chicago: Rand McNally, 1964.

Thomas, Jeoffrey. *Introduction to Political Philosophy*. London: Duckworth, 2000.

Wolff, Robert Paul. *In Defense of Anarchism*. New York: HarperCollins, 1976.

Chapter III

Berlin, Isaiah. *Four Essays on Liberty*. Oxford University Press, 1969.

Gray, J. *Mill on Liberty: A Defense*. London: Routledge, 1996.

Hayek, F. A. *The Road to Serfdom*. University of Chicago Press, 1944.

Nozick, Robert. *Anarchy, State and Utopia*. New York: Basic Books, 1974.

Popper, Karl R. *The Open Society and Its Enemies*. London: Routledge and Sons, 1944.

Rees, J. C. *John Stuart Mill On Liberty*. Oxford University Press, 1985.

Stephen, James Fitzjames. *Liberty, Equality, Fraternity*. University of Chicago Press, 1991.

Sterba, James P. *Justice For Here and Now*. Cambridge University Press, 1998.

Wolff, Jonathan. *An Introduction to Political Philosophy*. Oxford University Press, 1996.

Chapter IV

Bedau, Hugo, ed. *Justice and Equality*. Englewood Cliffs, N.J.: Prentice Hall, 1971.

Daniels, Norman, ed. *Reading Rawls*. New York: Basic Books, 1975.

Nagel, Thomas. *Equality and Partiality*. Oxford University Press, 1991.

Nielsen, Kai. "Radical Egalitarian Justice: Justice As Equality," *Social Theory and Practice* 5, no. 2 (1979).

Okin, Susan Moller. *Justice, Gender, and the Family*. New York: Basic Books, 1989.

Rawls, John. *Political Liberalism*. Columbia University Press, 1993.

Rawls, John. *A Theory of Justice*. Harvard University Press, 1971.

Reiman, Jeffrey. *Justice and Modern Moral Philosophy*. Yale University Press, 1990.

Rescher, Nicholas. *Distributive Justice*. Indianapolis, Indiana: Bobbs-Merrill, 1966.

Sandel, Michael. *Liberalism and the Limits of Justice*. Cambridge University Press, 1988.

Sterba, James. *The Demands of Justice*. University of Notre Dame Press, 1980.

Sterba, James. *How to Make People Just*. Lanham, Maryland: Rowman & Littlefield, 1992.

Veatch, Robert M. *The Foundations of Justice*. Oxford University Press, 1986.

Walzer, Michael. *Spheres of Justice: A Defense of Pluralism and Equality*. New York: Basic Books, 1983.

Wolgast, Elizabeth. *The Grammar of Justice*. Cornell University Press, 1987.

Chapter V

Aristotle. *The Politics of Aristotle*. Oxford University Press, 1946.

Bellamy, R., and Martin Hollis, eds. *Pluralism and Liberal Neutrality*. London: Cass Press, 1999.

Devlin, Patrick. *The Enforcement of Morals*. Oxford University Press, 1965.

Dworkin, Ronald. *The Law's Empire*. Harvard University Press, 1986.

Fuller, Lon. *The Morality of the Law*. Yale University Press, 1964.

George, Robert. *How to Make Men Moral*. Oxford, England: Clarendon Press, 1993.

Haksar, Vinet. *Equality, Liberty, and Perfectionism*. Oxford University Press, 1977.

Hart, H. L. A. *The Concept of Law*, Oxford University Press, 1961.

Hart, H. L. A. *Law, Liberty and Morality*. Oxford University Press, 1963.

Hart, H. L. A. *Punishment and Responsibility*. Oxford University Press, 1968.

Hurka, T. "Perfectionism." In *The Encyclopedia of Ethics*. Edited by Lawrence Becker. New York: Garland Press, 1992.

Kant, Immanuel, *The Foundations for the Metaphysics of Morals*. London: Random House, 1948.

Larmore, Charles. *Patterns of Moral Complexity*. Cambridge University Press, 1987.

Popper, Karl R. *The Open Society and Its Enemies*, London: Routledge & Kegan Paul, 1944.

Sher, George. *Beyond Neutrality*. Cambridge University Press, 1997.

Chapter VI

Ackerman, Bruce. *Social Justice in the Liberal State*. Yale University Press, 1980.

Alexander, Larry, and Maimon Schwarzchild. "Liberalism, Neutrality, and Equality of Welfare vs. Equality of Resource," *Philosophy & Public Affairs* 16, no. 1 (Winter 1987): 85–110.

Arneson, Richard J. "Equality and Equal of Opportunity for Welfare," *Philosophical Studies* (1989): 77–93.

Arneson, Richard J. "Liberalism, Distributive Subjectivism, and Equal Opportunity for Welfare," *Philosophy & Public Affairs* 19, no. 2 (Spring 1992): 158–194.

Baker, John. *Arguing for Equality*. Verso, 1987.

Beardsley, Monroe. "Equality and Obedience to Law." In *The Concept of Equality*. Edited by W. T. Blackstone. Minneapolis, Minnesota: Burgess International Group, Inc., 1960.

Bedau, Hugo Adam. "Egalitarianism and the Idea of Equality." In *Nomos IX: Equality*. Edited by J. Roland Pennock and John W. Chapman. New York: Atherton Press, 1967.

Benn, Stanley I. "Egalitarianism and the Equal Consideration of Interests." In *Nomos IX: Equality*. Edited by J. Roland Pennock and John W. Chapman. New York: Atherton Press, 1967.

Berlin, Isaiah. "Equality As an Ideal." In *Justice and Social Policy*. Edited by Frederick A. Olafson. Englewood Cliffs, N. J.: Prentice Hall, 1961.

Cohen, G. A. "Self-Ownership, World-Ownership, and Equality." In *Justice and Equality Here and Now*. Edited by F. Lucash. Cornell University Press, 1986.

Cohen, George A. "On the Currency of Egalitarian Justice," *Ethics* 99 (1989): 906–944.

Cranston, Maurice. *What Are Human Rights?* Jersey City, N.J.: Taplinger, 1973.

Dworkin, Ronald. "What Is Equality?" "Part 1, Equality of Welfare." "Part 2, Equality of Resources." *Philosophy and Public Affairs* 10, nos. 3, 4 (Summer and Fall 1981): 185–246, 283–345.

Dworkin, Ronald. "Comments on Narveson: In Defense of Equality," *Social Philosophy and Policy* 1 (1983): 24–40.

Finnis, J. *Natural Law and Natural Rights*. Oxford, England: Clarendon Press, 1980.

Flew, Antony. *The Politics of Procrustes: Contradictions of Enforced Equality*. Buffalo, N.Y.: Prometheus Books, 1981.

Green, S. J. D. "Competitive Equality of Opportunity: A Defense," *Ethics* 100 (1989): 5–32.

Hare, R. M. "Justice and Equality." In *Justice and Economic Distribution*. Edited by John Arthur and William H. Shaw. Englewood Cliffs, N. J.: Prentice Hall, 1978.

Kymlicka, Will. *Contemporary Political Philosophy*. Oxford University Press, 1990.

Landesman, Bruce. "Egalitarianism," *Canadian Journal of Philosophy* 8, no. 1 (March 1983).

Levin, Michael E. "Equality of Opportunity," *Philosophical Quarterly* 31, no. 123 (April 1981): 110–125.

Lucas, J. R. "Against Equality," *Philosophy* 40 (1965): 296–307.

Lucas, J. R. "Against Equality Again." In *Against Equality*. Edited by William Letwin. London: Macmillan, 1983.

Martin, Rex. *Rawls and Rights*. University of Kansas, 1985.

Norman, Richard. *Free and Equal: A Philosophical Examination of Political Values*. Oxford: Clarendon Press, 1987.

Machan, Tibor. *Individual Rights*. Chicago, Illinois: Open Court, 1989.

Oppenheim, Felix E. "Egalitarianism As a Descriptive Concept," *American Philosophical Quarterly* 7 (1970): 143–152.

Phelps Brown, Henry. *Egalitarianism and the Generation of Inequality*. Oxford University Press, 1988.

Pojman, Louis P. "Equality: A Plethora of Concepts." *Philosophy and Behavior* (1995).

Pojman, Louis P. and Westmoreland, R: *Equality: Selected Readings,* Oxford University Press, 1997.

Rae, Douglas. *Equalities*. Harvard University Press, 1981.

Rakowski, Eric. *Equal Justice*. Oxford University Press, 1992.

Raz, Joseph. "Principles of Equality," *Mind* 87 (1978): 321–342.

Rousseau, Jean-Jacques, *The Social Contract and Discourses*, London: Dent, 1983.

Sen, Amartya. *Inequality Reexamined*. Oxford: Clarendon Press, 1992.

Sher, George, *Desert*, Princeton University Press, 1987.

Sikora, R. I. "Six Viewpoints for Assessing Egalitarian Distribution Schemes," *Ethics* 99 (1989): 492–502.

Steiner, Hillel. "Capitalism, Justice and Equal Starts," *Social Philosophy and Policy* 5, no. 1 (Autumn 1987): 49–72.

Sowell, Thomas. *Preferential Policies: An International Perspective,* New York: Morrow, 1990.

Temkin, Larry S. *Inequality*. Oxford University Press, 1993.

Thomas, D. A. Lloyd. "Competitive Equality of Opportunity." *Mind* 86 (July 1977): 388–404.

Thomas, D. A. Lloyd. "Equality within the Limits of Reason Alone," *Mind* 88 (October 1979): 538–553.

Tocqueville, Alexis de. *Democracy in America*. Edited by J. P. Mayer. New York: HarperCollins, 1988.

Waldron, Jeremy, ed. *Theories of Rights*. Oxford University Press, 1984.

Westen, Peter. *Speaking of Equality*. Princeton University Press, 1990.

Westmoreland, Robert. "The Hobbesian Roots of Contemporary Liberalism," *Faith and Philosophy*, 8, no. 4 (October 1991).

Chapter VII

Dworkin, Ronald. *Taking Rights Seriously*. Harvard University Press, 1977.

Gewirth, Alan. *Human Rights*. University of Chicago Press, 1982.

Hohfeld, Wesley Newcomb. *Fundamental Legal Conceptions*. Edited by Walter Wheeler Cook. Yale University Press, 1964.

Lomasky, Loren. *Persons, Rights, and Moral Community*. Oxford University Press, 1987.

Lyons, David, ed. *Rights*. Belmont, Calif.: Wadsworth Publishing, 1979.

MacIntyre, Alasdair. *After Virtue*. Notre Dame, Indiana: Notre Dame University Press, 1981.

Nickel, James. *Making Sense of Human Rights*. University of California Press, 1987.

Paul, Ellen Frankl, Fred Miller, and Jeffery Paul, eds. *Human Rights*. New York: Basil Blackwell, 1984.

Pennock, J. Roland, and John W. Chapman, eds. *Human Rights*. New York University Press, 1981.

Smith, Tara. *Moral Rights and Political Freedom*. Lanham, Maryland: Rowman & Littlefield, 1995.

Sumner, L. W. *The Moral Foundation of Rights*. Oxford: Clarendon Press, 1987.

Thompson, Judith Garvis, Rights, *Restitution and Risk*, Harvard University Press, 1986.

Waldron, Jeremy. *The Right to Private Property*. Oxford: Clarendon Press, 1988.

Waldron, Jeremy, ed. *Theories of Rights*. Oxford University Press, 1984.

Wellman, Carl. *A Theory of Rights*. Rowman and Allenheld, 1985.

Wellman, Carl. *The Proliferation of Rights*. Boulder, Colorado: Westview Press, 1999.

Winston, Morton E., ed. *The Philosophy of Human Rights*. Belmont, Calif.: Wadsworth Publishing, 1989.

Chapter VIII

Beitz, Charles R. *Political Theory and International Relations*. Princeton University Press, 1999.

Barry, Brian. *The Liberal Theory of Justice*. Oxford University Press, 1973.

Borjas, George. *Heaven's Door: Immigration Policy and the American Economy*. Princeton University Press, 1999.

Mappel, D., and Terry Nadin, eds. *International Society*. Princeton University Press, 1998.

McKim, Robert, and Jeff McMahan, eds., *The Morality of Nationalism*. Oxford University Press, 1997.

Miller, David. *On Nationality*. Oxford University Press, 1995.

Myers, Robert J., ed. *International Ethics in the Nuclear Age*. University of America Press, 1987.

Nussbaum, Martha, et al., eds. *For Love of Country*. Boston: Beacon Press, 1996.

Sidgwick, Henry. *Elements of Politics*. 3rd ed. London: Macmillan, 1908; originally published in 1891.

Walzer, Michael. *Just and Unjust War*. New York: Basic Books, 1977.